W9-CKC-815

Reading the News About.....

▶ Supply and Demand *(p. 78)*

▶ Price Floors *(p. 83)*

▶ Monopoly *(p. 281)*

▶ Defection from the OPEC Cartel *(p. 307)*

▶ Household Labor Supply Decisions *(p. 328)*

▶ Stock Price Changes *(p. 361)*

▶ The 1996 Welfare Reform Act *(p. 391)*

▶ Government Objections to a Merger *(p. 442)*

▶ GDP Each Month *(p. 550)*

▶ Employment Each Month *(p. 576)*

▶ European Unemployment *(p. 584)*

▶ The Fed *(p. 734)*

▶ Purchasing Power Parity *(p. 831)*

Dairy price support defeat worries Vermont farmers

John Malcolm, Vermont's dairyman of the year, estimated the U.S. House defeat of milk price support legislation Thursday would cost him $10,000 this year, and would cost the state's economy $28 million.

"Anything is a lot of money," the Pawlet farmer said Friday. "We aren't even breaking even now."

Bulk prices for milk have dropped nearly 30 percent since August. Prices per hundred pounds of milk average $11.47, while the cost for Vermont farmers to produce that amount of milk averages $13.75. Leahy's plan would have temporarily fixed the price at $13.09.

Malcolm said he can keep farming for about a year with prices the way they are now, provided he makes cuts in equipment purchases. For some Vermont dairy families, the prospects are worse.

"We are just hanging on by a thread," said Helen Wilcox, who leases a farm in Alburg with her husband, Alvin. Of the couple's nine children, six are still at home, and the family has been selling bull calves for grocery money.

"I thought it was really sad," she said of the proposal's defeat, "because it would have helped drastically. . . . If (the price of milk) continues at $11.50,

we'll be out of farming by the year's end," she said.

"The Senate recognized that dairy farmers in virtually every state are suffering and acted to stop the hemorrhaging," Leahy, chairman of the Senate Agriculture Committee, said Friday. "This is a sad day for our nation's dairy farmers. The administration and House turned a deaf ear to their plight."

The Bush administration had threatened to veto the entire spending bill if it included the price support.

Economic Experiments and Tools

▶ Overview of Supply and Demand *(p. 66)*

▶ Experiments Demonstrate the Law of Diminishing Returns *(p. 163)*

▶ Experimental Tests of the Economic Theory of Taxation *(p. 191)*

▶ Helpful Hints for Drafting Cost Curves *(p. 210)*

▶ The Shutdown Point and the Firm's Supply Curve *(p. 216)*

▶ How to Manage the Divisions of a Large Firm *(p. 227)*

▶ Experimental Tests of the Model of Monopoly *(p. 277)*

▶ Variety Is the Spice of Life *(p. 294)*

▶ Selling the Airwaves *(p. 409)*

▶ Talking Points on the Gains from Trade *(p. 476)*

▶ Stocks and Flows *(p. 537)*

▶ Interest Rates and Exchange Rates *(p. 600)*

▶ Anticipation of Changes in Government Purchases *(p. 608)*

▶ A Graphical Illustration of Growth Accounting *(p. 633)*

▶ The Forecasting Industry *(p. 680)*

▶ Forecasting with Econometric Models *(p. 692)*

▶ The Fed Chairman Speaks on Principles of Monetary Policy *(p. 815)*

▶ Desert Storm and the Current Account *(p. 825)*

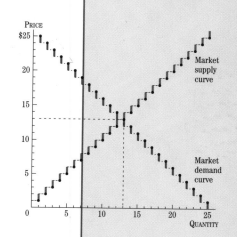

Book Number S-5-06-CSHS

Enter information in spaces below as instructed.

THIS BOOK IS THE PROPERTY OF:

State _Georgia_

Province _____

County _Clarke_

Parish _____

School District _Clarke County_

Other _____

Issued To	Year Used	Condition	
		Issued	Returned
Caroline Oates	06	new/fair	

FOLLETT
Educational Services ®
A Follett Corporation Company

Follett Educational Services, Inc.
1433 Internationale Parkway
Woodridge, IL 60517-4941
Phone (800) 621-4272
www.fes.follett.com

Economics

second edition

About the Author

John B. Taylor is the Raymond Professor of Economics at Stanford University and the director of Stanford's Introductory Economic Studies Center. Professor Taylor is a renowned teacher. Each year he teaches the introductory economics course about which students are wildly enthusiastic. As described in *The Stanford Daily*, "Many students say this course was their best experience in the classroom." Professor Taylor is known for his clear explanations and for his novel teaching ideas, including appearances by his family and a spiritual visitation by the voice of Adam Smith. In recognition of his teaching talents, he has received the Hoagland Prize, presented annually to Stanford's most outstanding teacher of undergraduate students, and the Rhodes Prize for excellent teaching in introductory courses. Professor Taylor studied economics at Princeton and received his Ph.D. at Stanford. He has also taught at Columbia, Yale, and Princeton.

Professor Taylor has published over 100 research papers and several books on economics, including his frequently cited work on wage setting and expectations. His book *Macroeconomics* is a best-selling intermediate text. His articles have appeared in the *Wall Street Journal,* the *Los Angeles Times,* and the *New York Times.* He has appeared on TV and radio shows, including CNN's *Crossfire,* ABC's *Nightline,* PBS's *NewsHour,* and NPR's *Talk of the Nation.* A formula he devised in 1993—now widely referred to as the Taylor Rule—is frequently used to predict Federal Reserve decisions, and "has attracted widening interest in recent years in the financial markets, the academic community, and at central banks," according to Alan Greenspan, chair of the Federal Reserve.

Professor Taylor served as a member of the President's Council of Economic Advisers from 1989 to 1991, where he helped put together the economic forecasts and was a trade negotiator at the Uruguay Round. In 1991 he returned to Stanford and his first loves, teaching and research. He directed the Stanford Center for Economic Policy Research from 1994 to 1997 and is now a member of the California Governor's Council of Economic Advisers and the Congressional Budget Office's Panel of Economic Advisers.

John Taylor currently lives on the Stanford campus with his wife and two children.

Economics

second edition

John B. Taylor
Stanford University

Houghton Mifflin Company   Boston   New York

Editor-in-Chief: Bonnie Binkert
Basic Book Editor: Ann West
Senior Project Editor: Margaret M. Kearney
Senior Production/Design Coordinator: Carol Merrigan
Senior Manufacturing Coordinator: Priscilla J. Abreu
Marketing Manager: Juli Bliss

Printed in the U.S.A.

Library of Congress Catalog Card Number: 97-72553

ISBN: 0-395-874521

23456789-VH-01 00 99 98

Brief Contents

Part 1 Introduction to Economics and Its Foundations 2

1. Observing and Explaining the Economy 4
2. Scarcity, Choice, and Economic Interaction 34
3. The Supply and Demand Model 54
4. Elasticity and Its Uses 88
5. The Demand Curve and the Behavior of Consumers 110
6. The Supply Curve and the Behavior of Firms 144
7. The Interaction of People in Markets 170

Part 2 Microeconomics over Time and Through Markets 198

8. Costs and the Evolution of Firms over Time 200
9. The Rise and Fall of Industries 238
10. Monopoly 262
11. Product Differentiation and Strategic Behavior 290
12. Labor Markets 316
13. Capital Markets 344

Part 3 The Role of Government 370

14. Taxes, Transfers, and Income Distribution 372
15. Public Goods, Externalities, and Government Behavior 404
16. Antitrust Policy and Regulation 436
17. The Gains from International Trade 458
18. International Trade Policy 486

Part 4 Introduction to Macroeconomics 506

19. A Preview of Macroeconomics 508
20. Measuring the Macroeconomy 532

Part 5 Long-Run Fundamentals and Economic Growth 562

21. Unemployment and Employment 564
22. Investment in New Capital 590
23. Technology and Economic Growth 616
24. The Monetary System and Inflation 644

Part 6 Economic Fluctuations 670

25. The First Steps Toward Recession or Boom 672
26. The Uncertain Multiplier 698
27. Aggregate Demand and Price Adjustment 726
28. Toward Recovery and Expansion 748

Part 7 Macroeconomic Policy 770

29. Fiscal Policy and the Budget Deficit 772
30. Monetary Policy 798
31. International Finance 820
32. Macroeconomic Debates 842
33. Economic Growth Around the World 856
34. Emerging Market Economies 876

Contents

Preface   xxiv

Part 1   INTRODUCTION TO ECONOMICS AND ITS FOUNDATIONS   2

Chapter 1   Observing and Explaining the Economy   4

Observations: What Economists Endeavor to Explain   5
Documenting and Quantifying Observations: A Case Study   6
Interpreting the Observations   11

Economic Models   15
What Are Economic Models?   15
Microeconomic Models versus Macroeconomic Models   17
The Use of Existing Models   19
The Development of New Models   19

Using Economics for Public Economic Policy   20
Positive versus Normative Economics   20
Economics as a Science versus a Partisan Policy Tool   21
Economics Is Not the Only Factor in Policy Issues   21

Conclusion: A Reader's Guide   21
Key Points 23 • Key Terms 23 • Questions for Review 23 • Problems 24

▶ *Using Economics to Explain Gender Pay Gaps   18*

Appendix to Chapter 1   Acquiring an Eye for Economics: Reading and
                        Understanding Graphs   25

Representing Observations with Graphs   25
Time-Series Graphs   25
Time-Series Graphs Showing Two or More Variables   28
Scatter Plots   29
Pie Charts   29

Representing Models with Graphs   30
Slopes of Curves   30
Graphs of Models with More than Two Variables   31
Key Terms and Definitions 32 • Questions for Review 32 • Problems 32

Chapter 2   Scarcity, Choice, and Economic Interaction   34

Scarcity, Choice, and Interaction for Individuals   35
Consumer Decisions   35
Producer Decisions   37
Trade Within a Country versus International Trade   38
Multilateral Trade and the Need for a Medium of Exchange   40

Scarcity and Choice for the Economy as a Whole   41
Production Possibilities   41
Increasing Opportunity Costs   42
The Production Possibilities Curve   42

Market Economies, Command Economies, and Prices 47
Three Questions 47
Key Elements of a Market Economy 48
Prices in Action: An Example 50

Conclusion 51
Key Points 51 • Key Terms 52 • Questions for Review 52 • Problems 52

▶ *Adam Smith, 1723–1790 39*
▶ *Using Economics to Explain Educational Choice and Economic Growth 45*

Chapter 3 The Supply and Demand Model 54

Demand 55
The Demand Curve 55
Shifts in Demand 56
Movements Along versus Shifts of the Demand Curve 59

Supply 60
The Supply Curve 61
Shifts in Supply 62
Movements Along versus Shifts of the Supply Curve 65

Market Equilibrium: Combining Supply and Demand 65
Determination of the Market Price 66
Finding the Equilibrium with a Supply and Demand Diagram 68
A Change in the Market 69

Using the Supply and Demand Model: A Case Study 73
Explaining and Predicting Peanut Prices 73

Interference with Market Prices 79
Price Ceilings and Price Floors 79
Shortages and Related Problems Resulting from Price Ceilings 79
Surpluses and Related Problems Resulting from Price Floors 81

Conclusion 84
Key Points 84 • Key Terms 85 • Questions for Review 85 • Problems 85

▶ *Overview of Supply and Demand 66*
▶ *Reading the News About Supply and Demand 78*
▶ *Reading the News About Price Floors 83*

Chapter 4 Elasticity and Its Uses 88

The Price Elasticity of Demand 89
The Importance of Knowing the Price Elasticity of Demand 89
Definition of the Price Elasticity of Demand 92
Terminology for Discussing Elasticities 93
Elasticities and Sketches of Demand Curves 95
Calculating the Elasticity with a Midpoint Formula 95
Revenue and the Price Elasticity of Demand 96
Differences in the Price Elasticity of Demand 98
Elasticities Related to Shifts in Demand 100

The Price Elasticity of Supply 101
Why the Price Elasticity of Supply Is Important 101
Definition of the Price Elasticity of Supply 102

Applications of Elasticity   105
The Size of the Oil Price Increase   105
Setting National Park Fees   105
Taxes and Labor Supply   107

Conclusion   107
Key Points 107 • Key Terms 108 • Questions for Review 108 • Problems 108

▶ *Alfred Marshall, 1842–1924   106*

Chapter 5   The Demand Curve and the Behavior of Consumers   110

Utility and Consumer Preferences   111
A Consumer's Utility Depends on the Consumption of Goods   111
Marginal Utility   112
Utility from More than One Good   114

The Budget Constraint and Utility Maximization   117
The Budget Constraint   117
Maximizing Utility Subject to the Budget Constraint   119
The Diamond–Water Paradox   123

Willingness to Pay and the Demand Curve   125
Measuring Willingness to Pay and Marginal Benefit   125
Graphical Derivation of the Demand Curve   126
The Price Equals Marginal Benefit Rule   129

The Market Demand Curve   129
Different Types of Individuals   129
Different Prices for the Same Good   130

Consumer Surplus   131

An Application: Saving   133
Price of Future Consumption versus Present Consumption   134
The Real Interest Rate   134
Saving and the Interest Rate   134

Conclusion   135
Key Points 135 • Key Terms 136 • Questions for Review 136 • Problems 136

▶ *Using Economics to Explain Family Decisions   124*
▶ *The Origin of Consumer Surplus   132*

Appendix to Chapter 5 Budget Lines and Indifference Curves   138

Part A: The Budget Line   138

Part B: The Indifference Curve   139
Getting to the Highest Indifference Curve Given the Budget Line   141
Effect of a Price Change on the Quantity of X Demanded   141
Effect of an Income Change on Demand   142

Conclusion   142
Key Points 142 • Key Terms and Definitions 143 • Questions for Review 143 •
Problems 143

Chapter 6 The Supply Curve and the Behavior of Firms 144

The Individual Firm 145
The Nature of Firms 145
An Example: Your Own Firm 147

The Firm's Profits 149
Total Revenue 150
Production and Costs 150

Profit Maximization and the Individual Firm's Supply Curve 155
Deriving a Firm's Supply Curve from Its Marginal Cost 156
Another Way to Look at Profit Maximization 158
A Comparison of the Two Approaches to Profit Maximization 161

The Market Supply Curve 162
The Slope of the Supply Curve 164
Shifts in the Supply Curve 164

Producer Surplus 165
A Graphical Representation of Producer Surplus 165
The Relationship Between Profits and Producer Surplus 166

Conclusion 167
Key Points 168 • Key Terms 168 • Questions for Review 169 • Problems 169

▶ *Experiments Demonstrate the Law of Diminishing Returns 163*

Chapter 7 The Interaction of People in Markets 170

Determining Production, Consumption, and Price in a Market 172
The Hard Way to Process Information, Coordinate, and Motivate 172
The Easy Way to Process Information, Coordinate, and Motivate 173
The Competitive Equilibrium Model 173

A Case Study: Setting Up a Market 176
A Double-Auction Market 176
Predictions of the Competitive Equilibrium Model 178
Other Types of Market Experiments 181

Are Competitive Markets Efficient? 182
The Meaning of Efficient 182
Is the Market Efficient? 184
Efficiency and Income Inequality 185

Measuring Waste from Inefficiency 186
Maximizing the Sum of Producer Plus Consumer Surplus 186
Deadweight Loss 186

The Deadweight Loss from Taxation 188
A Tax Paid by a Producer Shifts the Supply Curve 188
A New Equilibrium Price and Quantity 190
Deadweight Loss and Tax Revenue 191

Informational Efficiency 192

Conclusion 194
Key Points 195 • Key Terms 196 • Questions for Review 196 • Problems 196

▶ *Using Economics to Explain the Cost of Federal Farm Programs 189*
▶ *Experimental Tests of the Economic Theory of Taxation 191*

Part 2 MICROECONOMICS OVER TIME AND THROUGH MARKETS   198

Chapter 8   Costs and the Evolution of Firms over Time   200

Costs and Production at an Individual Firm   201
Total Costs, Fixed Costs, Variable Costs, and Marginal Cost   201
Average Cost   204
Costs Depend on the Firm's Production Function   205

Average Cost Curves for an Individual Firm   208
Marginal versus Average in the Classroom   209
Generic Cost Curves   209

Costs and Production: The Short Run   211
The Profit or Loss Rectangle   211
The Breakeven Point   214
The Shutdown Point   215

Costs and Production: The Long Run   217
The Effect of Capital Expansion on Total Costs   217
Effects of a Capital Expansion on Average Total Cost   219
The Long-Run *ATC* Curve   220
Capital Expansion and Production in the Long Run   221
The Mix of Capital and Labor   222

Economies of Scale   222

Acquisitions, Spinoffs, and Coordination of Divisions   224
Merging Two Firms: Economies of Scope   225
Market Prices as Transfer Prices   228

Conclusion   228
Key Points 229 • Key Terms 229 • Questions for Review 229 • Problems 230

▶ *Helpful Hints for Drafting Cost Curves   210*
▶ *The Shutdown Point and the Firm's Supply Curve   216*
▶ *Using Economics to Explain an Actual Firm's History   220*
▶ *How to Manage the Divisions of a Large Firm   227*

Appendix to Chapter 8 A Graphical Approach to Long-Run Capital and
                                            Labor Decisions   232

Adjusting the Mix of Capital and Labor   232
Isoquants   233
Isocost Lines   233
Minimizing Costs for a Given Quantity   235
A Change in the Relative Price of Labor   236
Key Terms and Definitions 237 • Questions for Review 237 • Problems 237

Chapter 9   The Rise and Fall of Industries   238

Change in Different Industries   239
The Rise and Fall of Broad Industry Groups   240
The Rise and Fall of More Narrowly Defined Industries   240
Global Industries   242
Case Study: Change in a Single Specific Industry   242

The Long-Run Competitive Equilibrium Model of an Industry   243
Setting Up the Model with Graphs   244
An Increase in Demand: The Effects on the Industry   246

How Does the Model Explain the Facts?   249
Entry Combined with Individual Firm Expansion   250
Industries in Decline   250
New Products and Changes in Costs   250

Minimum Costs per Unit and the Efficient Allocation of Capital   253
Average Total Cost Is Minimized   253
Efficient Allocation of Capital Among Industries   254

External Economies Are Diseconomies of Scale   254
External Diseconomies of Scale   254
External Economies of Scale   255

Conclusion   259
Key Points 259 • Key Terms 260 • Questions for Review 260 • Problems 260

▶ *Using Economics to Explain the Development of the Machine-Tool Industry   257*

Chapter 10   Monopoly   262

A Model of Monopoly   263
Getting an Intuitive Feel for the Market Power of a Monopoly   263
The Effects of a Monopoly's Decision on Revenues   265
Finding Output to Maximize Profits at the Monopoly   269

The Generic Diagram of a Monopoly and Its Profits   273
Determining Monopoly Output and Price on the Diagram   274
Determining the Monopoly's Profits   274

Competition, Monopoly, and Deadweight Loss   275
Comparison with Competition   275
Deadweight Loss from Monopoly   276
The Monopoly Price Is Greater than Marginal Cost   278

Monoplies and Government   279
Regulated Natural Monopolies   279
Patents and Copyrights   280
Licenses   282

Price Discrimination   283
Consumers with Different Price Elasticities of Demand   284
Quantity Discounts   285
Monopolies versus Other Firms with Market Power   286

Conclusion   287
Key Points 287 • Key Terms 288 • Questions for Review 288 • Problems 288

▶ *Experimental Tests of the Model of Monopoly   277*
▶ *Reading the News About Monopoly   281*

Chapter 11   Product Differentiation and Strategic Behavior   290

Product Differentiation   292
Product Differentiation and Variety in a Market Economy   292
Observations Explained by Product Differentiation   293
Ways That Products Are Differentiated   296
How Much Product Differentiation at a Firm?   296

The Model of Monopolistic Competition   298
A Typical Monopolistic Competitor   298
The Long-Run Monopolistically Competitive Equilibrium   301

Game Theory and Oligopoly **303**
An Overview of Game Theory 304
Applying Game Theory 305

Conjectural Variations and Oligopoly **308**
Strategic Demand Curves 309
Determining Quantity and Price 310

Measures of Market Power **311**
Estimates of Strategic Demand Curves 311
Concentration Ratios 312

Conclusion **312**
Key Points 313 • Key Terms 313 • Questions for Review 314 • Problems 314
▶ *Variety Is the Spice of Life* *294*
▶ *Reading the News About Defection from the OPEC Cartel* *307*

Chapter 12   Labor Markets   316

Terminology and Trends in Wages **317**
Measuring Workers' Pay 317

The Demand for Labor **319**
A Firm's Employment and Production Decisions 320
The Firm's Derived Demand and Market Demand 322
A Comparison of MRP=W with the Marginal Cost Equals Price Rule 324

The Labor Supply of Individuals and Households **326**
Work versus Two Alternatives: Home Work and Leisure 326
Work versus Another Alternative: Getting Human Capital 329

Explaining Wage Differences **330**
Labor Productivity 330
Compensating Wage Differentials 331
Discrimination 332
Minimum Wage Laws 334

Labor Contracts and Incentives **336**
Efficiency Wages 337

Labor Unions **338**
Union/Nonunion Wage Differentials 338
Monopsony and Bilateral Monopoly 340

Conclusion and Some Lessons **341**
Key Points 341 • Key Terms 342 • Questions for Review 342 • Problems 342
▶ *Reading the News About Household Labor Supply Decisions* *328*
▶ *Using Economics to Explain the Academic Wage Gap* *332*

Chapter 13   Capital Markets   344

Capital Market Terminology **345**
Physical Capital 345
Financial Capital 345

Markets for Physical Capital **346**
Rental Markets 346
The Ownership of Physical Capital 350
A Firm's Decision about Capital, Labor, and Output 351

Financial Capital 351
Stock Prices and Returns 351
Bond Prices and Returns 353

Risk versus Return 356
Behavior under Uncertainty 356
Risk and Rates of Return in Theory 358
Risk and Return in Reality 359
Diversification Reduces Risk 360
Efficient Market Theory: Speedy Entry and Exit 362

Corporate Governance Problems 363
Asymmetric Information: Moral Hazard and Adverse Selection 363
Incentives Through Profit Sharing 364
Incentives Through Threats of Takeovers 364

Conclusion and Some Lessons 364
Key Points 365 • Key Terms 365 • Questions for Review 365 • Problems 366

▶ *Reading the News About Stock Price Changes 361*

Appendix to Chapter 13 How to Discount Future Payments 368

The Discount Rate and the Present Discounted Value 368

Finding the Present Discounted Value 368
Key Points 369 • Key Terms and Definitions 369 • Questions for Review 369 •
Problems 369

Part 3 THE ROLE OF GOVERNMENT 370

Chapter 14 Taxes, Transfers, and Income Distribution 372

The Tax System 373
The Personal Income Tax 374
The Payroll Tax 378
Other Taxes 379
The Effects of Taxes 379
Tax Policy 385

Transfer Payments 386
Means-Tested Transfer Programs 386
The Earned Income Tax Credit (EITC) 387
Welfare Reform 388
Social Insurance Programs 392
Mandated Benefits 392

The Distribution of Income in the United States 394
The Personal Distribution of Income 394
The Lorenz Curve and Gini Coefficient 395
The Poor and the Poverty Rate 399
Effects of Taxes and Transfers on Income Distribution and Poverty 400

Conclusion 400
Key Points 401 • Key Terms 402 • Questions for Review 402 • Problems 402

▶ *Using Economics to Explain the Marriage Tax 377*
▶ *Reading the News About the 1996 Welfare Reform Act 391*
▶ *Using Economics to Explain Income Distribution Around the World 398*

Chapter 15   Public Goods, Externalities, and Government Behavior   404

A Brief Look at Government Production   405

Public Goods   406
Free Riders: A Difficulty for the Private Sector   407
Avoiding Free-Rider Problems   408
New Technology   408
Public Goods and Actual Government Production   408

Cost-Benefit Analysis   410
Marginal Cost and Marginal Benefit   410
Public Infrastructure Projects   411

Externalities: From the Environment to Education   412
Negative Externalities   413
Positive Externalities   414
Global Externalities   416

Remedies for Externalities   416
Private Remedies: Agreements Between the Affected Parties   417
Command and Control Remedies   419
Taxes and Subsidies   421
Tradable Permits   423
Balancing the Costs and Benefits of Reducing Externalities   424

Models of Government Behavior   425
Public Choice Models   426
Economic Policy Decisions Through Voting   426
Special Interest Groups   429
Time Inconsistency   430
Incentive Problems in Government   430
Better Government Through Market-Based Incentives   430

Conclusion   432
Key Points 432 • Key Terms 433 • Questions for Review 433 • Problems 433

▶ *Selling the Airwaves   409*
▶ *Using Economics to Explain the Tragedy of the Commons   418*
▶ *Using Economics to Explain Externalities from Biodiversity   420*

Chapter 16   Antitrust Policy and Regulation   436

Antitrust Policy   437
Attacking Existing Monopoly Power   437
Merger Policy   439
Price Fixing   443
Vertical Restraints   443

Regulating Natural Monopolies   445
Economies of Scale and Natural Monopolies   445
Alternative Methods of Regulation   445
Government-Run Monopolies   448

To Regulate or Not to Regulate   449
Borderline Cases   449
Regulators as Captives of Industry   450
Financial Market Regulation: Information and Risk   450

The Deregulation Movement   451

Economic Regulation versus Social Regulation   452

Conclusion   455
Key Points 455 • Key Terms 456 • Questions for Review 456 • Problems 456

▶ *Reading the News About Government Objections to a Merger   442*
▶ *Using Economics to Explain Insurance Regulations   451*

Chapter 17   The Gains from International Trade   458

Trade and Sovereignty   459
Sovereign National Governments   459
Recent Trends in International Trade 459

The Attack on Mercantilism 460
Mutual Gains from Voluntary Exchange of Existing Goods 461
Increased Competition 461
The Division of Labor 461
Better Use of Skills and Resources in Different Countries 462

Comparative Advantage   462
A Simple Example of Comparative Advantage   463
Trade Between Countries: Pharmaceuticals and Electronics   464
The Relative Price of Pharmaceutical Goods and Electronic Goods   466
Comparative Advantage and Gains from Trade   467
Graphical Illustration of the Gains from Trade   468

Reasons for Comparative Advantage   471
Dynamic Comparative Advantage   471
Factor Abundance of Countries and Factor Intensity of Industries   472

Gains from Expanded Markets   474
An Example of Gains from Trade Through Expanded Markets   474
Measuring the Gains from Expanded Markets   475

The Transition to Free Trade   482
Phaseout of Trade Restrictions   482
Trade Adjustment Assistance   482

Conclusion   483
Key Points 483 • Key Terms 484 • Questions for Review 484 • Problems 484

▶ *Talking Points on the Gains from Trade   476*
▶ *David Ricardo, 1772–1823   481*

Chapter 18   International Trade Policy   486

The Effects of Trade Restrictions   487
Tariffs   487
Quotas   488
Voluntary Restraint Agreements (VRAs)   490
Voluntary Import Expansion (VIE)   491
Trade Barriers Related to Domestic Policies   491

The History of Trade Restrictions   493
U.S. Tariffs   493
How Large Are the Gains from Reducing Current Trade Restrictions?   495
The Political Economy of Protectionist Pressures   496

Arguments for Trade Barriers   496
Restricting Supply and Strategic Trade Policy   496
The Infant Industry Argument   497
The National Security Argument   497
Retaliation Threats   498
What If Other Countries Subsidize Their Firms?   498
Unfair Competition from the Sun?   498

How to Reduce Trade Barriers   499
Unilateral Disarmament   499
Multilateral Negotiations   500
Regional Trading Areas   501
Managed Trade   502

Conclusion   503
Key Points 503 • Key Terms 504 • Questions for Review 504 • Problems 504
▶ *Using Economics to Explain the End of the Corn Laws   500*

Part 4   INTRODUCTION TO MACROECONOMICS   506

Chapter 19   A Preview of Macroeconomics   508

Economic Output over Time   509
Economic Growth: The Relentless Uphill Climb   509
Economic Fluctuations: Temporary Setbacks and Recoveries   511

Jobs, Inflation, and Interest Rates   515
Employment, Productivity, and Unemployment   515
Inflation   519
Interest Rates   520

Macroeconomic Theory and Policy   522
Economic Growth Theory and Economic Fluctuation Theory   522
Aggregate Supply and Long-Term Economic Growth   522
Government Policy for Long-Term Economic Growth   524
Economic Fluctuations Theory and Policy   525

Conclusion   526
Key Points 528 • Key Terms 528 • Questions for Review 528 • Problems 528
▶ *Using Economics to Explain a Recession's Pain Around the Country   518*

Appendix to Chapter 19   The Miracle of Compound Growth   531

Chapter 20   Measuring the Macroeconomy   532

Measuring GDP   533
A Precise Definition of GDP   533
The Spending Approach   535
The Income Approach   539
The Production Approach   541

Saving, Investment, and Net Exports   544
The Definition of a Country's Saving   544
Saving Equals Investment plus Net Exports   544

Real GDP and Nominal GDP   547
Adjusting GDP for Inflation   547

The GDP Deflator   549
Other Inflation Measures   552

Shortcomings of the GDP Measure   553
Revisions in GDP   554
Omissions from GDP   554
Other Measures of Well-Being   555

International Comparisons of GDP   556
The Problem with Using Market Exchange Rates for Comparisons   557
Purchasing Power Parity Exchange Rates   557

Conclusion   558
Key Points 559 • Key Terms 559 • Questions for Review 559 • Problems 560
▶ *Stocks and Flows   537*
▶ *Reading the News About GDP Each Month   550*

Part 5   LONG-RUN FUNDAMENTALS AND ECONOMIC GROWTH   562

Chapter 21   Unemployment and Employment   564

Employment and Unemployment Trends   565
Cyclical, Frictional, and Structural Unemployment   565
How Is Unemployment Measured?   566
Comparing Three Key Indicators   569
Aggregate Hours of Labor Input   570

The Nature of Unemployment   572
Reasons People Are Unemployed   572
Long-Term versus Short-Term Unemployment   575
Unemployment for Different Groups   577

Determination of Employment and Unemployment   578
Labor Demand and Labor Supply   578
Case Study: Explaining Long-Term Employment Trends   579
Why Is the Unemployment Rate Always Greater than Zero?   580
Policy Implications   582

Conclusion   586
Key Points 586 • Key Terms 586 • Questions for Review 587 • Problems 587
▶ *Reading the News About Employment Each Month   576*
▶ *Reading the News About European Unemployment   584*

Chapter 22   Investment in New Capital   590

Investment and the Accumulation of Productive Capital   591
Gross Investment, Net Investment, and Increases in Capital   591
Government Investment   593

Investment As a Share of GDP   594
The Investment Share versus the Other Shares of GDP   594
If One Share Goes Up, Another Must Go Down   595

Interest Rates and Consumption, Investment, and Net Exports   596
Consumption   596
Investment   598

Net Exports   599
Putting the Three Shares Together   601

Determining the Equilibrium Interest Rate   602
Adding the Nongovernment Shares Graphically   602
The Share of GDP Available for Nongovernment Use   602
Finding the Equilibrium Interest Rate Graphically   603

Impacts on the Investment Share   605
A Change in Government Purchases   605
Impact on Investment of a Shift in Consumption   606

The Saving Investment Approach   608
The National Saving Rate and the Interest Rate   609
Determination of the Equilibrium Interest Rate   609
Effect of a Downward Shift in the National Saving Rate   610

Determination of Government's Share of GDP   611
Arguments over the Appropriate Size of Government   611
Size of Government and Economic Growth   612

Conclusion   612
Key Points 613 • Key Terms 613 • Questions for Review 613 • Problems 614

▶ *Interest Rates and Exchange Rates   600*
▶ *Anticipation of Changes in Government Purchases   608*

Chapter 23   Technology and Economic Growth   616

How Economics Got the Nickname the "Dismal Science"   617
Labor Alone   618
Labor and Capital Only   623

Labor, Capital, and Technology   627
What Is Technology?   627
The Production of Technology: The Invention Factory   629
Special Features of the Technology Market   630

Growth Accounting   632
The Growth Accounting Formula   632
Case Studies: Using the Growth Accounting Formula   634

Technology Policy   636
Policy to Encourage Investment in Human Capital   636
Policy to Encourage Research and Innovation   636
Technology Embodied in New Capital   637
Is Government Intervention Appropriate?   637

Conclusion: Implications for Potential GDP   638
Key Points 639 • Key Terms 639 • Questions for Review 639 • Problems 640

▶ *Thomas Robert Malthus, 1766–1834   622*
▶ *A Graphical Illustration of Growth Accounting   633*

Appendix to Chapter 23 Deriving the Growth Accounting Formula   641

Key Points 642 • Key Term and Definition 642 • Questions for Review 643 •
Problems 643

Chapter 24   The Monetary System and Inflation   644

What Is Money?   645
Commodity Money   645
Three Functions of Money   645
From Coins to Paper Money to Deposits   646
Alternative Definitions of the Money Supply   647

The Fed and the Banks: Creators of Money   648
The Fed   649
The Balance Sheet of a Commercial Bank   651
The Role of Banks in Creating Money   652

How the Fed Controls Money Supply: Currency Plus Deposits   655
The Money Supply (M) and Bank Reserves (BR)   656
Currency versus Deposits   656
The Money Multiplier   657

Money Growth and Inflation   659
The Quantity Equation of Money   659
Some Key Episodes in Monetary History   660

Inflation: Effects on Unemployment and Productivity Growth   663
Effects on Unemployment   663
Effects on Productivity Growth   664
Why Is Inflation Almost Always Greater than Zero?   665

Conclusion   666
Key Points 667 • Key Terms 667 • Questions for Review 667 • Problems 668

Part 6   ECONOMIC FLUCTUATIONS   670

Chapter 25   The First Steps Toward Recession or Boom   672

Changes in Aggregate Demand First Lead to Changes in Output   673
Production and Demand at Individual Firms   675
Why Changes in Demand Are Translated into Changes in Production   676
Could Economic Fluctuations Also Be Due to Changes in Potential GDP?   678

Forecasting Real GDP   679
A Forecast for Next Year   679
A Conditional Forecast   681

The Response of Consumption to Income   682
The Consumption Function   682
What About Interest Rates and Other Influences on Consumption?   684

Finding Real GDP When Consumption and Income Move Together   685
The Logic of the Two-Way Link Between Consumption and Income   685
The 45-Degree Line   686
The Aggregate Expenditure Line   686
Determining Real GDP Through Spending Balance   689
A Better Forecast of Real GDP   690

Spending Balance and Departures of Real GDP from Potential GDP   693
Stepping Away from Potential GDP   693
Starting Away from Potential GDP   694

Conclusion   694
Key Points 695 • Key Terms 695 • Questions for Review 695 • Problems 696

▶ *The Forecasting Industry   680*
▶ *Forecasting with Econometric Models   692*

Chapter 26   The Uncertain Multiplier   698

How to Find the Multiplier   699
A Graphical Derivation of the Multiplier   699
An Algebraic Derivation of the Multiplier   701
Following the Multiplier Through the Economy   704

The Size of the Multiplier   707
The Multiplier and the Slope of the AE line   707
The Multiplier and the Marginal Propensity to Consume   708
Uncertainty about the Size of the Multiplier   710

A Key International Issue: Net Exports Depend on Income   710
How Do Net Exports Depend on Income?   710
The *AE* Line When Net Exports Depend on Income   712
Effects on the Size of Multiplier   713
The Impact on the Trade Deficit   716
Does Investment Depend on Income Too?   717

The Multiplier for a Tax Change   717

The Forward-Looking Consumption Model   719
Consumption Smoothing   720
The MPC for Permanent versus Temporary Changes in Income   720
Tests and Applications of the Forward-Looking Model   721

Conclusion   723
Key Points 723   •   Key Terms 723   •   Questions for Review 724   •   Problems 724
▶ *The Origins of the Multiplier   705*
▶ *John Maynard Keynes, 1883–1946   709*

Chapter 27   Aggregate Demand and Price Adjustment   726

The Aggregate Demand/Inflation Curve   728
Interest Rates and Real GDP   728
Interest Rates and Inflation   732
Derivation of the Aggregate Demand/Inflation Curve   735

The Price Adjustment Line   739
The Price Adjustment Line Is Flat   739
The Price Adjustment Line Shifts Gradually When Real GDP Departs from
    Potential GDP   741
Changes in Expectations or Commodity Prices Shift the Price Adjustment Line   742
Does the Price Adjustment Line Fit the Facts?   742

**Combining the Aggregate Demand/Inflation Curve and the Price
    Adjustment Line   744**

Conclusion   745
Key Points 745   •   Key Terms 746   •   Questions for Review 746   •   Problems 746
▶ *Reading the News About the Fed   734*

Chapter 28   Toward Recovery and Expansion   748

The End of Recessions and Booms   749
Real GDP and Inflation over Time   749

A More Detailed Report: Economic Behavior Behind the Scenes 751
The Return to Potential GDP after a Boom 754

Changes in Monetary Policy **755**
The Volcker Disinflation 757
Reinflation 759

The Case of a Price Shock or Supply Shock **759**
What Is a Price Shock? 760
The Effect of Price Shocks 760

Combining Different Scenarios **762**
A Monetary Policy Change with a Government Purchases Change 762
Monetary Errors and Reversals: A Boom-Bust Cycle 763

Conclusion **765**
Key Points 767 • Key Terms 767 • Questions for Review 767 • Problems 768
▶ *Using Economics to Explain the Recovery from the Great Depression* *758*
▶ *Brief History of Thought on Price Adjustment* *764*

Part 7 **MACROECONOMIC POLICY** **770**

Chapter 29 **Fiscal Policy and the Budget Deficit** **772**

The Government Budget: Taxes, Spending, the Deficit, and the Debt **773**
Setting the Annual Budget 773
A Look at the Federal Budget 776
The Federal Debt 777
State and Local Government Budgets 779

Discretionary and Automatic Countercyclical Fiscal Policy **780**
Impacts of the Instruments of Fiscal Policy 780
Countercyclical Fiscal Policy 783
The Discretion versus Rules Debate for Fiscal Policy 786

Economic Impact of the Budget Deficit **787**
Short-Run and Long-Run Impact of the Deficit 787
Credible Deficit Reduction Plans 788
The Structural versus the Cyclical Deficit 792

Budget Reforms **794**

Conclusion **795**
Key Points 795 • Key Terms 796 • Questions for Review 796 • Problems 796
▶ *Using Economics to Explain a Rise in Long-Term Interest Rates* *790*

Chapter 30 **Monetary Policy** **798**

Central Bank Independence **799**
Short-Run Gains versus Long-Run Pain 799
The Political Business Cycle 801
Time Inconsistency 801
Government Borrowing from the Central Bank 801
Possible Abuses of Independence 802

Money Demand, Money Supply, and the Interest Rate **803**
Money Demand 803
Money Supply 804
The Determination of the Interest Rate 805

Fed Policy Actions   806
Open Market Operations and Changes in the Federal Funds Rate   806
The Monetary Transmission Channel   808
Other Tools of Monetary Policy   809

Alternative Monetary Policies   810
The Constant Money Growth Rule   811
Real GDP in the Monetary Policy Rule   812
The Gold Standard   814

Gains from Credibility   814
Interpreting Policy Actions   814
Expectations and Credible Disinflation   817

Conclusion   817
Key Points 817 • Key Terms 818 • Questions for Review 818 • Problems 818

▶ *The Fed Chairman Speaks on Principles of Monetary Policy   815*

Chapter 31   International Finance   820

Balance of Trade Around the World   821
The Trade Deficit   821
Both Merchandise Trade and Services Trade Are Important   822
The Balance of Payments   823
Bilateral Surpluses and Deficits   827
Sectoral Deficits   828

Exchange Rate Determination   829
Purchasing Power Parity (PPP)   829
The Interest Rate: A Reason for Deviations from PPP   833

Fixed Exchange Rate Systems   834
International Gold Standard   834
The Bretton Woods System   834
The European Monetary System   835

Fixed Exchange Rates and International Independence   836
Loss of International Monetary Independence   836
Interventions in the Exchange Market   837
Reducing Exchange Rate Risk   837

Conclusion   838
Key Points 839 • Key Terms 840 • Questions for Review 840 • Problems 840

▶ *Desert Storm and the Current Account   825*
▶ *Reading the News About Purchasing Power Parity   831*

Chapter 32   Macroeconomic Debates   842

Schools of Thought in Macroeconomics   844
Developments from the 1930s Through the 1960s   844
Developments from the 1970s Through the Present   847
Macroeconomic Theory at the Turn of the Century   850

Debates about Macroeconomic Policy   851
The Bush Fiscal Package   851
The Clinton Fiscal Package   853
Lessons   853

Conclusion   854
Key Points 855 • Key Terms 855 • Questions for Review 855 • Problems 855

Chapter 33   Economic Growth Around the World   856

Catching Up or Not?   857
Catch-up Within the United States   857
Catch-up in the Advanced Countries   857
Catch-up in the Whole World   860

Economic Development   861
Billions Still in Poverty   861
Geographical Patterns   861
Terminology of Economic Development   862

Obstacles to the Spread of Technology   862
Reduction in Restrictions in the Eighteenth and Nineteenth Centuries   864
Remaining Restrictions in Developing Countries   865
Human Capital   866

Obstacles to Raising Capital per Worker   866
High Population Growth   866
Insufficient National Saving   867
The Lack of Foreign Investment in Developing Countries   867

Inward-Looking versus Outward-Looking Economic Policies   870

Conclusion   872
Key Points 873 • Key Terms 873 • Questions for Review 873 • Problems 874

▶ *Using Economics to Explain an Inadequacy of World Saving   868*

Chapter 34   Emerging Market Economies   876

Centrally Planned Economies   877
Central Planning in the Soviet Union 878
Trade Between the Soviet Union and Eastern Europe   881
Technological Change and the Quality of Goods   882
From Perestroika to the End of the Soviet Union   882
Soviet-Style Central Planning in China   883

Alternative Paths to a Market Economy   884
The Goals of Reform   884
Shock Therapy or Gradualism?   884

Economic Reform in Practice   885
Reforms in Poland   886
Reforms in China   887

Economic Freedom and Political Freedom   888

Conclusion   889
Key Points 890 • Key Terms 890 • Questions for Review 890 • Problems 890

▶ *Karl Marx, 1818–1883   879*

Glossary   893

Index   913

Preface

The goal of this book is to present modern economics in a form that is intuitive, interesting, and useful for students who have had no prior exposure to this fascinating subject. When I took the introductory economics course in college way back in the 1960s, I found the course and the textbook (Paul Samuelson's) fascinating. People called 1960s-vintage economics the "new economics," because many new ideas, including those put forth by John Maynard Keynes, were being applied for the first time in public policy. But during the 1970s, the 1980s, and the 1990s, economics underwent another tremendous wave of change. Now at the end of the 20th century, economics places much greater emphasis on incentives, on expectations, on long-run fundamentals, on the use of experiments, on rich surveys of individual experiences, on the theory of institutions, and on the importance of stable, predictable economic policies. These new ideas are both interesting and of great relevance to individuals, to firms, and to governments as we start the 21st century. The world economy has also changed radically in the last thirty years with market economies now being the preferred choice of virtually all countries around the world and with billions of more people linked together through international trade. With these changes economics is now more fascinating and more relevant than ever.

JOINING THE OLD WITH THE NEW

My strategy in developing the first edition of the textbook, published three years ago, was to give these changes a prominent, clearly explained place alongside the older parts of economics and thereby to make modern economics—with all its fascination and relevance—available to beginning students. The enthusiastic reaction of teachers and students to the first edition has validated this strategy. Teachers who have successfully taught from the first edition point to the clear demonstrations of how a market economy actually works, to the thorough explanation of why markets are efficient when incentives are right and inefficient when incentives are wrong, to the emphasis on long-run fundamentals, to the lively analysis and discussion of real-world public policy, and perhaps most crucial—and certainly the most gratifying to me—to the clear, intuitive explanation of basic economic principles through analogy, example, and user-friendly graphs and illustrations.

DEVELOPING THE SECOND EDITION

My strategy in developing the second edition of *Economics* was to produce a streamlined version of the first edition—with more efficient exposition, better organization, more visually effective page layouts, and with many new and updated real-world examples. Suggestions for the revision came from students in the introductory course I teach each year, from students and faculty who have used the book at many other colleges and universities, and from experts in specialized areas—such as experimental economics or international trade—whose advice we sought directly.

Armed with these suggestions we created a revised outline for the second edition. I then revisited every line of text, every graph, every box, every cartoon, and every photo, adding, deleting, or rewriting to streamline, clarify, and update. After faculty reviews of this draft and, of course, more editing and rewriting, the manuscript moved into production, during which layout—the size and placement of text, tables, and graphs on the page—became my paramount concern. One of the advantages of modern computer page-making techniques is that I could interact in real time with the production editor, experimenting with different layouts and making sure, for example, that the descriptions of the graphs in the text were placed at the most helpful positions relative to the graphs themselves. Though most time-consuming, this interaction was invaluable for making a user-friendly, visually efficient layout.

Key Text Revisions: Streamlining, Updating, and Enhancing Intuition

A few examples of the changes I made in the second edition will show how the discussion was streamlined, made more intuitive, and updated. A detailed account of all the additions, deletions, and modifications is found in the transition guide in the Instructor's Resource Manual and on the web site (http://www.hmco.com/college).

Major streamlining was achieved, for example, by eliminating Chapter 14, which had previewed the role of government, and by integrating the material on public choice into the chapter on public goods and externalities (now Chapter 15). Other examples of improved organization in the micro chapters include moving the material on the nature of firms from Chapter 8 to Chapter 6 (the first chapter on the theory of the firm) and moving some of the discussion of the role of government to Chapter 10 on monopoly so that instructors can discuss policy options before the more detailed treatment of antitrust and regulation in Chapter 16.

Examples of more intuitive explanations include the use of a new extended example of a student-run firm to derive the supply curve in Chapter 6. And by highlighting the analogy between the consumer decision in Chapter 5, and the firm decision in Chapter 6, the trio of Chapters 5, 6, and 7 (about which many faculty have been especially enthusiastic) now works better than ever. To make the double-auction market demonstration more useful to instructors (who may not have time to conduct experiments in class), we produced a short video to illustrate how experimental markets work.

Streamlining also occurred within the macro section of the book. The macroeconomic overview chapter (Chapter 19) now focuses more on a review of the key macroeconomic facts and less on previewing the theory. I also shortened the appendix on growth accounting accompanying Chapter 23, "Technology and Economic Growth," and moved some of the explanatory material on growth accounting into a new box in Chapter 23. The chapter on economic growth around the world (Chapter 25 in the first edition) was moved toward the end of the book, leaving four chapters on long-run fundamentals and economic growth and the same number of chapters on economic fluctuations. The description of the Fed was moved into the long-run oriented chapter on the monetary system (Chapter 24), with the later chapter on monetary policy (Chapter 30) now focusing more on monetary independence. The chapters that develop the model of the recovery of the economy after a recession were consolidated into a single chapter (27) in order to better exploit the analogy with supply and demand curves. Chapter 28, "Toward Recovery and Expansion," uses the model developed in Chapter 27 to illustrate the path the economy takes toward recovery after a recession. A streamlined description of the Fed's behavior in response to inflation is contained in Chapter 27, while the more detailed description of different policies is covered in Chapter 30. I also increased the number of teaching options by making it possible for instructors to skip Chapter 26,

"The Uncertain Multiplier," which discusses the multiplier calculations using the Keynesian Cross.

Examples of new material added to this edition include discussions of the 1996 Welfare Reform Act, the Federal Trade Commission analysis of the proposed merger of Office Depot and Staples, the new chain-weighted real GDP measures, the CPI bias problem, the world savings shortage, the new line-item veto authority used by President Clinton for the first time in 1997, pre-emptive monetary strikes, and, of course, all the new macroeconomic data and developments from the last three years.

New, Improved Boxes

As we revised, added, or updated boxes, we gave many of them special designations—"Reading the News About . . ." or "Using Economics to Explain . . ."—in order to help students use the material more effectively. Among the many new or revised boxes you'll find coverage of experimental results on the theory of taxation (Chapter 7) and the model of monopoly (Chapter 10), helpful hints for drafting costs curves (Chapter 8), and forecasting with econometric models (Chapter 25); you'll also find Reading the News boxes about price floors (Chapter 3), labor supply decisions in the household (Chapter 12), stock price changes (Chapter 13), GDP each month (Chapter 20), the Fed (Chapter 27), and Big Mac purchasing power parity (Chapter 31), among many others.

Enhanced Teaching and Learning Package

The package of teaching and learning aids (described below) has been completely revised with several new options. The teaching software has been expanded to match each chapter of the text. A web page is now available to provide additional help and information to both students and instructors. And a new series of teaching videos has been produced.

A BRIEF TOUR

Economics is designed for a two-term course. Parts 1 through 3 cover microeconomics, and Parts 4 through 7 cover macroeconomics. I recognize that teachers use a great variety of sequences and syllabi, and I have therefore taken great pains to allow for alternative plans of coverage. Furthermore, the text is available in two self-contained volumes, *Principles of Microeconomics* and *Principles of Macroeconomics*. International economic issues are considered throughout the text, with separate chapters on international economic policy.

PART 1
Introduction to Economics and Its Foundations

The basic workings of markets and the reasons they improve people's lives are the subjects of Part 1. Chapter 1 introduces the field of economics through a case study showing how economists observe and explain economic puzzles. Chapter 1 defines key terms and ideas, and Chapter 2 outlines the basic unifying themes of economics: scarcity, choice, and the production possibilities curve. The role of prices, the inherent international aspect of economics, the importance of property rights and incentives, and the difference between central planning and markets are some of the key ideas in these chapters. Chapters 3 and 4 cover the basic supply and demand model. I have tried to explain these basic ideas as fully and as clearly as I can, adding the extra sentence of clarification whenever it might help in understanding. The goal is to show how to use the supply and demand model and to learn to "think like an economist." A trio of chapters—5, 6, and 7—has the aim of explaining why competitive markets are efficient, perhaps the most important idea in economics. The parallel exposition of utility maximization (Chapter 5) and profit maximization (Chapter 6) culminates in a detailed description of why competitive markets are efficient (Chapter 7). These first seven chapters provide a complete, self-contained analysis of competitive markets before going on to develop more difficult concepts, such as long-run versus short-run cost curves or monopolist competition. This approach enables the student to learn, appreciate, and use important concepts such as efficiency and deadweight loss early in the course.

A modern market economy is not static; rather it grows and changes over time as firms add new and better machines and as people add to their skills and training. Part 2 describes how firms and markets grow and change over time. This part also shows how economists model the behavior of firms that are not perfectly competitive, such as monopolies. The models of dynamic behavior and imperfect competition developed here are used to explain the rise and fall of real-world firms and industries. Part 2 also delves into the special characteristics of labor markets.

PART 2
Microeconomics over Time and Through Markets

Different countries have taken widely different approaches to the economy. The policy of some countries has been to intervene in virtually every economic decision; other countries have followed more hands-off policies. Part 3, therefore, is devoted to the role of government in the economy. Tax policy, welfare reform, environmental policy, international trade policy, the regulation of industry, and the role of government in producing public goods are analyzed. The problem of government failure is analyzed using models of government behavior. International trade theory and policy are explored in Chapters 17 and 18.

PART 3
The Role of Government

Part 4 begins the study of macroeconomics. Chapter 19 is an overview of the facts emphasizing that macroeconomics is concerned with the growth and the fluctuations in the economy as a whole. Chapter 20 shows how GDP and other variables are measured.

PART 4
Introduction to Macroeconomics

Response to the first edition's treatment of long-run issues before developing the theory of economic fluctuations was overwhelmingly positive, and the second edition takes that approach one step further by streamlining the coverage of economic growth from five to four chapters so as to allow for a speedier introduction to fluctuations. Part 5 thus begins with an analysis of how the level of unemployment in the economy as a whole is determined and goes on to explore the accumulation of capital and technological progress. Labor, capital, and technology are presented here as the fundamental determinants of the economy's growth path. One clear advantage of this approach is that it allows students to focus first on issues about which there is general agreement among economists and in which many of the deep policy problems facing us at the start of the 21st century lie: long-term growth. Moreover, this ordering helps the student better understand short-term economic fluctuations.

PART 5
Long-Run Fundamentals and Economic Growth

As shown in the four chapters of Part 6, the economy does fluctuate as it grows over time. Declines in production and increases in unemployment (characteristics of the recessions of the early 1980s and early 1990s) have not vanished from the landscape as the problems of long-term growth have come to the fore. Part 6 delves into the causes of these fluctuations and an analysis of why they end. It begins by explaining why shifts in aggregate demand may cause the economy to fluctuate and ends by showing that price adjustment plays a significant role in the end of recessions.

PART 6
Economic Fluctuations

Countries have tried a variety of approaches to deal with economic growth and economic fluctuations. Part 7 examines these approaches to policy, about which there are many differing opinions. I have tried to explain these differences as clearly and as objectively as I can; there are also areas of agreement, which are stressed.

PART 7
Macroeconomic Policy

PEDAGOGICAL FEATURES

The following pedagogical features are designed to help the student learn economics.

Case studies within the text. This feature uses real-world situations to help motivate economic ideas and models. Examples include health care in Chapter 1, a recent drought in the U.S. peanut market in Chapter 3, and setting national park fees in Chapter 4.

Interesting economic puzzles to stimulate interest in economic models. Most chapters begin with a description of real-world phenomena which economics can help to explain. Examples include the opportunity costs of college for Tiger Woods in Chapter 1 and the sharp rise in oil prices during the Persian Gulf War in Chapter 4.

Integrating modern economic concepts in the context of substantive economic problems rather than in separate chapters. This approach demonstrates the relevance of the new ideas and keeps the text to a manageable size. For example, time inconsistency is described in the context of particular economic policy problems.

Use of experimental economics to help explain key ideas in ways that are helpful even to those who do not do such experiments. Details on how to set up and run 18 experiments are provided in an optional experiments manual. The double auction, described in Chapter 7, is one of the experiments featured in this manual and is also the subject of one of the video segments in the Economics Video series.

Brief reviews at the end of each major section (about four per chapter) summarize the key points in abbreviated form as the chapter evolves; these reviews are useful for preliminary skim reading as well as for review.

Boxes to give both current event and historical perspectives. Many of the text's boxes explain how to decipher recent news stories about economic policy. Others examine the contributions of the great economists such as Adam Smith and Alfred Marshall, the history of great ideas, and key historical events.

Functional use of full color to distinguish between curves and to show how the curves shift dynamically over time. An example of the effective use of multiple colors can be found in the discussion of increasing opportunity costs in Chapter 2.

Complete captions and small conversation boxes in graphs. The captions and the small yellow-shaded conversation boxes, such as in the graph in the margin, make many of the figures completely self-contained. In some graphs, sequential numbering of these conversation boxes stresses the dynamic nature of the curves.

Use of photos and cartoons to illustrate abstract ideas. Special care has gone into the selection of photos to illustrate difficult economic ideas such as inelastic supply curves or opportunity costs. Each text photo (many consisting of two or three parts) has a short title and caption to explain its relevance to the text discussion.

Key term definitions in the margin and a listing of the terms at the end of every chapter and appendix. There is also an alphabetized glossary at the end of the book.

Questions for review at the end of every chapter. These are tests of recall and require only short answers; they can be used for oral review or as a quick self-check.

Problems, an essential tool in learning economics, have been carefully selected and tested. An ample supply of these appear in every chapter and appendix. Some of these problems ask the reader to work out examples that are slightly different from

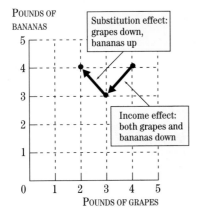

the ones in the text; others require a more critical thinking approach. A second set of problems which parallels those at the end of each chapter has been developed for the second edition. Included in the accompanying test bank, this problem set is also available to instructors via the web site.

A COMPLETE PACKAGE OF TEACHING AND LEARNING AIDS

The highly effective teaching and learning package prepared to accompany the text has been completely revised, updated, and expanded. It provides a full range of support for instructors and students.

Micro and Macro Study Guides.   David Papell of the University of Houston, John Solow of the University of Iowa, and Wm. Stewart Mounts, Jr. of Mercer University have prepared the study guides for the text. In my view, these study guides provide a wonderful learning opportunity that many students will value. Each chapter contains an overview, informal chapter reviews, and a section called "Zeroing In," which harnesses student intuition to explain the chapter's most important concepts. The study guides also provide ample means for practice in using the economic ideas and graphs introduced in each text chapter. A section called "Working It Out" provides worked problems that take students step by step through the analytical process needed to solve real-world applications of core concepts covered in the chapter. End-of-part quizzes offer students one last chance to test their retention of material before taking in-class exams.

Taylor Tutorial and Simulation Software.   A flexible, interactive computerized tutorial is available for students to review basic concepts covered in the text. A tutorial for each chapter in the text provides a second opportunity for students to review concepts and models and then to test themselves on what they've learned. A glossary and context-sensitive help are always available. The simulation component of the software includes more than 60 years of data on more than 20 key economic indicators, allowing students to graph and compare various measurement instruments and print out their results.

Micro and Macro Test Banks.   A reliable test bank is the most important resource for efficient and effective learning and teaching. Micro and Macro Test Banks have been prepared by Stuart Glosser of the University of Wisconsin, Whitewater, and myself. They contain more than 5,000 test questions—including multiple choice, true/false, short answer, and problems—many of which are based on graphs. The questions are coded for correct answer, question type, level of difficulty, and text topic. At the end of each test bank chapter is a set of problems that parallels the end-of-chapter problems from the text.

Computerized Testing Program.   A sophisticated and user-friendly program called ESA Test is available so that instructors can quickly create tests according to various selection criteria, including random selection. The program prints graphs as well as the text part of each question. Instructors can scramble the answer choices, edit questions, add their own questions to the pool, and customize their exams in various other ways. The program is available in Windows and Mac versions.

Instructor's Resource Manual.   Prepared by Wm. Stewart Mounts, Jr. of Mercer University, Denise Hixson of Midlands Technical College, Columbia, SC, and myself, the Instructor's Resource Manual provides both first-time and experienced instructors with a variety of additional resources for use with the text. Each chapter contains a brief overview, teaching objectives, key terms from the text, a section that orients instructors to the text's unique approach, and a suggested lecture outline with teaching tips that provide additional examples not found in the text and hints for teaching more difficult material. Discussion topics and solutions to end-of-chapter text problems are also provided.

Overhead Transparencies.   A set of full-color transparencies for all of the numbered figures used to describe the economic models or theories in the text is available for those who are using the text. I usually use two overhead projectors in class so that more than one figure or table can be shown simultaneously.

Power Presentation Manager.   This Windows-based software, developed by Houghton Mifflin, allows instructors to create customized lecture presentations that can be displayed on computer-based projection systems. The software, which includes a run-time version of Microsoft PowerPoint, makes available the figures, tables, and key equations from the text and also allows for access to laser disk sequences, instructors' own PowerPoint sets, and screens from other Windows-based software. With the Power Presentation Manager, instructors can quickly and easily integrate all these components—and create their own screens as well—to prepare a seamless classroom presentation with minimal in-class tinkering.

Classroom Experiments: A User's Guide.   As I mentioned previously, the text makes use of results from experimental economics to test models and to explain how markets work. I have regularly used experiments in my introductory economics classes—both small sections and large lectures—to illustrate how markets work, and it seems that more and more instructors are incorporating experiments into their classroom teaching. For those instructors who would like to do similar experiments, a lab manual has been prepared by Greg Delemeester of Marietta College and John Neral of Frostburg State University. Written with the first-time user in mind, the manual includes detailed step-by-step instructions for conducting 18 experiments, including the double auction experiment described in Chapter 7 of the text.

Economics Video Series.   This exciting teaching tool, which combines footage from my own classroom, animated charts and graphs, and additional narration, brings key economic ideas from the text to life. The video segments can be used as lecture launchers or as a review of material both inside and outside the classroom. The videos also serve as an introduction to some of the concepts that are unique to my text—such as the experimental auction or the development of the aggregate demand and price adjustment graph.

Web Site.   The web site (http://www.hmco.com/college), developed to accompany this text, provides an extended learning environment for students and a rich store of teaching resources for instructors. With materials carefully chosen to complement and supplement each chapter, students will find key economic links for every chapter as well as numerous ways to test their mastery of chapter content—including extended web-based assignments developed by John Kane of SUNY, Oswego. Another feature allows students and instructors to submit questions or comments about the text, which I will answer on-line. Instructors will find a complete set of parallel questions matching the end-of-chapter problems from the text (with answers), economic and teaching resource links, teaching tips, and the opportunity to view and demo the teaching and student software components of the teaching package.

ACKNOWLEDGMENTS

Completing a project like this is a team effort. I have had the chance to work with an excellent team of professionals at Houghton Mifflin. I worked closely with Bonnie Binkert, Ann West, and Margaret Kearney on this edition and I am grateful to them for their help and encouragement. I would also like to thank Priscilla Abreu, Juli Bliss, Patricia English, Carol Merrigan, Penny Peters, and Adrienne Vincent.

I am grateful to many of my colleagues at Stanford whom I consulted hundreds of times and to the Economics 1 students who used the book and gave me feedback that helped me determine when and where to add that extra sentence of explanation.

Many college teachers and researchers read all or part of the manuscript and gave very helpful comments that were incorporated into revisions. The book would not exist without the help of these reviewers, who are listed below. In particular, I wish to thank David Figlio, Denise Hixson, and David Spencer, who reviewed the text for accuracy during the last stages of production.

My family deserves very special thanks for putting up with me and with the seemingly endless early morning phone calls and piles of manuscript, news clippings, reviews, galleys, and page proof scattered about the house as I worked on the second edition. This book is dedicated to my family.

John B. Taylor
Stanford, California

REVIEWERS

Mark D. Agee
Pennsylvania State University, Altoona

Lee J. Alston
University of Illinois

Christine Amsler
Michigan State University

Charles Andrews
Mercer University

Dean Baim
Pepperdine University

Raymond S. Barnstone
Northeastern University and Lesley College

Kari Battaglia
University of North Texas

Klaus G. Becker
Texas Tech University

Valerie R. Bencivenga
Cornell University

Roger Bowles
University of Bath

Jozell Brister
Abilene Christian University

Paula Bracy
University of Toledo

Robert Brown
Texas Technical University

Robert Buchele
Smith College

Michael R. Butler
Texas Christian University

Richard Call
American River College

Leonard A. Carlson
Emory University

Michael J. Carter
University of Massachusetts, Lowell

Kenneth Chinn
Southeastern Oklahoma State University

Mike Cohick
Collin County Community College

Eric D. Craft
University of Richmond

William F. Chapel
University of Mississippi

Marcelo Clerici-Arias
Stanford University

Stephen L. Cobb
University of North Texas

Kathy L. Combs
California State University, Los Angeles

Joyce Cooper
Boston University

Steven Craig
University of Houston

Michael A. Curme
Miami University

Ward S. Curran
Trinity College

Audrey Davidson
University of Louisville

Joseph Daniels
Marquette University

Gregg Davis
Marshall University

Gregory E. DeFreitas
Hofstra University

Mary E. Deily
Lehigh University

David N. DeJong
University of Pittsburgh

David Denslow
University of Florida

Enrica Detragiache
Johns Hopkins University

Michael Devereux
University of British Columbia

Michael Dowd
University of Toledo

Douglas Downing
Seattle Pacific University

Dean Dudley
United States Military Academy

Mary E. Edwards
St. Cloud State University

David Figlio
University of Oregon

Gerald Friedman
University of Massachusetts, Amherst

Edwin T. Fujii
University of Hawaii

Mary Gade
Oklahoma State University

Janet Gerson
University of Michigan

J. Robert Gillette
University of Kentucky

Donna Ginther
Southern Methodist College

Mark Glick
University of Utah

Stuart M. Glosser
University of Wisconsin, Whitewater

Phil Graves
University of Colorado, Boulder

Paul W. Grimes
Mississippi State University

Lorna S. Gross
Worcester State College

Shoshana Grossbard-Shechtman
San Diego State University

Alan Haight
Bowling Green State University

David R. Hakes
University of Northern Iowa

Greg Hamilton
Marist College

David Hansen
Linfield College

Mehidi Harian
Bloomsburg University

Richard Harper
University of West Florida

Mitchell Harwitz
State University of New York, Buffalo

Mary Ann Hendryson
Western Washington University

James B. Herendeen
University of Texas, El Paso

Pershing J. Hill
University of Alaska, Anchorage

Denise Hixson
Midlands Technical College

Gail Mitchell Hoyt
University of Richmond

James M. Hvidding
Kutztown University

Beth Ingram
University of Iowa

Joyce Jacobsen
Wesleyan University

Syed Jafri
Tarleton State University

David Jaques
California Polytech University, Pomona

John Jascot
Capital Community Technical College

Allan Jenkins
University of Nebraska, Kearney

David Johnson
Wilfred Laurier University

Charles W. Johnston
University of Michigan, Flint

Nake Kamrany
University of Southern California

John Kane
State University of New York, Oswego

Manfred Keil
Claremont McKenna College

Elizabeth Kelly
University of Wisconsin, Madison

Kristen Keith
University of Alaska

John Klein
Georgia State University

Harry T. Kolendrianos
Danville Community College

Margaret Landman
Bridgewater State College

Philip J. Lane
Fairfield University

William Lang
Rutgers University

William D. Lastrapes
University of Georgia

Jim Lee
Fort Hays State University

Lawrence A. Leger
Loughborough University

David Li
University of Michigan

Susan Linz
Michigan State University

John K. Lodewijks
University of New South Wales

R. Ashley Lyman
University of Idaho

Craig MacPhee
University of Nebraska, Lincoln

Michael Magura
University of Toledo

Robert A. Margo
Vanderbilt University

John D. Mason
Gordon College

Robert McAuliffe
Babson College

Henry N. McCarl
University of Alabama, Birmingham

Laurence C. McCulloch
Ohio State University

Rob Roy McGregor
University of North Carolina, Charlotte

Richard McIntyre
University of Rhode Island

Gaminie Meepagala
Howard University

Douglas Morgan
University of California, Santa Barbara

Micke Meurs
American University

Khan A. Mohabbat
Northern Illinois University

Norma Morgan
Curry College

W. Douglas Morgan
University of California, Santa Barbara

Wm. Stewart Mounts, Jr.
Mercer University

Vai-Lam Mui
University of Southern California

David C. Murphy
Boston College

Ronald C. Necoechea
Ball State University

Hong V. Nguyen
University of Scranton

Rachel Nugent
Pacific Lutheran University

Anthony Patrick O'Brien
Lehigh University

William C. O'Connor
Western Montana College

Eliot S. Orton
New Mexico State University

David Papell
University of Houston

Walter Park
American University

Charles Parker
Wayne State College

James Payne
Eastern Kentucky University

E. Charles Pflanz
Scottsdale Community College

William A. Phillips
University of Southern Maine

Glenn J. Platt
Miami University

Charles Plott
California Institute of Technology

Lidija Polutnik
Babson College

David L. Prychitko
State University of New York, Oswego

Salim Rashid
University of Illinois, Urbana-Champaign

Margaret A. Ray
Mary Washington College

Geoffrey Renshaw
University of Warwick

John Ridpath
York University

Greg Rose
Sacramento City College

B. Peter Rosendorff
University of Southern California

Robert Rossana
Wayne State University

Marina Rosser
James Madison University

Kartic C. Roy
University of Queensland

Daniel Rubenson
Southern Oregon State College

Jeffrey Rubin
Rutgers University

Robert S. Rycroft
Mary Washington College

Jonathan Sandy
University of San Diego

Jeff Sarbaum
State University of New York, Binghamton

Gary Saxonhouse
University of Michigan

Edward Scahill
University of Scranton

James Byron Schlomach
Texas A&M University

Torsten Schmidt
University of New Hampshire

Thomas J. Shea
Springfield College

William J. Simeone
Providence College

Michael Smitka
Washington & Lee University

Ronald Soligo
Rice University

John L. Solow
University of Iowa

Clifford Sowell
Berea College

Michael Spagat
Brown University

David Spencer
Brigham Young University

J. R. Stanfield
Colorado State University

Ann B. Sternlicht
University of Richmond

Richard Stevenson
Liverpool University

James Stodder
Rensselaer Polytechnic Institute

Leslie S. Stratton
University of Arizona

Robert Stuart
Rutgers University

James Swoffard
University of South Alabama

Bette Lewis Tokar
Holy Family College

Paul Turner
University of Leeds

Gerald R. Visgilio
Connecticut College

Manhar Vyas
University of Pittsburgh

William V. Weber
Eastern Illinois University

Karl Wesolowski
Salem State College

Joseph Wesson
State University of New York, Potsdam

Geoff Whittam
University of Glasgow

Kenneth P. Wickman
State University of New York, Cortland

Catherine Winnett
University of Bath

Jennifer P. Wissink
Cornell University

Simon Wren-Lewis
University of Strathclyde

Peter R. Wyman
Spokane Falls Community College

Ali Zaker Shahrak
University of Santa Clara

1 part

Introduction to Economics and Its Foundations

A market economy is a social system in which most goods and services produced by people are sold to other people in markets at freely determined prices. But what exactly is a market? And how are prices determined? Does a market economy improve people's lives? If so, why, and by how much compared with other economic systems, such as the economies of primitive societies where little was bought or sold in markets, or those in modern societies where buying and selling has been severely restricted in some way? These are the most fundamental questions of economics and they are addressed in the first four chapters of the book. To answer these questions you must learn to "think like an economist."

Chapters 1 and 2 together define economics and present the first inklings of how economists think. In

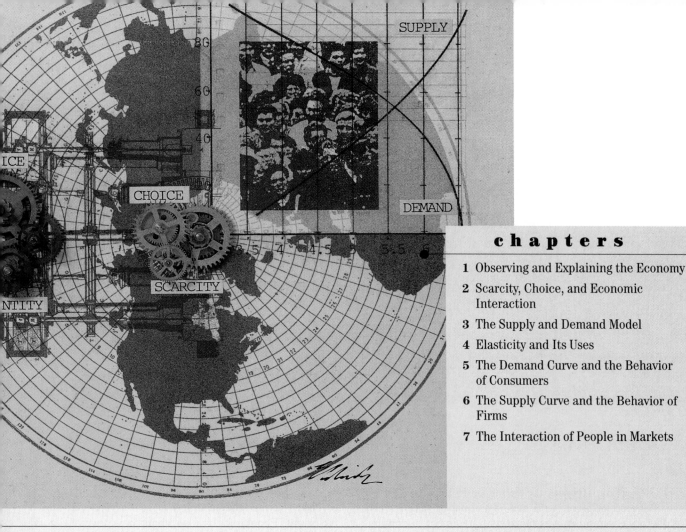

chapters

1 Observing and Explaining the Economy

2 Scarcity, Choice, and Economic Interaction

3 The Supply and Demand Model

4 Elasticity and Its Uses

5 The Demand Curve and the Behavior of Consumers

6 The Supply Curve and the Behavior of Firms

7 The Interaction of People in Markets

Chapter 1 we show how economists observe and explain economic facts. In Chapter 2 we delineate three unifying themes of economics: *scarcity* of time or resources, *choices* among several alternative ends, and the *interaction* of people in using the resources to achieve the ends. In Chapters 3 and 4 we reveal a one-hundred-year-old model—called the supply and demand model—which economists still use every day to explain how markets work. In the trio of Chapters 5, 6, and 7, we explain why and under what circumstances markets can improve people's lives. The discussion of consumer behavior in Chapter 5 and the behavior of firms in Chapter 6 leads to Chapter 7's description of how consumers and firms interact in markets. It is in Chapter 7 that we show why competitive markets—those with many buyers and sellers—are "efficient." We use results from experiments in economics to test the models and explain how they work.

These ideas and models are of great use to economists working for the government and for private business firms. When economists object to government controls on prices, they have these models in mind. When they argue that restrictions on the imports of foreign goods will cost consumers dearly, they use the supply and demand model to calculate the cost. When economists make recommendations for improving the operation of government or firms, they think about how markets provide incentives; they sometimes find ways for government or organizations to mimic the market. Once you understand the models you can use them to help form and defend your own ideas on these important issues.

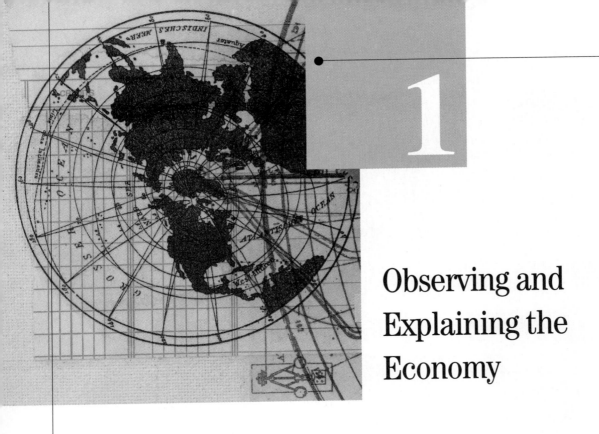

Observing and Explaining the Economy

1

This is a true story. In the spring of 1996, a 19-year-old college sophomore, who had just finished taking introductory economics, was faced with a *choice:* to continue college for an additional two years or to devote full time to a job. The job was being a professional golfer on the pro tour—a job for which the sophomore was uniquely qualified, having won three U.S. amateur titles. Doing both college and the pro tour was not an option because time is *scarce:* With only 24 hours in the day, he simply did not have time to do both. For this sophomore, completing college had a great cost: not only the two years of college expenses, but also the foregone tournament winnings and advertising endorsements (over $40 million) that a successful pro golf career would bring. The golfer—his name is Tiger Woods—made a choice. He became a pro. By the fall of 1996 he was selected Sportsman of the Year by *Sports Illustrated,* and in April 1997 he stunned the golfing world with a record-setting win of the venerable Masters Tournament—winning nearly half a million dollars.

More than anything else, economics is about such choices: whether to go to college or get a job after high school, to take economics or biology, to invest in one stock or another, to take one job or another, to go to work or stay home with children, or even whether to buy a cup of coffee at the student union or at a stylish café down the street. Economics is also about how to make good collective decisions as citizens of a community, state, or country. Decisions about what sort of taxes should be levied, whether bridges should be free or have tolls, or whether citizens of other countries should be allowed to trade freely with and migrate to your country are all informed by economics. Whether it is Tiger Woods, you, your best friend, your teacher, the president of a large firm, or even the president of the United States, the economic principles underlying the decisions are the same. Economics helps individuals and societies make choices about the challenges and opportunities they face.

The world faces a variety of economic challenges and opportunities as we move from the twentieth to the twenty-first century. Smaller improvements in living standards—a trend that started in the 1970s—are leaving many people in the current generation little better off than their parents, if better off at all. The gap between the wages of low-skilled and high-skilled workers has widened. Aside from a few notable exceptions in east Asia, many less-developed countries have not significantly reduced the gap between themselves and the more developed countries, such as the United States, in the last 50 years. People worry about losing their jobs to foreign workers in an increasingly global economy.

Yet, if we look around the world, we see tremendous economic opportunities. Political revolutions—symbolized by the tearing down of the Berlin Wall in 1989—have freed billions of people from tight government controls on their economies. Advances in information and transportation technologies have opened up new markets to sell and buy goods. Experience with a great inflation in the 1970s has taught us important lessons about how and why to keep inflation low, complementing the lessons about unemployment taught earlier by the Great Depression of the 1930s.

How we—workers, students, parents, consumers, retirees, politicians, voters—approach these economic challenges and opportunities will depend on our knowledge of how the economy works. If our economic knowledge is sound and if we apply it well, we can transform the challenges and opportunities into genuinely improved outcomes. Fifty years from now, historians will look back to the turn of the century to determine why the first decades of the twenty-first century were so good, or so bad. They will study how people applied their economic knowledge to decisions concerning jobs, education, child-rearing, consumption, retirement, and the role of government.

The purpose of this book is to introduce you to the field of economics and to help you understand the eco-

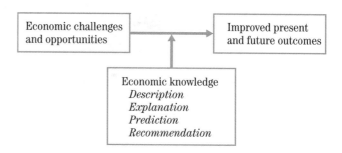

nomic challenges and opportunities you face as an individual and as a participant in the world economy. The objective is not to peek passively but to analyze actively. Economics is a way of thinking. It entails accurately *describing* economic events, *explaining* why the events occur, *predicting* under what circumstances such events might take place in the future, and *recommending* appropriate courses of action. To make use of economics, you will want to learn to do the describing, the explaining, and even the predicting and recommending yourself; that is, to reason and to think like an economist.

In answer to the question "What is economics?" a wisecracking economist once said, "It's what economists do." To get us started in our study of economics, this chapter examines two of the main things economists do: documenting and quantifying observations about the economy and developing and using models of how the economy works.

OBSERVATIONS: WHAT ECONOMISTS ENDEAVOR TO EXPLAIN

Just as physicists try to explain the existence of black holes in outer space or biologists try to explain why dinosaurs became extinct, economists try to explain puzzling observations and facts about the economy. Many observations come from everyday life. You might want to begin your study of economics by asking questions about economic observations—from your own experience, from recent news stories, from your history or political science courses. Perhaps some of your questions might be on topics like these:

▶ Why did health-care spending increase so rapidly compared to the rest of the U.S. economy in the last 20 years?

▶ Why did the price of health care increase more than most other prices?

▶ Why has the price of a college education also been increasing rapidly?

▶ Why have the wages of college-educated people increased much more rapidly than the wages of high school dropouts since the 1970s?

▶ What caused the Great Depression of the 1930s?

▶ Why is the average income of people in the United States about 30 times higher than that of people in China?

▶ Why is unemployment much higher in Europe than in the United States?

All these questions are based on observations about the economy. Some, like rising college tuition, are fairly obvious and are based on casual observation. But in order to answer such questions, economists, like physicists or biologists, need to systematically document and quantify their observations and look for patterns. If we can establish the date when dinosaurs became extinct, then we might test our hunch that a cataclysmic event such as an asteroid hitting the earth may have caused their extinction. To illustrate how economists document and quantify their observations, let us briefly focus on the first two of the preceding questions, the ones concerning health care and the economy.

Documenting and Quantifying Observations: A Case Study

Rising health-care spending and prices are more than a curiosity. The more a society spends on health care, the less it can spend on other things. Concerns about rising health-care spending have led to major proposals for changing how health care is provided and paid for in the United States. Throughout the 1990s, health care has been a major political issue. For example, debates about how to slow rising spending on Medicare—a government health-care program for the elderly—raged during the 1996 presidential and congressional elections. Let's see how the facts about health-care spending are put together.

In order to determine whether health-care spending has increased relative to the rest of the economy, as stated in the first question, we need a measure of health-care spending and a measure of the size of the overall economy.

GDP, Health Care, and the Health-Care Share

gross domestic product (GDP): a measure of the value of all the goods and services newly produced in an economy during a specified period of time.

The most comprehensive available measure of the size of an economy is the **gross domestic product (GDP).** For the United States, GDP is the total value of all products made in the United States during a specified period of time, such as a year. GDP includes all newly made goods, such as cars, trucks, shoes, airplanes, houses, and telephones; it also includes services, such as education, rock concerts, and health care. To measure the total value of all products made in the economy, economists add up all the dollars that people spend on the products.

How large is GDP in the United States? In 1995, it was $7,246 billion, or about $7.2 trillion. We can compute GDP in any year, and the question about health-care spending and the size of the economy requires that we look at the economy over time. In 1977, GDP was $2,027 billion. Column (1) of Table 1.1 provides a 20-year history of GDP.

economic history: the study of economic events and the collection of economic observations from the past.

In order to document observations and look for patterns, economists usually need to look back at some historical period and see what happened. The study of economic events of the past is called **economic history.** Economic historians frequently go back much more than 20 years to obtain observations. For example,

Year	(1) GDP	(2) Health-Care Spending	(3) Health-Care Share of GDP (percent)
1977	2,027	123	6.1
1978	2,291	140	6.1
1979	2,558	158	6.2
1980	2,784	181	6.5
1981	3,116	213	6.8
1982	3,242	239	7.4
1983	3,515	268	7.6
1984	3,902	294	7.5
1985	4,181	322	7.7
1986	4,422	346	7.8
1987	4,692	381	8.1
1988	5,050	429	8.5
1989	5,439	477	8.8
1990	5,744	538	9.4
1991	5,917	586	9.9
1992	6,244	647	10.4
1993	6,550	697	10.6
1994	6,931	739	10.7
1995	7,246	784	10.8
1996	7,576	816	10.8

TABLE 1.1
GDP and Health-Care Spending, 1977–1996

Note: GDP and health-care spending are measured in billions of dollars.
Source: U.S. Department of Commerce.

100 times column 2 divided by column 1

Robert Fogel, an economic historian who won the Nobel Prize in economics in 1993, has gone back over 300 years to collect data on nutrition and health, partly to better understand rising health-care spending today. As Fogel stated in his Nobel lecture, "Uncovering what actually happened in the past requires an enormous investment in time and effort."[1] Although covering a relatively short period, the observations shown in Table 1.1 are enough to illustrate how economists quantify their observations.

Economists frequently use graphs to present data like those shown in Table 1.1. For example, Figure 1.1 plots the data on GDP from column (1) of Table 1.1. The vertical axis is measured in billions of dollars; the horizontal axis is measured in years. For example, the point at the extreme lower left in Figure 1.1 represents GDP of $2,027 billion (on the vertical axis) in the year 1977 (on the horizontal axis). The points are connected by a line, which helps us visualize the steadily growing GDP during this period.

Now let us consider health-care spending, which includes payments for hospital services, lab tests, nursing homes, visits to the doctor or dentist, drugs, hearing aids, and eyeglasses. By adding up all spending on health care, we get $784 billion in 1995. This amount is about three times as large as the entire automobile industry, including cars, trucks, and parts.

1. Robert W. Fogel, "Economic Growth, Population Theory, and Physiology: The Bearing of Long-Term Processes on the Making of Economic Policy," *American Economic Review,* June 1994, p. 389.

FIGURE 1.1

Gross Domestic Product (GDP) in the United States, 1977–1996

GDP is the total dollar value of newly produced goods and services. It can be measured by adding up what people spend on everything from health care to cars. For each year from 1977 to 1996, GDP is plotted; the line connects all the points.

Source: U.S. Department of Commerce.

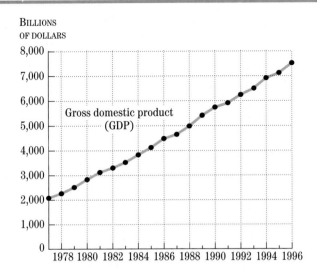

FIGURE 1.2

Spending on Health Care in the United States, 1977–1996

Health-care spending is the dollar value of payments for hospitals, doctors, dentists, nursing homes, drugs, and other items that provide medical care. Health care is one part of GDP.

Source: U.S. Department of Commerce.

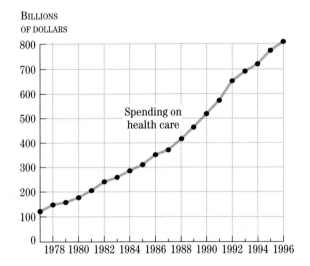

FIGURE 1.3

Health-Care Spending as a Percent of GDP

Each point in the graph is the ratio of spending on health care from Figure 1.2 to GDP from Figure 1.1, measured as a percent. For example, in 1995, health-care spending was $784 billion and GDP was $7,246 billion. The ratio is 784/7,246 = .108, or 10.8 percent.

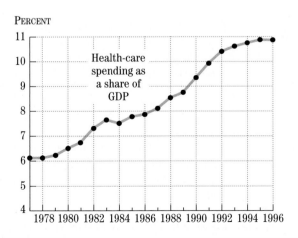

Health-care spending from 1977 to 1996 is listed in column (2) of Table 1.1 and is plotted in Figure 1.2. Figures 1.1 and 1.2 show that both GDP and health-care spending have grown since 1977. One way to assess the growth of health-care spending compared to spending on all goods and services is to look at health-care spending as a share, or percentage, of GDP. For example, health-care spending in 1995 was $784 billion; GDP was $7,246 billion. Thus, the share (in percentage terms) of GDP going to health care was

$$\frac{\text{Health-care spending}}{\text{GDP}} \times 100 = \begin{array}{l}\text{health-care spending}\\\text{as a share of GDP}\end{array}$$

$$\frac{784}{7,246} \times 100 = 10.8 \text{ percent}$$

Column (3) of Table 1.1 performs this calculation for all years from 1977 to 1996. Again, you can observe a pattern by plotting the shares, as in Figure 1.3. Health-care spending has been rising as a percent of GDP—or relative to the size of the economy, although it has recently started to slow down. Although both GDP and health-care spending have been increasing, health-care spending has been increasing more quickly, at least until recently. We have now quantified the observation about rising health-care spending. Now let us go on to consider the second question about health care and see whether the price of health care has risen compared with the price of other goods and services in the economy.

Overall Price Level, Health-Care Price, and Relative Price

Column (1) of Table 1.2 shows a measure of the average price of all the goods and services in GDP. Economists gather this information from surveys of prices of individual goods and services. They average these prices, giving greater weight to the prices of items on which more is spent. This average, plotted in Figure 1.4, is called the **overall price level.** A quick glance at the figure shows the increasing trend in the overall price level. There is a tendency for all prices to rise over time. The general increase in prices over time is called **inflation.** The **inflation rate** is defined as the percentage increase in the overall price level from one year to the next. The inflation rate has never fallen below zero during these years; in other words, the price level has never declined.

The tendency for the overall price level to rise over time affects our measure of GDP. Economists correct GDP for the rise in the overall price level and get a measure called **real GDP.** Real GDP can be computed by dividing GDP by the overall price level. Real GDP increases much less rapidly than GDP.

Having examined the overall price level, let us now determine whether the increase in the price of health care is greater than the increase in the overall price level. Column (2) of Table 1.2 shows a measure of the price of health care from lab tests to drugs. It is an average of the prices of all the items we included in our measure of health-care spending. Figure 1.5 plots the price of health care; like the overall price level, it has increased.

Now, to determine whether the price of health care has increased more or less rapidly than the overall price level, we look at the relative price of health care. The **relative price** is a measure of health-care prices compared with the average prices of all goods and services. It is computed by dividing the health-care price by the overall price level:

$$\frac{\text{Relative price}}{\text{of health care}} = \frac{\text{health-care price}}{\text{overall price level}}$$

overall price level: an average of the prices of all goods and services with greater weight given to items on which more is spent.

inflation: an increase in the overall price level.

inflation rate: the percentage increase in the overall price level from one year to the next.

real gross domestic product (real GDP): a measure of the value of all the goods and services newly produced in a country during some period of time, adjusted for inflation.

relative price: the price of a particular good compared to the price of other goods.

FIGURE 1.4
The Overall Price Level in the United States

The overall price level in the economy is like an average of prices of all goods and services in GDP. The overall price level has risen every year from 1977 to 1996.

Source: U.S. Department of Commerce.

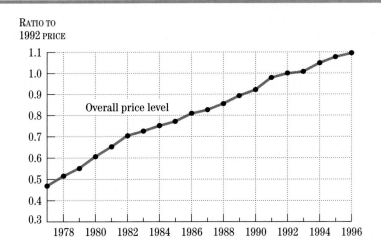

FIGURE 1.5
The Price of Health Care

The average price of health care has increased sharply since the 1970s, although the increase has slowed somewhat in the 1990s.

Source: U.S. Department of Commerce.

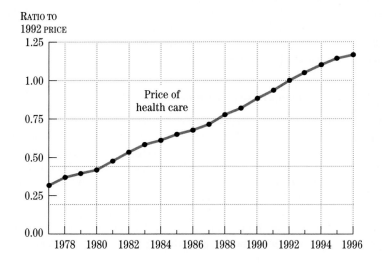

FIGURE 1.6
Relative Price of Health Care

The figure shows the ratio of the price of health care from Figure 1.5 to the overall price level from Figure 1.4. Health-care prices have risen more rapidly than the overall price level in most years. Hence, the relative price of health care has increased.

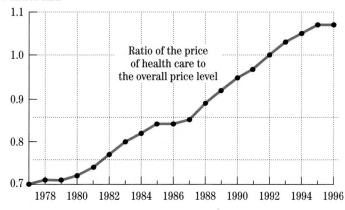

Year	(1) Overall Price Level	(2) Health-Care Price	(3) Relative Health-Care Price
1977	0.474	0.331	0.70
1978	0.510	0.363	0.71
1979	0.553	0.394	0.71
1980	0.604	0.436	0.72
1981	0.659	0.488	0.74
1982	0.701	0.541	0.77
1983	0.731	0.583	0.80
1984	0.759	0.623	0.82
1985	0.784	0.656	0.84
1986	0.806	0.678	0.84
1987	0.831	0.709	0.85
1988	0.861	0.764	0.89
1989	0.897	0.829	0.92
1990	0.936	0.892	0.95
1991	0.973	0.944	0.97
1992	1.000	1.000	1.00
1993	1.026	1.059	1.03
1994	1.050	1.105	1.05
1995	1.075	1.146	1.07
1996	1.097	1.170	1.07

TABLE 1.2
The Overall Price Level and the Price of Health Care

Note: The prices in columns (1) and (2) are given as a ratio to the price in 1992. This year is arbitrary: Using another year would not change the patterns of the relative price.
Source: U.S. Department of Commerce.

Column 2 divided by column 1

The relative price of health care is shown in column (3) of Table 1.2 and is plotted in Figure 1.6. Although the prices of all goods have increased on average, the price of health care has risen more rapidly in most years. Thus, we have quantified the second observation about health care: The price of health care has increased relative to the overall price level.

Interpreting the Observations

We have developed two economic variables to quantify our observations about health care in the United States. These variables are (1) the share of health-care spending in GDP and (2) the relative price of health care. An **economic variable** is any economic measure that can vary over a range of values. How have these two variables been related? Are there interesting patterns? How do we interpret the patterns?

Figure 1.7 shows how the relative price of health care and the health-care share of GDP have been related. Each point in the figure corresponds to a relative price and a health-care share taken from the last columns of Table 1.1 and Table 1.2. The relative price is on the vertical axis and the share of health care in GDP is on the horizontal axis.

economic variable: any economic measure that can vary over a range of values.

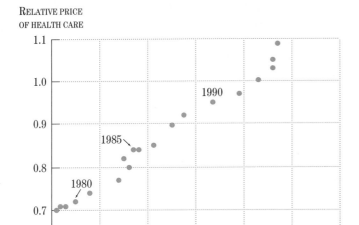

RELATIVE PRICE
OF HEALTH CARE

FIGURE 1.7
Relative Price of Health Care versus Health-Care Spending Share
The figure plots pairs of points: the relative price of health care on the vertical axis and health-care spending as a share of GDP on the horizontal axis. The observations come from the last columns of Table 1.1 and Table 1.2.

correlation: the degree to which economic variables are observed to move together: If they move in the same direction there is positive correlation; if they move in opposite directions there is negative correlation.

causation: a relation of cause and effect between variables in which one variable is a determinant of another variable.

controlled experiments: empirical tests of theories in a controlled setting in which particular effects can be isolated.

The points in Figure 1.7 trace out a close **correlation:** As the relative price of health care has increased, so has spending on health care as a share of GDP. Two variables are correlated if they tend to move up or down around the same time. There is a *positive correlation* if the two variables move in the same direction: When one goes up, the other goes up. The share of health-care spending in GDP and the relative price of health care are positively correlated.

Two variables are negatively correlated if they tend to move in opposite directions. If we had observed that the lower relative prices of health care were associated with higher spending shares, then there would have been a *negative correlation*.

Correlation versus Causation

Just because there is a correlation between two variables does not mean that one caused the other. There is a difference between *causation* and *correlation*. Correlation means that one event is usually observed to occur along with another. For example, high readings on a thermometer occur when it is hot outside. **Causation** means that one event brings about another event. But correlation does not imply causation. For example, the high reading on the thermometer does not cause the hot weather even though the high reading and the hot weather are correlated. In this example, we know that the causation goes the other way around: Hot weather causes the reading on the thermometer to be high.

More to the point of economics, if you look at the correlation in Figure 1.7, you might be tempted to say that the higher price of health care caused health-care spending to rise. But Figure 1.7 alone does not permit us to make such a conclusion about causation. The figure shows a correlation. Because we know a little about how thermometers work and the effects of the weather on temperature, we can draw a conclusion about causation. Similarly, we need to know more about how health care is produced and the effects of the price of health care on health-care spending before we can make statements about causality.

Controlled Experiments

In many sciences—certainly psychology, medicine, and biology—investigators perform **controlled experiments** to determine whether one event causes another event. An example of a controlled experiment is the clinical trial of new drugs. New drugs are tested by trying them out on two groups of individuals. One group gets the drug; the other group gets a placebo (a pill without the drug). If the experiment results in a significantly greater number of people in the group taking the drug being cured than in the control group not taking the drug, then investigators conclude that the drug causes the cure.

Unfortunately, such controlled experiments are rare in economics. In the case of health-care prices and health-care spending, we cannot go back and repeat the years from 1977 to 1996 with a different health-care price and see what happens. True, we could look at other countries' experience, or we could look at the experience of different states within the United States. Economists use such comparisons to help determine causation. For example, we could look at one state in which the price of medical care increased and one in which it did not. We could then look at the health-care spending in each state to see if higher prices caused health-care spending to increase. But, unfortunately, no two countries or states are alike in all respects. Thus, attempting to control for other factors is not as easy as in the case of clinical trials.

Experiments in Economics: A New Trend

In recent years economists have adapted some methods of experimental science and have begun to conduct economic experiments in laboratory settings that are similar to the real world. The experiments can be repeated, and various effects can be controlled for. **Experimental economics** is a growing area of economics. The findings of experimental economics have affected economists' understanding of how the economy works. Experiments in economics also provide an excellent way to *learn* how the economy works, much as experiments in science courses can help one learn about gravity or the structure of plant cells. But because it is difficult to replicate real-world settings exactly in such experiments, they have not yet been applied as widely as the clinical or laboratory experiments in other sciences.

experimental economics: a branch of economics that uses laboratory experiments to analyze economic behavior.

Faulty Data

Economic data are not always accurate. People sometimes do not understand the survey questions, are too busy to fill them out carefully, or do not have the correct information. Hospitals reporting data on health-care prices, for example, may not take account of changes in the quality of health care. When people purchase medical care, the quality of the service provided can vary widely over time and from doctor to doctor.

If the quality of health care is improving, then the higher relative prices we have observed might partly reflect better service rather than an increase in the price of the same service. The actual price of health care might have increased less rapidly if we measured the improved quality, such as reduced chances of serious stroke or depression because of better drugs.

The Behavior of People Underlying the Observations

Interpreting economic observations requires that one look behind the data to the behavior of the people whose economic decisions generate the data—for example, the people who consume health care (health-care consumers) and the people who produce health care (health-care producers).

Economists often group the people who consume goods and services into *households* (see Figure 1.8). A household is an individual or a group of individuals who share the same living quarters. For example, a household could be a group of recent college graduates sharing an apartment, a divorced person living alone, a family with four children, or a single retiree. Every individual in an economy belongs to a household, and each household must make decisions about the products and services it consumes.

FIGURE 1.8
A Circular Flow Diagram

This diagram shows how spending in general, and spending on health care in particular, equals production in general, and production of health care in particular. Buying and selling of goods and services takes place in the product market. The inputs to production—from tractors to magnetic resonance imagers—are supplied by households, either as workers or owners. Buying and selling take place in the labor and capital markets.

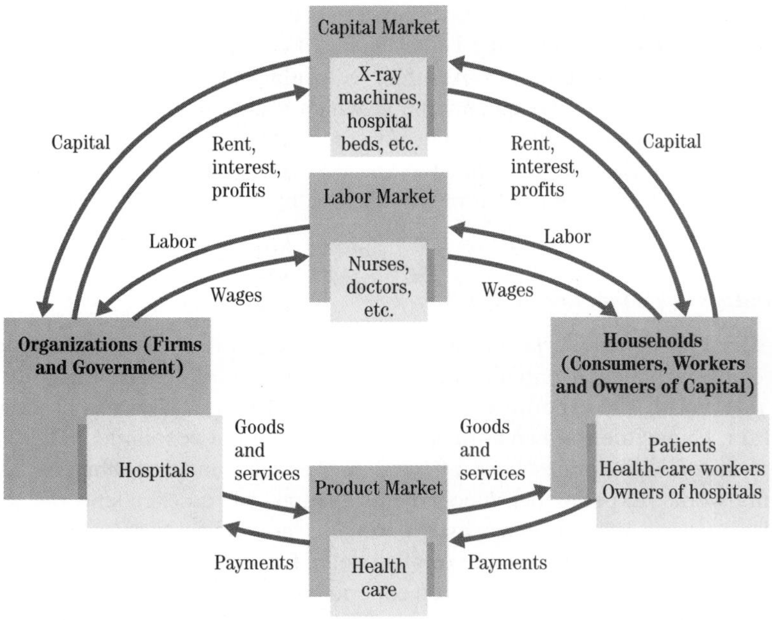

market: an arrangement by which economic exchanges between people take place.

labor: the number of hours people work in producing goods and services.

capital: the factories, improvements to cultivated land, machinery, and other tools, equipment, and structures used to produce goods and services.

inputs or factors of production: labor, capital, and other resources used in the production of goods and services.

Producers of goods and services are often referred to as *organizations,* which include firms and governments (see Figure 1.8). A private hospital, a health maintenance organization (HMO), or a small group practice of doctors are examples of firms producing health care. Governments also produce goods and services, such as national defense, police, education, and, occasionally, health care, but they serve other functions as well—such as the establishment and maintenance of laws and law enforcement. Government can play an important role in influencing economic decision-makers through the laws it sets on taxing and spending, but it is also one of the main tasks of economics to determine what role the government itself should play as a producer and consumer of goods in the economy.

Figure 1.8 also illustrates the working of markets. Households buy goods and services in markets. A **market** refers to an arrangement through which exchanges of goods or services between people take place. For example, HMOs produce health-care services and households purchase the health-care services in the health-care market, shown in the box labeled *product market* at the bottom of Figure 1.8.

Households also supply their **labor** to the firms who employ them; the buying and selling take place in the labor market, also shown in Figure 1.8. For example, a doctor or nurse may be employed by an HMO and receive wages in return. Households also supply other resources to firms—such as machines, land, and equipment—either by owning shares in the firms, renting equipment to the firms, or lending the firms funds to buy equipment. Resources, such as machines, used by firms to produce goods and services are called **capital.** In the health-care industry, capital includes such items as x-ray machines, hospital beds, and doctors' offices. For example, a young couple may rent out the first floor of their house as a doctor's office. They receive rent in return. Capital and labor are also called **inputs** or **factors of production** because they are used to produce goods and services.

Review

▶ Economists endeavor to explain facts and observations about the economy, but it is not always easy to establish what the facts are. Obtaining the relevant economic facts requires a study of economic history and surveys of firms and individuals. To establish patterns, it is necessary to carefully organize and present the information obtained, either in tables or graphs.

▶ GDP is a measure of all the goods and services produced in a country during a period of time. GDP is measured by adding up what people spend. The production of a type of good or service—such as health care—can be measured in the same way as GDP.

▶ Correlation does not imply causation. Because controlled experiments are rare in economics, establishing causation is more difficult than in other sciences.

▶ Recent advances in experimental economics are improving this situation.

▶ Economic observations are not always accurate. For example, the quality of a service such as medical care can be difficult to measure.

▶ Looking at the individual behavior of firms, households, and governments is an important part of interpreting economic observations.

ECONOMIC MODELS

In order to explain economic facts and observations, one needs an economic theory, or a *model*. An **economic model** is an explanation of how the economy or a part of the economy works. In practice, most economists use the terms *theory* and *model* interchangeably, although sometimes the term *theory* suggests a general explanation whereas the term *model* suggests a more specific explanation. The term *law* is also typically used interchangeably with the terms *model* or *theory* in economics.

economic model: an explanation of how the economy or part of the economy works.

What Are Economic Models?

Economic models are always abstractions, or simplifications, of the real world. They take very complicated phenomena, such as the behavior of people, firms, and governments, and simplify them, much like a model of a building used by architects is an abstraction, or simplification, of the actual building. Some models can be very detailed; others are just broad abstractions. Be sure to remember that the model and the phenomenon being explained by the model are different.

Do not be critical of economic models simply because they are simplifications. In every science, models are simplifications of reality. Models are successful if they explain reality reasonably well. In fact, if they were not simplifications, they would be hard to use effectively. Economic models differ from those in the physical sciences because they endeavor to explain human behavior, which is complex and often unpredictable. It is for this reason that the brilliant physicist Max Planck said that economics was harder than physics.

Economic models can be described with words, with numerical tables, with graphs, or with algebra. To use economics, it is important to be able to work with these different descriptions. Figures 1.9 and 1.10 show how models can be illustrated with graphs. By looking at graphs, we can see quickly whether the model has an inverse or direct relationship. If a model says that one variable varies inversely

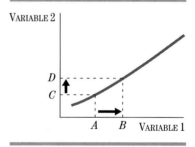

FIGURE 1.9
A Model with Two Positively Related Variables
The upward-sloping line shows how the variables are related. When one variable increases from A to B, the other variable increases from C to D. If one variable declines from B to A, the other variable declines from D to C. We say that variable 1 is positively related to variable 2, or that variable 1 varies directly with variable 2.

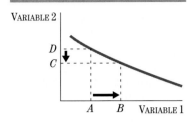

FIGURE 1.10
A Model with Two Negatively Related Variables

When one variable increases from *A* to *B,* the other variable decreases from *D* to *C.* Likewise, when one variable decreases from *B* to *A,* the other variable increases from *C* to *D.* We say variable 1 is negatively related to variable 2, or that variable 1 varies inversely with variable 2.

positively related: a situation in which an increase in one variable is associated with an increase in another variable; also called *directly related.*

negatively related: a situation in which an increase in one variable is associated with a decrease in another variable; also called *inversely related.*

with the other, this means that if the first variable rises, then the second falls. If a model says that one variable varies directly with another, this means that if one variable rises, the other also rises. In economics, the expression "is positively related to" is frequently used in place of the phrase "varies directly with," which is more common in other sciences. Similarly, the expression "is negatively related to" is frequently used in place of "varies inversely with."

In Figure 1.9, two variables—perhaps a relative price variable and a spending variable—are shown to be **positively related.** In other words, when variable 1 increases from *A* to *B,* variable 2 increases from *C* to *D* by the specific amount given by the curve. Likewise, when variable 1 decreases from *B* to *A,* variable 2 decreases from *D* to *C.* In Figure 1.10, a model with two variables that are **negatively related** is shown. Here, when variable 1 increases from *A* to *B,* variable 2 decreases from *D* to *C.* Likewise, when variable 1 decreases from *B* to *A,* variable 2 increases from *C* to *D.* Models have *constants* as well as variables. The constants in the models in Figures 1.9 and 1.10 are the positions and shapes of the curves.

An Example: A Model with Two Variables

Figure 1.11 shows an example of a model describing how doctors employed in a health maintenance organization provide physical examinations. The model states that the more doctors who are employed at the HMO, the more physical exams can be given. The model is represented in four different ways: (1) with words, (2) with a numerical table, (3) with a graph, and (4) with algebra.

On the lower right of Figure 1.11, we have the verbal description: more doctors, more physical exams, but with additional doctors increasing the number of exams by smaller amounts, presumably because the diagnostic facilities at the HMO are limited; for example, there are only so many rooms in the HMO available for physical exams.

On the upper left, we have a table with numbers showing how the number of examinations depends on the number of doctors. Exactly how many examinations are given by each number of doctors is shown in the table. Clearly this table is much more specific than the verbal description. Be sure to distinguish between the meaning of a table that presents a model—like the table in Figure 1.11—and a table that presents data—like Table 1.1. They look similar, but one represents observations about the real world and the other is a model of the real world.

On the upper right, we have a curve showing the relationship between doctors and physical examinations. The curve shows how many exams each number of doctors can perform. The points on the curve are plotted from the information in the table. The vertical axis has the number of examinations; the horizontal axis has the number of doctors. The points are connected with a line to help visualize the curve.

Finally, in the lower left we show the doctor-examination relationship in algebraic form. In this case the number of exams is equal to the square root of the number of doctors times 20. If we give a symbol (*y*) for the number of exams and (*x*) for the number of doctors, the model looks a lot like the equations in an algebra course.

All four representations of models have advantages and disadvantages. The advantage of the verbal representation is that we usually communicate to people in words, and if we want our economic models to have any use we need to communicate with people who have not studied economics. However, the verbal representation is not as precise as the other three. In addition to the verbal analysis, in this book we will focus on the tabular and graphical representations rather than on the algebraic descriptions.

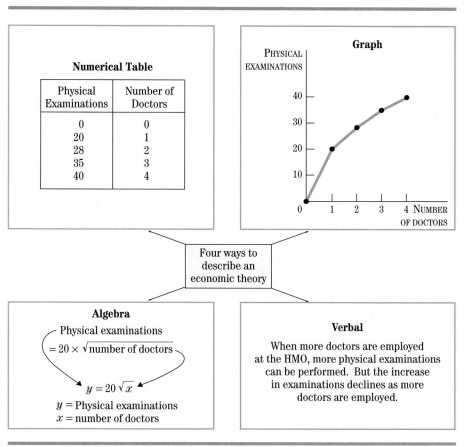

FIGURE 1.11
Economic Models in Four Ways
Each way has advantages and disadvantages; this book focuses mostly on verbal, graphical, and numerical tables, but occasionally some algebra will help to explain things.

Prediction and the Ceteris Paribus *Assumption*

Prediction is one of the most important uses of models. For example, using the model in Figure 1.10, we can predict that if variable 1 rises from *A* to *B*, then variable 2 will fall from *D* to *C*. Using the HMO model for physical exams, we might predict that more doctors at the HMO will increase the number of physicals that can be given. Economists use models to predict variables ranging from GDP next year to the price of medical care in the year 2000.

In order to use models for prediction, economists use the assumption of ***ceteris paribus,*** which means "all other things equal." For example, the prediction that variable 2 will fall from *D* to *C* assumes that the curve in Figure 1.10 does not shift: The position of the curve when variable 1 is at *A* is *equal* to the position of the curve when variable 1 is at *B*. If other things were not equal—if the curve shifted—then we could not predict that variable 2 would fall from *D* to *C* when variable 1 rose from *A* to *B*. Similarly, predicting that more doctors can produce more physical exams assumes that there is no power outage that would cause the diagnostic equipment to stop operating.

ceteris paribus: all other things being equal; refers to holding all other variables constant or keeping all other things the same when one variable is changed.

Microeconomic Models versus Macroeconomic Models

There are two main branches of economics: microeconomics and macroeconomics; thus, there are both microeconomic models and macroeconomic models.

Using Economics to Explain Gender Pay Gaps

Is there a gender pay gap in the United States? Although many people speak generally about the difference between the average pay of women and men in this country, labor economists such as Francine Blau of Cornell University and June O'Neill, formerly at Baruch University and now director of the Congressional Budget Office, have confirmed the existence of a significant gender pay gap—but one that has narrowed in recent years. Women earned 60 percent as much as men earned on average in 1980, but by 1990, women's wages were on average 71 percent that of men.

In order to explain the gender pay gap, labor economists look at the evidence and apply models. Such models indicate that the pay gap is due either to differences in the qualifications of workers (schooling or experience) or to discrimination. According to Francine Blau, "A large body of evidence . . . suggests that both gender differences in qualifications and labor market discrimination as conventionally measured play a role in explaining gender earnings differences. . . . Precisely determining the relative importance of each factor is difficult, however."[*]

Determining the relative importance of qualifications versus discrimination is crucial in court cases involving gender discrimination, in which women bring suit against firms for illegally discriminating. Such cases also illustrate how economics can be used in a partisan as well as a scientific way. Consider, for example, *Stender v. Lucky Stores Inc.,* a recent court case in which a California grocery store chain, Lucky Stores, was sued for discriminating against female workers.

Economists were called as expert witnesses for both sides. Labor economist John Pencavel testified for the plaintiffs, the women who brought the suit. He found that women at Lucky earned between 76 percent and 82 percent as much as Lucky's male workers earned. Pencavel found that women were regularly placed in jobs that paid less than jobs given male coworkers, although there was no significant difference between the education and experience of the workers. There was little difference in the wages of the male and female workers within each type of job; but some jobs paid more than others and women happened to be assigned to the lower-paying jobs.

Joan Haworth, another labor economist, was an expert witness for the defendant, Lucky Stores. She reported survey evidence showing that Lucky's assignment of women and men to different jobs reflected differences in the work preferences of men and women. Thus, Lucky justified its job assignments by arguing that there was a gender difference in attitudes toward work. Lucky argued that its employment policies were based on observed differences in the career aspirations of male and female employees. For example, one manager at Lucky testified that women were more interested in cash register work and men were more interested in floor work.

After weighing the facts and economic arguments, Judge Marilyn Hall Patel decided the case in favor of the plaintiffs. Although male and female employees received equal pay for equal work, she concluded that Lucky's employment policies

Labor economist June O'Neill, Director of the Congressional Budget Office, testifies before Congress in 1997.

involved discrimination. Judge Patel wrote: "The court finds defendant's explanation that the statistical disparities between men and women at Lucky are caused by differences in the work interests of men and women to be unpersuasive."[†]

The decision is a landmark because of the economic analysis that showed that discrimination could exist even if men and women were being paid the same wage for equal work. Of course, not all sex discrimination cases are decided in favor of the plaintiffs. But whoever wins a given case, economics is almost always a key consideration in the judge's decision.

*Francine Blau, "Gender and Economic Outcomes: The Role of Wage Structure," *Labour,* Vol. 7, 1993, pp. 73–92.

[†]*West's Federal Supplement,* Vol. 803 (St. Paul, Minn.: West Publishing Company, 1993), pp. 259–337.

Microeconomics studies the behavior of individual firms and households or specific markets like the health-care market or the college graduate market. It looks at variables such as the price of a college education or the reason for increased wages of college graduates. Microeconomic models explain why the price of gasoline varies from station to station or why there are discount airfares.

Macroeconomics focuses on the whole economy—the whole national economy or even the whole world economy. It tries to explain the changes in GDP over time rather than the changes in a part of GDP like health-care spending. It looks at questions such as what causes the overall price level to rise year after year, why many more workers are unemployed in Europe than in the United States, or why the Great Depression of the 1930s occurred.

microeconomics: the branch of economics that examines individual decision-making at firms and households and the way they interact in specific industries and markets.

macroeconomics: the branch of economics that examines the workings and problems of the economy as a whole—economic growth, inflation, unemployment, and economic fluctuations.

The Use of Existing Models

Because economics has been around for a long time, there are many existing models that can be applied to explain observations or make predictions that are useful to decision-makers. Much of what economists do in practice, whether in government or business or universities, is use models that are already in existence.

The models are used in many different types of applications, from determining the effects of discrimination in the workplace to evaluating the gains from lower health-care prices. Frequently the models are applied in new and clever ways.

The Development of New Models

Like models in other sciences, economic models change and new models are developed. Many of the models in this book are much different from the models in books published 40 years ago. New economic models evolve because some new observations cannot be explained by existing models.

The process of the development of new models or theories in economics proceeds much like any other science. First one develops a *hypothesis,* or a hunch, to explain a puzzling observation. Then one tests the hypothesis by seeing if it predicts well in explaining other observations. If the hypothesis passes this test, then it becomes accepted. In practice, however, this is at best a rough description of the process of scientific discovery in economics. Existing models are constantly being re-examined and tested. Some economists specialize in testing models; other specialize in developing them. There is an ongoing process of creating and testing of models in economics.

Review

▶ Economists use economic models to explain economic observations. Economic models are similar to models in other sciences. They are abstractions, or simplifications, of reality, and they have variables and constants. But economic models are different from models in the physical sciences because they must deal with human behavior. Models can be represented verbally, with numerical tables, with graphs, and with algebra.

▶ New economic models are developed in part because existing models cannot explain facts or observations.

USING ECONOMICS FOR PUBLIC ECONOMIC POLICY

market economy: an economy characterized by freely determined prices and the free exchange of goods and services in markets.

command economy: an economy in which the government determines prices and production; also called a centrally planned economy.

mixed economy: a market economy in which the government plays a very large role.

positive economics: economic analysis that explains what happens in the economy and why, without making recommendations about economic policy.

normative economics: economic analysis that makes recommendations about economic policy.

Council of Economic Advisers: a three-member group of economists appointed by the president of the United States to analyze the economy and make recommendations about economic policy.

One purpose of increasing our knowledge about the economy is to improve people's lives. People have used economic ideas to help reduce the likelihood of another Great Depression, to use scarce resources more efficiently, and to increase living standards. Your knowledge of economics will help you make better personal decisions about education, employment, and investments.

Ever since the birth of economics as a field—around 1776, when Adam Smith published the *Wealth of Nations*—economists have been concerned and motivated by a desire to improve the economic policy of governments. In fact, economics was originally called *political economy*. Much of the *Wealth of Nations* is about what the government should or should not do to affect the domestic and international economy.

Adam Smith argued for a system of *laissez faire*—little government control—where the role of the government is mainly to promote competition, provide for national defense, and reduce restrictions on the exchange of goods and services. Karl Marx, in contrast, argued in the nineteenth century against a laissez-faire approach. Marx's ideas led to a view that the government should essentially own and control all production. Partly as a result of these different views, two widely different types of economic systems existed for much of the twentieth century: **market economies,** where the vast majority of prices are free to vary, and **command economies,** where the vast majority of prices are determined by the central government. Command economies are also called *centrally planned* economies. The centrally planned economies of the former Soviet Union, Eastern Europe, and China can be traced to Marx's ideas. Today the debate about the role of government continues. Most countries have rejected the command economy and have moved toward market economies. But in many modern market economies, the government plays a large role, and for this reason such economies are sometimes called **mixed economies.** How great should the role of government be in a market economy? Should it provide health-care services? Should it react to the ups and downs in the economy? These are some of the questions we address in this book.

Positive versus Normative Economics

In debating the role of government in the economy, economists distinguish between positive and normative economics. **Positive economics** is about what is; **normative economics** is about what should be. For example, positive economics endeavors to explain why the Great Depression occurred. Normative economics aims to develop and recommend policies that will prevent another Great Depression. In general, normative economics is concerned with making recommendations about what the government should do—whether it should control the price of electricity or health care, or whether it should aim for a zero inflation rate or a 4 percent inflation rate. Economists who advise governments spend much of their time doing normative economics. For example, in the United States the president's **Council of Economic Advisers** has legal responsibility for advising the president about which economic policies are good and which are bad.

Positive economics can also be used to explain *why* governments do what they do. For example, why did the U.S. government control airfares and then stop? Why were tax rates cut in the 1980s and then increased in the 1990s? Positive analysis of

Economist Janet Yellen

In 1997 economist Janet Yellen became the chair of the Council of Economic Advisers, which gives advice to the President of the United States on all economic policy matters.

government policy requires a mixture of both political science and economic science, with a focus on what motivates voters and the politicians they elect.

Economics as a Science versus a Partisan Policy Tool

Although economics, like any other science, is based on facts and theories, it is not always used in a purely scientific way.

In political campaigns, economists put arguments forth in favor of one candidate, emphasizing the good side of their candidate and de-emphasizing the bad side. In a court of law, one economist will help a defendant—making the best case possible—and another economist might help the plaintiff—again, making the best case possible. In other words, economics is not always used objectively. A good reason to learn economics for yourself is to see through fallacious arguments.

But economics is not the only science that is used in these two entirely different modes. For example, there is currently a great controversy about the use of biology and chemistry to make estimates of the costs and benefits of different environmental policies. This is a politically controversial subject, and some on both sides of the controversy have been accused of using science in nonobjective ways.

Economics Is Not the Only Factor in Policy Issues

Although economics can be very useful in policy decisions, it is frequently not the only factor. For example, national security sometimes calls for a different recommendation on a policy issue than one based on a purely economic point of view. Although most economists recommend free exchange of goods between countries, the U.S. government restricted exports of high-technology goods such as computers during the cold war because defense specialists worried that the technology could help the military in the former Soviet Union, and this was viewed as more important than the economic argument. There are still heavy restrictions on trade in nuclear fuels for fear of the proliferation of nuclear weapons.

Review

▶ Economic theory can be used to make better economic decisions. Improving government policy decisions has long been a purpose of economics.

▶ The most basic economic policy questions concern the general role of government in a market economy.

CONCLUSION: A READER'S GUIDE

In this chapter, we have discussed how economic models can be used to answer important questions. But we have not answered the questions. To do so, we need the models themselves. In the following chapters, we will present the models. As you read more about economic models in these chapters, the following brief guide may prove useful. It brings together many of the ideas raised in this chapter.

First, economics—more than other sciences—requires a mixture of verbal and quantitative skills. Frequently those who come to economics with a good background in physical science and mathematics find the mix of formal models with more informal verbal descriptions of markets and institutions unusual and perhaps a little difficult. If you are one of these students, you might wish for a more cut-and-dried, or mathematical, approach.

In contrast, those who are good at history or philosophy may find the emphasis on formal models and graphs difficult and might even prefer a more historical approach that looks more at watershed events and famous individuals and less at formal models of how many individuals behave. If you are one of these students, you might wish economic models were less abstract.

In reality, however, economics is a mixture of formal modeling, historical analysis, and philosophy. If you are very good at math and think the symbols and graphs of elementary economics are too simple, think of Max Planck's comment about economics and focus on the complexity of the economic phenomena that these simple models and graphs are explaining. Then when you are asked an open-ended question about government policy that does not have a simple yes or no answer, you will not be caught off guard. Or if your advantage is in history or philosophy, you should spend more time honing your skills using models and graphs. Then when you are asked to solve a cut-and-dried economic problem with an exact answer requiring graphical analysis, you will not be caught off guard.

Second, the scope of economics is very wide. When your friends or relatives hear that you are taking economics, they might ask you for advice about what stock to buy. Economists' friends and relatives are always asking them for such advice. But economics alone offers no recommendations about the success of particular companies. Rather, economics gives you some tools to obtain information about companies and to analyze them yourself, perhaps to become an investment adviser.

Economics will also help you answer questions about whether to invest in the stock market or in a bank or how many stocks to buy. But the scope of economics is much, much broader than the stock market or banks, as the questions at the start of the chapter indicate. In fact, the scope of economics is even wider than these examples. Economists use their models, or theories, to study environmental pollution, crime, discrimination, and who should have the right to sue whom.

Third, there is less economic controversy than you may think. Watching economists debate issues on television or reading their opinions in a newspaper or magazine certainly gives the impression that they rarely agree. There are major controversies in economics, and we will examine these controversies in this book. But when people survey economists' beliefs, they find a surprising amount of agreement.

Why, then, the popular impression of disagreement? Because there are many economists, and one can always find some economist with a different viewpoint. When people sue other people in court and economics is an issue, it is always possible to find economists who will testify on each side, even if 99 percent of economists would agree with one side. Similarly, television interviews or news shows want to give both sides of public policy issues. Thus, even if 99 percent of economists agree with one side, it is possible to find at least one on the other side.

Economists are human beings with varying moral beliefs and different backgrounds and political views that are frequently unrelated to economic models. For example, an economist who is very concerned about the importation of drugs into the United States might appear to be more willing to condone a restriction on coffee exports, which might give Colombia a higher price for its coffee to offset a loss in revenue from cocaine. Another economist who might feel less strongly about drug imports may argue strongly against such a restriction on coffee. But if asked about restrictions on trade in the abstract, both economists would probably argue for government policies that prevent them.

Fourth, and perhaps most important, the study of economics is an intellectually fascinating adventure in its own right. Yes, economics is highly relevant, and it affects people's lives. But once you learn how economic models work, you will find that they are actually fun to use. And they would be just as much fun if they were not so relevant. Every now and then, just after you have learned about a new economic model, put the book down and think of the economic model independent of its message or relevance to society, perhaps like you would an enjoyable movie. In this way, too, you will be learning to think like an economist.

KEY POINTS

1. Economics provides explanations of certain economic observations in a way that can be used to make decisions.

2. Economics is useful for personal, business, and government policy decisions.

3. Observations or facts about the economy are sometimes not easy to establish.

4. Spending on health care and the price of health care provides a good example of how economists document the facts and explain them with models.

5. Economic models are abstractions, or simplifications, of reality.

6. Economic models, like models in other sciences, can be described with words, with tables, with graphs, or with

mathematics. All four ways are important and complement one another.

7. Much of economics uses existing models. Such models have been developed over the last 200 years and are used by individuals, businesses, and government.

8. Sometimes the facts require that economists develop new models.

9. Improving economic policy has been a goal of economists since the time of Adam Smith.

10. Decisions about the role of government in areas from airfares to health care are influenced by economic analysis.

KEY TERMS

gross domestic product (GDP)
economic history
overall price level
inflation
inflation rate
real GDP
relative price
economic variable
correlation
causation

controlled experiments
experimental economics
market
labor
capital
inputs or factors of
    production
economic model
positively related
negatively related

ceteris paribus
microeconomics
macroeconomics
market economy
command economy
mixed economy
positive economics
normative economics
Council of Economic Advisers

QUESTIONS FOR REVIEW

1. How do the economic challenges and opportunities around the world in the 1990s differ from those of the 1940s?

2. Why do economists need to document and quantify observations about the economy?

3. What is the most comprehensive available measure of the size of an economy?

4. What is the overall price level? What is inflation?

5. What is meant by a relative price?

6. How do economic models differ from the economic phenomena they explain?

7. Why doesn't correlation imply causation?

8. What is the difference between a variable and a constant in economics?

9. What is the difference between positive and normative economics?

10. How do economists use the *ceteris paribus* assumption?

PROBLEMS

1. Which of the following issues are microeconomic, and which are macroeconomic?
   a) The overall unemployment rate
   b) A tax that affects workers in the auto industry
   c) Inflation
   d) Prices of agricultural commodities
   e) Real GDP

2. Identify whether the following policy statements are positive or normative. Explain.
   a) "The government fought inflation during the early 1980s because it felt the inflation was damaging potential long-term economic growth."
   b) "The government should cut taxes in order to stimulate GDP."
   c) "Increases in consumer spending improved the Japanese economy last year, which indicates stronger growth of real GDP for next year."
   d) "Balancing the federal budget would be good for the economy."

3. Interpret the data on housing spending in the table below by filling in the blanks.
   a) What has happened to housing spending as a share of GDP over this 30-year period? How does this differ from the figures for health care in Tables 1.1 and 1.2?
   b) What has happened to the relative price of housing over this period? How does this compare to the change in the relative price of health care over this period?

4. Draw a diagram like Figure 1.8 for the market for movies and give examples of capital, labor, and firms in that market. Show how there is a complete circular flow of funds and goods in the economy as a whole.

5. Why is it typical for economists to make the *ceteris paribus* assumption when making predictions?

6. Interpret the observations on food spending in the table at the bottom of the page by filling in the blanks.
   a) What has happened to spending on food as a share of GDP over this 30-year period? How does this differ from the figures for health care in Tables 1.1 and 1.2?
   b) What has happened to the relative price of food over this period? How does this compare to the change in the relative price of health care over this period?

7. What is the difference between the overall price level and relative price? Which information is more useful if you are interested in the change in spending on a particular good? Which measure is more useful if you are interested in inflation?

8. Indicate whether you expect positive or negative correlation for the following pairs of variables. What is required to show causation?
   a) Sunrise and crowing roosters
   b) Price of theater tickets and number of theatergoers
   c) Purchases of candy and purchases of Valentine's Day cards

Problem 3

Year	GDP (billions of dollars)	Spending on Housing	Housing as a Share of GDP	Overall Price	Housing Price	Relative Housing Price
1960	526.6	48.2	_____	0.233	0.234	_____
1970	1,035.6	94.0	_____	0.306	0.285	_____
1980	2,784.2	255.2	_____	0.604	0.524	_____
1990	5,743.8	586.3	_____	0.936	0.985	_____

Problem 6

Year	GDP (billions of dollars)	Spending on Food	Food as a Share of GDP	Overall Price	Food Price	Relative Food Price
1960	526.6	82.3	_____	0.233	0.229	_____
1970	1,035.6	143.8	_____	0.306	0.301	_____
1980	2,784.2	355.4	_____	0.604	0.636	_____
1990	5,743.8	634.5	_____	0.936	0.951	_____

appendix to chapter 1

Acquiring an Eye for Economics: Reading and Understanding Graphs

Frances M. James worked in the Executive Office of the President for more than thirty years, serving under seven presidents, from Harry Truman to Jimmy Carter. Her job was to make sure the economic statistics used by each president and his Council of Economic Advisers were accurate and were presented clearly and meaningfully. Her skills were rare and valuable. She could look at a table with hundreds of numbers and quickly see whether something was wrong. "There is a minus sign missing," or, "It's billions not millions," or, "You must have confused Austria's GDP with Australia's GDP" are the kinds of things she would say. Such skills are hard to acquire, and Frances admired people who had taken the time to acquire them. She called the skill "having a nose for numbers."

But because most people do not have such a highly developed sense for deciphering columns of numbers, economists rely on graphs to make visual pictures of a table of numbers or a formula. Developing an eye for economics as represented in graphs is easier than developing a nose for numbers in tables. Graphs help us see correlations, or patterns, in economic observations. Graphs and diagrams are also useful for understanding economic models. They help us see how variables in the model behave. They help us describe assumptions about what firms and consumers do.

This appendix reviews the rudiments of analytical geometry that are used to create graphs for representing observations and models.

REPRESENTING OBSERVATIONS WITH GRAPHS

Most economic graphs are drawn in two dimensions, like the surface of this page, and the graphs are constructed using a **Cartesian coordinate system.** The idea of Cartesian coordinates is that pairs of observations on variables can be represented in a plane by designating one axis for one variable and the other axis for the other variable. Each point, or coordinate, on the plane corresponds to a pair of observations.

Time-Series Graphs

In many instances, we want to see how a variable changes over time. For example, many people are interested in changes in the federal debt—all the outstanding borrowing of the federal government that has not yet been paid back. Table 1A.1 shows six observations of the U.S. federal debt in billions of dollars. The observations are for every 10 years and are taken from the budget of the U.S. government; the observation for the year 2000 is based on a government projection. Because there are so few observations in Table 1A.1, it is easy to graph them by hand, and we have done so in Figure 1A.1. The graph in Figure 1A.1 is called a **time-series graph** because it plots a series—that is, several values of the variable—over time. When there are many observations, as in Table 1.1, economists use computers to plot the graphs automatically. Figure 1.1 was plotted by computer.

Observe the scales on the horizontal and vertical axes in Figure 1A.1. The six years are put on the horizontal axis, spread evenly from the year 1950 to the year 2000. For the

TABLE 1A.1
U.S. Federal Government Debt

Year	Debt (billions of dollars)
1950	219
1960	237
1970	283
1980	709
1990	2,410
2000	4,873

Source: Budget of the U.S. Government, Fiscal Year 1993; The Economic and Budget Outlook, Congressional Budget Office, September 1993.

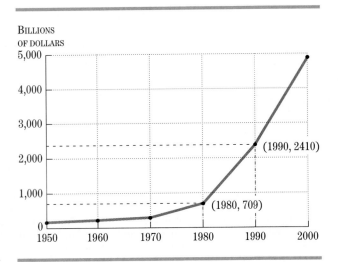

FIGURE 1A.1
U.S. Federal Debt
Each point corresponds to a pair of observations—the year and the debt—from Table 1A.1.

vertical axis, one needs to decide on a scale. The range of variation for the debt in Table 1A.1 is very wide—from a minimum of $219 billion to a maximum of $4,873 billion. Thus, the range of from $0 to $5,000 billion on the vertical axis in Figure 1A.1 is wide enough to contain all these points.

Now observe how each pair of points from Table 1A.1 is plotted in Figure 1A.1. The point for the pair of observations for the year 1950 and the debt of $219 billion is found by going over to 1950 on the horizontal axis, then going up to $219 billion and putting a dot there. The point for 1960 and $237 billion and all the other points are found in the same way. In order to better visualize the points, they can be connected with lines. These lines are not part of the observations; they are only a convenience to help eyeball the observations. The points for 1980 and 1990 are labeled with the pair of observations corresponding to Table 1A.1, but in general there is no need to put in such labels.

Now look at the pattern of points in Figure 1A.1. Some people feel that the pattern looks like a hockey stick. It is striking. The long handle of the hockey stick is the sharp increase in the debt in the 1980s and 1990s. The part of the hockey stick that you hit the ball or puck with represents slower increases in the debt in the earlier years. But the debt has increased throughout the period in the graph.

One could choose different scales than in Figure 1A.1, and if you plotted your own graph from Table 1A.1 with-

FIGURE 1A.2
Stretching the Debt Story in Two Ways
The points in both graphs are identical to Figure 1A.1, but by stretching or shrinking the scales the problem can be made to look either less alarming or more alarming.

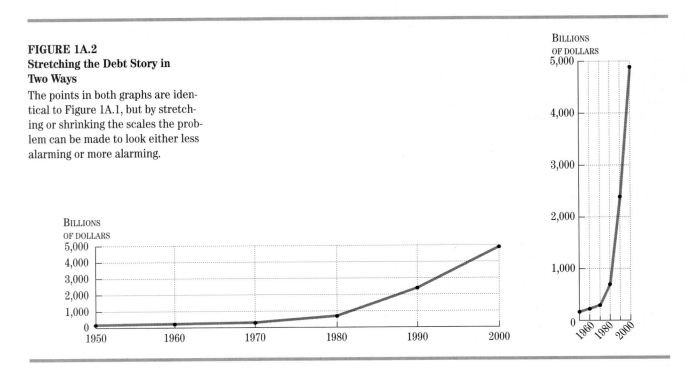

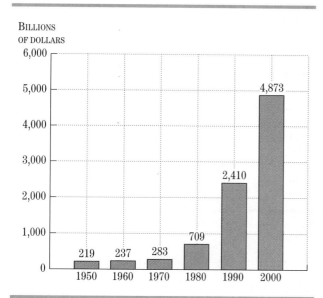

FIGURE 1A.3
U.S. Federal Debt in Bars
The observations are identical to
those in Figure 1A.1

Year	Debt (percent of GDP)
1950	82.5
1960	46.8
1970	28.7
1980	26.8
1990	44.2
2000	55.7

TABLE 1A.2
U.S. Federal Debt as a Percent of GDP

Source: U.S. Department of Commerce and Table 1A.1.

out looking at Figure 1A.1, your scales would probably be different. The scales determine how much movement there is in a time-series graph. For example, Figure 1A.2 shows two ways to stretch the scales to make the increase in the debt look either more alarming or less alarming. The diagram at the right looks even more like a hockey stick. But the diagram at the left looks less worrisome. So as not to be fooled by graphs, therefore, it is important to look at the scales and think about what they mean.

As an alternative to time-series graphs with dots connected by a line, the observations can be shown on a bar graph, as in Figure 1A.3. Some people prefer the visual look of a bar graph, but as is clear from a comparison of Figures 1A.1 and 1A.3, they provide the same information.

The debt as a percent of GDP is given in Table 1A.2 and graphed in Figure 1A.4. Note that this figure makes the debt look a lot different than the first one. For one thing, the line declines, reaches a minimum, and then begins to increase. As a percent of GDP, the debt fell from the end of the World War II (when it was very large because of the war debt) until around 1980. It increased again during the 1980s. As a percent of GDP, the debt is now less than after World War II, but it is still growing. When we consider the debt as a percentage of GDP, the recent increase appears less alarming. But that does not mean the increase is not a problem.

The scale in Figure 1A.4 for the debt as a percentage of GDP is from 0 to 90 percent. This leaves some wasted space at the bottom and the top of the graph. To eliminate this space and have more room to see the graph itself, we can start the range near the minimum value and end it near the maximum value. This is done in Figure 1A.5. Note, however, that cutting off the bottom of the scale could be misleading to people who do not look at the axis. In particular, 0 percent is no longer at the point where the horizontal and vertical axis intersect. To warn people about the missing part of the scale, a little cut is sometimes put on the

FIGURE 1A.4
U.S. Federal Debt as a Percent of GDP

Each point corresponds to a pair of observations from Table 1A.2.

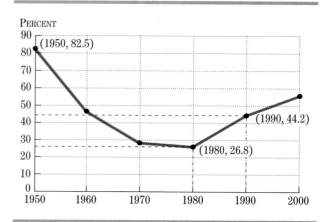

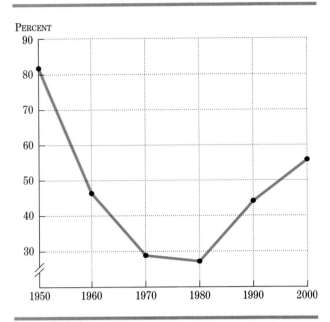

FIGURE 1A.5
**A Stretched-Scale Look at Debt as
a Percent of GDP**

To alert the reader that the bottom
part of the axis is not shown, a
break point is sometimes used, as
shown here.

axis, as shown in Figure 1A.5, but you have to look carefully at the scale.

Time-Series Graphs Showing Two or More Variables

So far we have shown how a graph can be used to show
observations on one variable over time. What if we want to
see how two or more variables change over time together?
Suppose, for example, we want to look at how observations
on debt as a percentage of GDP compare with the interest
rate the government must pay on its debt. The two variables
are shown in Table 1A.3.

The two sets of observations can easily be placed on
the same time-series graph. In other words, we could plot
the observations on the debt percentage and connect the
dots and then plot the interest rate observations and connect
the dots. If the scales of measurement of the two variables
are much different, then it might be hard to see each, however. For example, the interest rate ranges between 4 and 12
percent; it would not be very visible on a graph going all
the way from 0 to 100 percent, a range that is fine for the

TABLE 1A.3
**Interest Rate and Federal Debt as
a Percent of GDP**

Year	Debt (percent of GDP)	Interest Rate (percent)
1950	82.5	1.2
1960	46.8	2.9
1970	28.7	6.5
1980	26.8	11.5
1990	44.2	7.5
2000	55.7	4.5

Source: Federal Reserve Board and
Table 1A.2.

debt percentage. In this situation, a **dual scale** can be used,
as shown in Figure 1A.6. One scale is put on the left-hand
vertical axis and the other scale is put on the right-hand vertical axis. With a dual-scale diagram, it is very important to
be aware of the two scales. In this book we will emphasize
the different axes in dual-scale diagrams by the color line

FIGURE 1A.6
**Comparing Two Time Series with a
Dual Scale**

When two variables have different
scales, a dual scale is useful. Here
the interest rate and the debt as a
percent of GDP are plotted from
Table 1A.3.

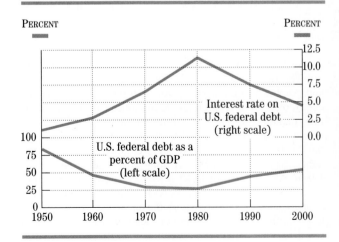

segment at the top of each vertical axis. The color line segment corresponds to the color of the curve plotted using that scale, as in Figure 1A.6.

Scatter Plots

Finally, two variables can be usefully compared with a **scatter plot.** The Cartesian coordinate method is used, as in the time-series graph, except that we do not put the year on one of the axes; rather, the horizontal axis is used for one of the variables and the vertical axis for the other variable. We do this for the debt percentage and the interest rate in Figure 1A.7. The interest rate is on the vertical axis and the debt percentage is on the horizontal axis. For example, the point at the upper left is 26.8 percent for the debt as a percent of GDP and 11.5 percent for the interest rate.

Note that this scatter plot reveals a negative correlation between the debt percentage and the interest rate. Recall that a negative correlation is when the points in a scatter plot tend to decline as you move from left to right. Note that this negative correlation is also apparent in a different way in Figure 1A.6 in which the debt percentage fell as the interest rate rose over time and then rose as the interest rate fell over time.

Remember that such a correlation does not imply causation or that there is an economic relation between the two variables. In particular it would be a serious mistake to conclude from Figure 1A.7 that there is a negative causal relationship between the debt ratio and the interest rate. The observed correlation could be caused by a third variable— such as inflation—that is affecting both the debt percentage and the interest rate.

Pie Charts

Time-series graphs, bar graphs, and scatter plots are not the only visual ways to observe economic data. For example, the *pie chart* in Figure 1A.8 is useful for comparing percentage shares for a small number of different groups or a small number of time periods. In this example, the pie chart is a visual representation of how the industrial countries produce more than half of the world's GDP while the developing countries produce 34 percent and the former communist countries in Eastern Europe and the former Soviet Union, now in transition toward market economies, produce about 11 percent.

FIGURE 1A.7
Scatter Plot

Interest rate and debt as a percent of GDP are shown.

INTEREST RATE
ON FEDERAL DEBT
(PERCENT)

FIGURE 1A.8
Pie Chart Showing the Shares of the World's GDP

The pie chart shows how the world's GDP is divided up into (1) the industrial countries, such as the United States, Germany, and Japan, (2) the developing countries, such as India, China, and Nigeria, and (3) countries in transition from communism to capitalism, such as Russia and Poland.

Source: International Monetary Fund.

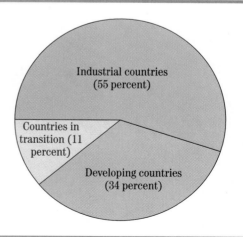

REPRESENTING MODELS WITH GRAPHS

Graphs can also represent models. As with graphs showing observations, graphs showing models are usually restricted to curves in two dimensions.

Slopes of Curves

Does a curve slope up or down? How steep is it? These questions are important in economics as in other sciences. The **slope** of a curve tells us how much the variable on the vertical axis changes when we change the variable on the horizontal axis by one unit.

The slope is computed as follows:

$$\text{Slope} = \frac{\text{change in variable on vertical axis}}{\text{change in variable on horizontal axis}}$$

In most algebra courses, the vertical axis is usually called the *y*-axis and the horizontal axis is called the *x*-axis. Thus,

the slope is sometime described as

$$\text{Slope} = \frac{\text{change in } y}{\text{change in } x} = \frac{\Delta y}{\Delta x}$$

where the Greek letter Δ (delta) means "change in." In other words, the slope is the ratio of the "rise" (vertical change) to the "run" (horizontal change).

Figure 1A.9 shows how to compute the slope. In this case, the slope declines as the variable on the *x*-axis increases.

Observe that *the steeper the curve, the larger the slope.* When the curve gets very flat, the slope gets close to zero. Curves can either be upward-sloping or downward-sloping. If the curve slopes up from left to right, as in Figure 1A.9, it has a **positive slope,** and we say the two variables are positively related. If the curve slopes down from left to right, it has a **negative slope,** and we say the two variables are negatively related. Figure 1A.10 shows a case where the slope is negative. When *x* increases by 1 unit (Δ*x* = 1), *y* declines by 2 units (Δ*y* = −2). Thus, the slope equals −2; it is negative. Observe how the curve slopes down from left to right.

FIGURE 1A.9
Measuring the Slope
The slope between two points is given by the change along the vertical axis divided by the change along the horizontal axis. In this example, the slope declines as *x* increases. Since the curve slopes up from left to right, it has a positive slope.

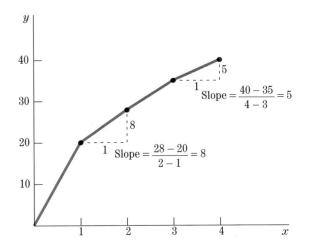

FIGURE 1A.10
A Relationship with a Negative Slope
Here the slope is negative: (Δ*y*)/(Δ*x*) = −2. As *x* increases, *y* falls. The line slopes down from left to right. In this case, *y* and *x* are inversely, or negatively, related.

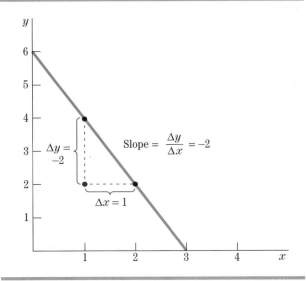

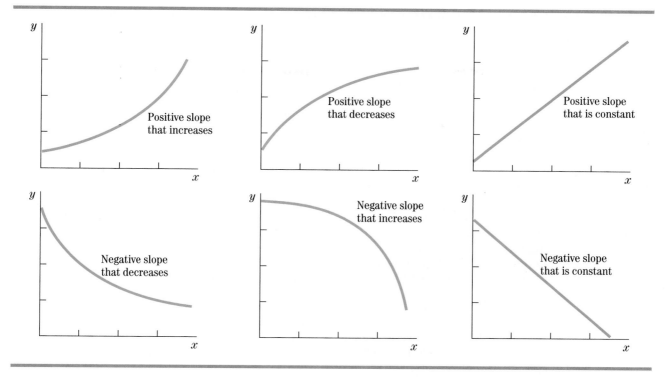

FIGURE 1A.11
Six Types of Relationships
In the top row, the variables are positively related. In the bottom row, they are negatively related.

If the curve is a straight line, then the slope is a constant. Curves that are straight lines—as in Figure 1A.10—are called **linear.** But economic relationships do not need to be linear, as the example in Figure 1A.9 makes clear. Figure 1A.11 shows six different examples of curves and indicates how they are described.

Graphs of Models with More Than Two Variables

In most cases, economic models involve more than two variables. For example, the number of physical examinations could depend on the number of nurses as well as the number of doctors. Or the amount of lemonade demanded might depend on the weather as well as on the price.

Economists have devised several methods to represent models with more than two variables with two-dimensional graphs. Suppose, for example, that the relationship between *y* and *x* in Figure 1A.10 depends on third variable *z*. For a given value for *x,* larger values of *z* lead to larger values of *y.* This example is graphed in Figure 1A.12. As in Figure 1A.10, when *x* increases, *y* falls. This is a **movement along**

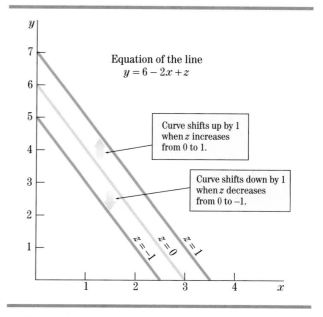

FIGURE 1A.12
A Third Variable Shifts the Curve
In order to represent models with three variables ($x,$ $y,$ and z) on a two-dimensional graph, economists distinguish between movements along the curve (when x and y change, holding z unchanged) and shifts of the curve (when z changes).

the curve. But what if z changes? We represent this as a **shift of the curve.** An increase in z shifts the curve up; a decrease in z shifts the curve down.

Thus, by distinguishing between shifts and movements along a curve, economists represent models with more than two variables in only two dimensions. Only two variables (x and y) are shown explicitly on the graph, and when the third (z) is fixed, changes in x and y are movements along the curve. When z changes, the curve shifts. The distinction between "movements along" and "shifts of" curves will come up many times in this book.

KEY TERMS AND DEFINITIONS

Cartesian coordinate system: a graphing system in which ordered pairs of numbers are represented on a plane by the distances from a point to two perpendicular lines, called axes.

time-series graph: a graph that plots a variable over time, usually with time on the horizontal axis.

dual scale: a graph that uses time on the horizontal axis and different scales on left and right vertical axes to compare the movements in two variables over time.

scatter plot: a graph in which points in a Cartesian coordinate system represent the values of two variables.

slope: refers to a curve and is defined as the change in the variable on the vertical axis divided by the change in the variable on the horizontal axis.

positive slope: a slope of a curve that is greater than zero, representing a positive or direct relationship between two variables.

negative slope: a slope of a curve that is less than zero, representing a negative or inverse relationship between two variables.

linear: a situation in which a curve is straight, with a constant slope.

movement along the curve: a situation in which a change in the variable on one axis causes a change in the variable on the other axis, but maintains the position of the curve.

shift of the curve: a change in the position of a curve usually caused by a change in a variable not represented on either axis.

QUESTIONS FOR REVIEW

1. What is the difference between a scatter plot and a time-series graph?

2. Why are dual scales sometimes necessary?

3. What is the advantage of graphs over verbal representations of models?

4. What does a curve with a negative slope look like?

5. What is the difference between a shift in a curve and a movement along a curve?

PROBLEMS

1. The table at the right presents data on the debt to GDP ratio and interest rates in the United Kingdom.
   a) Construct a time-series plot of the ratio of government debt to GDP.
   b) Construct a time-series plot of the interest rate.
   c) Construct a scatter plot of the debt ratio and the interest rate.

Year	Debt to GDP Ratio	Interest Rate
1984	47.3	9.9
1985	46.1	10.8
1986	45.0	10.5
1987	42.0	4.8
1988	35.7	10.0
1989	30.4	13.9
1990	28.7	14.8
1991	30.3	11.5
1992	35.6	9.5
1993	41.1	6.6

Source: Organization for Economic Cooperation and Development.

2. The following table presents data on U.S. turkey production and prices.

Year	Turkey Production (billions of pounds)	Price per Pound
1985	3.7	49.1
1986	4.1	47.1
1987	4.9	34.8
1988	5.1	38.6
1989	5.5	40.9
1990	6.0	39.4

Source: Statistical Abstract of the United States, 1993.

a) Construct a time-series plot of turkey production in the United States.

b) Construct a time-series plot of the price of turkey per pound.

c) Construct a scatter plot of turkey production and turkey prices.

3. The following table shows the number of physical examinations given by doctors at an HMO with three different-size clinics: small, medium, and large. The larger the clinic, the more patients the doctors can handle. (Observe that the small clinic is exactly like Figure 1.11.)

Exams per Small Clinic	Exams per Medium Clinic	Exams per Large Clinic	Number of Doctors
0	0	0	0
20	30	35	1
28	42	49	2
35	53	62	3
40	60	70	4

a) Show the relationship between doctors and physical exams given with *three* curves where the number of doctors is on the horizontal axis and the number of examinations is on the vertical axis.

b) Describe how the three relationships compare with one another.

c) Is a change in the number of doctors a shift or a movement along the curve?

d) Is a change in the size of the clinic a shift or a movement along the curve?

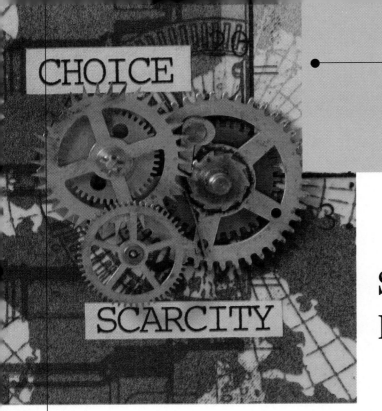

CHOICE
SCARCITY

2

Scarcity, Choice, and Economic Interaction

Boiled down to its essence, economics is the study of (1) the choices people make when there is a scarcity of resources, and (2) the economic interactions of people with other people when they make these choices. By exploring this brief definition, we can learn much about economics and about how economists think.

Scarcity is a situation where people's wants exceed their resources. People always face a scarcity of something, usually time or income. Scarcity implies that people must make a **choice**—to forego, or to give up, one thing in favor of another. For example, a college student who chooses to work during the school year has less time for studying, rollerblading, watching television, or something else. A college, with a given amount of tuition receipts or government grants, must choose between spending more on language instruction or more on mathematics instruction. A government, with a given amount of tax receipts, must choose between spending more on crime prevention or more on education. The people of a country, with a given amount of resources, must choose between spending more on health care or more on other things. Scarcity is a fact of economic life for individuals, for families, for colleges, for governments, for whole

economies, and even for the whole world. Scarcity is pervasive, and it forces us to pick and choose.

Economic interaction between people occurs when they trade or exchange goods or services with each other. For example, a college student buys education services from a college in exchange for tuition. A teenager sells labor services to Taco Bell in exchange for cash. Within a family, one spouse may agree to cook every day in exchange for the other spouse's doing the dishes every day. Within a university, workers at the university-owned copy center may provide copy services so that the faculty can give students lecture outlines.

As these examples indicate, economic interactions can occur either within an organizational structure, such as a university or a family, or in a market. Interactions *within* **organizations** include the cooking-washing arrangement between members of a family or the use of a university-owned copier, rather than a Kinko's copier, by faculty for lecture handouts. Interactions that take place *outside* of organizations take place in markets. Recall that a **market** is simply an arrangement where buyers and sellers can interact with each other. Interactions in markets include the buying and selling of a college education, of the labor services of Taco Bell workers, or of the copy services of firms like Kinko's. There are many other markets where economic interaction takes place, from the New York Stock Exchange to a local flea market.

Economic interaction, like scarcity and choice, is a fact of economic life. But economic interactions can make our lives much better. How an economy is set up to handle such interactions determines how well the economy as a whole works in providing for the well-being of the people in the economy.

In this chapter we look at the ways in which economists portray scarcity and choice for individuals and for whole economies. We show how people benefit from economic interactions, whether they occur within organizations or in markets. Many of the ideas and terms defined in this chapter will be used and studied in more detail in later chapters.

scarcity: the situation in which the quantity of resources is insufficient to meet all wants.

choice: a selection among alternative goods, services, or actions.

economic interaction: exchanges of goods and services between people.

organization: a human structure, such as a family, firm, government, or college, through which people may exchange goods and services.

market: an arrangement by which economic exchanges between people take place.

SCARCITY, CHOICE, AND INTERACTION FOR INDIVIDUALS

It is easy to find everyday examples of how scarcity affects individual choices. A choice that may be on your mind when you study economics is how much time to spend on it versus other activities. If you spend all your time on economics, you might get 100 on the final exam, but that might mean you get a zero in biology. If you spend all your time on biology, then you might get 100 in biology and a zero in economics. Most people resolve the choice by balancing out their time to get a decent grade in both subjects. If you are premed, then biology will probably get more time. If you are interested in business, then more time on economics might be appropriate.

Now let us apply this same idea to two economic problems: individual choices about what goods to *consume* and individual choices about what goods to *produce*. For each type of economic problem, we first show how scarcity forces one to make a choice; we then show how people gain from interacting with other people.

Consumer Decisions

Consider the choice made by a person deciding how much of a good or service to consume.

Scarcity and Choice for Individual Consumers

Consider Maria, who loves both ballet and opera. Suppose Maria has $500 to spend on entertainment. The $500 limit on her spending is an example of a *budget constraint,* because Maria is limited to spending no more than this budgeted amount for

Choice and Opportunity Cost

Choice creates opportunity costs. In this photograph, Coca-Cola appears to be the next best alternative to milk. Thus, the opportunity cost of choosing milk is the foregone consumption of Coca-Cola.

opportunity cost: the value of the next-best foregone alternative that was not chosen because something else was chosen.

gains from trade: improvements in income, production, or satisfaction owing to the exchange of goods or services.

entertainment. Suppose the price of a season ticket to 20 ballet performances is $500, and the price of a season ticket to 20 opera performances is also $500. Hence, the scarcity of funds for entertainment forces Maria to choose between two alternatives: a season ticket to the ballet or a season ticket to the opera. The decision depends on her tastes. Although she loves both ballet and opera, we assume that, if forced by scarcity to make a choice, she will choose the season opera tickets. She would prefer to buy both season tickets, but she cannot afford it. She would prefer to go to half of the operas and half of the ballets, but that choice is not open to her.

Maria's decision is an example of an economic problem that all people face. A budget constraint forces them to make a choice between different items that they want. Such choices create opportunity costs. The **opportunity cost** of a choice is the value of the foregone alternative that was not chosen. The opportunity cost of the opera season ticket is the loss from not being able to buy the ballet season ticket. An opportunity cost occurs every time there is a choice. For example, the opportunity cost of going to an 8 A.M. class rather than sleeping in is the lost sleep from getting up early.

In many cases involving choice and scarcity, there are many more than two things to choose from. If you choose vanilla ice cream out of a list of many possible flavors, then the opportunity cost is the loss from not being able to consume the *next best* flavor, perhaps strawberry. In addition to extending their choices, people may be able to increase the amount they have to spend by working more; then the opportunity cost is less leisure time. But the structure of the situation is much the same as Maria's choice.

Now, Maria is not the only consumer. Consider Adam, who also has $500 to spend. Adam also loves both ballet and opera. But he likes ballet slightly more than opera. If forced to make a choice between the season tickets, he will choose to buy season tickets to the ballet. His decisions are shaped by scarcity just as Maria's are: Scarcity comes from the budget constraint; he must make a choice, and there is an opportunity cost for each choice.

Gains from Trade

Now let us consider the possibility of economic interaction between Maria and Adam. Suppose that Maria and Adam can trade with each other. Maria decides to trade half (10) of her opera tickets for half (10) of Adam's ballet tickets, as shown in Figure 2.1. Through such a trade, both Maria and Adam can improve their situation. There are **gains from trade** because the trade reallocates goods between the two individuals in a way they both prefer. Trade occurs because Maria is willing to exchange 10 opera tickets for 10 ballet tickets, and Adam is willing to exchange 10 ballet tickets for 10 opera tickets. Because trade is mutually advantageous for both Maria and Adam, they will voluntarily do so if they are able to. In fact, if they did not gain from the trade, then neither would have bothered to make the trade.

Improvements Through Reallocation

This trade is an example of an economic interaction in which a reallocation of goods through trade makes both parties better off. There is no change in the total quantity of goods produced. The number of ballet and opera performances has remained the same. Trade simply reallocates existing goods.

The trade between Maria and Adam is typical of many economic interactions we will study in this book. Thinking like an economist in this example means recognizing that a voluntary exchange of goods between people must make them better off. Many economic exchanges are like this, even though they are more complicated than the exchange of season tickets to the opera and the ballet. In some cases one party might gain much more than the other. Maria, for example, might bargain with Adam and get him to give up 90 percent of his tickets for only 10 percent of hers. If we saw Adam after such a transaction, he might seem pretty angry; but, to an economist, if Adam made a voluntary trade, then he gained from the trade.

Producer Decisions

Now consider how scarcity, choice, and economic interaction might occur for people who produce goods. Again we consider an illustrative numerical example.

Scarcity and Choice for Individual Producers

Although all people face limitations on what they are able to produce, not all people face the same limitations. Consider Emily, a poet, and Johann, a printer, who both face scarcity and must make choices. Because of differences in training, abilities, or inclination, Emily is much better at writing poetry than Johann, but Johann is much better at printing books, pamphlets, and greeting cards than Emily. Suppose that Emily and Johann cannot interact with each other; perhaps they live on different islands and cannot communicate.

If Emily writes poetry full time, she could produce 10 poems in a day; but if Emily wants to make and sell greeting cards with her poems in them, she must spend some time printing cards and thereby spend less time writing poems. However, Emily is not very good at printing cards; it takes her so much time to print a card during the day that she has time to write only 1 poem rather than 10 poems during the day.

If Johann prints full time, he can produce 10 different greeting cards in a day. However, if he wants to sell greeting cards, he must write a poem to put inside them. Johann is so poor at writing poems that in order to write only 1 poem a day, his production of greeting cards drops from 10 to 1 per day.

Here is a summary of the choices Emily and Johann face because of a scarcity of time and resources.

	Emily, the Poet		**Johann, the Printer**	
	Write Full Time	Write and Print	Print Full Time	Write and Print
Cards	0	1	10	1
Poems	10	1	0	1

If Emily and Johann could not interact, then each could produce only 1 greeting card with a poem on the inside. Alternatively, Emily could produce 10 poems without the cards and Johann could produce 10 cards without the poems, but then neither would earn anything. We therefore assume that when confronted with this

---

Before Trade
Maria   *Adam*
20 opera tickets   20 ballet tickets

Two-way Trade

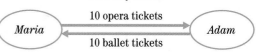

10 opera tickets
10 ballet tickets

After Trade
Maria   *Adam*
10 opera tickets   10 opera tickets
10 ballet tickets   10 ballet tickets

FIGURE 2.1
Gains from Trade Through a Better Allocation of Goods
Without economic interaction, Maria has more opera tickets than she would like, and Adam has more ballet tickets than he would like. By trading 10 ballet tickets for 10 opera tickets, they can both arrive at a more satisfactory situation.

choice, both Emily and Johann will each choose to produce 1 greeting card with a poem inside. In total, they produce 2 greeting cards.

Gains from Trade

Now suppose that Emily and Johann can trade. Johann could sell his printing services to Emily, agreeing to print her poems into nice greeting cards. Then Emily could sell the greeting cards to people. Under this arrangement, Emily could spend all day writing poetry and Johann could spend all day printing. In total, 10 different greeting cards could be produced with the same time and effort as only 2 greeting cards when Emily and Johann could not trade.

Note how in this example the interaction took place in a market; Emily sold her poems to Johann or Johann sold his print jobs to Emily. Another approach would be for Emily and Johann to go into business together, forming a firm, Dickinson and Gutenberg Greetings, Inc. Then their economic interaction would occur within the firm, without buying or selling in the market.

Whether in a market or within a firm, the gains from trade are huge in this example. By trading, Emily and Johann can increase production of greeting cards by five times, from 2 cards to 10 cards. In fact, the gains are so large that Emily and Johann would be very likely to trade unless they were prevented from doing so.

Specialization, Division of Labor, and Comparative Advantage

specialization: the situation in which a resource, such as labor, concentrates and develops efficiency at a particular task.

division of labor: the division of production into various parts in which different groups of workers specialize.

comparative advantage: a situation in which a person or country can produce one good more efficiently than another good in comparison with another person or country.

This example illustrates another reason economic interaction takes place and why there are gains from trade. Economic interaction allows for **specialization** by people in what they are good at. Emily specializes in poetry, and Johann specializes in printing. The example illustrates the idea of the division of labor. A **division of labor** occurs when some workers specialize in one task while others specialize in another task. They divide the overall production into parts, with some workers concentrating on one part (printing) and other workers concentrating on another part (writing). Adam Smith is usually given credit for developing the concept of division of labor; he placed great emphasis on it in the *Wealth of Nations.*

The poetry/printing example of Emily and Johann also illustrates another economic concept, **comparative advantage.** In general, a person or a group of people have a comparative advantage in producing one good relative to another good if they can produce that good with comparatively less time, effort, or resources than another person can produce that good. For example, compared with Johann, Emily has a comparative advantage in writing relative to printing. And compared with Emily, Johann has a comparative advantage in printing relative to writing. As this example shows, production can be increased if people specialize in the skill in which they have a comparative advantage.[1] That is, Emily specializes in writing and Johann in printing.

Trade Within a Country versus International Trade

Thus far, we have said nothing about where Maria, Adam, Emily, or Johann live or work. They could all reside in the same country, but they could also reside in different countries. Emily could live in the United States; Johann, in Germany. If so,

---

1. Other examples will be explored in the chapter "The Gains from International Trade," where we will see that comparative advantage can also occur when one person is absolutely better at both activities.

Adam Smith, 1723–1790

BORN:
Kircaldy, Scotland, 1723

EDUCATION:
M.A. degree, University of Glasgow, Scotland, 1740
Independent study, Oxford, 1741–1748

JOBS:
Independent study, Edinburgh, 1748–1751
Professor, University of Glasgow, 1751–1764
Tutor for a duke, traveling in Europe, 1764–1766
Independent study, Kircaldy, 1766–1776
Commissioner of Customs, Edinburgh, 1777–1790

MAJOR PUBLICATIONS:
The Theory of Moral Sentiments, 1759
An Inquiry into the Nature and Causes of the Wealth of Nations, 1776

In 1776, at the age of 53, Adam Smith published an amazing book that would eventually earn him the title "founder of modern economics." The *Wealth of Nations*—still relevant and widely quoted after 200 years—defined the landscape of economics. Its most revolutionary ideas, illustrated with hundreds of juicy examples, were that people's real incomes, rather than gold or silver, are the measure of a society's wealth and that real incomes would grow through the division of labor, trade, and the use of money.

What personal qualities enabled Smith to write such a classic? What does it take to start a whole new field? Clearly, Smith was bright. After all, he obtained a master's degree at age 17 at a time when few even went to college. But there were other factors that prepared Smith to write his great work. He spent 10 years in independent study, at Oxford and Edinburgh, before obtaining a job as a philosophy professor at the University of Glasgow, his alma mater. After about a dozen successful years at Glasgow, however, he resigned to follow a career path that would take him back to solitary study. In exchange for tutoring a young duke and traveling around Europe for two years, he was given a salary for life. After his tutoring job ended, Smith returned to the small town of his birth, Kircaldy, on the east coast of Scotland, and worked virtually alone for more than 10 years on economics. Thus, Smith spent nearly 25 years in independent study—observing facts, developing theories, imagining how to express the theories—a process that culminated in the *Wealth of Nations.* His intelligence and his love of independently pursuing ideas day after day, year after year are the sources of the *Wealth of Nations.*

Adam Smith is frequently associated with the idea that self-interest, rather than benevolence, should be the basis of society. But an earlier book by Smith, *The Theory of Moral Sentiments,* focused on people's compassion for others, and there is a continuity between this earlier book and the *Wealth of Nations.* Smith recognized the need for cooperation, but reasoned that people's compassion diminishes as they become remote from others in distance, time, or family relationship; and the complexity of a modern economy—the division of labor and the need for resources from all over the world—increases these distances between people, creating the need for alternatives to benevolence. Smith reasoned that self-interest and markets provide that alternative. He wrote that people are

. . . at all times in need of the co-operation and assistance of great multitudes. . . . The woolen coat, for example . . . is the produce of the joint labour of . . . [t]he shepherd, the sorter of the wool, the wool-comber or carder, the dyer, the scribbler, the spinner, the weaver, the fuller, the dresser, with many others. . . . [But man's] whole life is scarce sufficient to gain the friendship of a few persons . . . , and it is in vain for him to expect [help from] benevolence only. . . . It is not from the benevolence of the butcher, the brewer, or the baker, that we expect our dinner, but from their regard to their own interest. We address ourselves, not to their humanity but to their self-love, and never talk to them of our own necessities but of their advantages. [Man is] led by an invisible hand to promote an end which was no part of his intention. Nor is it always the worse for the society that it was no part of it. By pursuing his own interest he frequently promotes that of the society more effectually than when he really intends to promote it.

Source of quote: Adam Smith, *Wealth of Nations* (New York: Modern Library, 1994), pp. 12, 15, 485.

international trade: the exchange of goods and services between people or firms in different nations.

when Emily purchases Johann's printing service, **international trade** will take place because the trade is between people in two different countries. Similarly, Maria could live in Detroit, Michigan, and Adam, in Windsor, Ontario. If so, their trade would also be international.

The gains from international trade are thus of the same kind as the gains from trade within a country. Either people can better satisfy their preferences for goods by trading (as in the case of Maria and Adam), or they can better utilize their comparative advantage (as in the case of Emily and Johann). In either situation there is a gain from trade.

Multilateral Trade and the Need for a Medium of Exchange

multilateral trade: trade among more than two persons or nations.

Our examples have focused on the trade between only *two* people. But, in fact, thousands or even billions of people engage in trade. Such trade is called **multilateral trade,** rather than bilateral trade, because more than two parties participate.

medium of exchange: an item that is generally accepted as a means of payment for goods and services.

Multilateral trade between people requires a medium of exchange to facilitate such trades. A **medium of exchange** is a generally acceptable item that people can buy and sell goods for. Money—paper currency or coin—is such a medium of exchange.

Money facilitates trade by permitting people to exchange any good or service for money. The money can then be used to buy any other good or service—not only ballet or opera tickets—from anyone—not only Adam or Maria. Hence, money circulates among the buyers and sellers, facilitating the exchange of goods. Money is very handy when trade is multilateral.

Different Money in Different Countries

exchange rate: the price of one currency in terms of another.

Different countries use different forms of money: dollars in the United States, yen in Japan, marks in Germany, pesos in Mexico, and so on. The use of different monies is a custom or tradition much like the use of different languages. But just as different languages create a need for translators so that people can communicate, different monies create a need for exchanging one currency for another so that people can trade. In other words, trade between countries requires that people exchange the currency of one country for that of another.

Exchanging One Currency for Another

Cash machines are one way to exchange currency.

Exchange Rates

When Emily in the United States buys printing services from Johann in Germany, he will want to be paid in marks, but she will have dollars to pay. Thus, Emily will need to exchange her dollars for marks. The exchange rate tells us how many marks Emily can get for her dollars. The **exchange rate** is the price of one money in terms of another.

For example, if the dollar/mark exchange rate is 2 marks per dollar, then Emily could obtain 2 marks for each of her dollars when buying printing services from Johann. If the dollar/mark exchange rate fell to 1 mark per dollar, then Emily could obtain only 1 mark per dollar. If the exchange rate rose to 3 marks, she could get 3 marks per dollar.

Emily could exchange dollars for marks in many places: Most international airports offer travelers the opportunity to exchange dollars for several different currencies. There are also cash machines that change one currency into another. As long as there is a place where such exchanges can be carried out, people can trade goods and services in different countries, much as they can in the same country. However, the exchange rate can fluctuate from year to year or even day to day. Like most other prices, the exchange rate is determined by the forces of supply and demand. We will study supply and demand and their effect on prices in the next chapter.

Review

▶ All individuals face scarcity in one form or another. Scarcity forces people to make choices. When there is choice, there is also an opportunity cost of not doing one thing because another thing has been chosen.

▶ People benefit from economic interactions—trading goods and services—with other people. Gains from trade occur because goods and services can be allocated in ways that are more satisfactory to people.

▶ Gains from trade also occur because trade permits specialization through the division of labor. People should specialize in the production of goods they have a comparative advantage in.

▶ Money facilitates trade. Because different countries use different monies, international trade requires people to exchange foreign money. The price of one country's money in terms of another country's money is the exchange rate.

SCARCITY AND CHOICE FOR THE ECONOMY AS A WHOLE

Just as individuals face scarcity and choice, so does the economy as a whole. The total amount of resources in an economy—labor, land, capital, and technology—is limited. Thus, the economy cannot produce all the health care, crime prevention, education, or entertainment that people want. A choice must be made. Let us first consider how to represent scarcity and choice in the whole economy and then consider alternative ways to make the choices.

Production Possibilities

To simplify things, let us suppose that production in the economy can be divided into two broad categories. Suppose the economy can either produce computers (mainframes, PCs, hand calculators) or movies (thrillers, love stories, mysteries, musicals). The choice between computers and movies is symbolic of one of the most fundamental choices individuals in any society must face: how much to invest in order to produce more or better goods in the future versus how much to consume in the present. Computers help people produce more or better goods. Movies are a form of consumption. Other pairs of goods could also be used in our example. Another popular example is guns versus butter, representing defense goods versus nondefense goods.

With a scarcity of resources such as labor and capital, there is a choice between producing some goods, such as computers, versus other goods, such as movies. If the economy produces more of one then it must produce less of the other. Table 2.1

production possibilities: alternative combinations of production of various goods that are possible, given the economy's resources.

gives an example of the alternative choices, or the **production possibilities,** for computers and movies. Observe that there are six different choices, some with more computers and fewer movies, others with fewer computers and more movies.

Table 2.1 tells us what happens as available resources in the economy are moved from movie production to computer production or vice versa. If resources move from producing movies to producing computers, then fewer movies are produced. For example, if all resources are used to produce computers, then 25,000 computers and zero movies can be produced, according to the table. If all resources are used to produce movies, then no computers can be produced. These are two extremes, of course. If 100 movies are produced, then we produce 24,000 computers rather than 25,000 computers. If 200 movies are produced, then computer production must fall to 22,000.

TABLE 2.1
Production Possibilities

	Movies	Computers
A	0	25,000
B	100	24,000
C	200	22,000
D	300	18,000
E	400	13,000
F	500	0

Increasing Opportunity Costs

The production possibilities in Table 2.1 illustrate the concept of opportunity cost for the economy as a whole. The opportunity cost of producing more movies is the value of the foregone computers. For example, the opportunity cost of producing 200 movies rather than 100 movies is 2,000 computers.

An important economic idea about opportunity costs is demonstrated in Table 2.1. Observe that movie production increases as we move down the table. As we move from row to row, movie production increases by the same number: 100 movies. The decline in computer production between the first and second rows—from 25,000 to 24,000 computers—is 1,000 computers. The decline between the second and third rows—from 24,000 to 22,000 computers—is 2,000 computers. Thus, the decline in computer production gets greater as we produce more movies. As we move from 400 movies to 500 movies, we lose 13,000 computers. In other words, the opportunity cost, in terms of computers, of producing more movies increases as we produce more movies. Each extra movie requires a loss of more and more computers. What we have just described is called **increasing opportunity costs.**

increasing opportunity cost: a situation in which producing more of one good requires giving up producing an increasing amount of another good.

Why do increasing opportunity costs occur? You can think about it in the following way. Some of the available resources are better suited for movie production than computer production and vice versa. Workers who are good at building computers might not be so good at acting, for example, or moviemaking may require an area with a dry, sunny climate. As more and more resources go into making movies, we are forced to take resources that are much better at computer making and use them for moviemaking. Thus, more and more computer production must be lost to increase the production of movies by the same amount. Adding specialized computer designers to a movie cast would be very costly in terms of lost computers, and it might add little to movie production.

The Production Possibilities Curve

production possibilities curve: a curve showing the maximum combinations of production of two goods that are possible, given the economy's resources.

Figure 2.2 is a graphical representation of the production possibilities in Table 2.1 that nicely illustrates increasing opportunity costs. We put movies on the horizontal axis and computers on the vertical axis of the figure. Each pair of numbers in a row of the table becomes a point on the graph. For example, point *A* on the graph is from row A of the table. Point *B* is from row B, and so on.

When we connect the points in Figure 2.2, we obtain the **production possibilities curve.** It shows the maximum number of computers that can be produced for each quantity of movies produced. Note how the curve in Figure 2.2 slopes downward and is bowed out from the origin. That the curve is bowed out indicates that the opportunity cost of producing movies increases as more movies are produced. As resources move from computer making to moviemaking, each additional movie means a greater loss to computer production.

The connection between increasing opportunity costs and the production possibilities curve is further illustrated in Figure 2.3. The opportunity costs are shown on the left of the figure. For example, the opportunity cost of producing 100 rather than zero movies is 1,000 computers (24,000 rather than 25,000). As these opportunity costs increase, the production possibilities curve declines more and more sharply, as shown on the right.

Inefficient, Efficient, or Impossible?

The production possibilities curve shows the effects of scarcity and choice in the economy as a whole. Three situations can be distinguished in Figure 2.2, depending on whether production is in the shaded area, on the curve, or outside the curve.

First, imagine production at point *I*. This point is inside the curve with 100 movies and 18,000 computers. But the production possibilities curve tells us it is possible with the same amount of resources to produce more computers, more movies, or both. For some reason, the economy is not working well at point *I*. For example, instead of using movie film, people may be taking still photos and then sticking them together with tape to make the movie. Points inside the curve, like point *I*, are *inefficient* because the economy could produce larger numbers of movies, as at point *D*, or a larger number of computers, as at point *B*. Points inside the production possibilities curve are possible, but they are inefficient.

Second, consider points on the production possibilities curve. These points are *efficient*. They represent the maximum amount that can be produced with available resources. The only way to raise production of one good is to lower production of the other good.

Third, consider points to the right and above the production possibilities curve, like point *J* in Figure 2.2. These points are *impossible*. The economy does not have the resources to produce those quantities.

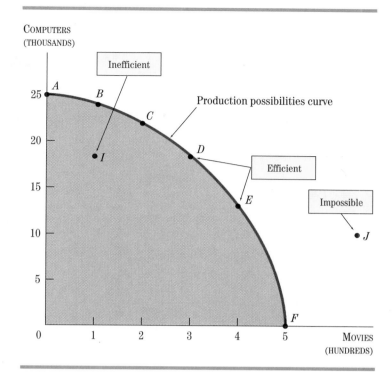

FIGURE 2.2
The Production Possibilities Curve
Each point on the curve shows the maximum amount of computers that can be produced when a given amount of movies is produced. The points with letters are the same as in Table 2.1 and are connected by smooth lines. Points in the shaded area inside the curve are inefficient. Points outside the curve are impossible. For the efficient points on the curve, the more movies that are produced, the fewer computers that are produced. The curve is bowed out because of increasing opportunity costs.

Economic Growth: Shifts in the Production Possibilities Curve

The production possibilities curve is not immovable. It can *shift* out or in. For example, the curve is shown to shift out in Figure 2.4. More resources—more labor, more capital, or more technology—shift the production possibilities curve out. A technological innovation that allowed one to edit movies faster would shift the curve outward. So would more moviemaking machinery: cameras, lights, studios.

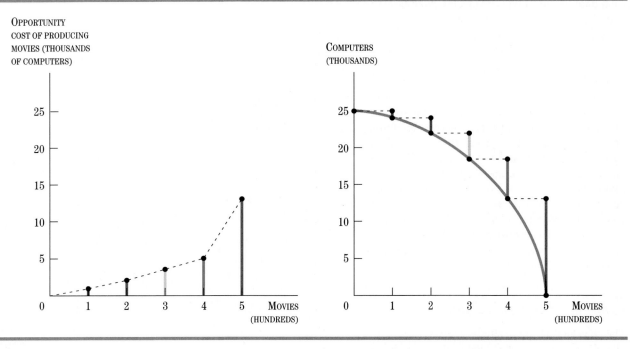

FIGURE 2.3   Increasing Opportunity Costs and the Production Possibilities Curve

As shown on the left, the opportunity cost of producing more movies increases with the number of movies produced. This is why the production possibilities curve declines more and more steeply and is bowed out from the origin. Each opportunity cost is designated by a different color, which is then shown along the production possibilities curve.

FIGURE 2.4
Shifts in the Production Possibilities Curve

The production possibilities curve shifts out as the economy grows. The maximum amount of movies and computers that can be produced increases. Improvements in technology, more machines, or more labor permit the economy to produce more.

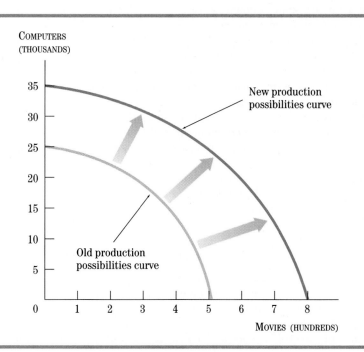

Using Economics to Explain Educational Choice and Economic Growth

More education raises economic growth—the outward shift of the production possibilities curve over time. Why? Because job skills obtained in elementary school, high school, or college enable workers to produce more goods and services. Economists consider education a type of *human capital.*

What type of education—elementary school, high school, or college—has contributed most to the shift in the production possibilities curve in the twentieth century? You might guess that the answer is college, but according to Claudia Goldin, an economic historian at Harvard University: "Increased high school attendance, not that of college nor elementary school, was responsible for the enormous increase in the human capital stock during this century."*

High school graduation rates rose dramatically from only 5 percent in 1910 to 65 percent in 1960, and the high school curriculum changed radically. In 1910, the typical high school focused on Latin and Greek, preparing most students for college. By the 1930s, high schools were teaching courses more useful for getting a job. The English curriculum was expanded. Vocational courses were introduced.

But why did so many more teenagers go to high school? Child labor laws and compulsory schooling laws might seem to be the obvious answer, but "evidence is mounting that legal change was not the spur it appears to be," according to Goldin's research, because most of these laws were passed or strictly enforced only after high school enrollment rates rose. Similarly, it appears that advertising campaigns including *The More You Learn the More You Earn* posters did not have much impact, according to Professor Goldin.

Changes in *opportunity cost* provide a better explanation. During the 1920s, the wages of those with a high school degree rose sharply compared to those without a high school degree. Increased mechanization and foreign immigrants reduced the demand for child and teenage labor, lowering the wage for those teenagers who dropped out of school. In other words, the opportunity cost of staying in school fell: A teenager would earn much less by dropping out of school and working than by graduating from high school. Thus, it is not surprising that many more teenagers chose to stay in high school, fueling economic growth for much of the century.

*Claudia Goldin, "How America Graduated from High School: 1910 to 1960," National Bureau of Economic Research, Working Paper No. 4762, June 1994.

When the production possibilities curve shifts out, more goods and services can be produced. When the economy's production increases, we say there is **economic growth.** The outward shift of the production possibilities curve, representing economic growth, need not be by the same amount in all directions. There can be more movement up than to the right, for example.

As the production possibilities curve shifts out, impossibilities are converted into possibilities. Some of what was impossible for the U.S. economy in 1970 is possible now. Some of what is impossible now will be possible in 2020, unless there is a complete halt to the growth of the economy. Hence, the economists' notion of possibilities is a temporary one. When we say that a certain combination of computers and movies is impossible, we do not mean "forever impossible" but only "impossible for a while."

> **economic growth:** an upward trend in real GDP, reflecting expansion in the economy over time; it can be represented as an outward shift in the production possibilities curve.

Scarcity, Choice, and Economic Growth

However, the conversion of impossibilities into possibilities is also an economic problem of choice and scarcity; if we do not invest in the future now—in machines, in education, in children, in technology—rather than consume everything, it is unlikely that economic growth will continue. If we take computers and movies as symbolic of investment and consumption, then choosing more investment will result in a larger outward shift of the production possibilities curve, as illustrated in

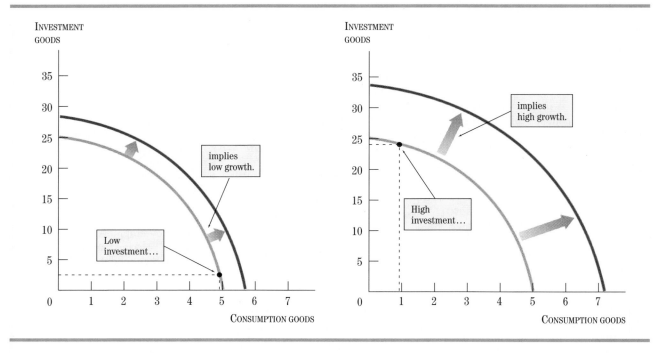

FIGURE 2.5
Shifts in the Production Possibilities Curve Depend on Choices
On the left, few resources are devoted to investment for the future; hence, the production possibilities curve shifts only a little over time. On the right, more resources are devoted to investment and less to consumption; hence, the production possibilities curve shifts out by a larger amount over time.

Figure 2.5. More investment in capital enables the economy to grow by a larger amount.

The production possibilities curve represents a tradeoff, but it does not mean that the economy is a *zero-sum game,* a term that means some people win only if others lose. First, it is not necessary for someone to lose in order for the production possibilities curve to shift out. When the curve shifts out, the production of both items increases. Although some people may fare better than others as the production possibilities curve is pushed out, no one necessarily loses. In principle, everyone can gain from economic growth. Second, if the economy is at an inefficient point (like point *I* in Figure 2.2), then production of both goods can be increased with no tradeoff. In general, therefore, the economy is more like a *positive-sum game*—one where everyone can win.

Review

▶ The production possibilities curve represents the choices open to a whole economy when confronted by a scarcity of resources. With a scarcity of technology, labor, and capital, as more of one item is produced, less of another item must be produced. The opportunity cost of producing more of one item is the reduced production of another item.

▶ The production possibilities curve is bowed out because of increasing opportunity costs.

▶ Points inside the curve are inefficient. Points on the curve are efficient. Points outside the curve are impossible.

▶ The production possibilities curve shifts out as labor, capital, and technology increase.

▶ Outward shifts of the production possibilities curve or moves from inefficient to efficient points are the reasons why the economy is not like a zero-sum game, despite the existence of scarcity and choice.

MARKET ECONOMIES, COMMAND ECONOMIES, AND PRICES

Although the production possibilities curve for the economy as a whole is a simplified representation of scarcity and choice, it enables us to discuss key questions about any economy.

Three Questions

Economists typically focus on three essential questions or problems that every economy must find a way to solve, whether it is a small island economy or a large economy like the United States.

▶ *What* is to be produced: movies, computers, guns, butter, greeting cards, rollerblades, health care, or something else? In other words, where on the production possibilities curve should an economy be?

▶ *How* are these goods to be produced? In other words, how can an economy use the available resources so that it is not at an inefficient point inside the production possibilities curve.

▶ *For whom* are the goods to be produced? We know from our ballet/opera tickets example that the allocation of goods in an economy affects people's well-being. An economy in which Maria cannot trade her opera tickets for ballet tickets would not work as well as one in which such trades and reallocations were possible. Moreover, an economy in which some people get everything and others get virtually nothing is also not working well.

Broadly speaking, the *market economy* and the *command economy* are two alternative approaches to these questions. In a market economy, most decisions about what, how, and for whom to produce are made by individual consumers, firms, governments, and other organizations interacting in markets. In a command,

The Three Fundamental Economic Questions
Any economic system has to answer three questions: What goods and services should be produced—cars, televisions, or something else? How should these goods or services be produced—in what type of factory, and with how much equipment and labor? And for whom should these goods be produced?

or centrally planned, economy, most decisions about what, how, and for whom to produce are made by those who control the government, which, through a central plan, commands and controls what people do.

Centrally planned economies are much less common today than they were in the mid-twentieth century, when nearly half the world's population lived in centrally planned economies, including Eastern Europe, the former Soviet Union, and China.

In recent years, the people of these countries have been trying to convert their command economies into market economies. After many decades, they became disillusioned with the way in which their command economies were working. By comparison the market economies in Western Europe, the United States, and Japan worked much better: These economies were more productive and offered greater quality and more variety of goods and services to consumers.

Key Elements of a Market Economy

Let us consider some of the key features of a market economy.

Freely Determined Prices

freely determined price: a price that is determined by the individuals and firms interacting in markets.

In a market economy, most prices—such as the price of computers or the price at which Maria and Adam trade ballet and opera tickets—are freely determined by individuals and firms. These **freely determined prices** are an essential characteristic of a market economy. In a command economy, most prices are set by government, and this leads to inefficiencies in the economy. For example, in the former Soviet Union, the price of bread was set so low that farmers had an incentive to feed the bread to the cows. Feeding bread to livestock is an enormous waste of resources. Livestock could eat plain grain. By feeding cows bread, farmers added the cost of the labor to bake the bread and the fuel to heat the bread ovens to the cost of livestock feed. This is inefficient, like point *I* in Figure 2.2.

In practice, not all prices in market economies are freely determined. For example, some cities control the price of rental apartments. We will look at these exceptions later. But the vast majority of prices are free to vary.

Property Rights and Incentives

property rights: rights over the use, sale, and proceeds from a good or resource.

Property rights are another key element of a market economy. **Property rights** give individuals the legal authority to keep or sell property, whether land, capital, or other resources. Property rights are needed for a market economy because they give people the ability to buy and sell goods. Without property rights, people could take whatever they wanted without paying. People would have to devote time and resources to protecting their earnings or goods.

incentive: a device that motivates people to take action, usually so as to increase economic efficiency.

Moreover, by giving people the rights to the earnings from their work, as well as letting them suffer some of the consequences or losses from their mistakes, property rights provide **incentives.** For example, if an inventor cannot get the property rights to an invention, then the incentive to produce the invention is low or even nonexistent. Hence there would be few inventions and we would all be worse off. If there were no property rights, people would not have incentives to specialize and reap the gains from the division of labor. Any extra earnings from specialization could be taken away.

Competitive Markets

Markets are competitive when there are many buyers and sellers and no single firm or group of firms dominates the market. When a market is dominated by a large firm, the outcome will most likely be inefficient. A single firm may be able to control the price, set it very high, and produce very little. With a high price, people will consume very little. Competitive markets mean that there are many milk companies or many automobile companies competing with each other.

Freedom to Trade at Home and Abroad

Economic interaction is a way to improve economic outcomes, as the examples in the previous section indicate. Allowing people to interact freely is thus another necessary ingredient of a market economy. Freedom to trade can be extended beyond national borders to other economies.

International trade increases the opportunities to gain from trade. This is especially important in small countries, where it is impossible to produce everything. But the gains from exchange and comparative advantage also exist for larger countries.

A Role for Government

Just because prices are freely determined and people are free to trade in a market economy does not mean there is no role for government. For example, in virtually all market economies, the government provides for defense and police protection. The government also helps establish property rights. But how far beyond that does it go? Should the government also address the "for whom" question by providing a safety net—a mechanism to deal with the individuals in the economy who are poor, who go bankrupt, who remain unemployed? Most would say yes, but what should the government's role be? As you will see, economics provides an analytical framework to answer such questions. In certain circumstances—called **market failure**—the market economy does not provide good enough answers to the "what, how, and for whom" questions, and the government has a role to play in improving on the market. However, the government, even in the case of market failure, may do worse than the market, in which case economists say there is **government failure.**

There is wide agreement among economists that the government has a role in keeping the overall price level stable in a market economy. A stable price level is necessary for a market economy to function well. Imagine how difficult it would be to set prices or decide what to buy if the overall price level rose by 50 percent one month and 100 percent the next month. There is also considerable agreement that the government has a role in keeping the overall economy stable and in preventing a repeat of the Great Depression of the 1930s or even less catastrophic increases in unemployment.

market failure: any situation in which the market does not lead to an efficient economic outcome and in which there is a potential role for government.

government failure: a situation in which the government makes things worse than the market, even though there may be market failure.

The Role of Nongovernment Organizations

It is an interesting feature of market economies that many economic interactions between people take place in organizations—firms, households, universities—rather than in markets. Some economic interactions that take place in organizations could take place in the market. In some circumstances, the same type of interaction takes place in a firm and in a market simultaneously. For example, many large firms employ lawyers as part of their permanent staff. Other firms simply purchase the services of such lawyers in the market; if the firm wants to sue someone or is being sued by someone, it hires an outside lawyer to represent it.

Economic interactions in firms differ from the market. Staff lawyers inside large firms are usually paid annual salaries that do not depend directly on the number of hours worked or their success in the lawsuits. In contrast, outside lawyers are paid an hourly fee and a contingency fee based on the number of hours worked and how successful they are.

Economic interactions within organizations take place at transfer prices. If your economics teacher wants to use special audiovisual equipment, the economics department may have to pay a price—called a *transfer price*—to the university's audiovisual department. A **transfer price** is a price that one department of an organization must pay to receive goods or services from another department in the same organization. The transfer price is usually set by the managers of the organization. If the shipping department of a large firm wants to use a lawyer in the firm's legal department, it will probably be charged a fee. If those same transactions occurred in the market, they would take place at a price or wage determined in the market.

Incentives within an organization are as important as incentives in markets. If the lawyers on a legal staff get to keep some of the damages the firm wins in a lawsuit, the lawyers will have more incentive to do a good job. Some firms even try to create marketlike competition between departments or workers in order to give more incentives.

Why do some economic interactions occur in markets and others in organizations? Ronald Coase of the University of Chicago won the Nobel Prize for showing that organizations such as firms are created to reduce market **transaction costs,** the costs of buying and selling that include finding a buyer or a seller and reaching agreement about a price. When market transaction costs are high, we see more transactions taking place within organizations. For example, the firm might have a legal staff rather than outside lawyers because searching for a good lawyer every time there is a lawsuit is too costly. In a crisis, a good lawyer may not be available.

transfer price: a price that one department of an organization must pay to receive goods or services from another department in the same organization.

transaction cost: the cost of buying or selling in a market including search, bargaining, and writing contracts.

Prices in Action: An Example

The previous discussion indicates that in market economies freely determined prices are important for determining what is produced, how, and for whom. In this section we examine the roles of prices in a market economy with an example demonstrating that (1) prices serve as *signals* about what should be produced and consumed when there are changes in tastes or changes in technology, (2) prices provide *incentives* to people to alter their production or consumption, and (3) prices affect the *distribution of income,* or who gets what in the economy.

Suppose that there is a sudden new trend for college students to ride bicycles more and drive cars less. How do prices help people in the economy decide what to do?

Signals.   First, consider how the information about the change in tastes is signaled to the producers of bicycles and cars. As people try to buy more bicycles, the price of bicycles rises. A higher price will signal that it is more profitable for firms to produce more bicycles. In addition, some bicycle components, like lightweight metal, will also increase in price. Increased lightweight metal prices signal that production should increase. As the price of metal rises, wages for metalworkers may increase. Thus, prices are a signal all the way from the consumer to the metalworkers that more bicycles should be produced. This is what is meant by the expression "prices are a signal."

It is important to note that no single individual knows the information that is transmitted by prices. Any economy is characterized by limited information, where people cannot know the exact reasons why prices for certain goods rise or fall. Hence, it is rather amazing that prices can signal this information.

Incentives. Now consider how prices provide incentives. A higher price for bicycles will increase the incentives for firms to produce bicycles. Because they receive more for each bicycle, they produce more. If there is a large price increase and it continues, new firms may enter the bicycle business. In contrast, the reduced prices for cars signals to car producers that production should decrease.

Distribution. How do prices affect the distribution of income? On the one hand, the workers who find the production of the good they make increasing because of the higher demand for bicycles will earn more. On the other hand, income will be reduced for those who make cars or who have to pay more for bicycles. Local delivery services that use bicycles will see their costs increase.

Review

▶ The market economy and the command economy are two alternative systems for addressing the questions any economy must face: what to produce, how to produce, and for whom to produce.

▶ A market economy is characterized by several key elements, such as freely determined prices, property rights, and freedom to trade at home and abroad.

▶ For a market economy to work well, markets should be competitive and the government should play a role, including keeping the overall price level and the overall economy stable.

▶ Prices are signals, they provide incentives, and they affect the distribution of income.

CONCLUSION

This chapter and Chapter 1 have given a broad overview of economics. In Chapter 1, we saw how economists document and quantify observations about the economy. We also saw that models—abstract simplifications of how the economy works—are used to explain observations and make predictions useful for decision-making in government, business, and everyday life.

In this chapter, we have learned about certain common characteristics of economic models and about how economists think, based on scarcity, choice, and interaction. We've looked at the three essential questions an economy must solve: what and how to produce and for whom. Now we are ready to actually do some economics. In the next chapter, we consider the most famous and frequently used model in economics: the basic supply and demand model.

KEY POINTS

1. Economics is the study of how people make choices when there is a scarcity of resources or time, and how people who make choices interact with each other.

2. Economic interactions occur in markets and in organizations.

3. Scarcity leads to choice, and choice leads to opportunity costs.

4. Trade leads to gains because it allows goods and services to be reallocated in a way that improves people's well-being and because it permits people to specialize in what they are relatively good at.

5. The production possibilities curve summarizes the tradeoffs in the whole economy due to scarcity. Economic production is efficient if the economy is on the production possibilities curve.

6. The three basic questions that any economy must face

are what, how, and for whom production should take place.

7. A well-functioning market system involves free prices, property rights, competition, freedom to trade, and a role for government and nongovernment organizations.

8. If prices are set at the wrong levels by government, waste and inefficiency—such as feeding bread to livestock—will result.

9. Prices transmit signals, provide incentives, and affect the distribution of income.

10. In organizations, transfer prices affect incentives for different departments within the organization.

KEY TERMS

scarcity	comparative advantage	freely determined prices
choice	international trade	property rights
economic interaction	multilateral trade	incentives
organizations	medium of exchange	market failure
market	exchange rate	government failure
opportunity cost	production possibilities	transfer price
gains from trade	increasing opportunity costs	transaction costs
specialization	production possibilities curve	
division of labor	economic growth	

QUESTIONS FOR REVIEW

1. How do scarcity, choice, and economic interaction fit into the definition of economics?

2. Why does scarcity imply a choice among alternatives?

3. Why does choice create opportunity costs?

4. What is the difference between economic interaction in markets and in organizations?

5. Why is there a gain from trade even if total production of goods and services does not change?

6. How can specialization lead to a gain from trade?

7. What is the principle of increasing opportunity costs?

8. What are the key ingredients of a market economy?

9. What are the three basic questions any economic system must address?

10. What are the three roles of prices?

PROBLEMS

1. Suppose you must divide your time between studying for economics and studying for biology. To make things simple, suppose there are only two choices. Suppose that the time and the grades on the finals are as follows:

Fraction of Time on Economics	Economics Grade	Biology Grade
100	100	0
80	97	40
60	90	75
40	75	90
20	40	97
0	0	100

a) Draw a production possibilities curve for the economics grade versus the biology grade.
b) What is the opportunity cost of increasing the time spent on economics from 80 percent to 100 percent? From 60 percent to 80 percent?
c) Are there increasing opportunity costs from spending more time studying economics? What about biology? Explain why this is the case using examples from your own study experience.

2. A small country produces only two goods, cars and cookies. Given its limited resources, this country has the following production possibilities:

Cars	Cookies
0	100
20	90
40	70
60	40
80	0

a) Draw the production possibilities curve.

b) Suppose the production of cars requires the use of large machinery and the production of cookies uses mostly labor. Show the change in the production possibilities curve when the number of machines increases but the amount of labor stays constant.

3. Suppose two countries have the production possibilities curve shown in Figure 2.2, where computers represent investment and movies represent consumption. However, one country chooses a combination that has more investment goods than the other country. How do you think the production possibilities curves of these two countries will differ 50 years from now?

4. Suppose that you are president of the student government, and you have $10,000 for guest speakers for the year. Spike Lee costs $10,000 per appearance. Former economic advisers to the government charge $1,000 per lecture. Hence, you cannot have both Spike Lee and the former economic advisers. Explain the economic problem of choice and scarcity in this case. What issues would you consider in arriving at a decision?

5. Compare two countries. In one country, the government sets prices and never adjusts them. In the other country, the government adjusts prices daily, endeavoring to allocate resources to consumers to satisfy their tastes. Are either of these a market economy? Why or why not?

6. Suppose there is a drought in Australia that causes a severe decline in the production of wheat and raises the price of wheat in the United States. Explain how this change in the price signals information to farmers, provides incentives to farmers in the United States, and affects the distribution of income.

7. Look at Figure 2.2 and compare points *I* and *D*. What is the opportunity cost of moving from *I* to *D*? What are some ways that the economy can move out of the inefficient area inside the production possibilities curve?

8. Suppose one country is more efficient at producing airplanes and another at producing computers. Should these two countries specialize and trade with each other? Why? Explain how specialization and trade is a positive-sum game.

9. Suppose Robert and Jennifer can produce the following combinations of apple pie and computer programs in a day:

Robert		Jennifer	
Pies	Programs	Pies	Programs
0	5	0	8
1	4	1	6
2	3	2	4
3	2	3	2
4	1	4	0
5	0	5	0

a) If Robert is currently producing 2 pies and Jennifer is currently producing 2 pies, then how many computer programs do they each produce? What is the total production of pies and computer programs between them?

b) Is it possible to increase the total production of pies and computer programs? Give an example of how they can change production to increase the total.

c) If they can increase total production, will there be gains from trade when they specialize and trade between themselves?

10. Consider a production possibilities curve showing the tradeoff a country faces in producing consumption goods (butter) and military equipment (guns). As the government decides to move production toward guns, there are increasing opportunity costs. Why?

11. "When you look at the economies in the United States, Europe, or Japan, you see most of the ingredients of a market economy. For example, consider bicycles. Prices in the bicycle market are free to vary; people have property rights to the bicycles they buy; many people sell bicycles; many bicycles sold in the United States, Europe, and Japan come from other countries; the government regulates bicycle use (no bicycles on the freeways, for example); and bicycle production takes place within firms with many workers." Replace bicycles with another good or service of your choosing in the previous quotation and comment on whether the sentence is still true.

12. Allison will graduate from high school next June. She has ranked her three possible postgraduation plans in the following order: (1) work for two years at a consulting job in her home town paying $20,000 per year, (2) attend a local community college for two years with tuition and expenses of $5,000 per year, and (3) travel around the world tutoring a rock star's child for pay of $5,000 per year. What is the opportunity cost of her choice?

13. Compare the opportunity cost of one more year of school versus working for one year for a (1) high school graduate, (2) college graduate, and (3) medical school graduate.

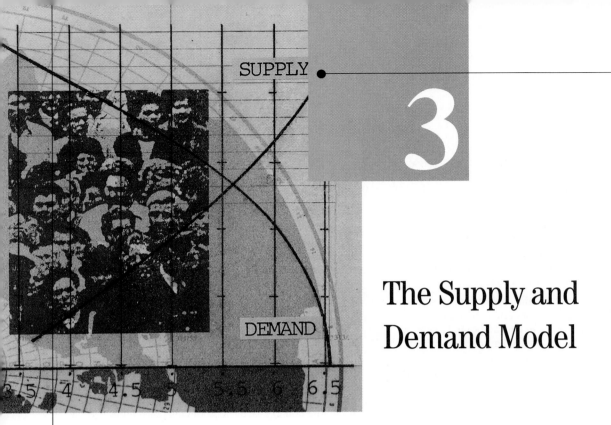

3

The Supply and Demand Model

Prices are both the lifeblood and the nervous system of a market economy. By transmitting vital information and providing incentives, prices enable a market economy to adjust to change and to thrive. But how are prices determined? What caused the price of health care to rise? What caused the price of computers to fall? What determines the price at which people buy or sell gasoline, electronic goods, printing services, or foreign currencies? The purpose of this chapter is to show how to find the answers to such questions.

To do so, we need to construct a model—a simplified description of how a market economy works. The model economists use to explain how prices are determined in a market economy is called the *supply and demand model.* This model describes how particular markets—such as the health-care market or the computer market—work. It

consists of three elements: *demand,* describing the behavior of consumers in the market; *supply,* describing the behavior of firms in the market; and *market equilibrium,* connecting supply and demand and describing how consumers and firms interact in the market.

Economists like to compare the supply and demand model to a pair of scissors. Demand is one blade of the scissors. Supply is the other. Either blade alone is incomplete and virtually useless; but when the two blades of a pair of scissors are connected to form the scissors, they become an amazingly useful, yet simple, tool. So it is with supply and demand.

In this chapter, we first describe each of the three elements of the model. We then show how to use the model to answer a host of questions about price determination in a market economy.

DEMAND

To an economist, the term *demand*—whether the demand for health care or the demand for computers—has a very specific meaning. **Demand** is a relationship between two economic variables: (1) *the price of a particular good,* and (2) *the quantity of the good consumers are willing to buy at that price during a specific time period,* all other things being equal. For short, we call the first variable the **price** and the second variable the **quantity demanded.** The phrase *all other things being equal,* or *ceteris paribus,* is appended to the definition of demand because the quantity consumers are willing to buy depends on many other things besides the price of the good; we want to hold these other things constant, or equal, while we examine the relationship between price and quantity demanded.

Demand can be represented either numerically with a table or graphically with a curve. In either case, demand describes how much of a good consumers will purchase at each price. Consider the demand for bicycles in the United States. An example of the demand for bicycles is shown in Table 3.1. Several prices for a typical bicycle are listed in the first column of the table, ranging from $140 to $300. Of course, there are many kinds of bicycles—mountain bikes, racing bikes, children's bikes, and inexpensive one-speed bikes with cruiser brakes—so you need to think about the price of an average, or typical, bike.

Listed in the second column of Table 3.1 is the quantity demanded (in millions of bicycles) each year in the United States at the price in the first column. This is the total demand in the bicycle market. For example, at a price of $180 per bicycle, consumers would buy 11 million bicycles. That is, the quantity demanded would be 11 million bicycles each year in the United States, according to Table 3.1.

Observe that, as the price rises, the quantity demanded by consumers goes down. If the price goes up from $180 to $200 per bicycle, for example, the quantity demanded goes down from 11 million to 9 million bicycles. On the other hand, if the price goes down, the quantity demanded goes up. If the price falls from $180 to $160, for example, the quantity demanded rises from 11 million to 14 million bicycles.

The relationship between price and quantity demanded in Table 3.1 is called a **demand schedule.** This relationship is an example of the law of demand. The **law of demand** says that the higher the price, the lower the quantity demanded in the market; and the lower the price, the higher the quantity demanded in the market. In other words, the law of demand says that the price and the quantity demanded are negatively related, all other things being equal.

The Demand Curve

Figure 3.1 represents demand graphically. It is a graph with the price of the good on the vertical axis and the quantity demanded of the good on the horizontal axis. It shows the demand for bicycles given in Table 3.1. Each of the nine rows in Table 3.1 corresponds to each of the nine points in Figure 3.1. For example, the point at the lower right part of the graph corresponds to the first row of the table, when the price is $140 and the quantity demanded is 18 million bicycles. The resulting curve showing all the combinations of price and quantity demanded is the **demand curve.**

demand: a relationship between **price** and **quantity demanded.**

TABLE 3.1
Demand Schedule for Bicycles
(millions of bicycles per year)

Price	Quantity Demanded
$140	18
$160	14
$180	11
$200	9
$220	7
$240	5
$260	3
$280	2
$300	1

demand schedule: a tabular presentation of demand showing the price and quantity demanded for a particular good, all else being equal.

law of demand: the tendency for the quantity demanded of a good in a market to decline as its price rises.

demand curve: a graph of demand showing the downward-sloping relationship between price and quantity demanded.

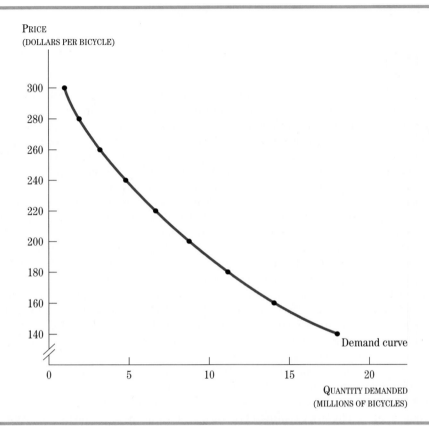

Price	Quantity Demanded
$140	18
$160	14
$180	11
$200	9
$220	7
$240	5
$260	3
$280	2
$300	1

FIGURE 3.1
The Demand Curve

The demand curve shows that the price of a good and the quantity demanded by consumers are negatively related. The curve slopes down. For each price, the demand curve gives the quantity demanded, or the quantity that consumers are willing to buy at that price. The points along the demand curve for bicycles shown here are the same as the pairs of numbers in Table 3.1.

It slopes downward from left to right because the quantity demanded is negatively related to the price. To remember that the *d*emand curve slopes *d*ownward, think of the *d* in *demand*.

Why does the demand curve slope downward? The demand curve tells us the quantity demanded by all consumers. If the price of bicycles falls, then some consumers who previously found the price of bicycles too high may decide to buy a bicycle. The lower price of bicycles gives them an incentive to buy bicycles rather than other goods. It is important to remember that when economists draw a demand curve, they hold constant the price of other goods: running shoes, rollerblades, motor scooters, etc. When the price of bicycles falls, bicycles become more attractive to people in comparison with these other goods. As a result, the quantity demanded rises when the price falls. Conversely, when the price of bicycles rises, some people may decide to buy rollerblades or motor scooters instead of bicycles. As a result, the quantity demanded declines when the price rises.

Shifts in Demand

Now price is not the only thing that affects the quantity of a good that people buy. The weather, people's concerns about the environment, or the availability of bike lanes on roads can influence people's decisions to purchase bicycles, for example. The quantity of bicycles bought might increase if a climate change brings on an extended period of dry weather. Because people would enjoy riding their bicycles

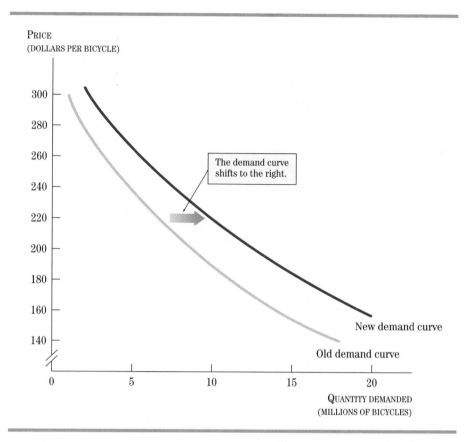

PRICE
(DOLLARS PER BICYCLE)

The demand curve shifts to the right.

New demand curve

Old demand curve

QUANTITY DEMANDED
(MILLIONS OF BICYCLES)

FIGURE 3.2
A Shift in the Demand Curve
The demand curve shows how the quantity demanded of a good is related to the price of the good, all other things being equal. A change in one of these other things—the weather or people's tastes, for example—will shift the demand curve as shown in the graph. In this case the demand for bicycles increases; the demand curve for bicycles shifts to the right.

more in dry weather, more bicycles would be purchased at any given price. Or perhaps there is a health trend leading people to get exercise by riding bicycles rather than driving their cars. This would also lead to more purchases of bicycles.

The demand curve is drawn assuming all other things equal, except the price of the good. A change in any one of these other things, previously assumed equal, will shift the demand curve. An increase in demand shifts the demand curve to the right. A decrease in demand shifts the demand curve to the left. This is illustrated in Figure 3.2. The lightly shaded curve labeled "old demand curve" is the same as the demand curve in Figure 3.1. The arrow shows how this curve has shifted to the right to the more darkly shaded curve labeled "new demand curve." Thus, Figure 3.2 shows that the demand curve for bicycles shifts to the right. When the demand curve shifts to the right, more bicycles are purchased than before at any given price. For example, before the shift in demand, a $200 price led to 9 million bicycles purchased. But when the demand curve shifts to the right because of drier weather, that same price leads to 13 million bicycles purchased. The demand curve would shift to the left if a climate change to wetter weather reduced people's purchases of bicycles at any given price.

There are many reasons the demand curve may shift. Most of them can be categorized into several sources: *consumers' preferences, consumers' information, consumers' incomes, the number of consumers in the population, consumers' expectations of future prices,* and *the price of related goods.* Let us briefly consider each source of shifts in demand.

Consumers' Preferences

In general, a change in people's tastes or preferences for a product compared to other products will change the amount of the product they purchase at any given price. The physical fitness craze leading to an increase in the demand for bicycles is an example. Other examples of changes in preferences that cause shifts in demand for other goods and services include an increase in the demand for over-the-counter cold remedies when the weather turns wet and chilly in the winter, an increase in the demand for taxis on rainy days, and a decline in the demand for travel on subways because of increasing concerns about crime.

Consumers' Information

A change in information relating to a product can also cause the demand curve to shift. For example, when people learned about the dangers of smoking, the demand for cigarettes declined. Similarly, information about the effects of cholesterol may have reduced the demand for beef and increased the demand for chicken. The demand curve for chicken shifted to the right. The demand curve for beef shifted to the left.

Consumers' Incomes

normal good: a good for which demand increases when income rises and decreases when income falls.

inferior good: a good for which demand decreases when income rises and increases when income falls.

If people's incomes change, then their purchases of goods usually change. An increase in income increases the demand for most goods. For example, higher incomes increase the demand for eating out, for cars, for movies. A decline in income reduces the demand for these goods. Goods for which demand increases when income rises, or for which demand decreases when income falls, are called **normal goods** by economists.

However, the demand for some goods—such as one-speed bicycles or day-old bread—may decline when income increases. Such goods are called **inferior goods** by economists. The demand for inferior goods declines when people's income increases because they can afford more attractive goods, such as fresh bread or 15-speed bicycles. But whether goods are normal or inferior, the demand for them usually shifts when consumers' incomes change.

Number of Consumers in the Population

Demand is a relationship between price and the quantity demanded by *all* consumers in the market. If the number of consumers increases, then demand will increase. If the number of consumers falls, then demand will decrease. For example, the number of teenagers in the U.S. population expanded sharply in the late 1990s. This increases the demand for *Seventeen* magazine, for rollerblades, for Clearasil, and for other goods that teenagers tend to buy. As the number of older people in the population increases in the early part of the twenty-first century, the demand for nursing homes is expected to increase.

Consumers' Expectations of the Future

If people expect the price of a good to increase, they will want to buy it before the price increases. Conversely, if people expect the price to decline, they will purchase less and wait for the decline. One sees this effect of expectations of future price changes often. "We better buy before the price goes up" is a common reason for purchasing items during a clearance sale. Or, "Let's put off buying that bicycle until the postholiday sales."

In general, it is difficult to forecast the future, but sometimes consumers know quite a bit about whether the price of a good will rise or fall, and they react accordingly. Thus, demand increases if people expect the *future* price of the good to rise. And demand decreases if people expect the *future* price of the good to fall.

Prices of Closely Related Goods

A sharp decrease in the price of motor scooters or rollerblades will decrease the demand for bicycles. Why? Because buying these related goods becomes relatively more attractive than buying bicycles. Motor scooters or rollerblades are examples of substitutes for bicycles. A **substitute** is a good that provides some of the same uses or enjoyment as another good. Butter and margarine are substitutes. In general, the demand for a good will increase if the price of a substitute for the good rises, and the demand for a good will decrease if the price of a substitute falls.

On the other hand, a sharp increase in the cost of bicycle helmets—another good closely related to bicycles—will decrease the demand for bicycles, especially if there is a law that requires that bicycle riders, but not rollerbladers, wear helmets. A bicycle helmet is an example of a good that is a complement to a bicycle. In general, a **complement** is a good that tends to be consumed together with another good. Coffee and sugar are complements. The demand for a good (sugar) increases if the price of a complement (coffee) decreases, and the demand for a good (sugar) decreases if the price of a complement (coffee) increases.

Movements Along versus Shifts of the Demand Curve

We have shown that the demand curve can shift, and we have given many possible reasons for such shifts. In using demand curves, it is very important to distinguish *shifts* of the demand curve from *movements along* the demand curve. This distinction is illustrated in Figure 3.3.

A *movement along* the demand curve occurs when the quantity demanded changes due to a *change in the price of the good*. For example, if the price of bicycles rises, causing the quantity demanded by consumers to fall, then there is a movement along the demand curve. A movement along the demand curve for bicycles occurs when the quantity demanded changes from point *A* to point *B* or from point *A* to point *C* in Figure 3.3. At point *A* the price is $200 and the quantity demanded is 9 million. At point *B* the price is $220 and the quantity demanded is 7 million. If the quantity changes because the price changes, economists say there is a *change in the quantity demanded.*

A *shift* of the demand curve, on the other hand, occurs if there is a change due to *any source except the price*. When the demand curve shifts, economists say there is a *change in demand*. Remember, the term *demand* refers to the entire curve or schedule relating price and quantity demanded, while the term *quantity demanded* refers to a single point on the demand curve. You should be able to tell whether any

Substitutes and Complements
Butter and margarine are examples of substitutes; they have similar characteristics. For example, margarine can be substituted for butter on toast. A *rise* in the price of butter will *increase* the demand for margarine. Hot dogs and hot dog buns are examples of complements; they tend to be consumed together. A *rise* in the price of hot dogs will *decrease* the demand for hot dog buns.

substitute: a good that has many of the same characteristics and can be used in place of another good.

complement: a good that is usually consumed or used together with another good.

FIGURE 3.3
Shifts versus Movements Along the Demand Curve

A *shift* in the demand curve occurs when there is a change in something (other than the good's own price) that affects the quantity of a good consumers are willing to buy. An increase in demand is a shift to the right of the demand curve. A decrease in demand is a shift to the left of the demand curve. A movement along the demand curve occurs when the price of the good changes, causing the quantity demanded to change as, for example, from point *A* to points *B* or *C*.

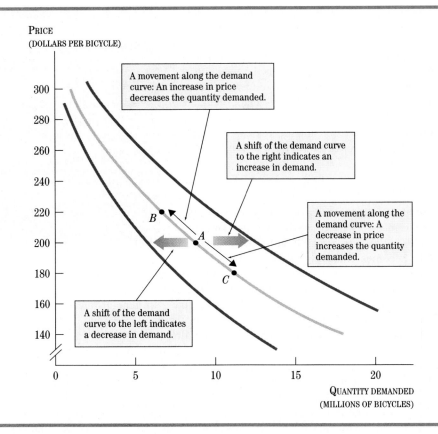

economic event causes (1) a change in demand or (2) a change in the quantity demanded; or, equivalently, (1) a shift in the demand curve or (2) a movement along the demand curve.

Review

▶ Demand is a relationship between the price of a good and the quantity people will buy at each price, all other things equal. The demand curve slopes down. The price and the quantity demanded are negatively related.

▶ When the price of a good changes, the quantity demanded changes and we have a movement along the demand curve.

▶ When something other than the price changes and affects demand, there is a shift in the demand curve or, simply, a change in demand.

SUPPLY

supply: a relationship between **price** and **quantity supplied.**

Whereas demand refers to the behavior of consumers, supply refers to the behavior of firms. The term *supply*—whether it is the supply of health care or computers—has a very specific meaning for economists. **Supply** is a relationship between two variables: (1) *the price of a particular good,* and (2) *the quantity of the good firms are willing to sell at that price,* all other things the same. For short, we call the first variable the **price** and the second variable the **quantity supplied.**

Supply can be represented with a numerical table or a graph. An example of the supply of bicycles is shown in Table 3.2. Listed in the first column of Table 3.2 is the price of bicycles; the range of prices is the same as for the demand schedule in Table 3.1. The second column lists the quantity supplied (in millions of bicycles) in the entire market by bicycle-producing firms at each price. For example, at a price of $180, the quantity supplied is 7 million bicycles. Observe that as the price increases, the quantity supplied increases, and that as the price decreases, the quantity supplied decreases. For example, if the price rises from $180 to $200, the quantity supplied increases from 7 to 9 million bicycles. The relationship between price and quantity supplied in Table 3.2 is a **supply schedule.** This relationship is an example of the law of supply. The **law of supply** says that the higher the price, the higher the quantity supplied, and the lower the price, the lower the quantity supplied. In other words, the law of supply says that the price and the quantity supplied are positively related.

The Supply Curve

We can represent the supply schedule in Table 3.2 graphically by plotting the price and quantity supplied on a graph, as shown in Figure 3.4. The scales of each axis in

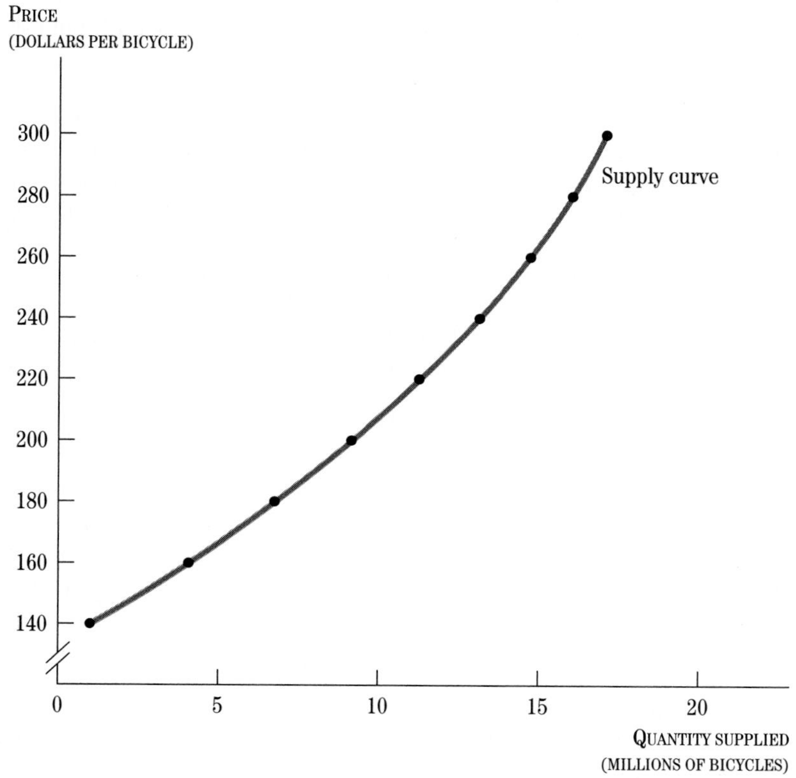

supply schedule: a tabular presentation of supply showing the price and quantity supplied of a particular good, all else being equal.

TABLE 3.2
Supply Schedule for Bicycles
(millions of bicycles per year)

Price	Quantity Supplied
$140	1
$160	4
$180	7
$200	9
$220	11
$240	13
$260	15
$280	16
$300	17

FIGURE 3.4
The Supply Curve
The supply curve shows that the price and the quantity supplied by firms in the market are positively related. The curve slopes up. For each price on the vertical axis, the supply curve shows the quantity that firms are willing to sell along the horizontal axis. The points along the supply curve for bicycles match the pairs of numbers in Table 3.2.

law of supply: the tendency for the quantity supplied of a good in a market to increase as its price rises.

supply curve: a graph of supply showing the upward-sloping relationship between price and quantity supplied.

Figure 3.4 are exactly the same as those in Figure 3.1, except that Figure 3.4 shows the quantity supplied, whereas Figure 3.1 shows the quantity demanded. Each pair of numbers in Table 3.2 is plotted as a point in Figure 3.4. The resulting curve showing all the combinations of prices and quantities supplied is the **supply curve.** Note that the curve slopes upward: $280 represents a high price, and there the quantity supplied is high—16 million bicycles. If the price is down at $160 a bicycle, then firms are willing to sell only 4 million bicycles.

Why does the supply curve slope upward? Imagine yourself running a firm that produces and sells bicycles. If the price of the bicycles goes up, from $180 to $280, then you can earn $100 more for each bicycle you produce and sell. Given your production costs, if you earn more from each bicycle, you will have a greater incentive to produce and sell more bicycles. If producing more bicycles increases the costs of producing each bicycle, perhaps because you must pay the bike assembly workers a higher wage for working overtime, the higher price will give you the incentive to incur these costs. Other bicycle firms will be thinking the same way. Thus, firms are willing to sell more bicycles as the price rises. Conversely, the incentive for firms to sell bicycles will decline as the price falls. Basically, that is why there is a positive relationship between price and quantity supplied.

Shifts in Supply

The supply curve is drawn assuming all other things equal, except the price of the good. If any one of these other things change, then the supply curve shifts. For example, suppose a new machine is invented that makes it less costly for firms to produce bicycles; then firms would have more incentive at any given price to produce and sell more bicycles. Supply would increase; the supply curve would shift to the right.

Figure 3.5 shows how the supply curve for bicycles would shift to the right because of a new cost-reducing machine. The supply curve would shift to the left when there is a decrease in supply. Supply would decrease, for example, if bicycle-producing firms suddenly found that their existing machines became too hot and had to be oiled with an expensive lubricant each time a bicycle was produced. This would raise costs, lower supply, and shift the supply curve to the left.

Many things can cause the supply curve to shift. Most of these can be categorized by the source of the change in supply: *technology, the price of goods used in production, the number of firms in the market, expectations of future prices,* and *government taxes, subsidies, and regulations.* Let us briefly consider the sources of shifts in supply.

Technology

Anything that changes the amount a firm can produce with a given amount of inputs to production can be considered a change in technology. Because of new discoveries and ideas for improving production, technology usually gets better over time. Better bicycle-making machinery is an example. Another example is the rapid improvement in the technology for producing computers. These technological improvements increase supply and shift the supply curve to the right.

Droughts, earthquakes, and terrorists' bombing of factories also affect the amount that can be produced with given inputs. A drought that reduces the amount of wheat that can be produced on a farm in the Midwest or a freeze that reduces the number of oranges yielded by trees in Florida orchards are examples. Because such

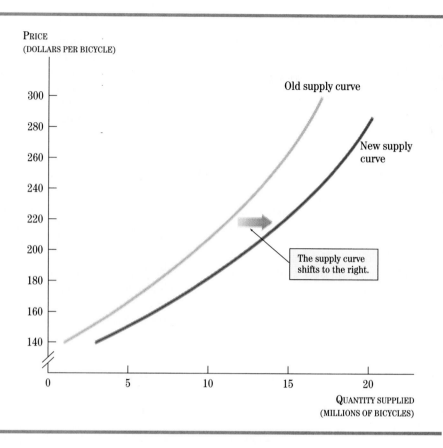

FIGURE 3.5
A Shift in the Supply Curve
The supply curve is a relationship between the quantity supplied of a good and the price of the good, all other things being equal. A change in one of these other things (other than the good's price) will shift the supply curve as shown in the graph. In this case the supply of bicycles increases; the supply curve for bicycles shifts to the right.

events change the amount that can be produced with a given amount of inputs, they are similar to changes in technology, though these examples reduce rather than increase supply. In these cases, the supply curve shifts to the left.

The Price of Goods Used in Production

If the prices of the inputs to production—raw materials, labor, or capital—increase, then it becomes more costly to produce goods, and firms would produce less at any given price; the supply curve would shift to the left. For example, if the price of fertilizer rises, then the cost of growing corn will rise, and the supply of corn will decrease. On the other hand, if the price of an input, such as fertilizer, falls, supply increases and the supply curve shifts to the right.

The Number of Firms in the Market

Remember that the supply curve refers to *all* the firms producing the product—all the corn farmers, for example. If the number of firms increases, then more goods will be produced at each price; supply increases, and the supply curve shifts to the right. For example, as more firms entered the overnight package delivery service in the 1980s and 1990s, the supply increased.

A decline in the number of firms would shift the supply curve to the left. For example, the number of drive-in movie theaters has declined sharply over the last 30 years; hence the supply curve has shifted.

Expectations of Future Price

If firms expect the price of the good they produce to rise in the future, then they will hold off selling at least part of production until the price rises. For example, farmers in the United States who anticipate an increase in wheat prices because of political turbulence in Russia may decide to store more wheat in silos and sell it later, when the price rises. Thus, expectations of *future* price increases tend to reduce supply. Conversely, expectations of *future* price decreases tend to increase supply.

Government Taxes, Subsidies, and Regulations

The government has the ability to affect the supply of particular goods produced by firms. For example, the government imposes taxes on firms to pay for such government services as education, police, and national defense. These taxes increase firms' costs and reduce supply. The supply curve shifts to the left when a tax on what firms sell in the market increases.

The government also makes payments—subsidies—to firms to encourage the firms to produce certain goods. Many farms now receive subsidies to produce certain food products. Such subsidies have the opposite effect of taxes on supply. An increase in subsidies reduces firms' costs and increases the supply.

FIGURE 3.6

Shifts versus Movements Along the Supply Curve

A *shift* in the supply curve occurs when there is a change in something (other than the price) that affects the amount of a good firms are willing to supply. An increase in supply is a shift to the right of the supply curve. A decrease in supply is a shift to the left of the supply curve. A movement along the supply curve occurs when the price of the good changes, causing the quantity supplied by firms to change; for example, from point D to points E or F.

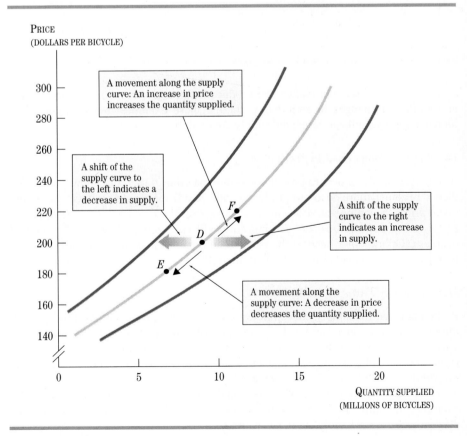

Governments also regulate firms. In some cases, such regulations can change the firms' costs of production and thereby affect supply. For example, when the government requires that firms install safety features on their products, the cost of producing the products rises, and thus supply declines.

Movements Along versus Shifts of the Supply Curve

Figure 3.6 compares *shifts* of the supply curve with *movements along* the supply curve. A *movement along* the supply curve occurs when a change in price causes a change in the quantity supplied. Economists then say there is a *change in the quantity supplied,* as, for example, when the quantity supplied changes from point *D* to point *F* or from point *D* to point *E* in Figure 3.6.

A *shift* of the supply curve occurs if there is a change due to *any source except the price.* When the supply curve shifts, economists say there is a *change in supply.* The term *supply* refers to the entire supply curve. The term *quantity supplied* refers to a point on the supply curve. As we will soon see, it is important to be able to tell whether a change in something causes (1) a change in supply or (2) a change in the quantity supplied; or, equivalently, (1) a shift in the supply curve or (2) a movement along the supply curve.

Review

▶ Supply is a positive relationship between the price of a good and the quantity supplied of the good by firms. The supply curve slopes upward because higher prices give firms more incentive to produce and sell more.

▶ When the quantity supplied changes because of a change in price, we have a movement along the supply curve. Other factors—such as technology, the number of firms, and expectations—affect supply. When these determinants change, the supply curve shifts.

MARKET EQUILIBRIUM: COMBINING SUPPLY AND DEMAND

Thus far, we have examined consumers' demand for goods in a market and firms' supply of goods in a market. Now we put supply and demand together to complete the supply and demand model. When consumers buy goods and firms sell goods, they interact in a market and a price is determined. Recall that a market does not need to be located at one place; the U.S. bicycle market consists of all the bicycle firms that sell bicycles and all the consumers who buy bicycles.

Although it may sound amazing, no single person or firm determines the price in the market. Instead the market determines the price. As buyers and sellers interact, prices might go up for a while and then go down. Alfred Marshall, the economist who did the most to develop the supply and demand model in the late nineteenth century, called this process the "higgling and bargaining" of the market. The assumption underlying the supply and demand model is that, in the give and take of the marketplace, prices adjust until they settle down to a level where the quantity supplied by firms equals the quantity demanded by consumers. Let's see how.

Overview of Supply and Demand

SUPPLY

Supply describes firms.

The supply curve looks like this:

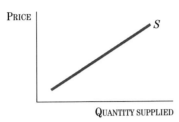

DEMAND

Demand describes consumers.

The demand curve looks like this:

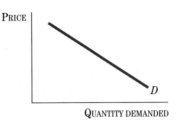

Law of Supply

Price and quantity supplied are positively related.

Movements along supply curve occur

when price rises and quantity supplied rises
or
when price falls and quantity supplied falls.

Shifts in supply are due to:

Technology (new inventions)

Number of firms in market

Price of goods used in production (inputs such as fertilizer, labor)

Government taxes, subsidies, regulations (commodity taxes, agricultural subsidies, safety regulations)

Expectations of future prices (firms will sell less now if prices are expected to rise; for example, farmers may store goods to sell next year)

Law of Demand

Price and quantity demanded are negatively related.

Movements along demand curve occur

when price rises and quantity demanded falls
or
when price falls and quantity demanded rises.

Shifts in demand are due to:

Preferences (nice weather or fitness craze changes tastes)

Number of consumers in market

Price of related goods (both substitutes, like butter and margarine, and complements, like coffee and sugar)

Consumers' income (normal goods versus inferior goods)

Expectations of future prices (consumers will buy more now if prices are expected to rise in the future)

Consumers' information (about cholesterol or smoking, for example)

Determination of the Market Price

To determine the market price, we combine the demand relationship between the price and the quantity demanded with the supply relationship between the price and the quantity supplied. We can do this using either a table or a diagram. First consider Table 3.3, which combines the demand schedule from Table 3.1 with the supply schedule from Table 3.2. The price is in the first column, the quantity demanded by consumers is in the second column, and the quantity supplied by firms is in the third column. Observe that the quantity consumers are willing to buy is shown to

Price	Quantity Demanded	Quantity Supplied	Shortage, Surplus, or Equilibrium	Price Rises or Falls
$140	18	1	Shortage = 17	Price rises
$160	14	4	Shortage = 10	Price rises
$180	11	7	Shortage = 4	Price rises
$200	9	9	Equilibrium	No change
$220	7	11	Surplus = 4	Price falls
$240	5	13	Surplus = 8	Price falls
$260	3	15	Surplus = 12	Price falls
$280	2	16	Surplus = 14	Price falls
$300	1	17	Surplus = 16	Price falls

TABLE 3.3
Finding the Market Equilibrium

Quantity supplied equals quantity demanded.

decline with the price, while the quantity firms are willing to sell is shown to increase with the price. In order to determine the price in the market, consider each of the prices in Table 3.3.

Finding the Market Price

Pick a price in Table 3.3, any price. Suppose the price you choose is $160. Then the quantity demanded by consumers (14 million bicycles) is greater than the quantity supplied by the firms (4 million bicycles). In other words, there is a shortage of 14 − 4 = 10 million bicycles. A **shortage** is a situation where the quantity demanded is greater than the quantity supplied.[1] With a shortage of bicycles, the price will quickly rise above $160; firms will charge higher prices, and consumers who are willing to pay more than $160 for a bicycle will pay higher prices to firms. Thus, $160 cannot last as the market price. Observe that as the price rises above $160, the quantity demanded falls, and the quantity supplied rises. Thus, as the price rises, the shortage begins to decline. If you choose any price below $200, the same thing will happen: There will be a shortage and the price will rise. The shortage disappears only when the price rises to $200, as shown in Table 3.3.

    Now pick a price above $200. Suppose you pick $260. Then the quantity demanded by consumers (3 million bicycles) is less than the quantity supplied by firms (15 million bicycles). In other words, there is a surplus of 12 million bicycles. A **surplus** is a situation in which the quantity supplied is greater than the quantity demanded.[2] With a surplus of bicycles, the price will fall: Firms that are willing to sell bicycles for less than $260 will offer to sell at lower prices to consumers. Thus, $260 cannot be the market price either. Observe that as the price falls below $260, the quantity demanded rises and the quantity supplied falls. Thus, the surplus declines. If you choose any price above $200, the same thing will happen: There will be a surplus and the price will fall. The surplus disappears only when the price falls to $200.

    Thus, we have shown that for any price below $200, there is a shortage and the price rises; while for any price above $200, there is a surplus and the price falls. What if the market price is $200? Then the quantity supplied equals the quantity demanded; there is neither a shortage nor a surplus, and there is no reason for the

shortage: the situation in which quantity demanded is greater than quantity supplied.

surplus: the situation in which quantity supplied is greater than quantity demanded.

1. *Excess demand* is another term for *shortage.*
2. *Excess supply* is another term for *surplus.*

equilibrium price: the price at which quantity supplied equals quantity demanded.

price to rise or fall. This price of $200 is therefore the most likely prediction of the market price. It is called the **equilibrium price** because at this price the quantity supplied equals the quantity demanded, and there is no tendency for price to change. There is no other price for which quantity supplied equals quantity demanded. By looking at all the other prices, you will see that there is either a shortage or a surplus, and there is a tendency for the price to either rise or fall.

equilibrium quantity: the quantity traded at the equilibrium price.

market equilibrium: the situation in which the price is equal to the equilibrium price and the quantity traded equals the equilibrium quantity.

The quantity bought and sold at the equilibrium price is 9 million bicycles. This is the **equilibrium quantity.** When the price equals the equilibrium price and the quantity bought and sold equals the equilibrium quantity, we say there is a **market equilibrium.**

Our discussion of the determination of the equilibrium price shows how the market price coordinates the buying and selling decisions of many firms and consumers. We see that the price serves a *rationing function;* that is, the price alleviates shortages: A higher price reduces the quantity demanded or increases the quantity supplied when necessary to eliminate a shortage. Similarly, a lower price increases the quantity demanded or decreases the quantity supplied when there is a surplus. Thus, both shortages and surpluses are eliminated by the forces of supply and demand.

Two Predictions

By combining supply and demand, we have completed the supply and demand model. The model can be applied to many markets, not just the example of the bicycle market. One prediction of the supply and demand model is that *the price in the market will be the price for which the quantity supplied equals the quantity demanded.* Thus, the model provides an answer to the question of what determines the price in the market. Another prediction of the model is that *the quantity bought and sold in the market is the quantity for which the quantity supplied equals the quantity demanded.*

Finding the Equilibrium with a Supply and Demand Diagram

The equilibrium price and quantity in a market can also be found with the help of a graph. Figure 3.7 combines the demand curve from Figure 3.1 and the supply curve from Figure 3.4 in the same diagram. Observe that the downward-sloping demand curve intersects the upward-sloping supply curve at a single point. At that point of intersection, the quantity supplied equals the quantity demanded. Hence, the *equilibrium price occurs at the intersection of the supply curve and the demand curve.* The equilibrium price of $200 is shown in Figure 3.7. At that price, the quantity demanded is 9 million bicycles and the quantity supplied is 9 million bicycles. This is the equilibrium quantity.

If the price were lower than this equilibrium price, say $160, then the quantity demanded would be greater than the quantity supplied. There would be a shortage and the price would begin to rise, as shown in the graph. On the other hand, if the price were above the equilibrium price, say $260, then there would be a surplus, as shown in the graph, and the price would begin to fall. Thus, the market price will tend to move toward the equilibrium price at the intersection of the supply curve and the demand curve. We can calculate exactly what the equilibrium price is on the graph by drawing a line over to the vertical axis. And we can calculate the equilibrium quantity by drawing a line down to the horizontal axis.

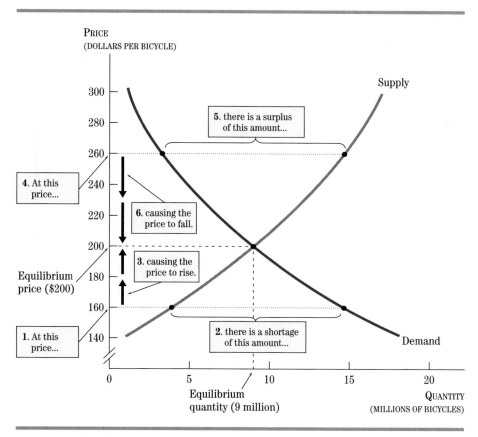

FIGURE 3.7
Equilibrium Price and Equilibrium Quantity
When buyers and sellers interact in the market, the equilibrium price is at the point of intersection of the supply curve and the demand curve. At this point, the quantity supplied equals the quantity demanded. The equilibrium quantity is also determined at that point. At a higher price, the quantity demanded will be less than the quantity supplied; there will be a surplus. At a lower price, the quantity demanded will be greater than the quantity supplied; there will be a shortage.

A Change in the Market

In order to use the supply and demand model to explain or predict changes in prices, we need to consider what happens to the equilibrium price when there is a change in supply or demand. We first consider a change in demand and then a change in supply.

Effects of a Change in Demand

Figure 3.8 shows the effects of a shift in the demand curve for bicycles. Suppose that a shift occurs because of a fitness craze that increases the demand for bicycles. The demand curve shifts to the right, as shown in graph (a) in Figure 3.8. The demand curve before the shift and the demand curve after the shift are labeled the "old demand curve" and the "new demand curve," respectively.

If you look at the graph you can see that something must happen to the equilibrium price when the demand curve shifts. The equilibrium price is determined at the intersection of the supply curve and the demand curve. With the new demand curve, there is a new intersection and, therefore, a new equilibrium price. The equilibrium price is no longer $200 in Figure 3.8(a). It is up to $220 per bicycle. Thus, the supply and demand model predicts that the price in the market will rise if there is an increase in demand. Note also that there is a change in the equilibrium

FIGURE 3.8
Effects of a Shift in Demand
When the demand increases, as in graph (a), the demand curve shifts to the right. The equilibrium price rises, and the equilibrium quantity also rises. When demand decreases, as in graph (b), the demand curve shifts to the left; the equilibrium price falls, and the equilibrium quantity also falls.

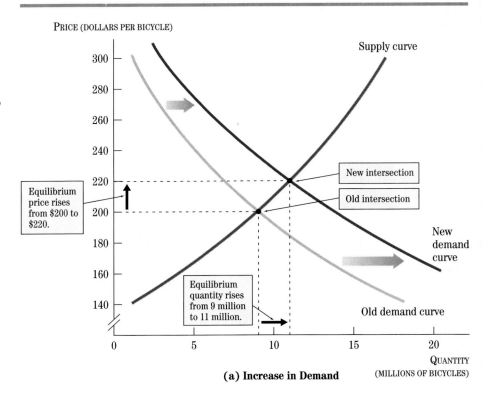

(a) Increase in Demand

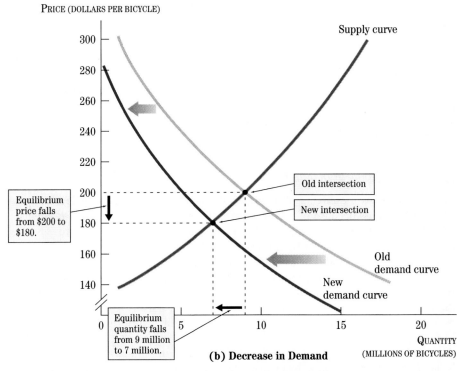

(b) Decrease in Demand

quantity of bicycles. The quantity of bicycles sold and bought has increased from 9 million to 11 million. Thus, the equilibrium quantity has increased along with the equilibrium price. The supply and demand model predicts that an increase in demand will raise both the price and the quantity sold in the market.

We can use the same method to find out what happens if demand decreases, as shown in graph (b) in Figure 3.8. In this case, the demand curve shifts to the left. At the new intersection of the supply and demand curve, the equilibrium price is lower and the quantity sold is also lower. Thus, the supply and demand model predicts that a decrease in demand will lower the price and lower the quantity sold in the market.

Note in these examples that when the demand curve shifts, it leads to a movement along the supply curve. First, the demand curve shifts to the right or to the left. Then there is movement along the supply curve because the change in the price affects the quantity of bicycles firms will sell.

Effects of a Change in Supply

Figure 3.9 shows what happens when there is a change in the market that shifts the supply curve. In graph (a) of Figure 3.9 we show the effect of an increase in supply, and in graph (b) we show the effect of a decrease in supply.

When the supply curve of bicycles shifts to the right, there is a new equilibrium price, which is lower than the old equilibrium price. In addition, the equilibrium quantity rises. Thus, the supply and demand model predicts that an increase in the supply of bicycles—perhaps because of better technology in bicycle production— will lower the price and raise the quantity of bicycles sold.

When the supply curve of bicycles shifts to the left, the equilibrium price rises, as shown in graph (b) of Figure 3.9, and the equilibrium quantity falls. Thus, the model predicts that anything that reduces supply will raise the price of bicycles and lower the quantity of bicycles produced.

Table 3.4 summarizes the results of this analysis of shifts in the supply and demand curve.

When Both Curves Shift

The supply and demand model is easiest to use when something shifts either demand or supply but not both. However, in reality, it is possible for something or several different things to simultaneously shift both supply and demand. To predict whether the price or the quantity rises or falls in such cases, we need to know whether demand or supply shifts by a larger amount. Dealing with the possibility of simultaneous shifts in demand and supply curves is important in practice, as we show in the next section.

Shift	Effect on Equilibrium Price	Effect on Equilibrium Quantity
Increase in demand	Up	Up
Decrease in demand	Down	Down
Increase in supply	Down	Up
Decrease in supply	Up	Down

TABLE 3.4
Effects of Shifts in Demand and Supply Curves

FIGURE 3.9
Effects of a Shift in Supply
When supply increases, as in graph (a), the supply curve shifts to the right; the equilibrium price falls and the equilibrium quantity rises. When supply decreases, as in graph (b), the supply curve shifts to the left; the equilibrium price rises and the equilibrium quantity falls.

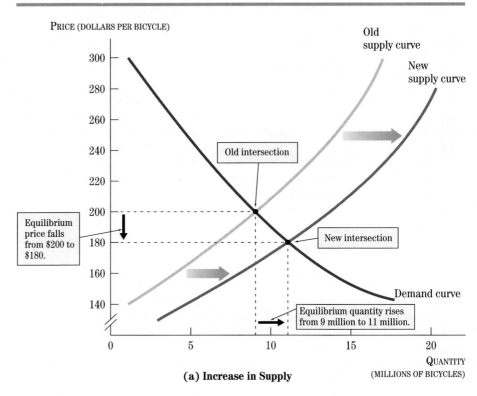

(a) Increase in Supply

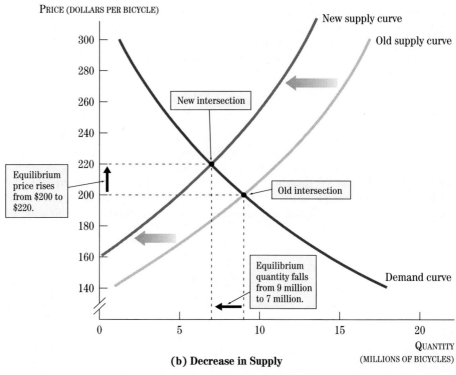

(b) Decrease in Supply

Review

▶ When firms and consumers interact in a market, a price is determined by the market.

▶ The supply and demand model predicts that the price is found at the intersection of the supply and demand curves. This price is called the equilibrium price.

▶ At this price, the quantity supplied equals the

quantity demanded, and there is no tendency for the price to change.

▶ A shift in the demand curve or the supply curve will change the equilibrium price and the equilibrium quantity. By considering changes in supply or demand, the model can be used to explain or predict price changes.

USING THE SUPPLY AND DEMAND MODEL: A CASE STUDY

Economists use the supply and demand model both to explain past observations about prices and to predict what would happen to prices under different scenarios. The hypothetical example of the bicycle market has been useful for defining and explaining general features of the supply and demand model. But now we want to show how to apply the model in real-world situations. In real-world applications, economists have to decide exactly what goods are included in the market and the time period for the application. To illustrate the application of the supply and demand model, we look in detail at some actual events in a specific market—the peanut market in the United States.

Explaining and Predicting Peanut Prices

To apply the supply and demand model to the peanut market, we need to know a little about where peanuts are produced and consumed. Figure 3.10 shows that most peanuts are produced on farms in the southeastern part of the United States. The biggest peanut-producing state is Georgia, but peanuts are also produced in Alabama, Florida, North Carolina, Texas, Oklahoma, and Virginia. The United States produces about 4 billion pounds of peanuts. Georgia produces over 1.8 billion of that 4 billion.

The demand for peanuts comes from consumers all over the United States. People from California to Maine eat peanuts and peanut butter. The U.S. government uses peanut butter in the school lunch program. In addition, Canadians buy U.S. peanuts. In sum, about 4 billion pounds of U.S.-produced peanuts are consumed each year in the United States and Canada.

Figure 3.11 shows a supply and demand model for peanuts. The model is an accurate description of the peanut market based on many observations over the years. You can see that the demand curve for peanuts is downward sloping. In the diagram, prices range from $.20 a pound all the way to $1.80 a pound for raw shelled peanuts. As you can see, when the price for peanuts is high, the quantity demanded is low. The supply curve shows that at a higher price farmers will want to produce more peanuts. The equilibrium price is shown to be $.60 a pound, and the equilibrium quantity about 4 billion pounds. These are close to the actual price and quantity of peanuts in early 1990.

FIGURE 3.10
Peanut Production in the United States

Most peanuts are produced in the Southeast. Hence, a drought in the Southeast will have a big effect on the supply of peanuts. The information in this map for 1989 is important for establishing that the 1990 drought did indeed shift the supply curve of peanuts to the left.

Source: U.S. Department of Agriculture.

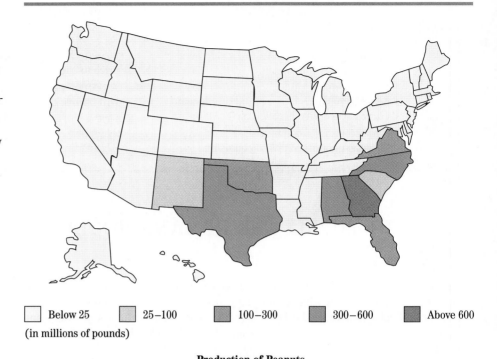

| ☐ Below 25 | ▨ 25–100 | ▨ 100–300 | ▨ 300–600 | ■ Above 600 |

(in millions of pounds)

Production of Peanuts

State	Quantity (million pounds)	Share of Total (percent)
Alabama	538	13.5
Florida	215	5.4
Georgia	1,850	46.3
New Mexico	44	1.1
North Carolina	370	9.3
Oklahoma	211	5.3
South Carolina	33	.8
Texas	485	12.1
Virginia	246	6.2
U.S. total	3,992	100.0

Drought in the Southeast

During 1990, there was a drought in the southeastern part of the United States, where most of the peanuts are grown. The drought meant that supply declined. Production dropped sharply in Georgia, Alabama, and Florida. In the supply and demand model, we would show that drought by a shift to the left in the supply curve for peanuts, as shown in Figure 3.12.

As you can see in Figure 3.12, the equilibrium price rises. In fact, the price of peanuts in the drought of 1990 did rise from about $.60 a pound to about $1.25 a pound. Thus, the supply and demand model can explain the rise in the peanut price.

Quite understandably, this price rise forced some hard choices on people who consume a lot of peanuts. Poor people tend to eat more peanut butter than rich people, so the price change affected the distribution of income. Further, the U.S.

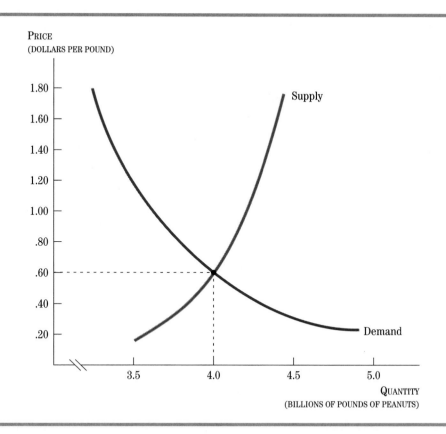

FIGURE 3.11
Supply and Demand for Peanuts
The quantity refers to the number of pounds produced in the United States. The price is the average price of raw peanuts in the United States.

Department of Agriculture (USDA) school lunch program that provides meals for poor children in the United States had to stop buying peanut butter because it got so expensive.

Thus, the price performed its three roles. The higher price lowered the quantity demanded by providing incentives for people to choose some other food. It transmitted information about the effects of the drought in the Southeast all over the country. It also affected the distribution of income because people who buy peanuts and peanut butter had less to spend on other things.

A Change in the Foreign Peanut Quota?

Although the market responded to the drought as predicted, the higher price made life difficult for some consumers. Was there anything to be done? Could the supply and demand model help in deciding what to do? Could it predict what would happen under various courses of action?

Believe it or not, the U.S. government prohibits virtually any imports of peanuts into the United States from other countries. There is a law limiting the amount of imported peanuts to a small quantity: about 1.7 million pounds, compared to the nearly 4 billion pounds consumed. This limit is called a **quota.** The United States allows only about a quarter of 1 percent of its peanut consumption to come from foreign countries.

quota: a governmental limit on the quantity of a particular good sold or imported.

FIGURE 3.12
Effects of a Drought in the Southeast

The drought reduces the supply of peanuts. Hence, the supply curve shifts to the left, raising the equilibrium price of peanuts and lowering the equilibrium quantity. The supply and demand model explains the observed increase in the price of peanuts.

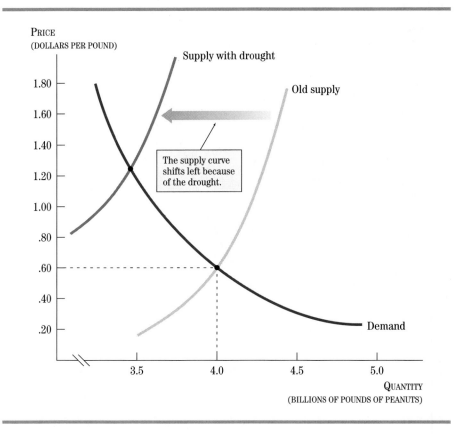

One simple way to lower the price would be to allow more foreign peanuts to come into the United States from Argentina, China, and other peanut-growing countries. In fact, the supply and demand model predicts that the price would fall if the quota was increased.

Allowing more foreign peanuts into the United States would shift the supply curve of peanuts to the right, as shown in Figure 3.13. That would lower the equilibrium price. For the size of the rightward shift in the diagram, the price would go down to about $.75 a pound, which would have helped the peanut consumers who were being hurt by the drought.

However, that is not what happened in 1990. The United States has a formal process to determine whether or not more foreign peanuts can be brought into the country. A committee, the International Trade Commission (ITC), decides whether the peanut farmers might be harmed by the lower price caused by such foreign peanuts. In 1990 it took many months for the ITC to make the decision. A majority of the commissioners determined that peanut farmers would not be affected a great deal if the U.S. government allowed more peanuts in. Economists who work for the ITC used a supply and demand model just like the one in Figure 3.13 to analyze the situation and make a recommendation to increase the quota. But others—including the peanut growers and some members of Congress—claimed there was no reason to increase the quota. They argued that the demand for peanuts had decreased after

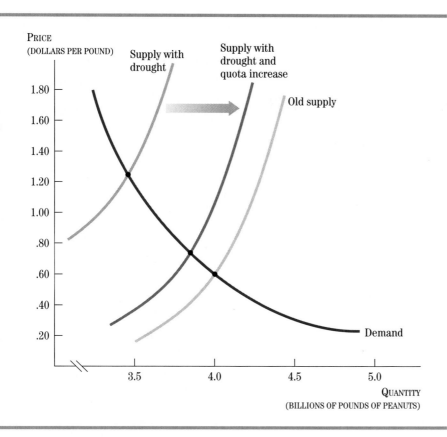

FIGURE 3.13
Predicted Effects of an Increase in the Peanut Quota
The supply and demand model can also be used to predict what would happen if more peanuts were allowed to enter the United States from abroad. The increase in supply would shift the supply curve to the right. The equilibrium price of peanuts would fall. Hence, the model predicts that increasing the quota would lower the price of peanuts and thereby tend to offset the effects of the drought.

the drought and that an increase in the supply of foreign peanuts was unnecessary. One peanut growers' group was quoted as saying, "Demand for peanut butter and peanut products will be less this year because the USDA has drastically reduced its purchases of peanut products."[3] Such statements confuse shifts of the demand curve and movements along the demand curve. As shown in Figure 3.12, the drought led to a movement along the demand curve because higher peanut prices forced people to reduce the quantity demanded. But this was not a decline in demand. Rather, consumers reduced the quantity demanded because the price was so high.

These debates led to delays. By the time the quota increase came, in July 1991, it was too little and too late. Ultimately, only about 16 million extra pounds of peanuts were imported. The supply and demand model predicts that such a small increase in supply will reduce the price only a small amount. Although the ultimate result may have been disappointing, the 1990 drought and peanut quota increase provide an excellent case study of how the supply and demand model is used in practice both to explain observations about prices and to make useful predictions about prices.

3. *Peanuts,* U.S. International Trade Commission Publication 2369, March 1991, p. A-70.

Reading the News About Supply and Demand

The following news account describes the situation in the peanut market after the drought of 1990. Observe how the supply and demand model corroborates ① the size of the price increase and the reason for the price increase, ② the effects on the price of increasing peanut imports by 300 million pounds, and ③ the typical rationalization on the part of growers that there was no reason to increase the quota because "supply was sufficient," while not mentioning that it was the doubling of prices that brought the quantity demanded down to equal the lower quantity supplied.

Peanuts could sell for peanuts again

By John Schmeltzer

Peanut butter, that staple of the American school lunch menu that all but disappeared last fall when peanut prices soared, may soon make a comeback, industry leaders say.

In recent months, prices for shelled peanuts more than doubled on the wholesale level, to $1.25 a pound from 60 cents a pound—a move that prompted the Department of Agriculture to substitute cholesterol-rich cheese in the school lunch program for the cholesterol-free peanut butter.

Analysts said the peanut shortfall was caused by severe import restrictions and last year's drought in the Southeast.

Peanut butter, which had been selling in the grocery store for about $3 for a 28-ounce jar, quickly skyrocketed to more than $4.

"You can import pistols but not peanuts," said James Mack on Wednesday, referring to restrictions that all but set quotas for how many goobers each U.S. peanut farmer is allowed to produce each year. Mack is general counsel for the Peanut Butter and Nut Processors Association.

'You can import pistols but not peanuts.'

—James Mack,
Peanut Butter and
Nut Processors Association

But processors say they expect a decision in as little as two weeks by President Bush on a temporary lifting of import restrictions, which would allow as much as 300 million pounds of peanuts to be imported between now and July 31. The temporary relaxation has been recommended by the U.S. International Trade Commission.

Since the ITC recommendation last week, prices for shelled peanuts have fallen to about $1 a pound, according to Mack. He said if the ITC recommendation is adopted, prices will probably drop to about 75 cents a pound—still 25 percent higher than before last year's poor crop hit the market.

The ITC recommendation is being opposed by growers and congressional leaders, who maintain there is sufficient supply for the domestic market and say Mack's association only represents 30 percent of the producers, none of whom are the major manufacturers of brands such as Planters or Skippy.

Sen. Wyche Fowler Jr. (D-Ga.), in a letter signed by 11 other senators, argued that opening the door to increased imports could end up costing U.S. taxpayers because of price-support programs.

"We don't think the importation of peanuts is necessary" said Emery Murphy, assistant executive director of the Georgia Peanut Commission. "We're certain there will be adverse effects to the industry and the government."

The nut processors association has been joined in its efforts to lift the import ban by the Consumer Alert Advocate Fund, whose president, Barbara Keating, said slow action by the government already has cost consumers $553 million.

Review

▶ The supply and demand model can be used in practical applications to explain price changes in many markets. It can also be used to predict what will happen to prices when certain actions—such as increasing a quota—are taken.

▶ In applying the model, economists consider shifts of the supply curve or the demand curve. In the case study of the drought, the supply curve for peanuts shifted.

INTERFERENCE WITH MARKET PRICES

Thus far we have used the supply and demand model in situations in which the price is freely determined without government control. But many times throughout history, and around the world today, governments have attempted to control market prices. The usual reason is that government leaders were not happy with the outcome of the market, or they were pressured by groups who would benefit from price controls.

Price controls were used widely by the U.S. government during World War II and again in the early 1970s. Price controls now exist in certain housing markets, agriculture markets, and labor markets in the United States. What are the effects of this government interference in the market? The supply and demand model can help answer this question.

price control: a government law or regulation that sets or limits the price to be charged for a particular good.

Price Ceilings and Price Floors

In general there are two broad types of government price controls. Controls can stipulate a **price ceiling,** or a maximum price, at which a good can be bought and sold. For example, the United States government controlled oil prices in the early 1970s, stipulating that firms could not charge more than a stated maximum price of $5.25 per barrel of crude oil; the equilibrium price was well over $10 per barrel at this time. Some cities in the United States have price controls on rental apartments. Landlords are not permitted to charge a rent higher than the maximum stipulated by the **rent control** law in these cities. Price ceilings are imposed by governments because of complaints that the market price is too high. The purpose is to help the consumers who must pay the prices. For example, rent controls exist in order to help people who must pay rent. However, as we will see, price controls have harmful side effects that can end up hurting those consumers the law is apparently trying to help.

Government price controls can also stipulate a **price floor,** or a minimum price. Price floors are imposed by governments in order to help the suppliers of goods and services. For example, the U.S. government requires that the price of sugar not fall below a certain amount in the United States. In the labor market, the U.S. government requires that firms pay workers a wage no less than a minimum, called the **minimum wage.**

price ceiling: a government price control that sets the maximum allowable price for a good.

rent control: a government price control that sets the maximum allowable rent on a house or apartment.

price floor: a government price control that sets the minimum allowable price for a good.

minimum wage: a wage per hour below which it is illegal to pay workers.

Shortages and Related Problems Resulting from Price Ceilings

If the government prevents firms from charging more than a certain amount for their products, then a shortage is likely to result, as illustrated in Figure 3.14. When the maximum price remains below the equilibrium price on the market, there is a persistent shortage; sellers are unwilling to supply as much as buyers want to buy. This is illustrated for the general case of any good in the top graph in Figure 3.14 and for the specific case of rent control in the bottom graph.

"I always wondered how the government set milk prices."

FIGURE 3.14
Effects of a Maximum Price Law
The top diagram shows the general
case when the government prevents
the market price from rising above
a particular maximum price, or sets
a price ceiling below the equilibrium price. The lower diagram
shows a particular example of a
price ceiling, rent controls on apartment units. The supply and demand
model predicts there will be a shortage. The shortage occurs because
the quantity supplied is less than
consumers are willing to buy at
that price. The shortage leads to
rationing, black markets, or lower
product quality.

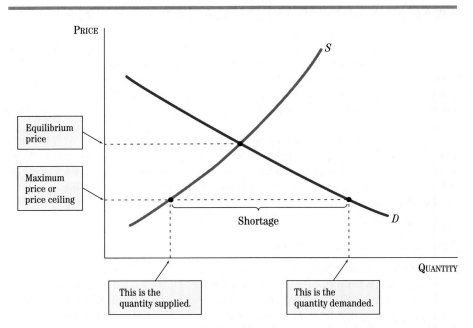

The General Case of a Price Ceiling

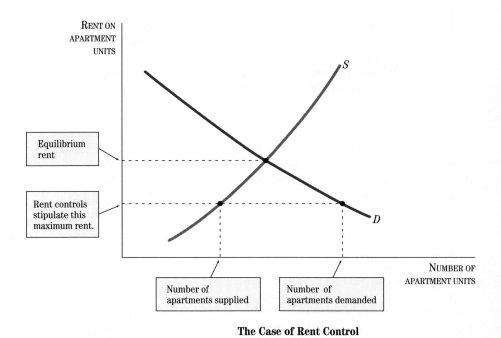

The Case of Rent Control

Dealing with Persistent Shortages

Because higher prices are not allowed, the shortage must be dealt with in other ways. Sometimes the government issues a limited amount of ration coupons to people to alleviate the shortage; this was done in World War II. The law required that people present these ration coupons at stores in order to buy goods. Thus, the total quantity demanded could not be greater than the amount of ration coupons. Alternatively, if there are no ration coupons, then the shortage might result in long waiting lines. In formerly centrally planned economies, long lines for bread were frequently observed because of price controls on bread. Sometimes black markets develop in which people buy and sell goods outside the watch of the government and charge whatever price they want. This typically happens in command economies. Black markets are also common in less-developed countries today when the governments in these countries impose price controls.

Another effect of price ceilings is a reduction in the quality of the good sold. By lowering the quality of the good, the producer can reduce the costs of producing it. Low-quality housing frequently results from rent control. By lowering the quality of the apartments—perhaps being slow to paint the walls or repair the elevator— landlords make the apartments shoddy and unattractive.

Making Things Worse

Although the stated purpose of price ceilings is to help people who have to pay high prices, the preceding examples indicate how they can make things worse. Issuing ration coupons raises difficult problems about who gets the coupons. In the case of a price ceiling on gasoline, for example, should the government give more coupons to those who commute by car than to those who do not? More generally, who is to decide who deserves the coupons? Rationing by waiting in line is also a poor outcome. People waiting in line could be doing more enjoyable or more useful things. Similarly, black markets, being illegal, encourage people to go outside the law; they thereby lose their rights to protection in the case of theft or fraud. Lowering the quality of the good is also a bad way to alleviate the problem of a high price. This simply eliminates the higher-quality good from production; consumers and producers lose.

Paradoxically, price ceilings frequently end up hurting those they try to help. Many people who benefit from controls, for example, are not poor at all. If rent controls reduce the supply of apartments, they make less housing available for everyone.

Surpluses and Related Problems Resulting from Price Floors

If the government imposes a price floor, then a surplus will occur, as shown in Figure 3.15. With the price above the equilibrium price, suppliers of goods and services want to sell more than people are willing to buy. Hence, there is a surplus. This is illustrated for the general case of any good in the top graph of Figure 3.15 and for the specific case of the minimum wage in the bottom graph.

How is this surplus dealt with in actual markets? In markets for farm products, the government usually has to buy the surplus and, perhaps, put it in storage; but buying farm products above the equilibrium price costs taxpayers money, and the higher price raises costs to consumers. For this reason, economists argue against

FIGURE 3.15
Effects of a Minimum Price Law

The top diagram shows the general case when the government prevents the market price from falling below a particular minimum price, or sets a price floor above the equilibrium price. The lower diagram shows a particular example when the price of labor—the wage—cannot fall below the minimum wage. The supply and demand model predicts that sellers are willing to sell a quantity greater than buyers are willing to buy at that price. Thus, there is a surplus of the good or, in the case of labor, unemployment for some of those who can be hired only at a lower wage.

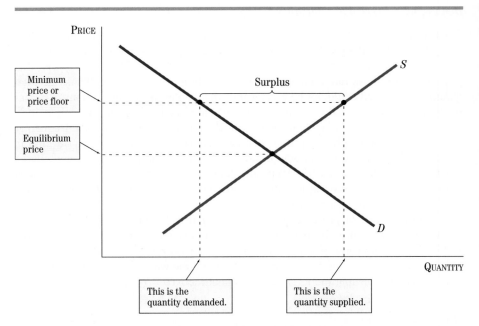

The General Case of a Price Floor

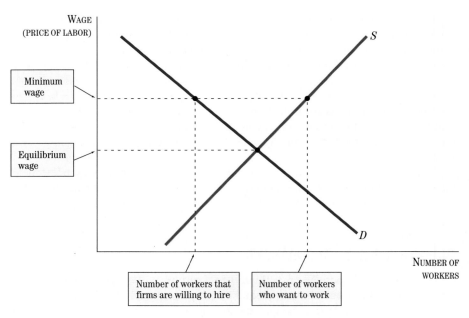

The Case of the Minimum Wage

Reading the News about Price Floors

The following news report depicts the pressures that sometimes lead governments to try to interfere with the prices that emerge from markets. As the price of milk dropped in August 1991, legislation was introduced into the U.S. Congress to put a floor on the price. At the time the market price for milk was $11.47 per hundred pounds; the legislation would have put a floor on

the price at a higher level, $13.09. Hence, if the legislation passed, the situation would be exactly like that in Figure 3.15. Consumers would have paid more for milk, and there would have been a milk surplus.

The article focuses on the hardships of milk farmers and their families, but it does not mention the cost to consumers. In this case the legisla-

tion did not pass. It is, therefore, an example where the government, through the political process, chose not to impose price controls, perhaps because of concerns about the harms from such controls, as illustrated in Figure 3.15.

Source of article: Burlington Free Press, March 23, 1991, pp. 1–2. Reprinted courtesy of the Burlington Free Press.

Dairy price support defeat worries Vermont farmers

John Malcolm, Vermont's dairyman of the year, estimated the U.S. House defeat of milk price support legislation Thursday would cost him $10,000 this year, and would cost the state's economy $28 million.

"Anything is a lot of money," the Pawlet farmer said Friday. "We aren't even breaking even now."

Bulk prices for milk have dropped nearly 30 percent since August. Prices per hundred pounds of milk average $11.47, while the cost for Vermont farmers to produce that amount of milk averages $13.75. Leahy's plan would have temporarily fixed the price at $13.09.

Malcolm said he can keep farming for about a year with prices the way they are now, provided he makes cuts in equipment purchases. For some Vermont dairy families, the prospects are worse.

"We are just hanging on by a thread," said Helen Wilcox, who leases a farm in Alburg with her husband, Alvin. Of the couple's nine children, six are still at home, and the family has been selling bull calves for grocery money.

"I thought it was really sad," she said of the proposal's defeat, "because it would have helped drastically. . . . If (the price of milk) continues at $11.50,

we'll be out of farming by the year's end," she said.

"The Senate recognized that dairy farmers in virtually every state are suffering and acted to stop the hemorrhaging," Leahy, chairman of the Senate Agriculture Committee, said Friday. "This is a sad day for our nation's dairy farmers. The administration and House turned a deaf ear to their plight."

The Bush administration had threatened to veto the entire spending bill if it included the price support.

price floors on agricultural goods. As an alternative, the government sometimes reduces the supply by telling firms to plant fewer acres or to destroy crops, or by restricting the amount that can come from abroad. In the United States, the federal government uses acreage restrictions in the case of wheat and other grains; it also uses import restrictions in the case of sugar. But government requirements to keep land idle or even destroy crops are particularly repugnant to most people.

As we will see in more detail later in this book, the supply and demand model can also be applied to labor markets. In that case, the price is the price of labor, or the wage. What does the supply and demand model predict about the effects of a minimum wage? In the case of labor markets, a minimum wage can cause unemployment. If the equilibrium wage is below the minimum wage, then some workers would be willing to work for less than the minimum wage. But employers are not permitted to pay them less than the minimum wage. Therefore, there is an oversupply of workers at the minimum wage. The number of workers demanded is less than the number of workers willing to work; thus, the supply and demand model predicts that the minimum wage causes unemployment.

The minimum wage would have no effect if the equilibrium wage were above the minimum wage. The supply and demand model predicts that the minimum wage affects workers whose wages would be below the minimum. Thus, a minimum wage would be most likely to increase unemployment for teenage workers with very few skills if their wages would otherwise be below the minimum.

Review

▶ Price ceilings cause persistent shortages, which, in turn, cause rationing, black markets, and a reduced quality of goods and services.

▶ Price floors cause persistent surpluses and unemployment, according to the supply and demand

model. In the case of price floors on agricultural products, the surpluses are bought by the government and put in storage. In the case of the minimum wage, the surpluses mean more unemployment for those who can only get jobs below the minimum wage.

CONCLUSION

This chapter has shown how prices are determined in markets where buyers and sellers interact freely. The supply and demand model is used to describe how prices are determined in such markets. It is probably the most frequently used model in economics and has been in existence for over a hundred years in pretty much the same form as economists use it now.

The key idea behind the model is that the price is found by the intersection of the supply and demand curves. To apply the model in practice, we need to look for factors that shift either the supply curve or the demand curve. In the most successful applications of the supply and demand model, the factors that affect supply and demand can be separated.

In the next chapter we show how economists measure "how much" quantity supplied and quantity demanded change when the price changes in the supply and demand model. Then, in later chapters we will see how the supply and demand model fits into the common economic problem of scarcity and choice, as defined in the previous chapter. By doing so, we will be able to take a closer look at the basic questions economists face: what, how, and for whom to produce.

KEY POINTS

1. Demand is a negative relationship between the price of a good and the quantity demanded by consumers. It can be shown graphically by a downward-sloping demand curve.

2. A movement along the demand curve occurs when a higher price reduces the quantity demanded or a lower price increases the quantity demanded.

3. A shift of the demand curve occurs when something besides the price causes the quantity people are willing to buy to change.

4. Supply is a positive relationship between the price of a good and the quantity supplied by firms. It can be shown graphically by an upward-sloping supply curve.

5. A movement along the supply curve occurs when a higher price increases the quantity supplied or a lower price decreases the quantity supplied.

6. A shift of the supply curve occurs when something besides the price causes the quantity firms are willing to sell to change.

7. The equilibrium price and equilibrium quantity are determined by the intersection of the supply curve and the demand curve where the quantity supplied equals the quantity demanded.

8. By shifting either the supply curve or the demand curve, observations on prices can be explained and predictions about prices can be made.

9. Price ceilings cause shortages, with the quantity supplied less than the quantity demanded. Shortages lead to rationing or black markets.

10. Price floors cause surpluses, with the quantity supplied greater than the quantity demanded.

KEY TERMS

demand	complement	equilibrium quantity
price	supply	market equilibrium
quantity demanded	quantity supplied	quota
demand schedule	supply schedule	price control
law of demand	law of supply	price ceiling
demand curve	supply curve	rent control
normal goods	shortage	price floor
inferior goods	surplus	minimum wage
substitute	equilibrium price	

QUESTIONS FOR REVIEW

1. Why does the demand curve slope downward?

2. Why does the supply curve slope upward?

3. What is the difference between a shift in the demand curve and a movement along the demand curve?

4. What are four things that cause a demand curve to shift?

5. What are four things that cause a supply curve to shift?

6. What is the difference between a shift in the supply curve and a movement along the supply curve?

7. What are the equilibrium price and equilibrium quantity?

8. What happens to the equilibrium price if the supply curve shifts to the right and the demand curve does not shift?

9. What happens to the equilibrium price if the demand curve shifts to the right and the supply curve does not shift?

10. Do price ceilings cause shortages or surpluses? What about price floors? Explain.

PROBLEMS

1. Consider the following supply and demand model of the world tea market (in billions of pounds).

Price per Pound	Quantity Supplied	Quantity Demanded
$.38	1,500	525
$.37	1,000	600
$.36	700	700
$.35	600	900
$.34	550	1,200

a) Is there a shortage or a surplus when the price is $.38? What about $.34?

b) What are the equilibrium price and the equilibrium quantity?
c) Graph the supply curve and the demand curve.
d) Show how the equilibrium price and quantity can be found on the graph.

2. Consider the supply and demand model in problem 1. Suppose that there is a drought in Sri Lanka that reduces the supply of tea by 400 billion pounds. Suppose demand does not change.

a) Write down in a table the new supply schedule for tea.

b) Find the new equilibrium price and the new equilibrium quantity.

c) Did the equilibrium quantity change by more or less than the change in supply?

d) Graph the new supply curve, along with the old supply curve and demand curve.

e) Show the change in the equilibrium price and the equilibrium quantity on the graph.

3. Use the supply and demand model to explain what happens to the equilibrium price and the equilibrium quantity in the orange juice market in each of the following cases.

a) The *New England Journal of Medicine* issues a widely publicized report that says vitamin C cures cancer, and orange juice is the best source of vitamin C.

b) A freeze in Florida destroys half the orange crop.

c) There is a sudden inflow of cheap orange juice imports from South America.

d) A major orange juice producer finds lead contamination in some containers, and this finding makes the nightly news.

4. For each of the following markets, indicate whether the stated change causes a shift in the supply curve, a shift in the demand curve, a movement along the supply curve, and/or a movement along the demand curve.

a) The housing market: Consumers' incomes increase.

b) The camera market: The price of film goes up.

c) The sugar market: There is a drought in the sugar cane fields in Hawaii.

d) The milk market: The price of milk increases, and the amount of milk people are willing to buy declines.

e) The fast food market: The number of fast food restaurants in the area increases.

f) The video rental market: The number of consumers in the area decreases.

g) The ice cream market: The price of frozen yogurt falls.

5. Draw a supply and demand diagram to indicate the market for Japanese cars in the United States, with the equilibrium price and quantity labeled. Suppose the government imposes a strict restriction on the quantity of Japanese cars sold in the United States. Show what happens in this market if the quantity restriction is less than the equilibrium quantity. What will happen if the quantity restriction is greater than the equilibrium quantity?

6. Consider the market for apartments in a town. The price for apartments is the rent.

a) Sketch the demand curve and the supply curve for apartments.

b) How is the equilibrium rent determined?

c) If the town council imposes a binding rent control below the equilibrium price, equivalent to a price ceiling in this market, what happens to quantity supplied and quantity demanded? How does the total amount of rent paid change?

d) Economists frequently argue against rent control because of the incentives it gives to landlords. Explain why this interference in the market may provide bad incentives.

7. In many countries there are price floors for agricultural commodities. Draw a supply and demand diagram that shows the market for a commodity that has a price fixed greater than the market equilibrium price. Will there be a shortage or a surplus?

8. Why is it necessary for people to stand in line for days before the sale of concert tickets for the most famous performers? Is the price mechanism working properly? Why are scalpers present on these occasions?

9. Assuming that either supply or demand, but not both, change, indicate the direction and change in either supply or demand that must have occurred to produce the following:

a) A decrease in the price and quantity of apples

b) A decrease in the price of bananas with an increase in the quantity of bananas

c) An increase in the price and quantity of cars

d) An increase in the quantity of computers with a decrease in the price

10. Draw a supply and demand diagram for each of the following changes in the bicycle market and show what happens.

a) Rollerblades replace bicycles as the most popular form of transportation for young people.

b) Incomes of people who like to ride bicycles increase.

c) Technology for producing bicycles improves.

d) The cost of the metal alloy used in producing bicycles increases.

11. Determine which of the following four sentences uses the terminology of the supply and demand model correctly.

a) "The price of bicycles rose, and therefore the demand for bicycles went down."

b) "The demand for bicycles increased, and therefore the price went up."

c) "The price of bicycles fell, decreasing the supply of bicycles."

d) "The supply of bicycles increased, and therefore the price of bicycles fell."

12. a) Suppose you find out that an increase in the price of first-class postage leads to an increase in the demand for overnight delivery service and a decrease in the demand for envelopes. For which good is postage a complement and for which is it a substitute?

b) Suppose someone tells you that a decrease in the price of pizza caused an increase in the demand for beer. Is this what you would expect? Why?

c) Suppose an increase in the price of coffee caused no change in the demand for tea. What can you conclude from this information?

13. Suppose an increase in consumers' incomes causes a rightward shift in the demand for computers and a leftward shift in the demand for radios. Which good is normal, and which is inferior? Draw a supply and demand diagram for each to explain how the price will change in each of these markets.

14. Straight-line demand and supply curves can be represented by algebraic equations. Given the following alge-braic expressions for supply and demand, calculate the equilibrium price and quantity by solving the two equations for P and Q.

Supply: $Q = 5 + 2P$

Demand: $Q = 10 - 2P$

Suppose that, due to an increase in consumers' incomes, the demand curve shifts. That is, the new demand equation is:

$Q = 13 - 2P$

Calculate the new equilibrium price and quantity.

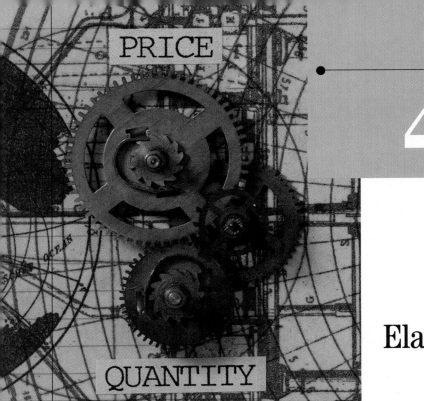

PRICE

QUANTITY

4

Elasticity and Its Uses

It was August 1990. Iraq had just invaded Kuwait. Military experts were holding meetings in the White House and the Pentagon to assess U.S. military options. Unbeknown to most people, economic experts were also holding meetings, mainly in the White House and the Treasury building next to the White House. The economic experts were assessing the seriousness of the world economic situation in the aftermath of the invasion. Iraq's invasion of Kuwait had eliminated about 7 percent of the world's daily oil supply of 60 million barrels. With Saudi Arabia's oil fields threatened by further Iraqi aggression and with Iran also possibly entering the conflict, the world's oil supply could have been reduced by another 18 percent, bringing the total reduction in supply to about 25 percent.

The supply and demand model tells us that such a reduction in supply should increase the price of oil. But by how much? By a negligible 3 percent? By a devastating 300 percent? Or by something in between? And what if Nigeria and Venezuela could be persuaded to increase

their oil production? By how much would oil prices rise then? These were the questions the economists were being asked. And they had to come up with quick answers.

There is an elegant, but remarkably useful, economic concept called *elasticity* that economists use to help answer such questions. In economics, elasticity is a measure of how sensitive one variable is to another. In particular, it measures how sensitive the quantity of a good that people demand or that firms supply is to the price of the good.

In this chapter we focus on elasticity. We first show why elasticity is important for making calculations such as the effects of a decline in oil supply. We then provide a formula for elasticity and show how it is calculated. Elasticity can apply to both demand and supply, and we consider both throughout the chapter. We also explain how elasticity is used in many different ways, from assessing the economic impact of a military invasion to determining an appropriate entrance fee to a national park.

THE PRICE ELASTICITY OF DEMAND

In general, *elasticity* is a measure of how sensitive one economic variable is to another economic variable. There are as many different types of elasticity as there are types of economic variables.

We first consider an elasticity called the price elasticity of demand. The price elasticity of demand is a measure of the sensitivity of the *quantity demanded* of a good to the *price* of the good. The "price elasticity of demand" is sometimes shortened to "elasticity of demand," the "demand elasticity," or even simply "elasticity," when the meaning is clear from the context. The price elasticity of demand always refers to a particular demand curve or demand schedule, such as the world demand for oil or the U.S. demand for bicycles. For a particular demand curve, all other things besides the price of the good being equal, the following relationships hold: As the price increases, the quantity demanded by consumers declines; as the price decreases, the quantity demanded by consumers increases. The price elasticity of demand is a measure of *how much* the quantity demanded changes when the price changes.

For example, when economists report that the price elasticity of demand for contact lenses is high, they mean that the quantity of contact lenses demanded by people changes by a large amount when the price changes. Or if they report that the price elasticity of demand for bread is low, they mean the quantity of bread demanded changes by only a small amount when the price of bread changes.

Before giving a formula for computing elasticity exactly, let us show intuitively why it is important to know how sensitive the quantity demanded is to the price, that is, to know a good's elasticity.

The Importance of Knowing the Price Elasticity of Demand

We began this chapter with questions about how much the price of oil would rise if the oil supply were reduced. The price elasticity of demand gives us the answers. Figure 4.1 illustrates how. It compares a high elasticity with a low elasticity.

High versus Low Elasticity

There are two graphs in Figure 4.1, each showing a different possible demand curve for oil in the world. We want to show why it is important to know which of these two demand curves is correct, or at least which one gives a better description of economic behavior in the oil market. Each graph has the price of oil on the vertical axis (in dollars per barrel) and the quantity of oil demanded on the horizontal axis (in millions of barrels of oil a day).

Both of the demand curves pass through the same point *A,* where the price of oil is $20 per barrel and the quantity demanded is 60 million barrels per day. But observe that the two different curves show different degrees of sensitivity of the quantity demanded to the price. In the top graph, where the demand curve is relatively flat, the quantity demanded of oil is very sensitive to the price; in other words, the demand curve has a high elasticity. For example, consider a change from point *A* to point *B* when the price rises by $2 from $20 to $22, or by 10 percent

FIGURE 4.1
Comparing Different Price Elasticities of Demand

Both sets of axes have exactly the same scale. In the top graph, the quantity demanded is very sensitive to the price; the elasticity is high. In the bottom graph, the quantity demanded is not very sensitive to the price; the elasticity is low. Thus, the same increase in price ($2, or 10 percent) reduces the quantity demanded much more when the elasticity is high (top graph) than when it is low (bottom graph).

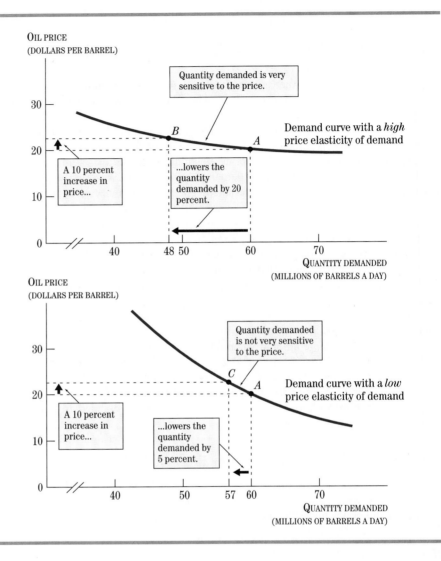

($2/$20 = .10, or 10 percent), and the quantity demanded falls by 12 million from 60 million to 48 million barrels a day, or by 20 percent (12/60 = .20 or 20 percent).

On the other hand, in the bottom graph the quantity demanded is not very sensitive to the price; in other words, the demand curve has a low elasticity. It is relatively steep. When the price rises by $2, or 10 percent, from point *A* to point *C,* the quantity demanded falls by 3 million barrels, or only 5 percent. Thus, the sensitivity of the quantity to the price, or the elasticity, is what distinguishes these two graphs.

The Impact of a Change in Supply on the Price of Oil

Now consider what happens when there is a decline in supply in the world oil market. In Figure 4.2 we combine the supply curve for oil with the two possible demand curves for oil from Figure 4.1. Initially the oil market is in equilibrium in Figure 4.2; in both graphs the quantity demanded equals the quantity supplied. The

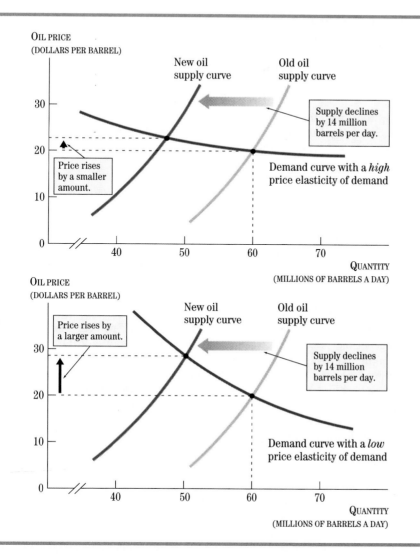

FIGURE 4.2
The Importance of the Price Elasticity of Demand
The impact on the oil price of a reduction in oil supply is shown for two different demand curves. The reduction in supply is the same for both graphs. When the price elasticity of demand is high (top graph), there is only a small increase in the price. When the price elasticity of demand is low (bottom graph), the price rises by much more.

equilibrium price is $20 per barrel and the equilibrium quantity is 60 million barrels per day, just like point *A* in Figure 4.1. A reduction in the supply of oil—perhaps because of the invasion of Kuwait by Iraq—is also shown. The exact same leftward shift in supply is shown in the top and bottom graphs of Figure 4.2.

Now, observe how the equilibrium price changes in the two graphs. Recall that this change is our prediction—using the supply and demand model—of what would happen to the price of oil if the supply declined. There is a huge difference in the size of the predicted price increase in the two graphs. In the top graph the oil price increases only a little. If the elasticity is very high, then only a small increase in the price is enough to get people to reduce their use of oil and thereby bring the quantity demanded down to a lower quantity supplied. On the other hand, in the bottom diagram the price rises by much more. Here the elasticity is very low, so that a large increase in price is needed to get people to reduce their use of oil and bring the quantity demanded down to quantity supplied.

Thus, in order to determine how much the price will rise in response to a shift in oil supply, we need to know the sensitivity of the quantity demanded to the price, or the elasticity of the demand curve.

Definition of the Price Elasticity of Demand

price elasticity of demand: the percentage change in the quantity demanded of a good divided by the percentage change in the price of that good.

Having demonstrated the practical importance of elasticity, let us now show exactly how it is defined and measured. **Price elasticity of demand** is defined as the percentage change in quantity demanded divided by the percentage change in the price. That is,

$$\begin{array}{c}\text{Price}\\\text{elasticity}\\\text{of demand}\end{array} = \frac{\text{percentage change in quantity demanded}}{\text{percentage change in the price}}$$

We emphasize that the price elasticity of demand refers to a particular demand curve; thus the numerator of this formula is the percentage change in quantity demanded when the price changes by the percentage amount shown in the denominator. All the other factors that affect demand are held constant when we compute the price elasticity of demand.

For example, as we move from point A to point B in the top graph of Figure 4.1, the percentage change in the quantity demanded is 20 percent and the percentage change in the price is 10 percent. Hence, the elasticity is 2. Or consider the example in the bottom graph of Figure 4.1. As we move from point A to point C in the bottom graph, the percentage change in the quantity demanded is 5 percent while the percentage change in the price is 10 percent. Hence, the elasticity is 1/2. Thus, the formula gives us a quantitative measure of sensitivity. Rather than simply saying an elasticity is high or low, we can calculate its value. An elasticity of 2 is much greater than an elasticity of 1/2, and now we can compare these two with other values.

If we let the symbol e_d represent the price elasticity of demand, then we can write the formula more compactly as

$$e_d = \frac{\Delta Q_d}{Q_d} \div \frac{\Delta P}{P} = \frac{\Delta Q_d / Q_d}{\Delta P / P}$$

where Q_d is the quantity demanded, P is the price, and Δ means "change in." Observe that to compute the percentage change in the numerator and the denominator, we need to divide the change in each variable (ΔP or ΔQ_d) by the variable (P or Q_d).

The Minus Sign Is Implicit

Because the quantity demanded is negatively related to the price along a demand curve, the elasticity of demand is a negative number: When $\Delta P/P$ is positive, $\Delta Q_d/Q_d$ is negative. But when economists write or talk about elasticity, they usually ignore the negative sign and report the absolute value of the number. For example, a 10 percent *increase* in the price of oil *decreases* the quantity demanded by 20 percent; thus, $\Delta P/P = +.10$ and $\Delta Q_d/Q_d = -.20$, so that the ratio of $\Delta Q_d/Q_d$ to $\Delta P/P$ is -2. But economists would say that the price elasticity of demand for oil is 2 in this case. Because the demand curve always slopes downward, this nearly universal convention need not cause any confusion, as long as you remember it.

The Advantage of a Unit-Free Measure

An attractive feature of the price elasticity of demand is that it does not depend on the units of measurement of the quantity demanded—whether barrels of oil or pounds of peanuts—or on the measure of price—whether in U.S. dollars or Mexican pesos. It is a **unit-free measure** because it uses *percentage changes* in price and quantity demanded. Thus, it provides a way to compare the price sensitivity of the demand for many different goods. It even allows us to compare the price sensitivity of cheap goods—like lard—with more expensive goods—like wool.

unit-free measure: a measure that does not depend on a unit of measurement.

For example, suppose that when the price of lard rises from 10 cents to 12 cents per pound, the quantity demanded falls from 20 tons to 19 tons: That is a decline of 1 ton for a 2 *cent* price increase.

In contrast, suppose that when the price of wool rises by $2, from $10 to $12 per pound, the quantity demanded falls by 1 ton, from 20 tons to 19 tons of wool. That would be a decline of 1 ton for a 2 *dollar* price increase.

Using these numbers, the price sensitivity of the demand for wool and lard might appear to be much different: 2 cents to get a ton of reduced purchases versus $2 to get a ton of reduced purchases. Yet the elasticities are the same. The percentage change in price is 20 percent in each case ($2/$10 = $.02/$.10 = .20, or 20 percent), and the percentage change in quantity is 5 percent in each case: 1 ton of lard/20 tons of lard = 1 ton of wool/20 tons of wool = .05, or 5 percent. Hence, the elasticity is 5/20 = 1/4 in both cases.

By looking at ratios of percentage changes, elasticity allows us to compare the price sensitivity of different goods regardless of the units for measuring either price or quantity. With hundreds of different currencies and hundreds of different units of measurement, this is indeed a major advantage.

Elasticity versus Slope

The *elasticity of the demand curve* is not the same as the *slope of the demand curve.* The slope of the demand curve is defined as the change in price divided by the change in quantity demanded: $\Delta P/\Delta Q$. The slope is not unit free; it depends on how the price and quantity are measured. Thus, it is not a good measure of price sensitivity when we compare different goods.

To illustrate the difference between slope and elasticity, we show in Figure 4.3 a demand curve for lard and a demand curve for wool. The two demand curves have different slopes because the prices are so different. In fact, the slope of the wool demand curve is 100 times greater than the slope of the lard demand curve. Yet the elasticity is the same for the change from *A* to *B* for both demand curves.

Terminology for Discussing Elasticities

Economists classify demand curves by the size of the price elasticities of demand, and they have developed a very precise terminology for doing so.

Elastic versus Inelastic Demand

Goods for which the price elasticity is greater than 1 have an **elastic demand.** For example, the quantity of foreign travel demanded decreases by more than 1 percent when the price rises by 1 percent because many people tend to travel at home rather than abroad when the price of foreign travel rises.

elastic demand: demand for which price elasticity is greater than 1.

FIGURE 4.3
Different Slopes and Same Elasticities

The slope of the wool demand curve in the bottom graph is greater than the slope of the lard demand curve in the top graph. The price elasticity of demand for lard and wool from point *A* to point *B* is the same, however. From point *A* to point *B* the price rises by 20 percent and the quantity demanded decreases by 5 percent. Thus, the elasticity is 1/4 for both lard and wool at these points.

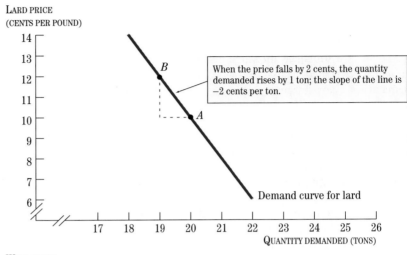

LARD PRICE
(CENTS PER POUND)

When the price falls by 2 cents, the quantity demanded rises by 1 ton; the slope of the line is −2 cents per ton.

Demand curve for lard

QUANTITY DEMANDED (TONS)

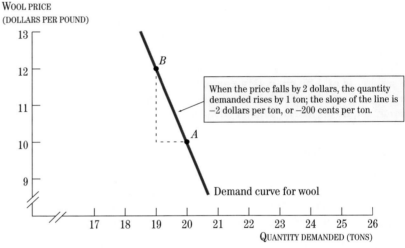

WOOL PRICE
(DOLLARS PER POUND)

When the price falls by 2 dollars, the quantity demanded rises by 1 ton; the slope of the line is −2 dollars per ton, or −200 cents per ton.

Demand curve for wool

QUANTITY DEMANDED (TONS)

inelastic demand: demand for which the price elasticity is less than 1.

unit elastic demand: demand for which price elasticity equals 1.

relatively elastic: a situation in which the elasticity of one good is greater than the elasticity of another good.

Goods for which the price elasticity of demand is less than 1 have an **inelastic demand.** For example, the quantity of eggs demanded decreases by less than 1 percent when the price of eggs rises by 1 percent because many people do not want to substitute other things for eggs at breakfast.

A good with an elasticity of 1 is called **unit elastic.** This distinction between elastic demand, unit elastic demand, and inelastic demand depends solely on whether the elasticity is greater than 1, equal to 1, or less than 1.

Relatively Elastic versus Relatively Inelastic Demand

Sometimes one wants to compare two elasticities, whether or not they are less than 1 or greater than 1. When doing so, economists frequently say a demand curve is **relatively elastic** compared with another demand curve if the elasticity of the first one is larger. For example, a good that has an elasticity of 1.8 is relatively elastic compared with a good with an elasticity of 1.2, or a good with an elasticity of .3 is relatively inelastic compared with a good with elasticity of .7. By using the modifier *relatively,* we are making a comparative statement that one price elasticity of demand is greater than another, regardless of whether it is less than 1 or greater than 1.

Perfectly Elastic versus Perfectly Inelastic Demand

A demand curve that is vertical is called **perfectly inelastic.** Figure 4.4 shows a perfectly inelastic demand curve. The elasticity is zero because when the price changes, the quantity demanded does not change at all. No matter what the price, the same quantity is demanded. People who need insulin would have a perfectly inelastic demand for insulin. As long as there are no substitutes for insulin, they will pay whatever they have to in order to get the insulin.

A demand curve that is horizontal is called **perfectly elastic.** Figure 4.4 also shows a perfectly elastic demand curve. The elasticity is infinite. The perfectly flat demand curve is sometimes hard to imagine because it entails infinitely large movements of quantity for tiny changes in price. In order to better visualize this case you can imagine that the curve is tilted ever so slightly. The infinity case is extreme and is used to approximate demand curves with very high elasticities.

Table 4.1 summarizes the terminology about elasticities.

Elasticities and Sketches of Demand Curves

After looking at Figure 4.1 or Figure 4.4, you might be tempted to say that demand curves that are very steep have a low elasticity, and demand curves that are very flat have a high elasticity. However, because the slope and the elasticity are such different concepts, we must be careful not to simply look at a steep curve and say it has a high elasticity. Recall, for example, that in Figure 4.3 we showed how different slopes can have the same elasticity. Moreover, as we show shortly, a curve with a constant slope has different elasticities at all points on the curve!

Calculating the Elasticity with a Midpoint Formula

To calculate the elasticity, we need to find the percentage change in the quantity demanded and divide it by the percentage change in the price. As we have already illustrated with examples, to get the percentage change in the price or quantity, we need to divide the change in price (ΔP) by the price (P), and the change in quantity (ΔQ_d) by the quantity demanded (Q_d). But when price and quantity demanded

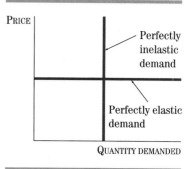

FIGURE 4.4
Perfectly Elastic and Perfectly Inelastic Demand
A perfectly inelastic demand curve is a vertical line at a certain quantity; the quantity demanded is completely insensitive to the price: No matter what happens to the price, the quantity demanded does not change. A perfectly elastic demand curve is a flat line at a certain price; an increase in price reduces the quantity demanded to zero; a small decrease in price raises the quantity demanded by a huge (literally infinite) amount.

perfectly inelastic demand: demand for which the price elasticity is zero, indicating no response to a change in price and therefore a vertical demand curve.

perfectly elastic demand: demand for which the price elasticity is infinite, indicating an infinite response to a change in the price and therefore a horizontal demand curve.

TABLE 4.1
Terminology for Price Elasticity of Demand

Term	Value of Price Elasticity of Demand (e_d)
Perfectly inelastic	0 (vertical demand curve)
Inelastic	Less than 1
Unit elastic	1
Elastic	Greater than 1
Perfectly elastic	Infinity (horizontal demand curve)
Good A is relatively elastic compared with good B.	Good A has a higher elasticity than good B.

change, there is a question about what to use for P and Q_d. Should we use the old price and old quantity demanded before the change, or should we use the new price and new quantity demanded after the change?

The most common convention economists use is a compromise between these two alternatives. They take the *average,* or the *midpoint,* of the old and new quantities demanded and the old and new prices. That is, they compute the elasticity using the following formula, called the *midpoint formula:*

$$\text{Price elasticity of demand} = \frac{\text{change in quantity}}{\text{average of old and new quantity}} \div \frac{\text{change in price}}{\text{average of old and new price}}$$

For example, if we use the midpoint formula to calculate the price elasticity of demand for oil when the price changes from $20 to $22 and the quantity demanded changes from 60 million to 48 million barrels a day, we get

$$\frac{60 - 48}{(60 + 48)/2} \div \frac{\$20 - \$22}{(\$20 + \$22)/2} = .2222 \div (-.0952) = -2.33$$

That is, the price elasticity of demand is 2.33 using the midpoint formula. In this case, this is close to the value of 2 we obtained by using the old price ($20) rather than the average $21 = ($20 + $22)/2, and the old quantity demanded (60) rather than the average quantity 54 = (60 + 48)/2.

Revenue and the Price Elasticity of Demand

When people purchase 60 million barrels of oil at $20 a barrel, they must pay a total of $1,200 million ($20 times 60 million). This is a payment to the oil producers and is the producers' revenue. In general, revenue is the price (P) times the quantity (Q), or $P \times Q$.

The Two Effects of Price on Revenue

Because revenue is defined as price times quantity, an increase or a decrease in the price has an effect on revenue. However, there are two opposite effects. Consider an increase in the price. An increase in the price raises the payment per unit but also reduces the number of units. In other words, when the price increases, people pay more for each item and this increases revenue; but they buy fewer items, and this decrease in the quantity demanded reduces revenue. The elasticity determines which of these two opposite effects dominates.

Figure 4.5 illustrates how the price elasticity determines the effect of a price change on revenue for the special case of a demand curve that is a straight line. Look first at the demand curve shown in the top panel of Figure 4.5. Observe that the elasticity is greater than 1 on the left part of the demand curve and less than 1 on the right part of the demand curve.

Now look at the lower panel in Figure 4.5; it shows how revenue is related to price in the case of this same straight-line demand curve. Observe how revenue changes as the price increases. When the price elasticity is greater than 1—in the region on the left—an increase in the price will lower revenue. For example, an increase in the price from $8 per unit to $9 per unit reduces the quantity demanded from 4 units to 2 units and revenue falls from $32 to $18; the gain in revenue from the higher price per unit is offset by the loss in revenue from the decline in the number of units sold. However, when the price elasticity is greater than 1—in the

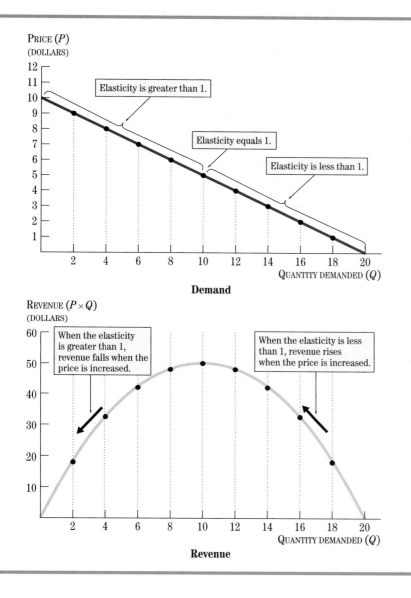

FIGURE 4.5
Revenue and Elasticity of a Straight-Line Demand Curve
Along the straight-line demand curve at the top, the price elasticity ranges from above 1 (to the left) to below 1 (to the right). When the price elasticity is greater than 1, an increase in the price will reduce revenue as shown in the lower panel.

region on the right—an increase in the price will raise revenue. For example, an increase in the price from $1 to $2 per unit reduces the quantity demanded from 18 units to 16 units and revenue rises from $18 to $32; in this case, the loss in revenue from the decline in number of units sold is not large enough to offset the gain in revenue from the higher price per unit.

Another illustration of the relationship between elasticity and revenue changes is found in Figure 4.6, which is a replica of Figure 4.1 with the scales changed to better illustrate the effects on revenue. We now know that the elasticity in the top graph is greater than 1 and the elasticity in the bottom graph is less than 1. We can see that the same price increase leads to a large decline in the quantity demanded when the elasticity is large and to a small decline in the quantity demanded when

FIGURE 4.6

Effects of an Increase in the Price of Oil on Revenue

These graphs are replicas of the demand curves for oil shown in Figure 4.1, with the scale changed to show the change in revenue when the price of oil is increased. An increase in the price has two effects on revenue, as shown by the gray- and pink-shaded rectangles. The increase in revenue (gray rectangle) is due to the higher price. The decrease in revenue (pink rectangle) is due to the decline in the quantity demanded as the price is increased. In the top graph, where elasticity is greater than 1, the net effect is a decline in revenue; in the bottom graph, where elasticity is less than 1, the net effect is an increase in revenue.

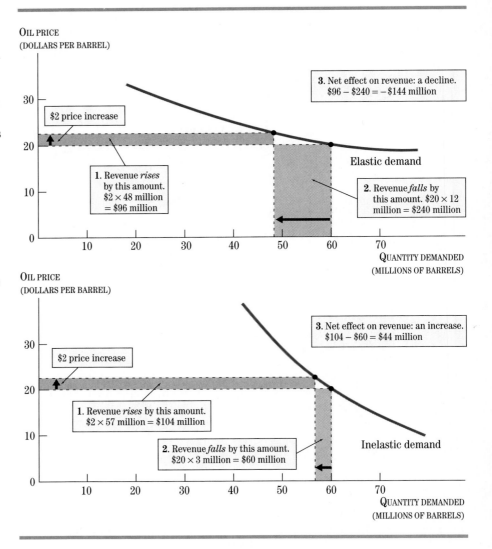

the elasticity is small. The two effects of a price increase are illustrated in the graphs. Revenue falls when the price is increased in the top graph and rises when the price is increased in the bottom graph.

Table 4.2 summarizes the relationship between revenue and the price elasticity of demand. Observe that an increase in price will raise revenue if the elasticity is less than 1 and will lower revenue if the elasticity is greater than 1.

Differences in the Price Elasticity of Demand

Table 4.3 shows some price elasticities of demand obtained by observing patterns of prices and quantities for several different goods and services. The price elasticity of demand for jewelry, for example, is 2.6. This means that for each percentage increase in the price of jewelry, the quantity demanded will fall by 2.6 percent. Compared with other elasticities, this is large. The price elasticity for alcoholic bev-

Elasticity Is	Terminology	Effect of a Price Increase on Revenue	Effect of a Price Decrease on Revenue
Less than 1	Inelastic	Revenue increases	Revenue decreases
1	Unit elastic	No change in revenue	No change in revenue
Greater than 1	Elastic	Revenue decreases	Revenue increases

● —————————
TABLE 4.2
Revenue and the Price Elasticity of Demand

erages is also large. On the other hand, the price elasticity for eggs is very small. For each percentage increase in the price of eggs, the quantity of eggs demanded falls by only .10 percent. The elasticity for gasoline is also low.

Why do these elasticities differ? Several factors affect elasticity.

● —————————
TABLE 4.3
Estimated Price Elasticities of Demand

Type of Good or Service	Price Elasticity
Eggs	.1
Gasoline	.2
Shoes	.9
Foreign travel	1.2
Alcoholic beverages	1.5
Jewelry	2.6

The Degree of Substitutability

A key factor is whether there are good substitutes for the item in question. Can people easily find a substitute when the price goes up? If the answer is yes, then the price elasticity will be high. Foreign travel has a very high elasticity because there is a reasonably good substitute: domestic travel.

On the other hand, the low price elasticity for eggs can be explained by the lack of good substitutes. As many egg fans know, these items are unique; synthetic eggs are not good substitutes for many people. Hence, the price elasticity of eggs is small. People will continue to buy them even if the price rises a lot.

The degree of substitutability depends in part on whether a good is a necessity or a luxury. Necessities cannot easily be substituted for and thus have a smaller price elasticity. Food is a necessity and tends to have a lower price elasticity than luxury items like jewelry.

Big-Ticket versus Little-Ticket Items

If a good represents a large fraction of people's income, then the price elasticity will be high. If the price of foreign travel doubles, many people will not be able to afford to travel abroad. On the other hand, if the good represents a small fraction of income, the elasticity will be low. For example, if the price of eggs doubles, most people can still afford to buy as many eggs as before the price rise. This is another reason why the price elasticity of the demand for foreign travel is larger than the price elasticity of the demand for eggs.

Temporary versus Permanent Price Changes

If a change in price is known to be temporary, the price elasticity of demand will tend to be high because many people can easily shift their purchases either later or earlier. For example, suppose a fabric and sewing machine store announces a discount price to last only one day. Then people will shift their purchase of the fabric or sewing machine they were thinking about buying to the sale day.

On the other hand, if the price cut is permanent, the price elasticity will be smaller. People who expect the price decrease to be permanent will not find it advantageous to buy sooner rather than later.

Long-Run versus Short-Run Elasticity

Frequently the price elasticity of demand is low immediately after a price change but then increases after a period of time has passed. In order to analyze these changes, economists distinguish between the *short run* and the *long run*. The short run is simply a period of time before people have made all their adjustments or changed their habits; the long run is a period of time long enough for people to make such adjustments or change their habits.

Many personal adjustments to a change in prices take a long time. For example, when the price of gasoline increases, people can reduce the quantity demanded in the short run only by driving less and using other transportation more. This might be inconvenient or impossible. In the long run, however, when it comes time to buy a new car, they can buy a more fuel-efficient one. Thus, the quantity of gasoline demanded falls by larger amounts in the long run than in the short run. In fact, the long-run price elasticity of the demand for gasoline is more than twice the short-run elasticity.

Habits that are difficult to break also cause differences between short-run and long-run elasticity. Even a large increase in the price of tobacco may have a small effect on the quantity purchased because people cannot break the smoking habit quickly. But after a period of time, the high price of cigarettes may encourage them to break the habit. Thus, the long-run elasticity for tobacco is higher than the short-run elasticity.

Elasticities Related to Shifts in Demand

income elasticity of demand: the percentage change in quantity demanded of one good divided by the percentage change in income.

Before moving on to supply, we briefly compare the price elasticity of demand with some other elasticities related to demand. Recall that the price elasticity of demand refers to movements along the demand curve. We emphasized in the previous chapter the difference between a shift in the demand curve and a movement along the demand curve. A *shift* in the demand curve occurs when there is a change in the quantity people are willing to buy due to a change in anything except the price; for example, a change in income, the price of other goods, or expectations will shift the demand curve.

The concept of elasticity can be applied to changes in the quantity consumers are willing to buy caused by changes in variables other than price. These elasticities must be distinguished from the price elasticity of demand. The **income elasticity of demand** is the percentage change in the quantity of a good demanded at any given price divided by a percentage change in income. That is,

$$\text{Income elasticity of demand} = \frac{\text{percentage change in quantity demanded}}{\text{percentage change in income}}$$

For example, if incomes rise by 10 percent and, as a result, people purchase 15 percent more health care at a given price, the income elasticity of health care is 1.5. Table 4.4 lists some income elasticities of demand for several different goods and services.

As discussed in Chapter 3, the demand for most goods increases when people's incomes increase. If you have more income, your demand for movies will probably

●━━━━━━━━━━━━━━━━━━━━━

TABLE 4.4
Estimated Income Elasticities of Demand

Type of Good or Service	Income Elasticity
Food	.3
Beer	.4
Wine	1.0
Automobiles	1.2
Air travel	6.0

increase at each price. Recall that a normal good is a good or service whose demand increases as income increases. But every good is not a normal good; if the demand for a good declines when income increases, the good is called an inferior good. The income elasticity of demand for an inferior good is negative and is reported as a negative number by economists.

Another type of elasticity relating to shifts in the demand curve is the **cross-price elasticity of demand,** which is defined as the percentage change in the quantity demanded divided by the percentage change in the price of another good. For example, an increase in the price of rollerblades would *increase* the quantity demanded of bicycles at every price as people shift away from rollerblading to bicycle riding. Rollerblades are a substitute for bicycles. A cross-price elasticity can also go in the other direction. An increase in the price of bicycle helmets may *reduce* the demand for bicycles. Recall that bicycle helmets and bicycles are complements. For a complement, the cross-price elasticity of demand is negative.

cross-price elasticity of demand: the percentage change in the quantity demanded of one good divided by the percentage change in the price of another good.

Review

▶ The price elasticity of demand is a unit-free number that tells us how sensitive the quantity demanded is to the price. It is defined as the percentage change in the quantity demanded divided by the percentage change in the price.

▶ The elasticity also helps determine how much of a price increase will occur as a result of a shift in supply, and how much revenue will change when the price rises.

▶ Horizontal demand curves have infinite price elasticity. Vertical demand curves have zero price elasticity. Most products have a price elasticity between these two extremes.

▶ The size of the price elasticity of demand depends on the availability of substitutes for the item, whether the item represents a large fraction of income, and whether the price change is temporary or permanent. There are also important differences

THE PRICE ELASTICITY OF SUPPLY

Knowing how sensitive the quantity supplied is to a change in price is just as important as knowing how sensitive the quantity demanded is. The price elasticity of supply measures this sensitivity. Recall that supply describes the behavior of those who produce goods. A high price elasticity of supply means that producers raise their production by a large amount if the price increases. A low price elasticity of supply means that producers raise their production only a little if the price increases. Let us briefly see why knowing this elasticity is important.

Why the Price Elasticity of Supply Is Important

Figure 4.7 shows two different supply curves for coffee. The horizontal axis shows the quantity of coffee supplied around the world in billions of pounds; the vertical axis shows the price in dollars per pound of coffee. For the supply curve in the top graph, the quantity supplied is very sensitive to the price; the price elasticity of supply is high. For the supply curve in the bottom graph, the price elasticity of supply is much lower.

FIGURE 4.7
Comparing Different Price Elasticities of Supply

In the top graph, the quantity supplied is much more sensitive to price than in the bottom graph. The price elasticity of supply is greater between points *A* and *B* at the top than between points *A* and *C* at the bottom.

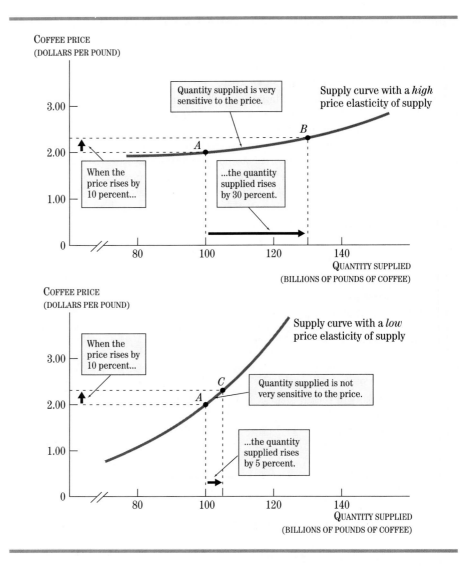

The price elasticity of supply is important for finding out the response of price to shifts in demand. This is shown in Figure 4.8, where the demand for coffee declines, perhaps because of concerns about the effect of the caffeine in coffee or because of a decrease in the price of caffeine-free substitutes for coffee. In any case, if the price elasticity of supply is high, as in the top graph, the price does not change as much as when the price elasticity of supply is low, as in the bottom graph. With a high price elasticity, a small change in price is enough to get firms to bring the quantity supplied down to the lower quantity demanded.

price elasticity of supply: the percentage change in quantity supplied divided by the percentage change in price.

Definition of the Price Elasticity of Supply

The price elasticity of supply can be calculated in much the same way as the price elasticity of demand. The **price elasticity of supply** is defined as the percentage

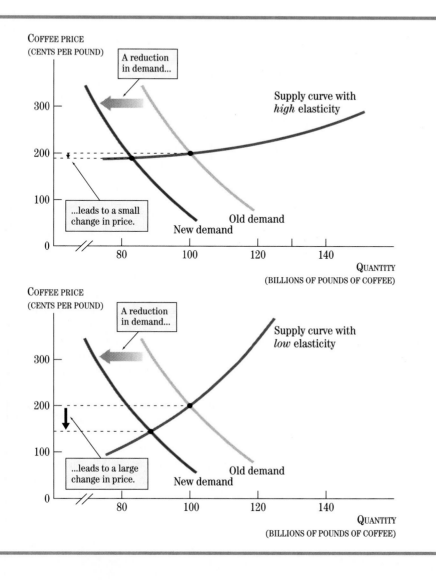

FIGURE 4.8
Importance of Knowing the Price Elasticity of Supply
When demand changes, the price will also change. If the price elasticity of supply is high, there will be a small change in price. If the price elasticity of supply is low, there will be a large change in price.

change in the quantity supplied divided by the percentage change in the price. That is,

$$\text{Price elasticity of supply} = \frac{\text{percentage change in quantity supplied}}{\text{percentage change in the price}}$$

The price elasticity of supply refers to movements of price and quantity supplied on a given supply curve, all other things being equal. Sometimes the "price elasticity of supply" is simply called the "supply elasticity" for short. If we let the symbol e_s be the price elasticity of supply, then

$$e_s = \frac{\Delta Q_s}{Q_s} \div \frac{\Delta P}{P} = \frac{\Delta Q_s / Q_s}{\Delta P / P}$$

where Q_s is the quantity supplied and P is the price. The price elasticity of supply is a positive number because the price and quantity supplied are positively related.

FIGURE 4.9
Perfectly Elastic and Perfectly Inelastic Supply
When the quantity supplied is completely unresponsive to the price, the supply curve is vertical and the price elasticity of supply is zero; this case is called perfectly inelastic supply. When the quantity supplied responds by large amounts to a price change, the supply curve is horizontal; economists then say supply is perfectly elastic.

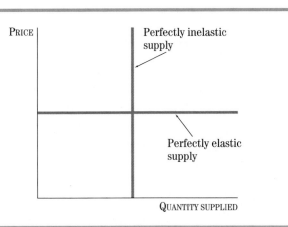

perfectly elastic supply: supply for which the price elasticity is infinite, indicating an infinite response of quantity supplied to a change in price and thereby a horizontal supply curve.

perfectly inelastic supply: supply for which the price elasticity is zero, indicating no response of quantity supplied to a change in price and thereby a vertical supply curve.

All of the attractive features of the price elasticity of demand apply to the price elasticity of supply. The price elasticity of supply is a unit-free measure. It differs from the slope. It does not depend on how the price or quantity is measured.

As in the case of demand, there can be **perfectly elastic supply** or **perfectly inelastic supply,** as shown in Figure 4.9. The vertical supply curve is perfectly inelastic; it has zero elasticity. Such supply curves are not unusual. For example, there is only one *Mona Lisa*. A higher price cannot bring about a higher quantity supplied, not even one more *Mona Lisa.* But the supply of most goods is not vertical. Higher prices will encourage coffee producers to use more fertilizer, hire more workers, and eventually plant more coffee trees. Thus the quantity supplied increases when the price rises.

The horizontal supply curve is perfectly elastic. In this case the price does not change at all. It is the same regardless of the quantity supplied. It is easier to understand the horizontal supply curve if you view it as an approximation to a supply curve that is *nearly* horizontal, one with a very high elasticity. Then only a small increase in price brings forth a huge increase in the quantity supplied by firms.

Perfectly Inelastic Supply
The *Mona Lisa* is an example of a good with a perfectly inelastic supply. The supply curve is vertical because no matter how high the price, no more *Mona Lisas* can be produced. However, the demand to see the *Mona Lisa* is *not* perfectly inelastic; raising the price of admission charged by the Louvre Museum in Paris would reduce the number of people coming to see the painting.

> ### Review
>
> ▶ The price elasticity of supply is a unit-free measure of how sensitive the quantity supplied is to the price. It is defined as the percentage change in the quantity supplied divided by the percentage change in the price.
>
> ▶ The price elasticity of supply is useful for determining how much prices will change when there is a change in demand.

APPLICATIONS OF ELASTICITY

We began the chapter by discussing a wartime application of the price elasticity of demand. Having defined elasticity for both demand and supply, let us now finish reviewing that wartime application and also apply elasticity to some everyday economic problems.

The Size of the Oil Price Increase

As stated in the introduction to this chapter, the 1990 military invasion of Kuwait by Iraq reduced the world oil supply by 7 percent. Economists estimated that the price elasticity of demand for oil was about .1 percent (that is, $e_d = .1$). Thus, with this small elasticity, they predicted that the oil price would rise by a large amount—about 70 percent. (Here's the calculation, using the symbols in the definition of the price elasticity of demand on page 92: $\Delta P/P = \Delta Q_d/Q_d \times 1/e_d = .07 \times 10 = .70$, or 70 percent.) In fact, the actual rise in the price of oil in 1990 *was* large, even larger than 70 percent: The price of oil rose from $17 per barrel in July 1990 to $36 in October 1990, or about 112 percent. (The larger than predicted price increase may have been due to worries that Iraq would also invade Saudi Arabia and reduce the oil supply even further.)

Hence, the oil supply and demand analysis helped explain the price effects of the reduction in oil supply. This economic model—showing that a huge oil price increase could be caused by the 7 percent reduction in oil supply—was a factor in the decision by the United States and its allies to send troops to the Middle East to halt the Iraqi invasion of Saudi Arabia and to eventually force Iraq out of Kuwait.

Setting National Park Fees

In 1994, the federal government proposed to increase the fees charged at national parks, from Yosemite to Yellowstone to the Great Smoky Mountains. It estimated that an increase in fees would raise revenue that could then be used to make repairs and improve facilities at the parks. However, an increase in fees could reduce the use of parks—decrease the quantity demanded—as you have seen. If the demand was elastic, then the higher fees would reduce revenue.

Why did the government estimate that revenue would go up? For one thing, a survey found that most users of parks had incomes in excess of $50,000 per year. Hence, park fees—even the higher ones—are a relatively small part of their income. In this way, the federal government figured that the elasticity of demand is less than one.

Alfred Marshall, 1842–1924

BORN:
Bermondsey (south of London), England, 1842

EDUCATION:
Cambridge University, graduated 1865

JOBS:
Professor, University College, Bristol, 1877–1883
Fellow, Oxford University, 1883–1885
Professor of political economy, Cambridge University, 1885–1908

MAJOR PUBLICATIONS:
Principles of Economics, 1890
Money, Credit and Commerce, 1923

Alfred Marshall was the first economist to define the powerful unit-free concept called elasticity, for which other economists are eternally grateful. The great economist John Maynard Keynes said, "I do not think Marshall did economists any greater service." Marshall defined elasticity in a remarkable book, *Principles of Economics,* published in 1890, when he was 48 years old. Here is how Marshall put it:

The elasticity of demand *in a market is great or small according as the amount demanded increases much or little for a given fall in price, and diminishes much or little for a given rise in price.*

Marshall's *Principles of Economics* contains many other innovations. The book was used in advanced economics courses for many decades; the economist Milton Friedman was still assigning the book to his students at the University of Chicago in the 1970s.

Why was the book so popular? It demonstrated the tremendous usefulness of the supply and demand model, in which the effects of economic policies are analyzed in a diagram by shifting supply or demand curves and considering their elasticities. Curiously, Marshall chose to make his diagrams the size of postage stamps and place them in small-print footnotes!

Marshall's *Principles of Economics* was not the first book to use demand or supply curves. Nearly 20 years earlier, in 1871, W. Stanley Jevons published a book of similar ideas. But more than anyone else, Marshall developed the supply and demand diagram into a powerful tool for analyzing real-world problems. Many economists credit Marshall with developing the *style* of economic reasoning that is routinely followed in applied economics work today. Marshall taught economists how to think like economists.

What was Alfred Marshall like? He spent much of his life as a professor, lecturing regularly and holding frequent

office hours at his home. He trained a whole generation of economists, including John Maynard Keynes. For enjoyment, he loved to hike in the Alps in the summer. He lectured about the material in his *Principles of Economics* many years before the book was published, and he waited until he was over 80 to publish his major work on macroeconomics, which he had lectured about in his 30s! Many have wondered about the reasons for "Marshall's delay," looking into his personal life for answers.

Marshall was born south of London to a family that was not particularly well-off; his father was a dominating figure and forbade Alfred to study mathematics, which Marshall loved but his father did not understand. Rather than go to Oxford, where his father wanted him to go, Marshall went to Cambridge and financed his education with a loan from one of his uncles.

Marshall did not decide to become an economist until after college. The reason for his choice? He said he saw economics as a way to help the poor and unfortunate in society.

Marshall was the greatest economist of the neoclassical school of the late 19th and early 20th century. The neoclassical school maintained most of the principles of the classical school founded by Adam Smith, but improved on them with the supply and demand model and its underlying foundation.

Marshall's simple, yet broad, definition of economics has itself become a classic. To Marshall,

Political Economy or Economics is a study of mankind in the ordinary business of life; it examines that part of individual and social action which is most closely connected with the attainment and with the use of the material requisites of wellbeing.

Source of quotes: Alfred Marshall, *Principles of Economics,* 8th ed. (New York: Macmillan, 1920), pp. 1, 102.

Taxes and Labor Supply

One of the most important supply curves is the supply curve of an individual's or a family's labor. Just as a firm decides how much to produce at each price of the good it sells, workers may decide how much to work at each price (wage) of the good they sell (labor). For example, a freelance editor may decide whether to take on a book-editing job depending on how high a wage the book publisher offers. At a very low wage, the editor may decide that there are better things to do than edit the book. At a higher wage, the editor may take the job—or even two jobs if the wage gets high enough. Thus, there is a labor supply curve for book-editing services.

A major source of revenue for the government is income taxes on the wages earned from working. The higher the tax rate, the less the worker can take home and, therefore, the less labor will be supplied. A higher tax rate increases the amount collected from each hour worked, but if fewer hours are worked as a result of the tax, then tax revenues may go down. The key factor is the labor supply elasticity—the percentage change in the quantity of labor supplied divided by the percentage change in take-home wage. If labor supply has a very low elasticity, then a higher tax rate will increase tax revenue. On the other hand, if labor supply has a very high elasticity, then a higher tax will decrease revenue.

Review

▶ Demand and supply elasticities help make decisions in government, business, and in our personal lives. Knowing the size of the elasticity is essential.

▶ Many decisions depend simply on whether the price elasticity of demand is greater or less than 1. Others depend on the elasticity of supply.

CONCLUSION

In this chapter we have provided a quantitative basis for the supply and demand model. We have seen that *how much* the equilibrium price and quantity change in response to a change in supply and demand depends on the elasticity of the supply and demand curves. Armed with these elasticities, we can predict what will happen to prices after a drop in the supply of a good. We can also predict what will happen to prices after a change in demand. And we can predict whether revenue will increase or decrease when prices, fees, or taxes are cut or raised.

Distinguishing between movements along and shifts of the curves, knowing the importance of the elasticity, and describing in words what happens when the intersection of the curves change are all important parts of economic thinking.

KEY POINTS

1. Elasticity is a measure of the sensitivity of one economic variable to another. For example, the price elasticity of demand measures how much the quantity demanded changes when the price changes.

2. The price elasticity of demand is the percentage change in the quantity demanded divided by the percentage change

in price. It refers to changes in price and quantity demanded along the demand curve, all other things being equal.

3. Elasticity is a unit-free measure.

4. Demand is elastic if the price elasticity of demand is greater than 1 and inelastic if the price elasticity of demand is less than 1.

5. When the elasticity is greater than 1, an increase in the price reduces the quantity demanded by a percentage greater than the percentage increase in the price, thereby reducing revenue. When the elasticity is less than 1, an increase in the price reduces the quantity demanded by a percentage less than the percentage increase in the price, thereby increasing revenue.

6. The elasticity of demand for a good depends on whether the good has close substitutes, whether its value is a large or small fraction of total income, and the time period of the change.

7. If a good has a low price elasticity of demand, then a change in supply will cause a big change in price. Con-

versely, if a good has a high price elasticity of demand, then a change in supply will cause a small change in price.

8. The price elasticity of supply is defined as the percentage change in the quantity supplied divided by the percentage change in the price.

9. In the short run, the price elasticity of supply is very low. In the long run, the price elasticity of supply is higher.

10. If a good has a low price elasticity of supply, then a change in demand will cause a big change in price. Conversely, if a good has a high price elasticity of supply, then a change in demand will cause a small change in price.

KEY TERMS

price elasticity of demand	relatively elastic	price elasticity of supply
unit-free measure	perfectly inelastic demand	perfectly elastic supply
elastic demand	perfectly elastic demand	perfectly inelastic supply
inelastic demand	income elasticity of demand	
unit elastic demand	cross-price elasticity of demand	

QUESTIONS FOR REVIEW

1. Why is the price elasticity of demand a unit-free measure of the sensitivity of the quantity demanded to a price change?

2. What factors determine whether the price elasticity of demand is high or low?

3. What is the difference between the price elasticity of demand, the income elasticity of demand, and the cross-price elasticity of demand?

4. Why is the price elasticity of demand useful for finding the size of the price change that occurs when supply shifts?

5. What is the difference between elastic and inelastic demand?

6. For what values of the price elasticity of demand do increases in the price increase revenue?

7. What is the slope of a perfectly elastic supply curve?

8. Why is the price elasticity of demand lower in the short run than in the long run?

9. Why is price elasticity of supply lower in the short run than in the long run?

10. What is the income elasticity of demand?

PROBLEMS

1. Assume that demand can be characterized by a perfectly elastic demand curve. How will the price change as the supply curve shifts? Why does it behave in this way? How does total revenue change as the supply curve shifts?

2. Suppose a city government decides that it wants to increase revenue by raising the price of parking tickets.

  a) When government officials increase the price of a ticket from $40 to $50, they are surprised that their revenue actually falls. What happened? What does this say about the responsiveness of people to the price of illegal parking? Is it elastic or inelastic?

  b) Suppose the city government collects the following data:

Price of Parking Ticket	Number of Tickets per Week
$10	100
$20	80
$30	60
$40	40
$50	20

Calculate revenue for each price-quantity combination. At what point does the demand for illegal parking go from the inelastic to the elastic portion of the curve? Use the midpoint formula for computing elasticities.

c) Given the preceding data, what ticket price will maximize the revenue received from parking tickets?

3. What does it mean for the supply curve to be perfectly inelastic? How does revenue change as the demand curve shifts?

4. Compare a market where supply and demand are very (but not perfectly) inelastic to one where supply and demand are very (but not perfectly) elastic. Suppose the government decides to impose a price floor $1 above the equilibrium prices in each of these markets. Compare, diagrammatically, the surpluses that result. Explain the difference between these two cases.

5. Using the following data for a demand curve, calculate the price elasticity of demand between a price of $9 and $10, and between $4 and $5. Use the midpoint formula.

Price	Quantity Demanded
10	10
9	20
8	30
7	40
6	50
5	60
4	70
3	80

a) Since this is a linear demand curve with a constant slope, why does the elasticity change?

b) At what point is price times quantity maximized? What is the elasticity *at that point?*

6. Use the following data to calculate the price elasticity of supply for the price between $7 and $8, and between $3 and $4. Use the midpoint formula. How does supply elasticity change as you move up the supply curve?

Price	Quantity Supplied
2	10
3	20
4	30
5	40
6	50
7	60
8	70
9	80

7. Suppose that the demand for cigarettes is very inelastic. If the government imposes a tax per pack of cigarettes, it is equivalent to the supply curve shifting up vertically by the amount of the tax. Show this in a diagram. If the demand is perfectly inelastic, by how much does the price, including the tax, increase? Why?

8. Calculate the cross-price elasticity for the following goods. Are they substitutes or complements?

a) The price of movie theater tickets goes up by 10 percent, causing the quantity demanded for video rentals to go up by 4 percent.

b) Computer prices fall by 20 percent, causing the quantity demanded of software to increase by 15 percent.

c) The price of apples falls by 5 percent, causing the quantity demanded of pears to fall by 5 percent.

d) The price of ice cream falls by 6 percent, causing the quantity demanded of frozen yogurt to fall by 1 percent.

9. Given the following income elasticities of demand, would you classify the following goods as luxury, necessity, or inferior goods?

a) Potatoes: elasticity = 0.5

b) Pinto beans: elasticity = −0.1

c) Bottled water: elasticity = 1.1

d) Video cameras: elasticity = 1.4

10. In 1992, the federal government placed a tax of 10 percent on goods like luxury automobiles and yachts. The boat-manufacturing industry had huge declines in orders for boats and laid off many workers, whereas the reaction in the auto industry was much milder. (The tax on yachts was subsequently removed.) Explain this situation using two supply and demand diagrams. Compare the elasticity of demand for luxury autos with that for yachts based on the experience with the luxury tax.

11. The following data on world coffee production from 1985 to 1987 come from the *CRB Commodity Year Book.*

	Production (millions of bags)	Price (dollars / pound)
1985	96	1.42
1986	80	2.01
1987	103	1.09

a) Plot the observations on a scatter diagram with price on the vertical axis and production on the horizontal axis.

b) Assume that production equals the quantity demanded around the world and that the coffee demand curve did not change between 1985 and 1987. First, calculate the price elasticity of demand for 1985 to 1986 using the midpoint formula. Next, calculate the same elasticities from 1986 to 1987. Would you say the demand for coffee is elastic or inelastic?

c) If the two calculations in part (b) differ by much, explain why.

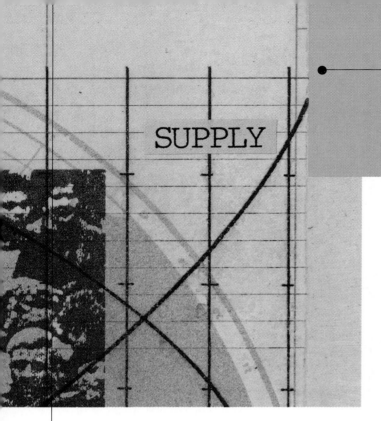

SUPPLY

5

The Demand Curve and the Behavior of Consumers

There is a demand curve for every item in the yellow pages: from automobile insurance to zinc etchings, from accounts at banks to yoga instructors, and from aircraft to ZIP code directories. There are demand curves for the thousands of items not listed in the yellow pages as well: foreign currencies, movie stars, oil tankers, stolen merchandise, and, of course, the many items invented since the yellow pages last went to print. For all these items, the demand curve describes the intuitive idea discussed in the previous two chapters that the quantity demanded depends on the price: A higher price for an item reduces the amount of the item that people are willing to buy; a lower price does the opposite, increasing the amount that people are willing to buy. Other factors besides the price—such as consumers' preferences and incomes—influence demand; the demand curve shifts when these other factors change. Figure 5.1 shows a typical demand curve with price on the vertical axis and the quantity demanded on the horizontal axis. The demand curve is for an entire market, which might consist of millions of consumers.

In this chapter we look under the surface of the demand curve and examine the behavior of these consumers. This examination has two purposes. The first is

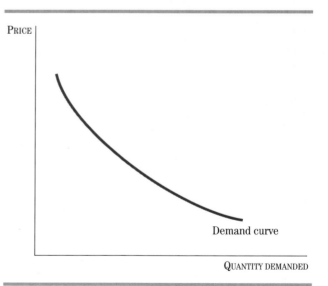

FIGURE 5.1
A Typical Demand Curve
Demand curves typically slope downward. The main job of this chapter is to explain the behavior of consumers that underlies the demand curve.

to see exactly what determines the slope and position of the demand curve: why it slopes downward and why changes in people's preferences or income cause it to shift.

The second purpose of examining the behavior of consumers is to see how well a market economy actually works. When we study the interactions of people in markets, it is the foundation of demand curves—people's preferences and choices—that we are investigating, not the demand curves themselves. Consumers do not go to the market with a demand curve; they go with certain preferences and objectives. One of the most important conclusions of the study of economics is that, under certain circumstances, a market economy works better than alternative systems to produce and allocate goods and resources. In order to understand that conclusion—to question it, to criticize it, to prove it, to defend it—we must look at the consumer behavior beneath the demand curve.

Our examination of consumer behavior in this chapter involves constructing a model. The main assumption of the model is that people make purposeful choices with limited resources to increase their satisfaction and better their lives. To make this assumption operational, economists have developed the idea of *utility*, which represents people's preferences for different items (products, jobs, leisure time) among a set of alternatives. We first define utility explicitly. We then show how economists use utility to derive the slope and position of the demand curve and to measure the performance of the market system.

UTILITY AND CONSUMER PREFERENCES

The model of consumer behavior starts with the basic idea that people have preferences or tastes for some goods relative to others. Not all of the millions of people who underlie a typical demand curve have the same tastes and preferences, of course. Some like Brussels sprouts; some hate Brussels sprouts. In developing the model of consumer behavior we first focus on individual consumers and then show how the behavior of the millions of individuals adds up.

Utility is a numerical indicator of a person's preference for some goods compared to others. If one prefers partaking in some activity, such as eating a pizza, to some other activity, such as going to a movie, then the utility from the pizza is greater than the utility from the movie. In general, if one item is preferred to some alternative, then the utility from the item is greater than the alternative.

utility: a numerical indicator of a person's preferences in which higher levels of utility indicate a greater preference.

Be careful not to confuse the economist's definition of utility with the everyday meaning. If you look up *utility* in the dictionary, you will probably see the word *usefulness,* but to an economist, higher *utility* does not mean greater "usefulness"; it simply means that the item is preferred to another item. Watching "The Oscars" or "The NCAA Final Four" might give you more utility than attending a review session for your economics course, even though it is not as useful for studying for the final.

A Consumer's Utility Depends on the Consumption of Goods

First, consider some examples of utility. Grapes are a product with which we have a lot of experience. They have been grown for more than 4,000 years, at least since 2400 B.C. in ancient Egypt, and in one form or another, they are still consumed around the world. Table 5.1 shows an example of the utility that one individual

TABLE 5.1
Example of Utility from Grapes for an Individual

Pounds of Grapes	Utility from Grapes	Marginal Utility
0	0	–
1	6	6
2	10	4
3	13	3
4	15	2
5	16	1

> The connecting lines emphasize how marginal utility is the *change* in utility as one more unit of a good is consumed.

might get from consuming table grapes. Because every person is different, Table 5.1 is just an example. You might imagine that the person is you, standing in front of a bin of fresh grapes at the grocery store, deciding how many pounds to buy. Or you can imagine an ancient Egyptian making the same choice thousands of years ago during a break in the construction of the Great Pyramid in Giza.

First look at the first two columns of Table 5.1. The first column shows the amount of grapes in pounds. The second column shows the utility that an individual gets from consuming that many pounds of grapes during a particular time period, perhaps next week. Various possibilities ranging from consuming no grapes to consuming 5 pounds of grapes are shown. Don't worry that there are many different types of grapes—green, red, seedless—just imagine your favorite type of grape.

Think about how much utility this individual might get from consuming different amounts of grapes, starting with no grapes. If the individual consumes no grapes, there is no utility. What about 1 pound of grapes? Let us assume that the utility from consuming 1 pound of grapes is 6 units of utility, as shown in the second row of column 2 of Table 5.1.

Continuing with the grape example, what is the utility from 2 pounds of grapes? Presumably, if you like 1 pound of grapes, you like 2 pounds of grapes more. Table 5.1 shows that the utility of 2 pounds of grapes is 10 units; the utility from 3 pounds of grapes is 13 units, and so on. Utility increases as more grapes are consumed.

Of course, grapes are not the only things people consume; the purpose of utility is to represent people's preference for goods like grapes in comparison with alternatives. Consider, for example, one possible alternative to grapes: bananas, another fruit consumed around the world. Table 5.2 shows the utility from bananas for the same individual—yourself, the ancient Egyptian, or someone else—whose utility from grapes is shown in Table 5.1. Note how the utility from bananas increases with the amount of bananas consumed, though not necessarily by the same amount as grapes.

Modeling a Consumer's Choice
This consumer, with a limited amount to spend, makes a choice that maximizes her utility. The combination of grapes and bananas that she prefers to other possible combinations of grapes and bananas must have a higher utility for her than the other combinations might have.

Marginal Utility

Column 3 of Tables 5.1 and 5.2 shows how much additional utility the person gets from consuming more grapes or bananas. In general, the additional utility a person gets from consuming one more unit

Pounds of Bananas	Utility from Bananas	Marginal Utility
0	0	–
1	10	10
2	18	8
3	22	4
4	24	2
5	25	1

Again, marginal utility is the change in utility as one more unit of a good is consumed.

TABLE 5.2

Example of Utility from Bananas for an Individual

of an item is called **marginal utility.** For example, the additional utility the individual gets from consuming 1 pound of grapes rather than no pounds is 6 units. The additional utility the individual gets from consuming 2 pounds of grapes rather than 1 pound is 4 units. The marginal utility for all the different amounts of grapes is shown in column 3 of Table 5.1. There is no entry for marginal utility in the first row because there is no entry less than zero. Observe how each number in column 3 is the difference between each pair of entries in column 2. Marginal utility can be computed the same way for other goods.

The idea of something being "marginal" is pervasive in economics, and it will come at you in many different ways throughout this book. Sometimes it may seem trivial, sometimes it may seem a bit complicated, but it is worth learning well. *Marginal* means "additional." The word conveys the idea of change in utility at the margin between two and three items or between four and five items.

The adjective *marginal* in front of utility is very important. If the adjective is absent, then we mean *utility* as in the second column of Tables 5.1 and 5.2. Sometimes the adjective *total* is used to emphasize the absence of marginal. Thus, *total utility* means utility rather than marginal utility. But economists do not usually use the word *total* in front of *utility;* they simply say *utility.*

Observe that the marginal utility in both Table 5.1 and Table 5.2 declines as more grapes or bananas are consumed. For example, consider what happens in Table 5.1 when consumption of grapes increases from 1 to 2 pounds and then from 2 to 3 pounds. We see that the individual's marginal utility from the second pound of grapes, once the individual already has 1 pound, equals 4. The marginal utility from the third pound of grapes equals 3. Thus, marginal utility declines from 4 to 3 as grape consumption increases to 2 pounds and then to 3 pounds. Now think about even more grape consumption and note the pattern of marginal utility that develops. As we go from 3 to 4 pounds of grapes, the marginal utility is 2. As we go from 4 to 5 pounds, marginal utility from grapes is only 1. A similar decline in marginal utilities is shown for bananas in Table 5.2.

The decline in utility as more and more of something is consumed is called **diminishing marginal utility.** As one consumes more and more grapes or bananas, the marginal utility declines. In other words, as more grapes are consumed, the individual's utility increases by less and less for each additional pound of grapes. At the extreme point in the tables—5 pounds of grapes or bananas—the individual gets very little additional utility from more grapes or bananas; eating more may make the person sick, so one has to find noneating uses for grapes and bananas—such as feeding grapes or banana nut bread to the birds.

Diminishing marginal utility occurs for virtually every good. Suppose that you like to eat popcorn at movies. Then the first bag might be quite tasty. The second bag will probably not taste quite as good, and as you eat more and more popcorn,

marginal utility: the additional utility from an additional unit of consumption of a good.

"It's been fun, Dave, but I think we're entering the diminished marginal utility phase of our relationship."

diminishing marginal utility: the decline in additional utility from consumption of an additional unit of a good as more and more of the good is consumed.

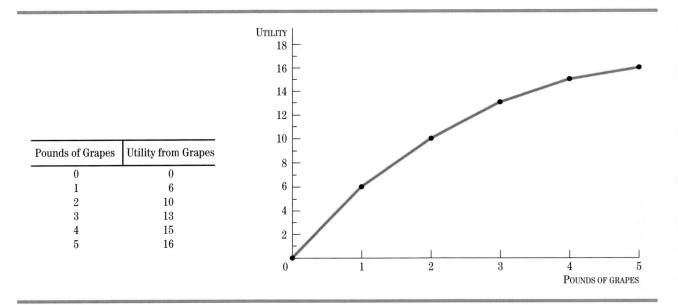

Pounds of Grapes	Utility from Grapes
0	0
1	6
2	10
3	13
4	15
5	16

FIGURE 5.2
Utility

Utility from a good increases as more of the good is consumed, but the size of the increase gets smaller, as shown in the example of grapes in this figure.

you will enjoy each bag less and less. Similarly, the marginal utility of owning a second bicycle if you already have one is less than the marginal utility of the first. The marginal utility of a second telephone in your house is less than the first, and the marginal utility of the third is less than the second, and so on.

We can illustrate graphically how utility and marginal utility depend on the consumption of different goods. Figure 5.2 shows in graphical form information from Table 5.1. Utility is on the vertical axis and pounds of grapes is on the horizontal axis. The pairs of numbers in columns 1 and 2 of Table 5.1 are plotted as points in Figure 5.2. (The numbers are reprinted in the margin close to the figure.) The points are connected to indicate that it is possible to consume fractions of pounds of grapes; the utility from doing so is between the integer amounts. Note that the slope of the curve showing utility gets less steep as more grapes are consumed. The slope of the curve is the change in utility divided by the change in the number of pounds of grapes consumed. In other words, the slope is the additional utility from each additional quantity of grapes consumed, or what we have called marginal utility. The declining slope—the gradual flattening out of the curve—is another way to think about diminishing marginal utility.

Marginal utility is plotted in Figure 5.3. Marginal utility is on the vertical axis and the number of pounds of grapes is on the horizontal axis. The points in Figure 5.3 are the pairs of numbers in columns 1 and 3 of Table 5.1. (Again, the numbers are reprinted close to the figure.) Observe that the relationship between marginal utility and the amount of grapes consumed in Figure 5.3 is downward-sloping. In other words, as more is consumed, marginal utility declines. This illustrates the principle of diminishing marginal utility again.

Utility from More than One Good

So far we have shown how different goods, such as grapes and bananas, separately affect a person's utility. To determine how a person decides between different goods, we must combine the effects of both of these goods on the person's utility.

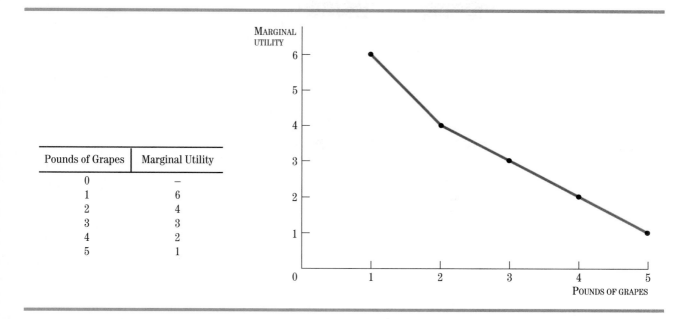

Pounds of Grapes	Marginal Utility
0	–
1	6
2	4
3	3
4	2
5	1

FIGURE 5.3
Marginal Utility
The change in utility as one more unit of a good is consumed is called the marginal utility. Marginal utility diminishes as more is consumed, as shown in the example of grapes in this figure.

An easy way to combine the two effects is simply to add them together. For example, looking back at Tables 5.1 and 5.2, we see that the utility from 2 pounds of grapes equals 10, and the utility from 3 pounds of bananas equals 22; thus, the utility from consuming 2 pounds of grapes *and* 3 pounds of bananas equals 32. We can use this approach to represent the utility from any combination of grape and banana consumption.

Table 5.3 shows the utility for different combinations of grapes and bananas, ranging from 1 pound to 5 pounds for each. A total of 25 rows are in the table to represent all the different combinations of pounds of grapes and bananas. Observe how the utility ranges from 16, when 1 pound of grapes and 1 pound of bananas are consumed, up to 41, when 5 pounds of grapes and 5 pounds of bananas are consumed.

Utility Indicates Preference

With two different goods affecting utility in Table 5.3, we can now show exactly how utility is a numerical indicator of a person's preference for one good compared with another. Recall that when utility from one activity is greater than utility from an alternative, the activity is preferred to the alternative. According to Table 5.3, the consumer prefers a combination of 4 pounds of grapes and 1 pound of bananas to a combination of 1 pound of grapes and 2 pounds of bananas because the utility of the former (25) is more than the latter (24). Other combinations can be ranked similarly. In some cases there are ties; for example, the consumer is *indifferent* between 3 pounds of grapes and 2 pounds of bananas versus 1 pound of grapes and 5 pounds of bananas because the utility of both is 31.

By ranking different combinations of goods in this way, a consumer's utility describes the consumer's preference for one good compared with another. Of all possible combinations, the one with the highest (maximum) utility is the one that is preferred to all the others. Thus, by maximizing utility the consumer can be said to be making decisions that lead to the most preferred outcome from the viewpoint of

TABLE 5.3
Utility from Grapes and Bananas

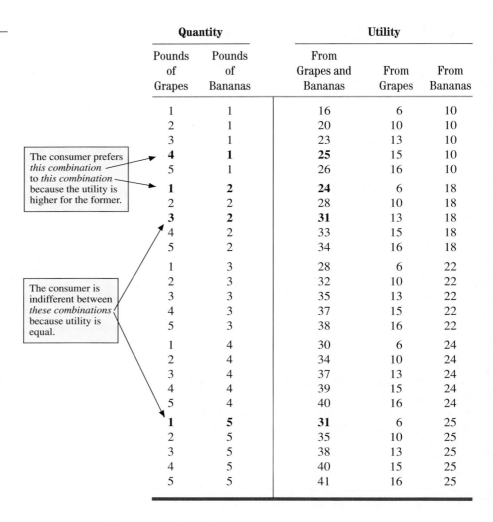

Quantity		Utility		
Pounds of Grapes	Pounds of Bananas	From Grapes and Bananas	From Grapes	From Bananas
1	1	16	6	10
2	1	20	10	10
3	1	23	13	10
4	**1**	**25**	15	10
5	1	26	16	10
1	**2**	**24**	6	18
2	2	28	10	18
3	**2**	**31**	13	18
4	2	33	15	18
5	2	34	16	18
1	3	28	6	22
2	3	32	10	22
3	3	35	13	22
4	3	37	15	22
5	3	38	16	22
1	4	30	6	24
2	4	34	10	24
3	4	37	13	24
4	4	39	15	24
5	4	40	16	24
1	**5**	**31**	6	25
2	5	35	10	25
3	5	38	13	25
4	5	40	15	25
5	5	41	16	25

The consumer prefers *this combination* to *this combination* because the utility is higher for the former.

The consumer is indifferent between *these combinations* because utility is equal.

the consumer. In this way, utility maximization makes operational the assumption that people make purposeful choices to increase their satisfaction.

An important fact about utility as exemplified in Table 5.3 is that the units for measuring it do not matter. For example, suppose we multiply utility from grapes and utility from bananas by 2, in Table 5.3, and then re-examine what utility implies about preferences. In Table 5.3 we would double the entries in the three columns on the right. Rather than 24 units of utility, we would have 48 units of utility from 1 pound of grapes and 2 pounds of bananas. But rather than this combination, the consumer would still prefer 4 pounds of grapes and 1 pound of bananas, which would have a utility of $2 \times 25 = 50$. In fact, you can multiply utility by any positive number—even a billion or a billionth—and as long as the same number multiplies both the utility due to grapes and the utility due to bananas, you get the same ordering of one combination compared to another.

The fact that the description of people's preferences does not depend on the units by which we measure utility is very important because in reality economists have no way to measure utility. That is why the tables and charts in this chapter do not give units by which utility is measured. In particular, no one can say that one person's utility is higher or lower than another person's utility. The utility of different people cannot be compared. An important feature of economists' use of utility is that it does not require or imply that utility of different people can be compared. Only the preference of a particular person for one type of good in comparison with another type of good is represented by utility.

More General Representations of Utility

Table 5.3 is a simple example of how a person's utility depends on the amount of consumption of different combinations of goods. More generally, a person's utility depends on thousands of different goods, but it is much simpler to focus on two.

In some cases, it might not be appropriate to add together the effects of grapes and bananas on utility, as in Table 5.3. For example, if you like to eat grapes and bananas together, then your utility from grapes would be higher if you consumed more bananas. If you had no grapes, your utility from 1 pound of bananas might be 10, but if you had a pound of grapes, your utility from bananas might be 20. If so, the effect of grapes and bananas on your utility could not simply be added together, as in the example. To allow for such possibilities, economists use more general representations of utility than in Table 5.3.

Review

▶ Utility is an indicator of a person's preferences for different goods. Combinations of goods with a higher utility are preferred to combinations of goods with a lower utility.

▶ The marginal utility of a good is the change in utility from an additional amount of the good.

▶ Diminishing marginal utility refers to the principle that as more of an item is consumed, its utility increases by smaller and smaller amounts. In other words, marginal utility declines as more is consumed.

THE BUDGET CONSTRAINT AND UTILITY MAXIMIZATION

We have now shown how a consumer's preferences can be described by utility. We have also shown that maximizing utility is an assumption equivalent to making choices to purposefully improve one's satisfaction. Now let us introduce the limits on the consumer's choice and explain how utility maximization works.

The Budget Constraint

Consumers are limited in how much they can spend when they choose between grapes or bananas or other goods. For example, suppose that the individual choosing between grapes and bananas is limited to spending a total of $8. That is, total spending on grapes plus bananas must be less than or equal to $8. This limit on total spending is called the **budget constraint.** In general, a budget constraint tells us that total expenditures on all goods and services must be less than a certain amount, perhaps the person's income for the year. The budget constraint is what limits the consumer's choices.

budget constraint: an income limitation on a person's expenditure on goods and services.

TABLE 5.4
The Budget Constraint and Expenditures at Different Prices

Pounds of Grapes	Pounds of Bananas	Expenditures: Price of Grapes = $1 Price of Bananas = $1	Expenditures: Price of Grapes = $2 Price of Bananas = $1
1	1	2	3
2	1	3	5
3	1	4	7
4	1	5	9
5	1	6	11
1	2	3	4
2	2	4	6
3	2	5	8
4	2	6	10
5	2	7	12
1	3	4	5
2	3	5	7
3	3	6	9
4	3	7	11
5	3	8	13
1	4	5	6
2	4	6	8
3	4	7	10
4	4	8	12
5	4	9	14
1	5	6	7
2	5	7	9
3	5	8	11
4	5	9	13
5	5	10	15

Note: The red numbers are outside the budget constraint (the sum is greater than $8). The black numbers are within the budget constraint (the sum is less than or equal to $8).

How much a consumer can spend and still remain within the budget constraint depends on the prices of the goods. For the example of grapes and bananas, if the consumer buys 1 pound of grapes at $2 and 2 pounds of bananas at $1, then expenditures are $4, well within the budget constraint of $8. But if 5 pounds of each are purchased at these prices, expenditures would be $15, a sum outside the budget constraint and, therefore, not possible.

The third and fourth columns of Table 5.4 show expenditures on grapes and bananas for two different situations. In both situations the price of bananas is $1; but in the situation in the third column the price of grapes is $1 while in the fourth column the price of grapes is $2. All the combinations of grapes and bananas from Table 5.3 are shown in Table 5.4. Several of the combinations are not within the $8 budget constraint; these are shown in red. Observe that when the price of grapes rises from $1 to $2, more combinations are outside the budget constraint and fewer are within the budget constraint. In general, a higher price for a good reduces the set of consumption opportunities for the individual. (Part A of the appendix to this chapter provides a graphical representation of the budget constraint.)

Maximizing Utility Subject to the Budget Constraint

Given utility in Table 5.3 and the budget constraint in Table 5.4, we can now show what happens when the individual maximizes utility subject to the budget constraint. **Utility maximization** means that people choose the highest possible level of utility given their budget constraint. In Table 5.5, we put utility, from Table 5.3, together with the budget constraint, from Table 5.4, to show how utility maximization subject to a budget constraint takes place.

Suppose first that the price of grapes is $1 per pound and the price of bananas is $1 per pound. By scanning down column 4 in Table 5.5, we see that the total of $8 can be spent on three different combinations. One of these is the highest level of utility achievable by the consumer with an $8 budget constraint. It is 39 units of

utility maximization: an assumption that people try to achieve the highest level of utility given their budget constraint.

●————————————————

TABLE 5.5
Maximizing Utility at Different Prices

Pounds of Grapes	Pounds of Bananas	Utility from Grapes and Bananas	Expenditures: Price of Grapes = $1 Price of Bananas = $1	Expenditures: Price of Grapes = $2 Price of Bananas = $1
1	1	16	2	3
2	1	20	3	5
3	1	23	4	7
4	1	25	5	9
5	1	26	6	11
1	2	24	3	4
2	2	28	4	6
3	2	31	5	8
4	2	33	6	10
5	2	34	7	12
1	3	28	4	5
2	3	32	5	7
3	3	35	6	9
4	3	37	7	11
5	3	38	8	13
1	4	30	5	6
2	4	34	6	8
3	4	37	7	10
4	4	39	8	12
5	4	40	9	14
1	5	31	6	7
2	5	35	7	9
3	5	38	8	11
4	5	40	9	13
5	5	41	10	15

A maximum utility of 39 can be obtained with an $8 budget at these prices.

A maximum utility of 34 can be obtained with an $8 budget at these prices.

utility from 4 pounds of grapes and 4 pounds of bananas. This is the most preferred combination that the individual can buy and remain within the budget constraint. Thus, utility maximization predicts that the consumer will purchase 4 pounds of grapes and 4 pounds of bananas at these prices. There is no other combination that will yield greater utility and still be within the $8 budget constraint.

Effect of a Change in Price: A Movement Along a Demand Curve

Price of Grapes	Quantity of Grapes Demanded by the Consumer
$1	4 pounds
$2	2 pounds

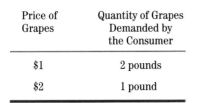

PRICE OF GRAPES (DOLLARS)

QUANTITY OF GRAPES DEMANDED BY THE CONSUMER (POUNDS)

Now suppose that the price of grapes rises from $1 to $2 per pound with the price of bananas staying the same. The new options for expenditures are shown in the last column of Table 5.5. You can see that there are two combinations for which expenditures equal the $8 budget constraint. For one of these combinations—2 pounds of grapes and 4 pounds of bananas—the maximum utility (34) is reached.

Now observe something very important. The quantity of grapes demanded at the higher price of grapes is less than the quantity demanded at the lower price of grapes: When the price of grapes is $1 per pound, the model predicts that 4 pounds of grapes are purchased; at the price of $2 per pound, the model predicts that 2 pounds of grapes are purchased. Thus, we have shown that the model of consumer behavior—in which people maximize utility subject to a budget constraint—predicts that a higher price leads to a reduced quantity demanded. In other words, as shown in the margin, we have derived, using this model, two points on a demand curve for the consumer. When the price goes up, the quantity demanded goes down; when the price goes down, the quantity demanded goes up. These are *movements along* a demand curve as shown in the small graph above, which indicates the two prices and the quantity demanded at each price; a line is drawn through the points to illustrate the downward-sloping demand curve.

Effect of a Change in Income: A Shift in the Demand Curve

Now consider the effect of a change in the individual's income on the quantity of grapes that the individual will purchase. Suppose that the individual now has $5 to spend rather than $8; in other words, there is a $3 reduction in the individual's income. What does the model predict will happen to the quantity of grapes the consumer is willing to buy? If the price is again $1 per pound of grapes and $1 per pound of bananas, then column 4 in Table 5.5 applies: Scanning down this column we see that, if expenditures are limited to $5, then the maximum utility (32) occurs when 2 pounds of grapes and 3 pounds of bananas are purchased. Recall that with $8 to spend the consumer was willing to buy 4 pounds of grapes. Thus, at a price of grapes of $1 per pound, the decrease in income leads to a reduction in the amount of grapes the consumer is willing to buy.

Price of Grapes	Quantity of Grapes Demanded by the Consumer
$1	2 pounds
$2	1 pound

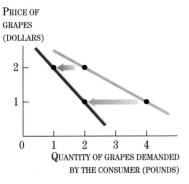

PRICE OF GRAPES (DOLLARS)

QUANTITY OF GRAPES DEMANDED BY THE CONSUMER (POUNDS)

We can also calculate the effects of the income change at a different set of prices. If the price is $2 for grapes and $1 for bananas, then the last column of Table 5.5 applies: With a limit of $5 to spend, the consumer maximizes utility when 1 pound of grapes and 3 pounds of bananas are purchased. The decrease in income leads to a decrease in the amount of grapes the consumer will purchase at each price of grapes. Thus, as shown in the margin, using the model of utility maximization, we have derived another demand curve corresponding to the decreased amount of income. Observe that the demand curve with the lower amount of income ($5) is shifted to the left compared with the demand curve with the higher amount of income ($8). Thus, we have shown explicitly that a change in income will *shift* the consumer's demand curve.

Income and Substitution Effects of a Price Change

The model of consumer behavior allows economists to do more than explain movements along and shifts of a consumer's demand curve. Using the concepts of utility and the budget constraint, economists distinguish between two separate reasons why an increase in the price leads to a decrease in the quantity demanded. These are (1) the income effect, and (2) the substitution effect.

The Income Effect of a Change in the Price We noted how an increase in the price reduces the number of options available to the consumer. When the price of grapes rises from $1 to $2 per pound, choices such as 4 pounds of grapes and 4 pounds of bananas are no longer within the budget constraint, although they were within the budget constraint at a grape price of $1 per pound. A total of fourteen options in Table 5.5 are outside the budget constraint when the price of grapes is $2, whereas only three are outside the budget constraint when the price is $1. This reduction in the options when the price rises is similar to what would happen if the consumer suddenly had less income to spend on both goods. In other words, the increase in the price reduces the amount of real income, which leads consumers to reduce the amount they will purchase.

The **income effect** is the amount by which quantity demanded falls because of the decline in real income from the price increase. Of course, a reduction in the grape price will have the opposite effect: It will increase the real income the consumer has to spend on both goods and in particular on grapes. The income effect is a general phenomenon that applies to all normal goods; for example, when the price of gasoline rises people will spend less on gasoline in part because their real income has declined. With less real income, they will spend less on most goods and services.

income effect: the amount by which the quantity demanded falls because of the decline in real income from a price increase.

The Substitution Effect of a Change in the Price An increase in the price of grapes with no change in the price of other goods causes an increase in the relative price of grapes. Because grapes become relatively more expensive people will switch their purchases away from grapes toward other goods even if there were no income effect. The **substitution effect** is the amount by which the quantity demanded falls when the price rises, exclusive of the income effect.

substitution effect: the amount by which quantity demanded falls when the price rises, exclusive of the income effect.

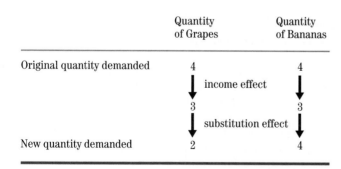

	Quantity of Grapes	Quantity of Bananas
Original quantity demanded	4	4
	↓ income effect	↓
	3	3
	↓ substitution effect	↓
New quantity demanded	2	4

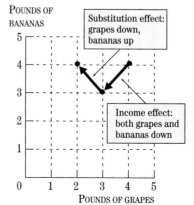

Visualizing the Income and Substitution Effects

Plotting the quantities from the above table in a graph with one good on the vertical axis and another on the horizontal axis helps visualize the income and substitution effects.

The income effect and the substitution effect can be illustrated in the grape-banana example. We already noted that a price increase from $1 to $2 reduces the quantity demanded of grapes by 2 pounds.

The total reduction in grape consumption of 2 pounds can be split, in this example, into 1 pound due to the income effect and 1 pound due to the substitution effect. The income effect reduces both grape and banana consumption; the substitution effect reduces grape consumption but it raises banana consumption, as illustrated in the table and graph on the previous page. The exact size of the income and substitution effects differs from example to example. In some cases the income effect is larger than the substitution effect; in other cases the substitution effect is larger.

Rules for Utility Maximization

The description of utility maximization with the example of Table 5.5 is straightforward. One scans the columns searching for the maximum value of utility for which expenditures are equal to or less than the budget constraint. Such a scan and search process is similar to how research economists find the maximum utility in practical applications when there are many different goods, though they are assisted by computers to help find the maximum.

utility maximizing rule: a condition that a consumer maximizes utility by choosing to purchase a combination of two goods such that the ratio of marginal utilities for the two goods equals the ratio of the market prices or, alternatively, such that the ratio of the marginal utility to the price of each of the two goods is equal.

There is another less direct approach to utility maximization that provides additional insights. The approach makes use of the **utility maximizing rule,** which states that when a consumer maximizes utility, the ratio of the marginal utilities of any two goods equals the ratio of the prices of the two goods. Thus, in the case of grapes and bananas:

$$\frac{MU_G}{MU_B} = \frac{P_G}{P_B} \text{ (utility maximizing rule)}$$

where MU_G is the marginal utility of grapes, MU_B is the marginal utility of bananas, P_G is the price of grapes, and P_B is the price of bananas.

Note how the rule works when the prices are $1 per pound of grapes and $1 per pound of bananas. We already showed that the consumer with an $8 budget constraint chooses to consume 4 pounds of grapes and 4 pounds of bananas to maximize utility. At this amount of consumption the marginal utility of grapes is 2 and the marginal utility of bananas is 2 (see Tables 5.1 and 5.2), so that the ratio of marginal utilities is 1 ($2 \div 2 = 1$), and the ratio of the prices is 1 ($\$1 \div \$1 = 1$). For the case when $P_G = \$2$ and $P_B = \$1$, the price ratio is 2; in this case the utility maximization choice is 2 pounds of grapes and 4 pounds of bananas, and the ratio of the marginal utilities is 2.

To see why the rule works, first imagine that the rule was violated. Suppose that the price ratio is 1 and that the $8 is being spent in such a way that the marginal utility ratio was 4, as would occur when 2 pounds of grapes and 5 pounds of bananas are consumed. Then the individual could buy 1 more pound of grapes and 1 less pound of bananas and increase utility. Because the marginal utility ratio is 4, the increase in utility from grapes is greater than the loss in utility from 1 less pound of bananas. When the utility maximizing rule holds, this kind of thing can't happen. If the ratio of marginal utility was 1, then the increased utility from more grapes would exactly equal the decreased utility from fewer bananas. So we know the consumer is maximizing utility.

A second way to see why the utility maximizing rule works is to write it in an alternative form:

$$\frac{MU_G}{P_G} = \frac{MU_B}{P_B} \text{ (utility maximizing rule—alternative form)}$$

In words, this expression states that if the consumer is maximizing utility, then the *marginal utility per additional dollar spent on one good must equal the marginal utility per additional dollar* spent on another good. For example, if P_G = \$2 and P_B = \$1, then MU_G = 2 and MU_B = 1 for the utility maximization, and MU_G/P_G = 2/2 = 1 with MU_B/P_B = 1/1 = 1. The rule holds. If, to the contrary, the rule were violated, then the consumer could change consumption and increase utility. If the marginal utility per additional dollar spent on grapes was 4 and the marginal utility per additional dollar spent on bananas was only 1, the consumer could increase utility by buying more grapes and fewer bananas. This would reduce the marginal utility of grapes and raise the marginal utility of bananas until the two were equal.

Putting the utility maximizing rule in this alternative form shows how it can be used to describe many decisions people make every day. For example, suppose you are interested in maximizing your GPA. Then in balancing your time spent studying for biology versus economics, you will want to make sure that more time spent on economics would not improve your economics grade by more than the time lost studying biology would worsen your biology grade. If spending more time on economics would increase your economics grade by more than it worsens your biology grade, then you should increase the time spent on economics. When the additional minute spent studying economics affects your grade by the same amount that it reduces your biology grade then you are maximizing your GPA. By equating the marginal change in your biology grade and your economics grade, you are allocating your time to achieve the highest GPA.

The Diamond–Water Paradox

The consumer behavior model just discussed can explain a number of otherwise puzzling observations. For example, one of the most quoted passages of Adam Smith's *Wealth of Nations* was the observation that "Nothing is more useful than water: but it will purchase scarce any thing; scarce any thing can be had in exchange for it. A diamond, on the contrary, has scarce any value in use; but a very great quantity of other goods may frequently be had in exchange for it."[1] Why are diamonds expensive and water cheap even though diamonds are less "useful" to the world's population than water?

The utility maximizing rule helps explain the paradox. The ratio of the price of diamonds to the price of water will be high if the ratio of the marginal utility of diamonds to the marginal utility of water is high. As we saw earlier in the chapter, the marginal utility of something declines the more people consume of it. Thus, water has relatively low marginal utility because, with water being so plentiful, people consume much of it every day. The marginal utility is low even though the total utility from water consumption in the world is very high. On the other hand, diamonds have a high marginal utility because, with diamonds being so scarce, people consume relatively little of them. The marginal utility of diamonds is high even

---

1. Adam Smith, *Wealth of Nations* (New York: Modern Library Edition, 1994), pp. 31–32.

Using Economics to Explain Family Decisions

Economics has traditionally studied the behavior of consumers as individuals rather than as members of families. Thus, the text's utility of grapes and bananas example applies to an individual.

How do economists modify the theory of consumer behavior to deal with the existence of families? One approach would be to treat the family rather than the individual as a decision-making unit. However, this approach either requires that the family have utility for particular goods, which ignores the differences between family members, or it assumes that there is one head of the family who makes all of the family's decisions. Neither assumption captures the complexity of real-world families, where individual members of the family may have widely differing tastes or preferences.

Another approach, initiated by Nobel Prize-winning economist Gary Becker, treats members of families as individuals who interact in an organization (the family) rather than in markets. The individuals are assumed to maximize utility, but consumption decisions within the family, such as an agreement to consume more Brussels sprouts and fewer potatoes at dinner, are made by implicit agreement—perhaps after some bargaining—between the family members. Using this approach, even marriage and divorce become part of the utility maximization exercise.

Nobel Prize-winning economist Gary S. Becker

The assumption of utility maximization in this context does not mean that each family member selfishly tries to improve his or her own satisfaction, because the utility of one family member can affect another. For example, the utility that children get from increased consumption of goods can raise the utility of the parents. When utility of some people positively affects the utility of others, utility displays *altruism.* In principle, there is no reason why the economists' concept of utility cannot include altruism, though the traditional assumption is that it does not.

One implication of utility maximization when applied to the family is the concept of a "demand curve for children." This concept has been used to explain certain observations about fertility. The "price" of chil-

dren is the whole range of costs parents must incur to raise a child: day-care costs, medical costs, opportunity costs from reducing the time spent at work, and so on. The demand curve for children has the price of children on the vertical axis and the number of children in the family on the horizontal axis. The demand curve is downward-sloping: the higher the "price"—for example, the higher the opportunity cost—the smaller will be the number of children.

How well does the demand for children work in explaining fertility? When one looks at different countries, one sees a strong negative correlation between wage levels and the fertility rate. For example, as wages in Europe, the United States, and Japan have increased, fertility rates have declined. Fertility rates are higher in poor countries than in richer countries. Thus, the concept of a demand curve for children appears to be consistent with some of the major observations about fertility.

Though the utility maximization approach can be used to study family decisions, economists do not believe it can explain everything. Psychology, moral values, love, and religion affect how family members interact with each other. Economists disagree on how much can be explained with utility maximization, but virtually no one feels it can explain everything about families or consumer behavior in general.

though the total utility of diamonds may be low. With the marginal utility of water low compared with the marginal utility of diamonds, the price of water must be low compared with the price of diamonds. Thus, by distinguishing utility from marginal utility—the latter concept was not known to Smith—we can explain the diamond–water paradox.

The diamond-water paradox is important because it is an extreme example of a very common occurrence. A similar paradox appears in the grape and banana example. We saw that when the price of grapes was $1 per pound and the price of bananas was $1 per pound, the marginal utility of grapes was equal to that of bananas, and the consumer bought 4 pounds of bananas and 4 pounds of grapes. Yet at this level of consumption, the utility from the grapes is much lower (15) than from the bananas (24).

Review

▶ By assuming that consumers maximize utility subject to a budget constraint, economists can show why higher prices lead to a smaller quantity demanded and why demand shifts when income changes.

▶ The same model of consumer behavior allows economists to distinguish between an income effect and a substitution effect from the price change.

▶ A rule for utility maximization is that the ratio of the marginal utilities of two goods must equal the ratio of the prices for the two goods or, alternatively stated, the ratio of the marginal utility to the price for any two goods must be equal.

▶ That prices are related to marginal utilities rather than total utilities explains many economic puzzles, such as the diamond-water paradox.

WILLINGNESS TO PAY AND THE DEMAND CURVE

The example of two goods in the previous section is useful for showing how the model of consumer behavior based on utility maximization gives an explicit rationale for the negative slope and the shift of the demand curve. A second purpose of developing a model of consumer behavior is to show how well the market system works. For this purpose, we need to extract some additional information from the model of consumer behavior.

Measuring Willingness to Pay and Marginal Benefit

Suppose we asked an individual who is consuming a zero amount of good *X,* "How much money would you be willing to pay for one unit of *X*?" Because the money, which the individual would pay, can be used to buy all other goods, not just one good, the question implicitly asks the individual to compare *X* with all other goods. In general, the answer to this question would depend on how much utility would increase with one unit of *X* and on how much utility would decrease because less would be spent on other goods given the budget constraint. In other words, the answer would depend on the person's preferences for *X* and all other goods as represented by utility.

Suppose that the answer is $5. Let us assume that the answer to the question gives us the true measure of the consumer's preferences. Then, once we get an answer to the first question, we could ask, "How much would you be willing to pay for two units of X?" Again, the answer would depend on how much utility would increase with another unit of X and on how much utility would decrease with less to spend on other goods. Suppose the answer is, "I would be willing to pay $8." We could then continue to ask the consumer about more and more units of X. We summarize the hypothetical answers in Table 5.6. The column labeled "Willingness to Pay" tabulates the answers to the question.

Assuming that the answers to the questions are true, willingness to pay measures how much the consumer would benefit from different amounts of X. We can define the *marginal benefit* from X in the same way we defined marginal utility. **Marginal benefit** is the increase in the willingness to pay to consume one more unit of a good. As a person consumes more and more of a good, the marginal benefit from additional amounts is likely to diminish. Thus, diminishing marginal benefit is as pervasive a phenomenon as diminishing marginal utility. An important advantage of marginal benefit as a representation of people's preferences is that it can be measured in dollars, whereas marginal utility cannot. Marginal benefit is therefore useful for assessing how well the market system works in providing benefits to consumers.

This method of obtaining information about people's preferences is sometimes used in practice. For example, a recent survey of people in the United States endeavored to obtain information about people's preferences for the 1.3 million-acre Selway Bitterroot Wilderness area in northern Idaho versus other goods. The survey question read, "If you could be sure the Selway Bitterroot Wilderness would not be opened for the proposed timber harvest and would be preserved as a 'wilderness area' indefinitely, what is the most that your household would pay each year through a federal income tax surcharge designated for preservation of the Selway Bitterroot Wilderness?" In this example, X is the "wilderness area."

But the answers to such questions are not always reliable, and economists prefer to estimate people's willingness to pay by looking at their decisions to purchase goods at different prices in the market. Regardless of how information about people's willingness to pay is obtained, willingness to pay provides a useful dollar measure of the benefits people receive from consumption.

marginal benefit: the increase in the willingness to pay to consume one more unit of a good.

TABLE 5.6
Willingness to Pay and Marginal Benefit

Quantity of X	Willingness to Pay for X (benefit from X)	Marginal Benefit from X
0	$0.00	—
1	$5.00	$5.00
2	$8.00	$3.00
3	$9.50	$1.50
4	$10.50	$1.00
5	$11.00	$.50

Graphical Derivation of the Demand Curve

A demand curve can be derived from the information about willingness to pay and marginal benefit of X in Table 5.6. Suppose that X is raisins (rice, salt, tea, orange juice, CDs, movies, or any other good will serve just as well as an example). We want to ask how many pounds of raisins the person would buy at different prices. We imagine different hypothetical prices for raisins from astronomical levels like $7 a pound to bargain basement levels like $.50 a pound.

To proceed graphically, we first plot the marginal benefit from Table 5.6 in Figure 5.4. Focus first on the black dots in Figure 5.4. The lines will be explained in the next few paragraphs. The horizontal axis in Figure 5.4 measures the quantity of raisins. On the vertical axis we want to indicate the price as well as the marginal benefit, so we measure the scale of the vertical axis in dollars. The black dots in Figure 5.4 represent the marginal benefit an individual gets from consuming different amounts of raisins.

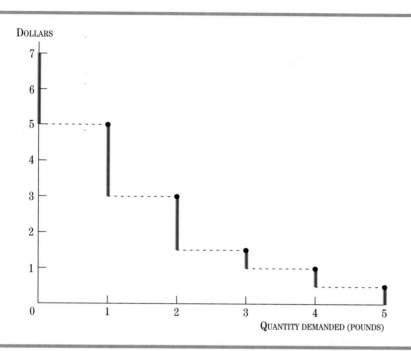

FIGURE 5.4
Derivation of the Individual Demand Curve
The dots are exactly the same as the marginal benefit in Table 5.6. At each dot, price equals marginal benefit. The vertical lines indicate how much is demanded at each price if the consumer is restricted to purchasing whole pounds.

How many pounds of raisins would this person consume at different prices for raisins? First suppose that the price is very high—$7 a pound. Draw an arrow pointing to this $7 price in Figure 5.4. We are going to derive a demand curve for this individual by gradually lowering the price from this high value and seeing how many pounds would be purchased at each price. As the price declines, you can slide your arrow down the vertical axis. For each price we ask the same question: How many pounds would the person buy? To make things simple at the start, assume that the person buys only whole pounds of raisins. You might want to imagine that the raisins come in 1-pound cellophane packages. We consider fractions of pounds later.

Suppose then that the price is $7 a pound. The marginal benefit from 1 pound of raisins is $5. Thus, the price is greater than the marginal benefit. Would the person buy a pound of raisins at this price? Because the price the consumers would have to pay is greater than the marginal benefit, the answer would be no: The person would not buy a pound of raisins at a price of $7. If the minimum amount of raisins that can be purchased is 1 pound, then the person will buy no pounds at a price of $7 per pound. The person might buy something else, like a magazine, but we know that no raisins will be consumed. We have shown, therefore, that the quantity demanded of raisins is zero when the price is $7.

Now start to lower the price. As long as the price is more than $5, the person will not buy any raisins. Hence, the quantity demanded at all prices higher than $5 is zero. We indicate this by the red line on the vertical axis above the $5 mark.

Now watch what happens when the price drops to $5. The marginal benefit from a pound of raisins is $5 and the price is $5. Now will a pound of raisins be purchased? Yes, because the marginal benefit from raisins is just equal to the price. Hence, the quantity demanded increases to 1 pound when the price falls to $5. In

Figure 5.4, the quantity demanded when the price is $5 is given by the black dot at 1 pound.

Continue lowering the price, slipping the arrow down the axis. The quantity demanded will stay at 1 pound as long as the price remains above the marginal benefit of buying another pound of raisins, or $3. We therefore extend the red line down at 1 pound as the price falls from $5 down to $3. Consider, for example, a price of $4. The person has already decided that 1 pound will be bought and the question is whether a second pound of raisins is worthwhile. Another pound has a marginal benefit of $3 (willingness to pay goes from $5 to $8 as the quantity increases from 1 to 2 pounds). The person has to pay $4, which is more than the marginal benefit. Hence, the quantity demanded stays at 1 pound when the price is $4. However, when the price falls to $3, another pound is purchased. That is, when the price is $3, the quantity demanded is 2 pounds, which is shown graphically by the black dot at 2 pounds.

Now suppose the price falls below $3, perhaps to $2. Is a third pound purchased? The marginal benefit of a third pound is $1.50; is it worth it to buy a third pound at $2 per pound? No. The quantity demanded stays at 3 pounds when the price is between $3 and $1.50, which we denote by extending the red line down from the black dot at 2 pounds. This story can be continued. As the price continues to fall, more pounds of raisins are demanded.

By considering various prices from over $5 to under $.50, we have traced out an **individual demand curve** that slopes downward. As the price is lowered, more raisins are purchased. The demand curve is downward-sloping because of diminishing marginal benefit. At each black dot in the diagram, price equals the marginal benefit.

The jagged shape of the demand curve in Figure 5.4 may look strange. It is due to the assumption that only 1-pound packages of raisins are considered by the consumer. In the case of raisins, it is usually possible to buy fractions of a pound, and if the marginal benefit of the fractions are between the values of the whole pounds, then the demand curve will be a smooth line, as shown in Figure 5.5. Then price would equal marginal benefit not only at the black dots but also on the lines con-

individual demand curve: a curve showing the relationship between quantity demanded of a good by an individual and the price of the good.

FIGURE 5.5
A Smooth Individual Demand Curve

If the consumer can buy fractions of a pound and if the marginal benefits of these fractions are between the whole pound amounts, the demand curve becomes a smooth line, as in the figure, rather than the series of steps in Figure 5.4. In some cases, such as the demand for cars, we cannot consider fractions, and individual demand curves will look like steps.

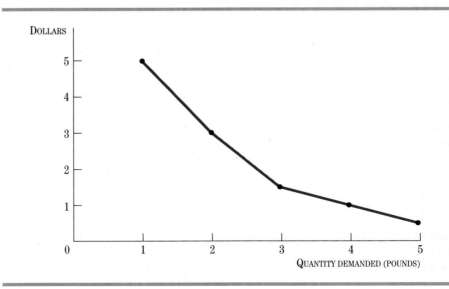

necting the dots. If you are unsure of this, imagine creating a new Table 5.6 and Figure 5.4 with *ounces* of raisins. There will be a point at each ounce and with 16 ounces per pound there will be so many points that the curve will be as smooth as Figure 5.5.

The Price Equals Marginal Benefit Rule

We have discovered another important principle of consumer behavior. If the consumer can adjust consumption of a good in small increments—such as fractions of a pound—then the consumer maximizes utility by buying an amount for which the *price equals marginal benefit*. This condition can be applied to any good—apples, peanuts, comic books, the number of movies you see each year—not just raisins.

Review

▶ Another way to study people's preferences is through their willingness to pay for different amounts of a good. Because dollars can be used to buy other goods, willingness to pay compares one good with all other goods.

▶ The marginal benefit from a good is the increase in the willingness to pay for one additional unit of a good.

▶ The condition that the price equals marginal benefit is key to microeconomic theory. We will use it later to demonstrate how a market system works.

▶ The individual demand curve slopes downward because of diminishing marginal benefits from consuming more of a good. As the price falls the individual will choose a quantity with a lower marginal benefit. Hence, the quantity demanded goes up as the price falls.

THE MARKET DEMAND CURVE

Thus far, we have graphically derived the *individual* demand curve. Now we consider the **market demand curve,** which is the sum of the individual demand curves. Figure 5.6 shows how we do the summing up. The figure shows the demand curve for raisins for two individuals, Ann and Pete. To get the market demand curve, add up, at any given price, the total amount demanded by Pete and Ann. For example, at a price of $5, Pete's demand is 1 pound and Ann's demand is 1 pound. The market demand is then 2 pounds. When the price is $3 a pound, the demand is 2 pounds for Pete and 2 pounds for Ann, or 4 pounds for the market as a whole. Obviously, the market for raisins consists of more than just Pete and Ann. To get the whole market, you would have to sum up the demands for millions of people.

market demand curve: the horizontal summation of all the individual demand curves for a good; also simply called the demand curve.

Different Types of Individuals

In Figure 5.6, both Pete's and Ann's demand curves are the same. They do not have to be. In fact, it is most likely that Ann and Pete have different preferences. Pete could be a peanut fan and be willing to pay less for raisins than Ann. It is incorrect to assume that everyone would be willing to pay the same for any good. There are all kinds of people in the world with different preferences. But you can still add up the demands of these people at any given price to get the market demand curve. As you add up many individual demand curves for different types of people, the

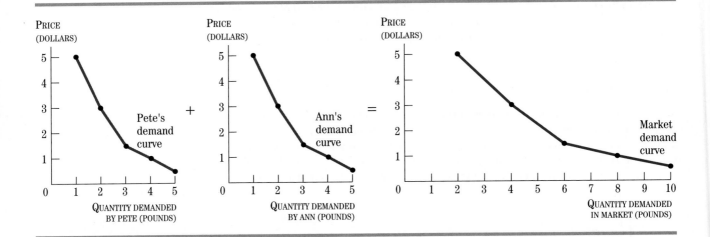

FIGURE 5.6
Derivation of the Market Demand Curve
The market demand curve is the sum of the demand curves of many individuals. The figure shows this for only two individuals with the same preferences. As more individuals are added with a diversity of tastes, the market demand curve becomes smoother and looks more like Figure 5.1.

market demand curve gets smoother, even when the product cannot be bought in fractions of a unit. For example, the market demand for cars is smooth even though most individuals buy either zero, one, or perhaps two cars. When you add in millions of people, the market demand curve for cars looks like the market demand curve in Figure 5.1 that we typically draw—smooth and downward-sloping.

Different Prices for the Same Good

When economists derive the market demand curve from the individual demand curves, they add up the quantity demanded at each price. What we are imagining here is that the price of the good at every location where it is sold is the same. You tabulate the total quantity demanded at that price. If there is a change in the price, then you get the market demand at that new price by summing up all the individual demands at the new price.

In reality, of course, the price of most goods is not the same at every location in the country or even in your neighborhood. Different grocery stores charge different prices for fruit. Some of these price differences may be due to differences in the quality: nicer shopping conditions, better service, or other factors that differ from store to store. Discount stores charge less for electronic equipment but provide fewer services. The price for a gallon of unleaded regular gasoline in 1996 ranged from $1.30 to $1.60 in different parts of California, partly because gas stations have higher expenses in the central cities than in the country. But for each location we can still add up the individual demand curves to get the market demand curve.

Review

▶ The market demand curve is derived from individual demand curves. At each price we add up how much is demanded by all individuals; the total is the market demand at that price.

▶ Even if the individual demand curves are not smooth, the market demand curve will be smooth because people have different tastes and preferences and prefer different benefits.

CONSUMER SURPLUS

In many cases people are willing to pay more for an item consumed than they have to pay for it. You may love going to see your favorite movie and would be willing to pay five times the $6 admission price to see it. But just like everyone else in line, you pay only $6 even if it is worth $30 to you. The difference between the $30 and the $6 is called *consumer surplus.*

In general, **consumer surplus** is the difference between the willingness to pay for an additional item (say $30 for a movie)—its marginal benefit—and the price paid for it (say $6 for a movie). Suppose the price of raisins is $4 per pound. Then the consumer in our previous example purchases 1 pound and the marginal benefit of the pound is $5. In that situation the consumer gets a consumer surplus because the marginal benefit of the raisins to the consumer is $5 but the price paid is only $4 per pound. Consumer surplus is the difference, or $1. If the price were $3.50, then the consumer surplus would be greater, or $1.50.

Suppose the price falls further so that two items are purchased. Consumer surplus is then defined as the sum of differences between the marginal benefits of each item and the price paid for the item. For example, if the price per pound of raisins is $2, as in Figure 5.7, then 2 pounds of raisins will be purchased and the consumer surplus will be $5 − $2 = $3 for the first pound plus $3 − $2 = $1 for the second pound for a total of $4. That is, the consumer surplus is $4.

Figure 5.7 shows graphically how consumer surplus is the area between the demand curve and the line indicating the price. In Figure 5.7 the total shaded area is equal to 4, consisting of two rectangular blocks, one with an area of 3 and the other with an area of 1. The area is the extra amount that the consumer is getting because the market price is lower than what the consumer is willing to pay.

Consumer surplus for the entire market is the sum of the consumer surpluses of all individuals who have purchased goods in the market. In Figure 5.8, consumer surplus is the area between the market demand curve and the market price line.

consumer surplus: the difference between what a person is willing to pay for an additional unit of a good—the marginal benefit—and the market price of the good; for the market as a whole, it is the sum of all the individual consumer surpluses, or the area below the market demand curve and above the market price.

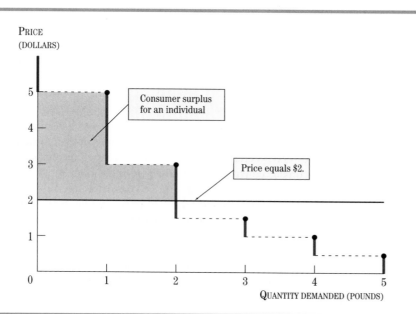

FIGURE 5.7
Consumer Surplus for an Individual
The consumer surplus is the difference between the marginal benefit a person gets from consuming a good and the price. It is given by the area between the demand curve and the price.

The Origin of Consumer Surplus

The great British economist Alfred Marshall did the most to develop and communicate the idea of consumer surplus; he put it this way in 1890: "The price which a person pays for a thing can never exceed, and seldom comes up to that which he would be willing to pay rather than go without it . . . he thus derives from the purchases a surplus of satisfaction. . . . It may be called consumer's surplus."*

However, it was Jules Dupuit, a French engineer, who first came up with the idea. He argued in 1844 that consumer surplus could be used as a way to estimate the benefit of public works, such as roads and bridges. Dupuit also offered a more visual description of consumer surplus: "If society is paying 500 million for the services rendered by the road, that only proves one thing—that their utility is at least 500 million. But it may be a hundred times or a thousand times greater. . . . If you take the [500 million] as the figure . . . you are acting like a man who, wishing to measure the height of a wall in the dark and finding that he cannot reach the top with this raised arm says: 'This wall is two meters high, for if it were not, my hand would reach above it.' In daylight and equipped with a ladder . . . our alleged two-meter wall is fifty meters high."†

*Alfred Marshall, *Principles of Economics,* 8th ed. (New York: Macmillan, 1920), p. 124.

† English translation of Jules Dupuit, "De la Mesure de l'Utilité des Travaux Publics," translated and reprinted in K. J. Arrow and T. Skitovsky, eds., *Readings in Welfare Economics* (Homewood, Ill.: Irwin, 1969).

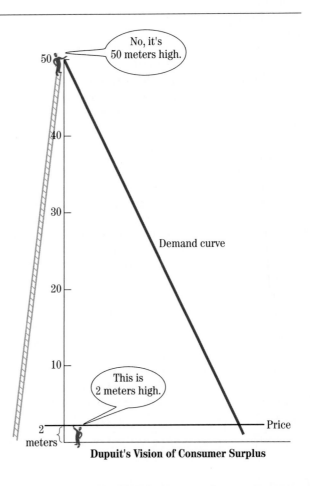

Dupuit's Vision of Consumer Surplus

Consumer surplus has many uses in economics. It is used to measure how well the market system works. We will show in Chapter 6 that the market system maximizes consumer surplus under certain circumstances. Consumer surplus can also be used to measure the gains to consumers that come from an innovation. For example, if a new production technique lowers the price of raisins, then the consumer surplus will increase: The area between the demand curve and the market price line increases. This increase is a measure of how much the new technique is worth to society.

Consumer surplus is also used to evaluate the benefits of government policies, such as building a new bridge or creating a new wilderness area. These policies will increase or decrease consumer surplus, and their value to society can be estimated using the concept of consumer surplus.

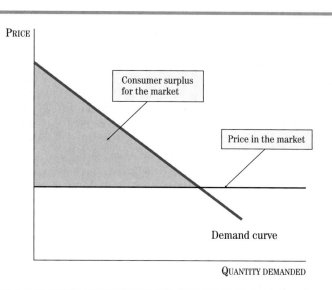

FIGURE 5.8
Consumer Surplus for the Market
The sum of the consumer surplus for all individuals in the market is the area between the demand curve and the price.

Review

▶ Consumer surplus is the area between the demand curve and the market price line. It is a measure of how much the consumer gains from buying goods in the market.

▶ The consumer surplus for the market is the sum of the individual consumer surpluses.

▶ Consumer surplus is an important tool for measuring the performance of an economic system or for assessing the impact of alternative government policies in that system.

AN APPLICATION: SAVING

The true beauty of the model of consumer behavior is found in its many diverse applications. In applying the model to different situations, economists think in terms of analogies. For example, to apply the model to movies rather than raisins, we make an analogy like: "Raisins are to the price of raisins as movies are to _____." The answer, of course, is "the price of movies." Other situations do not sound so simple, and part of learning to think like an economist is learning how to make these analogies.

A less simple application of the model of consumer behavior occurs in situations where individuals are deciding whether or not to save for the future. (Saving is defined as income less total consumption.)

How can we apply our model of consumer behavior to the saving decision? Make analogies. First, let us set up the problem. For a limited amount of income, as your saving increases, your consumption must go down. But more savings means you can have more consumption in the future. We can restate the question "How much do people choose to save?" as "How much do people choose to consume in the present versus consume in the future?" Let consumption in the future be good X and let consumption in the present be good Y.

The analogy is beginning to take shape. We know that for any two goods the ratio of their marginal utilities must be equal to the ratio of their prices. Thus, the ratio of the marginal utility of consumption in the future (MU_{future}) to the marginal utility of consumption in the present ($MU_{present}$) must equal the ratio of the price of consumption in the future (P_{future}) to the price of consumption in the present ($P_{present}$). That last sentence is long, which sometimes happens in analogies. Here is the formula:

$$\frac{MU_{future}}{MU_{present}} = \frac{P_{future}}{P_{present}}$$

There are really no new concepts, but we do need to say what we mean by the price of present and future consumption.

Price of Future Consumption versus Present Consumption

To pay for consumption in the future—a retirement, a college education for a child—many people put their dollars in a savings account. The savings account pays interest, say 5 percent per year. Thus $100 put in a savings account today becomes $105 next year. If there is no rise in the price of goods during the year, then the goods are effectively cheaper by the amount of the interest rate: by saving your $100 this year you can buy $105 worth of goods next year. It is like a sign in the store window announcing a sale on pens that says, "Buy 100 pens, get 5 free." The pens are 5 percent cheaper. If the interest rate rises to 10 percent, then the price of goods is even cheaper next year than this year. Thus, we have arrived at another part of the analogy. The interest rate measures the relative price of future goods compared with present goods. Higher interest rates make present goods more expensive compared with future goods. A higher interest rate raises the price of consumption today versus consumption tomorrow.

The Real Interest Rate

We need to make one adjustment to this idea because the price of goods—shirts, watches, etc.—may increase during the year. If the price of goods increases by 5 percent, then the 5 percent interest is wiped out, and 10 percent interest would mean you really have only 5 percent more to spend. This general increase in prices is inflation.

To correct for inflation we need to use the *real interest rate,* which is defined as the stated interest rate minus the expected rate of inflation. If inflation is expected to be 4 percent and the stated interest rate at banks is 5 percent, then the real rate of interest is 1 percent ($5 - 4 = 1$). Thus, the price of consumption today versus consumption tomorrow increases if the real interest rate increases.

Saving and the Interest Rate

We are almost finished with the analogy. Consumption today is like the raisins in our earlier example. Raisins are to the price of raisins as consumption in the present is to the price of consumption in the present. If our model of consumer behavior implies that the quantity demanded of raisins declines as the price of raisins rises, it also implies that consumption in the present will decline as the price of consumption in the present rises—that is, as the interest rate rises. Thus, we have a new application of the model of consumer behavior. A higher interest rate will reduce consumption in the present in favor of consumption in the future. In other words, a higher interest rate will raise saving, and a lower interest rate will lower saving.

Review

▶ The application of the model of consumer behavior to saving explains why saving may increase when the interest rate increases.

▶ When applying the model to saving, we make an analogy: Consumption in the present is one good; consumption in the future is another good.

▶ The price of present consumption rises relative to the price of future consumption when the interest rate increases.

CONCLUSION

This chapter is the first of three that looks at the individual behavior that underlies the economist's demand and supply curves. This chapter focused on consumers, Chapter 6 looks at firms, and Chapter 7 looks at the interaction of consumers and firms in markets. The payoffs in terms of understanding how and how well the market system works will not be fully realized until we have completed all three chapters, but we have already derived a number of useful results.

The basic economic principle that people make purposeful choices with limited resources to increase their well-being has led to an operational model of consumer behavior. Using the model, we showed why higher prices reduce the quantity demanded and why changes in income change demand. We also illustrated the income and substitution effects and explained the famous diamond-water paradox. None of these uses of the model requires that utility—the indicator of preferences—be measurable.

We also developed a measure of how much consumers gain from buying goods in the market. By looking at consumers' willingness to pay, we showed how to derive a complete demand curve. Along each consumer's demand curve, the marginal benefit of the last good purchased is equal to the price. Finally, consumer surplus—which we will make heavy use of in Chapter 7—is the difference between a consumer's willingness to pay and the amount actually paid.

KEY POINTS

1. The idea of utility makes operational the assumption that people make purposeful choices with limited resources.

2. Utility indicates the preferences people have for one item compared with other items.

3. Marginal utility is the change in utility as one consumes one more unit of an item.

4. Diminishing marginal utility means that people get smaller increases in utility the more they consume of an item.

5. Economists assume—at least as an approximation—that people maximize their utility. To do so, people adjust their consumption of every good to the point where the ratio of the marginal utilities equals the ratio of the price of any two goods.

6. The utility maximization rule also states that the ratio of the marginal utility to the price is equal for any two goods.

7. Utility maximization shows that higher prices reduce the quantity demanded.

8. Market demand curves are derived from individual demand curves.

9. Even though some individual demand curves may have sharp edges, differences between individuals will make the market demand curves for these items smooth.

10. Consumer surplus is the area between the demand curve and the market price line. Because a demand curve can be derived from willingness to pay and marginal benefits, consumer surplus is a measure of how much benefit a consumer gains from buying a product.

KEY TERMS

utility
marginal utility
diminishing marginal utility
budget constraint

utility maximization
income effect
substitution effect
utility maximizing rule

marginal benefit
individual demand curve
market demand curve
consumer surplus

QUESTIONS FOR REVIEW

1. What is the relationship between utility and marginal utility?

2. Why does marginal utility decrease as more is consumed?

3. Why is diminishing marginal utility a good assumption?

4. What is the relationship between utility maximization subject to a budget constraint and purposeful choice with limited resources?

5. Why does the rule that the ratio of the marginal utilities equals the price ratio of any two goods imply that utility is maximized?

6. What is the difference between the income effect and the substitution effect?

7. Why is the marginal benefit equal to the price of a good?

8. Why are market demand curves usually smoother than individual demand curves?

9. What is the explanation of Adam Smith's diamond-water paradox?

10. Why is consumer surplus equal to the area below the demand curve and above the price?

PROBLEMS

1. Using the example in Table 5.5, find the quantity of each good the consumer will purchase in the following cases. (*Note:* For case C you will need to add another expenditure column to Table 5.5.)

Case	Budget	Price of Grapes	Price of Bananas
A	$7	$1	$1
B	$6	$2	$1
C	$8	$1	$2

2. In the table in the right column consider the information on utility from consumption of CDs and magazines.
  a) Determine how much of each Sarah will consume if the price of CDs is $9 and the price of magazines is $3.
  b) Suppose the price of magazines goes up to $4.50.

	Sarah's Utility from CDs	Sarah's Utility from Magazines
1	27	8
2	51	14
3	71	16
4	87	17

How much of each will Sarah consume now? Why does it change?

3. Show that the units by which we measure utility do not matter by multiplying the utility from grapes and bananas by 100 and showing that you get the same answers as in Table 5.5.

4. Suppose that college tuition rises in the year 2001. Explain how both the income effect and the substitution effect would contribute to the change in the quantity of college education demanded.

5. The following table shows Andrew's willingness to pay for ice cream.

Gallons of Ice Cream	Willingness to Pay
0	$0
1	$10
2	$17
3	$22
4	$25
5	$27
6	$28

a) Calculate Andrew's marginal benefit from ice cream.
b) Draw Andrew's individual demand curve to scale.
c) Suppose the price of 1 gallon of ice cream is $3. How much would Andrew consume, and what is his consumer surplus? Show your answer graphically.

6. Suppose Beth's willingness to pay for ice cream is exactly twice that of Andrew's for every gallon, as shown in problem 5.
a) Draw Andrew's and Beth's demand curves to scale next to each other, assuming they can consume fractions of gallons of ice cream.
b) Draw the market demand curve if only Andrew and Beth are in the market.

7. Consider the example of willingness to pay for X (raisins) in Table 5.6. Compute the payment for raisins and differences between willingness to pay and payment for 0 to 5 pounds when the price is $.75. How many pounds of raisins will maximize the willingness to pay minus the payment? How does the answer compare to that using the price equals marginal benefit condition?

8. The data in the following table show the willingness to pay for cookies for Margaret and Dennis.

Willingness to Pay for Cookies ($)

Quantity	Margaret	Dennis
1	7	15
2	13	25
3	18	34
4	21	42
5	23	45

a) Calculate the marginal benefits for both people and both goods.
b) Derive Margaret's and Dennis's individual demand curves for cookies. Derive the market demand curve if only Margaret and Dennis are in the market.
c) Suppose that the price of cookies is $4.50. How many cookies will Margaret and Dennis buy? Calculate their consumer surplus. Draw a diagram like Figure 5.7 to show the area representing consumer surplus.
d) Show the consumer surplus for the whole market using the market demand curve. Draw a diagram like Figure 5.8.

9. Suppose you get a gift for which your willingness to pay is less than the price of the gift. In what sense is the consumer surplus negative—that is, there is a "consumer loss"? Draw this situation using a demand curve and a horizontal line showing the market price for the product. If consumer surplus is negative, why does gift giving persist?

Budget Lines and Indifference Curves

The model of consumer behavior in which utility is maximized subject to a budget constraint can be illustrated with a diagram, as described in this appendix.

We consider a single consumer deciding how much of two items to buy. Let one of the items be X and the other be Y. In Part A we show that the consumer budget constraint can be represented by a budget line, and then in Part B we show that the consumer's preferences can be represented by indifference curves.

PART A: THE BUDGET LINE

Suppose that the consumer has $20 to spend on X and Y and suppose that the price of X is $2 per unit and price of Y is $4 per unit. How much of X and Y can the consumer buy? If the consumer spends all $20 on Y, then 5 units of Y and no units of X are consumed. If the consumer buys 4 units of Y at $4 per unit, then $16 will be spent on Y and the remaining $4 can be spent buying 2 units of X. These and several other amounts of X and Y that can be bought with $20 are shown in the following table.

Units of Y	Units of X	Expenditures
5	0	$5 \times \$4 + 0 \times \$2 = \$20$
4	2	$4 \times \$4 + 2 \times \$2 = \$20$
3	4	$3 \times \$4 + 4 \times \$2 = \$20$
2	6	$2 \times \$4 + 6 \times \$2 = \$20$
1	8	$1 \times \$4 + 8 \times \$2 = \$20$
0	10	$0 \times \$4 + 10 \times \$2 = \$20$

These combinations represent the maximum amounts that can be purchased with $20. Note how the amounts are inversely related; as more is spent on X, less must be spent on Y. This inverse relationship is shown graphically in Figure 5A.1. We put units of Y on the vertical axis and units of X on the horizontal axis, and then plot the pairs of points from the table. The points are then connected with a line. The points trace a downward-sloping line starting in the

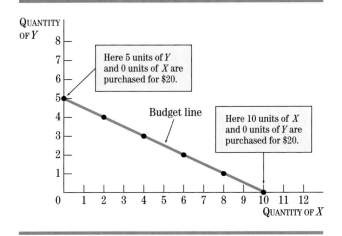

FIGURE 5A.1
Budget Line for a Consumer
The line shows how much a consumer with $20 can consume of quantity X at a price of $2 per unit and quantity Y at $4 per unit. If $20 is spent on Y and nothing on X, then 5 units of Y can be purchased, as shown on the vertical axis. If $20 is spent on X and nothing on Y, then 10 units of X can be purchased. Other combinations are shown on the line.

upper left at $X = 0$ and $Y = 5$ and ending on the right with $X = 10$ and $Y = 0$. All the other combinations of X and Y in the table, such as $X = 4$ and $Y = 3$, are shown on the line. If it is possible to consume fractions of X and Y, then all the points on the line between the plotted points can also be purchased with the $20. (For example, 2.5 units of Y and 5 units of X would cost $20: $2.5 \times \$4 + 5 \times \$2 = \$20$.) Because all these pairs of X and Y on this line can be pur-

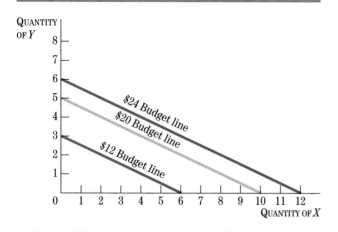

FIGURE 5A.2
Effect of a Change in Income on the Budget Line
If the consumer has more to spend, then the budget line is farther out. If the consumer has less to spend, then the budget line is farther in. Here a higher and lower budget line are compared with the $20 budget line in Figure 5A.1.

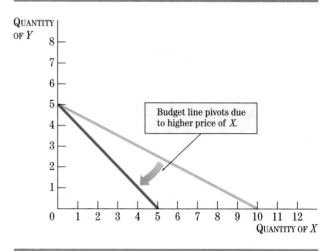

FIGURE 5A.3
Effect of a Higher Price of X on the Budget Line
The budget line pivots if the price of X changes. Here the price of X rises from $2 to $4 and the budget line twists down.

chased with a $20 budget, we call it the **budget line.** The consumer is constrained to buy combinations of X and Y either on or below the budget line. Amounts of X and Y consumed below the budget line cost less than $20. Points above the line require more than $20 and are not feasible.

The budget line will shift out if the consumer has more to spend, as shown in Figure 5A.2. For example, if the consumer has $24 rather than $20, then the budget line will shift up by 1 unit because the extra $4 permits the consumer to buy 1 more unit of Y. Alternatively, we could say that the budget line shifts to the right by 2 units in this case because the consumer can buy 2 more units of X with $4 more.

The steepness of the budget line depends on the prices of X and Y. In particular, the slope of the budget line is equal to -1 times the ratio of the price of X to the price of Y. That is, slope $= -[P_X/P_Y]$, which is $-\frac{1}{2}$ in this example. Why is the slope determined by the price ratio? Recall that the slope is the change in Y divided by the change in X. Along the budget line as X is increased by 1 unit, Y must fall by $\frac{1}{2}$ unit: buying 1 more unit of X costs $2 and requires selling $\frac{1}{2}$ unit of Y. Thus, the slope is $-\frac{1}{2}$.

In order to derive the demand curve for X, we need to find out what happens when the price of X changes. What

happens to the budget line when the price of X increases from $2 to $4, for example? The budget line twists down, as shown in Figure 5A.3. You can show this by creating a new table with pairs of X and Y that can be purchased with $20 at the new price and then plotting the points. The intuitive rationale for the twist is that the slope steepens to $-[P_X/P_Y] = -\$4/\$4 = -1$, and the position of X = 0 and Y = 5 on the vertical axis does not change, because 5 units of X can still be purchased.

To summarize, we have shown how a budget line can be used to represent the budget constraint for the consumer; now consider how we represent the consumer's preferences.

PART B: THE INDIFFERENCE CURVE

Recall from the chapter that utility is an indication of how a consumer prefers one item in comparison with another. If the level of utility is the same for two combinations of X and Y, then the consumer is *indifferent* between the two combinations. Suppose that the utility is the same for the combinations of X and Y that appear on the next page.

Units of *Y*	Units of *X*
6	1
4	2
2	6
1	12

The consumer is indifferent between any of these combinations. Observe how these amounts are inversely related. As consumption of *Y* declines, the consumer must be compensated with more *X* if the level of utility is not to decline.

We can plot these different amounts on the same type of graph we used for the budget line, as shown in Figure 5A.4. The consumer is indifferent between all four points. We have connected the points with a curve to represent other combinations of *X* and *Y* about which the consumer is indifferent. The curve is called an **indifference curve** because the consumer is indifferent between all the points on the curve.

The indifference curve slopes downward from left to right and is bowed in at the origin. Note how the indiffer-

FIGURE 5A.4
An Indifference Curve for a Consumer

The consumer is indifferent to *A* or *B* or any other point on an indifference curve. For example, the consumer is indifferent between consuming 4 of *Y* and 2 of *X* or 2 of *Y* and 6 of *X*.

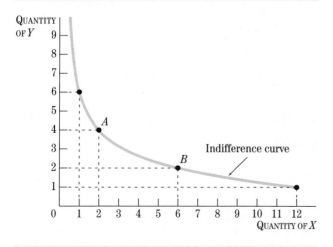

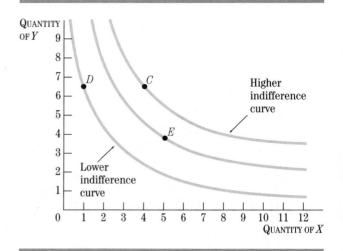

FIGURE 5A.5
Higher and Lower Indifference Curves

Amounts of *X* and *Y* on indifference curves that are higher are preferred to amounts lower on the indifference curves. The combination at *D* is the least preferred and the combination at *C* is the most preferred of the three combinations—*C, D,* and *E*.

ence curve is steep when a small amount of *X* is consumed and flat when a small amount of *Y* is consumed. This curvature is due to declining marginal utility. When the consumer is consuming only a little bit of one good, a large amount of the other good is required for compensation of a reduction in the first good.

The slope of the indifference curve is equal to negative 1 times the ratio of the marginal utility of *X* to the marginal utility of *Y;* that is, slope $= -[MU_X/MU_Y]$. The reason is that utility is the same for all points on an indifference curve. In other words, the decline in utility as *X* falls $(-MU_X \times \Delta X)$ must equal the increase in utility as *Y* rises $(MU_Y \times \Delta Y)$. Thus, $(MU_X \times \Delta X) = -(MU_Y \times \Delta Y)$, which implies that $\Delta Y/\Delta X = -MU_X/MU_Y$, which is the slope of the indifference curve.

We can represent higher levels of utility or more preferred combinations of *X* and *Y* by higher indifference curves, as shown in Figure 5A.5. Any point on a higher indifference curve is preferred to any point on a lower indifference curve.

Getting to the Highest Indifference Curve Given the Budget Line

Now we can combine the budget line and the indifference curve on the same diagram to illustrate the model of consumer behavior. Utility maximization subject to the budget constraint means getting to the highest possible indifference curve without going above the budget line. The process is shown in Figure 5A.6. The budget line from Figure 5A.1 and the indifference curves from Figure 5A.5 are shown in the diagram. The consumer cannot go beyond the budget line, and any point inside the budget line is inferior to points on the budget line. Thus, the combination of X and Y with the highest utility must be on the budget line. The highest indifference curve with points on the budget line is the one that just touches—is tangent to—the budget line. This occurs at point T in Figure 5A.6. The **tangency point** is the highest level of utility the consumer can achieve subject to the budget constraint. It is the combination of X and

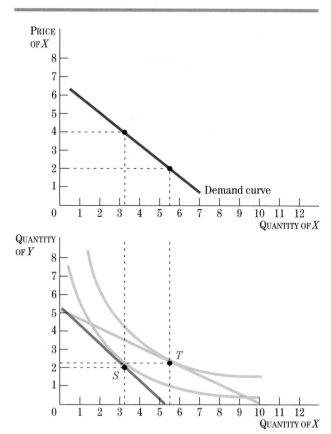

FIGURE 5A.6

The Best Choice for the Consumer

When the budget line is tangent to the indifference curve, the consumer cannot do any better. The point of tangency is at point T. Compare this with the other points. Point U is not the best point because it is inside the budget line. Point V is not the best point because there are other points on the budget line that are preferred. Point W is preferred to point T, but it is not feasible.

FIGURE 5A.7

An Increase in the Price of X

If the price of X rises, the budget line pivots down and the consumer's choice changes from point T to point S in the lower panel. The quantity of X consumed goes down; the price of X and the quantity of X are plotted in the top panel, showing the negative relationship between price and quantity demanded.

Y that the consumer chooses. The diagram shows that, in this example, the consumer buys 2¼ units of Y and 5½ units of X.

Effect of a Price Change on the Quantity of X Demanded

Now suppose the price of X increases; then the budget line twists down, as shown in the lower panel of Figure 5A.7.

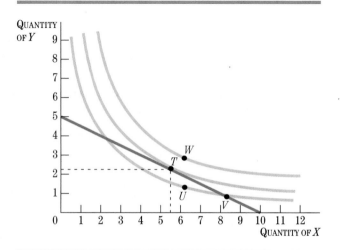

With the new budget line, the old consumer choice of 2¼ units of *X* and 5½ units of *Y* is no longer feasible: Point *T* is outside the new budget line. The highest level of utility the consumer can now achieve is at point *S* in the lower panel of Figure 5A.7. At point *S* the quantity of *X* has declined. Thus, a higher price of *X* has reduced the quantity of *X* demanded.

In the top panel, we show the relationship between the price of *X* and the reduction in the quantity of *X* demanded. The price of *X* is put on the vertical axis and the quantity of *X* demanded is put on the horizontal axis. The lower quantity demanded at the higher price shows the negative slope of the demand curve.

Effect of an Income Change on Demand

We can also examine what happens when the consumer's income changes but the price remains constant. This is illustrated in Figure 5A.8, where income declines. The lower income leads to less consumption of *X* and *Y*. In this case, both *X* and *Y* are normal goods because consumption goes down when income goes down (see Chapter 3). If the consumption of *X* increases as the budget curve shifts in, then *X* would be an inferior good.

CONCLUSION

The indifference curve is a convenient graphical device used by economists to derive demand curves. The device was first proposed by a British economist, F. Y. Edgeworth, over 100 years ago. It is now widely used by economists to study consumer behavior.

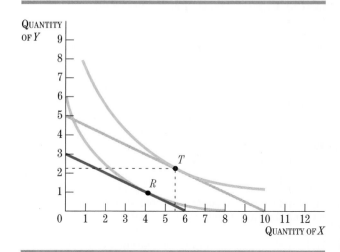

FIGURE 5A.8
A Decrease in Income
If the consumer's income falls, there is a new point where utility is maximized: The consumer moves from point *T* to point *R*. In this case, consumption of both *X* and *Y* decline. Neither good is an inferior good in this example.

KEY POINTS

1. The budget line represents the consumer's budget constraint in a diagram with the quantity consumed of each of two goods on the axes.

2. The budget line is downward-sloping with the slope equal to negative 1 times the ratio of the price of the good on the horizontal axis to the price of the good on the vertical axis.

3. A higher price of the good on the horizontal axis twists the budget line down.

4. An indifference curve shows the combinations of goods about which the consumer is indifferent.

5. Combinations of goods on higher indifference curves are preferred to combinations of goods on lower indifference curves.

6. The model of consumer behavior assumes that the consumer tries to get to the highest possible indifference curve without going beyond the budget line.

7. The consumer chooses the combination at the tangency of the budget line and the indifference curve.

8. A higher price of a good lowers the quantity demanded, according to the indifference curve and budget line diagram.

KEY TERMS AND DEFINITIONS

budget line: a line showing the maximum combinations of two goods that it is possible for a consumer to buy, given a budget constraint and the market prices of the two goods.

indifference curve: a curve showing the combinations of two goods that leave the consumer with the same level of utility.

tangency point: the only point in common for two curves, showing the point where the two curves just touch.

QUESTIONS FOR REVIEW

1. Why does the budget line slope downward?
2. What determines the slope of the budget line?
3. Why does the indifference curve slope downward?

4. Why does the consumer choose a point where the indifference curve is tangent to the budget line?

PROBLEMS

1. Draw a diagram like Figure 5A.7.
   a) Show what happens to the budget line if the price of X falls from $2 to $1.60. What is the maximum amount of X that can be purchased?
   b) Illustrate the new point of consumer choice (by drawing the appropriate indifference curve).
   c) Show the demand curve for the consumer.

2. Suppose the consumer in Figure 5A.7 has $24 to spend rather than $20. Draw two diagrams—one where X is a normal good and one where X is an inferior good.

3. Explain why the tangency of the indifference curve and the budget line implies that $P_Y/P_X = MU_Y/MU_X$, which is the utility maximizing rule discussed in the chapter.

The Supply Curve and the Behavior of Firms

The supply curve has as many applications as the demand curve. There is a supply curve for wheat, grapes, gasoline, pagers, cars, health insurance, telephone answering services, and millions of other goods and services. Whereas the demand curve describes the behavior of people buying and consuming goods and services, the supply curve describes the behavior of firms producing and selling the goods and services. The supply curve conveys the intuitive idea that a higher price for a good will increase the amount that firms are willing to produce and a lower price will do the opposite. In other words, the supply curve slopes upward, as illustrated in Figure 6.1. The supply curve tells us how much all the firms in the market— whether 5, 10, 100, 1,000, or 10,000—would produce at each price. Technology, the weather, and other things also affect a firm's production decisions, and when these things change, the supply curve shifts.

In this chapter we look under the surface of the supply curve and study the behavior of these firms. As with our study of the demand curve in the previous chapter, there are two important reasons to study the underlying foundations of the supply curve. First, we want to show why the supply curve is upward-sloping and what determines its position. Such information enables economists to

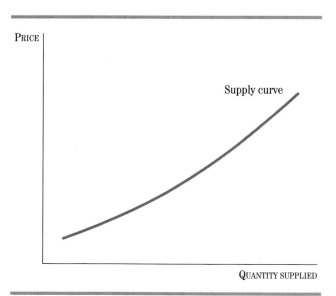

FIGURE 6.1
A Typical Supply Curve for a Market
Supply curves typically slope upward. In this chapter we look at the factors that motivate firms in the market to increase the quantity supplied as the price rises.

FIGURE 6.2

Basic Economic Principle	When Applied to the Behavior of Consumers	When Applied to the Behavior of Firms
People...	*Consumers...*	*Firms...*
make purposeful choices...	maximize utility...	maximize profits...
with limited resources.	subject to a budget constraint relating expenditure to income.	subject to a production function relating output to input.

FIGURE 6.2
The Basic Economic Principle Applies to Consumers and Firms
Both the model of consumer behavior discussed in Chapter 5 and the model of firm behavior introduced in this chapter are based on the basic economic principle that people make purposeful choices with limited resources.

assess how a change in technology or a new government policy—such as a change in taxes or regulations—affects the supply curve. Second, we want to show how, and how well, a real market economy works. The reality of a market is firms interacting with consumers. Hence, we need to look at the behavior of the firms as well as the behavior of the consumers to understand how the market works.

This chapter on supply parallels the previous chapter on demand, and we will exploit that parallel to make our analysis easier. In order to study the behavior of firms, we build a model. We construct the model by looking first at a single firm, just as we looked first at an individual consumer in the previous chapter. The model rests on the basic economic principle that people make purposeful choices with limited resources. In the previous chapter we made this principle operational by assuming that people maximize utility subject to a budget constraint. In this chapter, we make the principle operational by assuming

that firms maximize profits subject to a production relationship that describes how a firm's output of goods and services depends on inputs. Figure 6.2 illustrates how the basic economic principle applies both to firms and to consumers.

The new terms introduced in this chapter have analogies with terms introduced in the previous chapter. For example, we will derive a supply curve for a single firm, which will tell us how much of a good the firm would supply at different prices. The supply curve for an individual firm is analogous to the demand curve for an individual consumer, which tells us the quantity of a good the individual consumer demands at different prices. Another important concept in this chapter is marginal cost, the change in a firm's cost of producing a good when production is changed by one unit. We show how the supply curve for the individual firm comes from that firm's marginal cost of producing the good.

THE INDIVIDUAL FIRM

We start by looking at the behavior of a single firm. A **firm,** by definition, is an organization that produces goods or services. Just as no two consumers are exactly alike, no two firms are exactly alike.

firm: an organization that produces goods or services.

The Nature of Firms

Some firms are very small—a firm can be a small family farm in the country or a grocery store in the city. Bakeries, restaurants, auto dealers, and bicycle shops are all examples of firms that are usually relatively small. Other firms—such as General Electric or Exxon—are very large, producing many different products in large volume.

The terms *firm, company, business,* or *business enterprise* are used interchangeably. A firm may include several *establishments,* which are separate physical locations, such as an office, a factory, or a store, where work is done. For example, the toymaker Mattel is a firm with headquarters in California and manufacturing establishments in China, Italy, Malaysia, and Mexico. The U.S.-based grocery chain Kroger is a firm with over 2,000 establishments—more than 1,000 supermarkets and more than 1,000 convenience stores, including 208 Kwik-Starts and 105 Mini-Marts. Of course, many small firms have only one establishment.

Different Legal Forms of Firms

sole proprietorship: a firm owned by a single person.

There are three different legal forms of firms: sole proprietorships, partnerships, and corporations. A **sole proprietorship** is a firm owned by one person. The *manager* of the firm and the *owner* are usually the same person, though sometimes the owner may hire managers to make day-to-day decisions. The income earned by the business becomes the owner's personal income and is reported to the government on a personal income tax form along with any other income of the owner. When the same person owns and manages the firm, there is little question about who makes decisions: the owner-manager does. But even when the owner of a sole proprietorship hires managers, there is usually frequent contact, and the managers closely follow the decisions of the owner.

partnership: a firm owned by more than one person in which the partners decide the division of the firm's income among them and are jointly liable for losses the firm incurs.

A **partnership** is essentially the same as a sole proprietorship except there is more than one owner. The partners agree on the division of the income from the firm; partnership income is also reported on a personal income tax form. In a partnership, one of the partners or hired managers may be given responsibility to make day-to-day decisions while more major decisions, such as a decision to shut down or acquire another firm, may require agreement from all or a majority of the partners.

corporation: a firm characterized by limited liability on the part of owners and the separation of ownership and management.

A **corporation** is unlike a sole proprietorship or partnership in that the managers, including the chief executive officer (CEO), are usually somewhat removed from the owners. Moreover, the owners of the corporation are liable only for a limited amount of any losses the corporation incurs. For example, if the corporation runs losses for several years and cannot repay all its debts, the owners do not have to sell their cars or give up their houses to pay the lenders. At most, the owners lose the value of their share of ownership in the firm. This feature of a corporation is called *limited liability.* Limiting the liability of the owners of a corporation reduces the risks of the owners and makes owning shares of a corporation more attractive.

A corporation pays a tax on its profits—called the corporate income tax—that is separate from the personal income tax paid by the owners. The corporation pays out part of its profits to the owners of the corporation and can use the remaining profits to expand the firm by buying additional capital, equipment, or even other firms. This payout to the owners is called a *dividend.*

Owners of a corporation own stock—certificates of ownership—in the corporation. The owners elect a board of directors, which is supposed to watch over the management of the corporation and look out for the owners' interests. Owners can sell the stock in a stock market, such as the New York Stock Exchange. The corporation can exist long after the original owners and their heirs are deceased. If a corporation is doing well, it can live on and on.

The CEO and the other managers of a corporation make many of the day-to-day decisions about hiring workers or buying equipment. Big decisions, such as a major expansion or a downsizing, are usually made with the board of directors closely involved. Bigger decisions, such as mergers with other firms, require the vote of the owners. A host of important issues that pertain to the relationships between the managers and the owners of corporations fall under the heading *corporate governance.* Do the managers have the interests of the owners in mind? Or do the managers look out for their own interest, perhaps trying to get their friends on the board of directors, thereby getting more generous salaries or benefits such as a corporate jet?

These are difficult questions. When economists study such questions, they emphasize the *principal-agent* relationship that distinguishes sharply between the owners of the firm and the managers of the firm. The managers are viewed as *agents* for the owners; the owners are viewed as the *principals* who want the agents to carry out certain actions. In general, the job of an agent is to carry out the wishes of the principal. But in situations where the principal (the owner) does not have much information about the actions of the agents (the managers), difficult governance issues arise. One of the difficulties is finding ways to give the managers incentives to make decisions in the interest of the owners. One approach is to give the managers a share of the corporation so that they share in the firm's profits. Such an approach is called *profit sharing* and has been used frequently. In some cases, profit sharing is extended to all workers of a firm, not only the managers, in order to give the workers incentives to improve the profitability of the firm.

How Many Firms Are There?

In the United States about 80 percent of all businesses—about 15 million firms— are sole proprietorships and partnerships. Most of them are small businesses; the sales of all of them together are only about one-seventh of total sales in the United States. You probably have never heard of most of these firms except for the ones that are located in your local community. Most are tiny in comparison with the 500 largest corporations, such as GM, IBM, and 3M, which sell products in countries all over the world.

There are about 3.5 million corporations in the United States but most of these are also relatively small, with less than $1 million in revenues, on average. There are only about 14,000 corporations with revenues greater than $50 million per year. The 500 largest of these—frequently called the Fortune 500 after a list *Fortune* magazine publishes each year—have revenues ranging from $168 billion for number one—General Motors—to about $3 billion for number 500—Vencor, a health-care firm in Louisville, Kentucky. Although there are fewer large firms than small firms, the large firms account for most of the sales of goods and services. Revenues of the 14,000 largest corporations together amount to about $6 trillion, while revenues of the 15 million proprietorships and partnerships total about $1 trillion.

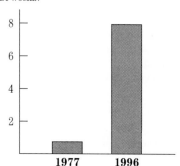

MILLIONS OF FIRMS OWNED BY WOMEN

A large number of firms in the United States are now owned by women.

Source: U.S. Bureau of the Census.

An Example: Your Own Firm

Are the decisions firms make anything like the decisions consumers make? Given the great variety of firms that exists in the marketplace, you might expect that the firms' decisions are much more complicated—and consequently more difficult to understand. Of course, many more people have had the experience of being a consumer than have had the experience of managing a firm. But if you can picture yourself as the owner/manager of your own firm, you will see that the economics of a firm's decision about how much to sell is analogous to the economics of a consumer's decision about how much to buy.

For example, imagine that you are the owner of a firm that grows pumpkins on a pumpkin patch; the patch has good soil and gets plenty of rain. The firm is one of many specializing in growing and selling pumpkins—in other words, there are many other firms with which you must compete. During the spring and summer you grow the pumpkins, and in the fall you sell them. As owner and manager of the firm you must pay rent at the start of each growing season to the landlord who owns the pumpkin patch. During the season you hire workers (perhaps college students) to tend the patch. The more workers tending the pumpkins, the more pumpkins you can grow on the patch.

The firm in our example, though hypothetical, is typical of many small firms and has features that apply to larger firms as well. This example firm is one with a single product (pumpkins) and two factors of production—land (the patch) and labor (the workers). One of the factors of production, land, cannot be changed during the season because the rent was paid in advance; this makes land a *fixed factor.* The other factor, labor, can be varied during the season, because you can choose to hire more or fewer workers; this makes labor a *variable factor.*

The Firm as a Price-Taker in a Competitive Market

Our aim is to determine the supply curve for a firm like this pumpkin firm. *A supply curve for a single firm tells us the quantity of a good that firm will produce at different prices.* To find the supply curve, we imagine that the firm looks at the price of the good it is selling and then decides how much to produce. For example, a baker considers the price of a loaf of bread prevailing in the market when deciding how many loaves of bread to produce. Because the firm takes the price in the market as a given when it makes a decision about production, we say that the firm is a **price-taker.** We assume that your pumpkin firm is a price-taker. This means that you decide how much to produce and sell after looking at the price of pumpkins in the market.

This description of a firm as price-taker may seem odd to you. After all, if the firm doesn't set the price, then who does? Of course, in some sense, each firm does. If you go to a bakery for a loaf of bread, a price tag states the price of the loaf, so the baker is clearly determining the price. But this is not the way economists look at it; there is a subtlety here in the way economists describe the market. With many bakers selling bread, in an important sense, the individual bakers do not have the ability to affect the price by much. If one baker charges $3 for a loaf of bread, and all the other bakers in the community charge $1.50 for the same loaf, no one will buy bread from the first baker. People will not even go to the store if they know the price is that high. They will go to other bakeries, where bread sells for $1.50 a loaf. Although in principle an individual firm has the ability to set any price it wants, in reality a firm cannot charge a price far from the price that prevails in the market without soon losing all its customers.

A market in which a single firm cannot affect the market price is called a **competitive market.** The market for fresh bread, with many bakeries in any reasonably sized community, is competitive. Because many firms are producing pumpkins along with our example pumpkin firm, the pumpkin market is also competitive. A competitive market requires that there be at least several firms competing with each other. Exactly how many firms are required to make a market competitive is difficult to say without studying the market carefully—as we do in later chapters. If a

price-taker: any firm that takes the market price as given; this firm cannot affect the market price because the market is competitive.

competitive market: a market where no firm has the power to affect the market price of a good.

market is competitive so that firms are price-takers, then we can derive a supply curve by asking, "How much bread would the baker produce if the price of bread were $1 a loaf? $1.50 a loaf? $2 a loaf? and so on. Or, in the case of your pumpkin firm, "How many pumpkins would the pumpkin firm produce if the price of pumpkins were $35 a crate? $70 a crate? and so on.

Other Types of Markets

Not all markets are as competitive as the fresh bread market or the pumpkin market, and part of our job later in the book is to study these markets. The exact opposite of a competitive market is where there is only one firm, in which case the firm is called a *monopoly*. Strictly speaking, a monopoly does not have a supply curve because the monopoly does not take the price as given. Instead, the monopoly can dictate the price (it is a *price-maker*). The question "How much does the monopoly produce at a given price?" has no meaning because the monopoly need not take the price as given. We consider monopolies in Chapter 10. For now we focus on the price-taking firms in a competitive market.

This subtlety about firms taking prices as given does not seem to arise in the case of the consumer. In deriving the demand curve in the previous chapter, we assumed that the individual consumer could not affect the price. This seems natural because we do not usually see buyers setting the price for bread or other commodities. As long as there are at least several buyers and several sellers in the market, we can assume that the price is taken as given by both buyers and sellers. In the next chapter, when we study the interaction of buyers and sellers in markets, we will show how the market price is determined.

Review

▶ Firms use inputs to produce goods and services; there are a great variety of sizes and types of firms.

▶ About 80 percent of U.S. firms are sole proprietorships or partnerships. The remaining 20 percent are corporations.

▶ In a competitive market with many firms, each firm is a price-taker.

▶ The supply curve of a firm describes how the quantity produced depends on the price.

THE FIRM'S PROFITS

Profits for any firm—a bakery producing bread or a farm producing pumpkins—are defined as the *total revenue* received from selling the product minus the *total costs* of producing the product. That is,

Profits = total revenue − total costs

When profits are negative—total revenue is less than total costs—the firm runs a *loss*. When profits are zero—total revenue is equal to total costs—the firm is breaking even.

We assume that the firm *maximizes* profits. That is, the firm decides on a quantity of production that will make profits as high as possible. To see how this is done,

profits: total revenue received from selling the product minus the total costs of producing the product.

we must examine how profits depend on the quantity produced. To do this, we must consider how total revenue and total costs—the two determinants of profits—depend on the quantity produced. We first consider total revenue and then total costs.

Total Revenue

total revenue: the price per unit times the quantity the firm sells.

Total revenue is the total number of dollars the firm receives from people who buy its product. Total revenue can be computed by multiplying the price of each unit sold by the quantity sold. That is,

$$\text{Total revenue} = \text{price} \times \text{quantity}$$
$$= P \times Q$$

where we use the letter P to stand for price and Q to stand for quantity. Because we are looking at an individual firm and a particular product, P is the price of the particular product the individual firm is selling and Q is the number of items the firm sells. There are a variety of ways to measure the quantity sold: numbers of crates of pumpkins, slices of pizza, loaves of bread, quarts of milk, kilowatts of electricity, etc. In the United States pounds and tons are usually used to measure items like coal, grapes, wheat, and sugar, but kilos would do as well.

Note that total revenue depends both on the price of the item being sold and on the number of items sold. For example, if the price of bread is $1.50 per loaf and 100 loaves are sold, then total revenue is $150. If the price rises to $2 a loaf and 200 loaves are sold, then total revenue is $400. The more items sold at a given price, the higher total revenue is. Thus, the firm can increase total revenue by producing and selling more goods.

Table 6.1 shows how total revenue increases with the quantity produced for the example firm producing pumpkins. Each row of the table shows the total revenue the firm receives from selling varying amounts of pumpkins. Each column showing total revenue corresponds to a different price: $35 per crate, $70 per crate, and $100 per crate. For example, when the firm can get $70 per crate, it receives $280 for selling 4 crates.

Production and Costs

total costs: the sum of variable costs and fixed costs.

Now that we have seen how total revenue depends on the quantity produced, let's examine how total costs depend on the quantity produced. **Total costs** are what the firm has to incur to produce the product. For the pumpkin firm example, total

---

TABLE 6.1
Total Revenue from Pumpkin Production at Three Prices

	Total Revenue		
Quantity Produced (crates)	Price = $35/crate	Price = $70/crate	Price = $100/crate
0	0	0	0
1	35	70	100
2	70	140	200
3	105	210	300
4	140	280	400
5	175	350	500

costs include the workers' salaries and the rent on the land. To see how total costs depend on the quantity produced, we must look at what happens to the quantity of labor and land used by the firm when the quantity produced increases or decreases.

The Time Period

We look at the firm's production decisions over a short period of time—such as one growing season—rather than over a long period of time—such as several growing seasons. Because we focus on the short run, we assume that only labor input to production can be varied. Our analysis of the firm in this chapter is called a *short-run* analysis because the time is too short to change the other factors of production, such as land; only labor can be changed. We make this assumption simply because it is easier to examine the firm's decisions when only one factor of production can be changed. It is a simplifying assumption that we will modify. In chapter 8 we take up the *long run,* when other factors of production—such as the size of the pumpkin patch—can change as well as labor.

The Production Function

Figure 6.3 plots the relationship between pumpkin production and labor input. The number of hours of work is on the horizontal axis, and the quantity produced is on the vertical axis. Each point in Figure 6.3 shows the number of hours of work and the quantity of pumpkins produced: to produce 3 crates requires 10 hours of work; to produce 5 crates requires 30 hours of work. Clearly, more pumpkin production requires more labor input. The graph in Figure 6.3 is called the firm's **production function** because it tells us how much is produced for each amount of labor input. This production function is for a given size of pumpkin patch.

The **marginal product of labor** is defined as the increase in production that comes from an additional unit of labor. Figure 6.3 shows that the marginal product of labor *declines* as labor input increases. Because of the curvature of the

Reminder

In Chapter 2 we saw that costs include *opportunity cost.* Thus, total costs for the pumpkin firm would include the opportunity cost of any time you spent operating the firm rather than doing something else, like study for an exam. To emphasize that opportunity cost is included in total costs when computing profits, economists sometimes use the term *economic profits* rather than simply profits.

production function: a relationship that shows the quantity of output for any given amount of input.

marginal product of labor: the change in production due to a one-unit increase in labor input.

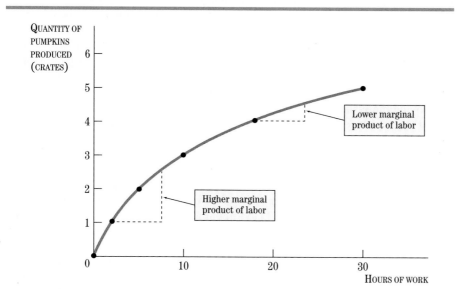

FIGURE 6.3
A Production Function Relating Output to Labor Input

As more workers are employed, production increases. But the increase in production added by each additional hour of work declines as more workers are hired because the capital the workers have to work with does not increase. Thus, there is a decreasing marginal product of labor, or diminishing returns to labor.

Diminishing Returns to Labor
Adding the second worker to this machine in a French vineyard increased the quantity of grapes produced by much less than the first worker did. Adding a third worker to the machine would increase the quantity of grapes produced by even less than adding the second worker did. Thus, this is an example of a decreasing marginal product of labor, or diminishing returns to labor.

diminishing returns to labor: a situation in which the incremental increase in output due to a unit increase in labor declines with increasing labor input; a decreasing marginal product of labor.

production function, the same increase in hours of work leads to a smaller increase in production when labor input is large than when labor input is small.

Another term for the phenomenon of declining marginal product of labor is **diminishing returns to labor.** In the pumpkin example, diminishing returns to labor occur as additional workers are employed. As more and more workers are employed on a given amount of land, each additional worker adds less and less additional output. Diminishing returns is a general phenomenon that occurs when some inputs to production—such as land or machines—are fixed. Because the size of the pumpkin patch is fixed, additional workers must eventually add less to production. Otherwise a single plot of land could produce all the world's pumpkins by employing huge numbers of workers. Thus, the return to each additional worker declines. Diminishing returns to labor occur in nonagricultural examples as well. Employing more and more workers at a single McDonalds will increase the amount of fast food produced by less and less.

Costs

Table 6.2 shows how total costs depend on the quantity of pumpkins produced at the pumpkin firm. The first column shows the quantity of pumpkins produced. The second column shows the required labor input to produce that quantity of pumpkins using the production function from Figure 6.3. The other columns show how total costs are determined.

The first row shows how much it costs if you decide to produce zero pumpkins. We assume that you have to pay $50 up front for rent on the patch even if a decision is made to produce no pumpkins. These payments are considered *fixed*

Quantity Produced (crates)	Hours of Labor Input	Variable Costs at $10 Wage (dollars)	Fixed Costs (dollars)	Total Costs (dollars)
0	0	0	50	50
1	2	20	50	70
2	5	50	50	100
3	10	100	50	150
4	18	180	50	230
5	30	300	50	350

TABLE 6.2
Example of Costs for a Single Firm

costs because they must be paid no matter how many pumpkins are produced. By definition, **fixed costs** are the part of total costs that do not depend on how much is produced.

fixed costs: costs of production that do not depend on the quantity of production.

The next row of Table 6.2 shows the costs of producing 1 crate of pumpkins. The additional costs of producing 1 crate compared to zero crates are $20. That payment is for 2 hours of work at $10 per hour. The $20 in payments are **variable costs** because they vary according to how much is produced. These costs are variable because more workers are hired as more is produced. Variable costs and fixed costs together constitute all the costs of producing the product and must be subtracted from revenue to get profits. Hence, *the sum of fixed costs and variable costs equals total costs,* as shown in the last column of Table 6.2.

variable costs: costs of production that vary with the quantity of production.

The third row of Table 6.2 shows the costs of producing 2 crates of pumpkins; clearly 2 crates are more costly to produce than 1 crate because more workers are needed. Variable costs, with 5 hours of work at $10 per hour, rise to $50. As more pumpkins are harvested, more workers must be hired, and the total costs increase. The remaining rows of Table 6.2 show what happens to costs as the quantity produced increases further.

Marginal cost is defined as the increase in total costs associated with an additional unit of production. Table 6.3 shows how marginal cost is calculated for the example in Table 6.2. For example, the marginal cost of increasing production from 1 crate to 2 crates is $30 ($100 − $70 = $30), and the marginal cost of increasing production from 2 crates to 3 crates is $50 ($150 − $100 = $50).

marginal cost: the change in total cost due to a one-unit change in quantity produced.

Notice how marginal cost increases as production increases. Marginal cost is greater when we go from 2 to 3 crates ($50) than from 1 to 2 crates ($30). The pattern of *increasing marginal cost* is apparent throughout the range of production in Table 6.3.

Quantity Produced (crates)	Total Costs (dollars)	Marginal Cost (dollars)
0	50	—
1	70	20
2	100	30
3	150	50
4	230	80
5	350	120

TABLE 6.3
Total Costs and Marginal Cost

The connecting lines emphasize how marginal cost is the change in total costs as the quantity produced increases by one unit.

Observe that *increasing marginal cost is due to the diminishing marginal product of labor:* marginal cost of going from 2 crates to 3 crates is greater than going from 1 crate to 2 crates because more worker hours are required to raise production from 2 crates to 3 crates than are required to raise production from 1 crate to 2 crates.

Increasing marginal cost is a general phenomenon that occurs in many production processes. It is essential for deriving the supply curve. In fact, as we will see, increasing marginal cost is the whole reason that the supply curve for an individual firm slopes upward.

There are exceptions to the principle of increasing marginal cost. One important exception is that marginal cost need not be increasing over the entire range of production. For example, there might be a decrease in marginal cost at very low levels of production. If a team of at least two workers is needed to harvest pumpkins, for example, then the marginal product of a second worker might be greater than the marginal product of a first worker. One worker might add very little while the second worker might add a lot. But diminishing returns to labor and increasing marginal cost eventually set in as more workers are hired and more pumpkins are produced.

This chapter assumes that marginal cost increases over the whole range of production. This a common assumption used by economists and is a good approximation except for very low levels of production. In Chapter 8, we will see what happens when marginal cost declines at low levels of production.

Graphical Representation of Total Costs and Marginal Cost

A better understanding of how a firm's total costs depend on production can be obtained by representing the total costs graphically. Figure 6.4 plots the pairs of numbers on total costs and quantity produced from the first two columns of Table 6.3. Dollars are on the vertical axis and the quantity of pumpkins produced is on the horizontal axis. Note how the total costs curve bends up: As marginal cost increases the curve gets steeper, or the slope increases. The marginal cost is the slope of the total cost curve. The increasing slope is a visual way to show the increasing marginal cost.

FIGURE 6.4
Total Costs

In order to produce goods, a firm incurs costs. For example, more workers must be paid to produce more goods. As more goods are produced, the firm's total costs rise, as shown here. At higher levels of production, costs increase by larger amounts for each additional item produced.

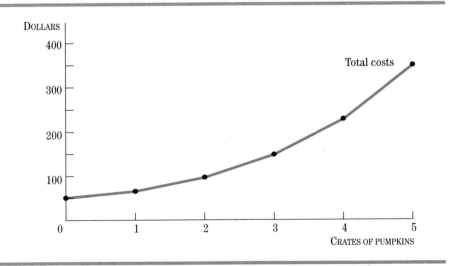

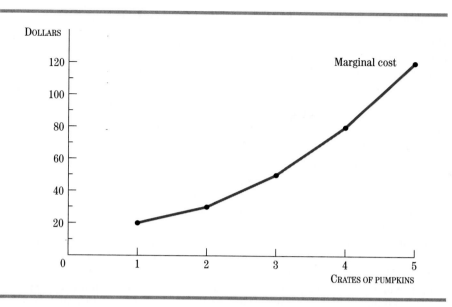

FIGURE 6.5
Marginal Cost
The change in total costs as more units of the good are produced is called marginal cost. Marginal cost increases as more units are produced, as illustrated here.

Figure 6.5 shows the relationship between marginal cost and number of crates of pumpkins produced. The points in Figure 6.5 correspond to the pairs of numbers in the first and third columns of Table 6.3. Note that the marginal cost curve slopes upward, illustrating how marginal cost increases. The upward-sloping supply curve can be derived from Figure 6.5, as we explain in the next section.

Review

▶ Profits are defined as the difference between total revenue and total costs.

▶ Profits depend on the quantity produced because both total revenue and total costs depend on the quantity produced.

▶ Total revenue is defined as the price (*P*) times the quantity (*Q*) produced and sold. Total revenue increases as the quantity produced increases.

▶ Total costs increase with the quantity produced because it takes more inputs—such as workers—to produce more output.

▶ Marginal cost increases as more is produced because of diminishing returns to labor. As labor is increased with a fixed amount of capital, the increase in output from each additional unit of labor declines.

PROFIT MAXIMIZATION AND THE INDIVIDUAL FIRM'S SUPPLY CURVE

To derive the firm's supply curve we assume that the firm chooses a quantity of production that maximizes profits. This is the assumption of **profit maximization.** Now that we have seen how profits depend on the quantity produced, we can proceed to show how the firm chooses a quantity to maximize profits.

profit maximization: an assumption that firms try to achieve the highest possible level of profits—total revenue minus total costs—given their production function.

Deriving a Firm's Supply Curve from Its Marginal Cost

Continuing with the pumpkin example, we first plot the marginal cost from Table 6.3 in Figure 6.6. Focus for now on the black dots in Figure 6.6; we derive the lines in the next few paragraphs. Each dot in Figure 6.6 represents the marginal cost of producing pumpkins at different levels of production. Figure 6.6 summarizes all that we need to know in order to find the quantity a profit-maximizing firm will produce.

Finding the Quantity Supplied at Different Prices

Suppose the price of pumpkins is $10 a crate. Mark this point on the vertical axis of the diagram in Figure 6.6 with an arrow. We are going to derive the supply curve for your pumpkin firm by gradually raising the price from the low $10 value and determining how much you would produce at each price. At $10, the price is less than the marginal cost of producing 1 unit, which is $20, according to Figure 6.6. Would it make sense to produce pumpkins at this price? No, because producing 1 crate of pumpkins has a marginal cost of $20. The *additional* revenue that comes from producing one more crate is $10. The additional, or extra, revenue that results from producing and selling one more unit of output is called **marginal revenue.** Because laying out $20 and getting back $10 reduces profits, you would not bother to produce any pumpkins. In other words, the marginal cost of increasing production from 0 to 1 crate would be greater than the marginal revenue from selling 1 crate. Producing nothing would be the profit-maximizing thing to do.

Suppose the price of pumpkins rises. Move your arrow up the vertical axis of Figure 6.6. As long as the price is below $20, there is no production. Thus, the amount supplied at prices from $0 to $20 is given by the thick line at the bottom of the vertical axis where quantity supplied equals zero.

Suppose the price rises to $20. Now the price equals the marginal cost, and the additional, or marginal, revenue from selling a crate of pumpkins will just cover the marginal cost of producing the crate. You now have sufficient incentive to produce

marginal revenue: the change in total revenue due to a one-unit increase in quantity sold.

FIGURE 6.6
Derivation of the Individual Firm's Supply Curve
The dots represent the marginal cost from Table 6.3. At each dot, price equals marginal cost. These dots and the thick vertical lines indicate the quantity the firm is willing to supply at each price. Along the vertical lines, the firm produces the quantity that keeps marginal cost close to price without exceeding it.

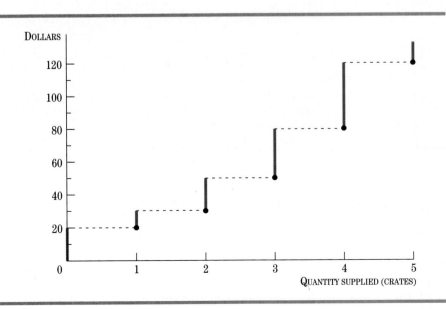

some pumpkins. Strictly speaking, the price would have to be a little bit greater than $20 (say $20.01) for you to earn more producing 1 crate rather than 0 crates. At a price of exactly $20, you may be indifferent between 0 crates and 1 crate. At a price of $19.99, you would definitely produce nothing. At a price of $20.01, you would definitely produce 1 crate. The price of $20 is right between, but let's assume that you produce 1 crate rather than 0 crates at a price of $20. We indicate this in Figure 6.6 by showing that the quantity supplied is given by the black dot at 1 crate and $20.

Now consider further increases in the price. At prices above $20 up to $30, you would produce 1 crate because the price received for producing an extra crate is less than the marginal cost of $30. However, at a price of $30, the quantity supplied increases to 2 crates because price just equals the marginal cost of increasing production from 1 to 2 crates. A supply curve is now beginning to take shape. You can complete the curve by continuing to raise the price and watch what happens.

To shorten the story, let us move toward the other end of the scale. Suppose the price of pumpkins is $100. At $100, the price is greater than the marginal cost of producing the fourth crate, which is $80, but it is less than the marginal cost of producing the fifth crate, which is $120. Suppose that you are producing 4 crates of pumpkins. Would it make sense to produce another crate? No, because increasing production from 4 crates to 5 crates has a marginal cost of $120. The marginal revenue that comes from producing one more crate is $100. Because laying out $120 and getting back $100 is a losing proposition, you would not do it. Production would stay at 4 crates. If production went up to 5 crates, profits would go down because the marginal cost of producing the fifth crate is greater than the marginal revenue. Producing 5 crates would not be a profit-maximizing thing to do.

What happens if the price rises to $110? At $110 the marginal cost is still less than the price so it still makes sense to produce 4 crates. What if the price rises to $120? Then at 5 crates, the price just equals the marginal cost and you would produce 5 crates. When the price rises to the marginal cost at five units, then production increases to five units.

We have traced out the complete *individual* supply curve for your firm using Figure 6.6 with the assumption of profit maximization and the concept of marginal cost. The supply curve in Figure 6.6 is steplike; it consists of small vertical segments shooting up from the dots. Strictly speaking, it is only at the dots that price equals marginal cost. On the vertical segments above the dots, the price is actually greater than the marginal cost of production, but the price is not great enough to move on to a higher level of production.

In reality, however, for most products it is possible to divide production into smaller units—half crates, quarter crates, even a single pumpkin. As we do so, the jaggedness of the diagram disappears. If marginal cost between the whole-crate intervals is between the marginal cost at each crate, then the supply curve will be smooth, as shown in Figure 6.7. It is the simple numerical example with production limited to whole-crate amounts that leads to steps in the supply curve. In reality, the diagram would consist of hundreds of dots rather than five dots. With hundreds of dots, the vertical segments would be too small to see and the firm's supply curve would be a smooth line. Price would equal marginal cost at every single point.

The Price Equals Marginal Cost Rule

In deriving the supply curve with Figure 6.6, we have discovered the key condition for profit maximization for a firm in a competitive market: *The firm will choose its*

FIGURE 6.7

A Smooth Individual Supply Curve
If the firm can adjust its production by small amounts, the supply curve becomes a smooth line, as in this figure, rather than a series of steps, as in Figure 6.6. In some cases, such as the building of an airport, a dam, or a suspension bridge, fractions are not possible and the supply curves will still have steps.

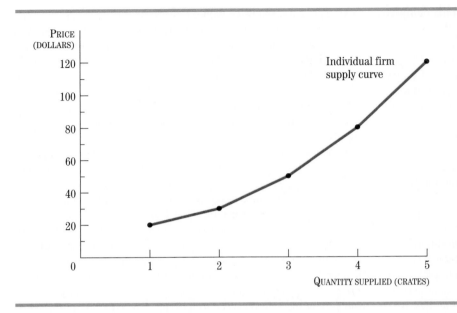

quantity such that price equals marginal cost. You can see that from Figure 6.6. When the price is $80, the firm chooses a level of production for which the marginal cost equals $80 and produces 4 crates.

The price equals marginal cost rule for a competitive firm is a special case of a more general profit-maximization rule that we used, without calling it a rule, in our derivation of the supply curve. This more general rule is that *the firm will choose a quantity to produce so that marginal revenue equals marginal cost.* This more general rule makes intuitive sense for any profit-maximizing firm, whether it is a competitive firm or a monopoly. If the marginal revenue from producing an additional quantity of output is greater than the marginal cost, then the firm should produce that quantity; by doing so it will increase total revenue by more than it increases total costs, and therefore it will increase profits. However, if the marginal revenue from an additional quantity is less than the marginal cost, then the firm should not produce that quantity. The firm maximizes profits by choosing the quantity of production for which marginal revenue equals marginal cost. Why is the price equals marginal cost rule a special case of the marginal revenue equals marginal cost rule? Because *for the case of a price-taking firm in a competitive market, the marginal revenue is equal to the price.* For example, as we showed above, if the price of pumpkins is $10 per crate, then the marginal, or additional, revenue from producing 1 crate of pumpkins is $10. Later, in Chapter 10, we will show that for a *monopoly,* marginal revenue does not equal the price, so that even though marginal revenue equals marginal cost, the price does not equal marginal cost.

Another Way to Look at Profit Maximization

Rather than considering marginal cost, you can also maximize profits by simply choosing the quantity of production that gives the highest level of profits. We can show how this is done either with a table or a graph.

A Profit Table

Table 6.4 shows profits for the pumpkin firm. Total revenue, shown in the third column, increases with the number of pumpkins sold. Because total revenue depends on the price, we need a separate panel showing profits for each price. Table 6.4 has three panels, one for each of three possible prices. (The prices are the same as in Table 6.1.) Suppose the price of pumpkins is $35 a crate. Then if you sell 1 crate, the revenue is $35; if you sell 2 crates, the revenue is $70, and so on. Total revenue equals the price ($35) times the number of crates sold. Clearly, if no pumpkins are sold, the total revenue will be zero. Panels II and III show total revenue for two higher prices—$70 per crate and $100 per crate. For each total price, revenue increases as more is produced and sold.

Table 6.4 also shows how total costs increase with production. This is the same information already presented in Table 6.2. We repeat it here so that total costs can easily be compared with total revenue to calculate profits. Note how total costs, like

TABLE 6.4
Profit Tables Showing Total Costs and Total Revenue at Different Prices

PANEL I
If price equals $35 per crate, then production equals 2 crates.

Crates	Total Costs	Total Revenue	Profits
0	50	0	−50
1	70	35	−35
2	100	70	−30
3	150	105	−45
4	230	140	−90
5	350	175	−175

PANEL II
If price equals $70 per crate, then production equals 3 crates.

Crates	Total Costs	Total Revenue	Profits
0	50	0	−50
1	70	70	0
2	100	140	40
3	150	210	60
4	230	280	50
5	350	350	0

PANEL III
If price equals $100 per crate, then production equals 4 crates.

Crates	Total Costs	Total Revenue	Profits
0	50	0	−50
1	70	100	30
2	100	200	100
3	150	300	150
4	230	400	170
5	350	500	150

total revenue, increase with production, from $50 for no pumpkins to $350 for 5 crates of pumpkins. The range of total costs is the same for all these panels because total costs do not depend on the price.

The last column of Table 6.4 shows profits: Total revenue minus total costs. Consider the $35 per crate price first in panel I. When no pumpkins are produced, profits are −$50. You lose $50 because $50 is paid for the land and total revenue is zero. If you produce 1 crate, the loss is $35; in other words, profits are −$35; the total cost of producing 1 crate ($70) minus the revenue from 1 crate ($35) equals −$35. For 2 crates, profits are still negative. Total revenue is $70 while total costs are $100, leaving a loss of $30. Three crates of pumpkins yields a loss of $45.

A glance down the last column in panel I shows that profits are negative at all production levels. In this case any production at all may seem fruitless. But remember that you already paid $50 for the use of the pumpkin patch. Hence, it is best to produce 2 crates and cut the losses to $30. You still lose but not as much as by producing only zero or 1 crate. This may seem strange because profits are negative. But the profit-maximizing level of production is 2 crates. The maximum of profits would be −$30. Stated differently, the minimum loss would be $30.

The same type of profit-maximizing exercise with a different price is illustrated in panel II of Table 6.4. Here the price of pumpkins is $70, so that the total revenue is higher. If you sell nothing, then total revenue is zero and the loss is $50. If you sell 1 crate, total revenue is $70 and profits are zero. But if you sell 2 crates, total costs are $100 and total revenue is $140. Finally, some positive profit can be seen. But profits can be increased further: The profit-maximizing level of production is 3 crates.

Panel III shows profits for a higher price of $100 a crate. At this price, you would produce 4 crates. Profits would be $170. More or less production would lower profits.

In these three cases you maximize profits by adjusting the quantity supplied. As the price rises from $35 to $70 to $100, the profit-maximizing quantity of pumpkins supplied goes from 2 crates to 3 crates to 4 crates. Thus, the price and the quantity supplied are positively related. This is the positively sloped supply curve derived in a different way.

A Profit Graph

The relationship between profits and production for the pumpkin firm in Table 6.4 can be illustrated with a graph that compares total costs and total revenue. This is done in Figure 6.8. The curved line in the top graph of Figure 6.8 is the total cost curve. It corresponds to the total costs listed in Table 6.4 and is the same as the total cost curve in Figure 6.4. The upward-sloping straight line shows what total revenue would be for a price of $70 per crate. This line corresponds to the total revenue column in panel II of Table 6.4.

Profits are given by the gap between the total revenue line and the total cost curve. The gap—profits—is plotted in the lower panel of Figure 6.8. Note how profits first increase and then decrease as more is produced. The profit-maximizing firm chooses a quantity to produce that leads to the biggest gap, or the biggest level of profits. That quantity is 3 crates of pumpkins.

Figure 6.8 illustrates why the price equals marginal cost condition gives exactly the same answer. Observe that at the point where profits are largest, the slope of the total revenue line equals the slope of the total cost line. Now, the slope

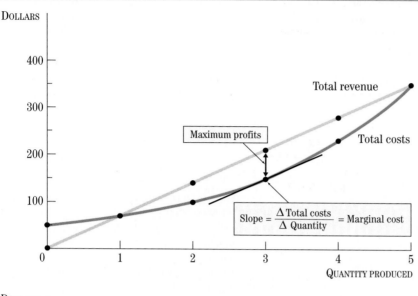

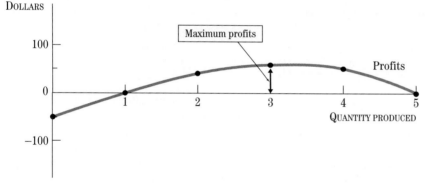

FIGURE 6.8
An Alternative Look at Profit Maximization
The top panel shows total costs and total revenue for a price of $70 per crate of pumpkins. Profits are the gap between total revenue and total costs. At the profit-maximizing point, the slope of the total cost curve equals the slope of the revenue line. Hence, price equals marginal cost. The bottom panel shows explicitly how profits first increase and then decrease with production.

of the total revenue line equals the price because the change in revenue ($P \times Q$) associated with a change in production is the price (P). For example, if the price is $70, then increasing production by one unit—from 2 to 3 crates—would raise revenue from $140 to $210, or by $70. Moreover, the slope of the total cost curve at any point is the marginal cost. When the gap between total revenue and total costs is widest—the profit-maximizing point—these two slopes are equal. In other words, price equals marginal cost.

A Comparison of the Two Approaches to Profit Maximization

We have now considered two different approaches to profit maximization. One approach compares the price to the marginal cost. The other approach looks at the explicit relationship between profits and production. Both approaches give the same answer. How do the approaches compare?

In Table 6.4 we looked at several prices; we derived the profit-maximizing level of production by looking at profits for different levels of production at these prices. To do so, we had to create a new table for each price. This is quite time consuming. In contrast, with the marginal cost approach, we only had to look at marginal cost for each unit of production and compare it with the price. Thus, the price equals marginal cost approach is considerably easier. Moreover, because marginal cost increases as the number of items produced increases, the price equals marginal cost approach tells us why the supply curve slopes upward. It is for these two reasons that economists usually use the price equals marginal cost approach.

Review

▶ Profit-maximizing firms respond to higher prices by increasing the quantity they are willing to produce. Their response is the supply curve.

▶ The supply curve can be derived by comparing price and marginal cost. A profit-maximizing firm will produce a quantity that equates price and marginal cost.

▶ The upward-sloping marginal cost curve implies an upward-sloping supply curve.

▶ The supply curve can also be derived by looking at the relationship between profits and production. The profit-maximizing quantity is the same as that determined by the price equals marginal cost approach.

THE MARKET SUPPLY CURVE

The *market* supply curve can be obtained by adding up all the *individual* firms' supply curves in the market. Figure 6.9 gives an example where there are two individual firm supply curves for pumpkins: One curve corresponds to your pumpkin firm and the other, which is identical to yours, corresponds to the firm of your competitor, Fred, who is growing pumpkins on the other side of town. You and Fred have the same marginal cost for pumpkin growing, so your supply curves are exactly the same. You will both choose to produce the same number of pumpkins if the price is the same.

If only you and Fred are in the market, the market supply curve is the sum of just your two supplies. You get the market curve by adding in the horizontal direction, as shown in Figure 6.9. For example, if the price is $30, the quantity supplied by Fred will be 2 crates and the quantity you supply will be 2 crates; thus the quantity supplied in the market at $30 is 4 crates. If the price rises to $50, Fred will produce 3 crates and you will also produce 3 crates; thus the quantity supplied in the market rises to 6 crates.

In reality, of course, there are more than two firms in a competitive market, and the individual supply curve for different firms in the market is usually different. But the concept of deriving the market supply curve is the same whether there are only two or 2,000 firms, and whether they are all the same or are all different. After adding up the individual supply curves for all the firms in the market, we arrive at a market supply curve like Figure 6.1. Thus, we have fulfilled one of the objectives of this chapter—deriving the market supply curve.

If there are many different firms in the market, the market supply curve can be much smoother than the individual supply curves. For example, a novelist may be

Experiments Demonstrate the Law of Diminishing Returns

Diminishing returns to labor means that the marginal product of labor declines as more workers are added to a fixed amount of land or capital. More generally, diminishing returns occur any time one factor of production increases while some other factor is fixed. Diminishing returns applies in so many situations— from the use of fertilizer in the production of potatoes to the use of labor in the production of French fries that economists sometimes refer to it as the *law* of diminishing returns.

Experiments provide evidence on diminishing returns. The table shows data on potato production obtained from experiments in Maine. The variable input to the production of potatoes is fertilizer; land, capital, labor, and other inputs to production are fixed in the experiments.

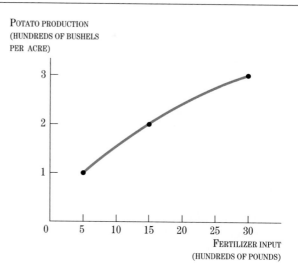

POTATO PRODUCTION
(HUNDREDS OF BUSHELS
PER ACRE)

FERTILIZER INPUT
(HUNDREDS OF POUNDS)

Potato Production (hundreds of bushels per acre)	Fertilizer Input (hundreds of pounds)	Variable Costs (dollars at $1 per pound)	Marginal Cost (dollars)
1	5	500	—
2	15	1,500	1,000
3	30	3,000	1,500

The first column of the table shows the number of bushels of potatoes that can be obtained from an acre; observe how potato production increases as more fertilizer is used. Observe the decreasing marginal product of fertilizer: Additional pounds of fertilizer result in smaller increases in potato production. A plot of this relationship is shown in the graph.

What does this data imply about the marginal cost of potatoes? Assuming that fertilizer costs $1 per pound, the variable costs of potato production are shown in the third column. Variable costs are given by the price of fertilizer times the amount of fertilizer used in production.

Marginal cost can be computed from the change in variable costs; (fixed costs, which do not change and therefore do not matter in the calculation of marginal cost, are not shown). With three observations on variable cost, we can compute two values for the marginal cost of potato production as shown in the table. Observe how marginal cost increases with the amount of potato production.

able to write only one novel a year. If a publisher offers a contract to write the novel that is above the marginal cost of producing the novel, then the novelist will write the novel. Otherwise, the novel will not be written. But the market in novels in any one year consists of many authors with many different marginal costs. As the price of novels rises, more and more authors will decide to write novels, and the market supply curve for novels will look very smooth.

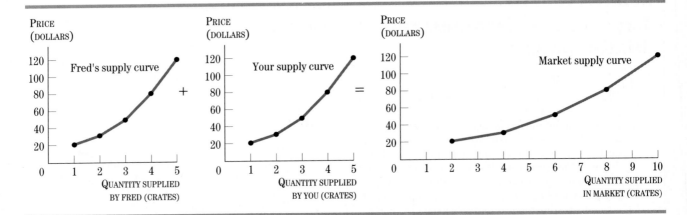

FIGURE 6.9
Derivation of the Market Supply Curve
The market supply curve is the sum of individual firms' supply curves for all the firms in the market. The figure shows how the supply curves of two firms—Fred's and yours—sum to a market supply curve.

The Slope of the Supply Curve

We have shown that the slope and position of the individual firms' supply curves depend on the marginal cost at the different firms. If marginal cost rises very sharply with more production, then the supply curve will be very steep. If marginal cost increases more gradually, then the supply curve will be flatter.

Because the market supply curve is the sum of the individual firms' supply curves, its slope will also depend on marginal cost. The market supply curve can get very steep at high levels of production because marginal cost gets very high when production is high.

Shifts in the Supply Curve

Because the supply curve for the individual firm is given by its marginal cost, anything that decreases marginal cost will shift down the individual supply curves and therefore the market supply curve. For example, a new technology might reduce the marginal cost at every level of production. If so, then the market supply curve will shift down by the amount that marginal cost declines. Observe that a downward shift of a supply curve is equivalent to a rightward shift. Similarly, an increase in marginal cost—perhaps because of a disease affecting the pumpkins that requires more labor for each crate of pumpkins—would shift the supply curve upward or to the left.

Review

▶ The market supply curve is derived by adding up all the individual supply curves of firms in the market.

▶ When the price rises, the individual firms in the market increase the quantity supplied. Hence, the market supply curve is upward-sloping.

▶ The slope of the supply curve depends on how sharply marginal cost increases.

▶ Anything that raises or lowers marginal cost will shift the market supply curve.

PRODUCER SURPLUS

A firm would not produce and sell an item if it could not get a price at least as high as the marginal cost of producing it. The **producer surplus** is the difference between the marginal cost of an item and the price received for it. For example, your marginal cost of washing cars on the weekend might be $4 per car. If the car-washing price in your area is $9 per car and this is the price you receive, then your producer surplus would be $5 per car. Or suppose, in the pumpkin example, that the price of pumpkins is $25. Then you get $25 for producing 1 crate and incur $20 in marginal cost. The difference, $5, is your producer surplus. If the price is $35 in the pumpkin example, 2 crates are produced and producer surplus is $15 ($35 − $20) at 1 crate plus $5 ($35 − $30) at 2 crates for a total of $20 producer surplus.

producer surplus: the difference between the price received by a firm for an additional item sold and the marginal cost of the item's production; for the market as a whole, it is the sum of all the individual firms' producer surpluses, or the area above the market supply curve and below the market price.

A Graphical Representation of Producer Surplus

The producer surplus can be represented graphically as the area above the individual firm supply curve and below the price line, as illustrated in Figure 6.10. The producer surplus is analogous to the consumer surplus, the area below the demand curve and above the price line derived in the previous chapter.

The producer surplus in the whole market can be obtained by adding up the producer surplus for all producers, or by looking at the area above the market supply curve and below the price. This is illustrated in Figure 6.11.

The applications of producer surplus are similar to consumer surplus. Producer surplus provides a measure of how much a producer gains from the market. The sum of producer surplus plus consumer surplus is a comprehensive measure of how well a market economy works, as we will see in the next chapter.

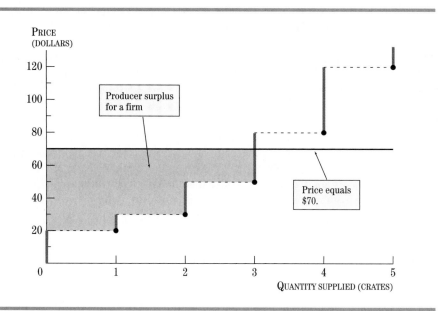

FIGURE 6.10
Producer Surplus for an Individual Firm

As shown here, for an individual firm, the producer surplus is the area between the price line and the supply curve.

FIGURE 6.11
Producer Surplus for the Market
If we add up producer surplus for each firm, we get the producer surplus for the whole market. This is given by the area between the price and the market supply curve.

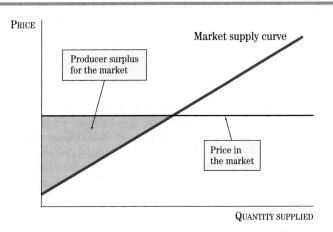

The Relationship Between Profits and Producer Surplus

Profits and producer surplus are not the same thing. Profits are the difference between total revenue and total costs, while the producer surplus measures the difference between the price and the marginal cost of every unit. How can we compare these two measures?

Suppose again the price of pumpkins is $35 per crate; then you are willing to produce 2 crates of pumpkins. Total revenue is $70 and total costs are $100; thus, you are losing $30 (profit $= -\$30$). (See panel I of Table 6.4.) How much is your producer surplus when 2 crates are sold at $35? As just defined,

$$\text{Producer surplus} = (P - MC_1) + (P - MC_2)$$
$$= (\$35 - \$20) + (\$35 - \$30) = \$20$$

where MC_1 is the marginal cost of the first crate and MC_2 is the marginal cost of the second crate. Thus, profits are $-\$30$ and producer surplus is $20.

Notice that there is a difference of $50 between profits and producer surplus. That number happens to be equal to the fixed costs of the firm. Thus, producer surplus equals profit plus fixed costs. Try the same method for different prices and quantities sold and you will arrive at the same result: Producer surplus always equals profits plus fixed costs. We now show that this is no coincidence.

Consider Table 6.5. The first four columns of Table 6.5 are already familiar from the earlier tables. The fifth column shows the sum of marginal costs for all that is produced. For example, the sum of marginal costs when production is 3 crates is $20 plus $30 plus $50 equals $100. The last column shows the difference between total costs and fixed costs. Notice that the last two columns are equal.

Thus, as we sum up marginal costs for any quantity Q produced, we count all costs except fixed costs. In other words,

Sum of marginal costs = total costs − fixed costs

When the producer sells a quantity Q, we can say that

$$\text{Producer surplus} = (P - MC_1) + (P - MC_2) + (P - MC_3) + \ldots + (P - MC_Q)$$

We can translate this definition of producer surplus into the price (P) of the good times the quantity (Q) sold minus the sum of the marginal costs of all units. That is,

TABLE 6.5
Summing Up Marginal Costs

Crates of Pumpkins	Fixed Costs	Total Costs	Marginal Cost	Sum of Marginal Costs	Total Costs Less Fixed Costs
1	50	70	20	20	20
2	50	100	30	50	50
3	50	150	50	100	100
4	50	230	80	180	180
5	50	350	120	300	300

Producer surplus $= (P \times Q) -$ sum of marginal costs

As we now know, $P \times Q$ is the total revenue, and the sum of marginal costs equals the difference between total costs and fixed costs. Substituting these relationships into the preceding gives

Producer surplus $=$ total revenue $-$ (total costs $-$ fixed costs)

Finally, since profits equal total revenue minus total costs, we obtain the relationship between producer surplus and profits:

Producer surplus $=$ profits $+$ fixed costs

Review

▶ Producer surplus is the price a firm receives for selling a unit of a product minus the marginal cost of producing it.

▶ The producer surplus for a firm is the area below the price line and above the firm's supply curve.

▶ For all the firms in a market, the producer surplus is the area below the price line and above the market supply curve.

▶ Producer surplus is different from profits. Producer surplus is greater than profits by the amount of fixed costs.

CONCLUSION

In this chapter we have derived the supply curve for a firm in a competitive market by constructing a model of the behavior of firms. The model assumes that a firm decides how much to produce by maximizing profits. The firm makes this decision taking prices as given and considering its production function, which relates the number of hours of work at the firm to the output of the firm. The production function enters the firm's profit calculations through its effects on the firm's costs. Because the production function has diminishing returns to labor, the firm faces increasing marginal cost. From the firm's marginal cost we can quickly find the firm's supply curve. Profit maximization implies that the firm will produce the quantity where price equals marginal cost.

The connection between marginal cost and the supply curve is fundamental to understanding how markets work. We will make use of this connection many times throughout this book, especially when we consider public policy issues, such as the efficiency of markets, taxation, and regulation of firms. When economists see or draw a supply curve, they are usually thinking about the marginal cost of the firms that underlie the supply curve. The supply curve and the marginal cost curve are virtually synonymous for economists.

The price equals marginal cost rule for a profit-maximizing firm is fundamental for understanding how well markets work. When, in the next chapter, we combine this rule with the analogous rule that the price equals the marginal benefit of a good for a consumer, we will discover an attractive feature of competitive markets.

Having developed a model of firm behavior in this chapter and a model of consumer behavior in the previous chapter, the next step in our analysis of markets is to examine the interaction of these firms and consumers. Building a model of this interaction is the first objective of the next chapter.

KEY POINTS

1. A firm is an organization that uses inputs to produce goods or services.

2. About 20 percent of firms are corporations; the rest are sole proprietorships or partnerships.

3. The foundations of supply are found in the profit-maximizing behavior of firms.

4. Profits are defined as total revenue minus total costs.

5. Marginal cost increases as more is produced because of diminishing returns to labor.

6. The production function shows how production increases with more labor; the marginal product of labor declines as more labor is added and capital is not changed.

7. A price-taking firm in a competitive market produces up to the point where price equals marginal cost, which is the key rule for profit maximization.

8. The reason the supply curve slopes upward is that marginal cost is increasing. A higher price enables the firm to produce at higher levels of marginal cost.

9. We can also determine the profit-maximizing quantity of production by looking at how profits depend on production and finding the highest level of profits.

10. The market supply curve is obtained by adding up the individual supply curves. The market supply curve can be smooth even if the individual supply curves are not.

11. Producer surplus is the area above either the individual or the market supply curves and below the price line.

12. Producer surplus and profit are not the same thing. Producer surplus equals profits plus fixed costs.

KEY TERMS

firm
sole proprietorship
partnership
corporation
price-taker
competitive market

profits
total revenue
total costs
production function
marginal product of labor
diminishing returns to labor

fixed costs
variable costs
marginal cost
profit maximization
marginal revenue
producer surplus

QUESTIONS FOR REVIEW

1. What is a firm?

2. What are the differences between a corporation and a partnership?

3. Why do total costs increase as more is produced?

4. Why does marginal cost increase as more is produced?

5. What is the relationship between individual supply curves and marginal cost?

6. Why does profit maximization imply that price equals marginal cost?

7. Why would a firm never choose to produce at a point when the price of an item is less than the marginal cost of the item?

8. What does it mean to say that firms are price-takers?

9. When does it make sense to assume firms are price-takers?

10. How is the market supply curve derived from individual supply curves?

11. Why might the market supply curve be smoother than the individual supply curves?

12. What is producer surplus?

PROBLEMS

1. The following table shows the total costs of producing pumpkins in a small patch of land.

Number of Pumpkins	Total Costs (dollars)
0	20
1	21
2	23
3	27
4	31
5	37
6	44
7	52
8	63
9	79
10	98

a) Calculate the marginal cost.
b) Draw the firm's supply curve.
c) Suppose the price of 1 pumpkin is $5. How much would this firm produce? What is its producer surplus? Show your answer graphically. Answer the same questions for a price of $17.

2. Consider the example of the cost of pumpkins in Table 6.4. Compute the total revenue, total costs, and profits when the price of a crate of pumpkins is $50. How many crates of pumpkins will maximize profits? How does the answer compare to that using the price equals marginal cost condition?

3. Consider the following information:

Daily Production and Costs at Jill's Bread Bakers

Quantity Produced (dozens of loaves)	Total Costs (dollars)
0	20
1	22
2	26
3	32
4	40
5	50
6	62
7	76

a) Calculate the marginal cost for Jill's bread production.
b) Draw the supply curve for this firm.
c) Jill can sell as many loaves as she wants in the market at a price of $12 for a dozen loaves. How many loaves will she sell each day? Use your diagram to show how much producer surplus she receives.

4. Suppose you have the opportunity to sell used books and can sell 1 book per hour at a price of $15. The only cost to you is the opportunity cost of your time. For the first 5 hours, the opportunity cost of your time is $10 per hour. But after 5 hours, you value your time at $20 per hour, because you have to study. Draw the marginal cost to you of supplying books. Draw in the price you receive for books. How many books will you sell? Calculate your producer surplus.

5. Sketch two new diagrams like the diagram in Figure 6.8, but assume the price is $35 and $100. Compare and contrast your two diagrams with Figure 6.8. How do the slopes of the total cost curve differ at the profit maximizing quantity?

6. Suppose a price-taking firm has the following total costs:

Quantity	Total Costs (dollars)
0	10
1	15
2	25
3	40
4	60
5	85
6	115

a) Calculate marginal cost. If the price in the market is $20, how many units will the firm produce?
b) Suppose the price in the market falls to $10 per unit. How much will the firm produce? What are profits? Will the firm still produce? Why?
c) Suppose that the price is still $10, but that total costs are lower by $5 at every level of production. How much will the firm produce now? Explain.

7

The Interaction of People in Markets

An economy is nothing more than the interaction of people producing, consuming, buying, and selling goods and services. Some economic interactions—purchases, sales, or other exchanges—occur in markets, such as a local flea market, the New York stock market, the Chicago pork belly market, the California earthquake insurance market, or the world computer chip market. Other economic interactions occur in organizations, such as the New York Times Company, the Chicago Police Department, the University of California, IBM, and NEC. Markets and organizations vary in size and structure, and they differ in the way that people interact within them. This chapter focuses on the economic interactions of people in markets.

In Chapter 5 we showed how the utility-maximizing behavior of buyers can be described by individual demand curves. In Chapter 6 we showed how the profit-maximizing behavior of sellers can be described by individual supply curves. In this chapter we show how the economic interactions of buyers and sellers in competitive markets can be explained by a model that combines individual demand curves and individual supply curves. Figure 7.1 is a schematic illustration of this interaction and the model to explain it. The model, called the **competitive equilibrium model,** is an embellishment of the supply and demand model discussed in Chapters 3 and 4, but now with the behavior of consumers and the behavior of firms explicit.

We show—using logic, empirical evidence, and experiments—that the free interaction of buyers and sellers in markets results in a price predicted by the competitive equilibrium model. We also use the model to explain how an **invisible hand**—the term coined by Adam Smith—works in these markets; that is, without any formal coordination, the buyers, who are trying to increase their utility, and the sellers, who are trying to increase their profits, end up producing and consuming a quantity that is efficient. In this chapter, we define what economists mean by efficient and we show why, in what sense, and under what circumstances, the quantity produced and consumed is efficient.

We also show how economists measure the economic gains from producing and consuming the efficient quantity and the economic loss from producing and consuming more or less than that quantity. These measures are used every day to evaluate the impact of different government policies, such as a tax on gasoline, a subsidy for research and development, a free trade agreement, or a restriction on peanuts or sugar production.

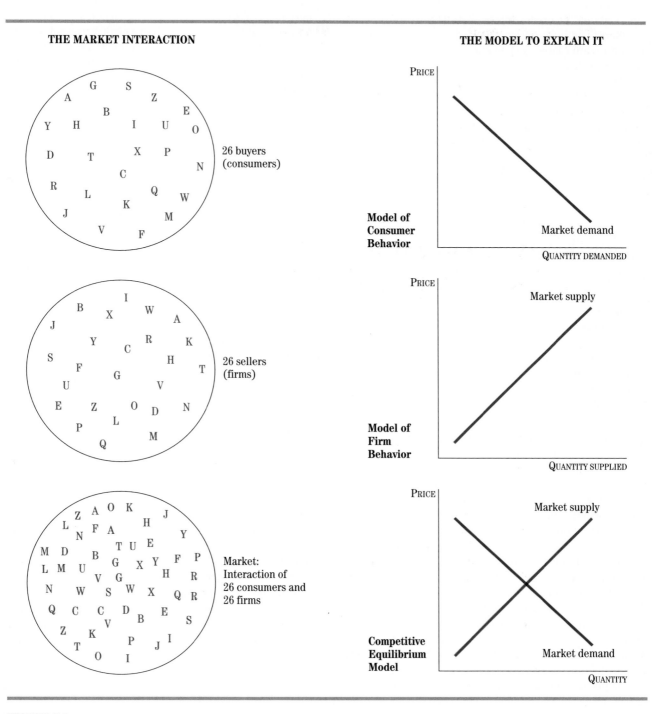

FIGURE 7.1

The Market Interaction and the Model to Explain It

In this chapter we explain how individual buyers and sellers interact in a market (on the left) by combining the model of the behavior of consumers (Chapter 5) with the model of the behavior of firms (Chapter 6) to get a model of competitive equilibrium (Chapter 7).

Although this chapter focuses on markets, it has implications for organizations that we will study in later chapters. The information requirements for efficient production within large organizations are daunting, pointing to another advantage of a market system where no one needs to have complete information and where prices—determined freely by the interaction of buyers and sellers—signal all the information that people need to know. However, using prices to coordinate activity within organizations is sometimes difficult, as we will see.

competitive equilibrium model: a model that assumes utility maximization on the part of consumers and profit maximization on the part of firms, along with competitive markets and freely determined prices.

invisible hand: the idea that the free interaction of people in a market economy leads to a desirable social outcome; the term was coined by Adam Smith.

DETERMINING PRODUCTION, CONSUMPTION, AND PRICE IN A MARKET

To begin the analysis of economic interaction, consider an example of consumers and producers of the same commodity: long-stem roses. Maria and Ken are two of many potential rose consumers who are deciding how many roses to buy. Both are willing to pay a certain amount for roses but not necessarily the same amount. Hugo and Mimi are two of many rose producers who are deciding how many roses to produce in their gardens. Both have marginal costs for producing roses but not necessarily the same marginal costs.

The Hard Way to Process Information, Coordinate, and Motivate

The rose decisions of Maria, Ken, Hugo, Mimi, and all the others in the market clearly interact with each other. For example, an increase in Hugo's marginal costs—perhaps because of an extra rose-processing expense to ward off a new insect—will probably reduce the amount of roses he decides to produce; this means either less rose consumption for Ken, Maria, and other consumers, or it means more rose production for Mimi and other producers. Similarly, if Ken decides to purchase more roses, someone else must decide to decrease consumption or increase production. How are all these decisions worked out? What *information* is needed to determine whether it is better for Mimi's garden to produce more or for Hugo's garden to produce more? What *coordinates* a change in consumption or production by one person with an offsetting change in consumption or production by other people? What *motivates* some people to consume less and others to produce more if one person decides to consume more?

Suppose you had to work this out. To make your job easier, suppose that Maria, Ken, Hugo, and Mimi were the whole world as far as roses go. If you and they were all in one place together, you might imagine conducting their consumption and production activities like the leader of a marching band would conduct the band members. You raise your baton toward Maria to signal more consumption;

you shake your head at Ken to signal less consumption; you point your finger at Hugo to signal more production; you turn your back on Mimi to signal no change in production; you blow your whistle to signal when to begin consuming and producing.

To provide motivation, you might change your facial expression when you look at Maria; a frown or perhaps a smile may help to motivate her to purchase more roses. Your choice of which finger to point at Hugo may affect his motivation, and the shrill of your whistle might serve to motivate them all to do what you say.

To do your job right, you will also need to have information about rose production for Mimi's and Hugo's gardens. For example, to know whether it is appropriate to point your finger at Hugo and turn your back on Mimi, you need to know which garden has lower marginal costs of rose production.

If this is not already beginning to sound ridiculously impossible, remember that if you had this job in the real world, you would have to coordinate, motivate, and know intimately millions of consumers and producers. This is an amazingly complex job even for this single, relatively simple commodity.

The Easy Way to Process Information, Coordinate, and Motivate

Fortunately, you do not need to worry about being called on to do such an impossible task. There is a remarkable device that does the information processing, coordinating, and motivating for us. No one person invented this device; it evolved slowly over thousands of years and is probably still evolving. It is called *the market* or, in this case, the long-stem-rose market. Of course, like many markets, the rose market does not take place in any one location. It consists of all the florists, street carts, or farmers' markets where roses are sold and all the gardens or greenhouses where roses are grown, whether in the United States, Europe, Latin America, Africa, Australia, or Asia. Fortunately, a market can serve as an information-processing, coordinating, and motivating device even if it does not take place at any one location. Buyers and sellers never have to see one another.

How does the market work? What will be the total quantity of roses consumed? Who will consume what amount? What will be the total quantity of roses produced? Which garden will produce what amount? Let us see how economists answer these questions about how people interact in a market.

The Competitive Equilibrium Model

Economists use the individual demand curves and the individual supply curves derived in the previous two chapters to describe what happens when consumers and firms interact in a market.

Recall that each of these individual demand curves depends on the marginal benefit—the willingness to pay for additional consumption—the individual gets from consuming the goods. Together these marginal benefits create a market demand curve for roses. The demand curve shows how much these consumers in total are willing to buy at each price.

Recall also that individual supply curves depend on the marginal costs of the firms. Together their marginal costs create a market supply curve of roses. The supply curve shows the total quantity supplied by all these firms at each price.

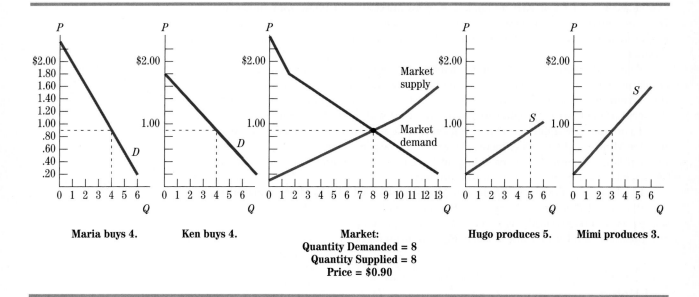

| Maria buys 4. | Ken buys 4. | Market:
Quantity Demanded = 8
Quantity Supplied = 8
Price = $0.90 | Hugo produces 5. | Mimi produces 3. |

FIGURE 7.2

Price and Quantity Determination

The market demand curve is the sum of the individual demand curves of the consumers in the market. The market supply curve is the sum of the individual supply curves for the producers. When quantity demanded equals quantity supplied, the two curves intersect. The equilibrium price and quantity will be given by this intersection. The individual consumer decisions can then be read off the individual supply and demand curves at those prices.

The resulting market demand and supply curves are shown in the center of Figure 7.2, flanked by Maria and Ken's individual demand curves and by Hugo and Mimi's individual supply curves. Note that we have used the same units for the quantity supplied and the quantity demanded in Figure 7.2; the price (*P*, measured in dollars per rose) is on the vertical axis and the quantity (*Q*, the number of roses) is on the horizontal axis. We continue to assume that Ken, Mimi, Hugo, and Maria are the whole market so that we can show the market in one diagram. A competitive market would typically require more buyers and sellers.

We have seen supply and demand curves like those in the center of Figure 7.2 before in Chapter 3. But now—after Chapters 5 and 6—we know much more about what the demand and supply curves mean. The model of consumer behavior and the model of firm behavior developed in Chapters 5 and 6 are now seen as underlying the supply and demand model. In order to emphasize that the supply and demand model incorporates utility-maximizing consumers and profit-maximizing firms in competitive markets, we refer to it as the *competitive equilibrium model.* The competitive equilibrium model, as we have said, is simply the supply and demand model with the behavior of consumers and firms made explicit. Because the competitive equilibrium model has more to it than the supply and demand model, we can do more with it.

Individual Production and Consumption Decisions

A key prediction of the competitive equilibrium model is that a price will emerge from the interaction of people in the market such that the quantity supplied *equals* the quantity demanded. This is the *equilibrium price.* Graphically, the price is given at the point of intersection of the market supply curve and the market demand curve; here the quantity supplied in the market equals the quantity demanded in the market. For the example shown in Figure 7.2, the equilibrium price is $.90 a rose.

equilibrium price: the price at which quantity supplied equals quantity demanded. (Ch. 3)

Once we determine the price in this way, the supply and demand curves tell us how much in total will be consumed and produced at that price. We look at the market demand curve and see how much is demanded at that price, and we look at the market supply curve and see how much is supplied at that price. Because the curves intersect at the market price, the quantity demanded and the quantity supplied are the same. They are at the point on the horizontal axis directly below the intersection. As shown in Figure 7.2, the quantity bought and sold is 8 roses.

Thus far, we have not done anything more with the competitive equilibrium model than we did with the supply and demand model. But now, armed with the price, we can go to the individual demand curves to see how much Maria and Ken will buy. Look to the left in Figure 7.2 to find the quantity demanded by Maria and Ken when the price is $.90 a rose. They each buy 4 roses. Maria and Ken are motivated to buy this amount—without any central coordinator—because, at $.90 a rose, they maximize their respective utilities by consuming this amount. Observe that Maria and Ken do not have the same individual demand curves. Nevertheless, the quantity demanded by each can still be determined from their demand curve, as shown in Figure 7.2.

The individual supply curves tell us how much Hugo and Mimi will produce. Look to the right in Figure 7.2 to see how much Hugo and Mimi produce when the price is $.90 a rose. Hugo produces 5 roses, and Mimi produces 3 roses. Hugo and Mimi are motivated to produce this amount—again without any central coordinator—because, at $.90 a rose, they maximize their profits by producing this amount.

In sum, the competitive equilibrium model, which includes the behavior of the consumers and the firms, predicts the price, the quantity consumed by each person, and the quantity produced by each firm. It also predicts a certain marginal benefit of consumption for each consumer and a certain marginal cost for each producer. Hence, the model provides answers to all the questions posed earlier.

Price Adjustment to the Equilibrium Price: Theory and Reality

As shown in Figure 7.2, if the price is higher than the predicted market price at the intersection of the supply curve and the demand curve, then the quantity supplied is greater than the quantity demanded; we say there is a *surplus*. Lowering the price will decrease the quantity supplied and increase quantity demanded until the surplus disappears. However, if the price is lower than the predicted market price, then the quantity demanded is greater than the quantity supplied; we say there is a *shortage*. Raising the price will decrease the quantity demanded and increase the quantity supplied until the shortage disappears. Thus, if the price falls when there is a surplus and rises when there is a shortage, the price will converge to the equilibrium price.

Although this description of the price adjusting up or down to reach an equilibrium between the quantity supplied and the quantity demanded has some intuitive appeal, it is not, taken literally, an accurate description of actual markets. In most markets, no one can even observe the supply and demand curves, let alone raise and lower the market price according to whether there is a surplus or a shortage of the commodity. No one looks over the rose market in that way, adjusting the price to balance out supply and demand. No one looks over the cotton market, the computer market, or most other markets. Instead, many individuals post prices or make bids to buy or give discounts, etc. Thus, the competitive equilibrium model cannot be taken as a literal description of how markets operate. The model's validity and usefulness depend on how well it performs in predicting the prices and quantities in

Be sure to distinguish between *surplus* and *consumer surplus* or *producer surplus:*

surplus: the situation in which quantity supplied is greater than quantity demanded. (Ch. 3)

consumer surplus: the difference between what a person is willing to pay for an additional unit of a good —the marginal benefit—and the market price of the good. (Ch. 5)

producer surplus: the difference between the price received by a firm for an additional item sold and the marginal cost of the item's production. (Ch. 6)

markets where real people interact buying and selling goods and services. We consider the model's validity in the next section.

Review

▶ Centrally coordinating and motivating the thousands of consumers and producers of any good would be an amazingly complex task requiring a vast amount of information.

▶ The market is a device that provides information and coordinates and motivates consumers and producers in a decentralized way. The market does this job in a way that no one individual can.

▶ Economists describe the interactions of people in the market through the competitive equilibrium model. According to the model, the equilibrium price and total quantity are given by the intersection of the market supply and demand curves; individual decisions about consumption and production are given through the individual demand and supply curves, which are based on utility maximization and profit maximization.

A CASE STUDY: SETTING UP A MARKET

How well does the competitive equilibrium model work in explaining the amount individual firms produce and the amount people consume? One answer to this question comes from observing markets in which one can see exactly what all the buyers and sellers do. Because it is difficult, if not impossible, to observe all the participants in actual markets, economists have set up experimental markets for this purpose. Traditionally, economics has not been a lab science, but new techniques are emerging that allow the principles of economics to be studied in labs much as they operate in the real world. Observing or participating in simple experiments can also improve one's understanding of economics. In this section we describe how experimental markets are used to test models like the competitive equilibrium model. To do so we need to show how an experimental market is set up.

A Double-Auction Market

double-auction market: a market in which several buyers and several sellers state prices at which they are willing to buy or sell a good.

The simplest kind of market that demonstrates how many markets work is one in which several buyers and several sellers make offers to buy or sell a commodity. Such markets are called **double-auction markets.** In many auctions—the kind you probably have seen at the county fair or on television, where cattle or art are sold—only the buyers call out bids. An auctioneer repeats the bids at rapid speeds and listens for higher bids. The highest bid gets the good.

A double auction works differently. *Both* buyers and sellers call out prices. Buyers bid a certain price for items they want to buy, and sellers ask a certain price for items they want to sell. The price the buyers call out is called a **bid,** and the price the sellers call out is called an **ask.** A market manager keeps track of the bids and asks. For example, the buyers and sellers may be a group of student volunteers. Four or five buyers and four or five sellers are enough to make the market work, but many more can also participate. One of the students, or perhaps the person conducting the market experiment, may be the market manager in charge of keeping track of the bids and asks to buy and sell.

bid: the price that buyers say they are willing to pay for a good in an auction market.

ask: the price that sellers say they are willing to sell a good for in an auction market.

Many real-world markets are double-auction markets. For example, the New York Stock Exchange and the exchanges in Chicago trading farm commodities, metals, and various financial securities are double-auction markets. In Chicago, traders in trading pits call out bids and asks to buy and sell. Sometimes these double-auction markets are called "open outcry" markets.

Trading Periods

All bids, asks, and transactions in a double-auction market take place during *trading periods*. At the start of the trading period the market opens; at the end of the trading period the market closes. A trading period is six and a half hours on the New York Stock Exchange, but not that much time is needed for a demonstration market. Ten minutes may be enough time.

As soon as the market opens, buyers can bid and sellers can ask certain prices. All the buyers and sellers are close enough to hear the bids and asks, or at least see the bids and asks recorded and displayed by the market manager. A transaction takes place any time a buyer accepts a price a seller asks or a seller accepts a price a buyer bids.

In order to make this demonstration market work like markets found to operate throughout the world, the buyers and sellers must be given an incentive to take their actions seriously. Both buyers and sellers earn a reward depending on how well they do in the market. Buyers' rewards are like a marginal benefit schedule (that is, an individual demand curve) described in Chapter 5. Sellers' rewards are like a marginal cost schedule (that is, a firm supply curve) described in Chapter 6. Small sheets of paper describing these marginal benefits and marginal costs are given to the buyers and sellers who participate in the market. An example of both a seller's marginal cost sheet and a buyer's marginal benefit sheet is shown in Table 7.1. The incentive to supply and demand goods according to these schedules comes from the opportunity to earn cash, as described next.

Buyers

During each trading period, buyers may purchase any number of items but can only bid for one unit at a time. For each item successfully purchased, the buyer receives the amount listed on the sheet under the column marked "marginal benefit." Thus, the buyer's personal gain on each item purchased is the difference between the marginal benefit of that item and the amount paid for it. Notice that a motivated buyer would want to get the lowest price possible. Other buyers will be competing to do the same thing. It would not be wise for a buyer to buy an item for more than the marginal benefit because that would result in a loss.

For example, suppose you have the buyer's sheet shown in Table 7.1 and you buy two items. The marginal benefit from the first item is \$25 and the marginal benefit from the second item is \$20. If you pay \$15 for the first item and \$10 for the second item, then your total gain is (\$25 − \$15) + (\$20 − \$10) = \$20.

Sellers

During each trading period, sellers are free to sell any number of items but can only ask a price for one item at a time. Each item sold costs the amount listed on the sheet under the column marked "marginal cost." The seller's personal gain on each item sold is the difference between the price the item sold for and the marginal cost

TABLE 7.1

Marginal Benefit and Marginal Cost for a Demonstration Market

Example Buyer Sheet

Number of Items	Marginal Benefit (dollars)
1	25
2	20
3	15
4	10
5	5

Example Seller Sheet

Number of Items	Marginal Cost (dollars)
1	1
2	6
3	11
4	16
5	21

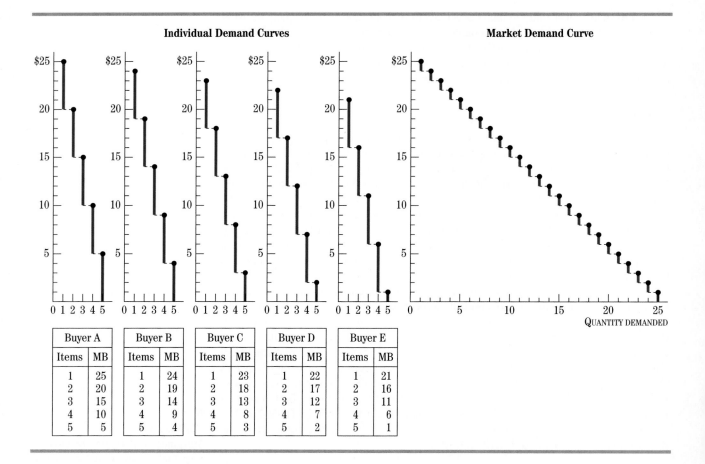

Individual Demand Curves

Market Demand Curve

Buyer A		Buyer B		Buyer C		Buyer D		Buyer E	
Items	MB	Items	MB	Items	MB	Items	MB	Items	MB
1	25	1	24	1	23	1	22	1	21
2	20	2	19	2	18	2	17	2	16
3	15	3	14	3	13	3	12	3	11
4	10	4	9	4	8	4	7	4	6
5	5	5	4	5	3	5	2	5	1

FIGURE 7.3
Information About the Demand Side of the Demonstration Market
There are five buyers in the market. The marginal benefits (*MB*) of each buyer are shown on each buyer's sheet. The corresponding individual demand curve is above the sheet. The market demand curve is shown on the right. It is the sum of all the items demanded at each price. No buyer in the demonstration market gets to see the other buyers' marginal benefits or the market demand curve.

of the item. Notice that a seller is motivated to get the highest price but is competing with other sellers who may be asking lower prices. It would not be wise for a seller to accept a price lower than the marginal cost, because that would result in a loss.

For example, suppose you have the seller's sheet shown in Table 7.1 and you sell two items. The marginal cost of the first item is $1 and the marginal cost of the second item is $6. If you sell the first item for $15 and the second item for $10, your gain is ($15 − $1) + ($10 − $6) = $18.

Trading Rules

The rules are simple. (1) Any new bid must be higher than an outstanding bid. (2) Any new ask must be lower than an outstanding ask. (3) Buyers or sellers are not to reveal their private information about their marginal benefits or their marginal costs.

Predictions of the Competitive Equilibrium Model

Observe that the stage is now set for a market. Buyers are motivated; sellers are motivated. Buyers and sellers can hear or see all the bids and asks. Now what would you predict would happen in this market? Does the outcome depend on the personalities, culture, or intelligence of the buyers and sellers? Does the competitive equilibrium model of consumers (buyers) and firms (sellers) predict the outcome?

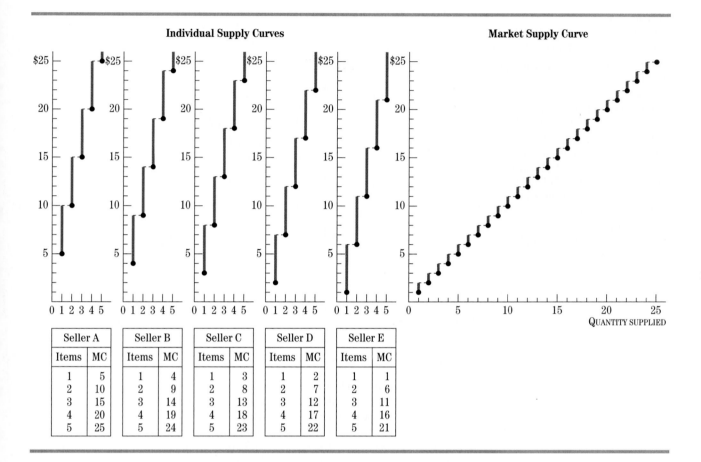

Individual Supply Curves

Market Supply Curve

QUANTITY SUPPLIED

Seller A		Seller B		Seller C		Seller D		Seller E	
Items	MC	Items	MC	Items	MC	Items	MC	Items	MC
1	5	1	4	1	3	1	2	1	1
2	10	2	9	2	8	2	7	2	6
3	15	3	14	3	13	3	12	3	11
4	20	4	19	4	18	4	17	4	16
5	25	5	24	5	23	5	22	5	21

Figures 7.3, 7.4, and 7.5 show the information about this market. The marginal benefits for the buyers, marginal costs for the sellers, the individual demand curves, the individual supply curves, and the market supply and demand curves are shown. On the bottom of Figure 7.3 are the marginal benefit sheets of the buyers. Each buyer has one sheet. The graph above each sheet is the individual demand curve, derived from the sheet, using the methods of Chapter 5. The market demand curve appears on the right. Figure 7.4 shows comparable information for the sellers. There are marginal costs and upward-sloping individual supply curves. The market supply curve is on the right.

Individual buyers and sellers in the market have information only about their own marginal costs or marginal benefits. They do not see what you see in Figures 7.3 and 7.4. In real markets, this is *imperfect information:* People know about their own preferences or their own costs, but typically they do not know about anyone else's. Information is similarly imperfect in this double-auction market.

Figure 7.5 shows the prediction of the competitive equilibrium model about the price and the quantity that will come out of this market. The demand curve of Figure 7.3 is combined with the supply curve of Figure 7.4. The two curves intersect at a price of $13 and a quantity of 13 items. In other words, the model predicts that when these 10 people interact in the market, the sellers will sell a total of 13 units, the buyers will buy a total of 13 units, and the market price will be $13. Is the prediction correct?

FIGURE 7.4
Information About the Supply Side of the Demonstration Market
There are five sellers in the market. The marginal costs (*MC*) of each seller are shown on each seller's sheet. The corresponding individual supply curve is shown above each sheet. The market supply curve is shown on the right. It is the sum of all items supplied at each price.

FIGURE 7.5
Predicted Price and Quantity in the Demonstration Market
The competitive equilibrium model predicts that the price and quantity traded will be at the intersection of the market supply and demand curves, as shown in the figure. The market demand curve is from Figure 7.3, and the market supply curve is from Figure 7.4. The predicted market price is $13 and the predicted quantity traded is 13 units. Neither buyers nor sellers in the demonstration market know about these market supply and demand curves.

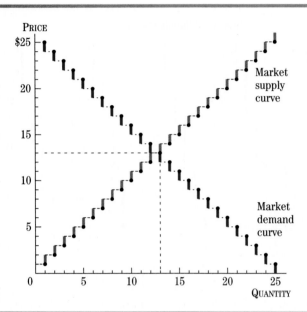

Results

The most convincing and memorable way to answer this question is to watch or to participate in an experimental demonstration market. One would want to use different marginal cost and marginal benefit sheets than those in Figures 7.3 and 7.4 so that market participants do not know the outcome. However, because the experiment has been tried many times before, we can simply examine what the results of such an experiment usually look like. First, after one or two trading periods, the price will settle down to about $13. Sometimes it will be $12 or $14, but rarely does it deviate much from $13. Second, after one or two trading periods, the quantity traded will be very close to 13 units. Again, sometimes it will be slightly more or slightly less.

In other words, the model as shown in Figure 7.5 comes very close to predicting the outcome of the double-auction market. Of course, if you gave different marginal costs or marginal benefits to the buyers and sellers, you would have different supply and demand curves and therefore get different answers, but the answers would be very close to those predicted by the model. Even though no one individual sets the price—the buyers and sellers are calling out prices in intense competition—the price settles down to the price predicted by the model.

In fact, experimental economists such as Vernon Smith at the University of Arizona and Charles Plott of the California Institute of Technology have found that the model works surprisingly well in predicting the outcome of these experiments. The finding that the model predicts so well for a very small number of buyers and sellers who have so little information about supply and demand in the market has been called a "scientific mystery" by Vernon Smith.[1]

Surprise or not, the double-auction market demonstrates both how a market works and how a model works at predicting the outcome of the market. In the next

1. Vernon L. Smith, "Microeconomic Systems as an Experimental Science," *American Economic Review,* Vol. 72, 1982.

few sections of this chapter, we use this model to measure the gains from trading in the market system. That the model works well in such experiments gives us more confidence in using it for these purposes.

To be sure, even though experiments are set up to mimic the operation of actual markets, they are still done in a laboratory setting. Market participants in the real world may be more or less sophisticated than those in the experiments, and the rules—if there are any—may be more complex in the real world. Thus, even though the experimental confirmation of the model is reassuring, we must remember that it is a model, not reality.

Price Discovery and Price-Taking

It is fascinating to watch how prices are determined in the double-auction market with a small number of sellers. Although individual buyers and sellers can call out prices, the market effectively finds the price. The process through which the double-auction market finds a price is called **price discovery,** and it is an important function of real-world markets.

Recall in Chapter 6 that we said a competitive market is one where there are enough sellers so that no one seller can affect the price. All sellers are *price-takers* in a competitive market. In the double-auction market with only five sellers, it is difficult for any one seller to sell a product at a price above the market price. Competition from only four other sellers keeps each seller in line. Thus, the price-taking assumption is surprisingly accurate. Competition also keeps the buyers in line. Any one buyer will find it difficult to hold out for a very low price when other buyers are competing to buy the product.

price discovery: the process by which a market finds the equilibrium market price.

Other Types of Market Experiments

Not all real-world markets are like the double-auction market. To mimic these other markets, the experiments can be modified. For example, in many markets, firms post their prices in store windows, in catalogues, or on menus rather than calling them out like the sellers in the double auction. More sophisticated market experiments in which buyers and sellers post prices rather than call them out indicate that this type of pricing behavior leads to outcomes somewhat different from those just described. Prices do not adjust as rapidly, and, therefore, the equilibrium quantity may be slightly different from that implied by the competitive equilibrium model. But even in posted price markets, experiments show that the market price converges to near the price predicted by the competitive equilibrium model.

Review

▶ Experiments can be used to test economic theories and to demonstrate how markets work.

▶ The double-auction market is a good type of market for experiments. Many real-world markets are double-auction markets, and others have similar characteristics.

▶ The competitive equilibrium model works remarkably well to predict the outcomes from these markets. The price and quantity sold are usually very close to those predicted by the model.

ARE COMPETITIVE MARKETS EFFICIENT?

We have shown how a market works and how to use the competitive equilibrium model. Now let's use the competitive equilibrium model to see how *well* the market works. Are the quantities produced and consumed in the market efficient?

The Meaning of Efficient

In general an inefficient outcome is one that wastes scarce resources, and an efficient outcome is one that does not waste scarce resources. Extremely inefficient economic outcomes are easy to spot. Constructing 250 million new video rental stores each year in the United States (or approximately one store per person) would obviously be wasteful. The workers building the new stores could be building other things that people wanted. If the U.S. economy produced such an outcome, everyone would say it was inefficient; shifting production to fewer video rental stores would clearly make many people better off.

An equally inefficient situation would occur if only one new video rental store a year was built; at that rate it would take more than 2,000 years to build the number of Blockbuster video rental stores that now exist in the United States. In such a situation, shifting production toward more video rental stores would clearly make many people better off.

Both these situations are inefficient because a change in production could make people better off. We might, therefore, define an efficient outcome as one that is so good that there is no change that would make people better off.

The Need for a More Precise Definition

However, because the economy consists of many different people, we need to be more careful in defining efficiency. For *every* economic outcome, it is possible to make someone better off at the expense of someone else. For example, suppose in the demonstration market described earlier that the market trading period ends in a situation in which buyer A gets 3 items and buyer C gets 2 items. If we take an item from buyer A and give it to buyer C, the benefits for buyer C would increase. However, the benefits of the good to buyer A would decrease. That such a transfer is possible does not indicate that the outcome of the market is wasteful or inefficient. More generally, the possibility of transferring a good from one person to another, thereby making someone better off at the expense of another, is not an indication that an economic situation is inefficient or wasteful.

However, if it were possible to change consumption or production in a way that would make someone better off *without* hurting someone else, then the initial situation would be inefficient. In such a situation resources are being wasted, because someone, perhaps many people, could have a better life without someone else being harmed.

Based on such considerations, economists have developed the following definition: An *efficient* outcome is one for which it is not possible to make someone better off without hurting someone else. This definition of an efficient outcome is called **Pareto efficiency,** after the Italian economist Vilfredo Pareto, who developed the idea.

Pareto efficiency: a situation in which it is not possible to make someone better off without making someone else worse off.

Three Conditions for Efficient Economic Outcomes

There are three conditions that must hold if an economic outcome is to be efficient.

First, *the marginal benefit (MB) must equal the marginal cost (MC) of the last item produced.* That is,

$$MB = MC$$

Why is this condition needed for efficiency? Suppose it did not hold. If the marginal cost is greater than the marginal benefit, then too much is being produced. In the example of producing 250 million video rental stores a year, the marginal cost is much greater than the marginal benefit of producing the 250 millionth video rental store. Reducing production (by a lot) would be appropriate. If the marginal cost is less than the marginal benefit of the product, then too little is being produced. In the example of producing only one video rental store a year, the marginal cost is certainly much less than the marginal benefit; more production would be appropriate. Only when marginal benefit is equal to marginal cost is the economic outcome efficient. This must occur for all goods from video rental stores to roses.

One way to better appreciate this condition is to imagine that you grew your own roses in your own garden. Clearly you would never produce more roses if the marginal cost to you was greater than the marginal benefit to you. But you would produce more roses if your marginal benefit of more roses was greater than your marginal cost. Only when marginal benefit equals marginal cost would you stop producing and consuming more.

The second condition for efficiency relates to the production of goods at different firms. It is that *the marginal cost of a good should be equal for every producer.* Again, if this were not the case then production could be increased without cost. For example, if Hugo's rose garden could produce an extra dozen roses at a marginal cost of $10 and Mimi's garden could produce an extra dozen roses at a marginal cost of $50, then it would make sense for Hugo's garden to increase production and for Mimi's garden to decrease production. Mimi could take the $50 she saved by producing less and have more than enough to pay Hugo's costs of producing an extra dozen. Only when the marginal costs are the same is there no way to increase production without cost. Note that it is not necessary for Hugo or Mimi or any other producer to be the same or even to have the same total costs; all that we require for efficiency is that the *marginal* costs be the same.

The third condition for efficiency relates to the allocation of goods to different consumers. It is that *the marginal benefit of consuming the same good should be equal for all consumers.* If the marginal benefits were not equal then there could be a gain for some people with no loss for anyone else. For example, suppose Ken's marginal benefit of roses was $3 and Maria's was $1; then if Maria sold roses to Ken for $2 both would be better off. But if their marginal benefits were the same then no improvement for one without harming the other would be possible.

In sum there are three conditions for efficiency: (1) the marginal benefit equals the marginal cost for the last item produced; (2) the marginal cost of producing each good is equal for all producers; and (3) the marginal benefit from consuming each good is equal for all consumers.

Is the Market Efficient?

Given the three conditions for efficiency, can we say that the market is efficient? The competitive equilibrium model provides us with a quick answer to that question.

According to the model of consumer behavior in Chapter 5, an individual consumer chooses a quantity of a good such that *price equals marginal benefit* that is, $P = MB$. This equality holds for every consumer at every point on the market demand curve. Remember that the marginal benefit is the willingness to pay dollars to consume an additional amount of a good. According to the model of firm behavior in Chapter 6, a firm produces a quantity of a good such that *price equals marginal cost.* That is, $P = MC$. This equality holds for every firm at every point on the market supply curve. At a point of intersection of the supply curve and the demand curve, both of these conditions must hold because the point of intersection is on both the supply curve and the demand curve. That is, $P = MB$ and $P = MC$ simultaneously. This implies that at the quantity produced by the market, *marginal benefit equals marginal cost.* That is $MB = MC$. This is true of every good.

Thus we have proven that a competitive market satisfies the first condition of efficiency. The marginal cost of producing roses, grapes, bread, peanuts, or automobiles is equal to the marginal benefit that people get from consuming them. This occurs without any person coordinating consumers and producers. Producing more or less of the item will only lead to a violation of this key equality between marginal cost and marginal benefit.

To better appreciate the result, again imagine that you grew your own roses in your own garden. Clearly, you would never grow more roses if the marginal benefit to you was less than your marginal cost. What is striking is that when you do not grow your own roses or even when you do not know anything about growing roses, the marginal benefit of more roses to you will be equal to the marginal cost of producing more roses.

The result is illustrated in Figure 7.6. At the market equilibrium quantity (point E), the marginal cost (the point on the supply curve) is equal to marginal benefit (the point on the demand curve). At any other point either marginal benefit will be greater than marginal cost or marginal benefit will be less than marginal cost.

The other two criteria for efficiency also hold in a competitive market. To see this, observe that in a market equilibrium the marginal cost for the producers is the same, because *they all face the same price;* along each of their individual supply curves they set marginal cost equal to the price. Similarly, in a market equilibrium, *all consumers*—Maria, Ken, and others—*face the same market price.* Hence, their marginal benefits are all equal, because on each of their individual demand curves the marginal benefit equals the price. Thus, it is not possible to make one person better off without hurting someone else. In a competitive market, the marginal benefits are equal. Thus, there is no improvement for one that does not hurt someone else.

In sum, for each good produced in a competitive market, (1) the marginal benefit equals the marginal cost of the last item produced; (2) the marginal cost is equal for all producers in the market, and (3) the marginal benefit is equal for all consumers in the market. Thus, we can say that the competitive market is Pareto efficient.

The proposition that competitive markets are efficient is one of the most important in economics, so much so that when proven with the mathematics necessary to keep track of many different goods and time periods, it is called the **first theorem of welfare economics.** The word *theorem* reflects the mathematics used in the advanced proof of the idea. The word *welfare* means that the theorem is about the overall well-being of people in the economy (the word *welfare* is synonymous with "well-being," not with a transfer payment to a poor person). The word *first* is used to distinguish this theorem from the second theorem of welfare economics, which states the converse of the first: Any Pareto efficient outcome can be obtained via a competitive market.

first theorem of welfare economics: the conclusion that a competitive market results in an efficient outcome; sometimes called the "invisible hand theorem"; the definition of efficiency used in the theorem is Pareto efficiency.

Efficiency and Income Inequality

Efficiency is one goal of an economic system, but it is not the only one. Another goal is that no one, or at least as few people as possible, ought to fall into dire economic circumstances. For example, reducing **income inequality** to an amount that makes poverty a rare occurrence is also a desirable goal in most economic systems.

income inequality: disparity in levels of income among individuals in the economy.

It is important to emphasize that efficiency and income equality are not the same thing. An allocation of bread between Hugo and Mimi is efficient if their marginal benefit of bread is the same and if the marginal benefits equal the marginal cost of bread. Then there is no mutually advantageous trade of bread between Hugo and Mimi that will make one better off without hurting the other.

However, suppose that Hugo has a low income, earning only $7,000 per year, and that Mimi has a high income, earning $70,000 per year. Suppose a severe drought raises the price of wheat and thus the price of bread. If the price of bread in the market gets very high, say $3 a loaf, then Hugo will be able to buy few loaves of bread and may go hungry, especially if he has a family. In this case, the economy gets good marks on efficiency grounds but fails miserably on income inequality grounds.

To remedy the situation, a common suggestion is to put price controls on bread. For example, to help Hugo and other less fortunate individuals, a law might be passed that bread prices cannot exceed $.50 a loaf. Although this may help the income inequality problem, it will unfortunately cause great inefficiency because it interferes with the market. At $.50 a loaf, bread producers will not produce very much, and Mimi will probably start buying bread to feed the birds, wasting scarce resources.

A better solution to the income inequality problem is to transfer income to Hugo and other low-income people from Mimi and other high-income people. With a transfer of income—say, through a tax and an income-support payment to the poor—the market would be able to function and the gross inefficiencies of price controls on bread would not occur. Even at the high price of bread, Hugo will be able to eat, perhaps buying some rice or a bread substitute. Then the bread, which is so expensive to produce, would not be wasted on the birds. Transfers of income are studied in more detail in Chapter 15 of this book.

FIGURE 7.6
The Efficiency of the Market: Marginal Benefit Equals Marginal Cost
Only at quantity *E* is the marginal benefit of an extra unit equal to the marginal cost of an extra unit. Point *D* is not efficient because the marginal benefit of an extra unit is greater than the marginal cost of producing it. Part *F* is also not efficient because the marginal cost of producing an extra unit is greater than the marginal benefit.

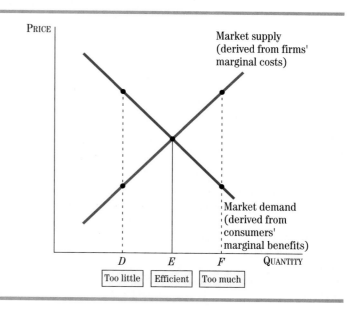

We will see that such transfers have advantages and disadvantages. Compared to price controls, their main advantage is that the market is allowed to operate efficiently.

The temptation to deal with income inequality problems in ways that interfere with the efficiency of the market is great in all societies. Price ceilings (rent controls) on rental apartments in some U.S. cities are one example, which we examined in Chapter 3. But this interference wastes economic resources.

Review

▶ Economic inefficiency implies a waste of resources. An efficient outcome is one in which no person's situation can be improved without hurting someone else. A key criterion for economic efficiency is that production and consumption be such that the marginal benefit of a good equals its marginal cost.

▶ One of the most desirable features of competitive markets is that at the equilibrium level of production, marginal benefit equals marginal cost. On the demand curve, marginal benefit equals the market price. On the supply curve, marginal cost equals the market price. Because the quantity demanded equals the quantity supplied in equilibrium, together these imply that marginal benefit equals marginal cost.

▶ Thus competitive markets are efficient. Any change in consumption or production that makes one person better off must make someone else worse off.

▶ Efficiency is not the same thing as income equality. An efficient outcome can coexist with an unequal outcome.

MEASURING WASTE FROM INEFFICIENCY

We know from Chapters 5 and 6 that consumer surplus and producer surplus are measures of how much consumers and producers gain from buying and selling in a market. The larger these two surpluses are, the better off people are in the society. The amount of consumer surplus plus producer surplus is a measure of economic well-being.

Maximizing the Sum of Producer Plus Consumer Surplus

Another way to think about the lightly shaded areas in the graphs The sum of consumer surplus plus producer surplus is the triangular area between the demand curve and the supply curve—shown by the lightly shaded area in the middle graph of Figure 7.7. The graph shows another way to think about this sum: The sum of consumer surplus plus producer surplus equals the marginal benefit minus the marginal cost of all the items produced.

An attractive feature of competitive markets is that they maximize the sum of consumer and producer surplus. Producer and consumer surplus are shown with the market supply and market demand diagram in Figure 7.7. Recall that the producer surplus for all producers is the area above the supply curve and below the market price line. The consumer surplus for all consumers is the area below the demand curve and above the market price line. Both the consumer surplus and the producer surplus are shown in Figure 7.7. The equilibrium quantity is at the intersection of the two curves. At this point consumer surplus plus producer surplus is maximized.

Deadweight Loss

Figure 7.7 also shows what happens to consumer surplus plus producer surplus when the efficient level of production does not occur. The top panel of Figure 7.7

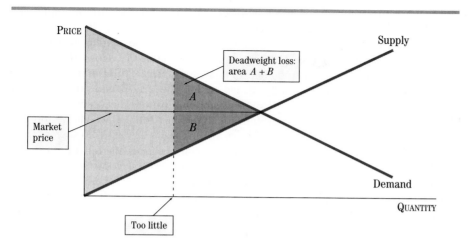

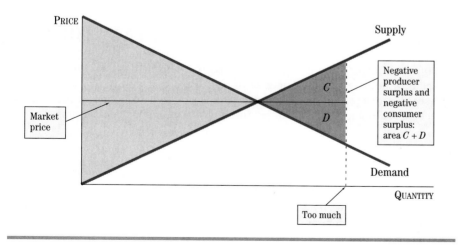

FIGURE 7.7
Measuring Economic Loss
When production is less or more than the market equilibrium amount, the economic loss is measured by the loss of consumer surplus plus producer surplus. In the top diagram, production is too small. In the bottom diagram, it is too large. In the middle diagram, it is efficient.

shows a situation where production is lower than the market equilibrium quantity, and clearly the sum of consumer and producer surplus is lower. By producing a smaller amount, we lose some of the consumer and producer surplus in the darkly shaded triangular area $A + B$. The bottom panel of Figure 7.7 shows the opposite situation, where production is too high. In this case, we have to subtract out the triangular area $C + D$ from the lightly shaded area on the left because price is greater than marginal benefit and lower than marginal cost, which means that consumer surplus and producer surplus are negative in the area $C + D$. In both the top and bottom panels of the figure, these darkly shaded triangles are a loss to society from producing more or less than the efficient amount. Economists call this loss the **deadweight loss.** It is a measure of the waste from inefficient production.

deadweight loss: the loss in producer and consumer surplus due to an inefficient level of production.

Deadweight loss is not simply a theoretical curiosity with a gruesome name; it is used by economists to measure the size of the waste to society of deviations from the competitive equilibrium. By calculating deadweight loss, economists can estimate the benefits and costs of many government programs. When you hear or read that the cost of U.S. agricultural programs is billions of dollars or that the benefit of a world-trade agreement is trillions of dollars, it is the increase or decrease in deadweight loss that is being referred to. (See the box on the opposite page.) In order to compute the deadweight loss all we need is the demand curve and the supply curve.

Review

▶ Competitive markets maximize producer surplus plus consumer surplus.

▶ If the quantity produced is either greater or less than the market equilibrium amount, the sum of consumer surplus plus producer surplus is less than

at the market equilibrium. The decline in consumer plus producer surplus measures the waste from producing the wrong amount. It is called deadweight loss.

THE DEADWEIGHT LOSS FROM TAXATION

An important application of deadweight loss is in estimating the impact of a tax. To see how, let's examine the impact of a tax on a commodity like gasoline. We will see that the tax shifts the supply curve, leads to a reduction in the quantity produced, and reduces the sum of producer surplus plus consumer surplus.

A Tax Paid by a Producer Shifts the Supply Curve

ad valorem tax: a tax that is proportional to the value of expenditures.

specific tax: a tax that is proportional to the number of items sold.

A tax on sales is a payment that must be made to the government by the seller of a product. The tax may be proportional to the dollar value of the products sold, in which case it is called an **ad valorem tax.** Or it may be proportional to the number of items sold (the number of gallons of gasoline), in which case the tax is called a **specific tax.**

Using Economics to Explain the Cost of Federal Farm Programs

For many years, the U.S. government has supported U.S. agriculture by instituting a minimum price for sugar, wool, wheat, peanuts, honey, and other farm products. These price floors raise the price of these products to U.S. consumers. The figure in panel A shows how a minimum price causes a surplus of any one of these products due to the combination of increased quantity supplied and lower quantity demanded at the higher price. The government would have to buy this surplus to keep the price high—at a large cost to the taxpayer.

However, in order to reduce the taxpayers' cost, in most cases the government attempts to reduce the surplus by limiting the cultivated acreage. For example, the U.S.

government has used *set-aside* or *acreage allotment* programs in which farmers agree to limit the acres they plant in order to qualify for price supports. This reduces the surplus and the government does not have to pay farmers as much for their production.

The effect of set-asides is shown in panel B. The limit on the amount that can be produced is shown by the solid vertical line. The government limits production to the amount Q_1. This limit leads to a market price P_1 equal to the support price but higher than the free market price without supports. In fact, the U.S. government calculates Q_1 by estimating the demand curve and finding the quantity demanded by consumers at the support price P_1.

But these programs are still very costly because people consume fewer farm products at a higher price. There is a deadweight loss, as shown in panel B.

Compared to the free market, consumers lose much more than the deadweight loss. They also lose the blue rectangular area in panel B. However, that loss in consumer surplus is a gain in producer surplus and is not a net loss to society. But if the typical farmer is richer than the typical consumer, then this transfer makes the income distribution more unequal. (Note how the term *surplus* is used differently from *consumer surplus* or *producer surplus*.)

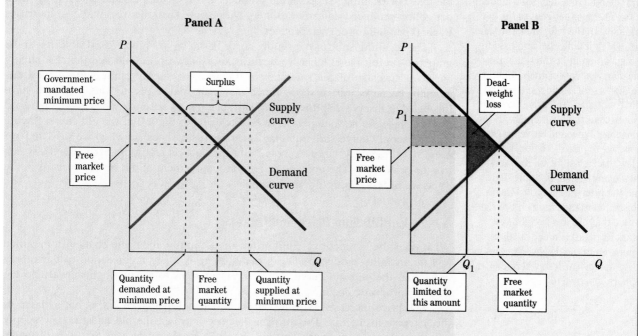

Panel A   **Panel B**

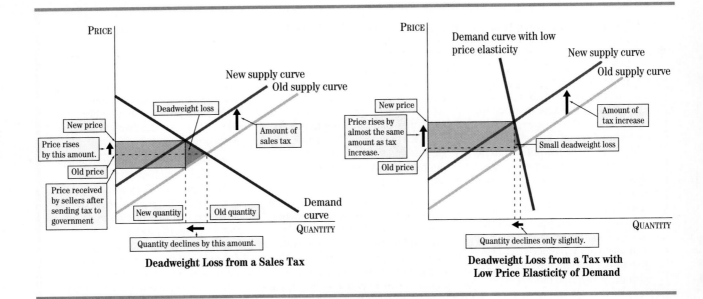

Deadweight Loss from a Sales Tax

Deadweight Loss from a Tax with Low Price Elasticity of Demand

FIGURE 7.8
Deadweight Loss from a Tax

In these two graphs the dark triangles represent the deadweight loss and the blue rectangles the amount of tax revenue that goes to the government. In the left panel, the sales tax, which is collected and paid to the government by the seller, raises the marginal cost of each item the producer sells. Hence, the supply curve shifts up. The price rises but by less than the tax increase. If the consumer's demand curve is very insensitive to price—that is, if there is a low price elasticity of demand—then quantity changes only slightly and the price rise is large. This is illustrated in the graph on the right; notice that the deadweight loss (dark triangle) is much smaller compared to the deadweight loss in the graph on the left, where demand is more sensitive to price.

Because the tax payment is made by the producer or the seller to the government, the immediate impact of the tax is to increase the marginal cost of producing the product. Hence, the immediate impact of the tax will be to shift the supply curve. In the case of gasoline, the producer's costs have increased by the amount of the tax. For example, suppose the producer has to send a certain amount, say $.50 per gallon produced and sold, to the government. Then the marginal cost increases by $.50 per gallon for each producer.

The resulting shift of the supply curve is shown in Figure 7.8. (Look first at the graph in the left panel.) The vertical distance between the old and the new supply curves is the size of the sales tax in dollars. The supply curve shifts up by this amount because this is how much the marginal costs to the producer have increased. (Observe that this upward shift can just as accurately be called a leftward shift because the new supply curve is above and to the left of the old curve. Saying that the supply curve shifts up may seem confusing because when we say "up," we seem to be meaning "more supply." But the "up" is along the vertical axis, which has the price on it. The upward, or leftward, movement of the supply curve is in the direction of less supply, not more supply.)

A New Equilibrium Price and Quantity

What does the competitive equilibrium model imply about the change in the price and the quantity produced? Observe that there is a new intersection of the supply curve and the demand curve. Thus, the price rises to a new, higher level and the quantity produced declines.

The price increase, as shown in the left panel of Figure 7.8, is not as large as the increase in the tax. The vertical distance between the old and the new supply curves is the amount of the tax, but the price increased by less than this distance. Thus the producers are not able to "pass on" the entire tax to the consumers in the form of higher prices. If the tax increase was $.50, then the price increase is less than $.50, perhaps $.40. The producers have been forced by the market—by the movement along the demand curve—to reduce their production, and thereby they have absorbed some of the tax increase.

The amount by which the price rises depends on the price elasticity of the supply and demand curves. For example, if the demand curve has a low price elasticity, there would be a larger increase in the price. If the demand curve has a higher price elasticity, there would be a smaller increase in the price. This is shown in the right panel of Figure 7.8, which illustrates a demand curve with low price elasticity. If the price elasticity is low, then large changes in the price make very little difference for demand. People are insensitive to price. When the quantity demanded is insensitive to the price—that is, when people do not reduce their consumption by much when the price rises—then the price rise is about the same as the tax increase, as shown in the right panel of Figure 7.8.

Deadweight Loss and Tax Revenue

Now consider what happens to consumer surplus and producer surplus with the sales tax. Because the total quantity produced is lower, there is a loss in consumer surplus and producer surplus. The right part of the triangle of consumer plus producer surplus has been cut off, and this measures the deadweight loss to society, as shown in the graphs in Figure 7.8. This loss occurs despite the fact that the tax

Experimental Tests of the Economic Theory of Taxation

A useful way to test the economic theory of a tax is to perform a market experiment similar to the one described earlier in this chapter. By increasing the marginal cost of all the sellers in the market, one can incorporate the tax into an experimental market. For example, replacing the original sellers' sheets in Figure 7.4 with new sheets in which marginal cost is $6 higher would show the impact of a $6 tax.

The effect of such a change on the market supply curve is shown on the graph. It shifts up by exactly $6. According to the competitive equilibrium model, the price should rise by $3 and production should fall by 3 units. The price increase should be less than the tax increase with about half the increase passed on to the buyers, according to the model.

Economists who run such experimental markets find that after one or two trading periods, the price rises to about $16 and the quantity falls to 10 units, compared with $13 and 13 units without the tax, much as predicted by the model. This occurs even if the buyers know nothing about the tax. The interaction of only a few sellers and buyers in the market with very limited information again results in the outcome predicted by the competitive equilibrium model.

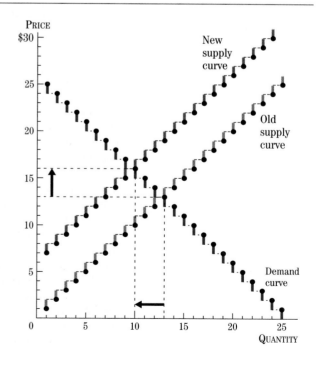

revenue going to the government is used for financing government activity. The deadweight loss is incurred because there is a movement of production away from the efficient level. Taxes may be necessary to finance the government, but they cause a deadweight loss to society. The size of the loss depends on the price elasticity of demand, as a comparison of the left and right panels of Figure 7.8 shows. If the price elasticity of demand is low, then the quantity demanded does not change by much and the deadweight loss is small. In Chapter 15, where we study the effects of different types of taxes, we will show that their impact depends on the price elasticity of supply as well as demand.

Figure 7.8 also tells us how much tax revenue goes to the government in the case of a specific tax. The tax revenue is the tax times the number of items sold. If the tax is $1 and 100 items are sold, the tax revenue is $100. This amount is shown by the blue rectangle. Some of what we call producer surplus and consumer surplus thus goes to the government. Another portion, the deadweight loss, is no longer available. No one gets it.

Review

▶ The impact of a tax on the economy can be analyzed using consumer surplus and producer surplus.

▶ Taxes are necessary to finance government expenditures, but they lower the production of the item being taxed.

▶ The loss to society from the decline in production is measured by the reduction in consumer surplus and producer surplus, the deadweight loss due to the tax.

INFORMATIONAL EFFICIENCY

We have shown that a competitive market works well in that the outcome is Pareto efficient. For every good, the sum of consumer surplus and producer surplus is maximized. These are important and attractive characteristics of a competitive market.

Another important and attractive characteristic of a competitive market is that the market processes information very efficiently. For example, in the double-auction market, the price reflects the marginal benefit for every buyer and the marginal cost for every seller. If a government official were asked to set the price in a real market, there would be no way that such information could be obtained, especially with millions of buyers and sellers. In other words, the market seems to be informationally efficient. Pareto efficiency is different from this *informational efficiency*.

In the 1930s and 1940s, as the government of the Soviet Union tried to centrally plan production in the entire economy, economists became more interested in the informational efficiency of markets. One of the most outspoken critics of central planning, and a strong advocate of the market system, was Friedrich Hayek, who emphasized the importance of informational efficiencies of the market. In Hayek's view, a major disadvantage of central planning—where the government sets all the prices and the quantities—is that it is informationally inefficient.

Coordination Without a Market
Although prices provide a valuable coordination role in a market economy, some activities are better coordinated without the market. It would not be efficient to coordinate each of the hand and foot movements of these 100 skydivers with prices.

If you had all the information about the buyers and sellers in the double-auction market, you could set the price to achieve a Pareto efficient outcome. To see Hayek's point, it is perhaps enough to observe such experimental markets and see that without private information about every buyer and seller, you or any government official would not know where to set the price. Complicate this with millions of buyers, millions of different products, and rapidly changing tastes and technology, and you can quickly comprehend Hayek's arguments. However, economists do not have results as neat as the first theorem of welfare economics to prove Hayek's point. The reason is that in some situations, the market would be unwieldy, and it is difficult to describe these situations with any generality.

Consider an example of coordinating the members of a marching band consisting of several different instruments and several different players. Suppose you were asked how to coordinate the members of a marching band through a price system in a market! You might set a price for playing loud versus soft and then vary the price according to how loud you wanted the band to play. But using the price system to conduct a real band would be an impossible task. It would be better to conduct the marching band without prices and without a market, just as all marching bands in the world are conducted. Coordinating millions of producers and consumers of roses by a central conductor is just as difficult as coordinating the members of a marching band by a price system. Rose production and consumption is handled well by the market and poorly by a central conductor. On the other hand, a marching band is handled poorly by the market and well by a central conductor.

Two obvious difficulties arise in using a market system to coordinate activities like a marching band. First, prices will not bring about a sufficiently precise or speedy response. It is essential that the flute and sax start playing at the same moment; a one-second delay will turn music into noise. It is better to tell the musicians to play this note at this volume at this time. Second, it is possible for the conductor to get information about each band member. A band leader knows which band member is capable of doing what.

In most situations where the informational advantage of the price system and the market is not large and where great precision in coordination is required, organizations spring up. Musicians form a band, a community forms a police force, and so on. Because economists have not been able to isolate the general informational or coordination characteristics that favor markets over organizations, they have not been able to formalize or measure informational efficiencies of the market. Examples like experimental markets show how the market can process information very efficiently. But there are examples—like the band—where the market system and prices have few informational advantages.

Review

▶ The market has the ability to process information efficiently. Market experiments demonstrate informational efficiency. The lack of informational efficiency is a key reason why central planning does not work well in complex and changing environments.

▶ For some activities, however, the market has few informational advantages. A production process where exact timing is essential will be poorly coordinated through prices. In almost all these situations, firms or organizations form and replace market transactions.

CONCLUSION

Adam Smith's idea of the "invisible hand" is perhaps the most important idea in economics: Individuals, by freely pursuing their own interests in a market economy, are led as if by an invisible hand to an outcome that is best overall. The first theorem of welfare economics, which we examined in this chapter, is the modern statement of Adam Smith's famous principle; in tribute to Smith's seminal idea we might call it the "invisible hand theorem," though the theorem was not actually proved by economists until the mid-twentieth century. Understanding why, and under what circumstances, the invisible hand theorem is true is an important part of understanding economics.

Understanding the theorem has required an investment in economic model building: In Chapter 5 we built a model of the behavior of consumers; in Chapter 6 we built a model of the behavior of firms; and now, in Chapter 7, we have combined these into a competitive equilibrium model describing how consumers and firms interact in markets. This model has provided the foundation for the supply and demand model we used in Chapters 3 and 4. Experimental markets, which are set up to behave in ways that are close to other markets, demonstrate that the model works well in predicting actual outcomes. Such experimental markets are also useful for demonstrating how markets work. When one watches such a market, one can almost see the invisible hand working!

Building the competitive equilibrium model has had payoffs beyond understanding this most important theorem in economics. Armed with the ideas of consumer surplus and producer surplus we can now measure the costs of deviations from the competitive market equilibrium. Such measures are used by economists to

Corporate leaders gather in a field outside Darien, Connecticut, where one of them claims
to have seen the invisible hand of the marketplace.

assess the costs and benefits of government programs that interfere, for bad or
good, with the market outcomes. Starting with Chapter 10, we will see that deviations from the competitive market equilibrium are caused by monopolies and other
factors. But first we need to look more closely at how costs and production within
individual firms and competitive industries change over time. We do this in Chapters 8 and 9.

KEY POINTS

1. The interaction of producers and consumers or buyers
and sellers in a market can be explained by the competitive
equilibrium model.

2. Processing information and coordinating and motivating
millions of consumption and production decisions is difficult, but the market is a device that can do the job remarkably well.

3. The competitive equilibrium model predicts that certain
prices, production decisions, and consumption decisions
will emerge from a market.

4. Experiments, which mimic many real-world markets,
demonstrate that the competitive equilibrium model works
well even though it is not a literal description of how markets operate.

5. Even with only a few sellers and buyers, the experimental markets appear to be well explained by the competitive
equilibrium model.

6. Competitive markets are Pareto efficient. In a competitive market it is not possible to change production or consumption in a way that will make one person better off
without hurting someone else.

7. Marginal benefit equals marginal cost for the last item
produced, and the sum of producer surplus and consumer
surplus is maximized in a competitive market.

8. Deviations from the efficient outcome create a loss to
society called deadweight loss.

9. Deadweight loss is caused by a tax that reduces the
quantity produced.

10. The market system is also informationally efficient.
However, there are no general theorems that prove the
informational efficiency of the market.

KEY TERMS

competitive equilibrium model	ask	income inequality
invisible hand	price discovery	deadweight loss
double-auction market	Pareto efficiency	ad valorem tax
bid	first theorem of welfare economics	specific tax

QUESTIONS FOR REVIEW

1. What are the information-processing, coordination, and motivation functions that arise when buyers and sellers interact?

2. Why is it difficult for one person or group of persons to perform these functions?

3. How does the market perform these functions?

4. What is an equilibrium price?

5. What is a double-auction market?

6. Do experimental markets validate the competitive equilibrium model?

7. What is the meaning of Pareto efficiency, and how does it differ from informational efficiency?

8. Why is it efficient for marginal benefit to equal marginal cost?

9. Why is the sum of consumer surplus and producer surplus maximized in the market?

10. What is deadweight loss, and how do taxes cause it?

PROBLEMS

1. Suppose a root disease destroys 80 percent of vineyards in the United States. Suppose the U.S. government observes that the price of grapes is increasing rapidly and imposes a price ceiling.

   a) Sketch a market demand and supply graph that shows the situation before and after the vineyard destruction, assuming that the government did not impose a price ceiling. For simplicity, assume that the demand curve does not shift.

   b) Now show the effect of the price ceiling on the quantity demanded and supplied. Indicate how many grapes are actually traded with the price ceiling.

   c) Show the effect of the price ceiling on economic efficiency using consumer and producer surplus.

   d) Is marginal cost higher or lower than marginal benefit with the price ceiling? Give a practical example of the use of grapes that illustrates the kind of economic inefficiency or waste that might occur because marginal cost differs from marginal benefit as a result of the grape price ceiling.

2. In 1975, 18 million calculators were produced and sold at an average price of $60. In 1983, 31 million calculators were produced and sold at an average price of $30. Assume that the demand curve for calculators did not shift between 1975 and 1983.

   a) Sketch a market demand and market supply curve for calculators in 1975 and in 1983 to illustrate the change in price and quantity. Mark the 1975 and 1983 prices and quantities on the axes.

   b) Describe an event that could have led to the changes you just illustrated.

   c) Show the gain to consumers from this event on your sketch.

3. The following figure shows the demand and supply for baby powder.

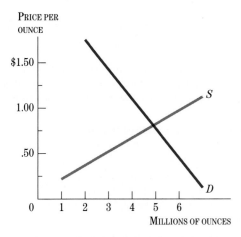

   a) Show equilibrium price, quantity, consumer surplus, and producer surplus.

b) Describe what would happen to the price of baby powder if a $.50 tax per ounce of baby powder were enacted by the federal government. Show your answer graphically.

c) Show the deadweight loss due to the tax on your diagram.

4. Calculate the consumer surplus using the market demand curve in Figure 7.3. Assume the market price is $10. Show how you get the same answer by adding up the consumer surplus for all five buyers. How much does consumer surplus increase for the market as a whole and for each individual when the market price falls to $5?

5. Calculate the producer surplus using the market supply curve in Figure 7.4. Assume that the market price is $10. Show how you get the same answer by adding up the producer surplus for all five sellers. How much does producer surplus increase for the market as a whole and for each seller when the market price rises to $15?

6. Consider the $6 tax increase in the demonstration market as shown in the box "Experimental Tests of the Economic Theory of Taxation."

a) Calculate the deadweight loss from the $6 tax, assuming the predicted new price and quantity.

b) Calculate the consumer surplus and the producer surplus after the tax is imposed.

c) Calculate the amount of revenue collected by the government.

7. For which of the following items—milk, wine, coffee, bread, gasoline, 100 percent wool sweaters, sports cars, VCRs—do you think the deadweight loss of a sales tax would be the largest? The smallest? Explain.

8. What would the competitive equilibrium model predict about the quantity sold if people were not allowed to bid or ask more than $8 for any good in the market illustrated in Figure 7.5? What if they were not allowed to bid or ask less than $20? Illustrate your answers in a graph and show the deadweight loss in each case.

9. Firm A and firm B both produce the same product with the following total costs:

Firm A		Firm B	
Quantity Produced	Total Costs	Quantity Produced	Total Costs
0	5	0	2
1	6	1	5
2	8	2	9
3	11	3	14
4	15	4	20

Consider a situation where 4 units are produced: Firm A produces 2 units and firm B produces 2 units. Explain why this situation is not Pareto efficient. Could such a situation occur in competitive markets if both firms maximized profits? How could production be changed at the two firms in order to produce the 4 items at lower cost? Suppose the price is $3. How much would each firm produce?

10. Design your own market experiment by creating five marginal cost curves, five marginal benefit curves, and the market supply and demand curves, as in Figures 7.3, 7.4, and 7.5.

part 2

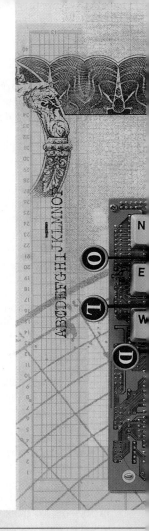

Microeconomics over Time and Through Markets

A modern market economy is in perpetual motion. People discover new techniques and build more and better machines. They go to school to improve their skills. Their tastes change. Many move from one part of the country to another, or they move to a different country altogether. New firms are created and grow while others shrink, shut down, or merge with other firms. Whole industries expand rapidly. Others contract. Industries become more competitive because of foreign trade, or less competitive because of a change in technology. Change takes place in many different types of markets—labor markets, rental markets, stock and bond markets, natural resource markets. Each type of market works and handles change in a slightly different way. The purpose of these six chapters is to explain how firms and industries react to change and to describe the workings of these different types of markets.

chapters

8 Costs and the Evolution of Firms over Time

9 The Rise and Fall of Industries

10 Monopoly

11 Product Differentiation and Strategic Behavior

12 Labor Markets

13 Capital Markets

In Chapter 8 we develop models of how firms behave over time—whether expanding, shutting down, or merging. In Chapter 9 we show how industries consisting of many firms respond to changes in people's tastes or to a new technology. In Chapter 10 we explore the intriguing case of monopoly where there is only one firm in an industry. In Chapter 11 we visit the half-way house between monopoly and competition—called monopolistic competition—and look into the game-like markets where only a few firms strategically interact. In Chapter 12 we investigate the unique characteristics of the most significant market in the world for most people—the labor market—where you sell your services to firms. In Chapter 13 we analyze the risky world of the stock and bond markets and try to explain how large publicly owned firms are controlled.

What are all these ideas and models good for? To economists interested in solving real-world puzzles,

they explain the behavior observed in different markets. But the models have many practical uses. Government policy makers use them to determine when a merger of two firms will reduce competition. Business firms use them to determine the value of a new or different product or to assess how different corporate strategies affect other firms in the industry. If you have funds to invest in the stock market, then the models can teach you some useful financial investment strategies such as the importance of diversification. And, perhaps most important, the models have lessons for anyone planning to enter the labor market, including the means to assess the factors that determine wages and salaries.

Costs and the Evolution of Firms over Time

Firms naturally evolve over time. Changes in technology, consumer tastes, or government policy require that firms change or eventually fail. Changes at firms—start-ups, expansions, downsizings, shutdowns—are of great interest to workers, customers, and investors. News about these changes fills much of the financial pages and the television business news. Sun Microsystems, United Airlines, Blockbuster Video, and Home Depot are examples of firms that have grown rapidly in recent years. IBM, Union Carbide, and Westinghouse are examples of firms that have downsized. About 1 percent of businesses shut down each year in the United States, but many more firms start up, so that the number of firms in existence continues to increase year after year.

In the United States about 700,000 new firms start up each year. Some are successful and expand. But others fail to make profits, and their losses are large enough that they decide to *shut down*. To an economist, shutdown means ceasing production. Shutdown is different from *bankruptcy*. Many firms go bankrupt and continue to produce. In such cases, bankruptcy is a legal definition that means the firm is working with the courts to find a way

to settle its debts while remaining open for business. Eventually, bankrupt firms may shut down, but many keep producing or are acquired by other firms.

The purpose of this chapter is to develop a model for analyzing such changes at firms over time. To do so, we will extend the model of firm behavior developed in Chapter 6 to examine the issues involved in a decision to start up, expand, or shut down a firm.

Costs, as we will see, are of vital importance to a firm's decision to start up, expand, or shut down. We will look carefully at firms' costs in this chapter. Some of the most rapidly growing firms in the United States have prospered because of new technologies that cut costs. For example, Wal-Mart—a rapidly expanding firm in the 1980s and 1990s—developed a system whereby salesclerks electronically scan a bar code on each item purchased and automatically transmit the information back to the manufacturer, who can then immediately begin producing more of that item. This reduced costs. Firms that competed with Wal-Mart, like Kmart and Sears, saw their profits adversely affected until they adopted similar cost-cutting technologies.

Costs determine how large firms should be. Differences in the costs of manufacturing cement versus haircuts, for example, mean that cement firms are usually large and barbershops are usually small. Costs also determine how firms should expand. For example, when firms choose between expanding their manufacturing facilities in the United States or acquiring another company abroad, they take into account the costs of labor and transportation as well as the effects of government policy toward firms.

Costs are such a crucial determinant of firm behavior that economists can capture the whole essence of a firm with a graph of its costs. By looking at such a graph, economists can determine the profitability of a firm and whether it should shut down or expand. This chapter shows how.

COSTS AND PRODUCTION AT AN INDIVIDUAL FIRM

In this section we develop a model of the behavior of firms over time. The model shows how a firm's costs determine its level of output. Average cost at the firm plays an important role in the model. To understand average cost, we must first review the ideas of total, fixed, variable, and marginal cost and show how these are related to the firm's production function.

Total Costs, Fixed Costs, Variable Costs, and Marginal Cost

Total costs (*TC*) are the sum of all costs incurred by a firm in producing goods or services. The more that is produced, the larger are total costs. Recall from Chapter 6 that *fixed costs* (*FC*) and *variable costs* (*VC*) are the two key components of total costs.

Fixed costs are the part of total costs that do not vary with the amount produced in the short run; fixed costs include the cost of the factories, land, machines, and all other things that do not change when production changes in the short run. *Variable costs* are the part of total costs that vary in the short run as production changes. Variable costs include wage payments for workers, gasoline for trucks, fertilizer for crops, and all other things that change when the amount produced changes. By definition, total costs equal fixed costs plus variable costs; or, in symbols, $TC = FC + VC$.

total costs: the sum of variable costs and fixed costs. (Ch. 6)

fixed costs: costs of production that do not depend on the quantity of production. (Ch. 6)

variable costs: costs of production that vary with the quantity of production. (Ch. 6)

The Short Run and the Long Run

Distinguishing the short run from the long run is the key to distinguishing fixed costs from variable costs. The *short run* and the *long run* are two broad categories into which economists parcel time. The **short run** is the period of time during which it is not possible to change all the inputs to production; only some inputs, such as labor, can be changed in the short run. The short run is too short, for example, to build a new factory or apartment building, to lay a fiber optic cable, to launch a new communications satellite, or to get out of a lease on a storefront. The **long run,** in contrast, is long enough that all inputs, including capital, can be changed. Hence, the cost of each of the items that cannot be changed in the short

short run: the period of time during which it is not possible to change all inputs to production; only some inputs, such as labor, can be changed.

long run: the minimum period of time during which all inputs to production can be changed.

run—factories, buildings, satellites—is fixed in the short run but can be changed in the long run.

Economists frequently use *capital* as an example of a factor that does not change in the short run, and they use *labor* as an example of a factor that can change in the short run. However, salaries paid to certain types of workers who have special skills and knowledge about the firm are better viewed as being fixed costs, and rents on certain capital items such as laptop computers or sewing machines are better viewed as being variable costs. Nevertheless, in the examples in this chapter, we refer to the cost of labor as the main variable cost and the cost of capital as the main fixed cost.

An Example

Table 8.1 illustrates these definitions with cost data for a hypothetical but typical transportation services firm located in Houston, Texas, called On-the-Move. The firm specializes in the strenuous but delicate job of moving pianos from one part of Houston to another. We use these hypothetical data rather than actual data to keep the example simple, but it is important to realize that the same analysis can be applied to data from any firm. Table 8.1 lists the total costs, fixed costs, and variable costs for different levels of output at the firm. Observe how fixed costs do not change but variable costs increase with output.

Figure 8.1 gives a visual perspective on total costs, fixed costs, and variable costs. It shows that fixed costs do not change in the short run at On-the-Move. Fixed costs are $300 per day regardless of how many pianos are moved during the day. Fixed costs are shown in Figure 8.1 to be the cost for four trucks and two terminals where the trucks are serviced and parked. Figure 8.1 also shows that variable costs increase with the amount produced. They increase from $600 to $1,660 as the number of pianos delivered per day rises from 5 to 10. Variable costs are

TABLE 8.1

Finding Average and Marginal Cost for an Example Firm: On-the-Move

(costs measured in dollars per day)

Quantity (pianos moved per day) (Q)	Total Costs (TC)	Fixed Costs (FC)	Variable Costs (VC)	Average Total Cost (ATC)	Average Fixed Cost (AFC)	Average Variable Cost (AVC)	Marginal Cost (MC)
0	300	300	0	—	—	—	—
1	450	300	150	450	300	150	150
2	570	300	270	285	150	135	120
3	670	300	370	223	100	123	100
4	780	300	480	195	75	120	110
5	900	300	600	180	60	120	120
6	1,040	300	740	173	50	123	140
7	1,200	300	900	171	43	128	160
8	1,390	300	1,090	174	38	136	190
9	1,640	300	1,340	182	33	149	250
10	1,960	300	1,660	196	30	166	320
11	2,460	300	2,160	223	27	196	500

$TC = FC + VC$

$ATC = \dfrac{TC}{Q}$

$AFC = \dfrac{FC}{Q}$

$AVC = \dfrac{VC}{Q}$

Change in TC / Change in Q

shown in Figure 8.1 to rise because additional workers are hired to carry the goods and drive and service the trucks. Thus, total costs rise from $900 to $1,960 as the number of pianos delivered rises from 5 to 10.

Figure 8.2 shows the same type of information as Figure 8.1 in graph form. Pairs of numbers on total costs and quantity from Table 8.1 are plotted in Figure 8.2. Connecting these dots results in the total costs curve. You can see how the total costs of moving the pianos steadily increase with the number of pianos moved. Fixed costs are shown to be unchanged at all levels of output. Figure 8.2 shows variable costs by the distance between the total cost curve and the fixed cost curve.

Marginal Cost

Table 8.1 also shows how the *marginal cost* of On-the-Move depends on the quantity of services produced (the number of pianos moved). Recall from Chapter 6 that

marginal cost: the change in total costs due to a one-unit change in quantity produced. (Ch. 6)

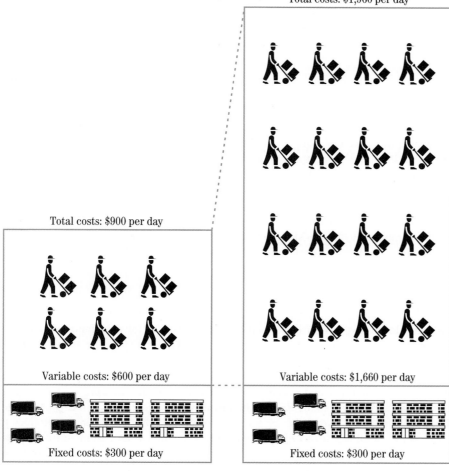

Five Moves per Day **Ten Moves per Day**

FIGURE 8.1
Fixed Costs versus Variable Costs
Fixed costs remain constant as the output of the firm increases in the short run. In the example of On-the-Move, fixed costs are the daily rental or interest costs for trucks and terminals under long-term lease or owned by the firm. Variable costs change with the level of output. In the case of On-the-Move, more workers must be hired to move more pianos.

FIGURE 8.2
Total Costs Minus Fixed Costs Equal Variable Costs
The two lines on the diagram show total costs and fixed costs for On-the-Move. Variable costs are the difference between the two lines. Variable costs rise with production, but fixed costs are constant.

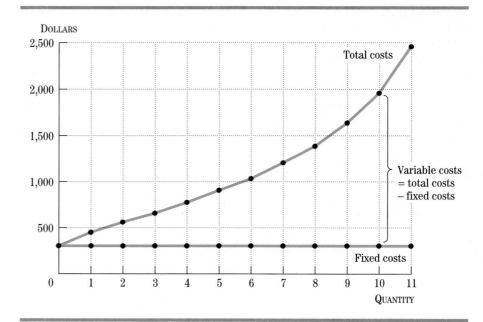

marginal cost is the change in total costs due to a one-unit change in the quantity produced. For example, the marginal cost of increasing production from 5 moves to 6 moves a day is $140, or the change in total costs ($1,040 − $900 = $140) divided by the change in production (6 − 5 = 1). The last column of Table 8.1 shows the marginal cost for each additional piano moved by On-the-Move, ranging from the first to the eleventh piano.

Observe that marginal cost declines at low levels of production in Table 8.1 and then begins to increase again. Marginal cost reaches a minimum of $100 when production increases from 2 to 3 units of output. Recall in the examples in Chapter 6 (Table 6.3) that marginal cost increased throughout the whole range of production. In the example of On-the-Move, marginal cost declines over part of the range of production. We will explain the reason for the difference, but we first need to define average cost.

Average Cost

average total cost (*ATC*): total costs of production divided by the quantity produced (also called cost per unit).

average variable cost (*AVC*): variable costs divided by the quantity produced.

average fixed cost (*AFC*): fixed cost divided by the quantity produced.

Average total cost (*ATC*) is defined as total costs (*TC*) of production divided by the quantity (*Q*) produced. We write in symbols: $ATC = TC/Q$. For example, if the total costs of producing 4 items are $3,000, then the average total cost is $750 ($3,000/4). Another name for average total cost is *cost per unit*. We can also define average cost for fixed and variable costs. Thus, **average variable cost (*AVC*)** is defined as variable costs divided by the quantity produced: $AVC = VC/Q$. **Average fixed cost (*AFC*)** is defined as fixed costs divided by the quantity produced: $AFC = FC/Q$. Of the three averages, we will use average total cost most frequently; the other two averages are important for knowing when to shut down a firm or keep it open when it is losing money.

Average total cost for On-the-Move is shown in Table 8.1. For example, total costs for 2 pianos moved (*Q* = 2) is $570; dividing $570 by 2 gives an average total cost of $285. For 3 pianos moved ($Q = 3$) total costs are $670; dividing by 3 gives $223 for average total cost. Notice that average total cost declines as production increases from low levels. Then average total cost starts to increase. In the example, average total cost starts to increase at 8 units: $1,390 divided by 8 is $174 and $1,200 divided by 7 is $171. That average total cost first decreases and then increases as production increases is a common pattern for most firms.

Average variable cost is also illustrated in Table 8.1. For 2 pianos moved ($Q = 2$), for example, average variable cost is $270 divided by 2, or $135. You can see that average variable cost, in this example, first declines and then increases throughout the rest of the range of production.

Finally, observe in Table 8.1 that average fixed cost gets smaller as production rises. Because average fixed cost is calculated by dividing fixed costs by the quantity produced, average fixed cost must decline as the quantity produced rises.

Costs Depend on the Firm's Production Function

The cost information in Table 8.1 is determined by how much *input* of labor and capital it takes to produce *output* and by the price of capital and labor. First consider some illustrative calculations of costs as the firm increases production from Q equals zero to 1 and then to 2.

Varying Labor Input but not Capital Input in the Short Run

According to Table 8.1, it costs On-the-Move $300 a day for capital, which is 4 trucks and 2 terminals. Let's assume that the $300 consists of $25 per day for each of the 4 trucks and $100 per day for each of the 2 terminals ($25 × 4 + $100 × 2 = $300). These are the fixed costs that will be incurred even if zero pianos are moved. If the trucks and terminals were leased for one year, then the fixed costs would include the rental payment on the lease. If the trucks and the terminals were purchased on credit by On-the-Move, then the fixed costs would include interest payments on the loans. If the trucks and the terminals were bought outright, then the fixed costs would include the opportunity cost—the foregone interest payments—on the funds used to buy the trucks and the terminals.

To move pianos, however, On-the-Move needs labor. To move one piano it might be enough to have one driver, one mechanic to service the truck, plus another worker to carry and load the piano. The example assumes the cost of labor input is $150, which might consist of 15 hours of work at $10 per hour; perhaps 5 hours of work for each of the 3 workers. As production increases from $Q = 0$ to $Q = 1$, variable costs increase from zero to $150 and total costs increase from $300 to $450. Thus, the marginal cost of moving 1 piano rather than zero pianos is $150.

To move to a higher level of production, On-the-Move requires more workers. According to Table 8.1, if production rises from 1 piano moved to 2 pianos moved, then total costs increase from $450 to $570; marginal cost is $120. With wages of $10 an hour, this marginal cost would be the cost of 12 more hours of work; perhaps another driver and loader each working 5 hours a day plus increasing the hours of the mechanic by 2. As we observed already, marginal cost *declines* as production increases from 1 to 2 units of output. Now we are beginning to see why. Marginal cost decreases because labor input rises by less when increasing production from 1 to 2 units than it does when increasing production from zero to 1 unit. The reason has to do with the nature of the firm's production; perhaps the mechanic can service two trucks at less than twice the time it takes to service one truck (5 hours for one, 7 hours for two). Although these calculations illustrate how costs depend on the inputs to production, to see what is going on throughout the whole range of production, we need to look at the firm's production function.

The Production Function

production function: a relationship that shows the quantity of output for any given amount of input. (Ch. 6)

Table 8.2 shows the number of hours of work required to move different numbers of pianos at On-the-Move. It is On-the-Move's short-run *production function,* showing how much output can be produced for each amount of labor input. To calculate the variable costs at On-the-Move, using the information in Table 8.2, continue to assume that the wage is $10 per hour. Then to move 1 piano takes 15 hours of work; at $10 per hour, variable costs are $150. To move 10 pianos takes 166 hours of work; at $10 per hour, variable costs are $1,660. Similar calculations are shown in the third column of Table 8.2 for all levels of output. Note that the variable costs in Table 8.2 are the same as those in Table 8.1. Thus, we have shown explicitly how the firm's costs depend on its production function.

Recall from Chapter 6 that the *marginal product of labor* is the change in production that can be obtained with an additional unit of labor. Decreasing marginal product of labor is called *diminishing returns to labor.* Increasing marginal product of labor is called *increasing returns to labor.*

The marginal product of labor is illustrated in Figure 8.3, which shows a graph of the production function from Table 8.2. Figure 8.3 shows how, for low levels of labor input, the marginal product of labor increases: Output increases by more from a given change in labor input as labor input increases. At low levels of production, increasing marginal product of labor is a possibility because the firm's capital can be better utilized: During an oil change, for example, the mechanic can work on the other truck as oil drains from the first truck. At high levels of labor input, marginal product starts to decline; diminishing returns set in. The same increase in labor input results in smaller and smaller increases in output.

TABLE 8.2

Using the Production Function to Compute Variable Costs

(Observe that increasing marginal product of labor exists at low levels of production; for example, it only takes 10 hours of labor to increase production [by 1 unit] from 2 to 3 units, whereas it takes 12 hours of labor to increase production [by 1 unit] from 1 to 2 units. At higher levels of production, decreasing marginal product of labor exists.)

Quantity (pianos moved)	Hours of Work	Labor Costs at $10 Wage (variable costs)
0	0	0
1	15	150
2	27	270
3	37	370
4	48	480
5	60	600
6	74	740
7	90	900
8	109	1,090
9	134	1,340
10	166	1,660
11	216	2,160

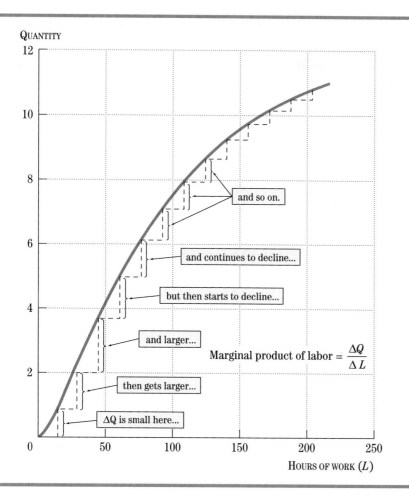

QUANTITY

Marginal product of labor $= \dfrac{\Delta Q}{\Delta L}$

and so on.

and continues to decline...

but then starts to decline...

and larger...

then gets larger...

ΔQ is small here...

HOURS OF WORK (L)

FIGURE 8.3
On-the-Move's Production Function

The curve shows the production function in which more labor input gives more output. Capital (trucks and terminals) is not changed. Observe that the marginal product of labor first increases and then decreases with more labor input.

Table 8.2 shows increasing marginal product of labor up to 3 units of output produced. Then diminishing returns begin. This pattern of increasing marginal product of labor up to 3 units of output and then decreasing marginal product is what causes the pattern of decreasing marginal cost up to 3 units of output produced followed by increasing marginal cost. More generally, if the marginal product of labor is increasing, then marginal cost is decreasing and vice versa. With more and more workers required to produce a given amount of output, the marginal cost of producing that amount would increase. To summarize:

Increasing marginal product of labor   ⟶   Decreasing marginal cost

Decreasing marginal product of labor   ⟶   Increasing marginal cost

Be sure to distinguish between the marginal product of labor and the average product of labor. The **average product of labor** is the quantity produced, or *total product*, divided by the amount of labor input. Thus, the average product of labor is Q/L, where Q is total product and L is labor input. On the other hand, the marginal product of labor is $\Delta Q/\Delta L$, where ΔQ is the change in the quantity produced and ΔL is the change in labor input.

average product of labor: the quantity produced divided by the amount of labor input.

Review

▶ The short run is the period of time in which it is not possible to change all inputs to production; only some inputs, such as labor, can be changed. The long run is the period of time in which the firm can vary all inputs to production, including capital.

▶ Fixed costs are constant in the short run for all levels of production. Variable costs increase in the short run as more is produced. Total costs are fixed costs plus variable costs.

▶ Useful information about a firm comes from looking at average cost, or cost per unit. There are three types of average cost:

1. Average total cost is defined as total costs divided by quantity, or $ATC = TC/Q$.
2. Average variable cost is defined as variable costs divided by quantity, or $AVC = VC/Q$.
3. Average fixed cost is defined as fixed costs divided by quantity, or $AFC = FC/Q$.

▶ Costs depend on the firm's production function. When marginal product of labor is decreasing, marginal cost is increasing.

AVERAGE COST CURVES FOR AN INDIVIDUAL FIRM

The information about average cost in Table 8.1 can be turned into an informative graph, as shown in Figure 8.4. The vertical axis of Figure 8.4 shows the dollar cost, and the horizontal axis shows the quantity produced. The pairs of points from Table 8.1 are plotted as dots in Figure 8.4, and the dots have been connected to help visualize the curves. Although the curves use exactly the same information as in Table 8.1, they are more useful. The curves are called the *marginal cost curve,* the *average total cost curve,* and the *average variable cost curve.* We label the curves *MC, ATC,* and *AVC,* respectively.

It is very clear from Figure 8.4 that marginal cost first decreases and then increases, as observed in Table 8.1. We now know the reason: The marginal product of each additional worker increases at lower levels of production and then decreases at higher levels of production, as shown in Figure 8.3.

Figure 8.4 also makes it very clear that average total cost first declines and then increases. In other words, the average total cost curve is *U-shaped.*

The relative positions of the average total cost curve and the marginal cost curve in Figure 8.4 are important and will come up repeatedly. Observe that when the marginal cost curve is below the average total cost curve, average total cost is declining. For example, when production rises from $Q = 1$ to $Q = 2$ in Figure 8.4, marginal cost is less than average total cost and average total cost declines. However, look at the right-hand side of Figure 8.4, where marginal cost is greater than average total cost; then average total cost increases. For example, a marginal cost of $250 is greater than the average total cost of $182, and average total cost goes up to $196. This is a general and important result: *When marginal cost is less than average total cost, then average total cost is declining; when marginal cost is greater than average total cost, then average total cost is increasing.*

This result also holds for average variable cost: If marginal cost is greater than average variable cost, then average variable cost is increasing; if marginal cost is less than average variable cost, then average variable cost is decreasing. These

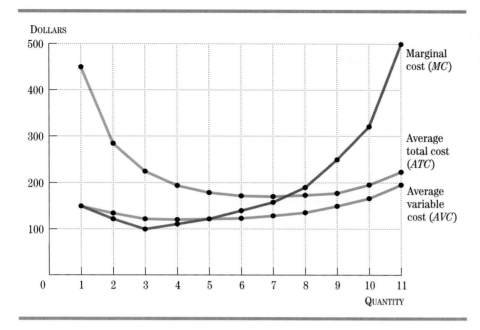

FIGURE 8.4
Average Cost and Marginal Cost from a Numerical Example
Average total cost first declines then increases as more is produced. Marginal cost is below average cost when average cost is falling and above average cost when average cost is rising. This is true for both average variable cost and average total cost. These cost curves are plotted from the data given in Table 8.1.

relationships between the two average cost curves and the marginal cost curve are essential to the analysis that follows.

Marginal versus Average in the Classroom

The reason for the relationship between marginal cost and average total cost or average variable cost can be seen with an analogy. Consider another example of averages, say average grades on the midterm exam in an economics class. Suppose that the average grade of people in the classroom the day after an exam is 64. Now imagine that another person enters the classroom with a midterm grade of 100. We know that 100 is greater than the average grade of 64. In other words, the "marginal grade" of 100 is greater than the average grade; when the person with the grade of 100 enters the room, the average grade in the classroom increases. Now suppose that a different person comes in who has never attended any lectures and that person's midterm grade is zero. The "marginal grade" of zero is less than the average grade of 64; hence, the average grade declines. This is a property of averaging and applies to grades, heights, weights, as well as to costs. When you bring someone into a group whose grade is less than the group's average, then the average declines. A below-average contribution causes the average to fall; on the other hand, an above-average contribution causes the average to rise. The relationships between marginal cost and average total cost or average variable cost say nothing more than this.

Generic Cost Curves

The relationship between marginal and average allows us to sketch a *generic* cost curve diagram, the general properties of which characterize virtually all firms, not just On-the-Move. Such a diagram is shown in Figure 8.5. Again, the vertical axis is the dollar cost and the horizontal axis is the quantity, but in a generic picture, we do not scale the axes because they apply to any firm, whether in textiles, moving, or

Helpful Hints for Drafting Cost Curves

When you are called on to draft diagrams of generic cost curves, you should:

1. Make sure the marginal cost curve cuts through the average total cost curve and the average variable cost curve at their minimum points and understand the reason for this.

2. Make sure the distance between average total cost and average variable cost gets smaller as you increase the amount of production.

3. Put a small dip on the left-hand side of the marginal cost curve before the upward slope begins. This makes your curve look more interesting and allows for the possibility of decreasing marginal cost at very low levels of production.

electronics. Note how the marginal cost curve cuts both the average variable cost curve and the average total cost curve at their minimum points. To the left of the point where the curves cross, marginal cost is less than average total cost, so average total cost declines. As the marginal cost curve passes through the minimum, average total cost begins to increase. Try drawing your own diagram. If the marginal cost curve does not go through the lowest point of both the average total cost curve and the average variable cost curve, you have made an error.

There is another important relationship in Figure 8.5. The distance between the average total cost curve and the average variable cost curve gets smaller as production increases because fixed costs are a smaller and smaller proportion of total costs as production increases. Recall that fixed costs are the difference between total costs and variable costs. Thus, the gap between average total cost and average variable cost is average fixed cost, or fixed costs divided by quantity, FC/Q. Since fixed costs (FC) do not change, the ratio FC/Q declines as Q increases. The distance between the average total cost curve and the average variable cost curve is this distance FC/Q, which declines as quantity increases. Hence, the distance between the ATC curve and the AVC curve grows smaller as you move to the right in the diagram. Any picture you draw should show this relationship.

FIGURE 8.5
Generic Sketch of Average Cost and Marginal Cost

Every firm can be described by cost curves of the type drawn here. Compare these generic curves with the specific curves in Figure 8.4. Be sure to follow the helpful hints (above) when you draw your own cost curves.

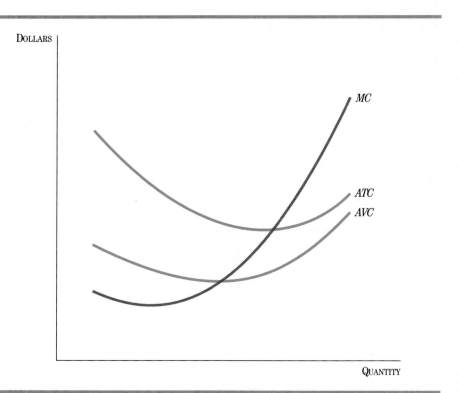

Observe that the marginal cost curve in the generic picture of Figure 8.5 has a region of declining marginal cost at low production levels. The graph allows for the possibility that at low production levels, the marginal product of labor increases and, therefore, marginal cost declines. This was true for On-the-Move, which had increasing marginal product of labor up to 3 pianos moved, and we allow for it in the generic case.

You may have noticed that for the cost curves for On-the-Move in Figure 8.4, the marginal cost curve and the average variable cost curve touch at 1 unit of output. This occurs because the marginal cost of producing 1 rather than zero units of output must equal the variable cost of producing 1 unit, as shown in Table 8.1. Thus, if the generic cost curve were drawn all the way over to 1 unit of output on the left of Figure 8.5, the marginal cost and the average variable cost curve would start at the same point. Because we do not usually draw generic cost curves that go all the way over to the vertical axis, we do not usually show them starting at the same point.

Review

▶ The marginal cost curve and the average cost curves are closely related. The marginal cost (*MC*) curve cuts through both the average total cost (*ATC*) curve and the average variable cost (*AVC*) curve at their lowest points.

▶ Another important property of a cost curve diagram is that the gap between average total cost and average variable cost gets smaller as more is produced.

COSTS AND PRODUCTION: THE SHORT RUN

As we saw in Chapter 6, a competitive firm takes the market price as given. If it is maximizing profits, it will choose a quantity to produce in the short run so that its marginal cost equals the market price ($P = MC$). The resulting level of production for a competitive firm with the cost curves in Figure 8.5 is shown in Figure 8.6. The quantity produced is determined by the intersection of the marginal cost (*MC*) curve and the market price line (*P*). We draw a dashed vertical line to mark the quantity (*Q*) produced. But when the firm produces this quantity, are this firm's profits positive, or is the firm running a loss? If it is running a loss, should it shut down in the short run? To answer these questions, we need to use the cost curves to find the firm's profits.

The Profit or Loss Rectangle

Profits equal total revenue minus total costs. To calculate profits with the average cost diagram, we need to represent total revenue and total costs on the average cost diagram.

The Total Revenue Area

Figure 8.6 shows a particular market price *P* and the corresponding level of production *Q* chosen by the firm. The total revenue that the firm gets from selling quantity

FIGURE 8.6
Price Equals Marginal Cost
If firms are maximizing profits, then they choose a quantity (*Q*) such that price equals marginal cost. Thus, the quantity is determined by the intersection of the market price line and the marginal cost curve as shown on the diagram. In the picture the *ATC* and *AVC* curves are a sideshow, but they enter the main act in Figure 8.7, when we look at the firm's level of profits.

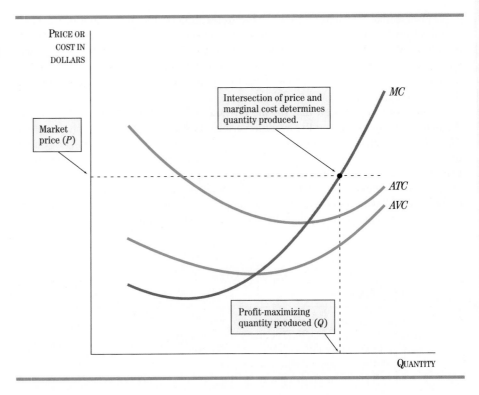

Q is price *P* times quantity *Q*. Figure 8.7 shows that this total revenue can be represented by the area of a rectangle with width *Q* and height *P*. This rectangle is shown by the shaded area in Figure 8.7. Because the width of this rectangle is the quantity produced *Q* and the height of this rectangle is the market price *P*, the area is $P \times Q$, or total revenue.

The Total Costs Area

Total costs can also be represented in Figure 8.7. First, observe the dashed vertical line in Figure 8.7 marking the profit-maximizing quantity produced. Next observe the point where the average total cost curve intersects this dashed vertical line. This point tells us what the firm's average total cost is when it produces the profit-maximizing quantity. The area of the rectangle with the hash marks shows the firm's total costs. Why? Remember that average total cost is defined as total costs divided by quantity. If we take average total cost and multiply by quantity, we get total costs: $ATC \times Q = TC$. The quantity produced (*Q*) is the width of the rectangle, and average total cost (*ATC*) is the height of the rectangle. Hence, total costs are given by the area of the rectangle with the hash marks.

Profits or Losses

Since profits are total revenue less total costs, we compute profits by looking at the difference between the two rectangles. The difference is itself a rectangle, shown by the part of the revenue rectangle that rises above the total costs rectangle. *Profits are positive* because total revenue is greater than total costs in Figure 8.7. But profits can also be negative, as shown in Figure 8.8.

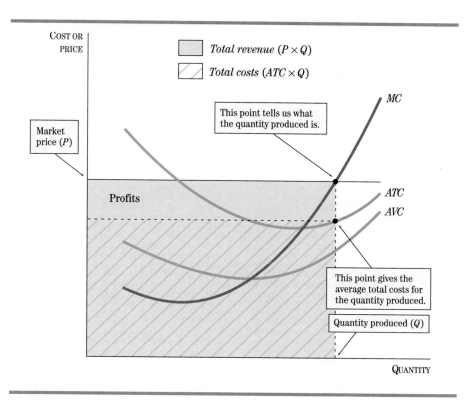

FIGURE 8.7
Showing Profits on the Cost Curve Diagram

The price and quantity produced are the same as those in Figure 8.6. The area of the shaded rectangle is total revenue. We use the *ATC* curve to find total costs in order to compute profits. First we mark where the *ATC* curve intersects the dashed vertical line showing the quantity produced. The area of the rectangle with the hash marks is total costs because the total costs (*TC*) equal average total cost (*ATC*) times quantity produced, $TC = ATC \times Q$. The part of the shaded rectangle rising above the hash-marked area is profits.

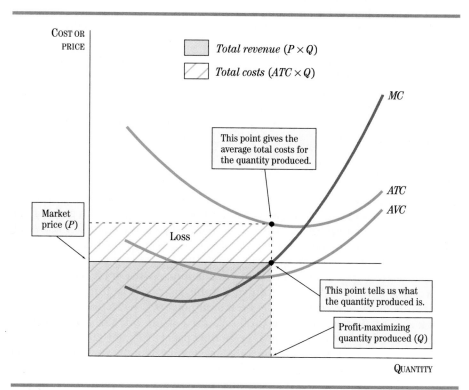

FIGURE 8.8
Showing a Loss on the Cost Curve Diagram

Here the market price is lower than in Figure 8.7. The market price line intersects the marginal cost curve at a point below the average total cost curve. Thus, the area of the total costs rectangle is larger than the area of the total revenue rectangle. Profits are less than zero, and the loss is shown in the diagram.

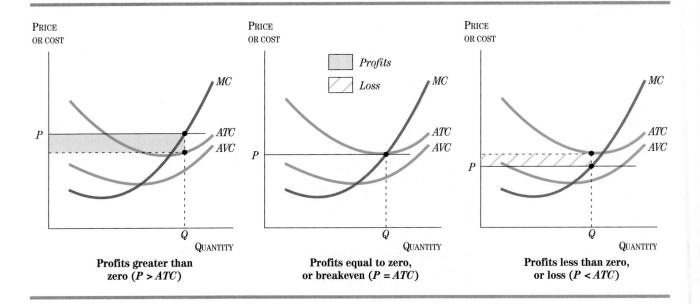

| Profits greater than zero (P > ATC) | Profits equal to zero, or breakeven (P = ATC) | Profits less than zero, or loss (P < ATC) |

FIGURE 8.9
The Breakeven Point

When profits are zero, we are at the breakeven point, as shown in the middle panel. In this case the market price line intersects the marginal cost curve exactly where it crosses the average total cost curve. The left panel shows a higher market price, and profits are greater than zero. The right panel shows a lower market price, and profits are less than zero—there is a loss. The cost curves are exactly the same in each diagram.

Suppose that the market price is at a point where the intersection of marginal cost curve and market price line gives a quantity of production for which average total cost is *above* the price. This situation is shown in Figure 8.8. At this lower price, we still have the necessary condition for profit maximization. The firm will produce the quantity that equates price and marginal cost, as shown by the intersection of the price line and the marginal cost curve.

The amount of total revenue at this price is again price times quantity ($P \times Q$), or the shaded rectangle.

Total costs are average total cost times the quantity produced, that is, $ATC \times Q$, or the area of the rectangle with the hash marks.

The difference between total revenue and total costs is profit, but in this case *profits are negative,* or there is a loss. Total revenue is less than total costs, as shown by the cost rectangle extending above the revenue rectangle. The extent of cost overhang is the loss.

The Breakeven Point

Now draw the market price line through the point where the marginal cost curve intersects the average total cost curve. Recall that this is the minimum point on the average total cost curve. This situation is shown in the middle panel of Figure 8.9. At that price, the firm chooses a quantity for which average total cost equals the price, so that the total revenue rectangle and the total cost rectangle are exactly the same. Thus, the difference between their areas is zero. At that price, the firm is at a **breakeven point:** $P = ATC,$ and economic profits are zero. The firm earns positive profits if the price is greater than the breakeven point ($P > ATC$), as shown in the left panel. The firm has negative profits (a loss) if the price is lower than the breakeven point ($P < ATC$), as shown in the right panel of Figure 8.9.

The case of negative profits raises the question of why the firm does not shut down. Every day we hear of businesses losing money. In 1993, for example,

breakeven point: the point at which price equals the minimum of average total cost.

Adidas, the running shoe company, lost $100,000,000 but it did not shut down. Why does a firm with negative profits stay in business? One reason is that if the firm shuts down, losses would be even larger. In the short run, the fixed costs have to be paid. By continuing operations, the firm can minimize its losses. Let's examine this more carefully and determine when exactly the firm should shut down.

The Shutdown Point

The firm should shut down if the price falls below the minimum point of the average variable cost curve and is not expected to rise again. In this case, the market price equals marginal cost at a quantity where total revenue ($P \times Q$) is smaller than the variable costs ($AVC \times Q$) of producing at that point.

When total revenue is less than variable costs, it makes sense to stop producing. For example, if the price of moving pianos is so low that the revenue from moving the pianos is less than the workers are paid to move the pianos, it is best not to move any pianos. It is better to shut down production. The fixed costs for the trucks and the garage would have been paid, but with the price so low, revenues cannot cover the payment to the workers.

The right panel of Figure 8.10 shows the case where the price is below average variable cost ($P < AVC$) and the firm should shut down. However, if the price is above average variable cost ($P > AVC$), as shown in the left panel of Figure 8.10, the firm should not shut down, even if the price is below average total cost and profits are negative. Because total revenue is greater than variable costs, shutting down would eliminate this extra revenue. It is better to keep producing in the short run. We assume that the firm must pay the fixed costs, as it is obligated for them over the short run. Only in the long run, when the firm can get out of its lease or other obligations, should it leave the business.

FIGURE 8.10
The Shutdown Point
When price is above average variable cost, the firm should keep producing even if profits are negative. But if price is less than average variable cost, losses will be smaller if the firm shuts down and stops producing. Hence, the shutdown point is when price equals average variable cost.

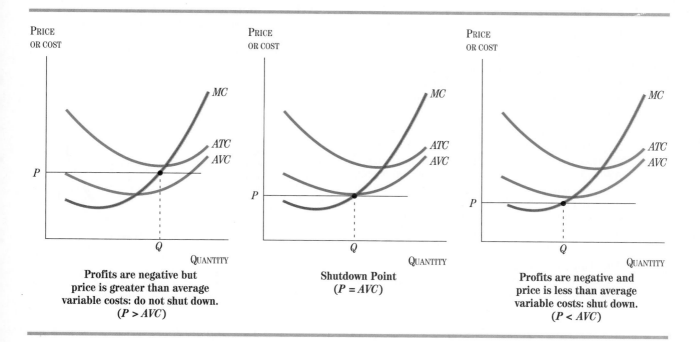

Profits are negative but price is greater than average variable costs: do not shut down.
($P > AVC$)

Shutdown Point
($P = AVC$)

Profits are negative and price is less than average variable costs: shut down.
($P < AVC$)

The middle panel of Figure 8.10 shows the case where price exactly equals the minimum point of the average variable cost curve. In this case, price equals marginal cost at a quantity where total revenue equals variable costs and price equals average variable cost ($P = AVC$). This is called the **shutdown point.** If the price falls below the shutdown point, the firm should shut down. If the price is above the shutdown point, the firm should continue producing.

shutdown point: the point at which price equals the minimum of average variable cost.

The Shutdown Point and the Firm's Supply Curve

If you are running a firm, it pays to know your shutdown point. You should stop producing if the price you can get for your product is less than average variable cost: $P < AVC$. To see this, note that

Profits = total revenue − total costs
$$= P \times Q - TC$$

Because total costs equal variable costs plus fixed costs,

$$TC = VC + FC$$

we can replace total costs to get:

Profits = $P \times Q - VC - FC$

Now, since $VC = AVC \times Q$, we have

Profits = $P \times Q - AVC \times Q - FC$

Rearranging this gives

Profits = $(P - AVC) \times Q - FC$

Thus, if $P < AVC$, the first term in the last expression is negative unless $Q = 0$. Thus, if $P < AVC$, the best your firm can do is set $Q = 0$. This eliminates the negative drain on profits in the first term in the last expression. You minimize your loss.

Suppose you are running a pizza delivery service with a fixed cost of $100 per day. If the price of pizza in your neighborhood falls to $10 and your minimum AVC is $15, then your loss will always be greater than $100 if you produce any pizzas. For example, if you make 10 pizzas, your loss is ($15 − $10) × 10 + $100 or $50 + $100 = $150. If you make no pizzas, you do not have to pay any workers to make or deliver pizza, and you limit your losses to $100 per day.

The shutdown point has interesting implications for the firm's supply curve. Recall that the supply curve of a single firm tells us the quantity of a good the firm will produce at different prices. As long as the price is

above average variable cost, the firm will produce a quantity such that marginal cost equals the price. Thus, for prices above average variable cost the marginal cost curve is the firm's supply curve, as shown in the figure.

However, if the price falls below average variable cost then the firm will shut down; in other words, the quantity produced will equal zero ($Q = 0$). Thus, for prices below average variable cost the supply curve jumps over to the vertical axis where $Q = 0$, as shown in the figure.

For the examples we considered in Chapter 6, the marginal cost was never decreasing and therefore marginal cost was always greater than average variable cost. Hence, the supply curve did not jump over to the vertical axis as in this figure.

As long as there is at least a small quantity produced, we know that the price equals marginal cost condition holds. Thus, price equals marginal cost for any profit-maximizing firm that is producing goods in a competitive market.

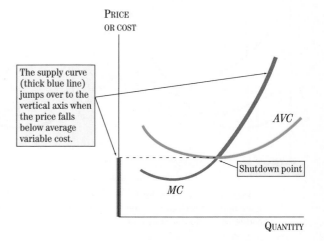

In thinking about the shutdown point, the time period is important. We are looking at the firm during the short run, when it is obligated to pay its fixed costs and cannot alter its capital. The question for On-the-Move is what to do when it has already committed to paying for trucks and the terminals but the price of moving pianos falls to such a low level that it does not cover variable costs. The shutdown rule says to stop in that situation. However, if profits are negative and the price is greater than average variable cost, then it is best to keep producing.

Be sure that you understand the difference between the shutdown point and the breakeven point. The shutdown point is where price equals the minimum average variable cost (Figure 8.10). The breakeven point is where price equals the minimum average total cost (Figure 8.9). If the price is between average total cost and average variable cost, then the firm is not breaking even; it is losing money. However, it does not make sense to shut down if the price is above the shutdown point.

Shutdown point
$P = \text{minimum } AVC$

Breakeven point
$P = \text{minimum } ATC$

Review

▶ Profits can be represented as a rectangle on the cost curve diagram. So can losses. The profit or loss rectangle is the difference between the revenue rectangle and the loss rectangle.

▶ At the breakeven point, profits are zero ($P = ATC$). At the shutdown point, $P = AVC$. When $P < AVC$, profits are maximized by ceasing operations.

COSTS AND PRODUCTION: THE LONG RUN

Thus far we have focused our analysis on the short run. By definition the short run is the period of time during which it is not possible for firms to adjust certain inputs to production. But what happens in the long run, when it *is* possible for firms to make such adjustments? For example, what happens to On-the-Move when it opens new terminals or takes out a lease on a fleet of new trucks? To answer this question, we need to show how the firm can adjust its fixed costs as well as its variable costs in the long run. All costs can be adjusted in the long run.

The Effect of Capital Expansion on Total Costs

First, consider what happens to fixed costs when the firm increases its capital. Suppose On-the-Move increases the size of its fleet from 4 trucks to 8 trucks and raises the number of terminals from 2 to 4. Then its fixed costs would increase because more rent would have to be paid for 4 terminals and 8 trucks than for 2 terminals and 4 trucks. To obtain the increase in fixed costs, we need to use the price of capital. Again, suppose trucks cost $25 per day and a terminal costs $100 per day. Then 4 trucks and 2 terminals would cost $300 and 8 trucks and 4 terminals would cost $600. Fixed costs would rise from $300 to $600.

Second, consider what happens to variable costs when the firm increases its capital. An increase in capital increases the amount that each additional worker can

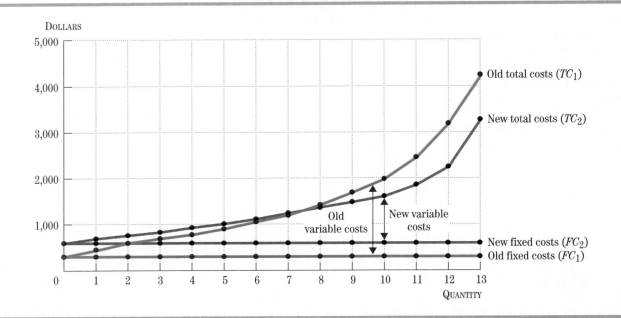

FIGURE 8.11

Shifts in Total Costs as a Firm Increases Its Capital

When a firm increases its capital, its fixed costs increase; as shown in the diagram, fixed costs rise from FC_1 to FC_2. However, its variable costs decrease, which is also shown. Thus, the new total cost curve (TC_2) will be above the old total cost curve (TC_1) for low-level output and below the old total cost curve (TC_1) for high-level output.

produce. For example, according to Table 8.2, 166 worker-hours were required for On-the-Move to move 10 pianos when there were 4 trucks and 2 terminals. With more capital (8 trucks and 4 terminals), it will take fewer hours of work to move the pianos. Assume, for example, that it takes only 120 worker-hours to deliver 10 pianos. Then with the wage equal to $10 per hour, the variable cost of moving 10 pianos falls from $1,660 to $1,200. In other words, variable costs decline as the firm expands its capital.

Now consider total costs. With fixed costs larger and variable costs smaller as a result of the increase in capital, what is the effect on total costs, which are the sum of fixed costs and variable costs? After the expansion, total costs will be higher at very low levels of output, where fixed costs dominate, but will be lower at high levels of output, where variable costs dominate. Figure 8.11 illustrates this using the total cost curve. Figure 8.11 is essentially the same as Figure 8.2 except that the green curves show the old costs before the expansion of capital and the purple curves show the new costs with the additional capital. The diagram shows that the new fixed costs are higher and the new variable costs are lower. The new total cost curve (TC_2) is twisted relative to the old total cost curve (TC_1). The new total cost curve is above the old curve at low levels of output and below the old total cost curve at high levels of output.

Table 8.3 provides the numerical information about costs that appear in Figure 8.11. To see the effect of the firm's expansion on average total cost, compare fixed costs, variable costs, and average total cost in Table 8.3 with those in Table 8.1. Observe that fixed costs are higher: $600 rather than $300. Variable costs are lower through the range of production. As a result, total costs are higher in Table 8.3 than Table 8.1 for production of less than 8 units, and lower in Table 8.3 than Table 8.1 for production of 8 units or more.

Quantity	Total Costs	Fixed Costs	Variable Costs	Average Total Cost
0	600	600	0	—
1	690	600	90	690
2	770	600	170	385
3	840	600	240	280
4	920	600	320	230
5	1010	600	410	202
6	1110	600	510	185
7	1220	600	620	174
8	1340	600	740	168
9	1470	600	870	163
10	1610	600	1010	161
11	1880	600	1280	171
12	2300	600	1700	192

TABLE 8.3
Costs with More Capital
(Compared with Table 8.1, fixed costs are higher and variable costs are lower in this table because capital is higher than in Table 8.1. Costs are measured in dollars.)

Effects of a Capital Expansion on Average Total Cost

Our analysis of the effects of the firm's capital expansion on total costs can be used to derive the effects on average total cost. Remember, average total cost (ATC) is total costs (TC) divided by the quantity (Q). Thus, if total costs increase at a given quantity of output, so will average total cost. And if total costs decrease at a given level of output, so will average total cost.

This is illustrated in Figure 8.12. An average total cost curve, labeled ATC_1, corresponding to average total cost in Table 8.1, is plotted. Another average total

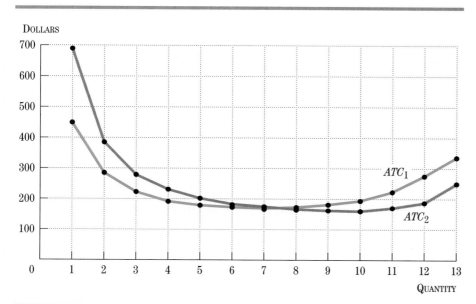

FIGURE 8.12
Shifts in Average Total Cost Curves When a Firm Expands Its Capital
The effects on average total cost follow directly from the effects on total costs in Figure 8.11. Here ATC_1 is the average total cost curve with a lower amount of capital, and ATC_2 is the average total cost curve with a higher amount of capital. To the left, at lower levels of output, higher fixed costs raise average total cost; to the right, at higher levels of output, lower variable costs tend to lower average total cost.

cost curve, labeled ATC_2, corresponding to average total cost in Table 8.3, is also plotted. The new average total cost curve (ATC_2) is above the old average total cost curve (ATC_1) at low levels of output and below the old average total cost curve (ATC_1) at higher levels of output. Average total cost is higher for production of less than 8 units and lower for production of 8 units or more. This is precisely what is shown for total costs in Figure 8.11.

The Long-Run *ATC* Curve

Now that we have seen what happens at On-the-Move when capital is expanded by a certain amount, we can see what happens when capital increases by even larger amounts. For example, suppose On-the-Move expands throughout Houston and even beyond Houston by expanding the size of its fleet of trucks and the terminals to park and service the trucks.

Figure 8.13 shows four different average total cost curves. Each of the average total cost curves corresponds to increased capital expansion at On-the-Move. The first two of these, ATC_1 and ATC_2, are the average total cost curves from Figure 8.12. Note that the second curve (ATC_2) is above the first (ATC_1) at low levels of output and below the first at high levels of output. The third and fourth are for even more trucks and terminals. The third average total cost curve (ATC_3) is above the second (ATC_2) at lower levels of output and below the second (ATC_2) at higher levels of output. The same is true of the fourth compared to the third.

The thick light green curve tracing out the bottoms of the four average total cost curves gives the lowest average total cost at any quantity produced. For example, at 11 pianos moved, the lowest average total cost is $164. This occurs on the average total cost curve ATC_3. This thick line tells us what average total cost is when the firm can expand (or contract) its capital; in other words, this is the average total cost curve for the long run. For this reason we call the curve that traces out

Using Economics to Explain an Actual Firm's History

The behavior of the hypothetical firm On-the-Move becomes more vivid if we look at the behavior of an actual moving firm over many years.

In 1930 the moving firm Roadway Express was founded by two brothers, Galen and Carroll Roush. At the start, it had 10 trucks and 3 terminals in Houston, Chicago, and Kansas City, Missouri. In 1975, when both Galen and Carroll Roush had retired from the business,

Roadway had 300 terminals in 40 states. In the early 1980s, it was the largest freight carrier in the country. By the 1990s, it had a fleet of 38,501 vehicles and 805 terminals all over the United States, Mexico, and Canada. Thus, in the long run, Roadway Express, like On-the-Move, could vary all inputs to production, not just workers.

But each year for the last 60 years, Roadway Express had certain costs

that were considered fixed in the short run, again just like On-the-Move. For example, when business conditions got bad in the early 1970s, the firm reduced its production by reducing labor input. This reduced its variable costs, which were nearly equal to 60 percent of expenses, but the expenses on its long-term leases for terminals and trucks could not be reduced in the short run.

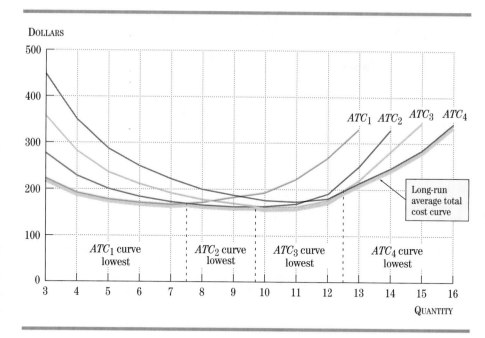

FIGURE 8.13
Long-Run versus Short-Run Average Total Cost
In the short run, it is not possible to change certain inputs, like the size of the factory or the number of machines. In the long run, these can be changed. For example, in the long run On-the-Move can build more terminals around town. This means the *ATC* curve shifts. The diagram shows four different *ATC* curves for On-the-Move; each new *ATC* curve represents more terminals, buildings, and machines than the *ATC* curve to its left. The long-run average total cost curve is shown by the thicker light green line.

the points on the lowest average total cost curves the **long-run average total cost curve.** The other average total cost curve that we have been discussing is called the *short-run average total cost curve,* or simply, the average total cost curve.

The long-run average total cost curve is one way that economists study the behavior of a firm over time. Frequently economists will simply draw a generic long-run average total cost curve without the short-run curves. Whether the long-run average total cost curve slopes up or down, and over what range, is crucial for understanding the nature of a firm, the industry in which it operates, and the role of government.

The lack of smoothness in the long-run average total cost curve may seem strange. It occurs in Figure 8.13 because we have drawn only four short-run average total cost curves. If it is possible to expand capital in smaller amounts, then the curve will look smoother. For example, between the first and second short-run average total cost curves (ATC_1 and ATC_2) in Figure 8.13 might be an average total cost curve for 6 trucks and 3 terminals. When we put in more and more short-run average total cost curves, the long-run average total cost curve gets smoother and smoother. But it still simply traces out the points of lowest cost for each level of output.

long-run average total cost curve: the curve that traces out the short-run average total cost curves, showing the lowest average total cost for each quantity produced as the firm expands in the long run.

Capital Expansion and Production in the Long Run

How does a firm like On-the-Move decide whether to expand or contract its capital in the long run? How much does it produce in the long run? The decision is very similar to the short-run decision about whether to hire more workers to move more pianos. Again, the firm sets the quantity produced to maximize profits. But now the quantity produced and profits can be affected by changes in capital as well as labor.

At any level of capital and labor input, we can compute profits. For each level of capital, there is a short-run average total cost curve. Profits can be computed from this average total cost curve as described in Figure 8.7. Hence, for any level of capital, profits can be computed by the firm.

If by expanding its capital and its output, the firm can increase its profits, then we predict that it will do so. If by reducing its capital and its output, we find that the firm can increase its profits, then we predict that it will do so. In other words, the firm adjusts the amount of capital to maximize profits.

The Mix of Capital and Labor

In the long run the firm adjusts both its capital and its labor. Both inputs are variable in the long run. What determines the mix of labor and capital when both are variable? The relative price of labor compared to capital will be the deciding factor.

In deriving the cost curves for On-the-Move, we assumed that the cost of labor was $10 per hour and that the cost of capital, consisting of trucks and terminals, was $25 a day for trucks and $100 a day for terminals. If the cost of labor was higher, say $20 per day, then On-the-Move would have the incentive to rent more trucks rather than hire more workers, at least to the extent that this was feasible.

However, if the cost of capital rose relative to labor, then the firm would have incentive to hire more workers. In general, the firm will use more capital relative to labor if the cost of capital declines relative to labor. And conversely, the firm will use less capital relative to labor if the cost of capital rises relative to labor.

Review

▶ In the long run, the firm can expand by increasing its capital. Fixed costs increase and variable costs decline at each level of production as the firm expands its capital. Thus, total costs, and average total cost, are higher at low levels of production and lower at high levels of production.

▶ The long-run average total cost curve traces out the points on the lowest short-run average total cost curve for each level of production.

ECONOMIES OF SCALE

The long-run average total cost curve describes a situation where the firm can expand all its inputs—both its capital and labor. When all inputs increase, we say that the *scale* of the firm increases. For example, if the number of workers at the firm doubles, the number of trucks doubles, the number of terminals doubles, and so on, then we would say the scale of the firm doubles. Thus, the long-run average total cost curve describes what happens to a firm's average total cost when its scale increases. There is some specialized terminology about different shapes of the long-run average total cost.

economies of scale: also called increasing returns to scale; a situation in which long-run average total cost declines as the output of a firm increases.

We say that there are **economies of scale,** or *increasing returns to scale,* if long-run average total cost falls as the scale of the firm increases. We say that there

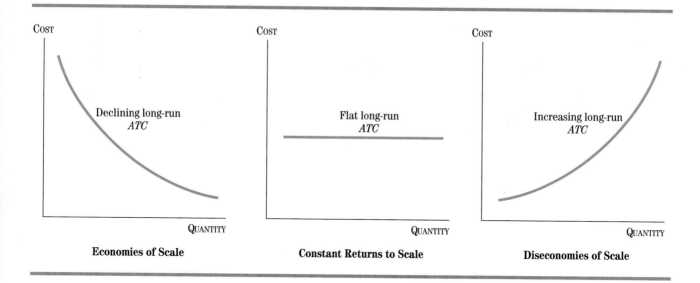

Economies of Scale   **Constant Returns to Scale**   **Diseconomies of Scale**

are **diseconomies of scale,** or *decreasing returns to scale,* if long-run average total cost rises as the scale of the firm increases. The situation in the middle, where long-run average total cost neither rises or falls, is called **constant returns to scale.** Figure 8.14 illustrates these three possible shapes for the long-run average total cost curve.

Whether there are increasing, decreasing, or constant returns to scale depends on the type of firm and the type of product. Consider a firm like On-the-Move. One can imagine that there would be economies of scale as the firm expanded the number of terminals around the city of Houston; then trucks could be serviced at many different locations and would not have to be driven so far at the end of the day or towed so far in the case of a breakdown. With a larger work force, On-the-Move could have workers who *specialize* in moving different types of pianos or who specialize in servicing different parts of the trucks. Some might specialize in moves to high-rise buildings. In other words, as the scale of a firm increases, the labor force can be divided into different tasks and specialize in each task.

Is there a limit to economies of scale? What about expanding beyond Houston to Galveston, Dallas, Tulsa, Mexico City, or even Lima, Peru? In the case of piano moving, returns to scale would probably begin to decline at some point. The extra administrative costs of organizing a large interstate or worldwide piano-moving firm would probably raise average total cost. Thus, one could imagine that the long-run average total cost curve for On-the-Move first declines and then increases as the firm grows in size.

Although no two firms are alike, the long-run average total cost curve for most firms probably declines at low levels of output, then remains flat, and finally begins to increase at high levels of output. As a firm gets very large, administrative expenses, as well as coordination and incentive problems, will begin to raise average total cost. The smallest scale of production, for which long-run average total cost is at a minimum, is called the **minimum efficient scale.** A typical long-run average cost curve and its minimum efficient scale are shown in Figure 8.15.

FIGURE 8.14
Economies and Diseconomies of Scale

If the long-run average total cost curve slopes downward, we say there are economies of scale. If the long-run average total cost curve slopes upward, we say there are diseconomies of scale. If the long-run average total cost curve is flat, we say there are constant returns to scale, as shown in the middle panel.

diseconomies of scale: also called decreasing returns to scale; a situation in which long-run average total cost increases as the output of a firm increases.

constant returns to scale: a situation in which long-run average total cost is constant as the output of a firm changes.

minimum efficient scale: the smallest scale of production for which long-run average total cost is at a minimum.

FIGURE 8.15
Typical Shape of the Long-Run Average Total Cost Curve
For many types of firms, the long-run *ATC* curve slopes down at low levels of output, then reaches a flat area, and finally begins to slope up at high levels. The minimum efficient scale is shown.

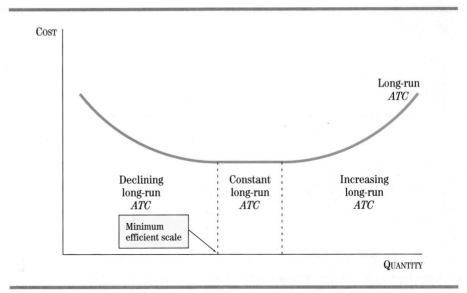

Review

▶ Economies of scale are nothing more than a downward-sloping long-run average total cost curve. Economies of scale may occur because of specialization that the division of labor in larger firms permits.

▶ Although economies of scale probably exist over some regions of production, the evidence indicates that as firms grow very large, diseconomies of scale set in.

ACQUISITIONS, SPINOFFS, AND COORDINATION OF DIVISIONS

An increase or decrease in the scale of a firm through capital expansion or contraction—as described in the previous two sections—is one kind of change in the firm over time. Firms can also change over time in other ways. They can grow through *acquisitions,* in which one firm buys, or acquires, another firm or division of a firm. If the product lines of the two firms are similar, then such acquisitions might be a way to reduce costs. That is one reason why the two large office supply firms—Staples and Office Depot—wanted to merge in 1997. Acquisition is also a common way for firms to adjust to change. As defense spending declined in the United States in the early 1990s, firms in the defense industry merged.

In recent years many large firms have tried to sell, or *spin off,* whole divisions in an effort to cut costs; they found that coordinating different product lines was not always cost efficient. Cutting costs by spinning off divisions of a firm is also called *restructuring.* Many large businesses in the United States have restructured in the

Changes in a Firm over Time
The first general merchandise "five and dime" store was opened by Woolworth in 1879. By building new stores and merging with other firms over time, Woolworth expanded greatly in size. By 1919 it had 1,081 stores in the United States, France, England, and Germany. Through the development of discount stores (Woolco) and specialty stores (including the Lady Foot Locker shown here), this firm continued to expand.

1980s and 1990s. For example, IBM sold its copier division to Kodak in 1988 and part of its defense division to Loral in 1993.

Merging Two Firms: Economies of Scope

When two firms merge into one firm after an acquisition, each firm may become a division within the same firm. Or, in the case of a spinoff, two divisions of a firm become two different firms. To the extent that the different divisions of a firm work together to produce a product, a spinoff of a division means that coordination of production that was done within the firm now must be done in the market. An acquisition of one firm by another means that the coordination of production moves from the market to within the organization. For example, Sony Corporation acquired CBS Records in 1988 in an effort to integrate the production of musical software products, such as sound or video recordings, with the production of hardware products such as compact disks. Previously Sony would have had to buy the recordings from CBS Records in the market; now that transaction is done within the larger firm.

"The Chloride Co. wants to merge with us. They think we can make salt together."

TABLE 8.4
Marginal Benefits and Costs for M-Division
(dollars)

Pianos Moved	Marginal Benefit	Marginal Cost
1	330	150
2	320	120
3	290	100
4	270	110
5	250	120
6	230	140
7	210	160
8	190	190
9	170	250
10	160	320

Consider a simpler example of an acquisition. Suppose there is an acquisition that involves the Houston piano-moving firm On-the-Move. Suppose that Uh-huh is another Houston firm specializing in Ray Charles look-alike productions. Uh-huh usually produces about 10 live gigs a day at birthday parties, weddings, and office parties throughout the greater Houston area. Uh-huh can make its products more attractive and competitive with its entertainment competitors by using exactly the same kind of piano that Ray Charles uses, but that requires moving pianos all over Houston. Uh-huh had been buying the services of On-the-Move in the market, but decides it can reduce costs and become more competitive by acquiring On-the-Move and dedicating that company to moving real Ray Charles pianos from gig to gig. Thus, the coordination of activities that had been done within the market now must be done within the new organization. The resulting new company is called Uh-huh; the previous name, On-the-Move, was painted over on the trucks and terminals; the former workers, trucks, and terminals of On-the-Move are now called the M-Division of Uh-huh.

Table 8.4 provides the relevant information about the new firm. The second column shows the *marginal benefit* to Uh-huh from moving real Ray Charles pianos to various events around the city. *Marginal benefit* for a firm is similar to marginal benefit for a consumer: It is the increase in Uh-huh's profits due to an additional piano moved. The third column shows the marginal cost of moving pianos. It is the same as the marginal cost for On-the-Move as shown in the last column of Table 8.1, when it was an independent firm.

Average total cost at On-the-Move may have declined as a result of the acquisition, but, if so, we assume that fixed costs declined without affecting marginal cost. Indeed, one reason for the merger may have been to reduce fixed costs. When average total cost declines as a result of a merger of two firms that are not producing the same type of product, they experience *economies of scope*. Average total cost may decline as a result of a merger of two different types of firms because of a synergy in the production process. For example, by having pianists and piano movers working together, the movers may learn how to pack more pianos on the truck. This would reduce the number of trucks needed to move the pianos and reduce fixed costs.

When Uh-huh purchased piano-moving services from On-the-Move, like any buyer, it bought a quantity such that its marginal benefit equaled the price. We know that when On-the-Move sold piano-moving services, it chose to sell a quantity that equated marginal cost and price. Thus, in the market, marginal cost equaled marginal benefit. Suppose that the market price for moving pianos was $190; then the resulting quantity was 8 pianos. It is best for the newly merged firm to move the same number of pianos because that is where the marginal benefit equals the marginal cost for the merged firm.

How to Manage the Divisions of a Large Firm

Which approach to managing the divisions of a large firm is better—the price-directed approach or the quantity-directed approach? There is no difference between the two approaches if the CEO has full information about the marginal benefit and marginal cost. But in reality the CEO does not have perfect information; especially in a large firm there is *imperfect information* about what goes on in each division. Changes in technology or other external events can change costs from day to day. When the marginal cost curve shifts in ways unknown to the CEO, it makes a difference whether the coordination is price-directed or quantity-directed.

To see why, consider the adjacent graph, which plots a marginal benefit curve, along with two marginal cost curves. The old marginal cost curve from Table 8.4 for On-the-Move (now M-Division) is shown, along with a new higher marginal cost curve. The CEO does not know about the shift in marginal cost but still must decide whether to direct M-Division by price or by quantity.

The price-directed approach is shown by the horizontal price line. The vertical quantity line shows the quantity-directed approach. The loss from each approach due to a higher marginal cost is shown by the deadweight loss; recall that *deadweight loss* is the decline in the area between the marginal benefit curve and the marginal cost curve. Neither the price nor the quantity is adjusted when the marginal cost curve shifts.

Note that the two deadweight losses are different. In the graph, the deadweight loss is slightly larger for the

quantity-directed approach than for the price-directed approach. Thus, in this case the price-directed approach would be preferable. This particular result depends on the slopes of the marginal cost and marginal benefit curves; in general, we cannot conclude that coordination by either a price-directed approach or by a quantity-directed approach is better in all cases.

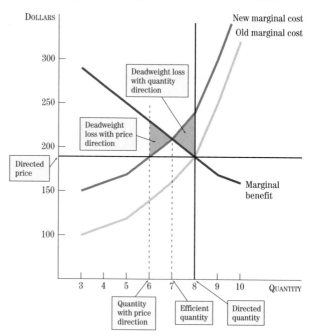

quantity-directed approach: a management technique in which decisions handed down by executives instruct a division to produce a given quantity.

price-directed approach: a management technique in which the instructions to a division of a firm are to maximize profits given transfer prices set by executives.

How should the merged firm determine this level of production? There are two possible approaches. First, the CEO of Uh-huh could instruct the workers in the M-Division to move 8 pianos. This is called the **quantity-directed approach.** Second, the CEO of Uh-huh could establish a *transfer price* for the use of M-Division's services within the firm. M-Division would then be instructed to maximize division profits. It would do so by choosing a quantity such that the transfer price equals marginal cost. This is the **price-directed approach.** If the CEO set a transfer price of $190 per piano moved, then M-Division would move 8 pianos.

Market Prices as Transfer Prices

Note that if other piano-moving firms in the Houston area stayed open after the merger—as seems likely—then there would still be a market price for piano moving. Uh-huh could use the market price as a transfer price. Management experts frequently suggest that firms use market prices, when available, as a guide for setting their transfer prices within the firm.

Without the market price as a guide, the managers might set the transfer price too high. With this high price the services of the firm's division would not be used enough. A too-low transfer price might encourage wasteful uses of the division's services.

Review

▶ When one firm acquires another, transactions that took place in the market must take place in the firm. Conversely, a restructuring that involves a spinoff moves transactions to the market.

▶ Coordination of different divisions within a merged firm can be directed either by prices or quantities.

▶ Management experts recommend that firms use market prices as a guide when setting transfer prices.

CONCLUSION

In this chapter we have developed a model for studying why firms shut down, expand, contract, or acquire other firms. This long-term analysis of the evolution of firms over time is an extension of the analysis of a firm's short-run behavior in Chapter 6.

A centerpiece of the model is a graph that shows the firm's average total cost. Using this graph, we can determine if a firm will shut down in the short run. We can also determine whether the firm will expand or contract in the long run. By looking at a firm's long-run average total cost curve, we can tell if a firm has economies of scale. We will use the average total cost curve extensively in the next several chapters of this book.

This chapter also considered cases where marginal cost declines at low levels of production. Marginal cost may decline if the marginal product of labor increases when output rises from low levels. But at higher levels of production the marginal product of labor decreases and marginal cost starts to increase. By deriving the firm's marginal cost from the production function, we showed why marginal cost is related to the marginal product of labor.

In the next chapter, we will use the cost curves derived in this chapter to study how whole industries—consisting of many firms—evolve over time. The average total cost curve will also prove useful when we study how monopolies operate and how government policy toward monopolies is formulated.

KEY POINTS

1. Firms start up, expand, contract, or shut down when conditions in the economy change.

2. The short run and the long run are two broad categories into which economists categorize time periods. The short run is the period of time during which it is not possible for the firm to change all the inputs to production; only some inputs, such as labor, can be changed. The long run is the minimum period of time in which the firm can vary all inputs to production, including capital.

3. Average total cost, or cost per unit, is widely used by economists, accountants, and investors to assess a firm's cost behavior.

4. When the market price equals the minimum of average total cost, the firm breaks even. At higher prices, profits are positive. At lower prices, profits are negative.

5. When the market price equals the minimum of average variable cost, the firm is just at the point of shutting down. If the price is below average variable cost, the firm should shut down.

6. The long-run average total cost curve describes how a firm's costs behave when the firm expands its capital.

7. If long-run average total cost declines, then there are economies of scale. For many firms, there is a range over which the long-run average total cost curve is flat, and we say there are constant returns to scale. When firms get very large, diseconomies of scale set in.

8. When firms split apart, transactions that were formerly undertaken in the firm take place in the market. The opposite occurs when firms merge: More transactions take place within the firm.

KEY TERMS

short run
long run
average total cost (*ATC*)
average variable cost (*AVC*)
average fixed cost (*AFC*)

average product of labor
breakeven point
shutdown point
long-run average total cost curve
economies of scale

diseconomies of scale
constant returns to scale
minimum efficient scale
quantity-directed approach
price-directed approach

QUESTIONS FOR REVIEW

1. What is the difference between average total cost and average variable cost?

2. Why does the marginal cost curve cut through the average total cost curve exactly at the minimum of the average total cost curve?

3. Why are total revenue, total costs, and profits given by areas of rectangles in the cost curve diagram?

4. What is the difference between the breakeven point and the shutdown point?

5. Why do average total cost curves shift as the firm expands, and how does the shift relate to economies of scale?

6. Why might a merger lower average total cost?

7. What is the minimum efficient scale of a firm?

8. What is the difference between price-directed and quantity-directed management of a firm's division?

PROBLEMS

1. Compare and contrast the following: short run/long run, fixed costs/variable costs, marginal cost/average variable cost, average total cost curve/long-run average total cost curve, average product of labor/marginal product of labor, breakeven point/shutdown point, economies of scale/diseconomies of scale, price-directed/quantity directed.

2. Draw the typical average total cost, average variable cost, and marginal cost curves for a profit-maximizing, price-taking firm like the one in Figure 8.6.

a) Show the market price at which the firm just breaks even. What is true of marginal cost at the profit-making quantity?

b) Show the rectangles that represent fixed costs and variable costs. What happens to the size of these areas as the market price increases? Show this in your diagram.

3. Draw a diagram of a competitive firm in which the price is at shutdown point, where $P = AVC$. Show that total revenue equals variable costs at this quantity. Also show that losses equal fixed costs.

4. The relationship between marginal and average can be illustrated with the marginal and average height of any group of people. Consider students as they walk into the student union. Suppose the first person is 6 feet tall. The second and third are 5½ and 5 feet tall, respectively. Graph the marginal and average height of people in the student union, placing height on the vertical axis and quantity of people on the horizontal axis, in order of their arrival. What do you notice about the relationship between marginal and average height? Suppose the fourth person coming into the student union is 6 feet tall. What happens to the average height?

5. Fill out the following table, showing total costs (TC) in dollars for various quantities (Q), and then draw a diagram showing marginal cost, average total cost, and average variable cost.

Q	TC	FC	VC	ATC	AFC	AVC	MC
0	10	___	___	___	___	___	___
1	13	___	___	___	___	___	___
2	15	___	___	___	___	___	___
3	16	___	___	___	___	___	___
4	20	___	___	___	___	___	___
5	30	___	___	___	___	___	___
6	42	___	___	___	___	___	___

a) Suppose this firm is a price-taker, that is, it is in a perfectly competitive market. If the price is $10 per unit, will this firm be earning profits? How much? What quantity will it produce?

b) What is the breakeven price? What is the shutdown price?

6. Suppose the firm in problem 5 can buy an additional machine that changes its total cost as shown in the following table. Calculate the costs in the table and sketch the ATC curve and MC curve. Compare these curves with the ATC curve and MC curve from problem 5. Does this expansion of the firm involve economies or diseconomies of scale?

Q	TC	FC	VC	ATC	AFC	AVC	MC
0	12	___	___	___	___	___	___
1	15	___	___	___	___	___	___
2	16	___	___	___	___	___	___
3	17	___	___	___	___	___	___
4	18	___	___	___	___	___	___
5	20	___	___	___	___	___	___
6	26	___	___	___	___	___	___

7. Plot the following data on quantity of production and long-run average total cost for a firm. Show the areas of economies and diseconomies of scale, and constant returns to scale. What is the minimum efficient scale? Will this firm have diminishing marginal returns to labor in these three regions? Explain.

Quantity	Long-Run ATC
1	45
2	38
3	34
4	32
5	30
6	30
7	33
8	36
9	40
10	44

8. Suppose a firm is deciding whether to invest in a new branch office with new employees or to hire more people to work in its current office. In which case will the firm be concerned about diminishing returns to labor, and in which will returns to scale come into play? If the firm can double its output by opening the new office and doubling the size of its work force, does this mean that diminishing returns to labor will not occur?

9. In a diagram like the one in the box "How to Manage the Divisions of a Large Firm," show the marginal cost and marginal benefit of a division of a firm. Show the dead-weight loss that occurs when the marginal cost of the division turns out to be surprisingly low rather than surprisingly high. Compare the price-directed and quantity-directing methods of managing the division.

10. Suppose a corporation uses the price-directed approach to encourage a division to produce the correct quantity. If the marginal benefit curve is very steep, would it be better to use a quantity-directed approach? Show the different possibilities for the size of the deadweight loss based on different slopes of the marginal benefit curve.

A Graphical Approach to Long-Run Capital and Labor Decisions

In this chapter we have emphasized that in the short run the firm can adjust some of its inputs, such as labor, but it cannot adjust other inputs, such as capital. In the long run, on the other hand, the firm can adjust all its inputs to production, capital as well as labor. When making decisions for the long run, the firm is free to choose any combination of labor and capital. The firm's choice will depend on the relative costs of the inputs and their relative marginal products. If the cost of labor increases, for example, the firm will utilize less labor and more capital.

In this appendix, we focus on the firm's choice between labor and capital in the long run. We introduce a graphical device similar to the indifference curves used to describe consumer choice in the appendix to Chapter 5. We use this graphical device to show exactly how a firm's choice between labor and capital depends on the relative price and the relative marginal productivities of labor and capital.

ADJUSTING THE MIX OF CAPITAL AND LABOR

Consider an example of a firm with two inputs to production: capital and labor. Table 8A.1 shows the possible combinations of inputs available to firms. For example, if the firm has 2 units of capital and uses 24 hours of labor, it can produce 3 units of output. The hypothetical numbers in Table 8A.1 could represent a wide variety of firms producing different types of products, but observe that we have chosen the units in the table to be the same as those for the hypothetical firm On-the-Move shown in Table 8.2 of the chapter. To make a comparison between Table 8A.1 and Table 8.2, you can think of a "unit" of capital corresponding to 4 trucks and 2 terminals with a cost of $300; 2 units of capital is 8 trucks and 4 terminals at a cost of $600. But

TABLE 8A.1
Production with Four Levels of Capital

		Labor Input (hours)		
Quantity Produced	With 1 Unit of Capital	With 2 Units of Capital	With 3 Units of Capital	With 4 Units of Capital
0	0	0	0	0
1	15	9	6	5
2	27	17	12	10
3	37	24	17	13
4	48	32	22	18
5	60	41	29	23
6	74	51	36	29
7	90	62	43	35
8	109	74	52	41
9	134	87	61	49
10	166	101	71	57
11	216	128	90	72
12	290	170	119	95
13	400	270	189	151
14	—	400	300	220
15	—	—	425	300
16	—	—	—	430

Note: The column showing labor input with one unit of capital corresponds to the production function for On-the-Move discussed in the text. (See Table 8.2.) The omitted entries in the table represent quantities of production that cannot be achieved without more capital.

Table 8A.1 could refer to many other firms with capital consisting of computers, machine tools, telephones, or pizza ovens; to allow for all these possibilities, we therefore refer to capital as a "unit" of capital.

The information in Table 8A.1 can be represented graphically, as shown in Figure 8A.1. Each column is plotted with labor input on the horizontal axis and the quantity produced on the vertical axis. Each column represents a production function for a given level of capital. Note how higher levels of capital increase the amount that can be produced with a given amount of labor. In other words, as we add more capital, the relationship between labor and output shifts up.

The information in Table 8A.1 and Figure 8A.1 can be displayed in another graph, Figure 8A.2, which provides a visual picture of how labor and capital jointly help a firm produce its product. Figure 8A.2 puts capital on the vertical axis and labor on the horizontal axis. We represent the quantity produced in Figure 8A.2 by writing a number in a circle equal to the amount produced with each amount of labor and capital. For example, with 1 unit of capital and 60 hours of labor, the firm can produce 5 units of output, according to Table 8A.1. Thus, we write the number 5 at

the point in Figure 8A.2 that represents labor input equal to 60 and capital input equal to 1.

Isoquants

Observe in Figure 8A.2 how the same amount of output can be produced using different combinations of capital and labor. We illustrate this in the figure by connecting points with the same quantity by a curved line. Each curve gives the combinations of labor and capital that produce the same quantity of output. The curves in Figure 8A.2 are called *isoquants*, where "iso" means "the same" and "quant" stands for "quantity produced." Thus, an **isoquant** is a curve that shows all the possible combinations of labor and capital that result in the same quantity of production. Isoquants convey a lot of information visually. Higher isoquants—those up and to the right—represent higher levels of output. Each isoquant slopes down because as capital input declines, labor input must increase if the quantity produced is to remain the same. The slope of the isoquants tells us how much labor must be substituted for capital (or vice versa) to leave production unchanged. Thus, the isoquants are good for studying how firms substitute one input for another when the prices of the inputs change. The slope of the isoquant is called the **rate of technical substitution,** because it tells us how much capital needs to be substituted for labor to give the same amount of production when labor is reduced by one unit.

Remember that the points in Figure 8A.2 do not display any information not in Table 8A.1 or Figure 8A.1. The same information appears in a different and convenient way.

Isocost Lines

A firm's total costs can also be shown on a diagram like Figure 8A.2. In considering the choice between capital and labor, the firm needs to consider the price of both. Suppose that labor costs $10 per hour and capital costs $300 per unit. Then if the firm uses 1 unit of capital and 150 hours of labor, its total costs will be $1 \times \$300 + 150 \times \$10 = \$1,800$. For the same total cost, the firm can pay for other combinations of labor and capital. For example, 2 units of capital and 120 hours of labor also cost $1,800. Other combinations are as follows:

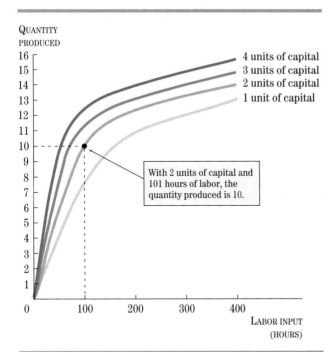

QUANTITY
PRODUCED

4 units of capital
3 units of capital
2 units of capital
1 unit of capital

With 2 units of capital and 101 hours of labor, the quantity produced is 10.

LABOR INPUT
(HOURS)

FIGURE 8A.1

The Production Function with Four Levels of Capital

As the amount of labor input increases, so does the amount of output. Each curve corresponds to a different level of capital. Higher curves represent higher capital. The points on these four curves are obtained from the four columns of Table 8A.1.

Hours of Labor	Units of Capital	Total Cost
180	0	$180 \times \$10 + 0 \times \$300 = \$1,800$
150	1	$150 \times \$10 + 1 \times \$300 = \$1,800$
120	2	$120 \times \$10 + 2 \times \$300 = \$1,800$
90	3	$90 \times \$10 + 3 \times \$300 = \$1,800$
60	4	$60 \times \$10 + 4 \times \$300 = \$1,800$
30	5	$30 \times \$10 + 5 \times \$300 = \$1,800$
0	6	$0 \times \$10 + 6 \times \$300 = \$1,800$

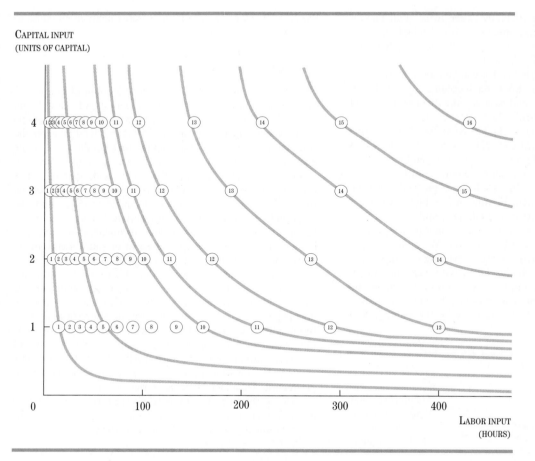

CAPITAL INPUT
(UNITS OF CAPITAL)

FIGURE 8A.2
Isoquants

The number in each circled point gives the quantity produced for the amount of labor and capital on the axes. The lines connecting equal quantities are called *isoquants*.

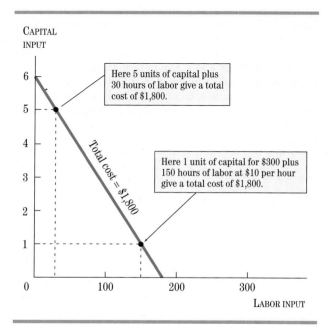

CAPITAL
INPUT

Here 5 units of capital plus 30 hours of labor give a total cost of $1,800.

Here 1 unit of capital for $300 plus 150 hours of labor at $10 per hour give a total cost of $1,800.

Total cost = $1,800

LABOR INPUT

FIGURE 8A.3
An Isocost Line

Each isocost line shows all the combinations of labor and capital that give the same total costs. In this case, the price of capital is $300 per unit and the price of labor is $10 per hour. Total costs are $1,800. For example, if 1 unit of capital is employed and 150 hours of labor are employed, total costs are $1,800 = $(1 \times \$300) + (150 \times \$10)$.

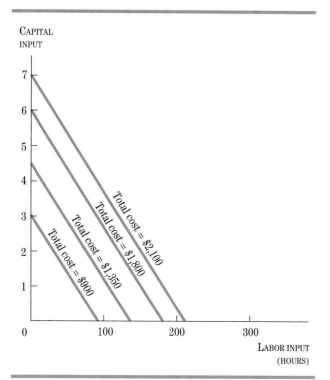

FIGURE 8A.4
Several Isocost Lines with Different Total Costs

Isocost lines with higher total costs are above and to the right of those with lower total costs. All the isocost lines in this diagram have a capital cost of $300 per unit and a labor cost of $10 per hour.

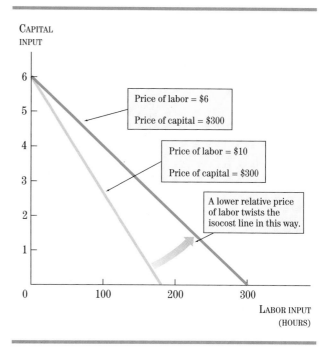

FIGURE 8A.5
Effect of a Change in Relative Prices on the Isocost Line

When the price of labor falls relative to the price of capital, the isocost line gets flatter, as in this diagram. In this case the price of labor falls from $10 per hour to $6 per hour while the price of capital remains at $300 per unit. Total costs remain equal to $1,800 in this case.

In other words, the $1,800 can be spent on any of these combinations of labor and capital. With $1,800, the firm can use 6 units of capital, but that would not permit the firm to hire any workers.

These different combinations of labor and capital that have a total cost of $1,800 are plotted in Figure 8A.3. Each combination of labor and capital in the table is plotted and the points are connected by a line. The line is called an **isocost** line. An isocost line shows the combinations of capital and labor that have the same total costs.

The position of the isocost line depends on the amount of total costs. Higher total costs are represented by higher isocost lines. This is shown in Figure 8A.4. Observe that the isocost line for total costs of $2,100 is above the one for $1,800.

The slope of the isocost line depends on the ratio of the price of labor to the price of capital. In particular, the slope equals −1 times the ratio of the price of labor to the price of capital. This is illustrated in Figure 8A.5 for the case where

total costs equal $1,800. If the price of labor falls from $10 to $6, then the isocost line gets flatter. Thus, if the hourly wage were $6 instead of $10, the firm would be able to pay for 250 hours of work and 1 unit of capital, compared with only 150 hours and 1 unit of capital, and still have a total cost of $1,800. Thus, as the price of labor (the wage) falls relative to the price of capital, the isocost line gets flatter.

Minimizing Costs for a Given Quantity

The isoquant and isocost lines can be used to determine the least-cost combination of capital and labor for any given quantity of production. Figure 8A.6 shows how. In Figure 8A.6 we show three isocost lines, along with an isoquant representing 11 units of output. For the isocost lines, the price of labor is $10 and the price of capital is $300. The point where the isocost line just touches the isoquant is a *tangency point*. It is labeled A.

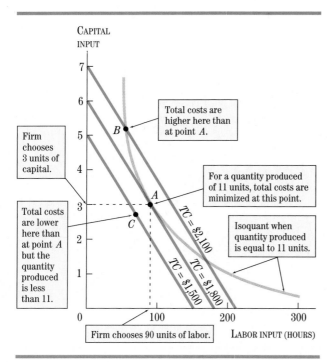

FIGURE 8A.6
Choosing Capital and Labor to Minimize Total Costs
The diagram illustrates how a firm chooses a mix of labor and capital to minimize total costs for a given level of output. Here the given level of output is 11 units, as shown by the single isoquant. Total costs are minimized by choosing a combination of labor and capital given by the tangency (point *A*) between the isocost line and the isoquant. Any other point on the isoquant would have the same quantity but higher total costs.

Point *A* is where the firm minimizes the cost of producing 11 units of output. To see this, suppose you are at point *A* and you move to the left and up along the same isoquant to point *B*. This means that the firm increases capital and decreases hours of labor, keeping quantity produced constant at 11 units; that is, the firm would substitute capital for labor. But such a substitution would increase the firm's costs, as shown in the figure. The payment for the extra capital will be greater than the saving from reduced labor. Thus, moving along the isoquant from *A* to *B* would increase the total costs to the firm.

A similar reasoning applies to moving from point *A* to point *C*. The firm uses fewer labor hours and less capital at point *C*, so that total costs are lower than at point *A*. But at

point *C* it does not have enough inputs to produce 11 units of output. Thus, point *A* is the lowest-cost point at which the firm can produce 11 units of output. It is the point at which the lowest isocost line is touching.

The rate of technical substitution of capital for labor and the ratio of the price of labor to the price of capital coincide at point *A*, because the slope of the isoquant and the isocost line are equal at point *A*. When the rate of technical substitution differs from the input price ratio, the firm is not minimizing its costs. (Observe how isoquants are analogous to indifference curves, and the isocost lines are analogous to the budget line described in the appendix to Chapter 5.)

A Change in the Relative Price of Labor

Now we show how isoquants and isocost lines can be used to predict how a firm will adjust its mix of inputs when there is a change in input prices. For example, suppose that

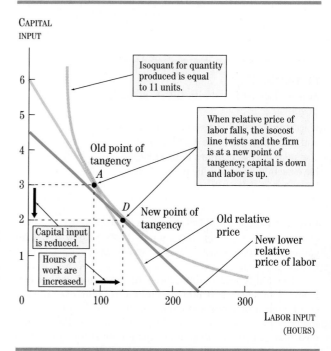

FIGURE 8A.7
Effect of a Lower Price of Labor Relative to Capital
The dark green isocost line has a lower price of labor relative to capital than the light green line. Hence, the amount of capital used by the firm decreases from 3 to 2, and the amount of labor rises from 90 hours to 130 hours.

the hourly wage falls from $10 to $6 and the price of capital rises from $300 to $600. That is, labor becomes cheaper relative to capital. Originally, the ratio of the price of labor to capital was $10/300 = .033$; now it is $6/600 = .010$. This is a big reduction, and we would expect the firm to adjust by changing capital and labor input. Figure 8A.7 shows how it would adjust the mix of capital and labor for a given quantity of output. Figure 8A.7 keeps the isoquant fixed but includes a new isocost line that reflects the lower relative price of labor and that is tangent to the isoquant. Since the new isocost line is flatter, the point of tangency with the

given isoquant no longer occurs at point *A*, where 3 units of capital were combined with 90 hours of labor. Now tangency occurs at point *D*, where there is a combination of 2 units of capital and 130 hours of labor. In other words, the firm has substituted labor for capital when the relative price of labor fell. At the new point *D*, the firm would use 1 less unit of capital and 40 more hours of labor.

In summary, common sense tells us that the firm will hire more labor and use less capital when the price of labor falls relative to the price of capital. The isoquants and isocost lines confirm this and tell us by exactly how much.

KEY TERMS AND DEFINITIONS

isoquant: a curve showing the combinations of two inputs that yield the same quantity of output.

isocost line: a line showing the combinations of two inputs that result in the same total costs.

rate of technical substitution: the rate at which one input must be substituted for another input to maintain the same production; it is the slope of the isoquant.

QUESTIONS FOR REVIEW

1. Why does the isoquant slope downward?

2. Why does the isocost line slope downward?

3. What determines the slope of the isocost line?

4. Why does the firm minimize cost for a given level of output by choosing capital and labor at the point where the isocost line is tangent to the isoquant?

PROBLEMS

1. Graph the isocost line associated with a wage of $10 per hour and a price of capital of $50 for total costs of $200, $240, and $300. Suppose the wage rises to $15 and the price of capital stays at $50. Show how the isocost line moves if total costs are $300.

2. Sketch a typical isocost line and isoquant where the firm has chosen the combination of capital and labor that minimizes total costs for a given quantity of output. Now suppose the price of capital rises and the wage does not change. What must the firm do to maintain the same level

of output as before the increase in the price of capital and still minimize costs? Will it substitute away from capital?

3. Draw a diagram with an isocost line and an isoquant next to a diagram with a budget line and an indifference curve from the appendix to Chapter 5. List the similarities and differences. How are the isocost and budget lines analogous to each other? How are the isoquant and the indifference curve analogous to each other? What is the importance of the tangency point in each case?

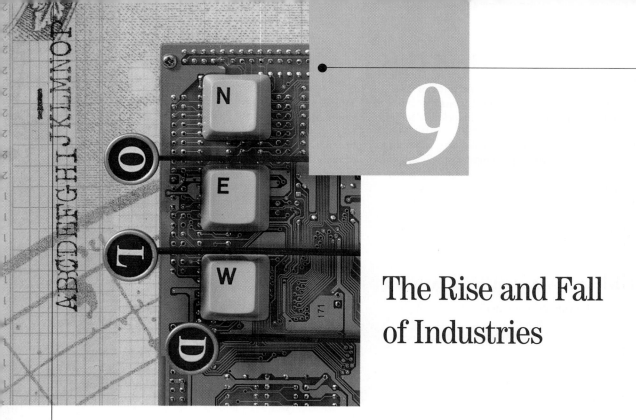

The Rise and Fall
of Industries

9

Fred Smith's college term paper led to the birth of a new industry. In the paper he described his idea for a new product: reliable overnight mail service. Although he got only a C on the paper, Fred Smith pursued his idea. He became an entrepreneur. After college, in 1973, he started a business firm that guaranteed next-day delivery of a letter or a package virtually anywhere in the United States. The firm, Federal Express, was successful, very successful; its sales reached $1 billion by 1982, $4 billion by 1988, $8 billion by 1992, and over $10 billion by 1996.

Seeing high profits at Federal Express, many other firms entered the industry, which government statisticians soon began calling the "expedited package express" industry. In the late 1970s, United Parcel Service (UPS) entered; in the early 1980s the U.S. Postal Service entered; many small local firms you've probably never heard of also got into the act. Thus, as shown in Figure 9.1, the entire industry expanded together with Federal Express. In 1988, when industry sales hit $21 billion, these other firms were doing four times as much business as Federal Express.

The expedited package express industry is an example of an industry on the rise. Many other examples of fast-growing industries exist in the annals of economic history. The aspirin industry was born 100 years ago in Germany when Felix Hoffman, working for the Bayer Company, invented aspirin to ease the pain of his father's rheumatism; despite efforts to limit entry by other firms, Bayer soon found itself in a rapidly growing industry with firms selling aspirin all over the world. Estée Lauder founded a cosmetic firm 50 years ago; it grew, along with a huge cosmetics industry, to be a $2 billion company by

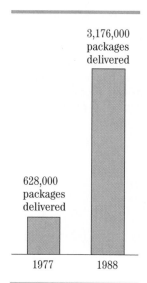

3,176,000 packages delivered

628,000 packages delivered

1977   1988

FIGURE 9.1
The Rise of an Industry

The growth of the expedited package express industry was very rapid in the 1980s. Measured by the number of packages delivered, the industry grew by over 400 percent from 1977 to 1988.

Source: Data from *Statistical Abstract of the United States,* 1993, Table 1006.

1990 with manufacturing plants in seven countries and sales all over the world. Kemmons Wilson started the motel franchising industry when he saw the potential demand for clean, reliable rooms for travelers and opened his first Holiday Inn in Memphis in 1952; by 1968, there were 1,000 Holiday Inns and now the industry includes other motel firms such as Days Inn and Motel 6.

Of course, industries do not always grow. Although aspirin is still the most widely used pain reliever in the world, its growth is now held back by new pain relievers like Tylenol, Advil, and Aleve. The U.S. beef industry has declined as the U.S. chicken industry has risen. The mainframe computer industry has declined as the personal computer industry has risen. Even the growth of the expedited package express industry is threatened by faster and cheaper fax machines and increased Internet access.

The cause of the rise and fall of industries can be traced to new ideas such as overnight delivery, to new cost-reducing technologies such as checkout counter scanners, or to changes in consumer tastes, such as a shift in preference toward foods with less fat. This latter shift, for example, is behind the rise of the chicken industry and the fall of the beef industry, as shown in Figure 9.2. Some industries have recurring ups and downs. The oil tanker shipping industry, for example, regularly expands when oil demand increases and declines when oil demand falls.

In this chapter we develop a model to explain the behavior of whole industries over time. We examine how economic forces cause industries to adjust to new technologies and to shifts in consumer tastes. Our analysis makes use of the tools introduced in the last chapter. The model continues to assume that the firms are operating in competitive markets. The initial forces causing an industry to rise or fall are described by shifts in a cost curve or a demand curve. Changes in the industry then occur as

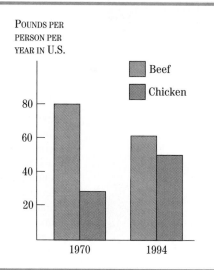

FIGURE 9.2

Taste Shifts and the Rise and Fall of Different Industries

Changes in tastes cause some industries to grow and others to contract. Concerns about fat in the diet may have been one reason that consumer tastes shifted from beef to chicken in the United States. In any case, the chicken industry flourished and the beef industry suffered as a result of the taste shift.

Source: Statistical Abstract of the United States, 1996, Table 226.

firms either enter or exit the industry. The central task of this chapter is to show how an industry grows or contracts as firms enter or exit the industry. Do profits fall or rise? Do the prices consumers pay increase or decrease? Before addressing these questions, we begin by examining some facts about changes in industries around the world today.

CHANGE IN DIFFERENT INDUSTRIES

An **industry** is a group of firms producing a similar product. The cosmetics industry, for example, refers to the firms producing cosmetics. The term *market* is sometimes used instead of industry. For example, the phrases "the firms in the cosmetic industry" and "the firms in the cosmetic market" mean the same thing. But the term *market* can also refer to the consumers who buy the goods as well as to the

industry: a group of firms producing a similar product.

TABLE 9.1
Changes in Production for Major Industry Groups as a Share of Total U.S. Production

Industry Group	Production as a Percent of GDP		
	1950	1970	1990
Goods Producing			
Agriculture, forestry, and fisheries	7	3	2
Mining	4	2	2
Construction	5	5	4
Manufacturing	29	25	19
Service Producing			
Transportation, communications, and public utilities	9	9	9
Wholesale trade	7	7	7
Retail trade	11	10	9
Finance, insurance, and real estate	12	14	18
Other services	8	12	18
Government	8	13	12

Note: Production in each industry is defined as the industry's sales less the costs of the materials that go into the product. For example, for automobile firms in the manufacturing industry, production is the sales of finished cars less the costs of the steel, tires, glass, upholstery, electronic equipment, and other items that went into the cars.
Source: U.S. Department of Commerce.

interaction of the producers and the consumers. Both firms and consumers are in the cosmetics market, but only firms are in the cosmetics industry.

Manufacturing is the making of goods by mechanical or chemical processes. In economics the word *industry* is much broader than manufacturing. Firms in an industry can produce *services* such as overnight delivery or overnight accommodations as well as manufactured goods.

The Rise and Fall of Broad Industry Groups

Table 9.1 divides all the firms in the economy into ten broad industries. The first four of these industries produce "goods," such as wheat, lumber, tuna, copper, houses, televisions, and cars. The last six of these industries produce "services," such as health, legal, and educational services.

Table 9.1 shows that, as a share of GDP, goods-producing industries have been declining while service-producing industries have been rising. About 73 percent of GDP now consists of services, compared to 54 percent in 1950. Growth of services has been particularly strong in the health, financial, and insurance industries. Every one of the goods-producing industry groups has declined as a share of GDP.

The Rise and Fall of More Narrowly Defined Industries

The industry groups in Table 9.1 are very broad and hide much that is going on within each industry. Within manufacturing, for example, the personal computer industry rose while the mainframe computer industry declined. Within services,

| | Level of Detail | | | |
Broad Industry Group	Two-Digit Industry Level	Three-Digit Industry Level	Four-Digit Industry Level	Firm Level
Manufac-turing	20 Food and kindred products	208 Beverages	2086 Bottled and canned soft drinks	Coca-Cola, PepsiCo
Services	73 Business services	737 Computer and data processing	7372 Prepackaged software	Microsoft, Netscape, Oracle
Finance, insurance, and real estate	63 Insurance carriers	632 Medical services and health insurance	6324 Hospital and medical insurance plans	Blue Cross, Travelers

TABLE 9.2

Examples of Different Levels of Industry Detail

(The numbers are the Standard Industrial Classification (SIC) codes of the U.S. government. Only three of the ten industry groups from Table 9.1 are shown.)

Source: Standard Industrial Classification Manual, 1987, Executive Office of the President, Office of Management and Budget.

videotape rentals rose while drive-in movies declined. Economists who study the behavior of industries must therefore use a more detailed classification.

The **Standard Industrial Classification (SIC)** is the most commonly used classification. Each of the ten major industry groups is divided into smaller groups; each of these smaller groups is divided into still smaller groups, and so on. For example, the manufacturing industry group is first divided into twenty different industries. Each of these twenty industries is called a "two-digit" industry because the Standard Industrial Classification assigns a two-digit code to each industry. For example, two of the two-digit industries within manufacturing are transportation equipment (code 37) and food processing (code 20). Railroads (code 40) and motor freight transport (code 42) are two of the two-digit industries in the transportation, communications, and public utilities group.

Each of the two-digit industries is then divided further into smaller groups called "three-digit" industries; the "three-digit" industries are divided into "four-digit" industries. Table 9.2 shows how the division works for several examples.

There are more than 1,000 four-digit industries, some of which have grown rapidly, some of which have shrunk, and some of which have recently been born. Because of rapid technological change and the development of new industries, the Standard Industrial Classification needs to be revised frequently. One newly created industry is the videotape rental industry (7841).

In what industry are large, diversified firms placed? Different establishments within a firm are placed in different industries depending on what they produce. For example, IBM produces computers and semiconductors; the IBM plants that produce computers are placed in the four-digit computer industry, while the plants that produce semiconductors are placed in the four-digit semiconductor industry.

Standard Industrial Classification (SIC): a taxonomy used to label and group industries for statistical purposes; each industry is given an SIC code.

TABLE 9.3
The Top Global Firms Within
Selected Industries

Industry	Largest Firm/Country	Fortune Global 500 Ranking
Aerospace	Lockheed Martin/U.S.	132
Building materials, Glass	Saint-Gobain/France	269
Chemicals	E.I. Dupont de Nemours/U.S.	58
Computers	IBM/U.S.	18
Electrical equipment	Hitachi/Japan	13
Energy	Teneo/Spain	204
Entertainment	Walt Disney/U.S.	350
Food	Unilever/Britain/Netherlands	38
Hotels, Casinos, Resorts	Japan Travel Bureau/Japan	240
Industrial equipment	Mitsubishi Heavy Ind./Japan	85
Mail and freight delivery	U.S. Postal Service/U.S.	29
Metals	Nippon Steel/Japan	88
Motor vehicles and parts	General Motors/U.S.	4
Publishing, Printing	Bertelsmann/Germany	144
Soaps, Cosmetics	Procter & Gamble/U.S.	71
Telecommunications	AT&T/U.S.	15
Tobacco	Philip Morris/U.S.	31
Trading	Mitsubishi/Japan	1

Note: The ranking is by size of revenues.
Source: Fortune, Global 500. Copyright © 1996 Time, Inc. All rights reserved.

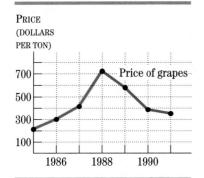

FIGURE 9.3
The Price of Grapes, 1985–1991
The price of Zinfandel grapes rose in the early 1980s because tastes shifted in favor of white wine made from these grapes. The higher price raised profits at Zinfandel vineyards and the number of vineyard acres increased as a result, as shown in Figure 9.4.

Source: Data from the Wine Institute.

Global Industries

Many industries are global. Firms in the United States sell or produce many of their goods in other countries. U.S. firms compete with firms in Japan, Europe, and elsewhere. The aspirin industry has been a global industry for 100 years. Reduced transportation and communication costs in recent years have made most other industries global. Until competition from Europe and Japan intensified 25 years ago, the U.S. automobile industry in the United States consisted mainly of three firms—General Motors, Ford, and Chrysler. Now the industry is truly global with Honda, Toyota, Hyundai, Fiat, and Volvo selling cars in the United States, and Ford and General Motors selling cars in Europe.

Table 9.3 classifies the world's largest firms into broad industry groups. For each industry, the largest firm and the country of origin are listed. Without a doubt, the industries and firms shown in Table 9.3 are global. Observe that the industry groups are very broad—much broader than the four-digit industries in the U.S. Standard Industrial Classification.

Case Study: Change in a Single Specific Industry

For the purpose of analyzing the effects of shifts in costs or demand, even the four-digit industries are frequently too broad. For example, within carbonated soft drinks, there are colas, root beer, ginger ale, etc. In order to analyze the rise and fall of an industry, economists usually need to narrow their focus further.

Consider, for example, changes in the grape industry, which is four-digit industry number 0172 of the agriculture, forestry, and fisheries industry group. The four-digit-level grape industry includes many different types of products. Some grape types are used to make raisins; other grapes are grown to be table grapes, and many different grape types are used for wine. Even within each of these categories, there are particular styles of grapes.

Consider the Zinfandel grape. This is one grape that is still largely confined to the United States, so we do not need to consider developments throughout the world. It is used to produce a particular type of wine, also called Zinfandel. Figure 9.3 shows a recent rise and fall in the price of Zinfandel grapes. The price more than tripled from 1985 to 1988. Then, nearly as sharply, the price declined from 1989 to 1991.

Figure 9.4 shows what happened to production in the Zinfandel grape industry during this period. The industry grew rapidly from 1985 to 1988: New vineyards entering the industry each year more than tripled. In 1988, industry growth slowed and the number of new vineyards entering the industry declined sharply. By 1991, growth was close to zero with only a handful of new vineyards entering.

How can we explain this huge rise and subsequent slowdown of the grape industry? The most likely explanation, as we will see in the next section, centers around the discovery of a new product. In the mid-1980s, it was discovered that Zinfandel grapes could be used to produce a new type of wine called "white Zinfandel," which proved to be very popular. Previously the grape was only used to produce a heavy red wine that was less popular. This discovery greatly increased the demand for the Zinfandel grape. In the next section, we develop a model to explain such changes in industries, and we illustrate how the model works with the Zinfandel grape industry.

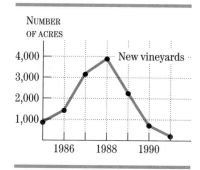

FIGURE 9.4
New Vineyards in the Grape Market, 1985–1991

As profits rose from growing Zinfandel grapes, the number of vineyards increased. The resulting increase in supply eventually lowered the price, which lowered profits, and the number of new vineyards declined. It takes several years for a new vineyard to start producing grapes.

Source: Data from California Agricultural Statistics Service.

Review

▶ The economy can be divided into ten broad industry groups. The service-producing industry groups have been growing while goods-producing industry groups have been shrinking relative to total production in the economy.

▶ The economy can also be divided into more than 1,000 detailed four-digit industries, or into even more detailed industries.

▶ Many industries are now global. U.S. firms routinely produce and sell goods in other countries and compete with foreign firms.

▶ The rise and fall of industries occurs in response to economic forces such as shifts in technology, consumer tastes, or new product ideas.

THE LONG-RUN COMPETITIVE EQUILIBRIUM MODEL OF AN INDUSTRY

The model we develop assumes that firms in the industry maximize profits and that they are competitive. As in the competitive equilibrium model of Chapter 7, individual firms are price-takers; that is, they cannot affect the price. But in order to explain how the industry changes over time, in this chapter we add something to the competitive equilibrium model: Over time some firms will enter an industry and

long-run competitive equilibrium model: a model of firms in an industry in which free entry and exit produce an equilibrium such that price equals the minimum of average total cost.

other firms will exit an industry. Because the entry and exit of firms takes time, we call this model the **long-run competitive equilibrium model.**

When we use the long-run competitive equilibrium model to explain the behavior of an actual industry, we do not necessarily mean that the industry itself conforms to the assumptions of the model exactly. A model is a means of explaining events in real-world industries; it is not the real world itself. In fact, some industries are very competitive and some are not very competitive. But the model can work well as an approximation in many industries. In the next two chapters we will develop alternative models of industry behavior that describe monopoly and the gray area between monopoly and competitive markets. But for this chapter, we focus on the competitive model. This model was one of the first developed by economists to explain the dynamic behavior of an industry; it has wide applicability and it works well. Moreover, understanding the model will make it easier to understand the alternative models developed in later chapters.

Setting Up the Model with Graphs

The assumption that a competitive firm cannot affect the price is illustrated in Figure 9.5. The left graph views the market from the perspective of a single typical firm in an industry. The price is on the vertical axis and the quantity produced by the single firm is on the horizontal axis. The market demand curve for the goods produced by the firms in the industry is shown in the right graph of Figure 9.5. The price is also on the vertical axis of the graph on the right, but the horizontal axis measures the *whole market or industry* production. Because the single firm cannot affect the price, the price, which represents the given market or industry price, is shown by a flat line drawn in the left graph. Notice that even though the single firm takes the price as given, the market demand curve is downward-sloping because it refers to the whole market. If the price in the market rises, then the quantity demanded of the product will fall. If the market price increases, then the quantity demanded will decline.

FIGURE 9.5
How a Competitive Firm Sees Demand in the Market

A competitive market is, by definition, one in which a single firm cannot affect the price. The firm takes the market price as given. Hence, the firm sees a flat demand curve, as shown in the graph on the left. Nevertheless, if all firms change production, the market price changes, as shown in the graph on the right. The two graphs are not alternatives. In a competitive market, they hold simultaneously. (In the graph on the right, a given length along the horizontal axis represents a much greater quantity than the same length in the graph on the left.)

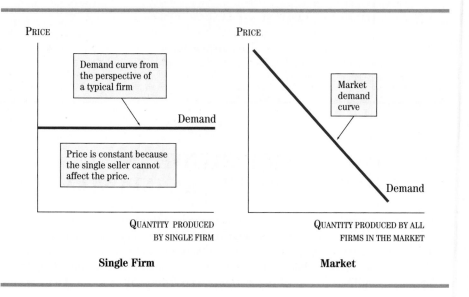

Entry and Exit

The new characteristic of competitive markets stressed in this chapter is the **free entry and exit** of firms in an industry. The question firms face is whether to *enter* an industry if they are not already in it, or whether to *exit* from the industry they are in. The decisions are based on profits—total revenue less total costs. If profits are positive, there is incentive to enter the industry. If profits are negative, there is incentive to exit the industry. When profits are equal to zero there is no incentive for either entry or exit.

When firms enter or exit an industry, the entire market or industry supply curve is affected. Recall that the market or industry supply curve is the sum of all the individual firms' supply curves. With more firms supplying goods, the total quantity of goods supplied increases at every price. Thus, more firms in the industry means that the market supply curve shifts to the right; fewer firms in the industry means that the market supply curve shifts to the left.

free entry and exit: movement of firms in and out of an industry that is not blocked by regulation, other firms, or any other barriers.

Long-Run Equilibrium

Figure 9.6 is a two-part diagram that shows the profit-maximizing behavior of a typical firm along with the market supply and demand curves. This diagram is generic; it could be drawn to correspond to the numerical specifications of the grape industry or any other industry. In the left graph are the cost curves of the typical firm in the industry with their typical positions: Marginal cost cuts through the average total cost curve at its lowest point. We do not draw in the average variable cost curve in order to keep the diagram from getting too cluttered.

The price line represents the current market price in the industry, for example, the price of a ton of grapes. Because the price line just touches the average total cost curve, we know from Chapter 8 that profits are zero. There is no incentive for

FIGURE 9.6
Long-Run Equilibrium in a Competitive Market
The left graph shows the typical firm's cost curves and the market price. The right graph shows the market supply and demand curves. The price is the same in both graphs because there is a single price in the market. The price is at a level where profits are zero because price equals average total cost.

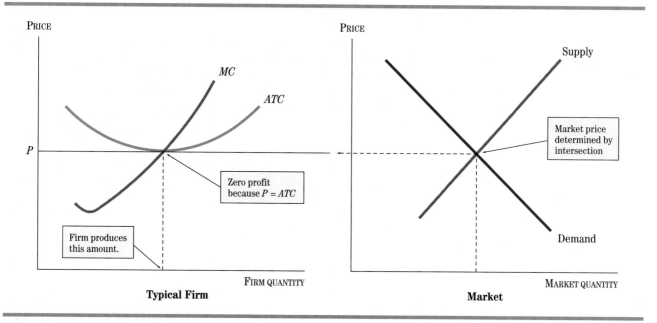

Typical Firm   **Market**

long-run equilibrium: a situation in which entry and exit from an industry is complete and economic profits are zero with price (*P*) equal to average total cost (*ATC*).

firms to either enter or exit the industry. A situation in which profits are zero and there is no incentive to enter or exit—as shown in Figure 9.6—is called a **long-run equilibrium.**

The market supply and demand curves are to the right of the cost curve diagram in Figure 9.6. The horizontal axis for the market supply and demand curves has a much different scale than the individual supply curves. An inch in the right-hand diagram represents much more production than an inch in the left-hand diagram because the diagram on the right is the sum of all the production of all the firms in the market. The market demand curve is downward-sloping: The higher the price, the less the quantity demanded. The intersection of the market supply curve and market demand curve determines the market price.

The left and the right graphs of Figure 9.6 are drawn with the same market price, and this price links the two graphs together. The price touches the bottom of the average total cost curve on the left graph, and this is the price that is at the intersection of the market supply and demand curves. The graphs are set up this way. They are meant to represent a situation of long-run equilibrium: The quantity demanded equals the quantity supplied in the market *and* profits are zero.

An Increase in Demand: The Effects on the Industry

Suppose there is a shift in demand as, for example, when the demand for Zinfandel grapes increased in the case study of the previous section. We show this increase in demand in the top right graph of Figure 9.7; the market demand curve shifts out from *D* to *D'*.

Short-Run Effects

Focus first on the top part of Figure 9.7 representing the short run. With the shift in the demand curve, we move up along the supply curve to a new intersection of the market supply curve and the market demand curve at a higher price. An increase in demand causes the rise in the market price.

Now note in the top left graph that we have moved the price line up from *P* to *P'*. Profit-maximizing firms already in the industry will produce more because the market price is higher. This is seen in the upper left of Figure 9.7, where the higher price intersects the marginal cost curve at a higher quantity of production. As production increases, marginal cost rises until it equals the new price.

Note also—and this is crucial—that at this higher price and higher level of production, the typical firm is now earning profits, as shown by the shaded rectangle in the top left graph. Price is above average total cost, so that profits have risen above zero. We have gone from a situation where profits were zero for firms in the industry to a situation where profits are positive. Thus, we have moved away from a long-run equilibrium because of the disturbance that shifts the market demand curve. This shift has created a situation in the market where there is a profit opportunity, encouraging new firms to enter the industry.

Toward a New Long-Run Equilibrium

Now focus on the two graphs in the bottom part of Figure 9.7 representing the long run. They show what happens as new firms enter the industry. In the lower right-hand graph, the supply curve for the whole industry or market shifts to the right

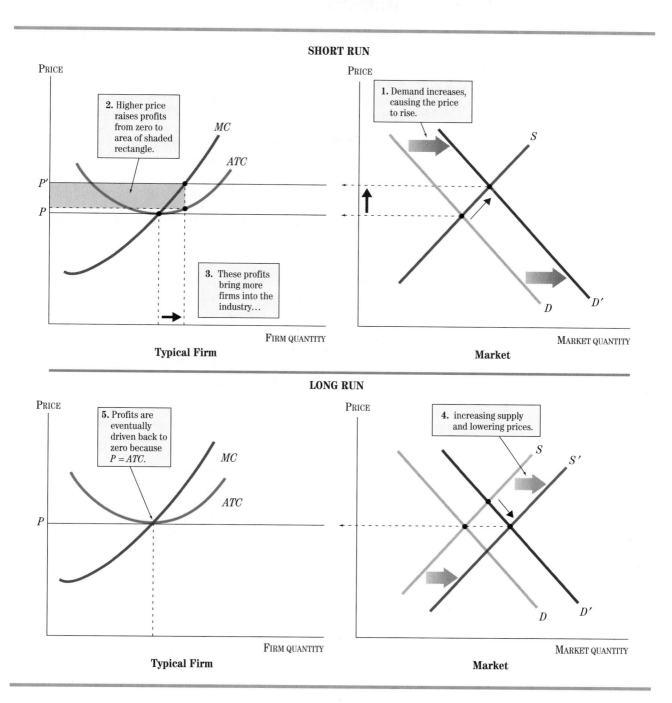

FIGURE 9.7

The Rise of an Industry after a Shift in Demand

The diagrams at the top show the short run. A shift in the demand curve to the right causes the price to rise from P to P'; each firm produces more and profits rise. Higher profits cause firms to enter the industry. The diagrams at the bottom show the long run. As firms enter, the market supply curve shifts to the right and the price falls back to P. New entry does not stop until profits return to zero in the long run.

from S to S'. Why? Because the market supply curve is the sum of the individual supply curves, and now there are firms entering the industry and adding to supply.

The rightward shift in the supply curve causes a reduction in the price below P', where it was in the short run. The price will continue adjusting until the price line just touches the bottom of the average total cost curve, where average total cost equals marginal cost. At this point, profits will again be zero and the industry will be in long-run equilibrium. Of course, this adjustment to a new long-run equilibrium takes time. It takes time for firms to decide whether or not to go into business, and it takes time to set up the firm once a decision is made.

The new long-run equilibrium for the typical firm is shown in the lower-left graph. It may take several years for an industry to move from the top of Figure 9.7 to the bottom. In fact, it would be more accurate to draw several rows of diagrams between the top and the bottom, showing how the process occurs gradually over time. These additional rows could show more and more firms entering the industry with the price falling until eventually profits are zero again and the incentive to enter the market disappears. The market supply curve will shift to the right until the price comes back to the point where average total cost is at a minimum, where profits are zero, and where no firms will enter or exit the industry.

Economic Profits versus Accounting Profits

It is important at this point to emphasize that the economist's definition of profits is different from an accountant's definition. When you read about the profits of General Motors in the newspaper, it is the accountant's definition that is being reported. There is nothing wrong with the accountant's definition of profits, but it is different from the economist's definition. When an accountant calculates profits for a firm, the total costs do not include the opportunity cost of the owner's time or the owner's funds. Such opportunity costs are *implicit:* The wage the owner could get elsewhere or the interest that could be earned on the funds if invested elsewhere are not explicitly paid, and the accountant therefore ignores them. When computing **accounting profits,** such implicit opportunity costs are not included in total costs. On the other hand, when computing **economic profits**—the measure of profits economists use—implicit opportunity costs are included in total costs. Economic profits are equal to accounting profits less any opportunity costs the accountants did not include when measuring total costs.

accounting profits: total revenue minus total costs where total costs exclude the implicit opportunity costs; this is the definition of profits usually reported by firms.

economic profits: total revenue minus total costs, where total costs include opportunity costs whether implicit or explicit.

For example, suppose accounting profits for a bakery are $40,000 a year. Suppose the owner of a bakery could earn $35,000 a year working as a manager at a video rental store. Suppose also that the owner could sell the bakery business for $50,000 and invest the money in a bank, where it would earn interest at 6 percent per year, or $3,000. Then the opportunity cost—which the accountant would not include in total costs—is $38,000 ($35,000 plus $3,000). To get economic profits, we have to subtract this opportunity cost from accounting profits. Thus, economic profits would be only $2,000.

Economic profits are used by economists because they measure the incentive the owner of the firm has to stay in business versus doing something else. In this case, with $2,000 in economic profits, the owner has an incentive to stay in the business. But if the owner could earn $39,000 running a video rental store, then economic profits for the bakery would be −$2,000 (40,000 − 39,000 − 3,000), and the owner would have incentive to run the video store. Even though accounting profits at the bakery were $40,000, the owner would have incentive to go to work elsewhere because economic profits are −$2,000. Thus, economic profits are a better measure of incentives than accounting profits, and this is why economists focus on economic profits. When we refer to profits in this book, we mean economic profits because we are interested in the incentives firms have either to enter or exit an industry.

Observe that if the bakery owner could earn exactly $37,000 at the video rental store, then economic profits at the bakery would be zero. Then the owner would be indifferent on economic considerations alone between staying in the bakery business or going to work for the video rental company. The term **normal profits** refers to the amount of accounting profits that exist when economic profits are equal to zero. In this last case, normal profits would be $40,000.

normal profits: the amount of accounting profits when economic profits are equal to zero.

The Equilibrium Number of Firms

The long-run equilibrium model predicts that a certain number of firms will be in the industry. The equilibrium number of firms will be such that there is no incentive for more firms to enter the industry or for others to leave. But how many firms is this? If the minimum point on the average cost curve of the typical firm represents production at a very small scale, then there will be many firms. That is, many firms will each produce a very small amount. If the minimum point represents production at a large scale, then there will be fewer firms; that is, a few firms will each produce a large amount.

To see this, consider the hypothetical case where all firms are identical. For example, if the minimum point on the average total cost curve for each firm in the grape industry occurs at 10,000 tons and the size of the whole market is 100,000 tons, then the model predicts 10 firms in the industry. If the quantity where average total cost is at a minimum is 1,000 tons, then there will be 100 firms. If in the latter case the demand for grapes increases and brings about a new long-run equilibrium of 130,000 tons, then the number of firms in the industry will rise from 100 to 130.

How Does the Model Explain the Facts?

Now let us consider the case study of the grape industry in Figures 9.3 and 9.4 in light of the long-run competitive equilibrium model. Recall that there was a shift in the demand for grapes around 1985. As predicted by the model, the price rose from 1985 to 1988 after the demand curve shifted. The price rise is shown in Figure 9.3. With the higher price, the profits from Zinfandel grape production will increase; thus, the model predicts the entry of new firms. In fact, as shown in Figure 9.4, Zinfandel vineyards did increase sharply in this same time period.

According to the model, in the long run, the increased supply from the new entrants to the industry should lower the price. As shown in Figure 9.3, the price did fall after 1988.

Again, according to the model, the lower price will reduce profit opportunities, and the number of new entrants should decline. Sure enough, the data show that the number of new entrants peaked and then declined after 1988.

At the end of this process, the price had returned to near the original price and the number of new entrants was close to zero. Apparently a new equilibrium was reached. Overall, the facts during this episode of change in the industry seem to be explained quite well by the model.

Entry Combined with Individual Firm Expansion

Thus far we have described the growth of an industry in terms of the increase in the number of firms. In the short run, immediately after a change in demand, there is no entry or exit; then entry takes place and the industry moves toward a new equilibrium in the long run. Recall from the last chapter that something else can occur in the long run but not in the short run. In the short run, a firm cannot expand its size by investing in new capital, but in the long run it can expand.

Is there any reason why we could not have both aspects of long-run behavior operating simultaneously? That is, could not new firms enter and existing firms expand at the same time? The answer, of course, is yes. In the case of grapes, the number of acres of vineyards can increase either when an existing grape firm increases the size of its cultivated vineyards (an expansion) or when new grape farmers enter the business (new firm entry). In either instance, the industry grows.

In reality, industries grow by a combination of the expansion of existing firms and the entry of new firms. For example, this was what happened in the expedited package express industry, which grew both because UPS and other firms entered and because Federal Express expanded.

Industries in Decline

The long-run competitive equilibrium model can also be used to explain the decline of an industry. Suppose there is a shift in the demand curve from D to D', as illustrated in the top right graph in Figure 9.8. This causes the market price to fall. The lower market price (P') causes existing firms to cut back on production in the short run: As production decreases, marginal cost falls until it equals the new lower price for each firm. However, the firms are now running losses. As shown in the top left graph of Figure 9.8, profits drop below zero.

With profits less than zero, firms now have incentive to leave the industry. As they leave, the market supply curve shifts to the left; from S to S' as shown in the bottom right graph of Figure 9.8. This causes the price to rise again. The end of the process is a new long-run equilibrium, as shown in the bottom left of Figure 9.8. In the long run, fewer firms are in the industry, total production in the industry is lower, and profits are back to zero.

New Products and Changes in Costs

Our analysis of the rise and fall of an industry thus far has centered around a shift in demand. But new technologies and ideas for new products that reduce costs can also cause an industry to change. The long-run competitive equilibrium model can also be used to explain these changes, as shown in Figure 9.9.

The case of cost-reducing technologies—say when Wal-Mart introduced checkout counter scanners—can be handled by shifting down the average total cost curve along with the marginal cost curve, as shown in Figure 9.9. This will lead to a situation of positive profits because average total cost falls below the original market price P. If other firms already in the industry adopt similar cost-cutting strategies, the market price will fall to P' but profits will still be positive, as shown in Figure 9.9. With positive profits, other firms will have incentives to enter the industry with similar technologies. As the market supply curve shifts out after more firms enter the industry, the price falls further to P'', and eventually competition brings economic profits back to zero.

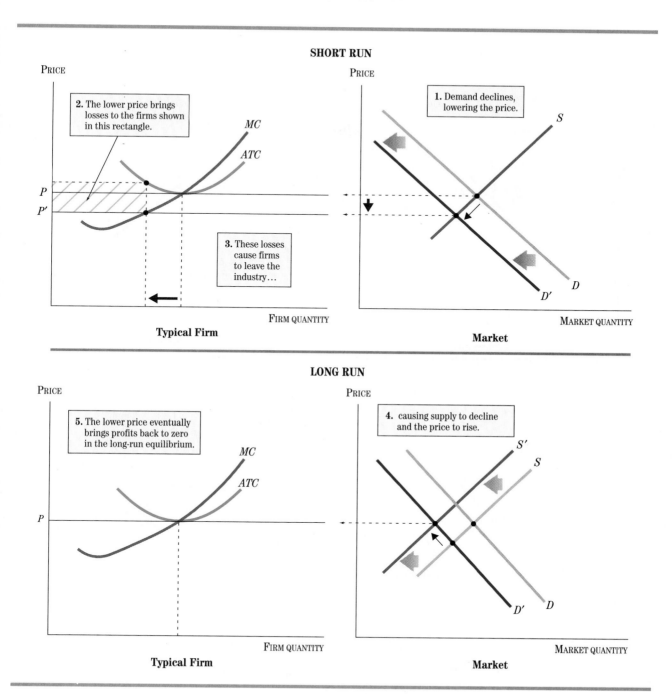

FIGURE 9.8

The Decline of an Industry after a Shift in Demand

In the short run, a reduction in demand lowers price from P to P' and causes losses. Firms leave the industry, causing prices to rise back to P. In the long run, profits return to zero, the number of firms in the industry has declined, and the total quantity produced has fallen in the industry.

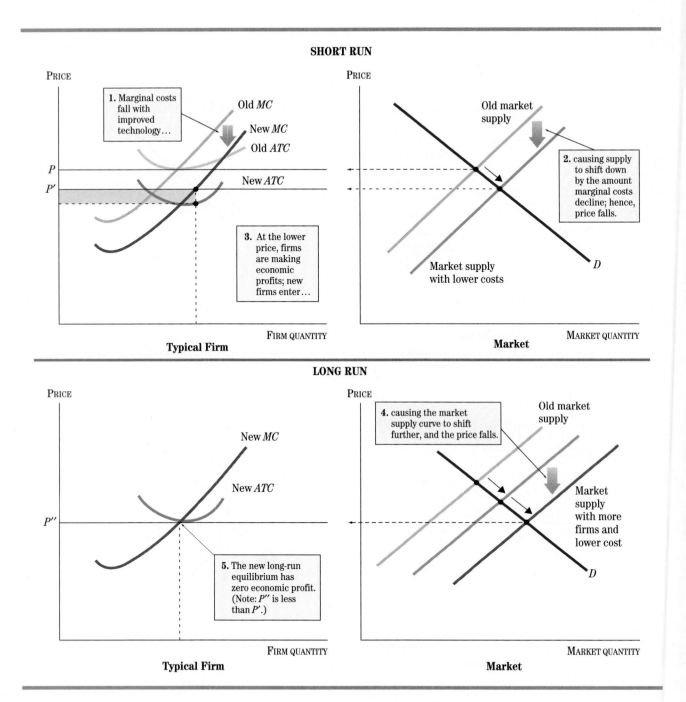

FIGURE 9.9
Effect of a Reduction in Costs

A new technology reduces costs and shifts the typical firm's *ATC* and *MC* curves down. The market supply curve shifts down by the same amount as the shift in marginal cost if other firms in the industry adopt the new technology right away. But because there are economic profits, new firms have incentives to enter the industry. As shown in the lower left graph, in the long run profits return to zero.

In the case of a new product, the firm introducing the product will earn economic profits for a while. For example, Fred Smith, who founded Federal Express, started a business making positive profits; average total cost was below the price. But this is a situation of profit opportunity for potential new entrants. As new entrants—such as UPS—enter the market, the supply curve shifts out and the market price falls. It will keep falling until price equals the minimum of average total cost and economic profits are zero. Perhaps that is the situation in the expedited package express industry today.

If new entrants drive economic profits to zero in the long run, then what incentives do firms have to introduce new products or develop cost-cutting technologies? The answer is that the economic profits in the short run can be substantial. Federal Express may have made hundreds of millions of dollars of economic profits before the competition eroded them. Wal-Mart also benefited for a while from cost-cutting innovations. No idea will generate economic profits forever in a competitive market, but the short-run profits can still provide plenty of incentive.

Review

▶ Entry and exit of firms in search of profit opportunities play a key role in the long-run competitive equilibrium model. The decision to enter versus exit an industry is determined by profit potential. Positive economic profits will attract new firms. Negative economic profits will cause firms to exit the industry. In long-run equilibrium, economic profits are zero.

▶ The market supply curve shifts as firms enter or exit the industry. With more firms the market supply curve shifts to the right. With fewer firms, the market supply curve shifts to the left.

▶ The model works well in practice, as illustrated by the case study of the Zinfandel grape industry. An increase in demand caused the price of Zinfandel grapes to rise. Grape-producing firms saw a profit opportunity and entered the industry, transforming existing land into vineyards. The supply of grapes began to increase. As a result, the price started to come back down again.

▶ The model can be used to explain the rise and fall of many different industries, whether due to new product ideas, innovative technology, or shifts in demand.

MINIMUM COSTS PER UNIT AND THE EFFICIENT ALLOCATION OF CAPITAL

If firms can enter or exit a competitive industry as assumed in this model, then there are several other attractive features of the competitive market that we can add to those discussed in Chapter 7.

Average Total Cost Is Minimized

In the long-run equilibrium, average total cost is as low as technology will permit. You can see this in Figures 9.6, 9.7, 9.8, or 9.9. In each case, the typical firm produces a quantity at which average total cost is at the *minimum point* of the firm's average total cost curve. This amount of production must occur in the long-run equilibrium because profits are zero. For profits to be zero, price must equal average total cost ($P = ATC$). The only place where $P = MC$ and $P = ATC$ is at the lowest point on the ATC curve. At this point, costs per unit are at a minimum.

In the long run, firms can expand or contract as well as enter or exit an industry. As they expand or contract, their costs are described by the long-run *ATC* curve. Thus, in the long-run competitive equilibrium, firms operate at the lowest point of the long-run average total cost curve.

That average total cost is at a minimum is an attractive feature of a competitive market where firms are free to enter and exit. It means that goods are produced at the lowest cost with the price consumers pay equal to that lowest cost. If firms could not enter and exit, this attractive feature would be lost.

Efficient Allocation of Capital Among Industries

An efficient allocation of capital among industries is also achieved by entry and exit in competitive markets. Entry of firms into the Zinfandel grape industry, for example, means that more capital has gone into that industry, where it can better satisfy consumer tastes, and less capital has gone into some other industry.

In the case of a declining industry, capital moves out of the industry to other industries, where it is more efficiently used. For example, capital moved away from the beef industry toward the chicken industry when the former contracted and the latter expanded in recent years. Thus, the long-run competitive equilibrium has another attractive property: Capital is allocated to its most efficient use. Again, this property is due to the free entry and exit of firms. If entry and exit were limited or if the market were not competitive for some other reason, this advantage would be lost.

Review

▶ In a long-run competitive equilibrium, firms operate at the minimum point on their long-run average total cost curves and capital is allocated efficiently across different industries.

▶ Minimum-cost production is a benefit to society of the competitive market with free entry and exit.

EXTERNAL ECONOMIES AND DISECONOMIES OF SCALE

In Chapter 8 we introduced the concept of economies and diseconomies of scale for a firm. A firm whose long-run average total cost declines as the firm expands has economies of scale. If long-run average total cost rises as the firm expands, there are diseconomies of scale. Economies and diseconomies of scale may exist for whole industries as well as for firms, as we now show.

External Diseconomies of Scale

When the number of firms in the Zinfandel grape industry increases, the demand for water for irrigation in grape-growing regions also increases, and this may raise the price of water in these regions. If so, then the cost of producing grapes increases. With the marginal cost of each grape producer increasing, the supply

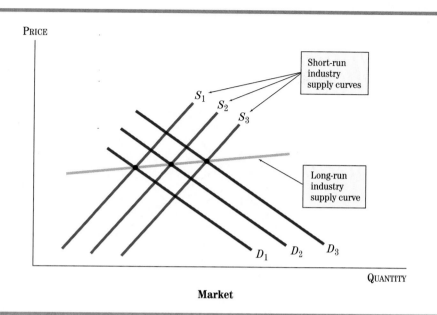

PRICE

S_1

S_2

S_3

Short-run industry supply curves

Long-run industry supply curve

D_1 D_2 D_3

QUANTITY

Market

FIGURE 9.10
External Diseconomies of Scale
As demand increases and more firms enter the industry, each firm's costs increase, perhaps because the prices of inputs to production rise. The higher costs tend to shift the market supply curve upward and to the left; thus the market supply curves do not shift to the right so much when new firms enter. The long-run industry supply curve slopes up, a phenomenon that is called external diseconomies of scale.

curve for each firm and for the industry or the market would shift up and to the left. Even though no single firm's decision affects the price of water for irrigation, the expansion of the industry does.

This is shown in the market supply and demand curves in Figure 9.10. Suppose there is a shift in the demand curve from D_1 to D_2. As the industry expands, more firms enter the industry and the supply curve shifts to the right from S_1 to S_2. Because the marginal cost at each firm rises as the industry expands, the supply curve does not shift to the right by as much as the demand curve shifts. Thus, the intersection of the demand curve D_2 and the supply curve S_2 occurs at a higher price than the intersection of S_1 and D_1.

We could consider a further shift in demand to D_3, leading to a shift in supply to S_3. This would be yet a new long-run equilibrium at a higher price because average total cost is higher. Observe that as successive market demand curves intersect successive market supply curves, the price rises and quantity rises; an upward-sloping **long-run industry supply curve** is traced out. We call the phenomenon of an upward-sloping long-run industry supply curve **external diseconomies of scale.** The word *external* indicates that cost increases are external to the firm, due, for example, to a higher price for inputs (such as water) to production. In contrast, the diseconomies of scale considered in Chapter 8 were internal to the firm due, for example, to increased costs of managing a larger firm; they can be called *internal diseconomies of scale* to distinguish them from the external case.

External Economies of Scale

External economies of scale are also possible. For example, the expansion of the Zinfandel grape industry might make it worthwhile for the students at agricultural schools to become specialists in Zinfandel grapes. With a smaller industry, such specialization would not have been worthwhile. The expertise that comes from that

long-run industry supply curve: a curve traced out by the intersections of demand curves shifting to the right and the corresponding short-run supply curves.

external diseconomies of scale: a situation in which growth in an industry causes average total cost for the individual firm to rise because of some factor external to the firm; it corresponds to an upward-sloping long-run industry supply curve.

external economies of scale: a situation in which growth in an industry causes average total cost for the individual firm to fall because of some factor external to the firm; it corresponds to a downward-sloping long-run industry supply curve.

FIGURE 9.11

External Economies of Scale

As demand expands and more firms enter the industry, each firm's costs decline, which causes the supply curve to shift to the right by even more than it would due to the increase in the number of firms. The long-run industry supply curve is thus downward-sloping, a phenomenon that is called external economies of scale.

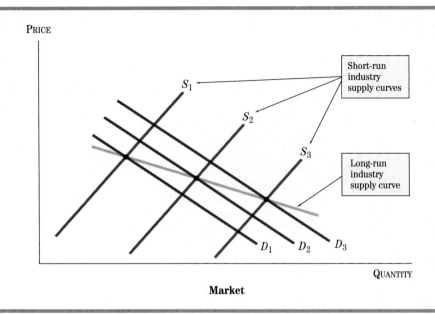

Market

specialization could reduce the cost of grape production by more than the cost of hiring the specialist. Then as the industry expands, both the average total cost and the marginal cost for individual firms may decline.

The case of external economies of scale is shown in Figure 9.11. Again, suppose there is a shift in the demand curve from D_1 to D_2. When the industry expands, the market supply curve shifts out from S_1 to S_2, or by *more* than the increase in demand so that the price falls. The reason the market supply curve shifts more than the market demand curve is that marginal cost at each firm has declined as the number of firms in the industry has increased. This larger shift in supply compared to demand is shown in Figure 9.11. Thus, the price falls as the industry expands.

With additional shifts in demand from D_2 to D_3, the market demand curves intersect with successive market supply curves at lower prices, resulting in a long-run industry supply curve that is downward-sloping. Again, the word *external* is used to distinguish these economies that occur outside the firm from those that are internal to the firm.

Our example of the reason why external economies occur is that a larger industry allows for opportunities for *specialization*—grape-growing specialists—who then provide services to the industry. There are other such examples. The expansion of the personal computer industry made it worthwhile for many small specialized firms servicing personal computer manufacturers to emerge. With a smaller-scale industry, this would not have been possible.

Note the contrast between internal and external economies of scale. The expansion of a single firm can generate internal economies of scale with the number of firms in the industry fixed because individuals within the firm can specialize. The expansion of an industry can generate external economies of scale even if the size of each firm in the industry does not increase. As an industry expands, firms might even split up into different firms, each dividing up the specialized work and concentrating on that.

Using Economics to Explain the Development of the Machine-Tool Industry

The machine-tool industry is an important one. Machine tools are the lathes and milling machines that create car bodies, bicycles, and high-tech military equipment out of steel, aluminum, and other metals. Today there are thousands of machine-tool factories around the world. One indicator of the importance of the machine-tool industry is that governments have tried—usually unsuccessfully—to protect the industry from foreign competition. Almost 200 years ago the government of England prohibited the export of machine tools because it was concerned other countries would learn how to make them. The U.S. government now has an agreement with foreign governments to restrict the amount of foreign-made machine tools brought into the United States.

The rapid growth of the machine-tool industry in the United States provides one of the classic examples of external economies of scale. There was no machine-tool industry in the United States in 1820. It began to grow rapidly when the firearm industry expanded in the mid-1820s. As rifle production increased, it became worthwhile for

firms to specialize in the production of lathes and milling machines to produce gunstocks. Eli Whitney, the famous inventor of the cotton gin, invented the milling machine around this time, which was a key factor in industry growth.

Of course, the development of the machine-tool industry reduced the costs in firearm manufacturing. Eli Whitney may have had the incentive to concentrate his thinking on inventing machine tools for firearm production, much as students at agricultural schools would have the incentive to specialize in Zinfandel grapes when grape production expands, as mentioned in the text.

The story of external economies of scale due to machine tools goes beyond the firearm industry. The expertise developed in the machine-tool industry became useful in the production of other goods. As the bicycle industry rose sharply in the 1890s, the need for lightweight, sturdy parts increased, and the machine-tool industry was able to make them. New machine tools were invented—such as the oil tube drill—as the bicycle industry expanded. Further growth and specialization in the machine-tool

industry was made possible by the growth of the bicycle industry. The cost of bicycles in turn was reduced.

The story continues. The automobile industry started to rise just as the bicycle industry was declining. The automobile industry was aided by the existence of machine tools and as it grew, the machine-tool industry could specialize even further. Thus, the external economies of scale reduced costs in the automobile industry. The same thing happened in the aircraft industry.

This continuing story of the role of the machine-tool industry in leading to external economies of scale first in firearm production, then bicycles, then automobiles, then aircraft is fascinating. It is tempting to imagine a *Back to the Future* or *It's a Wonderful Life* type of scenario. If the firearm industry had not expanded in the United States, then Eli Whitney's milling machine and the whole machine-tool industry may not have developed. What would this have implied for the bicycle? For the automobile? For the airplane?

The Standard Assumption: A Flat Long-Run Industry Supply Curve

In the examples used in the previous sections of this chapter, there were neither external economies of scale nor external diseconomies of scale. To convince yourself of this, look back to the graphs in the lower right-hand panels of Figures 9.7 and 9.8. You will see that the market price is the same in the long-run equilibrium after the shift in demand as before the shift in demand. If you draw a line between the intersection points of the supply and demand curves in those graphs, you will get a flat line. Thus, the long-run industry curve will be perfectly horizontal, in

External Economies of Scale

As an industry expands in size, firms in other industries have incentives to develop new products to service the industry. These new products reduce average total cost in the industry, thereby giving rise to economies of scale, as illustrated by the development of special electronic scanners for use by the expanding overnight delivery service industry (left). The new ideas may in turn be used to reduce costs in other industries, as illustrated by the use of electronic scanners in the retail food industry (right).

contrast to the upward slope in Figure 9.10 and the downward slope in Figure 9.11. The intersections of the shifting demand and supply curves trace out neither an upward-sloping long-run industry supply curve—the case of external diseconomies of scale—nor a downward-sloping long-run industry supply curve—the case of external economies of scale. The assumption of a flat long-run industry supply curve is the standard one economists use to study industries where neither type of external scale effect is known to occur.

External and Internal Economies of Scale Together

In practice it is possible for external and internal economies of scale to occur at the same time in one industry. When an industry grows in scale through the addition of new firms, it is common for the typical firm in the industry to expand its scale. Federal Express has grown in size at the same time that more firms have entered the industry. Through its larger size, Federal Express has achieved internal economies of scale (for example, by spreading the costs of its computer tracking system over more deliveries), and the larger industry as a whole has benefited from external economies of scale (as illustrated by the hand-held scanners shown in the photo).

Review

▶ External diseconomies of scale occur when an expansion of an industry raises costs at individual firms, perhaps because of a rise in input prices.

▶ External economies of scale arise when expansion of an industry lowers costs at individual firms in the industry. Opportunities for specialization for individuals and firms serving the industry are one reason for external economies of scale.

CONCLUSION

In this chapter we have addressed one of the most pervasive and perplexing realities of a market economy: the changes that occur when whole industries rise or fall over time. As consumer tastes change and new ideas are discovered, such changes are an ever-present phenomenon in modern economies around the world.

The model we have developed in this chapter to explain such changes extends the competitive equilibrium model we developed in Chapters 5, 6, 7, and 8 to allow for the entry or exit of firms in an industry. Because such entry usually takes time, we emphasize that this modification applies to the long run. Profits motivate firms to enter or exit an industry. Profits draw firms into the industry over time, whereas losses cause firms to leave. As firms enter, the industry expands. As firms leave, the industry declines. In the long-run equilibrium, profit opportunities have disappeared, and entry or exit stops.

In the next two chapters we begin to leave the realm of the competitive market. We will develop models of the behavior of monopolies and other firms for which the assumption of a competitive market is not accurate. In the process, we will see that many of the results we have obtained with competitive markets in this chapter are no longer true.

However, many of the ideas and concepts developed in this and the previous few chapters on the competitive model will be used in these chapters. The cost curve diagram will reappear in the model of monopoly in the next chapter; the idea of entry and exit will reappear in the chapter after that.

As we consider these new models and new results, we will use the models of this chapter as a basis of comparison. A central question will be: "How different are the results from those of the long-run competitive equilibrium model?" Keep that question in mind as you proceed to the following chapters.

KEY POINTS

1. New industries usually begin with new ideas for products that either create or fulfill consumer demand.

2. Economic history is filled with stories about the rise and fall of industries. Industries grow rapidly when cost-reducing technologies are discovered or demand increases. They decline when demand decreases, perhaps because of a cost-reduction technology in a competing product.

3. Economists divide the economy into broad industry groups such as agriculture, manufacturing, and services as well as into over 1,000 specific industries in the Standard Industrial Classification.

4. To study the rise and fall of industries it is frequently necessary to look at particular products within four-digit industries.

5. Because of reduced transportation and communication costs, most industries today are global.

6. The economists' competitive equilibrium model assumes that firms are price-takers.

7. The long-run competitive equilibrium model also assumes that firms enter or exit an industry until economic profits are driven to zero.

8. The long-run competitive equilibrium model can be used to explain many facts about the rise and fall of industries over time.

9. In the long run, the competitive equilibrium model implies that after entry and exit have taken place, average total costs are minimized and capital is allocated efficiently among industries.

10. Industries may exhibit either external economies of scale, when the long-run industry supply curve slopes down, or external diseconomies of scale, when the long-run industry supply curve slopes up.

KEY TERMS

industry

Standard Industrial Classification (SIC)

long-run competitive equilibrium
  model

free entry and exit

long-run equilibrium

accounting profits

economic profits

normal profits

long-run industry supply curve

external diseconomies of scale

external economies of scale

QUESTIONS FOR REVIEW

1. What are three possible sources of the rise of industries? Of the fall of industries?

2. What are the ten main industry groups into which an economy is typically divided? Which have risen and which have fallen most sharply as a share of GDP in the United States?

3. What is the difference between economic profits and accounting profits?

4. Why do firms enter an industry? Why do they exit?

5. Why does the market supply curve shift to the right when there are positive profits in an industry?

6. Why is "zero profits" a condition of long-run equilibrium?

7. What does the demand curve look like to a single firm in a competitive industry?

8. Why are average total costs minimized in a long-run competitive equilibrium?

9. What are external economies of scale? How do they differ from internal economies of scale?

10. How does the long-run/short-run distinction differ when applied to a firm versus an industry?

PROBLEMS

1. Assign each of the firms and industries mentioned in the introductory section of this chapter to one of the broad industry groups listed in Table 9.1.

2. Consider a competitive industry with a large number of textile-producing firms. Describe how that industry would adjust to a decline in demand for textiles. Explain your answer graphically, showing both the typical textile firm's marginal cost and average total cost curves as well as market supply and demand curves. Distinguish between the short run and the long run.

3. Sketch a diagram showing the costs and price of the typical price-taking firm in long-run equilibrium. Suppose a technology is invented that reduces average total cost and marginal cost. Draw this new situation. Describe how the industry adjusts. How will the long-run equilibrium price change? What happens to the number of firms in the industry?

4. Suppose the government imposes a sales tax on the good sold by firms in a competitive industry. Describe what happens to the price of the good in the short run and in the long run when firms are free to enter and exit. What happens to the number of firms in the industry and to total production in the industry?

5. Consider a typical carpet cleaning firm that currently faces $24 in fixed costs and an $8 hourly wage for workers. The price it gets for each office cleaned in a large office

building is $48 at the present long-run equilibrium. The production function of the firm is shown in the following table.

Number of Offices Cleaned	Hours of Work
0	0
1	5
2	9
3	15
4	22
5	30

a) Find marginal costs and average total costs for the typical firm.

b) How many offices are cleaned by the typical firm in long-run equilibrium?

c) Suppose there is an increase in demand. Describe the process that leads to a new long-run equilibrium. What is the new price in the long-run equilibrium? What is the quantity produced by the typical firm? Draw the market demand and supply curves before and after the shift. (Assume that the hourly wage remains at $8 per hour.)

d) Now assume that the increased number of cleaning firms causes a rise in the hourly wage from $8 to $9.

How would your answer differ from part (c)? In particular, compare the equilibrium price and the market demand and supply curves.

6. Compare and contrast economic profits, accounting profits, and normal profits.

7. Suppose that as an industry grows, each firm must maintain progressively higher government inspection standards for its products. Will this cause external economies or diseconomies of scale? Draw a diagram to explain.

8. What is the difference between the short run and long run for a firm (as in Chapter 8) and the short run and long run for an industry (described in this chapter)?

9. In some industries, firms learn how to produce a good more efficiently by improving products sold by rival firms. Computer software is an example of such an industry. Draw a diagram and explain how economies of scale could result in these industries.

10. Rank the following industries according to (1) how fast firms would be able to adjust their capital or other inputs fixed in the short run, and (2) how fast they would be able to enter or exit the industry.
  a) Video rental stores
  b) Automobile manufacturing firms
  c) Computer software producers
  d) Wheat farms
  e) Airplane manufacturing firms
  f) Airline transportation firms

11. This problem combines changes in capital at each firm over the long run with entry and exit of firms into or out of an industry in the long run. Given the data in the table for a typical firm in a competitive industry (with identical firms), sketch the two short-run average total cost curves (ATC_1 and ATC_2) and the two marginal cost curves (MC_1 and MC_2).

Quantity	Costs with 1 Unit of Capital		Costs with 2 Units of Capital	
	ATC_1	MC_1	ATC_2	MC_2
1	7.0	5	10.0	6
2	5.5	4	7.5	5
3	4.7	3	6.3	4
4	4.5	4	5.5	3
5	4.6	5	5.0	3
6	4.8	6	4.8	4
7	5.1	7	4.9	5
8	5.5	8	5.0	6
9	5.9	9	5.2	7
10	6.3	10	5.5	8
11	6.7	11	5.8	9
12	7.2	12	6.2	10

a) Suppose the price is $9 per unit. How much will the firm produce and with what level of capital?

b) Suppose the firm currently has costs on the ATC_2 curve. If the price falls to $7 per unit, will the firm contract when it is able to change its capital? Why?

c) What is the long-run industry equilibrium price and quantity for the typical firm? If there is a market demand of 4,000 units at that price, how many of these identical firms will there be in the industry?

d) Why might the firm operate with 2 units of capital in the short run if the long-run equilibrium implies 1 unit of capital?

$$\frac{(\Delta Q/Q)}{(\Delta P/P)} < 1$$

10

Monopoly

Sending the board game Monopoly to prospective customers at the start of 1991 was how Advanced Micro Devices called attention to Intel's monopoly. Both Advanced Micro Devices and Intel produce the central processor—the brains—of personal computers. Intel had a monopoly because it was the sole producer of the 386 computer chip, the most popular central processor for personal computers in the late 1980s and early 1990s. Intel's monopoly began in 1985, when its researchers invented the 386 chip. The company created the monopoly legally by obtaining patents and copyrights from the government that gave it the sole right to produce the 386 chip. No other firm could compete with Intel unless Intel gave permission, and Intel did not want to give permission to Advanced Micro Devices. As frequently happens, however, Advanced Micro Devices designed its own 386 chip, a clone of Intel's that did not infringe on Intel's patents. By 1991, Advanced Micro Devices was ready to compete with Intel and used the Monopoly game to help launch its product. Chips and Technologies, another chip firm, also designed a 386 clone. With their 386 clones, these firms were eventually able to break Intel's monopoly. But by the time they had done so, Intel had invented a more advanced chip—the 486—and created yet another

monopoly. Nevertheless, both Advanced Micro Devices and Chips and Technologies soon got into the act, developing chips that virtually replicated Intel's 486. Today the story continues with yet newer and faster chips.

When one firm, like Intel, is the sole producer of a good like the 386 chip it is by definition a monopoly in the market for that good. An important feature of today's economy is that monopolies, as in the computer chip example, frequently do not last very long. Rapid changes in technology can make patents and copyrights useless well before their life is over. The 386 monopoly lasted at most six years. Even local telephone companies—which are monopolies because they are the only provider of local telephone service—may find competition from cellular telephones or newer technologies.

Monopolies can be large global firms or small local firms. De Beers is a global firm that controls at least 80 percent of the world's diamond supply and, therefore, is virtually a monopoly; it has maintained its monopoly position since 1929, which shows that in some cases monopolies can last a long time. B & W Riverview Estates is a very small local monopoly in the little town of Los Molinos, California, providing water to only nine customers and earning revenue of $450 per year in the early 1990s. Because it is the only firm servicing the local market, by definition, it also is a monopoly. There are many small water companies in the United States, and each one is a monopoly.

Monopolies operate much differently from firms in competitive markets. The biggest difference is that monopolies have the power to set the price in their market. They use this power to charge higher prices than competitive firms would.

The aim of this chapter is to develop a model of monopoly that can be used to explain this behavior and thereby understand how real-world monopolies—such as De Beers and B & W Riverview Estates—operate. The model explains how a monopoly decides what price to charge its customers and what quantity to sell. It shows that monopolies cause a loss to society when compared with firms providing goods in competitive markets; the model also provides a way to measure that loss. We also use the model to explain some puzzling pricing behavior, such as why airlines charge a lower fare to travelers who stay over on a Saturday night.

Monopolies and the reasons for their existence raise important public policy questions about the role of government in the economy. For example, the loss that monopolies cause to society creates a potential role for government: It may step in to reduce this loss.

A MODEL OF MONOPOLY

A **monopoly** occurs when there is only one firm in an industry selling a product for which there are no close substitutes. Thus, implicit in the definition of monopoly are **barriers to entry**—other firms are not free to enter the industry. For example, De Beers creates barriers to entry by maintaining exclusive rights to the diamonds in virtually all the world's diamond mines.

monopoly: one firm in an industry selling a product for which there are no close substitutes.

barriers to entry: anything that prevents firms from entering a market.

The economist's model of a monopoly assumes that the monopoly will choose a level of output that maximizes profits. In this respect, the model of a monopoly is like that of a competitive firm. If increasing production will increase a monopoly's profits, then the monopoly will raise production, just as a competitive firm would. If cutting production will increase a monopoly's profits, then the monopoly will cut its production, just as a competitive firm would.

The difference between a monopoly and a competitive firm is not what motivates them, but rather how their actions affect the market price. The most important difference is that a monopoly has **market power.** That is, a monopoly has the power to set the price in the market, while a competitor does not. This is why a monopoly is called a **price-maker** rather than a *price-taker,* the term used to refer to a competitive firm.

market power: a firm's power to set its price without losing its entire share of the market.

price-maker: a firm that has the power to set its price, rather than taking the price set by the market.

Getting an Intuitive Feel for the Market Power of a Monopoly

We can demonstrate the monopoly's power to affect the price in the market by looking at either what happens when the monopoly changes its price or at what happens when the monopoly changes the quantity it produces. We consider the price decision first.

The Impact of Price Decisions

Market experiments provide a vivid illustration of the impact of a competitive firm's price decision on the market. When there are several sellers competing with each other in an experimental market, one seller can try to sell at a higher price, but no one buys because another seller is always nearby who will try to undercut that price. If a seller calls out a higher price, everyone ignores the seller; there is no effect on the market price. The same thing happens to a competitive firm in a real-world competitive market; the firm will not sell anything if it raises its price above the price in the market. Effectively, the competitive firm has no power to affect the price.

The monopoly's situation is much different. Again, consider a market experiment. Suppose that instead of having several sellers and several buyers, there is only one seller and several buyers. If the single seller sets a high price, there is no need to worry about being undercut by other sellers. There are no other sellers. Thus, the single seller—the monopoly—has the power to set a high price. True, the buyers will probably buy less at the higher price—that is, as the price rises, the quantity demanded declines—but because there are no other sellers, they will probably buy something from the lone seller. The same is true for monopolies operating in the real world. If the De Beers diamond company raises the price of diamonds, the quantity of diamonds demanded will go down, but De Beers will not lose all its business to another producer because there are virtually no other producers.

The Impact of Quantity Decisions

Another way to see this important difference between a monopoly and a competitor is to examine what happens to the price when the supplier of a good changes the quantity it produces and sells. Suppose that there are 100 firms competing in the bagel-baking market in a large city, each producing about the same quantity of bagels each day. Suppose that one of the firms—Bageloaf—decides to cut its production in half. Although this is a huge cut for one firm, it is a small cut compared to the whole market—only one-half a percent. Thus the market price will rise very little. Suppose, for example, the price elasticity of demand for bagels is 2, and the price of a bagel is \$.50 in the city. Then the price of a bagel would increase by only about a tenth of a cent, which is too small to affect the market price of a bagel at all. (Here's the calculation: The change in quantity $\Delta Q/Q = -.005$ and the elasticity $[(\Delta Q/Q) \div (\Delta P/P)] = -2$ together imply that $\Delta P/P = .0025$; then the price $P = \$.50$ times $.0025$ gives $.00125$, or $.125$ cents.) Moreover, if this little price increase affects the behavior at the other 99 firms at all, it will motivate them to increase their production slightly. As they increase the quantity they supply, they partially offset the cut in supply by Bageloaf and there will be even a smaller change in market price. Thus, by any measure, the overall impact on the price from the change in Bageloaf's production is negligible. Bageloaf has essentially no power to affect the price of bagels in the city.

But now suppose that Bageloaf and the 99 other firms are taken over by Bagelopoly, which then becomes the only bagel bakery in the city. Now if Bagelopoly cuts production in half, the total quantity of bagels supplied to the whole market is cut in half, and this will have a big effect on the price in the market. With the same price elasticity of demand of 2, the price of a bagel will increase from \$.50 to \$.62. ($\Delta Q/Q = -.5$, so that $\Delta P/P = .25$, or a 12.5 cent increase in the price.) If Bagelopoly cut its production even further, the price would rise further. However, if Bagelopoly increased the quantity it produced, the price of bagels would fall. Thus, Bagelopoly has immense power to affect the price. Even if Bagelopoly does not know exactly what the price elasticity of demand for bagels is, it can adjust the quantity it will produce either up or down to change the price.

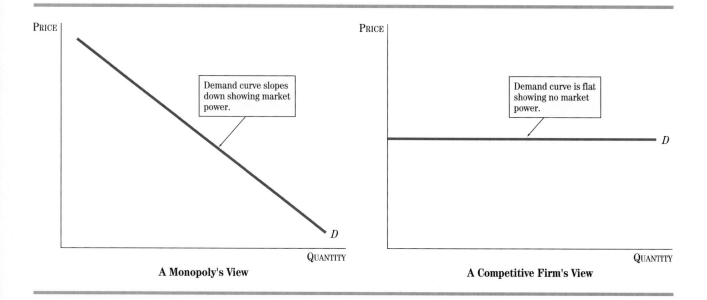

FIGURE 10.1

A Monopoly's View

A Competitive Firm's View

Demand curve slopes down showing market power.

Demand curve is flat showing no market power.

Showing Market Power with a Graph

Figure 10.1 contrasts the market power of a monopoly with a competitive firm. The right-hand graph shows that the competitive firm views the market price as essentially out of its control. The market price is shown by the flat line and is thus the same regardless of how much the firm produces. If the competitive firm tried to charge a higher price, nobody would buy because there are many competitors around charging a lower price, so, effectively, the competitive firm cannot charge a higher price.

To a monopoly, on the other hand, things look quite different. Because the monopoly is the sole producer of the product, it represents the entire market. The monopoly—shown in the left-hand graph—sees a downward-sloping market demand curve for its product. *The downward-sloping demand seen by the monopoly is the same as the market demand curve.* If the monopoly charges a higher price, the quantity demanded declines along the demand curve. With a higher price, fewer people buy the item, but with no competitors to undercut that higher price, there is still some demand for the product.

The difference in market power of a monopoly and a competitive firm—illustrated by the slope of the demand curve each faces—causes the difference in the behavior of the two types of firms.

The Effects of a Monopoly's Decision on Revenues

Now that we have seen how the monopoly can affect the price in its market by changing the quantity it produces, let's see how its revenues, and thus profits, are affected by the quantity produced.

Table 10.1 gives a specific numerical example of a monopoly. Depending on the units for measuring the quantity Q, the monopoly could be producing computer chips or diamonds or supplying water to homes in a city.

FIGURE 10.1

How the Market Power of a Monopoly and a Competitor Differ

A monopoly is the only firm in the market. Thus, the market demand curve and the demand curve of the monopoly are the same. By raising the price, the monopoly sells less. In contrast, the competitive firm has no impact on the market price. If the competitive firm charges a higher price, its sales will drop to zero.

TABLE 10.1

Revenue, Costs, and Profits for a Monopoly

(price, revenue, and cost measured in dollars)

Market Demand

Quantity Produced and Sold (Q)	Price (P)	Total Revenue (TR)	Marginal Revenue (MR)	Total Costs (TC)	Marginal Cost (MC)	Profits
0	160	0	—	70	—	−70
1	150	150	150	79	9	71
2	140	280	130	84	5	196
3	130	390	110	94	10	296
4	120	480	90	114	20	366
5	110	550	70	148	34	402
6	100	600	50	196	48	404
7	90	630	30	261	65	369
8	80	640	10	351	90	289
9	70	630	−10	481	130	149
10	60	600	−30	656	175	−56

$TR = P \times Q$

$\dfrac{\text{Change in } TR}{\text{Change in } Q}$

$\dfrac{\text{Change in } TR}{\text{Change in } Q}$

$TR - TC$

The two columns on the left represent the market demand curve, showing that there is a negative relationship between the price and the quantity sold: As the quantity sold rises from 3 to 4, for example, the price falls from $130 to $120 per unit.

The third column of Table 10.1 shows what happens to the monopoly's total revenue, or price times quantity, as the quantity of output increases. Observe that as the monopoly starts to increase the quantity produced, total revenue starts to rise: When zero units are sold, total revenue is clearly zero; when 1 unit is sold, total revenue is 1 × $150, or $150; when 2 units are sold, total revenue is 2 × $140, or $280, and so on. However, as the quantity sold increases, total revenue rises by smaller and smaller amounts and eventually starts to fall. In Table 10.1, total revenue reaches a peak of $640 at 8 units sold and then starts to decline.

The left-hand graph in Figure 10.2 shows how total revenue changes with the quantity of output for the example in Table 10.1. It shows that total revenue reaches a maximum. Although a monopolist has the power to influence the price, this does not mean that it can get as high a level of total revenue as it wants. Why does total revenue increase by smaller and smaller amounts and then decline as production increases? Because in order to sell more output, the monopolist must lower the price in order to get people to buy the increased output. As it raises output, it must lower the price more and more, and this causes the increase in total revenue to get smaller. As the price falls to very low levels, revenue actually declines.

Declining Marginal Revenue

In order to determine the quantity the monopolist produces to maximize profits, we must measure marginal revenue. *Marginal revenue,* introduced in Chapter 6, is the change in total revenue from one more unit of output sold. For example, if total

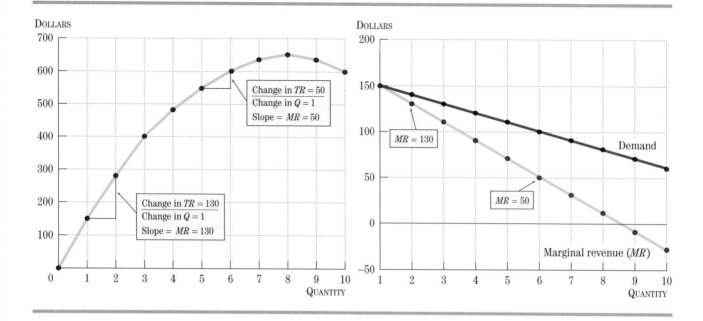

FIGURE 10.2
Total Revenue, Marginal Revenue, and Demand

revenue increases from $480 to $550, as output rises by 1 unit, marginal revenue is $70 ($550 − $480 = $70). Marginal revenue for the monopolist in Table 10.1 is shown in the fourth column, next to total revenue. In addition, marginal revenue is plotted in the right-hand graph of Figure 10.2, where it is labeled *MR*.

An important relationship between marginal revenue and price, shown in Table 10.1 and Figure 10.2, is that *marginal revenue declines as the quantity of output rises*. This is just another way to say that the changes in total revenue get smaller and smaller as output increases, as we already noted.

Marginal Revenue Is Less than the Price

Another important relationship between marginal revenue and price is that, for every level of output, *marginal revenue is less than the price* (except at the first unit of output, where it equals the price). To observe this, compare the price (*P*) and marginal revenue (*MR*) in Table 10.1 or in the right-hand panel of Figure 10.2.

Note that the red line in Figure 10.2 showing the price and the quantity of output demanded is simply the demand curve facing the monopolist. Thus, another way to say that marginal revenue is less than the price at a given level of output is that the *marginal revenue curve lies below the demand curve*.

Why is the marginal revenue curve below the demand curve? When the monopolist increases output by one unit, there are two effects on total revenue: (1) a positive effect, which equals the price *P* times the additional unit sold, and (2) a negative effect, which equals the reduction in the price on all items previously sold times the number of such items sold. For example, as the monopolist in Table 10.1 increases production from 4 to 5 units and the price falls from $120 to $110, marginal revenue is $70; this $70 is equal to $110 − $40. The increased revenue from the extra unit produced is $110, less $40, the decreased revenue from the reduction in the price ($10 times the 4 units previously produced). Marginal

The graph on the left plots total revenue for each level of output for Table 10.1. Total revenue first rises and then declines as the quantity of output increases. Marginal revenue is the change in total revenue for each additional increase in the quantity of output and is shown by the yellow curve at the right. Observe that the marginal revenue curve lies below the demand curve at each level of output except *Q* = 1.

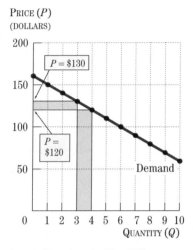

PRICE (*P*)
(DOLLARS)

Quantity Sold	Marginal Revenue (*MR*)		$\text{Price} \times \left(\begin{array}{c}\text{Change in}\\\text{Quantity}\end{array}\right)$ $(P \times \Delta Q)$		$\left(\begin{array}{c}\text{Change}\\\text{in}\\\text{Price}\end{array}\right) \times \left(\begin{array}{c}\text{Previous}\\\text{Quantity}\\\text{Sold}\end{array}\right)$ $(\Delta P \times Q)$
1	150	=	\$150 × 1	−	\$10 × 0
2	130	=	\$140 × 1	−	\$10 × 1
3	110	=	\$130 × 1	−	\$10 × 2
4	90	=	\$120 × 1	−	\$10 × 3
5	70	=	\$110 × 1	−	\$10 × 4
6	50	=	\$100 × 1	−	\$10 × 5
7	30	=	\$90 × 1	−	\$10 × 6
8	10	=	\$80 × 1	−	\$10 × 7
9	−10	=	\$70 × 1	−	\$10 × 8
10	−30	=	\$60 × 1	−	\$10 × 9

Graph Showing the Two Effects on Marginal Revenue

When the monopoly raises output from 3 units to 4 units, revenue increases; that is, marginal revenue is greater than zero. There is a positive effect (blue rectangle) because one more item is sold and a negative effect (red rectangle) because prices fall on previously sold items. Here the positive effect (area of blue rectangle is \$120) is greater than the negative effect (area of red rectangle is \$30), so marginal revenue is \$90.

revenue (*MR* = \$70) is thus less than the price (*P* = \$110). The two effects on marginal revenue are shown in the table above and the graph in the margin. Because the second effect—the reduction in revenue due to the lower price on the items previously produced—is subtracted from the first, the price is always greater than marginal revenue.

An Observation on Marginal Revenue and the Elasticity of Demand

The relationship between marginal revenue and price just described can be used to show that a monopolist will always produce where the price elasticity of demand is greater than 1. To see this, note that when marginal revenue is negative—as it is when output is 9 or 10 units in the example—total revenue falls as additional units are produced. It would be crazy for a monopolist to produce so much that its revenue is declining or marginal revenue is negative. Marginal revenue turns negative when the effect of the lower price on previous items sold is greater than the positive effect of an additional item sold: that is, when

$$\text{Price} \times \left(\begin{array}{c}\text{change in}\\\text{quantity}\end{array}\right) < \left(\begin{array}{c}\text{change in}\\\text{price}\end{array}\right) \times \left(\begin{array}{c}\text{previous}\\\text{quantity}\\\text{sold}\end{array}\right)$$

or

$$P \times \Delta Q < \Delta P \times Q$$

Recall the Greek letter Δ is short for "change in." By dividing both sides of the preceding expression by *Q* and then by *P*, it can be rewritten as

$$\Delta Q/Q < \Delta P/P$$

Now, if you divide both sides of this inequality by (Δ*P/P*), you get

$$\frac{(\Delta Q/Q)}{(\Delta P/P)} < 1$$

which states that the price elasticity of demand is less than 1. Thus, we conclude that a monopoly would never produce a level of output where demand is inelastic (that is, where the price elasticity of demand is less than 1). On the contrary, a monopoly always operates on the elastic part of the demand curve where the price elasticity of demand is greater than or equal to 1.

Average Revenue

We can also use average revenue to show that marginal revenue is less than the price. **Average revenue** is defined as total revenue divided by the quantity of output. That is, $AR = TR/Q$. Because total revenue (TR) equals price times quantity ($P \times Q$), we can write average revenue (AR) as ($P \times Q$)/Q or, simply, the price P. In other words, the demand curve—which shows price at each level of output—also shows average revenue for each level of output.

average revenue: total revenue divided by quantity.

Now recall from Chapter 8 that when the average of anything (costs, grades, heights, or revenues) declines, the marginal must be less than the average. Thus, because average revenues decline (that is, the demand curve slopes down), the marginal revenue curve must lie below the demand curve.

Finding Output to Maximize Profits at the Monopoly

Now that we have seen how a monopoly's revenues depend on its output decision, let's see how its profits depend on its output decision. Once we identify the relationship between profit and the quantity the monopoly will produce, we can locate the level of output that maximizes the monopoly's profits. To determine profits, we must look at the costs of the monopoly and then subtract total costs from total revenue.

Observe that the last three columns of Table 10.1 on page 266 show the costs and profits for the example monopoly. There are no new concepts about a monopoly's costs compared to a competitive firm's costs, so we can use the cost measures we developed in the previous three chapters. The most important concepts are that total costs increase as more is produced and that marginal cost also increases, at least for high levels of output.

Comparing Total Revenue and Total Costs

The difference between total revenue and total costs is profits. Observe in Table 10.1 that as output increases, both the total revenue from selling the product and the total costs of producing the product increase. However, at some level of output, total costs start to increase more than revenue increases, so that eventually profits must reach a maximum.

A quick glance at the profits in Table 10.1 will show that this maximum level of profits is $404 and is reached when the monopoly produces 6 units of output. The price the monopoly must charge so that people will buy 6 units of output is $100, according to the second column of Table 10.1.

To help you visualize how profits change with quantity produced and to locate the maximum level of profits, Figure 10.3 plots total costs, total revenue, and profits from Table 10.1. Profits are shown as the gap between total costs and total revenue. The gap realizes a maximum when output Q equals 6.

Equating Marginal Cost and Marginal Revenue

There is an alternative, more intuitive, approach to finding the level of output that maximizes a monopolist's profits. This approach looks at marginal revenue and marginal cost and employs a rule that economists use extensively.

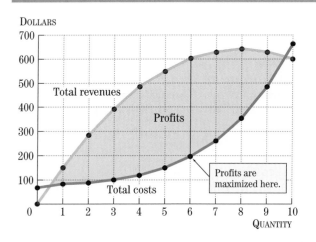

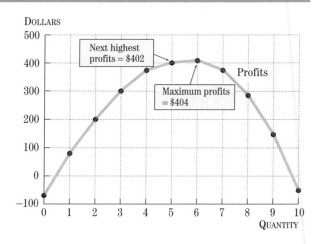

FIGURE 10.3
Finding Output to Maximize Profits

Profits are shown as the gap between total revenue and total costs in the graph on the left and are plotted on the graph on the right. Profits are at a maximum when the quantity of output is 6.

Consider producing different levels of output, starting at 1 unit and then rising unit by unit. Compare the marginal revenue from selling each additional unit of output with the marginal cost of producing it. If the marginal revenue is greater than the marginal cost of the additional unit, then profits will increase if the unit is produced. Thus, the unit should be produced, because total revenue rises by more than total costs. For example, in Table 10.1, the marginal revenue for producing 1 unit of output is $150 and the marginal cost is $9. Thus, at least 1 unit should be produced. What about 2 units? Then marginal revenue equals $130 and marginal cost equals $5, so it makes sense to produce 2 units. Continuing this way, the monopolist should increase its output as long as marginal revenue is greater than marginal cost. But because marginal revenue is decreasing and eventually marginal cost is increasing, at some level of output marginal revenue will drop below marginal cost. The monopolist should not produce at that level. For example, in Table 10.1, the marginal revenue for selling 7 units of output is less than the marginal cost of producing it. Thus, the monopolist should not produce 7 units; instead, 6 units of production, with $MR = 50$ and $MC = 48$, is the profit-maximization level; this is the highest level of output for which marginal revenue is greater than marginal cost. Note that this level of output is exactly what we obtain by looking at the gap between total revenue and total costs.

Thus, *the monopolist should produce up to the level of output where marginal cost equals marginal revenue* ($MC = MR$). If the level of production cannot be adjusted so exactly as to make marginal revenue precisely equal to marginal cost, then the firm should produce at the highest level of output for which marginal revenue exceeds marginal cost, as in Table 10.1. In most cases, the monopoly will be able to adjust its output by smaller fractional amounts (for example, pounds of diamonds rather than tons of diamonds) and, therefore, marginal revenue will equal marginal cost.

A picture of how this marginal revenue equals marginal cost rule works is shown in Figure 10.4. The marginal revenue curve is plotted, along with the marginal cost curve. As output increases above very low levels, the marginal cost curve slopes up and the marginal revenue curve slopes down. Marginal revenue equals marginal cost at the level of output where the two curves intersect.

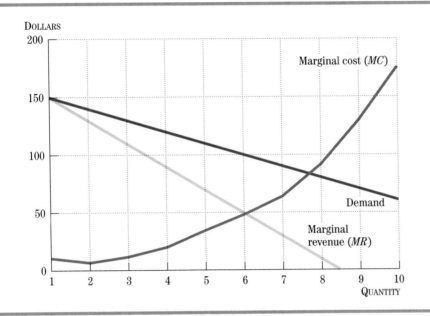

FIGURE 10.4
Marginal Revenue and Marginal Cost

The profit-maximizing monopoly will produce up to the point where marginal revenue equals marginal cost, as shown in the diagram. If fractional units cannot be produced, then the monopoly will produce at the highest level of output for which marginal revenue is greater than marginal cost. These curves are drawn for the monopoly in Table 10.1.

$MC = MR$ at a Monopoly versus $MC = P$ at a Competitive Firm

It is useful to compare the $MC = MR$ rule for the monopolist with the $MC = P$ rule for the competitive firm that we derived in Chapter 6.

Marginal Revenue Equals the Price for a Price-Taker

For a competitive firm, total revenue is equal to the quantity sold (Q) multiplied by the market price (P), but the competitive firm cannot affect the price. Thus, when the quantity sold is increased by one unit, revenue is increased by the price. In other words, marginal revenue equals the price for a competitive firm; to say that a competitive firm sets its marginal cost equal to marginal revenue is to say it sets its marginal cost equal to the price. Thus, the $MC = MR$ rule applies to both monopolies and competitive firms that maximize profits.

A Graphical Comparison

Figure 10.5 is a visual comparison of the two rules. A monopoly is shown on the right graph of Figure 10.5. This is the kind of graph we drew in Figure 10.3 except that it applies to any firm, so we do not show the units. A competitive firm is shown in the left graph of Figure 10.5. This is exactly like the graph showing a competitive firm in Figure 8.6. The scale on these two figures might be quite different; only the shapes are important for this comparison.

Look carefully at the shape of the total revenue curve for the monopoly and contrast it with the total revenue curve for the competitive firm. The total revenue curve for the monopoly starts to turn down at higher levels of output, while the total revenue curve for the competitive firm keeps rising as a straight line.

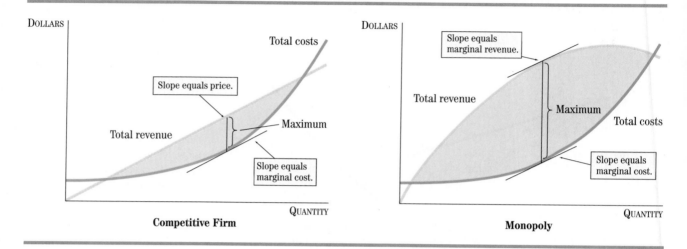

Competitive Firm   **Monopoly**

FIGURE 10.5
Profit Maximization for a
Monopoly and a Competitive Firm
Total revenue for a competitive firm
rises steadily with the amount sold;
total revenue for a monopoly first
rises and then falls. However, both
the monopolist and the competitor
maximize profits by making the gap
between the total costs curve and
the total revenue curve as large as
possible or by setting the slope of
the total revenue curve equal to the
slope of the total costs curve. Thus,
marginal revenue equals marginal
cost. For the competitive firm, marginal revenue equals the price.

To illustrate the maximization of profits, we have put the same total costs curve
on both graphs in Figure 10.5. Both types of firms maximize profits by setting production so that the gap between the total revenue and the total costs curve is as
large as possible. That level of output, the profit-maximizing level, is shown for
both firms. Higher or lower levels of output will reduce profits, as shown by the
gaps between total revenue and total costs in the diagrams.

Observe that at the profit-maximizing level of output, the slope of the total
costs curve is equal to the slope of the total revenue line. The slope of the total costs
curve is the marginal cost of changing production from one level of output to a
higher level. The slope of the total revenue curve is marginal revenue, because it is,
by the definition of slope, the ratio of the change in total revenue to each unit
change in output. Thus, we have another way of seeing that marginal revenue
equals marginal cost for profit maximization.

For the competitive firm, marginal revenue is the price, which implies the condition of profit maximization at a competitive firm derived in Chapter 6: Marginal
cost equals price. However, for the monopolist, marginal revenue and price are not
the same thing.

Review

▶ When one firm is the sole producer of a product
with no close substitutes, it is a monopoly. Most
monopolies do not last forever. They come and go
as technology changes. Barriers to the entry of new
firms are needed to maintain a monopoly.

▶ A monopoly is like a competitive firm in that it tries
to maximize profits. But unlike a competitive firm,
a monopoly has market power; it can affect the
market price. The demand curve the monopoly
faces is the same as the market demand curve.

▶ Marginal revenue is the change in total revenue as
output increases by one unit. Marginal revenue is
less than the price at each level of output (except
the first). If a firm maximizes profits, then marginal
revenue equals marginal cost ($MR = MC$).

▶ For a competitive firm, marginal revenue equals
marginal cost equals price ($MR = MC = P$).

▶ For a monopoly, marginal revenue also equals
marginal cost, but marginal revenue does not equal
the price. Hence, for the monopolist, price is not
necessarily equal to marginal cost.

THE GENERIC DIAGRAM OF A MONOPOLY AND ITS PROFITS

Look at Figure 10.6, which combines the monopoly's demand and marginal revenue curves with its average total cost curve and marginal cost curve. The diagram is the workhorse of the model of a monopoly, just as Figure 8.6 on page 212 is the workhorse of the model of a competitive firm. Like the diagram for a competitive firm, you should be able to draw it in your sleep. It is a generic diagram that applies to any monopolist, not just the one in Table 10.1, so we do not put scales on the axes.

Observe that Figure 10.6 shows four curves: a downward-sloping demand curve (*D*), a marginal revenue curve (*MR*), an average total cost curve (*ATC*), and a marginal cost curve (*MC*). The position of these curves is very important. First, the marginal cost curve cuts through the average total cost curve at the lowest point on the average total cost curve. Second, the marginal revenue curve is below the demand curve over the entire range of production (except at the vertical axis near 1, where they are equal).

We have already given the reasons for these two relationships (in Chapter 8 and in the previous section of this chapter), but it would be a good idea to practice sketching your own diagram like Figure 10.6 to make sure the positions of your curves meet these requirements.[1]

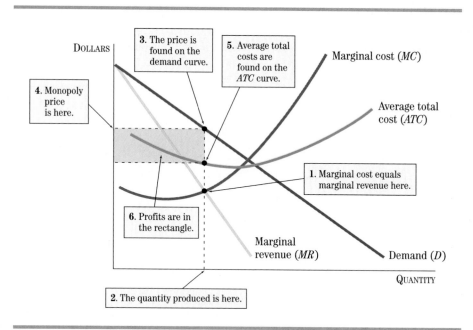

FIGURE 10.6

The Generic Diagram for a Monopoly

The marginal revenue and demand curves are superimposed on the monopoly's cost curves. The monopoly's production, price, and profits can be seen on the same diagram. Quantity is given by the intersection of the marginal revenue curve and the marginal cost curve. Price is given by the demand curve at the point where the quantity is produced, and average total cost is given by the *ATC* curve at that quantity. Monopoly profits are given by the rectangle that is the difference between total revenue and total costs.

1. When sketching diagrams, it is useful to know that when the demand curve is a straight line, the marginal revenue curve is always twice as steep as the demand curve and, if extended, would cut the horizontal axis exactly halfway between zero and the point where the demand curve would cut the horizontal axis.

Determining Monopoly Output and Price on the Diagram

In Figure 10.6 we show how to calculate the monopoly output and price. First, find the point of intersection of the marginal revenue curve and the marginal cost curve. Second, draw a dashed vertical line through this point and look down the dashed line at the horizontal axis to see what the quantity produced is. Producing a larger quantity would lower marginal revenue below marginal cost. Producing a smaller quantity would raise marginal revenue above marginal cost. The quantity shown is the profit-maximizing level. It is the amount the monopolist produces.

What price will the monopolist charge? We again use Figure 10.6, but be careful: Unlike the quantity, the monopolist's price is *not* determined by the intersection of the marginal revenue curve and the marginal cost curve. The price has to be such that the quantity demanded is equal to the quantity that the monopolist decides to produce. To find the price, we need to look up at the demand curve in Figure 10.6. The demand curve gives the relationship between price and quantity demanded. It tells how much the monopolist will need to charge for its product in order to sell the amount produced.

To calculate the price, extend the dashed vertical line upward from the point of intersection of the marginal cost curve and the marginal revenue curve until it intersects the demand curve. At the intersection of the demand curve and the vertical line, we find the price that will generate a quantity demanded equal to the quantity produced. Now draw a horizontal line over to the left from the point of intersection to mark the price on the vertical axis. This is the monopoly's price, about which we will have more to say later.

Determining the Monopoly's Profits

Profits can also be shown on the diagram in Figure 10.6. Profits are given by the difference between the area of two rectangles, a total revenue rectangle and a total

FIGURE 10.7

A Monopoly with Negative Profits

If a monopoly finds that average total cost is greater than the price where marginal revenue equals marginal cost, then it runs losses. If price is also less than average variable cost, then the monopoly should shut down, just like a competitive firm.

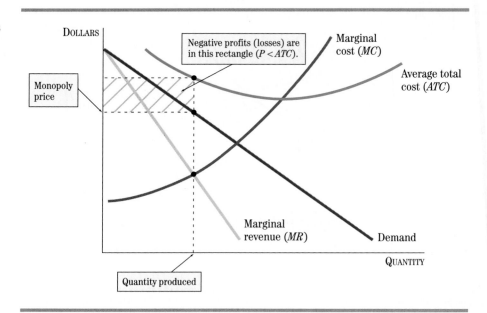

costs rectangle. Total revenue is price times quantity and is thus equal to the area of the rectangle with the height equal to the monopoly price and the length equal to the quantity produced. Total costs are average total cost times quantity and are thus equal to the area of the rectangle with height equal to *ATC* and length equal to the quantity produced. Profits are then equal to the green shaded area that is the difference between these two rectangles.

It is possible for a monopoly to have negative profits, or losses, as shown in Figure 10.7. In this case, the price is below average total cost and, therefore, total revenue is less than total costs. Like a competitive firm, a monopolist with negative profits will shut down if the price is less than average variable cost. It will eventually exit the market if negative profits persist.

Review

▶ A monopolist's profit-maximizing output and price can be determined graphically. The diagram shows four curves: the marginal revenue curve, the demand curve, the marginal cost curve, and the average total cost curve. The marginal revenue curve is always below the demand curve.

▶ The monopoly's production is determined at the point where marginal revenue equals marginal cost.

▶ The monopoly's price is determined from the demand curve at the point where quantity produced equals the quantity demanded.

▶ The monopoly's profits are determined by subtracting the total costs rectangle from the total revenue rectangle. The total revenue rectangle is given by the price times the quantity produced. The total costs rectangle is given by the average total cost times the quantity produced.

COMPETITION, MONOPOLY, AND DEADWEIGHT LOSS

Are monopolies harmful to society? Do they reduce consumer surplus? Can we measure these effects? To answer these questions, economists compare the price and output of a monopoly with those of a competitive industry. First observe in Figure 10.6 or Figure 10.7 that the monopoly does not operate at the minimum point on the average total cost curve even in the long run. Recall that firms in a competitive industry do operate at the lowest point on the average total cost curve in the long run.

To go further in our comparison, we use Figure 10.8, which is a repeat of Figure 10.6, except that the average total cost curve is removed to reduce the clutter. All the other curves are the same.

Comparison with Competition

Suppose that instead of only one firm in the market, there are now many competitive firms. For example, suppose Bagelopoly—a single firm producing bagels in a large city—is broken down into 100 different bagel bakeries like Bageloaf. Before the breakup, the production point for the monopolistic firm and its price are marked

FIGURE 10.8
Deadweight Loss from Monopoly

The monopolist's output and price are determined as in Figure 10.6. To get the competitive price, we imagine that competitive firms make up an industry supply curve that is the same as the monopolist's marginal cost curve. The competitive price and quantity are given by the intersection of the supply curve and the demand curve. The monopoly quantity is lower than the competitive quantity. The monopoly price is higher than the competitive price. The deadweight loss is the reduction in consumer plus producer surplus due to the lower level of production by the monopolist.

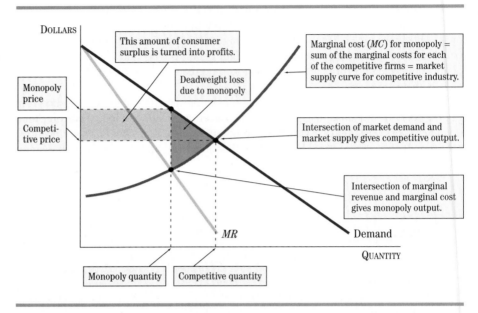

Numerical Example of Deadweight Loss Calculation

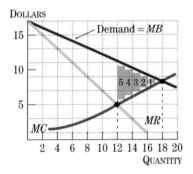

The monopoly above produces only 12 items, but a competitive industry would produce 18 items. For the 13th through the 17th items, which are not produced by the monopoly, the marginal benefit is greater than the marginal cost by the amounts $5, $4, $3, $2, and $1, respectively, as shown by the areas between the demand curve and the supply curve for the competitive industry. Hence, the deadweight loss caused by the monopoly is the sum $5 + $4 + $3 + $2 + $1 = $15.

as "monopoly quantity" and "monopoly price" in Figure 10.8. What are production and price after the breakup?

The market supply curve for the new competitive industry would be Bagelopoly's old marginal cost curve because this is the sum of all the marginal cost curves of all the newly created firms in the industry. Equilibrium in the competitive industry is where this market supply curve crosses the market demand curve. The amount of production at that point is marked in Figure 10.8 by "competitive quantity." The price at that equilibrium is marked by "competitive price" on the vertical axis.

Compare the quantity and price for the monopolist and the competitive industry. It is clear from the diagram that the quantity produced by the monopolist is less than the quantity produced by the competitive industry. It is also clear that the monopoly will charge a higher price than will emerge from a competitive industry. In sum, the monopoly produces less and charges a higher price than the competitive industry would.

This is a very important result. The monopoly exploits its market power by holding back on quantity produced and causing the price to rise compared with the competitive equilibrium. This is always the case. Convince yourself by drawing different diagrams. For example, when De Beers exercises its market power, it holds back production of diamonds, thereby raising the price and earning economic profits.

Note that even though the monopoly has the power to do so, it does not increase its price without limit. When the price is set very high, marginal revenue rises above marginal cost. That behavior is not profit-maximizing.

Deadweight Loss from Monopoly

The economic harm caused by a monopoly occurs because it produces less than a competitive industry would. How harmful, then, is a monopoly?

Experimental Tests of the Model of Monopoly

How well does the model of monopoly work? Market experiments help provide an answer. In experiments where a single seller—the monopoly—sets a price that *stays constant for the whole trading period*, with all buyers free to buy at that price during the trading period, the model of monopoly predicts the outcome accurately. After a few trading periods, during which the monopoly searches for the profit-maximizing price, the number of items sold and the price settle down to exactly what is predicted by the model of monopoly.

A surprising result occurs, however, when the single seller is allowed to call out different bids within the trading period, as in the double-auction market described in Chapter 7. In these types of experiments, after several trading periods, the price tends to settle down near the competitive price rather than near the

monopoly price. The reason is instructive. The single seller tries to charge different prices to different buyers, but ends up only being able to charge the competitive price! The monopoly figures that some buyers are willing to pay high prices. The monopoly thus asks high prices and sells some goods at these high prices. The monopoly then begins to lower the price to get the buyers who are only willing to pay less for the good. Working down the market demand curve, the monopoly sells the good to the last buyer at close to the competitive price.

The problem with this strategy is that when the trading period is repeated several times, the buyers learn that the monopoly will eventually lower the price, and they therefore refuse to buy at the higher prices. The monopoly ends up losing most of its market power, only able to charge near the competitive price.

Consumer Surplus and Producer Surplus Again

Economists measure the harm caused by monopolies by the decline in the sum of consumer surplus plus producer surplus. Recall that *consumer surplus* is the area above the market price line and below the demand curve, the demand curve being a measure of consumers' marginal benefit from consuming the good. The *producer surplus* is the area above the marginal cost curve and below the market price line. Consumer surplus plus producer surplus is thus the area between the demand curve and the marginal cost curve. It measures the sum of the marginal benefits to consumers of the good less the sum of the marginal costs to the producers of the good. A competitive market will maximize the sum of consumer plus producer surplus.

With a lower quantity produced by a monopoly, however, the sum of consumer surplus and producer surplus is reduced, as shown in Figure 10.8 and in the numerical example on the opposite page. This reduction in consumer plus producer surplus is called the *deadweight loss due to monopoly*. It is a quantitative measure of the harm a monopoly causes the economy.

How large is the deadweight loss in the U.S. economy? Using the method illustrated in Figure 10.8, empirical economists estimate the loss is between .5 and 2 percent of GDP, or between $40 billion and $150 billion per year. Of course, the deadweight loss is a larger percent of production in industries where monopolies are a greater presence.

Figure 10.8 also shows that the monopoly takes, in the form of profits, some of the consumer surplus that would have gone to the consumers in competitive markets. Now consumer surplus is the area below the demand curve and above the monopoly price, which is higher than the competitive price. However, this transfer of consumer surplus to the monopoly is not a deadweight loss, because what the

deadweight loss: the loss in producer and consumer surplus due to an inefficient level of production. (Ch. 7)

consumers lose, the monopoly gains. This transfer affects the distribution of income, but it is not a net loss to society.

Meaningful Comparisons

In any given application, one needs to be careful that the comparison of monopoly and competition makes sense. For example, some industries cannot be broken up into many competitive firms like bagel bakeries can. Having one hundred water companies serving one local area, for example, would be very costly. The choice to society is not between a monopolistic water industry and a competitive water industry. Although we might try to affect monopoly's decision by government actions, we should not try to break up water services within each community.

History provides many other examples. Western settlers in the United States during the nineteenth century had a larger consumer surplus from the monopolist railroads—in spite of the monopolists' profits—than they did from competitive wagon trains. Modern-day users of the information highway—computers and telecommunications—reap a larger consumer surplus from Intel's computer chips, even if they are produced monopolistically, than they would from a competitive abacus industry.

The Monopoly Price Is Greater than Marginal Cost

Another way to think about the loss to society from monopoly is to observe the difference between price and marginal cost. Figure 10.8, for example, shows that the monopoly price is well above the marginal cost at the quantity where the monopoly chooses to produce.

Marginal Benefit Is More than Marginal Cost

Because consumers will consume up to the point where the marginal benefit of a good equals its price, the excessive price means that marginal benefit of a good is greater than marginal cost. This is inefficient because producing more of the good would increase benefits to consumers by more than the cost of producing it.

The size of the difference between price and marginal cost depends on the elasticity of the monopoly's demand curve. If the demand curve is highly elastic (close to a competitive firm's view as shown in Figure 10.1), then the difference between price and marginal cost is small.

The Price-Cost Margin

price-cost margin: the difference between price and marginal cost divided by the price. This index is an indicator of market power, where an index of 0 indicates no market power and a higher price-cost margin indicates greater market power.

A common measure of the difference between price and the marginal cost is the **price-cost margin.** It is defined as

$$\frac{\text{Price minus marginal cost}}{\text{Price}}$$

For example, if the price is \$4 and the marginal cost is \$2, the price-cost margin is $(4 - 2)/4 = .5$. The price-cost margin for a competitive firm is zero because price equals marginal cost.

Economists use a rule of thumb to show how the price-cost margin depends on the price elasticity of demand. The rule of thumb is

$$\text{Price-cost margin} = \frac{1}{\text{price elasticity of demand}}$$

For example, when the elasticity of demand is 2, the price-cost margin is .5. The flat demand curve has an infinite elasticity, in which case the price-cost margin is zero; in other words, price equals marginal cost.

Review

▶ A monopoly creates a deadweight loss because it restricts output below what the competitive market would produce. The cost is measured by the deadweight loss, which is the reduction in the sum of consumer plus producer surplus.

▶ Another way to measure the impact of a monopoly is by the difference between price and marginal cost. Monopolies always charge a price higher than

marginal cost. The difference—summarized in the price-cost margin—depends inversely on the elasticity of demand.

▶ Sometimes the comparison between monopoly and competition is only hypothetical because it would either be impossible or make no sense to break up the monopoly into competitive firms.

MONOPOLIES AND GOVERNMENT

Given this demonstration that monopolies lead to high prices and a deadweight loss to society, you may be wondering why monopolies exist. In this section we consider four reasons for the existence of monopolies. In each case, we will see that government plays a role, either in reducing the costs of monopoly by regulating its price, in preventing the monopoly, or in creating the monopoly in the first place.

Regulated Natural Monopolies

The nature of production is a key factor in determining the number of firms in the industry. If big firms are needed to produce at low cost, it may be natural for a few firms or only one firm to exist. In particular, *economies of scale*—a declining long-run average total cost curve over some range of production—can lead to a monopoly. Recall from Chapter 8 that the *minimum efficient scale* of a firm is the minimum size of the firm for which average total costs are lowest. If the minimum efficient scale is only a small fraction of the size of the market, then there will be many firms.

For example, suppose the minimum efficient scale for beauty salons in a city is a size that serves 30 customers a day at each salon. Suppose the quantity of hair stylings demanded in the city is 300 per day. We can then expect there will be 10 beauty salons (300/30 = 10) in the city. But if the minimum efficient scale is larger (for example, 60 customers per day), then the number of firms in the industry will be smaller (for example, 300/60 = 5 salons). At the extreme case where the minimum efficient scale of the firm is as large or larger than the size of the market (for example, 300 per day), there would probably be only one firm (300/300 = 1), which would be a monopoly.

A water company in a small town, for example, has a minimum efficient scale larger than the number of houses and businesses in the town. There are huge fixed costs to lay pipe down the street but each house connection has a relatively low cost, so average total cost declines as more houses are connected. Other firms that

natural monopoly: a single firm in an industry in which average total cost is declining over the entire range of demand and the minimum efficient scale is larger than the size of the market.

usually have a very large minimum efficient scale are electricity and local telephone. In each of these industries, average total cost is lowest if one firm delivers the service. **Natural monopolies** exist when average total cost is declining and the minimum efficient scale is larger than the size of the market.

The prices charged by many natural monopolies are regulated by government. The purpose of the regulation is to keep the price below the monopoly price and closer to the competitive price. Such regulation can thereby reduce the deadweight loss of the monopoly. Alternative methods of regulating natural monopolies are discussed in Chapter 16. Water companies, electric companies, and local telephone companies are all regulated by government.

A change in technology that changes the minimum efficient scale of firms can radically alter the number of firms in the industry. For example, AT&T used to be viewed as a natural monopoly in long-distance telephone service. Because laying copper wire across the United States required a huge cost, it made little sense to have more than one firm. The U.S. government regulated the prices that AT&T charged its customers, endeavoring to keep the price of calls below the monopoly price and closer to the competitive price. But when the technology for transmitting signals by microwave developed, it became easier for other firms also to provide services. Thus, MCI and Sprint, as well as AT&T, could provide services at least as cheaply as one firm. Because of this technological change, the government decided to end the AT&T monopoly by allowing MCI and Sprint to compete with AT&T. Nationwide telephone service is no longer a monopoly.

Future changes in technology could eventually eliminate the natural monopoly and the need for government regulation in local telephone service as well. For example, cellular phone service does not require any wires to individual customers, and the minimum efficient scale for firms delivering such a service could be quite small.

Patents and Copyrights

Another way monopolies arise is through the granting of patents and copyrights by the government. Intel's patent was the source of its monopoly on its computer chips. The U.S. Constitution and the laws of many other countries require that government grant patents to inventors. If a firm registers an invention with the U.S. government, it can be granted a monopoly in the production of that item for 17 years. In other words, the government prohibits other firms from producing the good without the permission of the patent holder. Patents are given for many inventions, including the discovery of new drugs. Pharmaceutical companies hold patents on many of their products, giving them a monopoly to produce and sell the product. Copyrights on computer software, chips, movies, and books also give firms the sole right to market the products. Thus, patents and copyrights can create monopolies.

The award of monopoly rights through patents and copyrights serves a useful purpose. It can stimulate innovation by rewarding the inventor. In other words, the chance to get a patent or copyright gives the inventor more incentive to devote time and resources to invent new products or to take a risk and try out new ideas. Pharmaceutical companies, for example, argue that their patents on drugs are a reward for inventing the drugs. The higher prices and deadweight loss caused by the patent can be viewed as the cost of the new ideas and products. By passing laws to control drug prices, government could lower the prices of drugs to today's sick people. This would be popular, but doing so would reduce the incentive for the firms to invent new drugs. Society—and in particular, people in future years—could suffer a loss.

Reading the News About Monopoly

The U.S. Postal Service is an independent agency of the federal government. With revenue of over $50 billion per year, it would rank in the top ten firms in the United States if it were a private firm. The Postal Service has a monopoly in the delivery of first-class mail. How does it maintain this monopoly?

As the examples in the following article indicate, the Postal Service maintains barriers to the entry of private firms into its business by fining people who use private couri-ers in violation of the 1872 law that established the monopoly. Anyone who uses a private mail service for nonurgent first-class mail can be fined, and quite a few have been.

Maintaining barriers to entry this way is controversial. People pay more for mail service, and the quantity of service is reduced. Hence, legislation has been proposed to end the Postal Service fines.

In arguing against such legislation, the Postal Service maintains that it will have to raise postal rates if it loses customers to private carriers. Evidently, the Postal Service feels that higher postal rates will raise revenue. But with the development of fax machines, electronic mail, and other forms of communication, the price elasticity of demand for first-class mail may be above 1. If this is so, raising postal rates could lower revenue.

Source of article: "Private Couriers and Postal Service Slug It Out," *The New York Times,* February 14, 1994. Copyright © 1994 by the New York Times Company. Reprinted with permission.

Private Couriers and Postal Service Slug It Out

Special to the New York Times

WASHINGTON—Over the last three years the United States Postal Service has collected more than $500,000 in fines from companies that sent "nonurgent" mail by private couriers like Federal Express or DHL.

Now private couriers and their customers—outraged that the postal service could abuse its monopoly position in an effort to win back some of the express mail business—are fighting back.

Legislation has been introduced in Congress that stops the Postal Service from being able to investigate and intimidate companies into using the Postal Service instead of private couriers.

"This is a classic case of a Government agency that is 30 years behind the curve," said Senator Paul Coverdell, Republican of Georgia, who introduced the legislation in the Senate. "The entire subject should be moot. Are you going to fine people for using the fax machine?"

The legislation . . . states that a nongovernmental person may use a private express for the private carriage of certain letters and packets without being penalized by the Postal Service. . . .

The Postal Service has fined 21 companies for violating the 1872 law that established the Postal Service monopoly on mail delivery. A 1979 amendment to the law broke the monopoly on urgent mail, establishing as the definition of urgent, mail that must arrive by noon the next day or lose its value. The Postal Service has the right to decide what is urgent and what is not.

Postal officials say they lose millions to private companies, and without the ability to collect this revenue, they might have to raise first-class rates. The fines collected equal the amount the Postal Service would have earned if it had delivered the mail. . . .

The Postal Service cracked down on Federal agencies after discovering that the General Services Administration had worked out a deal with Federal Express to deliver overnight mail for $3.75, well below the Postal Service's overnight rate of $9.95, and well below Federal Express's standard rate of $15.50.

The Federal agencies did not have to pay lost revenue. Instead postal officials have been pressing the agencies to train their mailroom workers in the art of determining what is—and is not—urgent.

But private companies like Equifax Inc., a credit-reporting agency based in Atlanta, have not been so lucky. In September 1991 postal inspectors looked over their mail room. Eventually, in May 1992, Equifax paid $30,000 in fees, and since then, said David Mooney, Equifax public relations director, the company has made "minor adjustments" in its mailing policy. . . .

The Postal Service denies it has been using strong-arm tactics. "There has been no bullying at all" said Lou Eberhardt, a Postal Service spokesman. He said each company agreed to be audited after it was approached by postal inspectors. . . .

According to one Congressional aide, the Postal Service did not adhere to the 1872 law when it delivered a document recently, a report to Congress on its 1993 performance. Jay Morgan, an aide to Representative Mac Collins, a Georgia Republican, said the Congressman's copy of the "1993 Annual Report and Comprehensive Statement on Postal Operations" was delivered by a private bicycle messenger.

When patents expire, we usually see a major shift toward competition. In general, when assessing the deadweight loss due to monopoly, one must consider the benefits of the research and the new products that monopoly profits may create.

As technology has advanced, patents and copyrights have had to become increasingly complex in order to prevent firms from getting around them. Nevertheless, patent and copyright protection does not always work in maintaining the monopoly. Many times potential competing firms get around copyrights on computer software and chips by "reverse engineering" in which specialists look carefully at how each part of a product works, starting with the final output. Elaborate mechanisms have been developed, such as "clean rooms," in which one group of scientists and programmers tells another group what each subfunction of the invention does but does not tell them how it is done. The other group then tries to invent an alternative way to perform the task. Because they cannot see how it is done, they avoid violating the copyright.

Licenses

Sometimes the government or other organizations create a monopoly by giving or selling a license to one firm to produce the product. The U.S. Postal Service, for example, is a government-sponsored monopoly. A law makes it illegal to use a firm other than the U.S. Postal Service for first-class mail. However, even this monopoly is diminishing with competition from overnight mail services and fax technology.

National parks sometimes grant or sell licenses to single firms to provide food and lodging services. The Curry Company, for example, was granted a monopoly to provide services in Yosemite National Park. For a long time the Pennsylvania Turnpike—a toll road running the width of the state—licensed a monopoly to Howard Johnson Company to provide food for travelers on the long stretches of the road. In recent years, seeing the advantage of competition, the turnpike authorities have allowed several different fast food chains to get licenses.

Barriers to Entry in the Van Transportation Industry

Many U.S. cities limit the number of taxis and vans by requiring that each vehicle have a special license and then restricting the number of licenses. In New York City recently, these people applied for licenses to provide transportation services by vans to inner city neighborhoods. Their entry was denied, thereby giving the existing transit companies monopoly power to raise prices well above marginal cost.

Attempts to Monopolize and Erect Barriers to Entry

Adam Smith warned that firms would try to create monopolies in order to raise their prices. One of the reasons Smith favored free trade between countries is that it would reduce the ability of firms in one country to form a monopoly; if they did form a monopoly and there were no restrictions on trade serving as barriers to entry from firms in other countries, then foreign firms would break the monopoly.

History shows us many examples of firms attempting to monopolize an industry by merging with other firms and then erecting barriers to entry. De Beers is one example where such a strategy has apparently been successful on a global level. In the last part of the nineteenth century, several large firms were viewed as monopolies. Standard Oil, started by John D. Rockefeller in the 1880s, is a well-known example. The firm had control of most of the oil-refining capacity in the United States. Thus, Standard Oil was close to having a monopoly in oil refining. However, the federal government forced Standard Oil to break up into smaller firms. We will consider other examples of the government breaking up monopolies or preventing them from forming in Chapter 16.

Barriers to entry allow a monopoly to persist, so for a firm to maintain a monopoly, it needs barriers to entry. The box "Reading the News About Monopoly" on page 281 discusses one way in which such barriers are maintained: by fining people who use other firms. De Beers maintained its diamond monopoly by not allowing other firms to buy or get control of the diamond mines.

Barriers to entry can also be created by professional certification. For example, economists have argued that the medical and legal professions in the United States erect barriers to the entry of new doctors and lawyers by having tough standards for admittance to medical school or to the bar and by restricting the types of services that can be performed by nurses or paralegals. Doctors' and lawyers' fees might be lower if there were lower barriers to entry and, therefore, more competition.

Simply observing that a firm has no competitors is not enough to prove that there are barriers to entry. Sometimes the threat of potential entry into a market may be enough to get a monopolist to act like a competitive firm. For example, the possibility of a new bookstore opening up off campus may put pressure on the campus bookstore to keep its prices low. When other firms, such as off-campus bookstores, can potentially and easily enter the market, they create what economists call a **contestable market.** In general, the threat of competition in contestable markets can induce monopolists to act like competitors.

contestable market: a market in which the threat of competition is enough to encourage firms to act like competitors.

Review

▷ Economies of scale, patents, copyrights, and licenses are some of the reasons monopolies exist.

▷ Natural monopolies are frequently regulated by government.

▷ Many large monopolies in the United States, such as Standard Oil and AT&T, have been broken apart by government action.

PRICE DISCRIMINATION

In the model of monopoly we have studied in this chapter, the monopolists charge a single price for the good they sell. In some cases, however, firms charge different people different prices for the same item. This is called **price discrimination.** Price discrimination is common and is likely to become more common in the future as firms become more sophisticated in their price setting. Everyday examples include senior citizen discounts at movie theaters and discounts on airline tickets for Saturday-night stayovers.

Some price discrimination is less noticeable because it occurs in geographically separated markets. Charging different prices in foreign markets compared

price discrimination: a situation in which different groups of consumers are charged different prices for the same good.

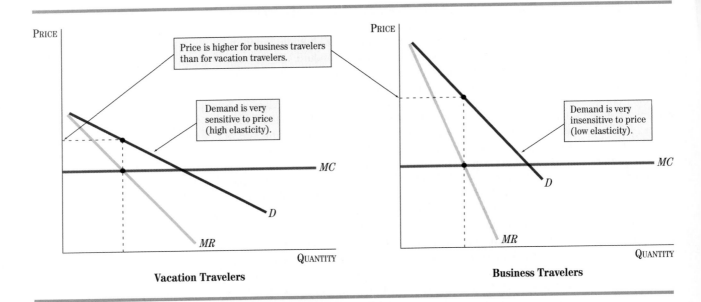

Vacation Travelers   **Business Travelers**

FIGURE 10.9

Price Discrimination Targeted at Different Groups

The monopolist has two groups of potential buyers for its travel services. For convenience we assume the marginal cost curve is flat. The group on the left has a high price elasticity of demand. The group on the right has a low price elasticity of demand. If the monopolist can discriminate between the buyers, then it is optimal to charge a lower price to the high-elasticity group and a higher price to the low-elasticity group.

with domestic markets is common. For example, Japanese cameras are less expensive in the United States than in Japan. In contrast, the price of luxury German cars in the United States is frequently higher than in Germany.

Volume or quantity discounts are another form of price discrimination. Higher prices are sometimes charged to customers who buy smaller amounts of an item. For example, electric utility firms sometimes charge more per kilowatt-hour to customers who use only a little electricity.

Consumers with Different Price Elasticities of Demand

Why is there price discrimination? Figure 10.9 shows a diagram of a monopoly that gives one explanation. Suppose the good being sold is airline travel between two remote islands, and suppose there is only one airline between the two islands. The two graphs in Figure 10.9 represent demand curves with different elasticities. On the left is the demand for vacation air travel. Vacationers are frequently more price sensitive than business people. They can be more flexible with their time; they can take a boat rather than the plane; they can stay home and paint the house. Hence, the price elasticity of demand is high for vacationers. Business travelers, however, do not have much choice. As shown on the graph to the right, they are less sensitive to price. An important business meeting may require a business person to fly to the other island with little advance notice. The price elasticity of demand is low for business travel. Difference between price elasticities is a key reason why price discrimination occurs.

In Figure 10.9, notice that both groups have downward-sloping demand curves and downward-sloping marginal revenue curves. For simplicity, marginal cost is constant and is shown with a straight line.

Figure 10.9 predicts that business travelers will be charged a higher price than vacationers. Why? Marginal revenue equals marginal cost at a higher price for business travelers than for vacationers. The model of monopoly predicts that the firm will charge a higher price to those with a lower elasticity and a lower price to those with a higher elasticity.

In fact, this is the type of price discrimination we see on airlines. But how can the airlines distinguish a business traveler from a vacation traveler? Clothing will not work because a business traveler could easily change from a suit to an aloha shirt and shorts to get the low fare. One device used by the airlines is the Saturday night stayover. Business travelers prefer to work and travel during the week. They value being home with family or friends on a Saturday night. Vacationers frequently do not mind extending their travel by a day or two to include a Saturday night, and they might want to vacation over the weekend. Hence, there is a strong correlation between vacation travelers and those who do not mind staying over on a Saturday night. A good way to price-discriminate, therefore, is to charge a lower price to people who stay in their destination on a Saturday night and to charge a higher price to those who are unwilling to do so.

Price discrimination based on different price elasticity of demand requires that the firm be able to prevent people who buy at a lower price from selling the item to other people. Thus, price discrimination is much more common in services than in manufactured goods.

Would it bother you to hear how little I paid for this flight?

Quantity Discounts

Another important form of price discrimination involves setting prices according to how much is purchased. If a business makes 100 telephone calls a day, it probably has to pay a higher fee per call than if it makes 1,000 a day. Telephone monopolies can increase their profits by such a price scheme, as shown in Figure 10.10.

The single-price monopoly is shown in the bottom graph of Figure 10.10. Two ways in which the monopoly can make higher profits by charging different prices are shown in the top two panels. In both cases, there is no difference in the price elasticity of demand for different consumers. To make it easy, assume that all consumers are identical. The demand curve is the sum of the marginal benefits of all the consumers in the market.

On the upper left the firm sets a higher price for the first few items a consumer buys and a lower price for the remaining items. Frequent flier miles on airlines are an example of this kind of pricing. If you fly more than a certain number of miles a year, you get a free ticket. Thus, the per mile fare for 20,000 miles is less than the fare for 10,000 miles. As the diagram shows, profits for the firm are higher in such a situation. In the example at the left, the higher price is the fare without the discount.

On the upper right we see how profits can be increased if the firm gives even deeper discounts to high-volume purchasers. As long as the high-volume purchasers cannot sell the product to the low-volume purchasers, there are extra profits to be made.

The upper right graph in Figure 10.10 illustrates an important benefit of price discrimination. It can reduce deadweight loss. By price discrimination, a monopoly actually produces more. For example, those who get a lower price because of frequent flier discounts may actually end up buying more. The result is that the airline has more flights. As already noted, the deadweight loss from a monopolist occurs because production is too low. If price discrimination allows more production, then it reduces deadweight loss.

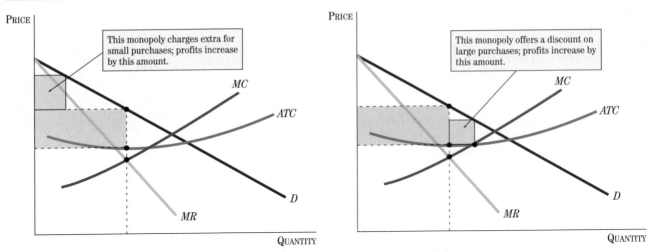

Two Examples of a Monopoly Charging Two Prices

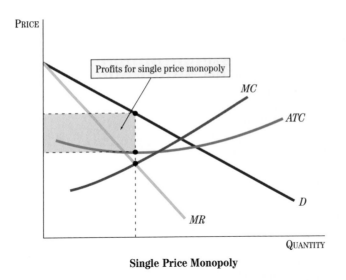

Single Price Monopoly

FIGURE 10.10
Price Discrimination Through Quantity Discounts or Premiums

The standard single-price monopoly is shown at the bottom. If the monopoly can charge a higher price to customers who buy only a little, profits can increase, as shown on the upper left. If the monopoly can give a discount to people who purchase a lot, it can also increase profits, as shown on the upper right. In this case, production increases.

Monopolies versus Other Firms with Market Power

The preceding examples of price discrimination involved monopolies—either the hypothetical airlines with sole control of travel between two remote islands or a telephone monopoly. But price discrimination also occurs in firms that are not monopolies. United, American, and TWA all offer different fares to customers based on different price elasticities when they fly the same routes. We will see in the next chapter that firms can have some monopoly power—face downward-sloping demand as shown in Figures 10.9 and 10.10—even if they are not monopolies. For example, firms in industries in which one firm's products are slightly different from other firms' products have market power. The preceding explanation of price discrimination can, therefore, apply to such firms.

Review

▶ Because a monopolist has market power, it can charge different prices to different consumers as long as it can prevent the consumers from reselling the good.

▶ Price discrimination explains telephone pricing as well as the complicated airfares on airlines.

▶ Deadweight loss is reduced by price discrimination.

CONCLUSION

The model of a monopoly we developed in this chapter centers on a key diagram, Figure 10.6 on page 273. Learning how to work with this diagram of a monopoly is very important. In fact, economists use this same diagram to describe any firm that has some market power, not just monopolies, as we show in the next chapter. Before proceeding, it is a good idea to practice sketching this generic diagram of a monopoly and finding output, price, and profits for different positions of the curve.

From the point of view of economic efficiency, the economic performance of monopolies is not nearly as good as that of competitive industries. Output is too low, marginal benefits are not equal to marginal costs, and consumer surplus plus producer surplus is diminished. But when assessing these losses, the fact that the expectation of monopoly profits—even if temporary—is the inducement for firms to do research and develop new products must also be considered.

Nevertheless the deadweight loss caused by monopolies provides a potential opportunity for government to intervene in the economy. In fact, the U.S. government actively intervenes in the economy to either prevent monopolies from forming or to regulate monopolies when it is not appropriate to break them apart. We look further into government preventing or regulating monopolies in Chapter 16.

KEY POINTS

1. A monopoly occurs when only one firm sells a product for which there are no close substitutes. The world diamond market is nearly a monopoly. Many local markets for water, sewage, electricity, and telephones are monopolies.

2. A monopolist possesses market power in the sense that it can lower the market price by producing more or raise the market price by producing less.

3. The model of a monopoly assumes that the monopoly tries to maximize profits and that it faces a downward-sloping demand curve.

4. A monopoly's total revenue increases and then decreases as it increases production.

5. The monopoly chooses a quantity such that marginal revenue equals marginal cost.

6. A monopoly produces a smaller quantity and charges a higher price than a competitive industry; the lower production causes a deadweight loss.

7. It is frequently not possible to create a competitive industry out of a monopoly, in which case the comparison between monopoly and competition is hypothetical.

8. Monopolies exist because of economies of scale that make the minimum efficient size of the firm larger than the market, and because of barriers to entry, including government patents and licenses.

9. Many monopolies are short lived; technological change can rapidly change a firm from a monopoly to a competitive firm, as exemplified by the long-distance telephone market.

10. A price-discriminating monopoly charges different prices to different customers depending on how elastic their demand is.

KEY TERMS

monopoly
barriers to entry
market power

price-maker
average revenue
price-cost margin

natural monopoly
contestable market
price discrimination

QUESTIONS FOR REVIEW

1. What is a monopoly?

2. What market power does a monopoly have?

3. How does a monopoly choose its profit-maximizing output and price?

4. Why does marginal revenue decline as more is produced by a monopoly?

5. Why is the marginal revenue curve below the demand curve for a monopoly but not for a competitive firm?

6. Why does a monopolist produce less than a competitive industry?

7. What forces tend to cause monopolies?

8. What is the deadweight loss from a monopoly?

9. What is price discrimination?

10. How does price discrimination reduce deadweight loss?

PROBLEMS

1. Suppose that the price elasticity of demand for diamonds is 1.
   a) Suppose only one monopolistic firm produces diamonds. If the monopolist cuts production by 10 percent, then by what percent does the price rise?
   b) Now suppose the market is competitive, with 100 firms each supplying 1 percent of the market. If one of the competitive firms cuts its own production by 10 percent and the 99 other firms do not change production, by what percentage does the price rise?
   c) Why is it likely that the other firms will in fact change production? Suppose each of the other firms increases its own production by .1 percent. By what percent will the price rise?
   d) How does your answer explain the difference between a monopolist's view and a competitor's view of the market?

2. The following table gives the total costs for a typical firm in a competitive industry. Suppose the price per unit of output is $25.

Quantity	Total Costs
0	22
1	40
2	60
3	87
4	120
5	155

a) What is the profit-maximizing level of production?
b) Suppose that through some means one firm buys up all the other firms. Sketch, using smooth curves not necessarily drawn to scale, a new diagram to illustrate the profit-maximizing price and level of production.
c) On the same graph, indicate the deadweight loss due to the transformation of the industry from competition to a monopoly.

3. The table below gives the total costs and total revenue schedule for a monopolist.

Quantity	Total Revenue	Total Costs
0	$0.00	$150
1	87.50	207
2	150.00	246
3	187.50	274
4	200.00	301
5	187.50	356
6	150.00	456
7	87.50	670

a) Calculate marginal revenue, marginal cost, and the demand curve.
b) Determine the profit-maximizing price and quantity, and calculate the resulting profit.

4. The following table gives the round-trip airfare from Los Angeles to New York on United Airlines on July 27, 1993.

Price	Advance Purchase	Minimum Stay	Cancellation Penalty
$418	14 days	Overnight on Saturday	100%
$683	3 days	Overnight on Saturday	100%
$1,366	None required	None required	None

Explain why United might want to charge different prices for the same route. Why are there minimum-stay requirements and cancellation penalties?

5. Sketch the diagram for a monopoly with an upward-sloping marginal cost curve that is earning economic profits. Suppose the government imposes a tax on each item the monopoly sells. Draw the diagram corresponding to this situation. How does this tax affect the monopoly's production and price? Show what happens to the area of deadweight loss.

6. Children, students, and senior citizens frequently are eligible for discounted tickets to movies. Is this an example of price discrimination? Explain the conditions necessary for price discrimination to occur and draw the graphs to describe this situation.

7. Why is it that firms need market power in order to price-discriminate? What other circumstances are required in order for a firm to price-discriminate? Give an example of a firm or industry that price-discriminates and explain how it is possible in that case.

8. Consider the following cost and demand information about a monopoly (in dollars). Fill out the table.

Quantity of Output	Price	Total Revenue	Marginal Revenue	Total Costs	Marginal Cost
1	14.00	———	———	16.00	———
2	12.00	———	———	20.00	———
3	10.00	———	———	25.00	———
4	8.50	———	———	33.00	———
5	7.00	———	———	41.00	———
6	5.50	———	———	50.00	———

a) Determine how much the monopoly will produce if it is maximizing profits. What price will the monopoly charge? What are its profits?

b) What quantity maximizes total revenue for the monopoly? Explain why producing this quantity will not maximize profits.

9. What is the price-cost margin for the typical competitive firm? What is the price-cost margin (at the profit-maximizing quantity) for the monopoly described in problem 8? If the government forced a breakup of the monopoly into three firms, in general what would happen to the price-cost margin? Why?

10. Suppose that the five sellers in the market described in Figure 7.4 merge together to form a monopoly. The buyers in the market described in Figure 7.3 continue to act independently. Assume that the marginal cost of the monopoly is given by the sum of the marginal costs of the five original sellers.

a) Compute the marginal revenue for the monopoly and plot it.

b) What output and what price do you predict the monopoly will choose?

c) What is the price-cost margin?

d) Calculate the loss of consumer surplus due to the monopoly.

e) Calculate the deadweight loss of the monopoly.

11. Calculate the deadweight loss of the monopoly described in Table 10.1.

Product Differentiation and Strategic Behavior

When John Johnson launched his magazine business in 1942, he differentiated his products from existing products in a way that was valued by millions of African Americans. As a result, the new product lines, the magazines *Ebony* and *Jet,* were huge successes. Johnson became a multimillionaire, and his firm became the second largest black-owned firm in the United States. Similarly, when Liz Claiborne started her new clothing firm in 1976, she differentiated her products from existing products in a way that was valued by millions of American women. She offered stylish yet affordable clothes for working women, and she too was successful: By 1991, Liz Claiborne, Inc., was the largest producer of women's clothing in the world. These stories of people finding ways to differentiate their products from existing products are told thousands of times a year, although not everyone is as successful as John Johnson and Liz Claiborne.

John Johnson's magazines and Liz Claiborne's suits and dresses were different in a way that was valued by consumers. Because their products were different from products made by the many other firms in their industries—magazine publishing and women's clothing, respectively—they each had market power in the sense

that they could charge a higher price for their products and not lose all their customers. Thus, neither Johnson Publishing nor Liz Claiborne, Inc., was just another firm entering a competitive industry where every firm sold the same product. But Johnson Publishing and Liz Claiborne, Inc., were not monopolies either; there were other firms in their industry, and they could not prevent entry into the industry by even more firms. As is typical of many firms, they seemed to be hybrids between a competitive firm and a monopoly.

In this chapter we develop a model widely used by economists to explain the behavior of such firms. It is called *the model of monopolistic competition.* **Monopolistic competition** occurs in an industry with many firms and free entry, where the product of each firm is slightly differentiated from the product of every other firm. We contrast the predictions of this model with the models of competition and monopoly developed in previous chapters.

We also develop a *model of oligopoly* in this chapter, because production differentiation is not the only reason many firms seem to fall between the models of monopoly and competition. In an **oligopoly,** there are very few firms in the industry. Because there are very few firms,

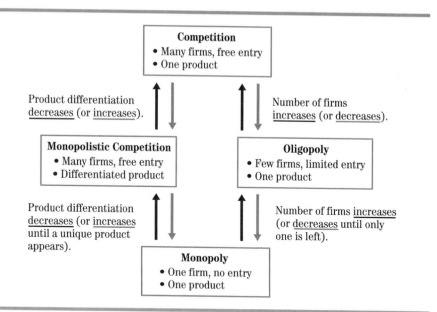

FIGURE 11.1
Four Types of Industries
The arrows show possible directions
of change: either from competition
toward monopoly (red arrows) or in
the other direction (black arrows).
Changes can occur simultaneously
on both the "product differentiation" and the "number of firms"
sides of the diagram.

Competition
• Many firms, free entry
• One product

Product differentiation
<u>decreases</u> (or <u>increases</u>).

Number of firms
<u>increases</u> (or <u>decreases</u>).

Monopolistic Competition
• Many firms, free entry
• Differentiated product

Oligopoly
• Few firms, limited entry
• One product

Product differentiation
<u>decreases</u> (or <u>increases</u>
until a unique product
appears).

Number of firms <u>increases</u>
(or <u>decreases</u> until only
one is left).

Monopoly
• One firm, no entry
• One product

each firm has market power. The actions of any one firm can significantly affect the market price. For example, suppose Bagelopoly, the monopoly bagel bakery in a large city discussed in the previous chapter, is broken up into two firms, Bageldum and Bageldee, which are then operated independently. Now both firms have market power. If Bageldum increases its price, it will lose some, but not all, of its customers; however, the decrease in the number of bagels sold will depend on what Bageldee does. If Bageldee increases its price also, then Bageldum will not see its sales fall by as much as if Bageldee does not increase its price.

Thus, much like two tennis players, Bageldee and Bageldum need to consider each others' actions. Their behavior is strategic in the sense that they need to anticipate what the other will do and develop a strategy to respond. Such situations, whether in games or in industry, are very complex. Neither the model of a competitive industry, where no one firm can affect the price, nor the model of monopoly, where one firm completely dominates the market, adequately describes such a situation. Hence, there is a need for a model of oligopoly to explain situations in which a few firms produce goods and services and engage in strategic behavior: thinking about, anticipating, and reacting to the other firm's moves.

Figure 11.1 compares the models of monopolistic competition, oligopoly, monopoly, and competition. Over time, industries can change from being a monopoly to monopolistic competition, to oligopoly, to competition, and back again, due to changes in the number of firms or the degree of product differentiation. For example, when Sprint and MCI broke into AT&T's monopoly, the market changed from a monopoly to either an oligopoly or competition, depending on how much power firms had to determine the price.

In order to emphasize the distinction between models of competition and monopolistic competition or between models of monopoly and monopolistic competition, the terms *pure competition* or *pure monopoly* are sometimes used. In this book, we simply use the terms *competition* and *monopoly*.

monopolistic competition:
an industry characterized by
many firms selling
differentiated products in an
industry in which there is
free entry and exit.

oligopoly: an industry
characterized by few firms
selling the same product
with limited entry of other
firms.

PRODUCT DIFFERENTIATION

product differentiation: the effort by firms to produce goods that are slightly different from other types of goods.

The effort by firms to fashion products different from other firms' products in ways that people value is called **product differentiation.** Product differentiation is pervasive in market economies. It leads to a great variety of consumer goods and capital goods. Goods for which there is no product differentiation, such as aluminum ingots or gold bullion, are called *homogenous products,* meaning that they are all exactly the same.

Product Differentiation and Variety in a Market Economy

Product differentiation is obvious in even a casual examination of a modern market economy.

Consumer Products

Consider, for example, the August 1993 issue of *Consumer Reports* magazine. It describes the pros and cons of 14 different types of sports drinks, like Gatorade and K-10; 18 different eyeglass chain stores, like Lenscrafters and Pearle Vision; 39 different brands of men's dress shirts, like Arrow and Van Heusen; 18 different types of kitchen knives, like Ginsu and Hoffritz; 19 different kinds of 8-inch adjustable wrenches; 15 different types of socket wrenches; and 9 different types of spot removers.

According to the characteristics used by *Consumer Reports* to rate the products—appearance, comfort, durability, strength, etc.—all these products were different. There is even product differentiation among the magazines that rate consumer products: *Consumer Reports* offers a differentiated product from *Consumers Digest.*

The wide variety of products in a market economy contrasts starkly with the absence of such variety in the former centrally planned economies of Eastern Europe and the former Soviet Union. Stores in Moscow or Warsaw would typically have only one type of each product—one type of wrench, for example—produced according to the specifications of the central planners. There was even relatively little variety in food or clothing. One of the first results of market economic reform in these countries has been an increase in the variety of goods available.

Product differentiation is a major activity of both existing firms and potential new firms. Business schools teach managers that product differentiation ranks together with cost cutting as one of the two basic ways that a firm can improve its performance. A budding entrepreneur can enter an existing industry either by finding a cheaper way to produce an existing product or by introducing a product that is differentiated from existing products in a way that will appeal to consumers. Prospective financial backers of the entrepreneur will want to know how the product is differentiated. The people who backed John Johnson and Liz Claiborne must have asked as much. (In both cases, their families helped in the financing; for example, John Johnson's mother mortgaged the family's furniture for $500.)

Product differentiation usually means something less than inventing an entirely new product. For example, the VCR—introduced in the late 1970s—was an entirely new product, but the voice-activated VCR is a differentiated product. Aspirin was an entirely new product when it was invented; wrapping aspirin in a special coating

Product Differentiation versus Homogenous Products

The wide variety of goods such as shoes (left) illustrates product differentiation in contrast to homogenous products such as wheat (right).

to make it easier to swallow is product differentiation. Coke, when it was invented in 1886, was a new product, while Pepsi, RC Cola, Jolt Cola, Yes Cola, and Mr. Cola, which followed over the years, are differentiated products.

Note that many differentiated products are sold by the same firm. For example, there are three Arrow shirts in the 1993 issue of *Consumer Reports*—one 100 percent cotton and two blends, each with a different weave.

Capital Goods

Product differentiation also exists for the capital goods—the machines and equipment—used by firms to produce their products. The large earthmoving equipment produced by Caterpillar is different from that produced by other firms such as Komatsu of Japan. One difference is the extensive spare parts and repair service that goes along with Caterpillar equipment. Bulldozers and road graders frequently break down and need quick repairs; by stationing parts distributorships and knowledgeable mechanics all over the world, Caterpillar can offer quick repairs in the case of costly breakdowns. In other words, the products are differentiated on the basis of service and a worldwide network.

The Caterpillar example indicates that product differentiation for producer goods can be an important source of cost reductions or quality improvements for the businesses that use these goods, such as the construction firms that use the earthmoving equipment.

Recent economic research has emphasized that product differentiation in the capital goods used by businesses has a key role in reducing the cost of production.

Observations Explained by Product Differentiation

Product differentiation explains certain facts about a market economy that could be puzzling if all goods were homogenous.

Intraindustry Trade

Differentiated products lead to trade between countries of goods in the same industry, called **intraindustry trade.** Trade between countries of goods in different industries, called **interindustry trade,** can be explained by comparative advantage.

intraindustry trade: trade between countries in goods from the same or similar industries.

interindustry trade: trade between countries in goods from different industries.

Variety Is the Spice of Life

The following table illustrates product differentiation. It shows 19 different 8-inch adjustable wrenches on the market in the United States. According to the three physical characteristics used in the ratings—strength, play in jaw, and adjustment—no two of these are alike. Hence, there is considerable product differentiation in this apparently homogenous tool. Note that the relationship between price and quality is positive but not strong. The worst wrench is the cheapest, but the best wrench is nearly as cheap.

Source of table: "Wrenches." Copyright 1993 by Consumers Union of U.S., Inc., Yonkers, NY 10703–1075. Adapted with permission from *Consumer Reports,* August 1993. Although this material originally appeared in *Consumer Reports,* the selective adaptation and resulting conclusions presented are those of the author and are not sanctioned or endorsed in any way by Consumers Union, the publisher of *Consumer Reports.*

Top-rated adjustable
Popular Mechanics 26637, $6 list

RATINGS

Better ← → Worse

Adjustable wrenches

Listed in order of estimated quality, based primarily on strength. Except where separated by a heavy line, closely ranked models differed little in quality. Bracketed models were judged approximately equal in quality and are listed in alphabetical order. The Ratings apply only to the eight-inch-size wrenches tested.

1 Brand and model. If you can't find a model, call the company. Phone numbers are listed on page 548.

2 Price. Manufacturer's suggested retail, rounded to the nearest dollar. A * denotes the price CU paid (a suggested retail price was not available).

3 Strength. Reflects the maximum turning force the wrench sustained before its jaws lost their grip. No wrench lost grip when turned hard by CU staffers; failures occurred only when extension pipes were fitted to the tools to increase turning leverage. This judgment, then, is useful mostly as an indication of the wrench's resistance to abuse.

4 Play in jaw. An appraisal of the slack (or "backlash") between each model's movable jaw and the worm screw that adjusts it. The less slack, the easier it is to set the jaw opening precisely.

5 Adjustment. We judged the smoothness of the worm screw in setting the jaw over its entire range of motion.

1 Brand and model	Price 2	Strength 3	Play in jaw 4	Adjustment 5	Comments
Popular Mechanics 26637 **A Best Buy**	$6	◉	◉	○	—
Ace 24485	9	◉	◒	○	A,E
Crescent AC18	17	◉	◒	◒	—
Craftsman 44603	14	◉	◒	◒	—
Channellock 808	19	◉	◉	◒	—
Diamond D78	13	◒	●	◒	A,C,D
Master Mechanic 139-584	14	◒	○	◉	—
NAPA AW-8	17	◒	◉	◉	B
Sears 30881	9	◒	○	◒	—
Vermont American 52508	9	◒	●	◒	—
Durex 7548	5	◒	○	◒	B
Olympia 01-008	5	◒	◒	●	B
Truecraft 208	12	◒	◒	○	—
Durabuilt TW148	7	○	○	◒	—
Great Neck AW8C	7	○	◒	◒	—
Thorsen Allied 56708	9	○	◒	◒	A
Bench Top 52814	6	○	○	●	B
Stanley 87-368	13*	◒	●	◉	—
Alltrade 140-B-8	5	●	◒	○	B

Features in Common
All are: ● About eight inches in length.
All have: ● A jaw-to-handle angle of 22.5°. ● Plated finish. ● Hole in handle for hanging in storage. ● Except when noted, a maximum jaw opening of 1 in.

Key to Comments
A–Plastic-clad handle; cushions hand.

B–Handle slightly narrower than most (and **NAPA** handle has more prominent edges than others); judged slightly less comfortable than most under heavy effort.
C–On one of three samples tested, jaw tended to bind when set at wide openings.
D–Maximum jaw opening of 1⅛ inches.
E–Discontinued; replaced by **Ace 20004240**, $9.

Bananas are traded for wheat because one good is grown better in warm climates and the other good is grown better in cooler climates. But why should intraindustry trade take place? Why should the United States both buy beer from Canada and sell beer to Canada? Beer is produced in many different countries, but a beer company in one country will differentiate its beer from a beer company in another country. In order for people to benefit from the variety of beer, we might see beer produced in the United States (for example, Budweiser) being exported to Canada and, at the same time, see beer produced in Canada (for example, Molson) being exported to the United States. If all beer were exactly the same (a homogenous commodity), such trade within the beer industry would make little sense, but it is easily understood when products are differentiated.

Advertising

Product differentiation also provides one explanation of why there appears to be so much advertising—the attempt by firms to tell consumers what is good about their product. If all products were homogenous, then advertising would make little sense: A bar of gold bullion is a bar of gold bullion, no matter who sells it. But if a firm has a newly differentiated product in which it has invested millions of dollars, then it needs to advertise it to prospective customers. You can have the greatest product in the world, but it will not sell if no one knows about it. Advertising is a way to provide information to consumers about how products differ.

Economists have debated the role of advertising in the economy for many years. Many have worried about the waste associated with advertising. It is hard to see how catchy phrases like "It's the right one, baby" are providing useful information about Diet Pepsi to consumers. One explanation is that the purpose of the advertising in these cases is to get people to try the product. If they like it, they will buy more; if they do not like it, they will not—but without the ad they might not ever try it. Whatever the reason, advertising will not sell an inferior product, at least not for long. For example, despite heavy advertising, Federal Express failed miserably with Zapmail—a product that guaranteed high-quality faxes of documents delivered around the country within hours—because of the superiority of inexpensive fax machines that even small businesses could buy.

Others say that advertising is wasteful partly because it is used to create a *perception* of product differentiation rather than genuine differences between products. For example, suppose Coke and Pepsi are homogenous products (for some people's tastes, they are identical). Then advertising simply has the purpose of creating a perception in people's minds that the products are different. If so, such product differentiation may be providing a false benefit, and the advertising used to promote it is a waste of people's time and effort.

Consumer Information Services

The existence of magazines such as *Consumer Reports* is also explained by product differentiation. These magazines would be of little use to consumers if all products were alike.

Such services may also help consumers sort through exaggerated claims in advertising or help them get a better perception of what the real differences between products are. It is hard to sell an expensive product that ends up last on a consumer-rating list, even with the most creative advertising.

Ways That Products Are Differentiated

Altering a product's *physical characteristics*—the sharpness of the knife, the calorie content of the sports drink, the mix of cotton and polyester in the shirt, etc.—is the most common method of product differentiation. However, as the example of Caterpillar shows, products can be differentiated for reasons other than the physical characteristics. Related features such as low installation costs, fast delivery, large inventory, and money-back guarantees also serve to differentiate products.

Location is another important way in which products are differentiated. A Blockbuster Video or a McDonald's down the block is a much different product for you than a Blockbuster Video or a McDonald's 100 miles away. Yet only the location differentiates the product.

Time is yet another way to differentiate products. An airline service with only one daily departure from Chicago to Dallas is different from a service with twelve departures a day. Adding more flights of exactly the same type of air service is a way to differentiate the product. A 24-hour supermarket provides a different service than one that is open only during the day.

How Much Product Differentiation at a Firm?

Product differentiation is costly. Developing a new variety of spot remover that will remove mustard from wool (no existing product is any good at this) would require chemical research, marketing research, and sales effort. Opening another Lenscrafters (there are already nearly five hundred in the United States) requires constructing and equipping a new store with eyeglass equipment, trained personnel, and inventory.

But product differentiation can bring in additional revenue for a firm. The new spot remover will be valued by ice skaters and football fans who want to keep warm with woolen blankets or scarves but who also like mustard on their hot dogs. The people in the neighborhood where the new Lenscrafters opens will value it because they do not have to drive or walk as far.

The assumption of profit maximization implies that firms will undertake an activity if it increases profits. Thus, firms will attempt to differentiate their products if the additional revenue from product differentiation is greater than the additional costs. This is exactly the advice given to managers in business school courses. "Create the largest gap between buyer value . . . and the cost of uniqueness" is the way Harvard Business School professor Michael Porter puts it in his book *Competitive Advantage*.[1] If the additional revenue is greater than the additional cost, then business firms will undertake a product-differentiation activity.

For a given firm, therefore, there is an *optimal* amount of product differentiation that balances out the additional revenue and the additional cost of the product differentiation. This is illustrated in Figure 11.2, which shows the number of differentiated products a firm chooses to develop on the horizontal axis. In the case of a chain like Lenscrafters, the horizontal axis would be the number of outlets. The additional revenue from developing another differentiated product is shown by the downward-sloping line. For example, as more and more Lenscrafters outlets are opened in a region, the additional revenue from each one declines because there is a

---

1. Michael Porter, *Competitive Advantage* (New York: Free Press, 1985), p. 153.

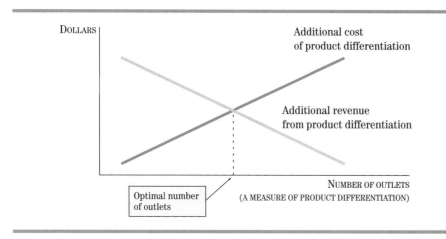

FIGURE 11.2
A Firm's Decision about Product Differentiation
Determining how much product differentiation a firm should undertake is a matter of equating the additional revenue and additional cost of another differentiated product. (Note that these "additional cost" and "additional revenue" curves are analogous to marginal cost and marginal revenue curves except that they depend on the *number* of differentiated products rather than the *quantity* of a particular product.)

fixed number of people who wear glasses in that region. The additional cost of developing another differentiated product is shown by the upward-sloping line. In the example of Lenscrafters, the additional cost of opening a new outlet might increase with the number of existing outlets because of the limited availability of good locations or trained opticians in the region. The optimal number of outlets (a measure of product differentiation) for Lenscrafters is at the point where the additional revenue from another outlet is just equal to the additional cost. Another outlet would reduce profits and would not be undertaken.

The idea applies equally well to other types of product differentiation. Consider, for example, the problem of an airline deciding how many flights to schedule on a given route. In this case the horizontal axis is the number of flights per day. The decision about how many types of shirts Arrow should offer is much the same.

Using this principle in practice is difficult because the revenue gains from product differentiation depend on what other firms do. For example, the revenue to Lenscrafters from a store in a new neighborhood depends on whether Pearle Vision also opens a new store in the neighborhood. Later in this chapter we look at some of the issues raised when there are strategic interactions between firms.

Review

▶ Product differentiation is evident in the variety of products we see every day, in the absence of such variety in centrally planned economies, and in the proliferation of such variety after market reforms.

▶ Intraindustry trade, advertising, and consumer information are some of the facts that can be better explained by product differentiation.

▶ Products can be differentiated by physical characteristics, location, and time, among other features.

▶ Profit-maximizing firms will fashion a differentiated product if the additional revenue from doing so is greater than the additional cost.

THE MODEL OF MONOPOLISTIC COMPETITION

The model of monopolistic competition, first developed by Edward Chamberlin of Harvard University in the 1930s, is designed to describe the behavior of firms operating in differentiated product markets. Monopolistic competition gets its name because it is a hybrid of monopoly and competition. Recall that monopoly has one seller facing a downward-sloping market demand curve with barriers to the entry of other firms. Competition has many sellers, each facing a horizontal demand curve with no barriers to entry and exit. Monopolistic competition, like competition, has many firms with free entry and exit, but, like monopoly, each firm faces a downward-sloping demand curve for its product.

The monopolistically competitive firm's demand curve slopes downward because of product differentiation. When a monopolistically competitive firm raises its price, the quantity demanded of its product goes down but does not plummet to zero, as in the case of a competitive firm. For example, if Nike raises the price of its running shoes, it will lose some sales to Reebok, but it will still sell a considerable number of running shoes because some people prefer Nike shoes to other brands. Nike running shoes and Reebok running shoes are differentiated products to many consumers. On the other hand, a competitive firm selling a product like wheat, which is a much more homogenous product, can expect to lose virtually all its customers to another firm if it raises its price above the market.

As we will see, free entry and exit is an important property of monopolistic competition. Because of it, firms can come into the market if there is a profit to be made or leave the market if they are running losses.

A Typical Monopolistic Competitor

Figure 11.3 illustrates the key features of the model of monopolistic competition. Each graph in Figure 11.3 shows a typical monopolistically competitive firm. At first glance, the graphs look exactly like the graph for a monopoly introduced in the last chapter. They should, because both monopolistic and monopolistically competitive firms face downward-sloping demand curves. However, the demand curve facing a monopolistically competitive firm has a different interpretation because there are other firms in the industry. The demand curve is not the market demand curve; rather it is the demand curve that is *specific* to each firm. When new firms enter the industry—for example, when L.A. Gear enters with Nike and Reebok—the demand curves specific to both Nike and Reebok shift to the left. When firms leave, the demand curves of the remaining firms shift to the right. The reason is that new firms take some of the quantity demanded away from existing firms, and when some firms exit, there is a greater quantity demanded for existing firms.

The difference between the graphs for a monopolist and a monopolistic competitor shows up when we move from the short run to the long run; that is, when firms enter and exit. This is illustrated in Figure 11.3. Note how the three graphs in the figure have exactly the same average total cost curves. The graphs differ from one another in that the location of the demand and marginal revenue curves relative to the average total cost curve is different in each. Graphs (a) and (b) represent the short run. Graph (c) represents the long run after the entry and exit of firms in the industry.

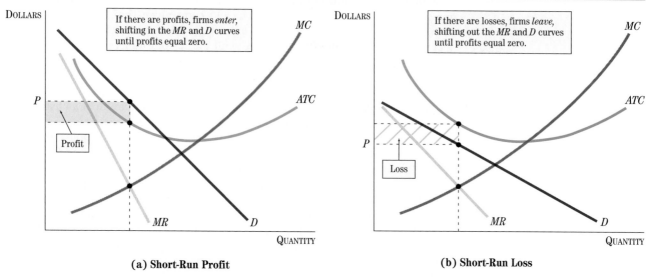

(a) Short-Run Profit

(b) Short-Run Loss

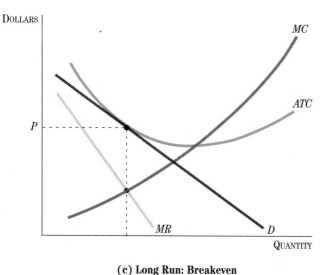

(c) Long Run: Breakeven

FIGURE 11.3
Monopolistic Competition
Each graph shows a typical firm in a monopolistically competitive industry. Firms enter the industry if there are profits, as in graph (a). This would shift the demand and marginal revenue curves to the left for the typical firm because some buyers switch to the new firms. Firms leave if there are losses, as in graph (b). This would shift the demand and marginal revenue curves to the right because the firms that stay in the industry get more buyers. In the long run, profits are driven to zero, as in graph (c).

Observe that the demand curve in graph (c) is drawn so that it just touches the average total cost curve. At this point, the profit-maximizing price equals average total cost. Thus, total revenue is equal to total costs, and profits are zero. On the other hand, in graphs (a) and (b), the demand curve is drawn so that there is either a positive profit or a negative profit (loss) because price is either greater than or less than average total cost.

The Short Run: Just Like a Monopoly

Consider the short-run situation before firms either enter or exit the industry. The monopolistic competitor's profit-maximization decision is like that of the monopoly. To maximize profits, it sets its quantity where marginal revenue equals marginal cost. Because the monopolistically competitive firm faces a downward-sloping demand curve, its profit-maximizing price and quantity balance the increased revenue from a higher price with the lost customers brought on by the higher price. The marginal-revenue-equals-marginal-cost condition achieves this balance. The profit-maximizing quantity of production is shown by the dashed vertical lines in graphs (a) and (b) of Figure 11.3.

For example, ForEyes, Lenscrafters, and Pearle Vision are monopolistic competitors in many shopping areas in the United States. Each local eyeglass store has an optometrist, but each offers slightly different services. At a shopping area with several of these eyeglass stores, one of them can raise prices slightly and fewer people will purchase glasses there. Some people will walk all the way to the other end of the mall to the store with the lower-priced glasses. Others will be happy to stay with the store that raised its prices because they like the service and location. These outlets are not monopolists, but the downward slope of their demand curves makes their pricing decision much like that of monopolists. The slope of the demand curve for a monopolistic competitor may be different than for a monopolist, but the qualitative relationship between demand, revenue, and costs—and the firm's decisions in setting quantity and price—are the same.

Entry and Exit: Just Like Competition

Now consider entry and exit, which can take place over time. In the model of long-run competitive equilibrium in Chapter 9, we showed that if there were economic profits to be made, new firms would enter the industry. If firms were running losses, then firms would exit the industry. Only when economic profits were zero would the industry be in long-run equilibrium with no tendency for firms either to enter or exit.

In monopolistic competition, the entry and exit decisions are driven by the same considerations. If profits are positive, as in graph (a) of Figure 11.3, firms have incentive to enter the industry. For example, in a shopping center or mall where existing eyeglass stores are earning economic profits, another such store would open. If profits are negative, as shown in graph (b) of Figure 11.3, firms have incentive to exit the industry. This represents a situation where there are too many eyeglass stores at the mall and each loses money.

As we move from the short run to the long run, the demand curve for each of the old firms will tend to shift to the point at which the demand curve and the average total cost curve are tangent; that is, at the point where the two curves just touch and have the same slope. Entry into the industry will shift the demand curve of each existing firm to the left, and exit will shift the demand curve of each remaining firm to the right.

We now know why the demand and marginal revenue curves shift in this way. With new firms entering the market, the existing firms will be sharing their sales with new firms. If ForEyes opens up a shop, then some of the customers who had been going to Lenscrafters and Pearle Vision will switch to the new firm. The demand at Lenscrafters and Pearle Vision will decline. Thus, the existing firms will see their demand curves shift to the left—each one will find it sells less at each price. The differences in the positions of the demand (and marginal revenue) curves in the short run and long run illustrate this shift. This shift in the demand curve occurs because new firms in the market are taking some of the demand, not because consumers have shifted their tastes away from the product. The shift in the demand curve causes each firm's profits to decline, and eventually profits decline to zero. (Recall that these are economic profits, not accounting profits, and are therefore a good measure of the incentive for firms to enter the industry.)

The case of negative profits and exit is similar. If demand is such that firms are running a loss, then some firms will exit the industry, causing the demand curve facing the remaining firms to shift to the right, until the losses (negative economic profits) are driven to zero. For example, Pearle Vision might decide to leave the shopping center; its customers then will go to Lenscrafters or ForEyes, increasing their demand. This is illustrated by comparing graph (b) of Figure 11.3, where there are losses in the short run, with graph (c), where there are zero profits.

The Long-Run Monopolistically Competitive Equilibrium

There are two differences between monopolistically competitive firms and competitive firms in the long run. To see these differences, consider Figure 11.4, which replicates graph (c) of Figure 11.3, showing the position of the typical monopolistic competitor in long-run equilibrium after entry and exit have taken place.

First, observe that price is greater than marginal cost for a monopolistically competitive firm. This was also true for the monopoly; it means that the market is not as efficient as a competitive market. Production is too low because the marginal benefit of additional production is greater than the marginal cost. Because each firm has some market power, it restricts output slightly and gets a higher price. The sum of producer plus consumer surplus is reduced relative to a competitive market. In other words, there is a loss of efficiency—a deadweight loss.

Second, as shown in Figure 11.4, the quantity produced is not at the minimum point on the average total cost curve, as it was for the competitive industry. That is, the quantity that the monopolistic competitor produces is at a higher-cost point than the quantity the perfect competitor would produce. Thus, monopolistically competitive firms operate in a situation of **excess costs.** If each firm expanded production

excess costs: costs of production that are higher than the minimum average total cost.

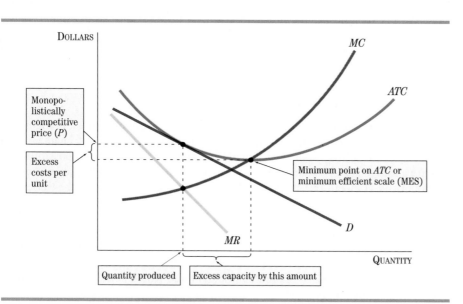

FIGURE 11.4
Excess Costs per Unit and Excess Capacity with Monopolistic Competition
In the long run, profits are zero for a monopolistically competitive firm, but the firm does not produce the quantity that minimizes average total cost. If the firm increases production, costs per unit will decline. In this sense, the firm operates at less than full capacity; it has excess capacity.

excess capacity: a situation in which a firm produces below the level that gives minimum average total cost.

and lowered its price, average total cost would decline. Each firm operates with some **excess capacity** in the sense that it could increase output and reduce average total cost. The firms choose not to do so because they have some market power to keep their prices a little higher and output a little lower than that. Their market power comes from the downward-sloping demand curve they face. For example, each optometry store charges a little more and sells slightly fewer eyeglasses than it would in a perfectly competitive market.

Comparing Monopoly, Competition, and Monopolistic Competition

The following table compares the different effects of competition, monopoly, and monopolistic competition.

Type of Model	Price	Deadweight Loss?	Average Total Cost Minimized?	Profit in Long Run?
Competition	$P = MC$	No	Yes	No
Monopolistic competition	$P > MC$	Yes	No	No
Monopoly	$P > MC$	Yes	No	Yes

A competitive firm will produce the quantity that equates price and marginal cost. A competitive market is efficient in that consumer surplus plus producer surplus is maximized and there is no deadweight loss. Average total cost is minimized.

In monopoly, price is greater than marginal cost. A monopoly is inefficient because consumer surplus plus producer surplus is not maximized, so there is deadweight loss. Moreover, average total cost is not minimized. Economic profits remain positive because firms cannot enter the market.

In monopolistic competition, price is also greater than marginal cost. Thus, consumer surplus plus producer surplus is not maximized and there is deadweight loss; average total cost is not minimized. However, profits are zero in the long-run equilibrium because of entry and exit. Monopolistic competition does not result in as efficient an outcome as competition. Monopolistic competition, as well as monopoly, is inefficient.

Product Variety versus Deadweight Loss

When comparing monopolistic competition with competition we must recognize—as with the comparison of monopoly and competition in the last chapter—that replacing monopolistic competition with competition may be an impossibility or require a loss to society. Remember that product differentiation is the key reason for monopolistic competition. We showed in the previous section why the variety of products that comes from product differentiation is usually something that consumers value. Some people like having both Pepsi and Coke. Roads and airports are better because of the different capabilities of earthmoving equipment sold by Caterpillar and Komatsu. Thus, eliminating monopolistic competition by having a single competitive product, whether Coksi or Catematsu, if even possible, would likely reduce consumer surplus by more than the gain that would come from competition over monopolistic competition.

More generally, product differentiation may be of sufficient value to consumers that it makes sense to have monopolistically competitive firms despite the deadweight loss. Or stated somewhat differently, the deadweight loss from monopolistic competition is part of the price consumers pay for the variety or the diversity of products.

Review

▶ The model of monopolistic competition is a hybrid of competition and monopoly. Entry and exit are possible, like competition, but firms see a downward-sloping demand curve, like monopoly, although there are many firms.

▶ The analysis of monopolistic competition in the short run is much like monopoly, but entry and exit lead to zero economic profits in the long run.

▶ Monopolistic competitors produce less than competitive firms and charge prices higher than marginal costs. Thus, there is a deadweight loss from monopolistic competition. In the long run, monopolistic competition produces less than the quantity that would minimize average total cost.

▶ The deadweight loss and excess costs can be viewed as the price of product variety.

GAME THEORY AND OLIGOPOLY

Thus far we have seen two situations where firms have market power: monopoly and monopolistic competition. But those are not the only two. When there are *very few* producers in an industry—a situation termed *oligopoly*—each firm can have an influence on the market price, even if the goods are homogenous. For example, if Saudi Arabia—one of the major producers of crude oil in the world and a member of the Organization of Petroleum Exporting Countries (OPEC)—decides to cut its production of crude oil, a relatively homogenous commodity, it can have a significant effect on the world price of oil. However, the effect on the price will depend on what other producers do. If the other producing countries—Iran, Kuwait, etc.—increase their production to offset the Saudi cuts, then the price does not change by much. Thus, Saudi Arabia, either through formal discussion with other oil-producing countries in OPEC or by guessing, must take account of what the other producers will do.

Such situations are not unusual. The managers of a firm in an industry with only a few other firms know their firm has market power. But they also know that the other firms in the industry have market power too. If the managers of a firm make the right assessment about how other firms will react to any course of action they take, then their firm will profit. This awareness and consideration of the market power and the reactions of other firms in the industry is called **strategic behavior.** Strategic behavior also may exist when there is product differentiation, as in monopolistically competitive industries, but to study and explain strategic behavior it is simpler to focus on oligopolies producing homogenous products.

There are two broad approaches to the study of the strategic behavior of firms in oligopolies. One approach uses **game theory,** an area of applied mathematics that studies games of strategy like poker or chess. Game theory has many applications in economics and the other behavioral sciences. Because oligopoly behavior has many

strategic behavior: firm behavior that takes into account the market power and reactions of other firms in the industry.

game theory: a branch of applied mathematics with many uses in economics including the analysis of the interaction of firms that take each other's actions into account.

of the features of games of strategy, game theory provides a precise framework to better understand oligopolies. The other approach is called the *conjectural variations* approach. We first discuss game theory and then conjectural variations.

An Overview of Game Theory

Game theory, like the basic economic theory of the firm and consumer (described in Chapters 5 and 6 of this book), makes the assumption that people make purposeful choices with limited resources. More precisely, game theory assumes that the players in a game try to maximize their payoffs—the amount they win or lose in the game. Depending on the application, a payoff might be measured by utility, if the player is a person, or by profits, if the player is a firm.

However, game theory endeavors to go beyond basic economic theory in that each player takes explicit account of the actions of each and every other player. It asks questions like: "What should Mary do if Deborah sees her and raises her by $10?" The aims of game theory are to analyze the choices facing each player and to design utility-maximizing actions, or strategies, that respond to every action of the other players.

prisoner's dilemma: a game in which individual incentives lead to a nonoptimal (noncooperative) outcome. If the players can credibly commit to cooperate, then they achieve the best (cooperative) outcome.

An important example in game theory is the game called **prisoner's dilemma,** illustrated in Figure 11.5. The game is between Ann and Pete, two prisoners who committed a crime. Figure 11.5 has two rows and two columns. The two columns for Ann show her options, which are labeled at the top "confess" or "remain silent." The two rows for Pete show his options; these are also labeled "confess" or "remain silent." Inside the boxes we see what happens to Ann and Pete for each option, confess or remain silent. The top right of each box shows what happens to Ann. The bottom left of each box shows what happens to Pete.

The police already have enough information to get a conviction for a lesser crime, in which case Ann and Pete would each get a 3-year jail sentence. Thus, if both Ann and Pete remain silent, they are sent to jail for 3 years each, as shown in the lower right-hand corner of the table.

But Ann and Pete each have the option of confessing to the more serious crime they committed. If Ann confesses and Pete does not, she gets a reward. If Pete confesses and Ann does not, he gets a reward. The reward is a reduced penalty: The jail sentence is only 1 year—not as severe as the 3 years it would be if the prosecutor had no confession. However, the penalty for the successful conviction of the more serious crime in the absence of a confession is 7 years. Thus, if Ann confesses and Pete does not, he gets a 7-year sentence. If both confess, they each get a 5-year sentence.

What should Pete and Ann do? The answer depends on their judgment about what the other person will do. And this is the point of the example. Ann can either confess or remain silent. The consequences of her actions depend on what Pete does. If Ann confesses and Pete confesses, she gets 5 years. If Ann confesses and Pete remains silent, Ann gets 1 year. If Ann remains silent and Pete remains silent, she gets 3 years. Finally, if Ann remains silent and Pete confesses, she gets 7 years. Pete is in the same situation that Ann is.

Think about a strategy for Ann. Ann is better off confessing, regardless of what Pete does. If Ann confesses and Pete confesses, Ann gets 5 years rather than 7

FIGURE 11.5
Two Prisoners Facing a Prisoner's Dilemma

Pete and Ann are in separate jail cells, held for a crime they *did* commit. The punishment for each—years in jail—is listed in the appropriate box and depends on whether they both confess or they both remain silent or on whether one confesses while the other remains silent. The top right of each box shows Ann's punishment; the bottom left of each box shows Pete's punishment.

years. If Ann confesses and Pete remains silent, then Ann gets 1 year rather than 3 years. Hence, there is a great incentive for Ann to confess because she does better in either case.

Pete is in the same situation. He can compare what his sentence would be whether Ann confesses or remains silent. In this case, Pete is better off confessing regardless of whether Ann confesses or remains silent.

What this reasoning suggests is that both Ann and Pete will confess. If they both had remained silent, they would only have gone to jail for 3 years, but the apparently sensible strategy is to confess and go to jail for 5 years. This is the prisoner's dilemma. The case where both remain silent is called the **cooperative outcome** of the game because to achieve this, they would somehow have to agree in advance not to confess and then keep their word. The case where both confess is called the **noncooperative outcome** of the game because Pete and Ann follow an "everyone for himself or herself" strategy. Note how the cooperative outcome is preferred by both Pete and Ann to the noncooperative outcome, yet both choose the option that results in the noncooperative outcome.

Applying Game Theory

How do we apply game theory to the strategy of firms in an oligopoly? To make the application easier, focus on the case where there are only two firms. This is a particular type of oligopoly called *duopoly.* As usual, we assume that the two firms behave in a way that will maximize their profits. The combined profits of both firms can be maximized if they act together as a monopolist.

There are three ways that these two firms might act together. The first is by **explicit collusion,** in which the managers communicate with each other and agree to fix prices or cut back on production. Although explicit collusion is illegal in the United States, it still happens. In the 1960s, executives of General Electric, Westinghouse, and other firms that produced electrical transformers and switching gear were sent to prison for secretly agreeing to fix prices. More recently, in the 1980s and 1990s, several firms in Florida and Texas have been found guilty of agreeing to fix prices for milk sold to schools. The OPEC producers outside of the United States routinely collude to cut back production and raise prices. A situation in which a group of producers coordinates its pricing and production decisions is called a **cartel.**

Second, there might be **tacit collusion,** where there is no explicit communication between firms, but firms keep prices high by regularly following the behavior of one firm in the industry. The dominant firm is sometimes called a **price leader.**

Third, the firms could merge, but that also might be illegal in the United States, as we discuss later in Chapter 16.

A Duopoly Game

Figure 11.6 shows the situation of two firms when acting like a monopoly is one of the options. Rather than Ann and Pete, we have two firms, Bageldee and Bageldum, which produce bagels. Instead of confess or remain silent, the options of the two firms are to collude and change the monopoly price or compete like competitive firms. Under competition, they earn zero economic profits and price equals marginal cost. If they collude, they charge a higher monopoly price and earn monopoly profits, which we assume to be $2 million.

cooperative outcome: an equilibrium in a game where the players agree to cooperate.

noncooperative outcome: an equilibrium in a game where the players cannot agree to cooperate and instead follow their individual incentives.

explicit collusion: open cooperation of firms to make mutually beneficial pricing or production decisions.

cartel: a group of producers in the same industry who coordinate pricing and production decisions.

tacit collusion: implicit or unstated cooperation of firms to make mutually beneficial pricing or production decisions.

price leader: the price-setting firm in a collusive industry where other firms follow the leader.

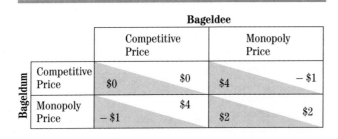

	Bageldee		
		Competitive Price	Monopoly Price
Bageldum	Competitive Price	$0 $0	$4 −$1
	Monopoly Price	−$1 $4	$2 $2

FIGURE 11.6

Two Firms Facing a Prisoner's Dilemma

The chart shows profits in millions of dollars for two firms that charge either the monopoly price or the competitive price in the market. The top right of each box shows Bageldee's profits; the bottom left of each box shows Bageldum's profits.

Consider the alternative outcomes of the game. The first outcome is where Bageldee and Bageldum act like competitive firms; they each earn zero economic profits. A second outcome is where they collude, agree to charge the monopoly price, and earn $2 million each. A third outcome is where Bageldum agrees to charge the monopoly price and Bageldee defects from the agreement. In other words, Bageldum charges the monopoly price and then gets wiped out of business because Bageldee cuts the price to the competitive level and everybody buys bagels from Bageldee. Negative economic profits of $1 million for Bageldum and a huge $4 million in profits for Bageldee are the result. The fourth outcome is where Bageldee sticks to the monopoly price and Bageldum cuts the price to the competitive level. Then Bageldee is wiped out.

Incentives to Defect

The duopoly situation is the same as the prisoner's dilemma. Just as there is an incentive for Pete and Ann to confess, there is an incentive for the firms Bageldum and Bageldee to defect from the agreement—that is, to charge the competitive price—because both Bageldee and Bageldum can do better by defecting regardless of what the other firm does. Thus, game theory predicts that unless there is a way to bind each firm to cooperate, there is going to be a tendency to defect. Since the defection results in the lower competitive price, the consumer gains from the defection. Deadweight loss is reduced.

Incentives to Cooperate: Repeated Games

Although the prisoner's dilemma suggests that there is a tendency to the noncooperative outcome for the firms—competition rather than monopoly—there is a difference between the situation of the prisoners Ann and Pete and the firms Bageldee and Bageldum. The firms will presumably have future opportunities to interact. The bagel market will be open next year and probably for many years. If the same game is to be played year after year—a repeated game—then the firms might be able to build up a reputation not to defect. For example, Bageldum will not defect because if it does so it will lose its reputation with Bageldee in the future.

Experimental economists have conducted experiments in which two people play the same prisoner's dilemma game over and over again. (The people in the experiments are given small monetary rewards rather than jail penalties!) These experiments indicate that people frequently end up using strategies that lead to a cooperative outcome. A typical strategy people use is called "tit-for-tat." Using a "tit-for-tat" strategy, one player regularly matches, *in the next game,* the actions of the other player *in the current game.* For example, Pete's tit-for-tat strategy would be to confess the next time the game is played if Ann confesses in the current game, and not to confess the next time the game is played if Ann does not confess in the current game. A tit-for-tat strategy gives the other player incentive to follow the cooperative action—not confess—and thereby leads to a cooperative outcome.

STEINER
USA

I BELIEVE IN LETTING MARKET FORCES DECIDE, AS LONG AS I'M A MARKET FORCE.

P. Steiner

Reading the News About Defection from the OPEC Cartel

This *Business Week* article explaining how producers defect from the OPEC cartel illustrates the game theory approach to oligopoly described in Figure 11.6.

The caption on the picture describes how "OPEC rebels" (that is, defectors from the agreement to restrict production) were producing "over their allocation." The agreement was for OPEC to produce a total of 23.6 million barrels a day. But Kuwait, Nigeria, and Iran produced an extra .75 million, raising total output to 24.35 million barrels.

The diagram of the world demand for oil shows how such increases in production would lower the price of oil. In fact, as shown in the time-series chart in the article, the price of crude oil did fall in the summer of 1993.

The article also discusses some of the practical difficulties of reining in defectors, illustrating the prisoner's dilemma faced by the OPEC producers. For example, Saudi Arabia is reported to be suspicious that Iran is cheating, and there is general bickering among the OPEC members, making collusion more difficult.

Source of article: Reprinted from August 9, 1993, issue of *Business Week* by special permission, copyright © 1993 by the McGraw-Hill Companies, Inc.

A BARREL OF TROUBLES FOR THE OIL MARKET

Iraqi exports and OPEC quota-busters could push prices even lower

For three years, oil traders around the world have dreaded the overthrow of Iraqi dictator Saddam Hussein. His ouster would likely put an end to the embargo slapped on exports of Iraqi oil following the invasion of Kuwait. And if huge quantities started hitting already flooded international markets, the price of crude would collapse.

Saddam is hanging in there. But Iraq and the U.N. are engaged in on-again-off-again talks to forge an agreement that would permit Baghdad to sell limited amounts of oil. Small wonder oil prices are skirting their lowest levels since July, 1990: Before ticking up slightly as July drew to its close, crude slipped below $16 a barrel, down 25% from two months before (chart).

QUOTA BUSTERS. . . . Kuwait, Nigeria, and Iran have been pumping far in excess of their allotted quotas, leaving OPEC at least 750,000 bbl. a day over its self-imposed output ceiling this quarter of 23.6 million bbl. a day. "The Iranians and the Kuwaitis are totally responsible for problems in the market," says a top Saudi official in Riyadh.

It will be an uphill battle to rein in the quota-busters. Saudi Arabia, OPEC's biggest producer at 8 million bbl. a day, is adamant about not cutting its output to make room for Iraqi exports—especially if traditional rivals like Iran continue to cheat. The standoff between Riyadh and Tehran means the downhill slide in oil prices is unlikely to be braked for long.

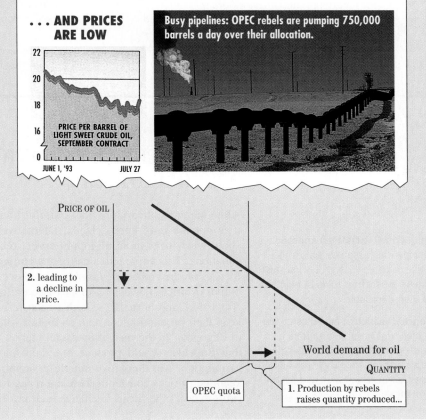

. . . AND PRICES ARE LOW

PRICE PER BARREL OF LIGHT SWEET CRUDE OIL, SEPTEMBER CONTRACT

22 · 20 · 18 · 16 · 0

JUNE 1, '93   JULY 27

Busy pipelines: OPEC rebels are pumping 750,000 barrels a day over their allocation.

PRICE OF OIL

2. leading to a decline in price.

World demand for oil

QUANTITY

OPEC quota

1. Production by rebels raises quantity produced...

Secret Defections

The incentive for one firm to defect from an agreement will depend on how likely it is that other firms will detect the defection. In the bagel example, it is very hard for Bageldee to cut prices without Bageldum knowing it. This makes defection less likely. If one firm can secretly cut prices or increase production, enforcing the agreement will be more difficult. This is the problem with the world coffee cartel; it is easy to ship coffee around the world or cut prices without being detected. Crude oil shipments are more easily seen, but a member of OPEC could try to sell oil secretly to China. This might go on for a long time without detection. The impact of such secret defection is much like the noncooperation solution to the game shown in Figure 11.5. Profits to the defector increase, and profits to the other producers decrease.

For a long time, Japanese construction firms operated a now well-known collusion scheme called *dango*. All firms submitted high-priced bids to the government and took turns offering slightly lower bids. Ironically, and unfortunately for consumers, making the bids public made it harder for any firm to defect because firms in the agreement would know at once which firm lowered its prices.

Review

▶ Game theory provides a framework for studying strategic behavior in an oligopoly. Games, including the prisoner's dilemma, describe the strategies firms can use when they have the options of charging a monopoly price or a lower price.

▶ Game theory illustrates why firms in an oligopoly will be tempted to defect from any agreement.

▶ To the extent a firm colludes, either explicitly or tacitly, it reduces economic efficiency by raising price above marginal cost.

CONJECTURAL VARIATIONS AND OLIGOPOLY

conjectural variations approach: a model that assumes that firms make decisions based on what they expect other firms to do in reaction to their decisions.

Cournot model: a model using the conjectural variations approach that assumes that each firm expects other firms to keep their production constant in response to actions the firm takes.

Although game theory provides a useful framework for studying strategic behavior, it is not the only approach. An alternative approach simply makes assumptions about what firms in an oligopoly expect other firms to do in response to different situations. This approach is called the **conjectural variations approach** because it focuses on the conjectures firms make about how much each other firm will vary its output or price. For example, one assumption, first made by the French economist Augustin Cournot in 1833, is that each firm expects other firms in the industry to keep their production constant no matter what happens. This is the **Cournot model** of oligopoly. In the case of the bagel market, for example, Bageldum would assume that Bageldee would produce a certain number of bagels. This is a very simple assumption. An alternative simple assumption is that firms expect other firms to keep their prices constant. There are many more complicated assumptions in which firms expect other firms to change their prices or outputs in particular ways.

Strategic Demand Curves

Figure 11.7 illustrates the conjectural variations approach to oligopoly. An ordinary marginal cost curve for an oligopolistic firm is shown in the figure. The downward-sloping curve is the **strategic demand curve.** It looks like an ordinary demand curve but is different from an ordinary demand curve. It is not the market demand curve, and it is unique to each firm in the oligopoly. It incorporates the expectations of each firm about what the other firms will do.

Associated with each strategic demand curve is a *strategic marginal revenue curve.* It is obtained in the usual way by finding total revenue ($P \times Q$) and calculating how total revenue changes as output changes, but it is based on the strategic demand curve and therefore takes into account the expectations of what other firms will do.

How does the strategic demand curve incorporate the firm's estimates or conjectures about the variation of the other firms' prices or quantity produced in response to its behavior? Suppose first that we assume, like Cournot, that each firm expects that the other firms will not change their production. Then the strategic demand curve simply is shifted to the left of the market demand curve by the amount that the other firms in the industry are expected to produce. The firm's strategic demand curve is what is left over after the other firms' production is removed. This is illustrated in Figure 11.8.

But this Cournot assumption is very unrealistic because the other firms would most likely react by changing their production. Let's consider a more realistic alternative. Again, suppose the firm is considering raising its price and reducing production. But now suppose the firm conjectures that other firms in its industry will also raise their prices. The impact on the quantity demanded of the firm's product will be smaller than if those firms did not change their prices. For example, if the price of Coca-Cola is raised, the quantity demanded of it will fall less if Pepsi also raises its price than if Pepsi's price remains unchanged. Thus, Coca-Cola's strategic demand curve—which takes account of Coca-Cola's conjecture

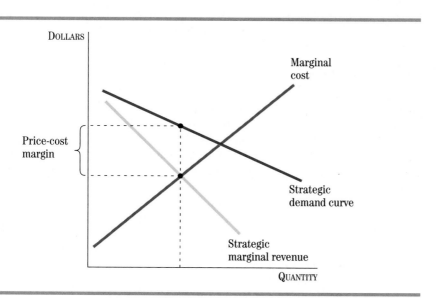

FIGURE 11.7
Strategic Demand Curve

An oligopolistic firm's strategic demand curve lies above its strategic marginal revenue curve. The quantity produced by the firm is found by equating marginal cost and strategic marginal revenue.

FIGURE 11.8
Strategic Demand Curve for a Conjecture of No Change in Output at the Other Firms
The graph shows how the strategic demand curve is derived from the market demand curve for a duopoly in the simple case where one firm (Bageldee) conjectures that the other firm (Bageldum) will keep its production constant at 100 units. The strategic demand curve describes how much the firm (Bageldee) expects its price to change as it adjusts its own output. In this case, the strategic demand curve is to the left of the market demand curve with the same slope. This is the assumption used by Cournot.

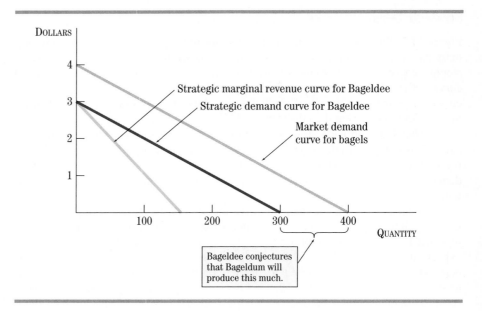

of Pepsi's response—has a smaller price elasticity than a demand curve that ignores Pepsi's response. The effect of Coca-Cola's price increase is altered by its conjecture about other firms' price increases. Alternatively, if the other firms in the industry are not expected to change their price by very much, the firm will lose a lot of customers; its strategic demand curve has a very large elasticity: A given percentage change in price reduces the quantity demanded by a large percentage.

The same basic issues arise in the case of a price cut by the typical firm. If it thinks other firms are employing a strategy to match its price cut, the firm will not expect to see much of an increase in quantity demanded; its strategic demand curve is relatively inelastic. If the firm believes that each other firm's strategy is not to match the price cut, then the strategic demand curve is relatively elastic.

Determining Quantity and Price

How do economists use the strategic demand curve? The profit-maximizing firm will produce an amount to set its marginal cost equal to its marginal revenue, where in this case marginal revenue is *strategic marginal revenue,* as shown in Figure 11.7. The strategic marginal revenue curve shows how much the firm perceives its revenue will change, taking into account its conjectures about the behavior of the other firms. Hence the quantity produced is determined by the intersection of the marginal cost curve and the strategic marginal revenue curve as shown in Figure 11.7. The firm's price is then found in the strategic demand curve.

price-cost margin: the difference between price and marginal cost divided by the price. This index is an indicator of market power, where an index of 0 indicates no market power and a higher price-cost margin indicates greater market power. (Ch. 10)

We can relate the size of the *price-cost margin* [$(P - MC)/P$] of an oligopolistic firm to the elasticity of its strategic demand curve. The smaller the elasticity of the strategic demand curve, the greater the price-cost margin. In fact, the formula for the price-cost margin presented in Chapter 10 applies here: The price-cost margin is equal to the inverse of the elasticity of the strategic demand curve.

Review

▶ Another approach to strategic behavior—called the conjectural variations approach—considers the conjecture of firms about other firms' behavior.

▶ These conjectures can be represented graphically in a strategic demand curve. A more elastic strategic demand curve means a smaller price-cost margin.

MEASURES OF MARKET POWER

The strategic demand curves are useful because they can be determined for real-world firms by observing their behavior over time. The curves enable economists to assess the amount of market power in real-world markets.

Estimates of Strategic Demand Curves

Table 11.1 gives some estimates of price elasticity of the strategic demand curve and the price-cost margin for firms in several different industries. The higher the price-cost margin the more market power the firm has. Observe in Table 11.1 that the price cost margin is very small for firms in coffee roasting, rubber, textiles, retail gasoline, and standard automobiles. The firms in these markets have little market power. In contrast, the price-cost margin is very high for firms in food processing and tobacco.

The price-cost margins depend on the strategic behavior of firms. Luxury cars, for which there are fewer producers and less competition than standard cars, have a larger price-cost margin; their strategic demand curves are less elastic, perhaps because, with fewer firms in the industry, other firms' prices are more likely to change when any one firm changes its prices.

Industry	Price-Cost Margin	Price Elasticity of Strategic Demand Curves
Food processing	.50	2.0
Coffee roasting	.04	25.0
Rubber	.05	20.0
Textiles	.07	14.3
Electrical machinery	.20	5.0
Tobacco	.65	1.5
Retail gasoline	.10	10.0
Standard automobiles	.10	10.0
Luxury automobiles	.34	2.9

TABLE 11.1
Price-Cost Margins in Several Industries

Source: Various empirical studies as summarized in T. F. Bresnahan, "Empirical Studies of Industries with Market Power," *Handbook of Industrial Organization,* Vol. II, ed. R. Schmalensee and R. D. Willig (Amsterdam: Elsevier Science Publishers, 1989).

TABLE 11.2

Concentration Ratios in Selected Manufacturing Industries

Industry	Four-Firm Ratio
Motor vehicles	90
Cereal breakfast foods	87
Primary aluminum	74
Prerecorded records and tapes	63
Metal cans	54
Shipbuilding and repairing	49
Dolls and stuffed toys	34
Pharmaceuticals	22
Precious jewelry	12
Women's dresses	6

structure-conduct-performance method: a method of analyzing the market power in an industry by looking at the structure of the industry.

Another interesting example is Anheuser-Busch, the producer of Budweiser beer. Before the introduction of Lite Beer by Miller, Anheuser-Busch had considerable market power; the price-cost margin was .3. After Lite Beer was introduced, the firm lost market power: The price-cost margin dropped to .03. Evidently Miller's Lite Beer made it a more visible player in the beer market and thus increased competition in the market in the sense that Anheuser-Busch's market power declined.

Concentration Ratios

Another way to assess the amount of market power of firms in an industry is to look at how concentrated the industry is. Collusive-type activity—whether explicit or tacit—would seem to be easier in an industry with only a handful of large firms producing most of the output. There are several measures of concentration. For example, the percent of an industry's output produced by the largest four firms is called the *four-firm concentration ratio*. This varies from 90 percent in domestic automobiles to about 50 percent in pet food to less than 5 percent in commercial printing. The four largest firms in the soft-drink industry—Coca-Cola, PepsiCo, Dr. Pepper/Seven-up and Cadbury Schweppes—account for 85 percent of the industry sales. See Table 11.2 for concentration ratios in some other industries.

The use of industry structure measures like concentration ratios to analyze the market power of industries is called the **structure-conduct-performance method.** It attempts to infer the conduct and performance of firms in an industry from the structure of the industry. For example, high concentration ratios are believed to lead to collusive conduct and, therefore, to a large amount of market power and inefficient economic performance.

Review

▶ The strategic demand curve provides useful empirical measures of market power. A sampling of estimates indicates that the elasticity of the strategic demand curve is very low in food processing and high in rubber, for example.

▶ The structure-conduct-performance method assesses market power by looking at concentration ratios and possibilities for entry and exit.

CONCLUSION

In this chapter we have explored two different types of models—monopolistic competition and oligopoly—which lie in the complex terrain between competition and monopoly. The models were motivated by the need to explain how real-world firms—Johnson Publications, Liz Claiborne, Nike, PepsiCo, the producers of OPEC, and the members of the coffee cartel—operate in markets with differentiated products or with a small number of other firms.

In the models introduced in this chapter, firms have market power in that they can affect the price of the good in their market. Market power enables a firm to charge a price higher than marginal cost. It is a source of deadweight loss. Observations of the behavior of actual firms show a wide variation in market power among firms.

The ideas about monopolistic competition and oligopoly discussed in this chapter are used by economists in government, businesses, and universities. Economists working in the U.S. Department of Justice use them to determine whether the government should intervene in certain industries, as we will explore in Chapter 16. Consultants to business use them to help firms decide how to differentiate their products from those of other firms.

Having concluded our discussion of the four basic types of models of markets in this chapter, it is useful to remember the important distinction between *models* and the *facts* the models endeavor to explain or predict. None of the assumptions of models—such as homogenous products or free entry—hold exactly in reality. For example, when contrasted with the monopolistic competition model of this chapter, the model of competition with its assumption of homogenous goods might seem not to apply to very many markets at all. Very few goods are exactly homogenous. But when economists apply their models they realize they are approximations of reality. How close an approximation comes to reality depends much on the application. The model of competition can be helpful in explaining the behavior of firms in industries that are approximately competitive, just as the model of monopoly can be helpful in explaining the behavior of firms in industries that are approximately monopolistic. Now we have a richer set of models that apply to situations far removed from competition or monopoly.

KEY POINTS

1. Firms that can differentiate their product and act strategically are in industries that fall between competition and monopoly.

2. Product differentiation—the effort by firms to create different products of value to consumers—is pervasive in a modern market economy. It helps explain intraindustry trade, advertising, and information services.

3. Monopolistic competition arises because of product differentiation. With monopolistic competition, firms have market power, but exit and entry into the industry lead to a situation of zero profits in the long run.

4. With monopolistic competition, the firm sets the quantity produced so that price exceeds marginal cost. As a result, there is a deadweight loss, and average total cost is not minimized.

5. The deadweight loss and excess costs of monopolistic competition are part of the price paid for product variety.

6. Strategic behavior occurs in industries with a small number of firms because each firm has market power to affect the price, and each firm cannot ignore the response of other firms to its own actions.

7. Game theory suggests that noncooperative outcomes are likely, implying that collusive behavior will frequently break down, unless firms acquire a reputation for not defecting and secret defections can be prevented.

8. Strategic demand curves incorporate the conjectures of firms about other firms' actions.

9. Estimates of strategic demand curves show large differences in market power between firms and industries and large changes in market power over time.

KEY TERMS

monopolistic competition
oligopoly
product differentiation
intraindustry trade
interindustry trade
excess costs
excess capacity

strategic behavior
game theory
prisoner's dilemma
cooperative outcome
noncooperative outcome
explicit collusion
cartel

tacit collusion
price leader
conjectural variations approach
Cournot model
strategic demand curve
structure-conduct-performance
    method

QUESTIONS FOR REVIEW

1. What is product differentiation?

2. What factors are relevant to the determination of optimal product differentiation?

3. Why is product differentiation an important reason for monopolistic competition?

4. What are two key differences between monopolistic competition and monopoly?

5. Why don't monopolistic competitors keep their average total cost at a minimum?

6. Why is the noncooperative outcome of a prisoner's dilemma game likely?

7. Why is duopoly like a prisoner's dilemma?

8. What is the difference between explicit and tacit collusion?

9. Why are secret defections a problem for cartels?

10. Why does the strategic marginal revenue curve depend on the strategic demand curve?

11. What are two alternative ways to assess the market power of firms in an industry?

PROBLEMS

1. Which of the following conditions will tend to induce collusion among sellers in a market?
   a) The transactions are publicly announced.
   b) There are few sellers.
   c) Some sellers have lower costs than other sellers.
   d) The market is open only for one year.
   e) The sellers cannot meet each other.

2. The following table shows the profits (in millions of dollars) of two firms (a duopoly) when they follow two different strategies in their market. Which is the cooperative outcome? What outcome does game theory predict? How would the result change if the game were repeated?

Firm A

		Defect	Collude
Firm B	**Defect**	$10 $10	$400 −$100
	Collude	−$100 $400	$200 $200

3. How does a firm decide whether to develop or sell a differentiated product? Does profit maximization play a role? Use your answer to explain why product differentiation is more common in market economies than in centrally planned economies.

4. Suppose the government places a sales tax on firms in a monopolistically competitive industry. Draw a diagram showing the short-run impact and the adjustment to the new long-run industry equilibrium. What happens to the equilibrium price and number of firms in the industry?

5. Compare the long-run equilibrium of a competitive firm with a monopolistically competitive one with the same cost structure. Why is the long-run price different in these two

models? Does the monopolistically competitive firm operate at minimum cost? Draw a diagram and explain.

6. Suppose an industry consists of two firms. Firm B conjectures that firm A will always produce 2 units, no matter what firm B produces. Firm B maximizes profits based on the remaining demand in the industry and has a constant marginal cost of 5.
   a) Use the following data to derive the strategic demand curve facing firm B, calculate marginal revenue for this firm, and determine the profit-maximizing level of production.

Market Demand	Strategic Demand for Firm B	Price (dollars)	Total Revenue for Firm B	Marginal Revenue for Firm B
2	____	10	____	____
3	____	9	____	____
4	____	8	____	____
5	____	7	____	____
6	____	6	____	____
7	____	5	____	____
8	____	4	____	____

   b) Compare this price and level of production to the situation where a monopolist controls this market.
   c) If firms A and B were both adjusting their production in order to compete, would their strategic demand curve be flatter or steeper than in part (a)? Explain.

7. Match the following characteristics with the appropriate models of firm behavior and explain the long-run efficiency (or inefficiency) of each.
   a) Many firms, differentiated product, free entry
   b) Patents, licenses, or barriers to entry, one firm
   c) Many firms, homogenous product, free entry
   d) Few firms, strategic behavior

8. Suppose monopolistically competitive firms in the software industry make a technological improvement that shifts down average total cost but does not affect marginal cost. What will happen to the equilibrium number of firms, the quantity produced, and the long-run price of software?

9. Suppose there are 10 monopolistically competitive restaurants in your town with identical costs. Given the following information, calculate the long-run price and quantity produced by each of the firms.

Each Firm's Demand		Each Firm's Costs	
Quantity	Price	Average Total Cost	Marginal Cost
1	10.00	12	—
2	8.00	9	6
3	6.00	7	3
4	4.00	6	3
5	2.00	7	11
6	1.50	8	13
7	1.00	9	15
8	.50	10	17

a) Calculate the price-cost margin. Approximately what is the price elasticity of demand based on this calculation?

b) What would be the level of production if this industry were a competitive industry? If there is free entry and exit in both monopolistic competition and competition, why is there a difference in the quantity the typical firm produces?

c) Suppose each firm's demand curve shifts to the right by 4 units and in the short run new firms cannot enter. Calculate the new level of production for the typical firm. (*Hint:* At every price, the quantity of production for each firm will increase by 4 units, but costs will remain as before.) Are they making profits in the short run? What will happen in the long run?

10. Strategic demand curves do not always have to be smooth. In this problem, the strategic demand curve has a *kink* in it. Suppose Actmore is a firm in an oligopoly with several other firms. Actmore is currently producing Q_1 units of output and charging price P_1. It makes conjectures about what the other firms in its industry will do. Actmore conjectures that

▶ if it *raises* its price above P_1, the other firms *will not raise* their prices.

▶ if it *lowers* its price below P_1, the other firms *will lower* their prices.

a) Sketch a diagram with price (P) on the vertical axis and quantity (Q) on the horizontal axis and show the points P_1 and Q_1 on Actmore's strategic demand curve.

b) Draw the part of the strategic demand curve for prices above P_1, taking into account Actmore's conjectures. Now draw the part of the strategic demand curve for prices below P_1, again taking into account Actmore's conjectures.

c) What do you notice about Actmore's strategic demand curve?

d) Now draw Actmore's strategic marginal revenue curve. (*Hint:* The strategic marginal revenue curve breaks apart at the kink.)

e) Draw a marginal cost curve that would be consistent with Actmore producing Q_1 units. What happens to Actmore's production if the marginal cost curve shifts up or down a little bit?

12

Labor Markets

What occupation will offer the best jobs in the future? What college major will provide the best chance of getting one of those jobs? Is graduate school worth it, or is it better to start work right away? Will women's earnings catch up to or exceed men's earnings in the future?

All these questions pertain to labor markets. For most people, labor markets are the most important markets in the world, much more important than stock markets. All the dividends paid on all the stock of U.S. firms amount to only 4 percent of the wages and salaries people earn in the labor market. It is not surprising, therefore, that many beginning economics students ask their teachers more questions about labor markets, such as the ones in the first paragraph, than they do about stock markets, even though many originally choose to take economics to learn more about the stock market.

In analyzing labor markets, economists stress their likeness with other markets, thus enabling them to use the standard supply and demand model. To see the analogy, consider Figure 12.1, which illustrates a typical *labor market*. It shows a typical labor supply curve and typical labor demand curve. On the vertical axis is the price of labor, or the wage. On the horizontal axis is the quantity of labor, either the number of workers or the number of hours worked. People work at many different types of jobs—nurses, mechanics, teachers, secretaries, judges, taxi drivers, hair stylists—and there is a labor market for each type. The labor market diagram in Figure 12.1 could refer to any one of these particular types of labor. The first thing to remember about the labor demand curve and the labor supply curve is that firms demand labor and people supply it. Labor—like other factors of production—is demanded by firms because it can be used to produce goods and services that firms can sell in markets for these goods and services; the labor demand curve tells us the quantity of labor demanded by firms at each wage. The labor supply curve tells the quantity of labor supplied by workers at each wage.

Note how the labor demand curve slopes downward and the labor supply curve slopes upward, just like other demand and supply curves. Thus, a higher wage reduces the quantity of labor demanded by firms, and a higher wage increases the quantity of labor supplied by people. Note also that the curves intersect at a particular wage and a particular quantity of labor. As with any other market, this intersection predicts the quantity of something (in this case, labor) and its price (in this case, the wage).

In this chapter we show how the labor demand and supply model rests on the basic economic principle that people make purposeful choices with limited resources. We will see that the model can be used to explain why wages change over time or why there are gaps between the wages of skilled and unskilled workers, between the wages of women and men, or between the wages of union and nonunion workers. Even some of the problems caused by discrimination can be better understood by the standard tools of supply and demand.

FIGURE 12.1
Labor Demand Curve and Labor Supply Curve

The basic economic approach to the labor market is to make an analogy with other markets. Labor is what is bought or sold on the labor market. The demand curve shows how much labor firms are willing to buy at a particular wage. The supply curve shows how much labor workers are willing to sell at a particular wage.

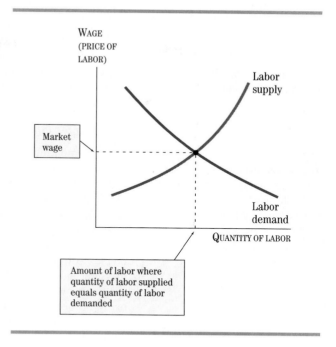

TERMINOLOGY AND TRENDS IN WAGES

It is easy enough to say that the price of labor is the wage. But defining exactly what is meant by the wage and assessing trends in wages is tricky. Hence, we start by reviewing some terminology.

Measuring Workers' Pay

When examining data on workers' pay, we must be specific about (1) what is included in the measure of pay, (2) whether inflation may be distorting the measure, and (3) the interval of time over which workers receive pay.

Pay Includes Fringe Benefits

Pay for work includes not only the direct payment to a worker—whether in the form of a paycheck, currency in a pay envelope, or a deposit in the worker's bank account—it also includes **fringe benefits.** Fringe benefits may consist of many different items: health or life insurance where the employer buys part or all of the insurance for the employee; retirement benefits where the employer puts aside funds for the employee's retirement; paid time off such as vacations and sick or maternity leave; and discounts on the company's products.

In recent years fringe benefits have become an increasingly larger share of total compensation in the United States and many other countries. In the United States

fringe benefit: compensation that a worker receives excluding direct money payments for time worked: insurance, retirement benefits, vacation time, and maternity and sick leave.

317

fringe benefits in the mid-1990s were about 18 percent of total pay. In 1960, fringe benefits were only about 8 percent of total pay.

The term *wage* sometimes refers to the part of the payment for work that excludes fringe benefits. For example, the minimum wage of $5.15 per hour does not usually include fringe benefits. But in most economics textbooks, the term **wage** refers to the *total* amount a firm pays workers, *including* fringe benefits. This book uses the usual textbook terminology. Thus, the wage is the price of labor.

wage: the price of labor defined over a period of time worked.

Adjusting for Inflation: Real Wages versus Nominal Wages

When comparing wages in different years, it is necessary to adjust for inflation, the general increase in prices over time. The **real wage** is a measure of the wage that has been adjusted for changes in inflation. The real wage is computed by dividing the stated wage by a measure of the price of goods and services workers buy. The most commonly used measure for this purpose is the consumer price index (CPI), which gives the price of a fixed collection, or market basket, of goods and services each year compared to some base year. For example, the CPI increased from about 1.00 in the 1983 base year to 1.47 in 1994. This means that the same goods and services that cost $100 in 1983 cost $147 in 1994. Suppose the hourly wage for a truck driver increased from $10 to $15 from 1983 to 1994, or by 50 percent; then the real wage increased from $10 (= $10/1.00) to $10.20 (= $15/1.47), or an increase of only 2 percent. Thus, because of the increase in prices, the real wage gain for the truck driver was far less than the 50 percent stated wage gain would suggest. The term *nominal wage* is used to emphasize that the wage has not been corrected for inflation. The real wage is the best way to compare wages in different years.

real wage: the wage or price of labor adjusted for inflation; in contrast, the nominal wage has not been adjusted for inflation.

The Time Interval: Hourly versus Weekly Measures of Pay

It is also important to distinguish between *hourly* and *weekly* measures of workers' pay. Weekly earnings are the total amount a worker earns during a week. Clearly, weekly earnings will be less for part-time work than for full-time work (usually 40 hours per week) if hourly earnings are the same.

Because part-time work has increased and the average number of hours per week has declined in the last 30 years in the United States, weekly earnings for the average worker have increased less rapidly than hourly earnings.

Wage Trends

Having introduced the terminology, let's look briefly at what has happened to wages in the United States in recent years. Figure 12.2 shows average real hourly wages in the United States from the mid-1950s through the mid-1990s.

What is most noticeable in Figure 12.2 is that workers' pay has generally increased over this period, but that a sharp decline in the rate of increase occurred sometime in the mid-1970s. The average American is not earning less in real terms, but the growth rate has diminished greatly. This slowdown is one of the most important economic problems facing the United States. It is a long-term trend that spans many ups and downs in the economy.

The dispersion, or distribution, of wages across the population is another issue about which economic analysis of labor markets can provide insights. Casual observation reveals large differences in the earnings of some people or groups compared to others. Sports celebrities and corporate executives are paid in the millions, many times the average wage in the United States. Workers with higher skills are paid more than workers with lower skills. College graduates earn more on average than those with a high school education or less. But there are other types of wage dispersions. For example, women on average earn less than men.

The distribution of wages across workers has changed substantially in recent years. One development that has received much attention from economists is that the pay gap between skilled and less skilled workers has increased. In the mid-1970s, college graduates earned about 45 percent more than high school graduates. In the 1990s, it was up to about 65 percent.

Another change is the wage difference between women and men, which, though still wide, has been narrowing in recent years. In the mid-1970s, women on average earned less than 60 cents for each dollar men earned. By the early 1990s it was over 70 cents.

What causes these changes? Can the economists' model of labor markets explain them? After developing the model in the next section, we will endeavor to answer these questions.

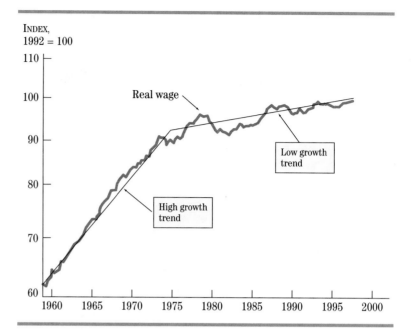

FIGURE 12.2
Growth of Real Wages
In the United States, average real hourly wages (including fringe benefits) grew rapidly from the 1950s to the mid-1970s. Starting in the mid-1970s, the growth rate slowed down.

Source: U.S. Department of Commerce.

Review

▶ Workers' pay includes fringe benefits, which are one-fifth of workers' pay in the United States.

▶ The real wage is an adjustment of the nominal wage to account for inflation.

▶ Real hourly wages have increased at a less rapid rate since the mid-1970s, after very rapid growth in the 1950s and 1960s.

▶ The dispersion of wages between skilled and unskilled workers has increased, with college-educated workers gaining over those without a college education. The gap between the average wage of women and men is substantial, although it has declined in recent years.

THE DEMAND FOR LABOR

The **labor market** consists of firms that have a demand for labor and people who supply the labor. In this section we look at **labor demand,** the relationship between the quantity of labor demanded by firms and the wage. In the next section we look at **labor supply,** the relationship between the quantity of labor supplied by people

labor market: the market in which individuals supply their labor time to firms in exchange for wages and salaries.

labor demand: the relationship between the quantity of labor demanded by firms and the wage.

labor supply: the relationship between the quantity of labor supplied by individuals and the wage.

derived demand: demand for an input derived from the demand for the product produced with that input.

and the wage. We start with a single firm's demand for labor and then sum up all the firms that are in the labor market to get the market demand for labor.

In deriving a firm's labor demand, economists assume that the firm's decision about how many workers to employ, like its decision about how much of a good or service to produce, is based on profit maximization. The demand for labor is a **derived demand;** that is, it is derived from the goods or services that the firm produces with the labor. The firm sells these goods and services to consumers in product markets, which are distinct from the labor market. Labor and other factors of production are not directly demanded by consumers; the goods and services labor produces are what is demanded by consumers. Thus, the demand for labor derives from these goods and services.

A Firm's Employment and Production Decisions

Recall how the idea of profit maximization was applied to a firm's decision about the quantity to produce: If producing another ton of steel will increase a steel firm's profits—that is, if the marginal revenue from producing a ton is greater than the marginal cost of producing the ton—then the firm will produce that ton of output. However, if producing another ton of steel reduces the firm's profits, then the firm will not produce that ton.

The idea of profit maximization is applied in a very similar way to a firm's decision about how many workers to employ: If employing another worker increases the firm's profits, then the firm will employ that worker. If employing another worker reduces the firm's profits, then the firm will not employ the worker.

We have already seen that a firm produces a quantity that equates marginal revenue to marginal cost ($MR = MC$). The firm satisfies an analogous condition in deciding how much labor to employ, as we discuss next.

From Marginal Product to Marginal Revenue Product

To determine a firm's demand curve for labor we must examine how the firm uses labor to produce its output of goods and services. We start by assuming that the firm sells its output in a *competitive market;* that is, the firm is a *price-taker.* We also assume that the firm takes the wage as given in the labor market; in otherwords, the firm is hiring such a small proportion of workers in the labor market that it cannot affect the market wage for those workers. Table 12.1 gives an example of such a competitive firm. It shows the weekly production and labor input of a firm called Getajob, which produces professional-looking job résumés in a college town. To produce a résumé, workers at Getajob talk to each of their clients—usually college seniors—give advice on what should go into their résumé, and then produce the résumé.

The first two columns of Table 12.1 show how Getajob can increase its production of résumés each week by employing more workers. This is the *production function* for the firm; it assumes the firm has a certain amount of capital—word-processing equipment, a small office near the campus, etc. We assume that labor is the only variable input to production in the short run, so that the cost of increasing the production of résumés depends only on the additional cost of employing more workers. Observe that the *marginal product (MP) of labor*—which we defined in Chapter 6 as the change in the quantity produced when one additional unit of labor is employed—declines as more workers are employed. In other words there is a

marginal product of labor: the change in production due to a one-unit increase in labor input. (Ch. 6)

Workers Employed Each Week (L)	Quantity Produced (Q)	Marginal Product of Labor (MP)	Price of Output (dollars) (P)	Total Revenue (dollars) (TR)	Marginal Revenue Product of Labor (dollars) (MRP)
0	0	—	100	0	—
1	17	17	100	1,700	1,700
2	31	14	100	3,100	1,400
3	42	11	100	4,200	1,100
4	51	9	100	5,100	900
5	58	7	100	5,800	700
6	63	5	100	6,300	500
7	66	3	100	6,600	300
8	68	2	100	6,800	200
9	69	1	100	6,900	100

TABLE 12.1
Labor Input and Marginal Revenue Product at a Competitive Firm

$$\frac{\text{Change in } Q}{\text{Change in } L} \qquad \begin{array}{c}P \text{ does not} \\ \text{depend on } Q.\end{array} \qquad P \times Q \qquad \frac{\text{Change in } TR}{\text{Change in } L} \text{ or } P \times MP$$

diminishing marginal product of labor, or diminishing return to labor: As more workers are hired with office space and equipment fixed, each additional worker adds less and less to production. For example, the first worker employed can produce 17 résumés a week, but if there are already 8 workers at Getajob, hiring a ninth worker will increase production by only 1 résumé.

Suppose that the market price for producing this type of résumé service is $100 per résumé, as shown in the fourth column of Table 12.1. Because Getajob is assumed to be a *competitive firm,* it cannot affect this price. Then, the total revenue of the firm for each amount of labor employed can be computed by multiplying the price (P) times the quantity produced (Q) with each amount of labor (L). This is shown in the next-to-last column. For example, total revenue with $L = 3$ workers employed is $P = \$100$ times $Q = 42$, or $4,200.

The last column of Table 12.1 shows the **marginal revenue product (MRP) of labor**. *The marginal revenue product of labor is defined as the change in total revenue when one additional unit of labor is employed.* For example, the marginal revenue product of labor from hiring a third worker is the total revenue with 3 workers ($4,200) minus the total revenue with 2 workers ($3,100), or $4,200 - $3,100 = $1,100. The marginal revenue product of labor is used to find the demand curve for labor, as we will soon see.

Before you read any further, stop and make sure you understand the difference between the marginal product (MP) and the marginal revenue product (MRP). The marginal product is the increase in the *quantity produced* when labor is increased by one unit. The marginal revenue product is the increase in *total revenue* when labor is increased by one unit. For a *competitive firm* taking the market price as given, the marginal revenue product (MRP) can be calculated by multiplying the marginal product (MP) by the price of output (P). For example, the marginal product when the third worker is hired is 11 résumés; thus the additional revenue that the third worker will generate for the firm is $100 per résumé times 11, or $1,100.

marginal revenue product of labor: the change in total revenue due to a one-unit increase in labor input.

Observe in Table 12.1 that the marginal revenue product of labor declines as more workers are employed. This is because the marginal product of labor declines.

The Marginal Revenue Product of Labor Equals the Wage (MRP = W)

Now we are almost ready to derive the firm's demand curve for labor. Suppose first that the wage for workers with the type of skills Getajob needs to produce résumés is $600 per week (for example, $15 per hour for 40 hours). Then, hiring 1 worker certainly makes sense because the marginal revenue product of labor is $1,700, or much greater than the $600 wage cost of hiring the worker. How about 2 workers? The marginal revenue product from employing a second worker is $1,400, still greater than $600; so it makes sense to hire a second worker. Continuing this way, we will see that the *firm will hire a total of 5 workers when the wage is $600 per week,* because hiring a sixth worker would result in a marginal revenue product of only $500, less than the $600 per week wage. Thus, if a firm maximizes profits it will hire the largest number of workers for which the marginal revenue product of labor is greater than the wage; if fractional units of labor input (for example, hours rather than weeks of work) are possible, then the firm will keep hiring workers until the marginal revenue product of labor exactly equals the wage. Thus, we have derived a key rule of profit maximization: Firms will hire workers up to the point where the *marginal revenue product of labor equals the wage.*

The rule that the marginal revenue product of labor equals the wage can be written in symbols as

$$MRP = W$$

The Firm's Derived Demand and Market Demand

Now, to find the demand curve for labor we need to determine how many workers the firm will hire at *different* wages. We know that Getajob will hire 5 workers if the wage is $600 per week. What if the wage were $800 per week? Then the firm will hire only 4 workers; the marginal revenue product of the fifth worker ($700) is now less than the wage ($800), so the firm will not be maximizing its profits if it hires 5 workers. Thus we have shown that a higher wage reduces the quantity of labor demanded by the firm. What if the wage is lower than $600? Suppose the wage is $250 a week, for example. Then the firm will hire 7 workers. Thus a lower wage increases the quantity of labor demanded by the firm.

Figure 12.3 shows how to determine the entire demand curve for labor. It shows the wage on the vertical axis and the quantity of labor on the horizontal axis. The plotted points are the marginal revenue products from Table 12.1. To find the demand curve we ask how much labor the firm would employ at each wage. Starting with a high wage we reduce the wage gradually, asking at each wage how much labor the firm would employ. At a weekly wage of $2,000 the marginal revenue product is less than the wage, so it does not make sense to hire any workers. Therefore, the quantity demanded is zero at wages above $2,000. At a weekly wage of $1,500 it makes sense to hire one worker, and so on. As the wage is gradually lowered, the quantity of labor demanded rises, as shown by the red line in Figure 12.3. The steplike downward-sloping curve is the labor demand curve. There would be more black dots and the curve would be very smooth if we measured work in fractions of a week rather than in whole weeks.

Observe in Figure 12.3 that a firm's demand curve for labor is completely determined by the firm's marginal revenue product of labor curve. We have shown why the demand curve for labor is downward-sloping: because the marginal revenue product of labor curve is downward-sloping. A higher wage will reduce the quantity of labor demanded and a lower wage will increase the quantity of labor demanded; these are *movements along* the downward-sloping labor demand curve. We also can explain why a firm's labor demand curve would *shift*. For example, if the price (*P*) of the good (résumés) rises—perhaps because the demand curve for résumés shifts outward—then the marginal revenue product of labor (*MRP* = *P* × *MP*) would rise and the demand curve for labor would shift outward. Similarly, a rise in the marginal product of labor (*MP*) would shift the labor demand curve outward. On the other hand, a decline in the price (*P*) or a decline in the marginal product (*MP*) would shift the labor demand curve to the left.

What If the Firm Is Not a Price-Taker?

This approach to deriving the demand curve for labor works equally well for the case of a firm that is not a price-taker but is instead a monopoly, a monopolistic competitor, or a firm in an oligopoly. Table 12.2 shows an example of such a firm. The key difference between the firm in Table 12.1 and the firm in Table 12.2 is in the column for the price. Rather than facing a constant price for its output and thus a horizontal demand curve, this firm faces a downward-sloping demand curve: It can increase the quantity of résumés demanded by lowering its price. For example, if Getajob's résumés are a slightly differentiated product from other résumé producers in town, then the demand curve it faces when selling résumés may be downward-sloping.

Once we observe that the price and output are inversely related, we can continue just as we did with the competitive firm. Again, total revenue is equal to the price times the quantity, and marginal revenue product is the change in total revenue as 1 more worker is hired. Again the marginal revenue product declines as more workers are hired, as shown in the last column of Table 12.2. However, now the marginal revenue product declines more sharply as more workers are employed, and it even turns negative. The reason is that as more workers are hired and more output is produced and sold, the price of output must fall. This cuts into revenue, even though output increases, because the lower price on items previously sold reduces revenue. But the principle of labor demand is the same: Firms hire up to the point when the marginal revenue product of labor equals the wage. The marginal revenue product determines the labor demand curve.

In the case of a firm with market power, the simple relationship *MRP* = *P* × *MP* no longer holds, however, because the firm does not take the market price as given. Instead we replace the price (*P*) by the more general marginal revenue (*MR*) in that relationship. This implies that the marginal revenue product is equal to the marginal revenue (*MR*) times the marginal product (*MP*). The relationship *MRP* = *MR* × *MP* holds for all firms whether they have market power or not. Only for a competitive firm is *MR* = *P*.

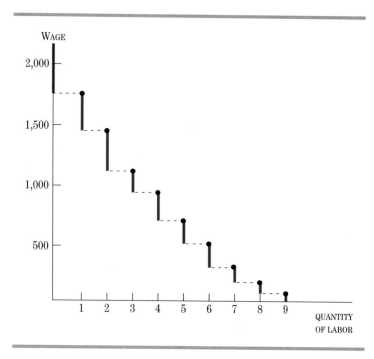

FIGURE 12.3
Determining a Firm's Demand Curve for Labor
The black dots are exactly the same as the marginal revenue product of labor in Table 12.1. The red line indicates the quantity of labor demanded at each wage. (If there were more dots the curve would smooth out into a typical looking labor demand curve.)

TABLE 12.2
Labor Input and Marginal Revenue Product for a Firm with Power to Affect the Market Price

Workers Employed Each Week (L)	Quantity Produced (Q)	Marginal Product of Labor (dollars) (MP)	Price of Output (dollars) (P)	Total Revenue (dollars) (TR)	Marginal Revenue Product of Labor (dollars) (MRP)
0	0	—	100	0	—
1	17	17	92	1,564	1,564
2	31	14	85	2,635	1,071
3	42	11	79	3,318	683
4	51	9	75	3,825	507
5	58	7	71	4,118	293
6	63	5	69	4,347	229
7	66	3	67	4,422	75
8	68	2	66	4,488	66
9	69	1	65	4,485	−3

$\dfrac{\text{Change in } Q}{\text{Change in } L}$ | P declines with Q. | $P \times Q$ | $\dfrac{\text{Change in } TR}{\text{Change in } L}$

Market Demand

To get the demand for labor in the market as a whole we must add up the labor demand curve for each firm demanding workers in the labor market. At each wage we sum the total quantity of labor demanded by all firms in the market; this is illustrated in Figure 12.4 for the case of two firms producing résumés. The two curves on the left are labor demand curves for two résumé-producing firms, Getajob and Careerpro. (The curves are smoothed out compared with Figure 12.3 so that they are easier to see.) The process of summing individual firms' demands for labor to get the market demand is analogous to summing individual demand curves for goods to get the market demand curve for goods. At each wage we sum the labor demand at all the firms to get the market demand.

A Comparison of *MRP* = *W* with the Marginal Cost Equals Price Rule

Note that a firm's decision to employ workers is closely tied to its decision about how much to produce. We have emphasized the former decision here and the latter decision in earlier chapters. To draw attention to this connection, we show in Table 12.3 the marginal cost when the wage is $600. Marginal cost is equal to the change in variable costs divided by the change in quantity produced. Variable costs are the wage times the amount of labor employed.

Now, consider the quantity of output the firm would produce if it compared price and marginal cost as discussed in earlier chapters. If the price of output is $100, the firm will produce 58 résumés: the highest level of output for which price is greater than marginal cost. This is exactly what we found using the *MRP* = *W*

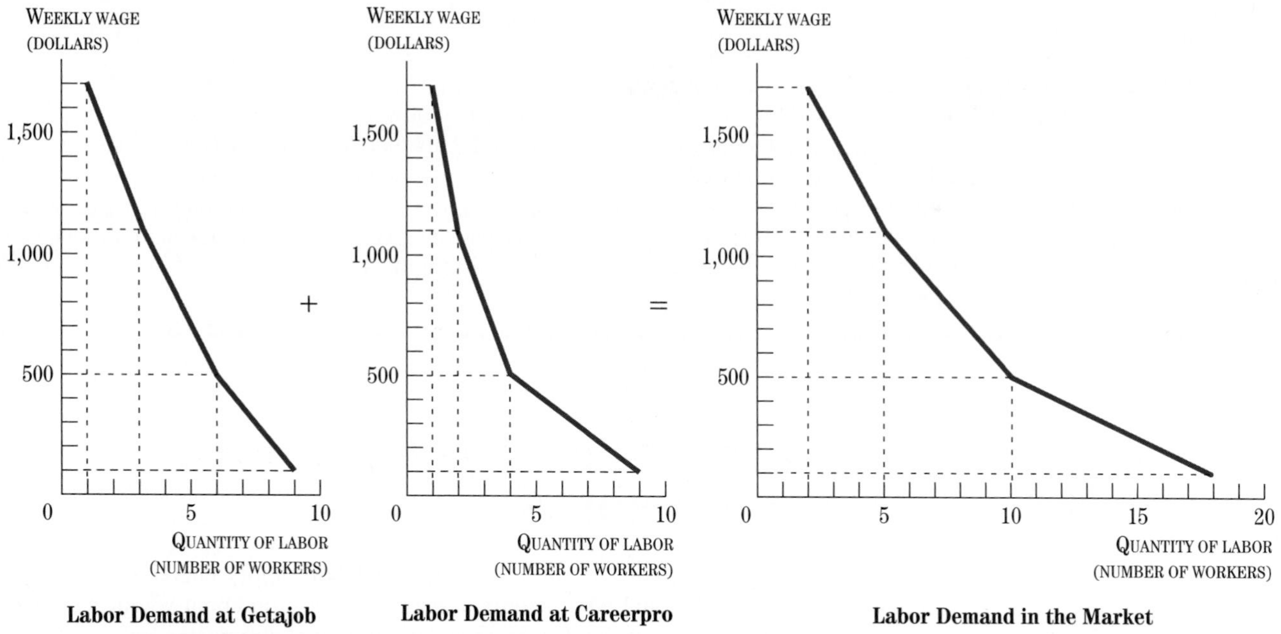

FIGURE 12.4
Summing Firms' Demands to Get the Labor Market Demand Curve
The labor demand curve in the market is obtained by summing the quantity of labor demanded by each firm at each wage.

rule, because 58 units of output requires 5 workers. Recall that employing 5 workers is the profit-maximizing labor choice when the wage is $600.

If the profit-maximizing firm could produce fractional units, then it would set marginal cost exactly equal to price. The resulting production decision would be exactly the same as implied by the rule that the marginal revenue product of labor equals the wage.

TABLE 12.3
Marginal Cost and the Production Decision at Getajob

Workers Employed Each Week (L)	Quantity Produced (Q)	Variable Costs (dollars) (VC)	Marginal Cost (dollars) (MC)
0	0	0	0
1	17	600	35
2	31	1,200	42
3	42	1,800	54
4	51	2,400	66
5	58	3,000	85
6	63	3,600	120
7	66	4,200	200
8	68	4,800	300
9	69	5,400	600

$600 wage × L

$\frac{\text{Change in } VC}{\text{Change in } Q.}$

Review

▶ The demand for labor is a relationship between the quantity of labor a firm will employ and the wage.

▶ The demand for labor is a derived demand because it is derived from the goods and services produced by labor. When the quantity of labor is the decision variable, the firm maximizes profits by setting the marginal revenue product of labor equal to the wage.

▶ When the wage rises, the quantity of labor demanded by firms declines. When the wage falls, the quantity of labor demanded increases. These are movements along the labor demand curve.

▶ When the price of a commodity produced by a particular type of labor rises, the demand curve for that type of labor shifts outward.

THE LABOR SUPPLY OF INDIVIDUALS AND HOUSEHOLDS

We now focus on *supply of labor*. The market labor supply curve is the sum of many people's individual labor supply curves. The decision about whether to work and how much to work depends very much on individual circumstances.

Work versus Two Alternatives: Home Work and Leisure

Consider a person deciding how much to work—either how many hours a week or how many weeks a year. As with any economic decision, we need to consider the alternative to work. Economists have traditionally called the alternative *leisure*, although many of the alternatives to work are not normally thought of as leisure. The alternatives to work include "home work" like painting the house or caring for children at home, as well as pure leisure time such as simply talking to friends on the telephone, going bowling, or hiking in the country. The price of leisure is the opportunity cost of not working, that is, the wage. If a person's marginal benefit of more leisure is greater than the wage, then the person will choose more leisure. The decision to consume more leisure is thus like the decision to consume more of any other good. This may seem strange, but the analogy works quite well in practice.

Effects of Wage Changes: Income and Substitution Effects

As with the decision to consume a commodity, the decision to work can be analyzed with the concepts of the *substitution effect* and the *income effect*.

The *substitution effect* says that the higher the wage, the more attractive work will seem compared to its alternatives: home work or leisure. A higher wage makes work more rewarding compared to the alternatives. Think about your own work opportunities. You may have many nonwork choices—including studying, sleeping, or watching TV. Although you enjoy these activities, suppose that the wage paid for part-time student employment triples. Then you might decide to work an extra hour each day. The sacrifice—less time to study, sleep, watch TV, etc.—will be worth the higher wage. The inducement to work a little more due to the higher wage is the substitution effect. The quantity of labor supplied tends to increase when the wage rises because of the substitution effect.

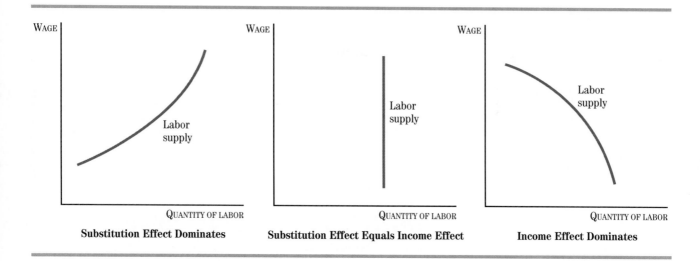

FIGURE 12.5
Three Labor Supply Curves
The three curves differ in the relative strength of the income and substitution effects. The labor supply curve on the left slopes upward because the substitution effect is stronger than the income effect. For the curve on the right, the income effect is stronger than the substitution effect. For the vertical curve in the middle, the two effects are the same.

The *income effect*, as in the demand for goods, reflects the effect of the price change on your real income. For example, if the wage for student employment triples, and if you are already working, you might think that you can work less. With a higher wage you can earn the same amount by working less. You may even have more money to do other things than work. Note that the income effect works in the opposite direction to the substitution effect: The quantity of labor supplied tends to decrease, rather than increase, when the wage rises because of the income effect.

The Shape of Supply Curves

Because the substitution effect and income effect work in opposite directions, the labor supply curve can slope either upward or downward. The supply curve slopes up if the substitution effect dominates but slopes down if the income effect dominates. Several possibilities for labor supply are illustrated in Figure 12.5.

Moreover, the same supply curve may slope upward for some range of wages and downward for another range. For example, at high levels of the wage—when people earn enough to take long vacations—the income effect may dominate. At lower wages, the substitution effect may be dominant. This would then result in a **backward-bending labor supply curve,** as shown in Figure 12.6.

This derivation of the labor supply curve may seem unrealistic. After all, the workweek is 40 hours for many jobs; you may not have much choice about the number of hours per week. In fact, the sensitivity of the quantity of labor supplied to the wage is probably small for many workers. But economists have shown that the effect is large for some workers, and it is useful therefore to distinguish one worker's supply curve from another's.

In a family with two adults and children, for example, one of the adults may already have a job and the other may be choosing between working at home or working outside the home. This decision may be very sensitive to the wage and perhaps the cost of child care or consuming more prepared meals. In fact, the increased number of women working outside the home may be due to the increased opportunities and wages for women. The increase in the wage induces

backward-bending labor supply curve: the situation in which the income effect outweighs the substitution effect of an increase in the wage, causing the labor supply curve to bend back and take on a negative slope at higher levels of income.

Reading the News About Household Labor Supply Decisions

As more and more families have two potential workers, the decision about labor supply has become a household decision. The following newspaper article tells a story that pairs the human side of the decision with the economic side. According to the calculations in the table, the net earnings from work—after taxes and all other expenses—may be very small.

Source of article: "The Daycare Dilemma: When Money Matters, Parents Must Decide Whether Working or Staying Home Pays," *San Jose Mercury News,* Sunday, February 14, 1993, Business, p. 1E. Copyright © 1993 San Jose Mercury News. All rights reserved. Reprinted with permission.

By Mark Schwanhausser
Mercury News Staff Writer

For Yolanda Achanzar, going to work was like listening to an old-fashioned cash register ring. She'd drop off her two toddlers with a sitter *(ka-ching:* $29 a day). She'd commute to the office in her Mercury Villager *(ka-ching:* $8). She'd dig into her purse for breakfast and lunch *(ka-ching:* $10). And she'd dress up for work (*ka-ching:* $5 a day, $8.50 if she snagged her hose, $12.50 if you include the dry-cleaning bills). "If you add all that up," she said, "it's just not worth it, vs. the time you could have spent with your children, loving them, rearing them, nurturing them."

And so, although she loved her job and co-workers, although her $25,000 paycheck accounted for nearly 40 percent of her family's total income, she chucked her job Friday to stay home with 27-month-old Marissa and 14-month-old Jordan. She felt she simply couldn't afford her job any longer.

Unlike the tiny minority of parents who, like Zoë Baird and Kimba Wood, don't have to worry about the financial strain of paying for child care, Achanzar and her husband, Gil, are among the millions of American parents who agonize trying to discover the proper mix for a family's financial welfare, the children's care and the parents' careers. For them, money is an issue—and something has to give.

For many parents, the decision starts with a bottom-line analysis of dollars in and dollars out. But next comes the long-term equation that consists of nothing but variables. How much is it worth to stay home with the kids? What lifestyle will we have?

DOES IT PAY TO STAY HOME?

Many parents finally decide it doesn't pay to have two incomes any longer, once they account for the cost of child care and other work-related expenses. Here are budget comparisons for two hypothetical couples trying to decide if the lower-paid spouse should stay home with their one child—and the fiscal impact the decision will have on their current standard of living.

	Both spouses work	One stays home	Both spouses work	One stays home
Income				
Spouse A	$35,600	$35,600	$67,000	$67,000
Spouse B	24,000	0	35,000	0
Total	**59,600**	**35,600**	**102,000**	**67,000**
Taxes[1]				
Taxable income	46,700	22,700	89,100	54,100
Federal	7,949	2,929	19,900	10,091
State	1,938	383	5,866	2,564
Social Security	4,559	2,723	7,091	4,413
Total taxes	**14,446**	**6,035**	**32,857**	**17,068**
Work expenses[2]				
Child care	5,000	0	10,000	0
Transportation	1,500	0	2,250	0
Meals	1,250	0	2,000	0
Wardrobe	900	0	1,200	0
Dry cleaning	360	0	500	0
Total expenses	**9,010**	**0**	**15,950**	**0**
Total income	59,600	35,600	102,000	67,000
Total taxes	14,446	6,035	32,857	17,068
Total expenses	9,010	0	15,950	0
Left to spend	**$36,144**	**$29,565**	**$53,193**	**$49,932**
Decreases in spendable cash		**$6,579**		**$3,261**
Percentage change		**18%**		**6%**

[1]Includes $480 federal child-care credit and variable state credit.
[2]Work expenses are for the lower-paid spouse only. Although that spouse's work expenses would be erased by staying home, bills at home would rise and should be included in a full-cost analysis.
Source: Mercury News

workers to work more in the labor market. Economists have observed a fairly strong wage effect on the amount women work.

One also needs to distinguish between the effects of a temporary change in the wage and a more permanent change. Empirical studies show that the quantity of labor supplied rises more in response to a temporary increase in the wage than to a permanent increase. What's the explanation? Consider an example. If you have a special one-time opportunity tomorrow to earn $100 an hour rather than your usual $6 an hour, you are likely to put off some leisure for one day; the substitution effect dominates. But if you are lucky enough to land a lifetime job of $100 an hour rather than $6 an hour, you may decide to work fewer hours and have more leisure time; the income effect dominates.

This difference between temporary and permanent changes helps explain the dramatic decline in the average hours per week in the United States as wages have risen over the last century. These are more permanent changes for which the income effect dominates.

Work versus Another Alternative: Getting Human Capital

The skills of a worker depend in part on how much schooling and training the worker has. The decision to obtain these skills—to finish high school and attend a community college or obtain a four-year college degree—is much like the choice between work and leisure. In fact, an important decision for many young people is whether to go to work or finish high school; if they have finished high school, the choice is whether to go to work or go to college.

Economists view the education and training that raise skills and productivity as a form of *investment*, a decision to spend funds or time on something now because it pays off in the future. Continuing the analogy, an investment in a college education raises the amount of **human capital**—a person's knowledge and skills—in the same way that the investment in a factory or machine by a business firm raises physical capital.

The decision to invest in human capital can be approached like any other economic choice. Suppose the decision is whether Angela should go to college or get a job. If she does not go to college, she saves on tuition and can begin earning an income right away. If she goes to college, she pays tuition and foregoes the opportunity to earn income at a full-time job. However, if Angela is like most people, college will improve her skills and land her a better job at a higher pay. The returns to college education are the extra pay. Angela ought to go to college—invest in human capital—if the returns are greater than the cost.

People can increase their skills at work as well as in school. In fact, **on-the-job training** is one of the most important ways that workers' productivity increases. On-the-job training can either be *firm specific*, when the skills are useful only at one firm, or *general purpose*, where the skills are transferable to other jobs.

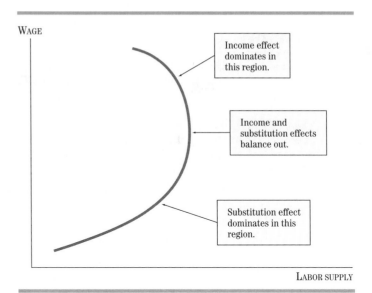

WAGE

Income effect dominates in this region.

Income and substitution effects balance out.

Substitution effect dominates in this region.

LABOR SUPPLY

FIGURE 12.6
Backward-Bending Labor Supply Curve
A person may have a labor supply curve that is positively sloped for a low wage, is steeper for a higher wage, and then bends backward for a high wage.

human capital: a person's accumulated knowledge and skills.

on-the-job training: the building of the skills of a firm's employees while they work for the firm.

THE FAR SIDE   By GARY LARSON

Hopeful parents

Review

▶ The labor supply curve can be viewed as the outcome of an individual's choice between work and some other activity, whether home work, schooling, or leisure.

▶ There is both a substitution effect and an income effect in the labor supply. The substitution effect is the increased attractiveness of work relative to its alternative as the wage rises. The income effect is

the increased attractiveness of leisure because there is more to spend when the wage rises. In some situations the income effect dominates. In other situations the substitution effect dominates.

▶ Human capital is the knowledge and skills that a person accumulates from going to school and receiving on-the-job training. The return on human capital has increased in recent years.

EXPLAINING WAGE DIFFERENCES

When we combine the labor demand and labor supply curves derived in the previous two sections, we get the model of the labor market summarized in Figure 12.1. The model predicts that the wage in the labor market will be at the intersection of the supply and demand curves. The point of intersection where the quantity of labor supplied equals the quantity of labor demanded, is the **labor market equilibrium.**

labor market equilibrium: the situation in which the quantity supplied of labor equals the quantity demanded of labor.

Labor Productivity

The model of the labor market predicts that the wage equals the marginal revenue product. If the marginal product of labor employed at a firm increases, then the model predicts that the wage will rise. Suppose the marginal product of labor rises for the economy as a whole; then wages should also rise. Is this what occurs in reality?

Wage Changes and Labor Productivity over Time

labor productivity: output per hour of work.

Figure 12.7 shows the trend in output per hour of work in the United States in the last 40 years. Output per hour of work is called **labor productivity** and is a good indication of trends in the marginal product of labor on average in the United States. The labor market model predicts that wages in the United States should increase when labor productivity increases. Do they?

Compare Figure 12.7 on labor productivity with Figure 12.2 on growth of real wages. Note that a change in the labor productivity trend occurred in the mid-1970s almost at the same time as the change in the trend of real wage growth. The close empirical association between wages and labor productivity that is evident in these two charts suggests that labor productivity is a key explanation of wage differences over time.

Wage Dispersion and Productivity

Can labor productivity also explain wage differences between people? If the marginal product of labor increases with additional skills from investment in human capital, then, on average, wages for people with a college education should be higher than they are for people without a college education. Hence, productivity differences are an explanation for the wage gap between workers who do not receive education beyond high school and those who are college educated.

Although human capital differences undoubtedly explain some of the dispersion of wages, some have argued that the greater productivity of college-educated workers is not due to the skills learned in college but to the fact that colleges screen applicants. For example, people who are not highly motivated or who have difficulty communicating have trouble getting into college. Hence, college graduates would earn higher wages even if they learned nothing in college. If so, a college degree *signals* to employers that the graduate is likely to be a productive worker.

Unfortunately, it is difficult to distinguish the skill-enhancing from the signaling effects of college. Certainly your grades and major in college affect the kind of job you get and how much you earn, suggesting that more than signaling is important to employers. In reality signaling and human capital both probably have a role to play in explaining the higher wages of college graduates.

Whether it is signaling or human capital that explains the higher wages of college graduates, labor productivity differences are still the underlying explanation for the wage differences. However, labor productivity does not explain everything about wages. Consider now some other factors.

Compensating Wage Differentials

Not all jobs that require workers with the same level of skill and productivity are alike. Some jobs are more pleasant, less stressful, or safer than other jobs. For example, the skills necessary to be a deep-sea salvage diver and a lifeguard are similar—good at swimming, good judgment, and good health. But the risks—such as decompression sickness—for a deep-sea diver are greater and the opportunity for social interaction is less. If the pay for both jobs were the same, say $10 per hour, most people would prefer the lifeguard job.

But this situation could not last. With many lifeguard applicants, the beach authorities would be unlikely to raise the wage above $10 and might even try to cut the wage if budget cuts occurred. With few applicants, the deep-sea salvage companies would have to raise the wage. After a while it would not be surprising to see the wage for lifeguards at $9 per hour and the wage for deep-sea divers at $12 per hour; these wages would be labor market equilibrium wages in the supply and demand model for lifeguards and deep-sea divers. Thus, we would be in a situation where the skills of the workers were identical but their wages were much different. The higher-risk job pays a higher wage than the lower-risk job.

Situations where wages differ because of the characteristics of the job are widespread. Hazardous duty pay is common in the military. Wage data show that night workers in manufacturing plants get wages that are about 3 percent higher on average than daytime workers, presumably to compensate for the inconvenience.

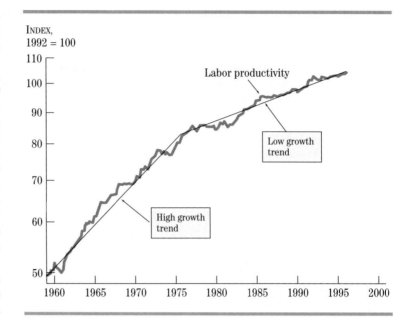

FIGURE 12.7
Labor Productivity in the United States

Productivity (output per hour of work in the whole economy) grew more rapidly before the mid-1970s than after. The slowdown in productivity growth occurred at about the same time as the slowdown in the growth of wages shown in Figure 12.2, much as would be predicted by the labor supply and demand model.

Source: U.S. Department of Commerce.

Using Economics to Explain the Academic Wage Gap

People with Ph.D.'s who teach or do research at colleges and universities are paid 10 percent less than people with Ph.D.'s who work for government and 20 percent less than people with Ph.D.'s who work for business firms. Why?

Consider these two possibilities: (1) people with Ph.D.'s who work in academia are less skilled and relatively unproductive, or (2) people with Ph.D.'s in business and government are paid a compensating wage differential because the job is less pleasant. (They don't have the pleasure of teaching students or the flexible academic hours.)

How can we tell which is the right explanation? Looking at what happens to people with Ph.D.'s when they move provides an answer. If their wages increase when they move to a nonacademic job, then compensating wage differentials rather than productivity differences would be the correct explanation.

The following table shows the average salary increases between 1985 and 1987 of people with Ph.D.'s who either (1) did not move, (2) moved to another college or

university, or (3) moved to business or government. The salary increases are largest for those who left academia. For example, the average salary for engineering Ph.D.'s nearly doubled when they moved from academia to work in a business firm or government. This indicates that the differences are not due to skill but to compensating wage differentials.

This is one of the rare cases where economists have actually been able to obtain data that distinguish compensating wage differentials from productivity or other explanations for wage differences. But if the case is representative, compensating wage differentials might play a big part in wage dispersion.

> Largest increase for every type of Ph.D.

	Increase in Salary (dollars)		
	Did Not Move	Moved to Another College	Left Academia
Physical science	7,303	10,216	15,330
Mathematical science	6,523	9,716	15,727
Environmental science	6,292	4,688	11,333
Life science	5,870	6,710	8,115
Psychology	5,920	6,559	10,371
Social science	5,796	7,687	12,485
Engineering	7,294	6,724	14,025
Humanities	5,042	5,380	8,204

Source: Adapted from Albert Rees, "The Salaries of Ph.D.'s in Academia and Elsewhere," *Journal of Economic Perspectives,* Winter 1993. Used with permission.

---

compensating wage differential: a difference in wages for people with similar skills based on some characteristic of the job, such as riskiness, discomfort, or convenience of the time schedule.

Such differences in wages are called **compensating wage differentials.** They are an important source of differences in wages that are not based on marginal product. With compensating differentials, workers may seek out riskier jobs in order to be paid more.

Discrimination

The ratio of the average wage of women to men was .5 in the 1950s. Although it is now about .7, it still shows a pay gap. The ratio of wages of blacks to whites was only .6 in the 1950s, and although it too has risen to .7, it is still quite low. Wage differences between white and minority workers or between men and women are an indication of discrimination if the wage differences cannot be explained by differences in marginal product or other factors unrelated to race or gender.

Wage Differences for Workers with the Same Marginal Products

Some, but not all, of these differences may be attributed to differences in human capital. The wage gap between blacks and whites or between men and women with comparable education and job experience is smaller than the ratios in the preceding paragraph. But a gap still exists.

Discrimination on the basis of race or gender prejudice can explain such differences. This is shown in Figure 12.8. *Discrimination* can be defined in the supply and demand model as not hiring women or minority workers even though their marginal product is just as high as other workers, or paying a lower wage to such workers even though their marginal product is equal to that of other workers. Either way, discrimination can be interpreted as a leftward shift of the labor demand curve for women or minority workers. As shown in Figure 12.8, this reduces the wages and employment for those discriminated against.

Competitive Markets and Discrimination

An important implication of this supply and demand interpretation of the effects of discrimination is that competition among firms may reduce it. This is an advantage of competitive markets that should be added to the advantages already mentioned. Why might competition reduce discrimination? Because firms in competitive markets that discriminate will lose out to firms that do not. Much like firms that do not keep their costs as low as other firms, they will eventually be driven out of the industry.

If markets are competitive, then firms that discriminate against women or minorities will pay them a wage lower than their marginal revenue products, as shown in Figure 12.8. In this situation, any profit-maximizing firm will see that it can raise its profits by paying these workers a little more—but still less than their

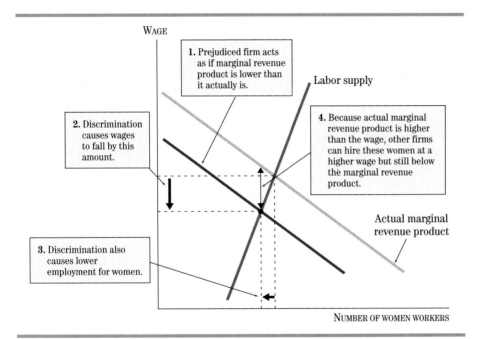

FIGURE 12.8
Discrimination in the Labor Market
Firms that discriminate against women pay them a wage that is less than their marginal product. But this gives other firms an opportunity to recruit workers from prejudiced firms by paying higher wages.

marginal revenue product—and hiring them away from firms that discriminate. As long as the discriminating firms pay less than the marginal product of labor, other firms can hire the workers and raise profits. Remember a firm will increase profits if the wage is less than the marginal revenue product. But eventually competition for workers will raise wages until the wages are equal to the marginal products of labor.

This description of events relies on a market being competitive. If firms have monopoly power or entry is limited so that economic profits are not driven to zero, then discrimination can continue to exist. That discrimination effects on wages do persist may be a sign that there is market power and barriers to entry. In any case, there are laws against discrimination that give those who are discriminated against for race, gender, or other reasons the right to sue those who are discriminating.

Some laws have been proposed requiring that employers pay the same wage to comparable skilled workers. Such proposals are called *comparable worth proposals.* The intent of such proposals is to bring wages of different groups into line. However, such laws might force wages to be the same in situations where wages are different for reasons other than discrimination, such as compensating wage differentials. If so, this would lead to shortages or surpluses, much as price ceilings or price floors in any market. In the lifeguard/deep-sea diver example, a law requiring employers to pay lifeguards and deep-sea divers the same wage would cause a surplus of lifeguards and a shortage of deep-sea divers. For example, suppose that with comparable worth legislation the wage for both lifeguards and deep-sea divers was $10 per hour. Because the labor market equilibrium wage for life guards, $9 per hour, is less than $10 per hour, there is a surplus of lifeguards: More people are willing to be lifeguards than employers are willing to hire. And because the labor market equilibrium wage for deep-sea divers, $12 per hour, is greater than $10, there is a shortage of deep-sea divers: Firms are willing to hire more deep sea divers than the number of deep-sea divers willing to dive for the $10 per hour wage.

Minimum Wage Laws

minimum wage legislation: a law that sets a floor on the wage, or price of labor.

Another example where the government stipulates a wage that employers must pay is **minimum wage legislation,** which is common in many countries and which was discussed in Chapter 3. The minimum wage sets a floor for the price of labor. Because wages differ due to skills, the impact of the minimum wage depends on the skills of the workers. Figure 12.9 shows what the supply and demand model predicts about the impact of the minimum wage on skilled and unskilled workers. A labor market for unskilled workers is shown on the left; the minimum wage is shown to be above the labor market equilibrium wage. There is thus a surplus, or unemployment: The quantity of labor demanded by firms at the minimum wage is less than the quantity of labor workers are willing to supply at that wage. A labor market for skilled workers is shown on the right: The minimum wage is shown to be below the market equilibrium wage for skilled workers. Thus a minimum wage at the level shown in the graph would not cause unemployment among skilled workers.

Therefore, the labor supply and demand model predicts that the minimum wage is a cause of unemployment among less skilled or less experienced workers, and thereby ends up hurting some of the least well off in society. This is why many economists are concerned about the impact of minimum wage legislation.

In interpreting this result remember that the supply and demand model is a *model* of reality, not reality itself. Although the model explains much about wages,

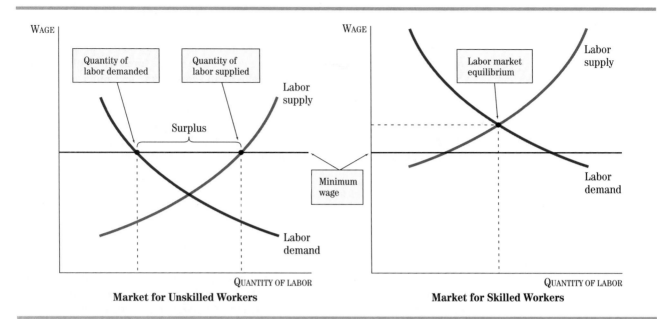

Market for Unskilled Workers   **Market for Skilled Workers**

its predictions about minimum wage laws should be verified like the predictions of any other economic model. In fact, labor economists have been trying to check the predictions of the model for the minimum wage for many years. Some, such as Jacob Mincer of Columbia University, have provided evidence that the predicted minimum wage impact is verified in real-world labor markets; others, such as David Card of the University of California at Berkeley and Alan Krueger of Princeton University, have provided evidence to the contrary: When they looked at the impact on low-skilled fast-food workers of different minimum wage laws in different states, they did not find the predicted impact on unemployment of the minimum wage. Because of this controversy, testing the supply and demand model of labor is currently a hot topic in economics.

FIGURE 12.9
Effects of a Minimum Wage
If there are government restrictions on wages that hold them below the labor market equilibrium, then a surplus (unemployment) will arise. Unemployment is more likely for unskilled workers because the equilibrium wage is lower.

Review

▶ Labor productivity differences are an explanation for some of the differences in wages.

▶ Compensating wage differentials occur because some jobs are more attractive than others. They are another source of wage disparity.

▶ Discrimination reduces the wages of those who are discriminated against below their marginal revenue product.

▶ Data suggest that the wage effects of discrimination continue to exist but have declined in recent years. The female-male wage gap and the black-white wage gap have declined but are still large.

▶ Competition can be a force against the effects of discrimination.

LABOR CONTRACTS AND INCENTIVES

The agreement to buy or sell labor is frequently a long-term one. The job-specific training and the difficulty of changing jobs make quick turnover costly for both firms and workers. **Long-term employment contracts** are either *explicit* or *implicit* agreements between workers and firms. Once a good match is found, both worker and employer have an incentive to preserve the match. Thus, employment relations need to be governed by some type of contract, even if it is not written down in a formal way. The contract needs to specify what will happen in the future when, for example, the marginal product of labor at the firm increases or decreases.

long-term employment contract: an agreement, either explicit or implicit, between employers and workers that sets conditions concerning the work relationship for a long period of time.

Contracts with Fixed Wages

Most workers would prefer a certain wage to an uncertain one; such workers may prefer a contract that gives a fixed wage that does not change when the marginal revenue product changes. Paying the same wage whether the workers are more or less productive reduces the risk to the worker.

Thus, many employment contracts make the wage the same whether the marginal revenue product is high or low. Workers will get the same pay in both cases, perhaps equal to the average of the high and low marginal revenue product.

Long-term employment contracts of this kind are quite common. A worker—a person working at Getajob, for example—is hired at a given weekly wage. If marginal revenue product declines because of a week of stormy winter weather with frequent power outages, Getajob will not reduce the weekly wage. On the other hand, when a crowd of college seniors arrives at the shop in May, the Getajob workers will have to work harder—their marginal revenue product rises—but they are not paid a higher wage. Thus, the weekly wage does not change with the actual week-to-week changes in marginal revenue product of the worker. The wage reflects marginal revenue product over a longer period. Most workers in the United States are paid with a fixed wage in this way.

Contracts with Piece-Rate Wages

An alternative type of labor contract endeavors to match productivity with the wage much more closely. Such contracts are used when the weekly or hourly wage does not provide sufficient *incentive* or where the manager cannot observe the worker carefully. Under a **piece-rate system,** workers are paid a specific amount depending on how much they produce. Thus, if their marginal product drops off, for whatever reason, they are paid less. Piece rates are common in the apparel and agriculture industries.

piece-rate system: a system by which workers are paid a specific amount per unit they produce.

Consider California lettuce growers, for example. The growers hire crews of workers to cut and pack the lettuce. A typical crew consists of two cutters and one packer who split their earnings equally. The crew is paid a piece rate, about $1.20 for a box of lettuce that might contain two dozen heads. A three-person crew can pick and pack about 75 boxes an hour. Thus, each worker can earn about $30 an hour. But if they slack off, their wages decline rapidly.

On the same lettuce farms, the growers may pay other workers on an hourly or weekly basis. Workers who wash the lettuce are paid an hourly wage. Truck drivers and the workers who carry the boxes to the trucks are also paid by the hour.

Why the difference? Piece rates are used when incentives are important and it is difficult to monitor the workers. This would apply to small crews of lettuce workers out in the fields but not to workers washing lettuce at the main building. Another reason is that some jobs, like washing lettuce or driving a truck, require particular care and safety. Driving the truck too fast or washing the lettuce carelessly might occur under a piece-rate system.

Deferred Payment Contracts

Yet another form of contract pays workers below their marginal revenue product when they are young and more than their marginal revenue product in the future as a reward for working hard. Lawyers and accountants frequently work hard at their firms when they are young; if they do well, they make partner and are then paid much more than the marginal revenue product when they are older. Such contracts are called **deferred payment contracts.**

Generous retirement plans are another form of deferred payment contract. A reward for staying at the firm and working hard is a nice retirement package.

Efficiency Wages

In cases where workers are difficult to monitor and motivation is a problem, workers are sometimes paid a wage higher than they would receive at other firms in order to motivate them. By getting a little more than they would at another firm, the workers are given an incentive to work more efficiently. The extra pay increases the cost of being fired. An **efficiency wage** is a wage that is higher than the worker would get at another job and is aimed at making the worker more *productive, or efficient.*

Efficiency wages might explain why wages are sometimes higher at larger firms than at smaller firms. At a small firm, the owner might know and be able to monitor the workers. At larger firms, where monitoring is difficult, the extra pay might be an efficiency wage. But compensating wage differentials could also explain the higher wages at larger firms, perhaps compensating for a less friendly work environment. In general, it is hard to distinguish efficiency wages from compensating wage differentials.

deferred payment contract: an agreement between a worker and an employer whereby the worker is paid less than the marginal revenue product when young, and subsequently paid more than the marginal revenue product when old.

efficiency wage: a wage higher than one that would equate quantity supplied and quantity demanded set by employers to increase worker efficiency, for example, by decreasing shirking by workers.

Compensating Wage Differentials versus Efficiency Wages
Compensating wage differentials are illustrated by the relatively high wages paid to someone for performing risky jobs like window washing on a skyscraper. Efficiency wages are illustrated by the relatively high wages (for then) paid by Henry Ford in order to give workers the incentive to work efficiently for fear of losing their jobs and having to accept lower-paying jobs. In many cases it is hard to distinguish between these two explanations for differences in wages.

'GOLD RUSH' IS STARTED BY FORD'S $5 OFFER

Thousands of Men Seek Employment in Detroit Factory.

Will Distribute $10,000,000 in Semi-Monthly Bonuses.

No Employee to Receive Less Than Five Dollars a Day.

Review

▶ Many labor market transactions are long term. Long-term relationships between workers and firms require implicit or explicit contracts.

▶ Most employment contracts have a fixed hourly or weekly wage, even though the marginal product of the worker fluctuates.

▶ Piece-rate contracts adjust the payment directly according to actual marginal product; they are a way to increase incentives to be more productive.

▶ Deferred compensation and efficiency wages are other forms of payment that aim at improving incentives and worker motivation.

LABOR UNIONS

labor union: a coalition of workers, organized to improve wages and working conditions of their members.

industrial union: a union organized within a given industry, whose members come from a variety of occupations.

craft union: a union organized to represent a single occupation, whose members come from a variety of industries.

The model of labor supply and demand can also help us understand the impact of labor unions. **Labor unions** such as the United Auto Workers or the United Farm Workers are organizations with the stated aim of improving wages and working conditions of their members. There are two types of unions: **industrial unions** represent most of the workers in an industry—such as the rubber workers, farm workers, or steelworkers—regardless of their occupation; **craft unions** represent workers in a single occupation or group of occupations, such as printers or dock-workers. In the 1930s and 1940s, there were disputes between those organizing craft unions and industrial unions. John L. Lewis, a labor union leader, argued that craft unions were not suitable for large numbers of unskilled workers. Hence, he and other union leaders split in 1936 from the American Federation of Labor (AFL), a group representing many labor unions, and formed the Congress of Industrial Organizations (CIO). It was not until 1955 that the AFL and CIO resolved their disputes and merged; one of the reasons for their resolution was that union membership was beginning to decline.

But the decline continued. About 17 percent of the U.S. labor force is currently unionized, down from about 25 percent in the mid-1950s. The fraction is much higher in other countries.

Unions negotiate with firms on behalf of their members in a collective bargaining process. Federal law, including the National Labor Relations Act (1935), gives workers the right to organize into unions and bargain with employers. The National Labor Relations Board is set up to make sure that firms do not illegally prevent workers from organizing and to monitor union elections of leaders.

In studying unions, it is important to distinguish between the union leaders who speak for the union members and the union members themselves. Like politicians, union leaders must be elected, and as is the case with politicians, we can sometimes better understand the actions of union leaders by assuming that they are motivated by the desire to be elected or re-elected.

Union/Nonunion Wage Differentials

Studies of the wages of union workers and nonunion workers have shown that union wages are about 15 percent higher than nonunion wages, even when workers' skills are the same. There are two different explanations of how unions raise wages.

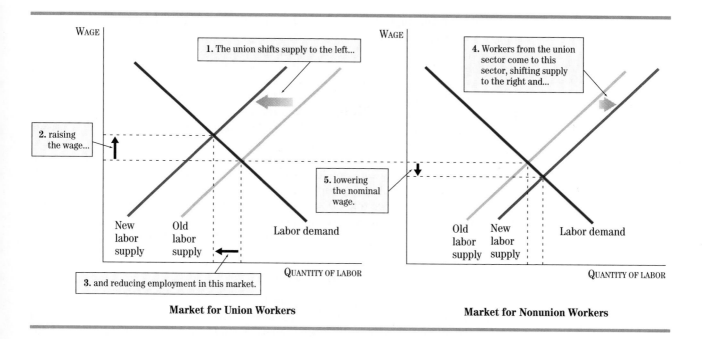

WAGE

1. The union shifts supply to the left...

2. raising the wage...

4. Workers from the union sector come to this sector, shifting supply to the right and...

5. lowering the nominal wage.

New labor supply | Old labor supply | Labor demand

3. and reducing employment in this market.

QUANTITY OF LABOR

Old labor supply | New labor supply | Labor demand

QUANTITY OF LABOR

Market for Union Workers

Market for Nonunion Workers

The Restricted Supply Explanation

One theory is that unions raise wages by restricting supply. By restricting membership, for example, they shift the labor supply curve to the left, raising wages, just as a monopolist raises the price of the good it sells by restricting supply. But by restricting supply, workers outside the union in another industry get paid less.

This effect of unions is illustrated in Figure 12.10. The graph on the right is one industry; the graph on the left is another industry. Suppose both industries require workers of the same skill level. Imagine the situation before the union is formed. Then the wages for the workers on the left and on the right in Figure 12.10 would be the same.

Now suppose a union organizes the industry on the left. Wages rise in the industry on the left, but the quantity of labor demanded in the industry falls. The workers who become unemployed on the left will likely move to the industry on the right. As they do so, the labor supply curve in the right-hand graph of Figure 12.10 shifts and the wage in that industry declines. Thus, a wage gap between the similarly skilled union and nonunion workers is created.

The Increased Productivity Explanation

Another theory, which was developed extensively in the book *What Do Unions Do?* by Richard Freeman and James Medoff of Harvard University, is that labor unions raise wages of workers by increasing their marginal product. They do so by providing a channel of communication with management, motivating workers, and providing a democratic means of resolving disputes.

A worker who has a dispute with the management of a firm or who sees the opportunity to get a higher wage at another firm could, in principle, move. But such moves can have huge costs: The firm may have invested in job-specific training and

FIGURE 12.10
The Effect of Unions on Wages
According to one view of labor unions, the union wage is increased relative to nonunion wages as a result of restricting the supply of workers. The supply in the union sector is reduced, but the supply in the nonunion sector is increased.

the worker might like the area where the firm is located. In situations where exit from a firm is costly, people find other ways to improve their situation without exiting. The economist Albert Hirschman in a famous book called *Exit, Voice, and Loyalty* has called this alternative "voice." Rather than exit or quit, the worker may try to show the firm that a raise is deserved. Or the worker can discuss with the employer how conditions can be changed. The choice between exit versus voice arises in many contexts: Should you transfer to a new college or tell the dean how the teaching might be improved? Should parents send their children to a private school or work to improve the local public school?

In many situations, exercising your voice requires collective action. If you complain only to the dean, nothing much will happen, but if you organize a "students against lousy teaching" group, you might see some changes. Those who emphasize this collective-voice role of labor unions argue that unions provide a means through which workers improve their productivity. This explains why the wages of union workers are higher than those of nonunion workers with the same skills and training.

Monopsony and Bilateral Monopoly

The analysis of labor unions in Figure 12.10 stresses the market power of unions as *sellers* of their members' labor in the labor market: By restricting supply, the union can raise the price of its members' wages, much like a monopolist or a group of oligopolists with market power can raise the price of the goods they sell.

However, the *buyers* in the labor market—that is, the firms that purchase the labor—may also have market power to affect the wage, contrary to the assumption we have made throughout this chapter that firms do not have such market power in the labor market. **Monopsony** is a situation where there is only one buyer. By reducing its demand, a monopsony can reduce the price in the market; it moves down along the supply curve, with both quantity and price lower.

The situation where there is only one seller (a monopoly) and one buyer (a monopsony) in a market is called a **bilateral monopoly.** A labor market with one labor union deciding the labor supply and one firm deciding the labor demand is an example of a bilateral monopoly.

In fact, there are few examples of monopsony; for most types of workers—sales clerks, accountants, engineers—there are typically many potential employers. Exceptions are found in small towns, where, for example, there may be only one auto repair shop. Then, if auto mechanics do not want to move, the auto repair shop is effectively the only employer. Another exception is found in professional sports leagues, where team owners form agreements with each other restricting workers' (that is, the players') mobility between teams. Such restrictions have been loosened significantly in recent years but still exist. If players had more freedom to move between teams, the teams' monopsony power would be reduced. Indeed, the loosening of restrictions that has already occurred has led to huge increases in players' salaries.

The outcome of a bilateral monopoly is difficult to predict. Compared to a situation where a monopsony faces competitive sellers, however, the bilateral monopoly can lead to a more efficient outcome. A firm with a monopsony facing many competitive sellers would buy *less* than a group of competitive buyers, in order to drive down the wage. By banding together, the sellers can confront this monopsony power with their own monopoly power. For example, they could refuse to work for less than the competitive wage. If their refusal is credible, they could take away the incentive for the monopsony to reduce labor demand because doing so would not reduce the wage.

monopsony: a situation in which there is a single buyer of a particular good or service in a given market.

bilateral monopoly: the situation in which there is one buyer and one seller in a market.

Review

▶ About 17 percent of U.S. workers belong to either industrial or craft unions.

▶ Workers who belong to unions are paid about 15 percent more on average than workers with the same skills who are not in unions. There are two conflicting explanations about why.

▶ One explanation is that labor unions improve productivity by improving worker motivation and providing workers with a collective voice.

▶ Another view is that labor unions raise productivity by restricting supply, much like a monopolist would, rather than by increasing productivity.

CONCLUSION AND SOME LESSONS

In this chapter we have shown how the labor supply and demand model is a powerful tool with many applications. In reviewing the key lessons of the labor supply and demand model, it is helpful to consider how these lessons may apply to you personally.

First, increasing your own labor productivity is a good way to increase your earnings. Many of the large differences in wages across individuals and across time are due to differences in productivity. Productivity is enhanced by increases in human capital, whether obtained in school or on the job. Such human capital will also prove useful if your firm shuts down and you need to find another job.

Second, if you are choosing between two occupations that you like equally well, choose the one that is less popular with other students of your generation and where it looks like demand will be increasing. Both the supply and the demand for labor affect the wage, and if the supply is expected to grow more rapidly than the demand in the occupation you are training for, wages will not be as high as in the occupation in relatively short supply.

Third, be sure to think about the wage you receive or the raises you get in real terms, not nominal terms, and make sure you are aware of fringe benefits offered or not offered.

Fourth, think about your job in a longer perspective. Partly for incentive reasons, some jobs pay little at the start, with the promise of higher payments later.

All these principles follow from the supply and demand model for labor.

KEY POINTS

1. Wage growth in the United States, which is defined by the real hourly average pay (including fringe benefits), has been increasing at a slower rate since the mid-1970s than in the 1950s and 1960s. Wage dispersion has also increased.

2. The demand for labor is a derived demand that comes from the profit-maximizing decisions of firms. Firms adjust their employment to make the marginal revenue product of labor equal to the wage. For a competitive firm, the marginal product equals the wage divided by the price.

3. The supply curve for labor can be explained by looking at the choices of individuals or households. A person will work more hours if the wage is greater than the marginal benefit of more leisure.

4. The substitution effect and the income effect work in opposite directions so that the labor supply curve can either be upward-sloping, vertical, downward-sloping, or backward-bending.

5. Long-term movements in wages are closely correlated with changes in labor productivity. Labor productivity difference also explains some of the differences in wages paid to different people.

6. Productivity does not explain everything. Compensating wage differentials and discrimination are other reasons wages differ.

7. Labor contracts—whether explicit or implicit—govern the long-term relationship between firms and workers.

8. Contracts explain why workers' hourly wages do not adjust for every up and down in marginal productivity.

9. When worker incentives or motivation are a problem, piece rates and deferred compensation can be used as alternative forms of labor contracts.

10. Union workers earn more than nonunion workers who have the same skills. This occurs either because unions increase labor productivity or because they restrict the supply of workers in an industry.

KEY TERMS

fringe benefits	backward-bending labor supply curve	piece-rate system
wage	human capital	deferred payment contracts
real wage	on-the-job training	efficiency wage
labor market	labor market equilibrium	labor unions
labor demand	labor productivity	industrial unions
labor supply	compensating wage differentials	craft unions
derived demand	minimum wage legislation	monopsony
marginal revenue product of labor	long-term employment contracts	bilateral monopoly

QUESTIONS FOR REVIEW

1. Are fringe benefits a significant part of average pay in the United States?

2. Why is labor demand a derived demand?

3. What is the marginal revenue product, and why must it equal the wage if a firm is maximizing profits?

4. Why is the demand for labor downward-sloping?

5. Why do the substitution effect and the income effect in labor supply work in opposite directions?

6. How can compensating wage differentials explain why workers with the same skills are paid different amounts?

7. Why does discrimination against women and minorities reduce their wage, and why does competition reduce the effects of discrimination?

8. Why are efficiency wages more common when workers can't be monitored?

9. Why are piece rates sometimes used instead of weekly wages?

10. What is the difference between the two main views of labor unions?

PROBLEMS

1. Ceres, Inc., is a 300-acre profit-maximizing farm that produces wheat. The wheat industry is competitive, and there are many other wheat firms in the industry like Ceres. The price of wheat is $5 per bushel. The following table shows wheat production per year and the number of workers employed at Ceres during the year.

Number of Workers	Wheat Production (bushels per year)
1	20,000
2	35,000
3	42,000
4	45,000
5	47,000
6	48,000

a) Draw to scale the demand curve for labor at Ceres. Label the axes, show the units, and draw the demand curve as accurately as possible.

b) If the wage for wheat-farm workers is $14,000 per year, how many workers will Ceres employ? Explain your answer.

c) Assume that labor with a wage rate of $14,000 per year is the only variable factor of production and that land with an annual rental rate of $100 per acre is the only fixed factor. How much profit is Ceres earning at this price, wage, and rent?

d) Will the price of wheat rise or fall from $5 per bushel in the long run as firms enter or exit the wheat industry? Explain your answer by sketching the industry supply and demand curves for wheat and the marginal cost and average total cost curves for a typical firm like Ceres.

2. Real wages grew less rapidly in the U. S. after the mid-1970s than before. Using the supply and demand model for labor, explain this development. Name one other factor that may have caused this development and explain its effect.

3. Draw a typical supply and demand for labor diagram to represent the market for doctors. Suppose a government regulation does not allow the wage rate for this profession to go as high as the market-determined wage rate. Depict this in your diagram. Will there be a shortage or surplus of doctors at that wage rate? How might a private hospital or health maintenance organization react with regard to fringe benefits to counteract the impact of this regulation?

4. Use the definition for the demand for labor as the marginal revenue product to argue that the increasing wage dispersion between skilled and unskilled workers could come from (1) increases in the relative productivity of skilled workers, and (2) increases in the demand for the products produced by skilled workers.

5. Given your answer to problem 4, what policies can the government pursue to correct this wage dispersion by affecting labor demand? What kinds of policies would the government pursue if it wanted to affect the supply of labor to correct excessive wage dispersion?

6. People often complain that sanitation workers are overpaid based on their level of education. Use the idea of compensating differentials to explain why those wages are relatively high.

7. Lincoln Electric Company, a well-known U.S. manufacturer of arc welding and electrical equipment, uses the following compensation policies: wages based on piece rates for factory jobs, year-end bonuses based on the profitability of the company and employees' merit ratings, and guaranteed employment for all workers. Explain the possible effectiveness of this scheme, using the information on labor contracts in the text.

8. Analyze the labor supply schedules for Ann and Margaret below:
a) Draw the labor supply schedules for the two women.
b) Which of these women probably has a higher level of education? Why?
c) For whom is the elasticity of supply of labor higher? What does this mean?
d) At what point does the income effect begin to outweigh the substitution effect for Margaret?

9. A competitive firm has the following production function. Calculate the marginal product of labor and draw the marginal revenue product schedule when the market price of the good it produces equals $10 per ton.

Quantity of Labor	Tons of Output
1	10
2	18
3	25
4	30
5	34
6	37
7	38

a) If the wage is $40, how many workers will the firm hire? Explain the reasoning behind the firm's decision.
b) If the price of the product this firm produces goes up to $15 per ton, how many workers will the firm hire? (Assume the market wage stays the same.) Why does it make sense for the firm to hire more workers?

10. Suppose a firm with some market power faces a downward-sloping demand curve for the product it produces. Given the following information on demand, fill in the table below and draw the resulting demand curve for labor.

Problem 8

	Ann		Margaret	
	Wage Rate per Hour	Hours Worked per Week	Wage Rate per Hour	Hours Worked per Week
	$5	10	$8	0
	$6	20	$10	20
	$7	30	$12	30
	$8	40	$14	40
	$9	45	$16	50
	$10	50	$18	60
	$11	55	$20	55

Problem 10

Quantity of Labor	Quantity of Output	Marginal Product	Price of Output	Total Revenue	Marginal Revenue	Marginal Revenue Product
2	10	_____	8.0	_____	_____	_____
4	18	_____	7.0	_____	_____	_____
6	24	_____	6.0	_____	_____	_____
8	28	_____	5.0	_____	_____	_____
10	30	_____	4.5	_____	_____	_____

Capital Markets

Now we complete our analysis of different types of markets by examining capital markets, including the stock market, perhaps the most actively watched and exciting market in the world. By one popular measure—the Dow Jones Industrial Index—the average price of stocks rose nearly 10 times during the 1980s and 1990s, from about 800 in 1982 to over 8,000 in 1997. But stock prices did not rise much at all in the 1970s, and in some years stock prices have fallen sharply.

In this chapter we take a broad look at capital markets. We examine markets in physical capital—such as the airplanes Federal Express might rent or buy—and markets in financial capital—such as the stocks or bonds Federal Express might issue to get funds to purchase new airplanes. Although physical capital and financial capital are conceptually distinct, they are closely connected. As the Federal Express example suggests, firms may obtain financial capital in order to purchase physical capital.

To examine the operation of capital markets we will use some of the basic tools of economics, including the supply and demand model and the idea of marginal revenue product introduced in the previous chapter. However, because prices in capital markets are very volatile and uncertain, to study these markets we need to consider risk and uncertainty. Moreover, capital raises important ownership and responsibility issues about who actually controls corporations—the owners or the managers—that we also need to consider.

We show in this chapter that a firm's demand for physical capital can be analyzed in much the same way that we analyzed the demand for labor in the previous chapter. We then go on to consider markets in financial capital, including the stock and bond markets. A major objective of this chapter is to give you the vocabulary and know-how to read key financial pages of the *Wall Street Journal* and other newspapers.

CAPITAL MARKET TERMINOLOGY

Some basic terminology about physical and financial capital is useful in studying capital markets.

Physical Capital

Physical capital refers to all the machines, factories, computers, trucks, cultivated farmland, and other physical resources held by organizations or individuals and used in the production of goods or services. In previous chapters we simply used the term *capital* when referring to "physical capital" because we were not contrasting it with financial capital. Firms combine physical capital with labor inputs to produce goods and services. Businesses obtain physical capital either by building it, buying it, or renting it. For example, McDonald's might hire a construction firm to build a new facility near a highway, buy an old Burger King and renovate it, or rent a storefront in a shopping center.

Not all physical capital is used by firms. Residential housing—single-family homes, apartments, trailers—is also a form of physical capital. It provides productive services in the form of living space that people can enjoy year after year. Government-owned roads, schools, and military equipment are also physical capital. It is useful to think of government capital as helping to produce services, whether transportation services, educational services, or national security.

An important characteristic of physical capital is that it lasts for a number of years. However, it does not remain in new condition permanently. Rather, it depreciates each year. **Depreciation** is the gradual decline in the productive usefulness of capital. Trucks, trailers, and even buildings wear out and must eventually be either replaced or refurbished.

depreciation: the decrease in an asset's value over time; for capital, it is the amount by which physical capital wears out over a given period of time.

Financial Capital

When a firm starts a new business, it needs to obtain funds. These funds are called **financial capital.** The new firm needs these funds to purchase, rent, or build physical capital. It may also need funds to pay workers for a while until the firm starts to earn a profit. Older existing firms also need to obtain funds to expand or to buy physical capital.

Firms can obtain financial capital in two different ways: by issuing debt and by issuing equity. Examples of debt are bank loans and bonds. Loans and bonds are a type of contract called a **debt contract** in which the lender agrees to provide funds today in exchange for a promise that the borrower will pay back the funds at a future date with interest. The amount of interest is determined by the *interest rate.* If the amount borrowed is $10,000 and is due in one year and the interest rate is 10 percent per year, then the borrower pays the lender $11,000 at the end of the year. The $11,000 includes the *principal* on the loan ($10,000) plus the *interest payment* ($1,000 = .1 times $10,000). Firms typically obtain loans from banks but larger firms also issue *corporate bonds.*

Firms are not the only issuers of debt. Most people who buy a house get a *mortgage,* which is a loan of funds to purchase real estate. In addition, many people get loans from banks to buy cars and consumer appliances. The biggest single

financial capital: funds used to purchase, rent, or build physical capital.

debt contract: a contract in which a lender agrees to provide funds today in exchange for a promise from the borrower, who will repay that amount plus interest at some point in the future.

issuer of debt in the United States is the federal government. The federal government borrows funds by selling *government bonds.*

Firms also obtain financial capital by issuing *stock,* or shares of ownership in the firm. Shares of ownership are a type of contract called an **equity contract.** In contrast to a debt contract, where the payment by the firm (the interest payment) does not depend on the profits of the firm, in an equity contract the payment by the firm does depend on the firm's profits. Sometimes the payment is a *dividend,* but shareholders can also benefit if the firm increases in value and their shares are worth more when they are sold.

Once bonds or stock have been issued, they can be exchanged or traded. There are highly organized financial markets for trading stocks and bonds. The government and corporate bond markets are located in New York City, London, Tokyo, and other large financial centers. The stock markets include the New York Stock Exchange, the American Stock Exchange, several regional stock exchanges in the United States, and many stock exchanges in other countries.

Having defined some key terms, we now proceed to discuss both types of capital markets. We begin with markets for physical capital.

equity contract: shares of ownership in a firm in which payments to the owners of the shares depend on the firm's profits.

Review

▶ Physical capital and financial capital are distinct but closely related. To expand their physical capital firms need to raise financial capital in some way.

▶ Debt contracts, such as bonds or loans, specify interest payments that do not depend on the profits

of the firm. Equity contracts, such as stocks, pay dividends that do depend on the profits of the firm.

▶ The bonds or stocks that firms issue can be traded. Organized markets for trading bonds and stocks are found in all the world's financial centers.

MARKETS FOR PHYSICAL CAPITAL

The demand for physical capital is a relationship between the quantity of capital demanded by firms and the price of this capital. The demand for capital is a *derived demand* in the same sense that the demand for labor is a derived demand; that is, the demand for capital derives from the goods and services that firms produce with capital. In this section we show that just as the quantity of labor the firm employs depends on the marginal revenue product of labor, the quantity of capital the firm employs depends on the marginal revenue product of capital.

Rental Markets

rental price of capital: the amount that a rental company charges for the use of capital equipment for a specified period of time.

The firm's capital decision is best understood if we first assume that the firm *rents* capital in a competitive rental market. In fact, it is common for firms to rent capital; for many types of equipment there is a rental market in which many rental firms specialize in renting the equipment to other firms. For example, a construction firm could rent a dump truck, a clothing store could rent a storefront at a mall, or an airline could lease an airplane. The price in the rental market is called the **rental price**

of capital. It is the amount a rental firm charges for the use of capital equipment for a specified period of time, such as a month.

Consider a hypothetical construction company, called Perma, deciding whether to rent a dump truck from a rental company called A-1 Rental. To show how much capital a firm like Perma would rent we need to consider the effect of this capital on the firm's profits. The marginal revenue product of capital can be used to assess this effect on profits. The **marginal revenue product of capital** is defined as the change in total revenue as the firm increases its capital by one unit. We assume that the marginal revenue product of capital declines as more capital is employed at the firm. For example, suppose the marginal revenue product of capital is $3,000 as capital rises from zero trucks to 1 truck, $1,500 as capital rises from 1 truck to 2 trucks, and $500 as capital rises from 2 trucks to 3 trucks.

Suppose the rental price of a dump truck is $1,000 a month. This is what A-1 Rental charges, and all other rental firms in the area charge essentially the same price. Because it is a competitive rental market, neither A-1 Rental nor Perma have enough market power to affect the rental price. How many dump trucks would the firm, Perma, use? With the marginal product of capital from 1 dump truck equal to $3,000 a month, the firm will employ at least 1 dump truck. In other words, if the firm's total revenue increases by $3,000 and the rental price is $1,000 for the truck, then it makes sense to rent the dump truck. With the marginal revenue product of capital from a second dump truck equal to $1,500, the firm will employ a second dump truck; by doing so, it can increase its profits by $500. However, with the marginal revenue product of capital from a third dump truck equal to only $500, the firm will lower its profits by renting a third dump truck. Hence, if the rental price of the dump truck is $1,000, the firm will employ exactly 2 dump trucks. The firm rents the largest amount of capital for which the marginal revenue product of capital is greater than the rental price; if fractional units of capital were possible, then the firm would keep renting more capital until *the marginal revenue product of capital exactly equals the rental price.*

Rental Market Advertising
Capital used by firms can frequently be rented, as illustrated by this advertisement for computers. The rental price is determined by supply and demand in the rental market.

marginal revenue product of capital: the change in total revenue due to a one-unit increase in capital.

The Demand Curve for Capital

To derive the demand curve for capital, we must determine the quantity of capital demanded by the firm as the rental price of capital changes. For example, if the rental price of dump trucks declines to $400, then the quantity of dump trucks demanded by the firm will increase; a third dump truck will be rented because the price is now below the marginal revenue product of capital. In other words, as the rental price of capital falls, the quantity of capital demanded increases. Similarly, as the rental price of capital rises, the quantity of capital demanded decreases.

Figure 13.1 illustrates this general principle. It shows the marginal revenue product of capital for any firm. As more capital is employed, the marginal revenue product declines. For profit maximization, the firm will rent capital to the point where the marginal revenue product of capital equals the rental price. Thus, as we lower the rental price, the quantity of capital demanded increases. In other words, the demand curve for capital is downward-sloping.

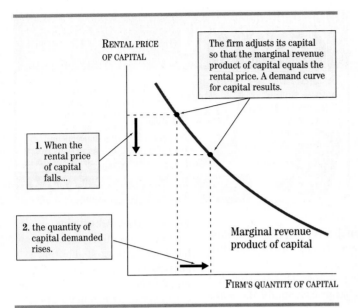

RENTAL PRICE
OF CAPITAL

The firm adjusts its capital so that the marginal revenue product of capital equals the rental price. A demand curve for capital results.

1. When the rental price of capital falls...

2. the quantity of capital demanded rises.

Marginal revenue product of capital

FIRM'S QUANTITY OF CAPITAL

FIGURE 13.1
Demand for Physical Capital by One Firm

A profit-maximizing firm chooses a quantity of capital that gives a marginal revenue product of capital equal to the rental price. Because the marginal revenue product of capital declines as more capital is used, a lower rental price of capital results in a larger quantity of capital demanded.

The demand curve for capital is determined by the marginal revenue product of capital. If the marginal revenue product changes, the demand curve for capital will shift. For example, if the marginal product of dump trucks rises, the demand for dump trucks by Perma will shift outward.

Demand for Factors of Production in General

Observe how similar this description of the demand for capital is to the description of the demand for labor in the previous chapter, in which we showed that the marginal revenue product of labor equals the wage. Here we showed that the marginal revenue product of capital equals the rental price. This same principle applies to any factor of production for which the market in that factor is competitive. *For any input to production, a profit-maximizing firm will choose a quantity of that input such that the marginal revenue product equals the price of that input.*

The Market Demand and Supply

The market demand for physical capital is found by adding up the demand for physical capital by many firms. Figure 13.2 shows such a market demand curve.

On the same diagram, we show the market supply curve. It is the sum of the supply curves for all the firms in the industry providing capital for rent, such as A-1 Rental. The equilibrium rental price and the equilibrium quantity of capital rented are shown in the diagram.

The supply and demand model for capital illustrated in Figure 13.2 can be used to predict the effects of tax changes or other changes in the capital market in much the same way as any other supply and demand model. For example, if the government places a tax on construction firms like Perma proportional to the quantity of trucks they rent, then the marginal revenue product of capital will decline and the demand curve for capital will shift to the left. This will lower the equilibrium rental price received by A-1 and reduce the quantity of capital rented. Alternatively, a government subsidy on the rental of capital by construction firms would shift the demand curve for capital to the right and increase the quantity of capital rented.

The Case of Fixed Supply: Economic Rents

An important special case of a market for physical capital occurs when the supply is completely fixed. Alfred Marshall gave the following famous example of physical capital with a completely fixed supply: "Let us suppose that a meteoric shower of a few thousand large stones harder than diamonds fell all in one place, so that they were all picked up at once, and no amount of search could find any more. These stones, able to cut every material, would revolutionize many branches of industry. . . ."[1]

1. Alfred Marshall, *Principles of Economics,* 8th ed. (New York: MacMillan, 1920), p. 415.

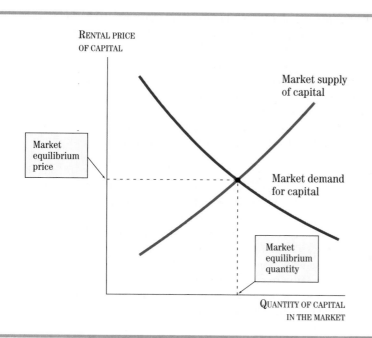

FIGURE 13.2
Market Supply and Demand for Physical Capital
The market demand for capital is the sum of the demands of the individual firms that use the equipment. The market supply is the sum of the supplies at the individual firms that provide the equipment. Market equilibrium occurs where the quantity of capital demanded equals the quantity of capital supplied.

The quantity of Marshall's stones cannot be increased or decreased regardless of the price of the stones. In other words, the supply curve for Marshall's stones is perfectly vertical, or perfectly inelastic, as shown in Figure 13.3.

Figure 13.3 shows what happens when there is a shift in demand for capital that is in fixed supply, such as Marshall's stones. A change in demand will change

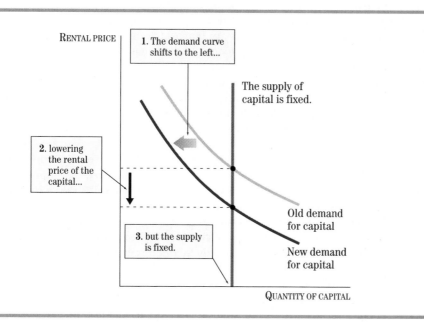

FIGURE 13.3
The Case of a Fixed Supply of Capital
When the supply of capital is perfectly inelastic, a shift in demand changes the rental price but not the quantity supplied. Marshall's stones are a hypothetical example of capital with a perfectly inelastic supply.

economic rent: the price of something that has a fixed supply.

the price, but will not change the quantity. Demand completely determines the price in this case because the quantity supplied cannot change.

Economists have a special terminology for the price in this circumstance: **Economic rent** is the price of anything that has a fixed supply. Economic rent is also sometimes called *pure rent.* Economic rent is a significant concept in economics precisely because the quantity supplied does not depend on the price. Thus, a tax on economic rents would not change the amount supplied; it would not affect economic efficiency or cause a deadweight loss. For example, if the government passed a tax (even a 99.9 percent tax) on the rental payments charged by the lucky owners of Marshall's stones, there would be no change in the quantity of stones supplied.

Marshall's stones are of course a hypothetical example. In practice, certain types of land may come close to an item in fixed supply, but it is always possible to improve land or clear land and thereby change its supply to some degree. The perfectly inelastic supply of Marshall's stones or the near perfectly inelastic supply of certain types of land is in sharp contrast to the higher elasticity of the supply of most capital goods. The supply of dump trucks, apartment buildings, and other types of capital is sensitive to changes in the price. Increases in the price provide an incentive to increase the quantity supplied, and decreases in the price provide an incentive to decrease the quantity supplied. In reality, therefore, taxes on capital would be expected to change the quantity of capital supplied.

The Ownership of Physical Capital

Rental markets for capital are common, but they are not the only way that firms obtain capital. The same construction firm that rents dump trucks might own the warehouse where it stores its building materials and the office where it keeps its books and meets prospective customers. Although there are legal and tax differences between renting and ownership, the economic principles are similar. In fact, even though owners of physical capital do not pay a rental price, economic considerations indicate that they pay an *implicit* rental price.

When a firm buys equipment, it must either use funds that it could have put in a bank, where they would earn interest, or borrow the funds. If it borrows the funds, the monthly interest payment on the loan is like a rental payment. If it uses its own funds, the interest it would have received at the bank is an opportunity cost and is considered to be similar to a rental payment. In addition to these payments, the firm that owns the equipment must factor in the wear and tear, or depreciation, on the equipment. The amount by which the firm's equipment deteriorates is also a cost.

implicit rental price: the interest payments on the funds borrowed to buy the capital plus the depreciation of the capital over a given period of time.

In sum, the **implicit rental price** of capital for a year equals the interest payments for the year plus the amount of depreciation during the year. For example, suppose the interest rate is 10 percent, the purchase price of a dump truck is $40,000, and the dump truck depreciates $8,000 per year. Then the implicit rental price is $12,000 per year (.10 times $40,000, plus $8,000), or $1,000 a month, the same as the rental price in our dump truck example. It is important to note that the implicit rental price depends on the interest rate. The higher the interest rate, the higher the interest payments during the year and thus the higher the implicit rental price. When the interest rate rises, the implicit rental price rises. When interest rates fall, the implicit rental price falls.

The concept of the implicit rental price makes the firm's decision to buy a dump truck, or any other piece of capital, analogous to the decision to rent. The demand curve looks the same as in Figure 13.1, except that it is the implicit rental price rather than the actual rental price that is on the vertical axis.

A Firm's Decision about Capital, Labor, and Output

There is an important link among the decisions about the quantity of *output* the firm produces (the focus of Chapters 8 and 9), the quantity of *labor* the firm employs (the focus of Chapter 12), and the quantity of *capital* the firm uses (the focus of this chapter). We focused on each of these decisions separately because the markets for the output of goods and services, for labor, and for capital are so different. But for a given firm the decisions are interrelated because the quantity of output depends on the quantity of labor and capital inputs as described by the firm's production function. The three decisions are all part of one profit-maximizing decision. For firms that obtain labor and capital in competitive markets for labor and physical capital, the decision involves three interrelated profit-maximizing rules: *The marginal revenue product of labor equals the wage; the marginal revenue product of capital equals the rental price;* and *the marginal revenue equals marginal cost.* Coordinating these decisions in a large organization may be difficult, and some firms are better at it than others, but any firm, no matter how small, must make decisions about producing output, employing workers, and using capital. A firm's decision to employ capital may involve a substitution of capital for labor. For example, if the rental price of dump trucks falls very low and the price of labor increases, then the firm will try to use more dump trucks and fewer workers.

Review

▶ The demand for physical capital at a firm is a derived demand.

▶ In a rental market when the rental price goes up, the quantity of capital demanded goes down because the marginal revenue product of capital curve slopes down.

▶ If capital is purchased rather than rented, then the rental price is replaced by the implicit rental price. The implicit rental price for a year is equal to the yearly interest payment on the loan to buy the equipment plus the amount of depreciation on the equipment during the year.

FINANCIAL CAPITAL

Having seen how markets for physical capital work, let us turn to the examination of markets in financial capital: stocks and bonds. Stocks and bonds are also called securities. Once firms issue stocks or bonds, these securities can be traded on the financial markets. Their prices are determined by the actions of buyers and sellers, like prices in any other market.

Stock Prices and Returns

The price of stocks for most large firms can be found in many daily newspapers. For example, the top part of Figure 13.4 shows the listing for the price of Pennzoil stock, for Friday, July 1, 1994. For another example, you may want to look up a similar listing in today's newspaper. The annual **return** from holding a stock is defined as the *dividend* plus the *capital gain* during the year. The dividend, you will

return: the income received from the ownership of an asset; for a stock, the return is the dividend plus the capital gain.

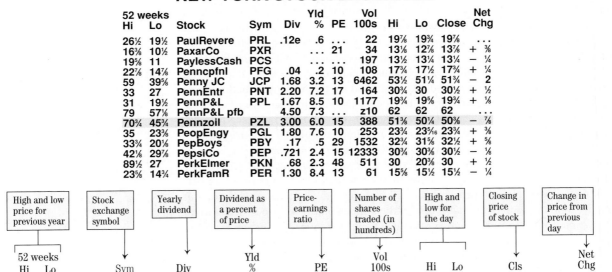

NEW YORK STOCK EXCHANGE

52 weeks Hi	Lo	Stock	Sym	Div	Yld %	PE	Vol 100s	Hi	Lo	Close	Net Chg
26½	19½	PaulRevere	PRL	.12e	.6	...	22	19⅞	19¾	19⅞	...
16¾	10½	PaxarCo	PXR	...	...	21	34	13⅛	12⅞	13¾	+ ⅜
19⅝	11	PaylessCash	PCS	...	...	...	197	13½	13¼	13¼	− ¼
22⅞	14⅞	Penncpfnl	PFG	.04	.2	10	108	17¾	17½	17¾	+ ¼
59	39⅝	Penny JC	JCP	1.68	3.2	13	6462	53½	51¼	51¾	− 2
33	27	PennEntr	PNT	2.20	7.2	17	164	30¾	30	30½	+ ½
31	19½	PennP&L	PPL	1.67	8.5	10	1177	19¾	19⅝	19¾	+ ⅛
79	57½	PennP&L pfb		4.50	7.3	...	z10	62	62	62	...
70¾	45¾	Pennzoil	PZL	3.00	6.0	15	388	51⅜	50¼	50⅜	− ⅞
35	23⅜	PeopEngy	PGL	1.80	7.6	10	253	23¾	23⁵⁄₁₆	23¾	+ ⅜
33¾	20⅛	PepBoys	PBY	.17	.5	29	1532	32¾	31⅝	32½	+ ⅝
42⅛	29⅞	PepsiCo	PEP	.72‡	2.4	15	12333	30¾	30⅜	30½	− ⅛
89½	27	PerkElmer	PKN	.68	2.3	48	511	30	20⅜	30	+ ½
23⅝	14¾	PerkFamR	PER	1.30	8.4	13	61	15⅝	15½	15½	− ¼

High and low price for previous year	Stock exchange symbol	Yearly dividend	Dividend as a percent of price	Price-earnings ratio	Number of shares traded (in hundreds)	High and low for the day	Closing price of stock	Change in price from previous day
52 weeks Hi Lo	Sym	Div	Yld %	PE	Vol 100s	Hi Lo	Cls	Net Chg
70³/4 45³/4 Pennzoil PZL		3.00	6.0	15	388	51³/8 50¹/4	50³/8	-7/8

NEW YORK EXCHANGE BONDS

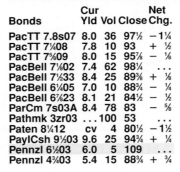

Bonds	Cur Yld	Vol	Close	Net Chg.
PacTT 7.8s07	8.0	36	97½	− 1¼
PacTT 7¼08	7.8	10	93	+ ½
PacTT 7⅝09	8.0	15	95⅝	− ⅛
PacBell 7⅜02	7.4	62	98¼	...
PacBell 7½33	8.4	25	89⅜	+ ⅛
PacBell 6¼05	7.0	10	88¾	− ¼
PacBell 6⅞23	8.1	21	84½	− ½
ParCm 7s03A	8.4	78	83	− ⅝
Pathmk 3zr03	...	100	53	...
Paten 8¼12	cv	4	80½	− 1½
PaylCsh 9⅛03	9.6	25	94¾	+ ¼
Pennzl 6½03	6.0	5	109	...
Pennzl 4¾03	5.4	15	88¾	+ ¾

Coupon rate	Year bond matures (2003)	Yield to maturity	Number of bonds traded	Closing price	Change in price from previous day
Rate	Maturity	Yld	Vol	Close	Net Chg
Pennzl 6½	03	6.0	5	109	—

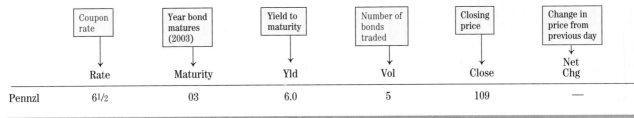

FIGURE 13.4
Stocks versus Bonds

The newspaper listings show how companies such as Pennzoil issue both stocks and bonds. The firm pays interest on the bonds and dividends on the stock. Dividends can be, and are, adjusted more frequently than interest payments, which are fixed as part of the bond agreement.

Source: Reprinted by permission of the *Wall Street Journal,* © 1994 Dow Jones & Company, Inc. All rights reserved worldwide.

recall, is the amount the firm pays out to the owners of the stock each year. The **capital gain** during the year is the increase in the price of the share during the year. A **capital loss** is a negative capital gain: a decrease in the price. The **rate of return** is the return stated as a percent of the price of the share.

The **dividend yield** is defined as the dividend stated as a percent of the price. For example, the dividend for Pennzoil in 1994 was $3 per year. For Pennzoil the dividend yield is 6.0 percent; .060 equals $3 divided by $50⅜, the closing price at the end of the day on July 1. The rate of return equals the percentage capital gain plus the dividend yield. For example, if the price of Pennzoil stock went from $50⅜ to $55⅜ in a year, then the percentage capital gain would be $5 divided by $50⅜, or about 10.0 percent. Combined with a dividend yield of 6.0 percent, this would be a rate of return of 16.0 percent.

Earnings is another word for the accounting profits of a firm. Firms do not pay out all of their profits as dividends; some of the profits are retained and invested in physical capital or research. Stock tables also list the **price-earnings ratio:** the price of the stock divided by the annual earnings per share. Observe in Figure 13.4 that the price-earnings ratio is 15 for Pennzoil. With a price of the stock of $50⅜, this means that earnings for the year were $3.36 per share (50.375/3.36 = 15). A firm's earnings ultimately influence the return on stock, so the price-earnings ratio, or its inverse, which is ⅟₁₅, or .067, for Pennzoil, is closely watched.

capital gain: the increase in the value of an asset through an increase in its price.

capital loss: the decrease in the value of an asset through a decrease in its price.

rate of return: the return on an asset stated as a percentage of the price of the asset.

dividend yield: the dividend stated as a percentage of the price of the stock.

earnings: accounting profits of a firm.

price-earnings ratio: the price of a stock divided by its annual earnings per share.

Bond Prices and Returns

Bond prices for both corporate and government bonds can also be found in the financial pages of the newspaper. The lower part of Figure 13.4 shows a newspaper table describing the prices on corporate bonds. Observe that one of the bonds was issued by Pennzoil, illustrating how firms issue both debt and equity.

Figure 13.5 shows newspaper reports on two different dates for bonds issued by the U.S. government. The bond reports displayed in Figures 13.4 and 13.5 illustrate quite a bit about how bonds and bond markets work.

Face Value, Maturity, Coupon, and Yield

There are four key characteristics of a bond: *coupon, maturity date, face value,* and *yield.* The **coupon** is the fixed amount that the borrower—in the case of Figure 13.5, the government—agrees to pay to the bondholder each year. The **maturity date** is the time when the coupon payments end and the principal is paid back. The **face value** is the amount of principal that will be paid back when the bond matures. Observe that the bond highlighted in Figure 13.5 has a maturity date of November 2021 and a coupon equal to 8 percent of the face value of the bond. That is, 8 percent, or $8 a year on a bond with a face value of $100, will be paid until 2021, and in November 2021, the $100 face value will be paid back. (The coupon is called a "rate" in Figures 13.4 and 13.5 because it is measured as a percent of the face value.)

The government issues bonds several times each year. The most recently issued 30-year government bond, which is called the "benchmark" bond, is always the focus of much press comment, as the quote in the margin on the next page exemplifies.

Once bonds are issued by the government, they can be sold or bought in the bond market. In the bond market, there are bond traders who make a living buying and selling bonds. The bond traders will *bid* a certain price at which they buy and *ask* a certain price at which they sell, just as in other markets with buyers and

coupon: the fixed amount that a borrower agrees to pay to the bond-holder each year.

maturity date: the date when the principal on a loan is paid back.

face value: the principal that will be paid back when a bond matures.

TREASURY BONDS, NOTES & BILLS

Monday, April 14, 1997   Wednesday, August 11, 1993

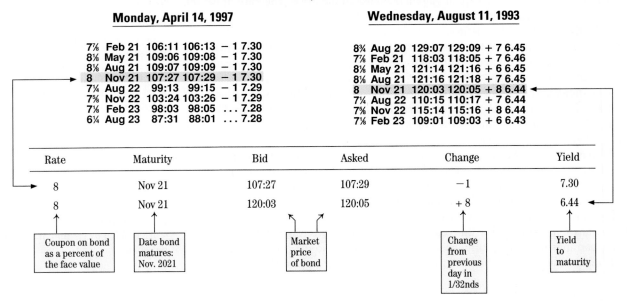

Rate	Maturity	Bid	Asked	Change	Yield
8	Nov 21	107:27	107:29	−1	7.30
8	Nov 21	120:03	120:05	+8	6.44

| Coupon on bond as a percent of the face value | Date bond matures: Nov. 2021 | Market price of bond | Change from previous day in 1/32nds | Yield to maturity |

FIGURE 13.5
Bond Prices and Yields

These two government bond tables at two different dates illustrate how bond prices and yields move in opposite directions. Between August 11, 1993, and April 14, 1997, the price of the highlighted bond fell from about $120 to about $107 while the yield rose from 6.44 to 7.30. The percentage price fall is almost the same as the percentage interest rate rise.

Source: Reprinted by permission of the *Wall Street Journal,* © 1997 Dow Jones & Company, Inc. All rights reserved worldwide.

yield: the annual rate of return on a bond if the bond were held to maturity.

A Typical Newspaper Discussion of Bond Yields

"The price of the benchmark 30-year Treasury bond rose less than ⅛ point, or less than $1.25 for a bond with $1,000 face value, to 84½₂. Its yield, which moves in the opposite direction of its price, dropped to 7.60% from 7.61% on Thursday."

Source: Thomas T. Vogel, Jr., "Bond Yield, Like Heat, Keeps Rising," *Wall Street Journal,* July 5, 1994, p. C17.

sellers such as the double-auction market described in Chapter 7. The bid price is slightly lower than the ask price, which enables the bond traders to earn a profit, buying at a slightly lower price than the price at which they sell. For example, on April 14, 1997, the bid price on the bond in Figure 13.5 was $107 27/32 and the ask price was $107 29/32. (Note how bond prices are rounded to the nearest 32nd of a dollar.)

The **yield,** or yield to maturity, is defined as the annual rate of return on the bond if the bond were held to maturity. When people refer to the current interest rate on bonds, they are referring to the yield on the bond. Observe that the yield on the highlighted bond in Figure 13.5 was 7.30 percent on April 14, 1997, slightly below the 8 percent coupon.

Bond Prices and Bond Yields

There is an inverse, or negative, relationship between the yield and the price. Why should this be? Suppose you just bought a 1-year bond for $100 that says the gov-

•

One-year maturity:	$P = \dfrac{R}{1 + i} + \dfrac{F}{1 + i}$	**TABLE 13.1**
		Bond Price Formula
Two-year maturity:	$P = \dfrac{R}{1 + i} + \dfrac{R}{(1 + i)^2} + \dfrac{F}{(1 + i)^2}$	
Three-year maturity:	$P = \dfrac{R}{1 + i} + \dfrac{R}{(1 + i)^2} + \dfrac{R}{(1 + i)^3} + \dfrac{F}{(1 + i)^3}$	
For very long term:	$P = \dfrac{R}{i}$	

P = price of bond
R = coupon
F = face value
i = yield

ernment will pay 5 percent of the face value, or $5, plus $100 at the end of the 1-year period. Now suppose that just after you bought the bond, interest rates on bank deposits suddenly jump to 10 percent. Your bond says you earn 5 percent per year, so if you hold it for the entire year, your rate of return is less than you could get in a bank deposit. Suddenly the bond looks much less attractive. You would probably want to sell it, but everyone else knows the bond is less attractive, also. You would not be able to get $100 for the bond. The price would decline until the rate of return on the bond just equaled the interest rate at the bank. For example, if the price fell to $95.45, then the payment of $105 at the end of the year would result in a 10 percent rate of return [that is, $.10 = (105 - 95.45)/95.45$]. In other words, the yield on the bond would rise until it equaled 10 percent rather than 5 percent.

Based on these considerations, there is a formula that gives the relationship between the price and the yield for bonds of any maturity. Let P be the price of the bond. Let R be the coupon. Let F be the face value. Let i be the yield. The formula relating to the price and the yield is indicated in the case of a 1-year bond in the first row of Table 13.1.

For a 1-year bond, a coupon payment of R is paid at the end of 1 year together with the face value of the bond. The price P is what you would be willing to pay *now, in the present,* for these future payments. It is the *present discounted value* of the coupon payment plus the face value at the end of the year. (The appendix at the end of this chapter discusses the present discounted value formula in greater detail.) By looking at the formula in the first row of Table 13.1, you can see the negative relationship between the price (P) of the bond and the yield (i) on the bond. The higher the yield, the lower the price; and conversely, the lower the yield, the higher the price.

A 2-year maturity bond is similar. You get R at the end of the first year and R plus the face value at the end of the second year. Now you want to divide the first year payment by $1 + i$ and the second year by $(1 + i)^2$. The formula still shows the inverse relationship between the yield and the price. A bond with a 3-year or higher maturity is similar. Computers do the calculation for the news reports, so even 30-year bond yields can easily be found from their price.

There is a convenient and simple approximation method for determining the price or yield on bonds with very long maturity dates. It says the price is equal to the coupon divided by the yield: $P = R/i$. This is the easiest way to remember the inverse relationship between the price and the yield. It is a close approximation for the long-term bonds like the 30-year bond.

RISK VERSUS RETURN

The prices of individual stocks traded in the financial markets are volatile. The price of Pennzoil, for example, fluctuated between about $85 and $45 a share in 1996 and 1997. A change in price of 10 or 20 percent in one day is not uncommon. Because of such variability, buying stocks is a risky activity. The price of bonds can also change by a large amount. For example, from mid-1996 to mid-1997, the price of government bonds rose by nearly 20 percent, but from mid-1993 to mid-1994, the price of government bonds *fell* by nearly 20 percent! Thus, government bonds are also a risky investment.

In this section we show that the riskiness of stocks and bonds affects their return. To do so we first examine how individuals behave when they face risk.

Behavior under Uncertainty

Most people do not like uncertainty. They are *risk averse* in most of their activities. Given a choice between two jobs that pay the same wage, most people will be averse to choosing the riskier job where there is a good chance of being laid off. Similarly, given a choice between two investments that pay the same return, people will choose the less risky one.

Let us examine this idea of risk aversion further. To be more precise, suppose that Melissa has a choice between the two alternatives shown in Table 13.2. She must decide what to do with her life savings of $10,000 for the next year. At the end of the year, she plans to buy a house, and she will need some money for a down payment. She can put her $10,000 in a bank account, where the interest rate is 5 percent, or she can buy $10,000 worth of a stock that pays a dividend of 5 percent and either a capital gain or loss. In the bank, the value of her savings is safe, but if

TABLE 13.2
Two Options: Different Risks, Same Expected Return

Low-Risk Option	High-Risk Option
A bank deposit with	A corporate stock with
5 percent interest	5 percent dividend and either a
	30 percent price decline or a 30 percent price increase

she buys the stock, there is a 50 percent chance that the price of the stock will fall by 30 percent and a 50 percent chance that the price of the stock will rise by 30 percent. In other words, the risky stock will leave Melissa with the possibility of a return of −$2,500 (a loss) or a return of $3,500 (a gain). (Here's the calculation: $10,000 × .05 − $10,000 × .30 = −$2,500 and $10,000 × .05 + $10,000 × .30 = $3,500.) The bank account leaves her with a guaranteed $500 return.

If Melissa were a risk-averse person, she would choose the less risky of these two options. It is easy to see that Melissa might be miserable in the case of a loss, so she would want to avoid it completely and take the safe option. This example illustrates the fundamental difference between more risky and less risky investments. Because the prices of stocks fluctuate, they are riskier than bank accounts when held for short periods like a year.

Both the options in Table 13.2 have the same **expected return.** The expected return on an investment weighs the different gains or losses according to how probable they are. In the case of the safe bank account, there is a 100 percent chance that the return is $500, so the expected return is $500. In the case of the stock, the expected return would be −$2,500 times the probability of this loss (1/2) plus $3,500 times the probability of this gain (also 1/2). Thus, the expected return is $500 (−2,500/2 + 3,500/2 = −1,250 + 1,750 = 500), the same as the return in the bank account.

expected return: the return on an uncertain investment calculated by weighting the gains or losses by the probability that they will occur.

The expected return is one way to measure how attractive an investment is. The word *expected* might appear misleading, since in the risky option $500 is not "expected" in the everyday use of the word. You do not expect $500; you expect either a loss of $2,500 or a gain of $3,500. If the term is confusing, think of the expected return as the average return that Melissa would get if she could take the second option year after year for many years. The loss of $2,500 and gain of $3,500 would average out to $500 per year after many years. (The term *expected return* has been carried over by economists and investment analysts from probability and statistics, where the term *expected value* is used to describe the mean, or the average, of a random variable.)

Although it is clear that Melissa would choose the less risky option of the two in Table 13.2, perhaps there is some compensation that Melissa would accept to offset her risk aversion. Although most people are averse to risk, they are willing to take on some risk if they are compensated for it. In the case of a risky financial investment, the compensation for higher risk could take the form of a higher expected return.

How could we make Melissa's expected return higher in the risky investment? Suppose Melissa had the choice between the same safe option in Table 13.2 and a high-risk stock that paid a dividend of 20 percent. This new choice is shown in Table 13.3; the difference is that the risky stock now offers a dividend of 20 percent, much

Low-Risk Option	High-Risk Option
A bank deposit with	A corporate stock with
5 percent interest	20 percent dividend
	and either a
	30 percent price decline or a
	30 percent price increase

TABLE 13.3
Two Options: Different Risks, Different Expected Returns

greater than the 5 percent in the first example and much greater than the 5 percent on the bank account. With the greater chance of a higher return on the stock, Melissa might be willing to buy the stock. Even in the worst situation, she loses just $1,000, which may still leave her with enough for the down payment on her new house. The expected return in the high-risk option is now $2,000, much greater than $500 on the bank account $(2,000 = -1,000/2 + 5,000/2 = -500 + 2,500)$.

In other words, Melissa would likely be willing to take on the risky investment. And if the 20 percent dividend in the example is not enough for her, some higher dividend (25 percent? 30 percent?) would be. This particular example illustrates the general point that risk-averse people are willing to take risks if they are paid for it.

Before we develop the implication of our analysis of individual behavior under uncertainty, we should pause to ask about the possibility that some people might be risk lovers rather than risk avoiders. The billions of dollars that are made in state lotteries in the United States and in private gambling casinos in Las Vegas, Atlantic City, and Monte Carlo indicate that some people enjoy risk. However, with few exceptions, most of the gambling in lotteries, slot machines, and even roulette wheels represents a small portion of the income or wealth of the gambler. Thus, you might be willing to spend $.50 or even $5 on lottery tickets or a slot machine for the chance of winning big, even if the odds are against you. Many people get enjoyment out of such wagers; but if the stakes are large compared to one's income or wealth, then few people want to play. For small sums, some people are risk lovers, but for large sums, virtually everybody becomes a risk avoider to some degree or another.

Risk and Rates of Return in Theory

What are the implications of our conclusion that investors will be willing to take risks if they are compensated with higher return on the stock or bond market? In the stock market the prices of individual stocks are determined by the bidding of buyers and sellers. Suppose a stock, QED, had a price that gave it the same expected rate of return as a bank account. Now QED, being a common stock, clearly has more risk than a bank account because its price could change. Hence, no risk-averse investor will want to buy QED. Just as Melissa will prefer to put her funds in a bank account in the example of Table 13.2 rather than into the risky option, investors will put their funds in a bank rather than buy QED. People owning shares of QED will sell and put their funds into a bank. With everybody wanting to sell QED and no one wanting to buy it, the price of QED will start to fall.

Now, the price and the expected rate of return are inversely related—recall that for a stock the rate of return is the return divided by the price. Thus, if the price falls and the dividend does not change, the rate of return will rise. This fall in the price will drive up the expected rate of return on QED. As the expected rate of return increases, it will eventually reach a point where it is high enough to compensate risk-averse investors. In other words, when the expected rate of return rises far enough above the bank account rate to compensate people for holding the risk, the price fall will stop. We will have an equilibrium where the expected rate of return on the stock is higher than the interest rate on the safe bank account. The higher rate of return will be associated with the higher risk.

Now some stocks are more risky than others. For example, the risk on the stock of small firms tends to be higher than the risk on the stock of larger firms, because small firms tend to be those that are just starting up. Not having yet proved them-

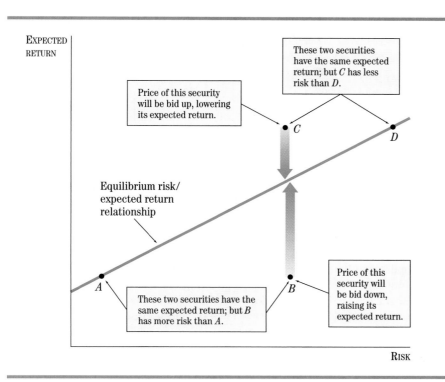

EXPECTED RETURN

These two securities have the same expected return; but C has less risk than D.

Price of this security will be bid up, lowering its expected return.

C

D

Equilibrium risk/ expected return relationship

A

These two securities have the same expected return; but B has more risk than A.

B

Price of this security will be bid down, raising its expected return.

RISK

FIGURE 13.6
The Equilibrium Relationship Between Return and Risk
More risky securities tend to have higher returns on average over the long term. For example, bank deposits are low risk and have a low expected return. Corporate stocks are higher risk—their price fluctuates—but on average over the long term have a higher return. The higher return is like a compensating wage differential in the labor market. It compensates those who take on more risk.

selves, small firms have a higher risk. People like Melissa will sell the more risky, smaller company stocks until the expected rate of return on those stocks is high enough compared with the less risky stocks of larger companies.

In equilibrium, we therefore expect to see a positive relationship between risk and the expected rate of return on securities. Securities with higher risks will have higher returns than securities with lower risks. Figure 13.6 shows the resulting **equilibrium risk-return relationship.**

There is probably no more important lesson about capital markets than this relationship. Individual investors should know it well. It says that to get a higher rate of return *on average over the long run* you have to accept a higher risk. Again, the market forces at work are the same as the ones that led to the compensating wage differentials in the labor market. In the labor market the higher wage in some jobs is the price that workers accept to take on the greater risk, or more generally, the less pleasant aspects of the job.

equilibrium risk-return relationship: the positive relationship between the risk and the expected rate of return on an asset derived from the fact that, on average, risk-averse investors who take on more risk must be compensated with a higher return.

Risk and Return in Reality

How well does this theoretical relationship work in reality? Very well. A tremendous amount of data over long periods of time on the financial markets support it. Table 13.4 presents data on the average return over 60 years for the four important types of securities we have mentioned in the theoretical discussion. The most risky of the four—the stocks of small firms—has the highest rate of return. Next highest in risk is the common stock of large firms. The least risky—short-term Treasury bills that are as safe as bank deposits—have the smallest rate of return. Long-term

●━━━━━━━━━━━━━━━━━━━━

TABLE 13.4
Average Rates of Return for
Different Risks, 1926–1993

	Average Rate of Return per Year (percent)	Risk (average size of price fluctuations)
U.S. Treasury bills	4	3
Long-term corporate bonds	6	8
Large-company stocks	12	21
Small-company stocks	18	35

Source: Data from Ibbotson Associates, *Stocks, Bonds, Bills, and Inflation,* 1994 yearbook, p. 31.

Note: These rates of return are not adjusted for inflation. The average rate of inflation was about 3 percent, which can be subtracted from each of the average returns to get the real return. The risk is the "standard deviation," a measure of volatility commonly used in probability and statistics.

bonds, where price changes can be large, have a rate of return greater than Treasury bills. Although the relative risks of these four types of securities may seem obvious, a measure of the differences in the sizes of their price volatility is shown in the second column and confirms the intuitive risk rankings.

In general, Table 13.4 is a striking confirmation of this fundamental result of financial markets that higher expected rates of return are associated with higher risk.

Diversification Reduces Risk

The familiar saying "Don't put all your eggs in one basket" is particularly relevant to stock markets. Rather than a basket of eggs you have a portfolio of stocks. A *portfolio* is a collection of stocks. Putting your funds into a portfolio of two or more stocks, whose prices do not always move in the same direction, rather than one stock, is called **portfolio diversification.** The risks from holding a single stock can be reduced significantly by putting half your funds in one stock and half in another. If one stock falls in price, the other stock may fall less, may not fall at all, or may even rise.

portfolio diversification: spreading the collection of assets owned to limit exposure to risk.

Holding two stocks in equal amounts is the most elementary form of diversification. With thousands of stocks to choose from, diversification is not limited to two. Figure 13.7 shows how sharply risk declines from diversification. By holding 10 different stocks rather than one, you can reduce your risk to about 30 percent of what it would be with one stock. If you hold some international stocks, whose behavior will be even more different than any one U.S. stock, you can reduce the risk even further. Mutual fund companies provide a way for an investor with only limited funds to diversify by holding 500 or even 5,000 stocks along with other investors. Some mutual funds—called *index funds*—consist of all the stocks in an index like the Standard and Poors (S&P) 500 Index, a weighted average of the stocks of 500 major companies. The Dow-Jones industrial index of 30 companies, which draws headlines every time it passes through a 1,000-point mark, is less frequently used as an index for mutual funds because it has a smaller number of stocks.

If you do not diversify, you are taking unneeded risks. But diversification cannot eliminate risk. A certain amount of risk cannot be diversified away. **Systematic risk** is what remains after diversification has reduced risk as much as it can. It is due to the ups and downs in the economy, which affect all stocks to some degree.

systematic risk: the level of risk in asset markets that investors cannot reduce by diversification.

Reading the News About Stock Price Changes

The following excerpt from the *New York Times* shows how fast prices adjust to eliminate profit opportunities in the stock market. As soon as the U.S. government announced that most tariffs on foreign steel imported into the United States would be reduced, investors realized the negative effect of this decision on the profits of domestic steel companies. More competition from foreign steel would lower the profits of steel producers in the United States. People immediately began selling their shares of domestic steel companies such as U.S. Steel. Within an hour, these steel stocks had fallen by as much as 27

percent; the size of the price decline depended on how much each firm was likely to be hurt by the import of foreign steel.

If you held steel stocks and heard about the decision on the evening news, you might think about selling the stocks the next day. But that might not be such a good idea, because the price already reflected the bad news.

The effect of such news on financial markets is so important that it is announced at a particular hour, sometimes when the markets are closed.

Another type of news that affects a broad spectrum of stocks is new

data about the state of the economy collected and released by the U.S. government. Because of its impact on markets, the government publishes a calendar that states in advance the date and exact time—precise to the minute—when inflation and unemployment statistics are going to be publicly released. The government distributes the news at the specified time to ensure that nobody has an unfair advantage.

Source of article: "Ruling Spurs an Industrywide Selloff" by Alison Leigh Cowan, *The New York Times*, July 28, 1993. Copyright © 1993 by The New York Times Company. Reprinted by permission.

Ruling Spurs an Industrywide Selloff

By ALISON LEIGH COWAN

The unfavorable resolution of some long-running trade disputes involving foreign steel imports sent the stocks of

major American steel companies reeling yesterday amid signs that the country's largest steelmaker, USX, had a turbulent quarter.

The USX U.S. Steel Group, whose stock is traded separately from its par-

ent's other subsidiaries, fell 13 percent. Bethlehem Steel skidded nearly 21 percent and National Steel plunged 27 percent.

Steel Stocks Take a Beating . . .

Trading yesterday for three major United States steel companies.

FIGURE 13.7
Risk Declines Sharply with Diversification

By holding more than one stock, the risk can be reduced. By holding 10 U.S. securities, the risk is reduced to 30 percent of the risk of holding one security. Diversifying internationally permits one to reduce risk further. (The risk is measured by the standard deviation.)

Source: "The Advantages of Domestic and International Diversification" by Bruno Solnick from *Finance as a Dynamic Process* by E.J. Elton and M.J. Gruber. Copyright © 1975. Used with permission.

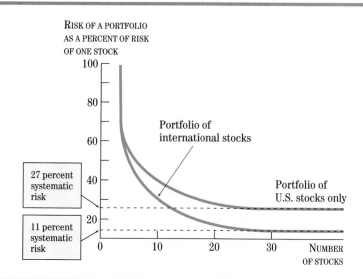

Efficient Market Theory: Speedy Entry and Exit

The shares of firms' stock on the market can be traded quickly any time of day. For most large and medium-sized companies, some people are always willing to buy and sell. If people hear that Intel made a discovery that is expected to raise its profits, they rush to buy Intel stock. If a court rules against a company, which will reduce its profits, then people rush to sell that company's stock. This rush to buy and sell changes prices instantaneously, so that the price adjusts rapidly to good news or bad news.The rapid adjustment means that there are rarely any unexploited profit opportunities for regular investors without inside information or a special ability to anticipate news, whether good or bad. The **efficient market hypothesis** is that there is an elimination of profit opportunities in financial markets as stock prices adjust quickly to new information. Rates of return greater than those due to the price of risk disappear soon after any good news about a stock appears.

efficient market hypothesis:
the idea that markets adjust rapidly enough to eliminate profit opportunities immediately.

Many tests over the years have found the efficient market hypothesis to be a close approximation of security price determination. It has led to the growth in popularity of index funds, where investors do not pay advisers to tell them when to buy and sell stock. They simply put their savings in a fund that includes a large number of stocks.

Review

▶ Risk-averse investors require compensation to hold risky assets. This compensation may take the form of a higher expected return.

▶ When buyers and sellers trade stocks or bonds in the market, a relationship between return and risk emerges: Higher risk is associated with higher returns.

▶ Diversification reduces risk but not below a bare minimum called systematic risk.

▶ The efficient market hypothesis predicts that stock prices adjust to eliminate rates of return in excess of those required to compensate for systematic risk.

CORPORATE GOVERNANCE PROBLEMS

When corporations issue stock to buy physical capital or start up operations, a separation between the owners of the corporation—the stockholders—and the managers of the corporation is created. This separation leads to incentive problems—the manager might not act in the interest of the shareholder. Here we show how these problems can be analyzed with a theory called *asymmetric information theory*.

Consider a start-up firm. When an entrepreneur at a start-up firm obtains financial capital by issuing stock, a special relationship is formed. Those who supplied the financial capital by buying the stock become owners or at least part owners of the company. If the entrepreneur does well and the company is a success, they reap large returns.

Asymmetric Information: Moral Hazard and Adverse Selection

Shareholders of a firm have less information than the managers about how the firm is doing even though the shareholders put a considerable amount of funds in the firm. These differences in information, called **asymmetric information,** can cause several problems. First, the manager might not act in the interest of the owners. Taking unnecessary business trips on the company's aircraft to exotic areas or not working hard to find the right employees are harmful to the shareholders' interests. Such actions are against the interest of the shareholders. They are called **moral hazard,** a term borrowed from research on the insurance industry, where asymmetric information is also a problem. Moral hazard in insurance occurs when people are less careful about trying to prevent fires after they get fire insurance. In the case of the firm, the manager may be less careful about the firm after the shareholders' or investors' funds have been obtained.

Another problem is that those entrepreneurs who have more risky projects would seek equity financing—where dividend payments to shareholders would be optional—rather than debt financing, where interest payments are required. This is called **adverse selection,** another term borrowed from insurance. In insurance, adverse selection occurs when people who are unhealthy select health insurance while healthy people do not. In this case, managers who have more risky projects select equity financing more than those who have less risky projects. This makes

asymmetric information: different levels of information available to different people in an economic interaction or exchange.

moral hazard: in insurance markets, a situation in which a person buys insurance against some risk and subsequently takes actions that increase the risks; analogous situations arise when there is asymmetric information in other markets.

adverse selection: in insurance markets, a situation in which the people who choose to buy insurance will be the riskiest group in the population; analogous situations apply in other markets.

A Shareholder Meeting: Principals, Agents, Asymmetric Information
Theories of corporate governance view a firm's shareholders (shown in the crowd) as the *principals* and the managers (shown on the stage) as the *agents.* Management incentive plans such as profit sharing are seen as ways of fostering good management performance when the principals have little information about what the agents actually do—a situation called *asymmetric information.*

potential shareholders or investors less willing to supply funds to equity markets. Finding ways to write contracts between principals (the owners or shareholders) and agents (the managers) to reduce the problems of moral hazard or adverse selection requires paying attention to incentives.

Incentives Through Profit Sharing

Adverse selection and moral hazard can be so serious that business relationships between principals and agents don't develop. For example, people may be unwilling to take a risky position in a firm for fear of either adverse selection or moral hazard. If so, the firm would not be able to issue equity. Finding relationships that give better incentives to managers is a way to revive equity financing. One way to prevent moral hazard in equity markets, for example, is to make sure that managers put their own funds into the firm. Then the managers gain if the company does well or lose if the company does poorly. Such arrangements are called **profit sharing** and can be extended to all employees of a firm, not just the top managers.

profit sharing: programs in which managers and employees receive a share of profits earned by the firm.

Incentives Through Threats of Takeovers

hostile takeover: a situation in which investors buy a large share of a company and replace the management.

The **hostile takeover,** where a group of investors tries to take over a company and replace the management, also may provide incentives. The mere threat of being taken over may be sufficient to give managers enough incentive to run the firm well. There are also cases where takeovers have improved a firm's performance.

One takeover case was the 1986 acquisition of Safeway, the grocery store chain, by KKR, a firm specializing in takeovers. According to some analysts, before the takeover, Safeway was poorly run. When KKR took over, the managers were given contracts in which their pay depended on the performance of the company. This changed the incentives facing management, and performance improved.

However, such takeovers have also been criticized. Some say they force management to take a short-term focus. To ward off takeovers, firms' managers have to watch day-to-day profits more carefully; this could make them avoid an investment that would raise profits in the future.

Review

▶ Equity contracts create a situation of asymmetric information in which the owners or shareholders do not have complete information about the manager's actions.

▶ The asymmetric information in these relationships leads to moral hazard, where the managers take actions that may not be in the best interests of the shareholders, and to adverse selection, in which those with high risk seek equity financing.

▶ Remedies to these problems include profit-sharing programs that give management incentives to take the owners' interests into account.

CONCLUSION AND SOME LESSONS

In this chapter we have seen how to employ some basic economic tools to analyze capital markets. In reviewing the lessons learned, it is helpful to see how they may apply to you personally.

First, by diversifying a portfolio of stocks, you can reduce risk substantially. Conversely, by holding an undiversified portfolio you are needlessly incurring risk.

Second, be aware of the efficient market hypothesis that profit opportunity disappears quickly in financial markets. Trading securities frequently to seek out profits can result in high transaction costs. Diversification in a mutual fund—perhaps an index fund—can reduce the transaction costs of frequent buying and selling.

Third, if you do try to pick your own portfolio rather than use a mutual fund, concentrate on areas you are familiar with. If you're an electrical engineer, you may know more than even the best investors about the promise of a new telecommunications or computer firm.

Fourth, over the short run, holding corporate stocks is more risky than putting your funds in a bank account, but over the long term, the higher rate of return on stocks outweighs the risks for most people. However, if you need money in the short term—to pay tuition, for example—stocks may not be worth the risk.

KEY POINTS

1. Physical capital is a form of capital used to produce goods and services.

2. Financial capital, including the stocks and bonds traded on the exchanges, is used by firms to obtain funds to invest in physical capital.

3. A firm's demand for physical capital is a derived demand. A firm will use capital up to the point where the marginal revenue product of capital equals the rental price.

4. The supply and demand for capital determines the rental price or the implicit rental price.

5. Once stocks and bonds are issued by firms, the shares trade on financial markets.

6. The rate of return on stocks is equal to the dividend plus the change in the price as a percent of the price. The rate of

return on bonds is the coupon plus the change in the price as a percent of the price.

7. Risk-averse investors will buy more risky stocks or bonds only if the expected rate of return is higher.

8. In market equilibrium, there is a positive relationship between risk and rate of return. If you want to get a higher rate of return, you have to accept higher risk. In any case, diversification reduces risk.

9. The equity contracts between managers and owners are frequently beset with moral hazard problems due to asymmetric information.

10. Profit-sharing contracts or takeovers can improve management incentives to use labor and capital in the most efficient way.

KEY TERMS

depreciation	capital loss	equilibrium risk-return relationship
financial capital	rate of return	portfolio diversification
debt contract	dividend yield	systematic risk
equity contract	earnings	efficient market hypothesis
rental price of capital	price-earnings ratio	asymmetric information
marginal revenue product of capital	coupon	moral hazard
economic rent	maturity date	adverse selection
implicit rental price	face value	profit sharing
return	yield	hostile takeover
capital gain	expected return	

QUESTIONS FOR REVIEW

1. Why is the quantity of capital demanded negatively related to the rental price of capital?

2. What is economic rent, and what is its usefulness?

3. How does the implicit rental price of capital depend on the interest rate and depreciation?

4. What three interrelated profit-maximization rules connect a firm's labor, capital, and output decisions?

5. Why are the price and yield on bonds inversely related?

6. What is the rate of return on stocks? On bonds?

7. Why do stocks have higher rates of return than bank deposits over the long term?

8. What is the effect of diversification on risk?

9. What is the difference between moral hazard and adverse selection?

10. What do corporate takeovers and profit-sharing plans have in common?

PROBLEMS

1. Which of the following are physical capital, and which are financial capital?
   a) A bond issued by American Airlines
   b) A loan you take out to start a newspaper business
   c) New desktop publishing equipment
   d) A 30-year bond issued by the U.S. government
   e) A pizza oven at Pizza Hut

2. Draw a diagram like that in Figure 13.2. Show what happens to the demand for capital and the equilibrium rental price if the marginal revenue product of capital falls.

3. Suppose that Marshall's stones were dropped all over the earth and finding them was difficult. Would the supply curve of capital still be perfectly inelastic? Would there be economic rent?

4. Suppose your company owns a piece of equipment that cost $100,000 and depreciates at 10 percent per year. If the current interest rate is 7 percent, what is its implicit rental price? Why does the implicit rental price depend on the interest rate?

5. The U.S. government issues a 1-year bill with a face value of $1,000 and with a zero coupon. If the market interest rate is 8 percent, what will the market price of the bond be? Now suppose you observe that the bond price falls 10 percent. What happens to its yield?

6. You are considering the purchase of stocks of two firms: a biotechnology corporation and a supermarket chain. Due to the uncertainty in the biotechnology industry, you estimate there is a 50-50 chance of either earning an 80 percent return on your investment or losing 80 percent of it within a year. The food industry is more stable, so you estimate that you have a 50-50 chance of either earning 10 percent or losing 10 percent. Suppose that both stocks have equal expected returns. Which stock would you buy? Why? What do you think other investors would do? What would be the effect of these actions on the relative price of the two stocks?

7. Identify which of the following situations might create moral hazard, adverse selection, neither, or both:
   a) Badly Managed Corporation notices that there is unemployment due to the recession and decides to save some money by lowering the wages offered to new employees, since there is a surplus of labor at the current wage.

   b) Badly Managed Corporation tries to steal workers from a rival firm by offering anyone who switches jobs lifetime employment. Some of the workers of the rival firm switch to Badly Managed Corporation and are now employed for life.
   c) The salespeople of Badly Managed Corporation receive wages based on the sales of the company as a whole, not on their individual sales.
   d) The stockholders of Badly Managed Corporation decide to pay the managers a percentage of revenues to give them an incentive to sell more.

8. Suppose you have $10,000 and must choose between investing in your own human capital or investing in physical or financial capital. What factors will enter into your decision-making process? How much risk will be involved with each investment? What would you do? Why?

9. What is the expected return of the following stock market investment portfolio?

	Good Market	Bad Market	Disastrous Market
Probability	.50	.30	.20
Rate of Return	.25	.10	−.25

   a) Would you choose this expected return or take a safe return of 7 percent from a savings deposit in your bank? Why?
   b) Suppose your teacher chooses the safe return from the bank. Is your teacher risk averse? How can you tell?

10. Graph the data on risk and expected return (in percent) for the following securities.

Asset	Expected Rate of Return	Risk
Bank deposit	3	0
U.S. Treasury bills	4	3
Goodcorp bonds	9	10
ABC stock	11	24
XYZ stock	13	24
Riskyco stock	16	39

Draw an equilibrium risk-return line through the points. Which two assets should have changes in their prices in the near future? In which direction will their prices change?

11. a) Suppose a 2-year bond has a 5 percent coupon, $1,000 face value, and the current market interest rate is 5 percent. What is the price of the bond?

b) Now suppose that you believe that the interest rate will remain 5 percent this year, but next year will fall to 3 percent. How much are you willing to pay for the 2-year bond today? Why?

12. What are the benefits of buying a mutual fund? Is there any risk involved in this investment?

How to Discount Future Payments

Decisions about buying physical assets or financial assets involve comparisons of payments of money at different points of time. But the same amount of money at two dates is worth different amounts, and to make such comparisons you need to calculate how large or small this difference is. The purpose of this appendix is to show you how to calculate that difference.

THE DISCOUNT RATE AND THE PRESENT DISCOUNTED VALUE

In general, the value today of a dollar paid in the future is less than a dollar. Why? Because you can earn interest on money by putting it in a bank. Suppose a person you trust completely to pay off a debt gives you an IOU promising to pay you $100 in one year; how much is that IOU worth to you today? How much would you be willing to pay for the IOU today? It would be less than $100, because you could put an amount less than $100 in a bank and get $100 at the end of a year. The exact amount depends on the interest rate. If the interest rate is 10 percent, the $100 should be worth $90.91 because, if you put $90.91 in a bank earning 10 percent per year, at the end of the year you will have exactly $100. That is, $90.91 plus interest payments of $9.09 ($90.91 times .1 rounded to the nearest penny) equals $100.

The process of translating a future payment into a value in the present is called **discounting.** The value in the present of a future payment is called the **present discounted value.** The interest rate used to do the discounting is called the **discount rate.** In the preceding example, a future payment of $100 has a present discounted value of $90.91, and the discount rate is 10 percent. If the discount rate were 20 percent, the present discounted value would be $83.33 (because if you put $83.33 in a bank for a year at a 20 percent interest rate, you would have, rounding to the nearest penny, $100 at the end of the year). The term *discount* is used because the value in the present is *less* than the future payment; in other words, the payment is "discounted," much like a $100 bicycle on sale might be "discounted" to $83.33.

FINDING THE PRESENT DISCOUNTED VALUE

The previous examples suggest that there is a formula for calculating present value and indeed there is. Let

the present discounted value be PDV

the discount rate be i

the future payment be F

The symbol i is measured as a fraction, but we speak of the discount rate in percentage terms; thus we would say "the discount rate is 10 percent" and write "$i = .1$."

Now, the present discounted value PDV is an amount, which, if you put it in a bank today at an interest rate i, you would get an amount in the future equal to the future payment F. For example, if the future date is one year from now, then if you put the amount PDV in a bank for one year you would get PDV times $(1 + i)$ at the end of the year. Thus, the PDV should be such that

$$PDV \times (1 + i) = F$$

Now divide both sides by $(1 + i)$ and you get

$$PDV = \frac{F}{(1 + i)}$$

which is the formula for the present discounted value in the case of a payment made one year in the future. That is,

$$\text{Present discounted value} = \frac{\text{payment in one year}}{(1 + \text{the discount rate})}$$

For example, if the payment in one year is $100 and the discount rate $i = .1$, then the present discounted value is $90.91 [$100/(1 + .1)], just as we reasoned previously.

To obtain the formula for the case where the payment is made more than one year in the future, we must recognize that the amount in the present can be put in a bank for more than one year earning interest at the discount rate. For example, if the interest rate is 10 percent, we could get $100 at the end of 2 years by investing $82.64 today. That is, putting $82.64 in the bank would give $82.64 times (1.1) at the end of one year; keeping all this in the bank for another year would give $82.64 times (1.1) times (1.1) or $82.64 times 1.21 or $100.00, again rounding off. Thus, in the case of a future payment in 2 years, we would have

$$PDV = \frac{F}{(1 + i)^2}$$

Analogous reasoning implies that the present discounted value of a payment made N years in the future would be

$$PDV = \frac{F}{(1 + i)^N}$$

For example, the present discounted value of a $100 payment to be made 20 years in the future is $14.86 if the discount rate is 10 percent. In other words, if you put $14.86 in the bank today at an interest rate of 10 percent, you would have about $100 at the end of 20 years. What is the

present discounted value of a $100 payment to be made 100 years in the future? The above formula tells us that the *PDV* is only $.00726, less than a penny! All of these examples indicate that the higher the discount rate, the lower the present discounted value of a future payment.

In many cases, we need to find the present discounted value of a *series* of payments made in several different years. We can do ths by combining the previous formulas. For example, the present discounted value of a payment F made in 1 year and again in 2 years would be

$$PDV = \frac{F}{(1 + i)} + \frac{F}{(1 + i)^2}$$

For example, the present discounted value of $100 paid in one year and $100 paid in 2 years would be $90.91 plus $82.64 or $173.55.

KEY POINTS

1. A dollar to be paid in the future is worth less than a dollar today.

2. The present discounted value of a future payment is the amount you would have to put in a bank today to get that same payment in the future.

3. The higher the discount rate, the lower the present discounted value of a future payment.

KEY TERMS AND DEFINITIONS

discounting: the process of translating a future payment into a value in the present.

present discounted value: the value in the present of future payments.

discount rate: an interest rate used to discount future payment when computing present discounted value.

QUESTIONS FOR REVIEW

1. Why is the present discounted value of a future payment of $1 less than $1?

2. What is the relationship between the discount rate and the interest rate?

3. What happens to the present discounted value of a future payment as the payment date stretches into the future?

4. Why is discounting important for decisions about physical and financial capital?

PROBLEMS

1. Find the present discounted value of
   a) $100 to be paid at the end of 3 years.
   b) $1,000 to be paid at the end of 1 year plus $1,000 to be paid at the end of 2 years.
   c) $10 to paid at the end of 1 year, $10 at the end of 2 years, and $100 at the end of 3 years.

2. The Disney Company issued corporate bonds, sometimes called "Mickey Mouse" bonds, which simply promised to pay $1,000 in 100 years with no payments of

interest. What is the present discounted value of one of these bonds on the date issued if the interest rate is 10 percent? How about 5 percent?

3. Suppose you win $1,000,000 in a lottery and your winnings are scheduled to be paid as follows: $300,000 at the end of 1 year, $300,000 at the end of 2 years, and $400,000 at the end of 3 years. If the interest rate is 10 percent, what is the present discounted value of your winnings?

part

3

The Role of Government

Throughout the twentieth century we have observed many approaches to government policy as it affects the economy. Some governments have directly intervened in virtually every economic decision, the extreme cases being the centrally planned economies of the former Soviet Union and China. Others, such as the United States and Western Europe, have followed more hands-off policies, giving their market economies more freedom to operate. But even in market economies there have been differences in the degree of government involvement, and the approaches in each country have changed over time. The purpose of these five chapters is to explore the role of the government in the economy. In the process, we show that the tools of economics can be applied to governments as well as to firms and consumers.

In Chapter 14 we look at income inequality in the United States and examine how government taxation

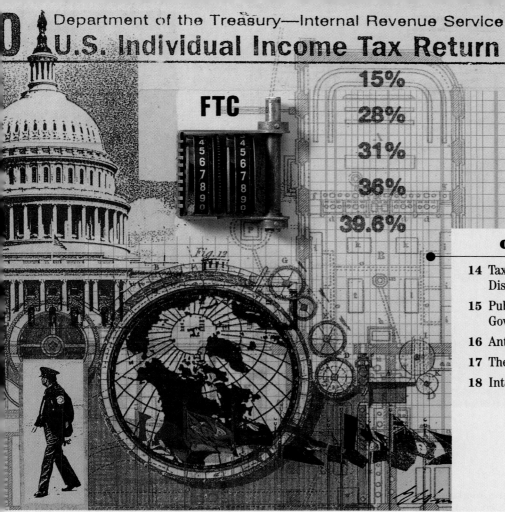

Department of the Treasury—Internal Revenue Service

U.S. Individual Income Tax Return

FTC

15%
28%
31%
36%
39.6%

chapters

14 Taxes, Transfers, and Income Distribution

15 Public Goods, Externalities, and Government Behavior

16 Antitrust Policy and Regulation

17 The Gains from International Trade

18 International Trade Policy

and welfare programs affect it. In Chapter 15 we see why public goods such as national defense are special, and we learn why competitive markets produce too much pollution and too little education and research. In Chapter 16 we delve into government policies to restrict market power either by promoting competition or by regulating the price charged by monopolies. In Chapter 17 we show that international trade between people in different countries is based on the same economic principles as trade between people in the same country. In Chapter 18 we investigate international trade policy—tariffs, quotas, trade agreements, and even trade wars.

From the time of Adam Smith's attack against bad government policy more than 200 years ago to the passionate pleas for tax reform, welfare reform, or regulatory reform heard today, the application of economics to government policy has been exciting and at the forefront of great intellectual debates. Economics has had more of an impact on public policy than many people, including many policymakers, realize. As you read these chapters, look for the more innovative ways in which economics has affected public policy in recent years, whether it is auctioning off the airwaves, finding creative solutions to the world problem of loss of biodiversity, controlling pollution by issuing tradable permits, providing incentives to reduce costs in cases where government regulates monopolies, or devising a political strategy to help reduce barriers to international trade.

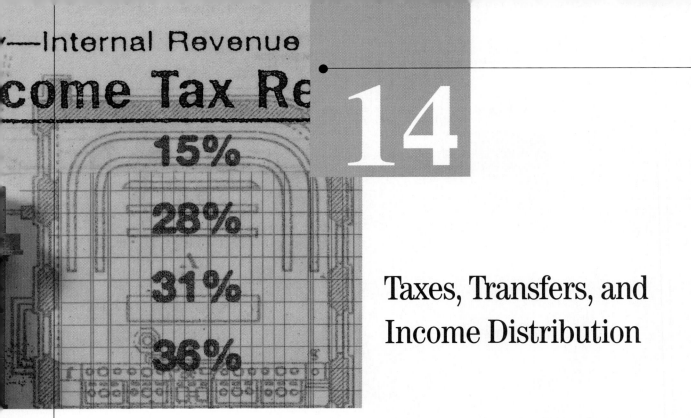

14

Taxes, Transfers, and Income Distribution

There is no reason to think that a market economy will automatically result in an equal distribution of income. Differences in ability, in health, in inheritance, in market power, in simple luck, and in the willingness to work, save, go to school, or take risks can cause differences in income. So can racial, sex, and religious discrimination. Natural disasters, as well as man-made disasters, can also leave some people in poverty and starvation. Shifts in the demands for certain products can benefit some and harm others, as can changes in technology. For example, as defense spending declined in the 1990s, workers in the defense industry suffered layoffs, unemployment, and reduced incomes. At the same time greater demand for personal computers created more jobs and higher wages for workers in that industry.

Of course, unequal income distribution is not unique to market economies. Under feudalism, the vast majority of individuals were poor and only very few—the royalty and the nobility—were well off. Under communism as practiced in the former Soviet Union and Eastern Europe, the ruling elite—the members of the high-level bureaucracy and the political leaders—received more income, typically in the form of services such as chauffeur-driven cars, fancy apartments, country homes, and good schools for their children, than the vast majority of the people.

There is a wide range of individual opinion about the causes of income inequality and what government should do about it. Many feel compassion and a moral obligation to help the very poor. Others feel it is unfair that some people make more in one day than others do in an entire year. Others see nothing unfair about a very unequal income distribution as long as there is equality of opportunity. Still others worry that a very unequal distribution of income can cause social unrest and deter a society from other goals, including an efficient economy.

Throughout the twentieth century all the world's democracies have chosen to set up government-run redistribution systems aimed at either reducing income inequality or helping the poor. Taxes and transfers lie at the heart of any government redistribution system. By taxing individuals who are relatively well off and making transfer payments to those who are relatively less well off, the aim is to make income distribution less unequal.

The purpose of this chapter is to provide an economic analysis of taxes and transfers. We begin the chapter with an analysis of taxes, which are used not only for transfer payments to the poor but also to pay for government spending of all types—military, police, road building, schools. We then go on to consider transfers, such as social security payments to the old and welfare payments to the poor. Finally, we examine the actual distribution of income and discuss how it has been affected by the tax and transfer system in the United States.

Today is an exciting time to study taxes, transfers, and income distribution. Debates have raged with passion about whether taxes should be increased or decreased or whether the rich should pay more or less in taxes. A major issue in the 1996 presidential election was whether tax rates should be reduced. There have also been great debates about government transfer programs. In 1996, President Clinton signed a welfare reform bill that gave vast discretion to the states to set work requirements for and time limits on public assistance.

This chapter endeavors to provide you with some of the economic principles to help you form and defend your opinions about these controversial matters.

THE TAX SYSTEM

We first consider the several different types of taxes used in the United States. Then we review the effects of these taxes and consider some proposals for reforming the tax system.

The major types of taxes that exist in the United States are the *personal income tax* on people's total income, the *payroll tax* on wage and salary income, the *corporate income tax* on corporate profit income, *excise taxes* on goods and services purchased, *estate* and *gift taxes* on inheritance and gifts from one person to another, and *tariffs,* which are taxes on goods imported into the country. In addition, many local governments raise revenue through *property taxes*.

As shown in Figure 14.1, the personal income tax and the payroll tax are by far the largest sources of tax revenue for the federal government. Together they account

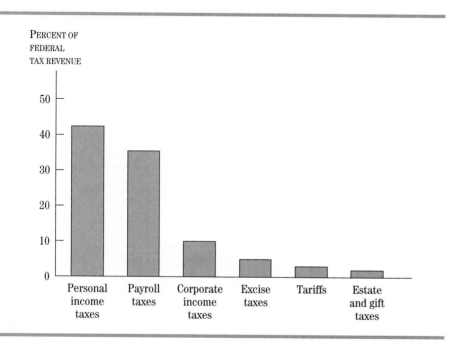

PERCENT OF FEDERAL TAX REVENUE

FIGURE 14.1
Taxes Paid to the Federal Government
Nearly 80 percent of federal taxes comes from the personal income tax and the payroll tax. The corporate income tax is about 10 percent of the total, with excise taxes, tariffs, and estate and gift taxes totaling about another 10 percent.

Taxes and Government Spending

Tax revenue raised by the tax system described in this chapter is used to pay for government purchases for the military, education, and roads, as illustrated in this typical sign. Taxes are also used to pay for transfer payments, as described later in the chapter.

personal income tax: a tax on all forms of income an individual or household receives.

taxable income: a household's income minus exemptions and deductions.

for nearly 80 percent of federal tax revenue. Hence, we focus most of our attention on these two taxes in the following discussion.

The Personal Income Tax

The **personal income tax** is a tax on all the income an individual or household receives, including wage and salary income, interest and dividend income, income from a small business, rents on property, royalties, and capital gains. (A *capital gain,* discussed in Chapter 13, is the increase in the value of an asset like a corporate stock. When the asset is sold, the capital gain—equal to the difference between the original purchase price and the selling price of the asset—is treated as income and is taxed.) The personal income tax was introduced in 1917 in the United States, soon after the ratification of the Sixteenth Amendment to the U.S. Constitution, which authorized income taxes.

Both the federal and state governments collect personal income taxes; most of the taxes are withheld from people by their employers, who send the tax payments directly to the government and notify the employee about how much is sent. We focus our discussion here on the federal income tax. Each April 15 a tax return—the Internal Revenue Service 1040 form—must be filed stating each individual's income for the previous year and the tax on that income; if an individual owes less in taxes than has been withheld during the past year, then the individual gets a refund; if an individual owes more than has been withheld, then the individual must pay an additional amount and perhaps a tax penalty.

Computing the Personal Income Tax

To explain the economic effects of the personal income tax, we must examine how people actually compute their own tax. The amount of tax a household owes depends on the tax rate and the amount of taxable income. **Taxable income** is defined as a household's income minus certain exemptions and deductions. An *exemption* is a dollar amount—$2,550 in 1996—that can be subtracted for each person in the household. *Deductions* are other items—such as interest payments on a home mortgage, charitable contributions, moving expenses—that can be subtracted. A single taxpayer is entitled to a deduction of *at least* $4,000 and a married couple to *at least* $6,700; these two amounts are called the *standard deduction.*

Consider, for example, the Lee family, which has four members: a wife, a husband, and two children. They can subtract $2,550 as a personal exemption for each of the four people in the family, for a total of $10,200, and they are entitled to a standard deduction of $6,700. Thus, they can subtract a total of $16,900 ($10,200 + $6,700) from their income. Suppose that the husband and wife each earn $28,000 per year in wages, and together they earn $4,000 in interest on a joint bank account, for a total income of $60,000. Thus, their taxable income is $43,100 ($60,000 − $16,900).

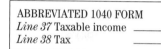

ABBREVIATED 1040 FORM
Line 37 Taxable income _____
Line 38 Tax _____

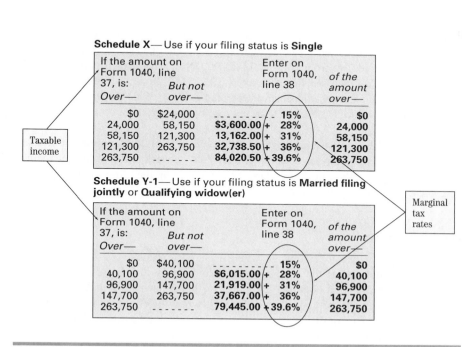

Taxable income

Marginal tax rates

FIGURE 14.2

Two Tax Rate Schedules from the 1040 Form

The tables show how to compute the tax for each amount of taxable income. Observe how the marginal rates rise from one tax bracket to the next. (The 1040 form also includes "tax tables," which give the taxes owed in dollars without stating the tax brackets explicitly.)

Now let us see how we combine taxable income with the tax rate to compute the tax. Figure 14.2 shows two different tax rate schedules copied exactly as they appeared in the 1996 IRS 1040 form. We do not need to consider the whole 1040 form. The IRS estimates that the average person takes 2 hours and 32 minutes to learn about the form—probably more time than you have to spend on this whole chapter. We will focus on only two lines: the line where taxable income is entered (called line 37) and the line where the tax is entered (called line 38) showing the dollar amount that the taxpayer owes the government. The tax rate schedule labeled "Schedule X" in the figure is for a taxpayer who is single; the tax rate schedule labeled "Schedule Y-1" is for two married taxpayers who are paying their taxes together. The first two columns give a range for taxable income, or the "amount on Form 1040, line 37." The next two columns tell how to compute the tax. The percentages in the tax rate schedule are the tax rates.

Look first at Schedule Y-1; the 15 percent tax rate in the schedule applies to all taxable income up to $40,100, at which point any additional income up to $96,900 is taxed at 28 percent. Any additional income over $96,900 but less than $147,700 is taxed at 31 percent, and so on for tax rates of 36 percent and 39.6 percent. Each of the rows in these schedules corresponds to a different tax rate; the range of taxable income in each row is called a **tax bracket.**

tax bracket: a range of taxable income that is taxed at the same rate.

"That's *INTERNAL,* as you well know!
Now go ahead and do it right!"

Let us compute the Lees' tax. Recall that their taxable income is $43,100. They are married and filing jointly, so we look at Schedule Y-1. We go to the second line because $43,100 is between $40,100 and $96,900. In other words, the Lees are in the 28 percent tax bracket. We find that they must pay $6,015 plus 28 percent of the amount their income is over $40,100, that is, plus .28 × ($43,100 − $40,100) = $840. Thus, the amount of tax they must pay is $6,015 + $840 = $6,855.

Now consider what happens when the Lees' income changes. Suppose that one of the Lees decides to earn more income by working 5½ days a week rather than 5 days a week. As a result, their income rises by 10 percent of $28,000, or $2,800. Thus, their taxable income rises from $43,100 to $45,900. Now what is their tax? Again looking at Schedule Y-1, we see that the tax is $6,015 + .28 × ($45,900 − $40,100) = $7,639. Thus, the Lees' tax has increased from $6,855 to $7,639, or by $784, as their income rose by $2,800. Observe that the tax rose by exactly 28 percent of the increase in income.

One can do the same exercise to find the change in the Lees' tax if one of the Lees had decided to work 4½ days a week rather than 5 days a week and their income thereby fell by $2,800. Then their tax would have been reduced by the same amount, $784, or 28 percent of the decline in income.

The Marginal Tax Rate

marginal tax rate: the change in total tax divided by the change in income.

The amount by which taxes change when one's income changes is the **marginal tax rate.** It is defined as the change in taxes divided by the change in income. In examining how the Lees compute their tax, we have discovered that the marginal tax rate for them is 28 percent. In other words, when their income increased, their taxes rose by 28 percent of the increase in income. As long as they stay within the 28 percent tax bracket, their marginal tax rate is 28 percent.

Observe that the marginal tax rate depends on one's income. The marginal rate varies from 15 percent for low incomes up to 39.6 percent for very high incomes. If one of the Lees decides to stop working, then their taxable income will fall by $28,000 to $15,100, in which case their marginal tax rate will decline as they enter the 15 percent bracket.

average tax rate: the total tax paid divided by the total taxable income.

In contrast to the marginal tax rate, the **average tax rate** is the total tax paid divided by the total taxable income. For example, the Lees' average tax rate before we considered changes in their income was $6,855/$43,100 = .159, or 15.9 percent, much lower than the 28 percent marginal tax rate. In other words, the Lees pay 15.9 percent of their total taxable income in taxes but must pay 28 percent of any additional income in taxes. The average tax rate is less than the marginal tax rate because the Lees pay only 15 percent on the first $40,100 of taxable income.

Economists feel that the marginal rate is important for assessing the effects of taxes on individual behavior. Their reasoning can be illustrated with the Lees again. Suppose that the Lees' marginal tax rate was 15 percent rather than 28 percent. Then, when one of the Lees decided to work an additional half day a week, they would be able to keep 85 cents for each extra dollar earned, sending 15 cents to the government. But with a marginal tax rate of 28 percent, the Lees could keep only 72 cents on the dollar. If the marginal tax rate for the Lees was 39.6 percent, then they could keep only 60.4 cents for each dollar earned. To take the example to an even greater extreme, suppose the marginal rate was 91 percent, which was the highest marginal rate before President Kennedy proposed reducing tax rates. Then, for each extra dollar earned, one could only keep 9 cents! Clearly, the marginal tax

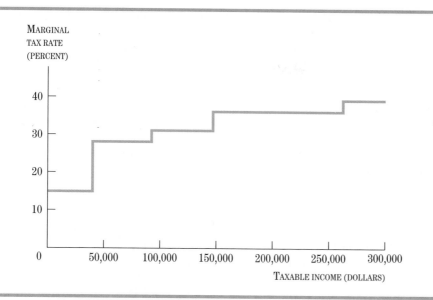

FIGURE 14.3
Marginal Tax Rates
As an example, the marginal tax rates from the IRS tax rate schedule Y-1 are plotted. The marginal tax rate is the change in the amount of tax paid for an extra dollar earned. The marginal tax rate increases with income. Each step takes the taxpayer to a higher tax bracket. Thus, higher-income people have a higher marginal tax rate than lower-income people. Under a flat tax, the marginal tax rate would be constant for all taxable income levels.

rate is going to influence people's choices about how much to work if they have a choice. The marginal tax rate has a significant effect on what people gain from working additional hours. This is why economists stress the marginal tax rate rather than the average tax rate when looking at the impact of the personal income tax on people's behavior.

Figure 14.3 provides a visual perspective on marginal tax rates. It plots the marginal tax rate from IRS Schedule Y-1 in Figure 14.2; the marginal tax rate is on

Using Economics to Explain the Marriage Tax

The phrase *the marriage tax* refers to the fact that the income tax is higher if two working people are married than if they are not married. To see this we can use the tax rate schedules in Figure 14.2. Suppose that before two people were married each had taxable income of $21,500. To compute their tax you use Schedule X, shown in Figure 14.2. With a taxable income of $21,500 each, the first row is relevant. The tax is 15 percent of

$21,500, or $3,225 each. Thus, the two of them together pay a total of $6,450.

Now consider what happens when they get married. Their taxable income rises to $43,000, twice the taxable income before marriage. Now go to Schedule Y-1, where the second row is now relevant. Their tax rises to $6,827, an increase of $377 per year. Their taxes increased simply because they got married.

The marriage tax is an example of inequity in the tax system. People who earn exactly the same income have different taxes.

Why is there a marriage tax? Does this mean that the government is against marriage? No. The reason has to do with the progressivity of the income tax. A marriage puts the couple into a higher tax bracket with a higher marginal rate. Thus, they pay more taxes.

progressive tax: a tax for which the amount of an individual's taxes rises as a proportion of income as the person's income increases.

regressive tax: a tax for which the amount of an individual's taxes falls as a proportion of income as the person's income increases.

proportional tax: a tax for which the amount of an individual's taxes as a percentage of income is constant as the person's income rises.

the vertical axis, and taxable income is on the horizontal axis. Observe how the marginal tax rate rises with income.

  A tax is **progressive** *if the amount of the tax as a percentage of income rises as income increases.* If the marginal tax rate rises with income—in which case people with higher incomes pay a larger percentage of their income in taxes—then the tax is progressive. *A tax is* **regressive** *if the amount of the tax as a percentage of income falls as income rises.* An income tax would be regressive if the marginal tax rate declined as income rose, or if people with high incomes could use deductions or other schemes to reduce the tax they paid to a smaller percentage of income than people with lower incomes. *A tax is* **proportional** *if the amount of the tax as a percentage of income is constant as income rises.*

Zero Tax on Low Incomes

In assessing how progressive the income tax is, one needs to remember that the taxes are based on taxable income, which is less than the income a household actually receives. Taxable income can be zero even if a household's income is greater than zero. For example, if the Lee family earned only $16,900 for the year, then their taxable income would be zero, because $16,900 equals the sum of their exemptions and deductions. Thus, they would not have to pay any personal income tax on incomes up to $16,900, according to the tax rate schedule. In general, the personal income tax is zero for household incomes up to the sum of the exemptions and deductions.

flat tax: a tax system for which there is a constant marginal tax rate for all levels of taxable income.

  A **flat tax** occurs when the marginal tax rates are constant for all levels of taxable income, in which case the line in Figure 14.3 would become flat. Even a flat rate tax system would have a degree of progressivity: The tax paid would rise as a percentage of income from zero (for workers below the sum of exemptions and deductions) to a positive amount as income rises.

The Payroll Tax

payroll tax: a tax on wages and salaries of individuals.

The **payroll tax** is a tax on the wages and salaries of individuals; another name for the payroll tax is the social security tax because much of it goes to finance social security benefits.

  Payroll taxes are submitted to the government by employers. The payroll tax raises nearly as much revenue as the income tax in the United States. The payroll tax is currently 15.3 percent of wages and salaries up to $62,700, and 2.9 percent on amounts above $62,700. For example, the payroll tax on the Lees' wage and salary income of $56,000 would be $8,568 (that is, .153 × $56,000), greater than the total that the Lees would pay in personal income taxes!

  The tax law says that half of the 15.3 percent payroll tax is to be paid by the worker while half is to be paid by the employer. Thus, the Lees would only be notified of half, or $4,284, of the payroll tax, even though their employer would have sent $8,568 to the government. If a person is self-employed—a business consultant, say, or a freelance editor—then the person pays the full 15.3 percent, because a self-employed person is both the employee and the employer. One of the most important things to understand about the payroll tax is that, as we will soon prove, its economic effects do not depend on who is legally required to pay what share of the tax; only the total 15.3 percent matters.

Other Taxes

All other federal taxes together amount to about one-fifth of total revenue. **Corporate income taxes** are taxes on the accounting profits of corporations. Currently the corporate tax rate is 34 percent of profits, though corporations with earnings less than $75,000 pay a smaller rate.

Excise taxes are taxes on goods that are paid when the goods are purchased. The federal government taxes several specific items, including gasoline, tobacco, beer, wine, and hard liquor. A **sales tax** is a type of excise tax that applies to total expenditures on a broad group of goods. For example, if your expenditures total $100 on many different goods at a retail store and the sales tax rate is 5 percent, then you pay $5 in sales tax. There is no national sales tax in the United States, but sales taxes are a major source of revenue for many states and local governments.

Finally, the federal government raises revenue by imposing tariffs on goods as they enter the United States; until the Sixteenth Amendment was ratified and the personal income tax was introduced, tariffs were the major source of revenue for the U.S. government. Now revenue from tariffs is a minor portion of total revenue.

Local governments rely heavily on **property taxes**—taxes on residential homes and business real estate—to raise revenue. Recall that income taxes—both personal and corporate—are also used at the state level.

corporate income tax: a tax on the accounting profits of corporations.

excise tax: a tax paid on the value of goods at the time of purchase.

sales tax: a type of excise tax that applies to total expenditures on a broad group of goods.

property tax: a tax on the value of property owned.

The Effects of Taxes

The purpose of most of the taxes just described is to raise revenue, but the taxes have effects on people's behavior. To examine these effects, let us start with a tax we looked at before in Chapter 7: a tax on a good or service.

The Effect of a Tax on a Good

Recall that a tax on a good increases the marginal cost to the seller of the good by the amount of the tax. For example, a tax of $1 on a gallon of gasoline will increase the marginal cost of each gallon by $1. An increase in a tax therefore shifts the supply curve up by the amount of the tax, a result shown in Figure 7.8 on page 190. Once the supply curve shifts, the ultimate impact on price and quantity will depend on the price elasticities of supply and demand.

The four panels of Figure 14.4 are designed to enable us to show how the price elasticity of demand and the price elasticity of supply determine the impact of the tax. In each of the four panels of the figure, the supply curve shifts up due to a tax of the same amount, shown by the blue arrow on the outside of each vertical axis. And in each of the four panels the equilibrium price rises and the equilibrium quantity falls. The equilibrium quantity falls because people reduce the quantity demanded of the good as its price rises due to the tax. The decline in the equilibrium quantity creates a loss of consumer surplus plus producer surplus, which we have called the deadweight loss of the tax. The size of the deadweight loss and the relative size of the impact on the price and the quantity are different in each panel of Figure 14.4 because the supply curve and the demand curve have different price elasticities.

One key point illustrated in Figure 14.4 is that *when the price elasticity of demand or the price elasticity of supply is very low, the deadweight loss from the tax is small.* This is shown in the two graphs in the left part of Figure 14.4, which

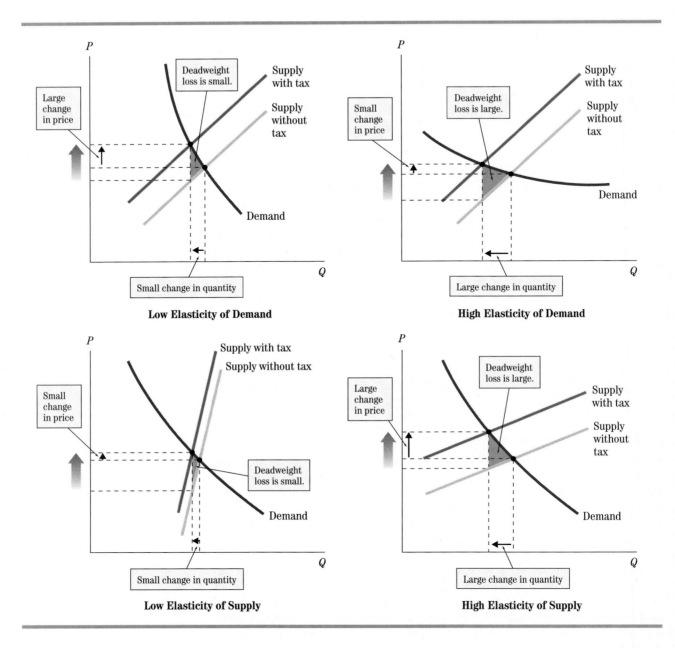

FIGURE 14.4
How Elasticities Determine the Effects of Taxes

1) *Deadweight loss effects:* When price elasticities are small, as in the left graphs, the deadweight loss is small and the change in equilibrium quantity is small. When price elasticities are high, as in the right graphs, the deadweight loss is large and the change in equilibrium quantity is large. 2) *Tax incidence and price effects:* When the price elasticity of demand is low or the price elasticity of supply is high, the tax is largely passed on to the consumer in higher prices. In contrast, when the price elasticity of demand is high or the price elasticity of supply is low, the burden of the tax falls on the producer because there is little price change.

have either a low elasticity of demand (top left) or a low elasticity of supply (bottom left). In either case the deadweight loss is small compared with the graphs at the right, which have higher elasticities.

The intuitive reason why low elasticities result in small deadweight losses is that the quantity of the good does not change very much when the price changes. Recall that a low price elasticity of demand means that quantity demanded is not very sensitive to a change in the price, as for example, in the case of a good like salt, which has few substitutes. A low elasticity of supply means that there is only a small change in the quantity supplied when the price changes. Thus, in the case of low elasticities, there is only a small difference between the efficient quantity of production and the quantity of production with the tax. There is little loss of efficiency. On the other hand, *when the price elasticity of demand or the price elasticity of supply is very high, the deadweight loss from the tax will be relatively large.* Here changes in price have big effects on either the quantity demanded or the quantity supplied, and the deadweight loss is large.

The price elasticities of supply and demand also affect how much the price changes in response to a tax. If the price rises by a large amount, then the tax is passed on to buyers in higher prices and the burden of the tax falls more on buyers. If the price rises little or not at all, then the seller absorbs the burden of the tax, and most of the tax is not passed on to buyers. **Tax incidence** refers to who actually bears the burden of the tax, the buyers or the sellers. By comparing the graphs of Figure 14.4, we see that *the smaller the price elasticity of demand and the larger the price elasticity of supply, the greater the rise in the price.* Comparing the upper two graphs of Figure 14.4, we see that the price rise is larger on the left, where the elasticity of demand is lower. For example, the price elasticity of demand for salt is very low. Thus, an increase in the tax on salt will have a large impact on the price; people will pay more for the salt with little reduction in the quantity demanded. In this case, the tax incidence falls mainly on the consumers of salt. The sellers can pass on the higher price to consumers when the elasticity of demand is low.

tax incidence: the allocation of the burden of the tax between buyer and seller.

Comparing the lower two graphs of Figure 14.4, we see that the price rise is smaller on the left, where the elasticity of supply is lower. Thus, taxing a good like land, which has a low elasticity of supply, will not affect the price very much. The suppliers of the land bear the burden of the tax.

Effects of the Personal Income Tax

We can apply our analysis of a tax on gasoline or salt to any other tax, including the personal income tax. The personal income tax is a tax on *labor* income (wages and salaries) as well as on *capital* income (interest, dividend, small business profits). However, labor income is by far the larger share of most people's income: For all 1040 forms filed, wages and salaries are over 75 percent of total income. Thus, we first focus on the personal income tax as a tax on labor income.

The analysis of the personal income tax is illustrated in Figure 14.5. Because the personal income tax is a tax on labor we need a model of the labor market to examine the effects of the tax. Figure 14.5 shows a labor demand curve and a labor supply curve. The wage paid to the worker is on the vertical axis, and the quantity of labor is on the horizontal axis. Figure 14.5 shows that the personal income tax shifts up the labor supply curve. The size of the upward shift depends on the marginal tax rate. For example, if a person were to supply more time working, the income received from work would be reduced by the marginal tax. If the person

FIGURE 14.5

Effects of a Higher Income Tax on Labor Supply

An income tax shifts the labor supply curve up by the amount of the tax on each extra hour of work because the worker must pay part of wage income to the government and thus receives less for each hour of work. Thus, the quantity of labor supplied declines. The decline in hours worked would be small if the supply curve had a low elasticity.

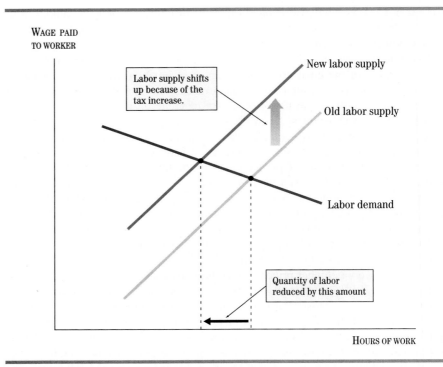

was in the 28 percent bracket, the income received from working would be 72 cents for each extra dollar earned working. Thus, to supply exactly the same quantity as without the tax, people require a higher wage. Because the wage paid to the worker is on the vertical axis, the labor supply curve shifts up to show this.

As the labor supply curve shifts up, the equilibrium quantity of labor declines. Thus, we predict that an income tax will reduce the amount of work. The reduced work will cause a deadweight loss just like the tax on a commodity. The size of the decline in hours of work will depend on the labor supply and labor demand elasticities. Figure 14.5 is not drawn to any particular scale, but the labor supply curve is shown to have a relatively low elasticity. The higher the labor supply elasticity, the greater the reduction in the quantity of labor supplied in response to the personal income tax.

Economists disagree about the size of the labor supply elasticity. One thing for sure is that the elasticity is different for different people. For example, the labor supply elasticity appears to be quite large for second earners in a two-person family such as the Lees. If so, a high marginal tax rate can reduce hours of work and thereby income. But if the labor supply curve has a low elasticity, there is little effect on hours of work.

The Effect of a Payroll Tax

We can use the same type of labor market diagram to analyze a payroll tax, as shown in Figure 14.6. Clearly, the payroll tax is a tax on labor in that it applies to wages and salaries. However, in the case of the payroll tax, we need to consider that the tax might be paid either by the employer or by the employee, as required by law. Figure 14.6 handles both cases.

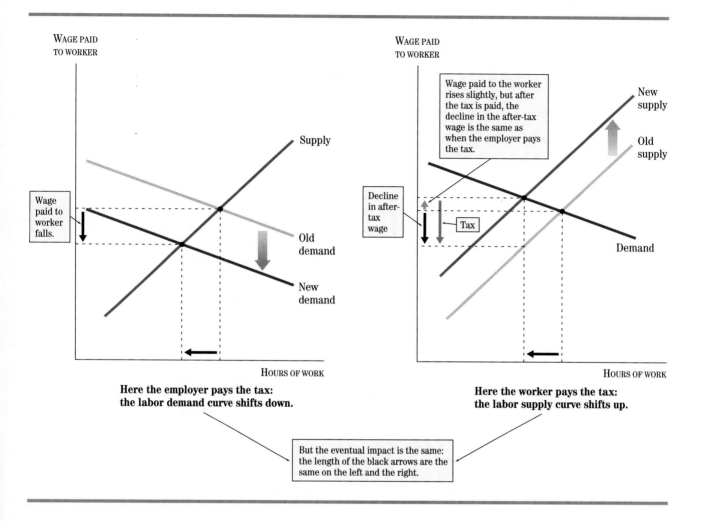

**Here the employer pays the tax:
the labor demand curve shifts down.**

**Here the worker pays the tax:
the labor supply curve shifts up.**

But the eventual impact is the same:
the length of the black arrows are the
same on the left and the right.

Suppose that the wage before the tax is $10 per hour and that the payroll tax is 10 percent, or $1 per hour. The case where the tax is paid by the employee is shown on the right of Figure 14.6. This picture looks much like Figure 14.5. The labor supply curve shifts up by the amount of the tax ($1) because the worker now has to pay a tax to the government for each hour worked. In other words, the worker will supply the same amount of work when the wage is $11 and the tax is $1 as when the wage is $10 and the tax is zero.

When the labor supply curve shifts up, we see in the right-hand panel of Figure 14.6 that the equilibrium quantity of labor employed declines. Observe that the wage paid by the employer rises because the reduced supply requires a reduction in the quantity of labor demanded, which is brought about by a higher wage. However, the "after-tax wage"—the wage less the tax—declines because the tax increases by more than the wage increases.

The case where the tax is paid by the employer is shown in the left graph of Figure 14.6. In this case the labor demand curve shifts down by the amount of the tax ($1) because the firm has to pay an additional $1 for each hour of work. When the labor demand curve shifts down, the equilibrium quantity of labor employed

FIGURE 14.6
Effect of Payroll Tax
If a payroll tax is paid by the employer, the labor demand curve shifts down by the amount of the tax because the firm's labor costs increase by the amount of the tax. Thus, the quantity of labor employed declines, as does the wage paid to the worker, as shown on the left. A payroll tax paid by the employee, shown on the right, causes the labor supply curve to rise by the amount of the tax, but the effects on after-tax wages received by the worker and the quantity of work are the same as when the employer pays.

Tax Revenues	Tax Rate	Wage	Hours Worked
$10,000	.50	$10/hour	2,000
$11,250	.75	$10/hour	1,500
$ 4,500	.90	$10/hour	500

TABLE 14.1
Tax Rates and Tax Revenue:
An Example

declines and the wage falls. Observe that the impact of the payroll tax is the same in both cases: There is a new equilibrium in the labor market with a lower wage and a lower quantity of labor.

Thus, a payroll tax has both an employment-reduction effect and a wage-reduction effect. Like any tax, the size of the quantity change and the price (wage) change depends on the supply and demand elasticities. For example, if the labor supply elasticity is low there will be a small reduction in employment, but the wage will fall by a large amount. However, if the labor supply elasticity is high, there will be a large employment effect, but the wage effect will be small.

tax revenue: the tax rate times the amount subject to tax.

The Possibility of a Perverse Effect on Tax Revenue

Tax revenue received by the government is equal to the tax rate times the amount that is subject to the tax. For example, in the case of a gasoline tax, the tax revenue is the tax per gallon times the number of gallons sold. As the tax rate increases, the amount subject to a tax will fall because the higher price due to the tax reduces the quantity demanded. If the quantity demanded falls sharply enough, then tax revenue could actually fall when the tax rate is increased.

The same possibility arises in the case of taxes on labor, either the payroll tax or the personal income tax. In the case of the payroll tax or the personal income tax for a worker, tax revenue is equal to the tax rate times the wage and salary income. As the tax rate rises, the amount of income subject to tax may fall if labor supply declines. Thus, in principle it is possible that a higher tax rate could result in reduced tax revenue. For example, consider the high marginal tax rates shown in Table 14.1: 50 percent, 75 percent, and 90 percent. If labor supply declines with a higher tax rate, as assumed in the table, then tax revenue first increases as the tax rate goes from 50 to 75 but then declines as the tax rate goes from 75 to 90.

The general relationship between tax rates and tax revenue is illustrated in Figure 14.7. As in the example of Table 14.1, tax revenue first rises and then falls as the tax rate increases. Figure 14.7 can apply to any tax on anything. At the two extremes of zero percent tax rate and 100 percent tax rate, tax revenue is zero. What happens between these two extremes depends on the elasticities. This relationship between the tax rate and the tax revenue, now frequently called the Laffer curve after the economist Arthur Laffer, who made it popular in the 1980s, has long been known to economists. It implies that if the tax rate is so high that we are on the downward-sloping part of the curve, then reducing the tax rate may increase tax revenue. However, there is great debate among economists about the tax rate at which the curve bends around (40 percent? 50 percent? 90 percent?) and how it applies in different situations.

Other factors influencing tax revenue when taxes get very high are tax avoidance and tax evasion. *Tax avoidance* means finding legal ways to reduce taxes, such as buying a home rather than renting in order to have a deduction for interest payments on a mortgage. *Tax evasion* is an illegal means of reducing one's tax. For

FIGURE 14.7
The Tax Rate and Tax Revenue
As the tax rate increases from low levels, tax revenue rises. At some point, however, the high tax rate reduces the quantity of the item that is taxed and encourages so much tax avoidance that the amount of tax revenue declines. The curve is frequently called the *Laffer curve.* The particular tax rate at which the curve bends depends on the price elasticities of the item being taxed and is a subject of great debate among economists.

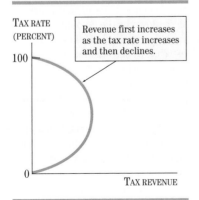

example, at high tax rates, people have incentives to evade the tax by not reporting income. Workers are tempted not to report tips. Or people resort to barter, which is difficult for the government to track down. For example, an employer may "pay" a little extra to a truck driver by allowing free use of the truck on weekends for fishing trips.

The Tradeoff Between Efficiency and Equality

We have observed in our analysis of each tax that the equilibrium quantity of the item taxed declines when the tax rate rises. This is where the inefficiency of the tax comes from. If the tax rate is very high, or the elasticities are very high, the inefficiency can be so severe that it could thwart one of the purposes of raising the taxes: to provide income support in order to raise the well-being of the least well off in the society. Why? Because the reduction in the quantity of labor supplied or goods produced could be so great that there would be less total income in the society. Thus, there would be less going to the poor even if they received a larger share of total income. In other words, there is a *tradeoff between equality and efficiency*. If one raises taxes too high for the purpose of making the income distribution more equal, the total amount of income may decline. In that event, there will be less available to redistribute.

Tax Policy

Our analysis of taxes has some implications for how the tax system—the combination of all the taxes in a society—should be designed or improved.

First, in order to reduce deadweight loss to a minimum, the ideal tax system should tax items with small price elasticities of supply and demand rather than items with large elasticities. We know that the deadweight loss is small when elasticities are small. The optimal tax system would have tax rates inversely related to the elasticities.

Second, the ideal tax system would try to keep the marginal tax rates low and the amount that is subject to tax high. For example, we saw that deductions reduce the amount subject to personal income tax by lowering taxable income. Some deductions are put in the tax system to encourage certain activities: A deduction for research expenses may encourage firms to fund research, for example. However, the more deductions, the higher the tax rate has to be to get the same tax revenue. By not allowing people to exclude so many items from income, a lower marginal tax rate could generate the same amount of revenue. And a lower marginal tax rate has the advantage of reducing the inefficiency of the tax.

Most tax reform efforts in the last 35 years have tried to reduce the number of deductions while lowering marginal tax rates. This was the idea behind the tax reform efforts in the 1960s under President Kennedy and in the 1980s under President Reagan. In the early 1990s the marginal tax rates on upper-income taxpayers were increased again, but they still remained below the high levels of the 1970s and certainly well below the high levels of the 1950s.

Third, the ideal tax system should be as simple and as fair as possible. If a tax system is not simple then valuable resources—people's time, computers, etc.—must be devoted to paying and processing taxes. The tax system is seen as unfair if it is regressive. Another view of fairness frequently used is the **ability-to-pay principle;** this view is that those with greater income should pay more in taxes than

ability-to-pay principle: the view that those with greater income should pay more in taxes than those with less income.

those with less income. The tax system is also viewed as unfair if people with the same incomes are taxed at different rates. For example, in the U.S. tax system a married couple pays a higher tax than an unmarried couple with exactly the same income. This is viewed by many as unfair.

Review

▶ Taxes are used to pay for transfers to low-income individuals as well as for government expenditures on military, police, roads, and bridges. Taxes are a necessary part of any modern market economy.

▶ Taxes cause inefficiencies in the form of reduced economic activity and deadweight loss.

▶ There is a tradeoff between efficiency and equality; raising taxes to reduce inequality may increase economic inefficiency and thereby reduce the amount of total income.

▶ To minimize the inefficiencies, items with low elasticities should be taxed more than items with high elasticities.

▶ In the case of taxes on labor income—a payroll tax or the income tax for most people—the amount of work declines as the tax is increased.

TRANSFER PAYMENTS

transfer payment: a grant of funds from the government to an individual.

A **transfer payment** is a payment from the government to an individual that is not in exchange for a good or service. Transfer payments can be either in cash or in kind. In-kind payments include vouchers to buy food or housing.

There are two types of government transfer payments in the United States: **means-tested transfers,** which depend on the income (the means) of the recipient and focus on helping poor people, and **social insurance transfers,** which do not depend on the income of the recipient. We will discuss each type of transfer, starting with the means-tested transfer programs.

means-tested transfer: a transfer payment that depends on the income of the recipient.

social insurance transfer: a transfer payment, such as social security, that does not depend on the income of the recipient.

Means-Tested Transfer Programs

Means-tested transfer payments are made to millions of people in the United States each year. The major programs are listed in Table 14.2.

In 1996 a new federal welfare law replaced Aid to Families with Dependent Children (AFDC)—a transfer program providing cash payments to poor families with children. Usually, AFDC has simply been called "welfare." Under the new **family support programs,** the federal government provides grants to states, which then decide which poor families are eligible. In contrast, under AFDC the federal government stipulated eligibility requirements.

family support programs: transfer programs through which the federal government makes grants to states to give cash to certain low-income families.

Medicaid: a health insurance program designed primarily for families with low incomes.

Medicaid is a health insurance program that is designed primarily to pay for health care for people with low incomes. Under the new welfare law, Medicaid eligibility is based substantially on the rules for eligibility under the former AFDC program, although it is no longer linked automatically to AFDC. Once income increases to a certain level, Medicaid support stops, so that the family must find another means of obtaining health insurance. **Supplemental security income (SSI)** is a program designed to help the neediest elderly as well as poor people who are disabled or blind. About 6 million people receive SSI assistance, including 4.4 million disabled, 1.5 million aged, and .1 million blind people.

supplemental security income (SSI): a means-tested transfer program designed primarily to help the poor who are disabled or blind.

TABLE 14.2
Means-Tested Transfer Programs in the United States
(Each of these federal programs requires that the recipient's income or assets be below a certain amount in order to receive payment.)

Family Support Programs (Welfare)
Payments to poor families with children

Medicaid
Health insurance primarily for welfare recipients

SSI (Supplemental Security Income)
Cash payments to poor people who are old, disabled, or blind

Food Stamp Program
Coupons for low-income people to buy food

Head Start
Preschool education for low-income children

Housing Assistance
Rental subsidies and aid for construction

The **food stamp program** is a major means-tested transfer program; it makes payment to as many as 27 million people each year. Like Medicaid, food stamps are an in-kind payment. People are not supposed to use the coupons to buy anything but food. This is a popular program because the intent of the money is to provide nutrition and because it is fairly inexpensive to run. The National School Lunch Program is similar to food stamps in that it aims to provide food to lower-income children. It provides school lunches for about 26 million children.

Head Start, another in-kind program, provides for preschool assistance to poor children to help them get a good start in school. It also is a popular program because there is evidence that it improves the performance, at least temporarily, of preschool children as they enter elementary school.

Housing assistance programs provide rental subsidies to people who cannot afford to buy a home. The programs sometimes provide aid to those whose business firms construct low-income housing. Many complain about waste and poor incentives in the housing programs and argue that they are in need of reform.

food stamp program: a government program that pays coupons (food stamps) to people with low incomes in order to buy food.

Head Start: a government transfer program that provides day care and nursery school training for poor children.

housing assistance programs: government programs that provide subsidies either to low-income families to rent housing or to contractors to build low-income housing.

The Earned Income Tax Credit (EITC)

A relatively new program aimed at helping the poor in the United States is the **earned income tax credit (EITC).** It is like a means-tested transfer payment in that people receive a cash payment from the government if their income is below a certain amount. However, it is actually part of the personal income tax (the form to obtain the payment is sent to people by the IRS along with the 1040 form).

The program provides assistance to about 18 million families. The EITC is for working people whose income is below a certain level, either because their wage is very low or because they work part time. They get a refundable credit that raises their take-home pay. For example, consider the four-person Lee family again. We know that if they earn less than $16,900, they pay no income tax. However, if the Lees earn between $0 and $8,425 in wages and salary and have no other income, then the EITC would pay 40 cents for each dollar they earned up to a maximum of about $3,370 per year ($3,370 = .4 × $8,425). To make sure that the EITC does not make payments to high-income people, the payments would decline if the Lees made more than $11,000. For each dollar they earn above $11,000 they lose 21 cents of their $3,370 until the benefits run out when their income reaches about $27,000.

earned income tax credit (EITC): a part of the personal income tax through which people with low income who work receive a payment from the government or a rebate on their taxes.

Observe that the EITC raises the incentive to work for incomes up to $8,425 and reduces the incentive to work for incomes greater than $11,000 and up to $27,000. With the EITC the marginal tax rate is effectively *negative* 40 percent for income below $8,425; that is, you *get* 40 cents rather than *pay* 40 cents for each dollar you earn. But the EITC adds 21 percent to the marginal tax rate for incomes over $11,000 up to $27,000.

Welfare Reform

The previous sections describe a variety of government programs that aim to transfer funds to the poor. As we will see, evidence suggests that they do have an impact in reducing income inequality. However, many people feel that the programs create a disincentive to work, since welfare payments are reduced when income from work rises.

Work Disincentives

The top panel of Figure 14.8 illustrates the first disincentive problem. The total income of an individual is plotted against the number of hours worked. Total income consists of wage income from work plus a welfare payment. The more steeply sloped solid black line shows the individual's wage income from work: the more hours worked, the more wage income the individual receives. This line intercepts the horizontal axis at zero income, so if there is no work and there is no welfare or charity, the person is in a state of extreme poverty.

The individual's total income is shown by the less steeply sloped dashed line in the top graph of Figure 14.8. It intercepts the vertical axis at an amount equal to the welfare payment the individual gets when not working at all. As the individual begins to work, the need for welfare declines and so the welfare payment declines. Observe that the amount of the welfare payment, which is represented by the shaded gap between the steep line and the less steep line, diminishes as the hours of work increase, and finally, after a certain number of hours worked, the welfare payment disappears.

Because the welfare payment is reduced when the individual's income from work rises, it creates a disincentive. The flatter the dashed line, the greater the disincentive. For example, if someone decided to work 10 hours a week for a total of $50 per week, but the welfare payment is reduced $30 per week, then effectively the marginal tax rate is 60 percent, high enough to discourage work.

Welfare reform endeavors to change the welfare system in order to reduce this disincentive. Looking at Figure 14.8, we see that there are two ways to make the dashed line steeper and thereby provide more incentive to work. One way is to reduce the amount of welfare paid at the zero income amount. Graphically, this is shown in the lower graph of Figure 14.8. This twists the dashed line because the intercept on the vertical axis is lower but the intersection of the dashed line and the solid line is at the same number of hours of work as the top graph. This will increase the slope of the dashed line and therefore provide more incentive to work. But the problem with this approach is that poor people get less welfare: The poverty rate could rise.

A second way to make the dashed line steeper is to raise the place at which it intersects the black solid line, as in the middle graph of Figure 14.8. But that might mean making welfare payments to people who do not need them at all, people who earn $50,000 or $60,000 annually.

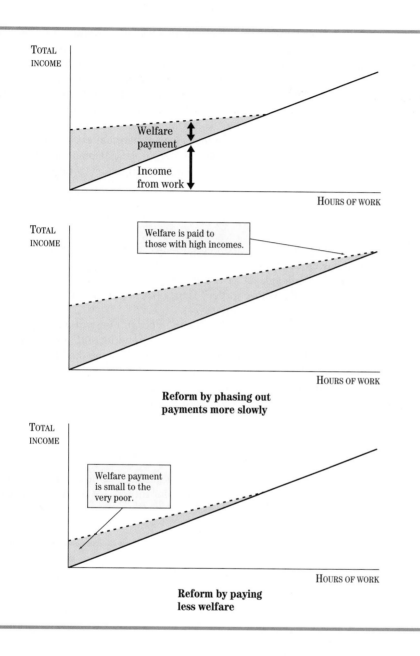

FIGURE 14.8
Welfare Reform to Improve Work Incentives
The top graph shows how welfare reduces the marginal earnings from working more hours because welfare payments are phased out. There are two basic approaches to reform: phasing out the payments more slowly (as in the middle graph) or lowering the welfare payment (as in the lower graph). Both have advantages and disadvantages.

The welfare reform act signed into law by President Clinton in 1996 leaves the decision of which welfare reform approach to take up to the states. As discussed in the box on page 391, the states are going off in different directions, some cutting welfare checks and others raising the amount that can be earned before welfare is reduced. Some states have taken other approaches to get around the disincentive difficulty. Florida, Tennessee, and Texas require adult welfare recipients to go to work immediately. Twenty-four states require that people work after two years on welfare. Other states require that a single parent finish high school in order to get the full welfare payment. These proposals are aimed at increasing the incentive to get off welfare and go to work.

The EITC can also be viewed as a way to increase the incentive to work. As stated in the *1994 Economic Report of the President*, "it provides positive work incentives for many of the lowest-paid employees in our society." As discussed earlier, it lowers the marginal tax rate by 40 percent for incomes up to $8,425. It has a disadvantage, however, in that it may increase the disincentive to work for incomes above $11,000 and up to $27,000. And recall that the marginal tax rate for the personal income tax starts at 15 percent (at $16,900 in income for a family of four, for example). The 21 percent plus the 15 percent gives a marginal tax rate of 36 percent, which is close to the highest marginal tax rate in the personal income tax. If we add in the payroll tax (15.3 percent), then the marginal tax rate rises even higher, to 51.3 percent!

The Problem of Welfare Notches

When welfare payments are not phased out smoothly, as in Figure 14.8, the disincentive to work can even be stronger. For example, when a family reaches a certain income level, it loses Medicaid, an insurance program that can be worth several thousand dollars to a family with children. Hence, there can actually be a fall in total income from working more hours per week.

This is illustrated in Figure 14.9. When the number of hours of work reaches a certain point, the Medicaid benefit drops. The drop in total income forms a wedge in the curve that is called a **welfare notch.** Clearly, there is some disincentive to do a few more hours of work if it will pull a family into the welfare notch. The problem is less severe if the income or hours of work take the family well beyond the notch, but if the choice is limited to a job with a few more hours, the disincentive can be severe.

welfare notch: a situation in which there is a decrease in total income for families on welfare when they increase the amount they work.

Payroll Subsidies and Empowerment, or Enterprise, Zones

Another proposal is to give more incentive to work through "empowerment zones," or "enterprise zones." Such programs give tax incentives for firms to increase

FIGURE 14.9
A Welfare Notch
If some welfare benefits decline sharply when income rises, a notch representing a decline in total income occurs. Such a notch causes a great disincentive to work more hours.

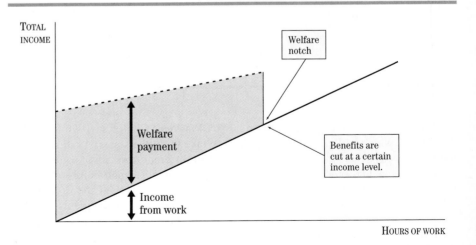

Reading the News About the 1996 Welfare Reform Act

The new federal welfare reform law lets states choose which approach to take to creating better work incentives in the welfare system. This news article describes the actual choices being made by various states after the welfare reform bill was signed into law by President Clinton. Some states allow for more earnings from work before welfare payments are phased out, while others reduce the amount of the payment. Both approaches will increase the incentives to work, as shown in Figure 14.8. Observe that some states plan to give firms financial subsidies to hire welfare recipients.

Experience with the different approaches on the state level will provide useful information about which approaches work better.

Source of article: "Rewards and Penalties Vary in States' Welfare Programs" by Robert Pear, *The New York Times,* February 23, 1997. Copyright © 1997 by The New York Times Company. Reprinted by permission.

Rewards and Penalties Vary in States' Welfare Programs

By ROBERT PEAR

WASHINGTON, Feb. 22 — Exercising the vast discretion given to them under the new welfare law, many states are adopting stricter work requirements and shorter time limits than Congress envisioned for public assistance.

But some states temper their stringent policies, allowing exemptions for parents who cannot find jobs or who are caring for disabled relatives.

Six months after President Clinton signed the welfare law, 40 governors have submitted state welfare plans to the Federal Government, and the Department of Health and Human Services has certified 37 as complete. Those states are allowed to run their own welfare and work programs with lump sums of Federal money that are, in many cases, greater than what the states would have received under the old welfare law.

States are, as Congress expected, going off in different directions, with different combinations of penalties and rewards. . . .

Some states encourage work by penalizing those who refuse to cooperate. Indiana has sharply increased the use of such penalties, which typically cut welfare checks by $90 a month.

Other states treat earned income in a new, more generous way, to make sure people are better off working than on welfare. In Pennsylvania, for example, a family of a mother and two children is now forced off welfare when the woman earns more than $10,300 a year. But under a new policy taking effect next month, the ceiling will be raised to $14,100.

At first, state welfare programs look like a crazy quilt. But separate reviews of state plans by the Federal Government, the National Governors' Association and The New York Times disclose some patterns.

TIME LIMITS Eighteen states — 45 percent of those that have filed plans — set time limits on welfare stricter than the five-year lifetime limit authorized by the Federal law. Twenty-two states plan to enforce the five-year limit.

Indiana and North Carolina have two-year limits. In North Carolina, people reaching the limit may reapply for benefits after three years off welfare. Montana has a two-year limit for single parents. Louisiana will pay welfare for no more than two years in any five-year period. Utah has a three-year limit. Connecticut has a 21-month limit, but makes exceptions and grants extensions in some cases — if, for example, a person is caring for an incapacitated child or spouse.

WORK REQUIREMENTS The Federal law requires adults to work within two years of receiving cash assistance, but 16 states, or 40 percent of those filing plans, have adopted more stringent work requirements. Twenty-four states intend to use the two-year work requirement.

Some states, including Florida, Tennessee and Texas, say that adult welfare recipients are expected to go to work immediately. Massachusetts requires work within two months. Virginia requires work in three months.

Michigan reduces welfare benefits by 25 percent if people do not meet work requirements within two months. In North Carolina, welfare recipients must obtain jobs or participate in job training within three months, or their benefits will be cut. Many states want to define "work" more broadly than Congress, so they can give credit for job-search activities or literacy classes.

SUBSIDIZED EMPLOYMENT
Twenty-seven states said they would subsidize jobs for welfare recipients. Typically, states take a portion of the money earmarked for welfare benefits or food stamps and give it to employers, who in turn pay wages to the welfare recipients.

Nineteen states, including New York and North Carolina, will make occasional payments to low-income families so they can cope with temporary setbacks and stay off welfare. People who are unexpectedly laid off or suffer brief illnesses may be eligible for such emergency grants.

employment in poor areas, which is the reason for the term *zone*. For example, in a pilot program enacted in 1993, a 20 percent payroll subsidy on wages and salaries up to $15,000 per worker is given to firms that are located in one of the zones and that employ workers who live in the zone.

A payroll subsidy is the opposite of a payroll tax. Rather than having to pay a tax, the firm receives a payment from the government. Such a tax will shift up the labor demand curve and either increase employment, raise wages, or a little of both, depending on the price elasticities of demand and supply.

Social Insurance Programs

social security: the system through which individuals make payments to the government when they work and receive payments from the government when they retire or become disabled.

Many transfer payments in the United States are not means-tested. The largest of these are social security, Medicare, and unemployment insurance. **Social security** is the system through which payments from the government are made to individuals over a certain age when they retire or become disabled. **Medicare** is a health insurance program for older people. **Unemployment insurance** pays money to individuals who are laid off from work.

Medicare: a government health insurance program for the elderly.

Social security, Medicare, and unemployment insurance are called *social insurance* because they make payments to anyone—rich or poor—under certain specific circumstances. Social security provides benefits when a worker becomes disabled or retires. Medicare provides payments when an older person requires medical care, and unemployment compensation is paid to workers when they are laid off from a job.

unemployment insurance: a program that makes payments to people who lose their jobs.

But these programs have features that make them much more than insurance programs. The programs have effects on income distribution because they transfer income between different groups. Consider social security and Medicare. Payroll taxes paid by workers pay for these programs. But the payroll taxes paid by an individual are only loosely related to the funds paid out to the same individual. In reality, each year the funds paid in by the workers are paid out to the current older people. In other words, social security is more like a transfer program from young people to older people than an insurance program.

However, because the social insurance programs are not means-tested, they also transfer income to middle-income and even wealthy individuals. In other words they are not well targeted at the lower-income groups. For this reason many people have suggested that these programs be means-tested. In fact, recent legislation has effectively reduced social security benefits to higher-income older people by requiring that a major part of the benefits be included in taxable income; social security benefits were formerly excluded from taxable income.

Mandated Benefits

mandated benefits: benefits that a firm is required by law to provide to its employees.

Mandated benefits occur when a firm is required by the government to provide a benefit for its workers. For example, a federal law requires firms to give unpaid leave to employees to care for a newborn baby or a sick relative. Such benefits are a cost to the firm (for example, the cost of finding and training a replacement or providing health insurance to the worker on leave). But, of course, they are a benefit to the worker. Another example of a mandated benefit is a proposal that would require that firms pay a portion of the health insurance costs of their workers.

The effects of mandated benefits can be analyzed using the supply and demand for labor diagram, much as we analyzed the effects of a payroll tax. As shown in Figure 14.10, the labor demand curve shifts down, as it did in Figure 14.6 for the

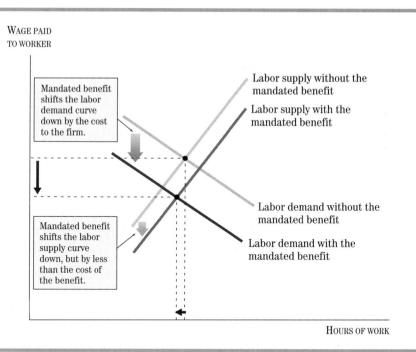

WAGE PAID
TO WORKER

Mandated benefit shifts the labor demand curve down by the cost to the firm.

Labor supply without the mandated benefit

Labor supply with the mandated benefit

Labor demand without the mandated benefit

Mandated benefit shifts the labor supply curve down, but by less than the cost of the benefit.

Labor demand with the mandated benefit

HOURS OF WORK

FIGURE 14.10
Effect of a Mandated Benefit
A mandated benefit is a cost to the firm; it shifts down the demand curve for labor just as payroll tax does. But in the case of a mandated benefit, the labor supply curve shifts down too. Hence, the wage paid to the worker falls, as does employment.

employer-paid payroll tax because the mandated benefits are a cost to the firm. But the mandated benefits provide a benefit to the workers, which shifts the labor supply curve down. The labor supply curve will probably not shift down as much as the labor demand curve because the worker will not value the benefit quite as much as its cost to the firm.

In any case, the new equilibrium in Figure 14.10 shows that the wage paid to the worker will fall by nearly the amount of the mandated benefit. In other words, despite the fact that the employer is "paying" for the mandated benefit, it is the worker who mainly pays. There will also be a reduction in employment.

If the workers valued the benefit exactly as much as it cost the firm, then the wage would fall by the full amount of the benefit. In this case employment would not fall at all.

Review

▶ There are two major types of transfer payments. Means-tested payments—family support, Medicaid, food stamps—depend on the income of the recipient. Social insurance—social security, unemployment compensation, and Medicare—does not depend on the income of the recipient.

▶ Means-tested transfer payments create disincentives. The purpose of welfare reform is to reduce those disincentives.

▶ Under welfare reform, states are trying different methods to reduce disincentives, including work requirements and time limits on payment of benefits to welfare recipients.

THE DISTRIBUTION OF INCOME IN THE UNITED STATES

What does the distribution of income in the United States actually look like? What effect does the tax and transfer system described in the previous two sections have on income distribution? Does the United States have a less equal income distribution than other countries? What has been happening to income distribution over time? To answer these questions, we need a quantitative measure of income distribution.

The Personal Distribution of Income

Current Population Survey: a monthly survey of a sample of households to obtain information about income and employment.

Data about people's income in the United States are collected by the Census Bureau in a monthly survey of about 60,000 households called the **Current Population Survey.** Using the information on the income of households in this survey, an estimate of the distribution of income for the entire country is made.

Economists and statisticians usually study the income distribution of families or households rather than individuals. A *family* is defined by the Census Bureau as a group of two or more people related by birth, marriage, or adoption who live in the same housing unit. A *household* consists of all related family members and unrelated individuals who live in the same housing unit. Because the members of a family or a household typically share their income, it is usually more sensible to consider families or households rather than individuals. One would not say that a young child who earns nothing is poor if the child's mother or father earns $100,000 a year. In a family without children where one spouse works and the other remains at home, one would not say that the working spouse is rich and the nonworking spouse is poor.

quintile: divisions or groupings of one-fifth of a population ordered by income, wealth, or some other statistic.

Because there are so many people in the population, it is necessary to have a simple way to summarize the income data. One way to do this is to arrange the population into a small number of groups ranging from the poorest to the richest. Most typically, the population is divided into fifths, called **quintiles,** with the same percentage of families or households in each quintile. For example, in Table 14.3 the 67 million families in the United States are divided into five quintiles, with 13.4 million families in each quintile. The first row shows the poorest 20 percent—the bottom quintile. The next several rows show the higher-income quintiles, with the last row showing the 20 percent with the highest incomes.

The second and third columns of Table 14.3 show how much income is earned by families in each of the five groups. The bottom 20 percent of families have incomes below $16,952, the families in the next quintile have incomes greater than $16,952 but less than $30,000, and so on. Note that the lower limit for families in

TABLE 14.3
Range of Annual Family Incomes for Five Quintiles, 1993

Quintile	Income Greater Than	Income Less Than
Bottom 20 percent	0	$16,952
Second 20 percent	$16,952	$30,000
Third 20 percent	$30,000	$45,020
Fourth 20 percent	$45,020	$66,794
Top 20 percent	$66,794	—

Source: Statistical Abstract of the United States, 1995, Table 733.

Quintile	Percent of Income	Cumulative Percent of Income
Bottom 20 percent	4	4
Second 20 percent	10	14
Third 20 percent	16	30
Fourth 20 percent	24	54
Top 20 percent	46	100

Source: Statistical Abstract of the United States, 1995, Table 733.

TABLE 14.4
Distribution of Family Income by Quintile

the top 20 percent is $66,794. The lower limit for the top 5 percent (not shown in the table) is $113,182. Table 14.3 indicates that there is an unequal distribution of income in the United States.

Inequality can be better measured by considering the total income in each quintile as a percentage of the total income in the country. Table 14.4 provides this information. The second column in Table 14.4 shows the income received by families in each quintile as a percent of total income in the United States.

A quick look at Table 14.4 again shows that the distribution of income is far from equal. Those in the lower 20 percent earn only 4 percent of total income. On the other hand, those in the top 20 percent earn 46 percent of total income. Thus, the amount of income earned by the rich is a large multiple of the amount of income earned by the poor.

These percentages are summed up in the third column of Table 14.4. This cumulative percent shows that the bottom 20 percent earn 4 percent of the income, the bottom 40 percent earn 14 percent of the income, the bottom 60 percent earn 30 percent of the income, and the bottom 80 percent earn 54 percent of the income.

The Lorenz Curve and Gini Coefficient

The data in Table 14.4 can be presented in a useful graphical form. Figure 14.11 shows the cumulative percent of income from the third column of Table 14.4 on the vertical axis and the percent representing each quintile from the first column on the horizontal axis. The five dots in the figure are the five pairs of observations from the table. For example, point *A* at the lower left corresponds to the 4 percent of income earned by the lowest 20 percent of people. Point *B* corresponds to the 14 percent of income earned by the lowest 40 percent of people. The other points are plotted the same way. The uppermost point is where 100 percent of the income is earned by 100 percent of the people.

If we connect these five points, we get a curve that is bowed out. This curve is called the **Lorenz curve.** To measure how bowed out the curve is, we draw the solid black 45-degree line. The 45-degree line is a line of perfect equality. On that line, the lowest 20 percent earn exactly 20 percent of the income, the lowest 40 percent earn exactly 40 percent of the income, and so on. Every household earns exactly the same amount.

The degree to which the Lorenz curve is bowed out from the 45-degree line provides a visual gauge of the inequality of income. The more bowed out the line is, the more unequal is the income distribution. The box on page 398 shows how the Lorenz curve in the United States compares with some other countries and with the world as a whole.

Lorenz curve: a curve showing the relation between the cumulative percentage of the population and the proportion of total income earned by each cumulative percentage. It measures income inequality.

FIGURE 14.11

The Lorenz Curve for the United States

Each point on the Lorenz curve gives the percent of income received by a percentage of households. The plotted points are for the United States. Point *A* shows that 4 percent of income is received by the lowest 20 percent of families. Point *B* shows that 14 percent of income is received by the lowest 40 percent of families. These two points and the others in the figure come from Table 14.4. In addition, the 45-degree line shows perfect equality, and the solid lines along the horizontal and right-hand vertical axis show perfect inequality. The shaded area between the 45-degree line and the Lorenz curve is a measure of inequality. The ratio of this area to the area of the triangle below the 45-degree line is the Gini coefficient.

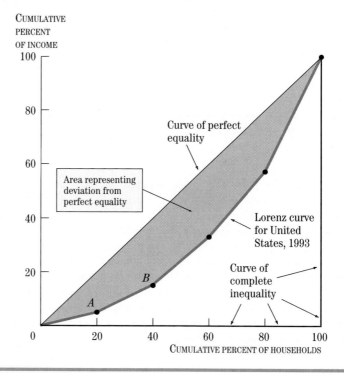

Gini coefficient: an index of income inequality ranging between 0 (for perfect equality) and 1 (for absolute inequality); it is defined as the ratio of the area between the Lorenz curve and the perfect equality line, divided by the area between the lines of perfect equality and perfect inequality.

The most unequal distribution possible would occur when only one person earns all the income. In that case, the curve could be so bowed out from the 45-degree line that it would consist of a straight line on the horizontal axis up to 100 and then a vertical line. For example, 99.9 percent of the households would earn zero percent of the income. Only when the richest person is included do we get 100 percent of the income.

The **Gini coefficient** is a useful numerical measure of how bowed out the Lorenz curve is. It is defined as the ratio of the area of the gap between the 45-degree line and the Lorenz curve to the area between the lines of perfect equality and perfect inequality. The Gini coefficient can range between 0 and 1. It has a value of zero if the area between the diagonal line and the Lorenz curve is zero. Thus, when the Gini coefficient is zero, we have perfect equality. The Gini coefficient would be 1 if only one person earned all the income in the economy.

Figure 14.12 shows how the Gini coefficient has changed in the United States over the last 40 years. The Gini coefficient has varied between a narrow range, from .35 to .40. The most notable feature of the Gini coefficient in Figure 14.12 is the decline after World War II until around 1970 and the subsequent increase. It is clear that in recent years income inequality has increased. Higher earnings of skilled and educated workers relative to the less unskilled and less educated may partly explain this change in income distribution. But the reason for these changes in income inequality is still a major unsettled question for economists.

It is important to note, however, that an increase in income inequality, as in Figure 14.12, does not necessarily mean that the rich got richer and the poor got poorer. For example, if one looks at average income in each quintile, one finds an increase for all groups from 1970 to 1990, even after adjusting for inflation. Average income in the bottom quintile increased by 25 percent from around 1970 to 1990, while average income in the top quintile increased by 35 percent. Thus, the top income group got richer by a larger amount than the bottom group—and so the income distribution widened—but the real income of those in the bottom group also increased over this long time span.

Income Mobility and Longer-Term Income Inequality

In interpreting income distribution statistics, it is important to recognize that the quintiles do not refer to the same people as the years go by. People move from quintile to quintile. People in the top quintile in one year may be in the bottom quintile the next year. And people in the bottom quintile one year may be in the top quintile the next year.

Distinguishing between income in any one year and income over several years is important. In a typical life span, people usually earn less when they are young than when they are middle-aged. As they grow older and become more experienced, their wages and salary increase. When people retire, their income usually declines again. Thus, even if everyone had the exact same lifetime income, one would see inequality in the income distribution every year. Middle-aged people would be relatively rich while young and old people would be relatively poor.

More generally, many people seem to move around the income distribution from year to year. Some undergo hardship such as a layoff or a permanent loss of job because of a change in the economy. Even if they are eventually rehired, in the short run they fall to the lower end of the income distribution when they are unemployed. On the other hand, some people do well and move quickly to the top of the income distribution.

How significant is income mobility? Economic research shows that about two-thirds of the people in any one quintile move to another over a 10-year period. About half of those in the top quintile move to a lower quintile, and about half of those in the bottom quintile move to a higher quintile. This degree of mobility has not changed in the last 20 years.

Changing Composition of Households

The formation or splitting up of households can also affect the distribution of income. For example, if two individuals who were living separately form a household, the household income doubles. Households splitting apart can also alter the income distribution drastically. If one adult leaves the family, perhaps because of divorce or desertion, and the other one stays home with the children, the income of the household declines substantially.

It appears that the splitting apart of households has had an impact on income distribution in the United States. According to some estimates, if household composition had not changed in the United States in the last 20 years, there would have been half as much an increase in inequality as measured by the Gini coefficient.

Distribution of Income versus the Distribution of Wealth

Another factor to keep in mind when interpreting data on the income distribution is the distinction between *income* and *wealth*. Your annual income is what you earn each year. Your wealth, or your net worth, is all you own minus what you owe

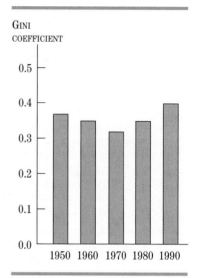

FIGURE 14.12
Changes in Income Inequality: The U.S. Gini Coefficient
The Gini coefficient is large when there is more inequality, as measured by the Lorenz curve in Figure 14.11. Thus, by this measure, inequality fell in the United States from 1950 to 1970 but increased from 1970 to 1990.

Using Economics to Explain Income Distribution Around the World

A Lorenz curve can be calculated for different countries or groups of countries. For most European countries the Lorenz curve is closer to equality than it is for the United States. Canada, Australia, and the United Kingdom have Lorenz curves very similar to that of the United States.

However, income distribution varies much more when we look beyond the developed countries. As the following figure shows, Bangladesh, a very poor country, has a more equal income distribution than the United States. Brazil, a middle-income country that is also much poorer than the United States, has a much less equal income distribution. Among individual countries, Bangladesh and Brazil are close to the extremes: 60 percent of the population receives 40 percent of the income in Bangladesh and 19 percent of the income in Brazil compared to 33 percent in the United States.

Income distribution in the world as a whole is far more unequal than for any one country because the very poor in some countries are combined with the very rich in other countries. For example, when West Germany united with East Germany to form one country, the income

distribution became more unequal for the unified country as a whole than it was for either country before unification. The Lorenz curve for the world as a whole—as illustrated

in the figure—shows far greater inequality than in any one country: 60 percent of the world's population receives only 5 percent of the income.

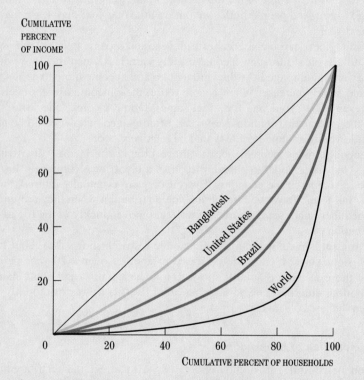

Source: World Development Report (Oxford University Press, 1992). (World curve computed from population data for low, lower-middle, upper-middle, and high-income countries.)

others. Wealth changes over a person's lifetime even more than income as people save for retirement. For example, a young person who has just graduated may have little wealth, or, with a college loan still to pay off, may have negative net worth. However, by saving a bit each year—perhaps through a retirement plan at work—the person's wealth gradually accumulates. By the time retirement age is reached the person may have a sizable retirement fund, and thus be relatively wealthy.

A survey of about 3,000 families in the United States in 1989 found that the top 10 percent of households held about 69 percent of the net worth in the United

States. Although such surveys are not as accurate as the regular monthly surveys of 60,000 households from which our information about income distribution is based, it is clear that the distribution of wealth is less equal than the distribution of income. About one-third of the net worth in this survey was in the form of net worth held in small businesses.

The Poor and the Poverty Rate

Many believe the main purpose of government redistribution of income is to help the poor. For this reason the term *social safety net* is sometimes used for an income redistribution system; the idea is that the programs try to prevent those who were born poor or who have become poor from falling too far down in income and therefore in nutrition, health, and general well-being.

Poverty can be observed virtually everywhere. The poor are visible in the blighted sections of cities and in remote rural areas. Most everyone has seen the serious problems of the homeless in cities of the United States. CNN has brought the agony of poverty around the world to our TV screens.

To gauge the success or failure of government policies to alleviate poverty, economists have developed quantitative measures of poverty. The **poverty rate** is the percentage of people who live in poverty. To calculate the poverty rate, one needs to define what it means to live in poverty. In the United States, poverty is usually quantitatively defined by a **poverty line,** an estimate of the minimal amount of annual income a family needs to avoid severe economic hardship. The poverty line in the United States is based on a survey showing that families spend on average one-third of their income on food. The poverty line is thus obtained by multiplying by 3 the Department of Agriculture's estimate of the amount of money needed to purchase a low-cost nutritionally adequate amount of food. In addition, adjustments are made for the size of the family. Table 14.5 shows the poverty line for several different family sizes. Since the 1960s, when it was first developed, the poverty line has been increased to adjust for inflation.

Using the poverty line and data on the income distribution, one can determine the number of people who live in poverty and the poverty rate.

The Overall Poverty Rate

Figure 14.13 shows the overall poverty rates in the United States over the last 30 years. The overall poverty rate declined sharply in the 1960s but increased slightly in the 1970s, 1980s, and 1990s. However, the poverty rate is still well below what it was around 1960.

Worse for Children, Better for the Elderly

There are important trends in poverty for different groups in the population. For example, the percent of children who live in poverty rose in the 1970s, 1980s, and 1990s. But the poverty rate for the elderly has declined, and this has held down the increase in the overall poverty rate.

Poverty rates have declined for the elderly mainly because of better retirement benefits, including social security payments, which prevent many elderly people from going into poverty.

The increase in poverty for children is troublesome, and it is difficult to explain. Some of it may have to do with the increase in single-headed households

poverty rate: the percentage of people living below the poverty line.

poverty line: an estimate of the mimimum amount of annual income required for a family to avoid severe economic hardship.

TABLE 14.5
The Poverty Line in the United States, 1993

Family Size	Poverty Line
Unrelated individuals	$ 7,363
Two persons	$ 9,414
Three persons	$11,522
Four persons	$14,763
Seven persons	$22,383

Source: Statistical Abstract of the United States, 1995, Table 746.

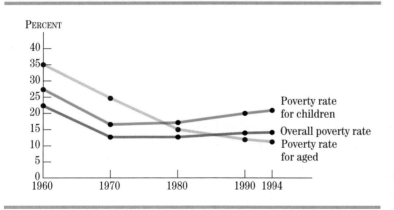

PERCENT

FIGURE 14.13
Poverty Rates in the United States
The overall poverty rate is the percentage of people with incomes below the poverty line. The poverty rate for children is the percent of all children in families with incomes below the poverty line. The poverty rate declined significantly for all three groups in the 1960s, but the poverty rate for children increased in the 1970s, 1980s, and 1990s while it continued to decline for the aged during the same period.

Source: Committee on Ways and Means, U.S. House of Representatives, *1991 Green Book*, May 1991, Table 2, pp. 1137–38; *Statistical Abstract of the United States, 1995.*

with children, which are usually poorer than two-adult households. Poverty rates in households with a single head and at least one child have ranged between 35 and 40 percent in the last 20 years—three times the overall poverty rate.

Effects of Taxes and Transfers on Income Distribution and Poverty

We have seen that two goals of the tax and transfer system are to redistribute income and reduce poverty. How successful is this redistribution effort? Estimates by the U.S. Census Bureau indicate that households in the bottom 20 percent have their average income increased by about $9,000 as a result of the tax and transfer system. Those in the second quintile have their average income increased by an average of about $4,000 as a result of the tax and transfer system. Those in the uppermost part of the income distribution have their average income reduced by about $22,000 as a result of the tax and transfer system.

To be sure, these estimates ignore any of the incentive effects mentioned earlier, such as the reduced work incentives that might result from the tax and transfer system. And they ignore any possible response of private efforts to redistribute income—such as charities—that might occur as a result of changes in the government's role.

How does the tax and transfer system affect the poverty rate? The same type of estimates indicate that without taxes and transfers, about 8 percent more of the U.S. population would be below the poverty line. Again, these estimates assume that there would be no response of people to the change in incentives caused by such a change in the tax and transfer system and thereby probably overstate the effect of the programs on poverty rates.

Review

▶ The distribution of income can be measured by the percentage of income earned by quintiles of households or families. The Lorenz curve and the Gini coefficient are computed from this distribution.

▶ The poverty rate is a quantitative measure of the amount of poverty in the United States.

▶ The distribution of income has become more unequal in the United States since the early 1970s. The change is partly due to a growing dispersion of wages between unskilled workers with little education and highly skilled workers with more education.

▶ In recent years, the poverty rate among children has increased while the poverty rate for the elderly has declined.

▶ Estimates indicate that the tax and transfer system currently makes the income distribution less unequal and the poverty rate lower than they would otherwise be.

▶ Nevertheless, the increase in poverty among children and the long period of time some people stay on welfare have raised serious concerns about the tax and transfer system in the United States.

CONCLUSION

In a democracy, the amount of government redistribution of income is decided by the people and their representatives. A majority seem to want some redistribution of income, but there is debate about how much the government should do.

Why doesn't a democracy lead to much more redistribution? After all, 60 percent of the people, according to Table 14.4, receive only 30 percent of the income. Since 60 percent of the voting population is enough to win an election, this 60 percent could vote to redistribute income much further. Why hasn't it?

There are probably a number of reasons. First, there is the tradeoff between equality and efficiency stressed in this chapter. People realize that taking away incentives to work will reduce the size of the pie for everyone.

Another reason is that most of us believe people should be rewarded for their work. Just as we can think of a fair income distribution, we can think about a fair reward system. If some students want to work hard in high school so they can attend college, why shouldn't they get the additional income that comes from that?

Some view inheritance as interfering with the idea of equal opportunity, and that is one reason for the inheritance tax. But many parents pass on human capital—education and training—rather than financial capital to their children. One may have advantages in life if one's parents encourage education and hard work. But one would not want to reduce incentives for parents to do so.

There is also the connection between personal freedom and economic freedom. Government involvement in income distribution means government involvement in people's lives. Those who cherish the idea of personal freedom worry about a system that taxes a large amount of income from people who work.

Finally, much income redistribution occurs through the private sector—private charities and churches. The distribution of food and the provision of health care have long been supported by nongovernment organizations. In times of floods or earthquakes it is common for people to volunteer to help those in distress. Private charity has certain advantages over government. Individuals become more personally involved if they perform a public service, whether volunteering at a soup kitchen or tutoring at an elementary school. But incentives for redistribution through private charity may be too small. People might give less to a charitable organization if they believe others are not giving. Thus, the private sector may not be sufficient.

KEY POINTS

1. The government in modern democracies plays a major role in trying to help the poor and provide a more equal income distribution.

2. Taxes are needed to pay for transfers and other government spending. In the United States the personal income tax and the payroll tax are by far the most significant sources of tax revenue at the federal level. Sales taxes and property taxes play a significant role at the local level.

3. Taxes cause inefficiencies, as measured by deadweight loss, because taxes reduce the amount of the economic activity being taxed—whether it is the production of a good or the labor of workers.

4. The incidence of a tax depends on the price elasticity of supply and demand. The deadweight loss from taxes on goods with low price elasticities is relatively small.

5. Transfer payments are classified into either means-tested programs—such as welfare and food stamps—or social insurance programs—such as social security and unemployment insurance.

6. Transfer payments can cause inefficiency due to disincentives to work or the incentive for families to split up.

7. There is a tradeoff between equality and efficiency. Tax reform and welfare reform try to improve incentives and reduce inefficiency.

8. The distribution of income has grown more unequal in recent years.

9. Poverty among children has increased, while poverty among the elderly has declined in recent years.

10. The tax and transfer system has reduced income inequality and lowered poverty rates, but there is much room for improvement and reform.

KEY TERMS

personal income tax
taxable income
tax bracket
marginal tax rate
average tax rate
progressive tax
regressive tax
proportional tax
flat tax
payroll tax
corporate income tax
excise tax
sales tax

property tax
tax incidence
tax revenue
ability-to-pay principle
transfer payment
means-tested transfer
social insurance transfer
family support programs
Medicaid
supplemental security income (SSI)
food stamp program
Head Start
housing assistance programs

earned income tax credit (EITC)
welfare notch
social security
Medicare
unemployment insurance
mandated benefits
Current Population Survey
quintile
Lorenz curve
Gini coefficient
poverty rate
poverty line

QUESTIONS FOR REVIEW

1. What are the two largest sources of tax revenue for the federal government?

2. What is the difference between income and taxable income?

3. Why is there a deadweight loss from the personal income tax?

4. Why are the effects of a payroll tax the same whether the employer or the worker pays it?

5. Why is deadweight loss from a payroll tax small when the elasticity of labor supply is small?

6. What is the difference between a marginal tax rate and an average tax rate? Why is the former more important for incentives?

7. What causes the tradeoff between equality and efficiency?

8. In what way do both welfare reform and tax reform focus on incentives?

9. What was the primary goal of the welfare reform law passed in 1996?

10. How is the distribution of income measured by the Lorenz curve and the Gini coefficient?

11. Why are income mobility and lifetime income important for interpreting the income distribution statistics?

PROBLEMS

1. The following table gives the income distribution in Sri Lanka and Belgium in 1990. Draw the Lorenz curve for each and compare them. Which country has the larger Gini coefficient?

Quintile	Income in Sri Lanka (%)	Income in Belgium (%)
Bottom 20 percent	5	8
Second 20 percent	9	14
Third 20 percent	12	18
Fourth 20 percent	18	24
Top 20 percent	56	36

2. Suppose the government decides to increase the payroll tax paid by employers. If the labor supply curve has a low elasticity, what will happen to the workers' wages? Who actually bears the burden of the tax, the workers or the firms? Would it be different if the labor supply has a high elasticity?

3. The table at the top of the next page gives hours worked and the welfare payment received.
 a) Calculate the missing data in the table, given that the hourly wage is $5 and total income is the sum of the wage payment and the welfare payment.

Hours Worked	Wage Payment	Welfare Payment	Total Income
0	———	10,000	———
500	———	8,000	———
1,000	———	6,000	———
1,500	———	4,000	———
2,000	———	2,000	———

b) Draw a graph that shows how much total income a worker earns with and without this welfare program. Put the number of hours worked on the horizontal axis and total income on the vertical axis.

c) What is the increase in total income for each additional hour worked without any welfare program? Compare it with the increase in total income for each additional hour worked under the welfare program.

d) How could the welfare program be changed to increase the incentive to work without reducing total income for a full-time worker (40 hours per week, 50 weeks per year, $5 per hour) below $12,000, which is already below the poverty line for a family of four?

4. Suppose that the labor demand curve is perfectly flat. What is the impact on a typical worker's hourly wage if the government increases the payroll tax paid by employers by 10 percent of the wage? Show what happens in a labor supply and labor demand graph like Figure 14.6. Why does the slope of the labor supply curve not affect your answer?

5. Suppose you are an economic adviser to a political candidate who wants to propose a particular tax policy. You analyze the effects of the policy and come up with the following data:

Quintile	Percent of Income without Tax	Percent of Income with Tax
Bottom 20 percent	5	5
Second 20 percent	11	8
Third 20 percent	20	16
Fourth 20 percent	23	27
Top 20 percent	41	44

Draw the Lorenz curve before and after the tax. Is this tax progressive or regressive? What will you recommend to your candidate?

6. Suppose it is mandated that health insurance be paid by employers.
   a) Draw a labor supply and labor demand diagram.

What happens to the labor demand curve? What happens to the labor supply curve?
   b) What happens to wages and employment relative to the initial situation?

7. Many states do not tax food items because that kind of tax is considered regressive. Explain. California tried to impose a "snack" tax—applying only to what the legislators thought was junk food. Suppose snack food has a higher elasticity of demand than nonsnack food. Draw a supply and demand diagram to explain which tax—on snack food or nonsnack food—will cause the price to rise more. Which will have a greater deadweight loss?

8. Some economists argue that we should use more progressive taxes, while others claim that we should adopt a flat tax. List some reasons for and against using progressive taxes.

9. Suppose the government is trying to decide between putting a sales tax on luxuries, which usually have very high demand elasticities, or on gasoline. Which tax will have a bigger effect on the market price? Which tax will cause the quantity traded in the market to decline the most? Draw a diagram to explain.

10. Suppose Fred, a bookkeeper, had taxable income of $21,000 last year. His doctor, Celia, had taxable income of $140,000 last year. Use the tax rate schedule in Figure 14.2 to figure out how much each owes in income taxes. What are their marginal tax rates? What are their average tax rates? (Assume that both are single.)

11. Analyze the distribution of income, using the household incomes in the following table. Rank the families by income. Compute the percentage of total income going to the poorest 20 percent of the families, the second 20 percent, and the richest 20 percent. Draw a Lorenz curve for the income distribution of these 10 families. Is their distribution more equal or less equal than the population of the United States as a whole?

Family	Income
Jones	$ 12,000
Pavlov	$100,000
Cohen	$ 24,000
Baker	$ 87,000
Dixon	$ 66,000
Sun	$ 72,000
Tanaka	$ 18,000
Bernardo	$ 45,000
Smith	$ 28,000
Lopez	$ 33,000

Public Goods, Externalities, and Government Behavior

The government produces a substantial amount of goods and services in today's market economies. More people are employed by the government in producing goods and services in the United States than are employed by all manufacturing firms, and this total doesn't even include the people in the armed forces. In addition to producing goods and services, like education, police, and national defense, the government pays private firms to produce goods and services. For example, it pays private construction firms to build bridges, insurance firms to administer Medicare, and private universities to educate students and do research. On top of that, the government mandates that people buy many goods and services, including fire alarms, automobile insurance, pollution control devices, car seats, and motorcycle helmets. Direct government involvement in the production of goods and services may seem extensive in the United States, but it is even greater in most other market economies.

One hundred years ago the government had a much smaller role in the production of goods and services than it does today. In the 1980s and 1990s there have been trends away from government production toward market production in many countries. Government production in formerly centrally planned economies in Russia and Eastern Europe is being scaled back in favor of the market. And in market economies as far south as New Zealand and as far north as Sweden the role of government has been reduced.

What economic principles determine whether a good or service should be provided by the government or left to the market? We have seen that competitive markets are remarkably efficient, but in some cases there is *market failure,* a situation in which the market is not efficient. The major sources of market failure are public goods, externalities, and monopoly power. This chapter will focus on the role of government in the cases of public goods and externalities, and the next chapter will focus on government policy toward monopoly power.

We first define public goods and externalities and show why competitive markets are inefficient when either is present. We then show how government can reduce the inefficiencies by producing goods and services or by taking actions to increase or decrease the private production of goods and services. Finally, we examine the problem of *government failure,* when, for political or bureaucratic reasons, government intervention in the market fails to improve the market outcome and may even make it worse.

market failure: any situation in which the market does not lead to an efficient outcome and in which there is a potential role for government (Ch. 2).

A BRIEF LOOK AT GOVERNMENT PRODUCTION

In the United States, goods and services are produced by literally thousands of governments—the federal government, 50 state governments, and 86,743 local governments, including counties, cities, towns, and school districts. Although the federal government and its chief executive officer, the president, get most of the publicity, state and local governments produce a much greater amount of goods and services than the federal government. The number of workers involved in production provides one measure of the relative size of the different parts of government. According to the 1990 census, of the 18.5 million government workers in the United States, 15.4 million, or 83 percent, worked for state and local governments. Total employment in the U.S. economy in 1990 was about 120 million.

Table 15.1 shows the range of goods and services produced by government. Observe the particular goods and services on the list. Education is by far the largest in terms of employment, followed by health and hospital services, national defense, police, the postal service, and highways. The figures for national defense include only civilian workers; if Table 15.1 included those serving in the armed forces— about 1.5 million—national defense would be second on the list. The other categories, from the judicial and legal system (federal, state, and county courts) to parks and recreation, are each significant but small relative to the total.

Observe also the types of goods and services not on the list because they are produced by the private sector of the economy. Manufacturing, mining, retail trade,

Function	Employment (millions)	Percent of Total
Education	8.4	45
Health and hospitals	1.9	10
National defense (civilian)	.9	5
Police protection	.9	5
Postal service	.8	4
Highways	.6	3
Judicial and legal	.4	2
Parks and recreation	.4	2
Fire protection	.3	2
Sanitation, sewage	.2	1
All other	4.0	21
Total	18.8	100

TABLE 15.1

Employment in Federal, State, and Local Government, 1993

Source: Statistical Abstract of the United States, 1996, p. 319.

405

wholesale trade, hotel services, and motion picture production are some of the items largely left to the private sector. Note also that for all the goods and services on the list in Table 15.1, the private sector provides at least some of the production. There are 6 million workers in the private health-care sector, for example, compared to the 1.9 million in government health care. The private sector is also involved in mail delivery, education, garbage collection, and even fire protection (volunteer fire departments).

The millions of government workers listed in Table 15.1 are employed in *producing* goods and services. In addition to producing goods and services, the government *pays for* or *requires* the private sector to produce certain goods and services. In other words, even if the government does not produce a good or a service, it may provide for its production. Consider military spending, for example. Including the armed forces, there are about 2.5 million government workers producing military goods and services. But there are another 2.5 million workers in private firms producing military goods and services. Thus, much of the production of military goods is purchased by the government from the private sector. Government contractors are employed by the government to produce missiles, bullets, food, clothing, etc.

Compared to many other countries with market economies, the governments in the United States produce or purchase a smaller amount of goods and services. The British have a national health service, for example, and most doctors are government employees. In France, telephone service is produced by the government. In Mexico, the national government produces and supplies oil products.

Partly because of dissatisfaction with government-produced goods and services, there has been a substantial reduction in the number and types of goods and services produced by governments around the world in recent years. The process of changing a government enterprise to a private enterprise is called **privatization.** For example, the British government sold British Airways to the public in 1987. The Mexicans privatized Telemex, the telephone company, in 1990. There has been a massive privatization of many businesses in Argentina and other Latin American countries. This privatization of formerly government-supplied goods and services has paralleled the transition from central planning to the market in Russia, Eastern Europe, and China, a transition that itself is the most massive privatization effort in history.

privatization: the process of changing a government enterprise into a privately owned enterprise.

Review

▶ Governments produce a substantial amount what we consume. State and local governments produce more than the federal government.

▶ Education is the largest government-produced item for the economy as a whole.

PUBLIC GOODS

Why is it necessary for governments to produce *any* goods and services? The concept of a public good helps us answer the question. A **public good** is a good or service having two characteristics, *nonrivalry in consumption* and *nonexcludability.* These characteristics lead to difficulties in production by private firms.

public good: a good or service that has two characteristics: nonrivalry in consumption and nonexcludability.

Nonrivalry in consumption means that more consumption of a good by one person does not mean less consumption of it by another person. For example, if you breathe more clean air by jogging rather than watching television, there is no less clean air for others to breathe. Or when a new baby is born, the baby immediately benefits from national defense without anyone else having to give up the benefits of national defense. Once a country's national defense—the military personnel, the strategic alliances, the missile defense system—is in place, the whole nation enjoys the security simultaneously; the total benefit is the sum of the benefits of every person. Clean air and national defense are examples of goods with nonrivalry. In contrast, for most goods, there is rivalry in consumption. For example, if you consume more grapes, then someone else must consume fewer grapes, or else more grapes must be produced. But for a good with nonrivalry in consumption, everybody can consume more if they want to. There is a collective aspect to the good.

nonrivalry: an aspect of a good for which increased consumption of the good by one person does not decrease the amount available for consumption by others.

Nonexcludability means that one cannot exclude people from consuming the good. For example, if the students at a college set up a crime-prevention program on campus consisting of all-night patrols, it is not possible to exclude from this service students who don't pay their class dues. Similarly, people cannot be excluded from the benefits of national defense. In contrast, most goods have the characteristic of excludability. For example, if you do not pay for grapes at the grocery store, the store owner can exclude you from consuming them.

nonexcludability: an aspect of a good for which no one can be excluded from consuming the good.

A public good is a good or service that has nonrivalry in consumption and nonexcludability. In contrast, a *private good* has excludability and rivalry.

Free Riders: A Difficulty for the Private Sector

Goods that have nonrivalry in consumption and nonexcludability create a **free-rider problem:** People can enjoy the good or service without reducing others' enjoyment even if they do not pay. To understand this concept, imagine you owned a huge bus with a broken rear door that allows people to get on and off without paying and without interfering with each other's travel. In that situation, you would have free riders. If you could not fix the door or do something else to exclude the free riders, you would not long be in the transportation business, because without fares, you would have losses.

free-rider problem: a problem arising in the case of public goods because those who do not contribute to the costs of providing the public good cannot be excluded from the benefits of the good.

National defense is like the huge bus with the broken rear door. You cannot exclude people from enjoying it, even if they do not pay, and one person's security does not reduce the security of others. It is clear that a private firm will have difficulty producing and selling national defense to the people of a country. For this reason, a collective action of government to provide the defense, requiring that people pay for it with taxes, is necessary. Similar actions are taken with other public goods such as police protection, fire protection, and the judicial system. That clean air has the property of a public good explains why government is involved in its "production." In this case, the government might help produce clean air by prohibiting the burning of leaves or the using of backyard barbecues. We will return to the government's role in air quality when we discuss the concept of externality.

Information also has the features of a public good. Everyone can benefit from information that a hurricane is on the way; there is no rivalry in consuming this information. Information about the state of the economy can also benefit everyone. For this reason, such information has been largely supplied by governments. In the United States, the Department of Commerce collects and distributes information about the economy, and the U.S. Weather Service collects information about the weather.

Avoiding Free-Rider Problems

Not all public goods are provided by the government. When they are not, some other means of dealing with the free-rider problem is needed. A classic example used by economists to explore the nature of public goods is the lighthouse that warns ships of nearby rocks and prevents them from running aground. A lighthouse has the feature of nonrivalry. If one ship goes safely by and enjoys the benefit of the light, this does not mean that another ship cannot go by. There is no rivalry in the consumption of the light provided by the lighthouse. Similarly, it is impossible to exclude ships from using the lighthouse because any ship can benefit from the light it projects.

However, lighthouse services are not always provided by the government. Early lighthouses were built by associations of shippers who charged fees to the ships in nearby ports. This system worked well because the fees could be collected from most shippers as they entered nearby ports. The free-rider problem was avoided; general tax revenue to pay for the lighthouse was not needed.

user fee: a fee charged for the use of a good normally provided by the government.

When the users of a government-provided service are charged for its use (some excludability is needed), the charge is called a **user fee.** In recent years, user fees have become more common in many government-provided services, including the national parks. The aim is to target the payments more closely to the users of the goods and services.

Although police services are almost always provided by government, there are many examples of security services provided by private firms. In these cases, the free-rider problem can be avoided. For example, a business firm may hire a guard to watch its premises. In these cases, the service is focused at a particular group, and excludability is possible.

New Technology

Modern technology is constantly changing the degree to which there is nonrivalry and nonexcludability for particular goods. When radio and television were invented, it became clear that once a radio or television program was broadcast, it was possible for anyone to tune in to the broadcast. A radio or television broadcast has both characteristics of a public good. But private firms have provided the vast majority of radio and television broadcasting services in the United States. The free-rider problem was partially avoided by using advertising to pay for the service. Paying directly would be impossible because of the inability to exclude individuals who do not pay.

More recently, technology is changing the public good features of television. Cable TV and the ability to scramble signals for those who use satellites to obtain their television signals have reduced the problem of nonexcludability. If one does not pay a cable television bill, the service can be turned off. If one does not pay the satellite fee, the signals can be scrambled so reception is impossible. Thus, it is now common to see cable television stations delivering specialized programming to small audiences that pay extra for the special service.

Public Goods and Actual Government Production

If we look at the types of goods produced by government in Table 15.1, we see many public goods, such as national defense, police protection, and the judicial and legal system. However, many of the goods in the list do not have features of public

Selling the Airwaves

The government not only buys goods, it sells them. One of the most valuable assets the government has been selling in recent years is found in thin air!

For a cellular telephone company or anyone else to send signals over the air it is necessary to have access to the radio spectrum, or the airwaves, over which the signals can be sent. Each section, or band, of the spectrum is like a piece of property. Just as a farmer needs a piece of land to grow crops, a telecommunications firm needs a piece of the airways to send signals. And just as a piece of land has a price, so does a piece of the airwaves. The price is determined by the laws of supply and demand.

The U.S. government is responsible for distributing the property rights to the spectrum in the United States. For many years the U.S. government had assigned rights to the radio spectrum through an administrative process that became increasingly inefficient over time. Economists had long recommended that the government use the market to remedy the inefficiencies caused by the bureaucratic process: They suggested the government sell—auction off—the spectrum rather than give it away. Finally, in 1993, Congress passed a bill giving the Federal Communications Commission (FCC) the authority to auction off the spectrum. Pieces of the spectrum for the use of new personal communication services, such as pocket telephones, were to be sold in the auction.

Auctioning off the airwaves is different than auctioning off art, rare wines, or many other forms of property, however, because the value of the piece of the spectrum to firms depends on whether they also have adjacent parts of the spectrum—either close geographically (like Florida and Georgia) or close in frequency (nearly the same megahertz number). For example, for travelers to use cellular telephones, the transmission must be able to roam from one geographical area to another.

Because spectrum auctions were different, economic experts were hired to help design the spectrum auction. Some were hired by the cellular telephone companies who would be doing the bidding. Others were hired by the FCC.

As a result of this input from economists, the auction design chosen by the FCC was a novel one. In most auctions goods are auctioned off *sequentially*—first one piece of art, then the next, and so on. In contrast,

The first auction of the radio spectrum by the FCC.

following the advice of the economists, bands of spectrum were auctioned off *simultaneously* by the FCC. In other words, firms could bid on several bands at the same time. It would be as if ten works of art were auctioned off at the same time with buyers able to offer different bids on each piece of art. Thus, if the bids on one piece were too high, a buyer could change the bid on another piece before the final sale was made. This simultaneous procedure dealt with the distinct characteristics of the spectrum, namely that many buyers wanted adjacent bands rather than a single band.

Because such a simultaneous auction had never taken place before, economic experiments were used to try it out. For example, Charles Plott of the California Institute of Technology conducted experiments on simultaneous auction proposals made by Paul Milgrom and Robert Wilson of Stanford University. Partly because the proposal worked well in the experiments, the FCC decided to use this approach. The auction process has been heralded as a great success.

(See John McMillan, "Selling Spectrum Rights," *Journal of Economic Perspectives,* Summer 1994.)

goods. Postal delivery, for example, is a service that has both rivalry in consumption and excludability. If you do not put a stamp on your letter, it is not delivered, and there is certainly rivalry in the consumption of a postal delivery worker's time. In principle, education also is characterized by rivalry in consumption and excludability. For a given-sized school, additional students reduce the education of other students, and it is technologically possible to exclude people. Although there are other reasons why the government might be involved in the production of these goods, it is important to note that the production of a good by the government does not make it a public good. Recall that in the formerly centrally planned economies the government produced virtually everything, private goods as well as public goods. The economist's definition of a public good is specific and is useful for determining when the government should produce something and when it is better left to the market. But actual decisions about production are made in the give and take of the political process and may or may not reflect the economic consideration emphasized here.

Review

▷ Public goods have two characteristics: nonrivalry, which means that greater consumption for one person does not mean less consumption for someone else, and nonexcludability, which means that it is not possible to exclude those who do not pay for the good.

▷ Public goods have a free-rider problem, which means that government production is frequently necessary.

▷ The private sector must deal with the free-rider problem if such goods are to be produced in the market.

COST-BENEFIT ANALYSIS

cost-benefit analysis: an appraisal of a project based on the costs and benefits derived from it.

Suppose that it is decided that a good or service is a public good and that if it is produced at all, government should provide it. Should the good be produced? How much of the good should be produced? Such decisions are ultimately made by voters and elected officials after much political debate. Some economic analysis of the costs and benefits of the goods and services should inform the participants in this debate. Balancing the costs and benefits of a good or service is called **cost-benefit analysis.**

Marginal Cost and Marginal Benefit

To determine the quantity of a government-provided service that should be produced, the marginal cost and marginal benefit of the service should be considered. In the case of police services, for example, a decision about whether to increase the size of the police force should consider both the marginal benefit to the people in the city—the reduction in loss of life and property from crime, the increased enjoyment from a secure environment, and safer schools—and the marginal cost—the increased payroll for the police. If the marginal benefit of more police is greater than the marginal cost of more police, then the police force should be increased. The optimal size of the police force should be such that the marginal cost of more police is equal to the marginal benefit of more police.

Measuring the costs of producing government-provided services is less difficult than measuring the benefits because government workers' wages or materials used in production have explicit dollar values. However, it is important to be sure to include all the costs. For example, the costs of any government services *ought* to include any deadweight losses from the increased taxes needed to finance these services. In other words, the costs are the dollar costs plus any deadweight loss from getting the additional tax revenue.

Measuring the benefits of government-provided services is difficult. How do we measure how much people value greater security in their community? How do we value the reduction in violence at schools or a reduced murder rate? Public opinion polls in which people are asked how much they would be willing to pay are a possibility. For example, people can be asked in surveys how much they would be willing to pay for more police in an area. Such estimates of willingness to pay are called **contingent valuations** because they give the value contingent on the public good existing and the person having to pay for it. Some economists think that contingent valuation is not reliable if people do not actually have to pay for the good or service. People may not give a good estimate of their true willingness to pay.

contingent valuation: an estimation of the willingness to pay for a project on the part of consumers who may benefit from the project.

Public Infrastructure Projects

In many cases, the decision to supply a public good involves large-scale public projects. There is a large initial expenditure and a payback in benefits that occurs over many years. For example, the construction of a road or bridge benefits those who use the road or bridge for many years. The term **public infrastructure project** describes public projects that last for many years in the future. Public infrastructure includes public airports, highways, computers, and government office buildings. Such a project should be undertaken if the benefits of the project exceed the costs of the project.

public infrastructure project: an investment project such as a bridge or jail funded by government designed to improve publicly provided services such as transportation or criminal justice.

Discounting Future Benefits

However, because the benefits of a public infrastructure project occur in the future, they must be discounted. For example, suppose the FBI is considering buying a new computer to help match fingerprints. The computer costs $800,000 and is expected to pay back benefits in terms of reduced crime of $550,000 at the end of one year and $605,000 at the end of two years. If the *discount rate,* the interest rate used to discount the future benefits, is 10 percent, then the present discounted value of the benefits is

$$\frac{\$550,000}{1 + .1} + \frac{\$605,000}{(1 + .1)^2} = \$1,000,000$$

(The appendix after Chapter 13 discusses present discounted value.) Because the costs ($800,000) are less than the benefits ($1,000,000), it makes sense for the FBI to buy the computer. If the computer cost $1,100,000, then the costs would be greater than the benefits and the FBI should not go ahead with the purchase. Of course, the example assumes the benefits are known and measured accurately, which, as just discussed, is not usually the case in practice.

Discount Rate (%)	Discounted Benefit ($)
1	1,137,600
2	1,120,700
3	1,104,300
4	1,088,200
5	1,072,600
6	1,057,300
7	1,042,400
8	1,027,900
9	1,013,800
10	1,000,000
11	986,500
12	973,400
13	960,500
14	948,000
15	935,700
16	923,800
17	912,000
18	900,600
19	889,400
20	878,500

The benefits of a project depend on the discount rate. At high discount rates, the benefit is low; at low discount rates, the benefit is high. In the example of the FBI computer, the table in the margin shows how the discount rate affects the benefits; this negative relationship between the discount rate and the benefits is true for any project.

What Discount Rate Should Be Used?

What discount rate should be used for public infrastructure projects? A private firm deciding whether to invest in a project would use the interest rate on other alternative investments. If the benefits and costs of a public investment have been measured accurately, then the discount rate on alternative uses of funds for the citizens in the community might be the appropriate discount rate. There is disagreement among economists about what discount rate is appropriate, however. When a government can borrow more cheaply than individuals, as the federal government can, then some argue that this lower interest rate is more appropriate. But others disagree, pointing to anomalies that would arise in such cases. Using a low discount rate would mean that more federal public projects would pass a cost-benefit analysis than would local government or private projects, because the federal government faces lower interest rates on its borrowing than local governments do. For example, the FBI could decide to buy a computer with the same costs and future benefits that the Miami police department would choose not to buy because it is cheaper for the federal government to borrow funds than the Miami government.

Review

▶ In deciding how much of a public good should be provided, cost-benefit analysis can be used. In deciding how large a police force should be, for example, the quantity of police services produced should be such that the marginal benefit of additional police equals marginal cost.

▶ In the case of large all-or-nothing public infrastructure projects, like bridges, the benefits may accrue over many years; they must be discounted when comparing them with the costs.

EXTERNALITIES: FROM THE ENVIRONMENT TO EDUCATION

externality: the situation in which the costs of producing or the benefits of consuming a good spill over onto those who are neither producing nor consuming the good.

We have seen that the existence of public goods provides an economic rationale for government involvement in the production of certain goods and services. Another rationale for government involvement in the production of certain goods and services is a market failure known as an externality. An **externality** occurs when the costs of producing a good or the benefits from consuming a good spill over to individuals who are not producing or consuming the good. The production of goods that cause pollution is the classic example of an externality. For example, when a coal-fired electric utility plant produces energy, it emits smoke that contains carbon dioxide, sulfur dioxide, and other pollutants into the air. These pollutants can make life miserable for people breathing the air and cause serious health concerns. Similarly, automobiles emit pollutants and reduce the quality of life for people in areas where cars are driven. Those who drive cars add a cost to others. These are examples of **negative externalities** because they have a negative effect—a cost—on the well-being of others. A **positive externality** occurs when a positive effect—a benefit—from producing or consuming a good spills over to others. For example, you might benefit if your neighbor plants a beautiful garden visible from your house or apartment. Let us first look at the effects of negative externalities and then consider positive externalities.

negative externality: the situation in which *costs* spill over onto someone not involved in producing or consuming the good.

positive externality: the situation in which *benefits* spill over onto someone not involved in producing or consuming the good.

Negative Externalities

In the case of negative externalities, a competitive market may not generate the efficient amount of production. The quantity produced is greater than the efficient quantity. For example, too much air-polluting electrical energy may be produced. The reason is that producers do not take account of the external costs when calculating their costs of production. If they did take these costs into account, they would produce less.

The reason why competitive markets are not efficient in the case of negative externalities can be illustrated using the supply and demand curves. For example, consider an example of a negative externality due to pollution caused by the production of electricity. A negative externality occurs because production of electricity raises pollution costs to other firms or individuals. The electrical utility plant pollutes the air and adds costs greater than the cost perceived by the electrical utility. The externality makes the marginal cost as perceived by the private firm, which we now call the **marginal private cost,** less than the true marginal cost that is incurred by society, which we call the **marginal social cost.** Marginal social cost is the sum of the firm's marginal private cost and the increase in external costs to society as more is produced. The marginal external cost is the change in external costs

marginal private cost: the marginal cost of production as viewed by the private firm or individual.

marginal social cost: the marginal cost of production as viewed by society as a whole.

A Negative Externality
The oil spilled into the ocean by this sinking oil tanker is an example of a negative externality: The production of goods by one firm (transportation of oil) raises costs or reduces benefits to people (the chance of an oil spill).

FIGURE 15.1

Illustration of a Typical Negative Externality

Because production of the good creates costs external to the firm (for example, pollution), the marginal social cost is greater than the marginal private cost to the firm. Thus, the equilibrium quantity that emerges from a competitive market is too large: Marginal benefit is less than marginal social cost.

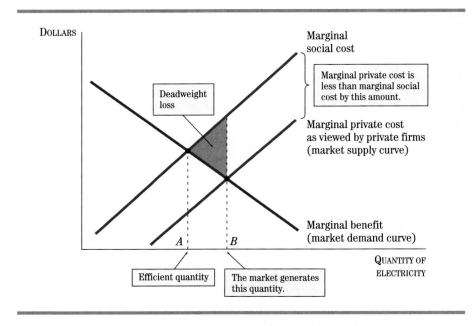

as more is produced. That is,

Marginal social cost = marginal private cost + marginal external cost

We illustrate this in Figure 15.1 by drawing a marginal private cost curve below the marginal social cost curve. We use the term *marginal private cost* to refer to what we have thus far called marginal cost in order to distinguish it from marginal social cost. Recall that adding up all the marginal (private) cost curves for the firms in a market gives the market supply curve, as labeled in the diagram.

Figure 15.1 also shows the marginal benefit to consumers from using the product, in this case electrical energy. This is the market demand curve for electricity. According to the supply and demand model, the interaction of firms and consumers in the market will result in a situation where the marginal cost of production—the marginal private cost—equals marginal benefit. This situation occurs at the market equilibrium where the quantity supplied equals the quantity demanded. The resulting quantity produced is indicated by point *B* in Figure 15.1.

However, at this amount of production, the marginal benefit of production is less than the marginal *social* cost of production. Marginal benefit equals marginal private cost but is less than marginal social cost. Only at point *A* in the figure is marginal benefit equal to marginal social cost. Thus, point *A* represents the efficient level of production. Because of the externality, too much is produced. Firms produce too much because they do not incur the external costs. There is a deadweight loss, as shown in Figure 15.1. Consumer surplus plus producer surplus is not maximized.

Positive Externalities

A positive externality occurs when the activity of one person makes another person better off, either reducing costs or increasing benefits. Let us examine what happens when a positive externality raises social benefits above private benefits. For exam-

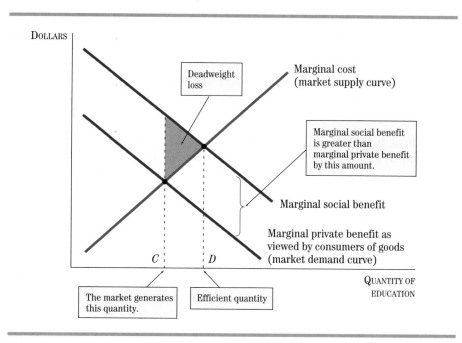

DOLLARS

Deadweight loss

Marginal cost (market supply curve)

Marginal social benefit is greater than marginal private benefit by this amount.

Marginal social benefit

Marginal private benefit as viewed by consumers of goods (market demand curve)

C   *D*

QUANTITY OF EDUCATION

The market generates this quantity.

Efficient quantity

FIGURE 15.2
Illustration of a Typical Positive Externality
Because consumption of the good (for example, education) gives benefits to others, the marginal social benefit is greater than the marginal private benefit. Hence, the equilibrium quantity that emerges from a competitive market is too low.

ple, increased earnings are a benefit from attending high school, college, graduate school, or continuing education. But the education also benefits society. The greater education that these individuals receive is spread to others. Going to school and learning to read and write makes people better citizens. Learning about hygiene and becoming health conscious puts less of a burden on the public health system.

Another example of a good with a positive externality is research. Firms that engage in research get some of the benefits of that research through the products that they can sell—maybe novel products. But in many cases the research spreads, and other people can take advantage of it as well. Research that spills over to other industries or other individuals is an externality. The benefit from the research expenditures goes beyond the individual; it creates inefficiencies just as negative externalities do.

To show how positive externalities affect the quantity produced in a competitive market, we need to look at the supply and demand curves. The externality makes the marginal benefit as perceived by the consumer, which we now call the **marginal private benefit**, less than the true benefit to society, which we call the **marginal social benefit**. With a positive externality, the marginal social benefit is greater than the marginal private benefit because there is a marginal external benefit from more consumption. That is,

Marginal social benefit = marginal private benefit + marginal external benefit

Figure 15.2 shows the impact of this difference between marginal social benefit and marginal private benefit. Suppose that Figure 15.2 refers to the market for education. Then the quantity of education is on the horizontal axis. The marginal social benefit curve is above the marginal private benefit curve in the figure. The marginal private benefit curve for consumers is the market demand curve. Consider the equilibrium quantity at point *C,* where the quantity supplied equals the quantity demanded in Figure 15.2. The market results in a quantity produced that is less than

marginal private benefit: the marginal benefit from consumption of a good as viewed by a private individual.

marginal social benefit: the marginal benefit from consumption of a good from the viewpoint of society as a whole.

the efficient quantity, which occurs when the marginal *social* benefit equals the marginal cost, as shown at point *D.* The quantity generated by the market is at a point where the marginal social benefit is greater than the marginal cost. Production and consumption of education would be inefficient; the quantity of education is too low. Again, there is a deadweight loss due to externality, as shown in Figure 15.2.

Global Externalities

Externalities have become international in recent years, paralleling the growth of international trade and finance. Sulfur dioxide emissions from electrical utility plants are an externality whose international effects have received much attention. The sulfur dioxide travels high into the air and is then dispersed by winds across long distances. Rainfall then brings the sulfur dioxide back to earth in the form of acid rain that lands on forests and lakes hundreds of miles away. In some cases, the acid rain occurs in countries different from the country where the sulfur dioxide was first emitted. In North America, acid rain may fall in Canada or upstate New York but results from burning fuel in the Midwest industrial centers. There is considerable disagreement among environmental experts about the significance of the pollution caused by acid rain. Some argue it is large; others argue it is small. In any case, it illustrates the global aspects of this externality.

Global warming is another example of an externality with international dimension. When too much carbon dioxide accumulates in the earth's atmosphere, it prevents the sun's warmth from escaping out of the atmosphere, causing a greenhouse effect. Global warming is caused by the emission of carbon dioxide by firms and individuals but has effects all over the world.

Review

▶ Externalities occur when the benefits or costs of producing and consuming spill over to others. Externalities cause the marginal private cost to be different from the marginal social cost, or the marginal private benefit to be different from the marginal social benefit.

▶ Externalities are a cause of market failure. Production of goods with negative externalities is more than the efficient amount. Production of goods with positive externalities is less than the efficient amount.

▶ Many externalities are global, occurring across borders, as when pollution emitted in one country has negative effects in other countries.

REMEDIES FOR EXTERNALITIES

As the previous section shows, competitive markets do not generate an efficient level of production when externalities exist. What are some of the ways in which a society can alleviate problems caused by these externalities? In some cases, the solution has been that government produces the good or service. In practice, elementary education is provided by governments all over the world with requirements that children attend school through a certain age. Education is by far the government-produced good or service with the most employment in the United States. But in most cases where externalities are present, production is left to the private sector, and government endeavors to influence the quantity produced. In fact, much of college education and some K-12 education is provided by the private sector in the United States.

How can production in the private sector be influenced by government so as to lead to a more efficient level of production of goods and services in the economy? We will see that the answer involves changing behavior so that the externalities are taken into account internally by firms and consumers. In other words, the challenge is to **internalize** the externalities.

internalize: the process of providing incentives so that externalities are taken into account internally by firms or consumers.

There are four alternative ways to bring about a more efficient level of production in the case of externalities. The first one discussed here, private remedies, does not require direct government intervention. The other three—command and control, taxes or subsidies, and tradable permits—do.

Private Remedies: Agreements Between the Affected Parties

In some cases people, through **private remedies,** can eliminate externalities themselves without government assistance. The 1991 Nobel Prize winner in economics, Ronald Coase of the University of Chicago, pointed out this possibility in a paper published in 1960.

private remedy: a procedure that eliminates or internalizes externalities without government action other than defining property rights.

Consider the following simple example similar to one used by Coase in his paper. Suppose that the externality relates to the production of two products: health care services and candy. Suppose that a hospital is built next door to a large candy factory. Making candy requires noisy pounding and vibrating machinery. Unfortunately, the walls of the new hospital are thin. The loud candy machinery can be heard right in the hospital. Thus, there is an externality that we might call noise pollution. It has a cost. It makes the hospital less effective, for example, because it is difficult for the doctors to hear their patients' hearts through the stethoscopes.

What can be done? The city mayor could adopt a rule prohibiting loud noise near the hospital, but that would severely impinge on the candy making in the city. Or, because the hospital was built after the candy factory, the mayor could say, "Too bad, doctors, candy is important too." Alternatively, it might be better for the candy workers and doctors to work this externality out themselves. The supervisor of the candy workers could negotiate with the doctors. Perhaps the candy workers could agree to use the loud machines only during the afternoon, during which the doctors would take an extended break. Or perhaps a thick wall could be built between the buildings. Thus, it is possible to resolve this externality more efficiently than the mayor could by negotiation between the two parties affected. Either of these privately negotiated alternatives seems more efficient than the mayor's rulings because the production of both candy and health-care services continues.

Note in these alternatives that both parties alter their behavior. For example, the doctors take a break, and the candy factory limits loud noise to each afternoon. Thus, the parties find a solution where the polluter does not make all the adjustments, as would be the case if the mayor adopted a "no loud noise" rule.

The Importance of Assigning Property Rights

For a negotiation like this to work, however, it is essential that property rights be well defined. *Property rights* determine who has the right to pollute or infringe on whom. Who, for example, is being infringed on in the case of the noise pollution?

property rights: rights over the use, sale, and proceeds from a good or resource. (Ch. 2)

Using Economics to Explain the Tragedy of the Commons

The key to reducing the harm caused by negative externalities in the environmental area is to get people to internalize the harm they cause to the environment.

One of the most powerful metaphors for this problem is a cattle-grazing example put forth by a biologist, Garrett Hardin, in an article called "The Tragedy of the Commons." Hardin wrote:

The tragedy of the commons develops this way. Picture a pasture open to all. It is to be expected that each herdsman will try to keep as many cattle as possible on the commons. . . . As a rational being, each herdsman seeks to maximize his gain.

Hardin assumes that the gain is +1, and then goes on to talk about the externality.

The effects of overgrazing are shared by all herdsmen, the negative utility for any particular decision-making herdsman is only a fraction of −1. . . . Therein is the tragedy. Each man is locked into a system that compels him to increase his herd without limitation—in a world that is limited. Ruin is the destination toward which all men rush, each pursuing his own best interest in a society that believes in freedom of the commons.

In history, the problem with the commons was frequently solved by

parceling out land to each herdsman and fencing each parcel. Then each herdsman had the incentive not to overgraze. Thus, defining property rights internalized the externality.

Source of quotes: Garrett Hardin, "The Tragedy of the Commons," *Science,* 1968, pp. 1243–1248.

Does the candy factory have the right to use loud machinery, or does the hospital have the right to peace and quiet? The mayor's ruling could establish who has the property right, but more likely the case would be taken to a court and the court would decide. After many such cases, precedent would establish who has the property rights in future cases.

     The property rights will determine who actually pays for the adjustment that remedies the externality. If the candy factory has the right, then the workers can demand some compensation (perhaps free health-care services) from the hospital to limit their noise to the afternoon. If the hospital has the right, then perhaps the doctors can get compensated with free candy during the break. The **Coase theorem** states that no matter who is assigned the property rights, the negotiations will lead to an efficient outcome as described in the candy/health-care example. The assignment of the property rights determines who makes the compensation.

Coase theorem: the idea that private negotiations between people will lead to an efficient resolution of externalities regardless of who has the property rights as long as the property rights are defined.

Transaction Costs

Even if property rights are well defined, for a private agreement like this to occur, transaction costs associated with the agreement must be small compared to the costs of the externality itself. *Transaction costs* are the time and effort needed to reach an agreement. As Coase put it, "In order to carry out a market transaction, it is necessary to discover who it is that one wishes to deal with, to inform people that one wishes to deal and on what terms, to conduct negotiations leading up to a bargain, to draw up the contract, to undertake the inspection needed to make sure that

transaction cost: the cost of buying or selling in a market including search, bargaining, and writing contracts. (Ch. 2)

the terms of the contract are being observed, and so on. These operations are often extremely costly."[1] Real-world negotiations are clearly time-consuming, requiring skilled and expensive lawyers in many cases. If these negotiation costs are large, then the private parties may not be able to reach an agreement. If the negotiation in the health-care/candy example took many years and had to be repeated many times, then it might be better to adopt a simple "no loud noise" rule.

The Free-Rider Problem Again

Free-rider problems can also prevent a private agreement from taking place. For example, a free-rider problem might occur if the hospital was very large, say 400 doctors. Suppose that the candy workers have the right to noise pollute, so that the candy workers require a payment in terms of health care. The hospital would need contributions from the doctors to provide the care. Thus, if each doctor worked in the hospital an extra day a year, this might be sufficient.

However, any one of the 400 doctors could refuse to work the extra day. Some of the doctors could say that they have other job opportunities where they do not have to work an extra day. In other words, doctors who did not pay could free-ride: work at the hospital and still benefit from the agreement. Because of this free-rider problem the hospital might find it hard to provide health care to the candy workers, and a private settlement might be impossible.

Thus, in the case where the transaction costs are high or free-rider problems exist, a private remedy may not be feasible. Then the role of government comes into play, much as it did in the case of public goods, where the free-rider problem was significant. Again, as Coase put it, "Instead of instituting a legal system of rights which can be modified by transactions on the market, the government may impose regulations which state what people must or must not do and which have to be obeyed."[2]

Command and Control Remedies

When private remedies to externalities are either too costly or not feasible because of free-rider problems, there is a role for government. One form of government intervention to solve the problem of externalities is the placement of restrictions or regulations on individuals or firms, often referred to as **command and control.** Such restrictions could make it illegal to pollute more than a certain amount. Firms that polluted more than a certain amount could then be fined. For example, in the United States the corporate average fleet efficiency (CAFE) standards require that the fleet of cars produced by automobile manufacturers each year must achieve a stated number of miles per gallon on the average. Another example is a government requirement that electrical utilities put "scrubbers" in their smokestacks to remove certain pollutants from the smoke they emit. In this case, the government regulates the technology that the firms use. Reducing pollution by regulating what firms or individuals produce is a classic example of command and control. Through commands the government controls what the private sector does. In principle, the externalities are made

command and control: the regulations and restrictions that the government uses to correct market imperfections.

1. Ronald Coase, "The Problem of Social Cost," *Journal of Law and Economics,* October 1960, Vol. 3, p. 15.
2. Ibid., p. 17.

Using Economics to Explain Externalities from Biodiversity

Biodiversity—the rich variety of plant and animal life in the world—has been recognized as having important benefits for pharmaceutical and medical research. Ideas for many important pharmaceutical products throughout history—from aspirin to life-saving drugs—have been discovered in the natural environment and then modified or improved by researchers. Preserving biodiversity is important for future discoveries and applications.

One of the great sources of biodiversity is the rain forests of South America. However, these rain forests are being cut and burned to make room for farms.

Observe that there is an externality here. Those governments or individuals who own the rain forests suffer little if any cost from cutting them down and losing the biodiversity. The cost is external to them,

spread around the world and, indeed, to future generations, who must forego the opportunity of better drugs or other benefits that the variety of plant and animal life might bring. This externality is global, not restricted to any one country. Thus, resolving it is even more difficult than in the case of a single country with one government. Political negotiations between governments are currently under way to try to resolve this global externality.

There are indications, however, that at least part of the externality is being reduced by private remedies—negotiations between affected parties. The pharmaceutical companies are beginning to offer the owners of the rain forests an opportunity to share in some of the patent and copyright royalties from the discovery of new drugs. In other words, the deal being worked out is that in exchange for

not cutting down the forests, the owners of the forests can share in any royalties from the drugs discovered with plant and animal life from the forests. If such royalties are available, then by cutting down the forests the owners forego the royalties; this raises the cost of cutting and burning and effectively internalizes at least part of the externality.

It is not yet clear whether the incentive will be great enough to slow the cutting and burning of the forests, or whether an international agreement between governments around the world is feasible. In fact, the difficulty of coordinating international government action in these cases may be the reason why interested private parties are looking for ways to resolve the externality themselves.

internal to the firm by requiring that the firm act as if it took the external costs into account.

Command and control methods are used widely by agencies such as the Environmental Protection Agency (EPA), which has responsibility for federal environmental policy in the United States. There are many disadvantages to command and control in the environmental area, however, and economists have criticized such methods. The most significant disadvantage is that command and control does not allow firms to find other, cheaper ways to reduce pollution. Command and control ignores the incentives firms might have to discover cheaper technologies. For example, under command and control, electrical utilities have to install a scrubber even if there is a better, cheaper alternative. New machinery without a scrubber might be more efficient than installing a scrubber. Similarly, developing alternative fuels or simply raising the price of gasoline might be a cheaper way to reduce pollution than the CAFE standards.

Taxes and Subsidies

Because of these disadvantages, economists usually recommend alternatives to command and control techniques to reduce pollution or to reduce the inefficiencies due to other externalities. Taxes and subsidies are one such alternative. How do they work?

Goods that have negative externalities are taxed. For example, if burning coal creates a pollution externality, a tax on coal would be imposed, perhaps $10 per ton. On the other hand, goods that have a positive externality are subsidized. For example, if going to college produces a positive externality, college education could be subsidized with government loans or grants. Taxes and subsidies internalize externalities by making the consumer feel the external benefits through the subsidy, or by making the firm pay for the external costs through the tax. Unlike command and control, taxes and subsidies allow firms or people to respond to price or cost changes. With changes in technology, a firm might find it could afford to pollute even less than allowed under a command and control guideline.

The way that taxes can be used to reduce pollution is illustrated graphically in Figure 15.3, which uses the same curves as Figure 15.1. Recall that the marginal social cost of production is greater than the marginal private cost, as viewed from the private firm, because the good pollutes. We know that taxes raise the marginal cost to the individual firm. They thereby shift up the market supply curve and lead to a market equilibrium with a smaller quantity produced. If the tax is chosen to exactly equal the difference between the marginal social cost and the marginal private cost, then the quantity produced will decline from the inefficient quantity shown at point *B* to the efficient quantity shown at point *A* in Figure 15.3.

There are many examples of taxes being used at least in part to reduce pollution. Gasoline taxes are widely viewed as being good for the environment because

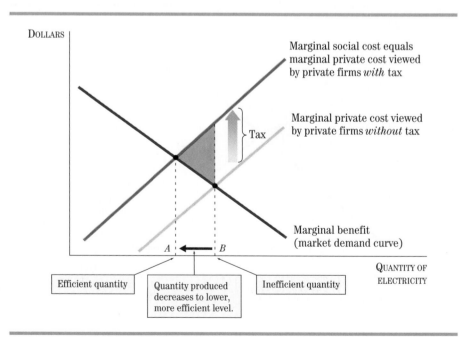

FIGURE 15.3
Using Taxes in the Case of a Negative Externality

A tax equal to the difference between the marginal private cost and the marginal social cost in Figure 15.1 shifts the supply curve up. This reduces the equilibrium quantity produced to the lower, more efficient level.

they reduce gasoline consumption, which pollutes the air. In the United States there is an average tax of 36 cents on each gallon of gasoline. The big advantage of taxes or subsidies compared with command and control is that the market is still being used. For example, if there is a shift in demand, the firm can adjust its technique of production as the price changes. But with command and control, adjustment must wait for the government to change its commands or controls.

In the case of positive externalities, subsidies rather than taxes can be used to increase production and bring marginal social benefits into line with marginal costs. For example, in Figure 15.4, which uses the same curve as Figure 15.2, a subsidy to encourage education, a good with a positive externality, is illustrated. In this case a subsidy to students raises the marginal benefit of education (as perceived by them) up to the marginal social benefit. As a result, the quantity of education rises from the inefficient level (*C*) to the efficient level (*D*), as illustrated in Figure 15.4.

In addition to subsidizing education, the government subsidizes research, another good with a positive externality, by providing research grants to private firms and individuals. The National Science Foundation supports basic research, and the National Institutes for Health support medical research. In supporting research with a limited budget, it is important for the government to place more emphasis on research with big externalities. Many view basic research as having larger positive externalities than applied research. The ideas in basic research, such as that of the structure of the atom, affect many parts of the economy. Applied research, such as that on a new lightweight metal for a bike, has more limited use, and the firm can prevent others from using it. Products developed in applied research can be sold for profit. This suggests that more government funds should go toward basic research than applied research. In fact, the federal government in the United States does spend more to subsidize basic research than applied research.

FIGURE 15.4
Using Subsidies in the Case of a Positive Externality

A subsidy equal to the difference between the marginal social benefit and the marginal private benefit of education or research shifts the demand curve up. This increases the equilibrium quantity produced to the higher, more efficient level and eliminates the deadweight loss due to the externality.

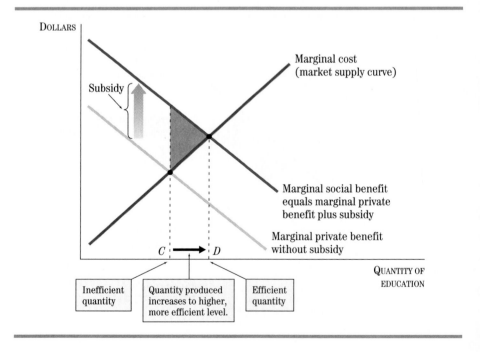

Emission Taxes

A more direct way to use taxes to deal with pollution externalities is to tax the firm based on the amount of pollution emitted. For example, an electrical utility could be charged fees depending on how many particles of sulfur dioxide it emits, rather than on how much electricity it produces. Such charges are called **emission taxes.** They are much like taxes on the amount of the product sold, but they focus directly on the amount of pollution.

    Emission taxes have an advantage over taxes on production in that the firm can use technology to change the amount of pollution associated with its production. Thus, rather than producing less electricity, the firm can reduce the amount of pollution associated with a given amount of electricity if it can find a cheaper way to do so. Emission taxes have an even greater advantage over command and control than a tax on the product has.

emission tax: a charge made to firms that pollute the environment based on the quantity of pollution they emit.

Why Is Command and Control Used More than Taxes?

There is one feature of command and control that many people like: The total amount of pollution can be better controlled than with a tax. This may explain why command and control is used more than taxes. Suppose, for example, that a tax is used to equate marginal social cost with marginal benefit, as in Figure 15.3. But suppose there is a sudden reduction in the private cost of producing electricity. Then, the private marginal cost curve shifts down and, with the tax unchanged, production (and pollution) increases. A regulation that stipulates a certain quantity to produce would not have this problem. The total amount of pollution would be fixed. Fortunately, in recent years, a new idea in pollution control has emerged that has both this advantage of command and control and the flexibility of the market. This new idea is tradable permits.

Tradable Permits

Tradable permits use the market to help achieve the standards set by the government. Rather than force a firm to meet a certain standard, the government issues a permit to firms that allows each firm to emit a certain limited amount of pollutants into the atmosphere. Firms have an incentive to lower their emissions because they can sell the permit if they do not use it. Firms that can lower their emissions cheaply will choose to do so and benefit by selling their permit to other firms for which it is more costly to reduce the pollution. Tradable permits not only allow the market system to work, they give incentive to firms to find the least costly form of pollution control.

tradable permit: a governmentally granted license to pollute that can be bought and sold.

Control over Firms as a Group Rather than Individual Firms

Tradable permits are ideal in certain circumstances. For example, they work well in the case of sulfur dioxide emissions. Recall that acid rain caused by sulfur dioxide falls over a wider area than that of the individual polluting firm. Acid rain has to do with the total amount of emissions and not with whether one firm pollutes more than another. It is the total amount of pollution of all firms in the country or the region that matters most. To reduce the total amount of pollution, the government issues a number of permits specifying permissible levels of pollution. Once these permits are issued, those firms that can reduce the emissions in the most cost-efficient manner will sell their permits to other firms. They can raise profits by reducing the pollution themselves and selling the permits to other firms with less efficient pollution-control methods. The total amount of pollution in the economy is equal to the total amount of permits issued and, therefore, is controlled perfectly.

Tradable permits are a new idea but are likely to be an increasingly common way to reduce pollution in the future. A tradable permit program called RECLAIM is being used in Los Angeles. Under the 1990 Clean Air Act, tradable permits can be used on a national basis.

Tradable permits could also work in global warming. The amount of global warming depends on the total amount of carbon dioxide emissions in the world's atmosphere. It does not matter whether a firm in Los Angeles or in Shanghai emits the carbon dioxide. Tradable permits could control the total amount of pollution. The permits would let firms or individuals decide on the most cost-effective way for them to reduce the total amount of pollution.

Assigning and Defining Property Rights

Tradable permits illustrate how important property rights are for resolving externalities. The role of government in this case is to create a market by defining certain rights to pollute and then allowing firms to buy and sell these rights. Once rights are assigned, the market can work and achieve efficiency.

Balancing the Costs and Benefits of Reducing Externalities

As with public goods, it is important to use a cost-benefit analysis when considering externalities. There are benefits to reducing pollution, but there are costs also. The costs of reducing pollution in the United States are about $120 billion per year, or about 2 percent of GDP. This percentage is expected to rise over time. These costs should be compared to the benefits associated with pollution control on a case-by-case basis. For example, the benefits of cleaning up a river should be compared with the costs of the cleanup.

Some people are concerned that a cost-benefit analysis will reduce spending on the environment too much. They argue that there is no tradeoff between costs and benefits. Environmental regulations can benefit rather than cost the economy, they argue, because requiring individuals to reduce pollution creates a demand for pollution-reducing devices and creates jobs in the pollution-reducing industry. But unless the pollution-reducing equipment is creating a benefit to society greater than the benefits of other goods, shifting more resources to pollution abatement will not be an efficient allocation of society's resources.

Many people argue that the surest way to reduce pollution around the world is to make sure the less-developed economies of the world improve their level of development. This will give them the resources to spend on pollution control since poor countries will not spend much on reducing pollution until the problems of poverty and hunger are reduced. Environmental degradation in the formerly centrally planned economies of Eastern Europe was severe. It is likely that the environment will improve when they have more resources to spend on it.

Review

▶ There are four basic ways to improve the efficiency of markets in the case of externalities: private remedies, command and control, taxes and subsidies, and tradable permits. The latter three involve direct government intervention and are needed when high transaction costs or free-rider problems rule private remedies out.

▶ Taxes and subsidies, as well as tradable permits, endeavor to use the market to help internalize the externality.

▶ Tradable permits require that the government define and assign property rights. Once the rights are defined and assigned, the market can allocate the resources to reduce pollution efficiently.

MODELS OF GOVERNMENT BEHAVIOR

The previous sections have outlined what government should do to correct market failure. Regardless of the reason market failure occurs, the outcomes are similar: Production may be too little or too much, and producer surplus plus consumer surplus is not maximized as shown in Figure 15.5. The result is deadweight loss, and the role of government is to change the level of production or employment so as to increase producer surplus plus consumer surplus. Using economics to explain the role of government in this way is considered a *normative* analysis of government policy. Recall from Chapter 1 that normative economics is the study of what *should be* done. But there is another way to look at government policy. It falls into the area of *positive* rather than normative economics and looks at what governments *actually do* rather than at what they should do.

FIGURE 15.5
Summarizing the Effects of Market Failure
Market failure results in too little (a) or too much (b) production of a good. When there is market failure, there is a role for government to provide incentives to change the market outcome and thereby reduce the deadweight loss.

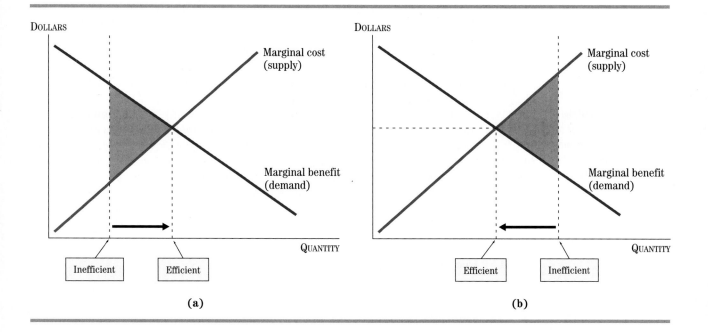

(a)

(b)

One of the reasons for studying what governments actually do is that frequently the normative recommendations are not followed, or government performs its role poorly. *Government failure* occurs when the government fails to improve on the market or even makes things worse. Sometimes government fails, and sometimes it succeeds. One objective of positive analysis of government is to understand why there is success and failure in different situations.

Public Choice Models

Government itself is run by people. Government behavior depends on the actions of voters, politicians, civil servants, and political appointees from judges to Cabinet officials. The work of government also depends on the large number of people who work in political campaigns, who are active in political parties, who lobby, and who participate in grassroots campaigns from letter writing to e-mail messages to political protests. Government organizations exist at the state and local levels as well as the federal level. What motivates the behavior of all these people?

The motivations of politicians and government workers are complex and varied. But the basic principle of economics that people try to improve their well-being given limited resources should apply to politics and government, as well as to consumers and firms. Many people enter politics for genuine patriotic reasons and are motivated by a desire to improve the well-being of people in their city, state, country, or even the world. Their motivations may be deeper than watching out for their own best interests, narrowly defined. For example, Alexander Hamilton, the first chief economic spokesman for the United States as the first secretary of the treasury, worked hard to put the newly formed country on a firm economic foundation by having the federal government assume the debts of the states after the Revolutionary War.

But the desire to get elected, or to get votes on issues after being elected, is also part of the motivation of all politicians. Alexander Hamilton would not have done his job if he had not made one of the great political deals of all time, trading his vote on one issue for another. In order to get the votes of the representatives from Virginia and Maryland for the federal government to assume the debts of the states, he agreed to vote to place the capital of the new country along the banks of the Potomac River between Maryland and Virginia, instead of selecting New York City.

public choice models: models of government behavior that assume that those in government take actions to maximize their own well-being, such as getting reelected.

Economic models of government behavior are called **public choice models.** They start from the premise that politicians are motivated by increasing their chances of getting themselves or the members of their party elected or reelected. And without explicit incentives to the contrary, government workers are presumed to be motivated by increasing their power or prestige, partly through increasing the size of their department or by getting promoted. By understanding this self-interest motivation, we can learn much about government, including the reasons for government failure and the reasons for government success.

Economic Policy Decisions Through Voting

Let us first examine how voting is used to make economic policy decisions in a political environment. We will use the assumption of public choice models: that getting elected is the primary motivation of politicians.

Single Issues with Unanimity

Let us start with the easiest case: There is only one economic policy decision to be made, and all the voters agree what it should be. For example, suppose that the issue is spending on national defense, a public good where the government has a key role to play according to the normative economic analysis discussed earlier.

Suppose the specific issue is how much to spend on national defense now that the cold war is over. Some alternatives are shown in Table 15.2.

Suppose that everyone agrees that a level of national defense around 4 percent of GDP in the United States is appropriate for the post-cold war period, in the absence of major world political changes. In reality, of course, opinions differ greatly about the appropriate level. But suppose that by looking at history or making international comparisons or by listening to experts on defense and world politics, everyone agrees that 4 percent of GDP is the right amount to spend.

Under these circumstances when there is only one issue on which all voters agree, voting will lead to the actions that everyone prefers, that is, 4 percent, even if politicians are motivated by nothing other than getting elected. Suppose that one politician or political party runs for election on a plank of 39 percent defense spending and that the other argues in favor of 2 percent; clearly, the party with 2 percent will win because it is much closer to the people's views. But then the other politician or party would see the need to move toward the consensus, to run on a 5 percent spending platform; if the other party stays at 2 percent, then the higher-spending party will win. But clearly the other party will then try to get closer to 4 percent, and eventually 4 percent will be the winner.

This example shows that the political system yields the preferred outcome. Of course after being elected, the politician might break the promise of the campaign. But if such a change cannot be justified on the basis of a change in circumstances, that politician may have difficulty getting reelected.

The Median Voter Theorem

What if people have different views? Suppose there is no unanimity about 4 percent defense as a share of GDP. Instead the country consists of people with many different opinions. Some want more than 4 percent; some want less than 4 percent. Suppose that about half of the people want more than 4 percent and half want less than 4 percent; in other words, 4 percent is the desire of the *median voter.*

If there is only one issue, there will be convergence of positions of the politicians or the parties toward the median voter's belief. For example, if one party or politician calls for 7 percent spending and the other party calls for 4 percent, then the party calling for 4 percent will attract more voters. Clearly, more than half of the voters are closer to 4 percent than to 7 percent. The **median voter theorem** predicts that the politicians who run on what the median voter wants will be elected. The views of the people at the extremes will not matter at all.

Convergence of Positions in a Two-Party System

An interesting corollary to the median voter theorem is that political parties or politicians will gravitate toward the center of opinion—toward the median voter. For example, in the case of national defense it makes no sense for any politician to run on a 39 percent recommendation. The parties will gravitate toward the median

TABLE 15.2
Alternative Levels of National Defense Spending

National Defense as a Share of GDP

1 percent	Japan's maximum
2 percent	U.S. in 1940
4 percent	Post-cold war
7 percent	U.S. in 1986
10 percent	U.S. in 1960
39 percent	U.S. in 1944

"As an anthropologist, I've been to tropic jungles and frozen tundras. I've seen primitive cultures and sophisticated societies. But this is the only place where I have been unable to figure out what's going on."

median voter theorem: a theorem stating that the median or middle of political preferences will be reflected in the government decisions.

convergence of positions: the concentration of the stances of political parties around the center of citizens' opinions.

voter. This **convergence of positions** may explain the tendency for Democrats and Republicans to take similar positions on many issues.

Voting Paradoxes

When there are many different issues—defense, taxes, welfare, health-care reform—and people have different opinions and views about each issue, the outcome of voting becomes more complicated. Certain decision-making problems arise. The simple example of the **voting paradox** illustrates some of these problems.

voting paradox: a decision-making dilemma caused by the fact that aggregate voting patterns will not consistently reflect citizens' preferences because of multiple issues on which people vote.

Suppose three voters have different preferences on three different economic policy options—A, B, and C. Ali likes A best, B second best, and C the least; Betty likes B best, C second best, and A the least; and Camilla likes C best, A second best, and B the least. The three policy options could be three different levels of defense spending (high, medium, and low) or three different pollution control plans (emission taxes, tradable permits, or command and control). Table 15.3 shows the three voters and their different preferences about each issue.

Consider three different elections held at different points in time, each with one issue paired up against the other. First, there is an election on A versus B, then on B versus C, and then on C versus A. The voting is by simple majority: The issue with the most votes wins. When the vote is on the alternatives A versus B, we see that A wins 2 to 1. That is, both Ali and Camilla like A better than B and vote for it, while only Betty likes B better than A and votes for B. When the vote is on B versus C, we see that B wins 2 to 1. Finally (this vote might be called for by a frustrated Camilla, who sees an opportunity), there is a vote on C versus A, and we see that now C wins 2 to 1. Although it looked like A was a winner over C—because A was preferred to B and B was preferred to C—we see that in the third vote C is preferred to A; this is the paradox.

The voting paradox suggests there might be instability in economic policies. Depending on how the votes were put together, the policy could shift from high defense to medium defense to low defense, or from one pollution control system to another, then to another, and then back again. Or taxes could be cut, then raised, and then raised again. All these changes could happen with nothing else in the world having changed. We could even imagine shifting between different economic systems involving different amounts of government intervention—from communism to capitalism to socialism to communism and back again!

This particular voting paradox has been known for two hundred years, but it is only relatively recently that we know that the problem is not unique to this example. Kenneth Arrow showed that this type of paradox is common to any voting

● ─────────────

TABLE 15.3
Preferences That Generate a Voting Paradox

Ranking	Ali	Betty	Camilla
First	A	B	C
Second	B	C	A
Third	C	A	B

In voting on one option versus another, we get:
on A versus B: A wins 2 to 1
on B versus C: B wins 2 to 1
on A versus C: C wins 2 to 1 ←

Paradox because
A wins over B and
B wins over C, yet
C wins over A

scheme. That no democratic voting scheme can avoid the inefficiencies of the type described in the voting paradox is called the **Arrow impossibility theorem.**

The voting paradox suggests a certain inherent degree of instability in decisions made by government. Clearly, shifting between different tax systems frequently is a source of uncertainty and inefficiency. The voting paradox may be a reason for government failure to arise in cases where the government takes on some activity such as correcting a market failure.

Arrow impossibility theorem: a theorem that says that no democratic voting scheme can avoid a voting paradox.

Special Interest Groups

The voting paradox is one reason for government failure. Special interest groups are another. It is not unusual for special interest groups to spend time and financial resources to influence legislation. They want policies that are good for them, even if the policies are not necessarily good for the country as a whole. For example, look at the farming industry, which has a great deal of government intervention. What is the explanation for the intervention? If you look back at the reasons for government intervention—income distribution, public goods, externalities—you will see that they do not apply to the farm sector. Food does not fit the definition of a public good, and many farmers who benefit from the intervention have higher incomes than other people in the society who do not benefit from such intervention. One can thus view the government regulation of agricultural markets as a form of government failure.

Concentrated Benefits and Diffuse Costs

One explanation for government failure in such situations is that special interest groups can have powerful effects on legislation that harms or benefits a small group of people a great deal but affects most everyone else only a little. For example, the federal subsidy to the sugar growers in the United States costs taxpayers and consumers somewhere between $800 million and $2.5 billion per year, or about $3.20 to $10 per person per year. However, the gain from the subsidy amounts to about $136,000 per sugar grower. Thus, the small cost is hardly enough for each consumer to spend time fighting Congress. However, the payments are certainly worth the sugar growers' effort to travel to Washington and to contribute to some political campaigns. When the costs are spread over millions of users and the benefits are concentrated on only a few, it is hard to eliminate government programs. Those who benefit have much more incentive to lobby and work hard for or against certain candidates. Thus the process of obtaining funds for election or getting support from the powerful interest groups can have large effects on policy.

Wasteful Lobbying

There is another economic harm from special interest lobbying. It is the waste of time and resources that the lobbying entails. Lobbyists are usually highly talented and skilled people, and millions of dollars in resources are spent on lobbying for legislation or other government actions.

In many less-developed countries—where special interest lobbying is more prevalent than in the United States—such activity occupies a significant amount of scarce resources.

Time Inconsistency

time inconsistency: the situation in which policymakers have the incentive to announce one economic policy but then change that policy after citizens have acted on the initial, stated policy.

Another possible source of government failure is **time inconsistency.** It occurs when government officials make statements or pass laws regarding future policy actions. People then make decisions and take actions with certain expectations regarding these government policies. In such situations there is frequently an incentive for the government to change the policy in the future from what was stated originally. A change in policy from what was originally announced is called time inconsistency.

For example, a local government might say that it has no intention of building a dam to protect a flood plain, and, therefore, people should not build their homes on the flood plain. But suppose that people start building their houses on the flood plain anyway, perhaps anticipating that the government will not do what it says. Once the houses are built and a community with schools, playgrounds, and offices has been established, a rainy season with flooding will make it likely that the government will build a dam despite its earlier policy. In other words, the government changes its policy. In fact, if you think about it for a while, you will realize that the government cannot commit itself to such a policy, and it makes perfect sense for people to assume that the government will change its mind and in fact build the dam. Whether it is because different politicians will be in charge in the future, or because it is hard to say no in the face of human misery, the government has difficulty committing itself to policies in the future. If the government could commit, then the policy would be much better. People would find almost as nice places to live away from the flood plain and the taxpayers would save millions by not having to build the dam. The challenge of dealing with the time inconsistency problem is to find ways for the government to develop a mechanism of commitment or to better establish its credibility.

Incentive Problems in Government

In any large government, many of the services are provided by civil servants rather than politicians and political appointees. In fact, it was to avoid the scandals of the spoils system—in which politicians would reward those who helped in a political campaign with jobs—that the civil service system set rules to protect against firing and established examinations and other criteria for job qualifications.

But what motivates government managers and workers? Profit maximization as in the case of business firms is not a factor. Perhaps increasing the size of the agency or the department of government is the goal of managers. But simply increasing the size of an agency is not likely to result in an efficient delivery of services. Profit motives and competition with other firms gives private firms an incentive to keep costs down and look for innovative production techniques and new products. But these incentives do not automatically arise in government. For this reason, it is likely that the government service, whether a public good or a regulation, will not be provided as efficiently as a good provided by the private sector. This is another possible reason for government failure.

Better Government Through Market-Based Incentives

In recent years there has been an effort to use incentives to improve the efficiency of government. Many of these ideas were summarized in a popular 1992 book,

Reinventing Government: How the Entrepreneurial Spirit Is Transforming the Public Sector, by David Osborne and Ted Gaebler, which lent its name to the "reinventing government" initiative promoted by the Clinton administration.

Admitting that "cynicism about government runs deep within the American soul" and that "our government is in deep trouble today," the authors give hundreds of examples of how the "entrepreneurial spirit" can be used to make police services, sanitation, and schools more efficient. In many cases, efficiency can be improved by having government workers rewarded for providing high-quality service with higher pay or other benefits. In other words, marketlike incentives would be used to encourage greater government efficiency.

A big part of improving government can come through providing competition. Vouchers—including food stamps, housing vouchers, college tuition grants, elementary school grants—have been suggested by economists as a way to add competition and improve government efficiency. For example, Osborne and Gaebler contrast two different systems of government support for World War II veterans: (1) the GI bill, where veterans were given vouchers to go to any college, private or public, and (2) the Veterans Administration hospitals, where the government itself provides medical service. They conclude that the first worked much better, and by analogy should be used in other cases where vouchers or government-produced services are the choices.

In the next chapter you will see some other examples of market-based remedies to government failure, including incentive regulation and market-based guidelines for policy to promote competition. Many of these ideas are new. They are clearly the way of the future, but it remains to be seen how effective they will be as a remedy for the government failure they endeavor to address.

Review

▶ Public choice models of government behavior assume that politicians and government workers endeavor to improve their own well-being much like models of firms and consumer behavior assume firms and consumers do.

▶ In cases where there is consensus among voters, voting will bring about the consensus government policy. When there is no consensus, the median voter theorem shows that the center of opinion is what matters for decisions. However, the voting paradox points out that in more complex decisions

with many options, the decisions can be unstable, leading to government failure.

▶ Other causes for government failure include special interest groups, time inconsistency, and poor incentives in government.

▶ Economic models of government behavior suggest ways to reduce the likelihood of government failure and increase government efficiency.

▶ Incentives and competition have been suggested as ways to improve the operation of government.

CONCLUSION

In this chapter we have explored market failure due to public goods and to externalities. A competitive market provides too little in the way of public goods such as national defense and too little in the way of goods for which there are positive externalities, such as education and research. A competitive market results in too much production of goods for which there are negative externalities, such as goods that pollute the environment.

Most of the remedies for market failure involve the action of government. The provision of public goods by the government should require a careful cost-benefit analysis to make sure that the benefits are greater than the cost of producing a public good. The opportunities for private parties to work out the externalities may be limited by transaction costs and free-rider problems. But there are ways in which the market system can aid the government, as in the case of tradable permits. In these cases, the main role of the government is to define and assign property rights.

It is very important, however, to develop models of government behavior and to recognize the possibility of government failure. In reality, political considerations enter into production of public goods. A member of Congress from one part of the country might push for a public works project in the local district in order to be reelected. Moreover, the externality argument emphasized in this chapter is frequently abused as a political device, providing justification for pork-barrel expenditures. Thus, finding ways to improve decision-making in government, such as through market-based incentives, is needed if government is to play its role in providing remedies for market failures.

KEY POINTS

1. The government produces a wide range of goods and services, employing over 15 percent of the work force in the United States. It also buys goods produced by private firms and provides them to the public.

2. Public goods are defined by two key characteristics, nonrivalry and nonexcludability. National defense and police services are the classic examples of public goods.

3. The existence of public goods provides a role for government because competitive markets frequently have difficulty producing such goods in the efficient amount.

4. Cost-benefit analysis is a technique to decide how much of a public good should be produced. Measuring benefits and deciding how to discount the future are difficult in the case of public goods.

5. Externalities occur when the costs or benefits of a good spill over to other parts of the economy. They create another potential role for government.

6. Goods may have a positive externality or a negative externality.

7. Externalities can sometimes be internalized in the private sector without government. But in many cases, externalities require some government action.

8. Taxes and subsidies or tradable permits are preferred to command and control because the market can still transmit information and provide incentives.

9. Models of government behavior are based on the economic assumption that people try to improve their well-being. In the case of politicians, this usually means taking actions to improve the chances of being elected or reelected.

10. The median voter theorem and the voting paradox are some of the results of the analysis of voting; the latter suggests a reason for government failure.

11. Special interest groups, time inconsistency, and poor incentives are some of the other reasons for government failure.

12. Marketlike incentives and competition are ways suggested by economists to reduce government failure.

KEY TERMS

privatization	contingent valuation	marginal private benefit	tradable permits
public good	public infrastructure project	marginal social benefit	public choice models
nonrivalry	externality	internalize	median voter theorem
nonexcludability	negative externality	private remedies	convergence of positions
free-rider problem	positive externality	Coase theorem	voting paradox
user fee	marginal private cost	command and control	Arrow impossibility theorem
cost-benefit analysis	marginal social cost	emission taxes	time inconsistency

QUESTIONS FOR REVIEW

1. What types of goods are produced or supplied by the government at the federal, state, and local levels?

2. Why do nonexcludability and nonrivalry make production by private firms in a market difficult?

3. Why is it difficult to measure the benefits of public goods when deciding how much to produce?

4. What is the use of cost-benefit analysis in the case of public goods?

5. What is the difference between a positive externality and a negative externality?

6. Why are private remedies for externalities not always feasible?

7. What is the advantage of emission taxes over command and control?

8. How do subsidies for education remedy a market failure?

9. What is the difference between the median voter theorem and the voting paradox?

10. What are the similarities and differences between market failure and government failure?

PROBLEMS

1. The following table shows the marginal benefit per year (in dollars) to all the households in a small community from the hiring of additional police officers to patrol the streets. The table also shows the marginal cost per year (in dollars) of hiring additional police per year.

Number of Police	Marginal Benefit	Marginal Cost
1	500,000	35,000
2	200,000	35,000
3	100,000	36,000
4	80,000	37,000
5	70,000	38,000
6	50,000	39,000
7	40,000	40,000
8	30,000	41,000
9	20,000	42,000
10	10,000	44,000

a) Is the service provided by the patrolling police officers a public good?

b) Why might the marginal benefit from an additional police officer decline with the number of police?

c) Plot the marginal benefit and the marginal cost in a graph with police on the horizontal axis.

d) What is the optimal amount of this public good (in terms of number of police officers)? Illustrate your answer in the graph in part (c).

e) Is this marginal benefit schedule the same as the town's demand curve for police? (*Hint:* Recall the exact definition of a market demand curve from Chapter 5).

2. Suppose that there are only three households in the town in problem 1 and that each one of them has marginal benefit in dollars from additional police as described in the following table.

Number of Police	Household A	Household B	Household C
1	200,000	200,000	100,000
2	100,000	60,000	40,000
3	50,000	30,000	20,000
4	40,000	25,000	15,000
5	36,000	20,000	14,000
6	25,000	15,000	10,000
7	20,000	14,000	6,000
8	15,000	13,000	2,000
9	10,000	9,000	1,000
10	5,000	4,500	500

a) Add up the marginal benefits of the three households for each number of police officers. Check that your addition gives the marginal benefit to all the households in the town as given in problem 1.

b) Plot each of the three marginal benefit schedules and the marginal benefit schedule for the whole town on the same graph with the number of police on the horizontal axis. (You will need a big vertical scale). What is the relationship between the three household curves and the curve for the whole town?

3. Australia requires its citizens to vote by imposing fines on those who do not vote. Does this policy help overcome a free-rider problem?

4. Public education is not a public good, but it has external effects. Explain.

5. Group projects—for example, when students are assigned to work together on the same term paper—can lead to a free-rider problem. Why? What are some methods teachers use to alleviate this free-rider problem?

6. Suppose that people value the continued existence of dolphins in the Pacific Ocean but that tuna fishing fleets kill large numbers of these mammals. Draw a graph showing the externality. Describe two alternative approaches to remedy the externality.

7. Suppose your neighbors across the street want you to help them tend the flower garden in the front of their house. Why is the flower garden an externality to you? What does this mean about the quantity of flowers that will be planted in the neighborhood? If you are planning to sell your house soon, will you be more or less likely to help your neighbors? Why?

8. Suppose that it costs $200,000 for a community to paint lines defining bike lanes on the sides of streets and that the paint lasts two years, after which it can no longer be seen. Suppose that the benefits to the community are estimated to be $100,000 in the first year and $110,000 in the second year. If the discount rate is 10 percent, should the community create bike lanes? What if the discount rate is 1 percent?

9. Property rights over the world's oceans are not well defined. Recently, experts have noted that fishing stocks are declining as the seas' resources are overused.

a) Explain, in economic terms, why this might have happened.

b) Commercial fishing firms in countries all over the world are complaining about the decline in their industry. The response of many governments has been to subsidize the fleets in their countries. Explain this as an example of government failure.

10. A sample of households was asked whether each would visit a proposed public recreation area if the price of entry to the area was set at different amounts ranging from as high as $100 to as low as $0 (no charge). A statistical

analysis of the sample determined that the recreation area would have the following number of visits for the given prices of entry:

Price per Visit (dollars)	Number of Visits (households per year)
100	0
90	5
80	10
70	20
60	30
50	50
40	100
30	500
20	800
16	1,000
12	2,000
10	3,000
8	5,000
6	10,000
4	30,000
2	40,000
1	50,000
0	100,000

a) What is the consumer surplus each year if the price is $30 per visit? What about $10 per visit?

b) Suppose that, if such an area is developed, the government charges a price of $5 per visit to cover the costs of maintaining the recreation area (sanitation, park rangers, etc). What are the benefits of the recreation area that must be compared with the cost of the land and development in a cost-benefit analysis?

11. List one specific example of a market failure and one of a government failure. What does the government do in the case of this market failure? Is the government successful? How might the market be used to reduce government failure? Is the government trying to correct this problem? What advice would you give to the government?

12. Cite one issue where Republicans and Democrats have had a convergence of positions and one where the parties' positions are quite different. Why is there a difference between the issues you have selected?

13. Suppose a government announces that the earnings on any fixed capital investment in the country will not be taxed for a certain period of time. Will investors generally be eager to invest? If the government has a problem financing its budget the following year, what will happen? Explain how this is an example of a time-inconsistent policy.

14. Use the median voter theorem to explain why the admission of a group of extreme right-wing students to a college replacing a more moderate group of right-wing graduates will not affect the election of class president.

15. Use the following set of preferences for Ali, Betty, and Camilla to show that the paradox of voting does not always occur:

	Ali	Betty	Camilla
First	A	B	C
Second	B	A	A
Third	C	C	B

How does this example differ from the one in Table 15.3?

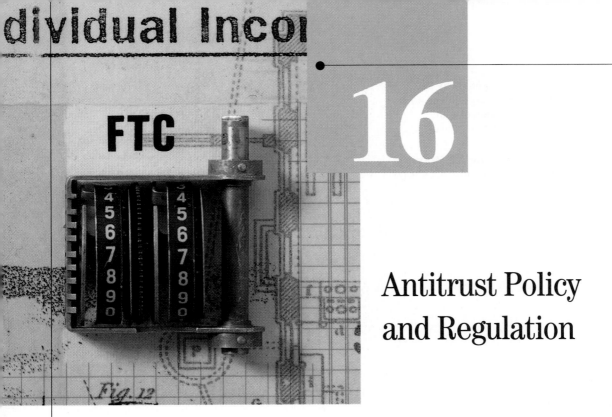

FTC

16

Antitrust Policy and Regulation

When Microsoft came to dominate the personal computer software industry, its founder, Bill Gates, was called before a U.S. government agency, the Federal Trade Commission, to defend the company against charges of unfair competition and monopoly power amid media comparisons with John D. Rockefeller's Standard Oil monopoly of the 1890s. When Microsoft wanted to buy Intuit, a personal finance software firm, the U.S. Justice Department blocked the purchase. When a new wireless communications device, the personal communications server, was developed, another government agency, the Federal Communications Commission, determined in advance the very structure of the new market—how many firms would be in each region and whether or not existing cellular phone companies would compete. When an orange juice company exaggerated its claim for freshness, yet another government agency, the Food and Drug Administration, told it to stop or penalties would be imposed.

These events represent just a few of the thousands of recent cases in which the government intervenes in the operations of firms. The intent of the government in many of these cases is to promote competition, which we

know is an essential ingredient of market efficiency. Recall from Chapter 10 on monopoly that when firms have market power they raise prices above marginal cost, reduce the quantity produced, and create a deadweight loss to society. In such cases, the government may be able to intervene to reduce the deadweight loss and increase economic efficiency.

This chapter uses the principle developed in Chapter 10 to explain the different ways the government can promote competition and regulate firms with market power. We consider two broad types of policy: (1) anti-trust policy, which is concerned with preventing anticompetitive practices like price fixing and with limiting firms' market power by preventing mergers or breaking up existing firms, and (2) regulatory policy, in which the government requires firms that have a natural monopoly to set prices at prescribed levels.

We will see in this chapter that there have been two conflicting trends in government regulation of firms in recent years. One trend is the deregulation movement, which occurred in response to growing evidence that regulation was being used in industries in which it was not appropriate. The deregulation movement began in the late 1970s and has reduced government regulation of prices in industries such as airlines, trucking, railroads, and telecommunications. The other trend is the increase in the number of government regulations and oversight in areas such as the environment and consumer safety.

ANTITRUST POLICY

Antitrust policy refers to the actions the government takes to promote competition among firms in the economy. Antitrust policy includes challenging and breaking up existing firms with significant market power, preventing mergers that would increase monopoly power significantly, prohibiting price fixing, and limiting anticompetitive arrangements between firms and their suppliers.

antitrust policy: government actions designed to promote competition among firms in the economy.

Attacking Existing Monopoly Power

Antitrust policy began in the United States just over 100 years ago in response to a massive wave of mergers and consolidations. Similar merger movements occurred in Europe at about the same time. These mergers were made possible by rapid innovations in transportation, communication, and management techniques. Railroads and telegraph lines expanded across the country, allowing large firms to place manufacturing facilities and sales offices in many different population centers. It was during this period that the Standard Oil Company grew rapidly, acquiring about 100 firms and gaining about 90 percent of U.S. oil refinery capacity. Similarly, the United States Steel Corporation was formed in 1901 by merging many smaller steel companies. It captured about 65 percent of the steel ingot market. These large firms were called *trusts*.

The **Sherman Antitrust Act** of 1890 was passed in an effort to prevent these large companies from using their monopoly power. Section 2 of the act focused on the large existing firms. It stated, "Every person who shall monopolize, or attempt to monopolize . . . any part of the trade or commerce among the several states, or with foreign nations, shall be deemed guilty of a felony."

Sherman Antitrust Act: a law passed in 1890 in the United States to reduce anticompetitive behavior; Section 1 makes price fixing illegal, and Section 2 makes attempts to monopolize illegal.

A Brief History: From Standard Oil to AT&T

It was on the basis of the Sherman Antitrust Act that Theodore Roosevelt's administration took action to break apart Standard Oil. After 10 years of litigation, the Supreme Court ruled in 1911 that Standard Oil monopolized the oil-refining industry illegally. To remedy the problem, the courts ordered that Standard Oil be broken into a number of separate entities. Many of these parts remain today. Standard Oil of New York became Mobil; Standard Oil of California became Chevron; Standard Oil of Indiana became Amoco. Exxon was the former Standard Oil of New Jersey. Competition among these companies was slow to develop since their shares were still controlled by Rockefeller. But as the shares were distributed to heirs and then sold, the companies began to compete against each other. Now the oil-producing companies have much less monopoly power.

437

Soon after its success in splitting apart Standard Oil, the U.S. government took successful action under the Sherman Act against the tobacco trust—splitting up the American Tobacco Company into sixteen different companies. It also broke up several monopolies in railroads, food processing, and chemicals. However, the government was not successful in using the Sherman Act against United States Steel. As part of the Standard Oil decision, the Supreme Court developed a rule of reason that required not only that a firm have monopoly power but also that it intend to use that power against other firms in a way that would restrict competition. Monopoly per se, in and of itself, was not enough, according to the Supreme Court in 1911. In other words, rather than issuing a **per se rule,** in which it is only necessary to show that a certain action occurred, the Supreme Court used a **rule of reason,** in which it is necessary to show that the action occurred *and* that there was purposeful intent and significant impact. Since most competitors and customers of United States Steel said that the company's actions did not restrain competition, the Supreme Court, applying its rule of reason, decided in 1920 that United States Steel was not guilty under the Sherman Act.

Twenty-five years later, a 1945 Supreme Court decision that found Alcoa Aluminum guilty of monopolization refined the rule of reason to make it easier to prove guilt. Although a monopoly per se was still not enough, the intent to willingly acquire and maintain a monopoly—easier to prove than an intent to restrict competition—was enough to establish guilt.

In 1969 the U.S. government brought antitrust action against IBM because of its dominance in the mainframe computer market. After a number of years of litigation, the government dropped the case. One reason was rapid change in the computer market. Mainframes were coming under competition from smaller computers. Firms such as Digital Equipment and Apple Computer were competing with IBM by 1982, when the government withdrew its case. Looking at the competition picture more broadly and recognizing that it had already spent millions, the government decided that antitrust action was no longer warranted.

The U.S. government took action against AT&T in the 1970s. It argued that AT&T was restraining trade as the only significant supplier of telephone service in the nation. As a result of that antitrust action, AT&T was broken apart into regional telephone companies. These regional companies have monopolies in their areas (and are regulated as described in the next section) but must now compete with each other in businesses such as telephone equipment. Moreover, AT&T now must compete with MCI and Sprint in providing long-distance telephone service nationwide. This increase in competition lowered the cost of long-distance calls.

Predatory Pricing

Attempts by firms to monopolize by predatory pricing have also been challenged by the government and other firms, though breakup is not usually the intended remedy. **Predatory pricing** refers to the attempt by a firm to charge a price below its shutdown point in order to drive its competitors out of business, after which it then forms a monopoly.

A 1986 Supreme Court decision, *Matsushita v. Zenith,* has made predatory pricing harder to prove. Matsushita and several other Japanese companies were accused by Zenith of predatory pricing of televisions in the U.S. market. After five years of litigation and appeals, the Court decided that there was not sufficient evidence for predatory pricing. The Court argued that the Japanese firms' share of the U.S. market was too small compared to Zenith's to make monopolization plausible.

---

per se rule: a standard in antitrust cases in which it is only necessary to show that an action occurred, not also that there was intent or significant impact.

rule of reason: an evolving standard by which antitrust cases are decided, requiring not only the existence of monopoly power but also the intent to restrict trade and the existence of significant impact.

predatory pricing: action on the part of one firm to set a price below its shutdown point to drive its competitors out of business.

Moreover, the low price of the Japanese televisions seemed to be based on low production costs. Thus, the Court's majority opinion stated that this predatory pricing case appeared to make "no economic sense."

Predatory pricing is difficult to distinguish from vigorous competition, which is essential to a well-functioning market economy. For example, Wal-Mart has been accused of predatory pricing by smaller retailers, who find it is hard to compete with Wal-Mart's low prices. Yet, in many of these cases, it is likely that Wal-Mart is more efficient. Its lower prices are due to lower costs. In 1993, Northwest Airlines sued American Airlines for predatory pricing in Texas but lost. The jury decided that although American Airlines was charging prices below its shutdown point, it was not attempting to monopolize the market.

Merger Policy

There have been thirty-three breakups of firms ordered by the courts since 1890, including those of Standard Oil, American Tobacco, Alcoa, and AT&T. Since the AT&T case, there have been no breakups. The relative infrequency of government-forced breakups in recent years may be due to greater international competition or to the effectiveness of merger policy, which we now consider. For firms to occupy a huge share of the market, they must either grow internally or merge with other firms. A merger policy that prevents mergers that create firms with huge market power reduces the need to break up firms.

The Legislation, the Antitrust Division, and the FTC

The Sherman Antitrust act dealt with monopolies already in existence. The **Clayton Antitrust Act** of 1914 aimed to prevent the creation of monopolies and, as amended in 1950, provides the legal basis for preventing mergers that would significantly reduce competition. The Federal Trade Commission Act of 1914 set up a new government agency called the **Federal Trade Commission (FTC),** which was to help enforce these acts along with the Justice Department.

To this day, the **Antitrust Division of the Justice Department** and the FTC have dual responsibility for competition policy in the United States. The Justice Department has more investigative power and can bring criminal charges, but for the most part, it is a dual responsibility.

Clayton Antitrust Act: a law passed in 1914 in the United States aimed at preventing monopolies from forming through mergers.

Federal Trade Commission (FTC): the government agency established to help enforce antitrust legislation in the United States; it shares this responsibility with the Antitrust Division of the Justice Department.

Antitrust Division of the Justice Department: the division of the Justice Department in the United States that enforces antitrust legislation, along with the Federal Trade Commission.

Economic Analysis

How does the government decide whether a merger by firms reduces competition in the market? The economists and lawyers in the Justice Department and the FTC provide much of the analysis. They focus on the market power of the firm. The more concentrated the firms in an industry, the more likely it is that the firms have significant market power. Concentration is usually measured by the Herfindahl-Hirschman index.

The "Herf"

The **Herfindahl-Hirschman index (HHI)** is used so frequently to analyze mergers that it has a nickname: the "Herf." The HHI is defined as the sum of the squares of the market shares of each firm in the industry. The more concentrated the industry, the larger the shares and, therefore, the larger the HHI. For example,

Herfindahl-Hirschman index (HHI): an index ranging in value from 0 to 10,000 indicating the concentration in an industry; it is calculated by summing the squares of the market shares of each firm in the industry.

if there is one firm, the HHI is $(100)^2 = 10,000$, the maximum value. If there are two firms each with a 50 percent share, the HHI is $(50)^2 + (50)^2 = 5,000$. If there are 10 firms with equal shares, the HHI is 1,000. Several other values of the HHI are listed in Table 16.1 for several hypothetical examples of firm shares in particular industries.

Observe that the HHI tends to be lower when there are more firms in the industry or when the shares of each firm are more equal. Even when the number of firms in the industry is very large, the HHI can be large if one or two firms have a large share. For example, an industry with 20 firms in which one firm has 81 percent of the market and the others each have 1 percent has a very large HHI of 6,580, even greater than a two-firm industry with equal shares.

According to the merger guidelines put forth by the Justice Department and the FTC, mergers in industries with a postmerger HHI above 1,800 would likely be challenged if the HHI rose by 50 points or more. When the HHI is below 1,000, a challenge is unlikely. Between 1,000 and 1,800, a challenge would occur if the HHI rose by 100 points. Table 16.2 shows the three key ranges for the HHI.

For example, suppose that the two smallest firms in the four-firm example industry C in Table 16.1 merged and the industry thereby took the form of example industry A; then the HHI would rise from 4,550 to 4,600 for an increase of 50. Hence, the merger would probably be challenged by the government. For another example, suppose that the two middle-sized firms with 20 percent shares in the five-firm example industry F in Table 16.1 merged and the industry thereby took the form of example industry D; then the HHI would increase by 800 (from 2,600 to 3,400), and the government would challenge the merger. In general, a 100-point change in the HHI corresponds roughly to a merger of two firms with a 7 percent share of the market.

The HHI is used because it indicates how likely it is that firms in the industry after the merger will have enough market power to raise prices well above marginal cost, reduce the quantity produced, and cause economic inefficiency. In 1986, the FTC did not permit a merger of Coca-Cola and Dr Pepper, which would have increased the HHI in carbonated soft drinks by 341 points, from 2,305 to 2,646.

The typical FTC or Justice Department decision goes beyond numerical concentration measures—especially if measures are in the uncertain region. Ease of

"This town isn't big enough for both of us—let's merge."

	Industry Example	Number of Firms	Shares (percent)	HHI
TABLE 16.1 **How the HHI Measures Industry Concentration: Examples**	A	3	60, 30, 10	4,600
	B	3	33, 33, 34	3,334
	C	4	60, 30, 5, 5	4,550
	D	4	40, 40, 10, 10	3,400
	E	4	25, 25, 25, 25	2,500
	F	5	40, 20, 20, 10, 10	2,600
	G	5	20, 20, 20, 20, 20	2,000
	H	10	19, others have 9	1,090
	I	10	all have 10	1,000
	J	20	24, others have 4	880
	K	20	all have 5	500
	L	25	all have 4	400
	M	50	all have 2	200

Postmerger HHI	Action
Above 1,800	Likely to challenge merger if HHI increases by 50 or more
Between 1,000 and 1,800	Likely to challenge merger if HHI increases by 100 or more
Less than 1,000	Unlikely to challenge

TABLE 16.2
The Merger Guidelines for the Herfindahl-Hirschman Index

entry of new firms into the industry is an important factor, as is the potential contestability of the market from other firms. Recall the idea of *contestable markets* discussed in Chapter 10; even if firms are highly concentrated in an industry, potential entry from other firms provides competitive pressure on the industry. Thus, an industry with a high degree of concentration may, in fact, be acting competitively because of the threat of new firms coming into the business.

contestable market: a market in which the threat of competition is enough to encourage firms to act like competitors. (Ch. 10)

Market Definition

When measuring concentration or ease of entry, the market definition is very important. **Market definition** is a description of the types of goods and services included in the market and the geographic area of the market. Table 16.3 shows the range of possibilities for market definition when considering the merger of soft drink producers. Should the market definition be narrow (carbonated soft drinks) or broad (all nonalcoholic beverages)? The market definition makes a big difference for concentration measures. The HHI for the carbonated soft drink market would have increased by 341 if Pepsi and Seven-Up had merged in 1986. In contrast, the

market definition: demarcation of a geographic region and a category of goods or services in which firms compete.

TABLE 16.3
Different Market Definitions in the Beverage Industry

						Milk
					Tea	Tea
				Coffee	Coffee	Coffee
			Juice drinks	Juice drinks	Juice drinks	Juice drinks
		Bottled water	Bottled water	Bottled water	Bottled water	Bottled water
	Powdered soft drinks	Powdered soft drinks	Powdered soft drinks	Powdered soft drinks	Powdered soft drinks	Powdered soft drinks
Carbonated soft drinks	Carbonated soft drinks	Carbonated soft drinks	Carbonated soft drinks	Carbonated soft drinks	Carbonated soft drinks	Carbonated soft drinks
Narrow Market Definition			**Medium Market Definition**			**Broad Market Definition**

Reading the News About Government Objections to a Merger

To get government approval of a merger, two merging firms frequently must promise to sell part of their business to a third firm in order to reduce the HHI index.

This article describes how a proposed merger between two big discount office supply firms—*Staples* and *Office Depot*—was blocked by the Federal Trade Commission (FTC), which stated that the merger would reduce competition and raise prices. In response to this FTC deci-

sion, the two firms then agreed to sell 63 stores to a third firm, *Officemax,* hoping that this action would lower the HHI index by enough to make the FTC change its mind.

Observe the areas of disagreement revealed in the article. First, even the FTC was not unanimous in its decision: One commissioner thought the merger was just fine. Second, even with the promise to sell stores, some critics, such as Ralph Nader, thought market power

would rise too much.

Why the differences of opinion? Different views about market definition, the relevance of changes in the HHI index, and the importance of contestable markets are the likely reasons for the different opinions about the merger.

Source of article: "Office Depot and Staples to Sell Stores," by John M. Broder, *The New York Times,* March 13, 1997. Copyright © 1997 by The New York Times Company. Reprinted by permission.

Office Depot And Staples To Sell Stores

Officemax Will Buy 63 In Bid to Save Merger

By John M. Broder

WASHINGTON, March 12—The office supply discounters Staples Inc. and Office Depot Inc., facing a threatened antitrust lawsuit to block their proposed merger, agreed today to sell 63 stores to their lone remaining competitor, Officemax Inc.

The $109 million deal is intended to overcome objections by the Federal Trade Commission to the $4 billion Staples-Office Depot deal. The commission voted 4 to 1 on Monday to seek a Federal court injunction to stop the deal on the ground that it would violate antitrust laws and bring higher office supply prices.

After the commission's threat to take Staples to court earlier this week, it is unlikely the agency will endorse the deal without careful study of the impact of the sale on competition and prices. That analysis can take days, or even weeks, and may involve new discussions with Staples about its plans.

The divestiture was engineered to answer F.T.C. staff worries about the 40 cities where only Staples and Office Depot have stores. Elimination of competition in those markets would allow the combined company to raise

prices with impunity, agency officials argued.

The 63 stores that Officemax will pick up are in many of those communities and will leave Staples with a head-to-head competitor and pressure to keep prices low, according to lawyers who helped structure the deal.

But consumer advocates said that the 63-store sale did not improve what they considered a bad deal.

Ralph Nader, who has lobbied against the office supply merger, said that Officemax's approval of the combination was evidence that the two remaining companies would see their competitive pressures ease and open the way for higher prices.

"Nothing irritates business executives more than competition," Mr. Nader said. "The willingness of Officemax to bail out the other two makes one very suspicious."

HHI would increase by only 74 if bottled water, powdered soft drinks, tea, juices, and coffee were also included in the market with carbonated soft drinks.

Defining the geographic area of a market is also a key aspect of defining the market for a good or service. In an integrated world economy, a significant amount of competition comes from firms in other countries. For example, in the automobile industry in the United States there have been only three major producers.

This is a highly concentrated industry. However, intense competition coming from Japanese cars, Korean cars, German cars, etc., increases the amount of competition. The rationale for challenging a merger is mitigated substantially by international competition.

Horizontal versus Vertical Mergers

Merger policy also distinguishes between **horizontal mergers,** in which two firms selling the same good, or same type of good, merge, and **vertical mergers,** in which a firm merges with its supplier, as, for example, when a clothing manufacturer merges with a retail clothing store chain. The merger guidelines in Table 16.2 refer to horizontal mergers. Virtually all economists agree that horizontal mergers have the potential to increase market power, all else the same.

There has been considerable disagreement among economists about the effects of vertical mergers, however. A vertical merger will seldom reduce competition if there are firms competing at each level of production. However, some feel a vertical merger may aid in reducing competition at the retail store level.

> **horizontal merger:** a combining of two firms that sell the same good or same type of good.

> **vertical merger:** a combining of two firms in which one supplies goods to the other.

Price Fixing

In addition to breaking up firms and preventing firms with a great amount of market power from forming, antitrust policy looks for specific forms of conspiracy to restrict competition among firms. For example, when two or more firms conspire to fix prices, they engage in an illegal anticompetitive practice. **Price fixing** is a serious, frequently criminal offense. Section 1 of the Sherman Antitrust Act makes price fixing illegal *per se.*

Laws against price fixing are enforced by bringing lawsuits against the alleged price fixers. Suits are brought both directly by the Justice Department and by individual firms that are harmed by price fixing. The number of private suits greatly exceeds the number of government suits. Individual firms can collect **treble damages** (a provision included in the Clayton Act)—three times the actual damages. The treble damage penalty aims to deter price fixing.

One of the most famous price-fixing cases in U.S. history occurred in the 1950s and involved Westinghouse and General Electric. Through an elaborate system of secret codes and secret meeting places, the executives of these two firms agreed together to set the price of electrical generators and other equipment they were selling in the same market. Through this agreement they set the price well above competitive levels, but they were discovered and found guilty of price fixing. Treble damages amounting to about $500 million were awarded, and criminal sentences were handed down; some executives went to prison.

A more recent price-fixing case involved the production of food additives. The large agricultural firm Archer-Daniels-Midland (ADM) was sued by the Justice Department for fixing prices with other international producers. In 1996, as part of the settlement in this case, ADM paid over $100 million in fines.

> **price fixing:** the situation in which firms conspire to set prices for goods sold in the same market.

> **treble damages:** penalties awarded to the injured party equal to three times the value of the injury.

Vertical Restraints

The price-fixing arrangements just described are an effort to restrict trade in one horizontal market, such as the electrical machinery market or the markets for food additives. Such restraints of trade clearly raise prices, reduce the quantity produced, and cause deadweight loss. But there are also efforts by firms to restrain

exclusive territories: the region over which a manufacturer limits the distribution or selling of its products to one retailer or wholesaler.

exclusive dealing: a condition of a contract by which a manufacturer does not allow a retailer to sell goods made by a competing manufacturer.

resale price maintenance: the situation in which a producer sets a list price and does not allow the retailer to offer a discount to consumers.

trade vertically. For example, **exclusive territories** occur when a manufacturer of a product gives certain retailers or wholesalers exclusive rights to sell the product in a given area. This practice is common in soft drink and beer distribution. **Exclusive dealing** is the practice by which a manufacturer does not allow a retailer to sell goods made by a competitor. **Resale price maintenance** is the practice of a manufacturer's setting a list price of a good and then forbidding the retailer to offer a discount.

Do vertical restraints reduce economic efficiency? There is considerable agreement among economists that manufacturers cannot increase their own market power by vertical restraints on the firms to which they supply goods. A manufacturer requiring that a retailer take a certain action does not give the manufacturer a greater ability to raise prices over competitors without losing sales. In addition, such restraints in some circumstances may actually increase economic efficiency. Consider resale price maintenance, for example.

The premium of the list price over a discount price may be considered payment for the service provided. Suppose that low-price discount stores compete with high-price retail stores that provide services to customers. If a discount store could offer the same product with little or no service, then people could go to the higher-price store, look the product over, get some useful advice from knowledgeable salespeople, and then buy at the discount store. They would be free-riding on the services of the higher-price store. Soon such services would disappear. Resale price maintenance can thus be viewed as a means of eliminating the free-rider problem by preventing the discount store from charging a lower price.

If a producer and retailer are vertically integrated into one firm, then clearly they coordinate the price decisions. For example, the Gap sells its own products in its retail outlets, and it obviously sets the retail price. Outlawing resale price maintenance would mean the firms that were not vertically integrated could not do the same thing as the Gap does. Why should Levi Strauss not be permitted to set the price of Levis sold at retail stores that compete with the Gap?

However, some argue that resale price maintenance is a way to reduce competition at the retail level. They see a value in retailers having competitive pressure to keep prices low as more important than avoiding the free-rider problem.

In sum, there is more controversy among economists about the effect of vertical restraints than about horizontal restraints.

Review

▷ Breaking up monopolies, preventing mergers that would create too much market power, and enforcing laws against price fixing are the main government actions that constitute antitrust policy.

▷ Section 1 of the Sherman Antitrust Act outlaws price fixing.

▷ Section 2 of the Sherman Antitrust Act allows the government to break up firms with monopoly power.

▷ The Clayton Act of 1914, as amended in 1950, provides the legal basis for merger policy.

▷ All these policies aim to increase competition and thus improve the efficiency of a market economy.

▷ There is more controversy about the effects of vertical mergers and vertical restraints than about horizontal mergers and horizontal restraints.

REGULATING NATURAL MONOPOLIES

The goal of antitrust policy is to increase competition and improve the efficiency of markets. Under some circumstances, however, breaking up a monopoly is not necessarily in the interest of economic efficiency. In the provision of certain public utilities, such as water, it is inefficient for more than one company to deliver the product to households. To provide its services, a water company must dig up the streets, lay the water pipes, and maintain them. It would be inefficient to have two companies supply the water because that would require two sets of pipes and would be a duplication of resources. Another example is electricity. It makes no sense to have two electric utility firms supply the same neighborhood with two sets of wires. A single supplier of electricity is more efficient.

natural monopoly: a single firm in an industry in which average total cost is declining over the entire range of production and the minimum efficient scale is larger than the size of the market. (Ch. 10)

economies of scale: also called increasing returns to scale; a situation in which long-run average total cost declines as the output of a firm increases. (Ch. 8)

Economies of Scale and Natural Monopolies

Water and electricity are examples of *natural monopolies,* industries where one firm can supply the entire market at a lower cost than two firms can. Recall from the discussion in Chapter 10 that the key characteristic of a natural monopoly is a declining average total cost curve. Average total cost declines as more is produced because fixed costs are very large compared to variable costs. Once the main line is laid for the water supply, it is relatively easy to hook up another house. Similarly, with electricity, once the main lines are installed, it is relatively easy to run wires into a house. A large initial outlay is necessary to lay the main water pipes or main electrical lines, but thereafter the cost is relatively low. The more houses that are hooked up, the less the average total cost is. Recall that when the long-run average total cost curve declines, there are *economies of scale.*

Figure 16.1 illustrates graphically why one firm can always produce more cheaply than more than one firm when the average total cost curve is downward-sloping. The figure shows quantity produced on the horizontal axis and dollars on the vertical axis; a downward-sloping average total cost curve is plotted. If two firms divide up the market (for example, if two water companies supply water to the neighborhood), then the average total cost is higher than if one firm produces for the entire market. It is more costly for two or more firms to produce a given quantity in the case of a declining average total cost curve than for one firm.

FIGURE 16.1
Natural Monopoly: Declining Average Total Cost
If two firms supply the market, dividing total production between them, costs are higher than if one firm supplies the market. The costs would be even greater if more than two firms split up the market.

Alternative Methods of Regulation

What is the best government policy toward a natural monopoly? Having one firm in an industry lowers the cost of production, but there will be inefficiencies associated with a monopoly: Price will be higher than marginal cost, and there will be a deadweight loss. To get both the advantages of one firm producing *and* competitionlike behavior, the government can either run the firm or regulate the firm. We consider regulation first.

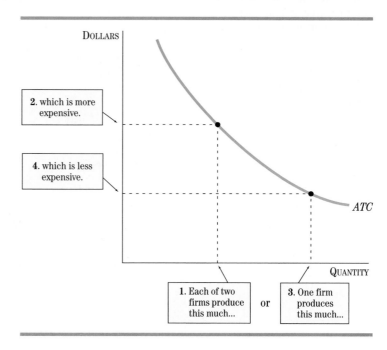

The monopoly price and quantity of a natural monopoly with declining average total cost are illustrated in Figure 16.2. The monopoly quantity occurs where marginal revenue equals marginal cost, the profit-maximizing point for the monopolist. The monopoly price is above marginal cost. If the firm's price was regulated, then the government could require the firm to set a lower price, thereby raising output and eliminating some of the deadweight loss associated with the monopoly. There are three ways for the government to regulate the price: marginal cost pricing, average total cost pricing, and incentive regulation.

Marginal Cost Pricing

We know that there is no deadweight loss with competition because firms choose a quantity of output such that marginal cost is equal to price. Hence, one possibility is for the government to require the monopoly to set its price equal to marginal cost. This method is called **marginal cost pricing.** However, with declining average total cost, the marginal cost is lower than average total cost. This is shown in Figure 16.2 for the case where marginal cost is constant. Thus, if price were equal to marginal cost, *the price would be less than average total cost,* and the monopoly's profits would be negative (a loss). There would be no incentive for any firm to come into the market.

For example, if the regulators of an electrical utility use a pricing rule with price equal to marginal cost, there will be no incentive for the electrical utility to

marginal cost pricing: a regulatory method that stipulates that the firm charge a price that equals marginal cost.

FIGURE 16.2
Monopoly Price versus Alternative Regulatory Schemes
Two alternatives, marginal cost pricing and average total cost pricing, are compared with the monopoly price. Marginal cost pricing gives the greatest quantity supplied, but because price is less than average total cost, the firm earns negative profits. Average total cost pricing results in a larger quantity supplied, and the firm earns zero economic profits.

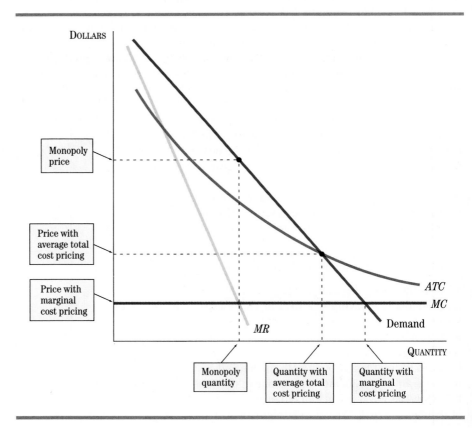

build a plant or produce electricity. Although the idea of mimicking a competitive firm by setting price equal to marginal cost might sound reasonable, it fails to work in practice.

Average Total Cost Pricing

Another method of regulation would have the firm set the price equal to average total cost. This is called **average total cost pricing,** or, sometimes, cost-of-service pricing. It is also illustrated in Figure 16.2. When price is equal to average total cost, we know that economic profits will be equal to zero. With the economic profits equal to zero, there will be enough to pay the managers and the investors in the firm their opportunity costs. Although price is still above marginal cost, it is less than the monopoly price; the deadweight loss will be smaller and more electricity will be produced compared with the monopoly.

average total cost pricing: a regulatory method that stipulates that the firm charge a price that equals average total cost.

But there are some serious problems with average total cost pricing. Suppose the firm knows that whatever its average total cost is, it will be allowed to charge a price equal to average total cost. In that situation, there is no incentive to reduce costs. Sloppy work or less innovative management could increase costs. With the regulatory scheme in which the price equals average total cost, the price would rise by any increase in cost. Inefficiencies could occur with no penalty whatsoever. This approach provides neither an incentive to reduce costs nor a penalty to avoid increasing costs on the part of the management and the workers of the regulated firm.

Incentive Regulation

The third regulation method endeavors to deal with the problem that average total cost pricing provides too little incentive to keep costs low. The method is called **incentive regulation.** It is a relatively new idea but it is quickly spreading, and most predict it is the way of the future. The method projects a regulated price out over a number of years. That price can be based on an estimate of average total cost. The regulated firm is told that the projected price will not be revised upward or downward for a number of years. If the regulated firm achieves average total cost lower than the price, it will be able to keep the profits, or perhaps pass on some of the profits to a worker who came up with the idea for the innovation. Similarly, if sloppy management causes average total cost to rise, then profits will fall because the regulatory agency will not revise the price.

incentive regulation: a regulatory method that sets prices for several years ahead and then allows the firm to keep any additional profits or suffer any losses over that period of time.

Thus, under incentive regulation, the regulated price is only imperfectly related to average total cost. The firm has a profit incentive to reduce costs. If a firm does poorly, it pays the penalty in terms of lower profits or losses.

Under incentive regulation, the incentives can be adjusted. For example, the California Public Utility Commission (the regulators of utility firms in California) has incentive schemes by which electrical utility firms and their customers share equally in the benefits of reduced costs and in the penalties from increased costs. This reduces the incentive to the firm in comparison to the case where the benefits and penalties are not shared.

Incentive regulation is sometimes made difficult by asymmetric information problems. The regulated firm knows more than the regulator about its equipment, technology, and workers. Thus, the firm can mislead the regulator and say its average total cost is higher than it actually is in order to get a higher price, as shown in Figure 16.3.

FIGURE 16.3
Asymmetric Information and Regulation
If a regulator uses average cost pricing but does not have complete information about costs at the firm, the firm could give misleading information about its costs in order to get a higher price from the regulator. In an extreme case, shown in this figure, the firm could say its costs were so high that it could get the monopoly price.

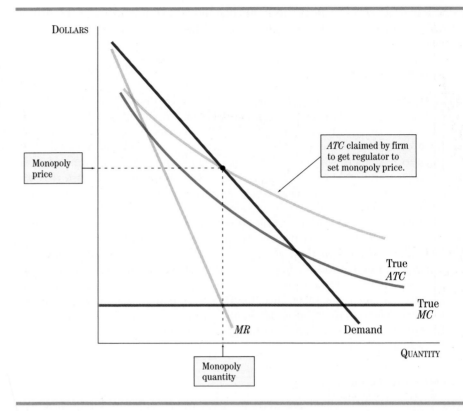

Government-Run Monopolies

In some cases, the government decides to run a natural monopoly itself rather than regulate a private firm. An example is the U.S. Postal Service monopoly in first-class mail. When the Postal Service was created, it seemed to make little sense to have two or three mail services delivering mail to individual houses. This decreasing average total cost feature was one justification for the government's role. An alternative is to regulate a private firm.

However, changes in technology have enabled a number of private firms, such as Federal Express, to enter the postal business in recent years, although U.S. law still does not permit any competition in first-class mail delivery. This competition from Federal Express in overnight delivery has resulted in improvement in the services of the U.S. Postal Service. The Postal Service now offers services that compete with Federal Express. Some are now questioning whether the Postal Service should maintain its monopoly in first-class mail delivery.

It has been more common in other countries for the government to run or own firms. For example, the French and Japanese telephone companies are largely government-owned. In recent years, there have been efforts to privatize such firms—sell them to the private sector. Telemex, the telephone company in Mexico, was sold in 1990; and about 40 percent of the Japanese telephone company has been sold in recent years.

Review

▸ In the case of natural monopoly, one firm can produce at lower average total cost than two or more firms, but a monopoly causes deadweight loss.

▸ There are two ways to reduce deadweight loss. Government can either regulate the monopoly or run the monopoly.

▸ If government regulates the monopoly through marginal cost pricing, the firm will run losses. Average total cost pricing leads to increased costs because it doesn't provide incentives to keep costs down. Incentive regulation is becoming the preferred method of regulation.

TO REGULATE OR NOT TO REGULATE

Our analysis thus far suggests that the government should regulate firms' prices in situations where natural monopolies exist. In practice, this requires deciding when a natural monopoly exists, which is frequently difficult.

There are many examples in American history where the government has regulated a firm's prices even when it is far-fetched to think about the firm as a natural monopoly. For example, for a long period of time, trucking was regulated by the federal government. Trucking regulation grew out of railroad regulation, which itself was originally justified when railroads were the only rapid form of transportation and thus were natural monopolies. Under trucking regulation, the federal government put a floor on the price that trucking companies could charge when shipping goods interstate. Federal regulation of trucking was disbanded in the early 1980s. Studies have shown that trucking rates fell as a result.

Borderline Cases

Clearly, trucking is not a natural monopoly. The trucking industry is at the opposite end of the spectrum from water or electrical utility companies, which are almost always regulated.

But there are many borderline cases that are more controversial. Many of these arise in high-technology industries such as telecommunications and computing. An important example is cable television. In 1992 there was considerable debate about whether the federal government should regulate cable television. On first thought, it may appear that cable television is no different from electricity or water. Once a cable television company lays the cable down in a neighborhood, it is a fairly small cost to connect each individual house to it. On the other hand, there are alternatives to cable television for many homes. For example, over-the-air television channels do provide some competition to cable television. If one lives in an area where there are few over-the-air channels, there is little competition. However, if there are six, seven, or eight over-the-air channels, then there is more competition.

Until 1992, the measure of effective competition used by the Federal Communications Commission (FCC), the federal agency that regulates the telecommunications industry, was whether there was a sufficient number of over-the-air channels. At first, the commission decided that three over-the-air channels represented effective competition. It did not regulate cable television companies in areas where there were more than three over-the-air channels. Later on, when it noticed that prices of cable television were rising and consumers were complaining, the FCC raised the limit to six over-the-air channels. In 1992, Congress passed a law saying it did not matter how many channels there were; the law required the FCC to regulate cable television firms in any case.

Over-the-air channels are not the only competition for cable television. People can use satellite dishes, which are coming down in cost. Eventually, it may be possible to use the telephone wires to transmit television signals, in which case the telephone companies could compete with the cable television companies.

High-tech industries change quickly, and it is difficult for government regulators to keep up with the changes. As mentioned in the opening paragraph of this chapter, the FCC has to plan way into the future to decide how to regulate new technologies like the personal communications server. Inflexible regulatory rules could slow innovation.

Regulators as Captives of Industry

Government or government agencies are run by people who have their own motivations, such as being reelected or increasing their influence. Thus, despite the economic advice about what government regulatory agencies should do, the agencies may end up doing something else. In fact, regulators have sometimes ended up helping the industry at the expense of the consumer. The railroad industry is an example. Originally, regulation of railroads was set up to reduce prices below the monopoly price. But as competition to the railroads from trucks and eventually airlines increased, the industry continued to be regulated. Eventually the regulators were helping the industry; they kept prices from falling to prevent railroad firms from failing. And by regulating trucking prices, they kept trucking firms from competing with the railroads. The Teamsters Union, which represents truck drivers, was one of the strongest supporters of regulation because it knew the regulations were keeping trucking prices high. In a sense, the regulators became captives of both the firms and the workers in the industry.

The Nobel Prize-winning economist George Stigler emphasized how regulatory agencies could become captive to the industry and therefore tend to thwart competition. The concerns that regulators will become captives is one reason some economists worry about allowing the government to regulate a new industry, like cable television. Eventually the government may try to protect the cable television operators in order to prevent them from failing. The government might limit competition in the future from satellite dishes or from the telephone company.

Financial Market Regulation: Information and Risk

The financial industry includes banks such as the Bank of America and Citibank, brokerage firms such as Merrill Lynch and Charles Schwab, and insurance firms like Allstate. Banks are regulated by three federal agencies: the Federal Reserve Board (Fed), the Federal Deposit Insurance Corporation (FDIC), and the Office of the Controller of the Currency (OCC), not to mention many state regulatory agencies. Brokerage firms are regulated by the Securities and Exchange Commission (SEC), which also enforces rules about what information corporations that issue

Using Economics to Explain Insurance Regulations

The insurance industry is one of the largest and fastest-growing industries in the United States. The products sold by firms in this industry are considered services and include health insurance, fire insurance, automobile insurance, life insurance, and many other types of insurance.

The insurance industry is also one of the most regulated industries in the economy. In the United States, insurance has been regulated by state governments since the end of the nineteenth century, after several massive bankruptcies followed major urban fires. States enforced a *price ceiling*—to prevent "excessive" prices and ensure the wide availability of insurance—and in

some cases a *price floor*—to provide adequate reserves to all insurance companies, including those that were inefficient and, thus, more likely to go bankrupt.

Insurance regulation, however, is more complicated than setting price floors and ceilings. It usually involves setting investment standards and nondiscriminatory risk classes. Other countries intervene even more actively in the insurance sector, limiting the entry of firms to the market or promoting a policy of transfer from wealthier individuals to poorer individuals.

Governments also sometimes require that people buy insurance. For example, many states require

drivers to buy automobile insurance. The federal government requires that all workers "buy" disability insurance through social security as well as unemployment insurance.

The problem of *adverse selection* explains some of these government requirements. With adverse selection, people with high risk (unobserved by the insurance firms) tend to buy insurance; but this tends to drive up insurance rates so that people with lower risks do not buy. In extreme cases of adverse selection, no insurance will be provided. Requiring that everyone buy eliminates the adverse selection problem.

publicly traded stock must disclose. Insurance firms are regulated by state agencies, not by the federal government.

Financial firms are not natural monopolies. The rationale for regulating financial firms has to do with externalities related to information and risk. For example, the regulatory agencies are supposed to examine banks, brokerage firms, and insurance companies to make sure they are financially sound. They provide a service that individuals would have difficulty performing on their own. Their supervision aims to reduce the risk to depositors and investors.

The Deregulation Movement

Starting in the late 1970s during the Carter administration and gaining force during the Reagan administration, the **deregulation movement**—the lifting of price regulations—radically changed several key industries. The list of initiatives that constitute this deregulation movement is impressive. For example, air cargo was deregulated in 1977, air travel was deregulated in 1978, satellite transmissions were deregulated in 1979, trucking was deregulated in 1980, cable television was deregulated in 1980 (although regulation was reimposed in 1992), crude oil prices and refined petroleum products were deregulated in 1981, and radio was deregulated in 1981. There was also deregulation of prices in the financial industry. Prior to the 1980s, the price—that is, the interest rate on deposits—was

deregulation movement: begun in the late 1970s, the drive to reduce the government regulations controlling prices and entry in many industries.

TABLE 16.4
Reductions in Deadweight Loss Due to Deregulation

Industry	Reduction in Deadweight Loss per Year (billions of dollars)
Airlines	17
Railroads	12
Trucking	11
Telecommunications	1
Cable television	1

Source: Data from Clifford Winston, "Economic Deregulation: Days of Reckoning for Microeconomists," *Journal of Economic Literature,* Sept. 1993, Table 6, p. 1284. (The numbers here are the averages of a range of estimates rounded to the nearest billion.)

controlled by the financial regulators. Regulation of brokerage fees was also eliminated.

This deregulation of prices reduced deadweight loss. Airline prices have declined for many travelers. It is now cheaper to ship goods by truck or by rail. Economists have estimated the size of this reduction in deadweight loss by calculating the increase in the area between the demand curve and the marginal cost curve as the quantity produced increased. Table 16.4 provides estimates of the elimination of the deadweight loss in several different industries. The reduction in the deadweight loss is about $42 billion per year, about ¼ percent of GDP.

Some people complain about deregulation. Business travelers complain that they have to pay more for air travel although vacation travelers can pay less. Another complaint is that there is too much monopoly power in regional hubs. For example, US Airways has a hub in Pittsburgh. TWA has a hub in St. Louis. Airlines that have a large share of the travel at hubs have market power at the hubs. One can, however, also find examples where increased competition has resulted in a decline in monopoly power at the hubs. For example, when Southwest Airlines started competing with TWA in the route between St. Louis and Kansas City, the cost of that trip fell.

Review

▶ In many cases it is clear that a natural monopoly exists and thus price regulation is needed. However, in certain industries like cable television, there is controversy about the need for regulation.

▶ There has frequently been price regulation where there is natural monopoly, as in trucking.

▶ The deregulation movement began in the late 1970s and continued well into the 1980s. It was in response to economic analysis that showed that it was harmful to regulate the prices of firms that are not natural monopolies.

▶ Trucking, airline, and railroad transportation prices are lower as a result of this deregulation. As with most economic changes, not everyone benefited. Business travelers saw the costs of some services increase.

ECONOMIC REGULATION VERSUS SOCIAL REGULATION

economic regulation: government regulation that sets prices or conditions on the entry of firms into an industry.

social regulation: government regulation, such as environmental, health, or safety regulation, that aims to overcome or correct externalities in which private costs differ from social costs.

The regulation of natural monopolies discussed in this chapter is an example of economic regulation. More generally, **economic regulation** is defined as a type of government regulation that sets prices or conditions on entry of firms into an industry. Economic regulation also includes the regulation of financial firms. However, economic regulation is not the only type of government regulation, as the discussion of the environmental regulations in the previous chapter indicates. This other type of regulation is called social regulation. Frequently, **social regulation,** which includes environmental controls, health and safety regulations, and restrictions on labeling and advertising, involves externalities. However, there is considerable disagreement about the exact economic rationale for much social regulation.

●————————————————————

TABLE 16.5
Key Federal Regulatory Agencies

Social Regulation
  Consumer Product Safety Commission (CPSC)
  Food and Drug Administration (FDA)
  Federal Aviation Administration (FAA)
  National Highway and Traffic Safety Administration (NHTSA)
  Occupational Safety and Health Administration (OSHA)
  Environmental Protection Agency (EPA)

Economic Regulation
  Nonfinancial
    Federal Communications Commission (FCC)
    Federal Energy Regulatory Commission (FERC)
  Financial
    Comptroller of the Currency (OCC)
    Federal Reserve System (Fed)
    Securities and Exchange Commission (SEC)

Table 16.5 provides a list of the key federal government agencies involved in social and economic regulation. We discussed the Environmental Protection Agency (EPA) in the previous chapter. Its role is to control pollution. The Food and Drug Administration (FDA) approves new drugs, regulates advertising for food and drugs, and provides standards for labeling on food packages. The Occupational Safety and Health Administration (OSHA) requires that employers inform workers about risks and mandates firms to reduce risks. The National Highway and Traffic Safety Administration (NHTSA) monitors risks and sets standards for automobiles and highways. The Federal Aviation Administration (FAA) sets standards for airline safety. The Consumer Product Safety Administration examines goods for risk. The Federal Trade Commission (FTC), discussed earlier, also regulates information in advertising. In the 1970s, for example, it challenged the ads for various aspirins, including Bayer, Anacin, and Bufferin.

Two Trends

One reason to distinguish economic regulation from social regulation is that the two have followed very different paths in recent years. There has been a rapid expansion of social regulation and a decline in economic regulation, as described earlier. Just as the economic deregulation movement was beginning in the 1970s, more social regulatory agencies—including the EPA and OSHA—were created. There appears to have been a great public demand for the federal government to take a more active role in social regulation. But the fact that such regulations appear to be popular does not mean that they are without fault.

Benefits and Costs Again

An analysis of the benefits of much social regulation can be cast in terms of information and risk. Recall that there are externalities associated with information and risk. If every person who flew on an airplane had to have it checked for safety, the costs would be huge. It is much cheaper to have an agency like the FAA check for airline safety. When the FAA sees a way to make a change in safety requirements that will reduce risk and thereby save lives, it has the authority to require that the

Economic Regulation and Social Regulation

The two photos are everyday reminders of economic and social regulation. On the left, the president of MTV must deal with government regulation of the price of cable TV—an example of *economic* regulation. On the right, a sign posts laws protecting endangered sea turtles—an example of *social* regulation.

airlines make these changes. Similarly, it would be costly for each consumer to check the accuracy of all advertising claims, or to test the efficacy of a new drug. By giving the FDA responsibility for testing new drugs, the public saves considerably on time and effort.

To be sure, without the government, private organizations would probably evolve to provide testing and information about products. Consumers Union is one such organization, and many industries have private watchdog organizations. But because of information externalities, the private actions would probably fall short of the efficient level.

The benefits from providing information about risks must be considered in light of the costs. The FDA might hold back a new drug for testing to reduce risks, but this is costly to the people whose lives could be saved if the drug were approved. The building code requirements for a construction site might raise the cost of construction significantly. Frequently, these costs are not visible. No one knows that an illness might have been prevented with a new drug, but everyone knows when a faulty new drug causes severe illness or death.

The actions of the FDA, OSHA, and other agencies involved in social regulation are frequently criticized because of the costs they impose on firms and consumers. Irate letters and critical editorials about the costs are common. It is very difficult to estimate the costs, but some economists have tried. The estimates range from around 3 to 5 percent of GDP per year for all programs. On the other side, the programs are popular, and they clearly do reduce risks and provide information.

Ultimately, the degree of government intervention will be decided in the give and take of the political process. But careful cost-benefit analysis on a program-by-program basis, as urged by many economists, would help in the decision-making process. For example, economists estimate that the cost of the FAA regulations on airplane cabin fire protection is $200,000 per life saved, which would appear to pass any reasonable cost-benefit analysis. On the other hand, the EPA land disposal regulations and the OSHA formaldehyde regulation cost $3.5 billion and $72 billion per life saved respectively. Most would say that scarce resources could be used to save lives in better ways. Estimates based on people's willingness to accept more risky jobs in comparison to less risky jobs indicate a value of between $1 million and $7 million per life.

Review

▶ Economic regulation and social regulation are the two major forms of government regulation. Economic regulation has declined, and social regulation has increased in recent years.

▶ Many have complained about the costs of social regulation. As in any question involving the role of government, intervention should be based on a cost-benefit analysis.

CONCLUSION

This chapter is the third on the role of government in a market economy. We considered the role of government in affecting income distribution in Chapter 14; in producing or providing for public goods in Chapter 15; in resolving externalities through social regulation, taxes/subsidies, or the assignment of property rights (tradable permits), also in Chapter 15; and in maintaining competitive markets through antitrust policy or the economic regulation of firms in this chapter.

This activity of government, of course, has to be paid for with taxes, ideally according to the principles of taxation discussed in Chapter 14, and with the recognition that taxes themselves cause deadweight loss just as market failure does.

This normative analysis of government policy must be placed in the context of what in reality motivates government policymakers. The example of regulators becoming captives of industry reminds us that having an analysis of what should be done is much different from getting it done. Government failure is a problem that must be confronted just like market failure. Reducing government failure requires designing the institutions of government to give government decision-makers the proper incentives.

We have considered international issues, such as international competition, throughout this discussion of government policy. We now continue our analysis of the role of government with a focus on international economic policy.

KEY POINTS

1. The government has an important role to play in maintaining competition in a market economy.

2. Part of antitrust policy is breaking apart firms with significant market power, although this technique is now used infrequently. Section 2 of the Sherman Antitrust Act provides the legal authority for challenging existing monopolies.

3. A more frequently used part of antitrust policy is preventing mergers that would cause significant market power. In the United States, the government must approve mergers.

4. Concentration measures such as the HHI are used to decide whether a merger should take place.

5. Price fixing is a serious antitrust offense in the United States, and the laws against it are enforced by allowing private firms to sue, providing for treble damages, and allowing the government to ask for criminal penalties.

6. In the case of natural monopolies, the government can either run the firm or regulate a private firm. In the United States, the latter route is usually taken.

7. Regulatory agencies have been using incentive regulation more frequently in order to give firms incentives to hold costs down.

8. The deregulation movement has consisted mainly of removing price regulations from firms that are not natural monopolies, such as trucking and airlines.

9. Overall the deregulation movement has significantly lowered costs to consumers, but it is controversial because services have been cut back in certain areas.

10. Social regulation includes environmental, health, and safety regulation. As economic regulation has been on the wane, social regulation has increased. This increase has had costs as well as benefits.

KEY TERMS

antitrust policy
Sherman Antitrust Act
per se rule
rule of reason
predatory pricing
Clayton Antitrust Act
Federal Trade Commission (FTC)
Antitrust Division of the Justice
   Department

Herfindahl-Hirschman index (HHI)
market definition
horizontal merger
vertical merger
price fixing
treble damages
exclusive territories
exclusive dealing
resale price maintenance

marginal cost pricing
average total cost pricing
incentive regulation
deregulation movement
economic regulation
social regulation

QUESTIONS FOR REVIEW

1. What historical development gave the impetus to the original antitrust legislation in the United States?

2. What is the difference between Section 1 and Section 2 of the Sherman Antitrust Act?

3. What is the difference between the rule of reason and the per se rule in the case of monopolization and in the case of price fixing?

4. What law gives the government the right to prevent mergers that would increase market power?

5. Why is the market definition crucial when calculating the HHI index in the case of mergers?

6. Why is marginal cost pricing a faulty pricing rule for regulatory agencies?

7. How does incentive regulation improve on average cost pricing?

8. Why is there more controversy about regulating cable television than about regulating water companies?

9. What is the difference between economic regulation and social regulation?

10. What is the rationale for regulating airline safety?

PROBLEMS

1. Which legislation—Section 1 of the Sherman Act, Section 2 of the Sherman Act, or the Clayton Act—gives the government the authority to take action in each of the following areas: prosecuting price fixing, preventing proposed mergers, breaking up existing monopolies, suing for predatory pricing?

2. Sketch a graph of a natural monopoly with declining average total cost and constant marginal cost.
  a) Show how the monopoly causes a deadweight loss with price not equal to marginal cost.
  b) Describe the pros and cons of three alternative ways

to regulate the monopoly and reduce deadweight loss: marginal cost pricing, average total cost pricing, and incentive regulation.

3. Historically, local telephone companies have been natural monopolies, but in the last few years cellular phones have started to offer services that are a substitute for wire connections.
  a) If traditional phone companies are under incentive regulation, how would the introduction of cellular phones affect them? Show it graphically.
  b) What should the regulatory agency do?

4. The demand schedule and total costs for a natural monopoly are given in the following table:

Price	Quantity	Total Costs
16	6	80
15	7	85
14	8	90
13	9	95
12	10	100
11	11	105
10	12	110
9	13	115
8	14	120
7	15	125
6	16	130
5	17	135
4	18	140

a) Why is this firm a natural monopoly? What will the monopoly price be? Calculate profits.

b) Suppose the government sees that this is a natural monopoly and decides to regulate it. If the regulators use average total cost pricing, what will the approximate price and quantity be? What should profits be when the regulators are using average total cost pricing?

c) If the regulators use marginal cost pricing, what will the price and quantity be? Why is this policy difficult for regulators to pursue in practice? What are profits in this situation?

d) Why might the government want to use incentive regulation?

5. In some states, regulatory authorities are beginning to allow some competition among electric power companies. What must the regulators think about the nature of this industry? What other industries have gone through this transformation? What are the benefits of deregulation?

6. A patent gives the owner of the patent a monopoly. Suppose firm A has a patent and firm B sues firm A for damages caused by the high price caused by the monopoly. Explain why breaking up the monopoly in order to reduce deadweight loss in the short run could raise deadweight loss in the long run.

7. The airline industry went through deregulation during the late 1970s and early 1980s. What changes in the airline industry would you expect to see after deregulation? How might the profits of airlines change with deregulation? Why?

8. Some people argue that coal mines are natural monopolies. In fact, until very recently, all coal mines in Great Britain were owned by the government. What conditions in the industry do you need to check in order to tell whether the industry is a natural monopoly?

9. Many countries, like Mexico and Russia, are now privatizing government-owned industries. If these industries are natural monopolies, what would you expect to see after privatization? If these industries would naturally have an oligopolistic structure, what would you expect to see after the privatization of a single government firm?

10. Why is it better to break up monopolies that are not natural monopolies rather than regulate them even if it is possible to regulate them?

11. If economies of scale are important, is it possible for consumers to be better off if the government allows more mergers? Explain.

12. Use the merger guidelines (Table 16.2) to decide whether the following changes in the industries in Table 16.1 would be permitted.

a) The nine small firms in example H merge into one firm.

b) Four of the small firms in example J merge into one firm.

c) The two largest firms in example D merge.

d) The two smallest firms in example A merge.

13. In reflecting on a recent term of service, a former head of the Antitrust Division said, "I was convinced that a little bit of efficiency outweighs a whole lot of market power." Evaluate this statement by considering two sources of efficiency—decreasing average total cost and research and development. Describe how these should be balanced against the deadweight loss from market power.

14. Compare the following two hypothetical cases of price fixing.

a) General Motors, Ford, and Chrysler are found to be coordinating their prices for Chevy Blazers, Ford Broncos, and Jeep Cherokees.

b) General Motors is coordinating with Chevy dealers around the country to set the price for Chevy Blazers. Which is more likely to raise prices and cause a deadweight loss? Explain.

17

The Gains from International Trade

On July 4, 1993, an explosion in a Sumitomo Chemical factory in Japan sent the price of computer memory chips soaring by 50 percent all over the world. Why? This factory made 65 percent of the world's supply of a special epoxy used to seal computer memory chips in their cases. When investigative reporters asked why the market was so concentrated at one firm, they found that the company was a low-cost producer; despite the small demand for this epoxy in Japan or in any one country, by producing for the world market, this factory could specialize, invest heavily in research, and achieve low-cost production. Such concentration and specialization are not unusual. The computer firm Intel dominates the world market for the computer memory chip, the brain of the PC. Another Japanese firm, Kyocera, supplies 70 percent of the market for the ceramic that surrounds the memory chip. In fact, inside the typical PC are parts of materials made in scores of different countries.

Later on that same day in the United States, Americans celebrated Independence Day. Many listened to tapes and CDs on electronic equipment made in Malaysia. Others played tennis wearing Nike shoes made in Korea or went swimming in Ocean Pacific swimsuits made in Sri Lanka. Still others looked at their Casio digital watches made in Mexico to be sure they would not miss the fireworks. A few even drove to the celebration in German cars. In the meantime, the people in other countries who had made the products Americans imported— such as the Malaysians, Koreans, Sri Lankans, Mexicans, and Germans—were buying American products: Caterpillar tractors, Motorola cellular phones, Microsoft Windows, Boeing 747s, and Merck pharmaceuticals to remove parasites from livestock or treat heart attacks.

These examples demonstrate two important reasons why people benefit from international trade. First, international trade allows firms such as Sumitomo Chemical and Intel to reduce costs by selling products to larger markets throughout the world. Second, international trade allows different countries to specialize in producing what they are relatively efficient at producing, such as pharmaceuticals in the United States and digital watches in Mexico.

This chapter explores the reasons for these gains from trade. After discussing some of the differences between international trade and within-country trade, we examine the arguments Adam Smith originally made in favor of international trade. We then develop models that economists use to study and measure the gains from international trade.

TRADE AND SOVEREIGNTY

International trade is trade between people or firms in different countries. Trade between people in Seattle and Vancouver, Canada, is international trade, whereas trade between Seattle and Anchorage is trade within a country. Thus, international trade is just another kind of economic interaction; it is subject to the same basic economic principles as trade between people in the same country.

Sovereign National Governments

International trade differs from trade in domestic markets, however, because countries are governed by their own laws and sovereign national governments. Sovereign national governments frequently place restrictions on trade between countries that they do not place on trade within countries. For example, the Texas legislature cannot prohibit the import of Florida oranges into Texas. The **commerce clause** of the U.S. Constitution forbids such restraint of trade between states. But the United States is a sovereign government. It can restrict or put taxes on the import of oranges from Brazil. Similarly, Japan can restrict the import of rice, and Australia can put taxes on the import of Japanese automobiles. The United States can also restrict the export of goods such as high-technology computers if it fears other countries may use the computers for military purposes. Many countries also have immigration laws that limit the movement of people between countries but not within countries.

Because each country has its own sovereign national government, intervention in the international economy—for good or for bad—may require international negotiation when policy actions taken in one country affect another country. Negotiations between governments may go beyond economics to areas such as national security. Dealing simultaneously with both economic and related noneconomic issues makes international economic policy challenging and interesting.

Recent Trends in International Trade

International trade has grown much faster than trade within countries in recent years. Figure 17.1 shows the trade in goods and services between countries for all countries in the world as a percent of world GDP. International trade has doubled as a proportion of world GDP during the last 30 or so years. Why has international trade grown so rapidly? There are two main reasons.

First, the cost of transportation and communication has been reduced dramatically. Air travel, telephone, and computer linkages have declined in price relative to

international trade: trade between people or firms in different countries.

commerce clause: the clause in the U.S. Constitution that prohibits restraint of trade between states.

FIGURE 17.1

Rapidly Expanding International Trade

International trade has increased faster than GDP in the last 30 or so years as trade restrictions and the cost of transportation and communications have gone down. International trade is measured as the sum of exports of all countries. The graph shows international trade as a percent of world GDP.

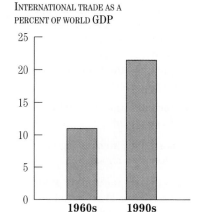

INTERNATIONAL TRADE AS A PERCENT OF WORLD GDP

other goods and services. The cost of air travel fell to 11 cents per mile in 1990 from 68 cents per mile in 1930, while the cost of a three-minute phone call from New York to London fell to $3 in 1990 from $245 in 1930 (adjusting the 1930 prices for general inflation).

Second, and perhaps even more important, government restrictions on trade between countries have come down. Western European countries are integrating into a single market. Canada, Mexico, and the United States have agreed to integrate their economies into a free trade area, where the term *free* indicates the elimination of restrictions on trade. Previously closed economies have opened themselves to world trade through major political and economic reforms. The formerly closed economies in Eastern Europe, Russia, and China, for example, are anxious to join the world trading system. Export-oriented countries in Asia are growing rapidly, and governments in South America such as Argentina and Chile are opening their economies to competition and foreign trade.

These countries are making these changes in an effort to help people. But why does international trade help them? Let's now consider that question.

Review

▶ The basic principles of economics apply to international trade between countries just as they apply to domestic trade within countries.

▶ A greater tendency for governments to interfere with trade between countries, national sovereignty, and restrictions on immigration are reasons international trade must be given special treatment by economists and economics textbooks.

▶ International trade has grown rapidly in recent years, most likely because of reduced transportation costs and lower government barriers to trade.

THE ATTACK ON MERCANTILISM

mercantilism: the notion, popular in the 1700s, that the wealth of a nation was based on how much it could export in excess of its imports, and thereby accumulate precious metals.

export: the sale of goods and services abroad.

import: the purchase of goods and services from abroad.

net exports: the value of goods and services sold abroad minus the value of goods and services bought from the rest of the world; exports minus imports.

Adam Smith was one of the first economists to show why the people of a country benefit from trade with other countries. International trade issues are woven throughout Smith's 1776 *Wealth of Nations,* and he devoted special chapters to international trade. Although the world and economics have changed substantially since the time of Adam Smith, many of his points still hold and are worth knowing.

The prevailing economic wisdom at the time Smith wrote his book was **mercantilism,** which held that countries would grow wealthy by accumulating gold and silver. They would do so by *exporting*—selling goods and services abroad—as much as possible, and by *importing*—buying goods and services abroad—as little as possible. In other words, a mercantilist policy tries to maximize **exports** minus **imports**—or what is called **net exports,** or the foreign trade balance. With exports greater than imports, so the mercantilist argument went, foreigners would have to pay the country gold and silver, which the country could then accumulate.

Adam Smith attacked mercantilism and, in contrast, put forth the revolutionary idea that the wealth of a nation depends on the incomes of the people in the country and what they are able to consume, not on the gold and silver held by the monarchs and nobles. According to Smith, imports rather than exports are the purpose of trade; imports of goods and services rather than the accumulation of gold and silver improve people's standard of living. The only reason to export is to pay for imports. Imposing **tariffs,** or taxes on imports, to limit imports for the purpose of accumulating gold and silver serves only to impoverish a nation. "It is not by the importation of gold and silver, that the discovery of America has enriched Europe," he wrote. "By the abundance of the American mines, those metals have become cheaper. A service of plate can now be purchased for about a third [of what] it would have cost in the fifteenth century."[1] Instead of the tariffs advocated by the mercantilists, Smith proposed a policy of **free trade**—the elimination of tariffs on imports. Smith put forth four specific reasons why a country could gain from trade: (1) mutual gains from voluntary exchange of existing goods, (2) increased competition, (3) the division of labor, and (4) better use of skills and resources in different countries. We briefly summarize all four and develop the last two in more detail in the remainder of the chapter.

tariff: a tax on imports.

free trade: a complete lack of restrictions on international trade.

Mutual Gains from Voluntary Exchange of Existing Goods

We have emphasized that when two people voluntarily exchange existing goods, they mutually gain, even though there is no increase in the amount of goods in the economy. People benefit from voluntary exchange by reaching a preferred combination of the different goods than before trade. Adam Smith emphasized this mutual benefit and argued that it applies just as well to people in different countries as to people in the same country.

But the gains from trade go beyond the benefits of exchanging existing goods. Trade can increase the amount of goods by making production more efficient.

Increased Competition

International trade makes the home market more competitive. This lowers prices. In Smith's words, "By restraining, either by high duties, or by absolute prohibitions, the importation of such goods from foreign countries as can be produced at home, the monopoly of the home market is more or less secured to the domestic industry . . ."[2]

Adam Smith's analysis of the competition effects of international trade applies very well to modern times. We see evidence of trade spurring on competition in many industries, from automobiles to steel to telecommunications. Competition from abroad helped improve the quality and reduce the price of cars in the United States. It also helped reduce the price and improve the quality of telephones and beef in Japan.

The Division of Labor

Smith identified the division of labor as a key reason for trade. The division of labor reduces costs since each worker can specialize and develop expertise in a certain area. But the division of labor requires that the market for the good be large. There is much less opportunity for the division of labor in an automobile firm producing 1,000 cars than in one producing 1,000,000 cars.

In other words, the size of the market is key to Smith's idea of the division of labor, and, with international trade, the markets can be larger. In fact, the title of one chapter in the *Wealth of Nations* is "That the division of labour is limited by the

1. Adam Smith, *Wealth of Nations* (New York: Modern Library, 1994), p. 476.
2. Ibid., p. 481.

extent of the market." In this chapter, Smith showed how international trade would increase the size of the market and allow for a greater division of labor. He argued, for example, that the nations along the shores of the Mediterranean Sea developed because of the ease of navigation on relatively calm waters. Trade with other nations over a vast area allowed for much larger markets.

Better Use of Skills and Resources in Different Countries

A fourth part of Smith's analysis of the gain from trade focused on the differences between countries. Smith argued that countries can gain from trade if they export things that they are good at producing and import things that other countries are good at producing. For example, the United States and Colombia can gain from trade if the United States produces wheat, which it can produce more cheaply than Colombia, and Colombia produces coffee, which it can produce more cheaply than the United States.

Smith supported this view with commonsense analogies: "It is the maxim of every prudent master of a family, never to attempt to make at home what it will cost him more to make than to buy." Or, "The taylor does not attempt to make his own shoes, but buys them from the shoemaker."[3]

Although correct as far as it goes, Smith's analysis of international differences did not go far enough. It was not until David Ricardo developed the theory of comparative advantage in 1817 that it was clear that the tailor could gain from trading with the shoemaker even if the tailor could produce both clothes and shoes better than the shoemaker. We examine comparative advantage in the next section and show that it is a powerful argument for international trade that goes well beyond examples like coffee and wheat.

Review

▶ The mercantilists argued that a country could grow wealthy by exporting more than it imports and thereby accumulating gold and silver. Adam Smith argued that rather than gold and silver, it is people's consumption of goods and services that makes a country wealthy.

▶ He proposed a policy of free trade rather than the high tariffs advocated by the mercantilists. He gave four reasons why there would be gains from trade: mutual benefits from exchanging existing goods, increased competition, lower costs through the division of labor, and better use of skills and resources in different countries.

COMPARATIVE ADVANTAGE

David Ricardo's theory of comparative advantage shows how a country can improve the income of its citizens by allowing them to trade with people in other countries, even if the people of the country are less efficient at producing all items.

---

3. Ibid., p. 485.

The United States, for example, may be more efficient than Korea in the production of both pharmaceutical goods and electronic goods. Even so, it may make sense for the United States to trade with Korea.

A Simple Example of Comparative Advantage

Consider first a parable to convey the general idea of comparative advantage. Rose is a highly skilled computer programmer who writes computer-assisted drawing programs. Rose owns a small firm that sells her programs to architects. She hires an experienced salesman, Sam, to contact the architects and sell her software. Thus, Rose specializes in programming, and Sam specializes in sales.

Let us complicate the story. Rose is a friendly, outgoing person and, because she knows her product better than Sam does, she is better at sales than Sam. We say that Rose has an **absolute advantage** over Sam in both programming and sales because she is better at both jobs. But it still makes sense for Rose to hire Sam because her efficiency at programming compared to Sam's is greater than her efficiency at sales compared to Sam's. We say that Rose has a *comparative advantage* over Sam in programming rather than in sales. If Rose sold her programs, then she would have to sacrifice her programming time, and her profits would fall. Thus, even though Rose is better at both programming and sales, she hires Sam to do the selling so she can program full time.

All this seems sensible. However, there is one additional part of the terminology that may at first seem confusing but is important. We said that Rose has the comparative advantage in programming, not in sales. But who does have the comparative advantage in sales? Sam does. Even though Sam is less efficient at both sales and programming, we say he has a comparative advantage in sales because, compared with Rose, he does relatively better at sales than he does at programming. A person cannot have a comparative advantage in both of only two activities.

absolute advantage: a situation in which a person or country is more efficient at producing a good in comparison with another person or country.

comparative advantage: a situation in which a person or country can produce one good more efficiently than another good in comparison with another person or country. (Ch. 2)

Opportunity Cost, Relative Efficiency, and Comparative Advantage

The idea of comparative advantage can also be explained in terms of *opportunity cost.* The opportunity cost of Rose or Sam spending more time selling is that she or he can produce fewer programs. Similarly, the opportunity cost of Rose or Sam spending more time writing programs is that she or he can make fewer sales.

Observe that, in the example, Sam has a lower opportunity cost of spending his time selling than Rose does; thus, it makes sense for Sam to do the selling rather than Rose. In contrast, Rose has a lower opportunity cost of spending her time writing computer programs than Sam does; thus, it makes sense for Rose to write computer programs rather than Sam.

Opportunity costs give us a way to define comparative advantage: A person with a lower opportunity cost of producing a good than another person has a comparative advantage in that good. Thus, Rose has a comparative advantage in computer programming, and Sam has a comparative advantage in sales.

Comparative advantage can also be explained in terms of relative efficiency: A person who is relatively more efficient at producing good X than good Y compared to another person has a comparative advantage in good X. Thus, again, we see that Rose has a comparative advantage in computer programming because she is relatively more efficient at producing computer programs than making sales compared to Sam.

opportunity cost: the value of the next-best foregone alternative that was not chosen because something else was chosen. (Ch. 2)

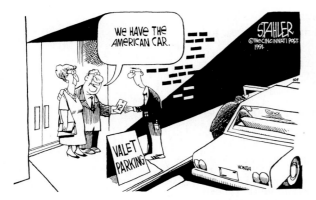

From People to Countries

Why is this story about Rose and Sam a parable? Because we can think of Rose and Sam as two countries that differ in efficiency at producing one product versus another. In the parable, Rose has a comparative advantage over Sam in programming, and Sam has a comparative advantage over Rose in sales. In general, *country A has a comparative advantage over country B in the production of a good if the opportunity cost of producing the good in country A is less than in country B*, or alternatively but equivalently stated, *if country A can produce the good relatively more efficiently than other goods compared to country B*. Thus, if you understand the Rose and Sam story, you should have no problems with the American and Korean story, which we now examine in more detail.

Trade Between Countries: Pharmaceuticals and Electronics

Consider the following two goods: (1) pharmaceutical goods—vaccines, antibiotics, antidepressants, analgesics, and treatments for high blood pressure or cholesterol; and (2) electronic goods—TV sets, boom boxes, portable stereos, electronic keyboards, and compact disk players. Different skills are required for the production of pharmaceuticals and electronic goods. Pharmaceutical production requires investment, knowledge of chemistry and biology, and the marketing of products where doctors make most of the choices. Producing electronic goods requires investment, knowledge of electrical engineering and microcircuitry, and the marketing of goods where consumers make most of the choices.

Table 17.1 provides an example of productivity differences in the production of pharmaceutical goods and electronic goods in two different countries, the United States and Korea. Productivity is measured by the amount of each good that can be produced by a worker per day of work. To be specific, let us suppose that the pharmaceutical goods are vaccines measured in vials, that the electronic goods are TV sets measured in numbers of TV sets, and that labor is the only factor of production in making vaccines and TV sets. The theory of comparative advantage does not depend on any of these assumptions, but they make the exposition much easier.

According to Table 17.1, in the United States it takes a worker one day of work to produce 6 vials of vaccines or 3 TV sets. In Korea one worker can produce 1 vial of vaccine or 2 TV sets. Thus, the United States is more productive than Korea in both vaccines and TV sets. We say that a country has an *absolute advantage* over another country in the production of a good if it is more efficient at producing that good. In this example, the United States has an absolute advantage in both vaccine and TV set production.

TABLE 17.1
Pharmaceutical and Electronic Goods Productivity in the United States and Korea
(hypothetical example)

	Output per Day of Work	
	Pharmaceutical Goods (vials of vaccine)	Electronic Goods (number of TV sets)
United States	6	3
Korea	1	2

 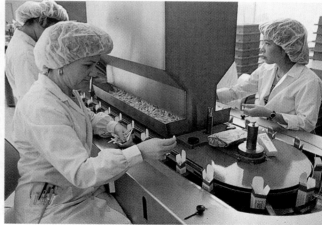

Electronics versus Pharmaceuticals

In the hypothetical example used in this chapter, Korea has a comparative advantage in electronics and the United States has a comparative advantage in pharmaceuticals. Thus, with trade between Korea and the United States, electronic goods will be produced in Korea, as shown in the left-hand photo, and pharmaceutical goods will be produced in the United States, as shown in the right-hand photo.

However, the United States has a comparative advantage over Korea in the production of vaccines rather than TV sets. To see this, note that a worker in the United States can produce 6 times as many vials of vaccine as a worker in Korea but only 1.5 times more TV sets. In other words, the United States is relatively more efficient in vaccines than in TV sets compared with Korea. Korea, being able to produce TV sets relatively more efficiently than vaccines compared to the United States, has a comparative advantage in TV sets.

Observe also how opportunity costs determine who has the comparative advantage. To produce 3 more TV sets, the United States must sacrifice 6 vials of vaccine; in other words, *in the United States the opportunity cost of 1 more TV set is 2 vials of vaccine.* In Korea, to produce 2 more TV sets, the Koreans must sacrifice 1 vial of vaccine; in other words, *in Korea, the opportunity cost of 1 more TV set is only ½ vial of vaccine.* Thus, we see that the opportunity cost of producing TV sets in Korea is lower than in the United States. By examining opportunity costs, we again see that Korea has a comparative advantage in TV sets.

An American Worker's View

Because labor productivity in both goods is higher in the United States than in Korea, wages are higher in the United States than in Korea in the example. Now think about the situation from the point of view of American workers who are paid more than Korean workers. They might wonder how they can compete with Korea. The Korean workers' wages seem very low compared to theirs. It doesn't seem fair. But as we will see, comparative advantage implies that American workers can gain from trade with the Koreans.

A Korean Worker's View

It is useful to think about Table 17.1 from the perspective of a Korean worker as well as a U.S. worker. From the Korean perspective, it might be noted that Korean workers are less productive in both electronic goods and pharmaceutical goods. Korean workers might wonder how they can ever compete with the United States, which looks like a productive powerhouse. The U.S. workers are more productive in both types of goods. Again, it doesn't seem fair. As we will see, however, the Koreans can also gain from trade with the Americans.

The Relative Price of Pharmaceutical Goods and Electronic Goods

To measure how much the Koreans and Americans can gain from trade we need to consider the *relative price* of pharmaceutical goods and electronic goods in Korea and the United States. The relative price describes how many pharmaceutical goods can be traded for electronic goods and, therefore, how much each country can gain from trade. For example, suppose the price of TV sets is $200 and the price of a vial of vaccine is $100. Then 2 vials of vaccine cost the same as 1 TV set; we say the relative price is 2 vials of vaccine per TV set. The next few paragraphs show how to determine the relative price from data on the costs of production.

Relative Price Without Trade

First, let us find the relative price with no trade between the countries. The relative price of two goods should depend on the relative costs of production. A good for which the cost of producing an additional quantity is relatively low will have a relatively low price.

Consider the United States. In this example, a day of work can produce either 6 vials of vaccine or 3 TV sets. With labor as the only factor of production, 6 vials of vaccine cost the same to produce as 3 TV sets; that is, 2 vials of vaccine cost the same to produce as 1 TV set. Therefore, the relative price should be 2 vials of vaccine per TV set.

Now consider Korea. Electronic goods should have a relatively low price in Korea because they are relatively cheap to produce. A day of work can produce either 1 vial of vaccine or 2 TV sets; thus 1 vial of vaccine costs the same to produce as 2 TV sets in Korea. Therefore, the relative price is ½ vial of vaccine per TV set.

Relative Price with Trade

Now consider what happens when both countries trade without government restrictions. If transportation costs are negligible and markets are competitive, then the price of a good must be the same whether it is in the United States or Korea. Why? Because any difference in price would quickly be eliminated by trade; if the price of TV sets is much less in Korea than in the United States, then traders would buy TV sets in Korea and sell them in the United States and make a profit; by doing so, however, they reduce the supply of TV sets in Korea and increase the supply in the United States. This would drive up the price in Korea and drive down the price in the United States until the price of TV sets in the two countries was the same. Thus, with trade, the price of vaccines and the price of TV sets will converge to the same levels in both countries. The relative price will therefore converge to the same value in both countries.

If the relative price is going to be the same in both countries, then we know the price must be somewhere between the price in each country before trade. That is, the price must be between 2 vials of vaccine per TV set (the U.S. relative price) and ½ vial of vaccine per TV set (the Korean relative price). We do not know exactly

Another example of relative prices:
Price of Phish concert = $45
Price of Phish T-shirt = $15
Relative price = 3 T-shirts per concert

	United States	Korea
Relative price before trade:	2 vials of vaccine per TV set	½ vial of vaccine per TV set
Relative price range after trade:	Between ½ and 2	Between ½ and 2
Relative price assumption:	1	1

TABLE 17.2
The Relative Price
The relative price must be the same in both countries with trade (vials of vaccine per TV set).

where the price will fall in between ½ and 2. It depends on the *demand* for vaccines and TV sets in Korea and the United States. Let us assume that the relative price is 1 vial of vaccine per TV set after trade, which is between ½ and 2 and a nice, easy number for making computations. The calculation of the price with trade is summarized in Table 17.2.

The relative price of vaccines and TV sets after trade—which we have assumed to be 1 vial per TV set—is called the *terms of trade*. In general, the **terms of trade** for a country are given by the quantity of imported goods that it can obtain per unit of exported goods. As we will see, Korea will be exporting TV sets and importing vaccines, while the United States will be exporting vaccines and importing TV sets.

terms of trade: quantity of imported goods a country can obtain in exchange for a unit of exported goods.

Comparative Advantage and Gains from Trade

What are the **gains from trade** due to comparative advantage? First, consider some examples.

gains from trade: improvements in income, production, or satisfaction owing to the exchange of goods or services.

One Country's Gain

Suppose that 10 American workers move out of electronics production and begin producing pharmaceuticals. We know from Table 17.1 that these 10 American workers can produce 60 vials of vaccine per day. Formerly, the 10 American workers were producing 30 TV sets per day. But their 60 vials of vaccine can be traded for TV sets produced in Korea. With the relative price of 1 vial per TV set, Americans will be able to exchange these 60 vials of vaccine for 60 TV sets. Thus, Americans gain 30 more TV sets by moving 10 more workers into vaccine production. This gain from trade is summarized in Table 17.3.

The Other Country's Gain

The same thing can happen in Korea. A Korean manufacturer can hire 30 workers who were formerly working in vaccine production to now produce TV sets. Vaccine production declines by 30 vials, but TV production increases by 60 TV sets. These 60 TV sets can be traded with Americans for 60 vials of vaccine. The reduction in the production of vaccine of 30 vials results in an import of vaccine of 60 vials; thus, the gain from trade is 30 vials of vaccine. The Koreans, by moving workers out of vaccine production and into TV set production, are getting more vaccine. This gain from trade for Korea is summarized in Table 17.3. Observe that the exports of TV sets from Korea equal the imports of TV sets to the United States.

TABLE 17.3
Changing Production and Gaining from Trade in the United States and Korea

United States

	Change in Production	Amount Traded	Net Gain from Trade
Vaccines	Up 60 vials	Export 60 vials	0
TV Sets	Down 30 sets	Import 60 sets	30 sets

Korea

	Change in Production	Amount Traded	Net Gain from Trade
Vaccines	Down 30 vials	Import 60 vials	30 vials
TV Sets	Up 60 sets	Export 60 sets	0

Just Like a New Technique

International trade is like the discovery of a new idea or technique that makes workers more productive. It is as if workers in the United States figure out how to produce more TV sets with the same amount of effort. Their trick is that they actually produce vaccines that are then traded for the TV sets. Like any other new technique, international trade improves the well-being of Americans. International trade also improves the well-being of the Koreans; it is as if they discovered a new technique, too.

Graphical Illustration of the Gains from Trade

The gains from trade due to comparative advantage can also be illustrated graphically with production possibilities curves, as shown in Figure 17.2. There are two graphs in the figure—one for the United States and the other for Korea. In both graphs the horizontal axis has the number of TV sets and the vertical axis has the number of vials of vaccine produced.

Production Possibilities Curves Without Trade

The solid purple lines in the two graphs show the production possibilities curves for vaccines and TV sets in the United States and in Korea before trade. To derive them we assume, for illustrative purposes, that there are 10,000 workers in the United States and 30,000 workers in Korea who can make either vaccines or TV sets.

If all the available workers in the United States produce vaccines, then total production will be 60,000 vials of vaccine (6 × 10,000) and zero TV sets. Alternatively, if 5,000 workers produce vaccines in the United States and 5,000 workers produce TV sets, then total production will be 30,000 vials of vaccine (6 × 5,000) and 15,000 TV sets (3 × 5,000). The solid line in the graph on the left of Figure 17.2 shows these possibilities and all other possibilities for producing vaccines and TV sets. It is the production possibilities curve without trade.

Korea's production possibilities curve without trade is shown by the solid purple line in the graph on the right of Figure 17.2. For example, if all 30,000 Korean workers produce TV sets, a total of 60,000 TV sets can be produced (2 × 30,000). This and other possibilities are on the curve.

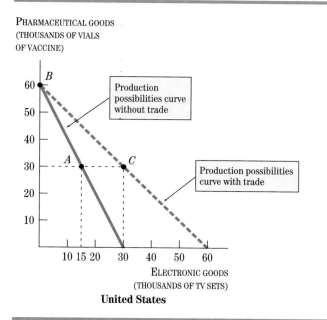

United States

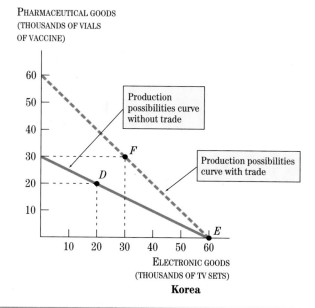

Korea

The slopes of the two production possibility curves without trade in Figure 17.2 show how many vials of vaccine can be transformed into TV sets in Korea and the United States. The production possibilities curve for the United States is steeper than for Korea because an increase in production of 1 TV set reduces vaccine production by 2 vials in the United States but by only ½ vial in Korea. The slope of the production possibilities curve is the opportunity cost; the opportunity cost of producing TV sets in the United States is higher than it is in Korea.

Production Possibilities Curves with Trade

The dashed purple lines in the two graphs in Figure 17.2 show the different combinations of vaccine and TV sets available in Korea and the United States when there is trade between the two countries at a relative price of 1 vial of vaccine for 1 TV set. These dashed lines are labeled "production possibilities curve with trade" to contrast them with the "production possibilities curve without trade" label on the solid line. The diagram shows that the production possibilities curves with trade are shifted out compared with the curves without trade.

To see how the production possibilities curve with trade is derived, consider how the United States could move from point A to point C in Figure 17.2. At point A Americans produce and consume without trade 15,000 TV sets and 30,000 vials of vaccine by having 5,000 workers in each industry. Now suppose all U.S. workers move out of TV set production into vaccine production, shifting U.S. production to zero TV sets and 60,000 vials of vaccine, as shown by point B. Then by trading some of the vaccine, Americans can obtain TV sets. As they trade more vaccine away, they move down the production possibilities curve with trade: 1 less vial of vaccine means 1 more TV set along the curve. If they move to point C in the diagram, they have traded 30,000 vials for 30,000 TV sets. Americans now have

FIGURE 17.2
Comparative Advantage
The production possibilities curves show electronic goods production (TV sets) versus pharmaceutical production (vaccines) in Korea and the United States. On the left, Americans are better off with trade because the production possibilities curve shifts out with trade; thus, with trade, Americans can reach a point like C rather than A. The gains from trade due to comparative advantage are shown by the distance between the two production possibilities curves—one with trade and the other without trade. On the right, Koreans are also better off because their production possibilities curve shifts out; thus, Koreans can reach point F, which is better than point D. To reach this outcome, Americans specialize in producing at point B and Koreans specialize in producing at point E.

30,000 TV sets and are left with 30,000 vials of vaccine. By producing more vaccine, the Americans get to purchase more TV sets. The distance from point *A* (before trade) to point *C* (after trade) in Figure 17.2 is the gain from trade: 15,000 more TV sets.

It would be possible, of course, to choose any other point on the production possibilities curve with trade. If Americans prefer more TV sets and fewer vaccines, they could move down along that dashed line, trading more of their vaccine for more TV sets. In general, the production possibilities curve *with* trade is further out than the production possibilities curve *without* trade, indicating the gain from trade.

Observe that the slope of the production possibilities curve with trade is given by the relative price: the number of vials of vaccine that can be obtained for a TV set. When the relative price is 1 vial per TV set, the slope is -1 because 1 less vial gives 1 more TV set. If the relative price were ½ vial per TV set, then the production possibilities curve with trade would be flatter.

The gains to Korea from trade are illustrated in the right-hand graph of Figure 17.2. For example, at point *D,* without trade, Koreans produce 20,000 TV sets with 10,000 workers and, with the remaining 20,000 workers, produce 20,000 vials of vaccine. With trade, they shift all production into TV sets, as at point *E* on the right graph. Then they trade the TV sets for vaccine. Such trade allows more consumption of vaccine in Korea. At point *F* in the right diagram the Koreans could consume 30,000 vials of vaccine and 30,000 TV sets, which is 10,000 more of each than before trade at point *D*. As in the case of the United States, the production possibilities curve shifts out with trade, and the size of the shift represents the gain from trade.

This example of Americans and Koreans consuming more than they were before trade illustrates the *principle of comparative advantage: By specializing in producing products in which they have a comparative advantage, countries can increase the amount of goods available for consumption.* Trade increases the amount of production in the world; it shifts out the production possibilities curves.

Increasing Opportunity Costs: Incomplete Specialization

One of the special assumptions in the example we have used to illustrate the theory of comparative advantage in Table 17.3 and Figure 17.2 is that opportunity costs are constant rather than increasing. It is because of this assumption that the production possibilities curves without trade in Figure 17.2 are straight lines rather than the bowed-out lines that we studied in Chapter 2. With increasing opportunity costs, the curves would be bowed out.

The straight-line production possibilities curves are the reason for complete specialization, with Korea producing no vaccines and the United States producing no TV sets. If there were increasing opportunity costs, as in the more typical example of the production possibilities curve, then complete specialization would not occur. Why? With increasing opportunity costs, as more and more workers are moved into the production of vaccines in the United States, the opportunity cost of producing more vaccine will rise. And as workers are moved out of vaccine production in Korea, the opportunity cost of vaccine production in Korea will fall. At some point the U.S. opportunity cost of vaccine production may rise to equal Korea's, at which point further specialization in vaccine production would cease in the United States. Thus, with increasing opportunity costs and bowed-out production possibilities curves there will most likely be incomplete specialization. But the principle of comparative advantage is not changed by increasing opportunity costs. By specializing to some degree in the goods they have a comparative advantage in, countries can increase world production. There are still substantial gains from trade, whether between Rose and Sam or between America and Korea.

Review

▶ Comparative advantage shows that a country can gain from trade even if it is more efficient at producing every product than another country. A country has a comparative advantage in a product if it is relatively more efficient at producing that product than the other country.

▶ The theory of comparative advantage predicts that there are gains from trade from increasing production in the good a country has a comparative advantage in and reducing production of the other good. By exporting the good it has a comparative advantage in, a country can increase consumption of both goods.

▶ Comparative advantage is like a new technology in which the country effectively produces more by having some goods produced in another country.

REASONS FOR COMPARATIVE ADVANTAGE

What determines a country's comparative advantage? There are some obvious answers. For example, Central America has a comparative advantage over North America in producing tropical fruit because of weather conditions: Bananas will not grow in Kansas or Nebraska outside of greenhouses.

In most cases, however, comparative advantage does not result from differences in climate and natural resources. More frequently, comparative advantage is due to decisions by individuals, by firms, or by the government in a given country. For example, a comparative advantage of the United States in pharmaceuticals might be due to investment in research and in physical and human capital in the areas of chemistry and biology. An enormous amount of research goes into developing technological know-how to produce pharmaceutical products.

In Korea, on the other hand, there may be less capital available for such huge expenditures on research in the pharmaceutical area. A Korean comparative advantage in electronic goods might be due to a large, well-trained work force that is well suited to electronics and small-scale assembly. For example, the excellent math and technical training in Korean high schools may provide a large labor force for the electronics industry.

Dynamic Comparative Advantage

Comparative advantages can change over time. In fact, the United States did have a comparative advantage in TV sets in the 1950s and early 1960s before the countries of east Asia developed skills and knowledge in these areas. A country may have a comparative advantage in a good it has recently developed, but then technology spreads to other countries, which develop the comparative advantage, and the first country goes on to something else.

Perhaps the United States's comparative advantage in pharmaceuticals will go to other countries in the future, and the United States will develop a comparative

dynamic comparative advantage: changes in comparative advantage over time from investment in physical and human capital and in technology.

advantage in other, yet unforeseen areas. The term **dynamic comparative advantage** describes changes in comparative advantage over time because of investment in physical and human capital and in technology.

Factor Abundance of Countries and Factor Intensity of Industries

To illustrate the importance of capital for comparative advantage, imagine a world in which all comparative advantage can be explained through differences between countries in the amount of physical capital that workers have to work with. It is such a world that is described by the Heckscher-Ohlin model, named after the two Swedish economists, Eli Heckscher and Bertil Ohlin, who developed it. Ohlin won a Nobel Prize for his work in international economics. The Heckscher-Ohlin model provides a particular explanation for comparative advantage.

capital abundant: a higher level of capital per worker in one country relative to another.

labor abundant: a lower level of capital per worker in one country relative to another.

capital intensive: production that uses a relatively high level of capital per worker.

labor intensive: production that uses a relatively low level of capital per worker.

Here is how comparative advantage develops in such a model. Suppose America has a higher level of capital per worker than Korea. In other words, America is **capital abundant** compared to Korea, and—what amounts to the same thing—Korea is **labor abundant** compared to America. We noted how pharmaceutical production uses more capital per worker than electronics production; in other words, pharmaceutical production is relatively **capital intensive,** while electronics production is relatively **labor intensive.** Hence, it makes sense that the United States has a comparative advantage in pharmaceuticals: The United States is relatively capital abundant, and pharmaceuticals are relatively capital intensive. On the other hand, Korea has a comparative advantage in electronics because Korea is relatively labor abundant, and electronics are relatively labor intensive. Thus, the Heckscher-Ohlin model predicts that if a country has a relative abundance of a factor (labor or capital), it will have a comparative advantage in those goods that require a greater amount of that factor.

The Leontief Paradox

Of course, the relative amount of physical capital compared to labor cannot explain all of comparative advantage: Human capital and research are also important. In fact, the economist Wassily Leontief (who also won a Nobel Prize) showed in a famous paper in 1953 that the United States tended to export goods that are more labor intensive than the goods it imports. At the time Leontief's paper was published, this finding was taken as a major puzzle because, by most measures, the United States had been a relatively capital-abundant country. His finding is still called the **Leontief paradox.**

Leontief paradox: the inconsistency that Wassily Leontief found between the data on U.S. trade and the Heckscher-Ohlin model.

However, it turned out that U.S. exports require more human capital—worker education and training—and more research than U.S. imports. For example, scientists and engineers were found to be more important in producing U.S. exports than they were in producing U.S. imports. And research and development expenditures were found to be more important in U.S. exports than in U.S. imports. Including these other factors helped explain the Leontief paradox because the United States had a relative abundance in these research and human capital factors.

Factor-Price Equalization

An important implication of the Heckscher-Ohlin model is that trade will tend to bring factor prices (the price of labor and the price of capital) into equality in different countries. In other words, if the comparative advantage between Korea and the

United States was due only to differences in relative capital and labor abundance, then trade would tend to increase real wages in Korea and lower real wages in the United States.

More generally, trade tends to increase demand for the factor that is relatively abundant in a country and decrease demand for the factor that is relatively scarce. This raises the price of the relatively abundant factor and lowers the price of the relatively scarce factor. Suppose the United States is more capital abundant than Korea and has a comparative advantage in pharmaceuticals, which are more capital intensive than electronics. Then with trade, the price of capital would rise relative to the price of labor in the United States. The intuition behind this prediction—which is called **factor-price equalization**—is that demand for labor (the relatively scarce factor) shifts down with trade as the United States increases production of pharmaceuticals and reduces its production of electronic goods. On the other hand, the demand for capital (the relatively abundant factor) shifts up with trade. Although there is no immigration, it is as if foreign workers compete with workers in the labor-scarce country and bid down the wage. Because technology also influences wages and productivity, it has been hard to detect such movements in wages. Wages in the developed world with high productivity due to high levels of technology remain well above wages in the less-developed world with low productivity due to low levels of technology.

In other words, changes in technology can offset the effects of factor-price equalization on wages. If trade raises technological know-how sufficiently, then no one has to suffer from greater trade. In our example of comparative advantage, American workers are paid more than Korean workers both before and after trade; that is because their overall level of productivity is higher. Workers in countries with higher productivity will be paid more than workers with lower productivity even in countries that trade.

Factor-price equalization can explain another phenomenon: growing wage disparity in the United States during the past 25 years in which the wages of high-skilled workers have risen relative to the wages of less-skilled workers. The United States is relatively abundant in high-skilled workers and developing countries are relatively abundant in low-skilled workers. Thus high-skilled workers' wages should rise and low-skilled workers' wages should fall in the United States, according to factor-price equalization. In this application of factor-price equalization, the two factors are high-skilled workers and low-skilled workers.

In the next section, we show that there are gains in efficiency and lower cost from trade that can benefit all workers.

factor-price equalization: the equalization of the price of labor and the price of capital across countries when they are engaging in free trade.

Review

▶ Comparative advantage changes over time and depends on the actions of individuals in a country. Comparative advantage is determined partly by physical and human capital and partly by technology in the country relative to other countries. It is not solely bestowed on the country through natural resources or a good climate. Thus, comparative advantage is a dynamic concept.

▶ International trade will tend to equalize wages in different countries. Technological differences, however, can keep wages high in high-productivity countries. The greater dispersion of wages in the developed countries in recent years may be partially due to international trade. Nevertheless, if trade increases productivity, wages can rise for all workers.

GAINS FROM EXPANDED MARKETS

In the introduction to this chapter and in the discussion of Adam Smith's writings, we stressed the gains from trade that come from larger-sized markets. Having discussed the principle of comparative advantage, we now examine this other source of the gains from trade.

An Example of Gains from Trade Through Expanded Markets

Let us start with a simple example. Consider two countries such as the United States and Germany that are similar in resources, capital, and skilled labor. Suppose there is a market in Germany and the United States for two medical diagnostic products—magnetic resonance imaging (MRI) machines and ultrasound scanners. Suppose the technology for producing each type of diagnostic device is the same in each country. We assume that the technology is identical because we want to show that trade will take place without differences between the countries.

Figure 17.3 illustrates the situation. Without trade, both Germany and the United States produce 1,000 MRIs and 1,000 ultrasound scanners. This amount of production meets the demand in the two separate markets. The cost per unit of producing each MRI unit is $300,000, while the cost per unit of producing each ultrasound scanner is $200,000. Again, these costs are the same in each country.

Effects of a Larger Market

Now suppose that the two countries trade. Observe in Figure 17.3—and this is very important—that the *cost per unit* of producing MRIs and ultrasound scanners *declines as more are produced.* Trade increases the size of the market for each product. In this example the market is twice as large with trade than without it: 2,000 MRIs rather than 1,000 and 2,000 ultrasound scanners rather than 1,000. The production of MRIs in the United States can expand, while the production of ultrasound scanners in the United States can contract. Similarly, the production of ultrasound scanners in Germany can expand, and the production of MRIs in Germany can contract. By specializing production of MRIs in the United States, the cost per unit of MRIs declines to $150,000. Similarly, the cost per unit of ultrasound scanners declines to $150,000. The United States exports MRIs to Germany so that the number of MRIs in Germany can be the same as without trade, and Germany exports ultrasound scanners to the United States. The gain from trade is the reduction in cost per unit. This gain from trade has occurred without any differences in the efficiency of production between each country.

Note that we could have set up the example differently. We could have had Germany specializing in MRIs and the United States specializing in ultrasound scanner production. Then the United States would have exported ultrasound scanners and Germany would have exported MRIs. But the gains from trade would have been exactly the same. Unlike the comparative advantage motive for trade, the expanded markets motive cannot alone predict what the direction of trade will be.

Intraindustry Trade versus Interindustry Trade

MRIs and ultrasound scanners are similar products; they are considered to be in the same industry, the medical diagnostic equipment industry. Thus, the trade between

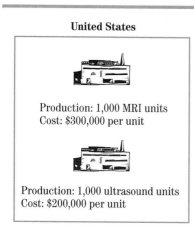
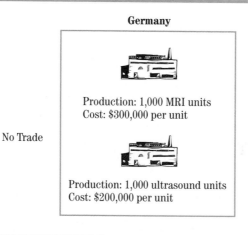

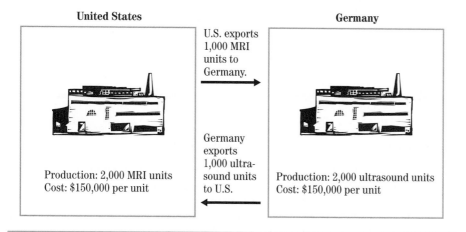

FIGURE 17.3
Gains from Global Markets
In this example, the technology of producing magnetic resonance imaging (MRI) machines and ultrasound scanners is assumed to be the same in the United States and Germany. In the top panel, with no trade between the United States and Germany, the quantity produced is low in each country and the cost per unit is high. With trade, the U.S. firm increases its production of MRIs and exports to Germany; the German firm increases its production of ultrasound scanners and exports to the United States. As a result, cost per unit comes down significantly.

Germany and the United States in MRIs and ultrasound scanners is called **intraindustry trade,** which means trade in goods in the same industry.

In contrast, the trade that took place in the example of comparative advantage was **interindustry trade,** because vaccines and TV sets are in different industries. In that example, the exports of vaccines from the United States greatly exceed imports of vaccines, producing a U.S. industry trade surplus in vaccines. Imports of TV sets into the United States are much greater than exports of TV sets, producing a U.S. industry trade deficit in TV sets.

These examples convey an important message about international trade. Trade due to comparative advantage tends to be interindustry, and trade due to expanded markets tends to be intraindustry. In reality, a huge amount of international trade is intraindustry trade. This indicates that creating larger markets is an important motive for trade.

intraindustry trade: trade between countries in goods from the same or similar industries.

interindustry trade: trade between countries in goods from different industries.

Measuring the Gains from Expanded Markets

The medical equipment example illustrates how larger markets can reduce costs. To fully describe the gains to trade from larger markets, we need to consider a model.

Talking Points on the Gains from Trade

Modern-day advocates of freer trade frequently emphasize that larger markets generate gains for consumers. To promote trade agreements in the 1990s, people who worked for Presidents Bush and Clinton made speeches and held meetings with members of Congress and many other interested groups. Many of their "talking points"—short phrases circulated around the administration that people can easily remember and repeat—focused on the gains from trade through larger markets. Examples of actual talking points used are:

▶   *The further integration of North American manufacturing facilities and the resulting product rationalizations would increase trade and the competitiveness of U.S. producers.*

▶   *U.S. companies operating in both Mexico and the United States will be able to reduce costs through product rationalization. They will no longer have to make the same vehicle, or the same parts for those vehicles, in two countries.*

▶   *Removal of internal distortions and economies of scale would enhance the international competitiveness of the North American automotive industry.*

Observe how close these talking points are to the model illustrated in Figure 17.4. The term *economies of scale* refers to the decline in cost per unit. *Product rationalization* refers to locating production in fewer factories in order to reduce cost per unit. (*Internal distortions* means that trade barriers had caused factories to be too small.)

The application of economics to gains from international trade due to larger markets is referred to as "new trade theory" because much of the research took place in the last 15 years. As the talking points indicate, the theory is already being used in practice.

A Relationship Between Cost per Unit and the Number of Firms

Let us first establish the principle exemplified in the medical equipment example: As the number of firms in a market of a given size increases, the cost per unit at each firm increases because each firm produces less. This is shown in the four graphs on the left of Figure 17.4, where four identical firms are shown. With one firm in the market, cost per unit is $10, but cost per unit rises to $30 when four firms are in the market.

Next observe the situation in the four graphs on the right of Figure 17.4. These graphs represent the same four firms, but now the size of the market is larger. By comparing the graphs on the left (smaller market) with those on the right (larger market) we see that an increase in the size of the market reduces cost per unit at each firm, holding the number of firms constant in the industry. For example, when there is one firm in the market, cost per unit is $5 for the larger market compared with $10 for the smaller market. Or with four firms, cost per unit is $25 for the larger market compared with $30 for the smaller market. Compare the little tables in Figure 17.4. As the market increases in size, each firm produces at a lower cost per unit.

Figure 17.5 summarizes the information in Figure 17.4. It shows the positive relationship between the number of firms in the market, shown on the horizontal axis, and the cost per unit at each firm. As the figure indicates, more firms mean a higher cost per unit at each firm. (Be careful to note that the horizontal axis in Figure 17.5 is the *number* of firms in a given *market,* not the quantity produced by a given firm.) When the size of the market increases, the relationship between the number of firms in the market and the cost per unit shifts down, as shown in Figure 17.5. In other words, as the market increases in size, cost per unit declines at each firm if the number of firms does not change.

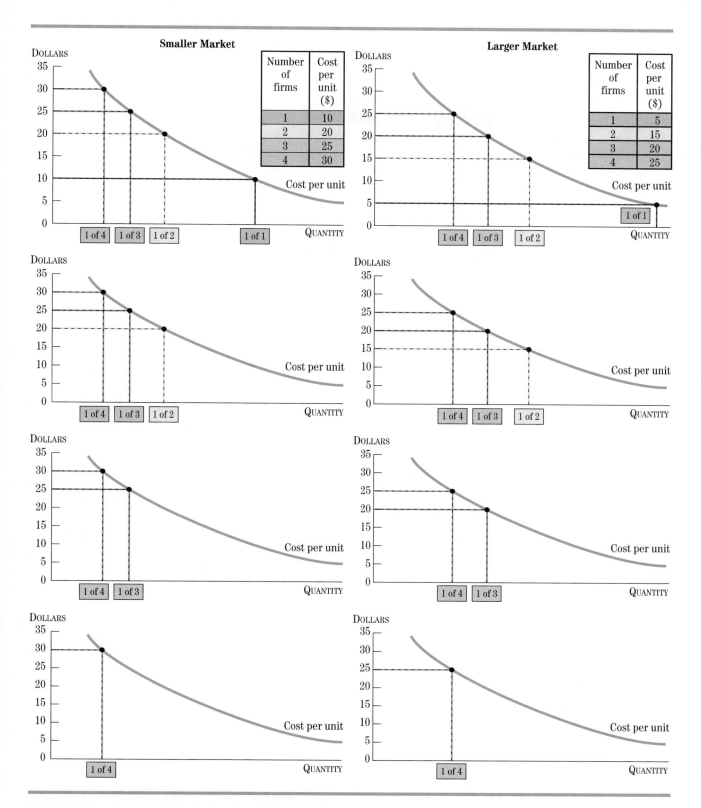

FIGURE 17.4   Cost per Unit: The Number of Firms and Market Size

FIGURE 17.5

The Relationship Between Cost per Unit and the Number of Firms

The first four points on each curve are plotted from the two tables in Figure 17.4 for 1 to 4 firms; the other points can be similarly obtained. Each curve shows how cost per unit at each firm rises as the number of firms increases in a market of a given size. The curve shifts down when the size of the market increases.

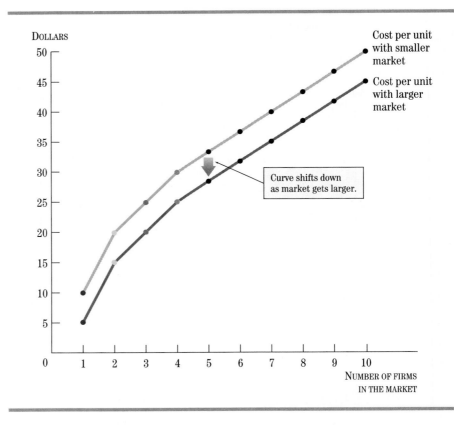

A Relationship Between the Price and the Number of Firms

A general feature of most markets is that as the number of firms in the market increases, the price at each firm declines. More firms make the market more competitive. Thus, there is a relationship between the price and the number of firms, as shown in Figure 17.6. As in Figure 17.5, the number of firms is on the horizontal axis. The curve in Figure 17.6 is downward-sloping because more firms mean a lower price.

FIGURE 17.6

The Relationship Between the Price and the Number of Firms

As the number of firms increases, the market price declines. This curve summarizes this relationship.

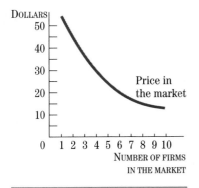

Equilibrium Price and Number of Firms

In the long run as firms either enter or exit an industry, price will tend to equal cost per unit. If the price for each unit were greater than the cost per unit, then there would be a profit opportunity for new firms; the number of firms in the industry would rise. If the price were less than the cost per unit, then firms would exit the industry. Only when price equals cost per unit is there a long-run equilibrium. Because price equals cost per unit, the curves in Figures 17.5 and 17.6 can be combined to determine the price and the number of firms in long-run equilibrium. As shown in Figure 17.7, there is a long-run equilibrium in the industry when the downward-sloping line for Figure 17.6 intersects the upward-sloping line (for the smaller market) from Figure 17.5. At this point, price equals cost per unit.

Corresponding to this long-run equilibrium is an equilibrium number of firms. More firms would lower the price below cost per unit, causing firms to leave the

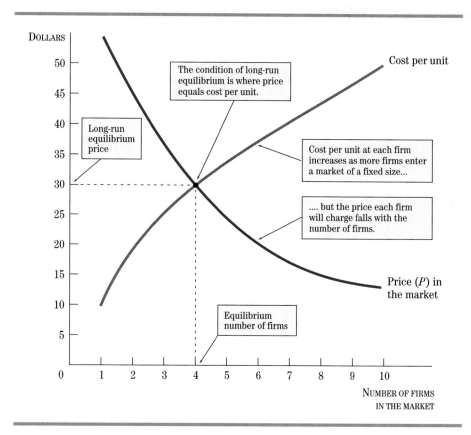

FIGURE 17.7
Long-Run Equilibrium Number of Firms and Cost per Unit
A condition for long-run equilibrium is that price equals cost per unit. In this diagram this condition is shown at the intersection of the two curves.

industry; fewer firms would raise price above cost per unit, attracting new firms to the industry. Figure 17.7 shows how the possibility of entry and exit results in a long-run equilibrium with price equal to cost per unit.

Increasing the Size of the Market

Now let us see how the industry equilibrium changes when the size of the market increases due to international trade. In Figure 17.8, we show how an increase in the size of the market, due perhaps to the creation of a free trade area, reduces the price and increases the number of firms. The curve showing the cost per unit of each firm shifts down and out as the market expands; that is, for each number of firms the cost per unit declines for each firm. This brings about a new intersection and a long-run equilibrium at a lower price. Moreover, the increase in the number of firms suggests that there will be more product variety, which is another part of the gain from trade.

The North American Automobile Market

The gains from trade due to larger markets arise in many real-world examples. Trade in cars between Canada and the United States now occurs even though

FIGURE 17.8
Gains from Trade Due to Larger Markets

When trade occurs, the market increases from the size of the market in one country to the combined size of the market in two or more countries. This larger market shifts the upward-sloping line down because cost per unit for each firm is lower when the market is bigger. In the long-run equilibrium at the intersection of the two new curves the price is lower and there are more firms. With more firms, there is more variety. Lower price and more variety are the gains from trade.

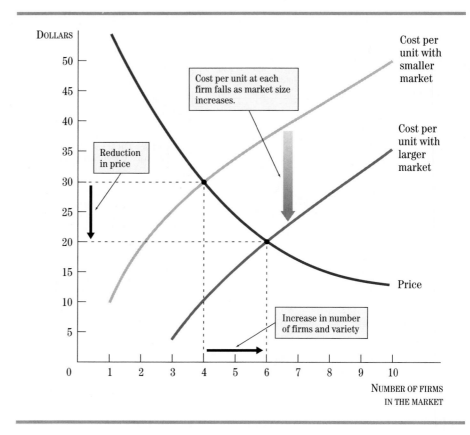

new trade theory: models of international trade in which cost per unit declines as the international market grows.

neither country has an obvious comparative advantage. Before 1964 trade in cars between Canada and the United States was restricted. Canadian factories thus had to limit their production to the Canadian market. This kept costs per unit high. When free trade in cars was permitted, the production in Canadian factories increased, and the Canadian factories began to export cars to the United States. By producing more cars, cost per unit declined. The term **new trade theory** refers to the models of international trade that emphasize the size of the market, and its effect on cost per unit.

Review

▶ Lowering costs per unit through the division of labor requires large markets. International trade creates large markets.

▶ A graphical model can be used to explain the gains from international trade; the model shows that a larger market reduces prices.

David Ricardo, 1772–1823

BORN:
London, 1772

EDUCATION:
Never attended college

JOBS:
Stockbroker, 1786–1815
Member of Parliament, 1819–1823

MAJOR PUBLICATIONS:
The High Price of Bullion, 1810; *On the Principles of Political Economy and Taxation,* 1817; *A Plan for a National Bank,* 1824

David Ricardo did not go to college. Instead, he went to work as a stockbroker at age 14 and eventually accumulated a vast fortune, including a beautiful country estate. Although Ricardo did not get interested in economics until he was 27, did not write on economics until he was 37, and then died young at age 51, he became one of the most influential economists of all time.

Ricardo continued the tradition of Adam Smith. In fact, he got interested in economics after reading Smith's *Wealth of Nations* during a vacation. But Ricardo greatly extended and improved on Smith's theories and made them more precise. Along with Smith and Robert Malthus—who was Ricardo's close friend but frequent intellectual opponent— Ricardo is considered by historians to be in the classical school, which argued for laissez-faire, free trade, and competitive markets in 18th- and 19th-century Britain.

Ricardo grappled with three of the most important policy issues in economics: inflation, taxes, and international trade. Both his first book, published in 1810, and his last book, published the year after his death, focused on inflation and what the government should do to keep inflation low.

Taxes were the subject of about one-third of the chapters of his major economics treatise, *On the Principles of Political Economy and Taxation.* In analyzing the effects of taxes—whether on corn, rent, land, gold, houses, profits, or wages—Ricardo emphasized how taxes affected people's incentives, and in particular the incentive to save for the future. He wrote:

There are no taxes which have not a tendency to lessen the power to accumulate. . . . It should be the policy of governments . . . never to lay such taxes as will inevitably fall on capital; since by so doing, they impair the funds for the maintenance of labour, and thereby diminish the future production of the country.

But perhaps Ricardo's most famous contribution is to international trade—in particular, his theory of comparative advantage. Ricardo used this theory to argue for repeal of the restrictions on agricultural imports known as the corn laws. Although he had a seat in the Parliament from which to argue his free trade position, it was not until 20 years after his death that the corn laws were repealed.

Ricardo's theory of comparative advantage is a good example of how he improved on the work of Adam Smith. Here is how Ricardo described comparative advantage in 1817:

Under a system of perfectly free commerce, each country naturally devotes its capital and labour to such employments as are most beneficial to each. . . . It will appear then, that a country possessing very considerable advantages in machinery and skill, and which may therefore be enabled to manufacture commodities with much less labour than her neighbors, may, in return for such commodities, import a portion of the corn required for its consumption, even if its land were more fertile, and corn could be grown with less labour than in the country from which it was imported. Two men can both make shoes and hats, and one is superior to the other in both employments; but in making hats, he can only exceed his competitor by one-fifth or 20 per cent., and in making shoes he can excel him by one-third or 33 per cent.;—will it not be for the interest of both, that the superior man should employ himself exclusively in making shoes, and the inferior man in making hats?

Ricardo then went on to compare his more powerful comparative advantage result with Adam Smith's simple examples where each country had an absolute advantage over the other in producing one good versus another good.

Source of quotes: David Ricardo, *On the Principles of Political Economy and Taxation,* 1817, pp. 136, 152–153, in *The Works and Correspondence of David Ricardo,* ed. Piero Sraffa (Cambridge University Press, 1962).

THE TRANSITION TO FREE TRADE

We have now seen how opening economies to international trade results in changes in production; TV sets and ultrasound scanner production in the United States declined as a result of opening the U.S. economy to trade in our examples. When one industry shrinks as a result of the removal of restrictions on trade, the cost of adjustment in the short run may be quite large, even if other industries grow. The problems of making a transition to free trade therefore deserve special examination, even if the gains from free trade unambiguously benefit all in the long run.

Although it is certainly possible for more workers in the United States to produce pharmaceuticals and for fewer workers to produce TV sets, those who lose their jobs in electronics, even temporarily, suffer. In the short run, it is difficult to retrain workers. Workers who are laid off as the electronics industry shrinks cannot move easily to the pharmaceutical industry. Many have to retire early. Retraining is possible, but it takes time and is difficult for older workers.

Phaseout of Trade Restrictions

phaseout: the gradual reduction of a government regulation or trade barrier.

These human costs of adjustment are a reason for a slow phaseout of trade barriers. **Phaseout** means that trade barriers are reduced a little bit each year. A slow phaseout of trade barriers was part of the North American Free Trade Agreement between Canada, Mexico, and the United States. It called for a phaseout period of 10 to 15 years depending on the product. For example, some tariffs were scheduled to be cut by 25 percent in the first year, 50 percent after 5 years, and 100 percent after 10 years. The purpose of the slow phaseout was to allow production to shift from one industry to another slowly. The intention was to adjust the work force through attrition as workers normally retired.

Trade Adjustment Assistance

trade adjustment assistance: transfer payments made to workers who will be hurt by the move to free trade.

Costs of transition are also the reason many people recommend **trade adjustment assistance,** which refers to transfer payments to workers who happen to be hurt because of a move to free trade. Unemployment insurance and other existing transfer programs might go a long way toward providing such assistance. However, because society as a whole benefits from free trade, some increased resources can be used to help the workers who bear the brunt of the adjustment. In other words, the extra income that can be obtained by trade may be used to ease the adjustment.

Transition costs are not a reason to avoid free trade. They are a reason to phase out the restrictions on trade gradually and to provide trade adjustment assistance to workers as needed.

Review

▶ Although free trade increases the well-being of a country's citizens, there may be a transition period during which some people lose their jobs and suffer a loss of income.

▶ Phasing out trade restrictions slowly and providing trade adjustment assistance eases the burden of this transition.

CONCLUSION

In this chapter, we have focused on the economic gains to the citizens of a country from international trade. We have mentioned four reasons for such gains: the mutual benefits from voluntary exchange, reduction in market power from greater competition, comparative advantage, and larger markets which reduce costs per unit. All four reasons apply to trade within a country as well as to international trade. Most of the chapter was spent showing how to measure the gains due to comparative advantage and larger markets.

In the next chapter, we will consider government policy toward international trade. In concluding this chapter, it is important to point out that the benefits of international trade go well beyond economic gains.

International trade sometimes puts competitive pressure on governments to deliver better policies. Within the United States, competition between states can make regulatory and tax policies more efficient. Similarly, competition can make regulatory policies in countries more efficient.

International trade can also improve international relations. Trade enables Americans to learn more about Southeast Asians or Europeans or Latin Americans. This improves understanding and reduces the possibilities for international conflict. Developing international trade with Russia and the other countries of the former Soviet Union might even reduce the possibility of another cold war or new international conflict in the future. If many people have an economic stake in a relationship, they will not like a military action that threatens that relationship.

International trade is, unfortunately, sometimes viewed as a war between countries. As the 1990s began, many worried about other countries, in particular Japan, catching up to the United States in income per capita. By the mid-1990s, this view changed radically as the Japanese economy faltered. But international trade is not a zero-sum game. If Japan grows more rapidly again, this need not have any detrimental effect on the well-being of Americans. Rather, international trade results in net gains for the citizens of both countries.

KEY POINTS

1. The principles of economics can be used to analyze international trade just as they can be used to analyze trade within a country.

2. International trade is different from within-country trade because national governments can place restrictions on the trade of goods and services between countries and on immigration.

3. According to the principle of comparative advantage, countries that specialize in producing goods that they have a comparative advantage in can increase world production and raise consumption in their own country.

4. The gains from trade due to comparative advantage can be shown graphically by shifting out the production possibilities curve.

5. Comparative advantage is a dynamic concept. If people in one country improve their skills or develop low-cost production methods through research, they will alter the comparative advantage.

6. If differences in the relative abundance of capital and labor are the reason for differences in comparative advantage, then international trade will tend to equalize real wages.

7. Lower cost per unit in larger markets is another key reason for gains from trade.

8. When the size of the market increases, cost per unit declines, there are more firms, and there is greater variety of products.

9. Opening an economy to trade by reducing trade barriers usually entails short-term adjustment costs for some workers, even though the long-term effects are beneficial. A slow phaseout of trade restrictions and trade adjustment assistance can reduce the harm from this adjustment.

10. The gains from international trade extend beyond economics to improving the operation of government and improving international relations. International trade is not a zero-sum game where one country wins only if another loses.

KEY TERMS

international trade	absolute advantage	Leontief paradox
commerce clause	terms of trade	factor-price equalization
mercantilism	gains from trade	intraindustry trade
exports	dynamic comparative advantage	interindustry trade
imports	capital abundant	new trade theory
net exports	labor abundant	phaseout
tariff	capital intensive	trade adjustment assistance
free trade	labor intensive	

QUESTIONS FOR REVIEW

1. What is the difference between absolute advantage and comparative advantage?

2. If the relative price of two goods is 4 in one country and 6 in another country before trade, in what range will the relative price be after trade?

3. What is the difference between the production possibilities curve before trade and after trade?

4. In what sense is comparative advantage a dynamic concept?

5. Why does trade take place even if one country does not have an absolute advantage over another?

6. Why might costs per unit decline when the market increases in size?

7. What is the difference between interindustry trade and intraindustry trade?

8. What explains the Leontief paradox?

9. Why are trade restrictions frequently phased out slowly?

10. What are four reasons for economic gains from trade?

PROBLEMS

1. Suppose the production of corn and cantaloupes per unit of labor in the United States and Mexico is as follows:

	Corn	Cantaloupes
United States	5 ears	1 melon
Mexico	1 ear	1 melon

a) Which country has a comparative advantage in corn production?
b) With free trade between the United States and Mexico, is it possible for 3 ears of corn to be worth the same as 1 melon? Explain.
c) Suppose that with free trade the price is 3 ears per melon. Suppose that the United States and Mexico both have 1 billion worker-hours that can be devoted to either corn production or cantaloupe production. Draw production possibilities curves between corn and cantaloupe production in the two countries with and without trade.
d) Is it possible for government policies in either the United States or Mexico to alter the comparative advantage? Explain and give two examples.

2. In the North American Free Trade Agreement between Canada, Mexico, and the United States, the phaseouts are slowest for American cantaloupes and Mexican corn. Explain the rationale for these phaseouts. Doesn't problem 1 say there is a gain from removing the barriers?

3. Suppose there are two goods, wheat and clothing, and two countries, the United States and Brazil, in the world. The production of wheat and clothing requires only labor. In the United States it takes 1 unit of labor to produce 4 bushels of wheat and 1 unit of labor to produce 2 items of clothing. In Brazil it takes 1 unit of labor to produce 1 bushel of wheat and 1 unit of labor to produce 1 item of clothing.

a) Suppose the United States has 100 units of labor and Brazil has 120. Draw the production possibilities curve for each country without trade. Which country has the absolute advantage in each good? Indicate each country's comparative advantage.
b) In what range would the world trading price ratio lie when these countries open up to free trade? Will both countries be better off? Why? Show this on your diagram.

4. Suppose France has 250 units of labor and Belgium has 100 units of labor. In France, 1 unit of labor can produce 1 shirt or 3 bottles of wine. In Belgium, 2 units of labor can produce 1 shirt or 3 bottles of wine. Draw the production possibilities curve for each country. If these countries open up to trade, what will happen? Why?

5. What is meant by factor-price equalization? Both opponents and supporters of the North American Free Trade Agreement used this theory to argue their positions. Explain how this is possible.

6. "Trade adjustment assistance is necessary for any government agreement that opens up trade." Comment.

7. Comparative advantage explains interindustry trade in different goods between countries. How do economists explain intraindustry trade, that is, trade in the same industry between countries? Why might people in the United States want to buy German cars, and Germans want to buy cars from the United States?

8. Suppose there are two countries, initially not trading with each other. Will prices fall when the two countries open up trade between them? Use both the comparative advantage and the expanded market models of trade to explain how prices will change.

9. Suppose an economics professor can type 15 pages in an hour or write half an economics lecture in an hour. Will she ever have a reason to hire an assistant who can type 10 pages per hour? Use the idea of comparative advantage to explain.

10. "Developing countries should exploit their own comparative advantage and quit trying to invest in physical and human capital to develop high-tech industries." Comment.

11. Suppose that each firm in an industry has total costs of production as follows:

Quantity of Output	Total Costs ($)
1	100
2	104
3	109
4	116
5	125
6	136
7	149
8	164
9	181
10	200
11	221
12	244

Suppose that the quantity demanded in the market is 6 units and that demand is perfectly inelastic.

a) Compute cost per unit for each firm in the industry for the cases when there are 2, 3, and 6 firms in the industry. Plot the relationship between cost per unit and the number of firms, with cost per unit on the vertical axis and number of firms on the horizontal axis.

b) Now suppose demand shifts out to 12 units because of an expansion of trade but is still perfectly inelastic. Find and plot cost per unit as in part (a) and compare the two plots.

12. How does the relative abundance of factors of production affect comparative advantage? Suppose you found that imports to the United States from Mexico were mainly goods, such as cement, that require much capital compared to labor, and that exports from the United States to Mexico were mainly goods, such as computer software, that require much labor compared to capital. Would your finding constitute evidence against the theory of comparative advantage?

13. The mercantilists advised that government always try to run trade surpluses (where exports are greater than imports) and avoid trade deficits (where exports are less than imports). What was Adam Smith's argument against this advice? Does his advice still apply today?

14. The following relationship between price, cost per unit, and the number of firms describes an industry in a single country.

Number of Firms	Cost per Unit ($)	Price ($)
1	10	90
2	20	80
3	30	70
4	40	60
5	50	50
6	60	46
7	70	43
8	80	40
9	90	38
10	100	36

a) Graph (1) the relationship between cost per unit and the number of firms, and (2) the relationship between price and the number of firms. Why does one slope up and the other slope down?

b) Find the long-run equilibrium price and number of firms.

c) Now suppose the country opens its borders to trade with other countries; as a result the relationship between cost per unit and the number of firms becomes as follows:

Number of Firms	Cost per Unit ($)
1	5
2	10
3	15
4	20
5	25
6	30
7	35
8	40
9	45
10	50

Find the new long-run equilibrium price and number of firms.

d) What are the gains from expanding the market through the reduction in trade barriers?

18

International
Trade Policy

Each year the U.S. government publishes a list hundreds of pages long, detailing the most significant restrictions that other governments place on international trade. The list includes Australia's 25 percent tariff on cars; Brazil's 70 percent tariff on motorcycles; France's ban on imports of U.S. poultry; India's 70 percent tariff on chocolate; Japan's restrictions on rice imports; Russia's 30 percent tariff on aircraft; and on and on.

The European countries and Japan publish their own long lists of restrictions the U.S. government places on international trade. These include import restrictions on textiles, apparel, cheese, ice cream, sugar syrup, cotton, and peanuts; the prohibition on foreign-made ships participating in U.S. coastal shipping; and on and on. Clearly, despite significant progress in trade agreements over the last 50 years, the world is still far from free trade. Why do we have a world with many trade barriers? The answer lies in politics as much as in economics.

In the United States, trade policy has changed course many times during the twentieth century as the political climate changed. Tariffs declined during the first part of the century, a trend that lasted until World War I. Then, soon after World War I, tariffs began to rise again, reaching record levels and causing economic damage during the Great Depression of the 1930s. Policy then changed direction yet again, with tariffs declining in the 1940s. This trend continued during the years after World War II, with the United States leading a multilateral effort to reduce barriers to trade around the world.

Trade policy has veered in other directions over the last 25 years, with greater emphasis placed on regional trade; the free trade agreement of the United States, Canada, and Mexico to cut tariffs among them to zero (NAFTA) is one example of this shift. New types of barriers to trade, such as voluntary agreements between countries to manage the volume of trade, have multiplied. At the same time, populist politicians such as Pat Buchanan and Ross Perot gained large followings by protesting free trade. As the twenty-first century begins, many worry that a powerful political movement demanding higher trade barriers could arise again.

This chapter considers both the economics and the politics of international trade policy. It examines the impact of the trade barriers that currently exist, the gains that could occur from eliminating them, the arguments given in favor of them, and the various policies that might be taken to reduce them.

THE EFFECTS OF TRADE RESTRICTIONS

Governments use many methods to restrict international trade. Policies that restrict trade are called **protectionist policies** because the restrictions usually protect industries from foreign imports. In addition to reducing imports, these policies raise prices, as we show next.

protectionist policy: a policy that restricts trade to protect domestic producers.

Tariffs

The oldest and most common method for a government to restrict trade is the *tariff,* a tax on goods imported into a country. The higher the tariff, the more trade is restricted. An **ad valorem tariff** is a tax equal to a certain percentage of the value of the good. For example, a 15 percent tariff on the value of goods imported is an ad valorem tariff. If $100,000 worth of goods are imported, the tariff revenue is $15,000. A **specific tariff** is a tax on the quantity sold, such as 50 cents for each kilogram of zinc.

ad valorem tariff: a tax on imports evaluated as a percentage of the value of the import.

specific tariff: a tax on imports that is proportional to the number of units or items imported.

The economic effects of a tariff are illustrated in Figure 18.1. We consider a particular good—automobiles, for example—that is exported from one country (Japan, for example) and imported by another country (the United States, for example). There is an *import demand curve* and an *export supply curve* shown in Figure 18.1. The **import demand curve** gives the quantity of imported goods that will be demanded at each price. The import demand curve shows that a higher price for imported goods will reduce the quantity of the goods demanded. A higher price on Nissans and Toyotas, for example, will lead to a smaller quantity of Nissans and Toyotas demanded by Americans. Like the standard demand curve, the import demand curve is downward-sloping.

import demand curve: a curve showing the quantity of imports demanded at various prices.

The **export supply curve** gives the quantity of exports that foreign firms are willing to sell at each price. In the case of Nissans and Toyotas, the export supply curve gives the quantity of Toyotas and Nissans that Japanese producers are willing to sell in the United States. The supply curve is upward-sloping because foreign producers are willing to supply more cars when the price is higher, just like an ordinary supply curve.

export supply curve: a curve showing the quantity of exports supplied at various prices.

In equilibrium, for any single type of good, the quantity of exports supplied must equal the quantity of imports demanded. Thus, the intersection of the export supply curve and import demand curve gives the amount imported into the country and the price.

When the government imposes a tariff, the supply curve shifts up, as shown in Figure 18.1. The tariff increases the marginal cost of supplying cars to the United

FIGURE 18.1
The Effects of a Tariff
A tariff shifts the export supply curve up by the amount of the tariff. Thus, the price paid for imports by consumers rises and the quantity imported declines. The price increase (upward-pointing black arrow) is less than the tariff (upward-pointing blue arrow). The revenue to the government is shown by the shaded area; it is the tariff times the amount imported.

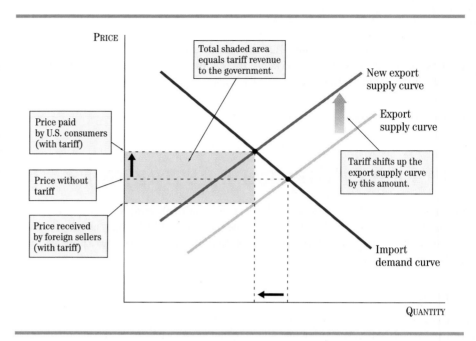

States. The amount of the tariff in dollars is the amount by which the supply curve shifts up; it is given by the length of the blue arrow in Figure 18.1.

The tariff changes the intersection of the export supply curve and the import demand curve. At the new equilibrium, a lower quantity is imported at a higher price. The price paid for cars by consumers rises, but the increase in the price is less than the tariff. In Figure 18.1, the black arrow shows the price increase. The blue arrow is longer than the upward-pointing black arrow along the vertical axis, which shows the tariff increase. The size of the price increase depends on the slopes of the demand curve and the supply curve.

The price received by suppliers equals the price paid by consumers less the tariff that must be paid to the government. Observe that the price received by the sellers declines due to the tariff.

The amount of revenue that the government collects is given by the quantity imported times the tariff, which is indicated by the shaded rectangle in Figure 18.1. For example, if the tariff is $1,000 per car and 1 million cars are imported, the revenue is $1 billion. Tariff revenues are called *duties* and are collected by customs.

The tariff also has an effect on U.S. car producers. Because the tariff reduces imports from abroad and raises their price, the demand for cars produced by import-competing companies in the United States—General Motors, Ford, or Chrysler—increases. This increase in demand will raise the price of U.S. cars. Thus, consumers pay more for both imported cars and domestically produced cars.

Quotas

quota: an upper limit on the quantity of a good that may be imported or sold.

Another method of government restriction of international trade is called a **quota.** A quota sets a limit, a maximum, on the amount of a given good that can be

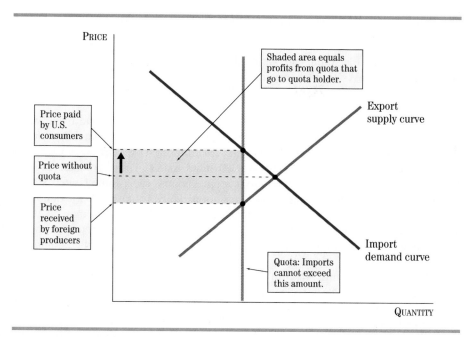

PRICE

Shaded area equals profits from quota that go to quota holder.

Export supply curve

Price paid by U.S. consumers

Price without quota

Price received by foreign producers

Import demand curve

Quota: Imports cannot exceed this amount.

QUANTITY

FIGURE 18.2
The Effects of a Quota
A quota can be set to allow the same quantity of imports as a tariff. The quota in this figure and the tariff in Figure 18.1 allow the same quantity of imports into the country. The price increase is the same for the quota and the tariff. But, in the case of a quota, the revenue goes to quota holders, not to the U.S. government.

imported. The United States has quotas on the import of ice cream, sugar, cotton, peanuts, and other commodities. Foreigners can supply only a limited amount to the United States.

The economic effect of a quota is illustrated in Figure 18.2. The export supply curve and the import demand curve are identical to Figure 18.1. The quota, the maximum that foreign firms can export to the United States, is indicated in Figure 18.2 by the solid purple vertical line labeled "quota." Exporters cannot supply more cars than the quota and, therefore, American consumers cannot buy more than this amount. We have chosen the quota amount to equal the quantity imported with the tariff in Figure 18.1. This shows that the government can achieve, if it wants to, the same effects on the quantity imported using a quota or a tariff. Moreover, the price increase in Figure 18.2, represented by the black arrow along the vertical axis, is the same as the price increase in Figure 18.1. Viewed from the domestic market, therefore, a quota and a tariff are equivalent: If the quota is set to allow in the same quantity of imports as the tariff, then the price increase will be the same. Consumers pay more for imports in both cases, and the demand for domestically produced goods that are substitutes for imports will increase. The price of domestically produced cars would also increase if there were a quota on foreign cars.

Then what is the difference in the effects of a tariff and a quota? Unlike a tariff, no revenue goes to the government with a quota. The difference between the price that the foreign suppliers get and the higher price that the consumers pay goes to the holders of the quota—the ones who are allowed to import into the country. Frequently foreign countries hold the quotas. The revenue the quota holders get is indicated by the shaded rectangle in Figure 18.2. It is equal to the quantity imported times the difference between the price paid by the consumers and the price received by the producers. The size of that rectangle is identical to the size of the rectangle showing the revenue paid to the government in the case of the tariff in Figure 18.1.

Voluntary Restraint Agreements (VRAs)

voluntary restraint agreement (VRA): a country's self-imposed government restriction on exports to a particular country.

A relatively new alternative to tariffs and quotas is the **voluntary restraint agreement (VRA).** These restraints are similar to quotas except that one country, such as the United States, asks another country to "volunteer" to restrict its firms' exports to the United States. Although a tariff or a quota must be passed by Congress, VRAs can be negotiated by the president without Congress approving.

The United States negotiated VRAs with Japan for automobiles in the early 1980s. The Japanese government agreed to limit the number of automobiles Japanese firms exported to the United States to 2.8 million. There are also VRAs on machine tools and textiles exported to the United States. These voluntary agreements usually occur because of pressure that one country, such as the United States, exerts on the other country. Hence, they are not actually voluntary. For example, a foreign government might agree to a VRA because the other country may be about to impose steep tariffs. Or there may be diplomatic pressures unrelated to economics that one country can use to pressure another country into the so-called voluntary actions.

What is the economic effect of a VRA? Figure 18.3 examines the impact. The supply and demand curves are identical to those in Figures 18.1 and 18.2. The amount of the VRA chosen for illustration is the same as the quota in Figure 18.2 and the resulting quantity from the tariff in Figure 18.1. This shows that the effect of the VRA on price and quantity can be made identical to the quota and the tariff. Consumers pay more under tariffs, quotas, or VRAs. The difference between VRAs and quotas is the recipient of the equivalent of the tariff revenue. In the case of the VRA, these revenues go to the foreign firms. As firms reduce their production, the price rises, and their profits rise. Thus, what would have been tariff revenue to the U.S. government in the case of a U.S. tariff becomes increased profits for foreign firms in the case of a VRA.

FIGURE 18.3
The Effects of a Voluntary Restraint Agreement (VRA)
The effects are just like the quota in Figure 18.2 except the revenue goes to foreign firms rather than quota holders. Because of the VRA, the foreign firms act as if they are in a cartel to restrict output and raise prices.

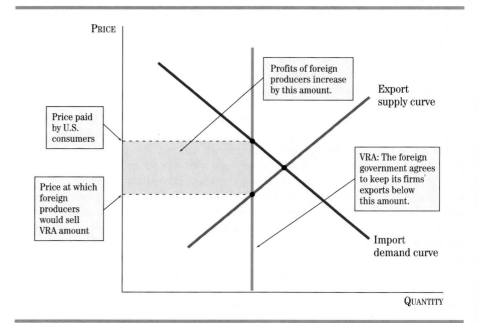

Studies show that the VRAs used in the United States in the 1980s for automobiles did lead to a higher price and additional revenue to the Japanese automobile producers. The price of Japanese cars sold in the United States rose by about $1,000, and the increase in demand for U.S. cars led to their price increasing by about $1,400 for the average car.

Voluntary Import Expansion (VIE)

A new type of intervention by the government in foreign trade is the **voluntary import expansion (VIE)**. With VIEs, a government agrees to have its firms expand their imports of foreign goods from another country. For example, the United States arranged for a VIE with Japan in semiconductors in 1986 and renewed it in 1991. Under this agreement, the Japanese government was to see to it that Japanese firms purchased foreign semiconductors in the amount of at least 20 percent of the Japanese market for semiconductors. The rationale given by the U.S. government was that Japanese firms had a preference for Japanese semiconductors, though the Japanese government denied it. To offset this preference, the U.S. government asked the Japanese government to volunteer to increase U.S. imports.

voluntary import expansion (VIE): a government agreement to expand imports from a particular country.

A VIE may seem rather benign; after all, trade is apparently being increased, not decreased. Although there is not a consensus among economists about the effects of VIEs, some economists estimate the effects on U.S. consumers to be much like that of VRAs or quotas. Consider a VIE with Japan in which the Japanese agree to import more U.S. cars. Suppose the Japanese government gets Japanese rental car companies to buy more U.S. automobiles. The "voluntary" increase in demand for U.S. cars in Japan causes an increase in the price of U.S. cars in Japan. This is likely to raise the price of Japanese cars in Japan as well.

Now consider what happens in the United States. The higher price of cars in Japan reduces the number of Japanese cars Japanese firms will want to export to the United States. As illustrated in Figure 18.4, this upward shift in the export supply curve will raise the price of cars in the U.S. market. Thus, a VIE has effects similar to a VRA, quota, or tariff.

The reason there is not a consensus about the effect of VIEs on U.S. consumer prices is that some economic analysts estimate that the price of cars in Japan will not rise. In their view, the Japanese are discriminating against foreign products, and offsetting the discrimination by government action will not raise prices.

Trade Barriers Related to Domestic Policies

Other government policies can restrict international trade even if their main purpose is related to domestic policy. Quality and performance standards, for example, may be biased against foreign products. The standards may have a good purpose, such as safety or compatibility with other products, but frequently they do not. Consider the Canadian plywood standards for building construction, which keep out U.S. plywood. The Canadians argue that the standards are needed to satisfy building requirements in Canada, but Americans argue that plywood that does not meet the Canadian standards works just as well. A safety restriction against American-made baseball bats in Japan during the 1980s is another example. Most Americans viewed the bats as perfectly safe and viewed the Japanese safety standard as a restriction on trade.

Standards, therefore, are a tricky problem because governments can argue that they are for the purpose of improving performance in their own country. The U.S.

FIGURE 18.4
The Effects of a Voluntary Import Expansion (VIE)
With a VIE, the export supply curve is likely to shift up if the price foreign producers receive in their home market (not shown on this diagram) rises when there is an expansion in demand due to the VIE. The upward shift in the export supply curve raises the price of cars in the United States.

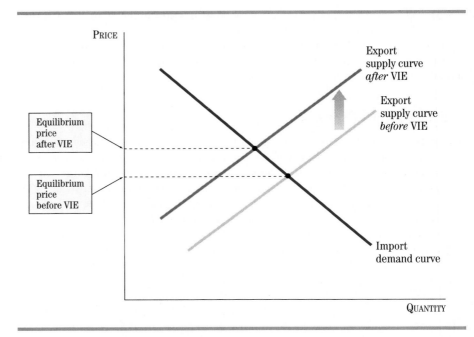

Food and Drug Administration does not allow untested drugs into the United States even though foreign governments deem them safe. The FDA argues that the restriction is necessary to protect consumers, but foreign governments view it as a trade restriction. Such a standard does seem like a trade barrier, but in reality it is a matter of dispute.

Another domestic policy that affects trade policy is government procurement, the process by which governments buy goods and services. If government procurement policy has a bias against foreign products, then it is considered a restriction on trade. For example, the U.S. government has a "Buy American" policy that gives a slight edge to American suppliers of goods and services. Federal employees must try to travel on domestic airlines even when traveling abroad. The government of Japan has had a policy of only buying Japanese supercomputers.

Any government procurement policy that is biased against lower-priced foreign goods in favor of more expensive domestic goods will either require higher taxes or will raise prices for the consumers of government services. Such a policy is like other trade restrictions.

Review

▶ The most common ways for government to restrict foreign trade are tariffs and quotas. Voluntary restraint agreements and voluntary import expansions have become more popular in recent years.

▶ Tariffs and quotas have the same effect on price and quantity. They differ in who gets the tariff revenue.

▶ Many government standards and regulations aimed at domestic trade affect international trade. They present a tricky problem for trade policy.

THE HISTORY OF TRADE RESTRICTIONS

As stated earlier, tariffs are the oldest form of trade restriction. Throughout history, governments have used tariffs to raise revenue. **Revenue tariffs,** whose main purpose is raising revenue, were by far the most significant source of federal revenue in the United States before the income tax was enacted in 1917 (see Figure 18.5). Revenue tariffs are still common in less-developed countries because they are easy for the government to collect as the goods come through a port or one of a few checkpoints.

U.S. Tariffs

Tariffs are a big part of U.S. history. Even before the United States was a country, a tariff on tea imported into the colonies led to the Boston Tea Party. One of the first acts of the U.S. Congress placed tariffs on imports. Figure 18.6 summarizes the history of tariffs in the United States since the early 1800s.

From the Tariff of Abominations to Smoot-Hawley

Tariffs were high throughout much of U.S. history, rarely getting below 20 percent in the nineteenth century. In addition to raising revenue, these tariffs had the purpose of reducing imports of manufactured goods. The tariffs offered protection to manufacturers in the North but raised prices for consumers. Since the South was mainly agricultural and a consumer of manufactured goods, there was a constant dispute between the North and the South over these tariffs.

The highest of these tariffs was nicknamed the "tariff of abominations." This tariff, passed in 1828, brought the average tariff level in the United States to over 60 percent. The tariff made purchases of farm equipment much more expensive in the southern states. It almost led to a civil war before the actual Civil War as the southern states threatened to secede. However, because the tariff was so high, it was soon repealed, and for the next 10 years tariffs were relatively low by nineteenth-century standards.

The most devastating increase in tariffs in U.S. history occurred during the Great Depression. The **Smoot-Hawley tariff** of 1930 raised average tariffs to 59 percent. Congress and President Hoover apparently hoped that raising tariffs would help stimulate U.S. production and offset the Great Depression. But the increase had precisely the opposite effect. Other countries retaliated by raising their tariffs on U.S. goods. Each country tried to beat the others with higher tariffs, a phenomenon known as a **trade war.** The Smoot-Hawley tariff had terrible consequences. Figure 18.7 is a dramatic illustration of the decline in trade that occurred at the time of these tariff increases during the Great Depression. The Smoot-Hawley tariff made the Great Depression worse than it would have otherwise been.

From the Reciprocal Trade Agreement Act to GATT

The only good thing about the Smoot-Hawley tariff was that it demonstrated to the whole world how harmful tariffs can be. In order to achieve lower tariffs, the Congress passed and President Roosevelt signed the **Reciprocal Trade Agreement Act** in 1934. This act was probably the most significant event in the history of U.S. trade policy. It authorized the president to cut U.S. tariffs by up to 50 percent if other countries would cut their tariffs on a reciprocating basis. The reciprocal trade

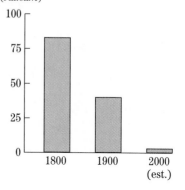

TARIFFS AS A SHARE OF
TOTAL FEDERAL RECEIPTS
(PERCENT)

FIGURE 18.5
Tariffs as a Share of Total Federal Revenue
The first tariff, passed in 1789, represented nearly all of the federal government's revenue; 200 years later, tariff revenues were only about 1 percent of the total.

Source: Historical Statistics of the United States, Colonial Times to 1957, series Y 259–260 and Budget of the U.S. Government, 1993.

revenue tariff: an import tax whose main purpose is to provide revenue to the government.

Smoot-Hawley tariff: a set of tariffs imposed in 1930 that raised the average tariff level to 59 percent by 1932.

trade war: a conflict among nations over trade policies caused by imposition of protectionist policies on the part of one country and subsequent retaliatory actions by other countries.

Reciprocal Trade Agreement Act: passed in 1934 by the U.S. Congress, it allowed cuts in tariff rates based on similar cuts in tariff rates in European countries.

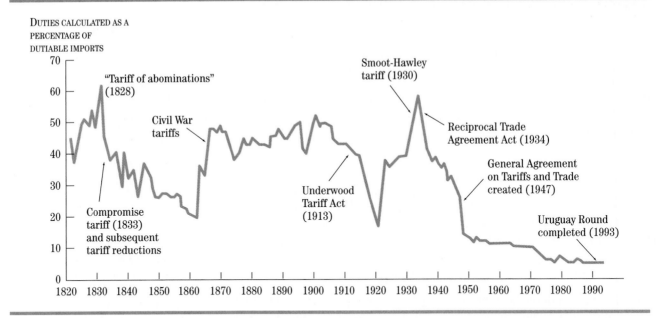

DUTIES CALCULATED AS A
PERCENTAGE OF
DUTIABLE IMPORTS

FIGURE 18.6
History of Tariffs in the United States

The chart shows the ratio of tariff revenues to the value of imports subject to tariffs measured as a percentage. This percentage is a measure of the average tariff excluding goods not subject to any tariff.

Source: Historical Statistics of the United States, Colonial Times to 1970 and *Statistical Abstract of the United States,* 1993, Table 1353.

General Agreement on Tariffs and Trade (GATT): an international treaty and organization designed to promote mutual reductions in tariffs and other trade barriers among countries.

antidumping duty: a tariff imposed on a country as a penalty for dumping goods.

dumping: the selling of goods by foreign firms at a price below average cost or below the price in the domestic country.

agreements resulted in a remarkable reduction in tariffs. By the end of World War II the average tariff level was down from a peak of 59 percent under Smoot-Hawley to 25 percent. The successful approach to tariff reduction under the Reciprocal Trade Agreement Act was made permanent in 1947 with the creation of a new international organization, the **General Agreement on Tariffs and Trade (GATT).** GATT was set up to continue the process of tariff reduction. During the half century since the end of World War II, tariffs have continued to decline on a reciprocating basis. By 1992 the average U.S. tariff level was down to 5.2 percent.

Antidumping Duties

No history of U.S. tariffs would be complete without a discussion of antidumping duties. **Antidumping duties** are tariffs put on foreign firms as a penalty for dumping. When a firm sells products in another country at prices below average cost or below the price in the home country, it is called **dumping.** Dumping can occur for many reasons. For example, the firm might want to sell at a lower price in the foreign market, where the demand is more elastic, than in the home market, where it is less elastic. If so, consumers in the foreign market benefit. But some people argue that dumping is a way for foreign firms to drive domestic firms out of business and thereby gain market share and market power. In any case, in the United States and other countries, dumping is illegal; the penalty is a high tariff—the antidumping duty—on the good that is being dumped.

Many economists are concerned that antidumping duties, or even the threat of such duties, are serious restrictions on trade. They reduce imports and raise consumer prices. Moreover, they are frequently used for protectionist purposes. Firms in industries that desire additional protection can file dumping charges and request that tariffs be raised. Frequently, they are successful. Thus, an important issue for the future is how to reduce the use of antidumping duties for restricting trade.

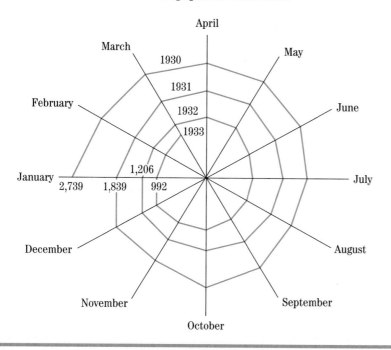

Contracting Spiral of World Trade

FIGURE 18.7
Decline in World Trade During the Great Depression
This circular graph, used by Charles Kindleberger of MIT, illustrates how world trade collapsed after tariffs increased during the Great Depression. The distance from the middle of the graph to the point in each spoke is the amount of trade (in millions of dollars) during each month. A time-series graph could show the same information but would look less dramatic.

Source: From Charles Kindleberger, *The World in Depression, 1929–39* (Berkeley: University of California Press, 1973). Data reprinted by permission from League of Nations, *Monthly Bulletin of Statistics,* February 1934.

The Rise of Nontariff Barriers

As tariffs were being reduced in the post–World War II period, a conflicting trend began to emerge. Some of the other methods to restrict trade—called **nontariff barriers** to trade—grew in popularity. Nontariff barriers include anything from quotas to quality standards aimed at reducing the import of foreign products. Nontariff barriers may have arisen as a replacement for tariffs in response to political pressure for protection of certain industries.

nontariff barrier: any government action other than a tariff that reduces imports, such as a quota or a standard.

The Multifiber Agreement (MFA) is an example. It grew from a small VRA program into a complex worldwide system of VRAs designed to limit the imports of textiles and apparel into the United States and Europe. The MFA limits imports of thousands of products, from men's and women's shirts to swimsuits. Reducing such nontariff barriers—whether in textiles or agriculture—is a major objective of trade policy today.

How Large Are the Gains from Reducing Trade Restrictions?

Restrictions on trade raise prices and reduce the quantity of products available to consumers. Estimates made in the late 1980s indicate that the gain from removing these restrictions could be as large as $60 billion per year.

To get a better understanding of the gains, consider three of the many goods and services that might be affected: textiles, cars, and sugar. The textile and apparel MFA is estimated to have cost consumers $11 billion in 1987, although domestic producers gained $4 billion. The net loss is thus $7 billion. VRAs on Japanese automobiles are estimated to have cost American consumers $5.8 billion in 1984, while

U.S. producers gained $2.6 billion; the net loss was thus $3.2 billion. Quotas on sugar imports were estimated to have cost American consumers $1.9 billion in 1987, while the gain to producers was $1 billion; the net loss was $.9 billion.

The Political Economy of Protectionist Pressures

These calculations of the gains from trade as well as the brief review of U.S. tariff history help explain why restrictions on trade that harm the overall economy continue to exist. Firms and workers in industries protected by import restrictions benefit from these restrictions. For example, the producers gain about $4 billion in textiles and $1 billion in sugar. Thus, removing protection has losers as well as winners within a country even though the winners benefit more than the losers are hurt.

In most cases, the people who benefit from protection are few and the people who lose are many. Individual firms or workers in textiles benefit from protection by thousands of dollars a year, while each consumer may lose hundreds of dollars a year. Thus, those who benefit from protection lobby their representatives heavily, while those who lose from protection are more diffuse and have less power.

Review

▷ Tariffs have been used by governments to raise revenue long before income taxes were invented.

▷ Tariffs have also been used for protectionist purposes in several important instances in U.S. history. Manufacturing firms in the North were protected by tariffs at the expense of consumers of manufactured goods, many of whom were in the South.

▷ The Smoot-Hawley tariff of the 1930s was one of the most harmful in U.S. history. It led to a trade war in which other countries raised tariffs in retaliation.

▷ Tariffs have come down since the 1930s. However, in recent years, nontariff barriers to trade have gone up.

▷ Although tariffs are now low on average by historical standards, tariffs and nontariff barriers still cost American consumers billions of dollars each year.

ARGUMENTS FOR TRADE BARRIERS

It appears that many trade barriers exist because of the political power of the interest groups that demand them. But aren't there any good economic rationales for trade barriers? Are trade barriers ever beneficial to the economy as a whole? Let's examine some arguments that say they are.

Restricting Supply and Strategic Trade Policy

If the firms in one country produce much of the world's supply of a good, then the country can gain by restricting trade. By restricting the amount that the firms supply to the world, the country can raise the world price and the firms' profits. In fact, this is precisely what oil exporting countries do. Even the whole country may benefit if some of the extra profits are taxed away.

This argument in favor of trade restrictions is an old one. However, it has two serious problems. First, it invites retaliation. Other countries may raise their tariffs in response. If one retaliation invites another retaliation, then a trade war might be started. Second, restricting trade to increase domestic firms' profits is a beggar-thy-neighbor policy because one country gains only at the expense of other countries.

In recent years more sophisticated versions of this rationale for trade restrictions have appeared. A **strategic trade policy** is a set of actions—subsidies or tax credits—that aims to encourage large firms to start up in a particular country. If those firms are able to capture most of the world market, then the policy of restricting supply and raising prices becomes a possibility. Strategic trade policy gets its name from the strategic interaction between governments that arises when they endeavor to subsidize firms. Here is how such strategic interaction arises.

strategic trade policy: a set of government actions designed to encourage large firms to locate or start up in that country.

Suppose European governments subsidize the production of a new aircraft at the European firm Airbus. By doing so, they may prevent a U.S. firm, perhaps Boeing, from producing the aircraft. Why? The world market might not be large enough for two aircraft of the same type. In other words, with two firms cost per unit may be greater than the expected purchase price of the aircraft. With only one firm producing, cost per unit might be lower.

If the subsidy is successful in keeping Boeing out, the eventual profits at the European firm may be greater than the subsidy. However, there is a risk to Europe. Boeing could produce the aircraft anyway, perhaps thinking that cost per unit will be low enough even with two aircraft of the same type. Then the profits in Europe would not cover the subsidy. Thus, Europe must try to guess what Boeing will do. The problem gets more complicated if the U.S. government gets involved and threatens to subsidize Boeing. Because of such strategic behavior, the European subsidy policy could fail as the United States retaliates with its own subsidy. Aside from being a beggar-thy-neighbor policy, strategic trade policy is difficult to carry out because of the strategic behavior.

The Infant Industry Argument

One of the earliest statements of the **infant industry argument** in favor of trade restrictions was put forth by Alexander Hamilton in 1791 in his *Report on Manufactures.* Hamilton argued that manufacturing firms in the newly created United States should be protected from imports. Once the industries were established, they could compete with foreign imports. But as they got started, they needed protection until they reached a certain scale.

infant industry argument: the view that a new industry may be helped by protectionist policies.

A danger with the infant industry argument is that the protection may last long after it was initially justified. In Latin America, for example, infant industry arguments were used to justify import protection in the 1950s. However, these barriers to trade lasted long after any kind of a reasonable infant industry argument could be made.

The National Security Argument

A nation's security is another argument for trade restrictions. The national security argument is that there are certain goods, such as special metals, computers, ships, or aircraft, the country needs to be able to produce in time of war. If it does not have an industry that produces them, it could be at a severe disadvantage.

However, national security arguments can be used by firms seeking protection from foreign imports. Japanese rice farmers, for example, made national security arguments for protection from rice imports. In fact, the rice restriction has little to do with national security because rice can be imported from many different countries. In the United States, the textile industry has argued on national security grounds that it needs protection because it provides military uniforms made from U.S. textiles.

It is important to examine whether there are alternatives to trade restrictions before applying the national security argument and restricting trade. For example, rather than restricting rice imports, the Japanese could store a large amount of rice in case of a war emergency. Or the United States could store millions of extra uniforms rather than restrict textile imports if one really thought that uniforms were a national security issue. In fact, the United States does have stockpiles of many rare minerals and metals needed for national defense production.

Retaliation Threats

Threatening other countries or retaliating against them when they have trade restrictions is another possible reason to deviate from free trade. If the United States threatens the Japanese by saying it will close U.S. markets, then it may encourage Japan to open its markets to the United States. Thus, by retaliating or threatening, there is a possibility of increasing international trade around the world.

However, the retaliation argument can also be used by those seeking protection. Those in the United States who are most vocal about retaliation against other countries are frequently those who want to protect an industry. Many economists worry about threats of retaliation because they fear that other countries will respond with further retaliation, and a trade war will occur.

What If Other Countries Subsidize Their Firms?

If foreign governments subsidize their firms' exports, does this justify U.S. government subsidies to U.S. firms to help them compete against the foreign firms?

Foreign subsidies to foreign producers are a particularly difficult issue. On the one hand, if foreign subsidies lower the price of U.S. imports, then U.S. consumers benefit. If Europe wants to use taxpayer funds to subsidize aircraft manufacturers, then why not enjoy the lower-cost aircraft? On the other hand, foreign subsidies enable industries to thrive more for political reasons than economic ones. From a global perspective, such government intervention should be avoided since it hurts consumers.

Unfair Competition from the Sun?

Firms seeking protection frequently complain about "unfair competition" from other countries. In a famous satire of such complaints, a French economist, Frédéric Bastiat, wrote about candlemakers complaining about a foreign rival—the sun! The candlemakers in Bastiat's satire petitioned French legislators to pass a law requiring the closing of all windows, dormers, skylights, shutters, curtains, and blinds to protect them from this competition. Though written more than 150 years ago, the behavior Bastiat described seems to apply to many modern producers who seek protection from competition.

Review

▶ An old rationale for trade restrictions is to raise the price of exports. But reducing supply through trade restrictions is a beggar-thy-neighbor policy that is likely to result in retaliation.

▶ National security, infant industry, and retaliation are other arguments in favor of trade restrictions. Each has the possibility of being used by protectionists.

HOW TO REDUCE TRADE BARRIERS

Viewed in their entirety, the economic arguments against trade restrictions seem to overwhelm the economic arguments in favor of trade restrictions. The economic arguments in favor of free trade have been in existence for over 200 years. The recommendation of early economists such as Adam Smith and David Ricardo was simple: Develop a policy to reduce trade barriers.

However, it was not until many years after Smith and Ricardo wrote that their recommendations were translated into a practical trade policy. Then, as now, political pressures favoring protection made the repeal of trade barriers difficult, as well as hazardous to political careers. (See the box "The End of the Corn Laws.") Today, a carefully formulated trade policy can include a variety of approaches.

Unilateral Disarmament

One approach to removing trade barriers in a country is simply to remove them unilaterally. Making an analogy with the arms race, we call this policy **unilateral disarmament.** When a country unilaterally reduces its arms, it does so without getting anything in arms reduction from other countries. With unilateral disarmament in trade policy, a country reduces its trade barriers without other countries also reducing their trade barriers. Unilateral disarmament is what Smith and Ricardo recommended for England.

It is difficult to achieve unilateral disarmament today. Consider, for example, the Trade-Enhancement Initiative started in 1990 to reduce American and European barriers to imports from the emerging democracies in Eastern Europe. Despite powerful arguments from economists that such reduction would spur the development of market economies in these areas, little reduction in trade barriers occurred as a result of this initiative. Strong protests from clothing manufacturers in the United States and dairy product manufacturers in Europe prevented any significant increase of the amount of Polish men's suits or Hungarian cheese allowed to be imported.

As the example shows, the difficulty of unilateral disarmament is that some individuals are hurt, if only temporarily, and it is hard to compensate them. The workers and producers in the textile industry benefit from the restriction on Polish suits; the removal of the barriers is a significant cost to them even if it is outweighed by gains to society. Of those who gain, each gains only a little. Of those who lose, each loses a lot. The political pressures they exert are significant. As a result, unilateral disarmament is rarely successful in the developed countries today as a means of reducing trade barriers.

unilateral disarmament: in trade policy, the removal of trade barriers by one country without reciprocal action on the part of other countries.

Using Economics to Explain the End of the Corn Laws

Corn laws, recorded back as far as the twelfth century, restricted imports of grains, including wheat, rye, and barley, into England. Adam Smith devoted an entire chapter of his 1776 *Wealth of Nations* to the corn laws, arguing that "the praises which have been bestowed upon the law . . . are altogether unmerited."* But legislation introduced in 1791 raised the grain import tariff even further. The corn laws were unpopular with everyone except the landowners and farmers.

The Anti-Corn League, founded in 1839 by Richard Cobden, was the most significant pressure group in nineteenth-century England. The Anti-Corn League used the arguments of Smith and Ricardo that the corn laws were an economic disaster and a moral tragedy: The laws impoverished and even starved the working class, constrained the growth of manufacturing, and

provided government support to the wealthy. The catalyst was the Irish potato famine of 1845, which raised agricultural prices even further.

Robert Peel, the Tory prime minister from 1841 to 1846, was reform minded. He introduced currency reform and reduced tariffs on many goods after reintroducing the income tax. Until 1845 he was against repeal of the corn laws, primarily because of strong support for them from landowners in the Tory party. But under pressure from Cobden and the Anti-Corn League, he changed his position after the potato famine and argued for the repeal of the corn laws.

In February 1846, Peel introduced a package of measures abolishing duties on imported corn over a three-year period. Only a minority of his party supported him, but the package passed. The split in the

Tory party ended Peel's career, and the party did not win an election until the emergence of the new Conservative party in 1868, when Benjamin Disraeli was elected.

The repeal of the corn laws and other protectionist measures ushered in the free trade era in England. The economist-philosopher John Stuart Mill's *Principles of Political Economy* was published in 1848 and became the handbook of free markets for nearly 50 years: "Laisserfaire, in short, should be the general practice: every departure from it, unless required by some great good, is a certain evil."†

---

*Adam Smith, *Wealth of Nations* (New York: Modern Library, 1994), p. 560.

†John Stuart Mill, *Principles of Political Economy,* 1848, p. 950, in *Reprints of Economic Classics,* ed. Augustus M. Kelley (New York: Bookseller, 1965).

Multilateral Negotiations

multilateral negotiation: simultaneous tariff reductions on the part of many countries.

An alternative to unilateral disarmament is **multilateral negotiation,** which involves simultaneous tariff reductions among many countries. The main example of the multilateral approach is the General Agreement on Tariffs and Trade (GATT). With multilateral negotiations, opposing political interests can cancel each other out. For example, import-competing domestic industries that will be hurt by the reduction of trade barriers, such as textiles in the United States or agriculture in Europe and Japan, can be countered by export interests that will gain from the reduction in trade barriers. Since consumers will gain, they are also a potential counter to protectionism, but they are too diffuse to make a difference, as we just discussed. With multilateral negotiations, interested exporters who gain from the reduction in barriers will push the political process to get the reductions.

Multilateral negotiations also balance international interests. For example, to get less-developed countries to remove their barriers on imports of financial and telecommunications services, the United States had to agree to remove agricultural trade barriers in the United States.

The Uruguay Round

Multilateral trade negotiations under GATT have taken place in a series of negotiating rounds, each of which lasts several years. During each round, the countries try to come to agreement on a list of tariff reductions and the removal of other trade restrictions. There have been eight rounds of negotiations since GATT was established in 1947. The most recent was the **Uruguay Round,** named after the country where the first negotiations occurred in 1986. After many years, the Uruguay Round negotiations ended in 1993. An important innovation of the Uruguay Round was that it created a new multilateral organization, called the **World Trade Organization (WTO),** to settle disputes between countries about unfair trade policies.

    The reduction in tariffs through multilateral negotiations under GATT has been dramatic. Tariffs are expected to go below 3 percent on average in the United States with the implementation of the Uruguay Round agreement. Recall that this compares with nearly 60 percent in the mid-1930s.

> **Uruguay Round:** the most recent round of negotiations on the General Agreement on Tariffs and Trade, begun in 1986 in Uruguay.
>
> **World Trade Organization (WTO):** an international organization that can mediate trade disputes.

Most-Favored Nation Policy

Multilateral negotiations are almost always conducted on a **most-favored nation (MFN)** basis. MFN means that when the United States or any other country reduces its tariffs under GATT, it reduces them for virtually everyone. Today, if a country is not granted MFN status, the United States imposes Smoot-Hawley–level tariffs on the country. For example, concern about human rights in China led some to argue that the United States should remove MFN status for China. Doing so would have raised tariffs on Chinese imports to about 60 percent.

> **most-favored nation (MFN):** the principle by which all countries involved in GATT negotiations receive the same tariff rates as the country with the lowest negotiated tariff rates.

Regional Trading Areas

Creating regional trading areas is an increasingly popular approach to reducing trade barriers. For example, in 1988 a free trade agreement between the United States and Canada called for removal of all trade restrictions between those two countries. The North American Free Trade Agreement (NAFTA) will reduce tariffs to zero between Canada, the United States, and Mexico. An even wider free trade area is proposed for the whole Western Hemisphere.

    Regional trading areas have some advantages over multilateral approaches. First, fewer countries are involved, so the negotiations are easier. Second, regional political factors can help offset protectionist pressures. For example, the political goal of European unity helped establish grassroots support to reduce trade barriers among the countries of Europe. More recently, the countries of Europe have formed a single market with even fewer restrictions on trade.

Trade Diversion versus Trade Creation

But there are disadvantages of regional trading areas in comparison with multilateral reductions in trade barriers under GATT. **Trade diversion** is one disadvantage. Trade is diverted when low-cost firms from countries outside the trading area are replaced by high-cost firms within the trading area. For example, as a result of NAFTA, producers of electronic equipment in Southeast Asia will have to pay a U.S. tariff, while producers of the same equipment in Mexico will not have to pay

> **trade diversion:** the shifting of trade away from the low-cost producer toward a higher-cost producer because of a reduction in trade barriers with the country of the higher-cost producer.

trade creation: the increase in trade due to a decrease in trade barriers.

the tariff. As a result, some production will shift from Southeast Asia to Mexico; that is viewed as a trade diversion from what might otherwise be a low-cost producer. The hope is that **trade creation**—the increase in trade due to the lower tariffs between the countries—outweighs trade diversion.

Free Trade Areas versus Customs Unions

free trade area (FTA): an area that has no trade barriers between the countries in the area.

customs union: a free trade area with a common external tariff.

There is an important difference between two types of regional trading areas: **free trade areas (FTAs)** and **customs unions.** In both, barriers to trade between countries in the area or the union are removed. But external tariffs are treated differently: Under a customs union, such as the European Union (EU), external tariffs are the same for all countries. For example, semiconductor tariffs are exactly the same in France, Germany, and the other members of the EU. Under a free trade area, external tariffs can differ for the different countries in the free trade area. For example, the United States's external tariffs on textiles are higher than Mexico's. These differences in external tariffs under an FTA cause complications because a good could be shipped into the country with the low tariff and then moved within the FTA to the country with the high tariff. To prevent such external tariff avoidance, **domestic content restrictions** must be incorporated into the agreement. These restrictions say that in order to qualify for the zero tariffs between the countries, a certain fraction of the product must be made within the FTA. For example, under NAFTA, the majority of parts in television sets and automobiles must be manufactured in Canada, Mexico, or the United States in order for the television or car to qualify for a zero tariff.

domestic content restriction: a requirement that a fraction of the product must be produced within the area to qualify for zero tariffs between the countries in the free trade area.

Managed Trade

managed trade: a situation in which a government takes actions to promote or restrict trade in certain goods, usually by setting targets for exports or imports.

Trade policymakers and news reporters frequently use the term **managed trade** to refer to the actions of government agencies to affect trade by persuading firms to buy or sell larger or smaller quantities of goods in other countries. The term means different things to different people. Most frequently, managed trade includes the VRAs and VIEs discussed earlier in the chapter. The semiconductor agreement between Japan and the United States is an example of managed trade. Managed trade actions like VRAs and VIEs stipulate certain numerical targets for exports or imports. The numerical target is usually stated as a percent of the market that must be imported or exported. For example, the semiconductor VIE called for imports equal to 20 percent of the Japanese market.

Some economic analysts in the United States argue that managed trade has the purpose of avoiding trade barriers such as tariffs or quotas. They believe managed trade is needed because governments intervene in the market in other countries. Managed trade is the way things are, they argue, and the U.S. government needs to face up to it. But others argue—and this is the more typical view among economists—that there are alternatives to managed trade that work better to improve economic efficiency. Many economists argue that managed trade is actually a form of trade barrier. For example, if a country should want to promote a certain economic activity—say, semiconductor production—then rather than requiring that foreigners buy that product, the government can provide tax credits or direct research subsidies. This is more transparent and does not have the side effect of raising U.S. consumer prices.

Review

▶ There are many different approaches to removing restrictions on international trade, including unilateral disarmament, multilateral negotiations under GATT, and regional trading areas—FTAs and custom unions.

▶ Managed trade—such as voluntary import expansions—is put forth as a way to increase rather than restrict trade. But many economists argue that it is an intervention in the market that can be handled in better ways.

CONCLUSION

Very few economists disagree with the proposition that tariffs and quotas usually reduce the general economic well-being of a society. In fact, polls of economists show that they disagree less on this proposition than virtually any other in economics, except perhaps the similar proposition that government price controls reduce economic well-being. This unanimity among economists was reflected in the debate over the North American Free Trade Agreement in 1993 in the United States. Every living Nobel Prize–winning economist endorsed the agreement to eliminate tariffs and quotas among Canada, Mexico, and the United States.

This chapter has shown that despite this unanimity, many restrictions on international trade still exist. True, there have been substantial reductions in tariffs in the last 50 years, and the recently completed Uruguay Round and North American Free Trade Agreement promise to continue this reduction in tariffs. But the use of nontariff barriers and antidumping laws has yet to show signs of diminishing. Trade disputes between the United States and Japan over domestic economic policies and particular products have worried some economists, who fear that a trade war with escalating trade restrictions could occur.

The need for cooperation in the formulation of trade policies is likely to increase rather than decrease in the future. The challenge is to develop a means for conducting international trade policy in a world in which many sovereign governments, each of which is free to formulate its own policy, coexist.

KEY POINTS

1. Despite the economic arguments put forth in support of free trade, there are still plenty of restrictions on trade in the world.

2. Tariffs and quotas are the two main forms of restricting international trade. They are equivalent in their effects on prices and imports.

3. Tariffs were originally a major source of government revenue but are relatively insignificant sources of revenue today.

4. Quotas do not generate any revenue for the government. The quota holders get all the revenue.

5. Voluntary export restraints are much like quotas except they can be negotiated without an act of Congress, and the revenue usually goes to the foreign producer in the form of increased profits.

6. Strategic trade, national security, and infant industry are arguments put forth in support of trade barriers. In most cases, they are overwhelmed by the arguments in favor of reduced trade barriers.

7. Eliminating restrictions on trade unilaterally is difficult because of the harm done to those who are protected by the restrictions.

8. Regional trading areas and multilateral tariff reductions endeavor to reduce trade barriers by balancing export interests against import-competing interests.

9. Free trade areas and customs unions both create trade and divert trade.

10. Quantitative estimates of the gains from eliminating trade barriers are large in the United States and even larger for the world as a whole.

KEY TERMS

protectionist policy
ad valorem tariff
specific tariff
import demand curve
export supply curve
quota
voluntary restraint agreement (VRA)
voluntary import expansion (VIE)
revenue tariffs
Smoot-Hawley tariff

trade war
Reciprocal Trade Agreement Act
General Agreement on Tariffs and
  Trade (GATT)
antidumping duties
dumping
nontariff barriers
strategic trade policy
infant industry argument
unilateral disarmament

multilateral negotiation
Uruguay Round
World Trade Organization (WTO)
most-favored nation (MFN)
trade diversion
trade creation
free trade area (FTA)
customs union
domestic content restrictions
managed trade

QUESTIONS FOR REVIEW

1. In what sense are a tariff and a quota equivalent?

2. Why might a tariff raise the price of the imported product by less than the amount of the tariff?

3. How does a voluntary restraint agreement encourage the restriction of supply in the foreign country?

4. What are some examples of government standards and government procurement being used as trade barriers?

5. Why is unilateral disarmament a difficult way to reduce trade barriers?

6. How do multilateral negotiations or regional trading areas make the reduction of trade barriers easier politically?

7. Why might a free trade area cause trade diversion?

8. What is the infant industry argument in favor of trade protection?

9. What are the disadvantages of using retaliation in trade policy?

10. How large are the gains from reducing trade barriers?

PROBLEMS

1. Estimates show that voluntary export restraints through which the government of Japan restricted automobile exports to the United States in the mid-1980s raised the price of Japanese cars in the United States by about $1,000. Sketch a diagram to show how this occurred and briefly explain the price increase.

2. Suppose the United States can produce steel domestically at $20,000 a ton, while Mexico can produce it at $15,000 and Brazil at $10,000. Assume the United States, Brazil, and Mexico currently impose a tariff of 60 percent on foreign steel. Given these assumptions, who produces the steel Americans consume? Would it be beneficial for the United States to form an economic union with Mexico if they keep the same tariff on Brazilian steel? Why?

3. Suppose the U.S. government decides to cut the quantity of textile imports in half by using quotas. Draw a diagram to illustrate this policy. Who benefits and who loses from this policy?

4. During the 1970s, several oil-producing countries restricted their exports of oil. What is the economic rationale for this restriction on trade? Why is it called a beggar-thy-neighbor policy?

5. "Maintaining a large trade surplus improves consumer welfare." Comment.

6. Suppose the U.S. government has decided for national security reasons that it must reduce the quantity of machine tools imported. What is the rationale? How can the United

States accomplish this goal? Which policy would you recommend? Why?

7. The United States imports lumber from Canada. Draw an export supply, import demand diagram to analyze this situation. Suppose Canada gives a new export subsidy to its lumber industry. What will happen to the price and quantity in the United States? Is the United States better off? Why does the United States government complain when foreign governments subsidize their export industries?

8. "Import tariffs are a blunt instrument for protecting industries. It would be better to try to support productivity improvements in these industries." Comment.

9. Suppose French wine suddenly becomes popular in the United States. How does this affect the price and quantity of imports of French wine? Suppose the U.S. wine industry lobbies for protection. If the government imposes a tariff in order to restore the original quantity of imports, what will happen to the price of French wine in the United States? Show how much tariff revenue the government will collect.

10. Suppose the United States decides to withdraw most-favored nation treatment from China. What would happen to the price and quantity of U.S. imports from China? Use a diagram to explain your answer.

4 part

Introduction to Macroeconomics

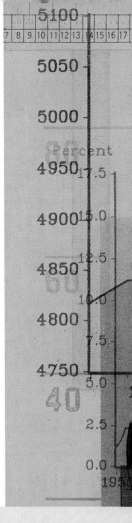

In the last 100 years the amount of goods and services that each person can produce on average has grown by more than five times in the United States. This *economic growth* is the single most important reason for improvements in living standards. Economic growth provides the means for people to reduce poverty and to achieve a better life. However, temporary fluctuations in production—such as the Great Depression of the 1930s or the much milder downturn in the early 1990s—sometimes interrupt this growth and cause great hardship. During such *economic fluctuations* people lose their jobs, poverty increases, and incomes fall until the economy returns to its upward growth path.

Patent No. 24,458,807

1990   1991   1995
Interest
Rate

1990   1995

chapters

19 A Preview of Macroeconomics
20 Measuring the Macroeconomy

Whereas economists use the supply and demand model and other microeconomic models to explain the behavior of firms and consumers in particular markets—the markets for bicycles, telephones, wheat—they use macroeconomic models to explain economic growth and fluctuations. When economists build macroeconomic models, they must look at the whole economy, which represents the sum of many individual markets.

With these two chapters we begin to take a look at the whole economy. In Chapter 19 we examine the history of the ups and downs in the U.S. economy, paying particular attention to national income, unemployment, inflation, and interest rates. We also provide an overview of macroeconomic models of growth and fluctuations. In Chapter 20 we examine how production of goods and services in the whole economy is measured, laying down basic principles for defining saving and the accumulation of capital.

These two chapters will serve as preparation for the discussion of long-run economic growth in Part 5 and fluctuations in total production and employment in Part 6.

19

A Preview of Macroeconomics

Macroeconomics is the study of how the economy as a whole grows and changes over time. It explains the miracles of economic growth: why, for example, young Americans living at the end of the twentieth century could choose to work only two months of the year, take a ten-month vacation each year, and still consume the same amount that their great-great-grandparents consumed 100 years ago. Macroeconomics also explains the dilemmas of economic growth: why a long-term economic slowdown that began in the mid-1970s is leaving many of these same young Americans no better off than their parents. Macroeconomics explains the dilemma of over 25 percent unemployment in the 1930s, and—another miracle—why we have not seen such high unemployment since. It explains why even in a good year about 5 percent of the workers are unemployed in the United States. Macroeconomics also explains why inflation—the mysterious increase in the price of virtually everything in the economy—caused a $100-a-month apartment in the 1950s to rent for $500 a month in the 1990s.

Macroeconomics concentrates on the *whole* economy—the whole national economy or even the whole world economy—rather than on particular parts of the economy, such as the health-care industry or the electronics industry. Determining what is produced and who gets it is closer to the subject of microeconomics than macroeconomics. Think of the economy as a pizza pie. Macroeconomics focuses on the size of the pie: Why does the size of the pie increase over the long haul? Why does the size shrink occasionally (a medium shows up when you ordered a large)? What can we do to increase the size of the pie and prevent it from shrinking occasionally?

Macroeconomics is important to you and your future. Your first job will be harder to find if unemployment is high. And if inflation picks up again, it may wipe out most of your savings. On a brighter note, increased economic growth would mean a better future for you, help alleviate poverty, and even provide funds to clean up the environment.

Good government policy can provide for high economic growth, low unemployment, and low inflation. But bad economic policy can lower growth and cause both high inflation and high unemployment. Macroeconomics is essential for determining what is good economic policy and how to achieve it.

This chapter first summarizes the recent historical performance of the economy, highlighting key facts to remember. It then gives a very short preview of the macroeconomic theory designed to explain these facts.

The theory will be developed in Parts 5 and 6, and, along with the facts, will provide a basis for making decisions about economic policy.

ECONOMIC OUTPUT OVER TIME

Real gross domestic product is the place to begin describing the subject matter of macroeconomics. You will recall from Chapter 1 that gross domestic product (GDP) is the total value of all goods and services produced in the economy during a specified period of time, such as a year or a quarter. The adjective *real* means that the measure of production is adjusted for the general increase in prices over time. This general increase in prices is called *inflation*. Although real GDP is not a perfect measure of how much is produced—for example, it does not include the value of a home-cooked meal or a garage painted by a do-it-yourselfer, and it does not subtract out pollution or environmental damage—it is the most comprehensive measure economists have to determine how the economy is doing. Real GDP is also called *output* or *production*.

Figure 19.1 shows the changes in real GDP over the last 40 years in the United States. When you look at real GDP over time, as in Figure 19.1, you notice two simultaneous patterns emerging. Over the long term, increases in real GDP demonstrate an upward trend, which economists call long-term **economic growth.** In the short term, there are **economic fluctuations**—more transient increases or decreases in real GDP. These short-term fluctuations in real GDP are also called **business cycles.** The difference between the long-term economic growth trend and the economic fluctuations can be better seen by drawing a relatively smooth line between the observations on real GDP. Such a smooth trend line is shown in Figure 19.1. Sometimes real GDP fluctuates above the trend line and sometimes it fluctuates below the trend line. In this section we look more closely at these two patterns: economic growth and economic fluctuations.

Economic Growth: The Relentless Uphill Climb

The large increase in real GDP shown in Figure 19.1 means that each year in the 1990s people in the United States produce a much greater amount of goods and services than they did 30 or 40 years ago. Improvements in the well-being of individuals in any society cannot occur without such increases in real GDP. To get a better measure of how individuals benefit from increases in real GDP, we consider average production per person, or *real GDP per capita*. Real GDP per capita is real GDP divided by the number of people in the economy. It is the total of all food, clothes, cars, houses, CDs, concerts, education, computers, etc., per person. When real GDP per capita is increasing, then the well-being—or the standard of living—of individuals in the economy, at least on average, is improving.

real gross domestic product (real GDP): a measure of the value of all the goods and services newly produced in a country during some period of time, adjusted for inflation.

economic growth: an upward trend in real GDP, reflecting expansion in the economy over time.

economic fluctuations: swings in real GDP that lead to deviations of the economy from its long-term growth trend.

business cycles: short-term fluctuations in real GDP and employment.

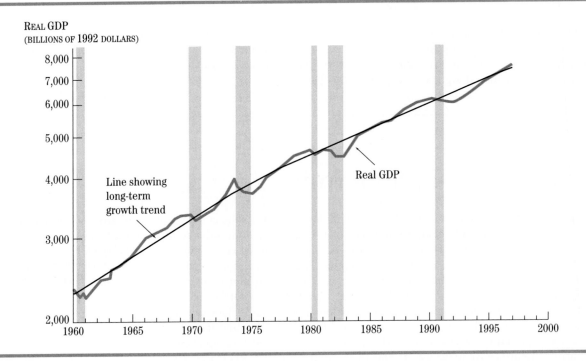

FIGURE 19.1
Economic Growth and Fluctuations During the Last 40 Years
Real GDP has tripled in the last 40 years. The trend in growth is shown by the black line. Real GDP is now more than $3 trillion higher than it was 40 years ago. At the same time, the economy has fluctuated up and down as it has grown, with six recessions—marked by the vertical shaded bars—and six subsequent recoveries since 1960.

Source: U.S. Department of Commerce.

The Economic Growth Record

How much economic growth has there been during the last 40 years in the United States? The annual *economic growth rate*—the percentage increase in real GDP each year—provides a good measure. On the average for the last 40 years, the annual economic growth rate has been about 3 percent. This may not sound like much, but it means that real GDP has more than tripled in the last 40 years. The United States now produces $3 trillion more goods and services than it did in the 1950s. The increase in production in the United States since the early 1960s is larger than what Japan and Germany now produce together. It is as if all the production of Japan and Germany—what is made by all the workers, machines, and technology in these countries—were annexed to the U.S. economy, as illustrated in Figure 19.2.

How much has real GDP *per capita* increased during this period? Because the U.S. population increased by about 100 million people during this period, the increase in real GDP per capita has been less dramatic than the increase in real GDP, but it is impressive nonetheless. The annual growth rate of real GDP per capita is the percentage increase in real GDP per capita each year. It has averaged about 1.7 percent per year. Again, this might not sound like much, but it has meant that real GDP per capita doubled from about $10,000 per person in the 1950s to about $20,000 per person in the 1990s. That extra $10,000 per person represents increased opportunities for travel, VCRs, housing, washing machines, aerobics classes, health care, antipollution devices for cars, and so on.

To be sure, not everyone benefited by the same amount from this increased average production per person; some did not benefit at all. And perhaps the production could be used for better purposes. Some feel that Americans spend too much

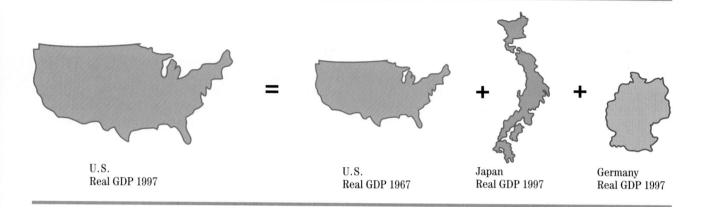

U.S.
Real GDP 1997

U.S.
Real GDP 1967

Japan
Real GDP 1997

Germany
Real GDP 1997

on health care and gasoline and not enough on child care and the criminal justice system.

The Economic Growth Slowdown

Long-term growth was more rapid in the period from the 1950s to the 1970s than it was from the 1970s to the 1990s. Economic growth in the former period was about 3½ percent per year, but in the latter period, it slowed to 2½ percent per year. A similar slowdown in economic growth also occurred in many other countries. This decline in economic growth means a loss of $1 trillion a year that might have been spent on other things, including cars, houses, better roads and bridges, aid to the poor, or environmental cleanup. If economic growth had remained at 3½ percent per year, real GDP would have been $1 trillion higher now than it is. This decline in economic growth is a problem because it slows improvements in economic well-being. But although we lament that we could have done better, we should not ignore that we have done as well as we have.

Over long spans of time, small differences in economic growth—even less than 1 percent per year—can transform societies. For example, economic growth in the southern states was only a fraction of a percent greater than in the North in the 100 years after the Civil War. Yet this enabled the South to rise from a real income per capita about half that of the North after the Civil War to about the same as the North today. Economic growth is the reason that Italy has caught up and even surpassed the United Kingdom in real GDP per capita; 100 years ago Italy had a real GDP per capita about half that of the United Kingdom. Economic growth is also key to improvements in the less-developed countries in Africa, Asia, and Latin America. Because economic growth has been lagging in many of these countries, real GDP per capita is considerably less than in the United States.

Economic Fluctuations: Temporary Setbacks and Recoveries

Clearly, real GDP grows over time, but every now and then real GDP stops growing, falls, and then starts increasing rapidly again. These ups and downs in the economy—that is, economic fluctuations or business cycles—can be viewed in Figure 19.1.

FIGURE 19.2
Visualizing Economic Growth
Over the last 30 years, production in the U.S. economy has increased by more than the total current production of the Japanese and German economies combined. It is as if the United States annexed Germany and Japan.

Source: International Monetary Fund.

recession: a decline in real GDP that lasts for at least six months.

peak: the highest point in real GDP before a recession.

trough: the lowest point of real GDP at the end of a recession.

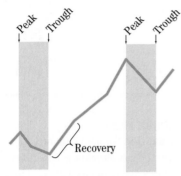

Two of these business cycles, one in the mid-1970s and the other in the early 1990s, are blown up for closer examination in Figure 19.3. As these two examples illustrate, no two business cycles are alike. The pattern of real GDP varies considerably. However, certain phases are common to all business cycles. These common phases are sketched in the margin. When real GDP falls, economists say there is a **recession;** a rule of thumb says that the fall in real GDP must last for a half year or more before it is considered a recession. The highest point before the start of the recession is called the **peak.** The lowest point at the end of a recession is called the **trough,** a term that may cause you to imagine water accumulating at the bottom of one of the dips.

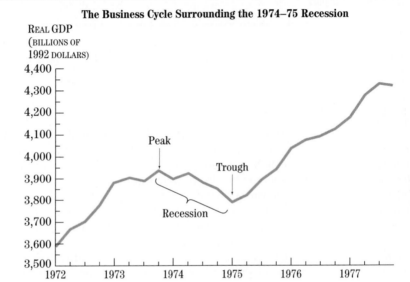

FIGURE 19.3
The Phases of Business Cycles
Although no two business cycles are alike, they have common features, including the four phases—*peak, recession, trough,* and *expansion,* which lasts until the next peak. The early part of the expansion is called the *recovery.* Note that the 1973–1975 recession was larger and deeper than the 1990–1991 recession.

Source: U.S. Department of Commerce.

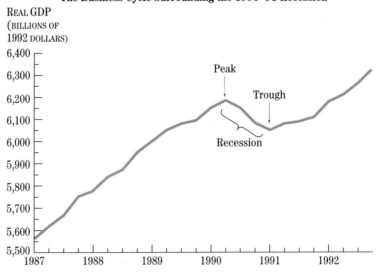

The period between recessions—from the trough to the next peak—is called an **expansion.** The early part of an expansion is usually called a **recovery** because the economy is just recovering from the recession.

The peaks and troughs of the six recessions since 1960 are shown by vertical bars in Figure 19.1. The shaded areas represent the recessions. The area between the shaded bars shows the expansions. The dates of all peaks and troughs back to 1920 are shown in Table 19.1. The average length of each business cycle from peak to peak is five years, but it is clear from Table 19.1 that business cycles are not regularly occurring ups and downs, like sunup and sundown. Recessions occur irregularly. There were only 12 months between the back-to-back recessions of the early 1980s, while 58 months of uninterrupted growth occurred between the 1973–1975 recession and the 1980 recession. The recession phases of business cycles also vary in duration and depth. The 1980 recession, for example, was not nearly as long or as deep as the 1973–1975 recession.

The 1990–1991 recession was one of the shortest recessions in U.S. history, and it was followed by a very long expansion. Before that recession, economic growth occurred almost uninterrupted for most of the 1980s from the trough of the previous recession in November 1982 to a peak in July 1990. The 1980s and 1990s saw the first- and second-longest peacetime expansions in U.S. history.

Economists debate whether economic policies were responsible for the expansions of the 1980s and 1990s. We will examine these debates in later chapters. Another debate is the cause of the recession that began in 1990. The first month of recession occurred just after Iraq invaded Kuwait, causing a disruption in the oil fields and a jump in world oil prices. Some argue that this jump in oil prices was a factor in the recession. Others point to an increase in taxes in 1990.

expansion: the period between the trough of a recession and the next peak, consisting of a general rise in output and employment.

recovery: the early part of an economic expansion, immediately after the trough of the recession.

**TABLE 19.1
Comparison of Recessions**

Recession		Duration of Recession (months from peak to trough)	Decline in Real GDP (percent from peak to trough)	Duration of Next Expansion (months from trough to peak)
Peak	Trough			
Jan 1920	Jul 1921	18	8.7	22
May 1923	Jul 1924	14	4.1	27
Oct 1926	Nov 1927	13	2.0	21
Aug 1929	Mar 1933	43	32.6	50
May 1937	Jun 1938	13	18.2	80
Feb 1945	Oct 1945	8	11.0	37
Nov 1948	Oct 1949	11	1.5	45
Jul 1953	May 1954	10	3.2	39
Aug 1957	Apr 1958	8	3.3	24
Apr 1960	Feb 1961	10	1.2	106
Dec 1969	Nov 1970	11	1.0	36
Nov 1973	Mar 1975	16	4.9	58
Jan 1980	Jul 1980	6	2.5	12
Jul 1981	Nov 1982	16	3.0	92
Jul 1990	Mar 1991	8	1.4	78*

*As of September 1997.

Source: National Bureau of Economic Research.

A Recession's Aftermath

The economy usually takes several years to return to normal after a recession. Thus, a period of bad economic times always follows a recession while the economy recovers. Remember that economists define recessions as periods when real GDP is declining, not as periods when real GDP is down. Despite the technical definition, many people still associate the word *recession* with bad economic times. For example, although the 1990–1991 recession ended in March 1991, most people felt that bad economic times extended beyond March 1991 well into 1992, and they were right. But, technically speaking, the recession was over in March 1991, well before the effects of an improving economy were felt by most people.

FIGURE 19.4
Growth and Fluctuations Throughout the Twentieth Century
Economic growth has continued, but the size of economic fluctuations has diminished remarkably. Recent ups and downs are minuscule in comparison with the Great Depression.

Source: U.S. Department of Commerce.

Recessions versus Depressions

Recessions have been observed for as long as economists have tracked the economy. Some past recessions have lasted so long and were so deep that they are called *depressions*. There is no formal definition of a depression. A depression is a huge recession.

Fortunately, we have not experienced a depression in the United States for a long time. Figure 19.4 shows the history of real GDP for about 100 years. The most

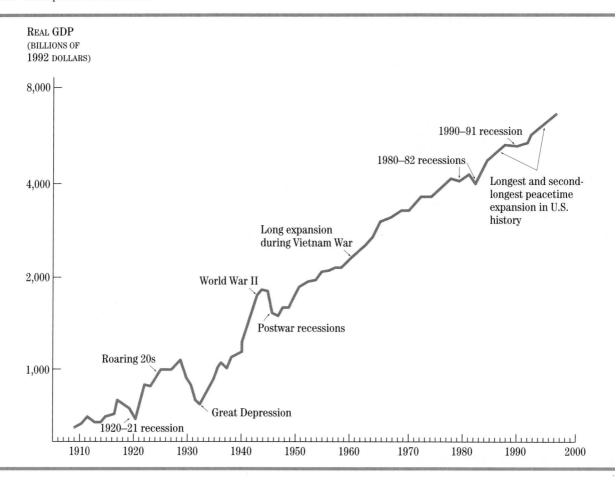

noticeable decline in real GDP occurred in the 1929–1933 recession. Real GDP fell by 32.6 percent in this period. This decline in real GDP was so large that it was given its own designation by economists and historians—the *Great Depression.* The recessions of recent years have had much smaller declines.

Table 19.1 shows how much real GDP fell in the fifteen recessions since the 1920s. The 1920–1921 recession and the 1937–1938 recession were big enough to be classified as depressions, but both are small compared to the Great Depression. Real GDP also declined substantially after World War II, when war production declined.

Clearly, recent recessions are not even remotely comparable in severity to the Great Depression or the other huge recessions of the 1920s and 1930s. The 1990–1991 recession, for example, had only one-twentieth the decline in real GDP that occurred during the Great Depression. But because any recession rivets attention on people's hardship and suffering, there is always a tendency to view a current recession as worse than all previous recessions. Some commentators reporting on the 1990–1991 recession wondered whether it should be compared with the Great Depression. For example, in September 1992, Louis Uchitelle of the *New York Times* wrote, "Technically, the recession is over, but spiritually, it continues. . . . The question is, what to call these hard times. What has been happening in America since 1989 seems momentous enough to enter history as a major economic event of the 20th century."[1]

Review

▶ Economic growth and economic fluctuations in real GDP occur simultaneously.

▶ Economic growth provides lasting improvements in the well-being of people. But recessions interrupt this growth.

▶ The Great Depression of the 1930s was a much larger downturn than recent recessions. It was about twenty times more severe than the 1990–1991 recession when measured by the decline in real GDP.

JOBS, INFLATION, AND INTEREST RATES

As real GDP changes over time, so do other economic variables, such as employment and inflation. Looking at these other economic variables gives us a better understanding of the human story behind the changes in real GDP. They also provide additional information about the economy's performance—just as a person's pulse rate or cholesterol level gives information different from the body temperature. No one variable is sufficient. We start with a look at employment, productivity, and unemployment.

Employment, Productivity, and Unemployment

When judging the success of an economy or the success of economic policies, many people look at how well the economy does in creating jobs. President Clinton set an economic policy goal of creating 8 million jobs in four years starting in 1993,

1. Louis Uchitelle, "Even Words Fail in This Economy," *New York Times,* September 8, 1992, p. C2.

and in his reelection campaign in 1996, he emphasized that this goal had been exceeded, with 10 million jobs created. President Reagan and President Bush pointed to the success of their economic policies by mentioning that 20 million jobs were created during the 1980s.

labor productivity: output per hour of work.

Although the number of jobs is important, so is the amount that each worker produces—what is called **labor productivity,** or sometimes simply *productivity.* More precisely, economists define labor productivity as real GDP per hour of work in the economy as a whole. As you will see, labor productivity is important because it ultimately determines how much workers are paid. Higher labor productivity leads to higher pay for work.

The Record on Jobs and Productivity

What is the long-term record on jobs in the United States economy? By any measure, the record is impressive. About 65 million more people have jobs now in the United States than 40 years ago. That amounts to an average of 1.6 million more people working each year. Figure 19.5 shows this large growth—a doubling of employment (the number of people working), from about 65 million to 130 million people.

This increase in the number of people holding jobs represents the net effect of new jobs being created and old jobs being lost. In a growing economy, many jobs are destroyed as tastes change and firms go out of business. But because even more new jobs are created by new and expanding businesses, there is a *net increase* in the number of jobs.

FIGURE 19.5
Number of People Holding Jobs
Employment in the United States has doubled during the last 40 years. During each recession, the number of people working declines and then increases during the expansion.

Source: U.S. Department of Labor.

A much greater fraction of the population is working now than was working 40 years ago, largely because more women are in the work force. Thus, the economy has been successful in creating jobs for a growing population as well as for the growing fraction of people who are working.

What is the record on labor productivity? The annual growth rate of labor productivity has averaged about 1.3 percent per year when measured by real GDP per

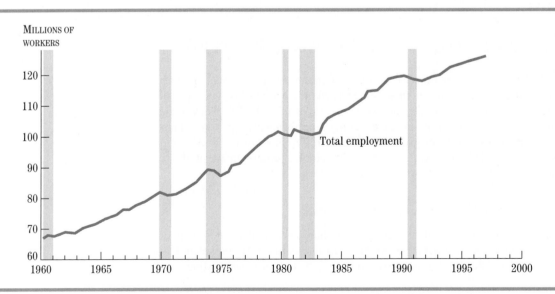

hour of work. However, just as there has been a slowdown in economic growth, there has been a slowdown in productivity growth over the longer term. Productivity growth averaged 2.0 percent from the 1950s to the 1970s and only 0.7 percent per year since then. Hence, the overall record on productivity growth is not as good as the record on job growth.

Unemployment During Recessions

There are fluctuations in employment just as there are fluctuations in real GDP. In fact, the timing is nearly identical. Observe in Figure 19.5 that employment declines during recessions: Firms lay off workers in recessions, and it is difficult to find a job. But when real GDP starts to grow again during recovery periods, the number of jobs starts to increase again. The decline in the number of jobs during recessions is one of the reasons that recessions create severe hardship for people.

The fluctuations in employment may appear small and insignificant in Figure 19.5, but they are not insignificant if you lose your job. Workers who lose their jobs during recessions usually become unemployed. The **unemployment rate** is the number of unemployed people as a percentage of the labor force; the labor force consists of those who are either working or looking for work. Every time the economy goes into a recession, the unemployment rate rises because people are laid off and new jobs are difficult to find. The individual stories behind the unemployment numbers frequently represent frustration and distress.

Figure 19.6 shows what happens to the unemployment rate as the economy goes through recessions and recoveries. The increase in the unemployment rate during recessions is eventually followed by a decline in unemployment during the recovery. Note, for example, how unemployment rose during the recessions of 1969–1970 and 1973–1975. Around the time of the 1990–1991 recession, the unemployment rate rose from 5.1 percent to 7.8 percent.

Figure 19.7 shows how high the unemployment rate got during the Great Depression. It rose to over 25 percent; one in four workers was out of work. Fortunately, recent increases in unemployment during recessions have been much smaller. The unemployment rate reached 10.8 percent in the early 1980s, the highest level since World War II.

unemployment rate: the percentage of the labor force that is unemployed.

FIGURE 19.6
The Unemployment Rate

The number of unemployed workers as a percentage of the labor force— the unemployment rate—increases during recessions because people are laid off and it is difficult to find work. Sometimes the unemployment rate continues to increase for a while after the recession is over, as in 1971 and 1991. But eventually unemployment declines during the economic recovery.

Source: U.S. Department of Labor.

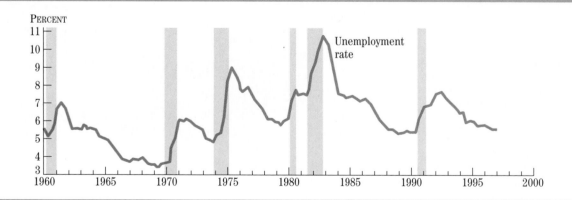

Using Economics to Explain a Recession's Pain
Around the Country

Although recessions, by definition, affect the whole economy, they have uneven effects on different regions. Some regions are hit at slightly different times and by different amounts. When the national recession is over, production and employment in certain regions of the country might still be falling.

The accompanying map shows the unemployment rate in each state of the United States in June 1992, a little over a year after the 1990–1991 recession ended. The national unemployment rate was 7.7 percent and coming down, but there was an enormous variety of unemployment experiences in different parts of the country. In California, Florida, Illinois, New York, New Jersey, Massachusetts, Michigan, Mississippi, and West Virginia, the unemployment rate was over 8.5 percent. But in several of the central and mountain states, the unemployment rate was less than 5.5 percent, below the national average in good times. Hence, while much of the country was still hurting from the recession, other parts had recovered.

The severity of the recession on California and New York may have had a significant impact on how people viewed the recession. For example, economic reporting about the recession may have depicted it as worse than it was for the economy as a whole, because many of the national media centers are in New York and California.

These regional differences also affect political strategy. When unemployment is high in a recession, people are less likely to vote for the incumbent; thus, states with very high unemployment rates might be given less attention when allocating scarce time and resources in a political campaign.

In the 1992 presidential election, which took place soon after the data shown on the map were collected, the incumbent president, George Bush, won only two of the nine states with unemployment over 8.5 percent. Bush lost in only two of the seven states with unemployment below 5.5 percent, and in both of these, Wisconsin and Iowa, he also lost in the 1988 election. Although the economy is not the only factor in elections, it seemed at least like a key factor in this case.

Why did high unemployment linger for so long in states like Massachusetts, California, and New York? One explanation helps us understand the causes of recessions. In the early 1990s, national defense expenditures were cut sharply. A large fraction of the California and Massachusetts economies produce military equipment. Hence, when national defense spending fell, employment in these regions fell sharply. There are other possible reasons. The California economy had an even stronger expansion than the rest of the national economy in the 1980s. This long expansion may have led to overbuilding, and when the expansion ended, people cut this back sharply. The construction business was particularly hard hit in this recession.

Another important example of regional differences is the Texas economy in the mid-1980s. While most of the national economy was expanding rapidly, the Texas economy went into a downturn because of a drop in the price of oil, a relatively large part of the Texas economy.

Similar regional differences exist in other countries. Unemployment has been higher in the south of Italy than in the north; and it has been higher in the north of the United Kingdom than in the south.

Unemployment rates in June 1992

- 10.0% or over
- 8.5–9.9%
- 7.0–8.4%
- 5.5–6.9%
- Under 5.5%

Source: U.S. Department of Labor.

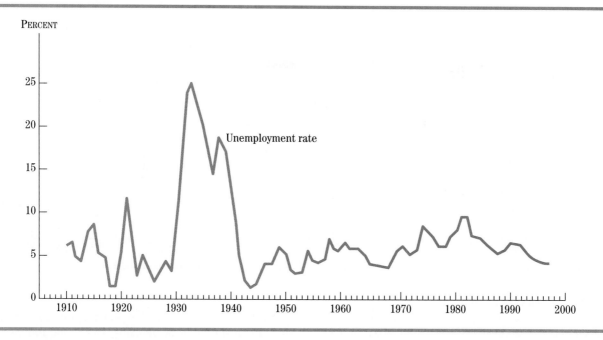

PERCENT

Unemployment rate

FIGURE 19.7
Unemployment During the Great Depression

The increase in unemployment in the United States during the Great Depression was huge compared with the increase in unemployment during more mild downturns in the economy. More than one in four workers were unemployed during the Great Depression.

Source: U.S. Department of Labor.

Inflation

As output and jobs in the economy have grown and fluctuated over time, there have also been large changes in inflation, the general increase from year to year in the average price of goods and services. When inflation rises, people start to complain about how expensive everything is getting. When inflation gets very high, it begins to interfere with the workings of the economy because people and business firms find it difficult to determine the price of goods and services and worry about how much the price will change in the future. Thus low and stable inflation is considered a plus for an economy.

How does inflation actually behave? The **inflation rate** is the percentage increase in the average price of all goods and services from one year to the next. Figure 19.8 shows the inflation rate for the same 40-year period we have focused on in our examination of real GDP and employment. Clearly, a low and stable inflation rate has not been a feature of the United States during this period. There are several useful facts to note about the behavior of inflation.

First, inflation is closely correlated with the ups and downs in real GDP and employment: Inflation increased prior to every recession in the last 40 years and then subsided during and after every recession. We will want to explore whether this close correlation between the ups and downs in inflation and the ups and downs in the economy helps explain economic fluctuations.

Second, there are longer-term trends in inflation. For example, inflation rose from a low point in the mid-1960s to a high point of double-digit inflation in 1980. This period of persistently high inflation from the mid-1960s until 1980 is called the *Great Inflation.* The Great Inflation ended in the early 1980s, when the inflation rate declined substantially. Such a decline in inflation is called *disinflation.* (When inflation is negative and the average price level falls, economists call it *deflation.*)

inflation rate: the percentage increase in the overall price level over a given period of time, usually one year.

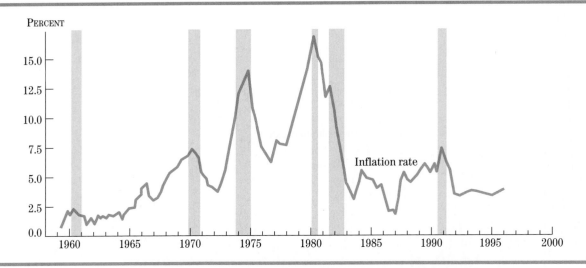

FIGURE 19.8
The Ups and Downs in Inflation
Inflation has increased before each
recession and then declined during
and immediately after each recession. In addition, a longer-term
upward trend in inflation began in
the mid-1960s and, after several ups
and downs, reached a peak in 1980.
In 1981–1983, America had a disinflation—a decline in the rate of
inflation.
Source: U.S. Department of Labor
(Consumer Price Index).

interest rate: the amount received
per dollar loaned per year, usually
expressed as a percentage (e.g., 6
percent) of the loan.

Third, judging by history, there is no reason to expect the inflation rate to be
zero, even on average. Since the disinflation of the early 1980s, the inflation rate
has remained around 3 or 4 percent in the United States.

Why does inflation increase before recessions? Why does inflation fall during
and after recessions? What caused the Great Inflation? Why is inflation not equal
to zero even in more normal times, when the economy is neither in recession nor
in boom? What can economic policy do to keep inflation low and stable? These
are some of the questions and policy issues about inflation addressed by macroeconomics.

Interest Rates

The **interest rate** is the amount that lenders charge when they lend money,
expressed as a percent of the amount loaned. For example, if you borrow $100 for a
year from a friend and the interest rate on the loan is 6 percent, then you must pay
your friend back $106 at the end of the year. The interest rate is another key eco-
nomic variable that is related to the growth and change in real GDP over time.

Different Types of Interest Rates and Their Behavior

There are many different interest rates in the economy: The *mortgage interest rate*
is the rate on loans to buy a house; the *savings deposit interest rate* is the rate people get on their savings deposits at banks; the *Treasury bill rate* is the interest rate
the government pays when it borrows money from people for a year or less; the *federal funds rate* is the interest rate banks charge each other on very short loans.
Interest rates influence people's economic behavior. When interest rates rise, for
example, it is more expensive to borrow funds to buy a house or a car, so many people postpone such purchases.

Figure 19.9 shows the behavior of a typical interest rate, the federal funds
rate, during the last 40 years. First, note how closely the ups and downs in the
interest rate are correlated with the ups and downs in the economy. Interest rates

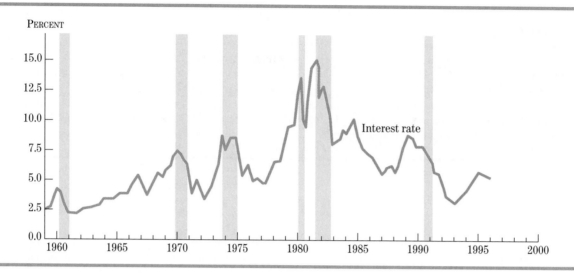

FIGURE 19.9
The Ups and Downs in Interest Rates

Interest rates generally rise just before a recession and then decline during and just after the recession. There was also a longer-term trend upward in interest rates in the 1960s and 1970s and a downward trend in the 1980s and 1990s. These longer-term trends are correlated with inflation, as shown in Figure 19.8. The interest rate shown here is the federal funds interest rate.

Source: Federal Reserve Board.

rise before each recession and then decline during and after each recession. Second, note that, like the inflation rate, there are longer-term trends in the interest rate. The interest rate rose from the mid-1960s until the 1980s. Each fluctuation in interest rates during this period brought forth a higher peak in interest rates. Then in the 1980s, the interest rate began a downward trend; each peak was lower than the previous peak. By the early 1990s, interest rates had returned to the levels of the 1960s.

The Concept of the Real Interest Rate

As we will see, the trends and fluctuations in interest rates are intimately connected with the trends and fluctuations in inflation and real GDP. In fact, the longer-term rise in interest rates in the 1960s and 1970s was partly due to the rise in the rate of inflation. When inflation rises, people who lend money will be paid back in funds that are worth less because the average price of goods rises more quickly. To compensate for this decline in the value of funds, lenders require a higher interest rate. For example, if the inflation rate is 20 percent and you lend someone $100 for a year at 6 percent, then you get back $106 at the end of the year. However, the *average* price of goods you can buy with your $106 is now 20 percent higher. Thus, your 6 percent gain in interest has been offset by a 20 percent loss. It is as if you receive *negative* 14 percent interest: 6 percent interest less 20 percent inflation. The difference between the stated interest rate and the inflation rate is thus a better measure of the real interest rate. Economists define the **real interest rate** as the interest rate less the inflation rate people expect. The term **nominal interest rate** is sometimes used to refer to the interest rate on a loan, making no adjustment for inflation. For example, the real interest rate is 2 percent if the nominal interest rate is 5 percent and inflation is expected to be 3 percent (5 − 3 = 2). To keep the real interest rate from changing by a large amount as inflation rises, the nominal interest rate has to increase with inflation. Thus, the concept of the real interest rate helps us understand why inflation and interest rates have moved together. We will make much more use of the real interest rate in later chapters.

real interest rate: the interest rate minus the expected rate of inflation; it adjusts the nominal interest rate for inflation.

nominal interest rate: the interest rate uncorrected for inflation.

MACROECONOMIC THEORY AND POLICY

Because strong economic growth raises living standards of people in an economy, and because increases in unemployment during recessions cause hardship, two goals of economic policy are to raise long-term growth and to reduce the size of short-term economic fluctuations. However, the facts—summarized above—about economic growth and fluctuations do not give economists a basis for making recommendations about economic policy. Before one can be confident about recommending a policy, one needs a coherent theory to explain the facts.

Economic Growth Theory and Economic Fluctuation Theory

Macroeconomic theory is divided into two branches. *Economic growth theory* aims to explain the long-term upward rise of real GDP over time. Why does real GDP grow? Why does its growth slow down for long periods of time as it did in the mid-1970s? Will the long-term growth rate of real GDP pick up again? *Economic fluctuations theory* tries to explain the shorter-term fluctuations in real GDP. Economic growth theory and economic fluctuations theory combine to form *macroeconomic theory,* which explains why the economy both grows and fluctuates over time.

Aggregate Supply and Long-Term Economic Growth

Economic growth theory starts by distinguishing the longer-term economic growth trend from the shorter-term fluctuations in the economy. This is not as easy as it may seem because the longer-term growth trend itself may change, as we have already seen from the long-term growth trend drawn in Figure 19.1. The trend line slows down in the mid-1970s. The growth trend could slow further or speed up in the future.

potential GDP: the economy's long-term growth trend for real GDP determined by the available supply of capital, labor, and technology. Real GDP fluctuates above and below potential GDP.

It will be useful to give a name to the upward trend line in real GDP shown in Figure 19.1. We will call it **potential GDP.** Potential GDP represents the long-run tendency of the economy to grow. Real GDP fluctuates around potential GDP. No one knows exactly where potential GDP lies and exactly what its growth rate is, but any trend line that has the same long-term increase as real GDP and intersects real GDP in several places is probably a good estimate.

Note that potential GDP as defined here and as used by most macroeconomists is not the maximum amount of real GDP. As Figure 19.1 shows, sometimes real GDP goes above potential GDP. Thus, potential GDP is more like the average or normal level of real GDP.

Economic growth theory postulates that the potential GDP of an economy is given by its **aggregate supply.** *Aggregate* means total. Aggregate supply is all goods and services produced by all the firms in the economy using the available labor, capital, and technology. **Labor** is the total number of hours workers are available to work in producing real GDP. **Capital** is the total number of factories, cultivated plots of land, machines, computers, and other tools available for the workers to use to produce real GDP. **Technology** is all the available know-how—from organizational schemes to improved telecommunications to better computer programming skills—that workers and firms can use when they produce real GDP. Labor, capital, and technology jointly determine aggregate supply.

The Production Function

We can summarize the relationship between the three determinants and the aggregate supply of real GDP as:

Real GDP = F (labor, capital, technology)

which we say in words as "real GDP is a function, F, of labor, capital, and technology." The function F means that there is some general relationship between these variables. For this relationship, we assume that higher capital, higher labor, and higher technology all mean higher real GDP; and lower capital, lower labor, and lower technology all mean less real GDP. We call this relationship the **production function** because it tells us how much production (real GDP) of goods and services can be obtained from a certain amount of labor, capital, and technological inputs. A higher long-term economic growth rate for the economy requires a higher growth rate for one or more of these three determinants. A lower long-term economic growth rate may be due to a slower growth rate for one or more of these three determinants.

The production function applies to the entire economy, but we also have production functions for individual firms in the economy. For example, consider the production of cars. The car factory and the machines in the factory are the capital. The workers who work in the factory are the labor. The assembly-line production method is the technology. The cars coming out of the factory are the output. The production function for the economy as a whole has real GDP as output, not just cars, and all available labor, capital, and technology as inputs, not just those producing cars.

aggregate supply: the total value of all goods and services produced in the economy by the available supply of capital, labor, and technology (also called potential GDP).

labor: the number of hours people work in producing goods and services.

capital: the factories, improvements to cultivated land, machinery, and other tools, equipment, and structures used to produce goods and services.

technology: anything that raises the amount of output that can be produced with a given amount of labor and capital.

production function: the relationship that describes output as a function of labor, capital, and technology.

Aggregate Supply and the Production Function

The theory of economic growth is based on the production function, which is a model of how labor (L), capital (K), and technology (T) jointly determine the aggregate supply of output in the economy. Here the workers at the automobile plant are part of the economy's labor (left), the tools that the workers are using to assemble the cars are the economy's capital (middle), and computer programming skills are part of the economy's technology (right), which raises the value of output for a given amount of labor and capital.

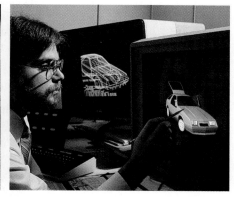

"That, in itself, is a breakthrough."

The production function can be written more compactly by introducing some symbols:

$$Y = F(L, K, T)$$

where the symbol Y means real GDP, the symbol L means labor, the symbol K means capital, and the symbol T means technology. This function tells us that an economy can increase its potential GDP by increasing labor (L), capital (K), and technology (T).

As we develop the theory of economic growth, we will consider each of these three determinants. But we can illustrate the use of the production function for explaining economic growth with what we have so far. For example, we noted earlier that the growth rate of real GDP slowed down in the 1970s. We now know that the slowdown must have been due to a slowdown of the growth of labor, capital, or technology. By the end of Chapter 23, we will be able to show that a large part, though not all, of the slowdown was due to technology.

Government Policy for Long-Term Economic Growth

Most governments have been interested in finding ways to increase economic growth. Economic policies that aim to increase long-term economic growth are sometimes called *supply side policies* because they concentrate on increasing the growth of potential GDP, which is the aggregate supply of the economy.

Fiscal Policy

Our preview of growth theory already tells us where policies to increase growth should focus: on increasing the available supply of labor, capital, and technology. The growth rate of capital depends on how much businesses invest in new capital each year. The amount that businesses choose to invest depends in part on the incentives they have to invest. We will see that the incentive to invest depends on the amount of taxing, spending, and borrowing by government. Hence, government policy can affect the incentive to invest and thereby stimulate long-term economic growth. Government policy concerning taxing, spending, and borrowing is called *fiscal policy.*

Labor supply also depends on incentives. In the case of labor, it is the incentive for firms to hire workers or for people to work harder or longer, or for workers who are not in the labor force to come into the labor force, or for people to retire later in life. Again, government policy toward taxing, spending, and borrowing affects these incentives.

Finally, technology growth can also be affected by government policy if the government gives incentives for researchers to invent new technologies or provides funds for education so workers can improve their skills and know-how.

Monetary Policy

Keeping inflation low and stable is another part of government policy to stimulate long-term economic growth. We will see that the government has an important role to play in determining the inflation rate, especially over the long term, because the inflation rate in the long term depends on the growth rate of the money supply, which can be controlled by the government. Government policy concerning the money supply and the control of inflation is called *monetary policy.* The institution of government assigned to conduct monetary policy is the central bank. In the United States the central bank is the Federal Reserve System.

Why should low and stable inflation be part of an economic growth policy? An examination of inflation and economic growth in a number of countries indicates that inflation is negatively correlated with long-term economic growth. The reason for this negative correlation over the long term may be that inflation raises uncertainty and thereby reduces incentives to invest in capital or improve technology. The theory of economic growth tells us that lower capital growth and lower technological growth reduce economic growth.

Economic Fluctuations Theory and Policy

Our review of the performance of the economy showed some of the hardships that come from economic fluctuations, especially the recessions and unemployment. Can government economic policy improve economic performance by reducing the size of the fluctuations? To answer these questions, we need a theory to interpret the facts of economic fluctuations.

The theory of economic fluctuations builds on the works of many economists—including John Maynard Keynes's 1936 book *The General Theory of Employment, Interest and Money;* Milton Friedman and Anna Schwartz's 1963 book *A Monetary History of the United States;* and a 1981 book, *Rational Expectations and Econometric Practice,* edited by Robert Lucas and Thomas Sargent.

Aggregate Demand and Economic Fluctuations

The theory of economic fluctuations emphasizes fluctuations in the demand for goods and services as the reason for the ups and downs in the economy. Because the focus is on the sum of the demand for all goods and services in the economy—not only the demand for peanuts or bicycles—we use the term *aggregate demand*. More precisely, **aggregate demand** is the sum of demands from the four groups that contribute to demand in the whole economy: consumers, business firms, government, and foreigners. Originally, due to the influence of Keynes, the theory placed great emphasis on fluctuations in aggregate demand brought about by changes in demand by business firms. But Friedman and Schwartz argued that other parts of the economy, especially government, play a crucial role through adjustments in the money supply.

According to this theory, the declines in real GDP below potential GDP during recessions are caused by declines in aggregate demand, and the increases in real GDP above potential GDP are caused by increases in aggregate demand. For example, the decrease in real GDP in the 1990–1991 recession may have been due to a decline in government demand. In fact, government military spending did decline sharply. Or the recession may have been due to a decline in demand by consumers as they learned about Iraq's invasion of Kuwait in August 1990, saw oil and gasoline prices rise, and worried about the threat of war.

Thus, a key assumption of the theory of economic fluctuations is that real GDP fluctuates around potential GDP. Why is this a good assumption? How do we know that the fluctuations in the economy are not due solely to fluctuations in potential GDP, that is, the economy's aggregate supply? The rationale for the assumption is that most of the determinants of potential GDP usually change rather smoothly. Clearly, population grows relatively smoothly. We do not have a sudden drop in the U.S. population every few years, nor is there a huge migration of people from the

aggregate demand: the total demand for goods and services by consumers, businesses, government, and foreigners.

United States during recessions. The same is true with factories and equipment in the economy. Unless there is a major war at home, we do not suddenly lose equipment or factories in the economy on a massive scale. Even the 1992 hurricane in Florida, the 1994 earthquake in California, or the 1997 flood in North Dakota, although devastating for those hit, took only a tiny fraction out of the potential GDP of the entire U.S. economy. Finally, technological know-how does not suddenly decline; we do not suddenly forget how to produce things. The steady upward movement of potential GDP thus represents gradual accumulations—growth of population, growth of capital, and growth of technology. However, although many economists place more emphasis on the role of aggregate demand in short-run economic fluctuations than on fluctuations in potential GDP, it is too extreme to insist that there are absolutely no fluctuations in potential GDP.

Macroeconomic Policy for Economic Fluctuations

Macroeconomic policy has huge effects on economic fluctuations. In particular, fiscal and monetary policy can influence the size of the ups and downs in the economy just as they can influence economic growth. For example, an increase in government spending in a recession might increase aggregate demand and mitigate other forces that reduce aggregate demand. When we look at fiscal and monetary policy, we address such questions as: Is there something the government can do to improve the performance of the economy to prevent recessions from occurring? Can monetary policy prevent another Great Depression and perhaps even reduce the likelihood of all recessions? How can we avoid in the future another bout of high inflation like the Great Inflation?

Review

▶ Economic growth theory concentrates on explaining the longer-term upward path of the economy.

▶ Economic growth depends on three factors: the growth of capital, labor, and technology.

▶ Government policy can influence long-term economic growth by affecting these three factors. To raise long-term economic growth, government fiscal policies can provide incentives for investment in capital, for research and development of new technologies, for education, and for increased labor

supply. A monetary policy of low and stable inflation can also have a positive effect on economic growth.

▶ Economic fluctuations theory assumes that fluctuations in GDP are due to fluctuations in aggregate demand.

▶ Monetary policy and fiscal policy can reduce the fluctuations in real GDP. Finding good rules for such policies is a major task of macroeconomics.

CONCLUSION

This chapter started with a brief history of economic growth and fluctuations in the United States. Although this history mentioned specific individuals (presidents, economists, journalists), institutions (the government, the Federal Reserve System), and episodes (the Great Depression and the Great Inflation), the most important facts to remember are the patterns formed by the major economic variables. The key facts, therefore, are that economic growth provides impressive gains in the well-being of

---

MACROECONOMIC FACTS

Long-Term Economic Growth

1. Real GDP per capita growth has been spectacular over the last 75 years.
2. The number of jobs rose dramatically too.
3. Real GDP per capita growth slowed in the 1970s.
4. Productivity growth also slowed in the 1970s.
5. Inflation is negatively correlated with economic growth in many countries.

Short-Term Economic Fluctuations

1. There have been 15 business cycles in 75 years, averaging 1 every 5 years.
2. Unemployment rose in every recession.
3. Inflation rose before recessions and fell during and after recessions.
4. Interest rates rose before recessions and fell during and after recessions.
5. The Great Depression was much worse than recent recessions.

↓

MACROECONOMIC THEORY

1. Long-term economic growth is due primarily to increases in aggregate supply.
   - Aggregate supply depends on the availability of labor, capital, and technology, whose relationship to one another is expressed by the production function.
   - Potential GDP gradually increases over time.

2. Short-term economic fluctuations are due primarily to fluctuations in aggregate demand.
   - Real GDP fluctuates around potential GDP.
   - Fluctuations in potential GDP play a smaller role.

↓

MACROECONOMIC POLICY

To Increase Long-Term Growth

1. Fiscal policy should provide incentives to invest in capital, technology, and labor.
2. Monetary policy should keep inflation low and stable.

To Reduce Short-Term Fluctuations

1. Fiscal and monetary policy should do no harm.
2. These policies should try to mitigate changes in aggregate demand.

---

individuals over the long term, that economic growth slowed down in the 1970s, that economic growth is temporarily interrupted by recessions, which have grown smaller in magnitude since the 1930s, that employment falls and unemployment rises in recessions, that all recessions end, that inflation rises before recessions and declines during and after recessions, and that interest rates also rise before recessions and then fall. These are the facts on which macroeconomic theory is based and about which macroeconomic policy is concerned. Remembering these facts not only helps you understand theory and make judgments about government policy, it prevents you from being fooled by people who try to distort economic history. Do not believe someone who tells you in the middle of the next recession—whenever it occurs—that it is the worst since the Great Depression—unless of course it is!

The connection between the facts, the theory, and the policy is shown schematically in Figure 19.10. After showing how we obtain the facts in the next chapter, we then go on to look at explanations for economic growth and economic fluctuations and proposals for macroeconomic policies.

FIGURE 19.10

Macroeconomic Facts, Theory, and Policy

This diagram summarizes some of the key ideas of macroeconomics that will be explored in later chapters. Looking through the diagram may help you see the forest of macroeconomics through the trees of facts and theory.

KEY POINTS

1. Macroeconomics is concerned with economic growth and fluctuations in the whole economy.

2. The U.S. economy and many other economies have grown dramatically over the last 40 years. Long-term growth has slowed among the most advanced countries in the last 20 years.

3. Economists agree that economic growth occurs because of increases in labor, capital, and technological know-how.

4. Economic policies that provide incentives to increase capital and resources devoted to improving technology can raise productivity growth.

5. Economic fluctuations consist of recessions—when real GDP falls and unemployment increases—followed by recoveries—when real GDP rises rapidly and unemployment falls.

6. Recent recessions have been much less severe than the Great Depression of the 1930s, when real GDP fell by over 30 percent.

7. The unemployment rate is well above zero even when the economy is booming.

8. The most popular theory of economic fluctuations is that they occur because of fluctuations in aggregate demand.

9. Macroeconomic policies include monetary and fiscal policies that are aimed at keeping business cycles small and inflation low.

10. Economic growth theory and economic fluctuations theory combine to form macroeconomic theory, which explains why the economy grows and fluctuates over time.

KEY TERMS

real gross domestic product (real GDP)	expansion	potential GDP
economic growth	recovery	aggregate supply
economic fluctuations	labor productivity	labor
business cycles	unemployment rate	capital
recession	inflation rate	technology
peak	interest rate	production function
trough	real interest rate	aggregate demand
	nominal interest rate	

QUESTIONS FOR REVIEW

1. By how much did real GDP grow in the last 40 years?

2. What is the economic growth slowdown, and when did .it occur?

3. Why do bad economic times continue after recessions end?

4. Why does unemployment rise in recessions?

5. How many recessions have there been since the Great Depression?

6. How do the 1981–1982 and the 1990–1991 recessions compare?

7. What happens to inflation and interest rates immediately before, during, and after a recession?

8. What are the two broad branches of macroeconomic theory?

9. What are the three determinants of economic growth?

10. What is potential GDP?

11. What is aggregate demand?

12. What is the difference between monetary policy and fiscal policy?

PROBLEMS

1. The chart at the top of the next page shows a business cycle that occurred in the United States in the early 1950s. The early 1950s were similar to the early 1990s in the sense that America was adjusting to the end of a war—World War II rather than the cold war, and to the return of a political party to the White House after a long absence—from Democrat to Republican rather than from Republican to Democrat. The economy expanded at a 2.5 percent growth rate in late 1951 and 1952, which appears to have been near the economy's potential growth rate. Draw in potential GDP and show the peak, recession, trough, and recovery phases of this business cycle. Compare this business cycle with the cycle in the early 1990s shown in Figure 19.3.

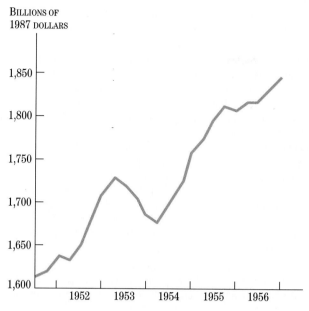

BILLIONS OF
1987 DOLLARS

Source: U.S. Department of Commerce.

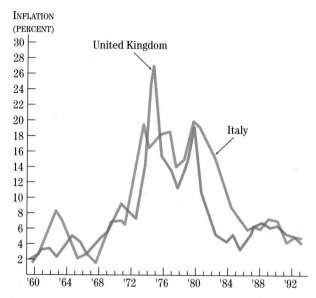

INFLATION
(PERCENT)

Source: Organization for Economic Cooperation and Development.

2. Suppose the U.S. economy is currently at the trough of a business cycle. What is the relationship between real and potential GDP? Is it likely that real GDP will stay in this relative position for a long period of time (say, 10 years)? Explain briefly.

3. List several economic topics from this week's newspapers that are examples of macroeconomic issues. Which of the issues are related to economic growth, and which are related to economic fluctuations? Which are related to economic policy?

4. The following charts show the inflation rate for the four largest countries in Europe. Compare inflation in these countries with that in the United States as discussed in the chapter. Is a Great Inflation observable in the other countries? Which countries had the best inflation performances, and which had the worst? In which country would you expect interest rates to be lowest in 1976?

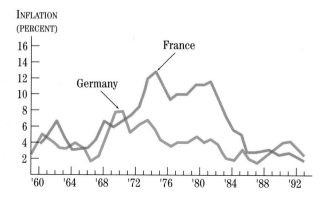

INFLATION
(PERCENT)

5. Using the following data from Great Britain, plot real GDP on the vertical axis and the year on the horizontal axis. Can you differentiate economic growth from economic fluctuations?

Year	Real GDP (billions of pounds)	Rate of Unemployment (percent)
1977	312	5.2
1978	324	4.9
1979	331	4.5
1980	324	6.1
1981	321	9.1
1982	325	10.4
1983	338	11.2
1984	343	11.4
1985	356	11.6
1986	370	11.8
1987	387	10.4
1988	404	8.2
1989	413	6.2
1990	417	5.9
1991	408	8.3
1992	404	10.1
1993	413	10.3
1994	429	9.3
1995	442	8.3
1996	455	8.1

a) Draw a line that shows the trend of potential GDP. Identify the years of the peaks, troughs, recessions, and expansions.

b) How does the timing of these business cycles compare with the U.S. business cycle shown in Figure 19.1?

c) Calculate the growth rate from 1989 to 1990 and from 1990 to 1991.

d) Calculate the average annual growth rate from 1977 to 1986 and from 1987 to 1996. (*Hint:* See the formula in the appendix to this chapter.) In which period was economic growth larger?

e) What relationship do you see between unemployment and real GDP?

6. Compare Figure 19.1 showing real GDP with Figure 19.5 showing employment for the same period in the United States. Describe how real GDP and employment are correlated over the long term and over the short term. Do employment and real GDP rise or fall over the long term? Explain why. Do they rise or fall during recessions? Try to explain why.

7. Suppose the annual rate of growth of real GDP per capita is 2 percent. How much will real GDP increase over a 10-year period? How much over a 50-year period? Answer the same questions for a growth rate of 1 percent. (*Hint:* See the formula in the appendix to this chapter.)

8. The shaded block in the following table shows the amount of output that can be produced using different combinations of capital and labor in a hypothetical economy with a particular technology. For example, 226 units of output are produced when 200 workers use 300 units of capital. The table is a numerical example of the production function described in the chapter. Hold capital constant at 300 while you increase labor. What happens to output? Now hold labor constant at 200 workers and raise the level of capital. What happens to output? Finally, what happens if you increase both capital and labor by the same amount?

9. Suppose there is a permanent decrease in the labor force. How does this affect the economy's potential GDP?

10. Suppose you had savings deposited in an account at an interest rate of 5 percent and your father tells you that he earned 10 percent interest 20 years ago. Which of you was getting the better return? Is that all the information you need? Suppose that the inflation rate in the United States was 12 percent 20 years ago and it is 3 percent now. Does this information change your answer? Be sure to use the concept of the real interest rate in your answer.

11. Suppose you have $1,000, which you can put in two different types of accounts at a bank. One account pays interest of 7 percent per year; the other pays interest at 1 percent per year plus the rate of inflation. Calculate the real return you will receive after 1 year if the inflation rate is 4 percent. Which account will you choose if you expect the rate of inflation to be 9 percent? Why?

12. Suppose people start retiring at a later age because of improved medical technology. How does this affect the economy's potential GDP? Why might the government want to encourage later retirement?

13. What factors can cause fluctuations in aggregate demand? Are these the same as the determinants of potential GDP? Why do economists think that changes in aggregate demand are the primary cause of short-term economic fluctuations?

14. What determines potential GDP? What factors could cause the growth rate of potential GDP to slow down? What economic policies can the government use to affect potential GDP?

15. What is the difference between increasing labor productivity and increasing real GDP? Why do governments want to pursue policies that improve labor productivity?

		Labor				
		100	200	300	400	500
	100	100	162	216	264	309
Capital	200	123	200	266	325	380
	300	139	226	300	367	429
	400	152	246	327	400	468
	500	162	263	350	428	500

The Miracle of Compound Growth

Compound growth explains why small differences in the annual economic growth rate make such huge differences to real GDP over time. This appendix explains this compounding effect and provides some simple formulas for computing growth rates with a hand calculator.

Compound growth works just like compound interest on a savings account. Compound interest is defined as the "interest on the interest" you earn in earlier periods. For example, suppose you have a savings account in a bank that pays 6 percent per year in interest. That is, if you put $100 in the account, then after one year you will get $100 times .06, or $6 in interest. If you leave the original $100 plus the $6—that is, $106—in the bank for a second year, then at the end of the second year you will get $106 times .06, or $6.36 in interest. The $.36 is the "interest on the interest," that is, $6 times .06.

At the end of the second year you have $100 + $6 + $6.36 = $112.36. If you leave that in the bank for a third year, you will get $6.74 in interest, of which $.74 is "interest on the interest" earned in the first two years. Note how the "interest on the interest" rises from $.36 in the second year to $.74 in the third year. Following the same calculations, the interest on the interest in the fourth year would be $1.15. After 13 years, "interest on the interest" is greater than the $6 interest on the original $100! As a result of this compound interest, the size of your account grows rapidly. At the end of 20 years it is $320.71; after 40 years your $100 has grown to $1,028.57.

This same idea applies to the growth of an economy. Suppose that real GDP is $100 billion, about the level of Taiwan's, and that the growth rate is 6 percent per year, about the Taiwan average in recent years. After one year, real GDP would increase $100 billion times .06, or by $6 billion. Real GDP rises from $100 billion to $106 billion. In the second year, real GDP increases $106 billion times .06, or by $6.36 billion. Real GDP rises from $106 billion to $112.36 billion. Continuing this way, here is how real GDP grows, rounding to the nearest $.1 billion:

	Real GDP (billions)		Real GDP (billions)
year 0	$ 100.0	year 20	$ 320.7
year 1	$ 106.0	year 30	$ 574.3
year 2	$ 112.4	year 40	$1,028.6
year 3	$ 119.1	year 50	$1,842.0
year 4	$ 126.2	year 60	$3,298.8
year 5	$ 133.3	year 70	$5,907.6
year 10	$ 179.1		

Thus, in less than the average life span, real GDP in Taiwan would increase by about 60 times and approach the current level of the United States.

There is a simple formula for computing these changes, which comes from multiplying 1.06 by the initial level year after year. For example, the level of real GDP after one year is $100 billion times .06 plus $100 billion, or $100 billion times 1.06; after two years, it is $106 billion times 1.06, or $100 billion times $(1.06)^2$. Thus, for n years the formula is

(Initial level) times $(1.06)^n$ = level at end of n years

where the initial level could be $100 in a bank, the $100 billion level of real GDP, or anything else. For example, real GDP at the end of 70 years in the table shown earlier is: $100 billion times $(1.06)^n$ = $100 billion times 59.076 = $5,907.6 billion, with $n = 70$. Here the growth rate (or the interest rate) is 6 percent. In general, the formula is:

(Initial level) times $(1 + g)^n$ = level at end of n years

where g is the annual growth rate, stated as a fraction: that is, 6 percent is .06. If you have a hand calculator with a key that does y^x, it is fairly easy to make these calculations, and if you try it you will see the power of compound growth.

When economists refer to average annual growth over time they include this compounding effect. The growth rate is computed by inverting the formula. That is, the growth rate, stated as a fraction, between some initial level and a level n years later is given by:

$$g = \left(\frac{\text{level at end of } n \text{ years}}{\text{initial level}}\right)^{1/n} - 1$$

For example, the growth rate from year 0 to year 20 in the table is:

$$g = \left(\frac{320.7}{100}\right)^{1/20} - 1$$
$$= (1.06) - 1$$
$$= .06$$

or 6 percent. Again, if your calculator has a key for y^x, you can make these calculations fairly easily. For a one-year growth rate, you simply need to divide the second year by the first and subtract 1 to get the growth rate. Problem 5 in Chapter 19 gives some exercises in computing growth rates.

You can use this formula to find how long it takes something to rise by a certain percentage. For example, to calculate how many years it takes something that grows at rate g to double, you solve $(1 + g)^n = 2$ for n. The answer is approximately $n = .72/g$. In other words, if you take 72 and divide it by the growth rate in percent, you get the number of years it takes to double the amount. This is called the *rule of 72*. If your bank account pays 7.2 percent interest, it doubles in 10 years.

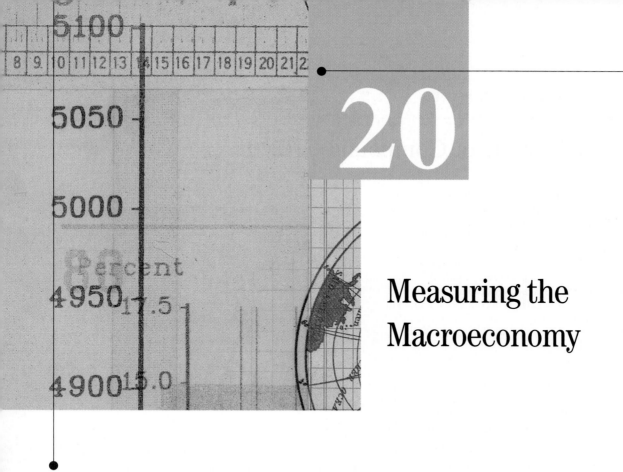

20

Measuring the Macroeconomy

Whether they measure the performance of a quarterback, the weather patterns over the past 100,000 years, the severity of an earthquake, or the balance in your bank account, statistics are seldom interesting in their own right. Their value lies in the information we derive from them. Economic statistics contain valuable information about how the economy works. Every Monday the *Wall Street Journal* and other papers publish a list of the dates on which key statistics will be released during the week; when they are released, the data are headlines in many newspapers, frequently on the first page. In fact, if we use headlines as a gauge, economic statistics are as newsworthy as sports, politics, or weather statistics.

For those who run private business firms or government agencies, measuring the economy accurately is essential. Faulty economic statistics can lead to bad decisions. For example, many economists argue that overestimates of inflation cause the government to spend much more than it otherwise would. Bond and stock traders in New York, Tokyo, London, and everywhere else, glue their eyes to their computer terminals when a new government statistic measuring the course of the economy is about to be released. By buying or selling quickly in

reaction to the new information, they can make millions or avoid losing millions. Economists in the government likewise await economic statistics eagerly; the data will determine what fiscal and monetary policy actions they should recommend. In fact, top officials at the White House (including the president) find the data so important that they make sure they get them the night before they are released to the public.

To economists, economic measurement is interesting in its own right, involving clever solutions to intriguing problems. One of the first Nobel Prizes in economics was given to Simon Kuznets for solving some of these measurement problems. Economics students cannot help but learn a little about how the economy works when they study how to measure it, just like geology students cannot help but learn a little about earthquakes when they study how the Richter scale measures them.

In this chapter we examine how economists measure a country's production and the income that is generated from this production. We stated in the previous chapter that real gross domestic product (real GDP) is the most comprehensive measure we have of a country's production. But before measuring *real* GDP, we must show how to measure GDP itself. In the process of describing the measurement of GDP, we will observe several key relationships and interpret what these relationships mean.

MEASURING GDP

To use GDP as a measure of production, we need to be precise about *what* is included in production, *where* production takes place, and *when* production takes place.

A Precise Definition of GDP

GDP is a measure of the value of all the final goods and services newly produced in a country during some period of time. Let us dissect this definition to determine what is in GDP and what is not, as well as where and when GDP is produced.

▶ *What?* Only *newly produced* goods and services are included. That 10-year-old baby carriage sold in a garage sale is not in this year's GDP; it was included in GDP 10 years ago, when it was produced. Both *goods*—such as automobiles and new houses—as well as *services*—such as bus rides or a college education—are included in GDP.

▶ *Where?* Only goods and services produced *within the borders* of a country are included in GDP. Goods produced by Americans working in another country are not part of U.S. GDP; they are part of the other country's GDP. Goods and services produced by foreigners working in the United States are part of U.S. GDP. There is another measure, gross national product (GNP), which is like GDP except that it includes goods produced by Americans working abroad and excludes goods produced in America by foreigners.

▶ *When?* Only goods and services produced *during some specified period* of time are included in GDP. We always need to specify the period during which we are measuring GDP. For example, U.S. GDP in 1998 is the production during 1998. Production during a year is 365 times larger than production for a typical day.

Rounded off to the nearest billion, GDP, or total production, was $7,576 billion in the United States in 1996. Rounded off to the nearest trillion, GDP was $8 trillion. That is an average production of about $21 billion worth of goods and services a day for each of the 365 days during the year. GDP grew by about 5 percent from 1995 to 1996.

Prices Determine the Importance of Goods and Services in GDP

GDP is a single number, but it measures the production of many different things, from apples to oranges, from car insurance to life insurance, from audio CDs to cassette tapes. How can we add up such different products? Is a CD more important than a tape? Each good is given a weight when we compute GDP and that weight is its *price*. If the price of a CD is greater than the price of a tape, then the CD will count more in GDP.

To see this, imagine that production consists entirely of CDs and tapes. If a CD costs $15 and a tape costs $5, then producing three CDs will add $45 to GDP while

TABLE 20.1
Adding Up Unlike Products: Audio CDs and Cassette Tapes

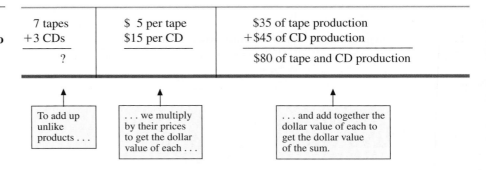

producing seven tapes will add $35 to GDP. Thus, producing three CDs plus seven tapes adds $80 to GDP, as shown in Table 20.1.

Although this method of weighting by price might not appeal to you personally—you might like tapes more than CDs—it is hard to imagine anything more workable. In a market system, prices tend to reflect the cost and value of the goods and services produced. One of the great problems of measuring GDP in the former centrally planned economies such as the Soviet Union was that the price of goods was set by the government; thus, each item was given a weight that may have had little to do with its cost or value to individuals. Without market prices, measuring GDP in the former Soviet Union was difficult.

Intermediate Goods Are Part of Final Goods

When measuring GDP, it is important not to count the same item more than once. This can occur if you are not careful. Consider bicycle tires. When you buy a $150 bicycle, the tires are considered part of the bicycle. Suppose the tires are worth $20. Then it would be a mistake to count the $20 value of the tires and the $150 value of the bicycle for a total value of $170. That would count the tires twice, which is called double counting. When a tire is part of a new bicycle, it is an example of an **intermediate good.** Intermediate goods are part of **final goods,** which by definition are goods that undergo no further processing. In this case, the final good is the bicycle. To avoid double counting, we never count intermediate goods; only final goods are part of GDP. If in a few years you bought a new $25 bicycle tire for your bicycle, then the tire would be a final good.

intermediate good: a good that undergoes further processing before it is sold to consumers.

final good: a new good that undergoes no further processing before it is sold to consumers.

Three Ways to Measure GDP

Economists have three different ways to measure GDP. All give the same answer, but they refer to conceptually different activities in the economy and provide different ways to think about GDP. All three are important in the development of macroeconomic theory and are reported in the **national income and product accounts,** the official U.S. government tabulation of GDP put together by economists and statisticians at the U.S. Department of Commerce.

The first way measures the total amount that people *spend* on goods and services made in America. This is the *spending* approach. The second way measures the total *income* that is earned by all the workers and businesses that produce American goods and services. This is the *income* approach. By this measure, your income is a measure of what you produce. The third way measures the total of all the goods and services as they are *produced,* or as they are shipped out of the fac-

national income and product accounts: official government tabulation of the components of GDP and aggregate income.

tory. This is the *production* approach. Note that each of the measures considers the whole economy, and thus, we frequently refer to them as aggregate spending, aggregate income, or aggregate production, where the word *aggregate* means total. Let us consider each of the three approaches in turn.

The Spending Approach

Typically, total spending in the economy is divided into four categories: *consumption, investment, government purchases,* and *net exports,* which equal exports minus imports. Each of the four categories corresponds closely to one of four groups into which the economy is divided: consumers, businesses, governments, and foreigners. Before considering each category and group, look at Table 20.2, which shows how the $7,576 billion of GDP in the United States in 1996 divided into the four categories.

Consumption

The first category—**consumption**—includes purchases of final goods and services by individuals. Government statisticians who collect the data in most countries survey department stores, discount stores, car dealers, and other sellers to see how much consumers purchase each year ($5,152 billion in 1996, as given in Table 20.2). They count consumption as anything purchased by consumers. Consumption does not include spending by business and government. Consumer purchases may be big-ticket items such as a new convertible, an operation to remove a cancerous tumor, a new stereo, a weekend vacation, or college tuition, as well as smaller-ticket items such as an oil change, a medical checkup, a rose for a friend, a bus ride, or a driver's education class.

Consumption is a whopping 68 percent of GDP in the United States (See Figure 20.1). By comparison, consumption is 58 percent of GDP in Japan and 55 percent of GDP in Germany. Many consider the high consumption rate of Americans to be a serious economic problem because it represents less saving for the future than in other countries.

Investment

The second item—**investment**—consists of purchases of final goods by business firms. When a business such as a pizza delivery firm buys a new car, economists consider that purchase as part of investment rather than consumption. The firm uses the car to make deliveries, which contributes to its production of delivered pizzas. Included in investment are all the new machines, new factories, and other tools that businesses use to produce goods and services. Purchases of intermediate goods that go directly into a manufactured product—such as the tire that is part of a bicycle—

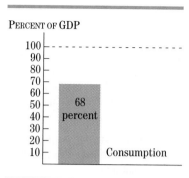

FIGURE 20.1
Consumption as a Share of GDP
Consumption is 68 percent of GDP in the United States.

consumption: purchases of final goods and services by individuals.

investment: purchases of final goods by firms plus purchases of newly produced residences by households.

Gross Domestic Product (GDP)	$7,576
Consumption	5,152
Investment	1,116
Government purchases	1,407
Net exports	−99

Source: U.S. Department of Commerce.

TABLE 20.2
Four Categories of Spending in 1996
(billions of dollars)

business fixed investment:
investment by firms in physical capital, such as factories and equipment.

inventory investment: a change in the stock of inventories from one date to another.

are not counted as investment. These items are part of the finished product—the bicycle, in this case—purchased by consumers. We do not want to count such items twice.

The new machines, factories, and other tools that are part of investment in any year are sometimes called **business fixed investment,** which amounted to $791 billion in 1996. There are two other items that government statisticians include as part of investment: inventory investment and residential investment.

Inventory investment is defined as the change in *inventories,* which are the goods on store shelves, on showroom floors, or in warehouses that have not yet been sold or assembled into a final form for sale. For example, cars on the lot of a car dealer are part of inventories. When inventory investment is positive, then inventories are rising. When inventory investment is negative, then inventories are falling. For example, if a car dealer has an inventory of 20 cars on September 30, gets 15 new cars shipped from the factory during the month of October, and sells no cars during the month, then the dealer's inventory will be 35 cars on October 31. Inventory investment is positive 15 cars, and inventory rises from 20 cars to 35 cars. If 22 cars are then sold during the month of November and there are no shipments from the factory, then the dealer's inventory will be 13 cars on November 30. Inventory investment is negative 22 cars, and inventory decreases from 35 cars to 13 cars.

Why is inventory investment included as a spending item when we compute GDP? The reason is that we want a measure of production. Consider the car example again. Car production rises by one car when a complete Jeep rolls out of the factory. But the Jeep is not usually instantaneously purchased by a consumer. First, the Jeep is shipped to the Jeep dealer, where it is put on the lot. If the government statisticians look at what consumers purchase, they will not count the Jeep because it has not been purchased yet. But if inventory investment is counted as part of investment spending, then the Jeep will get counted. That is why we include inventory investment in spending.

What happens when a consumer purchases the Jeep? Consumption will rise because the purchases of Jeeps have risen and the car dealer's inventory goes down by one car. Thus, inventory investment is negative one car. Adding one Jeep consumed to negative one Jeep of inventory investment gives zero, which is just what we want because there is no change in production.

In 1996 inventory investment throughout the economy was $14 billion. Some firms added inventories and others subtracted. Inventory investment tends to fluctuate up and down and therefore plays a big role in the business cycle.

residential investment: purchases of new houses and apartment buildings.

The other part of investment that is not business fixed investment is **residential investment,** the purchase of new houses and apartment buildings. About $311 billion worth of housing and apartments were constructed in 1996. Although much of this was purchased by consumers rather than businesses, it is included in investment because it produces services: shelter and, in some cases, a place to relax and enjoy life.

Combining the three parts of investment, we find that investment was $1,116 billion in 1996: $791 billion of business fixed investment, $311 billion of residential investment, and $14 billion of inventory investment. Thus, investment was about 15 percent of GDP in 1996 (see Figure 20.2).

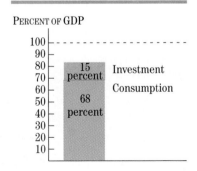

PERCENT OF GDP

FIGURE 20.2
Investment and Consumption as a Share of GDP

Investment is a much smaller share of GDP than is consumption.

Note the special way the term investment is used in this discussion. To an economist, investment means the purchase of new factories, houses, or equipment. But in everyday language, investment usually refers to an individual putting away some funds for the future, perhaps in the stock market, such as "I'll invest in the stock market." Be sure to stay aware of this distinction.

Stocks and Flows

The distinction between inventories and inventory investment (the change in inventories) illustrates an important idea in economics. It is the distinction between *stocks* and *flows*. The amount of inventories at a firm *at a particular date* is a *stock,* while the change in inventories *during a particular period* between two dates is a *flow.* To remember the distinction, notice that the expression "to take stock" means adding up all the inventories on the shelves. If a car dealer has 35 cars on the lot at the close of business on October 31, we say the stock of inventory is 35 cars. If the stock increases to 40 cars by the close of business on November 30, then the flow of inventory investment is 5 cars during the month of November.

The economist's distinction between stocks and flows can be illustrated by picturing water flowing into and out of a lake, for example, the Colorado River flowing into and out of Lake Powell behind Glen Canyon Dam. When more water flows in than flows out, the stock of water in Lake Powell rises. Similarly, a positive flow of inventory investment raises the stock of inventory at a firm. And just as when more water flows out than flows in and the stock of water falls, negative inventory investment lowers the stock of inventory.

The distinction between stocks and flows can be made for other economic measures as well. The factories in America on December 31, 1998, are a stock. The investment in the number of factories during 1998 is a flow. The money in your checking account is a stock. The deposit you made last week is a flow.

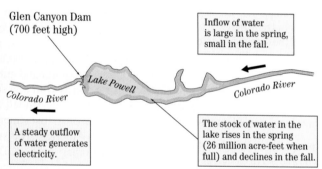

Glen Canyon Dam
(700 feet high)

Inflow of water is large in the spring, small in the fall.

Lake Powell

Colorado River

Colorado River

A steady outflow of water generates electricity.

The stock of water in the lake rises in the spring (26 million acre-feet when full) and declines in the fall.

Government Purchases

The third category of spending—**government purchases**—is spending by federal, state, and local governments on new goods and services. Most spending by the U.S. government is for the military. At the state and local level, education, roads, and police dominate government purchases. Government purchases of goods and services were equal to $1,407 billion in 1996 (see Figure 20.3).

   Not all government outlays are included in government purchases. A government welfare payment or retirement payment to an individual is not a purchase of a good or service; it is a *transfer payment* of income from the government to an individual. Transfer payments do not represent new production of anything, as would the purchase of a weapon or a new road or a new building. Because GDP measures the production of new goods and services, government outlays on transfer payments like social security, unemployment compensation, and welfare payments are excluded. Only purchases are counted because only these items represent something produced. Government *outlays* are purchases plus transfer payments.

government purchases: purchases by federal, state, and local governments of new goods and services.

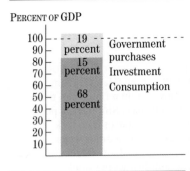

FIGURE 20.3
Government Purchases,
Investment, and Consumption as
a Share of GDP

Government purchases as a share
of GDP are greater than investment
and less than consumption. When
the stacked bar goes above the 100
percent line, there are negative net
exports (a trade deficit), as shown
here. If the stacked bar stops below
the 100 percent line, there is a
trade surplus.

net exports: the value of exports
minus the value of imports.

exports: the total value of the
goods and services that people in
one country sell to people in other
countries.

imports: the total value of the
goods and services that people in
one country buy from people in
other countries.

trade balance: the value of exports
minus the value of imports.

Net Exports

The final spending category is **net exports,** the difference between exports and imports. American **exports** are what Americans sell to foreigners, whether pharmaceuticals, computers, grain, or a vacation in Florida. American **imports** are what Americans buy from foreigners, whether cars, VCRs, shirts, or a vacation in France. Net exports are defined as exports minus imports. Net exports are a measure of how much more we sell to foreigners than we buy from foreigners. Another term for net exports is the **trade balance.** If net exports are positive, we have a trade surplus. If net exports are negative, we have a trade deficit. By these calculations, the United States had a trade deficit in 1996: $855 billion in exports and $954 billion in imports. Hence, net exports were a negative $99 billion, and appear in Table 20.2 as −$99 billion. The trade deficit got as high as $143 billion in 1987. The last time there was a trade surplus in the United States was in 1975, when it was $14 billion.

Why are net exports added in when computing GDP by the spending approach? There are two reasons. First, we included foreign goods in consumption and investment spending. For example, an imported Toyota purchased at a car dealer in the United States is included in consumption even though it is not produced in the United States. To measure what is produced in the United States, that Toyota must be deducted. Thus, imports must be subtracted to get a measure of total production in the economy. The second reason is that the exports Americans sell abroad are produced in the United States, but they are not counted in consumption or investment or government purchases in the United States. Thus, exports need to be added in to get a measure of production. Because, by definition, net exports are exports minus imports, adding net exports to spending is the same as adding in exports and subtracting out imports. Adding net exports to total spending kills two birds with one stone.

In 1996, the United States imported more than it exported, so the sum of consumption plus investment plus government purchases overstated what was produced in America. The sum of these three items exceeds GDP, as shown in Figure 20.3. In other words, GDP was $99 billion less than the sum of consumption plus investment plus government purchases.

A Key Equation

The notion that we can measure production by adding up consumption, investment, government purchases, and net exports is important enough to herald with some algebra.

Let the symbol C stand for consumption, I for investment, G for government spending, and X for net exports. Let Y stand for GDP because we use G for government purchases. We will use these symbols many times again. The idea that production equals spending can then be written as

$$Y = C + I + G + X$$

This equation states, using algebraic symbols, that production, Y, equals spending: consumption, C, plus investment, I, plus government purchases, G, plus net exports, X (meaning exports minus imports). In 1996 the values of these items (in billions of dollars) were:

$$7,576 = 5,152 + 1,116 + 1,407 + (-99)$$

This simple algebraic relationship plays a key role in later chapters.

The Income Approach

The income that people earn producing GDP in a country provides another measure of GDP. To see why, first consider a simple example of a single business firm.

Suppose you start a driver's education business. Your production and sales of driver's education services in your first year is $50,000; this is the amount you are paid in total by 500 people for the $100 service. To produce these services, you pay two driving teachers $20,000 each, or a total of $40,000, which is your total cost because the students use their own cars. Your profits are defined as the difference between sales and costs, or $50,000 − $40,000 = $10,000. Now, if you add the total amount of income earned in the production of your driver's education service—the amount earned by two teachers plus the profits you earn—you get $20,000 + $20,000 + $10,000. This sum of incomes is exactly equal to $50,000 which is the same as the amount produced. Thus, by adding up the income of the people who produce the output of the firm, you get a measure of the output. The same idea is true for the country as a whole, which consists of many such businesses and workers.

To show how this works, look at each of the income items in Table 20.3. We first describe each of these items and then show that when we add the items up we get GDP.

Labor Income

Economists classify wages, salaries, and fringe benefits paid to workers as **labor income,** signifying that it is payment to people for their labor. *Wages* usually refer to payments to workers paid by the hour; *salaries* refer to payments to workers paid by the month or year; and *fringe benefits* refer to retirement, health, and other benefits paid by firms on behalf of workers. As shown in Table 20.3, labor income was $4,449 billion in 1996.

labor income: the sum of wages, salaries, and fringe benefits paid to workers.

Capital Income

Economists classify profits, rental payments, and interest payments as **capital income.** *Profits* include the profits of large corporations like General Motors or Exxon and also the income of small businesses and farms. The royalties an independent screenwriter receives from selling a movie script are also part of profits. *Rental payments* are income to persons who own buildings and rent them out. The rents they receive from their tenants are rental payments. *Interest payments* are

capital income: the sum of profits, rental payments, and interest payments.

Aggregate Income	$7,576	**TABLE 20.3**
Labor income (wages, salaries, fringe benefits)	4,449	**Aggregate Income and GDP**
Capital income (profits, interest, rents)	1,588	**in 1996**
Depreciation	853	(billions of dollars)
Indirect business taxes	609	
Net income of foreigners	9	
Statistical discrepancy	68	
equals GDP	$7,576	

Source: U.S. Department of Commerce.

income received from lending to business firms. Interest payments are included in capital income because they represent part of the income generated by the firms' production. Because many individuals pay interest (on mortgages, car loans, etc.) as well as receive interest (on deposits at a bank, etc.), interest payments are defined as the difference between receipts and payments. Table 20.3 shows that capital income was $1,588 billion in 1996, much less than labor income. Capital income is about one-third as large as labor income.

Depreciation

depreciation: the decrease in an asset's value over time; for capital, it is the amount by which physical capital wears out over a given period of time.

Depreciation is the amount by which factories and machines wear out each year. A remarkably large part of investment that is part of GDP each year goes to replace worn-out factories and machines. Businesses need to replace depreciated equipment with investment in new equipment just to maintain productive capacity—the number of factories and machines available for use.

net investment: gross investment minus depreciation.

The difference between investment, the purchases of final goods by firms, and depreciation is called **net investment,** a measure of how much new investment there is each year after depreciation is subtracted. Net investment was $263 billion ($1,116 billion − $853 billion) in 1996, much smaller than the $1,116 billion in investment. Sometimes the $1,116 billion of investment, including depreciation, is called **gross investment.** The relationship between gross investment and net investment is thus

gross investment: the total amount of investment, including that which goes to replacing worn-out capital.

Gross investment − depreciation = net investment

The reason for the term *gross* in gross domestic product is that it includes gross investment, not only net investment. Another measure, called *net domestic product,* refers to gross domestic product less depreciation.

Profits and the other parts of capital income are reported to the government statisticians after subtracting out depreciation. But depreciation does represent part of GDP because the replacement of old equipment must be produced by someone. Thus, it is necessary to add in depreciation if we are to have a measure of GDP.

Indirect Business Taxes

indirect business taxes: taxes, such as sales taxes, that are levied on products when they are sold.

Indirect business taxes consist mainly of sales taxes sent directly by businesses to the government. For example, the price of gasoline at the pump includes a tax that people who buy gasoline pay as part of the price and that the gasoline station sends to the government. When we tabulate total production in the United States by adding up the value of what people spend, we use the prices businesses charge for a specific good—such as gasoline. Part of that price includes a sales tax that is sent to the government and, like depreciation, is not included in firms' profits. Thus, capital income does not include the sales taxes paid by businesses to the government. But those taxes are part of the income generated in producing GDP. We therefore must add sales taxes to capital and labor income.

Net Income of Foreigners

Foreigners produce part of the GDP in the United States. But their income is not included in labor income or capital income. For example, the salary of a Canadian hockey player who plays for the Pittsburgh Penguins and keeps his official residence as Canada would not be included in the U.S. labor income. But that income represents payment for services produced in the United States, which is part of U.S. GDP. We must add such income payments to foreigners for production in the United States because that production is part of GDP. Moreover, some of U.S. labor and capital income is earned producing GDP in other countries and to get a measure of income generated in producing U.S. GDP, we must subtract that out. For example, the salary of a U.S. baseball player who plays for the Toronto Blue Jays and keeps his official residence as the United States represents payment for services produced in Canada, which is not part of U.S. GDP. We must exclude such incomes paid for production in other countries. To account for both of these effects, we must add *net* income earned by foreigners in the United States—that is, the income earned by foreigners in the United States less what Americans earned abroad—to get GDP. In 1996, Americans earned less abroad ($223 billion) than foreigners earned in the United States ($232 billion); hence, in 1996 *net* income of foreigners was $9 billion as shown in Table 20.3.

Table 20.3 shows the effects of adding up these five items. The sum is close but not quite equal to GDP. The discrepancy reflects errors made in collecting data on income or spending. The discrepancy has a formal name: the **statistical discrepancy.** In percentage terms the amount is small, less than 1 percent of GDP, considering the different ways the data on income and spending are collected. If we add in the statistical discrepancy, then we have a measure of *aggregate income* that equals GDP. From now on we can use the same symbol (Y) to refer to GDP or to aggregate income, because GDP and aggregate income amount to the same thing.

The yellow "pipes" in Figure 20.4 illustrate the link between aggregate income and aggregate spending. People earn income from producing goods and services, and they spend this income (Y) to buy goods and services ($C, I, G,$ and X).

statistical discrepancy: the discrepancy between calculations of GDP using the spending approach and the income approach due to unreported data or errors in data collection.

$$\text{GDP} = \begin{matrix} \text{production} \\ \text{or} \\ \text{output} \end{matrix} = \text{income}$$

National Income and Personal Income

In addition to aggregate income, there are two other measures of income that are sometimes used by economists. **National income** is the sum of labor income and capital income, as we have already defined them. Thus, this measure excludes the income earned to pay indirect business taxes, depreciation, and foreigners in the United States. Labor income is about 73 percent of national income and capital income is the remaining 27 percent. **Personal income** is a measure of the income paid directly to individuals. In addition to labor income, it includes transfer payments from the government to individuals and the part of capital income paid out to individuals in the form of dividends, interest, rent, and small business earnings.

national income: the sum of labor income and capital income.

personal income: income paid directly to individuals; includes labor income, transfer payments, and the part of capital income that is paid out to individuals.

The Production Approach

The third measure of GDP adds up the production of each firm or industry in the economy. In order to make this method work, we must avoid the "double counting" problem discussed earlier. For example, if you try to compute GDP by adding new automobiles to new steel to new tires, you will count the steel and the tires that go into producing the new automobile twice. Thus, when we measure GDP by production, it is necessary to count only the **value added** by each manufacturer. Value added is the value of a firm's production less the value of the intermediate goods used in production. In other words, it is the value the firm adds to the intermediate inputs to get the final output. An automobile manufacturer buys the steel, tires, and

value added: the value of the firm's production minus the value of the intermediate goods used in production.

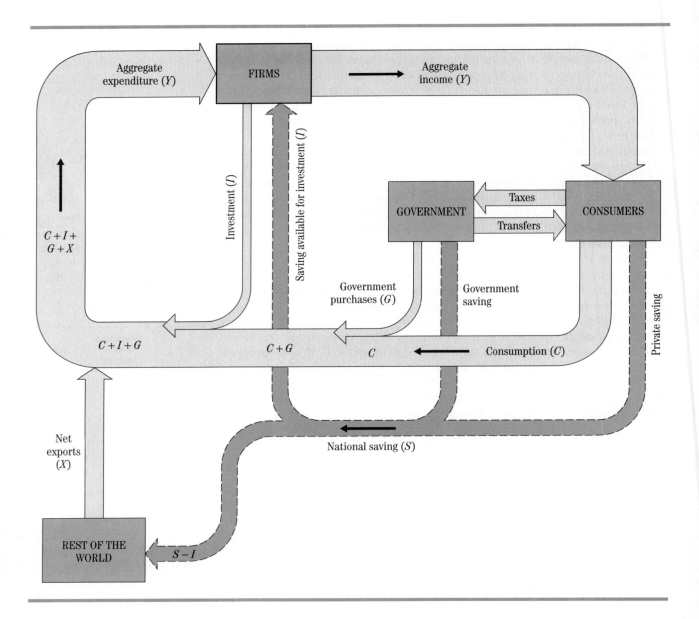

FIGURE 20.4

The Circular Flow of Income and Expenditure

This figure illustrates how aggregate expenditure equals aggregate income. First focus on the yellow "pipes." Starting at the bottom right part of the figure, consumption (C) is joined by government purchases (G), investment (I), and net exports (X) to sum to aggregate expenditures ($C + I + G + X$) on the left. At the top of the figure, this aggregate spending is received by firms that produce the goods and then pay out aggregate income (Y) to households in the form of rents, interest payments, and profits. The government takes in taxes and makes transfer payments in addition to government purchases.

The red pipes show the flows of saving as described in the section "Saving, Investment, and Net Exports." Private saving plus government saving add up to national saving (S). This saving then goes to finance investment by firms. If net exports are greater than zero, then some of the saving goes abroad.

FIGURE 20.5
Value Added in Coffee:
From Beans to Espresso

By adding up the value added at
each stage of production, from
coffee bean growing to espresso
making, we get a measure of the
value of a cup of espresso. Double
counting is avoided. Using the same
procedure for the whole economy
permits us to compute GDP by
adding up production.

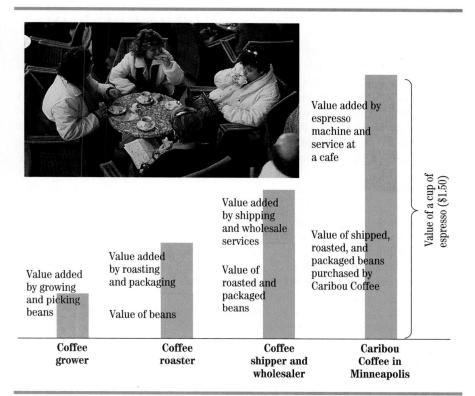

other inputs and adds value by assembling the car. When we measure GDP by production, we count only the value added at each level of production. Figure 20.5 shows how adding up the value added for each firm involved in producing a cup of espresso in the economy will automatically avoid double counting and give a measure of the final value of the cup of espresso when purchased at a coffeehouse or cafe. The same is true for the economy as a whole.

Review

► Adding up all the spending—consumption, investment, government purchases, and net exports—in the U.S. economy gives a measure of total annual production—gross domestic product (GDP). Inventory investment is treated as part of investment spending to ensure that we get a measure of production. Net exports are added to ensure that imported goods in consumption are not counted as U.S. production and that U.S. exports are counted as U.S. production.

► The sum of labor income, capital income, depreciation, sales taxes, and net income paid to foreigners gives another measure of GDP.

► GDP can also be measured by adding up production, but with this method we must be careful not to double count. By adding up only the value added of each firm or industry, we automatically prevent double counting. Value added is the difference between a firm's sales and its payments for intermediate inputs to production.

SAVING, INVESTMENT, AND NET EXPORTS

Armed with measures of aggregate spending, aggregate income, or aggregate production, economists often talk about a country's income or spending as if they were talking about a person's income or spending. Of course, the numbers are much larger for a country than for an individual. U.S. income of about $8 trillion is nearly unfathomable even compared with the income of the highest-paid movie stars or business executives. And, of course, the United States or any other country is not a person with one mind or set of plans. U.S. income and U.S. spending are simply the sums of incomes and spending of millions of individuals, even though we use single symbols like Y to represent these enormous quantities.

Nevertheless, analogies between countries and individuals are useful, especially when discussing economic growth and change over time. In this section we define saving and show how to measure saving for an entire country, using the definitions of income and spending we have derived thus far. Measuring a country's saving will be important in our study of economic growth and fluctuations in later chapters.

For an individual, saving is defined as income less consumption. If you earn $20,000 in income during the year and spend $18,000 on consumption—food, rent, movies—by definition your saving is $2,000 for the year. But if your consumption is $23,000 for the year, then your saving is negative $3,000, and you will either have to take $3,000 out of the bank or borrow $3,000.

The Definition of a Country's Saving

national saving: aggregate income minus consumption minus government purchases.

For a country, saving is defined the same way: by subtracting from the country's income what is consumed. For a country, however, there is also a government, and much (about 85 percent) of government purchases provide services that are like consumption—park services, police security services, and national defense services—rather than like investment, such as road building. Thus, **national saving** is defined as income less consumption and government purchases. That is,

National saving = income − consumption − government purchases

(An alternative definition would subtract only the part [85 percent] of government purchases that are clearly consumption.)

Using the symbol S for national saving and the symbols already introduced for income (Y), consumption (C), and government purchases (G), we define national saving as:

$$S = Y - C - G$$

Using the numbers from Table 20.2, national saving in 1996 was $1,017 = ($7,576 − $5,152 − $1,407), with all numbers in billions. Note that national saving, just like income, consumption, and government purchases, refers to a particular period of time, usually a year. National saving is what a country has left over in any one year for things other than consumption and government purchases.

Saving Equals Investment plus Net Exports

Where does this national saving go? An important principle of macroeconomics is that the national saving of a country is used either to finance the country's investment in factories, equipment, and housing or to finance the net purchases of the country's goods by foreigners. Net purchases by foreigners are equal to the difference between exports and imports, or net exports. Just as a furniture store provides funds (in the form of a credit card loan) to purchasers of furniture, the country provides funds to foreigners for purchases of its exports over its imports.

We can prove this important principle by simply looking carefully at the definition of national saving. First, write down the equation

$$Y = C + I + G + X$$

which, as already discussed, states that income (Y) equals consumption (C) plus investment (I) plus government purchases (G) plus net exports (X). Next, subtract consumption (C) and government purchases (G) from the left-hand side of the equation to get national saving; this means you must also subtract consumption (C) and government purchases (G) from the right-hand side. Here is what the subtraction gives you:

$$Y - C - G = I + X$$
$$S = I + X$$

where we have substituted national saving (S) for ($Y - C - G$), on the left. Thus, in words we have shown that

National saving = investment + net exports

Using the numbers from Table 20.2, national saving in 1996 equaled $1,017 = $1,116 + (−$99), with all numbers in billions.

This remarkable result says that the saving by all the millions of individuals in a country must be equal to the investment in new factories, equipment, and housing in the country plus the excess of exports over imports—net exports. If the country does not trade with the rest of the world, national saving must exactly equal investment.

What is the explanation for this result? By definition, national saving is what a country has left over after consumption and government purchases. What is left over can be used for other things, and there are only two other types of things possible: (1) investment in new factories, equipment, and housing, or (2) providing funds to foreigners equal to any purchases they make (exports) over and above what they sell (imports), or net exports. When more is saved than is invested, the excess saving shows up as a trade surplus—net exports will be positive. However, when less is saved than is invested, net exports are negative—there is a trade deficit.

To give further insights into this relationship between national saving, investment, and net exports, it is useful to consider the behavior of individuals and firms.

Saving by the Young, the Middle-Aged, and the Old

National saving is the sum of all saving in the economy. But some people are saving, some are not saving at all, and some even have negative saving, or *dissaving*. For example, when people are old they usually consume more than their income; they draw down their retirement savings. When people are middle-aged, they usually save for retirement—their income is greater than their consumption. And most young people save very little, or even dissave if they are able to borrow, perhaps from their friends or parents.

In most societies, there is a mixture of young, middle-aged, and old in the population. But the mixture is usually changing over time. National saving—the sum of everyone's saving—is affected by these changes. With the old tending to dissave, an increase in the number of old people in the society would therefore reduce the amount of national saving. For this reason, there is concern that national saving in the United States will decline as the post–World War II baby boom generation retires, starting around 2010.

Government Saving

Because the government is part of the economy, any saving by the government is part of national saving. What do we mean by saving by the government? The difference between the government's receipts from taxes and the government's expenditures—called the government *budget surplus*—is government saving. When the surplus is negative there is a *budget deficit,* and the government dissaves. In recent years the U.S. federal government has been a dissaver; that is, it has taken in less in income through tax receipts than it has spent. When the government runs a budget deficit, it lowers national saving unless saving by individuals increases.

The red "pipes" in Figure 20.4 illustrate how government saving can contribute to national saving, which in turn equals investment plus net exports.

People Saving and Investing

In general, the investing, exporting, and importing in the economy are not done by the same people who do the saving. Investment in factories and equipment in the economy is undertaken by firms. Investment in housing is done by individuals. Exporting and importing, which constitute net exports, are done by both firms and individuals. Saving is undertaken by other individuals as they save for retirement or other future events. Dissaving occurs if the government runs a budget deficit. There are some exceptions, where the same individuals do both the saving and investing. For example, you might decide to build your own house over a number of years. Each year you could use your savings to invest in part of the house. But typically investors and savers are different individuals.

Nevertheless, the link between national saving, investment, and net exports is maintained as millions of firms, individuals, and people in government go about their daily lives. There is a different story for everyone. Individuals who save might put their savings into a bank, and the bank in turn might lend out the funds to a firm that then uses the funds for investment in equipment. Or the bank might lend the money to another individual to build a house, or it might lend the funds to a firm in another country; that firm could use the funds to buy U.S. goods (exports).

The important point is that all these millions, even billions, of individual actions must adhere to the principle that national saving equals investment plus net exports.

Review

▶ For an individual, saving equals income minus consumption. For the United States, national saving is defined as income minus consumption minus government purchases. Government purchases are subtracted because many of them provide consumptionlike services to individuals.

▶ National saving always equals investment plus net exports. When national saving is less than investment, there is a trade deficit. When national saving is greater than investment, there is a trade surplus.

REAL GDP AND NOMINAL GDP

Economists use GDP to assess how the economy is changing over time. For example, they might want to know how rapidly the production of goods and services has grown and what that implies about economic growth in the future. However, the dollar value of the goods and services in GDP is determined by the price of these goods and services. Thus, an increase in the prices of all goods and services will make measured GDP grow, even if there is no real increase in the amount of production in the economy. Suppose, for example, that the prices of all goods in the economy double and that the number of items produced of every good remains the same. Then the dollar value of these items will double even though physical production does not change. A $10,000 car becomes a $20,000 car, a $7 haircut becomes a $14 haircut, and so on. Thus, GDP will double as well. At the other extreme, if the prices of all goods are cut in half, then measured GDP will fall by half even if there is no change in the number of items produced. Clearly, GDP is not useful for comparing production at different dates when there are increases in all prices. Although the examples of doubling or halving of all prices are extreme, we do know from Chapter 19 that there is a tendency for prices on the average to rise over time—a tendency that we have called inflation. Thus, when there is inflation, GDP becomes an unreliable measure of the changes in production over time.

Adjusting GDP for Inflation

Real GDP, as we discussed in Chapter 19, is a measure of production that corrects for this inflation. To emphasize the difference between GDP and real GDP, we will define **nominal GDP** as what has previously been referred to as GDP.

real gross domestic product (real GDP): a measure of the value of all the goods and services newly produced in a country during some period of time, adjusted for inflation.

nominal GDP: gross domestic product without any correction for inflation; the same as GDP; the value of all goods and services newly produced in a country during some period of time, usually a year.

Computing Real GDP Growth Between Two Years

To see how real GDP is calculated, consider an example. Suppose that total production consists entirely of the production of audio CDs and cassette tapes and that we want to compare this total production in two different years: 1997 and 1998.

	1997		1998	
	Price	Quantity	Price	Quantity
CDs	$15	1,000	$20	1,200
Tapes	$ 5	2,000	$10	2,200

Notice that the number of CDs produced increases by 20 percent and the number of tapes produced increases by 10 percent from 1997 to 1998. Notice also that the price of CDs is greater than the price of tapes, but both increase between the two years because of inflation. Nominal GDP is equal to the dollar amount spent on CDs, plus the dollar amount spent on tapes, or $25,000 in 1997 and $46,000 in 1998, a substantial 84 percent increase.

Nominal GDP in 1997 = $15 × 1,000 + $ 5 × 2,000 = $25,000

Nominal GDP in 1998 = $20 × 1,200 + $10 × 2,200 = $46,000

Clearly, nominal GDP is not a good measure of the increase in production: Nominal GDP increases by 84 percent, a much greater increase than the increase in either CD production (20 percent) or tape production (10 percent). Thus, failing to correct for inflation gives a misleading estimate.

To calculate real GDP we must use the *same* price for both years and, thereby, adjust for inflation. That is, the number of CDs and tapes produced in the two years must be evaluated at the same prices. For example, production could be calculated in both years using 1997 prices. That is,

Using 1997 prices, production in 1997 = $15 × 1,000 + $5 × 2,000 = $25,000

Using 1997 prices, production in 1998 = $15 × 1,200 + $5 × 2,200 = $29,000

Keeping prices constant at 1997 levels, we see that the increase in production is from $25,000 in 1997 to $29,000 in 1998, an increase of 16 percent.

However, production can also be calculated in both years using 1998 prices. That is,

Using 1998 prices, production in 1997 = $20 × 1,000 + $10 × 2,000 = $40,000

Using 1998 prices, production in 1998 = $20 × 1,200 + $10 × 2,200 = $46,000

Keeping prices constant at 1998 levels, we see that the increase in production is from $40,000 in 1997 to $46,000 in 1998, an increase of 15 percent.

Observe that the percentage increase in production is slightly different (16 percent versus 15 percent) depending on whether 1997 or 1998 prices are used. Such differences are inevitable, because there is no reason to prefer the prices in one year to those of another year when controlling for inflation. Economists arrive at a single percentage by simply *averaging* the two percentages.[1] In this example, they would conclude that the *increase in real GDP from 1997 to 1998 was 15.5 percent*, the average of 16 percent and 15 percent.

This 15.5 percent increase in real GDP is much less than the 84 percent increase in nominal GDP and much closer to the actual increase in the number of CDs and tapes produced. By adjusting for inflation in this way, real GDP gives a better picture of the increase in actual production in the economy.

A Year-to-Year Chain

This example shows how the growth rate of real GDP between the two years 1997 and 1998 is calculated in the case of two goods. The same approach is used for any other two years and more than two goods. To correct for inflation across more than two years, economists simply do a series of these two-year corrections and then "chain" them together. Each year is a link in the chain. For example, if the growth rate from 1998 to 1999 was found to be 13.5 percent, then chaining this together with the 15.5 percent from 1997 to 1998 would imply an average annual growth rate of 14.5 percent for the two years from 1997 to 1999. That is,

Observe that 13.5 percent and 15.5 percent are *chained* together to get 14.5 percent average for two years.

By chaining other years together, link by link, the chain can be made as long as we want.

---

1. A "geometric" average is used. The geometric average of two numbers is the square root of the product of the two numbers

From the 1992 Base Year to Other Years

To obtain real GDP in any one year, we start with a *base year* and then use these growth rates to compute GDP in another year. The base year is a year when real GDP is set equal to nominal GDP. Currently, 1992 is the base year for government statistical calculations of GDP in the United States. Thus, real GDP in 1992 and nominal GDP in 1992 are the same: $6,244 billion.

To get real GDP in other years economists start with the base year and use the real GDP growth rates to find GDP in any other year. Consider 1993. The growth rate of real GDP in 1993—calculated using the methods just described for the entire economy—is 2.27 percent. Thus, real GDP in 1993 was $6,386, or 2.27 percent greater than $6,244 billion. The $6,386 billion is 1993 real GDP measured in 1992 dollars. To emphasize that this number is calculated by chaining years together with growth rates, economists say that real GDP is measured in "chained 1992 dollars," a term that frequently appears in newspaper reports about real GDP.

Real GDP versus Nominal GDP over Time

Figure 20.6 compares real and nominal GDP over a 15-year period. Observe that for the 1992 base year, real GDP and nominal GDP are equal. However, by 1996 real GDP reached about $6.9 trillion with nominal GDP at $7.6 trillion. Thus, just as in the example, real GDP increased much less than nominal GDP. For the years prior to 1992, real GDP is more than nominal GDP because 1992 prices were higher than prices in earlier years. From Figure 20.6 you can see that nominal GDP would give a very misleading picture of the U.S. economy.

The GDP Deflator

Nominal GDP grows faster than real GDP because of inflation. The greater the difference between nominal GDP growth and real GDP growth, the greater is the inflation. If there were a deflation, with prices falling, then nominal GDP would increase less than real GDP. Hence, a by-product of computing real GDP is a measure of the rate of inflation.

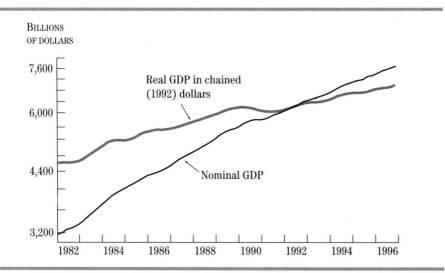

FIGURE 20.6
Real GDP versus Nominal GDP
Real GDP increases much less than nominal GDP because real GDP is adjusted for rising prices. Most of the increase in nominal GDP is due to rising prices. The chart shows real GDP for the 1992 base year, when real GDP and nominal GDP are equal. Nominal GDP is below real GDP in earlier years because prices are generally lower before 1992.

Source: U.S. Department of Commerce.

Reading the News About GDP Each Month

Near the end of every month, newspaper stories appear in most papers around the country (indeed, around the world) about the latest GDP measurement for the United States. The stories are generated by a release of data about GDP by economic statisticians at the U.S. Department of Commerce, where the national income and product accounts are tabulated.

Often the story appears on the first page of the newspaper with a big headline, as did the following story from the *New York Times* of October 31, 1996. Similar stories appeared in all the major newspapers, including the *Wall Street Journal*. Frequently the president of the United States or a high administration official comments on what the data mean for the economy, as did President Clinton's advisers in the story reproduced here. And because 1996 was an election year, presidential candidate Bob Dole also commented on the data.

The discussion of GDP in this chapter should give you the information

you need to read and understand these articles and to judge whether the headline, the reporter's interpretation of the GDP data, and the public official's comments make sense. The article reproduced here reported a slowdown for the economy, as reflected in its headline and general tone.

There are several points to keep in mind when reading news stories about GDP.

First, the measures of GDP are reported for each of the four quarters of the year. There is a news story each month because the data are revised twice. The first month after the quarter gives the first estimate of GDP; that is what is reported in the following article. In the second and third months, the estimates are revised as new data about the economy are obtained. Sometimes you have to read carefully to know whether what you are reading is a first-time report or a revision.

Second, the GDP measure for a quarter of a year represents the aggregate

production during the quarter, but the amount of production is stated at an *annual rate* to make the magnitude comparable to the annual GDP measure. For example, GDP was reported to be $7,616 billion in the third quarter at an annual rate in the attached article, but, in reality, GDP during the quarter was only one-fourth of that.

Third, the GDP measures for each quarter are *seasonally adjusted*. Some seasons of the year always involve more production than other seasons, and these differences have little to do with where the economy is going. For example, the fourth quarter (October–December) usually involves more production in anticipation of the holidays. Seasonal adjustments try to take out these fluctuations so that they do not show up in the reported measures of GDP.

Source of article: "Economic Growth Retreats to 2.2%," by David E. Sanger, *The New York Times*, October 31, 1996. Copyright © 1996 by The New York Times Company. Reprinted by permission.

ECONOMIC GROWTH RETREATS TO 2.2%

Refers to the growth rate of real GDP

Experts Differ on How Long Slowdown Is Likely to Last

By DAVID E. SANGER

WASHINGTON, Oct. 30 — In one of the last major indicators of the country's economic performance before the Presidential election, the Commerce Department today reported a sharp slowdown in economic growth in the third quarter of the year, but no sign of a revival of even modest inflation.

Today's news, that the growth rate fell to 2.2 percent in the third quarter, from 4.7 percent in the second, did not come as a surprise. Most economists had expected that the economy would cool off considerably. But they differ on whether this is the beginning of a longer downturn or a brief slowing of an expansion that can be sustained well into next year.

Both sides in that debate could pick out evidence from numbers reported today to support their arguments: Growth in personal spending by consumers slowed to a near standstill, but companies continued to buy equipment at a remarkable pace, a sign that they expect continued good times.

There was little question, however, that the combination of slower growth and continued low inflation wiped out the fears prevalent three months ago that the Federal Reserve would be forced to raise short-term interest rates.

And the figures put the economy on a path to grow 2.8 percent for the year, by most estimates — well ahead of what both Democrats and Republicans expected early in the year.

continued

Reading the News About GDP Each Month *(continued)*

Not surprisingly, both campaigns seized on today's numbers to bolster their sharply conflicting assessments of the nation's economic health. Commerce Secretary Mickey Kantor, carefully plucking out figures on the growth of the private economy, which exclude government spending, argued that the economy was growing faster than "in the so-called go-go 80's."

"We're in the midst of a balanced, sustained economic expansion that is delivering the goods for the American people," he said.

But Bob Dole, campaigning in Tennessee, referred to an economy that "is barely afloat," and said, "if this is a recovery, I can hardly wait for the recession." His staff compared today's numbers with those of the first quarter of 1993 — when Mr. Clinton was inaugurated and when the economy was climbing out of recession with growth at a rate of more than 4 percent — to support its argument that Mr. Clinton had been a lucky bystander to good times rather than a contributor to the economy's success. . . .

The biggest surprise in the figures was the paltry growth in consumer spending: a mere four-tenths of a percent at an annual rate. In the first half of the year the rate was closer to 3.5 percent. . . .

Inventories also increased sharply in the third quarter, suggesting that some of the G.D.P. gains were attributable to goods that were being produced but not yet consumed.

Buying habits historically wax and wane, so it is difficult to determine how much the spending slowdown really means. But the caution of consumers was in sharp contrast to the continued enthusiasm of American businesses, which spent 19 percent more than a year ago on equipment, largely computers, and built factories at a pace suggestive of a far more healthy expansion. . . .

One area that saw a significant downturn was exports, which until now have spurred the economy. Exports were up only six-tenths of a percent. Some of that slowdown is understandable: the United States economy has grown far faster than Europe's or Japan's, meaning that the country is in a position to take in more goods while demand for American exports lags. But it is an inconvenient turn of events for the Clinton Administration, which has made the export boom a centerpiece of its economic message. . . .

Data included in the gross domestic product for the third quarter of 1996 follow, with all dollar amounts in billions at seasonally adjusted annual rates. Percentage changes are from the previous quarter at seasonally adjusted annual rates.

Different interpretations of the data in a presidential election campaign

Nominal GDP

Chained refers to the year-by-year method of estimating real GDP.

Real GDP

Some of the key components of spending are discussed here

GDP deflator

Current Prices	Last Quarter	Pct. Chg.
Gross Domestic Product	$7,616.0	+3.8
Consumption	5,164.1	+1.9
Business investment	801.6	+15.2
Inventory change	42.4	N.A.
Housing	311.7	−3.1
Net exports	−115.7	N.A.
Government	1,412.0	+0.9
Memo: Final sales*	7,573.7	+2.0
Chained 1992 Dollars		
Gross Domestic Product	$6,929.7	+2.2
Consumption	4,692.8	+0.4
Business investment	776.6	+14.7
Inventory Change	39.6	N.A.
Housing	277.4	−5.8
Net exports	−132.2	N.A.
Government	1,273.7	−1.4
Memo: Final sales*	6,889.6	+0.3
G.D.P. price deflator		+1.6
G.D.P. chain-weighted price index		+1.9

*G.D.P. less inventory change.
N.A. Data Not applicable.
Source: Commerce Department

GDP deflator: nominal GDP divided by real GDP; it measures the level of prices of goods and services included in real GDP relative to a given base year.

price level: the average level of prices in the economy.

More precisely, if we divide nominal GDP by real GDP, we get the **GDP deflator,** a measure of the **price level,** which is the level of all the prices of the items in real GDP. That is,

$$\text{GDP deflator} = \frac{\text{nominal GDP}}{\text{real GDP}}$$

Here the GDP deflator is defined so that its value in the base year, such as 1992, is 1.00. (Sometimes it is scaled to equal 100 in the base year by multiplying by 100.)

The reason for the term *deflator* is that to get real GDP we can deflate nominal GDP by dividing it by the GDP deflator. That is,

$$\text{Real GDP} = \frac{\text{nominal GDP}}{\text{GDP deflator}}$$

The percentage change in the GDP deflator from one year to the next is a measure of the rate of inflation.

Other Inflation Measures

consumer price index (CPI): a price index equal to the current price of a fixed market basket of consumer goods and services in a base year.

There are other measures of inflation. A frequently cited one is based on the **consumer price index (CPI),** which is the price of a fixed collection—a "market basket"—of consumer goods and services in a given year divided by the price of the same collection in some base year. For example, if the market basket consists of one CD and two tapes, then the CPI for 1998 compared with the 1997 base year in the previous example would be

$$\frac{\$20 \times 1 + \$10 \times 2}{\$15 \times 1 + \$5 \times 2} = \frac{40}{25} = 1.60$$

The CPI inflation rate is the percent change in the CPI; it measures how fast the prices of the items in the basket increase in price.

Using a fixed collection of goods and services in the CPI is one of the reasons economists think the CPI overstates inflation. When the price of goods rises, the quantity demanded should decline; when the price falls, the quantity demanded rises. Thus, by not allowing the quantities to change when the price changes, the CPI puts too much weight on items with rising prices and too little weight on items with declining prices. The result is an overstatement of inflation.

In 1996, a group of economists appointed by the U.S. Senate and chaired by Michael Boskin of Stanford University, found that the government, by adjusting expenditures according to this overstated CPI, was spending billions of dollars more than it would with a correct CPI. Hence, getting the economic statistics right makes a big difference.

chain weighted price index: a price index using a changing basket of goods and services computed just as real GDP is computed.

Recently another measure of the average price of all goods and services in GDP has been developed. It is called the **chain weighted price index.** Unlike the CPI, it is not based on a fixed quantity of goods and services in some base year. Rather, the quantities in the index change each year, and the percentage changes in the index are chained together, just as in the calculation of real GDP. Moreover, the chain weighted price index includes consumption, investment, and government purchases, not just consumption. The chain weighted price index is usually mentioned as a measure of inflation in news reports about GDP.

Figure 20.7 shows how measures of inflation using the GDP deflator and the CPI compare. The general inflation movements are similar. The CPI is more volatile, however.

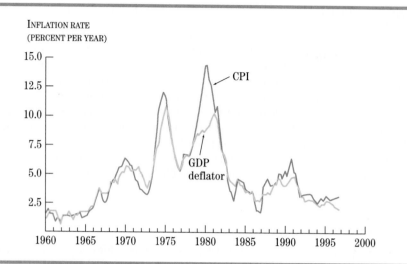

FIGURE 20.7
Comparison of Measures of Inflation
Measuring inflation with either the CPI or the GDP deflator shows the rise in inflation in the 1960s and 1970s and the lower inflation in the 1980s and early 1990s. The CPI is more volatile: It bounces around more. (The inflation rate is based on yearly percent changes in the stated variable.)

Source: U.S. Department of Commerce.

Although these three measures of prices provide the main statistics for inflation, there are still other measures. The producer price index (PPI), for example, measures the prices of raw materials and intermediate goods as well as the prices of final goods sold by producers. Services are excluded from the PPI, however. Raw materials prices—oil, wheat, copper—are sometimes watched carefully because they give early warning signs of increases in inflation.

Review

▶ Real GDP corrects nominal GDP for inflation. Real GDP measures the production of goods and services in the dollars of a given base year, such as 1992.

▶ Real GDP is a better measure of changes in the physical amount of production in the economy than is nominal GDP.

▶ The GDP deflator is a measure of the price level in the economy. It is defined as the ratio of nominal GDP to real GDP. The percentage change in the GDP deflator from year to year is a measure of the inflation rate.

SHORTCOMINGS OF THE GDP MEASURE

Although GDP is the best measure of overall production we have, it is deficient in several ways. First, there are revisions to GDP that can change the assessment of the economy. Second, GDP omits some production. Third, the production of goods and services, even on a per person or per capita basis, is only part of what affects the quality of life.

Revisions in GDP

Government statisticians obtain data on GDP from surveys of stores and businesses, and even income tax data from the Internal Revenue Service. Not all of the data are collected quickly. Data on sales at stores and large firms come in within a month; exports and imports take several months. Some income tax data are reported only once a year. Information about small firms comes in even more slowly.

For this reason, the statistics on GDP are frequently revised as new data come in. Every few years there is a big revision and the base year for computing real GDP is changed. For those who use the GDP data to make decisions, either in business or government, faulty data on GDP, which are apparent only when the data are revised, can lead to mistakes. Revisions of GDP are inevitable and occur in all countries.

Omissions from GDP

Most of the production that is omitted from GDP either does not occur in a formal market or government statisticians have a difficult time measuring it. Examples are work done in the home, illegal commerce, and quality improvements in goods.

Home Work and Production

Much of the production that people do at home—making dinner or a sweater, changing the car oil or a baby's diapers, cutting the grass or the kids' hair—is productive activity, but it is not included in GDP because the transactions are not recorded in markets where statisticians measure spending. Such production would be included in GDP if people hired and paid someone else to do any of these things.

Note that some home production is included in GDP. If you run a mail order or telemarketing business out of your home and pay taxes on your income, then this production is likely to be counted in GDP.

Government statisticians try to estimate some home production of final goods and include it in GDP. For example, if a person owns a house, the house provides services in the form of a place to live, eat, sleep, and entertain. An estimate of the value of these services is part of consumption even though there is no visible spending on them each year.

Leisure Activity

Much leisure activity is not included in GDP even though it may be enjoyable. Going to the beach or hiking in the mountains more often and working less might be something you decide to do as your income increases. If people start taking Friday afternoons off, GDP will go down but the level of well-being may increase. The consumption of leisure is omitted from GDP unless it involves a purchase in the market such as a movie or a ballgame ticket.

The Underground Economy

A large amount of production is not counted in GDP because it is purposely hidden from the view of the government. Illegal activity—growing marijuana in the California coastal range, selling pharmaceuticals not yet approved by the Food and Drug Administration—is excluded from GDP, because no one wants to report this activity to the government. People who get cash payments—perhaps in the form of tips at hotels or restaurants—may not report them in order to avoid taxes, and these are not counted either. If people do not report interest on a loan to a friend or relative, this is also omitted from GDP.

The sum of all the missing items is referred to as the *underground economy.* Estimates of the size of the underground economy are understandably uncertain. They range from about 10 percent of GDP in the United States to about 25 percent in Italy to over 40 percent in Peru.

The underground economy makes GDP a less useful measure of the size of an economy, and we should be aware of it when using GDP. But the underground economy does not render GDP a useless measure. It is unlikely that the underground economy grows much more or much less rapidly than the rest of the economy. Changes in laws can increase or decrease the incentives to produce outside the legal market economy, but these are unlikely to be large enough to change estimated growth rates of GDP by much. For example, the reduction of taxes in the United States in the 1980s encouraged more people to report more of their incomes to the government, and this increased both reported incomes and tax receipts. But it did not seem to have a major impact on the measurement of GDP.

Improved Products

Our measure of GDP sometimes misses improvements in the quality of goods and services. For example, a personal computer made in 1988 looks similar to a personal computer made in 1998. Yet, the 1998 computer is vastly superior; it can do computations much faster and store much more information. If personal computers in GDP are valued by their price times their number, then GDP will vastly understate the amount of production in terms of storage and speed.

In recent years, government statisticians have tried to measure the improved performance of computers and include this in GDP. However, the same problem exists for many other goods, from medical care, where microscopic surgery allows for knee surgery unheard of 20 years ago, to ski boots, which are far more comfortable than they were 20 years ago.

Other Measures of Well-Being

In the previous chapter, we described how improvements in the well-being of individuals in a society cannot occur without increases in real GDP per capita. However, even if real GDP per capita did include production in the underground economy, the value of home production, and all the improvements in goods and services, it would not alone serve as a measure of individual well-being. There are many other important aspects of the well-being of individuals: a long and healthy life expectancy, a clean environment, a small chance of war, crime, or the death of a child. The production of goods and services in a country can affect these other things, and indeed be affected by them, but it is not a measure of them.

Vital Statistics on the Quality of Life

Consider what has happened to some other measures of well-being as real GDP per capita has grown. During the last 40 years, we have seen life expectancy in the United States increase from about 69 years in the 1950s to 76 years in the 1990s.

This compares with a life expectancy of only 47 years in the early part of this century. Infant mortality has also declined, from about 2.6 infant deaths per 100 live births in the mid-1950s to .9 in the mid-1990s. In the early part of this century, infant mortality in the United States was 10 deaths for every 100 live births. The fraction of women who die in childbirth has also declined. So by some of these important measures, the quality of life has improved along with real GDP per capita.

But there are still serious problems and room for gains; as death rates from car accidents, heart disease, and stroke have decreased, death rates among young people from AIDS, suicide, and murder have been rising. Also of serious concern is the increasing percentage of children who live in poverty. Thus, the impressive gain in real GDP per capita has been correlated with both gains and losses in other measures of well-being.

Environmental Quality

A clean and safe environment is also a factor in the quality of life. Through much of the twentieth century, environmental pollution has increased as real GDP has grown. In the United States, Europe, and Japan in the last 40 years, however, some forms of pollution have been declining. For example, emissions of carbon monoxide, sulfur dioxide, and other air pollutants have declined. Part of the reason for these declines is that an increasing part of U.S. GDP has been devoted to reducing pollution. In the 1990s, about 2 percent per year of GDP has been spent on reducing pollution, from antipollution devices on cars to water-treatment plants.

As in other measures of the quality of life, however, there is room for improvement. There is a great debate about how much of GDP should be spent on improving the environment, just like there is debate about how much should be spent on police to reduce crime or on the military to defend the country. But GDP itself does not provide an indication of whether pollution or many of the other measures of the quality of life are improving or getting worse.

Review

▶ Real GDP per capita is not without its own shortcomings as an indicator of well-being in a society. Certain items are omitted—home production, leisure, the underground economy, and some quality improvements.

▶ There are other indicators of the quality of life, including vital statistics on mortality and the environment, that can be affected by GDP per capita but that are conceptually distinct and independently useful.

INTERNATIONAL COMPARISONS OF GDP

As we showed earlier, GDP can be adjusted for inflation in order to make comparisons of production in different years. A more difficult problem is comparing GDP in different countries, where the prices of individual goods differ. Making accurate comparisons of GDP in different countries is important for economic policy. Politicians frequently compare economic performance of the United States with other countries in order to show what is right or wrong with current economic policies. In this section, we show how economists adjust GDP to make such comparisons. To illustrate the problem, consider comparing real GDP in the United States with Japan.

The Problem with Using Market Exchange Rates for Comparisons

GDP in Japan was 470 trillion yen in 1994. In the United States, GDP was about $7 trillion in the same year. How do we compare these two numbers? One simple way would be to convert the yen to dollars using the exchange rate between yen and dollars in the foreign currency market. The market exchange rate in 1994 was about 100 yen per dollar. If we take the 470 trillion yen and convert it to dollars by dividing it by 100 yen per dollar, we get $4.7 trillion (470/100 = 4.7) as an estimate of GDP in Japan stated in dollars. The $4.7 trillion in Japan could then be compared with the $7 trillion in the United States. By this measure, Japanese production is approximately 67 percent of United States production—$4.7 trillion is 67 percent of $7 trillion. But is this comparison any good?

If we are interested in what a Japanese person can buy in Japan compared with what an American can buy in the United States, the answer is no. The prices of goods are much different in the two countries and the exchange rate is not a good guide to these price differences. Consider an example: Big Mac hamburgers sold by McDonald's. In fact, for those who trade in foreign currency markets, Big Macs are a favorite example; prices of Big Macs in different countries are printed in many magazines and newspapers. A Big Mac hamburger in Japan costs about 450 yen. If we convert that to dollars using the 1994 exchange rate, the cost of the Big Mac in dollars would be about $4.50 (450/100 = 4.50). But a Big Mac in the United States does not cost nearly that much; it costs about $2.50. Thus, the exchange rate overstates the price of Big Macs in Japan and, for the same reasons, overstates the value of GDP in Japan.

Purchasing Power Parity Exchange Rates

To account for these price differences, economists use an adjusted exchange rate that better reflects the different prices in the different countries. An exchange rate that makes Big Macs in Japan and the United States cost about the same would be 180 yen per dollar. Then a 450 yen hamburger in Japan would translate into about $2.50 (450/180 = 2.50). This exchange rate would make the power of yen and dollars to purchase Big Macs the same in both countries. For this reason, 180 yen per dollar is called the **purchasing power parity exchange rate.** In reality, purchasing power parity exchange rates are computed using the prices of thousands of goods, not only Big Macs. More formally, the purchasing power parity exchange rate between the yen and the dollar is the number of yen required to buy the same amount of goods that can be bought with a dollar. Of course, purchasing power parity exchange rates can be similarly defined and measured for French francs, German marks, and any other currency.

Let us compare U.S. and Japanese GDP, using 180 yen per dollar as the purchasing power parity exchange rate. The 470 trillion yen Japanese GDP now translates into $2.6 trillion, much less than the $4.7 trillion first estimated. According to this estimate, Japanese GDP is closer to 40 percent of U.S. GDP than to 67 percent.

purchasing power parity exchange rate: an exchange rate such that the prices of similar goods in different countries are the same when measured in the same currency.

Reversals of International Rankings

The difference this conversion makes for GDP per capita is even more striking. GDP per capita in Japan translated into dollars using the market exchange rate is $31,000, *greater* than the $25,000 GDP per capita in the United States. But if we make the translation using the purchasing power parity exchange rate, GDP per capita in Japan is $17,000, *less* than in the United States. Thus, depending on which exchange rate you use, it is possible to rank the United States either higher or lower than Japan. In fact, because the yen/dollar market exchange rate fluctuated so much in the 1980s and 1990s—it fell from 250 yen per dollar to 100 yen per dollar—it is possible to show that the United States rapidly fell behind Japan. At 250 yen per dollar, Japanese GDP per capita would be $12,000; at 130 yen per dollar it would be $24,000. Clearly, this increase does not mean that the Japanese rapidly overtook America or that America fell rapidly behind.

Despite the difficulties in measuring the purchasing power parity exchange rate, most economists feel that it gives a much better international comparison than the market exchange rate.

Review

▶ Comparing GDP in different countries is difficult because the prices are so different. Purchasing power parity is a method to compare GDP that takes into account the difference in prices.

▶ Serious mistakes about the relative performance of different countries can be made if market exchange rates are used for comparisons.

CONCLUSION

In this chapter we have shown how to measure the size of an economy in terms of its GDP. In the process, we have explained that income, spending, and production in a country are all equal, that a country's saving equals its investment plus its net exports, and that GDP can be adjusted to make comparisons over time or between countries.

Given this information, we can now proceed to develop a theory of why the economy—as measured by real GDP—grows and changes over time.

In conclusion, it is important to recall that aggregate income (or production or spending), the subject of our study, tells us much about the quality of life of people in a country but it does not tell us everything. As the economist-philosopher John Stuart Mill said of aggregate income in his *Principles of Political Economy*, first published in 1848: "The inquiries which relate to it are in no danger of being confounded with those relating to any other of the great human interests. All know that it is one thing to be rich, another to be enlightened, brave or humane . . . those things, indeed, are all indirectly connected, and react upon one another."[2]

2. John Stuart Mill, *Principles of Political Economy,* in *Reprints of Economic Classics,* ed. Augustus M. Kelley (New York: Bookseller, 1965), pp. 1–2.

KEY POINTS

1. U.S. gross domestic product (GDP) is the total production of new goods and services in the United States during a particular period.

2. GDP can be measured by adding all spending on new goods and services in the United States. Changes in inventories and net exports must be added to spending.

3. GDP can also be measured by adding labor income, capital income, depreciation, sales taxes, and net income of foreigners. Except for a small statistical discrepancy, the income approach gives the same answer as the spending approach.

4. Value added is a measure of a firm's production. Value added is defined as the difference between the value of the production sold and the cost of inputs to production. GDP can be measured by adding the value added of all firms in the economy.

5. National saving in the United States is defined as income less consumption less government purchases. National saving must be equal to investment plus net exports.

6. Real GDP is a measure of production adjusted for inflation. It is the best overall measure of changes in the production of goods and services over time.

7. GDP is not without its shortcomings. It does not include production in the underground economy or much work done in the home. And it is only one of many measures of well-being.

8. To compare real GDP in different countries, the exchange rate must be adjusted for differences in prices in the different countries using purchasing power parity.

KEY TERMS

intermediate good
final good
national income and product
  accounts
consumption
investment
business fixed investment
inventory investment
residential investment
government purchases
net exports

exports
imports
trade balance
labor income
capital income
depreciation
net investment
gross investment
indirect business taxes
statistical discrepancy
national income

personal income
value added
national saving
real GDP
nominal GDP
GDP deflator
price level
consumer price index (CPI)
chain weighted price index
purchasing power parity
  exchange rate

QUESTIONS FOR REVIEW

1. Why do we add up total spending in order to compute GDP when GDP is supposed to be a measure of production?

2. Approximately what were the percentages of consumption, investment, government purchases, and net exports in GDP in 1996 in the United States? How do they compare with Japan and Germany?

3. Why is the sum of all income equal to GDP?

4. What is national saving? Why is it always equal to investment plus net exports?

5. Under what assumptions about net exports will an increase in national saving increase investment?

6. What is the significance of value added, and how does one measure it for a single firm?

7. Why are increases in nominal GDP not a good measure of economic growth?

8. Why is the production of meals in the home not included in GDP? Should it be?

9. Why is the purchase of a used car not included in GDP? Should it be?

10. Why do we add inventory investment to spending when computing GDP?

PROBLEMS

1. Given the information in the table at the bottom of the page for three consecutive years in the U.S. economy, calculate the missing data.

2. Suppose the U.S. government is trying to bring underground activities into the legal economy so it can collect taxes on these activities.

   a) How is this campaign likely to affect the measure of GDP?

   b) Will this change in GDP reflect a change in well-being?

3. In market economies, prices reflect the value people place on goods and services, and therefore it makes sense to use them as weights when calculating GDP. In centrally planned economies, however, prices are controlled by the government instead of the market. Examine the following data for a centrally planned economy that subsequently frees prices:

Good	Quantity	Controlled Price	Market Price
Bread	1,000	$ 2	$10
Shirts	500	$20	$15

   a) Calculate GDP under the controlled prices and under market prices, assuming the quantities do not change. Did governmentally set prices mean an under- or overvaluation of production on the whole?

   b) How do people value each good in relation to previously controlled prices?

4. Look at the two scenarios for monthly inventories and sales for a company producing TV dinners. In both scenarios, the company's sales are the same. In scenario A, the company maintains production at a constant level. In scenario B, the company adjusts production within the month to match sales.

   a) Calculate the inventory investment in each month and resulting stock of inventory at the beginning of the following month for both scenarios.

   b) Does maintaining constant production lead to greater or lesser fluctuations in the stock of inventory? Explain.

Scenario A

Month	Start-of-the-Month Inventory Stock	Production	Sales	Inventory Investment
Jan.	80	80	80	_____
Feb.	_____	80	60	_____
Mar.	_____	80	40	_____
Apr.	_____	80	100	_____
May	_____	80	80	_____

Scenario B

Month	Start-of-the-Month Inventory Stock	Production	Sales	Inventory Investment
Jan.	80	80	80	_____
Feb.	_____	60	60	_____
Mar.	_____	40	40	_____
Apr.	_____	100	100	_____
May	_____	80	80	_____

5. Suppose there are only three goods in the economy:

Year	Good	Price	Quantity
1997	Apples	$1/lb.	500 lbs.
	Bananas	$2/lb.	250 lbs.
	Computers	$1,000	5
1998	Apples	$1.50/lb.	400 lbs.
	Bananas	$2.50/lb.	200 lbs.
	Computers	$1,000	7

   a) Calculate nominal GDP for 1997 and 1998.

   b) Calculate the percentage change in GDP from 1997 to 1998 using 1997 prices and 1998 prices.

   c) Calculate the percentage change in real GDP from 1997 to 1998 using your answers from (b).

   d) What is the GDP deflator for 1998 if it equals 1.0 in 1997?

Problem 1

Year	Nominal GDP (in billions of U.S. dollars)	Real GDP (in billions of 1992 dollars)	GDP Deflator (1992 = 100)	Inflation (percent change in GDP deflator)	Real GDP per Capita (in 1992 dollars)	Population (in millions)
1990	5,743.8	_____	93.6	4.3	_____	249.9
1991		6,079.0	_____	4.0	_____	252.7
1992	_____	_____	100.00	_____	24,449	255.4

6. Use the following data for a South Dakota wheat farm:

Revenue:	$1,000
Costs:	
Wages and salaries	$ 700
Rent on land	$ 50
Rental fee for tractor	$ 100
Seed, fertilizer	$ 100
Pesticide, irrigation	$ 50

a) Calculate value added by this farm.

b) Profits are revenue minus costs. Capital income consists of profits, rents, and interest. Show that value added equals capital income plus labor income paid by the farm.

c) Suppose that, due to flooding in Kansas, wheat prices increase suddenly and revenues rise to $1,100 but prices of intermediate inputs do not change. What happens to value added and profits in this case?

7. Suppose the following data describe the economic activity in a country for 1998.

Component of Spending	Value in Billions of Dollars
Consumption	500
Business fixed and residential investment	100
Inventory stock at the end of 1997	10
Inventory stock at the end of 1998	50
Depreciation	15
Government outlays	250
Government purchases	200
Total government tax receipts	190
Exports	150
Imports	120
Labor income	450
Capital income	250
Net income of foreigners	20
Sales taxes	100

Given these data, calculate the following:

a) Inventory investment

b) Net exports

c) Gross domestic product

d) Statistical discrepancy

e) National saving

f) Government saving

Verify that national saving equals investment plus net exports.

8. In 1991, investment in Japan was about 146 trillion yen and the trade surplus was 8 trillion yen. How much was national saving in Japan? If the government had neither a budget surplus nor a budget deficit, how much was saving by consumers and businesses in Japan?

9. When Americans travel to developing countries, they usually find their dollars buy much more than in the United States.

a) If purchasing power parity exchange rates are used instead of market exchange rates, what is likely to happen to estimates of GDP per capita for these developing countries?

b) GDP per capita is an imperfect measure of production because it doesn't include home production. In countries where a garden plot provides a significant portion of the family's food, is production likely to be overstated or understated by looking at GDP? Why?

10. Prices of Big Macs in various countries have been used to illustrate the purchasing power parity (PPP) exchange rates between the countries.

a) Suppose the price of a Big Mac in Moscow is 11,000 rubles, and in the United States the price is $2.50. What would be the PPP exchange rate according to Big Mac prices?

b) A friend of yours comes back from Moscow and tells you that he received 5,800 rubles for every dollar he traded on the street near Red Square. How does this exchange rate compare to the Big Mac PPP you calculated?

c) Suppose Russian GDP was 1,130 billion rubles in 1997. The price of a Big Mac in Moscow was about 11,000 rubles, while the street exchange rate at the end of the summer was about 5,800 rubles per dollar. Assuming a $2.50 U.S. price for a Big Mac, calculate Russian 1997 GDP in dollars using the Big Mac PPP rate. Compare this with the GDP using the street market exchange rate for 1997.

Long-Run Fundamentals and Economic Growth

Economic growth has long been a subject of economic research. It was the major subject of Adam Smith's *Wealth of Nations*, published in 1776, just as the first great wave of economic growth was gaining steam. The phrase *wealth of nations* was used to describe the economic growth of a nation. Labor, capital, and technology all played a role in Adam Smith's writings, but it was not until the 1950s that economists developed a theory sophisticated enough to distinguish between and measure the relative effects of labor, capital, and technology on economic growth. This new line of research is ongoing.

The theory of economic growth is based on a few fundamental economic principles that are particularly applicable to long-run issues. These long-run fundamentals pertain to four key areas: (1) the determination of employment through the supply and demand for labor, (2) the determination of the interest rate and

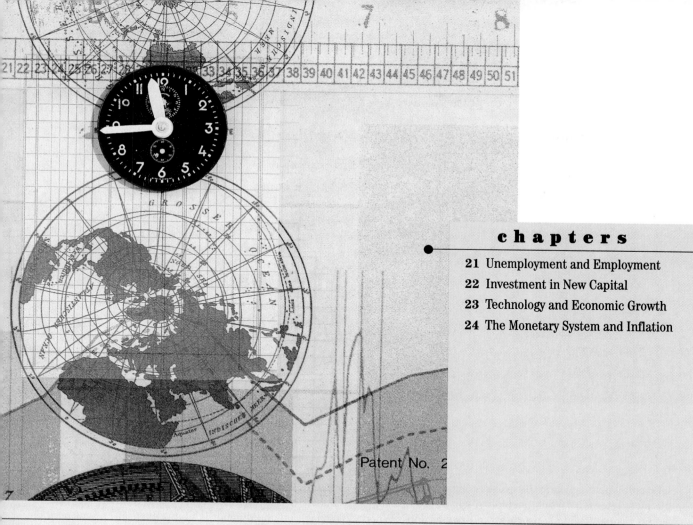

chapters

21 Unemployment and Employment

22 Investment in New Capital

23 Technology and Economic Growth

24 The Monetary System and Inflation

investment in the economy as a whole, (3) the production of technology through invention and innovation, and (4) the determination of the overall price level and inflation. The four chapters in this part of the book cover these four areas.

In Chapter 21 we look at what determines the number of jobs as well as the level of unemployment in the economy as a whole. In Chapter 22 we show how to determine the real interest rate and in doing so explain investment, saving, and capital accumulation. The level of well-being in an economy depends on the capital workers have to work with and on the growth of technology, including workers' skills. In Chapter 23 we illustrate how economists determine which factors are more important for economic growth. In Chapter 24 we examine the role of the monetary system in the economy and explain how the price level and inflation are determined in the long run.

There is considerable agreement among economists about the long-run macroeconomic principles discussed in these chapters. These principles address many of the deep problems the United States and other countries face at the end of the twentieth century, such as lower long-run economic growth than earlier in the century. The explanations for fluctuations in total production and employment—a more controversial but equally important topic—are discussed in the next part of the book, chapters 25–28.

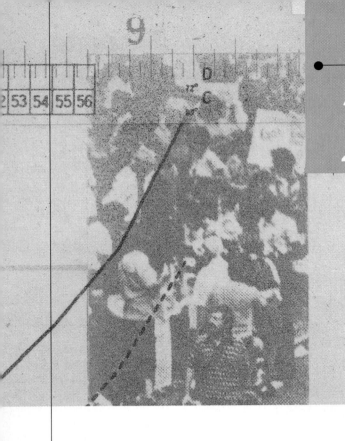

21

Unemployment and Employment

Unemployment is where the macroeconomy touches people most intensely. When unemployment is low, it is easier for people to find satisfying, well-paying jobs. When unemployment is high, jobs are harder to find, and people may accept jobs that do not closely match their skills. Unemployment rises during recessions and declines during recoveries. But even during normal periods when the economy is growing smoothly—neither in recession nor in boom—unemployment remains well above zero. In 1997, for example, a full six years away from the previous recession, about 7 million people were unemployed in the United States. Seven million!

Unemployment in years like 1997 can be as painful and cause as much hardship to those who experience it as unemployment in recessions. Beyond the obvious hardship of economic loss, unemployment can have other, even more devastating effects on the people involved. If unemployment persists, people may fall into poverty. The lack of a job for a long time is hard on an individual's self-respect—and it can destroy families. Young people who are consistently unemployed may never learn marketable job skills and can become disillusioned about their hopes for the future. The rate of teenage unemployment is high—even in normal periods the unemployment rate for teenagers rarely dips below 15 percent—and is even higher for black teenagers—over 30 percent.

Aside from the individual and family hardships, there is another reason to be interested in the rate of unemployment. When more workers are unemployed, aggregate production in the economy is less than if those same workers were employed. That is, there is an under-utilization of resources. In contrast, when employment is growing rapidly, the economy's production of goods and services is also growing rapidly, providing more resources to meet peoples' needs and wants.

This chapter examines unemployment, employment growth, and the effect of employment on the capacity of the economy to produce goods and services. It explains how unemployment is measured, and it examines the determinants of unemployment and the policy actions that can be taken to reduce unemployment.

EMPLOYMENT AND UNEMPLOYMENT TRENDS

In this section we show how unemployment and employment are defined and measured, examine recent employment trends in the United States, and develop a comprehensive measure of labor input to production.

Cyclical, Frictional, and Structural Unemployment

Figure 21.1 shows the unemployment rate and real GDP in the United States during a 15-year period that includes two recessions and two long expansions. Economists use the term **natural unemployment rate** to refer to the unemployment rate that exists when the economy is neither in a recession nor in a boom and real GDP is equal to potential GDP. Observe that the actual unemployment rate rises above the natural unemployment rate when the economy goes into a recession and real GDP falls below potential GDP. And the unemployment rate falls below the natural rate when the economy goes into a boom and real GDP rises above potential GDP. For example, as shown in Figure 21.1, the unemployment rate fell to 5 percent in 1989 as the economy boomed and then rose to over 7 percent when the economy went into a recession in 1991. Then the unemployment rate declined as real GDP moved closer to potential GDP in 1993 and 1994.

The increase in unemployment above the natural rate during and in the aftermath of recessions is called **cyclical unemployment** because it is related to the business cycle. For example, the increase in the unemployment rate from 1990 to 1992 was cyclical. The unemployment that exists in more normal times is due to a combination of **frictional unemployment** and **structural unemployment.** Frictional unemployment occurs as new workers enter the labor force and must look for work, or as workers change jobs for one reason or another and need some time to find another job. Most frictional unemployment is short lived. In contrast, some workers are unemployed for a long time, six months or more; they may have trouble finding work because they have insufficient skills, or their skills are no longer in demand because of a technological change or a shift in people's tastes toward new products. Such unemployment is called structural unemployment. The amount of frictional unemployment and structural unemployment in the economy is not a constant, so the natural unemployment rate may change over time. But such changes are more gradual and not directly related to business cycle fluctuations.

When economists use the term *natural* unemployment rate, they do not mean to say "okay" or "just fine," as when your doctor tells you that to have a higher temperature in the evening than in the morning is "natural." They simply mean that whenever the overall macroeconomy operates close to normal in the sense that real GDP is near potential GDP, the unemployment rate hovers around this natural rate.

The natural rate of unemployment appears to have been close to 5 percent in the 1950s. Some even claimed it was 4 percent. It increased slightly in the late 1960s and early 1970s. One possible reason for the increase was the influx of young baby boom workers into the labor force in the 1960s and 1970s. Young people tend to have higher unemployment rates than older people. There is a possibility that

natural unemployment rate: the unemployment rate that exists in normal times, when there is neither a recession nor a boom and real GDP is equal to potential GDP.

cyclical unemployment: unemployment due to a recession, when the rate of unemployment is above the natural rate of unemployment.

frictional unemployment: short-term unemployment arising from normal turnover in the labor market, such as when people change occupations or locations, or are new entrants.

structural unemployment: long-term unemployment due to structural problems such as poor skills or longer-term changes in demand or insufficient work incentives.

FIGURE 21.1
Real GDP, Potential GDP, and the Unemployment Rate

In periods like 1987 or early 1994 real GDP is equal to potential GDP and the unemployment rate is equal to the natural rate of unemployment, which appears to be somewhere around 6 percent. Note that when real GDP is above potential GDP, the unemployment rate is below the natural rate of unemployment; and when real GDP is below potential GDP, the unemployment rate is above the natural rate.

Source: U.S. Department of Commerce and U.S. Department of Labor.

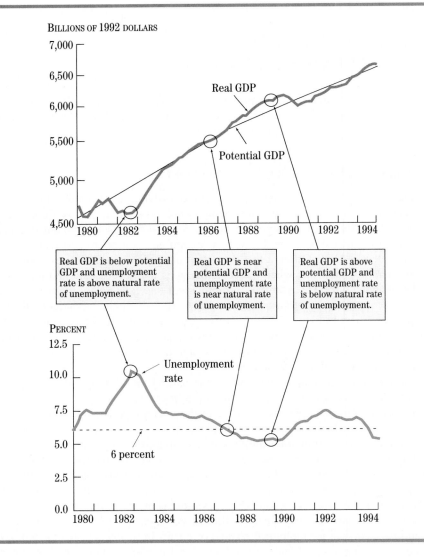

the natural rate is declining again as the labor force ages. Some economists believe that the natural rate fell to about 5.5 percent in the late 1990s, but it is unlikely to have fallen below 5 percent. It is important to remember that the natural unemployment rate is not a constant and that economists do not know its value precisely.

How Is Unemployment Measured?

current population survey:
a monthly survey of a sample of U.S. households done by the U.S. Census Bureau; it measures employment, unemployment, the labor force, and other characteristics of the U.S. population.

labor force: all those who are either employed or unemployed.

Each month the U.S. Census Bureau surveys a sample of about 60,000 households in the United States. The survey is called the **current population survey.** By asking the people in the survey a number of questions, the Census Bureau determines whether each person 16 years of age or over is employed or unemployed. The **labor force** consists of all people 16 years of age and over who are either employed or unemployed.

Who Is Employed and Who Is Unemployed?

To be counted as unemployed, a person must be looking for work, but not have a job. To be counted as employed a person must have a job, either a job outside the home—as in the case of a teaching job at a high school or a welding job at a factory—or a *paid* job inside the home—as in the case of a freelance editor or a telemarketer who works for pay at home. A person who has an *unpaid* job at home—for example, caring for children or working on the house—is not counted as employed. If a person is not counted either as unemployed or employed, then the person is not in the labor force. For example, a person who is working at home without pay and who is not looking for a paid job is considered not in the labor force.

Figure 21.2 illustrates the definitions of employment, unemployment, and the labor force. Using 1996 as an example, it shows that out of a total population of 265.5 million, about 200.5 million were in the **working-age population,** people 16 years of age or over (and not in jail or a hospital unable to work). Of this 200.5 million, about 126.7 million were employed and about 7.2 million were unemployed; the remaining 66.6 million were of working age but not in the labor force.

working-age population: persons over 16 years of age who are not in an institution such as a jail or hospital.

The Labor Force and Discouraged Workers

Judging who should be counted in the labor force and who should not be counted is difficult. For example, consider two retired people. One decided to retire at age 65 and is now enjoying retirement in Florida. The other was laid off from a job at age 55 and, after looking for a job for two years, got discouraged and stopped looking, feeling forced into retirement. You may feel that the second person, but not the first, should be counted as unemployed. However, according to the official statistics, neither is unemployed; they are not in the labor force because they are not looking for work. In general, workers, such as the second retired worker, who have left the labor force after not being able to find a job are called *discouraged workers.*

Defining and measuring the labor force is the most difficult part of measuring the amount of unemployment. In 1994 a slight change in the way the questions were phrased in the current population survey revealed that many women who were working at home without pay were actually looking for a paid job; as a result of the change in the question these women are now counted as unemployed rather than as out of the labor force. As a result of the change, the labor force and measured unemployment both rose.

Part-Time Work

A person is counted as employed in the current population survey if he or she has worked at all during the week of the survey. Thus, part-time workers are counted as employed. The official definition of a **part-time worker** is one who works between 1 and 34 hours per week. About 11 percent of U.S. workers are employed part time.

part-time worker: someone who works between 1 and 34 hours per week.

There is a big difference between the percentage of men who work part time and the percentage of women who work part time. About 20 percent of women work part time while only about 7 percent of men work part time. Women give personal choice rather than unavailability of full-time jobs as a reason for part-time work more frequently than men do. About 29 percent of employed women who have children under 6 work part time.

Because of part-time work, the average number of hours of work per worker each week is about 34 hours, less than the typical 40 hours a week.

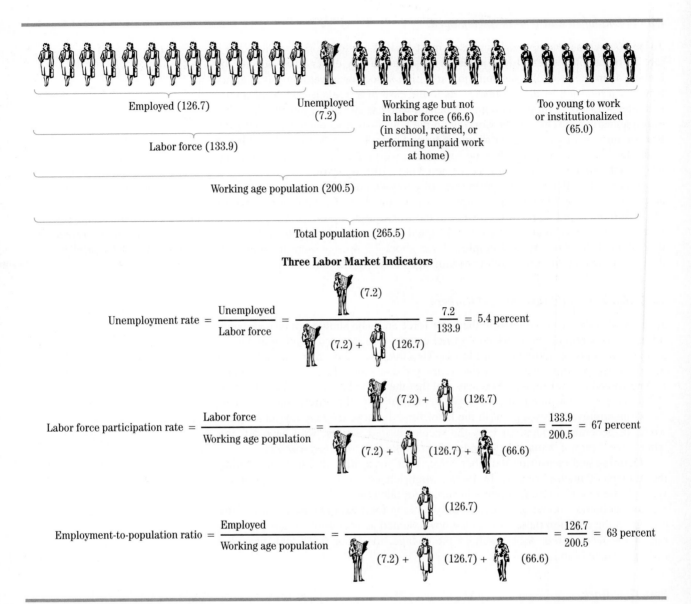

Three Labor Market Indicators

FIGURE 21.2

Placing the Population into Labor Market Categories

As shown at the top of this diagram, the total population is divided into four groups: employed, unemployed, working age but not in the labor force, and too young to work or institutionalized. Three key labor market indicators are then computed from these categories. For example, the unemployment rate is the number of unemployed divided by the number of people in the labor force. The employment-to-population ratio divides the number of employed workers by the working-age population. (The numbers in parentheses are millions and show statistics for 1996. Each pictograph represents approximately 10 million people.)

Source: U.S. Department of Labor.

Comparing Three Key Indicators

Now let us examine the three key indicators of conditions in the labor market. These are

1. the **unemployment rate,** the ratio of unemployed workers to the labor force;

2. the **labor force participation rate,** the ratio of people in the labor force to the working-age population;

3. the **employment-to-population ratio,** the ratio of employed workers to the working-age population.

All three are measured in percent as shown in Figure 21.2. Both the unemployment rate and the labor force participation rate depend on the labor force, and therefore have the same measurement difficulties that the labor force does. Only the employment-to-population ratio does not depend on the labor force.

The shaded panel of Table 21.1 shows the behavior of these indicators from the mid-1970s to the mid-1990s. Note how the unemployment rate fluctuated around an average of about 6 percent during these years as the economy went through recessions in the early 1980s and early 1990s. The unemployment rate rose to about

unemployment rate: the ratio (usually expressed as a percentage) of unemployed workers to the labor force.

labor force participation rate: the ratio (usually expressed as a percentage) of people in the labor force to the working-age population.

employment-to-population ratio: the ratio (usually expressed as a percentage) of employed workers to the working-age population.

●─────────────────

TABLE 21.1
Recent History of Labor Market Indicators

Year	Population (millions)	Working-Age Population (millions)	Labor Force (millions)	Employed (millions)	Unemployed (millions)	Unemployment Rate (percent)	Labor Force Participation Rate (percent)	Employment-to Population Ratio (percent)
1976	218.0	157.8	97.8	90.4	7.4	7.6	62	57
1977	220.2	160.7	100.7	93.7	7.0	7.0	63	58
1978	222.6	163.5	103.9	97.7	6.2	6.0	64	60
1979	225.1	166.5	106.6	100.4	6.2	5.8	64	60
1980	227.7	169.3	108.5	100.9	7.6	7.0	64	60
1981	223.0	171.8	110.3	102.0	8.3	7.5	64	60
1982	232.2	173.9	111.9	101.2	10.7	9.6	64	59
1983	234.3	175.9	113.2	102.5	10.7	9.5	64	58
1984	236.3	178.1	115.2	106.7	8.5	7.4	65	58
1985	238.5	179.9	117.2	108.9	8.3	7.1	65	60
1986	240.7	182.3	119.5	111.3	8.2	6.9	66	61
1987	242.8	184.5	121.6	114.2	7.4	6.1	66	61
1988	245.0	186.3	123.4	116.7	6.7	5.4	66	62
1989	247.3	188.1	125.6	119.0	6.6	5.3	67	63
1990	249.9	189.7	126.4	119.6	6.8	5.4	67	63
1991	252.7	191.3	126.9	118.4	8.5	6.7	66	63
1992	255.5	193.1	128.5	119.2	9.3	7.2	67	62
1993	258.2	195.0	129.5	120.8	8.7	6.7	66	62
1994	260.7	196.8	131.1	123.1	8.0	6.1	66	62
1995	263.0	198.6	132.3	124.9	7.4	5.6	67	63
1996	265.5	200.5	133.9	126.7	7.2	5.4	67	63

Source: U.S. Department of Labor, Bureau of Labor Statistics.

$$\frac{\text{Unemployed}}{\text{Labor force}} \qquad \frac{\text{Labor force}}{\text{Working-age population}} \qquad \frac{\text{Employed}}{\text{Working-age population}}$$

FIGURE 21.3

Employment-to-Population Ratio for Men, Women, and Everyone

The percentage of working-age women who work outside the home has increased steadily since the 1950s. At the same time, the percentage of working-age men who work outside the home has declined, until the late 1970s, when it leveled off. Since then the total employment-to-population ratio has increased. There are declines in all three ratios during recessions.

Source: U.S. Department of Labor.

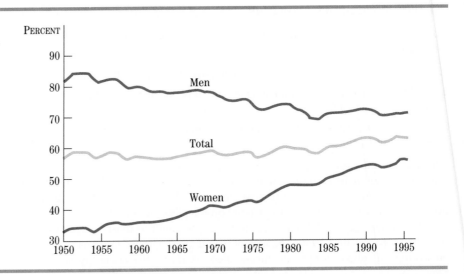

10 percent in 1982 after the 1981–1982 recession. In the absence of these business cycle fluctuations, the unemployment rate was about 6 percent. This indicates that the natural unemployment rate was about 6 percent during this period.

Table 21.1 shows a steady rise in the labor force participation rate, from 62 percent of the labor force in the mid-1970s to 67 percent of the labor force in the mid-1990s. This increase is mainly due to more women entering the labor force, a trend that has been going on since the 1950s. In the early 1950s about 30 percent of women were in the labor force, but now about 60 percent are. Possible explanations for this trend include reduced discrimination, increased opportunities and pay for women, the favorable experience of many women working for pay during World War II, and the women's movement, which emphasized the attractiveness of paid work outside the home.

The employment-to-population ratio fluctuates as real GDP fluctuates, but there is an important longer-term trend. The employment-to-population ratio has increased from about 57 percent in 1976 to about 63 percent in 1996. The employment-to-population ratio is higher than it has been at any time in U.S. history. In this sense the U.S. economy is creating more jobs now than at any time in its history. How does one explain this? Again, the rising percentage of women who are employed is a major factor, as shown in Figure 21.3.

Aggregate Hours of Labor Input

As we have seen, some people work part time. Others work full time; some work overtime. For these reasons, the number of people employed is not a good measure of the labor input to production in the economy. For example, consider two typists who both work half time; one works 4 hours in the morning and the other works 4 hours in the afternoon, both 5 days a week. Together they work as much as one full-time typist; to say that the labor input of these two typists is twice as much as the labor input of one full-time typist would be an obvious mistake. Rather, their combined labor input is the same as one full-time typist: 40 hours a week.

This example shows why economists consider the number of hours people work rather than the number of people who work when they measure labor input to production, whether it is typists at a firm or workers in the whole economy. Thus, the most comprehensive measure of labor input to the production of real GDP is the total number of hours worked by all workers, or **aggregate hours.** The number of aggregate hours of labor input depends on the average number of hours of work for each person and the number of people working.

aggregate hours: the total number of hours worked by all workers in the economy in a given period of time.

Effects of Unemployment on Labor Input

How does a change in the unemployment rate change the amount of labor input to production? Consider an example. Suppose that the rate of unemployment rises to 10 percent from 6 percent. With a labor force of 134 million this would lower the number of employed workers by about 5 million [(.10 − .06) × 134 = 5]. Thus, an increase in the unemployment rate clearly reduces labor input.

Case Study: CEA Forecasts of Future Aggregate Hours

The first row of Table 21.2 shows the growth rate of aggregate hours during the recent past and the near future. The information is taken from the 1997 *Economic Report of the President* and illustrates how aggregate hours are analyzed and projected by the Council of Economic Advisers (CEA), the group responsible for preparing the economic report and making economic forecasts for the president.

Observe in the second row of Table 21.2 that the growth of the working-age population slowed down in the 1990s to about 1 percent per year. This is the main reason the growth of aggregate hours also slowed down, as shown in the first row of Table 21.2.

How fast are aggregate hours likely to grow in the future? The President's Council of Economic Advisers predicts that the growth rate of aggregate hours during the late 1990s and early twenty-first century will be 1.2 percent per year, as shown in Table 21.2. It arrived at this estimate by considering three factors. Let us consider each in turn.

First, the CEA predicts that the growth rate of the working-age population will be *1.0 percent per year.* At least for the next 10 years there is little uncertainty about the growth of the working-age population because most of this population is already born and the number of people likely to immigrate can be estimated from U.S. limits on immigration.

Second, the CEA predicts that the employment-to-population ratio will increase slightly, contributing about *.2 percent per year* to the growth of aggregate hours.

	1973–1990	1990–1996	1996–2003
Growth rate of aggregate hours	1.7	1.4	1.2
Growth rate of working-age population	1.5	1.0	1.0

TABLE 21.2

Growth Rates of Aggregate Hours and Working-Age Population (percent per year)

Source: Economic Report of the President, 1997, Table 2–3, p. 86.

Third, the CEA predicts that there will be little or no change in the number of hours per worker; in other words the CEA estimates that this will contribute *0 percent per year* to the growth of aggregate hours. The growth in the number of hours per worker slowed down in recent years, partly because of the increase in part-time work in the economy. However, the CEA predicts that this slowdown will end and the hours per worker will remain steady.

Adding this all up (1.0 percent + .2 percent + 0 percent), the CEA forecasts that aggregate labor input will grow by 1.2 percent per year in the next few years.

Review

▶ Unemployment and employment in the United States are measured by a current population survey.

▶ Only working-age people can be unemployed, according to the official definition of unemployment, and to be counted as unemployed you have to be looking for work.

▶ The unemployment rate in the United States has averaged about 6 percent in the last 30 years, but the actual unemployment rate has fluctuated around this average. The unemployment rate in the absence of cyclical increases or decreases in unemployment is called the natural unemployment rate.

▶ The term *natural* in natural unemployment rate does not mean good or even satisfactory. The natural rate of unemployment is not a constant. It was around 5 percent in the 1950s and may return to 5 percent in the future.

▶ The employment-to-population ratio has risen in the 1970s and 1980s. More women have been entering the labor force since the early 1950s. Average hours worked per worker have declined.

▶ Aggregate hours is the most comprehensive measure of labor input. It is expected to grow by about 1.2 percent per year in the near future.

THE NATURE OF UNEMPLOYMENT

Having examined the aggregate data, let us now look at the circumstances of people who are unemployed. There are many reasons people become unemployed, and their experiences with unemployment vary widely.

Reasons People Are Unemployed

We can divide up the many reasons people become unemployed into three broad categories. People are unemployed because they have either *lost their previous job* (**job losers**), *quit their previous job* (**job leavers**), or *just entered the labor force to look for work* (**new entrants**).

Job Losers

job losers: people who are unemployed because they lost their previous job.

job leavers: people who are unemployed because they quit their previous job.

new entrants: people who are unemployed because they just entered the labor force and are still looking for work.

Among the people who lost their jobs in a typical recent year was a vice president of a large bank in New York City. When the vice president's financial services marketing department was eliminated, she lost her job. After three months of unemployment that were spent searching for work and waiting for responses from her letters and telephone calls, the former vice president took a freelance job, using her expertise in bank accounts to advise clients. Within a year, she was making three times her former salary.

The vice president's unemployment experience, although surely trying for her at the time, had a happy ending. In fact, you might say that the labor market worked pretty well. At least judging by her salary, she is more productive in her new job. Although one job was destroyed, another one—better, in this case—was created.

This transition from one job to another is part of the dynamism of any free market economy. The economist Joseph Schumpeter called this dynamism *creative destruction,* referring to the loss of whole business firms as well as jobs when new ideas and techniques replace the old. Creative destruction means that something better is created as something else is destroyed. In this case, a better job was created when another job was destroyed. On average, about 5 percent of jobs are destroyed each year by plant closings, bankruptcies, or downsizing of firms. In 1996 that amounted to about 6 million jobs destroyed. On balance, for an economy with growing employment more jobs are created than are destroyed. In 1996 enough jobs were created that on balance, employment increased by nearly 2 million jobs. But unemployment, at least part of it, is a by-product of these changes.

Many people who lose their job are probably not as lucky as the woman in our story. Among the unemployed in the 1990s were middle-aged engineers let go by McDonnell Douglas after many years of employment. Finding a new job is difficult for such workers because their skills are specific to a particular firm. The loss of such a job not only has disastrous effects on their incomes, but it can have psychological effects. It may mean that their children cannot go to college, or that they must sell their house. Unemployment compensation provides some relief—perhaps about $200 a week until it runs out. In many cases, though, this is well below what these workers were earning. Until they find a new job, they are obviously part of the millions of unemployed. Some may wait until a comparable job comes along; others may accept a lower-paying job. For example, one worker laid off from McDonnell Douglas took a job installing new kitchens at half the pay.

People may lose their jobs even when the economy is not in a recession. On average, about half of all unemployed workers are unemployed because they lost their job for one reason or another. The economy is always in a state of flux, with some firms going out of business or shrinking and other firms starting up or

Three Reasons People Are Unemployed

At any given time, people are unemployed for one of three reasons: They lost their job and are looking for another job (left), they quit their previous job and are still looking for a new job (middle), or they just entered the labor force and are unemployed while looking for work (right).

FIGURE 21.4
Unemployment According to Previous Job Status

On average, about half of unemployment consists of people who lost their jobs, either temporarily or permanently. The rest consists of people who left their jobs to look for another job or who were previously out of the labor force. The number of unemployed who are job losers increases in recessions and decreases in booms.

Source: U.S. Department of Labor.

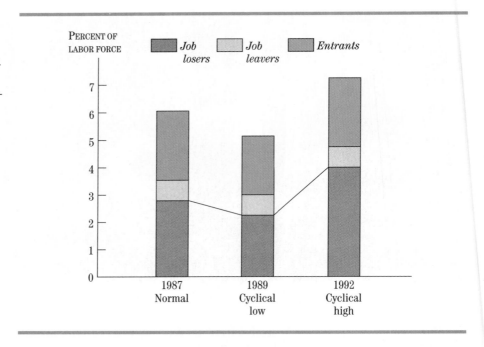

expanding. Tastes change, new discoveries are made, and competition improves productivity and changes the relative fortune of firms and workers.

job vacancies: positions that firms are trying to fill, but for which they have yet to find suitable workers.

Job vacancies are the jobs firms are trying to fill. Job vacancies and unemployment exist simultaneously. Unfortunately, many job vacancies require different skills, are in another part of the country, or are at lower wages than the skills, location, or former salaries of unemployed workers. This is especially true during periods of great change such as in the 1990s, when defense spending fell rapidly. Workers skilled at one job may be unemployed while firms cannot find workers with other skills.

The number of unemployed workers who have lost their job increases during recessions, when the unemployment rate is cyclically high, and declines in booms, when the unemployment rate is cyclically low, as shown in Figure 21.4. The main reason is that it is more difficult to find a new job in a recession, when fewer firms are hiring, than in a boom, when many firms are hiring. Figure 21.4 shows that increases and decreases in the number of unemployed workers who have lost their job is the only component of unemployment that moves up and down significantly during the business cycle. The proportion of people who are job leavers and new entrants is fairly constant.

Job Leavers

Some estimate that on average American workers change jobs every three or four years. Many of these job changes occur when people are young: Young workers are finding out what they are good at or what they enjoy or are rapidly accumulating skills that give them greater opportunities. A small part of unemployment—about 1 percentage point—consists of people who quit their previous job to look for another job. While they are looking for work they are counted as unemployed.

There is very little increase in unemployment due to quits in recessions. Why? Two opposing forces net out to little change. In a recession, when unemployment is high, fewer workers quit their job because they fear being unemployed for a long period of time. This reduces quit unemployment, but the lower number of job vacancies makes finding a job more difficult and raises unemployment.

New Entrants and Re-entrants

Figure 21.4 also shows that a large number of the unemployed workers in any year have just entered the work force. If you do not have a job lined up before you graduate, there is a good chance that you will be unemployed for a period of time while you look for work following graduation. In fact, there is a huge increase in unemployment each June when millions of students enter the labor force for the first time. This is called **seasonal unemployment** because it occurs each graduation "season." In contrast, unemployment is relatively low around the holiday season, when many businesses hire extra employees. Government statisticians smooth out this seasonal unemployment to help them see other trends in unemployment, so the newspaper reports on the unemployment rate rarely mention this phenomenon.

Some unemployed workers are re-entering the labor force. For example, a young person may decide to go back to school and then re-enter the labor force afterward. Others might choose to drop out of the labor force for several years to take care of small children at home—a job that is not counted in the employment statistics.

Some new entrants to the labor force find it very difficult to find a job. They remain unemployed for long periods of time. In fact, although the hardships of people who lose their jobs are severe, the hardships for many young people who seem to be endlessly looking for work are also severe.

seasonal unemployment: unemployment that varies with the seasons of the year due to seasonal fluctuations in supply or demand for labor.

Long-Term versus Short-Term Unemployment

The hardships associated with unemployment depend on its duration. Figure 21.5 shows how the unemployment rate divides up according to how long the unemployed workers have been unemployed. On average, about half of unemployment is very short term, less than 5 weeks. A market economy encompassing 265 million people exercising free choice could not possibly function without some very short-term unemployment as people changed jobs or looked for new opportunities.

Another 35 percent of unemployed workers have been unemployed for more than 5 weeks but less than 6 months, leaving about 15 percent of unemployed workers who have been unemployed for more than 6 months—the truly long-term unemployed. Although the number of short-term unemployed does not vary much over the business cycle, the number of long-term unemployed increases dramatically in recessions and falls during booms.

FIGURE 21.5
Unemployment by Duration
On average, about half of unemployment is very short term—less than 5 weeks. Longer-term unemployment increases in recessions and decreases in booms along with total unemployment.

Source: U.S. Department of Labor.

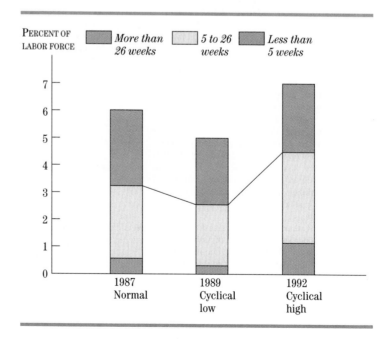

Reading the News About Employment Each Month

Each month—usually the first Friday of the month—the U.S. Department of Labor releases information about employment and unemployment in the previous month. There is a major news article about the report in most newspapers. The following article is a typical example. You should be able to find the terms discussed in this article in the text.

There is one frequent point of confusion in the monthly reports. The current population survey of *households* provides data on employment. However, there is another way the government gets data about employment: by asking *firms* directly about how many workers they employ in the so-called *payroll* or *establishment survey.*

The establishment survey is always released with the household survey each month, and this is the cause for confusion, as illustrated in the article below: Although employment rose by a large amount in the household survey, it only rose by a small amount in the payroll survey. This is why the headline mentioned a skewed picture. Over short periods of time the establishment survey is a better measure, but over the longer term—a year or more—the current population survey is better because it captures employment at new firms or self-employment.

Source of article: Yi-Hsin Chang, "Jobless Rate Skews Picture of Labor Market." Reprinted by permission of *The Wall Street Journal,* © 1994 Dow Jones Company, Inc. All rights reserved worldwide.

Jobless Rate Skews Picture of Labor Market

Big Drop Overstates Trend; Payroll Rise Suggests More Moderate Growth

ECONOMY

By YI-HSIN CHANG
Staff Reporter of THE WALL STREET JOURNAL

WASHINGTON – May's big drop in the unemployment rate to 6% from 6.4% from April overstates the rate at which the job market is improving.

Labor Department officials said the more moderate rise of employment recorded in its separate survey of business payrolls – which grew by 191,000 jobs last month – is probably a more accurate gauge of the economy. That number suggests the economy is growing at a moderate, but not excessive, rate.

Katharine G. Abraham, commissioner of the Bureau of Labor Statistics, said the sharp decline in the unemployment rate "probably overstates what's going on." . . .

The White House called a news conference to boast of the figures, but some analysts were concerned that the continued sizable increases in average hourly earnings might be a harbinger of inflation.

"There's a distinct possibility that inflation could worsen as the unemployment rate falls below 6%," said Michael Penzer, senior economist at Bank of America in San Francisco, who believes the natural rate of unemployment is 6%. When the unemployment rate falls below the natural rate – a number economists can't seem to agree on – companies sometimes have difficulty finding the workers they need, which could lead to higher prices.

But Audrey Freedman, an economist at Audrey Freedman & Associates, said she didn't see a threat of inflation because she believes the natural rate of unemployment is closer to 5%. . . .

Labor Secretary Robert Reich said the economy was in good shape for the summer. "This is good news for college graduates and even for high school graduates who face the best job markets in years."

Callouts:

- Here the administration emphasizes the good news.
- Here the natural unemployment rate is discussed, illustrating uncertainty about its level.
- A very large decline for one month . . .
- but . . .
- Data from current population survey
- Data from payroll or establishment survey
- Demographic data

EMPLOYMENT

Here are excerpts from the Labor Department's employment report. The figures are seasonally adjusted.

	May 1994	April 1994
	(millions of persons)	
Civilian labor force	130.8	130.7
Civilian employment	122.9	122.3
Unemployment	7.9	8.4
Payroll employment	112.8	112.7
Unemployment:	(percent of labor force)	
All civilian workers	6.0	6.4
Adult men	5.2	5.6
Adult women	5.4	5.6
Teen-agers	18.3	19.9
White	5.2	5.6
Black	11.5	11.8
Black teen-agers	39.9	36.2
Hispanic	9.5	10.8

	Unemployment Rates	
	1991	1996
Females over 19	5.7	4.8
Males over 19	6.4	4.6
Experienced persons	6.6	5.2
All persons	6.8	5.4
Blacks	11.1	9.3
Male teens, 16–19	19.8	18.1
Female teens, 16–19	17.5	15.2
Black male teens, 16–19	36.3	36.9
Black female teens, 16–19	36.0	30.3

TABLE 21.3
Unemployment Rates for Different Demographic Groups
(percent of labor force for each group)

Source: U.S. Department of Labor.

Unemployment for Different Groups

Regardless of how one interprets the numbers, certain groups of workers experience very long spells of unemployment and suffer great hardships as a result of the difficulty they have finding work. Table 21.3 shows the unemployment rates for several different demographic groups in the United States in two years, 1991 and 1996.

Unemployment is lowest for adult men and women. But unemployment is very high for teenagers. To some extent this is due to more frequent job changes and the period of time required to find work after graduating from school. But many teenagers who are looking for work have dropped out of school and are therefore unskilled and have little or no experience. Their unemployment rates are extremely high, especially for young minorities. The unemployment rate is between 30 and 40 percent for black teenagers. Thus, even when there is good news about the overall unemployment rate, the news may remain bleak for those with low skills and little experience. The overall unemployment rate does not capture the long-term hardships experienced by certain groups.

Review

▶ People become unemployed when they lose their job, quit their job, or decide to enter the labor force to look for a job. In a market economy, job loss occurs simultaneously with job creation.

▶ Quitting a job is the least likely reason that people are unemployed. Losing a job or looking for work after some time out of the labor force are more likely reasons to be unemployed. In a recession, job loss becomes the most common reason to be unemployed.

▶ Many unemployed people have been unemployed for a very short period of time. This frictional unemployment is probably not very harmful and is a necessary part of any market economy.

▶ But about 15 percent of unemployed people have been unemployed for 6 months or more, even in normal times. Long-term unemployment increases dramatically in recessions.

▶ Teenagers and minorities in the United States have very high unemployment rates, even in boom years.

DETERMINATION OF EMPLOYMENT AND UNEMPLOYMENT

The most logical place to look for an explanation of employment and unemployment is in the economist's standard tool kit: supply and demand.

Labor Demand and Labor Supply

labor demand curve: a downward-sloping relationship showing the quantity of labor firms are willing to hire at each wage.

labor supply curve: the relationship showing the quantity of labor workers are willing to supply at each wage.

real wage: the nominal wage adjusted for inflation. It is calculated by dividing the wage by the price level.

Figure 21.6 shows a labor demand curve and a labor supply curve. On the vertical axis is the price of labor (wage) and on the horizontal axis is the quantity of labor supplied or demanded. In a labor market, the **labor demand curve** describes the behavior of firms, indicating how much labor they would demand at a given wage. The **labor supply curve** describes the behavior of workers, showing how much labor they would supply at a given wage. The *wage,* usually measured in dollars per hour of work, is the price of labor. To explain employment in the whole economy, it is best to think of the wage relative to the average price of goods. In other words, the wage on the vertical axis is the **real wage,** which we define as:

$$\text{Real wage} = \frac{\text{wage}}{\text{price level}}$$

Firms consider the wages they must pay their workers in comparison with the price of the product they sell. The workers consider the wage in comparison with the price of goods they buy. Thus, in the whole economy, it is the real wage that affects the quantity of labor supplied and demanded.

The labor demand curve slopes downward because the higher the real wage, the less labor firms demand. A lower real wage gives firms an incentive to hire more workers.

FIGURE 21.6
Labor Supply, Labor Demand, and Equilibrium Employment
The intersection of the labor supply curve and the labor demand curve determines equilibrium employment and the real wage.

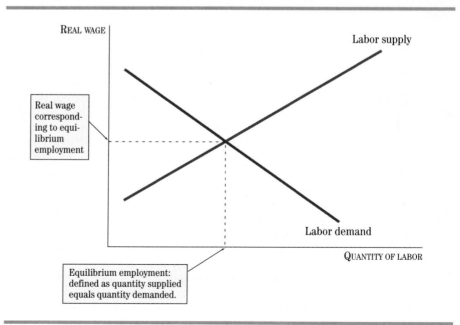

The labor supply curve slopes upward, showing that the higher the wage, the more labor workers are willing to supply. A higher real wage gives workers more incentive to work or to work longer hours.

Like any market, we would predict that the amount of labor traded—the number of workers employed—should be at the intersection of the labor demand curve and labor supply curve, as shown in Figure 21.6. The intersection also determines the equilibrium real wage that brings the quantity supplied into equality with the quantity demanded.

Case Study: Explaining Long-Term Employment Trends

Our review of employment trends in the United States in recent decades showed that the proportion of people working in the population has increased. The labor supply and demand analysis provides an explanation for this increase.

Throughout the post–World War II period, real wages have been rising, though since the mid-1970s the trend has slowed. Thus, we have a combination of an increased real wage and an increased proportion of the population working. This pattern is consistent with a shift in the labor demand curve and movement along the labor supply curve as shown in Figure 21.7.

As described by the upward-sloping supply curve, the higher wages could be attracting more people into the work force. In fact, as wages have increased, there has been an especially large increase in the percentage of women in the work force. But what could have caused this movement along the supply curve? And why would it have been especially strong for women?

One possibility is that the growth of the service industries—medical, legal, retail trade, telecommunications, transportation—caused an especially large increase in the demand for women. Economists have found that the labor supply of women is more sensitive to changes in the wage than men. Thus, the increase in labor demand in service industries could explain the especially large rise in the employment-to-population ratio for women as well as the increase in the real wage.

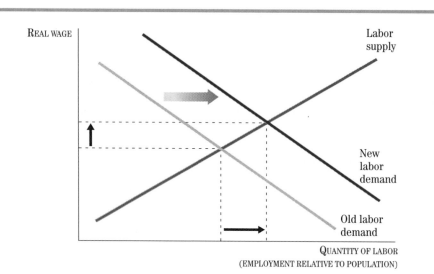

FIGURE 21.7
Explaining the Increase in the Employment-to-Population Ratio
One explanation for the rise in the employment-to-population ratio in recent decades is a shift in the labor demand curve, which would raise both the real wage and employment. For this purpose, interpret the horizontal axis as employment relative to the population.

Although the labor supply and demand analysis can explain this phenomenon, other factors also may have played a role, such as laws prohibiting discrimination and the women's movement. The point here is to show that the supply and demand model fits the facts.

Many other employment trends can be explained by the labor supply and labor demand analysis. The reduction in labor force participation of older men because of earlier retirement, for example, can be explained by the increased retirement pay due to private pensions and social security through which the government supports the elderly. Higher retirement payments make retirement more attractive compared to work and thus reduce labor supply.

Why Is the Unemployment Rate Always Greater than Zero?

Despite its usefulness in explaining employment trends, the supply and demand model must be modified if it is to explain unemployment. Having read about unemployment in this chapter, do you see something wrong with the picture in Figure 21.6? It seems inconsistent with the discussion of unemployment. With the quantity of labor supplied equal to the quantity of labor demanded, as in Figure 21.6, there seems to be no unemployment. The intersection of the supply and demand curves seems to predict a market situation that is contrary to the facts. Hence, in order to use the basic supply and demand analysis to explain why unemployment is greater than zero in the real world, we need to modify the story.

Economists have developed two different explanations that adapt the standard labor supply and demand analysis to account for unemployment. Though quite different, the explanations are complementary. In fact, it is essential to use both simultaneously if we are to understand unemployment. Some economists tend to emphasize one over the other, and this frequently turns discussions of the labor market into debates. We will refer to the two explanations as **job rationing** and **job search.**

job rationing: a reason for unemployment in which the quantity of labor supplied is greater than the quantity demanded because the real wage is too high.

job search: a reason for unemployment in which uncertainty in the labor market and workers' limited information requires people to spend time searching for a job.

Job Rationing

The job-rationing story has two parts. One is an assumption that *the wage is higher than what would equate the quantity supplied with the quantity demanded.* There are several reasons why this might be the case, but first consider the consequences for the labor supply and demand diagram. Figure 21.8 shows the same labor supply and demand curves as shown in Figure 21.6. However, in Figure 21.8 the wage is higher than the wage that would equate the quantity of labor supplied with the quantity of labor demanded. At this wage the number of workers demanded by firms is smaller than the number of workers willing to supply their labor at that wage.

The other part of the job-rationing story tells us how to determine the number of workers who are unemployed. This part of the story assumes that the number of workers employed equals the number of workers demanded by business firms. When the wage is too high, firms hire a smaller number of workers, and workers supply whatever the firms demand. Figure 21.8 shows the resulting amount of employment as point *A* on the labor demand curve at the given wage. With employment equal to the number of workers demanded, we see that the number of workers willing to supply their labor is greater than the number of workers employed; the excess supply therefore results in unemployment. The amount of unemployment measured in the horizontal direction is shown in the diagram.

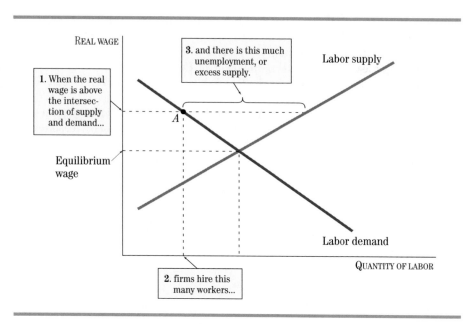

FIGURE 21.8
Excess Supply of Labor and Unemployment
The supply and demand curves are exactly as in Figure 21.6. Here, however, the real wage is too high to bring the quantity supplied into equality with the quantity demanded. The number of workers employed is given by point *A* on the demand curve, where the real wage is above the equilibrium wage. At this higher real wage, the quantity supplied is greater than the quantity demanded—a situation we can think of as unemployment.

This is a situation where workers would be willing to take a job at the wage that firms are paying, but there are not enough job offers at that wage. In effect the available jobs are rationed, for example, by a first-come-first-served rule or by seniority. It is as if, when enough workers are hired, the firms close their hiring offices and the remaining workers stay unemployed. If the wage were lower, then the firm would hire more workers, but the wage is not lower.

In most markets a situation of excess supply brings about a reduction in the price, or in this case the wage. Thus, if this explanation of unemployment is to work in practice, there has to be a force at work to prevent the wage from falling. If the theory is to be helpful in explaining unemployment, then the force has to be permanent, not only at work in a recession. Why doesn't the wage fall when there is an excess supply of workers?

Economists propose three key reasons to explain why the wage might be always too high to bring the quantity of labor demanded into balance with the quantity of labor supplied.

1. *Minimum wages.* Most countries have a legal **minimum wage,** or lowest possible wage, that employers can pay their employees. In the United States, the minimum wage is $5.15 per hour. A minimum wage could cause unemployment to be higher than it otherwise would be, as shown on the diagram in Figure 21.8: Employers would move down and to the right along their labor demand curve and hire more workers if the wage were lower.

minimum wage: a wage per hour below which it is illegal to pay workers.

One of the reasons teenage unemployment is high (as shown in Table 21.3) may be related to the minimum wage. Because many teenagers are unskilled, the wage firms would be willing to pay them is low. A minimum wage, therefore, may price them out of the market and cause them to be unemployed.

2. *Insiders versus outsiders.* Sometimes groups of workers—**insiders,** who have jobs—can prevent the wage from declining. If these workers have developed skills unique to the job, or if there is legislation preventing their firing without significant legal costs, then they have some power to keep wages up. Labor unions

insider: a person who already works for a firm and has some influence over wage and hiring policy.

outsider: someone who is not working for a particular firm, making it difficult for him or her to get a job with that firm although he or she is willing to work for a lower wage.

efficiency wage: a wage higher than that which would equate quantity supplied and quantity demanded set by employers in order to increase worker efficiency, for example, by decreasing shirking by workers.

may help them keep the wage higher than it would otherwise be. One consequence of the higher wage is to prevent the firm from hiring unemployed workers—the **outsiders**—who would be willing to work at a lower wage. This is a common explanation for the very high unemployment in Europe, and the theory has been developed and applied to Europe by the Swedish economist Assar Lindbeck and the British economist Dennis Snower.

3. *Efficiency wages.* Firms may choose to pay workers an **efficiency wage**—an extra amount to encourage them to be more efficient. There are many reasons why workers' efficiency or productivity might increase with the wage. Turnover will be lower with a higher wage because there is less reason for workers to look for another job: They are unlikely to find a position paying more than their current wage. Lower turnover means lower training costs. Moreover, workers might not shirk as much with a higher wage. This is particularly important to the firm when jobs are difficult to monitor. With efficiency wages, workers who are working are paid more than the wage that equates the quantity supplied with the quantity demanded. When workers are paid efficiency wages, unemployment will be greater than zero.

Job Search

We now turn to the second explanation that modifies the standard labor supply and demand analysis. The labor market is constantly in a state of flux, with jobs being created and destroyed and people moving from one job to another. The demand for one type of work falls and the demand for another type of work increases. Labor supply curves also shift.

In other words, the labor market is never truly in the state of rest conveyed by the fixed supply and demand curves in Figure 21.6. But how can we change the picture? Imagine labor demand and labor supply curves that constantly bounce around. The demand for labor, the supply of labor, and the wage would be different every period. Figure 21.6 would be in perpetual motion. Mathematicians use the adjective *stochastic* to describe this constant bouncing around. Economists apply the term *stochastic* to models of the labor market that are in perpetual motion. Rather than a fixed equilibrium of quantity and a fixed wage, there is a *stochastic equilibrium.* This stochastic equilibrium in the labor market is a way to characterize the constant job creation and job destruction that exist in the economy. People enter the work force, move from one job to another, lose their jobs, or drop out of the labor force. Wages change, inducing people to enter or re-enter the market. Figure 21.9 is a schematic representation of the flows of workers in and out of the labor market.

In a stochastic equilibrium, at any point in time people will be searching for a job. Many who do so will be unemployed for some time. They lost their job, quit their job, or came back to the job market after an absence from work. One of the reasons they remain unemployed for a while is that they find it to their advantage not to accept the first job that comes along. Rather, they wait for a possibly higher-paying job. While they wait they are unemployed.

Policy Implications

The theories of employment and unemployment that have been discussed above have implications for how economic policies affect the amount of employment and the unemployment rate.

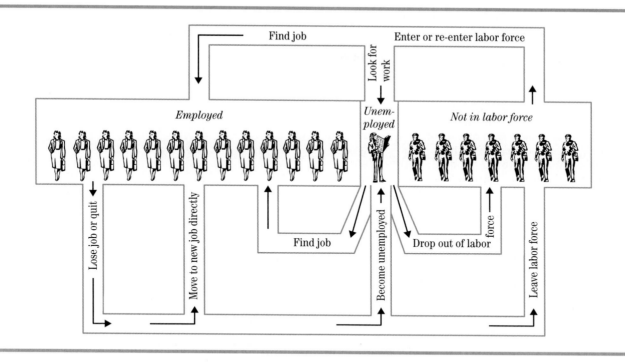

FIGURE 21.9
Labor Market Flows

The labor market is constantly in a state of flux, as people lose jobs, quit jobs, find jobs, and get in and out of the labor force. Most people pass through the unemployment box for a short period, but among the unemployed, some have not held jobs for a long time.

The Effects of Taxes

Consider first a tax on labor. An example of such a tax is a *payroll tax* that is collected in proportion to the workers' pay. In the United States there is a payroll tax to finance social security. A payroll tax can be paid either by the worker or by the firm, but its effects are the same.

Figure 21.10 shows the effect in the case where the tax is paid by the firm. The labor demand curve shifts down by the amount of the tax. For example, suppose a firm would employ 100 workers at $11 per hour without a tax. If there was a $1 tax, then the firm would demand 100 workers at a lower wage of $10. In either case the firm would be paying $11 per hour and would demand the same number of workers, but in one case the wage is $10 and in the other it is $11.

The effect of the tax is to lower employment, as shown in Figure 21.10. Thus, labor taxes reduce employment. Conversely, reducing labor taxes, or at least keeping them from rising, has a positive effect on employment.

Policies to Reduce the Natural Unemployment Rate

Both the job-rationing model and the job-search model have implications for how public policy can reduce the natural rate of unemployment. We already mentioned how a very high minimum wage could increase unemployment. Conversely, a lower minimum wage for young workers could reduce unemployment. And if information about jobs is increased through job-placement centers or improved communication about the labor market, we would expect unemployment from job search to go down.

Reading the News About European Unemployment

The following article from the *Economist* magazine gives a European perspective on unemployment. It begins by noting that the very high unemployment in Europe is not cyclical due to a recession but has persisted for many years. (See the bar chart showing the unemployment rate in several European countries and the United States in 1996.)

The *Economist* argues that it would be a mistake for the United States to follow European labor market policies such as a high minimum wage and generous unemployment benefits.

Most of the arguments in the article are consistent with either job rationing or job search.

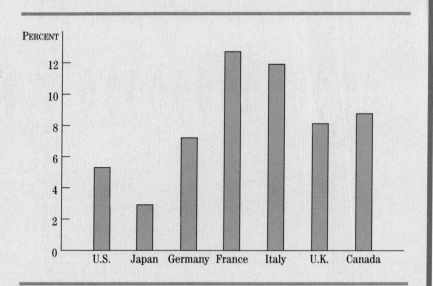

Doleful

Europe does indeed provide America with useful lessons about unemployment—about the policies to be avoided, not adopted

If the jobs of labour ministers and labour economists were tied to the success of their policies, most of them would be joining the 35m people—8.5% of the workforce—in the rich world's still-lengthening unemployment queues . . .

Unemployment in the [European] Community averages 12% of the labour force, compared with less than 7% in America. Worse still, almost half of Europe's jobless have been on the dole for more than a year; in America the equivalent figure is only 11%. It is even more striking that, while the number of American jobs has almost doubled since 1960, EC employment has risen by a paltry 10%. . . .

These figures suggest that Europe has more to learn from America than the other way around. . . . Europe's generous social-security benefits give the unemployed little incentive to seek work. Minimum wages, intended to protect the low-paid, instead cost young workers their jobs. France's minimum wage was increased sharply in the 1980s, to more than 50% of average earnings; America's has fallen to about 30%. It is no coincidence that a quarter of France's people under 25 years of age are unemployed, roughly twice the share in America.

Employers' social-security contributions and other non-wage costs add, on average, an extra 30% to wage costs in the EC (almost 50% in Germany). As with everything else, higher prices mean less demand—in this case, the demand of employers for workers. . . .

So look not to Europe for answers. . . . In the long term, the way to create more well-paid jobs in both America and in Europe is through better education and training. But this takes time. In the short term, there is no substitute for flexible wages.

Source of article: "Doleful," *Economist,* October 9, 1993, p. 17. Copyright © 1993 The Economist Newspaper Group, Inc. Reprinted with permission. Further reproduction prohibited.

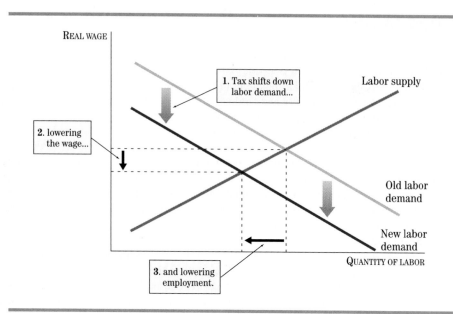

FIGURE 21.10
Effects of a Payroll Tax
A tax on labor lowers the labor demand curve by the amount of the tax because employers must pay more for workers. The new equilibrium has a lower wage and less employment.

Unemployment compensation, paid to workers who have been laid off from their job, also affects job search. Unemployment compensation enables workers to spend more time looking for a job or to hold out for a higher-paying job. But in the United States unemployment compensation does not last forever. In normal times it runs out after 26 weeks, and the evidence shows that many people stop searching and take a job just when their unemployment compensation runs out. Clearly, unemployment compensation not only helps mitigate the hardships associated with unemployment, it allows people more time to search. But as a by-product, unemployment compensation increases unemployment. In Europe, for example, generous unemployment benefits have been linked to persistent high unemployment. Thus, not allowing unemployment compensation to be paid for very long periods probably reduces unemployment.

Review

▶ The supply and demand for labor is the starting point for explaining long-term employment trends. The intersection of supply and demand curves determines the amount of employment, and shifts in demand can explain why the employment-to-population ratio has increased.

▶ But the basic supply and demand theory needs to be modified to account for unemployment. Economists use two approaches, job rationing or job search, to explain why unemployment occurs.

▶ Job rationing occurs when the wage is too high. Unemployment can be interpreted as the difference between the quantity supplied and the quantity demanded at that high wage. Wages can be too high because of minimum-wage laws, insiders, or efficiency wages.

▶ Job search is another reason for unemployment. It takes time to find a job and people have an incentive to wait for a good job.

CONCLUSION

Our analysis of aggregate employment and unemployment has put the spotlight on two different roles of labor. In one role, labor is simply an input to the production of real GDP. We showed that aggregate hours of all workers is the most comprehensive measure of labor input. We also showed that forecasts of the growth of aggregate hours in the future depend on forecasts of the growth rate of population, the employment-to-population ratio, and hours per worker.

In its other role, labor is the people doing the work. In this role the study of labor looks at the problems people face when they lose their job, decide to enter the labor force, or take a part-time job. It also looks at the effects of minimum wages and unemployment compensation on unemployment, at the serious problems that high rates of unemployment seem to cause (as evidenced by Europe in the 1980s and 1990s), and at the reasons why more women have entered the labor force in the past several decades.

In the next two chapters we consider the other inputs to production—capital and technology. But labor will continue to appear in these two different roles. For example, we will study human capital—education and training—both as something that raises the efficiency of labor in producing real GDP and as something that affects people and about which they make purposeful choices.

KEY POINTS

1. Unemployment data are collected in the monthly current population survey.

2. A person is unemployed if he or she is old enough to work, is looking for work, but does not have a job.

3. Unemployment is never zero in a market economy, even during booms. In normal times the unemployment rate in the United States has been somewhere around 6 percent, although this number is not a fixed constant and could change in the future.

4. The employment-to-population ratio has risen in the United States during recent decades, and the average number of hours each worker works has declined.

5. Aggregate hours of work by all workers is the most comprehensive measure of labor input to producing real GDP.

6. People are unemployed for three reasons: They have lost their job, they have quit their job, or they have just entered the labor force.

7. The labor supply and labor demand curves can be used to explain trends in employment in the economy.

8. Unemployment can be explained by both job rationing, in which the wage is too high to equate supply and demand, and by job search, in which unemployed people look for work.

9. Economic policies, such as exemptions for teenagers from the minimum-wage laws, time limits on unemployment compensation, or the provision of information about job openings to reduce job search time, can reduce the natural unemployment rate.

KEY TERMS

natural unemployment rate
cyclical unemployment
frictional unemployment
structural unemployment
current population survey
labor force
working-age population
part-time worker
unemployment rate

labor force participation rate
employment-to-population ratio
aggregate hours
job losers
job leavers
new entrants
job vacancies
seasonal unemployment
labor demand curve

labor supply curve
real wage
job rationing
job search
minimum wage
insiders
outsiders
efficiency wage

QUESTIONS FOR REVIEW

1. How is the working-age population defined?

2. How do economists define unemployment, and how do they measure how many people are unemployed?

3. What is the definition of the labor force?

4. What happened to the employment-to-population ratio from the late 1970s to the mid-1990s?

5. What is the difference between frictional and structural unemployment?

6. What factors determine the amount of labor input—aggregate labor hours—to producing real GDP?

7. Why isn't the unemployment rate equal to zero in normal times?

8. What fraction of unemployment is due to job loss, job quits, and new entrants in normal times?

9. What is the difference between unemployment due to job rationing and unemployment due to job search?

10. What do we mean by a stochastic equilibrium in the labor market?

11. What three economic policies would reduce the rate of unemployment in normal times?

PROBLEMS

1. Which of the following people would be unemployed according to official statistics? Which ones would *you* define as unemployed? Why?

   a) A person who is writing a book at home while seeking a permanent position on a newspaper

   b) A full-time student

   c) A recent graduate who is looking for a job

   d) A person who just wants to sit in front of the television all day

   e) A worker who quits his job because he thinks the pay is insufficient

   f) A teenager who gets discouraged looking for work and stops looking

2. The following table shows the demand and supply of labor at different hourly wages (in dollars).

Demand for Labor		Supply of Labor	
Wage/Hour	Quantity	Wage/Hour	Quantity
6	100	6	60
7	90	7	70
8	80	8	80
9	70	9	90
10	60	10	100
11	50	11	110

   a) Draw the supply and demand of labor.

   b) What is the wage and the quantity of labor at equilibrium?

   c) Suppose the government passes a minimum-wage law and nobody can earn less than $10 per hour. What would the new quantity of labor in the market be? Show what happens graphically. Who gains and who loses from this law?

3. a) Suppose the government decided to eliminate the minimum wage. What is likely to happen to the wages of unskilled workers in an area where the cost of living is very low? What is likely to happen to the wages of highly skilled computer programmers? Will this change in government policy significantly reduce unemployment? Why or why not?

   b) Now suppose instead that the government changes unemployment benefits so that they end after two weeks. What is likely to happen to the unemployment rate? Will this change in government policy lead to an increase in labor productivity? Why or why not?

4. In 1994 the *New York Times* computerized its help-wanted advertising, allowing people who were looking for work to put résumés on file with the paper. Then, whenever a person saw an interesting job ad, the résumé would be sent to the prospective employer by computer. Here is part of the *New York Times* advertisement for the service, which is called FasTrak.

ALL YOU DO IS . . .

1. Mail us your résumé.

2. Then, just keep up with the employment ads in the *New York Times* beginning January 9.

3. Anytime you see a FasTrak job that interests you, simply call the FasTrak phone number and punch in the code assigned to that particular job.

4. Your résumé will be sped to that employer via computer!

What would you predict this new service would do to the unemployment rate? Use one of the theories in this chapter to explain why unemployment will not be eliminated. What if the service became universally available in all parts of the country?

5. Suppose you own and run a bicycle repair shop with several employees. You decide to use your facilities at home to manage your business rather than hang around the bike shop while you do the books. You are surprised to discover that the productivity of your business falls. What happened? If you decide to keep your office at home, what will you have to do to increase the productivity of your business back to its previous level? If this same phenomenon is true of all businesses, then why may there be job rationing?

6. Use a supply and demand diagram to show the possible reduction in teenage unemployment from a lower minimum "training" wage for workers under 20 years of age. For what reasons might older, unskilled workers complain about such a policy?

7. Use the theories of job rationing and job search to try to explain why the natural rate of unemployment in the United States is below that in France. What can the French government do to try to remedy this situation? Might these remedies be politically unpopular?

8. Suppose in the year 2003 the economy is in "normal" times and the unemployment rate is 6 percent in the United States.

　a) If the working-age population is 205 million and the total labor force is 135 million, how many people are unemployed?
　b) What is the labor force participation rate in the year 2003?
　c) What change has occurred in the labor force participation rate since 1996? Give one reason this change might have occurred.
　d) What is the employment-to-population ratio? How has it changed since 1996?

9. Suppose that the natural rate of unemployment in the year 2003 has increased to 7 percent.

　a) If the total labor force is 135 million, then how many people are unemployed?

　b) If the situation is the same as in previous years, approximately how many of those people are job losers?
　c) Approximately how many of them have been unemployed for less than five weeks?
　d) If the population is 205 million, then what has happened to the employment-to-population ratio over the previous 6 years?

10. Average weekly hours per worker have fallen in the United States, as shown in the following table:

Year	Average Weekly Hours per Worker	Employment-to-Population Ratio
1960	38.6	56.1%
1970	37.1	57.4%
1980	35.3	59.2%
1990	34.5	62.7%

Source: U.S. Department of Labor.

　a) What is the likely cause of the fall in the average weekly hours of work per worker?
　b) If the employment-to-population ratio had remained constant over this period of time, what would have happened to the total hours of work per person in the United States?

11. Show that employment in the economy is equal to the working-age population times the labor force participation rate times (1 minus the unemployment rate) when both rates are measured as fractions. Use this equation to fill in the table below, which gives historical data for the United States. Calculate the employment-to-population ratio for 1950 and compare it with the figures given in Table 21.1. If the employment-to-population ratio for 1996 were the same as in 1950, what would total employment be in 1996, assuming the same 200.5 million for the working-age population?

Problem 11

Year	Total Employment (millions)	Unemployment Rate (percent)	Labor Force Participation Rate (percent)	Working-Age Population (millions)
1950	————	5.2	59.7	106.2
1960	67.6	5.4	60.0	————
1970	80.8	————	61.0	139.2

Source: U.S. Department of Labor.

12. The total employment in the economy is equal to the working-age population times (1 minus the unemployment rate) times the labor force participation rate.

a) Using the data, fill in the table below showing how many employed people there were in the United States at the turn of each decade.

b) Suppose the projection for the working-age population in the year 2020 for the United States is 255 million. If the unemployment rate and the labor force participation rate are the same in 2020 as they are in 1990, how much employment will there be?

c) Using the same projection of 255 million for working-age population in 2020, calculate employment with an unemployment rate of 6 percent and a labor force participation rate of 60 percent. Do the same for a labor force participation rate of 70 percent. Which of these estimates do you think is more realistic? Why?

13. The age distribution of the population changes over time—in the United States, better health care and smaller family size in recent years means that there are increasingly larger proportions of people over age 16. At the same time, there is likely to be a decline in the labor force participation rate as baby boomers retire. Using the same method as in the previous question, calculate total employment and the employment-to-population ratio based on the scenario in the table below.

a) Describe what happens to total employment and the employment-to-population ratio in this scenario.

b) Is it possible that labor force participation falls so much that total employment falls? How low would the labor force participation rate have to be in 2010 for total employment to be lower than in 1990?

Problem 12

Year	Total Employment (millions)	Unemployment Rate (percent)	Labor Force Participation Rate (percent)	Working-Age Population (millions)
1970	_____	4.8	61.0%	139.2
1980	_____	7.0	63.8%	169.3
1990	_____	5.4	66.6%	189.7

Source: U.S. Department of Labor.

Problem 13

Year	Unemployment Rate (percent)	Labor Force Participation Rate (percent)	Working-Age Population (millions)	Total Employment (millions)	Employment-to-Population Ratio
1990	5.5	66.4	188	_____	_____
2000	5.5	64.0	208	_____	_____
2010	5.5	62.0	230	_____	_____

Source: U.S. Department of Labor.

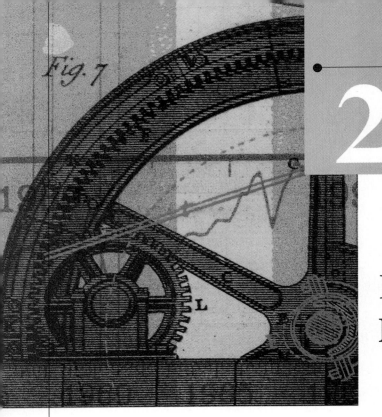

Fig. 7

22

Investment in New Capital

A good way to get a view of the role of capital in the economy is simply to take a bus ride and stare out the window. If your ride is in the country you may see silos, barns, tractors, harvesters, fences, water towers, and irrigation systems. In the suburbs you may see shopping centers, airports, moving vans, high schools, amusement parks, and earth-moving equipment. Closer to the city you may see machine shops, warehouses, truck depots, oil storage tanks, pipelines, and electric power plants. As the bus pulls into a downtown bus terminal, you will see office buildings, taxicabs, hotels, and storefronts with copy machines, computers, and dry cleaning equipment. And all the time you are traveling on roads, over bridges, through tunnels, and, of course, in the bus.

Every one of these items, and many more, constitutes *capital*—the factories, machinery, and other productive resources used to produce the goods and services that make up the economy's real GDP. All this capital did not appear overnight. It gradually accumulated as people invested in new capital each year for many years.

Capital increases the amount of goods and services that each worker can produce. Thus, with more capital in

an economy, real GDP per hour of work—labor productivity—is higher. Simply increasing the amount of labor—the number of workers or the number of hours of work—increases real GDP, as we saw in the previous chapter, but it does not increase labor productivity. Increasing technological know-how also raises labor productivity because workers become more effective at using capital. Thus, capital and technology are the two key driving forces behind labor productivity growth and rising standards of living. In this chapter we look at capital. We examine technology in the next chapter.

If capital in the economy is to increase, there must be *investment* because capital is nothing other than the accumulation of past investment. Investment is one component of GDP, together with consumption, government purchases, and net exports. To determine how much GDP is devoted to investment, we work with the equation introduced in Chapter 20: GDP (Y) = consumption (C) + investment (I) + government purchases (G) + net exports (X). After describing how investment must compete with the other sources of spending, we will show how the interest rate is one of the factors that influences investment. We then show how the interest rate is determined, and, using this interest rate, we predict the share of GDP that goes to investment.

The theory developed in this chapter has many practical uses. For example, the president's Council of Economic Advisers (CEA) argues that an economic plan to reduce the budget deficit would "increase the share of domestic investment in GDP by about 1 percent," because it would lower the interest rate. "Lower interest rates . . . are the way the market accomplishes . . . expenditure switching," in this case, "away from consumption and government purchases toward investment," the CEA reasons. The CEA also predicts that an "increase in the share of investment in GDP of 1 percentage point would have a substantial effect on the capital-labor ratio"—the amount of capital that workers have to work with.[1] How do economists make such predictions? What underlies the CEA's reasoning? The theory developed in this chapter will allow you to answer such questions.

The theory applies more to the long run than to short-run economic fluctuations. For this reason, the Council of Economic Advisers was careful to note that its predicted rise in investment would take several years. The theory is also useful for explaining why the share of investment in GDP fell during the 1970s and 1980s in the United States, or why the increase in government spending in Germany in the 1990s led to higher interest rates in Germany.

INVESTMENT AND THE ACCUMULATION OF PRODUCTIVE CAPITAL

Before we investigate what determines investment, we need to briefly review how investment is defined and consider how it increases the stock of capital over time.

Gross Investment, Net Investment, and Increases in Capital

Investment (I) consists of the purchases of goods by businesses for use in production, as well as the purchases of new residences by households. Consider some examples. Investment occurs at large business firms, such as when Hewlett-Packard builds a new assembly plant in California or Ford Motor builds a Taurus factory in Georgia. Investment also occurs at start-up companies. The founders of Hewlett-Packard, William Hewlett and David Packard, purchased new equipment to construct their first electronic instrument product, the Model 200A, in Packard's garage. Sometimes entrepreneurs invest in new residential capital on a grand scale. Arthur Levitt built 17,000 houses in the potato fields of Long Island, New York, and sold them to returning veterans after World War II. But most residential capital is created on a much smaller scale, as when a family living in Levittown in 1998 puts in a new kitchen sink or converts the attic into a third bedroom.

These examples illustrate how investment increases capital. But there is an important difference between gross investment and net investment, as we discussed in Chapter 20. Investment in the preceding examples refers to *gross investment*— the actual amount of purchases of new goods by businesses each year. However, much of this new investment is going to replace old capital that is wearing out. The

investment: purchases of final goods by firms plus purchases of newly produced residences by households.

1. *Economic Report of the President, 1994*, pp. 36, 83, 85.

Investment and the Accumulation of Capital over Time

Starting with an existing capital stock—illustrated by the few small buildings in New York City at the time of the American Revolution—and adding investment each year, year after year—illustrated by the construction of new buildings in New York City—results in a higher level of capital—illustrated by the New York City skyline today.

new assembly plant built by Hewlett-Packard may be replacing an old assembly plant that is being torn down. The increase in capital, then, is the value of the new assembly plant minus the value of the old assembly plant. Recall that the total amount of capital that wears out each year in the economy is called *depreciation.* Thus, it is only gross investment minus depreciation—or *net investment*—that adds to the total stock of capital in the economy. For example, $100 billion of net investment would be the difference between $770 billion gross investment and $670 billion in depreciation.

The total amount of capital in the economy increases each year by the amount of net investment during the year. More precisely:

$$\begin{array}{c} \text{Capital at the end} \\ \text{of this year} \end{array} = \begin{array}{c} \text{net investment} \\ \text{during this year} \end{array} + \begin{array}{c} \text{capital at the end} \\ \text{of last year} \end{array}$$

For example, if $10,000 billion is the value of all capital in the economy at the end of last year, then $100 billion of net investment during this year would raise the capital stock to $10,100 billion by the end of this year. This is a 1 percent increase in the capital stock. Figure 22.1 illustrates graphically, but with a different numerical example, how capital increases by the amount of net investment.

Although net investment is all that is added to the capital stock, the whole of gross investment must be produced and is thus part of real GDP. The economy's productive resources must be used to produce investment goods whether or not they are going to replace worn-out goods. When we use the symbol I for investment we always mean gross investment.

Keep in mind also that the new factories and machines that replace worn-out capital goods are frequently more efficient than old ones. For example, a new tractor may use less fuel than the old tractor it replaces. Thus, investment undertaken to replace an equal amount of worn-out capital, even though it does not raise the capital stock, may *improve* the existing capital stock. In fact, sometimes firms invest because they learn about an improved version of their old machine and want to acquire the new machine to improve productivity or the quality of production.

Government Investment

Some investment is undertaken by government. Although government investment is not included in investment (*I*) as measured by the national income and product accounts, it increases the amount of capital used in producing GDP and, therefore, needs to be considered when studying the role of capital in economic growth.

Public Infrastructure Investment

Part of government purchases (*G*) includes new highways, bridges, air-traffic control systems, courthouses, police cars, school buildings, water conservation projects, and computers to store patent and trademark information or process tax collections. Although not purchased by private firms or individuals, this type of capital is necessary for the provision of goods such as national defense, police protection, and education. Purchases of this type of capital are called **public infrastructure investment** because they add to the public infrastructure and thus contribute to the economy's productive potential. Public infrastructure investment is essential to the functioning of a modern economy. Without roads or highways for the transportation of goods, or without courts for the enforcement of laws, production would be much lower.

Public infrastructure investment increases the share of government purchases (*G*) in GDP, and the more GDP we devote to it, the less we have available to devote to something else, including the private investment that we defined by investment (*I*). Because investment (*I*) excludes public infrastructure investment, it is sometimes called *gross private domestic investment*.

Using Investment (I) in Practice

Even though investment (*I*) may not be a completely inclusive measure of the investment that adds to capital and contributes to economic growth, it is a close approximation for most purposes. Moreover, the value of investment (*I*) can be adjusted if we truly want to know how much investment adds to growth. We can still use investment (*I*), as long as we are aware that the actual investment that contributes to growth may be slightly different. Thus, for the remainder of this chapter we focus on what determines investment (*I*).

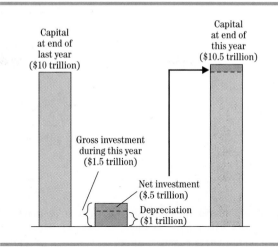

FIGURE 22.1
Net Investment Increases Capital: An Example
The figure illustrates how net investment—the difference between gross investment and depreciation—is added to the capital stock.

public infrastructure investment: purchases of capital by government for use as public goods, which add to the productive capacity of the economy.

Review

▶ Much of gross investment replaces depreciating capital. Only net investment adds to the capital stock.

▶ New capital that replaces old capital frequently embodies improved methods and new ideas.

▶ Some capital accumulation is done under the heading of government purchases. Part of government purchases is public infrastructure investment, which adds to the productive capital of the economy.

INVESTMENT AS A SHARE OF GDP

Investment is just one of the uses of GDP. We know that GDP is also used for consumption, government purchases, and net exports. Symbolically,

$$Y = C + I + G + X$$

where Y equals GDP, C equals consumption, I equals investment, G equals government purchases, and X equals net exports. This equation can help determine how much of GDP is devoted to investment.

The Investment Share versus the Other Shares of GDP

investment share: the proportion of GDP that is used for investment; equals investment divided by GDP, or I/Y.

The **investment share** of GDP is the proportion of GDP that is used for investment. The investment share of GDP is defined as investment (I) divided by GDP, or I/Y. When studying investment, economists frequently concentrate on the investment share of GDP. Sometimes the investment share is called the *investment rate*. For example, when the Council of Economic Advisers writes that the "investment rate is 13 percent," it means that $I/Y = .13$, or 13 percent.

As long as GDP is growing along with potential GDP and there is no recession that reduces GDP, an increase in the investment share means more investment and therefore a greater increase in capital. Because our focus in this chapter is on the long term rather than on short-term economic fluctuations, we concentrate on periods when GDP is close to potential GDP and look at what determines investment share. An increase in the share of GDP devoted to investment means an increase in the capital stock relative to GDP.

consumption share: the proportion of GDP that is used for consumption; equals consumption divided by GDP, or C/Y.

net exports share: the proportion of GDP that is equal to net exports; equals net exports divided by GDP, or X/Y.

government purchases share: the proportion of GDP that is used for government purchases; equals government purchases divided by GDP, or G/Y.

We can define the other shares of GDP analogously: C/Y is the **consumption share,** X/Y is the **net exports share,** and G/Y is the **government purchases share.** We can also establish a simple relationship between the investment share and the other shares of spending in GDP by taking the equation $Y = C + I + G + X$ and dividing both sides by Y. This simple division gives us a relationship that says the sum of the shares of spending in GDP must equal 1. Writing that algebraically yields:

$$1 = \frac{C}{Y} + \frac{I}{Y} + \frac{G}{Y} + \frac{X}{Y}$$

If we use the shares that existed in 1996 (see Table 20.2), we get:

$$1 = \frac{5,152}{7,576} + \frac{1,116}{7,576} + \frac{1,407}{7,576} + \frac{-99}{7,576}$$
$$1 = .680 + .147 + .186 + (-.013)$$

In other words, consumption accounted for 68.0 percent of GDP; investment for 14.7 percent of GDP; government purchases for 18.6 percent of GDP; and net exports, in deficit at negative $99 billion, accounted for about negative 1.3 percent of GDP. In this example from 1996, the sum of the four shares on the right equals 1. And, of course, this must be true for any year.

Figure 22.2 shows the four shares of spending in GDP for the last 65 years in the United States. A huge temporary fluctuation in the shares of spending in GDP occurred in World War II, when government spending on the military rose sharply.

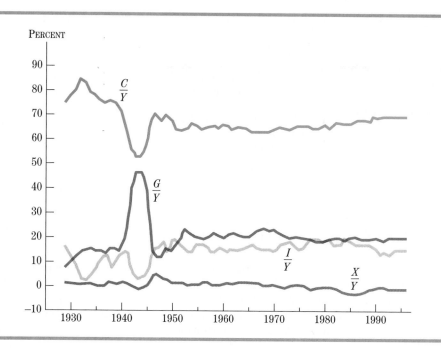

FIGURE 22.2
History of Spending Shares in GDP
The government purchases share rose sharply during World War II, and all three of the other shares declined. Since the mid-1950s, the changes in the shares have been much smaller. The consumption share rose, and net exports went from positive to negative.

Source: U.S. Department of Commerce.

Government purchases reached 50 percent of GDP, and the other three shares declined. Clearly, the movements in government spending as a share of GDP are a factor in determining the share of investment in GDP. Since World War II the shares have been much steadier. In recent years the consumption share has been higher than in the 1950s and 1960s and the net exports share has been negative as the United States has run trade deficits. (Recall that when net exports are negative, there is a trade deficit.)

If One Share Goes Up, Another Must Go Down

The share of spending equation demonstrates a simple but important point: A change in one of the shares implies a change in one or more of the other shares. That the shares must sum to 1 means that an increase in any of the shares must entail a reduction in one of the other shares. For example, an increase in the share of spending going to government purchases must result in a decrease in the share going to one or more of the other components of spending. Similarly, in a budget-cutting era, decreases in the government purchases share must result in an increase in some other share, such as the investment share. One cannot have an increase in government purchases as a share of GDP, going from, say, 19 percent to 25 percent, without a decline in the share of either consumption or investment or net exports.

What determines the investment share as well as the other shares of GDP? What is the mechanism through which a change in one share—such as the government share of GDP—brings about a change in one of the other shares? Does the investment share change? Or do the consumption or net exports shares change? To answer these questions, we need to consider the interest rate.

Review

▶ The share of investment in GDP determines how much new capital will be accumulated as the economy grows over time.

▶ Simple arithmetic tells us that the sum of all the shares of spending in GDP must equal 1.

▶ Thus, an increase in the share of GDP going to investment must be accompanied by a reduction in one or more of the other three shares—consumption, government purchases, or net exports.

INTEREST RATES AND CONSUMPTION, INVESTMENT, AND NET EXPORTS

In this section we show that the interest rate affects all three of the components of spending done by the private sector: consumption, investment, and net exports. Each component competes for a share of GDP along with government purchases, and the interest rate is a key factor in determining the amount that people in the economy are willing to devote to each component.

Consumption

If total consumption rises as a share of GDP, then the families and individuals in the economy on average raise their consumption relative to their income. For a family or an individual, saving is defined as income less consumption. Thus, if consumption increases, saving must decline for an individual or family with a given income. Because saving is used for future consumption, more consumption now means less consumption later.

However, if total consumption falls as a share of GDP, then families and individuals on average lower their consumption relative to their income. Therefore, they must save more. By saving more, they can consume more in the future. Less consumption now means more consumption later.

Consumption and the Interest Rate

People's decision to consume more or less today and thus less or more tomorrow depends on a relative price, much like any other economic decision. The relative price is defined as the price of consuming today relative to the price of consuming tomorrow.

Changes in the interest rate will change the relative price. A higher interest rate will raise the price of consumption today relative to the price of consumption tomorrow because it will enable a family to get more for its saving (either a bigger, more enjoyable home improvement, a larger retirement fund, or more college education). Because a higher interest rate raises the price of consuming today rather than tomorrow, it should reduce consumption today. A lower interest rate lowers the price of consuming today and thereby increases consumption relative to income. Thus, consumption is negatively related to the interest rate.

Why does the interest rate affect the relative price of consumption today? If the interest rate is higher, that means that any saving will deliver more funds in the future, which can then be used for consumption in the future. A higher interest rate makes consuming today more expensive compared to the future because it makes the return on saving higher. At a 6 percent interest rate, you can put $100 in the bank and receive $106 at the end of the year, whereas at 2 percent interest you will get only $102 at the end of the year. The change in the interest rate from 2 percent to 6 percent raises the price of consuming $100 worth of goods today by $4. Of course, $4 might seem like a small amount compared to $100, but imagine saving for a long period of time, say for retirement or a college education for one's children, and that small difference in interest rates builds up to quite a bit.

Stated somewhat differently, a higher interest rate gives people more incentive to save for the future, whether for home improvements, retirement, or a college education. With more saving, there is less consumption. The decision to consume is really a decision to consume at one time (today) rather than at another time (tomorrow). A higher interest rate makes consuming at this time relatively more costly compared to consuming at a later time.

What is true for individuals on average will be true for the economy as a whole. Figure 22.3 shows how the consumption share is negatively related to the interest rate. For this example, when the interest rate is 4 percent, the share of consumption in GDP will be about 65 percent. If the interest rate increases to 8 percent, then the share declines to 64 percent. Alternatively, if the interest rate declines, the consumption share increases.

Movements along versus Shifts of the Consumption Share Line

Observe that the relationship between the interest rate and consumption as a share of GDP in Figure 22.3 looks much like a demand curve. Like a demand curve, it is downward-sloping. And like a demand curve, it shows the quantity consumers are willing to consume at each interest rate. The interest rate is like a price: A higher price—that is, a higher interest rate—reduces the amount people will consume, and a lower price—that is, a lower interest rate—increases the amount of goods and services people will consume. When an increase in the interest rate leads to a decline in consumption, we see a *movement along* the consumption share line, as shown in Figure 22.3.

As with a demand curve, it is important to distinguish such movements along the consumption share line from *shifts of* the consumption share line. The interest rate is not the only thing that affects consumption as a share of GDP. When a factor other than the interest rate changes the consumption share of GDP, there is a shift in the consumption share line in Figure 22.3. For example, an increase in taxes on consumption—such as a national sales tax—would reduce the quantity of goods people would consume relative to their income. In other words, an increase in taxes on consumption would shift the consumption share line in Figure 22.3 to the left: Less would be consumed relative to

FIGURE 22.3
The Consumption Share and the Interest Rate
A higher interest rate lowers the amount of consumption relative to GDP. A higher interest rate discourages consumption and encourages saving.

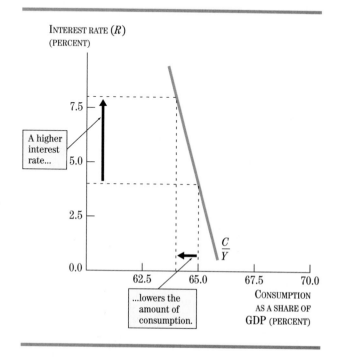

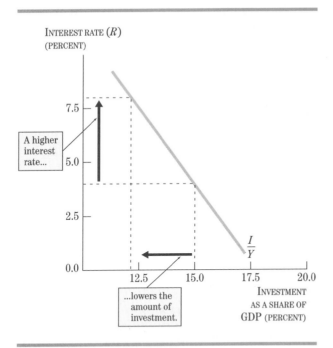

FIGURE 22.4

The Investment Share and the Interest Rate

A higher interest rate lowers investment. The sensitivity of investment to the interest rate is greater than the sensitivity of consumption to the interest rate, as shown in Figure 22.3.

GDP at every interest rate. Conversely, a decrease in taxes on consumption would shift the consumption share line in Figure 22.3 to the right.

Investment

A similar relationship exists for investment and interest rates. Figure 22.4 shows that there is a negative relationship between the interest rate and the investment share. For this example, when the interest rate rises from 4 percent to 8 percent, the investment share decreases from 15 percent to 12 percent. Economists have observed that investment is more sensitive than consumption to interest rates. Therefore, the line for I/Y in Figure 22.4 is less steep than the line for C/Y in Figure 22.3.

Why does this negative relationship exist in the case of investment? When businesses decide to invest, they frequently borrow the funds to buy the new machines and equipment or to build a new factory. The higher the interest rate, the more they must pay to borrow. Thus, higher interest rates discourage borrowing. Less borrowing means fewer purchases of new equipment. Investment projects that would be undertaken at lower interest rates are postponed or cancelled when interest rates rise. However, when interest rates fall, firms pay less to borrow. Thus, firms are willing to purchase more equipment or build factories that they would not build at higher interest rates.

Recall that investment also includes the purchases of new houses. Most people need to take out loans (mortgages) to purchase houses. When the interest rate on mortgages rises, people purchase fewer or smaller houses; when the interest rate falls, people purchase more or larger houses.

The negative relationship between investment as a share of GDP and the interest rate is observed in the economy for many years and it makes sense: A higher interest rate discourages investment, and a lower interest rate encourages investment.

Observe that the relationship between the investment share of GDP and the interest rate in Figure 22.4 looks like a demand curve. It is downward-sloping. The interest rate is like the price: A higher interest rate decreases the amount of investment firms will do, and a lower interest rate increases the amount of investment firms will do.

Other factors besides interest rates also affect investment; when these factors change, the investment share line in Figure 22.4 will *shift*. For example, an investment tax credit in which a firm's taxes are lowered if the firm buys new equipment would increase the amount that firms would invest at each interest rate. An investment tax credit would shift the investment share line in Figure 22.4 to the right: The investment that firms are willing to do as a share of GDP rises at a given interest rate. A change in firms' expectations of the future could also shift the investment share line; if firms feel that new computing or telecommunications equipment will lower their costs in the future, they will purchase the equip-

ment, thereby increasing their investment at a given interest rate; the investment share line will shift to the right. Conversely, pessimism on the part of firms about the benefits of investment could shift the line to the left.

Net Exports

Net exports are also negatively related to the interest rate. As you can see in Figure 22.5, a negative relationship exists that is much like the relationship of consumption and investment to the interest rate. For this example, when the interest rate goes up, from 4 percent to 8 percent, net exports go from zero to about −4 percent of GDP. Remember that when net exports are negative there is a trade deficit.

The story behind this relationship is unfortunately somewhat more involved than for investment or for consumption. However, you may find the story more interesting because it includes the role of foreign exchange rates in determining exports and imports, as well as the relationship between interest rates and exchange rates. In any case, it is important to grasp the key features. The story has three parts. (Recall that foreign exchange rates were discussed in Chapter 2.)

The Interest Rate and the Exchange Rate

Let us start with the relationship between the interest rate and the exchange rate. International investors must decide whether to put their funds in assets denominated in dollars—such as an account at a U.S. bank in New York City—or in assets denominated in foreign currencies—such as an account at a Japanese bank in Tokyo. If interest rates rise in the United States, then international investors are more interested in placing their funds in dollar-denominated assets. They can earn more by doing so. For example, suppose the interest rate paid on U.S. dollar deposits in New York rises and there is no change in the interest rates in Japan. Then international investors who are considering investing in Japanese yen versus U.S. dollars will start to shift their funds from Tokyo to New York in order to take advantage of the higher interest rate. As funds are shifted to the United States, the demand for dollar-denominated assets begins to increase. This increased demand puts upward pressure on the dollar exchange rate, and the exchange rate will rise. In other words, the higher interest rate will tend to bring about a higher level of the dollar exchange rate. For example, an increase in the interest rate in the United States might cause the dollar to increase from 100 yen per dollar to 120 yen per dollar. Conversely, a lower interest rate in the United States brings about a lower exchange rate for the dollar.

Thus, the interest rate and exchange rate are positively related. Such a relationship is confirmed by observing interest rates and exchange rates in the market over several years. When the interest rate increases compared to interest rates abroad, the exchange rate rises. See the box "Interest Rates and Exchange Rates," which discusses the significant rise of the U.S. dollar relative to the German mark in the mid 1980s when the U.S. interest rate rose.

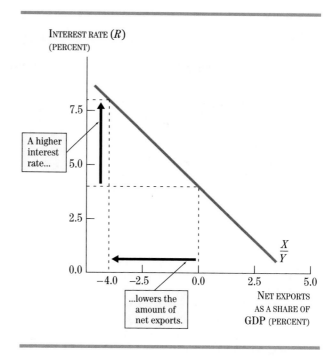

FIGURE 22.5
The Net Exports Share and the Interest Rate
A higher interest rate lowers net exports because it tends to raise the exchange rate. The higher exchange rate lowers exports and raises imports, thereby lowering net exports. When net exports are negative, there is a trade deficit. When net exports are positive, there is a trade surplus.

Interest Rates and Exchange Rates

In general, an increase in interest rates in the United States is associated with an increase in the dollar exchange rate because higher interest rates attract the funds of international investors.

The exchange rate between the U.S. dollar and the German mark in the 1980s and 1990s shows how well the theory works. The purple line in this graph shows the exchange rate in marks per dollar from 1978 through 1991 with the scale on the right-hand axis. The dollar appreciated—more marks per dollar—from 1978 to 1984 and then depreciated with a few ups and downs in between.

The green line in the graph is the interest rate on U.S. Treasury bonds measured relative to the interest rate on German bonds. (That is, the figure shows the difference between the two interest rates.) The scale is on the left-hand axis.

As the U.S. interest rate rose compared to Germany, the value of the dollar rose relative to the German mark. Although the relationship is not perfect, the direction is clear. The same type of relationship is true for other currencies.

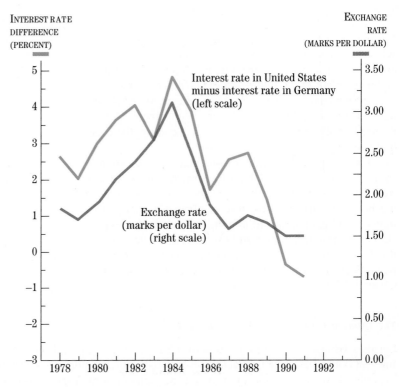

Source: Organization for Economic Cooperation and Development.

The Exchange Rate and Net Exports

A higher dollar exchange rate brought about by a higher interest rate will tend to make imported goods to the United States more attractive because it makes these foreign goods cheaper. For example, the dollar exchange rate against the yen was relatively high at 250 yen per dollar in 1985 and comparatively low at 100 yen per dollar in 1994. When the exchange rate between the dollar and the yen was 250 yen per dollar in 1985, one could buy a kimono costing 25,000 yen for $100 (25,000/250). This was much cheaper than in 1994, when the exchange rate was 100 yen per dollar and the kimono cost $250 (25,000/100). Thus, a higher exchange rate increases the quantity demanded of imported goods.

In addition, the higher exchange rate makes U.S. exports less attractive because it makes American goods more expensive. For example, a $20,000 Jeep Cherokee cost 5 million yen in Japan in 1985 and only 2 million yen in 1994 because the dollar was higher in 1985. Thus, the exchange rate affects exports.

We have shown that a higher exchange rate means more imports and fewer exports. Since net exports are the difference between exports and imports, a higher exchange rate must mean that net exports are going down. Conversely, a lower exchange rate must mean that net exports are going up. To arrive at this result, we used a combination of some simple arithmetic that emphasizes net exports as the difference between exports and imports as well as an economic rationale that says both exports and imports should depend on the exchange rate.

Combining the Two Relationships

Let us combine the two relationships. One relates the interest rate to the exchange rate and the other relates the exchange rate to net exports. Combining those two we get the relationship between the interest rate and net exports summarized below.

Interest Rate	Exchange Rate	Net Exports
up $\longrightarrow$	up $\longrightarrow$	down
down $\longrightarrow$	down $\longrightarrow$	up

If the interest rate goes up, then the exchange rate goes up and net exports go down. Thus, a higher interest rate reduces net exports. The link is the exchange rate, which is increased by the higher interest rate and which in turn makes net exports fall. Of course, all of this works in reverse too. If the interest rate goes down, then the exchange rate goes down and net exports go up. Thus, a lower interest rate increases net exports, because a lower interest rate means a lower exchange rate for the dollar, which stimulates U.S. exports and discourages imports.

By combining the relationships between the interest rate, the exchange rate, exports, and imports, we have derived the relationship between net exports as a share of GDP and the interest rate shown in Figure 22.5. Like the consumption share line and the investment share line, the net export line in the figure looks like a demand curve. It is downward-sloping. Changes in the interest rate lead to movements along the net export line in Figure 22.5. Changes in other factors—such as a shift in foreign demand for U.S. products—may cause the line to shift.

Putting the Three Shares Together

We have shown that the consumption, investment, and net exports shares are all negatively related to the interest rate. Our next task is to determine the interest rate and, thereby, a particular value for each share. To determine the interest rate, we will require that the sum of these three shares equals what is left over after the government takes its share. This will ensure that all shares sum to 1.

Review

▶ Consumption, investment, and net exports are negatively related to the interest rate.

▶ Higher interest rates raise the price of consumption this year relative to next year. This means fewer goods consumed this year.

▶ Business firms invest less when interest rates rise because higher interest rates raise borrowing costs.

▶ Higher interest rates raise the exchange rate and thereby discourage exports and encourage imports, leading to a decline in net exports.

▶ Other factors besides the interest rate may affect consumption, investment, and net exports. When one of these factors changes, the relationship between the interest rate and consumption, investment, or net exports shifts.

DETERMINING THE EQUILIBRIUM INTEREST RATE

The interest rate affects the three shares (consumption, investment, and net exports) and therefore affects the sum of the three shares. This is shown by the downward-sloping line in diagram (d) of Figure 22.6. In diagram (d), an increase in the interest rate reduces the sum of the three shares of GDP.

Adding the Nongovernment Shares Graphically

Note carefully how Figure 22.6 is put together and how the downward-sloping line in diagram (d) is derived. We have taken the graphs from Figures 22.3, 22.4, and 22.5 and assembled them horizontally in diagrams (a), (b), and (c) of Figure 22.6. The downward-sloping red line in diagram (d) is the sum of the three downward-sloping lines in diagrams (a), (b), and (c). It is the nongovernment share of GDP, or NG/Y, where $NG = C + I + X$ and as usual Y is GDP. For example, when the interest rate is 4 percent, the line in diagram (d) shows that the nongovernment share—the sum of investment, consumption, and net exports as a share of GDP—is 80 percent; this is the sum of 65 percent for the consumption share, 15 percent for the investment share, and zero percent for the net exports share. Similarly, the other points in diagram (d) are obtained by adding up the three shares at other levels of interest rates. For example, at an interest rate of 5 percent, we see that the sum of the share of consumption, investment, and net exports is down to about 78 percent.

The Share of GDP Available for Nongovernment Use

To determine the interest rate we must consider the fourth share: government. The share of GDP not used by the government is available for nongovernment use, that is, for either consumption, investment, or net exports. For example, if the government share is 22 percent of GDP, then the share available for nongovernment use is 78 percent. The sum of the consumption share, the investment share, and the net export share must equal 78 percent.

What brings this equality about? In a market economy, the government does not stipulate that consumption, investment, or net exports must equal 78 percent, or

**FIGURE 22.6
Summing Up Consumption, Investment, and Net Exports Shares**

Diagrams (a), (b), and (c) are reproductions of Figures 22.3, 22.4, and 22.5. For each interest rate, the three shares are added together to get the sum of shares shown in diagram (d). For example, when the interest rate is 4 percent, we get 65 percent for consumption share, 15 percent for investment share, and 0 percent for net exports, summing to 80 percent. The sum of the three nongovernment shares (NG/Y) is negatively related to the interest rate (R).

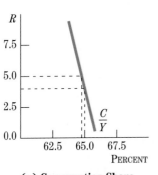

(a) Consumption Share

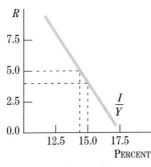

(b) Investment Share

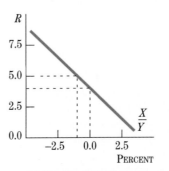

(c) Net Exports Share

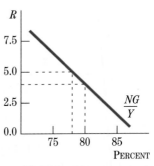

(d) Nongovernment Share

any other share of GDP. Instead, prices—in this case the interest rate—adjust to provide individual consumers or firms with the incentive to make the necessary adjustments. Recall from Chapter 2 that the price in a market serves as both a signal and an incentive to individuals. In a market economy as a whole, the interest rate adjusts to ensure equality between (1) the sum of investment, consumption, and net exports shares, and (2) the share of GDP available for investment, consumption, and net exports.

If the sum of consumption, investment, and net exports shares begins to rise above the share of GDP available after the government takes its share, then the interest rate will rise and will bring consumption, investment, net exports, or all three back down to what is available. Recall that a higher interest rate provides an incentive to people to reduce their consumption and for firms to reduce their investment. If the sum of consumption, investment, and net exports begins to fall below what was available, then the interest rate will fall, bringing the nongovernment shares up to what was available. Thus, in a market economy, changes in the interest rate bring consumption, investment, and net exports into equality with the amount of GDP available. Or, equivalently, changes in the interest rate ensure that the sum of all four shares of GDP is 1.

Finding the Equilibrium Interest Rate Graphically

Figure 22.7 illustrates how the interest rate brings about the equality. Look first at diagram (d). In diagram (d), the share of GDP available for nongovernment use is indicated by the vertical line. The government share of spending is assumed not to depend on the interest rate but rather on public decisions made by voters and politicians about the role of government in the economy. This is why the share of GDP available for nongovernment use does not depend on the interest rate and why it is represented by a vertical line. In the case where government purchases are 22

FIGURE 22.7
Determining the Equilibrium Interest Rate, Investment, and the Other Shares
In this case, government purchases are assumed to be 22 percent of GDP. Mark the implied share available for nongovernmental uses of 78 percent in diagram (d). The equilibrium interest rate is determined at the intersection of the two lines in diagram (d). Given this interest rate, we can compute investment and the other shares of spending in GDP using diagrams (a), (b), and (c).

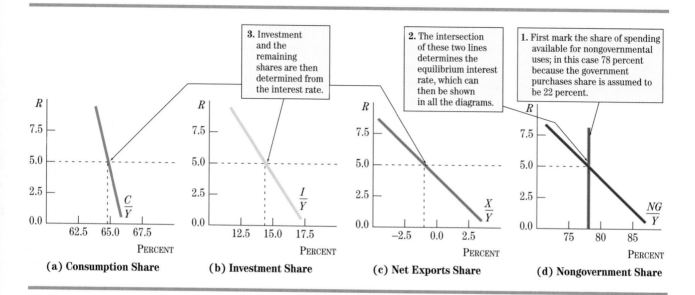

3. Investment and the remaining shares are then determined from the interest rate.

2. The intersection of these two lines determines the equilibrium interest rate, which can then be shown in all the diagrams.

1. First mark the share of spending available for nongovernmental uses; in this case 78 percent because the government purchases share is assumed to be 22 percent.

(a) Consumption Share **(b) Investment Share** **(c) Net Exports Share** **(d) Nongovernment Share**

equilibrium interest rate: the interest rate that equates the sum of consumption, investment, and net export shares to the share of GDP available for nongovernment use.

percent of GDP, the vertical line is at 78 percent, as shown in Figure 22.7 (d). If the government share were larger, we would draw the vertical line further to the left, showing that the share available for nongovernment use was smaller.

The sum of the three nongovernment shares is shown by the downward-sloping line in Figure 22.7 (d). This is the same line we derived in Figure 22.6 (d). At the intersection of this downward-sloping line and the vertical line, the sum of investment, consumption, and net exports is equal to the share that is available for nongovernment use. For example, when the share available is 78 percent, we see in diagram (d) of Figure 22.7 that the point of intersection occurs when the interest rate is 5 percent. This is the **equilibrium interest rate,** the interest rate that makes the sum of consumption, investment, and net export shares equal to the share of GDP available. It is also the interest rate for which the sum of all shares of GDP equals 1.

Once we determine the equilibrium interest rate, we can find each of the investment, consumption, and net exports shares. Each of these shares depends on the interest rate, as shown in diagrams (a), (b), and (c) of Figure 22.7. To determine each of the shares, simply draw a line across the three diagrams at the equilibrium interest rate. Then in diagram (a) we find the consumption share, in diagram (b) the investment share, and in diagram (c) the net exports share.

Analogy with Supply and Demand

Observe that the intersection of the two lines in diagram (d) of Figure 22.7 is much like the intersection of a demand curve and a supply curve. The red downward-sloping line—showing how the sum of investment, consumption, and net exports is negatively related to the interest rate—looks just like a demand curve. The blue vertical line—showing the share of GDP available for consumption, investment, and net exports—looks like a vertical supply curve. The intersection of the two curves determines the equilibrium price—in this case the equilibrium interest rate in the economy as a whole. In the next section, we show how shifts in one or both of these two curves lead to a new equilibrium interest rate, much like shifts in supply and demand curves lead to a new equilibrium price.

The Real Interest Rate in the Long Run

Having determined the equilibrium interest rate, it is important to mention once more that our analysis applies to the *long run*—perhaps three years or more—rather than to short-run economic fluctuations. It takes time for consumers and firms to completely respond to a change in interest rates.

Moreover, the interest rate in the analysis refers to the *real* interest rate, which, as defined in Chapter 19, is the interest rate on loans adjusted for inflation. The real interest rate is defined as the nominal interest rate less the expected inflation rate. If the inflation rate is low, there is little difference between the real interest rate and the nominal interest rate; but if inflation is high, there is a big difference and the real interest rate is a much better measure of the incentives affecting consumers and firms. An interest rate of 50 percent would seem high but would actually be quite low—2 percent in real terms—if people expected inflation to be 48 percent.

Broadly speaking, the analysis in this section shows that the real interest rate in the long run is determined by balancing people's demands for consumption, investment, and net exports with the available supply of goods and services in the economy.

Review

▶ The sum of consumption, investment, and net exports shares of GDP is negatively related to the interest rate, because each of the individual components is negatively related to the interest rate.

▶ The equilibrium interest rate is determined by the condition that the sum of the three nongovernment shares of GDP equal the share not used by government. Using the equilibrium interest rate, we can then find each of the nongovernment shares.

IMPACTS ON THE INVESTMENT SHARE

Now let us use this theory to examine how the investment share—and thereby the accumulation of capital—is affected by changes in the economy. We consider a shift in government purchases and a shift in consumption. Both reflect possible economic policy decisions.

A Change in Government Purchases

What happens when government purchases increase or decrease as a share of GDP? We know as a matter of arithmetic that some other share must move in a direction opposite to the government share. To find out what happens to investment we need to look at what happens to consumption and net exports too.

Suppose that the government share of GDP increases by 2 percent, perhaps as a result of an increase in defense spending, as in the early 1980s in the United States, or by an increased need for government infrastructure spending, as in the unification of Germany in the 1990s.

The effects of this change are shown in Figure 22.8. If government purchases as a share of GDP increase by 2 percent, then we know that the share of GDP available for nongovernmental use must *decrease* by 2 percent. Thus, in diagram (d) of Figure 22.8, we shift the vertical line marking the available share to the left by 2 percentage points. As Figure 22.8 (d) shows, there is now a new intersection of the two lines and a new higher equilibrium interest rate. The increase in the interest rate is the market mechanism that brings about a decline in consumption plus investment plus net exports as a share of GDP.

Diagram (d) of Figure 22.8, for example, shows that the new interest rate is 5 percent rather than 4 percent. That is, the interest rate has increased by 1 percentage point. Now we are prepared to answer the key question: What is the impact on investment?

To see the effect on investment share, we draw a horizontal line at 5 percent interest, as shown in Figure 22.8, and read off the implied amount of investment as well as consumption and net exports shares. According to the diagram, the share of consumption decreases by ¼ percent of GDP, the share of investment decreases by about ¾ percent of GDP, and the share of net exports decreases by about 1 percent of GDP. The sum is 2 percent, which is exactly the decrease in the share of government spending. It all adds up, and we have a particular prediction, not only about investment but also about consumption and net exports.

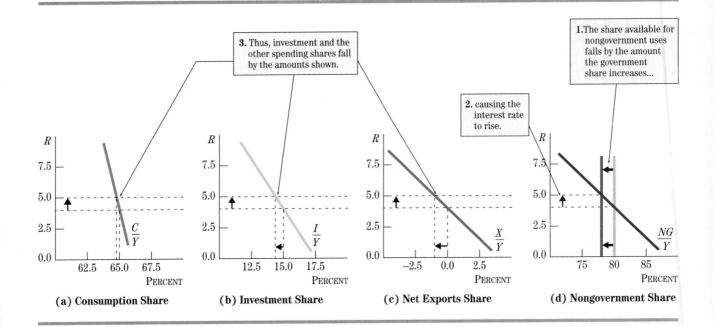

FIGURE 22.8
The Effect of an Increase in Government Purchases

If the government purchases share of GDP rises, then the share available for nongovernment uses must fall by the same amount. This causes a rise in interest rates, which reduces consumption, investment, and net exports as a share of GDP.

The same process could work in reverse if we decreased government purchases as a share of GDP. In Figure 22.8, the interest rates would have to fall. To find out the effect on the other components of spending, we would draw a horizontal line at a lower interest rate. That would show us that investment would rise as a share of GDP, and so would consumption and net exports.

Sometimes the decline in investment due to an increase in government purchases is called **crowding out** because investment is "crowded out" by the government purchases. Thus, we have shown that an increase in government purchases as a share of GDP causes a crowding out of investment in the long run. However, because net exports and consumption also fall, the crowding out of investment is not as large as it would otherwise be. All these effects are summarized in Figure 22.8.

crowding out: the decline in private investment owing to an increase in government purchases.

Impact on Investment of a Shift in Consumption

Suppose that there is an increase in the amount people want to consume at every interest rate. Such a shift seems to have taken place in the United States from the early 1970s to the late 1980s. In 1973, the consumption share of GDP was 63 percent, and in 1989 it was 67 percent.

Economic policy changes can bring about such shifts. For example, in the late 1980s, Individual Retirement Accounts (IRAs), which allowed people to reduce their taxes if they saved for retirement each year, were virtually eliminated. The elimination of the lower tax on savings through IRAs may have been an inducement for many people to consume more and save less.

The impact of a shift in consumption—whatever its cause—is analyzed in Figure 22.9. The relationship between the interest rate and consumption shifts out

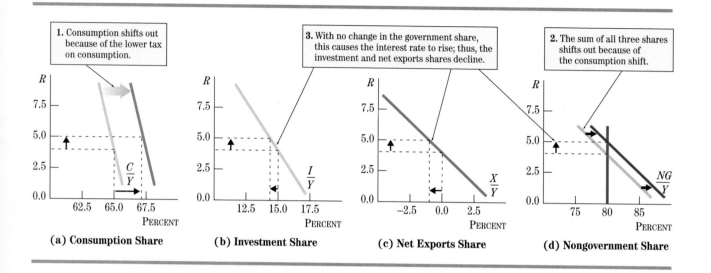

1. Consumption shifts out because of the lower tax on consumption.

3. With no change in the government share, this causes the interest rate to rise; thus, the investment and net exports shares decline.

2. The sum of all three shares shifts out because of the consumption shift.

(a) Consumption Share

(b) Investment Share

(c) Net Exports Share

(d) Nongovernment Share

in diagram (a); this causes the sum of investment, consumption, and net exports to shift out, as shown by the shift in the line in diagram (d).

The impact is an increase in the equilibrium interest rate and a decline in investment. However, because net exports decline, the impact on investment is much less than if net exports had not changed. The action of foreigners reduces substantially the effect of the increased consumption on capital formation.

The overall prediction of the effects of such a shift are very close to what has happened in the United States from the early 1970s to the late 1980s, as shown in Table 22.1. As the consumption share rose over this long period, the investment share and the net exports share fell. The government purchases share was unchanged. According to most estimates the real interest rate was higher in the 1980s than in the 1970s. Thus, the theory of investment put forth in this chapter explains the long-term trends in the shares of spending and interest rates very well under the assumption that there was a shift in consumption.

We can also investigate other policy changes. For example, what if there were an increase in the tax on consumption? In this case, the nongovernment share line in Figure 22.9 would shift to the left in diagram (d). Interest rates would fall and investment would rise; net exports would also rise. One of the reasons that taxes on consumption have been recommended by economists is that they would increase investment, as predicted by the theory.

FIGURE 22.9
Effect of a Shift in Consumption
If the amount of consumption relative to income rises at every interest rate—perhaps because of a tax change that reduces the tax on consumption—the interest rate will rise. Both investment and net exports decline.

	1973	1989
Consumption share	63	67
Investment share	18	16
Net exports share	0	−2
Government purchases share	19	19

TABLE 22.1
Shares of GDP: 1973 and 1989
(percent)

Anticipation of Changes in Government Purchases

The theory of investment predicts that an increase in the government share of GDP will raise interest rates and thereby crowd out investment, net exports, and even consumption as a share of GDP. This graph shows how this actually happened in Germany in late 1989 and 1990 after the Berlin Wall fell and German unification was expected. The purple line shows that government purchases in Germany rose in mid-1990. The green line shows that interest rates also rose.

Notice that interest rates rose *before* the increase in government purchases. Most economists explained the increase in interest rates in late 1989 as due to anticipation of the increase in government purchases that would be needed for the expected reunification of Germany. This is an example of how expectations of the future can affect events in the present. The long-term interest rates on bonds reflect expectations of interest rates in the future because the bonds will not mature for many years.

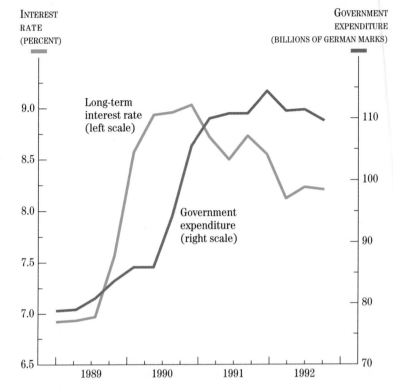

Source: Organization for Economic Cooperation and Development.

Review

▶ The impact of a change in government spending on capital accumulation can be analyzed by looking at what happens to the interest rate and each component of GDP.

▶ An increase in the government spending share reduces the share available for nongovernment use by exactly the same amount. This means that interest rates must rise. The rise in interest rates causes investment, consumption, and net exports to fall.

▶ An upward shift in consumption causes investment and net exports to fall and the interest rate to rise.

THE SAVING INVESTMENT APPROACH

In Chapter 20, we derived a relationship showing that national saving equals investment plus net exports. This relationship provides an alternative approach to determine investment and the interest rate. The alternative gives exactly the same answers, but it provides additional insights because it focuses on saving, the flip side of consumption.

National saving (S) is defined as aggregate income minus consumption minus government purchases, or

$$S = Y - C - G$$

National saving must always be equal to investment plus net exports; that is,

$$S = I + X$$

Now we show that this relationship can be used to determine the interest rate and investment share.

The National Saving Rate and the Interest Rate

The ratio of national saving to GDP is the **national saving rate.** If we divide each term in the definition of national saving by Y, we can write the national saving rate as 1 minus the share of consumption and government purchases in GDP. That is,

$$\frac{\text{National}}{\text{saving rate}} = 1 - \frac{\text{consumption}}{\text{share}} - \frac{\text{government}}{\text{purchases share}}$$

or

$$\frac{S}{Y} = 1 - \frac{C}{Y} - \frac{G}{Y}$$

We know that the consumption share (C/Y) depends on the interest rate. This equation tells us that the national saving rate also depends on the interest rate. In particular, the national saving rate is positively related to the interest rate because the consumption share is negatively related to the interest rate, as we showed earlier. In other words, when the interest rate rises, the consumption share falls, implying that the saving rate rises. The relationship between the national saving rate and the interest rate is shown in Figure 22.10.

The equation for S/Y also shows that an increase in government share reduces saving at every interest rate; thus, the relationship between the national saving rate and the interest rate shifts to the left when the government share increases.

Determination of the Equilibrium Interest Rate

If we divide both sides of the expression $S = I + X$ by Y, we get

$$\frac{S}{Y} = \frac{I}{Y} + \frac{X}{Y}$$

or, in other words, the national saving rate equals investment share plus net exports share. The terms on both sides of this equation depend on the interest rate. We can plot these two relationships in the same graph as Figure 22.10 to get a prediction of the equilibrium interest rate. This is done in Figure 22.11. The upward-sloping line in the figure shows the national saving

national saving rate: the proportion of GDP that is saved, neither consumed nor spent on government purchases; equals national saving (S) divided by GDP, or S/Y. It also equals 1 minus the consumption share minus the government purchases share of GDP.

FIGURE 22.10
The National Saving Rate and the Interest Rate
When the interest rate rises, national saving as a share of GDP rises because the consumption share falls. The sensitivity of the national saving rate to the interest rate is thought by most economists to be smaller than for the investment share.

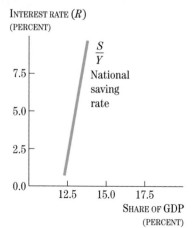

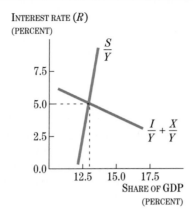

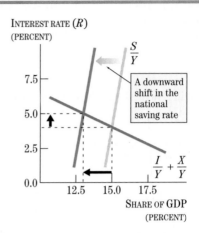

FIGURE 22.11
Determining the Interest Rate Using the Saving Relationship
The interest rate is determined at the point where national saving equals investment plus net exports, shown at the intersection of the two lines. The saving rate (and the sum of the investment and net exports shares) is shown on the horizontal axis.

FIGURE 22.12
The Effect of a Downward Shift in the Saving Rate
The effect is the same as the shift upward in the consumption share illustrated in Figure 22.9. The lower national saving rate raises interest rates and lowers the investment share and the net exports share.

rate. An increase in the interest rate causes the saving rate to rise. The downward-sloping line shows the sum of I/Y and X/Y; this sum is negatively related to the interest rate.

At the intersection of the two lines in Figure 22.11, the national saving rate equals the investment share plus the net exports share. The intersection, therefore, determines the equilibrium interest rate. The interest rate is exactly the same as that in Figure 22.7, which is based on exactly the same relationships. The national saving rate is shown on the horizontal axis, and the investment share can be determined by subtracting the net exports share.

Effect of a Downward Shift in the National Saving Rate

Now let us look at the same shift in consumption share considered in the previous section but with a focus on saving. An upward shift in the consumption share is equivalent to a downward shift in the saving rate. Thus, we shift the interest rate-saving rate relationship to the left in Figure 22.12, representing a downshift in the national saving rate. As shown in the figure, this leads to a higher interest rate and a lower share for investment and net exports. Hence the predictions are the same as the previous analysis in Figure 22.9. The decline in investment is less than the decline in the saving rate because net exports decline. (This is not shown in Figure 22.12.) If net exports fall by a large amount in response to the decline in the national saving rate, then investment does not change much at all.

Review

▶ The national saving rate is an increasing function of the interest rate. The sum of the investment and net exports shares is a decreasing function of the interest rate. The equality of the national saving rate and the sum of the two shares determines the interest rate.

▶ A downward shift in the national saving rate lowers the investment share and raises the interest rate. It also lowers the net exports share. These are the same results caused by an increase in consumption; thus, an upward shift in the consumption share is equivalent to a downward shift in the saving rate.

DETERMINATION OF GOVERNMENT'S SHARE OF GDP

Throughout this chapter we have said that government's share of GDP is determined by voters and politicians, and we looked at what impact a change in government share would have on investment and interest rates. A rise in the share of government purchases means that something else has to decline. A fall in the share of government purchases means that there is an opportunity for spending elsewhere. But what factors determine government's share?

Arguments over the Appropriate Size of Government

Government has a significant role in the economy, a role that is most forcefully illustrated in the case of providing for goods such as national defense and police. Government also has a role in education, either by subsidizing education or by providing it directly. In most countries primary and secondary education comprises a large part of government purchases. College education in the United States is partly provided by the private sector, but there is also a very large public sector in college education.

Over the years there have been debates among economists and noneconomists alike about whether the United States or other economies devote too much or too little to public spending versus private spending. John Kenneth Galbraith of Harvard University supported the view in the 1950s and 1960s that the United States was not spending enough on public goods and was spending too much on private goods. In the 1980s the trend appeared to shift substantially, and people argued that too much was spent on public goods, especially on nondefense public goods. Indeed, this was part of the Reagan revolution and represents a view supported by economists such as Milton Friedman.

By the 1990s, the trend appeared to be moving back in the other direction. Economists began to emphasize that economic growth depends on government spending on public infrastructure. But there is a substantial difference of opinion in the United States about what the government's share of GDP should be. These differences of opinion have led to an intense political debate that promises to continue for years into the future.

Size of Government and Economic Growth

This chapter has introduced an important macroeconomic factor to consider when assessing the appropriate size of government. Investment in new capital is affected by the size of government in the economy. Private investment is greater when purchases by the government are less. More investment spending raises productivity because there are more machines and factories for workers to work with. Higher government purchases are a negative for long-term growth on that account.

On the other hand, government spending is needed for the roads, education, and legal system that help produce economic growth. But even to the extent that government spending increases long-term growth, it reduces the share of GDP available for private investment. To the extent that consumption and net exports also shrink as government purchases increase, the effect on private investment is smaller.

Thus, there is a need for balance between government purchases and private investment. The mix will ultimately be determined in the political debate. This chapter provides some economic analysis, which is useful in that debate.

Review

▶ Debates have raged for years about the appropriate size of the share of government purchases in the economy.

▶ A higher share for government means less private investment, and this could reduce economic growth.

▶ However, some government spending is essential for economic growth.

▶ Getting the right balance between government purchases and private investment is one of the most important jobs of a political system.

CONCLUSION

In this chapter we have developed a theory that determines the equilibrium interest rate and the amount of investment in the whole economy. Because investment is only one of the uses of GDP, we needed to consider the other uses—consumption, government, and net exports—when we developed the theory.

For a given share of government purchases in GDP, the theory predicts the interest rate and the investment share as well as the consumption share and the net exports share. The theory can be used to analyze the impact on investment of a change in government purchases, a change in taxes, or a shift in consumption or saving. The theory applies to the economy in the long run as real GDP grows along the path of potential GDP.

The investment share of GDP determines how rapidly capital in the economy grows. With a higher investment share—or investment rate—the capital stock will grow more rapidly, and the amount of capital per worker will rise. With more capital to work with, workers will be able to produce more; in other words, productivity—real GDP per hour of work—will rise. Thus, understanding what determines investment is essential for understanding productivity growth. Here is how the

Council of Economic Advisers puts it: "The reasons for wanting to raise the investment share of GDP are straightforward: Workers are more productive when they are equipped with more and better capital, more productive workers earn higher real wages, and higher real wages are the mainspring of higher living standards. Few economic propositions are better supported than these—or more important."[2]

Productivity growth and rising living standards also depend on technological growth, which we turn to in the next chapter.

KEY POINTS

1. The accumulation of capital through investment is one of two key ways that long-term growth of productivity—output per hour of work—occurs. The other is technology.

2. To raise capital relative to the GDP the share of investment in GDP must rise.

3. Over the long term, investment competes with consumption, government purchases, and net exports for a share of GDP.

4. Higher interest rates raise the price of consumption and lead to a reduction of consumption as a share of GDP.

5. Higher interest rates also reduce investment.

6. Higher interest rates lower net exports by causing the exchange rate to rise. A higher exchange rate reduces exports and raises imports.

7. An equilibrium interest rate is found by equating the sum of the consumption, investment, and net exports shares to the share of GDP available for nongovernment use.

8. An increase in government purchases crowds out the share of investment in GDP by raising interest rates. Consumption and net exports also fall, making crowding out of investment less severe.

9. The choice between private investment on the one hand and government purchases on the other affects long-term economic growth.

KEY TERMS

investment	consumption share	equilibrium interest rate
public infrastructure investment	net exports share	crowding out
investment share	government purchases share	national saving rate

QUESTIONS FOR REVIEW

1. Why does an increase in investment share in GDP require a decrease in some other share?

2. What is the relationship between consumption and interest rates?

3. Why does investment fall when interest rates rise?

4. Why is there a relationship between the exchange rate and the interest rate?

5. How does the relationship between net exports and the exchange rate tie into the negative relationship between interest rates and net exports?

6. What determines the equilibrium interest rate?

7. Why should we care about achieving an increase in investment?

8. Are all investment goods accounted for in the investment component of GDP?

9. What is crowding out?

10. In what sense does the theory in this chapter apply to the long run rather than to short-run economic fluctuations?

2. *Economic Report of the President, 1994*, p. 36.

PROBLEMS

1. Describe the long-run impact of a decline of defense spending by 1 percent of GDP on interest rates and on consumption, investment, and net exports as a share of GDP. Consider two different cases:

a) No other changes in policy accompany the defense cut.

b) The funds saved from the defense cut are used to increase government expenditures on roads and bridges.

2. Suppose that there is a technological improvement that makes capital last longer—that is, wear out at a slower rate. What happens to depreciation? For a fixed level of saving, what happens to gross and net investment in this case? Explain.

3. a) As government's share in GDP decreases, the non-governmental share increases. Depict this in a diagram. What happens to interest rates?

b) As interest rates fall, what change is there in the exchange rate? What happens to net exports in this case? Does this match your earlier picture?

c) Suppose net exports are very sensitive to changes in interest rates. Does that mean a relatively big or relatively small change in net exports?

4. Suppose you have the following data for capital and investment in an economy:

Year	Capital Stock on Jan. 1	Depreciation	Gross Invest-ment	Net Invest-ment
1993	1000	———	200	———
1994	———	———	310	———
1995	———	———	120	———
1996	———	———	200	———

a) Assume that depreciation during any year is 10 percent of the January 1 level of the capital stock. Calculate the missing values in the table.

b) Is depreciation of capital a stock or a flow variable? Explain. (*Hint:* See the box "Stocks and Flows" in Chapter 20.)

c) Is net investment negative in any year? What does such a situation mean?

5. Suppose that the government wants to increase public infrastructure investment.

a) If government purchases increase, what happens to government's share in total spending? Is there crowding out?

b) Suppose instead that the government encourages private business to purchase the public infrastructure.

Where will it enter GDP? If government's share in spending is fixed, what happens to the other shares when this infrastructure is built?

6. Many people believe that the U.S. saving rate is too low. Suppose all private citizens save at a higher rate. Show what happens in this case in the savings and investment diagram where the S/Y curve shifts. Now show the same situation in the C/Y, I/Y, and X/Y diagrams. Which curve shifts? If government's share in GDP doesn't change, then what must happen to interest rates? Explain how this affects X/Y.

7. Draw two sets of diagrams like Figure 22.7 to depict two situations. In one set, draw investment and net exports being very sensitive to interest rates—that is, the I/Y and X/Y curves are very flat. In the other set, draw investment and net exports as insensitive to interest rates—that is, the I/Y and X/Y curves are nearly vertical. For the same increase in the government's share in GDP, in which set of diagrams will interest rates rise more? Why?

8. Suppose $C = 1,400, I = 400, G = 200, X = 0$.

a) What is GDP? Calculate each component's share of GDP.

b) Suppose government spending falls to 100 and GDP does not change. What is government spending's share of GDP now? What is the new nongovernment share?

c) What happens to C/Y, X/Y, and I/Y? (Do not calculate anything—just give a direction.) Explain the mechanism by which each of these changes happens.

9. Using the diagram at the top of the next page, find the equilibrium interest rate when the government share is 20 percent. What is the investment share? Show what happens to all the variables if there is an upward shift in the investment relation because of a new tax policy that encourages investment.

10. Suppose the government institutes an investment tax credit so that at every level of the interest rate, businesses will invest a greater share of GDP. Show how this change will affect the interest rate and the shares of consumption and net exports in GDP, assuming that the share of government spending of GDP remains constant.

11. Suppose that there is a leftward shift in the C/Y line due to higher consumption taxes, but at the same time, the government increases its share in GDP to maintain the same interest rate. Describe graphically how this affects each of the shares of GDP. If investment's share is the only thing that affects growth in this system, what will happen to growth as a result of this government policy?

12. Suppose the following equations describe the relationship between shares of spending in GDP (Y) and the inter-

Problem 9

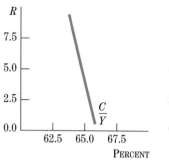

(a) Consumption Share

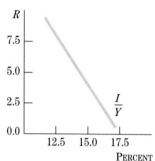

(b) Investment Share

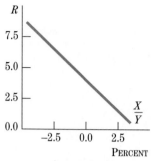

(c) Net Exports Share

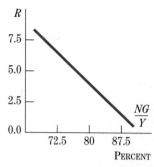

(d) Nongovernment Share

est rate (R), measured in decimal fractions (that is, $R = .04$ means that the interest rate is 4 percent).

$$\frac{C}{Y} = .65 - .25\,(R - .04)$$

$$\frac{I}{Y} = .15 - .75\,(R - .04)$$

$$\frac{X}{Y} = 0 - 1.00\,(R - .04)$$

$$\frac{G}{Y} = .18$$

a) Use algebra to determine the values of the interest rate and the shares of spending in GDP.
b) Do the calculations again for a government share of 20 percent rather than 18 percent (that is, $G/Y = .20$).

13. Graph the relationships defined in problem 12 to scale in a four-part diagram like Figure 22.6. Use the diagram to analyze each of the following situations.

a) Suppose there is a decrease in the foreign demand for U.S. goods that changes the coefficient in the net exports share equation from 0 to $-.02$. What happens to the interest rate and the shares of consumption, investment, net exports, and government purchases in the United States?
b) Determine how an increase in taxes that reduces the coefficient in the consumption share equation from .65 to .63 would affect the interest rate and the shares of consumption, investment, net exports, and government purchases.
c) Suppose firms are willing to invest 20 percent rather than 15 percent of GDP at an interest rate of 4 percent. How would this affect the interest rate and the shares of spending in GDP?

14. Derive and draw the national saving rate-interest rate relation (as in Figure 22.10) from the information on consumption, government spending, and net exports used in problem 12. In the same graph, draw investment plus net exports as a share of GDP. Determine the equilibrium level of saving and the interest rate using this graph.

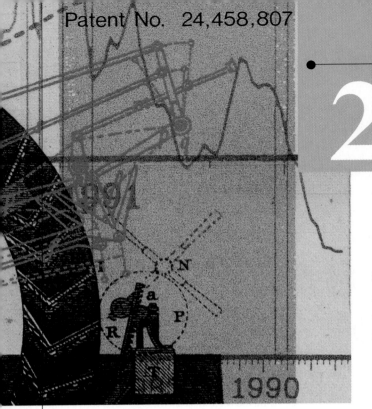

23

Technology and Economic Growth

For most of human history there was no economic growth. True, vast quantities of wealth were amassed by kings and queens through conquest and exploitation; coliseums, pyramids, and great walls were constructed by millions of slaves; and great works of art were produced by talented individuals on all continents. But output per hour of work—the productive power of labor that determines the well-being of most people—grew hardly at all for thousands of years. Except for the ruling classes, people lived in extreme poverty.

This situation changed dramatically around the eighteenth century. Table 23.1 shows the growth rates of *output per hour of work,* or *productivity,* for different periods during the last 300 years. Observe that there was no growth in output per hour of work for most of the 1700s, much like the thousands of years before. Then, in the late 1700s and early 1800s—the period historians call the Industrial Revolution—economic growth began to pick up. Growth accelerated in the early 1800s and then rose to historically unprecedented levels in the twentieth century.

The increase in economic growth during the last 200 years has taken the average person's income in the

advanced countries to a level never dreamed of in antiquity, except by the richest emperors and empresses. Although clearly dramatic to look at now, the growth rate

TABLE 23.1
Economic Growth During the Last 300 Years

Period	The Growth Rate in Real GDP per Hour of Work (percent per year)
1700–1785	0
1785–1820	½
1820–1890	1½
1890–1996	2¼

Note: In order to show productivity growth for the most advanced countries, rather than averaging over poorer countries and richer countries, the table reports growth for the country with the highest level of productivity in the given period: the Netherlands for the first period, the United Kingdom for the second, and the United States for the third and fourth periods.

Source: Angus Maddison, *Phases of Capitalist Development* (London: Oxford University Press, 1982); *Economic Report of the President,* 1997.

was not so rapid as to transform people from rags to riches literally overnight. At the ½ percent growth rate of the late 1700s, it would have taken five generations to double income per capita. At 1½ percent growth, it would still take two generations. At the 2¼ percent growth in much of the 1900s, it would take one generation.

Why did the growth of real GDP per hour of work begin to increase and then take off in the eighteenth century? The theory of economic growth tells us that increases in labor can increase the growth in real GDP but not the growth of real GDP per hour of work. To explain the growth of productivity, we must focus on the two other factors: the growth of capital and the growth of technology. Capital raises real GDP per hour of work by giving workers more tools and equipment to work with.

However, as we will show in this chapter, capital alone is not sufficient to achieve the growth we have seen over the past 200 years. Technology—the knowledge and methods that underlie the production process—must also have played a big role.

Understanding the role of technology enables economists to better evaluate the advantages and disadvantages of various economic policies to improve economic growth. For example, should economic policies to stimulate economic growth focus more on capital or more on technology? Perhaps the biggest economic problem the United States faces today is the slowdown in economic growth that began about 25 years ago. The right economic policies regarding technology might go a long way toward solving this problem.

HOW ECONOMICS GOT THE NICKNAME THE "DISMAL SCIENCE"

To prove why technology must have played a key role in the economic growth of the past two centuries, we first consider a theory of economic growth without either capital or technology. In this simplified theory, real GDP depends only on labor. That is, the amount of output in the economy can be described by the production function $Y = F(L)$, where Y is real GDP and L is labor input. When labor input increases, real GDP increases.

The proof that technology must have been a quantitatively important influence on economic growth goes as follows: First, we show why the theory without either capital or technology is too limited to explain growth. Second, we add only capital and show that, although the theory begins to look promising, it still fails to explain growth. Third, we add technology and show that the resulting theory explains the growth patterns in Table 23.1.

Surprisingly, the model without capital and technology has an important place in the history of economic thought, and it can teach us useful lessons about how economics as a science should be used for policy decisions today. The theory without capital and technology is actually very close to the economic theory proposed by some of the early economists. In particular, the economist Thomas Robert Malthus used such a theory to make predictions about economic growth and population growth over time in his famous *Essay on the Principle of Population,* published in 1798. Malthus's predictions about future economic growth were so pessimistic that people started to call all of economics the "dismal science," and the name stuck. Let's see why the predictions were so pessimistic.

The Contribution of Technology to Productivity Growth

Both improvements in technology and greater capital per hour of work can lead to growth in output per hour of work (productivity growth) over time. How quantitatively important has technology been? As these three photos illustrate, improvements in technology have played a very important role in productivity growth over the long term.

Labor Alone

First, consider the production of a single good. Imagine workers on a one-acre vineyard planting, maintaining, and harvesting grapes and suppose the only input that can be varied is labor. With more workers, the vineyard can produce more goods but, according to the simple story that output depends only on labor, the vineyard cannot increase capital because there is no capital. For example, the vineyard cannot buy wagons or wheelbarrows to haul fertilizer around. The only way the vineyard can increase output is by hiring more workers to haul the fertilizer.

Now, suppose all this is true for the economy as a whole. The firms in the economy can produce more output by hiring more workers, but they cannot increase capital. The situation is shown for the entire economy in Figure 23.1. On the vertical axis is output. On the horizontal axis is labor input to producing output. The curve shows that more labor can produce more output. The curve is a graphical plot of the aggregate production function $Y = F(L)$ for the whole economy.

Diminishing Returns to Labor

The slope of the curve in Figure 23.1 is important. The flattening out of the curve shows that there are **diminishing returns** to labor: The greater the number of workers used in producing output, the less additional output that comes from each additional worker. Why? Consider production of a single good again, such as grapes at the vineyard. Increasing employment at the one-acre vineyard from one to two workers raises production more than increasing employment from 1,001 to 1,002 workers. A second worker could take charge of irrigation or inspect the vines for insects while the first worker harvested grapes. But with 1,001 workers on the vineyard, the 1,002nd worker could find little to do to raise production. Diminishing returns to labor exist because labor is the only input to production that we are changing. As more workers are employed on the same one-acre plot, the contribution that each additional worker makes goes down. Adding one worker when only one worker is employed can increase production by a large amount. But adding one worker when there are already 1,001 on the acre plot cannot add as much! For the same reasons, diminishing returns to labor exist for the whole economy.

When early economists, such as Malthus, wrote about economics in the late eighteenth and early nineteenth century, agriculture was a large part of the economy, employing more than 75 percent of all workers, compared with about 2 per-

diminishing returns: a situation in which successive increases in the use of an input, holding other inputs constant, will eventually cause a decline in the additional production derived from one more unit of that input.

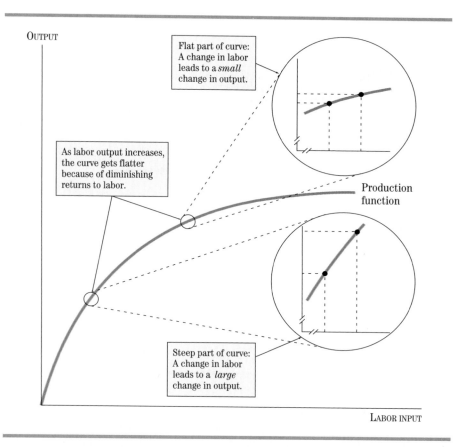

FIGURE 23.1
A Theory Where Only Changes in Labor Can Change Output
The curve shows the production function $Y = F(L)$ where Y is output and L is labor input (hours of work). In this theory, capital and technology are out of the picture. With more labor working on a fixed supply of land, there are diminishing returns, as shown by the curvature of the production function.

cent in the United States today. Farm product and gross domestic product were almost the same thing. Hence, agricultural examples such as the preceding one were very fitting. Although the amount of farmland could be increased somewhat by clearing more forests, the number of acres of land available for producing farm goods was limited, especially in England, where many early economists lived. It was not so unrealistic for them to think of labor as the only input to production that could be increased. Moreover, they saw only small improvements in farming methods in Europe for thousands of years, so they can be excused for underestimating the effects of capital and technology on output when they developed their economic theories.

Malthusian Predictions

One of the most influential ideas developed during this period was the pessimistic Malthusian prediction about population and economic growth. Malthus emphasized that workers and the population as a whole needed a certain amount of output to survive or subsist. If output in the economy, which was largely farm output, dropped below a certain amount, called the subsistence level, then people would begin to die of starvation. This is illustrated in Figure 23.2. The axes of Figure 23.2 are the same as Figure 23.1. The line in Figure 23.2—called the **subsistence line**— tells us how much output the population would need to subsist—to avoid starvation

subsistence line: a line representing the minimum amount of production the population needs to survive or subsist.

FIGURE 23.2

The Subsistence Line

Along the subsistence line, output per worker is just equal to what it takes for people to live. For the example shown, subsistence is 50 units of output per worker, so that 20 workers need to produce 1,000 units to survive, 100 workers need to produce 5,000 units, and so on. Below subsistence, people die and labor input declines. Above the line, population and labor input rise.

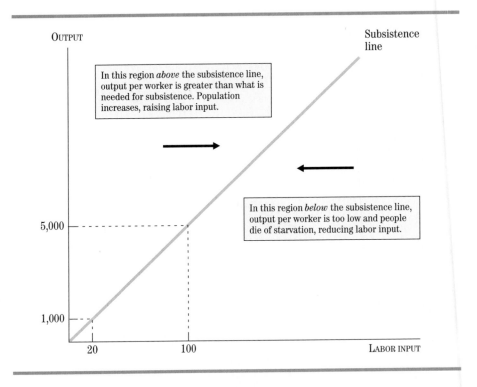

and death. A larger labor input corresponding to a larger population of workers requires more output to subsist; therefore, the line slopes upward. The subsistence level per worker—the minimum amount of output a worker and the worker's family would need to survive—is given by the slope of the subsistence line. For example, if it takes 50 units of output per worker to survive, then 100 workers require 5,000 units of output.

The subsistence line divides Figure 23.2 into two regions. Observe that in the region above the subsistence line, people have more than enough to survive. Malthus assumed that birthrates would increase and death rates would decline in this situation. Hence, the population and labor input would be increasing. This is shown by the arrow pointing to the right. In the region below the subsistence line, output is below the required amount; people do not have enough to live on, and starvation, health problems, and higher death rates reduce the population. Thus, the available labor input is declining, as shown by the arrow pointing to the left.

When the subsistence line is combined with the simple production function relating output to labor input, the Malthusian prediction about economic growth and population emerges. This is shown in Figure 23.3, which superimposes the subsistence line from Figure 23.2 on the production function from Figure 23.1. The amount of output for a particular amount of labor input is always given by the production function; that is, the economy is always at a point on the production function. If output is above the subsistence line, then there will be more output than people need to survive. In that case, the population of workers will grow, according to Malthus. An increase in the population will increase labor input and the economy will move back to the subsistence line. However, if output is below the subsistence line, then the labor input will decline and the economy will move back to the subsistence line.

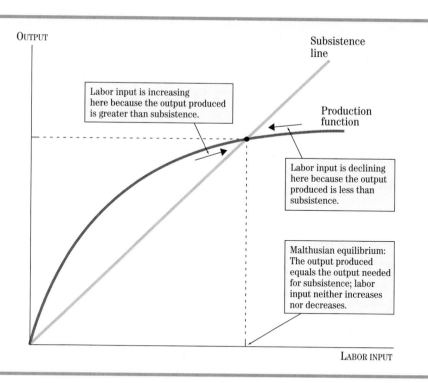

OUTPUT

Subsistence line

Labor input is increasing here because the output produced is greater than subsistence.

Production function

Labor input is declining here because the output produced is less than subsistence.

Malthusian equilibrium: The output produced equals the output needed for subsistence; labor input neither increases nor decreases.

LABOR INPUT

FIGURE 23.3
A Malthusian Equilibrium
There is only one equilibrium labor input, as indicated on the diagram. At a higher labor input, output will fall below subsistence, reducing the population and labor input. At a lower labor input, output will rise above subsistence, raising birthrates and increasing the population and labor input.

Thus, the Malthusian prediction is that real GDP will gravitate toward the subsistence level of output, limiting the well-being of all people—the workers and their children, their grandchildren, and so on for eternity. There is no long-term economic growth. The subsistence level of output is determined by the point of intersection of the production function and the subsistence line. This point is called a **Malthusian equilibrium** because the level of output given by the production function is exactly equal to the level of output needed for subsistence given by the subsistence line. Figure 23.3 shows the labor input corresponding to this Malthusian equilibrium.

Why is the Malthusian equilibrium a *stable* equilibrium? That is, why is there a tendency to move toward the equilibrium? If, starting at that equilibrium, the number of workers grew more rapidly, then output would not keep up and the economy would move into the starvation region; this would cause an automatic reduction in the labor input back to the equilibrium level. If, starting at that equilibrium, labor grew less rapidly, then output per worker would increase, which would stimulate population growth and again bring labor input back to the equilibrium level.

The Malthusian prediction was that the people of England would be forever limited to consuming a subsistence level of output. This prediction is called the **iron law of wages** because the total amount that workers could receive for their work—their wage—was limited to this subsistence amount. A science with that prediction and the associated world-view that most people would forever be struggling at the brink of starvation, with occasional bouts of hardship and mass starvation, seems to deserve the term *dismal science* it was given by the Scottish historian Thomas Carlyle. Malthus himself was less harsh when commenting on the theory,

Malthusian equilibrium: a situation in which production equals the subsistence level of output because population adjusts based on consumption of food.

iron law of wages: the prediction that wages will always tend to equal the subsistence level.

Thomas Robert Malthus, 1766–1834

BORN:
Surrey, England 1766

EDUCATION:
Cambridge University, 1784–1788

JOBS:
Parson, Church of England, 1788–1804
Fellow, Cambridge University, 1793–1804
Professor of history and political economy, East India Company College,
   in Haileybury, England, 1805–1834

MAJOR PUBLICATIONS:
An Essay on the Principle of Population as It Affects the Future Improvements of Society, 1798; *Principles of Political Economy,* 1820

Thomas Robert Malthus, called Bob by his dad and Pop by his students, published his *Essay on the Principles of Population* anonymously when he was 32 years old. Very short—only 137 pages—and wonderfully written, this book had an enormous impact on economists, public officials, and even biologists. Its pessimistic idea—that workers would be forever limited to a bare subsistence with intermittent periods of starvation—immediately attracted wide attention and made Malthus famous for all time.

Malthus did not argue that the supply of farmland was completely fixed. He did insist, however, that even if the supply of farmland could be increased through forest clearing, its growth would be far less rapid than population growth. Malthus argued that population growth is geometric, but that the growth of farm production is arithmetic. Thus he wrote:

. . . population, when unchecked, goes on doubling every twenty-five years, or increases in a geometrical ratio. . . . the means of subsistence increases in an arithmetical ratio.

   Let us now bring the effects of these two ratios together.

   Taking the population of the world at any number, a thousand millions, for instance, the human species would increase in the ratio of 1, 2, 4, 8, 16, 32, 64, 128, 256, 512, etc. and subsistence as 1, 2, 3, 4, 5, 6, 7, 8, 9, 10, etc. In two centuries and a quarter, the population would be to the means of subsistence as 512 to 10: in three centuries as 4096 to 13; and in two thousand years the difference would be incalculable. . . .

Malthus did not shy away from giving policy advice based on his theory. For example, he criticized Prime Minister William Pitt's "Poor Bill," which would have paid a small sum each week to workers with children.

I confess, that before the bill was brought into Parliament, and for some time after, I thought that such a regulation

would be highly beneficial; . . . but further reflection on the subject has convinced me, that if . . . it tend[s] to increase population, without increasing the produce, . . . a day's labour will purchase a smaller quantity of provisions, and the poor therefore in general must be more distressed.

Pitt was greatly influenced by Malthus's argument: After he heard the argument, he withdrew his support for the bill, arguing that helping the poor in this way would be futile and would only increase the population and lead to more suffering. For many years, the Malthusian prediction was cited as a reason not to give welfare to the poor.

Although Malthus used only elementary biology, his research helped stimulate one of the great discoveries in biology: Darwin's theory of evolution. Darwin wrote in his autobiography that he got the idea of natural selection while reading Malthus.

After Maltus wrote his famous *Essay,* he went on to a career as an economist with broad interests. He was the very first professor of economics (then called political economy) anywhere in the world. He was one of the classical economists, a friend and intellectual opponent of David Ricardo. We can use modern terminology to summarize their main difference: Malthus criticized Ricardo for ignoring short-run economic fluctuations and always focusing on the economy's long-run potential growth path; Ricardo criticized Malthus for ignoring the long-run growth path and always focusing on the short-run economic fluctuations. One can view the modern theory of economic growth and fluctuations described in this text as combining these two traditions.

Source of quotes: Thomas Robert Malthus, *An Essay on the Principle of Population as It Affects the Future Improvements of Society,* 1798, pp. 12–13, 50, in *The Works of Thomas Robert Malthus,* Vol. I, ed. E. A. Wrigley and D. Souden (London: William Pickering, 1986).

saying only that it had a "melancholy hue." But his depiction of the struggle for survival was one of unmistakable horror: "sickly seasons, epidemics, pestilence and plague advance in terrific array and sweep off their thousands and tens of thousands."[1]

Real GDP per worker was just beginning to grow rapidly as Malthus wrote (see Table 23.1). As growth continued, it gradually became clear that his dismal predictions were not coming true in England or in the other countries about which he wrote. In fact, the population was expanding, rather than stabilizing. Hence, the Malthusian prediction turned out to be wrong.

To be sure, starvation has not disappeared from the planet. Population growth in the underdeveloped parts of the world has frequently faced limited food supplies, resulting in struggles like those depicted by Malthus. And some twentieth-century writers, like Malthus, paint a bleak picture of the future—for example, in 1972 D. Meadows and others wrote *Limits to Growth,* which says that we are up against limited energy supplies and the only thing we can do is to stop economic growth. But since the problems of less-developed countries have occurred alongside a remarkable fiftyfold increase in living standards in the advanced countries, history suggests that there are non-Malthusian explanations for the Malthusian struggles we have observed in the less-developed countries. But what was missing from Malthus's theory? What can we add to the "labor only" theory to explain economic growth?

Labor and Capital Only

One thing missing from the simple "output depends only on labor" story is capital—an input to production that can increase over time, if some of GDP is devoted to investment. With capital, the production function becomes $Y = F(L, K)$, where K stands for capital. Output can be increased by using more capital, even if the amount of labor is not increased. Consider the vineyard example again. By buying a wheelbarrow to haul the fertilizer around the vineyard, the vineyard can produce more grapes with the same number of workers. More capital at the vineyard increases output. The same is true for the economy as a whole. By increasing the amount of capital in the economy, more real GDP can be produced with the same number of workers.

Figure 23.4 illustrates how more capital raises output. The axes are the same as Figure 23.1, and the curve again shows that more output can be produced by more labor. But, in addition, Figure 23.4 shows that if we add capital to the economy—by investing a certain amount each year—the relationship between output and labor shifts up: More capital provides more output at any level of labor input. To see this, pick a point on the horizontal axis, say point *A,* to designate a certain amount of labor input. Then draw a vertical line up from this point, such as the dashed line shown. The vertical distance between the curve marked "less capital" and the curve marked "more capital" shows how additional capital raises production.

The addition of capital to the growth model changes the Malthusian predictions. As the production function shifts up with more capital, the intersection of the production function and the subsistence line shifts out. Hence, it is possible for the population *and* labor input to increase, contrary to Malthus's prediction.

1. Thomas Robert Malthus, *An Essay on the Principle of Population as It Affects the Future Improvements of Society,* 1798, pp. ii, 52, in *The Works of Thomas Robert Malthus,* Vol. I, ed. E. A. Wrigley and D. Souden (London: William Pickering, 1986).

FIGURE 23.4
Capital Becomes a Factor of Production

The axes are just like those in Figure 23.1, but now if more capital is added to production, more output can be produced with the same labor input. For example, when labor input is at point *A,* more output can be produced with more capital.

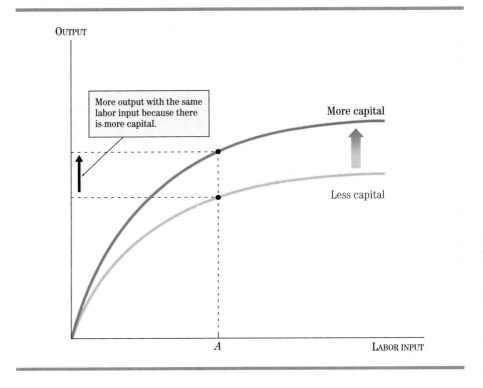

FIGURE 23.5
Output Growing above Subsistence with Capital

If capital grows along with labor input, output can remain above the subsistence line. Here labor input increases from *A* to *B,* the capital stock increases, and output moves away, rather than toward, the subsistence line, in contrast to Figure 23.3.

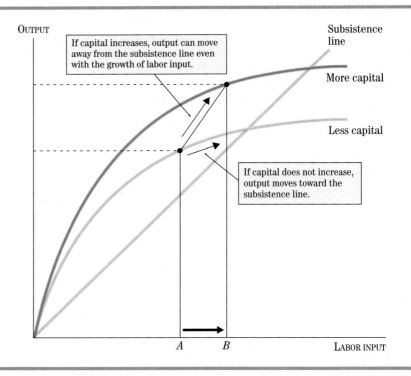

Output Can Rise above Subsistence

Something more is possible: The population can continually increase while output rises above the subsistence level. This is shown in Figure 23.5, in which the production function is shifted up because of investment in more capital, while at the same time the labor input is increasing from point *A* to point *B* along the horizontal axis. With capital and labor increasing together, output rises above the subsistence level. In fact, output can grow along a line with a slope greater than the subsistence line.

Adding capital as an input to production prevents an economy from getting stuck in a Malthusian equilibrium with a stable population and output equal to subsistence. Population can grow and real GDP can grow above subsistence. By taking some production and using it for investment, the ratio of capital to labor can be increased. With each worker having more capital with which to work, output per worker is higher.

Diminishing Returns to Capital

However, the addition of capital to the theory does not solve everything. If labor has diminishing returns, why would not capital? Figure 23.6 shows that there are *diminishing returns to capital* too. Each additional amount of capital—another wheelbarrow or another hoe—results in smaller and smaller additions to output. Hence, the gaps between the several production functions in Figure 23.6 get smaller and smaller as more capital is added. As more capital is added there is less ability to increase output per worker. Compare adding one wheelbarrow to the vineyard

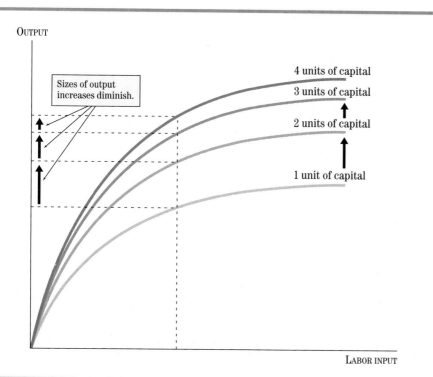

**FIGURE 23.6
Capital Has Diminishing Returns Also**

As capital per worker increases, each additional unit of capital produces less output. Thus, there is a limit to how much growth per worker additional capital per worker can bring.

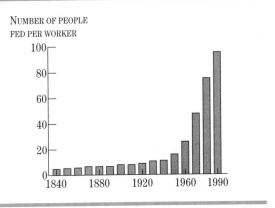

NUMBER OF PEOPLE
FED PER WORKER

FIGURE 23.7
Food Output per Worker

Farm productivity has risen dramatically. Simply adding more horse-drawn harvesting machines and threshers—the leading technology in 1840—would have led to diminishing returns and could not have produced this increased output. Technology—combines, gasoline-powered tractors, dry farming, etc.—was the key to sustained increases in output per worker.

Source: Statistical Abstract of the United States and Historical Statistics of the United States.

when there is already one with adding one wheelbarrow when there are already fifty. Clearly, the fifty-first wheelbarrow would increase farm output by only a minuscule amount, certainly much less than the second wheelbarrow. With a one-acre vineyard, there would not even be much room for the fifty-first wheelbarrow!

Diminishing returns to capital also occur for the economy as a whole. Thus, adding more capital per worker cannot raise real GDP per worker above some limit, and even getting close to that limit will require an enormous amount of capital. Investment would have to be such a large share of GDP that there would be little left for anything else. Thus, even with capital, the model yields a very pessimistic conclusion, not as devastating as Malthus's prediction, but not nearly as optimistic as the fiftyfold (and still counting) gain in productivity that we have observed. Eventually, growth in output per hour of work would stop. Economics still seems to deserve the nickname the "dismal science," even with capital.

Another way to prove that a model with capital and labor alone is not sufficient to explain the growth of productivity is to focus on one type of good, such as agricultural products. Figure 23.7 shows the increased farm output per worker in the past 150 years in the United States. Farm output per worker is measured by the number of people who could be fed on average by a single farm worker—the number of mouths fed per worker. Farm output per worker—a measure of labor productivity in agriculture—increased thirty times during this 150-year period—an average annual growth rate of productivity of 2¼ percent per year. Simply adding more of the type of capital goods available in 1840—for example, the horse-drawn grain harvesters or threshers—could not have produced this kind of growth. Increases in labor productivity required the increase in something else. We now know that "something else" is technology—for example, the invention of combines, which put harvesters and threshers together; the invention of gasoline-powered tractors; and the discovery of new methods of using farmland, such as the "dry farming" crop-rotation method for the plains of the United States.

Thus, labor and capital alone cannot explain the phenomenal growth in either farm output or real GDP during the last 200 years. We move on to the final step in our model construction and testing.

Review

▷ An economic growth theory with capital and labor alone cannot account for the sustained increase in real GDP per hour of work that began in the late 1700s and continues today.

▷ Malthus predicted that output would forever hover around a subsistence level and that whenever the population increased, it would be forced back to an equilibrium level. Sustained increases in real GDP per hour of work have contradicted Malthus's predictions.

▷ Adding capital to Malthus's theory can explain why real GDP can remain far above subsistence levels indefinitely, even with the population growing at a steady rate. However, it cannot explain the sustained *increases* in real GDP per hour of work that we have observed.

LABOR, CAPITAL, AND TECHNOLOGY

When we add technology to capital and labor we have the modern theory of economic growth. The theory can be summarized symbolically by the familiar aggregate production function:

$$Y = F(L, K, T)$$

where T now stands for technology. This function identifies labor, capital, *and* technology as inputs to production.

What Is Technology?

Technology is the most difficult of the three inputs to production to define and envision. Technology is a form of knowledge; it includes the knowledge needed to produce agricultural products from baby food to wine, the knowledge to make industrial products from penicillin to satellites, the knowledge to produce services from rock concerts to heart transplants, even the knowledge of how to get oil and minerals out of the ground.

Technology is defined as anything that raises the amount of real GDP that can be produced with a given amount of labor and capital. **Technological change** is simply the change in the existing technology between two dates. Technological progress is an improvement—an increase—in the technology, but since technology is usually increasing, the term *technological change* also usually means an improvement. Recall that real GDP is a measure that includes the quality of the goods produced (assuming that prices reflect quality) as well as the introduction of new products. Thus, technological progress also includes things that increase the quality and diversity of goods and services.

technology: anything that raises the amount of output that can be produced with a given level of capital and labor.

technological change: improvement in technology over time.

Invention, Innovation, and Diffusion

Technological change occurs when new ideas are developed into new products that increase production, such as the steel plow, the harvester, the combine, the automobile, radar, the telephone, the computer, the airplane, lasers, and fiber optic cable. Economists distinguish between an **invention,** which is the discovery of new knowledge or a new principle, such as electricity, and **innovation,** in which the new knowledge is brought into application with a new product, such as the electric light bulb. Economists also distinguish between the innovation itself and the **diffusion** of the innovation throughout the economy, a process that involves advertising, marketing, and spreading the innovation to new uses, such as the use of the electric light bulb to create night shifts in factories.

Thus, technology is much more than scientific knowledge. The discovery of DNA did not improve technology until it was applied to genetic engineering. The knowledge of mathematics made possible the invention and development of computers in the 1940s, a technology that has obviously improved productivity. Technology depends in part on scientific knowledge, and many people feel that science will become more and more important in future technological change.

The sewing machine is a good illustration of invention, innovation, and diffusion. In 1847, "17 machines capable of mechanically forming a stitch had been invented," according to Ross Thompson, an economic historian. But only one of these, Elias Howe's sewing machine, developed into a commercially successful

invention: a discovery of new knowledge.

innovation: applications of new knowledge in a way that creates new products or significantly changes old ones.

diffusion: the spreading of an innovation throughout the economy.

innovation. A Boston machinist turned entrepreneur, Howe tried to sell his invention. As he did so, he and others found out how to modify the invention to make it more useful and attractive to potential buyers. Soon the invention turned into a popular innovation used widely. Wide diffusion of the innovation occurred as others produced household versions of the sewing machine like the one marketed by the Singer Company. This story also illustrates that innovation and diffusion usually require the work of an entrepreneur who recognizes the potential of the invention.

Organization and Specialization

Technology also includes how firms are organized. Better organization schemes can mean a smaller bureaucracy and more output per hour of work without the addition of capital. More efficient organization can improve the flow of information within a firm and thereby affect labor productivity. Better incentive programs that encourage workers to communicate their ideas to management, for example, increase productivity.

Henry Ford's idea of the assembly line greatly increased the productivity of workers. The assembly line enabled the car to come to the worker rather than have the worker go to the car. Thus, each worker could specialize in a certain type of activity; through specialization, productivity increased. The assembly line alone is estimated to have reduced the time it took a group of workers to produce a car from 12½ hours to ½ hour. Productivity increased and so did wages.

New technology can affect how labor and capital are used at a firm. Economists distinguish between *labor-saving* and *capital-saving* technological change. **Labor-saving technological change** means that fewer workers are needed to produce the same amount of output; **capital-saving technological change** means that fewer machines are needed to produce the same amount of output. An example of a labor-saving technological change would be the gasoline-powered tractor replacing a horse-drawn plow, enabling the same worker to plow many more acres. An example of a capital-saving technological change is the night shift. By bringing a crew of workers to work in a steel mill from 4 P.M. to midnight and another to work from midnight to 8 A.M., the same steel-making furnaces are three times as productive as when the working hours are only from 8 A.M. to 4 P.M.

Specialization of workers at a firm adds to productivity. Adam Smith emphasized the importance of specialization in his *Wealth of Nations;* his phrase **division of labor** refers to how a manufacturing task could be divided up among a group of workers, each of whom would specialize in a part of the job. His famous example was pin making. He described how a group of 10 workers could make 48,000 pins a day, an output per worker of 4,800 pins a day: "One man draws out the wire, another straightens it, a third cuts it, a fourth points it, a fifth grinds it at the top for receiving the head, . . ." and so on. Smith argued that one worker working alone could not produce even 20 pins, not even "two-hundred fortieth" of the productivity of each worker in the 10-person operation.

Because specialization permits workers to repeat the same task many times, their productivity increases, as in the old adage "practice makes perfect." Each time the task is repeated the worker becomes more proficient—a phenomenon economists call **learning by doing.** The commonsense principle of learning by doing is that the more one does something, the more one learns about how to do it. For example, as the number of airplanes produced of a particular type—say a DC-10—increases, the workers become more and more skilled at producing that type of airplane. Careful studies of aircraft production have shown that productivity increases

---

labor-saving technological change: a technological innovation that reduces the amount of labor needed to produce a given amount of output with a given amount of capital.

capital-saving technological change: a technological innovation that reduces the amount of capital needed to produce a given amount of output with a given amount of labor.

division of labor: dividing work into different tasks with groups of workers specializing in each task.

learning by doing: a situation in which workers become more proficient by doing a particular task many times.

by 20 percent for each 100 percent increase in output of a particular type of plane. This relationship between learning and the amount of production is commonly called the "learning curve." Learning is a type of technological progress.

Human Capital

Many firms provide training courses for workers to increase their skills and their productivity. *On-the-job training* is a catchall term for any education, training, or skills a worker receives while at work.

Most workers receive much of their education and training before they begin working, whether in grade school, high school, college, or professional schools. Because increases in education and training can raise workers' productivity, such increases are considered another source of technological change.

The education and training of workers, called **human capital** by economists, is similar to physical capital—factories and equipment. In order to accumulate human capital—to become more educated or better trained—people must devote time and resources, much as a firm must devote resources to investment if physical capital is to increase.

human capital: accumulated education and training workers receive that increases their productivity.

The decision to invest in human capital is influenced by considerations similar to those that motivate a firm to invest in physical capital: the cost of the investment versus the expected return. For example, investing in a college education may require that one borrow the money for tuition; if the interest rate on the loan rises, then people will be less likely to invest in a college education. Thus, investment in education may be negatively related to the interest rate, much as physical investment is. This is one reason why, in order to encourage more education and thereby increase economic growth and productivity, the U.S. government provides low-interest loans to college students, making an investment in college more attractive. We will return to the government's role in education as part of its broader policy to increase economic growth later in the chapter.

The Production of Technology: The Invention Factory

Technology is sometimes discovered by chance by a lone inventor and sometimes by trial and error by an individual worker. A secretary who experiments with several different filing systems to reduce search time or with different locations for the computer, the printer, the telephone, and the photocopier is engaged in improving technology around the office. Frequently, technological progress is better thought of as a continuous process with a small adjustment here and a small adjustment there that add up to major improvements over time.

But more and more technological change is the result of huge expenditures of research and development funds by industry and government. Thomas Edison's "invention factory" in Menlo Park, New Jersey, is one of the first examples of a large industrial laboratory devoted to the production of technology. It in turn influenced the development of many other labs, such as the David Sarnoff research lab of RCA. Merck & Co., a drug company, spends nearly $1 billion per year on research and development for the production of new technology.

Cartoonists & Writers Syndicate

HARRIS
USA

THANK YOU FOR NOT DOING RESEARCH THAT HAS ALREADY BEEN DONE

S.Harris

Invention Factories

The amount of technology produced at Thomas Edison's invention factory (left) or at the research lab of a modern biotechnology firm like Cetus (right) can be explained by the laws of supply and demand. But technology is different from most private goods: If one person uses more technology, there is just as much available for others to use, and it is difficult to exclude people from using a new technology.

patent: a grant giving an inventor exclusive rights to use an invention for 17 years.

Edison's Menlo Park laboratory had about 25 technicians working in three or four different buildings. In the six years from 1876 to 1882, the laboratory invented the light bulb, the phonograph, the telephone transmitter, and electrical generators. Each of these inventions turned out to be a successful innovation that was diffused widely. For each innovation a **patent** was granted by the federal government. A patent indicates that the invention is original and that the inventor has the exclusive right to use it for 17 years. In order to obtain a patent for the rights to an invention, an inventor must apply to the Patent and Trademark Office of the federal government. Patents give inventors an inducement to invent. The number of patents granted is an indicator of how much technological progress is going on. Edison obtained patents at a pace of about 67 a year at his lab.

Edison's invention factory required both labor and capital input, much like factories producing other commodities. The workers in such laboratories are highly skilled, their own knowledge obtained through formal schooling or on-the-job training—human capital. A highly trained work force is an important prerequisite to the production of technology.

The supply of technology—the output of Edison's invention factory, for example—depends on the cost of producing the new technology, which must include the great risk that little or nothing will be invented, and the benefits from the new technology: how much Edison can charge for the rights to use his techniques for making light bulbs. Often inventive activity has changed as a result of shifts in the economy that change the costs and benefits. For example, increases in textile workers' wages stimulated the invention of the textile machines, because such machines then yielded greater profits.

Special Features of the Technology Market

nonrivalry: the situation in which more people can consume a good without reducing the amount available for others to consume.

When viewed as a commodity that can be produced, technology has two special qualities that affect how much will be produced. The first is **nonrivalry.** This means that one person's use of the technology does not reduce the amount that another person can use. If one university uses the same book-filing system as another university, that does not reduce the quality of the first university's system. In contrast, most goods are rivals in consumption: If you drink a bottle of Coke, there is one less bottle of Coke around for other people to drink.

The second feature of technology is **nonexcludability.** This means that the inventor or the owner of the technology cannot exclude other people from using it. For example, the system software for Apple computers shows a series of logos and pull-down menus that can be moved around the screen with a mouse. The idea could easily be adapted for use in other software programs by other companies. In fact, the Windows program of Microsoft has similar features to the Apple software, but, according to the court that ruled on Apple's complaint that Microsoft was illegally copying, the features were not so similar that Microsoft could not use them.

As the example of Apple and Microsoft shows, the legal system and the enforcement of **intellectual property laws** determine in part the degree of nonexcludability. Intellectual property laws provide for trademarks and copyrights as well as patents. These laws help inventors exclude others from using the invention without compensation. But it is impossible to exclude others from using much technology.

Thus, the technology may *spill over* from one activity to another. If your economics teacher invents a new way to teach economics on a computer, it might spill over to your chemistry teacher, who sees how the technology applies to a different subject. Sometimes spillovers occur because research personnel move from one firm to another. Henry Ford knew Thomas Edison and was stimulated to experiment on internal combustion engines by Edison. Hence, Edison's research spilled over to another industry, but Edison would find it very difficult to get compensation from Henry Ford even if he wanted to. Consider also the difficulty Malthus would have had trying to get compensation from Darwin for his ideas on natural selection (see the box on Malthus).

Because inventors cannot be fully compensated for the benefits their ideas provide to others, they might produce too little technology. The private incentives to invent are less than the gain from the inventions to society. If the incentives were higher—say through government subsidies to research and development—more inventions might be produced. Thus, there is a potential role for government in providing funds for research and development, both in industry and at universities. Before we consider this role, we must examine how to measure technological change in the economy as a whole.

> **nonexcludability:** the situation in which no one can be prevented from consuming a good.

> **intellectual property laws:** laws that protect ownership rights over ideas and inventions; includes patent laws, copyright laws, and trademark laws.

Review

▶ Technological change has a very broad definition. It is anything that increases production for a given level of labor and capital. Technological change has been an essential ingredient in the increase in the growth of real GDP per hour of work in the last 200 years.

▶ Technology can be improved by the education and training of workers—investment in human capital. Technology can also be improved through inventions produced in "invention factories" or industrial research laboratories, as well as by trial and error. In any case, the level of technology is determined by market forces.

▶ But technology exhibits nonrivalry in consumption and a high degree of nonexcludability. These are precisely the conditions in which there will be an underproduction of technology.

GROWTH ACCOUNTING

Both technological change and capital formation cause real GDP per hour of work to grow. Is it possible to determine how much growth has been due to technology as distinct from capital? Surprisingly, the answer is yes. A significant recent development in economics has been a technique to measure quantitatively how important capital versus technology has been for growth in the economy as a whole. Robert Solow of MIT made the pioneering contribution and won the Nobel Prize for his innovation. In 1957 he published a paper called "Technical Progress and the Aggregate Production Function" that contained a simple mathematical formula. It is this formula—called the **growth accounting formula**—that enables economists to estimate the relative contributions of capital versus technology.

growth accounting formula: an equation that states that the growth rate of real GDP per hour of work equals capital's share of income times the growth rate of capital per hour of work plus the growth rate of technology.

The Growth Accounting Formula

The growth accounting formula is remarkably simple. It can be written as follows:

$$\begin{pmatrix} \text{Growth rate of real} \\ \text{GDP per hour of work} \end{pmatrix} = \frac{1}{3}\begin{pmatrix} \text{growth rate of capital} \\ \text{per hour of work} \end{pmatrix} + \begin{pmatrix} \text{growth rate} \\ \text{of technology} \end{pmatrix}$$

The growth accounting formula can be derived from the aggregate production function. (The box on the next page contains a brief graphical explanation and the appendix to this chapter provides more details about the derivation.)

The two ingredients in the growth of real GDP per hour of work—the growth of *capital* and the growth of *technology*—are apparent in the formula. The growth accounting formula allows us to measure the importance of these two ingredients.

Here is how the formula works. The growth rates of real GDP per hour of work and capital per hour of work are readily determined from available data sources in most countries. Using the formula, we can express the growth rate of technology as follows:

$$\begin{pmatrix} \text{Growth rate} \\ \text{of technology} \end{pmatrix} = \begin{pmatrix} \text{growth rate of real} \\ \text{GDP per hour of work} \end{pmatrix} - \frac{1}{3}\begin{pmatrix} \text{growth rate of capital} \\ \text{per hour of work} \end{pmatrix}$$

Thus, the growth rate of technology can be determined by subtracting ⅓ times the growth rate of capital per hour of work from the growth rate of real GDP per hour of work. Consider an example. Suppose the growth rate of real GDP per hour of work is 2 percent per year. Suppose also that the growth rate of capital per hour of work is 3 percent per year. Then the growth rate of technology must be 1 percent per year: $2 - [(⅓) \times 3] = 1$. Thus, in the example, one-half of the growth of productivity is due to technological change and one-half to the growth of capital per hour of work.

Why is the growth of capital per hour multiplied by ⅓? The simplest reason is that economists view the production function for the economy as one in which output rises by only ⅓ of the percent by which capital increases. For example, a vineyard owner can estimate by what percent grape output will rise if the workers have more wheelbarrows to work with. If the number of wheelbarrows at the vineyard is increased by 100 percent and if the ⅓ coefficient applies to the vineyard, then grape production per hour of work will increase by 33 percent. In other words, this is a property of the grape production function. Statistical studies suggest that the ⅓ coefficient seems to apply to the production function in the economy as a whole.

Another reason for the ⅓ coefficient on capital growth is based on a basic principle of economics that inputs to production receive income according to their

A Graphical Illustration of Growth Accounting

The growth accounting formula splits up the growth of productivity into two sources: the growth of capital per hour of work and the growth of technological change. The figure on the left below explains this split graphically through the familiar distinction between the shifts of and movements along curves. The figure shows the relationship between productivity (Y/L) and capital per hour of work (K/L). Higher capital per hour leads to more output per hour, as shown by the purple curves in the figure. Technological change shifts the purple curve up because, by definition, technological change is anything that raises productivity for a given level of capital per hour of work.

The purple curves in the figure are much like a production function except productivity (Y/L), rather than output (Y), is what is being explained. Hence, we call each purple curve in the figure a *productivity curve*. The production function and the productivity curve are perfectly compatible with each other, but one focuses on output and the other on output per hour of work.

Actual productivity increases in the economy are due to a combination of *movements along* the productivity curve, because of more capital per hour, and of *shifts* of the productivity curve, because of technological

change. The purpose of the growth accounting formula is to determine how much is due to movement along and how much is due to a shift. This is illustrated by two observations on productivity and capital per hour in two different years (year 1 and year 2). Observe how the increase in productivity from year 1 to year 2 is due partly to an upward shift of the productivity curve and partly to a movement along the curve.

This graphical approach can be applied to the productivity slowdown, as shown in the graph on the lower right. This graph focuses on the upper portion of three U.S. productivity curves corresponding to the three years, 1955, 1975, and 1995 (the lower portions are cut away for better visibility of the relevant parts of the curves).

Observe on the horizontal axis how productivity increased by a smaller percentage from 1975 to 1995 than it did from 1955 to 1975. Observe also that the curve shifts up by a much smaller amount from 1975 to 1995 than it does from 1955 to 1975. In fact, the productivity slowdown is almost entirely due to smaller shifts in the curve rather than to smaller percentage increases in capital per worker. This finding is also shown in Table 23.2

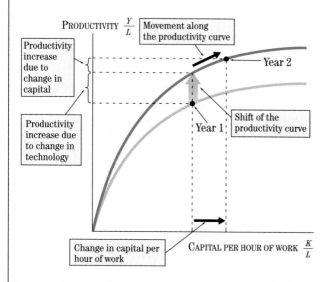

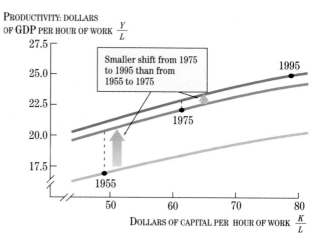

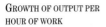

GROWTH OF OUTPUT PER
HOUR OF WORK

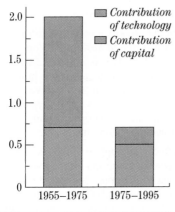

FIGURE 23.8
The Role of Capital and
Technology in the Growth of
Productivity
The slowdown in the growth rate
of labor productivity is due both to
capital and technology, but technology growth has slowed down by a
larger amount, according to the
growth accounting formula. (The
data for the bar chart come from
Table 23.2.)
Source: U.S. Department of Commerce.

contribution to production. If you look back at Table 20.3, you will find that capital income ($1,588 billion) plus depreciation ($853 billion) for the U.S. economy as a whole is about ⅓ of aggregate income ($7,576 billion). This provides statistical support for the ⅓ coefficient.

We should not give the impression, however, that economists know the coefficient on capital growth in the growth accounting formula with much precision. There is uncertainty about its size. It could be ¼ or even 5/12. In any case, the growth accounting formula is a helpful rule of thumb to assist policymakers in deciding what emphasis to place on capital versus technology when developing programs to stimulate economic growth.

Case Studies: Using the Growth Accounting Formula

Before describing what economic policies can be put in place to improve technology, let us briefly examine quantitatively what the growth accounting formula tells us about the actual importance of technology in economic growth.

Productivity Slowdown in the United States

Figure 23.8 and Table 23.2 show the breakdown between capital growth and technology growth during the productivity slowdown that began in the 1970s in the United States. Both capital growth and technology growth slowed down, but the slowdown in the growth of productivity seems to be largely due to a slowdown in the growth of technology.

The implication of this examination of the source of the productivity slowdown is that government policies to address the slowdown should pay particular attention to the slowdown in technological change due perhaps to insufficient research and development, education, rewards to inventors, or incentives to organize production efficiently.

Demise of the Soviet Union

Table 23.3 shows the growth accounting formula applied to the former Soviet Union. It shows the high rates of growth in the Soviet Union in the 1970s and early 1980s, a time when many Americans were still worried about the Soviet Union overtaking the United States, recalling former Soviet Premier Nikita Khrushchev's highly publicized statement "We will bury you."

But as the table shows, most of that growth was due to increases in capital per worker and not to technological change. Such high rates of capital growth could not be maintained without severe burden on the people. Eventually the Soviet citizens

TABLE 23.2
Accounting for the Productivity
Growth Slowdown in the United
States
(The numbers are average annual growth rates.)

Period	(1) Productivity Growth	(2) ⅓ Capital per Hour of Work	(3) Technology Growth
1955–1975	2.0	0.7	1.3
1975–1995	0.7	0.5	0.2

Source: U.S. Department of Commerce and Bureau of Labor Statistics.

Period	Productivity Growth	⅓ Capital per Hour of Work	Technology Growth
1971–1975	4.5	3.0	1.5
1976–1980	3.3	3.9	−0.6
1981–1985	2.7	3.5	−0.8

TABLE 23.3
Growth Accounting in the Former Soviet Union

Source: A Study of the Soviet Economy, International Monetary Fund, The World Bank, Organization for Economic Cooperation and Development, and European Bank for Reconstruction and Development, Paris, 1991, Table E.2, Volume 1, p. 100 and Table VI.I1, Volume 3, p. 370. (For technology growth, the average of upper and lower estimates are reported.)

complained that such a high share of their output was going to investment. They wanted the consumer goods that were being most visibly obtained in the market economies. One could have predicted problems and perhaps even the demise of the Soviet Union from an examination of the sources of growth.

A Tale of Two Countries

The growth accounting formula can also be used to examine the very high-growth economies of East Asia. Consider Hong Kong and Singapore, for example. Both had approximately the same high rate of 5 percent per year productivity growth over the 1970s and 1980s. But, by applying the growth accounting formula, Alwyn Young of MIT found that there is an enormous difference in how important technological change was compared to the growth of capital per worker in the two countries. On the one hand, Hong Kong had a growth rate of technology that contributed almost 35 percent of the growth rate of output. Capital per worker contributed about 65 percent of growth. On the other hand, the growth accounting formula shows that Singapore had virtually no technological change during this period. It was generating the high growth rate solely through a very high growth rate of capital per worker.

Why the large difference in the role of technological change? Alwyn Young argues that the Singapore government encouraged firms to produce the very latest products. Perhaps this policy caused firms to switch too rapidly from one leading product to another and prevented them from learning to be more efficient in producing any given product. Hong Kong did not follow such a policy. Moreover, Hong Kong had a better-educated labor force, and this may have improved technology.

Review

▶ With the growth accounting formula we can estimate the relative contributions of capital and technology to economic growth. In the growth accounting formula the weight given to capital growth is about ⅓, but it could be somewhat smaller or larger.

▶ The productivity slowdown in the United States during the last 20 years seems to be largely due to a slowdown in technology growth, although capital growth slowed down as well.

▶ Some countries depend more on capital for growth, and others depend more on technology.

TECHNOLOGY POLICY

The growth accounting formula tells us that if economic policy is to help restore the higher productivity growth that existed before the productivity slowdown in the United States, it must provide incentives for, or remove disincentives to, technological progress. What policies might the United States pursue in order to improve technological progress?

Policy to Encourage Investment in Human Capital

research and development (R & D): activities designed to further scientific knowledge and develop new products.

One policy is to improve education. A more highly trained work force is more productive. Better-educated workers are more able to make technological improvements. In other words, human capital can improve the production of technology. Hence, educational reform (higher standards, more local school autonomy, and school choice) as well as more funding would be ways to increase technological change. Some studies have shown that the U.S. educational system is falling behind other countries, especially in mathematics and science in the K–12 schools; hence, additional support seems warranted in order to raise economic growth.

Policy to Encourage Research and Innovation

FIGURE 23.9
Research and Development Expenditures in the United States
The United States devotes about 2.6 percent of its GDP to research and development. The funds come from the federal government and the private sector. Most of the R&D funds are used by private firms and universities.

Source: Statistical Abstract of the United States.

Today the United States and other advanced countries spend huge quantities on **research and development (R&D).** Some of the research supports pure science, but much of it is for applied research in engineering and medical technology. Figure 23.9 shows that about 2.6 percent of U.S. GDP goes to research and development. The government provides much of its R&D funds through research grants and contracts to private firms and universities through the National Science Foundation and the National Institutes of Health and through its own research labs. But private firms are the users of most of the research funds, as also shown in Figure 23.9.

The United States spends less on research and development as a share of GDP but more in total than the other countries. Total spending on research rather than spending as a share of GDP is a better measure of the usefulness of the spending if the benefits spill over to the whole economy.

During the cold war, much of U.S. research and development spending went for national defense. What should happen to those research dollars as overall defense spending has come down now that the cold war is over? Some argue that more civilian research should be supported. For many years the Defense Advanced Research Projects Agency (DARPA) funded research on computer networks and artificial intelligence. In 1993, the *D* in DARPA was dropped, signaling the new focus on civilian research. However, there is a debate about whether the government should directly support research in certain industries—say, computers or genetic engineering—at the expense of others. Such targeted technology policy is called *industrial policy.* Those who argue against it say that the private sector knows more than the government about which industries are promising for technological innovations.

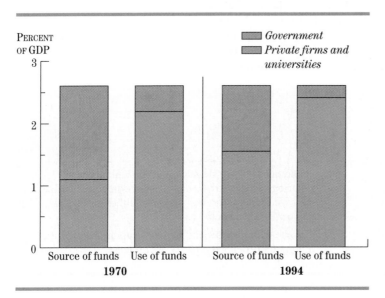

PERCENT OF GDP

Government
Private firms and universities

Source of funds   Use of funds
1970

Source of funds   Use of funds
1994

Increased government support for research and development regardless of industry can be achieved through tax credits. A *tax credit for research* allows firms to deduct a certain fraction of their research expenditures from their taxes in order to reduce their tax bill. This increases the incentive to engage in research and development. Another way to increase the incentive for inventors and innovators is to give them a more certain claim to the property rights from their invention. The government has a role here in defining and enforcing property rights, through patent laws, trademarks, and copyrights.

Technology Embodied in New Capital

Although we have emphasized that capital and technology have two distinct effects on the growth rate of productivity, it is not always possible to separate them in practice. In order to take advantage of a new technology, it may be necessary to invest in new capital. Consider the Thompson Bagel Machine, invented by Dan Thompson, which can automatically roll and shape bagels. Before the machine was invented, bakers rolled and shaped the bagels by hand. According to Dan Thompson, who in 1993 was running the Thompson Bagel Machine Manufacturing Corporation, headquartered in Los Angeles, "You used to have two guys handshaping and boiling and baking who could turn out maybe 120 bagels an hour. With the machine and now the new ovens, I have one baker putting out 400 bagels an hour."[2] That is a productivity increase of over 500 percent! But the new technology is inseparable from the capital. In order to take advantage of the technology, bagel producers have to buy the machine as well as the new ovens to go with it.

Economists call this *embodied technological change* because it is embodied in the capital. An example of *disembodied technological change* would be the discovery of a new way to forecast the demand for bagels at the shop each morning so that fewer people would be disappointed on popular days and fewer bagels would be wasted on slack days. Taking advantage of this technology might not require any new capital.

The relationship between capital and technology has implications for technology policies. For example, policies that remove disincentives to invest might indirectly improve technology as they encourage investment in new, more productive equipment.

Is Government Intervention Appropriate?

Any time there is a question about whether government should intervene in the economy, such as with the technology policies just discussed, the operation of the private market should be examined carefully. For example, we noted that incentives for technology production may be too low without government intervention. Certainly some research a business firm undertakes can be kept secret from others. In such cases, the firm may have sufficient incentive to do the research. But many research results are hard to keep secret. In that case, there is a role for government intervention in subsidizing the research. In general, policies to effect economic growth should be given the test for whether government intervention in the economy is necessary: Is the private market providing the right incentives? If not, can the government do better without a large risk of government failure? If the answers are "no" and "yes," respectively, then government intervention is appropriate.

2. *New York Times,* April 25, 1993.

Review

▶ Policy proposals to increase productivity growth by providing incentives to increase technology include educational reform, research tax credits, increased funding for research, moving government support toward areas that have significant spillovers, and improving intellectual property laws to better define the property rights of inventors and extend them globally.

▶ Many technologies are embodied in new capital. Hence, policies to stimulate capital formation could also increase technology.

FIGURE 23.10
Forecasting Potential GDP Growth: Now to 2003
This figure shows the key ingredients that go into an actual forecast of potential GDP growth. Observe that within each bracket the percents add up to the total. In the upper left part of the figure, a coefficient of ⅓ in the growth accounting formula is assumed.

CONCLUSION: IMPLICATIONS FOR POTENTIAL GDP

When we first examined the growth of the economy over time in Chapter 19, we noted the longer-term trend in real GDP. The long-run trend was called potential GDP. The growth of potential GDP depends on three factors: labor, which we studied in Chapter 21; capital, which we studied in Chapter 22; and finally technology, which we studied in this chapter.

To conclude our discussion of the three factors affecting economic growth, let us see how economists combine forecasts of labor growth, capital growth, and technology growth to project potential GDP growth in the future. For example, the president's Council of Economic Advisers forecasts potential GDP growth of 2.3 percent

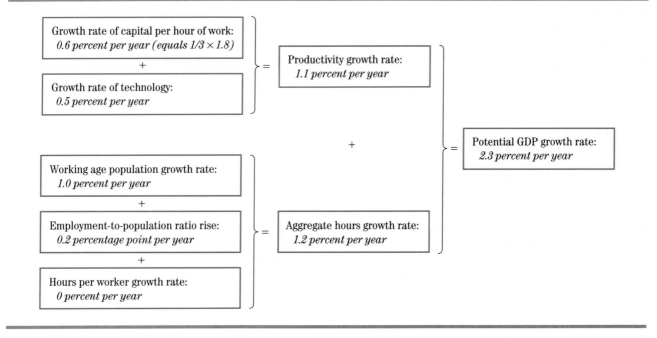

per year from now through the year 2003.[3] The assumptions that underlie this forecast are summarized in Figure 23.10. Observe that the 2.3 percent potential GDP growth rate is based on a growth rate of aggregate hours of 1.2 percent per year, as we discussed in Chapter 21, and a productivity growth rate of 1.1 percent per year. This estimate of productivity growth is less than in the 1950s and 1960s but greater than in the 1970s and 1980s. The growth rate of potential GDP is thus the sum of the growth rate of aggregate hours of work plus the productivity growth rate.

After discussing the monetary system in the next chapter, we will turn to the study of economic fluctuations around this potential GDP path.

KEY POINTS

1. Technology, along with labor and capital, determines economic growth. Technological progress explains the growth wave that started in the late 1700s and enabled the developed countries to get rich.

2. Malthus's pessimistic growth prediction was wrong because it omitted the effects of capital and, more important, technology.

3. Technology is defined by economists to be much broader than "high-tech" products or inventions. Technology includes such things as better organizational structure for a firm and better education for workers as much as innovations like fiber optic cables.

4. As a commodity, technology has the special features of nonexcludability and nonrivalry.

5. Patent laws attempt to make technology more excludable and thereby increase the incentives to invest.

6. The growth accounting formula is itself a great invention that has enabled economists to better understand the role of technology in the economy.

7. Technology policy has the goal of offsetting disincentives to invest and innovate that exist in the private market.

8. Government support for education and research is a key part of a modern technology policy.

KEY TERMS

diminishing returns	innovation	patent
subsistence line	diffusion	nonrivalry
Malthusian equilibrium	labor-saving technological change	nonexcludability
iron law of wages	capital-saving technological change	intellectual property laws
technology	division of labor	growth accounting formula
technological change	learning by doing	research and development (R&D)
invention	human capital	

QUESTIONS FOR REVIEW

1. Why did Malthus's predictions turn out to be wrong for England?

2. What is the essential difference between economic growth in the last 200 years and in the 2,000 years before that?

3. Why are economists so sure that technology played a big role in economic growth during the last 200 years?

4. Why does technology include different ways to organize a business firm?

5. How is technology produced?

6. What is the importance of nonrivalry and nonexcludability for technology?

7. Of what practical use is the growth accounting formula?

8. What is wrong with a growth policy that focuses on capital formation but not on technology?

9. What do intellectual property rights have to do with economic growth?

10. What is the rationale for government intervention in the production of technology?

3. *Economic Report of the President, 1997*, p. 86.

PROBLEMS

1. Consider a country in which capital per hour of work from 1950 to 1973 grew by 3 percent per year and output per hour of work grew by about 3 percent per year. Suppose that from 1973 to 1991 capital per hour of work did not grow at all and output per hour of work grew by about 1 percent per year. How much of the slowdown in productivity (output per hour of work) growth was due to technological change? Explain. (Assume that the coefficient on capital in the growth accounting formula is ⅓.)

2. In Chapter 22, you learned that a decrease in government spending results, among other things, in an increase in investment in the long run. Suppose the capital stock is $1 trillion and a fall in government spending causes a $50 billion rise in investment. Determine the effect of the change in government purchases on long-run output growth using the growth accounting formula. (Assume that the coefficient on capital in the growth accounting formula is ⅓.)

3. The following table shows how output (shaded) depends on capital and labor (it is the same table as in problem 8, Chapter 19). Using the data in the table, draw the production function $Y = F(L)$, when the capital stock (K) is 100 and when it is 200. What do you observe? Now draw the same curve when the capital stock is 300 and 400. Do you observe any difference in the resulting increase in output? What do economists call this phenomenon?

	Labor				
	100	200	300	400	500
100	100	162	216	264	309
200	123	200	266	325	380
300	139	226	300	367	429
400	152	246	327	400	468
500	162	263	350	428	500

(leftmost column label: **Capital**)

4. Using the table from problem 3, suppose the capital stock is 100 and the subsistence level is .8 units of output per unit of labor. How many units of labor will be employed in a Malthusian equilibrium? If the capital stock were 200, how many units would be employed? Draw a diagram to illustrate your answer.

5. Which of the following types of government spending are likely to help economic growth? Why?
  a) Military spending on advertising for recruits
  b) Military spending on laser research
  c) Funding for a nationwide computer network
  d) Subsidies for a national opera company
  e) Extra funding for educational programs

6. The former Soviet Union had high rates of economic growth, especially in the 1950s and 1960s, but could not maintain them. Why? What does this tell us about the limitations of capital and of government?

7. a) Suppose a country has no growth in technology, and capital and labor hours are growing at the same rate. What is the growth rate of real GDP per hour of work? Explain.
  b) Suppose that capital in the country described in part (a) continues to grow at its previous rate, technology growth is still zero, but growth in labor hours falls to half its previous rate. What happens to growth in real GDP per capita?

8. Suppose that in order to increase the rate of economic growth, the government is considering two options:
  1) A tax credit for research
  2) An increase in the life of patents
Write a one page memo presenting the economic case for either one of these two options over the other.

9. Identify the following as contributing to either capital, labor, or technological growth in the growth accounting equation:
  a) A business buys a computer.
  b) You take a course in computer programming.
  c) The government subsidizes joint research projects by Japanese and U.S. automakers to make more fuel-efficient cars.

10. Identify the following as either capital-saving or labor-saving technological change:
  a) A bagel baker buys a machine that rolls and shapes bagels automatically.
  b) An office reconfigures its computer network so more workers have access to the computers in the office.
  c) A university starts a summer program.

11. a) Draw a diagram for the Malthusian equilibrium, as in Figure 23.3, and explain the mechanism by which the economy gets to the equilibrium point.
  b) Instead of Malthus's assumption about population, assume that people choose how many children to have so that output is as far above the subsistence level as possible. How can you show this on the diagram? (*Hint:* Look at the point on the production function that has the same slope as the subsistence line.) Would this level of the population defy the dismal Malthusian prediction of people always living at the subsistence level?
  c) Suppose the subsistence level increases as a disease forces workers to eat more to stay alive. Show this situation on the diagram. What happens to the Malthusian equilibrium quantity of labor input?

12. If we incorrectly estimate the share of capital in income, it can affect our estimation of how large technological growth has been. Use the data from problem 1 to recalculate the change in output per hour of work when capital's share is ¼. Explain intuitively the difference in the importance of technology.

Deriving the Growth Accounting Formula

Figure 23A.1 shows the relationship between productivity (*Y/L*) and capital per hour of work (*K/L*). Because of diminishing returns to capital, the line is curved: As capital per hour of work increases, the increased productivity that comes from additional capital per hour diminishes.

The curve in Figure 23A.1 is called a **productivity curve;** it can be represented in symbols as $(Y/L) = f(K/L)$, or productivity is a function of capital per hour of work.

An upward shift in the productivity function due to an increase in technological change is shown in Figure 23A.2.

For example, with capital per hour constant at point *A* in the figure, more technology leads to more productivity.

We can derive the growth accounting formula using this graph in much the same way as Robert Solow did in 1957. Productivity increases in the economy are due to a combination of *movements along* the productivity function, because of more capital per hour, and of *shifts* of the productivity function, because of technological change.

FIGURE 23A.1
Productivity Curve

Productivity, or output per hour of work, is shown to increase with the amount of capital that workers have, as measured by capital per hour of work. The productivity curve gets flatter as output per hour of work increases because of diminishing returns to capital.

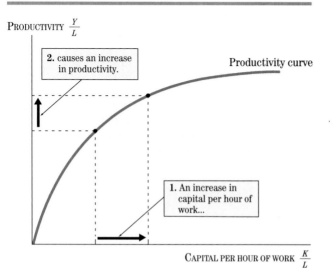

FIGURE 23A.2
A Shift in the Productivity Curve Due to Technology

An increase in technology permits an increase in productivity even if there is no change in capital per hour of work. For example, if capital per hour of work stays at *A*, productivity increases when the productivity curve shifts up.

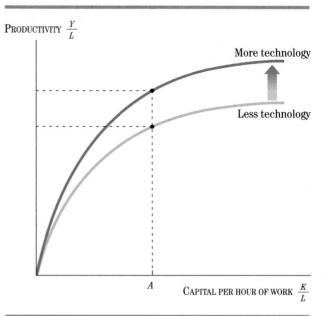

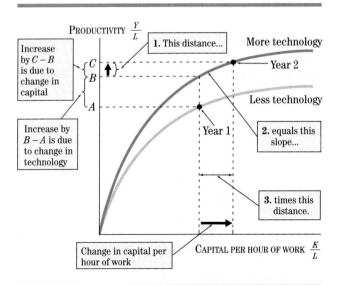

FIGURE 23A.3
Growth Accounting with Capital
per Hour and Technology
Increasing
Here a shift in the productivity curve and a
movement along the productivity curve due to
more capital per hour of work are combined.
Productivity increases. The part of the increase
due to capital and the part due to technological
change are shown in the diagram.

In Figure 23A.3, productivity and capital per hour in
two different years (year 1 and year 2) are shown. These
could be 1997 and 1998 or any other two years. In this
example, the growth rate of productivity is given by the

increase in productivity (C minus A) divided by the initial
level of productivity (A), or $(C - A)/A$. (The definition of
the growth rate of a variable is the change divided by the
initial level.) Observe in Figure 23A.3 how the increase in
productivity can be divided into the part due to technology
(B minus A) and the part due to higher capital per worker
hour (C minus B). Thus, we have

$$\underbrace{(C - A)/A}_{\substack{\text{Growth rate of} \\ \text{productivity}}} = \underbrace{(B - A)/A}_{\substack{\text{Growth rate} \\ \text{of technology}}} + \underbrace{(C - B)/A}_{\substack{\text{Term related to} \\ \text{capital per hour}}}$$

which is close to the growth accounting formula. To finish,
we need to examine the second term on the right. How does
this term relate to capital per hour of work? The boxes in
Figure 23A.3 show that $C - B$ equals the *change* in capital
per hour of work $\Delta(K/L)$ times the *slope* of the productivity
function. (The slope times the change along the horizontal
axis gives the changes along the vertical axis.) Let the symbol r be the slope, which measures how much additional
capital increases output. Thus, $(C - B)/A$ is given by:

$$\frac{\Delta(K/L)r}{Y/L} = \frac{\Delta(K/L)}{(K/L)}r(K/Y)$$

The expression on the right is obtained by multiplying the
numerator and the denominator of the expression on the left
by (K/Y). Now the term on the right is simply the growth
rate of capital per hour times $r(K/Y)$. The amount of
income paid to capital is r times K if capital is paid according to how much additional capital increases output. Aggregate income is given by Y. Thus, the term $r(K/Y)$ is the
share of capital income in aggregate income. As explained
in the text, $r(K/Y)$ is approximately ⅓ in the United States.
Thus, the expression $(C - B)/A$ is the growth rate of capital
per hour of work times the share of capital income in
aggregate income. Thus, the growth accounting formula is
derived.

KEY POINTS

1. The productivity curve describes how more capital per
hour of work increases productivity, or output per hour of
work.

2. The productivity curve shifts up if there is an increase in
technology.

3. The growth accounting formula is derived by dividing
an increase in productivity into (1) a shift in the productivity curve due to more technology, and (2) a movement
along the productivity curve due to more capital per worker.

KEY TERM AND DEFINITION

productivity curve: a relationship stating the output per
hour of work for each amount of capital per hour of work in
the economy.

QUESTIONS FOR REVIEW

1. What is the difference between the productivity curve and the production function?

2. What is the difference between a shift in the productivity curve and a movement along the curve?

3. Why does the share of capital income in total income appear in the growth accounting formula?

PROBLEMS

1. Consider the following relation between productivity and capital per hour for the economy:

Capital per Hour of Work (K/L) (dollars)	Output per Hour of Work (Y/L) (dollars)
10	5
20	9
30	12
40	14
50	15

a) Plot the productivity curve.
b) Suppose in year 1, $K/L = 30$ and $Y/L = 12$, but in year 2, $K/L = 40$ and $Y/L = 14$. How much has technol-

ogy contributed to the increase in productivity between the two years?

c) Suppose that between year 2 and year 3 the productivity curve shifts up by \$1 at each level of capital per hour of work. If $K/L = 50$ and $Y/L = 16$ in year 3, how many dollars did capital contribute to productivity growth between year 2 and year 3? How much was the contribution as a fraction of the growth rate of capital per worker?

2. Suppose the production function $Y = f(K,L)$ is such that Y equals the square root of the product (K times L). Plot the production function with Y on the vertical axis and L on the horizontal axis for the case where $K = 100$. Plot the productivity curve with Y/L on the vertical axis and K/L on the horizontal axis.

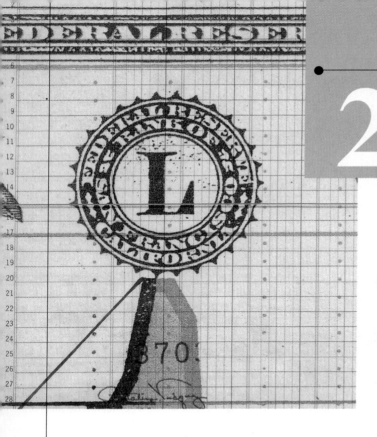

The Monetary System and Inflation

Working behind the scenes as the great drama of economic growth unfolds—with labor, capital, and technology in the leading roles—is the monetary system. The monetary system is the arrangement through which people carry out transactions with each other, whether buying or selling, saving or investing, borrowing or lending. Banks are part of the monetary system; they accept deposits, making it easier for people to lend, and they provide loans, making it easier for people to borrow; they channel funds from savers to investors; and they allow people to write checks on their deposits to make payments for goods and services, ranging from aircraft to photocopying. Coins and paper currency issued by governments are also part of the monetary system; these simple items also serve as a means of payment for goods and services. A well-functioning monetary system is essential for strong economic growth.

In this chapter we examine the monetary system. We first examine the role of coins, paper currency, and other forms of what we will define as money. We then consider commercial banks, one of the major providers of money. We will also consider the Federal Reserve System, the central bank of the United States, which has responsibility for controlling the amount of money in the economy. We will show that, in the long run, money is the cause of inflation, and inflation can influence economic growth. In doing so, we introduce a famous equation, called the quantity equation of money, which is, in the view of some economists, as fundamental for the monetary system as Einstein's equation $E = mc^2$ is for physics. We show how this equation provides a convenient way to organize one's thinking about the monetary system, inflation, and economic growth.

WHAT IS MONEY?

At the heart of the monetary system is **money.** Economists define money in a particular way. It is the part of a person's wealth that can be readily used for transactions, such as buying a lunch or selling a bicycle. Thus, money is anything that is generally accepted as payment for goods and services, not because it is inherently attractive or appealing, but because it can be used to pay for other goods and services. This definition of money is different from the more typical usage, which includes a person's total income or total wealth, as when we say, "She makes a lot of money," or "He has a lot of money." To an economist, money includes the dimes or quarters in a person's pocket but is not the amount the person earns each year.

Commodity Money

Many items have been used for money throughout history. Salt, cattle, furs, tobacco, shells, and arrowheads have been used as money. Traces of their former use can still be found in our vocabulary. The word *salary* derives from the Latin word for salt and the word *pecuniary* derives from the Latin word for cattle. In World War II prisoner of war camps, cigarettes were used for money. On the island of Yap in the Pacific Ocean, huge stones weighing several tons were used for money. Throughout history the most common form of money has been metallic coins, usually gold, silver, or bronze. Gold coins were used as early as the seventh century B.C. in Lydia (now western Turkey). The Chinese were issuing bronze coins with a hole in the middle in the fifth century B.C., and in the fourth century the Greeks issued silver coins called tetradrachmas that had the goddess Athena on one side and her sacred animal, the owl, on the other. All these examples of money are commodities and are therefore called **commodity money.** Metals proved to be the most common form of commodity money because they could be divided easily into smaller units, are very durable, and could be carried around.

   When gold, silver, and other commodities were used as money, changes in the supply of the commodities would change their price relative to all other goods. An increase in the supply of gold would reduce the price of gold relative to all other goods or, alternatively stated, raise the price of all other goods in terms of the number of gold coins required to purchase them. Recall that an increase in the price of all goods is called inflation. Thus, increases in the supply of gold or any other commodity used as money would cause inflation to increase. Whenever there were huge gold discoveries, the price of gold fell and there were increases in inflation in countries that used gold as money. Thus, inflation was determined largely by the supply of precious metals. This relationship between the supply of money and inflation, which seems so clear in the case of commodity money, has persisted into modern times even though there are now many other forms of money. Before examining modern money, let us look carefully at the functions of money.

Three Functions of Money

Money has three different functions: It is a medium of exchange, a unit of account, and a store of value. All three functions can be illustrated with the simple example of gold or silver coins.

Tetradrachmas

money: that part of a person's wealth that can be readily used for transactions; money also serves as a store of value and a unit of account.

commodity money: a good used as money that has some intrinsic value in a nonmonetary use.

Stone Money of Yap Island, Micronesia

Medium of Exchange

medium of exchange: something that is generally accepted as a means of payment.

Money serves as a **medium of exchange** in that it is an item that people are willing to accept as payment for what they are selling because they in turn can use it to pay for something else they want. For example, in ancient times people received coins for their work and then used these coins to buy the goods and services they wanted.

The use of coins was a great technological improvement over **barter,** in which goods are exchanged only for other goods. Under a barter system, there is no single medium of exchange. Thus, under a barter system, if you make shoes and want to buy apples, you have to find an apple seller who needs new shoes. The disadvantage of a barter system is that it requires a rare **coincidence of wants** in which the person who wants to consume what you want to sell (shoes, for example) has exactly what you want to consume (apples, for example).

barter: trade in goods or services without the use of money.

coincidence of wants: a condition required for exchange in a nonmonetary system; to accomplish a trade, it is necessary to find someone who has what you want and who also wants what you have.

Store of Value

store of value: something that will allow purchasing power to be carried from one period to the next.

Money also serves as a **store of value** from one period to another. For example, in ancient times people could sell their produce in September for gold coins and then use the coins to buy staples in January. In other words, they could store their purchasing power from one season to another.

Money is not the only thing that can provide a store of value. For example, rice or corn can also be stored from one season to the next. But if you are not a farmer with a large storage bin, money is a more convenient store of value.

Unit of Account

unit of account: a standard unit in which prices can be quoted and values of goods can be compared.

Money also serves a third function, providing a **unit of account.** The prices of goods are usually stated in the units of money. For example, prices of shoes or apples in ancient Greece were stated in a certain number of tetradrachmas because people using these coins were familiar with that unit. Originally, units of money were determined by the weight of the metal. The British pound, for example, was originally a pound of silver; a penny was originally a pennyweight of silver—$\frac{1}{20}$ th of an ounce, or $\frac{1}{240}$ th of a pound. That terminology stuck even though, as we will see, modern money is unrelated to silver or any other metal.

To better understand the difference between the unit of account and the medium of exchange, it is helpful to find examples where they are based on different monies. For example, when inflation got very high in Argentina in the early 1990s, the prices of many goods were quoted in U.S. dollars rather than Argentine pesos, but people usually exchanged pesos when they bought or sold goods. Thus, the U.S. dollar was the unit of account while the medium of exchange was still the peso. But such cases are the exception; the unit of account and the medium of exchange are usually the same money.

From Coins to Paper Money to Deposits

paper money: currency made of paper that has no intrinsic value.

Although coins and other commodity monies are improvements over barter, there are more efficient forms of money. Starting in the late eighteenth and early nineteenth century, **paper money** began to be used widely and supplemented or replaced coins as a form of money. Although there are a few examples where paper money was used earlier, it was at this time that it became generally recognized that paper money was easier to use and could save greatly on the use of precious metals.

Originally, the amount of paper currency was linked by law or convention to the supply of commodities. For example, the U.S. dollar was worth $22 per ounce of gold during the years before the Civil War. One reason for this link was the recognition that more money would cause inflation and that limiting the amount of paper money to the amount of some commodity like gold would limit the amount of paper money. Irving Fisher of Yale University, perhaps the most prolific and influential American economist of the early twentieth century, argued for linking paper money to commodities for precisely this reason. Many countries of the world linked their paper money to gold. They were on a **gold standard,** which meant that the price of gold in terms of paper money was fixed by the government. The government fixed the price by agreeing to buy and sell gold at that price. Occasionally, countries went off the gold standard—such as the United States during the Civil War. When this happened, the supply of paper money usually increased and inflation rose, just as when commodity money increased. The paper money issued during the Civil War was called *greenbacks.* During the years after the Civil War, the supply of greenbacks was reduced and the United States returned to the gold standard in 1879. The United States and most other countries went off the gold standard again during World War I. Today the United States and other countries have severed all links between their paper money and gold and apparently have no intention of returning. Governments now supply virtually all the coin and paper money—the two together are called **currency.**

> **gold standard:** a monetary standard in which the value of paper money is linked to gold.

Though paper money was much easier to make and to use than coins, it too has been surpassed by a more efficient form of money. Today money consists mainly of **checking deposits,** or checkable deposits, at banks or other financial institutions. These are deposits of funds on which an individual can write a check to make payment for goods and services. The deposits serve as money because people can write checks on them. For example, when a student pays $100 for books with a check, the student's checking deposit at the bank goes down by $100 and the bookstore's checking deposit at its bank goes up by $100. Checking deposits are used in much the same way as when a student pays with a $100 bill, which is then placed in the store's cash register. The student's holding of money goes down by $100 and the store's goes up by $100. Such deposits are used by many people at least as a partial payment for coin or paper money. Writing checks to pay for goods has become more common than using currency.

> **currency:** money in its physical form: coin and paper money.

> **checking deposit:** an account at a financial institution on which checks can be written; also called checkable deposit.

Alternative Definitions of the Money Supply

Today economists define the **money supply** as the sum of currency (coin and paper money) held by the public and deposits at banks. But there are differences of opinion about what types of deposits should be included.

> **money supply:** the sum of currency (coin and paper money) held by the public and deposits at banks.

The narrowest measure of the money supply is called **M1.** The M1 measure consists mainly of currency plus checking deposits (travelers checks are also part of M1 but constitute less than 1 percent of total M1). The items in M1 have a great degree of *liquidity,* which means that they can be quickly and easily used to purchase goods and services.

> **M1:** currency plus checking deposits plus travelers checks.

Many things that people would consider money, however, are not included in M1. For example, if you had no cash but wanted to buy a birthday gift for a relative, you could withdraw cash from your savings deposit. A **savings deposit** is a deposit that pays interest and from which funds can normally be easily withdrawn at anytime. In other words, a savings deposit is also liquid but not quite as liquid as a

> **savings deposit:** an account at a financial institution that is very liquid but generally cannot be easily used for transactions.

TABLE 24.1
Measures of Money in the United States, 1996
(billions of dollars)

Currency	396
M1: Currency plus checking deposits	1,077
M2: M1 plus time deposits, savings deposits, and other deposits on which check writing is limited or not allowed	3,826

Source: Federal Reserve Board.

time deposit: an account at a financial institution that requires that the money be left in the account for a specified period of time.

M2: M1 plus savings, time, and limited checking deposits.

checking deposit. Similarly, **time deposits**—which require the depositor to keep the money at the bank for a certain time or else lose interest—are not as liquid as checking deposits, but it is possible to withdraw funds from them. Economists have created a broader measure of the money supply called **M2,** which includes all that is in M1 plus savings deposits, time deposits, and certain accounts for which check writing is very limited. Still broader concepts of the money supply can be defined, but M1 and M2 are the most important ones. Table 24.1 shows the total amounts of different definitions of the money supply for the whole U.S. economy in 1996.

Only about one-third of the M1 definition of the money supply is currency and only about one-tenth of the M2 definition is currency. There is disagreement among economists about whether the more narrowly defined M1 or the more broadly defined M2 or something else is the best definition of the money supply. There is probably no best definition for all times and all purposes. For simplicity, in the rest of this chapter we make no distinction between the Ms but simply refer to the money supply, M, as currency plus deposits.

Review

▶ Commodity money—usually gold, silver, or bronze coins—originally served as the main type of money in most societies. Increases in the supply of these commodities would reduce their price relative to all other commodities and thereby cause inflation.

▶ Later, paper currency and deposits at banks became forms of money. Under the gold standard, the amount of paper currency was linked to gold. The United States and all other countries no longer link their money to any commodity, including gold.

▶ There are three roles for money—as a medium of exchange, as a store of value, and as a unit of account.

▶ The two main definitions of the money supply are M1 and M2.

THE FED AND THE BANKS: CREATORS OF MONEY

Federal Reserve System (the Fed): the central bank of the United States, which oversees the creation of money in the United States.

We have seen that increases in the supply of commodity money such as gold would increase inflation. So would printing paper money by governments. But in today's world, money consists mainly of deposits. In the United States, the **Federal Reserve System,** nicknamed the "Fed," determines the supply of currency and the supply of deposits and is thus a most powerful institution. To understand how the Fed determines the supply of currency and deposits, we must first look at how the Fed works and at how banks accept deposits and make loans.

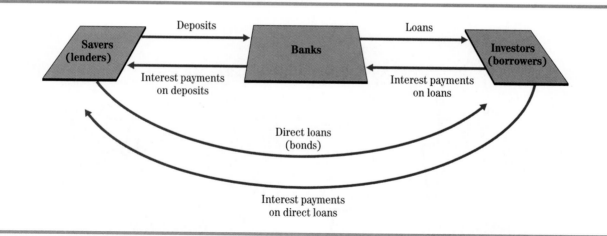

FIGURE 24.1
Channeling Funds from Savers to Investors
Savers, those whose income is greater than consumption, can supply funds to investors in two ways: through banks (and other types of financial intermediaries) or by making direct loans, perhaps by buying bonds issued by a business firm. The banks earn profits by charging a higher interest on their loans than they pay on their deposits.

A **bank**—such as BankBoston or Wells Fargo Bank—is a firm that channels funds from savers to investors by accepting deposits and making loans. Figure 24.1 illustrates this function of banks. Banks are a type of *financial intermediary* because they "intermediate" between savers and investors. Other examples of financial intermediaries are credit unions and savings and loan institutions. Banks are sometimes called *commercial banks* because many of their loans are to business firms engaged in commerce. Banks accept deposits from people who have funds and who want to earn interest and then lend the funds to other individuals who want to borrow and who are willing to pay interest. A bank earns profits by charging a higher interest rate to the borrowers than it pays to the depositors.

bank: a firm that channels funds from savers to investors by accepting deposits and making loans.

The Fed

The *central bank* of a country serves as a bank to other banks. In other words, commercial banks deposit funds at the central bank, and the central bank in turn makes loans to other commercial banks. We will see that the deposits of the commercial banks at the central bank are very important for controlling the money supply.

In the United States, the central bank is the Fed, which was established by the 1913 Federal Reserve Act and now consists of over 25,000 employees spread all over the country.

Board of Governors

At the core of the Fed is the *Board of Governors of the Federal Reserve System,* or the Federal Reserve Board, consisting of seven people appointed to fourteen-year terms by the president of the United States and confirmed by the Senate. The Federal Reserve Board is located in Washington, D.C.

One of the governors is appointed by the president to a four-year term as chair of the board; this appointment also requires Senate confirmation and can be renewed for additional terms. Alan Greenspan was appointed to the chair by President Reagan in 1987 and reappointed by Presidents Bush and Clinton. Greenspan took over from Paul Volcker, who was appointed by President Carter in 1979 and reappointed by President Reagan in 1983.

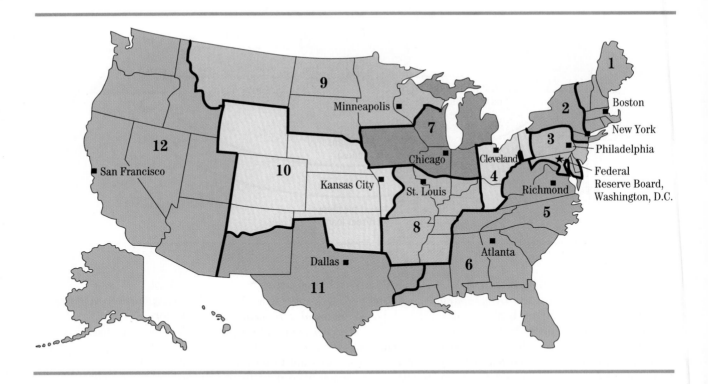

FIGURE 24.2
The Twelve Districts and Fed Independence

When the Fed was created by the Federal Reserve Act of 1913, the country was divided into twelve districts, each with a district Federal Reserve Bank. Each district bank is headed by a president who sits on the FOMC. Unlike the seven members of the Board of Governors, the presidents of the district banks are not selected by the president of the United States.

Federal Open Market Committee (FOMC): the committee, consisting of the seven members of the Board of Governors and the twelve presidents of the Fed district banks, that meets about eight times per year; only five of the presidents vote at any one time.

The District Federal Reserve Banks

The Federal Reserve System not only includes the Federal Reserve Board in Washington but also twelve Federal Reserve Banks in different regions of the country. A map defining the regions is shown in Figure 24.2. For example, the district bank for the southeastern states is the Federal Reserve Bank of Atlanta, and the district bank for the western states is the Federal Reserve Bank of San Francisco. When the Federal Reserve was established by the Federal Reserve Act of 1913, the population density was more concentrated in the Midwest and the East than it is now. Hence, almost all of the Federal Reserve district banks are in the Midwest and the East. Missouri has two district banks, located in St. Louis and Kansas City. The Federal Reserve Bank of New York is particularly significant because the major financial markets are located in New York City, and responsibility for carrying out decisions made by the Fed is given to the New York Federal Reserve Bank.

The term *Fed* refers to the whole Federal Reserve System, including the Board of Governors in Washington and the twelve district banks. Each district bank is headed by a president who is chosen by commercial bankers and other people in the district and approved by the Board of Governors.

The Federal Open Market Committee (FOMC)

The Fed makes decisions about the supply of currency and deposits through a committee called the **Federal Open Market Committee (FOMC).** The members of the FOMC are the seven governors and the twelve district bank presidents, but only five of the presidents vote at any one time. Thus, there are twelve voting members of the FOMC at any one time. The FOMC meets in Washington about eight times a

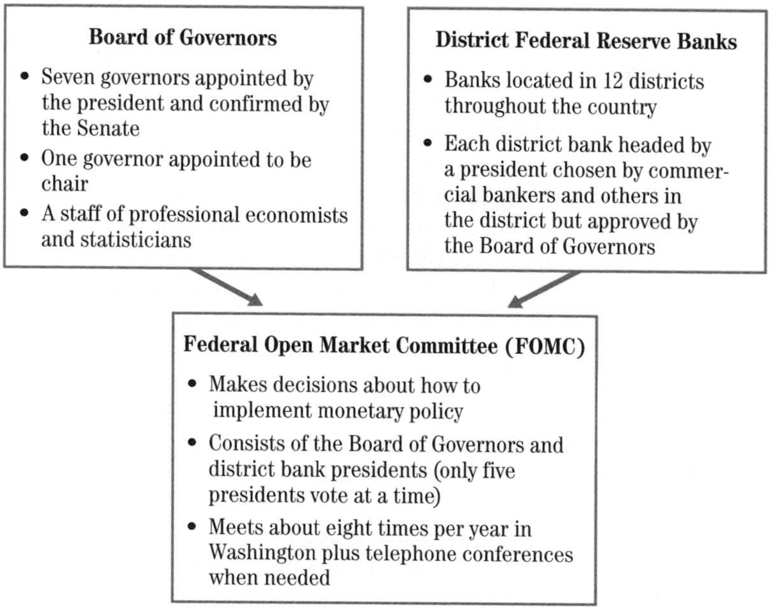

Board of Governors	District Federal Reserve Banks
• Seven governors appointed by the president and confirmed by the Senate • One governor appointed to be chair • A staff of professional economists and statisticians	• Banks located in 12 districts throughout the country • Each district bank headed by a president chosen by commercial bankers and others in the district but approved by the Board of Governors

Federal Open Market Committee (FOMC)

• Makes decisions about how to implement monetary policy

• Consists of the Board of Governors and district bank presidents (only five presidents vote at a time)

• Meets about eight times per year in Washington plus telephone conferences when needed

---

FIGURE 24.3
The Structure of the Federal Reserve System
Decisions about the money supply are made by the FOMC, which consists of the Fed governors and district Fed presidents.

year to decide how to implement monetary policy. Figure 24.3 shows the relationship between the FOMC, the Board of Governors, and the district banks.

Even though the chair of the Fed has only one vote among twelve on the FOMC, the position has considerably more power than that one vote might represent. Traditionally, the Fed has preferred to make decisions with a large degree of consensus, with only two or three dissenting votes. This consensus decision-making and the fact that the chair (1) has executive authority over the operations of the whole Federal Reserve System, (2) sets the agenda at the FOMC meetings, and (3) represents the Fed in testimony before Congress makes the position more powerful. Journalists in the popular press, writing about the Fed, usually act as if the chair has almost complete power over Fed decisions. Some view the chair of the Fed as the second most powerful person in America, after the president of the United States.

Now that we have described the Fed, let us examine the operation of banks and how they, along with the Fed, create money.

The Balance Sheet of a Commercial Bank

A commercial bank accepts deposits from individuals and makes loans to others. To understand how a bank functions, it is necessary to look at its balance sheet, which shows these deposits and loans. Table 24.2 is an example of a balance sheet for a bank, called BankOne, that has $100 million in deposits, $70 million in loans, $20 million in bonds, and $10 million in reserves.

The different items are divided into *assets* and *liabilities.* An **asset** is something of value owned by a person or firm. A **liability** is something of value a person or a firm owes, such as a debt, to someone else. Thus a bank's assets are anything the bank owns or any sum owed by someone else to the bank. A bank's liability is anything the bank owes to someone else. People's *deposits* at banks are the main

asset: something of value owned by a person or a firm.

liability: something of value a person or firm owes to someone else.

	Assets		Liabilities	
Loans	70	Deposits	100
Bonds	20		
Reserves	10		

> This is the initial situation. The ratio of reserves to deposits is .1.

TABLE 24.2
Balance Sheet of BankOne
(millions of dollars)

reserves: deposits that commercial banks hold at the Fed.

required reserve ratio: the fraction of a bank's deposits that it is required to hold at the Fed.

loan: an interest-bearing asset to the bank that lends money to an individual or firm.

bond: a promise by a firm or government to pay a certain amount of money to the bondholder on a fixed date in the future.

liability of banks, as shown in Table 24.2. Certain assets, such as the bank's building or furniture, are not shown in this balance sheet because they do not change when the money supply changes. Also, when a bank starts up, the owners must put in some funds, called the bank's capital stock, which can be used in case the bank needs cash in an emergency. This asset is not shown in the balance sheet either.

Consider each of the assets shown in the balance sheet in Table 24.2. **Reserves** are deposits that commercial banks hold at the Fed, much like people hold deposits at commercial banks. Remember, the Fed is the bank for the commercial banks. Just as you can hold a deposit at a commercial bank, a commercial bank can hold a deposit at the Fed. Reserves are simply a name for these deposits by commercial banks at the Fed.

Under U.S. law, a commercial bank is required to hold reserves at the Fed equal to a fraction of the deposits people hold at the commercial bank; this fraction is called the **required reserve ratio.** In this example, reserves are equal to 10 percent of deposits (10/100 = .1), and we will assume for now that this is the required reserve ratio.

The two other assets of the bank are loans and bonds. **Loans** are made by banks to individuals or firms for a period of time; the banks earn interest on these loans. **Bonds** are a promise of a firm or government to pay back a certain amount after a number years. Bonds can be issued by entities with a good reputation for repayment—such as the U.S. government or a large corporation. After bonds are issued, they can be bought or sold, and banks sometimes buy such bonds, as BankOne has done in the example. For simplicity, we assume the bonds here are government bonds, issued by the U.S. government.

Observe how the bank channels funds from savers to investors. The bank's deposits come from the savings of individuals, while the loans are made to individuals or business firms who may use the funds for investment. Thus, the bank is receiving funds from people who are saving and lending to people who are investing. For example, if you save and deposit the funds in a bank, someone else in the economy uses the funds to invest (buy equipment at a business firm), or someone abroad gets a loan to buy goods made in the United States (exports). Consider how inefficient the process would be without banks (or other financial intermediaries). Small savers would have to look for people who wanted to borrow money to invest, a tedious job. Thus, banks make saving much more attractive. Without banks, both saving and investment would probably be lower.

The Role of Banks in Creating Money

Because deposits at banks are a form of money, the banks play an important role in creating money. The Fed orchestrates this role. A link between the deposits at banks and the reserves at the Fed provides the key mechanism for the Fed to exert control over the amount of deposits at the commercial banks. To see this we first look at some examples and then show how this link between reserves and deposits works in the whole economy. To make the story simpler for now, we assume that everyone

Assets		Liabilities	
Loans	70	Deposits	100
Bonds	10		
Reserves	20		

Note the effect of the Fed's purchase of bonds: Compared with Table 24.2, bonds are lower and reserves are higher in Table 24.3. The ratio of reserves to deposits is .2.

TABLE 24.3
Balance Sheet of BankOne after Reserves Increase
(millions of dollars)

uses deposits rather than currency for their money. (We will take up currency again in the next section.)

Bank-by-Bank Deposit Expansion

To see how the Fed can change the deposit component of the money supply, let us examine a particular transaction in some detail. Suppose there is an increase in the amount of reserves BankOne holds at the Fed. The Fed can cause such an increase in reserves simply by buying something from BankOne and paying for it by increasing BankOne's reserves at the Fed. The Fed usually buys government bonds when it wants to increase reserves because banks have a lot of bonds. So let's assume that the Fed buys $10 million of government bonds from BankOne and pays for the bonds by increasing BankOne's reserves by $10 million. Thus, BankOne's holdings of bonds decline by $10 million, from $20 million to $10 million, and BankOne's reserves at the Fed increase by $10 million, from $10 million to $20 million. The balance sheet would then look like Table 24.3, a change from Table 24.2. The key point is that there are now $10 million more reserves in the economy than before the Fed purchased the government bonds from BankOne. The reserves are held by BankOne, but they will not be for long.

Recall that banks hold reserves equal to a certain fraction of their deposits, a fraction called the reserve ratio, which we are assuming is 10 percent in this example. But now, after the Fed's actions, BankOne has 20 percent of its deposits as reserves, or more than the required 10 percent. Because the reserves do not pay any interest, while loans and bonds do, the bank will have incentive to reduce its reserves and make more loans or buy more bonds.

Suppose BankOne decreases its reserves by making more loans; with the reserve ratio of .1, the bank can loan $10 million. Suppose the bank loans $10 million to UNO, a small oil company that uses the funds to buy an oil tanker from DOS, a shipbuilding firm. UNO pays DOS with a check from BankOne, and DOS deposits the check in its checking account at its own bank, BankTwo. Now BankTwo must ask BankOne for payment; BankOne will make the payment by lowering its reserve account at the Fed and increasing BankTwo's reserve account at the Fed by $10 million. At the end of these transactions, BankOne's balance sheet is shown in Table 24.4.

Hence, after BankOne makes the loan and transfers its reserves to BankTwo, its reserves are back to 10 percent of its deposits. This is the end of the story for

Assets		Liabilities	
Loans	80	Deposits	100
Bonds	10		
Reserves	10		

By making more loans, the bank reduces the ratio of reserves to deposits back to .1.

TABLE 24.4
Balance Sheet of BankOne after It Makes Loans

TABLE 24.5
Deposit Expansion
(millions of dollars)

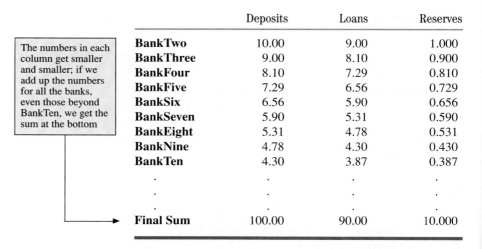

	Deposits	Loans	Reserves
The numbers in each column get smaller and smaller; if we add up the numbers for all the banks, even those beyond BankTen, we get the sum at the bottom			
BankTwo	10.00	9.00	1.000
BankThree	9.00	8.10	0.900
BankFour	8.10	7.29	0.810
BankFive	7.29	6.56	0.729
BankSix	6.56	5.90	0.656
BankSeven	5.90	5.31	0.590
BankEight	5.31	4.78	0.531
BankNine	4.78	4.30	0.430
BankTen	4.30	3.87	0.387
.	.	.	.
.	.	.	.
.	.	.	.
Final Sum	100.00	90.00	10.000

BankOne, but not for the economy as a whole because BankTwo now has $10 million more in reserves and this is going to affect BankTwo's decisions. Let us see how.

Now BankTwo finds itself with $10 million in additional deposits and $10 million in additional reserves at the Fed. (Remember that deposits are a liability to BankTwo and the reserves are an asset; thus, assets and liabilities each have risen by $10 million.) However, BankTwo only needs to hold $1 million in reserves for the additional $10 million in deposits. Thus, BankTwo will want to make more loans until its reserves equal 10 percent of its deposits. It will lend out to other people an amount equal to 90 percent of the $10 million, or $9 million. The increase in deposits, loans, and reserves at BankTwo is shown in the first row of Table 24.5. This is the end of the story for BankTwo but not for the economy as a whole.

The people who get loans from BankTwo will use these loans to pay others. Thus, the funds will likely end up in yet another bank, called BankThree. Then, BankThree will find itself with $9 million in additional deposits and $9 million in additional reserves. BankThree will then lend 90 percent of the $9 million, or $8.1 million, as shown in the second row of Table 24.5. This process will continue from bank to bank. We begin to see that the initial increase in reserves is leading to a much bigger expansion of deposits. The whole process is shown in Table 24.5. Each row shows what happens at each bank. The sum of each column shows the change for the whole economy. If we sum the columns through the end of the process, we will see that deposits and thus the money supply increases by $100 million as a result of the $10 million increase in reserves. The increase in deposits is 10 times the actual increase in reserves! In reality, the whole process takes a short period of time (days rather than weeks) because banks adjust their loans and reserves very quickly.

A Formula Linking Reserves and Deposits

It is no coincidence that the increase in deposits is 10 times the increase in reserves. With the reserve ratio equal to .1 for each bank in the economy, there is a formula linking reserves and deposits for the whole economy. It is given by

Reserves = (reserve ratio) × deposits

where reserves and deposits refer to the amount in the whole economy. If we divide both sides of this expression by the reserve ratio, we get

$$\text{Deposits} = \left(\frac{1}{\text{reserve ratio}}\right) \times \text{reserves}$$

Thus, any increase in reserves is multiplied by the inverse of the reserve ratio to get the increase in deposits. For example, if the $10 million change in reserves is multiplied by $(1/.1) = 10$, we get $100 million change in deposits, which is just what Table 24.5 shows in the detailed look at the expansion of deposits throughout the economy. This reasoning about what happens in the economy as a whole gives the same answer as the step-by-step analysis.

One could also analyze the effects of a decline in reserves using the same detailed examination of the process—or much more simply by using the formula linking reserves and deposits. A decrease in reserves occurs when the Fed sells bonds. For example, a decrease in reserves of $10 million would lead to a decrease in deposits by $100 million. Also, the relationship between deposits and reserves in the economy as a whole shows that there is nothing special about the detailed example; the same expansion would occur with more banks or fewer banks. Moreover, one could have started the example by assuming the Fed bought $10 million in government bonds from some person other than a bank. That person would deposit the check from the Fed in a bank and the process would play itself out just as in Table 24.5. In the end, the answer must be exactly the same: A $10 million increase in reserves leads to a $100 million increase in deposits.

Review

▶ Banks serve two important functions in the monetary system: They help channel funds from savers to investors, and their deposits can be used as money.

▶ The Fed is a bank for the commercial banks. Commercial banks hold deposits, called reserves, at the Fed.

▶ The Fed includes a Board of Governors and twelve District Federal Reserve Banks. The Fed's Federal Open Market Committee makes decisions about the money supply.

▶ Banks create more deposits and thus more money when the Fed increases reserves. The deposits at banks increase by a multiple of the increase in reserves where the multiple depends inversely on the reserve ratio.

HOW THE FED CONTROLS THE MONEY SUPPLY: CURRENCY PLUS DEPOSITS

We have now seen how the Fed, through an increase in reserves, can increase the amount of deposits, or, through a decrease in reserves, can reduce deposits. So far we have been ignoring currency. But the money supply includes currency as well as deposits. What determines the total money supply in the economy when currency is in the story? How does the Fed affect it? With currency in the picture, there are now three things to keep track of: deposits, reserves, and currency. We will find it useful to introduce some shorthand notation to keep track of all three.

The Money Supply (M) and Bank Reserves (BR)

The supply of money is currency plus deposits. (Recall that we are not distinguishing between the different definitions of the money supply or different types of deposits.) If we let CU stand for currency and D stand for deposits, then

$$M = CU + D$$

or, in words, the money supply equals currency plus deposits.

We already know that commercial banks hold a fraction of their deposits at the Fed. Let BR represent the reserves the commercial banks hold at the Fed and let r be the reserve ratio. Then the relationship between reserves and deposits described in the previous section can be written using symbols as

$$BR = rD$$

or, in words, bank reserves equal the reserve ratio (r) times deposits (D). For example, if banks are required to hold 10 percent of their deposits as reserves at the Fed, then $r = .1$. Remember, reserves, held at the central bank by the commercial banks, are just like any other deposit, such as a checking deposit. For example, CitiBank, a commercial bank headquartered in New York City, holds a large amount of reserves at the Fed.

Currency versus Deposits

Although currency and deposits are both part of the money supply, they have different characteristics. For some purposes, people prefer currency to checking deposits and vice versa. These preferences determine how much currency versus checking deposits is in the economy. If you want to hold more currency in your wallet because you find it is more convenient than a checking deposit, you just go to the bank and reduce your checking deposit and carry around more currency. If you are worried about crime and do not want to have much currency in your wallet, then you go to the bank and deposit a larger amount in your checking account. Thus, people decide on the amount of currency versus deposits in the economy. In Japan, where crime is less prevalent than in many other countries, people use much more currency compared to checking accounts than in other countries. Even Japanese business executives who earn the equivalent of $120,000 a year frequently are paid monthly with the equivalent of $10,000 in cash.

currency to deposit ratio: the proportion of currency that people in the economy want to hold relative to their deposits; it equals currency divided by deposits.

In order to determine the amount of currency versus deposits in the economy as a whole, we assume that people want to hold currency equal to a certain fraction of their deposits. More precisely, we assume that there is a ratio called the **currency to deposit ratio** that at any time describes how much currency people want to hold compared to their deposits. If people are happy holding an amount of currency equal to 40 percent of their deposits, then the currency to deposit ratio is .4. If deposits equal $700 billion and the currency to deposit ratio is .4, then currency would equal $280 billion and the money supply would equal $980 billion. Different individuals will have different tastes, but on the average, there will be an overall ratio of currency to deposits in the economy. That ratio depends on people's behavior, on custom, and, as already mentioned, on security in the community.

The ratio also depends on technology; for example, credit cards have reduced the currency to deposit ratio. Note, however, that credit cards are not money any more than a driver's license used for identification when cashing a check is money. Credit cards make more use of checking deposits relative to currency because people usually pay their credit card bills with a check.

At any given point in time, we can take the currency to deposit ratio as a fairly stable number. If the currency to deposit ratio is k, then we can write

Currency = (currency to deposit ratio) × deposits
$$= k \times \text{deposits}$$

Using the symbols we have already introduced, we can write this as

$$CU = kD$$

We now use this expression along with the previous two expressions for the money supply (M) and bank reserve (BR) to show how the Fed can control the money supply.

The Money Multiplier

We saw that the Fed can change the amount of bank reserves by buying and selling bonds. We also saw that when the Fed increases reserves, deposits expand. If currency held by people is equal to k times deposits, then currency will increase when deposits increase. Thus, by buying and selling bonds, the Fed can affect the supply of currency. The Fed can therefore control both currency and reserves. The sum of currency plus reserves is called the **monetary base** by economists. Because the Fed can control both currency and reserves it can control the monetary base. If we let MB stand for the monetary base, then

$$MB = CU + BR$$

monetary base: currency plus reserves.

Table 24.6 shows the size of the monetary base in the U.S. economy in 1996.

We now want to derive a link between the monetary base MB and the money supply M. That link can be used by the Fed to control the money supply. To derive the link we will use some algebra and equations just like the people at the Fed use. We can use the equation showing that the money supply equals currency plus deposits and the equation showing that currency is a certain fraction of deposits to get a relationship between the money supply and deposits. That is, substitute $CU = kD$ into the equation $M = CU + D$ to get $M = kD + D$, or

$$M = (k + 1)D$$

TABLE 24.6
The Monetary Base for the United States, 1996
(billions of dollars)

Currency	396
Reserves	57
Monetary Base	453

Source: Federal Reserve Board.

There is also the relationship that exists between bank reserves and deposits, $BR = rD$, which together with $CU = kD$ can be substituted into the equation $MB = CU + BR$ to get $MB = kD + rD$, or

$$MB = (k + r)D$$

Now, to find the link between MB and M, divide M by MB and cancel out D to get

$$\frac{M}{MB} = \frac{(k + 1)}{(r + k)}$$

We call this ratio, $(k + 1)/(r + k)$, the money multiplier. For example, suppose the reserve ratio r is .1 and the currency to deposit ratio k is .2, then the money

FIGURE 24.4

The Inverted Monetary Pyramid

The money supply, defined either as M1 or M2, is built on the monetary base. The money multiplier multiplies the monetary base to get either M1 or M2. These data are for the United States in 1996. The money multiplier for M1 is about 2.4 and for M2 it is about 8.4.

Source: Federal Reserve Board.

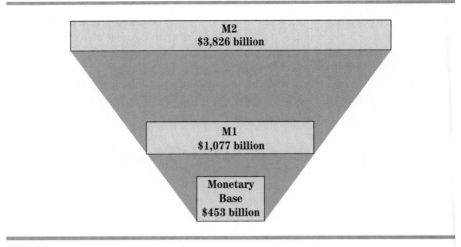

money multiplier: the multiple by which the money supply changes due to a change in the monetary base.

multiplier is $(.2 + 1)/(.1 + .2) = 1.2/.3 = 4$. An increase in the monetary base *MB* of $100 million would increase the money supply *M* by $400 million. This large increase is the reason for the term *multiplier*. In general, the **money multiplier** is the number you multiply the monetary base by to get the money supply.

To see how the money multiplier works in practice, suppose the Fed buys bonds so as to increase the monetary base by $1 billion; according to the money multiplier, the money supply in the economy should increase by $4 billion. The actual increase in the money supply occurs through a bank-by-bank process just like that shown in Table 24.5 with currency now changing as well. With currency in the story, the total effect on the money supply of a change in the monetary base is smaller than in Table 24.5 because people do not put all their money in banks. This reduces the amount of deposit expansion. Note that if $k = 0$, the case without currency, the money multiplier is 10 in this example. Thus, an increase in the monetary base of $10 million will increase money by $100 million, as in the previous section.

More important than the fact that the multiplier is greater than 1 is that it provides a link between the monetary base and the money supply in the economy. As long as the currency to deposit ratio and the reserve ratio do not change, the Fed can control the money supply by adjusting the monetary base. Remarkably, as illustrated by Figure 24.4, the whole money supply is built on the monetary base. Now let us look at the effects of changes in the money supply.

Review

▶ The monetary base is the sum of currency plus bank reserves. The Fed can change the money supply—currency plus deposits—by adjusting the monetary base. A change in the monetary base changes the money supply by a multiple of the increase in the monetary base. The multiple is called the money multiplier.

▶ The money multiplier depends on the reserve ratio and the currency to deposit ratio.

MONEY GROWTH AND INFLATION

Because people use money to buy and sell goods and services, the total money supply in the economy and the total value of goods and services in the economy are closely related. In the economy as a whole, nominal GDP is the dollar value of all goods and services. Thus, we would expect to see a close relationship between the money supply and nominal GDP.

Consider first a simple example. Suppose that all of your transactions are with food-vending machines and video game machines. You will need money in your pocket to carry out your transactions. If you use the vending and video game machines ten times a day, you will need ten times more money in your pocket than if you use the machines once a day. Hence, ten times more transactions means ten times more money. If the prices for vending machine items and minutes on a video game double, then you will need twice as much money for each day's activities, assuming the higher price does not cure your habit. Hence, whether the volume of transactions increases because the real number of items purchased increases or because the price of each item increases, the amount of money used for transactions will rise. What is true for you and the machines is true for the whole population and the whole economy. For the whole economy, the number of transactions is closely related to nominal GDP. Nominal GDP can be expressed as the price level (the GDP deflator) times real GDP. Thus, nominal GDP increases if the price level rises or if real GDP rises. In either case the money supply needed for transactions rises.

The Quantity Equation of Money

The relationship between money and nominal GDP in the economy as a whole can be summarized by the **quantity equation of money,** which is written:

> Money supply × velocity = price level × real GDP

or

> $MV = PY$

where V is velocity, P is the price level, and Y is real GDP. Remember the right-hand side of this equation also equals nominal GDP. Velocity is computed by dividing nominal GDP by the money supply. That is,

$$V = \frac{\text{nominal GDP}}{M}$$

Thus, in 1996 velocity was about 7 with the money supply (M1) at $1,077 billion and nominal GDP at $7,576 billion. Thus, **velocity** is simply the term one multiplies the money supply by to get nominal GDP. If velocity were higher, the same money supply would permit more transactions—more nominal GDP. If velocity were lower, fewer transactions would be carried out with the same amount of money.

Note that *velocity* can be thought of as measuring how fast money is used. It is the number of times a dollar is used on average to make purchases of final goods and services. To see this, suppose an automatic teller machine is installed in the room with the vending machines and video games from the preceding example. Each morning you get cash from the automatic teller machine for your morning games, and each day at midday you could get cash from the machine to pay for your afternoon use of the games and vending machines; then you would need to

quantity equation of money: the equation relating the price level and real GDP to the quantity of money and the velocity of money: The quantity of money times its velocity equals the price level times real GDP; in terms of growth rates it states that money growth plus velocity growth equals inflation plus real GDP growth.

velocity: a measure of how fast money is turned over in the economy: Velocity equals nominal GDP divided by the money supply.

carry only half as much currency in your pocket as before they installed the automatic teller machines and you had to bring enough cash to last all day. From your perspective, therefore, the velocity of money doubles. As this example shows, velocity in the economy depends on technology and, in particular, on how efficient we are at using money.

If you look carefully at the preceding quantity equation of money, you see that if velocity is not affected by a change in money, then an increase in the money supply must lead to an increase in nominal GDP. In this sense, the money supply in the economy and nominal GDP are closely related. If real GDP is also not affected by a change in money, then an increase in the money supply will increase the price level. Higher rates of money growth would thus lead to higher inflation, just as in the case of commodity money at the start of the chapter.

A restatement of the quantity equation using growth rates leads to a convenient relationship between money growth, inflation, real GDP growth, and velocity growth. In particular,

Inflation + real GDP growth = money growth + velocity growth

For example, if the money supply growth is 5 percent per year, velocity growth is 0 percent per year, and real GDP growth is 3 percent per year, then this equation says that inflation is 2 percent per year. This growth rate form of the quantity equation follows directly from the quantity equation itself; in general, the rate of growth of a product of two terms is approximately equal to the sum of the growth rates of the two terms. Thus, the growth rate of M times V equals the growth rate of M plus the growth rate of V, and the growth rate of P times Y equals the growth rate of P plus the growth rate of Y.

The quantity equation tells us that along a long-run economic growth path in which real GDP growth is equal to potential GDP growth, an increase in money growth by a certain number of percentage points will result in the long run in an increase in inflation of the same number of percentage points unless there is a change in velocity growth. Thus, higher money growth will lead to higher inflation in the long run. If velocity growth remains at zero, as in the previous example, and real GDP growth remains at 3 percent per year, then an increase in money growth by 10 percentage points, from 5 to 15 percent, will increase inflation by 10 percentage points, from 2 to 12 percent.

Figure 24.5 shows the close relationship between money growth and inflation in the seven largest developed economies over a recent 20-year period. Money growth is plotted on the vertical axis and inflation on the horizontal axis. Each point represents a country. For countries with higher money growth, inflation has been higher. The line drawn through the points shows that inflation increases by about the same number of percentage points as money growth increases, as predicted by the quantity equation. Because the countries are close to this line, the quantity equation seems to work fairly well in predicting the relationship between money growth and inflation.

Some Key Episodes in Monetary History

Figure 24.6 presents an overview of U.S. monetary history; it shows the U.S. price level during the past 200 years. Historical studies indicate that the supply of money has increased much more rapidly since World War II, and especially after the mid-1960s, than in any other period of similar length in U.S. history. This is why inflation has been worse, especially after the mid-1960s, as shown in Figure 24.6.

FIGURE 24.5
The Relation Between Money Growth and Inflation
As the data for these several countries show, higher money growth is associated with higher inflation. The data pertain to the period 1973–1991 and are stated as the average percent per year.

Source: Organization for Economic Cooperation and Development.

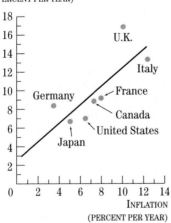

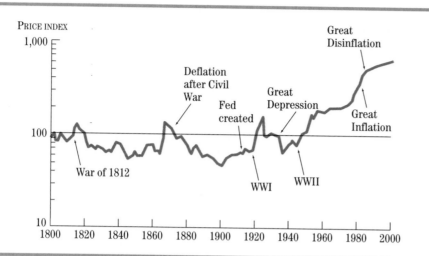

PRICE INDEX

Great
Disinflation

Deflation
after Civil
War

Great
Depression

Fed
created

Great
Inflation

100

War of 1812

WWI

WWII

10

1800 1820 1840 1860 1880 1900 1920 1940 1960 1980 2000

FIGURE 24.6

The Price Level in the United States, 1800–1996

For much of U.S. history, the average price fluctuated around a stable level, though there were several periods of deflation, such as after the Civil War. Since World War II, and especially since the mid-1960s, rising prices—inflation—have been the rule. In the 1980s, there was a disinflation that reduced the inflation rate but did not bring it to zero.

Source: Historical Statistics of the United States.

Because the rate of increase in the price level is inflation, the upward movements of the line showing the price indicate periods of inflation. In the 150 years before World War II there was much less long-term inflation than there has been in recent years.

The United States experienced an even higher inflation during the Revolutionary War: The paper currency issued at the time, the Continental, lost so much value that the phrase "not worth a continental" became part of the language.

Why does inflation get so high? The most common reason is that the government prints money to pay for its expenditures. Countries with very high inflation have trouble raising revenues from taxes because it is easy for people to avoid taxes. These governments also do not have the credibility to borrow funds. Thus, the central bank starts printing money and letting the government use the money to pay for goods and services. As money growth increases, inflation rises. As inflation rises, people are not willing to hold as much money because it is losing its value, so the government has to print even more money.

Although printing money is not *now* a significant source of government financing for lower-inflation countries like the United States and Germany, there have been episodes in the past when both of these countries resorted to printing money to finance deficits. We mentioned the U.S. Revolutionary War. The hyperinflation in Germany was even worse. Inflation rose to over 100 percent per week.

A very high inflation is called *hyperinflation.* Hyperinflation occurred in Germany in 1923. The German government incurred huge expenses during World War I, and after the war, Germany lost all of its colonies, 10 percent of its population, and almost 15 percent of its main territory, which included much of the iron- and coal-producing areas.

Huge demands for war reparations from the victors in World War I compounded the problem. The budget deficit

Hyperinflation and Nearly Worthless Money

So much money was printed during the period of German hyperinflation that it became cheaper to burn several million German marks to cook breakfast—as this woman was doing in 1923—than to buy kindling wood with the nearly worthless money.

FIGURE 24.7

German Hyperinflation of 1923

The chart shows the weekly percent change in the price level in Germany in 1923. Inflation rose to truly astronomical levels for several months.

Source: J.P. Young, *European Currency and Finance,* Vol. 1 (Washington, D.C.: Government Printing Office, 1925), p. 503.

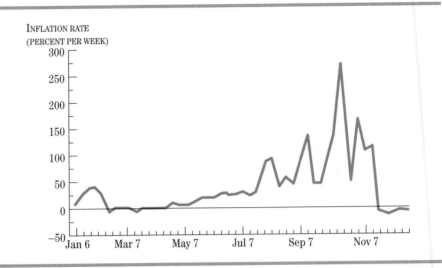

50,000,000 German Mark Reichsbank Note, 1923

could be financed only by printing money, which finally gave way to the hyperinflation of 1923. Figure 24.7 shows the *weekly* increase in German prices. Shop owners closed their shops at lunchtime to change the prices. Workers were paid twice weekly. People would rush to the stores and buy everything they needed for the next few days. Firms also set up barter systems with their workers, exchanging consumer goods directly for labor.

The hyperinflation was caused by a huge increase in money growth. Everyone tried to get rid of cash as soon as possible, thus accelerating the inflationary process. Also, by the time the government received its tax revenue, it was not worth much because prices had risen sharply, and the budget deficit grew even greater. The government needed to print even more money. In the last months of hyperinflation more than 30 paper mills worked at full capacity to deliver paper currency. One hundred fifty printing firms had 2,000 presses running 24 hours a day to print German marks, and they could not keep up with the need for new notes. On November 15, 1923, an economic reform stabilized the inflation rate. By then, the German price level was 100 billion times what it was before the hyperinflation.

The German hyperinflation of 1923 is not a unique historical episode, and it is not necessarily linked to war, as the hyperinflation in the early 1990s in Argentina makes clear. In the mid-1990s, an inflation in Russia was also caused by the creation of too much money. Money growth is the cause of all hyperinflations.

Review

▶ The money supply and the value of transactions in an economy are closely related. The quantity equation describes this relationship; it says that the money supply times velocity equals nominal GDP.

▶ Higher rates of money growth will eventually lead to higher inflation.

▶ A hyperinflation is a very high inflation.

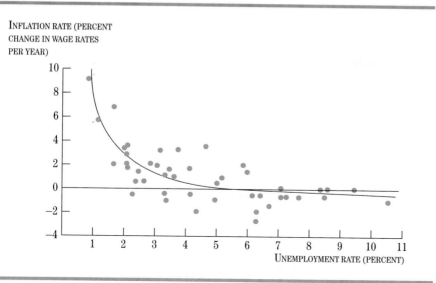

INFLATION RATE (PERCENT CHANGE IN WAGE RATES PER YEAR)

UNEMPLOYMENT RATE (PERCENT)

FIGURE 24.8

A Replica of an Original Phillips Curve

A.W. Phillips published this curve in a 1958 paper. The vertical axis measures inflation in terms of wages rather than prices, but the curve looks about the same with most measures of inflation. Each point represents one year. The curve drawn through the points had enormous influence and led many economists to argue that lower unemployment in normal times could be achieved by a higher inflation rate. But it did not work.

Source: A.W. Phillips, "The Relationship Between Unemployment and the Rate of Change of Money Wage Rates in the United Kingdom," from *Economica.* Copyright © 1958 by Basil Blackwell, Ltd. Used with permission. The data period is 1861–1913.

INFLATION: EFFECTS ON UNEMPLOYMENT AND PRODUCTIVITY GROWTH

We have seen that inflation is related to money growth and that money growth is determined by the government, in particular, by the Fed. What effects does inflation have on the economy and, in particular, on the long-run growth of the economy? Two effects of inflation have been studied in great detail by economists: its effect on unemployment and its effect on the long-run growth of real GDP.

Effects on Unemployment

In the late 1950s, the economist A. W. Phillips, then at the London School of Economics, published a paper showing that periods in British history with low unemployment were associated with high inflation and that periods with high unemployment were associated with low inflation.[1] In other words, if you place unemployment on the horizontal axis of a diagram and inflation on the vertical axis and plot pairs of observations from each year, you get a downward-sloping relationship. That relationship came to be called the **Phillips curve.** An original Phillips curve from Phillips's 1958 paper is shown in Figure 24.8.

The relationship led many to believe that lower unemployment could be achieved by having a higher inflation rate. In other words, the Phillips curve was taken to imply that there was a negative relationship between unemployment and inflation in the long run. However, basic economic reasoning—as first put forth in the late 1960s by economists Edmund Phelps and Milton Friedman—suggested otherwise.

Phillips curve: a downward-sloping relationship between inflation and unemployment; originally found by A.W. Phillips in data from the late 1800s and early 1900s.

1. A. W. Phillips "The Relationship Between Unemployment and the Rate of Change of Money Wage Rates in the United Kingdom," *Economica,* November 1958.

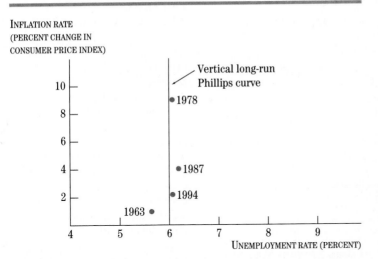

FIGURE 24.9
The Modern View of the Long-Run Phillips Curve

Economic theory and experience have shown that the Phillips curve is vertical in the long run. A higher inflation rate will not permanently lower the unemployment rate. The diagram shows four years in which real GDP is approximately equal to potential GDP. The points cluster around a line that is remarkably close to vertical.

Source: U.S. Department of Labor.

The hypothesis of Friedman and Phelps proved to be a remarkably accurate description of reality. They argued that the Phillips curve relationship between unemployment and inflation was only temporary. For example, suppose the central bank suddenly increases the rate of growth of the money supply and this causes a sudden increase in inflation. The rise in inflation might reduce the real wage (the wage divided by the price level) because wages might not adjust quickly enough to the higher inflation rate. The rate of unemployment would go down because firms would hire more workers at the lower real wage. But if the inflation persisted, people would begin to raise their expectation of inflation, and workers would soon demand higher wage increases to compensate for the lost purchasing power. These wage increases would raise the real wage again and the unemployment rate with it. Unemployment would return to normal. Thus, at best, the decline in unemployment would be temporary. In the long run, we would have a higher inflation rate, but the unemployment rate would remain at its natural rate.

According to Friedman and Phelps, therefore, the curve showing the relationship between inflation and unemloyment is vertical in the long run: that is, a higher inflation rate, as measured along the vertical axis of Phillips's diagram, would lead to about the same unemployment rate along the horizontal axis.

How well does this analysis of Friedman and Phelps describe the data in the long run? Figure 24.9 provides an answer. Four pairs of U.S. inflation and unemployment rates for four normal years when real GDP equals potential GDP are plotted. The points trace out a remarkably vertical curve, especially in comparison with the short-run curve in Figure 24.8. We have purposely only plotted points on the picture where real GDP is close to potential GDP because they exclude the economic fluctuations in the economy around potential GDP. But these points clearly show how the Phillips curve relationship between unemployment and inflation turned out to be wrong when applied to a situation of higher long-run inflation. Inflation did not lower the rate of unemployment. That there is no long-run tradeoff between inflation and unemployment has become a major principle of macroeconomics.

Effects on Productivity Growth

The effects of inflation on economic growth occur through its effects on productivity growth. According to the growth accounting formula of Chapter 23, high rates of inflation will reduce productivity growth by reducing investment in physical and human capital and by reducing the rate of technological change. But why would inflation reduce investment or technological change? Part of the answer is that highly volatile inflation rates from year to year and increased volatility of relative prices are usually associated with higher inflation.

Recall that our discussion of investment in Chapter 22 showed that investment is negatively related to the interest rate. Higher interest rates reduce the attractiveness of new investment projects that do not have high enough returns. When inflation rates are high they are often volatile. Thus, high inflation increases uncertainty about the future returns from investment. A higher rate of inflation than expected would reduce the real cost of borrowing, and a lower rate of inflation than expected would increase the real cost of borrowing. Thus, by increasing uncertainty, high inflation could reduce investment; the resulting lower growth in the capital to labor ratio would thus reduce productivity growth.

Higher inflation could reduce the rate of technological change for similar reasons. Investment in human capital and in research and development—both factors in technological change—might therefore be lower.

Observations on economic growth in different countries indicate that inflation is negatively correlated with economic growth. How large are the effects? According to one recent estimate by Brian Motley, an economist who works at the Fed, a reduction in the inflation rate of 5 percentage points would increase the long-run growth rate of productivity by from .1 to .3 percent per year. If the larger estimate is correct, then reducing the inflation rate from 12 percent—close to where it was in the late 1970s—to 2 percent would raise productivity growth by .6 percentage points, nearly doubling the rate of the last 20 years. The estimate is uncertain, but even with the lower estimate the increase in growth associated with lower inflation would be substantial. Motley's results also indicate that there is relatively less improvement in lowering the inflation rate from 2 percent to 0 percent, a range where we have very little experience.

Why Is Inflation Almost Always Greater than Zero?

If inflation does not lower unemployment and seems to be bad for long-term growth, then why is there inflation? If inflation can be reduced to zero simply by reducing money growth to the rate of real GDP growth less velocity growth, then why have governments not done it? What can we expect in the future?

Printing Money to Finance Government Expenditures

One reason, which was discussed earlier, is that inflation is caused by printing money to finance government expenditures. In countries where tax collection is difficult and tax revenue has not been enough to cover government expenditure, printing money is a significant source of financing government spending. Effectively these countries use inflation as another tax, sometimes called the *inflation tax.*

However, this explanation does not apply to countries like the United States. In the United States the inflation tax is a minor source of revenue, and the Federal Reserve System is not in the business of lending funds directly to government.

Bias in Measuring Inflation

In the 1990s inflation in the United States fell to around 3 percent for the first time in 25 years. But there is disagreement about whether it should be lowered further. Perhaps the main reason for not reducing inflation further is that many economists feel that inflation is measured with some upward bias and that when measured inflation is about 1 or 2 percent, actual inflation is essentially zero. One reason for the upward bias, discussed in Chapter 20, is that people tend to consume less of items that increase more rapidly in price.

It is hard to estimate how large this bias is, but 1 to 2 percent is a common view. If 2 percent is the bias, then the 3 percent inflation seen in America in the early 1990s was actually 1 percent, quite close to zero. Recall from Chapter 20 that a Senate-appointed commission of economists, chaired by Michael Boskin of Stanford, concluded that the bias was about 1 percent.

Concerns about Deflation or Disinflation

Another reason why zero inflation might not be the correct policy is that inflation is never perfectly steady. If zero is the average, then there will be some periods when inflation is negative, a situation of deflation. Historically, periods of deflation have been bad for the economy, and this raises concerns about deflation in the future.

Finally, even though low inflation may be good for long-term economic growth, the process of getting to low inflation from high inflation—a process called *disinflation*—may be costly to the economy. As we know from Chapter 19, periods when inflation *declines* are usually periods of high unemployment. If policymakers place a lot of emphasis on the short-run costs, they may be unwilling to make changes that provide benefits in the long run. We will take up this tradeoff between the long run and the short run in later chapters on economic fluctuations.

Review

▶ The Phillips curve helped create the view that there was a long-run tradeoff between inflation and unemployment.

▶ Modern macroeconomic theory indicates that there is no such long-range tradeoff. Higher inflation does not reduce the unemployment rate in the long run.

▶ High inflation does seem to reduce economic growth.

▶ The need for countries to print money to finance government spending is one reason inflation is greater than zero.

▶ An upward bias in measures of inflation indicates that 1 or 2 percent measured inflation may be very close to zero.

CONCLUSION

Money has fascinated economists for centuries. The famous quantity equation introduced in this chapter predates Adam Smith and was used by the economist-philosopher David Hume in the eighteenth century. Adam Smith placed money second only to the division of labor in the first chapters of the *Wealth of Nations*.

In this chapter we have seen how money and the whole monetary system fit into the theory of economic growth, helping to channel funds from savers to investors, providing an efficient way to exchange goods and services, and ultimately causing inflation, which in turn affects economic growth.

Although the role of money appears mysterious and has caused some great debates in economics and politics, most of the ideas presented in this chapter are relatively noncontroversial. The three functions of money, the deposit expansion process, the money multiplier, the technical ability of the central bank to control the monetary base, the fact that money is the cause of inflation in the long run, the conclusion that there is no long-run tradeoff between inflation and unemployment, and the belief that high inflation tends to lower productivity are things many economists now agree on.

Many of the controversies about money pertain to the short-run fluctuations in the economy and revolve around the effects changes in the money supply have on real GDP in the short run. After considering the reasons why real GDP may depart from potential GDP in the short run in the next two chapters, we will return to the relationship between money and the short-run fluctuations in the economy. When we do so we will make use of the analysis in this chapter that shows how the central bank controls the money supply.

KEY POINTS

1. Commodity money, ranging from salt to gold coins, has been used in place of barter for many centuries. Now paper money and deposits are also part of money.

2. Money has three roles: a medium of exchange, a store of value, and a unit of account.

3. The quantity equation describes the relationship between money growth, real GDP growth, and inflation.

4. Higher money growth leads to higher inflation in the long run.

5. Commercial banks are financial intermediaries; their deposits are part of the money supply.

6. The central bank controls the money supply by changing the monetary base.

7. The central bank in the United States is the Federal Reserve System (the Fed).

8. The money multiplier tells us how much the money supply increases when the monetary base increases.

9. There is no long-run relationship between inflation and unemployment.

10. Inflation, at least at high levels, reduces long-run economic growth.

11. There is some disagreement about exactly how low inflation should be; few argue for inflation less than zero.

KEY TERMS

money	money supply	reserves
commodity money	M1	required reserve ratio
medium of exchange	savings deposit	loan
barter	time deposit	bond
coincidence of wants	M2	currency to deposit ratio
store of value	Federal Reserve System (the Fed)	monetary base
unit of account	bank	money multiplier
paper money	Federal Open Market Committee	quantity equation of money
gold standard	(FOMC)	velocity
currency	asset	Phillips curve
checking deposit	liability	

QUESTIONS FOR REVIEW

1. What are some examples of commodity money?

2. What are the differences between the medium of exchange, store of value, and unit of account roles of money?

3. Why are bank deposits part of money but an expensive purse to put the money in is not?

4. Why does higher money growth cause inflation?

5. What is the quantity equation of money?

6. What is a bank?

7. How do banks create money?

8. What is the Fed, and how is the FOMC organized?

9. What is the money multiplier, and why does it depend on the required reserve ratio?

10. Why is the natural rate of unemployment unrelated to the inflation rate?

11. Why is the inflation rate rarely zero?

PROBLEMS

1. Which of the following are money, and which are not? Explain.
 a) A credit card
 b) A dollar bill
 c) A check in your checkbook
 d) Funds in a checking account

2. State whether each of the following statements is true or false. Explain your answers in one or two sentences.
 a) The larger the reserve ratio at banks, the smaller the money multiplier.
 b) The Federal Reserve increases reserves by selling government bonds.
 c) The same money is always used as both a unit of account and a medium of exchange at any one time in any one country.
 d) When commodity money is the only type of money, a decrease in the price of the commodity serving as money is inflation.

3. Suppose that, before the invention of the automatic teller machine, people held currency equal to 20 percent of their bank deposits. If the required reserve ratio is 20 percent, what is the money multiplier? Now suppose that, after the invention of the ATM, people hold only 10 percent of the value of their deposits in currency. What is the money multiplier now? Explain how the change in the money multiplier occurs.

4. Sam sells his government bond and it is bought by the Fed. Sam receives $10,000, which he promptly deposits in his checking account at his bank.
 a) For simplicity, suppose that $k = 0$: People hold all their money in the bank. If the required reserve ratio is 10 percent for all bank deposits, how much of this new deposit will Sam's bank lend out?
 b) Sam's bank lends this money to Jason, who uses it to pay the contractor, Karen, who remodeled his kitchen. Karen deposits this money into her checking account at a different bank than Sam's. How much will be lent out by Karen's bank?
 c) This process of lending and relending will continue through the banking system until there is nothing left to lend. At that point, how much is the total increase in deposits created by Sam's initial $10,000?
 d) How will the total increase in deposits change from part (c) if $k > 0$? Why?

5. Every year you negotiate with your employer over your wage rate.
 a) Suppose you expect inflation to be 5 percent. If your wage is now $10 per hour, what new wage will keep your expected real wage unchanged?
 b) Your employer agrees to raise your wage by enough to keep your expected real wage constant. The employer

agrees with your expectation of inflation. But during the next year there is much lower inflation than expected—1 percent. What has happened to your real wage? How will your employer react to this?
 c) You manage to keep your job, but some of your coworkers are laid off. How will this affect the negotiations for next year's wages? What will have happened to your expectation of inflation?

6. Use the quantity equation in its growth form to answer the following:
 a) Suppose there is no change in velocity and that there is zero growth in output. If inflation is 30 percent per month, what must be the monthly growth rate of the money supply based on the quantity equation? Explain.
 b) Now suppose that inflation is still 30 percent per month but that output is falling at a rate of 5 percent per month. What must be the growth rate of money now?
 c) In this situation, why would workers want their employer to pay their monthly salary in weekly installments rather than once a month? What effect will increasing the frequency of pay have on the velocity of money?
 d) As the pace of inflation increases, people want to spend their money more quickly because it is losing value. Use the quantity equation to explain what effect this increase in velocity has on inflation.

7. Fill out the following table using the quantity equation:

Year	Quantity of Money (M2) (billions of $)	Velocity	Real GDP (billions of 1992 $)	Price Level (GDP deflator 1992 = 100)
1989	3,164	_____	6,060	89.7
1990	3,282	_____	6,139	93.6
1991	3,384	_____	6,079	97.3

 a) Calculate the growth rates for each of the four variables between 1989 and 1990.
 b) Calculate nominal GDP for 1989 and 1990, and then calculate the growth rate of nominal GDP between 1989 and 1990. Compare this result with the sum of the growth rates of real GDP and the price level between those two years.
 c) The quantity equation of money in growth rates can be written as:

Growth in M + growth in V = growth in GDP
    + growth in P

Does the growth rate form of the quantity equation work for the time period from 1989 to 1990?

d) Compare the velocity in 1990 with velocity in 1991. Is this surprising? What are possible causes of this result?

8. Construct a balance sheet, with assets on the left and liabilities on the right, for two commercial banks (Combank and Mercbank) to show how banks create money. Assume that reserves are 10 percent of deposits and that people hold no currency—all their money is in their checking accounts.

a) Suppose Tony (a private citizen) sells a government bond that he owns back to the Fed and deposits all of the $10,000 sum into his account at Combank. Show how this creates both new assets and new liabilities for Combank.

b) How much of this new deposit can Combank lend out? Assume it lends this amount to Mark, who then deposits this amount in Mercbank. Show this on Mercbank's balance sheet.

c) Suppose a used car is bought with this loan. The former owner of the car, Leah, deposits the proceeds from the sale into her account at Combank. How much is this deposit? How much in new excess reserves are created when she makes this deposit?

d) This process of lending and relending creates money throughout the banking system. How much money (that is, in new deposits) has been created from the initial deposit of $10,000 due to the two subsequent loans?

e) Use the money multiplier for this example to calculate how much money will be created when the lending is allowed to continue forever.

9. Credit cards are not included in the money supply, but currency and deposits at banks are included. Explain why credit cards are excluded. (Hint: Credit cards are a form of identification that allows you to borrow.)

Economic Fluctuations

During the Great Depression of the 1930s, the production of goods and services in the United States fell by one-third and many people lost their jobs and faced prolonged hardship. More recent economic downturns have been much milder, but they also have caused harm to people. Fortunately, recessions appear to have become less frequent, but there is no evidence that they have been eliminated. Hence, recessions persist as an economic problem, even as the problem of low long-term economic growth has risen in importance, as described in the four preceding chapters.

In the four upcoming chapters, we delve into the causes of recessions and examine the forces that cause each recession to end. In Chapter 25 we start to unveil the model of economic fluctuations. The main aim of Chapter 25 is to show why real GDP initially

Real GDP

chapters

25 The First Steps Toward Recession or Boom

26 The Uncertain Multiplier

27 Aggregate Demand and Price Adjustment

28 Toward Recovery and Expansion

steps away from potential GDP at the start of a recession or a boom. In Chapter 26 we define the multiplier, which determines the size of the initial steps of real GDP away from potential GDP. In Chapter 27 we examine the dynamic patterns of real GDP and inflation that occur as real GDP returns to potential GDP after a recession. We also complete the economic fluctuations model, and show that the model is based on a diagram similar to the basic supply and demand model. In Chapter 28 we look at how the economic fluctuations model developed in the preceding chapters is used to determine the path the economy takes toward recovery after a recession.

The ideas and models introduced in these chapters are used on a daily basis by economists in the world's capitals and financial centers. Economic forecasters in private firms and the government use models like these to forecast the growth of the economy over several years. Central bankers, who control the money supply in the United States and other countries, use these ideas to help them decide how much money to supply; their decisions have enormous impact on the economy. Economic advisers to the president of the United States or members of Congress use the models to determine how large the budget deficit will be and to decide whether a change in taxes is advisable; their decisions also have a great impact on the economy. The exciting thing about these models is that you can learn to use them in essentially the same way they are used by those making these momentous decisions about monetary and fiscal policy.

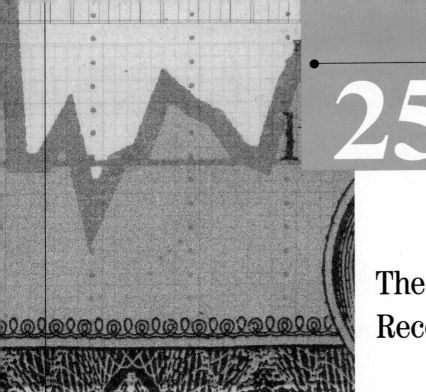

25

The First Steps Toward Recession or Boom

Economic fluctuations are departures of the economy from its long-term growth trend. These departures include recessions, such as the ones that occurred in the United States, Japan, and the European countries in the early 1980s and again in the early 1990s. They also include booms, such as the ones that occurred in the same countries in the mid-1980s. Economic fluctuations—also called business cycles—have been a common occurrence in all economies at least since the great economic growth wave began 200 years ago, but they have changed over time. One notable difference is that they seem to have diminished in severity.

One recent economic fluctuation is brought into focus in Figure 25.1. A boom in 1988 and 1989 raised real GDP above potential GDP. A recession in 1990 lowered real GDP below potential GDP, and a recovery starting in 1991 brought real GDP back toward potential GDP by 1994. Our purpose now is to focus, as does Figure 25.1, on economic fluctuations.

Economic fluctuations occur simultaneously with long-term economic growth, as shown by the longer history in Figure 25.1. Real GDP has fluctuated around what might otherwise have been a steady upward-moving trend. Although no two economic fluctuations are alike—some are long, some are short, some are deep, some are shallow—they have common features. Perhaps the most important one is that the recessions and booms end, and real GDP eventually returns to a more normal long-run growth path.

Although recessions eventually end, they bring unemployment and hardship to many people. Booms can also cause harm. Inflation usually rises in booms. When inflation gets too high, it reduces long-term growth and frequently leads to subsequent recessions.

In this chapter, we look at the first steps the economy takes as it moves into a recession or a boom. In other words, we examine the initial, or short-run, increase or decrease of real GDP above or below potential GDP. We will show that the first steps of real GDP away from potential GDP are usually caused by changes in aggregate demand. Aggregate demand is the total amount consumers, businesses, government, and foreigners are willing to spend on all goods and services in the economy. In contrast, the growth of potential GDP is caused by increases in the available supply of inputs to production: labor, capital, and technology.

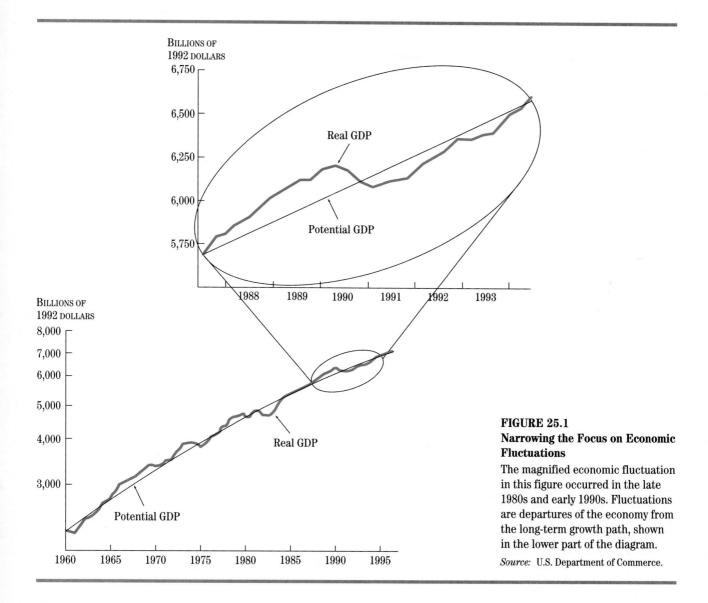

FIGURE 25.1
Narrowing the Focus on Economic Fluctuations
The magnified economic fluctuation in this figure occurred in the late 1980s and early 1990s. Fluctuations are departures of the economy from the long-term growth path, shown in the lower part of the diagram.

Source: U.S. Department of Commerce.

CHANGES IN AGGREGATE DEMAND FIRST LEAD TO CHANGES IN OUTPUT

Figure 25.2 illustrates the essential idea used to explain economic fluctuations: that increases or decreases in real GDP that are above or below potential GDP occur largely because of increases or decreases in aggregate demand in the economy. Changes in aggregate demand occur when consumers, business firms, government,

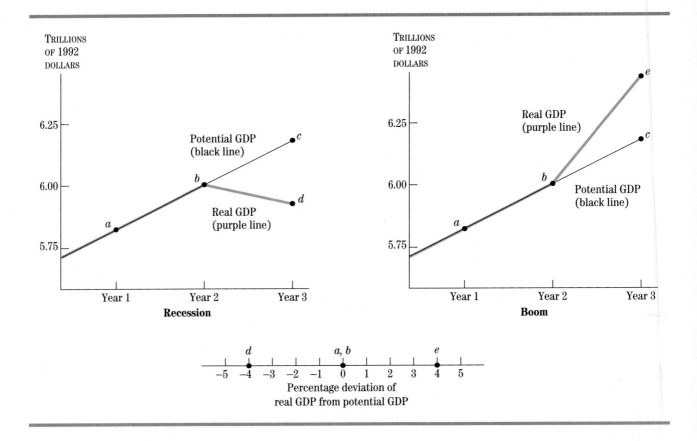

FIGURE 25.2
The First Step of an Economic Fluctuation

Potential GDP is shown by the black upward-sloping line in both diagrams. Points *a, b,* and *c* represent three different levels of potential GDP in three years. A recession is a downward departure of real GDP (shown in purple) from potential GDP, as illustrated by point *d* on the left. A boom is an upward departure of real GDP from potential GDP, as illustrated by point *e* on the right. The departures are explained by changes in aggregate demand. The line at the bottom shows the percent deviation of real GDP from potential GDP.

or foreigners expand or cut back their spending plans. Potential GDP in three years is marked by the points *a, b,* and *c* in Figure 25.2. These three values of potential GDP are part of the longer-term steady increase in potential GDP over time due to increases in the supply of labor and capital and improvements in technology. Potential GDP represents what firms would want to produce in "normal times," when the economy is neither in a recession nor in a boom. In normal times, real GDP is equal to potential GDP. Years 1 and 2 in Figure 25.2 are assumed to be normal years. However, year 3 is not a normal year. Point *d* in the left panel of the figure and point *e* in the right panel represent two alternative types of departures of real GDP from potential GDP that could occur in year 3: a recession and a boom.

In a boom, real GDP rises above potential GDP to a point like *e* in the right panel of Figure 25.2. Firms produce more in response to the increase in aggregate demand; they employ more workers, and unemployment declines. Eventually—this part of the story comes in later chapters—if demand for their products stays high, firms raise their prices, and real GDP returns toward potential GDP.

In a recession, all this works in reverse. Real GDP falls below potential GDP to a point like *d* in the left panel of Figure 25.2. Firms produce less and lay off workers. Unemployment rises. Eventually—again, this part of the story comes in later chapters—if demand stays low, firms begin to cut their prices, and real GDP moves back toward potential GDP. Thus, in both booms and recessions, changes in aggregate demand cause fluctuations in real GDP.

Economists frequently measure the departures of real GDP from potential GDP in percentages rather than dollar amounts. For example, if potential GDP is $6.20 trillion and real GDP is $6.45 trillion, then the percentage departure of real GDP from potential GDP is 4 percent: $(6.45 - 6.20)/6.20 = .04$. If real GDP were $5.95 trillion and potential GDP remained at $6.20 trillion, then the percentage departure would be -4 percent: $(5.95 - 6.20)/6.20 = -.04$. Percentages make it easier to compare economic fluctuations in different countries that have different sizes of real GDP. At the bottom of the two panels in Figure 25.2 is a horizontal line representing the size of the fluctuations in real GDP around potential GDP in each year.

Points *d* and *e* in Figure 25.2 represent the first steps of an economic fluctuation. These first steps occur in the short run.

Production and Demand at Individual Firms

Why do firms produce more—bringing real GDP above *potential GDP*—when the demand for their products rises? Why do firms produce less—bringing real GDP below potential GDP—when the demand for their products falls? These questions have probably occupied economists' time more than any other in macroeconomics. Although more work still needs to be done, substantial improvements in economists' understanding of the issues have been made in the last 20 years.

potential GDP: the economy's long-term growth trend for real GDP determined by the available supply of capital, labor and technology. Real GDP fluctuates above and below potential GDP. (Ch. 19)

Normal Capacity Utilization and the Natural Unemployment Rate

First consider some simple facts about how firms operate. In normal times, when real GDP is equal to potential GDP, most firms operate with some excess capacity so they can expand production without major bottlenecks. Small retail service businesses from taxi companies to dry cleaners can usually increase production when customer demand increases. Another taxi is added to a busy route and one of the drivers is asked to work overtime. One of the dry cleaning employees who has been working part time is happy to work full time. The same is true for large manufacturing firms. When asked what percent of capacity their production is in normal times, manufacturing firms typically answer about 80 percent. Thus, firms normally have room to expand production: In boom periods capacity utilization goes up to 90 percent or higher. If firms need more labor to expand production, they can ask workers to work overtime, call workers back from previous layoffs, or hire additional workers. With the unemployment rate equal to the *natural unemployment rate,* it is usually possible to find some workers to join the firm. That is why the unemployment rate drops below the natural unemployment rate in booms after real GDP rises above potential GDP.

natural unemployment rate: the unemployment rate that exists in normal times when there is neither a recession nor a boom and real GDP is equal to potential GDP. (Ch. 21)

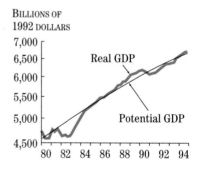

In recessions, when demand declines, these same firms clearly have the capability to reduce production, and they do. In recessions, capacity utilization goes down to 70 percent or lower. Firms ask workers to stop working overtime, they move some workers to part time, or they lay off some workers. Some institute hiring freezes to make sure the personnel office does not keep hiring workers. That is why the unemployment rate rises above the natural unemployment rate in recessions when real GDP falls below potential GDP. For example, the unemployment rate rose to more than 7 percent when the 1990–1991 recession brought real GDP below potential GDP. We illustrated the relationship between the unemployment rate and the movements of real GDP relative to potential GDP in Figure 21.1, which is repeated in the margin to the right.

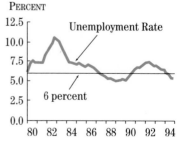

Production Decisions by Actual Firms

Individual firms—Mayflower moving services being just one example—raise production during booms when the demand for their goods or services rises, and lower production during recessions when the demand for their goods or services declines. These decisions by individual firms lead to fluctuations of real GDP above or below potential GDP.

Production and Employment Decisions at Actual Firms

Consider a typical service firm at the start of the 1990–1991 recession. Mayflower, the moving company named after the ship that moved the Pilgrims, found the demand for its moving and storage services growing rapidly in the boom of the late 1980s. The company expanded production by moving more households and, as a result, increased its employment from 6,800 workers in 1987 to 11,400 in 1989. In 1990, as the recession took hold, demand for Mayflower's services began to fall. The company reduced production—moved fewer households—and employment fell from 11,400 in 1989 to 10,900 in 1990, a decline of about 5 percent.

Consider the example of a construction firm at about the same time. As is typical in recessions, construction was hit hard in the 1990–1991 recession. Trammell Crow, the real estate construction company based in Dallas, Texas, found the demand for its construction services fall off dramatically in 1990. Hence, the firm produced fewer of these services. It built fewer shopping malls and convention centers. Total square feet under construction by Trammell Crow fell from 44 million in 1989 to 27 million in 1990. Employment at Trammell Crow also fell from the year 1989 to 1990. Employment had expanded rapidly during the 1988–1989 boom. Thus, Trammell Crow is another example showing how fluctuations in demand cause a change in production.

Why Changes in Demand Are Translated into Changes in Production

Economists apply theories of decision-making under uncertainty to explain the behavior of firms in such situations.

Limited Information and Implicit Contracts

When a business firm notices an increase in demand for its products, it frequently does not know whether the increase in demand is temporary or permanent, or whether it is common to all firms in the economy or the industry. The firm is uncertain about the reasons for the change in demand for its products because it operates under **limited information.** In such a situation, the firm could raise its prices and thereby reduce the quantity demanded of its products and perhaps make greater short-term profits. But rather than raise its prices to limit the quantity demanded, the typical firm matches the increase in demand with more production.

If it is possible for the firm to expand production by increasing employment or the utilization of its capital, the firm is unlikely to raise prices right away. Raising prices may require costly changes in catalogues, menus, or advertising brochures. In a well-known study of prices of major magazines, Stephen Cecchetti of Ohio State University found that the price stays constant for many months or even years in the face of changes in demand for the magazines. Moreover, if the change in demand is temporary, raising prices might result in the firm losing some of its regu-

limited information: a situation in which firms have incomplete knowledge about some market conditions, such as whether a change in demand for their product is temporary or permanent or whether the change is due to a recession or boom in the whole economy.

lar customers. Kmart has a reputation as a low-price retailer. If it raises its prices in an unusually busy spring, it might lose its reputation. Wal-Mart might be the winner. Although Kmart, or other firms in similar situations, does not make any explicit price pledge or contract with its customers, economists describe the relationship between the firm and its customers as involving an **implicit contract.** It is as if the firm has an unwritten and unspoken promise with its customers not to change prices frequently.

For similar reasons, wages do not immediately rise, although the demand for labor increases. The firm does not want to pay new workers more, disrupt its pay scales, and perhaps lower the morale of its current employees. Pay scales are typically only changed once a year or less. Again, it is as if the firm has an implicit contract not to change wages at the drop of a hat. In some cases, union wage contracts that fix pay scales are negotiated only every three years.

Similarly, in a recession, when the firm finds the demand for its product declining, it may not know for a while whether the decline in sales is temporary, permanent, unique to itself, or a common feature in the economy. Hence, it will not cut prices immediately or reduce its employees' wages. When it is clear that the demand change is lasting and is occurring throughout the economy, then prices and eventually wages will begin to adjust.

The limited-information explanation for the finding that changes in demand get translated into changes in production and employment was incorporated into macroeconomic theory by Robert Lucas of the University of Chicago in the early 1970s. That limited information is not the whole story but appears to share a role with implicit contracts concerning prices and wages was incorporated into macroeconomic theory by other economists, such as Stanley Fischer of Massachusetts Institute of Technology and Edmund Phelps of Columbia University. Although there have been heated academic debates between those who use these two approaches, reality seems to combine limited information and implicit contracts. In fact, the preceding description of implicit contracts used the idea that firms have limited information. Sometimes economists use the term **nominal rigidities** to refer to inflexibilities in price and wage behavior that are implied by both theories.

DAVE CARPENTER...

"We figure it was HERE when the recession officially began."

implicit contract: an informal agreement between a firm and its customers or between a firm and its employees.

nominal rigidities: inflexibilities in wages and prices.

A Graphical Illustration of the Typical Firm

Figure 25.3 illustrates how a change in demand gets translated into a change in the quantity produced at a typical firm. The firm's price is on the vertical axis and its production is on the horizontal axis. The firm faces a downward-sloping demand curve for its product. There are three downward-sloping demand curves: high, medium, and low, each corresponding to a different level of demand. Two types of assumptions for the behavior of the firm are illustrated: (1) the **sticky price assumption,** in which the firm does not immediately change its price when demand changes, and (2) the **flexible price assumption,** in which the firm raises its price immediately when demand increases and lowers its price immediately when demand falls. The ideas of limited information and implicit contracts imply that the firm will tend to change its price only after the change in demand is recognized as long-lasting.

sticky price assumption: an assumption that prices do not move quickly in response to a change in supply or demand; the assumption is used in the theory of economic fluctuations.

flexible price assumption: an assumption that prices adjust instantaneously in response to a change in supply or demand.

FIGURE 25.3
Alternative Short-Run Responses
of a Typical Firm to a Change
in Demand
The figure shows different demand
curves for the firm's product: high,
medium, and low. Two different production and price responses to the
change in demand are also shown.
With limited information or implicit
contracts, the firm changes production by the amount of the change in
demand. If the firm changes its production by a smaller amount, the
price must change.

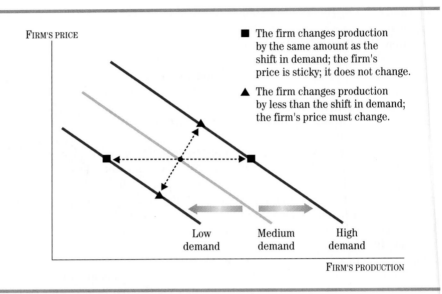

Could Economic Fluctuations Also Be Due to Changes in Potential GDP?

Our discussion thus far of the production decisions of individual firms has shown
why it is natural to identify fluctuations in real GDP with fluctuations in aggregate
demand. To be sure, economic fluctuations also occur because of changes in potential GDP. For example, when agriculture was a much larger fraction of real GDP,
drought and floods had more noticeable effects on real GDP. Although agriculture
is currently a very small fraction of total production, the possibility that increases or
decreases in potential GDP may still play a large role in economic fluctuations is a
topic currently being examined by economists. Economic theories that emphasize
changes in potential GDP as a source of economic fluctuations are called **real busi-**
ness cycle theories. Most frequently changes in technology are assumed to be the
reason for changes in potential GDP in real business cycle theories.

real business cycle theory:
a theory of macroeconomics that
stresses that shifts in potential GDP
are a primary cause of fluctuations
in real GDP; the shifts in potential
GDP are usually caused by changes
in technology.

    The factors that underlie potential GDP growth—population, capital, techno-
logical know-how—tend to evolve relatively smoothly. Population growth, for
example, is much steadier than real GDP growth. We do not have a drop in the population every few years and a sudden spurt the next year. Slowdowns in population
growth occur gradually over time as birthrates and death rates change. Similarly,
although individual factories or machines may be lost in a hurricane or flood, this
does not happen in such a massive way across the country that it would show up as
large as a recession or a boom in the whole economy. Thus, the amount of capital
changes slowly over time. Even technological change does not seem capable of
explaining most fluctuations. It is true that some inventions and innovations raise
productivity substantially in certain sectors of the economy over short periods of
time. The impact on the whole economy is more spread out and gradual, however.
Moreover, people do not suddenly forget how to use a technology. There do not
seem to be sudden decreases in technological know-how. For these reasons, potential GDP usually tends to grow relatively smoothly over time, compared to the fluctuations in aggregate demand.

FORECASTING REAL GDP

To illustrate how we use the idea that changes in aggregate demand lead to short-run fluctuations in real GDP, we will focus on an important macroeconomic task: short-term economic forecasting of real GDP about one year ahead. To **forecast** real GDP, economic forecasters divide aggregate demand into its four key components: consumption, investment, government purchases, and net exports. Remember that real GDP can be measured by adding together the four types of spending: what people *consume,* what firms *invest,* what *governments purchase,* and what *foreigners purchase* net of what they sell in the United States. In symbols, we have

forecast: a prediction of an economic variable such as real GDP.

$$Y = C + I + G + X$$

In other words, real GDP (Y) is the sum of consumption (C), investment (I), government purchases (G), and net exports (X).

The preceding equation is a central tool of analysis used by economic forecasters at macroeconomic forecasting firms. These firms are hired by other businesses to forecast real GDP and related economic variables. (See the box "The Forecasting Industry.") Business decisions to hire new workers are frequently based on such forecasts. In addition, forecasting is part of the job of the Federal Reserve, the Congressional Budget Office (CBO), and the President's Council of Economic Advisers (CEA). These government agencies regularly make forecasts of where real GDP is headed in the short run. The Fed uses such forecasts to make decisions about how much money growth to provide. Each December the CEA develops a forecast for the following year that is used to prepare the president's budget proposals, which are submitted to Congress. The CBO then does its own analysis of the president's budget using another forecast. Similar organizations and firms exist in other countries.

A Forecast for Next Year

Suppose that it is December 2004 and a forecast of real GDP (Y) is being prepared for the year 2005. Using the preceding equation, a reasonable way to proceed would be to forecast consumption for the next year, then forecast investment, then forecast government purchases, and, finally, forecast net exports. When forecasting each item, the forecaster would consider a range of issues: consumer confidence

The Forecasting Industry

Short-term forecasting of real GDP—usually one year ahead—has become a major industry employing thousands of economists, statisticians, and computer programmers. Each month the *Blue Chip Economic Indicators* tabulates the forecasts of the top forecasters. A summary of 52 different forecasts of real GDP for 1994 made in November 1993 is shown in the table. Observe that the forecast is stated as the growth rate of real GDP for 1994 over 1993. The average (called the Blue Chip Consensus) was 2.8 percent. The highest forecasts are labeled "H," and the lowest forecasts are labeled "L." Virtually all the forecasters in this group use some version of the method of forecasting real GDP described in this chapter.

How accurate was the Blue Chip Consensus in 1994? We now know that the actual growth rate of real GDP was 3.5 percent, slightly above the 2.8 percent forecast; this is a rather typical margin of error for economic forecasting.

Source: Blue Chip Economic Indicators, Capitol Publications, Inc., November 10, 1993, p. 3.

BLUE CHIP ECONOMIC INDICATORS

1994 Real GDP Consensus Estimate

Percent Change 1994 From 1993 (Year-Over-Year)

**NOVEMBER 1993
Forecast for 1994**

Morgan Guaranty Trust Co.	3.4H	Eggert Economic Enterprises, Inc.	2.8
UCLA Business Forecast	3.4H	DuPont	2.8
Sears Roebuck & Co.	3.4H	Comerica	2.8
Robert Genetski & Assoc., Inc.	3.3	CoreStates Financial Corp.	2.8
Morris Cohen & Associates	3.3	U.S. Trust Co.	2.7
Turning Points (Micrometrics)	3.3	PNC Bank	2.7
Bostonian Economic Research	3.2	SOM Economics, Inc.	2.7
Motorola, Inc.	3.2	National Assn. of Home Builders	2.7
Conference Board	3.1	Bank of America	2.7
Brown Brothers Harriman	3.1	Dun & Bradstreet	2.6
Prudential Securities	3.1	Morgan Stanley & Co.	2.6
Northern Trust Company	3.1	Nat'l. City Bank of Cleveland	2.6
NationsBanc Capital Markets, Inc.	3.1	U.S. Chamber of Commerce	2.6
Shawmut National Corp	3.0	Prudential Insurance Co.	2.6
Metropolitan Life Insurance Co.	3.0	Reeder Associates (Charles)	2.6
Chrysler Corporation	3.0	Cahners Economics	2.5
First Interstate Bancorp	3.0	Chase Manhattan Bank	2.5
General Motors	3.0	Bankers Trust Co.	2.5
Merrill Lynch	3.0	C. J. Lawrence, Inc.	2.5
Wayne Hummer & Co., Chicago	2.9	University of Michigan	2.5
Pennzoil Company	2.9	Arnhold & S. Bleichroeder	2.4
Ford Motor Co.	2.9	Evans Economics	2.4
Georgia State University	2.9	Econoclast	2.0
First National Bank of Chicago	2.9	Inforum - Univ. of Maryland	1.7L
Mortgage Bankers Assn. of Amer.	2.9	Chemical Banking	1.7L
Laurence H. Meyer & Assoc.	2.9		
Fairmodel	2.9	**1994 Consensus: November Avg.**	**2.8**

might affect consumption; business confidence might be a factor in investment; the mood of the country might be a factor in government purchases; and developments in foreign countries might affect the forecast for net exports. In any case, adding these four spending items together would give a forecast for real GDP for the year 2005. For example, one economist may forecast that $C = \$7,000$ billion, $I = \$900$ billion, $X = \$100$ billion, and $G = \$2,000$ billion. Then the forecast for real GDP is $\$10,000$ billion. If real GDP in 2004 is $\$9,700$, then the forecast would be for 3.1 percent growth for the year 2005. Forecasts are typically expressed as growth rates of real GDP from one year to the next.

Alternatively, the forecaster may be concerned about recessions in other countries and have a lower forecast for net exports, perhaps $X = \$50$ billion. This alternative and any others can be incorporated into the forecast of real GDP by using a different value for one of the components.

A Conditional Forecast

The preceding forecast is prepared by making the best assumption about what is likely for government purchases and the other three components of spending. Another type of forecast—called a **conditional forecast**—describes what real GDP will be under alternative assumptions about the components of spending. For example, the president of the United States in the year 2004 might want the CEA or the CBO to estimate the effect of a proposal to change government purchases on the economy in 2005. A conditional forecast would be a forecast of real GDP conditional on this change in government purchases. A conditional forecast for real GDP can be made using similar methods. Let's see how.

conditional forecast: a prediction that depends on assumed values for government purchases, taxes, or some other variable that affects the forecast.

Suppose the proposal is to cut federal government purchases by $\$100$ billion in real terms in one year. What is the effect of such a change in government purchases on aggregate demand in the short run? If the government demands $\$100$ billion less, then firms will produce $\$100$ billion less. A forecast conditional on a $\$100$ billion spending cut would be $\$100$ billion less for real GDP, or $\$9,900$ billion. Again, we just add up $\$7,000$ billion, $\$900$ billion, $\$100$ billion, and now $\$1,900$ billion. Real GDP growth for the year is now forecast to be about 2.1 percent, conditional on the policy proposal.

The forecast is based on the equation that $Y = C + I + G + X$ and the idea that changes in aggregate demand cause real GDP fluctuations. Although simple, it is specific and substantive. For example, this same type of reasoning led economists to forecast an economic slowdown in the United States in the early 1990s due to the reduction in government defense spending occurring at that time. According to this method of forecasting, changes in aggregate demand are responsible for most of the short-run ups and downs in the economy. It is this explanation that most economic forecasters use when they forecast real GDP for one year ahead.

Review

▶ The four components of spending can be added to make a forecast for real GDP. Making such a forecast is an important application of macroeconomics.

▶ Forecasts may be conditional on a particular event, such as a change in government purchases or a change in taxes.

THE RESPONSE OF CONSUMPTION TO INCOME

In the forecasting example we assumed that none of the components—neither consumption, investment, nor net exports—change in response to the decline in government purchases. For example, consumption (C) was unchanged at $7,000 billion when we altered G in our conditional forecast. But these components of spending are likely to change. Thus, something important is missing from the procedure for forecasting real GDP. To improve the forecast, we must describe how the components of aggregate demand—consumption, investment, or net exports—might change in response to other developments in the economy. We will eventually consider the response of consumption, investment, and net exports to many factors, including interest rates, exchange rates, and income. However, bringing all these factors into consideration at once is complicated, and we must start with a *simplifying assumption.* Here the simplifying assumption is that consumption is the only component of expenditures that responds to income, and that income is the only influence on consumption. Consumption is a good place to begin because it is by far the largest component. Before we finish developing a complete theory of economic fluctuations, we will consider the other components and the other influences. Let us begin by examining why consumption may be affected by income.

The Consumption Function

consumption function: the positive relationship between consumption and income.

The **consumption function** describes how consumption depends on income. The notion of a consumption function originated with John Maynard Keynes, who wrote about it during the 1930s. Research on the consumption function has been intense ever since. For each individual, the consumption function says that the more income one has, the more one consumes. For the national economy as a whole, it says that the more income Americans have, the more Americans consume. For the world economy as a whole, it says that the more income in the world, the more people in the world consume. Table 25.1 gives a simple example of how consumption depends on income in the United States economy.

As you can see from the table, as income increases from 1,000 to 2,000, consumption increases as well from 1,600 to 2,200, and as income increases from 3,000 to 4,000, consumption increases from 2,800 to 3,400. More income means more consumption, but the consumption function also tells us *how much* consumption increases when income increases. Each change in income by 1,000 causes an increase in consumption by 600. The changes in consumption are smaller than the changes in income. Notice that, in this example, at very low levels of income, consumption is greater than income. If consumption were greater than income for a particular individual, that individual would have to borrow. At higher levels of income, when consumption is less than income, the individual would be able to save.

The consumption function is supposed to describe the behavior of individuals because the economy is made up of individuals. Consequently, it summarizes the behavior of all people in the economy with respect to consumption. The simple consumption function is not meant to be the complete explanation of consumption. Recall that it is based on a simplifying assumption.

TABLE 25.1
An Example of the Consumption Function
(billions of dollars)

Consumption	Income
1,600	1,000
2,200	2,000
2,800	3,000
3,400	4,000
4,000	5,000
4,600	6,000
5,200	7,000
5,800	8,000
6,400	9,000
7,000	10,000
7,600	11,000
8,200	12,000
8,800	13,000
9,400	14,000

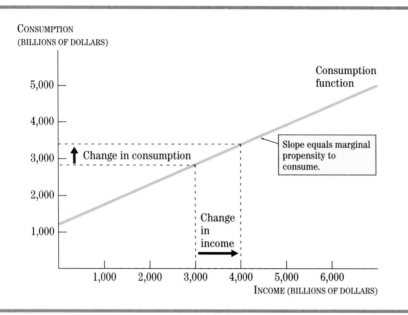

FIGURE 25.4
The Consumption Function
For the economy as a whole, more income leads to more consumption, as shown by the example of an upward-sloping consumption function in the figure. This represents the sum of all the individuals in the economy, many of whom consume more when their income rises. The graph is based on the numbers in Table 25.1.

The Marginal Propensity to Consume

A concept related to the consumption function is the **marginal propensity to consume,** or **MPC** for short. The marginal propensity to consume measures how much consumption changes for a given change in income. The term *marginal* refers to the additional amount of consumption that is due to a change in income. The term *propensity* refers to the inclination to consume. By definition,

$$\text{Marginal Propensity to Consume (MPC)} = \frac{\text{change in consumption}}{\text{change in income}}$$

What is the MPC for the consumption function in Table 25.1? Observe that the change in consumption from row to row is 600. The change in income from row to row is 1,000; thus the MPC = 600/1,000 = .6. Although this is only a simple example, it turns out that the MPC is around that magnitude for the U.S. economy.

Figure 25.4 graphs the consumption function by putting income on the horizontal axis and consumption on the vertical axis. We get the upward-sloping line by plotting the pairs of observations on consumption and income in Table 25.1 and connecting them with a line. This line, which demonstrates that consumption rises with income, is the consumption function. Its slope is equal to the MPC. For this example, the MPC = .6. The graph shows that at low levels of income, consumption is greater than income, but at high levels of income, consumption is less than income.

Which Measure of Income?

The consumption function is a straight-line relationship between consumption and income. Sometimes income in the relationship is measured by **aggregate income** (*Y*), which is also equal to real GDP, and sometimes by disposable income. **Disposable income** is the income that households receive in wages, dividends, and interest

marginal propensity to consume (MPC): the slope of the consumption function, showing the change in consumption that is due to a given change in income.

aggregate income: the total income received by all factors of production in the economy; also simply called "income."

disposable income: income that households have to spend after taxes have been paid and transfers from the government have been received.

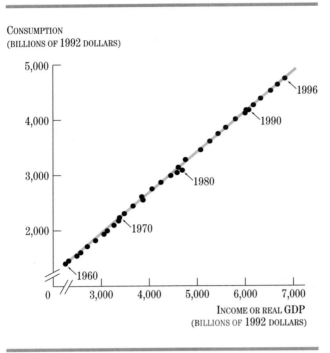

CONSUMPTION
(BILLIONS OF 1992 DOLLARS)

INCOME OR REAL GDP
(BILLIONS OF 1992 DOLLARS)

payments plus transfers they may get from the government minus any taxes they pay to the government. Disposable income is the preferred measure of income when one is interested in household consumption because this is what households have available to spend. But the consumption function for the whole economy looks similar for either aggregate income or disposable income because aggregate income and disposable income fluctuate and grow together. In the United States and most other countries, taxes and transfers are nearly proportional to income.

For the rest of this chapter, we will use aggregate income, or real GDP, as the measure of income in the consumption function. We put real GDP, or income (we drop the word *aggregate* in aggregate income), on the horizontal axis of the consumption function diagram, because real GDP and income are always equal. Figure 25.5 shows the actual relationship between consumption and income, or real GDP. Note, however, that when we consider an explicit change in taxes, we must take account of the difference between disposable income and income. (Remember, *income* means "aggregate income for the whole economy" in this chapter.)

FIGURE 25.5
Consumption versus Aggregate Income
The graph shows the close relationship between consumption and aggregate income, or real GDP, in the U.S. economy. The points fall close to the straight line drawn in the diagram.
Source: U.S. Department of Commerce.

What about Interest Rates and Other Influences on Consumption?

Other factors besides income affect consumption. For example, you may recall from Chapter 22 that people's consumption is affected by the interest rate. Also, people's wealth—including their savings in a bank and their house—may affect their consumption. A person with a large amount of savings in a bank might consume a considerable amount even if the person's income in any one year is very low. Why have we not brought the interest rate or wealth into the picture here?

The answer is simple. To keep the analysis manageable at the start, we are putting the interest rate and other influences aside. We eventually return to consider the effects of interest rates and other factors on consumption. But during economic fluctuations, the effects of changes in income on consumption are most important, and we focus on these now.

Review

▶ The consumption function describes the response of consumption to changes in income. The elementary consumption function ignores the effects of interest rates and wealth on consumption.

▶ The marginal propensity to consume (MPC) tells us *how much* consumption changes in response to a change in income.

▶ For the economy as a whole, the consumption function can be expressed in terms of aggregate income or disposable income. Aggregate income is always equal to real GDP. Here we use aggregate income.

FINDING REAL GDP WHEN CONSUMPTION AND INCOME MOVE TOGETHER

Now let us use the consumption function to get a better prediction of what happens to real GDP in the short run when government purchases change. In other words, we want to improve the conditional forecast of real GDP when there is a change in government purchases, taking the consumption function into account. Again, as in the earlier example of forecasting, let us assume that government spending will decline by $100 billion next year. Our goal is to find out what happens to real GDP in the short run.

The Logic of the Two-Way Link Between Consumption and Income

The consumption function is a relationship between consumption and income. But we also have another relationship between consumption and income: $Y = C + I + G + X$. Income is on the left-hand side of this identity because real GDP equals income. That is, Y equals income as well as real GDP. The two relationships together will enable us to find out what happens to real GDP.

How? Think about it logically. The first attempt at our forecasting analysis said that a reduction in government spending is going to reduce real GDP. But now we see that something else must happen because consumption depends on income, and real GDP is equal to income. A reduction in government spending will reduce income. The consumption function tells us a reduction in income must reduce consumption.

Here is the chain of logic in brief:

1. A cut in government spending reduces real GDP.

2. Real GDP is income.

3. Thus, income is reduced.

4. Consumption depends on income.

5. Thus, consumption is reduced.

In sum, consumption will decline when we reduce government spending.

For example, when the government reduces defense spending, the firms that produce the defense goods find demand falling and they produce less. Some of the defense workers are either going to work fewer hours a week or be laid off. Therefore, they will receive a reduced income or no income at all. In addition, the profits at the defense firms will decline; thus, the income of the owners of the firms will decline. With less income, the workers and the owners will spend less; that is, their consumption will decline. This is the connection between government spending and consumption that we are concerned about: The change in government purchases reduces defense workers' income, which results in less consumption.

Consider a specific case study. This type of logic was applied by economists to estimate the impact of closing Fort Ord, the military base near Monterey Bay in California, on the Monterey economy. When the estimates were made, the base employed 3,000 civilians and 14,000 military personnel. Payroll was $558 million. Thus, closing the base would reduce incomes by as much as $558 million as these workers were laid off or retired. Although some workers might find jobs quickly elsewhere, there would be a decline in income that would result in a reduction in consumption by those workers. Using an MPC of .6, consumption would decline by $335 million (.6 times 558) if income was reduced by $558 million. This would tend to throw others in the Monterey area out of work as spending in retail and service stores declined. This would further reduce consumption, and so on. Although this case study refers to a small region of the entire country, the same logic applies to the economy as a whole.

The 45-Degree Line

We can use a convenient graph to calculate how much income and consumption changes in the whole economy and thereby find out what happens to real GDP. In Figure 25.6 there is a line that shows graphically that income in the economy is equal to spending. That is, income (Y) equals spending ($C + I + G + X$). In Figure 25.6, income is on the horizontal axis and spending is on the vertical axis. All the points where spending equals income are on the upward-sloping line in Figure 25.6. The line has a slope of 1, or an angle of 45 degrees with the horizontal axis, because the distances from any point on the line to the horizontal axis and the vertical axis are equal. Along that line—which is called the **45-degree line**—spending and income are equal.

45-degree line: the line showing that aggregate expenditure equals aggregate income.

The Aggregate Expenditure Line

aggregate expenditure line: the relation between the sum of the four components of spending ($C + I + G + X$) and aggregate income.

Figure 25.7 shows another relationship called the **aggregate expenditure line.** Like Figure 25.6, income or real GDP is on the horizontal axis, and spending is on the vertical axis. The top line in Figure 25.7 is the aggregate expenditure line. It is called the aggregate expenditure line because it shows how aggregate expenditure, or spending, depends on income. The four components that make up the aggregate expenditure line are consumption, investment, government purchases, and net exports. However, the aggregate expenditure line shows how these four components

FIGURE 25.6
The 45-Degree Line
This simple line is a graphical representation of the income equals spending identity. The pairs of points on the 45-degree line have the same level of spending and income. For example, the level of spending at A is the same dollar amount as the level of income at A. Moreover, because income equals real GDP, we can put either income or real GDP on the horizontal axis.

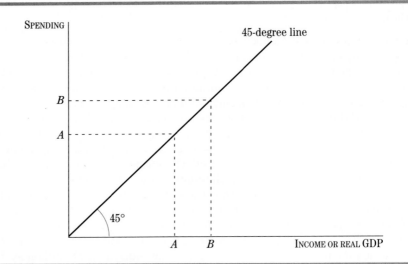

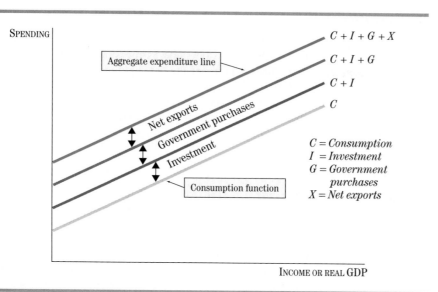

FIGURE 25.7

Aggregate Expenditure Line

By adding investment (I), government purchases (G), and net exports (X) to the consumption function, we build the aggregate expenditure line.

depend on income. It is this dependency of spending on income that is the defining characteristic of the aggregate expenditure line. Here is how the aggregate expenditure line is derived.

The consumption function is shown as the lowest line in Figure 25.7. It is simply the consumption function from Figure 25.4, which says that the higher income is, the more people want to consume. The next line above the consumption function in Figure 25.7 is parallel to the consumption function. This line represents the addition of investment to consumption at each level of income. It says investment is so many billions of dollars in the U.S. economy, and the distance between the lines is this amount of investment. For example, if investment equals $800 billion, the distance between the consumption function and this next line is $800 billion.

The reason the line is parallel to the consumption line is that we are starting our explanation by saying that investment does not depend on income. This simplifying assumption means that investment is a constant number, and the distance between the lines is the same regardless of income. We just add the same amount at each point.

The next line in Figure 25.7 adds in a constant level of government purchases. This next line is also parallel to the other lines because the increase at every level of income is the same. The distance between the lines represents a fixed level of government purchases, say $1,600 billion, at every level of income.

Finally, to get the top line in Figure 25.7, we add in net exports. For simplicity, we assume that net exports do not depend on income, an assumption that we will change soon. Thus, the top line is parallel to all the other lines. The top line is the sum of $C + I + G + X$. It is the aggregate expenditure (AE) line. The term *aggregate* is used because it refers to the whole economy. But the most important thing to remember about the AE line is that it shows how the sum of the four components depends on income.

Before we can use the AE line, we must know what determines its slope and what causes it to shift.

The Slope of the AE Line

Observe in Figure 25.7 that the *AE* line is parallel to the consumption function. Therefore, the slope of the *AE* line is the same as the slope of the consumption function. We already know that the slope of the consumption function is the MPC. Hence, the slope of the *AE* line is also equal to the MPC.

Because the MPC is less than 1, the aggregate expenditure line is flatter (the slope is smaller) than the 45-degree line, which has a slope of exactly 1. This fact will soon be used to find real GDP.

Shifts in the AE Line

The aggregate expenditure line can shift for several reasons. Consider first what happens to the aggregate expenditure line if government purchases fall because of a cut in defense spending. As shown in Figure 25.8, the *AE* line shifts downward in a parallel fashion. The *AE* line is simply the sum $C + I + G + X$. Because G is less at all income levels, the line shifts down. The aggregate expenditure line is lowered because the distance between the consumption function and the other lines declines (see Figure 25.7). The reverse of this, an increase in government purchases, will cause the aggregate expenditure line to shift up.

What happens to the aggregate expenditure line if investment falls? Investment, remember, is the gap between the first and second lines in Figure 25.7. If investment declines (as might happen if businesses get pessimistic about the future and invest less), then the aggregate expenditure line shifts downward. With less investment, the gap between the lines shrinks. The reverse of this, an increase in investment, will cause the aggregate expenditure line to shift up, as shown in Figure 25.8.

A change in net exports, perhaps because of a change in the demand for U.S. exports to other countries, will also shift the *AE* line. A downward shift in net exports lowers the *AE* line, and an upward shift in the net exports raises the *AE* line.

Finally, the aggregate expenditure line can also be shifted by changes in taxes. At any given level of income, an increase in taxes means people have less to spend,

FIGURE 25.8
Shifts in the Aggregate Expenditure Line
The aggregate expenditure line shifts down if (1) government purchases (*G*) fall, (2) investment (*I*) falls, (3) taxes (*T*) increase, or (4) net exports (*X*) fall. The aggregate expenditure line shifts up if (1) government purchases rise, (2) investment rises, (3) taxes are cut, or (4) net exports rise.

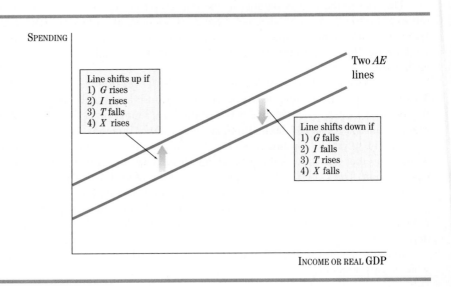

and this will cause people to consume less. Hence, the aggregate expenditure line shifts down when taxes rise. The reverse of this, a cut in taxes, causes the aggregate expenditure line to shift up. We will use the symbol T to refer to taxes. For example, if $T = \$1,500$ billion, then people pay and the government receives $1,500 billion in taxes.

Determining Real GDP Through Spending Balance

Having derived the aggregate expenditure line and the 45-degree line, we can combine the two to find real GDP. Figure 25.9 shows how the aggregate expenditure line and the 45-degree line combine in one diagram. Observe that the two lines intersect. They must intersect because they have different slopes. Real GDP is found at the point of intersection of these two lines. Why?

Income and spending are always equal and the 45-degree line is drawn to represent this equality. Therefore, at any point on the 45-degree line, income equals spending. Moreover, income and spending must be on the aggregate expenditure line, because only at points on that line do people consume according to the consumption function.

If both relationships hold, that is, income and spending are the same (we are on the 45-degree line) and people's consumption is described by the consumption function (we are on the *AE* line), then logically we must be at the intersection of these two lines. We call that point of intersection **spending balance.** The level of income determined by that point is just the right level to cause people to purchase an amount of consumption that—when added to investment, government purchases, and net exports—gives exactly the same level of income. We would not have spending balance at either a higher or lower level of income. The diagram in Figure 25.9 showing that the 45-degree line and the aggregate expenditure line cross is sometimes called the "Keynesian Cross" after John Maynard Keynes.

Table 25.2 provides an alternative way to determine spending balance. It uses a numerical tabulation of the consumption function rather than graphs. Aggregate

spending balance: the level of income or real GDP at which the 45-degree line and the aggregate expenditure line cross; also called equilibrium income.

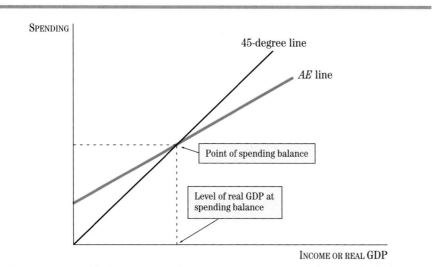

SPENDING

45-degree line

AE line

Point of spending balance

Level of real GDP at spending balance

INCOME OR REAL GDP

FIGURE 25.9
Spending Balance
Spending balance occurs when two relations are satisfied simultaneously: (1) income equals spending, and (2) spending equals consumption, which is a function of income, plus investment plus government purchases plus net exports. Only one level of income gives spending balance. That level of income is determined by the intersection of the 45-degree line and the *AE* line.

TABLE 25.2
A Numerical Example of Spending
Balance
(billions of dollars)

Income or Real GDP	Aggregate Expenditure	Consumption	Investment	Government Purchases	Net Exports
6,000	7,600	4,600	900	2,000	100
7,000	8,200	5,200	900	2,000	100
8,000	8,800	5,800	900	2,000	100
9,000	9,400	6,400	900	2,000	100
10,000	10,000	7,000	900	2,000	100
11,000	10,600	7,000	900	2,000	100
12,000	11,200	8,200	900	2,000	100
13,000	11,800	8,800	900	2,000	100
14,000	12,400	9,400	900	2,000	100

expenditure is obtained by adding the four columns on the right of Table 25.2. Consumption is shown to depend on income according to the same consumption function in Table 25.1. Observe that there is only one row where income equals aggregate expenditure. That row is where spending balance occurs. The row is shaded and corresponds to the point of intersection of the 45-degree line and the aggregate expenditure line in Figure 25.9.

Because the point of spending balance is at the intersection of two lines, we can think of it as an equilibrium, much as the intersection of a demand curve and a supply curve for wheat is an equilibrium. Because real GDP is not necessarily equal to potential GDP at this intersection, however, there is a sense in which the equilibrium is temporary; eventually real GDP will move back to potential GDP, as we will show in later chapters.

The point of spending balance is also an equilibrium in the sense that economic forces cause real GDP to be at that intersection. To see this, consider Table 25.2. As we noted, the shaded row corresponds to the intersection of the 45-degree line and the aggregate expenditure line: Income or real GDP equals aggregate expenditure. Suppose that income or real GDP were less than aggregate expenditure, as in one of the rows above the shaded row in Table 25.2. This would not be an equilibrium because firms would not be producing enough goods and services (real GDP) to satisfy people's aggregate expenditure on goods and services. Firms would increase their production, and real GDP would rise until it equaled aggregate expenditure. Similarly, if real GDP were greater than aggregate expenditure, as in one of the rows below the shaded row in Table 25.2, firms would be producing more than people would be buying. Hence, firms would reduce their production and real GDP would fall until it equaled aggregate expenditure.

A Better Forecast of Real GDP

Now let us return to forecasting real GDP using these new tools. Recall the example of making a forecast of real GDP for the year 2005 (from the vantage point of December 2004), conditional on a proposed decline in government purchases of $100 billion. Our new tools will enable us to take account of the effect of this decline on consumption, which we had previously ignored in the simple forecast.

Figure 25.10 shows two *AE* lines. The top *AE* line is without the change in government purchases. In this case, $G = \$2,000$ billion, $C = \$7,000$ billion, $I = \$900$ billion, and $X = \$100$ billion, yielding income, or real GDP, of $10,000

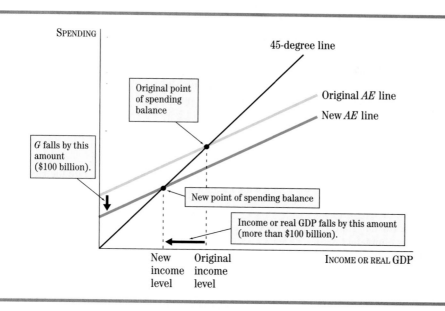

FIGURE 25.10
From One Point of Spending Balance to Another
The aggregate expenditure line shifts down because of a decline in government purchases. This shifts down the forecast for real GDP. A forecast of real GDP conditional on the decline in government purchases would therefore be lower.

billion. For the conditional forecast, we assume G is cut by $100 billion to $1,900 billion. In Figure 25.10, that causes the AE line to shift down to the "new" AE line. Observe that the AE line shifts down by $100 billion—a parallel shift. This new AE line cuts the 45-degree line at a lower point.

Logic tells us the economy will now operate at a different point of spending balance, where the aggregate expenditure line and the 45-degree line now intersect. Thus we move from one intersection to a new intersection as a result of the decline in the aggregate expenditure line. The new point of spending balance is at a lower level of real GDP.

We now have a prediction that real GDP will fall if government spending declines. Observe in Figure 25.10 that the decline in real GDP is larger than the $100 billion decline in government purchases and, therefore, larger than the $100 billion decline in real GDP in the simple forecast. The reason is that consumption has fallen as well as government purchases because income has declined. In Figure 25.10 the difference looks quite large. It is certainly large enough to influence a new administration's decision to reduce government purchases. The example and the application illustrate that it is not just for fun that we have derived the AE line. It is an essential tool of the practicing macroeconomist.

Review

▶ Spending balance occurs when the identity $Y = C + I + G + X$ and the consumption function relating C to Y hold simultaneously.

▶ Spending balance can be shown on a graph with the 45-degree line and the aggregate expenditure (AE) line. The intersection of the two lines determines a level of income, or real GDP, that gives spending balance.

▶ A shift in the aggregate expenditure line brings about a new level of spending balance.

Forecasting with Econometric Models

Economic forecasters use large mathematical models with hundreds of equations to help them forecast real GDP. Such models are called *econometric models*. They were first developed in the 1950s. Lawrence Klein of the University of Pennsylvania won a Nobel Prize for developing some of the first econometric models. Today, economists use high-speed computers to forecast real GDP with such models, but the basic ideas are no more difficult conceptually than those we use to find real GDP with the diagram of spending balance in this chapter. To see this, we show that finding real GDP through spending balance is equivalent to solving two equations. Once the idea is understood with two equations, the extension to hundreds of equations merely requires a computer.

The key idea behind spending balance is that two relationships, or equations, must hold simultaneously:

1. the consumption function relating income (Y) to consumption (C)

2. the income-spending identity relating income (3) to consumption (C)

Algebra provides a way to solve such relationships simultaneously. In the language of algebra, we have two equations in two unknowns.

The first equation is the consumption function. It can be written with algebra for the example given in Table 25.1 of the text as:

$$C = 1 + .6Y$$

where C is consumption and Y is income measured in trillions of dollars. For example, if $Y = \$5$ trillion, then $C = \$4$ trillion [$4 = 1 + (.6 \times 5)$]. Check to see that this is the fifth row of Table 25.1. Try some other values for Y.

The second equation is the income-spending identity. When investment (I) plus government purchases (G) plus net exports (X) equals $3 trillion, as in Table 25.2, the income-spending identity ($Y = C + I + G + X$) can be written as:

$$Y = C + 3$$

where we have set $I + G + X = 3$.

Spending balance occurs at the value of Y that satisfies both equations.

To solve for Y using algebra, first write the two equations next to each other:

$$C = 1 + .6Y$$
$$Y = C + 3$$

A two-equation model in two unknowns

Now substitute the first equation for C into the right-hand side of the second:

$$Y = \underbrace{1 + .6Y}{} + 3$$
$$Y = C + 3$$

to get

$$Y = \underbrace{1 + .6Y + 3}_{}$$

Aggregate expenditure

Note that the right-hand side of this equation is aggregate expenditure. It shows explicitly that aggregate expenditure depends on income (Y), which is the essential idea behind the aggregate expenditure line. The left-hand side of the equation is income. Spending balance occurs when the left equals the right. Gathering all the terms in Y together on the left-hand side gives

$$.4Y = 4$$

This tells you immediately that $Y = \$10$ trillion, which is the answer. Putting $Y = 10$ back into the consumption equation gives $C = 7$.

The value $Y = 10$ is the same answer as the one given in the shaded row of Table 25.2. It is also the same answer given by the intersection of the 45-degree line and the aggregate expenditure line.

Once one represents a model using algebra, it is possible to make interesting modifications. For example, to analyze the effect of taxes on their forecast, economists would change the consumption function to $C = 1 + .6(Y - T)$ where T is taxes (say $T = \$.8$ trillion); the analysis would be similar.

Some people find algebra easier to work with than the numerical examples and the graphs. If you are one of those people, you can use this algebra to help you, but you should still learn the graphs and the numerical examples because that is how economic forecasters and other economists communicate their ideas to others.

SPENDING BALANCE AND DEPARTURES OF REAL GDP FROM POTENTIAL GDP

We have shown how to compute a level of real GDP for the purpose of making short-term forecasts. This level of real GDP is determined by aggregate demand—consumption, investment, government purchases, and net exports. It is not necessarily equal to potential GDP, which depends on the supply of labor, capital, and technology. Thus, we can have real GDP departing from potential GDP, as it does in recessions and booms. Let's see how.

Stepping Away from Potential GDP

Figure 25.11 illustrates how the first steps of a boom or a recession can be explained by shifts in the aggregate expenditure line. The left panel of the figure shows three different aggregate expenditure lines. Each line corresponds to a different level of government purchases or a different level of net exports or investment. The right panel of Figure 25.11—which is much like Figure 25.2—shows real GDP and potential GDP during a three-year period. There is a close connection between the left and right panels of Figure 25.11. The vertical axes are identical, and the points *c, d,* and *e* represent the same level of spending in both panels.

Observe how the three *AE* lines intersect the 45-degree line at three different levels of real GDP. Let us suppose that the middle *AE* line intersects the 45-degree line at a level of real GDP that is the same as potential GDP in year 3. This is point *c.* The other two *AE* lines generate the first step of a recession or a boom. The lower *AE* line represents a recession; real GDP at the intersection of this *AE* line and the

FIGURE 25.11
Spending Balance and Departures of Real GDP from Potential GDP
This figure shows how the levels of real GDP found through spending balance can explain the first steps of a recession or boom. The left panel shows spending balance for three *AE* curves; one (*c*) gives real GDP equal to potential GDP, a second (*e*) gives real GDP above potential GDP, and a third (*d*) gives real GDP below potential GDP. As shown in the right panel, two of these entail departures of real GDP from potential GDP.

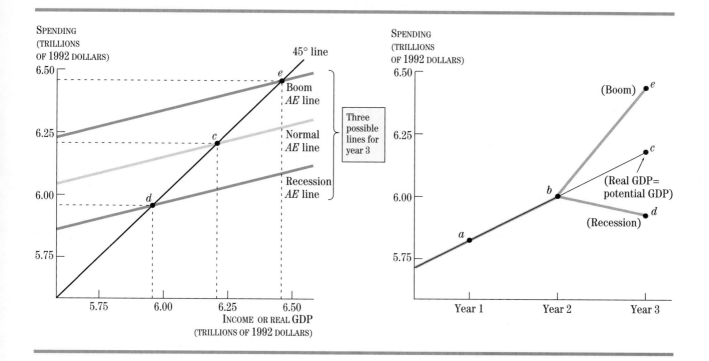

45-degree line (point *d*) is at a level below potential GDP and also below the level of real GDP in year 2. Thus, real GDP would decline from year 2 to year 3 with this aggregate expenditure line. On the other hand, the upper *AE* line corresponds to the first step of a boom. Real GDP at point *e* is above potential GDP in year 3.

By referring to these values of real GDP as the *first* steps of a boom or a recession, we are emphasizing that they are not the end of the story. We will see that there are forces in the economy that tend to bring real GDP back toward potential GDP. This calculation of real GDP gives only the short-run impact of changes in government spending, investment, net exports, or taxes.

Starting Away from Potential GDP

Thus far we have shown how a shift in the *AE* line can bring the economy away from potential GDP when we start with real GDP equal to potential GDP. We could also have started our analysis with real GDP away from potential GDP.

For example, suppose that real GDP turns out to be below potential GDP in year 3 in Figure 25.11. If, in this situation, there is a further downward shift in the aggregate expenditure line, say because of a further decline in net exports, then real GDP could fall even further below potential GDP before there are sufficient forces to bring real GDP back toward potential. During the Great Depression in the 1930s, real GDP declined for several years in a row before starting to recover. Such successive declines could be explained by several successive shifts downward in the aggregate expenditure line.

Moreover, it is possible for the aggregate expenditure line in Figure 25.11 to shift back up from position *d* in year 3, say because of a change in government purchases, bringing real GDP back to potential GDP. For example, during World War II, government purchases increased for several successive years, and real GDP rose from below potential GDP to well above potential GDP during this period.

As these examples show, shifts in the aggregate expenditure line, for whatever reason, can explain many types of movements of real GDP around potential GDP.

Review

▶ Shifts in the aggregate expenditure line can explain the departures of real GDP from potential GDP.

▶ When the aggregate expenditure line shifts down, real GDP declines, and, if it was previously equal to potential GDP, it will fall below potential GDP.

▶ Upward shifts in the aggregate expenditure line will bring real GDP above potential GDP.

▶ The aggregate expenditure line can shift for many reasons. Changes in taxes, government purchases, investment, and net exports will cause the *AE* line to shift.

CONCLUSION

With this chapter we have begun to develop a theory of economic fluctuations. We have shown how economists explain departures of real GDP from potential GDP using the idea that these fluctuations are due to changes in aggregate demand. We used this explanation to make short-term forecasts of real GDP. The aggregate expenditure line—showing how the demand for consumption, investment, and net exports depends on income—and the 45-degree line are key parts of the forecasting process. However, our analysis thus far has made several simplifying assumptions. For example, the only thing people's consumption decisions respond to is a change in income.

In later chapters we show that consumption as well as investment and net exports respond to interest rates and inflation. The responses to interest rates and inflation will explain why real GDP returns to potential GDP in the long run.

KEY POINTS

1. Economic fluctuations are temporary deviations of real GDP from potential GDP.

2. Employment and unemployment fluctuate with real GDP. Unemployment increases in recessions and decreases in booms.

3. The fluctuations in real GDP and potential GDP are mainly due to fluctuations in aggregate demand. Limited information and implicit contracts give a theoretical rationale for this fact, which appears to be an obvious feature of economic fluctuations when we look at individual firms and workers.

4. The idea that fluctuations in real GDP are mainly due to aggregate demand is used to find real GDP when making a short-term forecast.

5. Real GDP can be predicted on the basis of forecasts of consumption, investment, net exports, and government

purchases. But these items depend on income and, thus, on the forecast of real GDP itself.

6. The consumption function describes how consumption responds to income.

7. The aggregate expenditure line is built up from the consumption function.

8. The 45-degree line tells us that expenditures equal income.

9. Combining the aggregate expenditure line and the 45-degree line in a diagram enables us to determine the level of income or real GDP.

10. The level of real GDP that gives spending balance changes when government spending changes. Real GDP will decline in the short run when government purchases are cut.

KEY TERMS

limited information	real business cycle theory	aggregate income
implicit contract	forecast	disposable income
nominal rigidities	conditional forecast	45-degree line
sticky price assumption	consumption function	aggregate expenditure line
flexible price assumption	marginal propensity to consume (MPC)	spending balance

QUESTIONS FOR REVIEW

1. Why do theories of economic fluctuations focus on aggregate demand rather than potential GDP as the main source of the short-run economic fluctuations?

2. Why do theories of economic growth focus on potential GDP (with its three determinants) rather than aggregate demand as the main source of economic growth?

3. What is the role of implicit contracts in explaining why prices and wages are sticky?

4. Why does the unemployment rate rise above the natural unemployment rate when real GDP falls below potential GDP?

5. What is the normal rate of capacity utilization in manu-

facturing firms? What is the significance of this normal rate for explaining economic fluctuations?

6. What is a conditional forecast?

7. What accounting identity does the 45-degree line represent?

8. Why does the aggregate expenditure line have a slope less than 1?

9. Why do economic forecasters have to take into account the consumption function?

10. Why is real GDP given by the intersection of the 45-degree line and the aggregate expenditure line?

PROBLEMS

1. Sketch a diagram with a 45-degree line and an aggregate expenditure line that describes macroeconomic spending balance. What factors determine how steep the aggregate expenditure line is? What macroeconomic relationship is described by the 45-degree line? Show on the diagram what will happen to the level of income if there is a rise in government purchases. Does U.S. income increase by more or by less than the upward shift in government purchases? Explain.

2. Describe what happens to the aggregate expenditure line in each of the following cases:
  a) Government spending on highways rises.
  b) The Chinese decide to spend $10 billion on aircraft built in the United States.
  c) Firms become very pessimistic about the future.
  d) A law is enacted requiring that the government pay $10,000 to anyone who builds a new house.

3. The following table shows the relationship between income and consumption in an economy.

Income (Y) (in billions of dollars)	Consumption (C) (in billions of dollars)
0	1,000
1,000	1,500
2,000	2,000
3,000	2,500
4,000	3,000
5,000	3,500
6,000	4,000
7,000	4,500

Assume that investment (I) is $500 billion, government purchases (G) are $300 billion, and net exports (X) are $200 billion.
  a) What is the numerical value of the marginal propensity to consume?
  b) Construct a table analogous to Table 25.2 for this economy. What is the level of income that gives spending balance in the economy?
  c) For this level of income, calculate the level of national saving. Is national saving equal to investment plus net exports?
  d) Sketch a diagram with a 45-degree line and an aggregate expenditure curve that describes the preceding relationships. Show graphically what happens to income when the government raises taxes.

4. Suppose government purchases will increase by $100 billion, and a forecasting firm predicts that real GDP will rise in the short run by $100 billion as a result. Would you

say that forecast is accurate? Why? If you were running a business and subscribe to that forecasting service, what questions would you ask about the forecast?

5. Suppose that business executives are very optimistic, and they raise their investment spending. What happens to the AE line? How will this affect real GDP? Sketch a diagram to demonstrate your answer.

6. Suppose that American goods suddenly become unpopular in Europe. What happens to net exports? How will this shift the AE line? What happens to real GDP? Demonstrate this in a diagram.

7. Why are sticky prices important in explaining why changes in aggregate demand bring about large changes in production and real GDP? If firms have perfect (exact) information about whether changes in the demand for their products are temporary or permanent, will this increase or decrease the stickiness of prices? If all firms had perfect information, would there still be wide fluctuations of real GDP around potential GDP?

8. Suppose the information in the following table describes the economic situation in the United States at the end of 2004:

Year	Real GDP (billions of 2004 dollars)	Potential GDP (billions of 2004 dollars)
2002	9,613	9,613
2003	9,854	9,854
2004	10,100	10,100
2005 (optimistic forecast)	10,600	10,353
2005 (pessimistic forecast)	9,900	10,353

  a) Graph real GDP over time, placing the year on the horizontal axis. Calculate the growth rate of real GDP between 2003 and 2004.
  b) The optimistic forecast for the year 2005 is based on the possibility that businesses are optimistic about the economy. What will the growth rate of real GDP be if the optimistic forecast turns out to be true?
  c) The pessimistic forecast is based on the possibility that businesses will be pessimistic about the economy. What will the growth rate of real GDP be if this forecast is correct?
  d) What is the deviation (in terms of dollars and as a percentage) of real GDP from potential GDP in 2005 if the optimistic forecast is correct? What is the deviation (in terms of dollars and as a percentage) from potential GDP in 2005 if the pessimistic forecast is correct?

9. Given the following consumption function stated in algebraic form, calculate real GDP (Y) that results in spending balance in the economy:

$C = 100 + .5 (Y - T)$
$I = 200$
$G = 200$
$X = 100$
$T = 200$

a) Suppose you find out that government purchases will increase to 300 next year. What is your forecast of real GDP for next year? Which way did the *AE* line shift?

b) Suppose businesses are pessimistic about how the economy will do next year. They decide to decrease their spending on plant and equipment by 100. How will this shift the *AE* line and by how much? What is the new level of real GDP?

c) Now suppose that the marginal propensity to consume is .6 instead of .5. How does this affect the level of real GDP at spending balance? Why?

d) Explain what happens when the government decides to increase taxes by $50 per person. Which way does the

AE line shift? Why? How does this affect real GDP in the economy?

e) Suppose the government decides to increase taxes and government purchases by the same amount, that is, T and G both rise to 300. Calculate the new equilibrium Y and compare it to the original equilibrium with $G = T = 200$. Why did Y go up when both T and G rose by the same amount?

10. This problem incorporates taxes into the algebraic model described in the box "Forecasting with Econometric Models." Let the consumption function be given by

$C = 1 + .6(Y - T)$

where T is taxes. Suppose $I + G + X = 3$. Everything is measured in trillions of dollars.

a) Find real GDP (Y) when $T = 1$.

b) Now increase T to 1.2. What happens to Y compared to part (a)?

c) Now decrease T to .8. What happens to Y compared to part (a)?

d) Using these results, explain how changes in taxes would affect one's short-term forecast of real GDP.

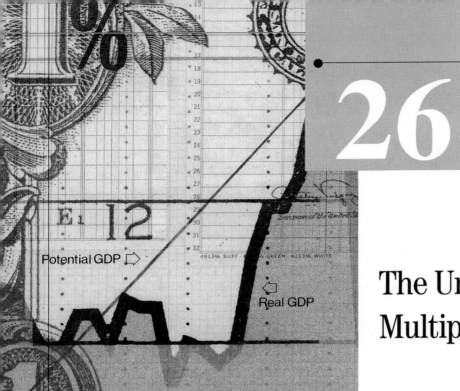

Potential GDP

Real GDP

The Uncertain Multiplier

How much does real GDP change in the short run when government purchases change, when taxes change, or when foreigners' demands for U.S. products change? Economists measure this change with the multiplier—the ratio of the change in real GDP to whatever is causing real GDP to change. If the economists at a forecasting firm report that the multiplier for a change in government purchases, for example, is 2, they mean that real GDP will change in the short run by twice as much as the change in government purchases. Another way to ask the opening question, then, is: How large is the multiplier?

We ended the last chapter with a partial answer when we showed that real GDP will depart from potential GDP in the short run when there is a change in government purchases. We showed that if consumption is positively related to income and if net exports are unrelated to income, then real GDP changes by more than the change in government purchases. In other words, the multiplier—in this case, the ratio of the change in real GDP to the change in government purchases—is greater than 1. In particular, we showed that a cut in government purchases of $100 billion would lead to a reduction in real GDP in the short run of more than $100 billion.

But there is considerable uncertainty about the exact size of the multiplier. DRI, a major forecasting firm, has put the multiplier for a change in government purchases in the United States at 2.1, meaning that a decrease in government purchases of $100 billion would decrease real GDP by $210 billion in the short run. Economists at the Federal Reserve Board put the multiplier at 1.7. The staff of the International Monetary Fund puts it at 1.2. Different assumptions about people's consumption behavior can lead to an even wider range of estimates of the size of the multiplier.

In this chapter we show how to measure the multiplier and we assess factors that affect its size. That the size of the multiplier is uncertain does not render it useless, and finding out why it is uncertain is far better than ignoring the multiplier. One way or another the multiplier must be taken into account in analyzing short-run fluctuations in real GDP, employment, and unemployment. Cuts in military purchases or a new federal program for construction of roads and bridges will have effects on the entire economy. Are the military cuts large enough to lead to a recession? Will the new construction program add too much to a booming economy? Assuming that such changes in government programs are good in the long run, how could we mitigate any adverse short-run effects on the economy?

For example, a decline in defense spending, made possible by the end of the cold war around 1989, was partly responsible for the slowdown in the U.S. economy in the early 1990s and is frequently mentioned as one of the possible causes of the recession that began in 1990. There was also a tax increase in 1990, aimed at reducing the U.S. budget deficit. Could the multiplier from this tax increase have been large enough to have caused the recession or made it worse? Should the tax increase have been delayed because of the recession? Or should the cuts in military spending have been delayed? To make judgments about when and by how much to change government programs, policymakers need to consider the short-run impact of changes in government purchases and taxes on real GDP. In other words, they need to consider the size of the multiplier.

HOW TO FIND THE MULTIPLIER

We first show how to use graphs to find the multiplier. We make use of the 45-degree line and the aggregate expenditure line introduced in the previous chapter. We then derive the multiplier algebraically. Last, but not least, we describe in words how the multiplier actually works its way through the economy.

A Graphical Derivation of the Multiplier

Figure 26.1 is a diagram like the one derived in the previous chapter with income or real GDP on the horizontal axis and spending on the vertical axis. The 45-degree line equates spending and income. There are two aggregate expenditure (AE) lines in Figure 26.1. Both AE lines show that aggregate expenditure in the economy—the sum of consumption plus investment plus government purchases plus net exports, or $C + I + G + X$—rises with income. Aggregate expenditure rises with income because consumption rises with income, according to the consumption function. We assume that the marginal propensity to consume is equal to .6. Thus, the slope of both aggregate expenditure lines is .6 in Figure 26.1.

The Multiplier for a General Shift in the Aggregate Expenditure Line

Observe that one aggregate expenditure line is labeled "old" and the other is labeled "new." Our objective is to analyze the impact on real GDP of a shift in the aggregate expenditure line, that is, a shift from the "old" AE line to the "new" AE line. The upward-pointing black arrow shows the size of the shift in the aggregate expenditure line. Such a shift can occur because of a change in government purchases, a change in taxes, a change in investment, or a change in net exports.

Note that the "new" aggregate expenditure line intersects the 45-degree line at a different point of spending balance than the "old" aggregate expenditure line. At this new point of spending balance, the level of income, or real GDP, is higher than at the old point of spending balance. On the horizontal axis the black arrow pointing to the right shows this shift to a higher level of real GDP. Look carefully at the

FIGURE 26.1
Graphical Calculation of the Multiplier

An upward shift in the *AE* line raises real GDP in the short run by a multiple of the shift in the *AE* line. The multiplier can be found graphically. It is the ratio of the length of the black horizontal arrow to the length of the black vertical arrow.

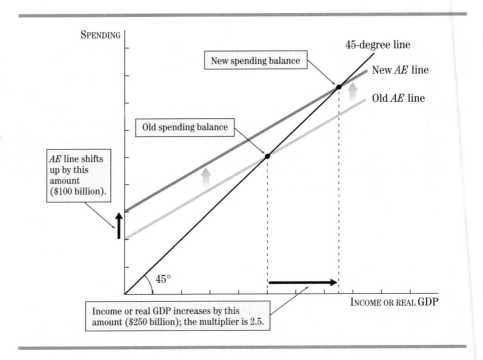

diagram to note the *size* of the change in real GDP along the horizontal axis and compare it with the change in the aggregate expenditure line. Observe that the horizontal change is *larger* than the vertical change. This is due to the multiplier. In fact, the term *multiplier* is used because the change in real GDP is a multiple of the shift in the aggregate expenditure line.

In general, we define the **multiplier** as the ratio of the change in real GDP to the shift in the aggregate expenditure line, regardless of the reason for the shift in the aggregate expenditure line (whether it is due to a change in government purchases, a change in taxes, a change in investment, or a change in foreign demand). That is, by definition,

multiplier: the ratio of the change in real GDP to the shift in the aggregate expenditure line.

$$\text{Multiplier} = \frac{\text{change in real GDP}}{\text{shift in the aggregate expenditure line}}$$

The multiplier is equal to the ratio of the length of the arrow along the horizontal axis to the length of the arrow along the vertical axis in Figure 26.1. You can calculate the multiplier by measuring these lengths. Observe that for the aggregate expenditure line with a slope of .6 drawn in Figure 26.1, the multiplier is 2.5.

Note that the multiplier is greater than 1 in this example. Draw your own version of Figure 26.1 in order to convince yourself that as long as the aggregate expenditure line is upward-sloping with a slope less than 1 (so that it is less steep than the 45-degree line), the multiplier is greater than 1. The multiplier expresses a key finding: A shift in the aggregate expenditure line results in a change in real GDP in the economy greater than the shift in the aggregate expenditure line.

Specific Cases of the Multiplier

The multiplier applies to anything that shifts the aggregate expenditure line. One example is an increase in government purchases. An increase in government purchases by $100 billion would shift the *AE* line up by $100 billion. This would increase real GDP by $250 billion if the multiplier for government purchases is 2.5. Another example would be a decrease in government purchases, which would shift the *AE* line down by the amount of the government purchases decrease. Thus, a $100 billion cut in government purchases would reduce real GDP by $250 billion in the short run if the multiplier is 2.5.

Another example is an increase in investment, which shifts the *AE* line. If there is a $20 billion increase in investment in new homes because of a new tax credit for first-time homebuyers, then the *AE* line will shift up by $20 billion, and real GDP rises by $50 billion if the multiplier is 2.5. Similarly, an increase in foreign demand for U.S. products shifts up the aggregate expenditure line.

The aggregate expenditure line will shift down if there is a drop in consumer confidence that leads people to consume less regardless of their income. This is called an *autonomous* change in consumption because it is independent of income. The *AE* line shifts down by the amount of the autonomous decline in consumption. The effect on real GDP is the multiplier times the shift in the *AE* line. Finally, there is the effect of income tax changes, a subject we take up later in the chapter.

An Algebraic Derivation of the Multiplier

The multiplier also can be computed directly without using a diagram. To demonstrate this, let us focus again on a case where the MPC is .6. To be specific, we suppose that the particular reason for a change in the aggregate expenditure line is an increase in government purchases. Then the multiplier is the ratio of the change in real GDP to the change in government purchases. We already showed graphically that the multiplier was 2.5 when the MPC was .6. How do we get 2.5 with algebra? We need to consider the algebra that corresponds to the lines in the graphs.

As you know, the identity that income or real GDP (Y) equals consumption (C) plus investment (I) plus government purchases (G) plus net exports (X) can be written algebraically as

$$Y = C + I + G + X$$

To find the multiplier, we want to determine the impact of a *change* in government purchases on real GDP. That is, we want to find the change in Y that occurs when G changes. Any change in Y must come either directly from a change in G or indirectly from a change in C, I, or X, according to the preceding identity. Denote the change in any of these items by the Greek letter Δ. Then we can write the identity in terms of changes:

$$\Delta Y = \Delta C + \Delta I + \Delta G + \Delta X$$

That is, the *change* in real GDP is equal to the *change* in consumption plus the *change* in investment plus the *change* in government purchases plus the *change* in net exports. Now consider each of the four terms on the right.

The change in government purchases (ΔG) equals $100 billion. For convenience, to make things simple, we continue to assume that there is no change in investment or in net exports. In other words, we assume that neither responds to changes in income. Expressed in symbols, $\Delta I = 0$ and $\Delta X = 0$.

On the other hand, we have assumed a consumption function that tells us how much consumption changes when income changes. The consumption function we use for the algebraic calculation has an MPC of .6. Using algebra, we write $\Delta C = .6\Delta Y$. That is, the change in consumption equals .6 times the change in income; for example, if the change in income $\Delta Y = \$10$ billion, then the change in consumption $\Delta C = \$6$ billion if the MPC is .6.

Now let us take our ingredients:

1. $\Delta Y = \Delta C + \Delta I + \Delta G + \Delta X$.

2. The changes in investment and net exports are zero ($\Delta I = \Delta X = 0$).

3. The change in consumption is .6 times the change in income ($\Delta C = .6\Delta Y$).

Replacing ΔI with zero and ΔX with zero removes ΔI and ΔX from the right-hand side of the identity. Replacing ΔC with $.6\Delta Y$ in the same identity results in

$$\Delta Y = .6\Delta Y + \Delta G$$

Note that the term ΔY appears on both sides of this equation. Gathering terms in ΔY on the left-hand side of the equation gives

$$(1 - .6)\Delta Y = \Delta G$$

Dividing both sides by ΔG and by $(1 - .6)$ results in

$$\begin{aligned}
\Delta Y/\Delta G &= 1/(1 - .6) \\
&= 1/.4 \\
&= 2.5
\end{aligned}$$

Thus, the change in income, or real GDP, that occurs when government purchases change, according to this calculation, is 2.5 times the change in government purchases. That is, $\Delta Y = 2.5\Delta G$. The number—2.5—is the multiplier. The calculations are summarized in Table 26.1. The algebraic calculation agrees with the graphical

---

TABLE 26.1
Derivation of the Multiplier for MPC = .6

The identity,

$$Y = C + I + G + X$$

when written in terms of changes, becomes

$$\Delta Y = \Delta C + \Delta I + \Delta G + \Delta X$$

We assume investment does not change,

$$\Delta I = 0$$

that net exports do not change either,

$$\Delta X = 0$$

and that consumption changes according to the equation

$$\Delta C = .6\Delta Y$$

Substituting ΔI, ΔX, and ΔC into the expression for ΔY gives

$$\Delta Y = .6\Delta Y + \Delta G$$

Solving for ΔY gives

$$\frac{\Delta Y}{\Delta G} = \frac{1}{1 - .6} = 2.5 \quad \text{(the multiplier)}$$

calculation. The $100 billion increase in government purchases is translated into a $250 billion increase in real GDP.

You can perform this same calculation for *any value* of the marginal propensity to consume (MPC), not just .6. To see this, again we focus on finding the change in income, or real GDP, associated with a change in government purchases. Assume that the change in investment and the change in net exports equal zero. The change in consumption equals the MPC times the change in income, where the MPC is any number. Using the same approach as in the case of MPC = .6 we find that the multiplier is

$$\frac{\Delta Y}{\Delta G} = \frac{1}{(1 - \text{MPC})} \quad \text{(the multiplier)}$$

The algebraic derivation of the multiplier with a general value for the MPC is shown in Table 26.2; the derivation is similar to the case of MPC = .6.

An alternative algebraic way to write the multiplier uses the concept of the **marginal propensity to save (MPS).** The marginal propensity to save for a person is the additional amount that person saves when the person's income rises. Since an individual must either consume or save any additional income, the marginal propensity to consume (MPC) plus the marginal propensity to save (MPS) must equal 1. Thus, the MPS equals $1 - \text{MPC}$. For example, if income increases by $100 and the MPC is .6, then consumption increases by $60 and saving must increase by $40. The MPS is .4.

The MPS can also be defined for the economy as a whole. Saving for the whole economy is defined as income (Y) minus consumption (C). Any increase in income that does not go to consumption must go to saving; as with an individual,

marginal propensity to save (MPS): the change in saving due to a given change in income; MPS = 1 − marginal propensity to consume (MPC).

Start with the identity

$$Y = C + I + G + X$$

and convert it to change form

$$\Delta Y = \Delta C + \Delta I + \Delta G + \Delta X$$

Substitute $\Delta I = 0$ and $\Delta X = 0$ and

$$\Delta C = \text{MPC} \times \Delta Y$$

into the change form of the identity to get

$$\Delta Y = \text{MPC} \times \Delta Y + \Delta G$$

Gather terms involving ΔY to get

$$(1 - \text{MPC}) \times \Delta Y = \Delta G$$

Divide both sides by ΔG and by $1 - \text{MPC}$ to get

$$\frac{\Delta Y}{\Delta G} = \frac{1}{1 - \text{MPC}} \quad \text{(the multiplier)}$$

TABLE 26.2
Derivation of the Multiplier for Any MPC

MPC + MPS = 1 for the whole economy. Thus, we can replace 1 − MPC with MPS in the preceding expression for the multiplier. Doing so, we get

$$\frac{\Delta Y}{\Delta G} = \frac{1}{MPS}$$

Thus, the multiplier is equal to the inverse of the marginal propensity to save.

Following the Multiplier Through the Economy

A third method to find the multiplier is to examine what happens when a change in government purchases winds its way through the economy. Such an economic narrative demonstrates how the multiplier works.

Assume that the government increases its military purchases, as it did in the early 1980s in the United States when President Reagan increased defense spending. In this example, the government increases purchases of jets and aircraft carriers. The immediate impact of the change in government purchases is an increase in production of jets and aircraft carriers. With an increase in demand, areospace and shipbuilding firms produce more, and real GDP rises. The initial increase in real GDP from an increase in government purchases of $100 billion is that same $100 billion. If the government is purchasing more jets, the production of jets increases. We call this initial increase in real GDP the *first-round* effect, which includes only the initial change in government purchases.

The first round is not the end of the story. A further increase in real GDP occurs when the workers employed in making the aircraft carriers and jets start working more hours and new workers are hired. As a result, the wage income workers get paid rises, and the profits made by the manufacturers increase. With both wage income and profit income rising, income in the economy as a whole rises by $100 billion. According to the consumption function, people will consume more. How much more? The consumption function tells us that .6 times the change in income, or $60 billion, will be the additional increase in consumption by the workers and owners of the defense firms. Real GDP rises by $60 billion, the increased production of the goods the workers and owners consume. This $60 billion increase in real GDP is the *second-round* effect. It is hard for anyone to know what the workers in the defense industry or the owners of the defense firms will start purchasing, but presumably it would be an array of goods: clothes, VCRs, movies, and restaurant meals. But with an MPC of .6, we do know they will purchase $60 billion more of these goods. The increase in production spreads throughout the economy. After this second round, real GDP has increased by $160 billion, the sum of $100 billion on the first round and $60 billion on the second round. This is shown in the first and second rows of Table 26.3.

The story continues. The workers who make the clothes, VCRs, and other goods and services for which there is $60 billion more in spending also have an increase in their income. Either they are no longer unemployed or they work more hours. Similarly, the profits of the owners of those firms increase. As a result, they consume more. How much more? According to the consumption function, .6 times the increase in their income. The increase in income outside of military production was $60 billion, so the increase in consumption must now be .6 times that, or a $36 billion increase. This increase is the *third-round* effect. As the increase permeates the economy, it is impossible to say what particular goods will increase in production, but we know that total production continues to increase. After three rounds, real GDP has increased by $196 billion, as shown in the third row of Table 26.3.

The Origins of the Multiplier

John Maynard Keynes credited the idea of the multiplier to another British economist, R. F. Kahn. Kahn focused on the change in employment that would accompany a change in real GDP in a 1931 paper on the multiplier. Interestingly, Kahn's description of the multiplier began with a situation where real GDP is near potential GDP. In such a situation, Kahn wrote, "If investment increases, the production of consumption-goods must diminish by an equal amount."

But Kahn, like Keynes, did not write in times when real GDP was equal to potential GDP. He wrote during the Great Depression, a case of a departure from potential GDP. Under such conditions, he argued,

". . . for each man placed in primary employment, the number who receive secondary employment is $k + k^2 + k^3 + k^4 + \ldots = k/(1 - k)$."

For Kahn, k was analogous to the marginal propensity to consume. By primary employment (of 1 man) he meant the first round of the multiplier process as described in this textbook; by secondary employment [of $k/(1 - k)$ men] he meant all the other rounds. Thus,

the value of Kahn's multiplier is $1 + k/(1 - k)$, which can be shown to equal $1/(1 - k)$, exactly the formula for the multiplier used in this chapter. But where does the long series involving k, k^2, k^3, and so on, which Kahn used to find the multiplier, come from?

Kahn observed that the impact on employment of successive rounds of the multiplier is like the terms in a geometric sum. A geometric sum, you may recall from your math courses, is a sum of terms each of which converges geometrically to zero. The terms in the sum are 1, k, k^2, k^3, k^4, k^5, and so on, where k is less than 1. For example, if $k = .6$, the value of the MPC in the examples in the text, then the terms are 1, .6, .36, .216, .1296, .07776, and so on. Compare these terms with those in the second column of Table 26.3. Each shows the amount of the change in real GDP on each round of the multiplier. The geometric sum adds up all these rounds and gives the value of the multiplier.

Source of quote: R. F. Kahn, "The Relation of Home Investment to Unemployment," *Economic Journal*, June 1931.

The increase does not stop there. Another $36 billion more in consumption means that there is $36 billion more in income for people somewhere in the economy. This increases consumption further, by .6 times the $36 billion, or $21.6 billion. According to the column on the right of Table 26.3, the cumulative effect on real GDP is now up to $217.6 billion after four rounds. Observe how each new entry in the first column is added to the previous total to get the cumulative effect on real GDP.

Round	Change in Real GDP	Cumulative Change in Real GDP
First round	100.000	100.000
Second round	60.000	160.000
Third round	36.000	196.000
Fourth round	21.600	217.600
Fifth round	12.960	230.560
.	.	.
.	.	.
.	.	.
After an infinite number of rounds	0.000	250.000

TABLE 26.3

A Numerical Illustration of the Multiplier Process

(billions of dollars)

The story is now getting repetitive. We multiply .6 times $21.6 billion to get $12.96 billion. The total effect on real GDP is now $230.56 billion at the fifth round. In fact, we are already almost at $250 billion. If we kept on going for more and more rounds, we would get closer and closer to the $250 billion amount obtained from the algebra and graphs.

Hence, tracing out each round in the multiplier process gives the same answer as the other two approaches to finding the multiplier. It also shows why the multiplier is greater than 1. The repetitive flow of spending and income spreads throughout the economy, multiplying the initial increase in government purchases into increased spending and income for many others in the economy. Figure 26.2 gives a

FIGURE 26.2

The Rounds of the Multiplier Process

The height of each bar shows the cumulative impact on real GDP for each round of the multiplier. The dark part of each bar shows what is added to real GDP in each round. The top panel shows the rounds of spending when the marginal propensity to consume is .6, as in Table 26.3. The bottom panel shows the rounds of spending for a smaller MPC, equal to .4. In both cases, government purchases rise by $100 billion.

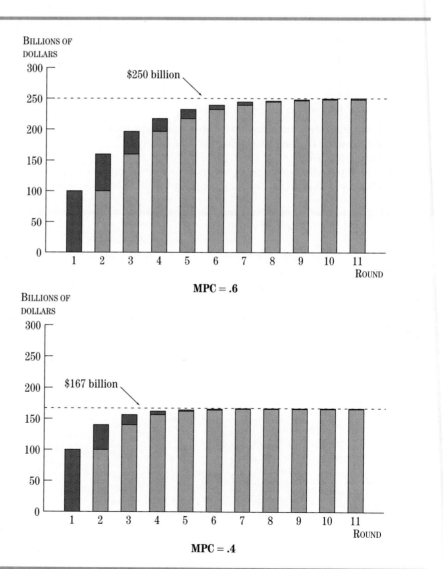

more visual perspective on the rounds of the multiplier. It shows in the bar chart in the top panel the same data presented in Table 26.3.

The successive rounds of the multiplier also occur when there is a decrease in government spending. Then the entries in Table 26.3 would decrease rather than increase. To test yourself, try following the multiplier through the economy after a *decrease* in military purchases of $100 billion.

In reality all the rounds of the multiplier occur very rapidly—getting close to the full value of the multiplier within a year or so. Thus, in looking at these rounds we are still considering what happens to real GDP in the short run, during the first step of real GDP away from potential GDP. Starting from a situation where real GDP equals potential GDP, an increase in military spending would raise real GDP above potential, and a decrease in military spending would lower real GDP below potential. In either case the multiplier tells us how large the change in real GDP will be.

Review

▶ The multiplier is defined as the ratio of the change in real GDP to a shift in the aggregate expenditure line. In the case where the aggregate expenditure line shifts because of a change in government purchases, the multiplier is equal to the change in real GDP divided by the change in government purchases.

▶ The multiplier can be found using graphical methods, algebraic methods, or by summing up the rounds of the multiplier process. All three methods give the same answer, but each illustrates different aspects of the multiplier.

▶ After only a few rounds of the multiplier process, the final value of the multiplier is nearly reached.

THE SIZE OF THE MULTIPLIER

What determines the size of the multiplier? Our graphical calculation of the multiplier indicates that the answer to this question can be found in the aggregate expenditure line, because the multiplier was derived from this line.

The Multiplier and the Slope of the *AE* line

The left and right panels of Figure 26.3 show two different calculations of the multiplier. The calculations differ only in the slope of the aggregate expenditure line. The size of the upward shift in the aggregate expenditure lines is exactly the same in the two panels, but the left panel has aggregate expenditure lines that are relatively steep, while the right panel has aggregate expenditure lines that are relatively flat.

Observe the difference in the multiplier in the two panels. The shift in the *AE* line is the same in both graphs, but the increase in real GDP in the left panel is larger than the increase in real GDP in the right panel. Therefore, the multiplier is larger in the left panel. In the left panel the multiplier is 2.5. In the right panel it is 1.3.

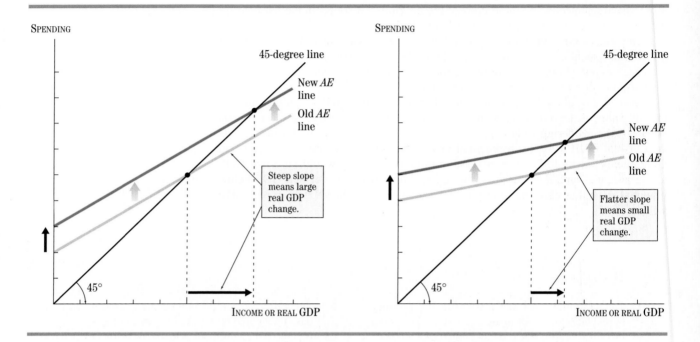

FIGURE 26.3

The Multiplier and the Slope of the *AE* Line

In the left panel the *AE* line is relatively steep. In the right panel the *AE* line is relatively flat. Observe that the multiplier is much larger in the left panel than in the right panel.

Figure 26.3 demonstrates that the multiplier is positively related to the slope of the aggregate expenditure line. Draw your own graphs with varying slopes of the aggregate expenditure line to convince yourself that the size of the multiplier depends on the slope of the *AE* line. The steeper the *AE* line, the larger the multiplier. The flatter the *AE* line, the smaller the multiplier.

The Multiplier and the Marginal Propensity to Consume

The slope of the *AE* line is equal to the marginal propensity to consume. Thus, one interpretation of the relatively steep *AE* line in the left panel of Figure 26.3 is that the marginal propensity to consume is high compared to the marginal propensity to consume in the right panel. This implies that a relatively large marginal propensity to consume leads to a relatively large multiplier.

The formula for the multiplier that was derived earlier—showing that the multiplier is related to the marginal propensity to consume—confirms this. In particular, the size of the multiplier equals $1/(1 - \text{MPC})$. For example, if the MPC is .6, then the multiplier is 2.5. If the MPC is .4, then the multiplier is $1/(1 - .4)$, or about 1.7. Lowering the MPC from .6 to .4 lowers the multiplier from 2.5 to 1.7. Therefore, if the MPC is lower, the multiplier is lower. And if the MPC is higher, the multiplier is higher. Thus, the algebra confirms the result that is illustrated graphically in Figure 26.3.

Is there any economic intuition behind the relationship between the multiplier and the marginal propensity to consume? Recall that in examining the rounds of the multiplier through the economy we found that the size of the second, third, and each subsequent round depended on the marginal propensity to consume. If the marginal propensity to consume is larger, then the increase in income from the first

John Maynard Keynes, 1883–1946

BORN:
Cambridge, England, 1883

EDUCATION:
Cambridge University, graduated 1906

JOBS:
India Office, London, 1906–1909
Cambridge University, 1909–1915
British Treasury, 1915–1919
Cambridge University, 1919–1946

MAJOR PUBLICATIONS:
The Economic Consequences of the Peace, 1919; *A Tract on Monetary Reform,* 1923; *A Treatise on Money,* 1930; *The General Theory of Employment, Interest and Money,* 1936

John Maynard Keynes—the inventor of the marginal propensity to consume and of the broader idea that a decline in aggregate demand could bring the economy below its potential—was one of the greatest economists of all time, of similar stature to Adam Smith, David Ricardo, and Alfred Marshall. Keynes put forth the marginal propensity to consume and the multiplier in *The General Theory of Employment, Interest and Money.* Written in the midst of the Great Depression, it provided an explanation for a worldwide tragedy that prevailing economic theory—with its microeconomic emphasis, as represented by Marshall's *Principles of Economics*—hardly addressed. Keynes's ideas spread rapidly and had a lasting influence; referring to them as the "Keynesian revolution" is no exaggeration. Many elements of Keynes's theory are contained in this and the previous chapter of this text.

Much of the *General Theory* is difficult to read. As Keynes put it, "This book is chiefly addressed to my fellow economists." But Keynes's well-developed writing skills emerge in some of the less technical passages, especially those on speculation and expectations in financial markets.

The *General Theory* is a highly theoretical book with very little data. In fact, until Keynes demonstrated the importance of aggregate demand very little data were available on aggregate income, consumption, or investment. But Keynes did give factual evidence about the marginal propensity to consume and the multiplier. He recognized that existing aggregate data for Britain were not sufficiently accurate to estimate the marginal propensity to consume, so he provided estimates for the United States using preliminary data that were soon to be published for the first time by Simon Kuznets of Harvard University. Keynes writes:

At present, however, our statistics are not accurate enough. . . . The best for the purpose, of which I am aware, are Mr. Kuznets' figures for the United States . . . , though they are, nevertheless, very precarious. . . . If single years are taken in isolation, the results look rather wild. But if they are grouped in pairs, the multiplier seems to have been less than 3 and probably fairly stable in the neighbourhood of 2.5. This suggests a marginal propensity to consume not exceeding 60 to 70 per cent. . . .

Note that Keynes's estimates of the MPC are very close to the example used in this chapter.

The *General Theory* was not Keynes's only book. Keynes gained notoriety in his thirties for a best-selling book called *The Economic Consequences of the Peace,* written in only two months during the summer of 1919. As an economic adviser to the British government, Keynes accompanied the prime minister to the Versailles Peace Conference in 1919 at the end of World War I. It was at that peace conference that the victors demanded heavy reparations from Germany, harming the German economy and thereby helping Hitler in his rise to power. In his 1919 book, Keynes predicted serious harm from the stiff reparations and ridiculed the heads of government at the conference, including his own prime minister, Lloyd George, and the American president Woodrow Wilson.

Keynes's *Tract on Monetary Reform* written in 1923 focused more on inflation than did the *General Theory.* Although Keynes has been criticized for not dealing with inflation in the *General Theory,* his earlier writings suggest that, if he had lived longer, he may have weighed in against the forces that led to the high inflation of the late 1960s and 1970s.

Source of quote: John Maynard Keynes, *The General Theory of Employment, Interest and Money,* first edition (1936), in *The Collected Writings of John Maynard Keynes,* Vol. VII (Cambridge: Cambridge University Press), pp. 154–155.

TABLE 26.4
The MPC and the Multiplier

MPC	Multiplier $1/(1 - MPC)$
.25	1.33
.30	1.42
.35	1.54
.40	1.67
.45	1.82
.50	2.00
.55	2.22
.60	2.50
.65	2.86
.70	3.33
.75	4.00
.80	5.00
.85	6.67
.90	10.00
.95	20.00

round generates a larger increase in consumption on the second round, and so on. If each successive round is larger, then the multiplier is larger, because the multiplier comes from summing up all the rounds. In order to visualize this concept, look back at the bar charts in the top and bottom panels of Figure 26.2. The top panel, which we already considered, has an MPC of .6; the bottom panel has an MPC of .4. They show that the marginal propensity to consume determines the size of the multiplier.

Uncertainty about the Size of the Multiplier

If there is uncertainty about the slope of the *AE* line or about the size of the MPC, then there is also uncertainty about the size of the multiplier. In order to see why, consider Table 26.4, which contains several different values of the MPC and the multiplier.

Uncertainty about the MPC might be described by a *range* of different values of the MPC. For example, if policymakers were uncertain about the MPC, they might say it was *around* .6, perhaps between .4 or .8, rather than exactly .6. According to Table 26.4, if the MPC is .8 rather than .6, then the multiplier is twice as large—5 rather than 2.5. If the MPC is .4, then the multiplier is 1.7. In reality, uncertainty about the size of the MPC in a given situation is one of the key reasons the multiplier itself is uncertain.

Review

▶ The size of the multiplier is positively related to the slope of the *AE* line. The steeper the *AE* line, the larger the multiplier.

▶ The size of the multiplier is also positively related to the marginal propensity to consume (MPC). The higher the MPC, the higher the multiplier.

▶ Uncertainty about the size of the MPC is a key reason that the size of the multiplier is uncertain.

A KEY INTERNATIONAL ISSUE: NET EXPORTS DEPEND ON INCOME

Thus far we have made the simplifying assumption that net exports do not respond to income. However, another influence on the size of the multiplier is the response of net exports to income; it is time to incorporate this response into our analysis.

How Do Net Exports Depend on Income?

To understand how the responsiveness of net exports to income affects the multiplier, we first need to consider how net exports depend on income. Recall that net exports are exports minus imports. To examine the effect of income on net exports, we first look at exports and then at imports.

Exports

Exports are goods and services we sell to other countries—aircraft, pharmaceuticals, telephones. Do U.S. exports depend on income in the United States? No, not much. If Americans earn a little more or a little less, the demand for U.S. exports is not going to increase or decrease. What is likely to make the demand for U.S. exports increase or decrease is a change in income abroad—changes in income in Japan, Europe, or Latin America will affect demand for U.S. exports. U.S. exports will not be affected even if the United States has a recession. Of course, if Japan or Europe has a recession, that is another story. In any case, we conclude that U.S. exports are unresponsive to the changes in U.S. income.

Imports

Imports are goods and services people in the United States purchase from abroad—automobiles, sweaters, vacations. Does the amount purchased of these goods and services change when our incomes change? Yes, because imports are part of consumption. Just as we argued that consumption responds to income, so must imports respond to income. Higher income will lead to higher consumption of both goods purchased in the United States and goods purchased abroad. That reasoning leads us to hypothesize that imports are positively related to income. The hypothesis turns out to be accurate when we look at observations on income and imports.

Figure 26.4 illustrates how higher income leads to higher imports. For example, if the slope of the line in Figure 26.4 is .2, then a rise of income in the United States by $10 billion raises imports by $2 billion. The effect of a change in income on imports is analogous to the marginal propensity to consume. When the MPC is .6, an increase in income by $10 billion leads consumption to rise by $6 billion. We are saying now that imports rise by .2 times the increase in income.

The **marginal propensity to import (MPI)** is the amount that imports change when income changes. Thus, the MPI is .2 in this example. The MPI is smaller than the MPC because most of the goods we consume when income rises are not imported. The United States imports less when U.S. income goes down and imports more when income goes up, but the changes are smaller than the change in consumption. For example, in the 1990–1991 recession when income in the United States fell, U.S. imports of cars from Japan declined, just as the consumption of cars produced in the United States declined. However, imports declined by a smaller amount than consumption.

Net Exports

If exports are unrelated to income and imports are positively related to income, then net exports—exports less imports—must be negatively related to income. A numerical example of income, exports, imports, and net exports in Table 26.5 shows why. Income is shown in the

marginal propensity to import (MPI): the change in imports because of a given change in income.

FIGURE 26.4
Relationship Between Imports and Income
The higher income is, the more foreign goods people want to buy. Thus, imports depend positively on income. The slope of the relationship is called the marginal propensity to import (MPI).

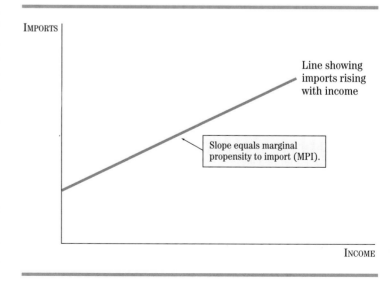

IMPORTS

Line showing imports rising with income

Slope equals marginal propensity to import (MPI).

INCOME

TABLE 26.5
Net Exports and Income:
A Numerical Example
(billions of dollars)

Income	Exports	Imports	Net Exports
6,000	2,100	1,200	900
7,000	2,100	1,400	700
8,000	2,100	1,600	500
9,000	2,100	1,800	300
10,000	2,100	2,000	100
11,000	2,100	2,200	−100
12,000	2,100	2,400	−300
13,000	2,100	2,600	−500
14,000	2,100	2,800	−700

first column. Exports, in the second column, are assumed to be constant—$2,100 billion—or unresponsive to income. Imports, in the third column, rise with income with a marginal propensity to import of .2. Net exports, in the fourth column, are negatively related to income, simply because we subtract imports from exports to get net exports.

Note that net exports respond to income in the opposite direction as consumption. Consumption is positively related to income while net exports are negatively related to income. The amount by which net exports changes with income is the marginal propensity to import. Observe in the example that each $1,000 billion increase in income lowers net exports by $200 billion.

The *AE* Line When Net Exports Depend on Income

How does this effect of income on net exports change our analysis? Table 26.6 shows how aggregate expenditure is determined when net exports depend on income. Net exports are shown in the far right column of the table. When net exports are added to consumption, investment, and government purchases, also shown in Table 26.6, we get aggregate expenditure. If you compare Table 26.6 with Table 25.2, you will see that aggregate expenditure rises less quickly with income. In Table 25.2 when net exports do not depend on income, aggregate expenditure increases by $600 billion for each $1,000 billion rise in income. In Table 26.6, aggregate expenditure rises by $400 billion for each $1,000 rise in income. Spending balance is achieved when real GDP is $10,000 billion.

TABLE 26.6
Aggregate Expenditure When Net
Exports Depend on Income

Income or Real GDP	Aggregate Expenditure	Consumption	Investment	Government Purchases	Net Exports
6,000	8,400	4,600	900	2,000	900
7,000	8,800	5,200	900	2,000	700
8,000	9,200	5,800	900	2,000	500
9,000	9,600	6,400	900	2,000	300
10,000	10,000	7,000	900	2,000	100
11,000	10,400	7,600	900	2,000	−100
12,000	10,800	8,200	900	2,000	−300
13,000	11,200	8,800	900	2,000	−500
14,000	11,600	9,400	900	2,000	−700

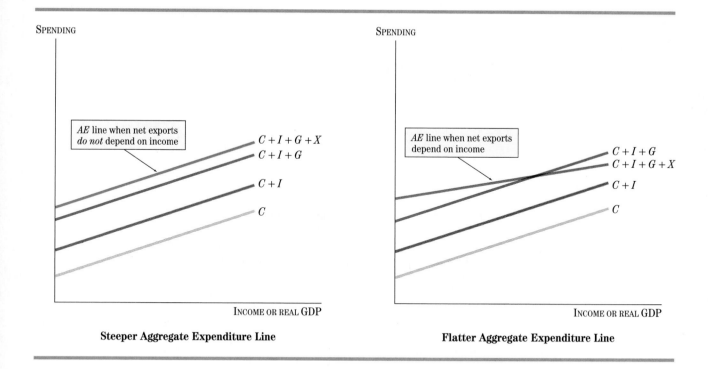

Steeper Aggregate Expenditure Line   **Flatter Aggregate Expenditure Line**

Figure 26.5 shows what happens graphically to the aggregate expenditure line when net exports depend on income. Compare the aggregate expenditure lines in both panels of Figure 26.5.

Note how the slope of the aggregate expenditure line is flatter when net exports depend on income. The reason is that the higher income, as shown in Table 26.6, results in the lower net exports. Recall that the aggregate expenditure line is built by adding up consumption, investment, government purchases, and net exports. Whereas investment and government purchases are still assumed to be unresponsive to income, net exports now depend on income. Thus, the higher income is, the less X there is to add to $C + I + G$. In fact, as income gets very high, X becomes negative, as shown in Table 26.5, so we must subtract dollars from $C + I + G$.

FIGURE 26.5
Net Exports and the Slope of the *AE* Line
When net exports depend on income, the aggregate expenditure line is flatter. The reason is that net exports are high at low levels of income and low at high levels of income, as shown in Table 26.6.

Effects on the Size of Multiplier

Now we have an answer to the question about how net exports affect the multiplier. Recall that Figure 26.3 proved that the flatter the aggregate expenditure line, the smaller the multiplier. Thus, because the aggregate expenditure line is flatter with net exports depending on income, we know that the multiplier is smaller. We can think of the right panel of Figure 26.3 as corresponding to a situation where net exports respond to income; the *AE* line is flatter and the multiplier is smaller. The responsiveness of imports to income makes the multiplier go down.

The intuitive reason that the multiplier is smaller when net exports respond to income is that some of the change in spending that occurs when income changes goes to goods and services produced abroad. In the case of an increase in military spending, for example, some of the increased income of defense workers is spent

TABLE 26.7
Derivation of the Multiplier When the MPI = .2 and the MPC = .6

The identity

$$Y = C + I + G + X$$

can be written in change form as

$$\Delta Y = \Delta C + \Delta I + \Delta G + \Delta X$$

We continue to assume that

$$\Delta I = 0$$

and

$$\Delta C = .6\Delta Y$$

But now the change in net exports is given by

$$\Delta X = -.2\Delta Y$$

Now put ΔI, ΔC, and ΔX into the identity to get

$$\Delta Y = .6\Delta Y + \Delta G - .2\Delta Y$$

Gather together the terms involving ΔY to get

$$(1 - .6 + .2)\Delta Y = \Delta G$$

Dividing both sides by ΔG, we get

$$\frac{\Delta Y}{\Delta G} = \frac{1}{1 - .6 + .2} = 1.7 \qquad \text{(the multiplier when MPI = .2)}$$

on Toyotas rather than Fords. A change in foreign production changes the income of workers in foreign countries, but not the workers at home. Thus, the multiplier process is partly cut off.

How the Multiplier Depends on the MPI and the MPC

Table 26.7 shows how the multiplier can be computed with algebra in the case where the marginal propensity to consume is .6 and the marginal propensity to import is .2. The multiplier is reduced from 2.5 to about 1.7. Hence, making net exports respond to income affects the size of the multiplier significantly.

We can also show explicitly how the multiplier depends on the MPI along with the MPC. The derivation, which is much like that in Table 26.7, is shown in Table 26.8. The result is

$$\frac{\Delta Y}{\Delta G} = \frac{1}{1 - \text{MPC} + \text{MPI}}$$

For example, if MPC = .6 and MPI = .2, the multiplier is 1.7.

The Rounds of the Multiplier When Net Exports Depend on Income

Let us now follow the multiplier through the economy when net exports depend on income using the example of an increase in defense spending. Table 26.9 provides the numerical example.

Start with

$$\Delta Y = \Delta C + \Delta I + \Delta G + \Delta X$$

Assume that

$$\Delta I = 0$$

and that

$$\Delta C = \text{MPC} \times \Delta Y$$

and that

$$\Delta X = - \text{MPI} \times \Delta Y$$

Putting the above expressions together we get

$$\Delta Y = (\text{MPC} \times \Delta Y) + \Delta G - (\text{MPI} \times \Delta Y)$$

and solving for the change in Y we get

$$\frac{\Delta Y}{\Delta G} = \frac{1}{1 - \text{MPC} + \text{MPI}}$$

TABLE 26.8
Derivation of the Multiplier for Any MPC and MPI

We start with an increase in purchases of military equipment of $100 billion. This causes an increase in real GDP in the first round by the same amount as in Table 26.3, the case where net exports did not depend on income.

There is a difference in the second and later rounds, however. Those workers in the defense industries who are working more are going to spend more for clothes, cars, and other things. But now part of their increased spending falls on foreign goods, like Japanese cars. The increase in purchases on foreign goods lessens the increase in production in the United States because the higher demand is spread, for example, from Ford to Toyota. This lessens the increase in real GDP in the U.S. economy by $20 billion. Fewer workers in the U.S. automobile industry work longer hours or are hired when net exports respond to income because some of the increased spending goes abroad. Thus, at the end of the second round, real GDP has increased by $140 billion compared with $160 billion in Table 26.3. Note that in

Round	Change in Real GDP	Change in Consumption	Change in Net Exports	Cumulative Change in Real GDP
First round	100.000	0.000	0.000	100.000
Second round	40.000	60.000	−20.000	140.000
Third round	16.000	24.000	−8.000	156.000
Fourth round	6.400	9.600	−3.200	162.400
Fifth round	2.560	3.840	−1.280	164.960
.	.	.	.	.
.	.	.	.	.
.	.	.	.	.
After an infinite number of rounds	0.000	0.000	0.000	166.667

TABLE 26.9
Multiplier Rounds with Net Exports
(billions of dollars)

Rounds of the Multiplier

These two rows of photos illustrate the initial two rounds of the multiplier. The top photo shows the first round: An increase in government purchases leads to increased production of aircraft. The photos in the second row illustrate the second round: Defense workers, whose incomes rise, will increase their consumption at retail stores (left), but some of this increased spending is on goods imported from abroad (right). These two rows of photos correspond to the first two rows of Table 26.9, but the multiplier process continues on and on for many more rounds.

twin deficits: a term referring to a situation in which a government budget deficit and an international trade deficit occur simultaneously.

each round the effect on real GDP is reduced by the decrease in net exports. In the end, the increase in real GDP is about $167 billion, considerably less than the $250 billion in Table 26.3.

The Impact on the Trade Deficit

An implication of net exports depending on income is that a change in government purchases—or any other shift in the *AE* line—affects the trade surplus or deficit. Recall that there is a trade surplus if net exports are positive and a trade deficit if net exports are negative.

Consider what happens to the trade surplus or deficit when government spending is cut in an effort to reduce the budget deficit. When we lower government purchases, income is reduced. This reduction of income causes imports to fall and, because net exports is defined as exports less imports, it causes net exports to rise, which will reduce the trade deficit. If there is a trade surplus, then it will increase the trade surplus.

Note also that lower government purchases will lower the budget deficit, which is defined as government receipts less government spending. The simultaneous occurence of a budget deficit and a trade deficit is sometimes called **twin deficits.** A lower budget deficit brought on by lower government purchases will lower the trade deficit.

Does Investment Depend on Income Too?

In this section we have shown that net exports depend on income and examined the implications of this dependence. Now we have both consumption (*C*) and net exports (*X*) depending on income. But what about the other component of private spending, investment (*I*)? Doesn't investment depend on income too?

There are indeed several reasons why investment might depend on income. Recall that the purchases of new equipment and new factories used for production by businesses are included in investment. Businesses may be more willing to make such purchases if people's incomes are high and they can therefore expect to sell more products to people. Similarly, if people's incomes are low, businesses may be less willing to purchase new equipment because they expect that people will be spending less. Thus, investment, like consumption and net exports, probably depends on income, and many economists worry about this dependence when explaining economic fluctuations.

Incorporating the responsiveness of investment into the aggregate expenditure line would be no more difficult than incorporating the responsiveness of net exports, as we have done in this section. But doing so does not change the analysis in fundamental ways. The basic spending balance and multiplier story remains the same. For this reason, we do not formally incorporate the responsiveness of investment to income.

Review

- ▶ U.S. exports to other countries are not affected by U.S. income. But U.S. imports from other countries depend positively on U.S. income. Thus, net exports—exports less imports—depend negatively on the level of income.
- ▶ The aggregate expenditure line is flatter with net exports depending on income.

- ▶ When net exports respond to income, the multiplier is smaller because the changes in income lead to spending on foreign goods.
- ▶ The marginal propensity to import and the size of the multiplier are negatively related.

THE MULTIPLIER FOR A TAX CHANGE

Another government policy change in addition to increases or decreases in government purchases that can affect the economy in the short run is a change in taxes. There are many cases where government officials have cut taxes in order to increase real GDP. In the early days of his administration, for example, President Kennedy proposed tax cuts to increase real GDP and help the economy recover from a recession. What is the short-run impact on real GDP of a change in taxes? Suppose, for example, the newly elected president in December 2004 proposes a tax cut of $100 billion in the year 2005. What is the likely impact on real GDP?

Before assessing this impact, it is important to distinguish between a change in tax rates and a change in taxes, or tax revenue. The **tax rate** is the percentage of

tax rate: the percentage of income or the value of a good paid to the government in the form of taxes.

tax revenue: the total amount the government receives in the form of taxes; equals the tax rate times income (also simply called taxes).

your income that you are required to pay to the government. **Tax revenue** is the total amount the government gets. For example, if the tax rate is 20 percent and your income is $30,000, then the tax revenue the government gets from you is $6,000.

Changes in tax rates may affect people's incentive to work and, therefore, may raise or lower potential GDP. But changes in tax revenue—whether caused by a change in the tax rate or a refund or rebate of past taxes—can cause real GDP to depart from potential GDP in the short run. Changes in taxes have effects on people's income and, therefore, can affect their consumption. Our focus here is on the effects of changes in tax revenues on real GDP in the short run.

A change in tax revenue will affect disposable income. For example, a tax cut of $100 billion will increase disposable income by $100 billion throughout the economy. If people have more disposable income, their consumption will rise. According to the consumption function, consumption will rise by the marginal propensity to consume (MPC) times the increase in disposable income. Thus, in this example, if the MPC = .6, consumption will shift up by $60 billion. This is a shift up in consumption at every level of real GDP.

The effect of this upward shift in consumption can now be analyzed using the aggregate expenditure line and the 45-degree line. Figure 26.6 shows that the *AE* line will shift up by the MPC times the tax cut, or by $60 billion. It is an upward shift of the *AE* line because consumption is part of aggregate expenditure, and consumption shifts up at every level of real GDP.

The upward shift in the *AE* line has the same multiplier effect as the earlier shifts we considered. (To keep the algebra simple, we assume that net exports are unrelated to income, or MPI = 0. If the MPI were not zero, we would use the expression for the multiplier in the previous section.) The ratio of the increase in real GDP to the size of the upward shift in the *AE* line is given by $1/(1 - \text{MPC})$, just as before. Thus, the total effect on real GDP of the tax increase is

$$\text{Change in GDP} = \left(\frac{1}{1 - \text{MPC}}\right) \times \underbrace{\text{MPC} \times \text{change in taxes}}_{\text{Size of shift in } AE \text{ line}}$$

For example, if the MPC is .6 and the tax cut is $100 billion, then the impact on real GDP will be $2.5 \times .6 \times 100 = \$150$ billion.

Note that the impact on real GDP for the $100 billion tax cut is smaller than the impact of a $100 billion increase in government purchases. The reason is that the initial impact on the aggregate expenditure line is smaller: Only 60 percent of the $100 billion tax cut is spent by consumers, while 100 percent of the $100 billion government purchases increase is spent by government.

balanced budget multiplier: the ratio of the change in real GDP to a change in government purchases when the change in government purchases is matched by an equivalent change in taxes.

Because of the different impacts of taxes and spending, it is possible for the government to increase spending *and* tax revenue by the same magnitude and still increase real GDP. For example, suppose government purchases are increased by $100 billion and simultaneously taxes are raised by $100 billion so that the budget deficit neither rises or falls. According to our analysis, the spending increase will raise real GDP by $250 billion in the short run and the tax increase will lower GDP by $150 billion. The total increase in real GDP is thus $100 billion even though the budget deficit is unchanged. The **balanced budget multiplier** is defined as the ratio of the change in real GDP to a change in government purchases when that change is matched by a change in taxes.

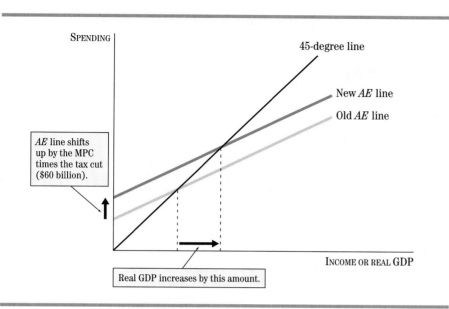

SPENDING

45-degree line

New *AE* line

Old *AE* line

AE line shifts up by the MPC times the tax cut ($60 billion).

INCOME OR REAL GDP

Real GDP increases by this amount.

FIGURE 26.6
The Multiplier for a Tax Cut
A reduction in tax payments will raise disposable income at every level of real GDP. This will raise consumption and the *AE* line at every level of real GDP by the MPC times the tax cut. If required tax payments are reduced by $100 billion, the *AE* line will shift up by $60 billion. Then the multiplier goes to work.

Review

▶ An increase in taxes reduces disposable income and thereby shifts the consumption function down. The downward shift in the consumption function equals the marginal propensity to consume times the tax increase.

▶ A cut in taxes works in reverse to raise consumption and real GDP.

▶ The total impact of a change in taxes on real GDP is less than the impact of a change in government purchases.

▶ It is essential to distinguish between taxes, or tax revenue, and tax rates. Tax revenue equals the tax rate times income. Tax rate changes affect potential GDP.

THE FORWARD-LOOKING CONSUMPTION MODEL

Our analysis of the multiplier shows that it depends on the MPC. One reason there is uncertainty about the size of the multiplier is that the MPC seems to change in certain situations. Although the consumption function with a constant MPC gives an adequate prediction of people's behavior in many situations, it sometimes works very poorly. For example, the MPC turned out to be very small when taxes were cut in 1975; people saved almost the entire increase in disposable income that resulted from the tax cut. However, the MPC turned out to be very large for the tax cuts in 1981, only six years later; people saved very little of the increase in disposable income in that case.

forward-looking consumption model: a model that explains consumer behavior by assuming that people anticipate future income when deciding on consumption spending today.

permanent income model: a type of forward-looking consumption model that assumes that people distinguish between temporary changes in their income and permanent changes in their income; the permanent changes have a larger effect on consumption.

life-cycle model: a type of forward-looking consumption model that assumes that people base their consumption decisions on their expected lifetime income rather than on their current income.

The **forward-looking consumption model** explains these changes in the MPC and identifies part of the uncertainty in the MPC. The forward-looking consumption model was developed independently and in different ways by two Nobel Prize-winning economists, Milton Friedman and Franco Modigliani. Friedman's version is called the **permanent income model,** and Modigliani's version is called the **life-cycle model.**

Consumption Smoothing

The forward-looking model starts with the idea that people attempt to look ahead to their future income prospects when deciding how much to consume. They do not simply consider their current income. For example, if a young medical doctor decides to take a year off from a high-paying suburban medical practice to do community service at little or no pay, that doctor's income will fall below the poverty line for a year. But the doctor is unlikely to cut consumption to a fraction of the poverty level of income. Even if the doctor were young enough to have little savings, borrowing or taking out a home equity loan would be a way to keep consumption high and even buy an occasional luxury item. The doctor is basing consumption decisions on expected income for several years—making an assessment of a more permanent income, or a life-cycle income—not just for one year.

There are many other examples. Farmers in poor rural areas of Asia try to save something in good years so that they will be able to maintain their consumption in bad years. They try not to consume a fixed fraction of their income. In many cases the saving is in storable farm goods like rice.

consumption smoothing: the idea that, although their incomes fluctuate, people try to stabilize consumption spending from year to year.

As these examples indicate, instead of allowing their consumption to vary with their income, which may be quite erratic, most people engage in **consumption smoothing** from year to year.

The MPC for Permanent versus Temporary Changes in Income

Once people estimate their future income prospects, they try to maintain their consumption at the same level from year to year. If their income temporarily falls, they do not cut their consumption by much; *the MPC is very small—maybe about .05—in the case of a temporary change in income.* But if they find out their income will increase permanently, they will increase their consumption a lot; *the MPC is very large—maybe .95—in the case of a permanent change in income.* For example, if a new fertilizer doubles permanently the rice yield of a rice farmer's land, we can expect that the farmer's consumption will about double.

The difference between the forward-looking consumption model and the simple consumption function is illustrated in Figure 26.7. In the right panel of Figure 26.7, income is expected to follow a typical life-cycle pattern: lower when young, higher when middle-aged, and very low when retired. However, consumption does not follow these ups and downs; it is flat. The left panel shows the opposite extreme of the standard consumption function with a fixed MPC. In that case people live well when middle-aged but have a tough time when young or old.

liquidity constraint: the situation in which people cannot borrow to smooth their consumption spending when their income is low.

Occasionally some people are prevented from completely smoothing their income because they have a **liquidity constraint;** that is, they cannot get a loan to consume more than their income. Such liquidity constraints do not appear to be important enough in the economy as a whole to thwart the forward-looking model completely. Of course not all people try to smooth their income; some people like to go on binges, spending everything, even if the binge is followed by a long lull.

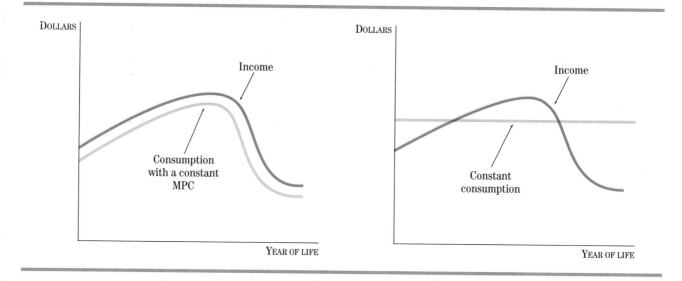

FIGURE 26.7
Two Extreme Forms of
Consumption Behavior
The right panel shows the future
outlook of a young person or family
described by the forward-looking
model of consumption. The left
panel shows the outlook of a young
family with a constant MPC. The
path of expected income (green
line) is the same in both cases.

Tests and Applications of the Forward-Looking Model

Observations on consumption and income for the economy as a whole indicate that
the forward-looking model significantly improves our understanding of observed
changes in the MPC. For example, economists have demonstrated that the measured MPC for the economy as a whole is lower for temporary changes in income
that occur during recessions and booms than for more permanent increases in
income that occur as potential GDP grows over time. Studies of thousands of individual families over time show that the individual MPC for temporary changes in
income is about one-third of the MPC for permanent changes in income.

Permanent versus Temporary Tax Cuts

The forward-looking model is also the most promising explanation for the low
MPC during the tax cut of 1975. That tax cut was explicitly temporary, a one-time
tax rebate, good for only one year. In contrast, the tax cut in the early 1980s was
explicitly permanent and was expected to apply for many years into the future. The
MPC was large in this case.

The effects of a permanent versus a temporary tax cut are illustrated using the
aggregate expenditure line in Figure 26.8. The left panel shows the effects of a permanent tax cut. With a permanent tax cut, the MPC is high, so the shift in the
aggregate expenditure line (the MPC times the tax cut) is big and the multiplier is
big. For a temporary tax cut, shown in the right panel, the MPC is low, the shift in
the aggregate expenditure line is small, and the multiplier is small. In estimating the
effects of various tax proposals on the economy, economic forecasters take these
changes in the MPC into account.

Anticipating Future Tax Cuts or Increases

The forward-looking model changes our estimate of the impact of changes in taxes
that are expected to occur in the future. For example, if people are certain of a tax
cut in the future, they may begin to increase their consumption right away, before

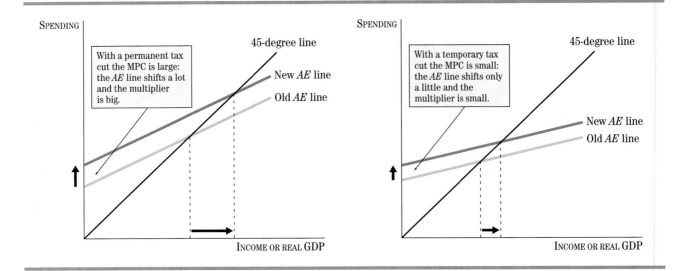

FIGURE 26.8
A Temporary versus a Permanent Tax Cut

The left diagram is for a permanent tax cut. Because people expect larger incomes over the long haul, the MPC is large, closer to 1. The right diagram is for a temporary tax cut. The MPC is small because people's long-term income has not changed much.

rational expectations assumption: the assumption that people forecast the future no better or no worse than economic forecasters.

the tax decreases. In this case the MPC is technically huge, because consumption increases with little or no observed change in current income. Conversely, they may reduce their consumption in anticipation of a tax increase.

It is difficult to know how large these effects are because we do not observe people's expectations of the future. Estimates based on the assumption that people forecast the future no better or no worse than economic forecasters—this is the **rational expectations assumption**—suggest that the effects are large and significant.

In situations where the expectations effects are obvious, we do see an impact. For example, in December 1992, after the 1992 presidential election when a tax increase became more likely, there was evidence that many people who could do so shifted their reported income for tax purposes from 1993 to 1992. But whether people held back their consumption in anticipation of future tax increases is difficult to say. In any case, because people's behavior is affected by their expectations of the future, attempts to estimate the impact of a policy proposal like a change in taxes need to take these expectations into account.

Review

▶ The forward-looking consumption model helps explain why the MPC is sometimes large and sometimes small. It enables policymakers to better assess the impact of proposed policy changes.

▶ Most people try to smooth their consumption over time. They respond to expectations of future income as well as to current income when making consumption decisions.

▶ The MPC is smaller for temporary changes in income than for permanent changes in income. Hence, the multiplier for a temporary tax cut is less than for a permanent tax cut.

▶ Anticipations of future tax changes are also a factor in consumption decisions. Although expectations are difficult to measure, economists predicting the effects of policy changes must include the expectations of individuals and firms about the future.

CONCLUSION

In this chapter we have shown how to find the size of the first step real GDP takes as it departs from potential GDP in the short run in response to several different events. The events we have described are increases or decreases in government purchases and increases or decreases in taxes. But the same approach can be used for anything that shifts the aggregate expenditure line: a change in investment, a change in net exports, or a shift in the consumption function.

The multiplier is the most common way economists describe how much real GDP changes in response to all these events. The size of the multiplier depends on the marginal propensity to consume. The size of the multiplier is uncertain because the marginal propensity to consume is uncertain. The forward-looking consumption model is an attempt to improve on the consumption function in order to reduce this uncertainty and better explain the departures of real GDP from potential GDP.

In this chapter we also allowed for net exports to depend on income, and in doing so brought key international factors into the theory of the fluctuations of real GDP that we have been developing.

But the theory of economic fluctuations is not yet finished. We have not yet begun to explain how and why real GDP returns to potential GDP in the long run. Our focus has remained on the short run in this chapter. The level of real GDP that gives spending balance is not a final equilibrium; it is not the end of the story. As explained in the next two chapters, spending balance itself automatically changes over time in response to economic forces. It is in these chapters that our story becomes dynamic—and where interest rates and inflation begin to play a formal role.

KEY POINTS

1. The multiplier can be found in three ways: graphs with the 45-degree line, the aggregate expenditure line, and spending balance; algebra using the consumption function; and numerical summation of the successive rounds of spending and real GDP changes. All three ways show that the size of the multiplier is positively related to the marginal propensity to consume (MPC).

2. The formula for the multiplier is $1/(1 - \text{MPC})$ or $1/\text{MPS}$, where MPS is the marginal propensity to save.

3. Uncertainty about the size of the multiplier can be traced to uncertainty about the size of the MPC.

4. Imports are positively related to income, and net exports are negatively related to income.

5. The size of the multiplier is negatively related to the marginal propensity to import.

6. The multiplier for tax changes is less than the multiplier for spending changes; part of a tax cut is saved.

7. The forward-looking consumption model explains why the MPC is low in some cases and high in others. It helps economists deal with the uncertainty in the multiplier.

8. The forward-looking consumption model also implies that anticipated changes in taxes affect consumption and are a further reason for uncertainty about the MPC. Although such effects have been observed, it is difficult to estimate their size in advance.

9. The rational expectations assumption, which suggests that people forecast the future no better or no worse than economic forecasters, is one method to make such estimates. With this assumption, the effects of anticipated tax changes on consumption are quite high.

KEY TERMS

multiplier
marginal propensity to save (MPS)
marginal propensity to import (MPI)
twin deficits
tax rate

tax revenue
balanced budget multiplier
forward-looking consumption model
permanent income model
life-cycle model

consumption smoothing
liquidity constraint
rational expectations assumption

QUESTIONS FOR REVIEW

1. What are the three ways to find the multiplier?

2. Why is the size of the multiplier positively related to the MPC?

3. To what degree is there uncertainty about the size of the multiplier for government purchases as judged by different economic forecasters?

4. Why is the size of the multiplier negatively related to the marginal propensity to import?

5. Why do imports depend on income while exports do not?

6. Why does real GDP change by a larger amount from changes in government purchases than from tax changes?

7. How does the forward-looking consumption model differ from the consumption function with a fixed MPC?

8. Why is the MPC for a temporary tax cut less than the MPC for a permanent tax cut? Are there examples that prove the point?

9. What is consumption smoothing?

10. Why do changes in future taxes that are anticipated in advance affect consumption?

PROBLEMS

1. Using an aggregate expenditure/45-degree diagram show the following situations:
   a) The multiplier is greater than 1 and rises if the marginal propensity to consume rises.
   b) The multiplier for an economy when net exports respond to income is smaller than the multiplier for an economy when net exports do not resond to income.
   c) An increase in the budget deficit will increase the trade deficit.
Be sure to label the axes and lines and explain briefly the economic reasoning that underlies your argument.

2. The following table shows real GDP and imports in billions of dollars for an economy.

Real GDP or Income	Imports
2,000	400
3,000	500
4,000	600
5,000	700
6,000	800
7,000	900

Suppose that exports are equal to $700 billion.
   a) Construct a graph showing how imports depend on income.
   b) Construct a graph showing how net exports depend on income.
   c) If the level of real GDP that occurs at spending balance is $6,000 billion, will there by a trade surplus or deficit? What type of policy regarding government purchases would bring the trade deficit or trade surplus closer to zero?
   d) If the marginal propensity to consume is .6, what is the size of the multiplier?

3. The following numerical example shows how an economy's consumption and net exports depends on income:

Real GDP or Income	Consumption	Net Exports
100	80	30
200	160	20
300	240	10
400	320	0
500	400	-10
600	480	-20
700	560	-30

   a) Find the marginal propensity to consume, the marginal propensity to save, the marginal propensity to import, and the multiplier.
   b) Suppose that $I = 60$ and $G = 50$ and taxes are zero. Find aggregate expenditures for each level of income listed in the table. What is the level of real GDP, consumption, and net exports where spending balance occurs? Is there a trade deficit or a trade surplus?
   c) Suppose that government purchases rise by 10. What happens to net exports?

4. Suppose that the marginal propensity to consume in a closed economy is estimated to be .6 but there is a 10 percent margin of error on either side. In other words, the MPC could be anywhere between .54 and .66. In what range will the multiplier lie? Quantify the range of impacts on real GDP of a $100 million increase in G. Do the same when the margin of error is 20 percent on either side of .6.

5. Suppose the marginal propensity to consume is .9 and that when income is zero, consumption is $100 billion. Assume $I = 200$, $G = 50$, $X = 0$, and $T = 50$.
   a) What would be the effect on income of a simultaneous increase in G and T of $10 billion? Why would income change at all?

b) Derive a multiplier that works for every case where the budget is balanced (that is, $G = T$).

6. Suppose Joe spends every additional dollar of income that he receives.

a) What is Joe's marginal propensity to consume? What does his consumption function look like?

b) Suppose that Jane spends half of each additional dollar of income that she receives. What is the slope of Jane's consumption function?

c) What differences in Joe's and Jane's incomes or jobs might explain the differences in their MPCs?

7. Plot values of the multiplier for different MPCs ranging from 0 to 1, putting the MPC on the horizontal axis and the multiplier on the vertical axis. What does it mean if the MPC is zero? What happens to the multiplier as the MPC approaches 1?

8. Given the following information, calculate the level of real GDP, which results in spending balance in the economy (T is taxes or tax revenue).

$$C = 100 + .7 (Y - T)$$
$$I = 100$$
$$G = 200$$
$$T = 200$$
$$X = 50 - .1Y$$

a) What is the marginal propensity to consume in this example? What is the marginal propensity to save? What is the marginal propensity to import? How does the marginal propensity to import affect the slope of the AE line, compared to the same model without imports or exports?

b) What is the multiplier? Explain why this multiplier is smaller than when the marginal propensity to import is zero.

c) Is there a trade deficit or surplus?

d) Verify that saving equals investment plus net exports.

e) Suppose the net export equation is $X = 100 - .1Y$. Calculate a new equilibrium level of spending balance. Did this change affect the multiplier?

9. This problem examines what happens when taxes depend on income.

a) Use the equation $T = 100 + .2Y$ for taxes in the previous problem and determine the multiplier. What is the level of real GDP at spending balance now?

b) Suppose the government implements a new tax system with $T = 150 + .1Y$, rather than the one in part (a). What happens to the multiplier? What is the new level of real GDP at spending balance? Is the government budget in surplus or deficit?

10. Consider the following economy.

$$C = 100 + .8 (Y - T)$$
$$I = 100 + .1Y$$
$$X = 50 - .2Y$$
$$G = 200$$
$$T = 200$$

a) Solve for real GDP at spending balance. (Note that investment as well as consumption and net exports is responsive to income.)

b) Calculate national saving.

c) Now suppose that people start saving more of their income. In particular, the consumption function shifts down to $C = 25 + .8 (Y - T)$. What is the new level of real GDP? Calculate national saving now. How does this compare to your answer to part (b)?

d) Explain why national saving has declined despite the efforts of individuals to increase saving.

11. Each month a certain fraction of employees' pay is withheld and sent to the government as part of what is owed for personal income taxes. If the taxes owed for the year are less than the amount withheld, then a refund is sent early in the following year. Otherwise additional taxes must be paid by April 15. In 1992 the amount of income *withheld* was lowered by about $10 billion to increase consumption and real GDP and thereby speed recovery from the 1990–1991 recession. However, the amount of taxes owed was not changed. Discuss why the impact of this 1992 change would be smaller than a cut in taxes of $10 billion during 1992.

12. The following cartoon presents a puzzle: Increased consumption might be good for the economy and bad for the economy. By distinguishing between the long run (e.g., Chapter 22) and the short run in this chapter, explain this puzzle.

Aggregate Demand and Price Adjustment

Why do recessions end? Why do booms end? Are there economic forces at work in market economies like that of the United States that bring real GDP back down toward potential GDP after a boom? Do these same forces work in a recession to halt the decline in real GDP and start a recovery, the period of relatively rapid growth that brings real GDP back up toward potential GDP? If such forces do exist, how fast can we expect them to work? Will recessions naturally end in one year or three years? Will recovery take three years or five years? These questions are important for economic policymaking.

To answer these questions, we need to construct an economic fluctuations model—a simplified description of how the whole economy adjusts over time after it moves away from potential GDP in a boom or in a recession. The purpose of this chapter is to construct, in graphical form, such an economic fluctuations model.

Although the economic fluctuations model pertains to the whole economy, it is analogous to the supply and demand model (Chapter 3), in which we used a graph to explain the behavior of particular markets such as the peanut market. Just as we presented the supply and demand model in a graph consisting of three elements:

▶ a *demand curve,*

▶ a *supply curve,* and

▶ an *equilibrium* at the intersection of the two curves,

we present the economic fluctuations model in a graph consisting of three elements:

▶ an *aggregate demand/inflation (ADI) curve,*

▶ a *price adjustment (PA) line,* and

▶ an *equilibrium* at the intersection of the curve and line.

The economic fluctuations model is based on ideas previously developed in this book. For example, in explaining the model we will use the idea that consumption, investment, and net exports depend negatively on the interest rate (Chapter 22), as well as the idea of spending balance (Chapter 25). We will also use observations of actual economic fluctuations presented in Chapter 19. One key observation—that fluctuations in inflation are closely associated with fluctuations in real GDP—is critical to this analysis. We observed in Chapter 19 that inflation typically increases just before a recession and subsides during and immediately after a recession as the

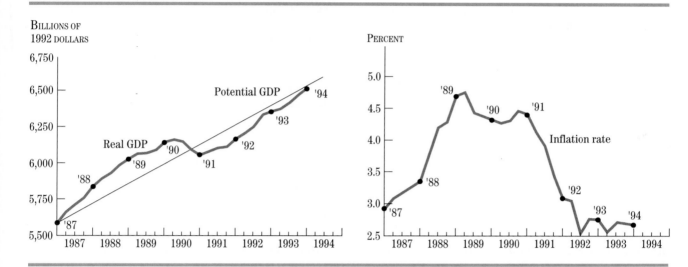

FIGURE 27.1

Two Time-Series Graphs Showing Real GDP and Inflation from 1987 to 1994

The economic fluctuation from 1987 through 1994 is shown in these diagrams. Inflation and real GDP appear to move together.

recovery gets started. You can see this in Figure 27.1 for the case of the economic fluctuation that occurred from 1987 to 1994. The graph on the left shows real GDP fluctuating around potential GDP. The graph on the right shows inflation. Notice that in 1988 and 1989, when real GDP is above potential GDP (before the recession begins), the inflation rate is rising; during and after the recession, when real GDP is less than potential GDP (from 1991 to 1994), the inflation rate is declining.

Figure 27.2 summarizes this relationship, enabling us to monitor the movements of real GDP and inflation over time. Real GDP is shown on the horizontal axis and the inflation rate is shown on the vertical axis. Each dot on the graph corresponds to a pair of observations from the two time-series graphs in Figure 27.1. When the economy is in a boom or recovering from a recession, the points in Figure 27.2 are moving to the right. In a recession, the points are moving to the left. Increases in inflation are upward, while decreases in inflation are downward. The arrows drawn between the dots in Figure 27.2 show these movements. Follow the path of the arrows starting in 1987 and going all the way to 1994. For this period, the arrows form a circular pattern starting with low inflation (1987), moving toward higher inflation (1988–1989), and then moving into recession (1990–1991) and recovery (1992–1994).

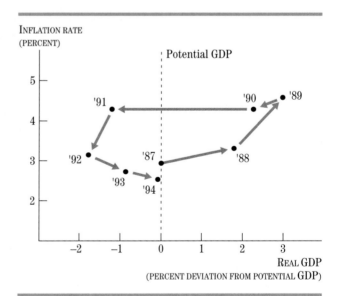

FIGURE 27.2

Real GDP and Inflation Movements in a Single Diagram

The dots represent real GDP and inflation rate points from Figure 27.1. Recessions are shown as leftward movements, and booms and recoveries as rightward movements.

Source: U.S. Department of Commerce.

The economic fluctuations model we develop in this chapter will help explain the pattern of these dots. We will do this much in the same way that we explained the pattern of price and quantity observations in the peanut or other microeconomic markets using supply and demand curves. In the microeconomic supply and demand model, the intersection of the *demand curve* and the *supply curve* gives us the *equilibrium* price and quantity. In the economic fluctuations model, the intersection of the

aggregate demand/inflation (ADI) curve and *the price adjustment (PA) line*—in a graph with the same axes used in Figure 27.2—gives us *equilibrium* real GDP and inflation.

We will start our construction of the economic fluctuations model by deriving the aggregate demand/inflation curve and then the price adjustment line. We will then show how their intersection determines real GDP and inflation.

THE AGGREGATE DEMAND/ INFLATION CURVE

aggregate demand/inflation (*ADI*) curve: a line showing a negative relationship between inflation and the aggregate quantity of goods and services demanded at that inflation rate.

The **aggregate demand/inflation (*ADI*) curve** is a relationship between two economic variables: real GDP and the inflation rate. Real GDP is usually measured as percentage deviation from potential GDP, and the inflation rate is usually measured as the annual percentage change in the overall price level from year to year. Figure 27.3 shows an aggregate demand/inflation curve for the United States. Observe that inflation is measured on the vertical axis, that real GDP is measured on the horizontal axis, and that we have drawn a vertical dashed line to mark the point where real GDP equals potential GDP. The aggregate demand/inflation curve shows different combinations of real GDP and inflation. It is downward-sloping from left to right because real GDP is negatively related to inflation along the curve. The term *aggregate demand* is used because we interpret the movements of real GDP away from potential GDP as due to fluctuations in the sum (aggregate) of the demand for consumption, investment, net exports, and government purchases.

Why does the aggregate demand/inflation curve slope downward? We will answer this question and derive the curve in three steps. First, we show that there is a negative relationship between the interest rate and real GDP. Second, we show that there is a positive relationship between inflation and the interest rate. Third, we show that these two relationships imply that there is a negative relationship between real GDP and inflation, and that relationship is the aggregate demand/inflation curve. The following schematic chart shows how the three steps fit together.

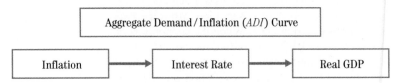

Interest Rates and Real GDP

Consumption, investment, and net exports are all components of aggregate expenditure that are negatively related to the interest rate. Combining these components provides an explanation of the negative relationship between real GDP and the interest

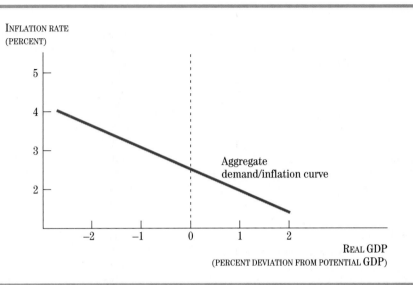

FIGURE 27.3
The Aggregate Demand/Inflation Curve

The aggregate demand/inflation curve shows that higher inflation and real GDP are negatively related.

rate. The negative effect of the interest rate on investment, net exports, and consumption is no different from the one discussed in Chapter 22 (pages 596-601). If you have already studied that chapter, the next few pages will serve as a brief review.

Investment

Investment is the component of aggregate expenditure that is probably most sensitive to the interest rate. Recall that part of investment is the purchase of new equipment or a new factory by a business firm. Many firms must borrow funds to pay for such investments. Higher interest rates make such borrowing more costly. Hence, businesses that are thinking about buying a new machine and need to borrow funds will be less inclined to purchase such an investment good if interest rates are higher. The additional profits the firm might expect to earn from purchasing a photocopier or truck are more likely to be lower than the interest costs on the loan if the interest rate is high. Thus, higher interest rates reduce investment spending by businesses. Also, remember that part of investment is the purchase of new houses. Most people need to take out a mortgage in order to buy a house. Like any loan, the mortgage has an interest rate, and higher interest rates make mortgages more costly. Hence, with higher interest rates fewer people take out mortgages and buy new houses. Spending for new housing declines.

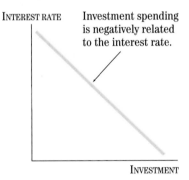

The same reasoning works to show why lower interest rates will increase investment spending: Lower interest rates reduce the cost of borrowing and make investment more attractive to firms and households.

To summarize, both business investment and housing investment decline when the interest rate rises, and they increase when the interest rate falls. At any time there are some firms or households deciding whether to buy a new machine or a new house, and they are going to be less inclined to buy such things when the interest rate is higher.

Net Exports

The negative relationship between net exports and the interest rate requires a somewhat more involved explanation than investment. The relationship exists because higher interest rates in the United States tend to lead to a higher dollar exchange rate and, in turn, a higher exchange rate reduces net exports.

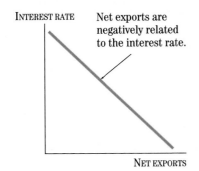

INTEREST RATE   Net exports are negatively related to the interest rate.

NET EXPORTS

A higher interest rate in the United States compared with other countries raises the exchange rate because it increases the demand for U.S. dollar bank accounts and other assets that pay interest. That increased demand bids up the price of dollars; hence, the exchange rate—the price of dollars—rises. Now, with a higher exchange rate, net exports will be lower because U.S.-produced exports become more expensive to foreigners, who must pay a higher price for dollars, and imported foreign goods become cheaper for Americans, who can get more foreign goods for higher-priced dollars. With exports falling and imports rising, net exports—exports less imports—must fall. In sum, higher interest rates reduce net exports.

The same reasoning works for lower interest rates as well. If the interest rate falls in the United States, then U.S. dollar bank accounts are less attractive compared with other countries such as Germany or Japan. This bids down the price of dollars, and the exchange rate falls. Now, with a lower exchange rate, net exports will be higher because U.S.-produced exports are less expensive to foreigners and imported foreign goods are more expensive for Americans. With exports rising and imports falling, net exports must rise. Thus, lower interest rates increase net exports.

To summarize, there is a negative relationship between the interest rate and the exchange rate that works through the exchange rate as follows:

Interest Rate	Exchange Rate	Net Exports
up ⟶	up ⟶	down
down ⟶	down ⟶	up

If the interest rate goes up, then the exchange rate goes up, causing net exports to go down. If the interest rate goes down, then the exchange rate goes down, causing net exports to go up.

Consumption

We have shown that two of the components of aggregate expenditure—investment and net exports—are sensitive to the interest rate. What about consumption?

Although consumption is probably less sensitive to the interest rate than the other components, there is some evidence that higher interest rates encourage people to save a larger fraction of their income. As explained in Chapter 22, higher interest rates encourage people to save, because they earn more on their savings. Because more saving means less consumption, this implies that consumption is negatively related to the interest rate. However, most economists feel that the effect of interest rates on consumption is much less than on investment and net exports.

Spending Balance

To summarize the discussion thus far, investment, net exports, and consumption are all negatively related to the interest rate. The overall effect of a change in interest rates on real GDP can now be assessed.

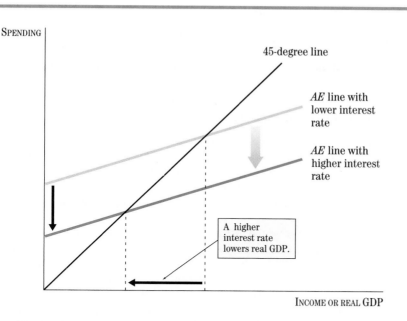

FIGURE 27.4
The Interest Rate, Spending Balance, and Real GDP
A higher interest rate shifts the *AE* line down because consumption, investment, and net exports depend negatively on the interest rate. Thus, real GDP declines with a higher interest rate. Conversely, a lower interest rate raises real GDP.

Figure 27.4 shows the 45-degree line and two different aggregate expenditure (*AE*) lines corresponding to two different interest rates. Higher interest rates shift down the *AE* line because a higher interest rate lowers investment, net exports, and consumption, which are all part of aggregate expenditure.

Observe how the downward shift of the *AE* line leads to a new point of spending balance. The intersection of the *AE* line with the 45-degree line occurs at a lower level of real GDP. Note that real GDP is lower not only because the higher interest rate lowers investment, net exports, and consumption, but also because a decline in income will lower consumption further. Real GDP declines by the amount shown on the horizontal axis, which is larger than the downward shift in the *AE* line. *Thus, an increase in the interest rate lowers real GDP.*

What about a decline in the interest rate? A lower interest rate will raise the *AE* line. In that case, the *AE* line would shift up, and the point of spending balance at the intersection with the 45-degree line would be at a higher level of real GDP. *Thus, a decrease in the interest rate raises real GDP.*

In sum, we have shown that there is a negative relationship between the interest rate and real GDP.

Keep in mind that the *real* interest rate is a better measure of the effect of interest rates on investment, net exports, and consumption than the *nominal* interest rate because it corrects for inflation. Recall from Chapter 19 that the *real* interest rate equals the stated, or *nominal,* interest rate (on loans or mortgages) minus the expected inflation rate. For example, if the nominal interest rate is 13 percent and inflation has been at 10 percent and is expected to remain there, the real interest rate is 3 percent. When inflation is low and stable, the real and nominal interest rates do not differ much from each other. But when inflation rates are high, it is important to look at the real interest rate when examining the impact of interest rates on real GDP.

Real interest rate =

nominal interest rate − **expected inflation rate.**

Interest Rates and Inflation

Now that we have seen why interest rates affect real GDP, let us proceed to the second step in our analysis. We want to show why a rise in inflation will increase the interest rate and thereby lower real GDP, or why a decline in inflation will decrease the interest rate and thereby raise real GDP.

Central Bank Interest Rate Policy

The easiest way to see why the interest rate rises when the inflation rate increases is to examine the behavior of the central bank. We discussed the U.S. central bank—the Fed—in Chapter 24. The Fed and central banks in other countries typically follow policies in which they respond to an increase in the inflation rate by raising the interest rate. By far the most widely followed and analyzed decision by the Fed is its interest rate decision.

Why does the Fed raise the interest rate when the inflation rate rises? The inflation rate is ultimately the responsibility of the Fed, and the goal of controlling inflation requires that the central bank raise the interest rate when the inflation rate rises. Suppose that the economy starts into a boom and inflation starts to rise. If the central bank takes actions to raise the interest rate, then the higher interest rate will slow the growth of real GDP and cut off the boom. If the rise in the interest rate is high enough and soon enough, cutting off the boom in real GDP will then reduce inflationary pressures and bring inflation back down again.

The goal of controlling inflation also requires that the central bank lower the interest rate when inflation falls. Suppose that the economy starts to slow down and inflation starts to fall. If the central bank takes action to reduce the interest rate, then the lower interest rate will increase the growth of real GDP. If the decline in the interest rate is large enough and soon enough, the increase in real GDP will end the slowdown and the downward pressure on inflation will be cut off.

The data in Table 27.1 illustrate these actions of the Fed. For each inflation rate, an interest rate decision by the Fed is shown. For example, when inflation is 2 percent, the interest rate decision is 4 percent. When inflation rises to 4 percent, the interest rate decision by the Fed is 7 percent. Thus, when inflation rises, the central bank raises the interest rate, and when inflation falls, the central bank lowers the interest rate.

Note that the interest rate rises more than inflation rises in Table 27.1. The reason is related to the distinction between the nominal interest rate and the real interest rate. If an increase in the interest rate is to reduce real GDP, then the real interest rate must rise because real GDP depends negatively on the real interest rate, as described in the previous section. If the nominal interest rate rises by more than the expected inflation rate, then the real interest rate will rise and real GDP should decline. Thus, for the interest rate decisions in the table, the nominal interest rate rises by more than inflation as a way to get the real interest rate to rise. If, instead, the nominal interest rate rose by less than the increase in the inflation rate, then the real interest rate would not rise; rather, it would fall.

The behavior of the central bank illustrated in Table 27.1 is called a **monetary policy rule** because it describes the systematic response of the interest rate to inflation as decided by the central bank. For a given level of real GDP the central bank, as a rule, takes actions to raise the interest rate when inflation rises. Keep in mind that the central bank does not set interest rates by decree or by direct control. Governments sometimes do control the price of goods; for example, some city governments control the rents on apartments. The central bank does not apply such

●————————————

TABLE 27.1

A Numerical Example of Central Bank Interest Rate Policy

Inflation Rate	Interest Rate Decision
0.0	1.0
1.0	2.5
2.0	4.0
3.0	5.5
4.0	7.0
5.0	8.5
6.0	10.0
7.0	11.5
8.0	13.0

monetary policy rule: a description of how much the interest rate or other instruments of monetary policy respond to inflation or other measures of the state of the economy.

controls to the interest rate. Rather it enters the markets in which short-term interest rates are determined by the usual forces of supply and demand. In the United States, the short-term interest rate the Fed focuses on is the interest rate on overnight loans between banks. It is called the **federal funds rate,** and the overnight interbank loan market is called the federal funds market. When the Fed wants to lower this interest rate, it supplies funds to this market. When it wants to raise the interest rate, it withdraws funds. This process is identical to the one the Fed uses to adjust bank reserves, as discussed in Chapter 24: It can supply funds by buying bonds and withdraw funds by selling bonds, a process that is illustrated with examples and case studies in Chapter 30.

federal funds rate: the interest rate on overnight loans between banks that the Federal Reserve influences by changing the supply of funds (bank reserves) in the market.

A Graph of the Response of the Interest Rate to Inflation

Figure 27.5 represents the monetary policy rule graphically, using the information in Table 27.1. When the inflation rate rises, the nominal interest rate rises along the purple upward-sloping line. When the inflation rate declines, the nominal interest rate declines. The nominal interest rate must rise by more than the inflation rate if the *real* interest rate is to rise when inflation rises; this requires that the slope of the monetary policy rule line in Figure 27.5 be greater than 1. We illustrate that the slope is greater than 1 by drawing in a dashed line with a slope of 1. Observe that the dashed line intersects the vertical axis at 2 percentage points for the interest rate. Thus, for points along this dashed line, the difference between the nominal interest rate and the inflation rate is 2 percent; that is, the real interest rate is a constant 2 percent.

target inflation rate: the central bank's goal for the average rate of inflation over the long run.

Most central banks have a **target inflation rate,** the inflation rate that the central bank tries to maintain on average over the long run. Because of various shocks to the economy, the central bank cannot control the inflation rate perfectly; sometimes the inflation rate will rise above the target inflation rate, and sometimes the inflation rate will fall below the target inflation rate. Some central banks, such as the Bank of England and the Reserve Bank of New Zealand, have explicit inflation targets. Other central banks, like the Fed or the German Bundesbank, have implicit target inflation rates that are not explicitly announced, but which can be assessed by observing central bank decisions over time. The target inflation rate for the Fed and the Bundesbank appears to be about 2 percent.

FIGURE 27.5
A Monetary Policy Rule
The monetary policy rule shows that the Fed lets the interest rate rise when inflation rises and lets the interest rate fall when inflation falls. The Fed's inflation target is assumed to be 2 percent. The dashed line has a slope of 1 and corresponds to a real interest rate of 2 percent. (The monetary policy rule is drawn using the information in Table 27.1.)

This 2 percent target inflation rate is shown in Figure 27.5. Observe that if the real interest rate is 2 percent, as in Figure 27.5, this target inflation rate implies that the average value of the nominal interest rate (the federal funds rate) will be about 4 percent. When the actual inflation rate rises above the target inflation rate of 2 percent, the Fed will raise the federal funds rate above the target of 4 percent.

A Simplifying Assumption

The behavior of the central bank described in this section provides the easiest explanation of the response of interest rates to inflation; but it is not the only possible explanation. Indeed, examples discussed in Chapter 30 show that the general upward-sloping relationship in Figure 27.5, which we call the monetary policy rule, is common to many different types of monetary policies, including policies in which the

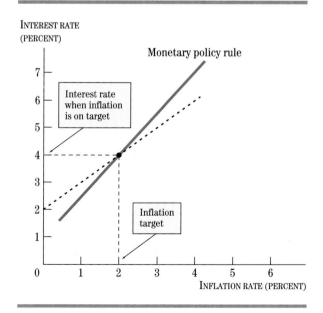

Reading the News About the Fed

This front-page *New York Times* headline illustrates the great importance attached to central bank policy. The news article describes how the Fed took actions on March 25, 1997, to increase the interest rate because of concerns that inflation was rising. Similar headlines appeared in most of the newspapers in the country. The Fed decision was also widely reported on television and radio. In this case, the interest rate rose to 5.5 percent; it was 5.25 percent through much of 1996 and early 1997.

Because the rise in the inflation rate that brought about the Fed's interest rate decision was small, some analysts disagreed with the Fed's decision.

Observe how many of the terms and concepts used in this article are discussed in this chapter: Federal Reserve, federal funds rate, effect of interest rates on investment and consumption, goals of the Fed in restraining inflation, overnight loans between banks.

Note also how the article sounds as if the Fed controls interest rates by decree. In reality, the Fed does not literally set interest rates. Rather, it buys and sells government bonds and thereby influences the interest rate in the market.

Source: From " Federal Reserve Lifts a Key Rate; First Rise Since '95," *The New York Times,* March 26, 1997. Copyright © 1997 by the New York Times Company. Reprinted by permission.

FEDERAL RESERVE LIFTS A KEY RATE; FIRST RISE SINCE '95

The Federal Reserve raised its short-term interest rate target—the Federal funds rate—for the first time since Feb. 1, 1995.

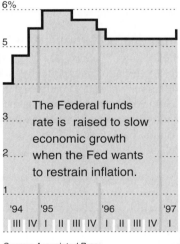

Yesterday: Up 0.25 point to 5.50%

The Federal funds rate is raised to slow economic growth when the Fed wants to restrain inflation.

Source: Associated Press

Here the federal funds rate is defined.

Here the Fed's decision is described.

Here the effect of the higher interest rate on investment and consumption is mentioned.

UP QUARTER-POINT

Move to 5.5% Is Aimed At Checking Inflation —Stocks Weaken

By Richard W. Stevenson

WASHINGTON, March 25 — The Federal Reserve voted today to raise interest rates for the first time in more than two years, firing a warning shot at an inflationary threat that remained hidden over the horizon.

The central bank took one of the smallest steps it could, nudging up the more important of the two short-term rates it controls — the Federal funds target rate for overnight loans between banks — by a quarter of a percentage point, to 5.5 percent. In doing so, it was trying to keep the economy from growing so fast that it generates wage and price pressures strong enough to threaten the nation's six-year economic expansion.

Because banks tie their benchmark loan rates to the Federal funds rate, today's action will ripple through the economy, probably curbing investment and consumption somewhat by increasing the rates charged for many business and personal loans and for credit cards.

central bank keeps money growth constant, or adheres to a gold standard, or reacts to other variables in addition to inflation, such as real GDP. Although the position and shape of the monetary policy rule will differ for these different types of policies, the overall response of interest rates to inflation will be similar, and the story of economic fluctuations that we discuss in this chapter will be similar. Our reason for using this particular derivation of the monetary policy rule is that it is the easiest to explain and is a close approximation of the actual behavior of the Fed and other central banks today. In other words, it is a good *simplifying assumption.*

Derivation of the Aggregate Demand/Inflation Curve

Thus far we have shown that the level of real GDP is negatively related to the interest rate and that the interest rate is positively related to the inflation rate through the central bank's policy rule. We now combine these two concepts to derive the aggregate demand/inflation (*ADI*) curve—the inverse relationship between the inflation rate and real GDP.

The chain of reasoning that brings about the aggregate demand/inflation curve can be explained by considering what would happen if the inflation rate rose. First, the interest rate would rise because the Fed raises the interest rate in response to a higher inflation rate. Next, the higher interest rate would mean less investment spending, a decline in net exports, and a decline in consumption. Lower investment spending occurs because investment is made more costly by the high interest rate. American goods become more expensive, and foreign goods become cheaper. Thus, net exports—exports minus imports—decline. We can represent this decrease in aggregate expenditure as a downward shift in the aggregate expenditure line. This leads to spending balance at a lower level of real GDP.

The opposite chain of events would occur if there were a fall in inflation below the target inflation rate. First, the Fed would lower the interest rate according to the monetary policy rule. The lower interest rate, in turn, would cause investment, net exports, and consumption to rise. Hence, the aggregate expenditure line would shift up, and the level of GDP would rise.

In sum, we see that when the inflation rate rises, real GDP decreases, and when the inflation rate falls, real GDP increases. In other words, there is a negative relationship between inflation and real GDP. When we graph this relationship in a diagram with real GDP on the horizontal axis and inflation on the vertical axis we get a downward-sloping curve like the one shown in Figure 27.3; this curve is the aggregate demand/inflation curve, which we have thus derived.

An alternative self-contained graphical derivation of the aggregate demand/ inflation curve is provided in Figure 27.6; the figure traces through the chain of events following an increase in inflation, including the Fed interest rate increase according to its policy rule, the change in spending balance, and finally the decline in real GDP.

Movements along the Aggregate Demand/Inflation Curve

Thus far, we have explained why the aggregate demand/inflation curve has a negative slope—that is, why higher inflation means lower real GDP. A *change in real GDP* due to a *change in inflation* is thus a *movement along* the aggregate demand/inflation curve. Recall that in microeconomics a similar movement along the demand curve occurs when a *change in the price* leads to a *change in quantity demanded.* When inflation rises and causes the Fed to raise the interest rate and real

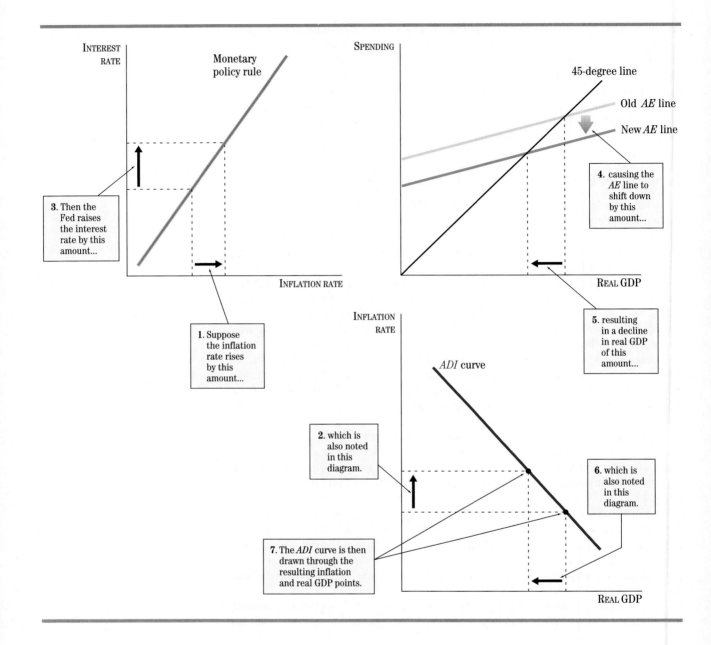

FIGURE 27.6
Graphical Derivation of the Aggregate Demand/Inflation Curve

When inflation rises, the central bank raises the interest rate and this lowers real GDP. Hence, we have the aggregate demand/inflation curve.

GDP declines, there is a movement up and to the left along the aggregate demand/inflation curve. When inflation declines and the Fed lowers the interest rate, causing real GDP to rise, there is a movement down and to the right along the aggregate demand/inflation curve.

Shifts of the Aggregate Demand/Inflation Curve

Now the inflation rate is not the only thing that affects aggregate demand. Changes in government purchases, shifts in the *target* for monetary policy, shifts in foreign demand for U.S. exports, changes in taxes, and changes in consumer confidence,

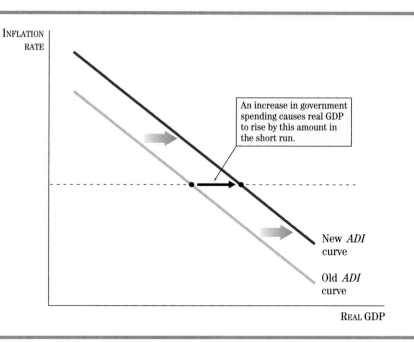

FIGURE 27.7
How Government Purchases Shift the Aggregate Demand/Inflation Curve
An increase in government purchases shifts the *ADI* curve to the right. Real GDP rises by the same amount at every level of inflation.

among other things, affect aggregate demand. When any of these factors changes aggregate demand, we say there is a *shift* in the aggregate demand/inflation curve. Let us briefly consider some of those sources of shifts in the aggregate demand/inflation curve.

Government Purchases Imagine that government purchases rise. We know from our analysis of spending balance in the previous chapter that an increase in government purchases will increase real GDP in the short run. This increase in real GDP occurs at any inflation rate: at 2 percent, at 4 percent, or at any other level. Now, if real GDP increases at a given inflation rate, the aggregate demand/inflation curve will shift to the right. This is shown in Figure 27.7. The new aggregate demand/inflation curve will be parallel to the original aggregate demand/inflation curve because no matter what the inflation rate is in the economy, the shift in government purchases is going to have the same effect on real GDP. The same reasoning implies that a decline in government spending shifts the aggregate demand/inflation curve to the left.

Changes in the Target Inflation Rate Now consider what happens if the Fed shifts to a higher target inflation rate. Suppose that the previous target inflation rate was 2 percent and the new target inflation rate is 4 percent. Figure 27.8 shows how this shifts the monetary policy rule line outward toward higher inflation. Observe that this will initially cause the interest rate to decline at every level of inflation. For example, if the inflation rate was 2 percent before the change in policy, the interest rate will drop from 4 percent to 3 percent, as shown in the diagram. These lower interest rates will increase real GDP, and thereby shift the aggregate demand/inflation curve out. The same reasoning implies that a lowering of the target inflation rate by the Fed will shift the monetary policy rule to the left, increase the interest rate, and shift the aggregate demand/inflation curve to the left.

FIGURE 27.8

A Change in the Monetary Policy Rule

A change in the policy rule to a higher inflation target initially implies a decline in the interest rate. The lower interest rate shifts up the *AE* line and increases real GDP in the short run. As a result, at a given inflation rate the *ADI* curve shifts to the right.

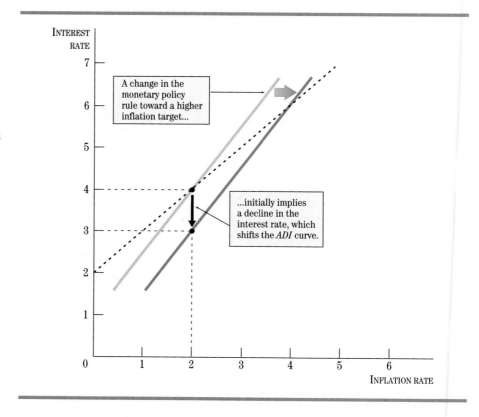

FIGURE 27.9

Shifts in the Aggregate Demand/Inflation Curve

Many things shift the *ADI* curve. For example, an increase in government purchases shifts the *ADI* curve to the right. A change in the monetary policy rule toward a higher inflation target shifts the *ADI* curve to the right. A decline in government purchases and a change in the monetary policy rule toward a lower inflation target shifts the curve to the left.

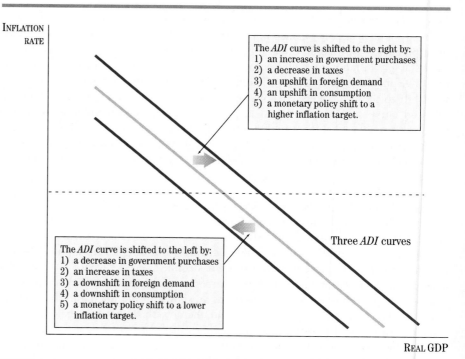

Other Changes   Any change in the economy (other than a change in the inflation rate) that shifts the aggregate expenditure line will also shift the aggregate demand/inflation curve. We considered many such possibilities in Chapter 25; their effects on the aggregate demand/inflation curve are shown in Figure 27.9. For example, an increase in the foreign demand for U.S. products will increase net exports, raise real GDP, and shift the aggregate demand/inflation curve to the right. A drop in consumer confidence that reduces the amount of consumption at every level of income will shift the aggregate demand/inflation curve to the left. Finally, an increase in taxes shifts the aggregate demand/inflation curve to the left, while a decrease in taxes shifts the aggregate demand/inflation curve to the right.

Review

▶ The aggregate demand/inflation curve is an inverse relationship between inflation and real GDP.

▶ Investment, net exports, and consumption are negatively related to the interest rate. Hence, real GDP falls when the interest rate rises.

▶ When inflation increases, the central bank raises the interest rate, and this lowers real GDP. Conversely, when inflation falls, the central bank lowers the interest rate, and this raises real GDP. These are movements along the aggregate demand/inflation curve.

▶ The aggregate demand/inflation curve shifts to the right when the central bank changes its monetary policy rule toward more inflation and shifts to the left when the central banks changes its policy rule toward less inflation.

▶ Higher government purchases shift the aggregate demand/inflation curve to the right. Lower government purchases shift the aggregate demand/inflation curve to the left.

THE PRICE ADJUSTMENT LINE

Having derived the aggregate demand/inflation curve and studied its properties, let us now look at the price adjustment line, the second element of the economic fluctuations model. The **price adjustment (*PA*) line** is a flat line showing the level of inflation in the economy at any point in time. Figure 27.10 shows an example of the price adjustment line in a diagram with inflation on the vertical axis and real GDP on the horizontal axis. For example, if the line touches 4 percent on the vertical axis, then it tells us that inflation is 4 percent.

The price adjustment line describes the economic behavior of firms and workers setting prices and wages in the economy. There are several important features about the slope and position of the price adjustment line.

price adjustment (*PA*) line: a flat line showing the level of inflation in the economy at a given point in time. It shifts up when real GDP is greater than potential GDP, and it shifts down when real GDP is less than potential GDP; it also shifts when expectations of inflation or raw materials prices change.

The Price Adjustment Line Is Flat

That the price adjustment line is flat indicates that firms and workers adjust their prices and wages in such a way that the inflation rate remains steady in the short run as real GDP changes. Only after time does inflation change significantly and the price adjustment line move. In the short run, inflation stays at 4 percent, or wherever the price adjustment line happens to be, when real GDP changes.

In interpreting the price adjustment line, it is helpful to remember that it is part of a *model* of the overall economy and is thus an approximation of reality. In fact,

FIGURE 27.10

Price Adjustment and Changes in Inflation

In the top panel, real GDP is above potential GDP and inflation is rising; thus, the price adjustment line shifts up. In the bottom panel, real GDP is below potential GDP and inflation is falling; thus, the price adjustment line shifts down.

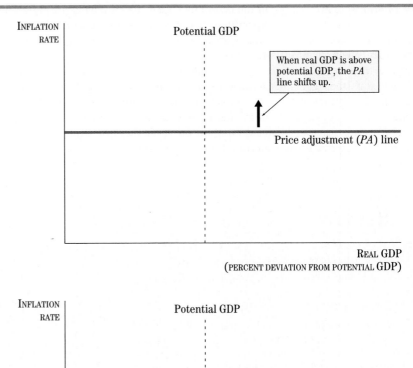

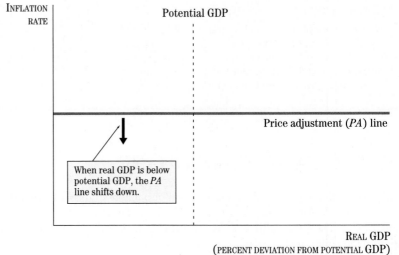

inflation does not remain *perfectly* steady, and the price adjustment line could have a small upward slope. But it is a good approximation to assume that the price adjustment line is flat.

There are two reasons why inflation does not change very much in the short run even if real GDP and the demand for firms' products changes: (1) expectations of steady inflation, and (2) staggered wage and price setting.

Expectations of Steady Inflation

Expectations about the price and wage decisions of other firms influence a firm's price and wage decisions. For example, if the overall inflation rate in the economy has been hovering around 10 percent year after year, then a firm can expect that its competitors' prices will probably increase by about 10 percent per year, unless circumstances change. To keep prices near the competition, this firm will need to increase its price by about 10 percent each year. Thus, the inflation rate stays steady at 10 percent per year.

Wage adjustments also must be undertaken with expectations of the future. If firms and workers expect that workers at other firms will be getting large wage increases, then meeting the competition will require similar large wage increases. A smaller wage increase would reduce the wage relative to other workers. Many firms base their wage decisions on the wages paid by other firms to workers whose skills and experience are similar to their workers. If they see the wages at other firms rising, they will be more willing to increase wages.

Firms and workers also look to expectations of inflation when deciding on wage increases. In an economy with 10 percent inflation, wages will have to increase by 10 percent for workers just to keep up with the cost of living. Lower wage increases would result in a decline in workers' real wages.

Staggered Price and Wage Setting

Not all wages and prices are changed at the same time throughout the economy. Rather, price setting and wage setting are staggered over months and even years. For example, autoworkers might negotiate three-year wage contracts in 1993, 1996, 1999, etc. Dockworkers might negotiate three-year contracts in 1994, 1997, 2000, etc. Bus companies and train companies do not adjust their prices at the same time, even though they may compete for the same riders. On any given day, we can be sure that there is a wage or price adjustment somewhere in the economy, but the vast majority of wages and prices do not change.

Staggered price and wage setting slows down the adjustment of prices in the economy. When considering what wage increases are likely in the next year, firms and workers know about the most recent three-year wage increase. For example, an agreement made by another firm to increase wages by 10 percent per year for three years into the future will affect the expectations of wages paid to competing workers in the future. This wage agreement will not change unless the firm is on the edge of bankruptcy and perhaps not even then. Hence, workers and firms deciding on wage increases will tend to match the wage increases recently made at other firms. Thus, price and wage decisions made today are directly influenced by price and wage decisions made yesterday.

As with many things in life, when today's decisions are influenced by yesterday's decisions, inertia sets in. The staggering of the decisions makes it difficult to break the inertia. Unless there is a reason to make a change—such as a persistent decline in demand or a change in expectations of inflation—the price increases or wage increases continue from year to year. The flat price adjustment line describes this inertia.

The Price Adjustment Line Shifts Gradually When Real GDP Departs from Potential GDP

The price adjustment line does not always stay put; rather it may shift up or down from year to year. If real GDP stays above potential GDP, then inflation starts to rise. Firms see that the demand for their products is remaining high, and they begin adjusting their prices. If the inflation rate was 10 percent, then the firms will have to raise their prices by more than 10 percent if they want their relative prices to increase. Hence, inflation starts to rise. The price adjustment line is shifted upward to illustrate this rise in inflation; it will keep shifting upward as long as real GDP is above potential GDP.

However, if real GDP is below potential GDP, then firms will see that the demand for their products is falling off, and they will adjust their prices. If inflation was 10 percent, the firms will raise their prices by less than 10 percent—perhaps by 7 percent—if they want the relative price of their goods to fall. Hence, inflation falls. The price adjustment line is shifted down to illustrate this fall in inflation. Figure 27.10 shows the direction of these shifts.

If real GDP stays at potential GDP, neither to the left nor to the right of the vertical potential GDP line in Figure 27.10, then inflation remains unchanged. For example, in the absence of a recession or a boom, the inflation rate would remain steady year after year. This steady inflation is represented by an unmoving price adjustment line year after year.

The following is a shorthand summary of price adjustment in the economy as a whole:

Real GDP = potential GDP $\longrightarrow$ inflation rate does not change (*PA* line does not shift)

Real GDP > potential GDP $\longrightarrow$ inflation rate increases (*PA* line shifts up)

Real GDP < potential GDP $\longrightarrow$ inflation rate decreases (*PA* line shifts down)

Changes in Expectations or Commodity Prices Shift the Price Adjustment Line

Even if real GDP is at potential GDP, some special events in the economy can cause the price adjustment line to shift up or down. One important example is *shifts in expectations* of inflation. If firms and workers expect inflation to rise, then they are likely to raise wages and prices to keep pace with inflation. Thus, an increase in expectations of inflation will cause the price adjustment line to shift up to a higher inflation rate. And a decrease in expectations of inflation will cause the price adjustment line to shift down.

Another example is a change in commodity prices that affects firms' costs of production. For example, we will examine the effects on inflation of an oil price increase in the next chapter. By raising firms' costs, such an oil price increase would lead firms to charge higher prices, and the price adjustment line would rise, at least temporarily.

Does the Price Adjustment Line Fit the Facts?

Are these assumptions about the price adjustment line accurate? Does inflation rise when real GDP is above potential GDP and fall when real GDP is below potential GDP? Figure 27.11 provides the relevant evidence. The points in the figure indicate the level of inflation and the percent deviation of real GDP from potential GDP for years when real GDP was more than 1 percent above or below potential GDP. (We only use deviations that are greater than 1 percent, because it is difficult to measure the deviations with better than 1 percent accuracy.) Up arrows indicate that inflation increased from the year before the labeled year.

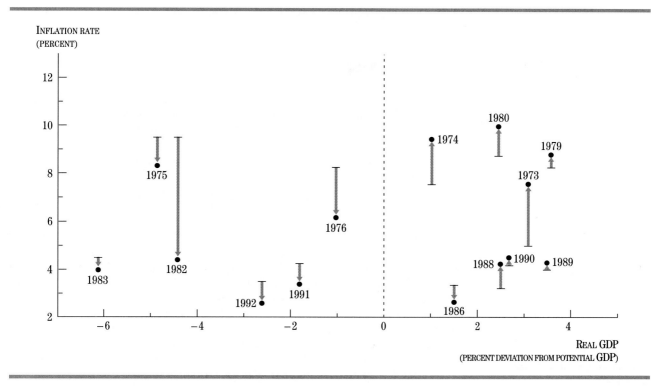

Down arrows indicate that inflation decreased. The length of the arrow is the size of the inflation increase or decrease.

Inflation declines when real GDP is less than—to the left of—potential GDP in Figure 27.11. The biggest decline in inflation occurred in 1982, when real GDP was far below potential GDP. When real GDP is greater than—to the right of—potential GDP, inflation is rising in the vast majority of cases. Figure 27.11 indicates that the theory of the price adjustment line shown in Figure 27.10 fits the facts very well.

FIGURE 27.11
Declines and Increases in Inflation
The data show that inflation falls when real GDP is below potential GDP; inflation rises when real GDP is above potential GDP.

Source: U.S. Department of Commerce.

Review

▶ The price adjustment line, the second element of the economic fluctuations model, is a flat line showing the level of inflation in the economy at any point in time. The price adjustment line describes the economic behavior of firms and workers setting prices and wages in the economy.

▶ Firms do not change their prices instantaneously when the demand for their product changes. Thus, when aggregate demand changes and real GDP departs from potential GDP, the inflation rate does not immediately change; the price adjustment line does not shift in response to such changes in the short run.

▶ Staggered price setting tends to slow down the adjustment of prices in the economy as a whole.

▶ Over time, however, inflation does respond to departures of real GDP from potential GDP. This response can be described by upward and downward shifts in the price adjustment (*PA*) line over time.

COMBINING THE AGGREGATE DEMAND/INFLATION CURVE AND THE PRICE ADJUSTMENT LINE

We have now derived two relationships—the aggregate demand/inflation curve and the price adjustment line—that describe real GDP and inflation in the economy as a whole. Both relationships can be combined to make predictions about real GDP and inflation.

Along the aggregate demand/inflation curve in Figure 27.3, real GDP and inflation are negatively related. This curve describes the behavior of firms and consumers as they respond to a higher interest rate caused by higher inflation. They respond by lowering consumption, investment, and net exports. This line presents a range of possible values of real GDP and inflation.

The price adjustment line in Figure 27.10, on the other hand, tells us what the inflation rate is at any point in time. Thus, we can use the price adjustment line to determine exactly what inflation rate applies to the aggregate demand/inflation curve. For example, if the price adjustment line tells us that the inflation rate for 2004 is 5 percent, then we can go right to the aggregate demand/inflation curve to determine what the level of real GDP will be at that 5 percent inflation rate. If the aggregate demand/inflation curve says that real GDP is 2 percent below potential GDP when inflation is 5 percent, then we predict that real GDP is 2 percent below potential GDP. The price adjustment line tells us the current location of inflation—and therefore real GDP—along the aggregate demand/inflation curve.

Figure 27.12 illustrates the determination of real GDP and inflation graphically. It combines the curve from Figure 27.3 with the price adjustment line from Figure 27.10. At any point in time, the price adjustment line is given as shown in Figure 27.12. The price adjustment line intersects the aggregate demand/inflation curve at a single point. It is at this point of intersection where inflation and real GDP are determined. The intersection gives an *equilibrium* level of real GDP and inflation. At that point we can look down to the horizontal axis of the diagram to determine the level of real GDP corresponding to that level of inflation. For ex-

FIGURE 27.12
Determining Real GDP and Inflation

Real GDP is determined at the intersection of the *ADI* curve and the *PA* line. All three panels have the same *ADI* curve and the same vertical line marking potential GDP. Three different levels of the *PA* line give three different levels of real GDP: less than, equal to, and greater than potential GDP.

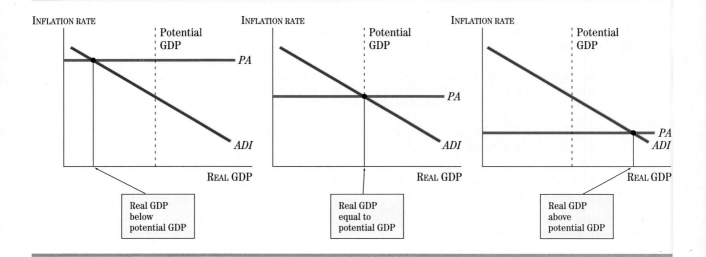

ample, the point of intersection in the left panel of Figure 27.12 might be when inflation is 5 percent and real GDP is 2 percent below potential GDP. The point of intersection in the right panel is at a lower inflation rate when real GDP is above potential GDP. The point of intersection in the middle panel of Figure 27.12 has real GDP equal to potential GDP.

As Figure 27.12 makes clear, the intersection of the price adjustment line and the aggregate demand/inflation curve may give values of real GDP that are either above or below potential GDP. But if real GDP is not equal to potential GDP, then the economy has not fully recovered from a recession, as on the left of Figure 27.12, or returned to potential GDP after a boom, as on the right. To describe dynamic movements of inflation and real GDP, we must consider how either the price adjustment line or the aggregate demand/inflation curve shift over time. That is the subject of the next chapter.

Review

▶ In any year, the price adjustment line tells us what the inflation rate is. Using the aggregate demand/inflation curve we can then make a prediction about what real GDP is.

▶ The intersection of the aggregate demand/inflation curve and the price adjustment line gives a pair of observations on real GDP and inflation at any point in time.

CONCLUSION

With the three elements of the economic fluctuations model—the aggregate/demand inflation curve, the price adjustment line, and their intersection—put together, we are now ready to use the model to explain the fluctuations of real GDP and inflation during recessions and booms. In reviewing the different elements it is useful to consider the scissors analogy mentioned in our discussion of the supply and demand model.

The aggregate demand/inflation curve is like one blade of the scissors. The price adjustment line is the other blade. Either blade alone is insufficient to explain economic fluctuations. Either blade alone is an incomplete story. But when the two blades of the scissors are put together to form a pair of scissors, they become a practical tool to explain the ups and downs in the economy. And compared to the complexity and vastness of the whole economy with millions of firms and consumers, this particular pair of scissors is amazingly simple.

KEY POINTS

1. Along the aggregate demand/inflation (*ADI*) curve, real GDP is negatively related to inflation.

2. Investment, net exports, and consumption depend negatively on the interest rate. Hence, aggregate expenditure, which includes investment, net exports, and consumption, depends negatively on the interest rate.

3. An increase in the interest rate causes the aggregate expenditure line to shift down.

4. The level of real GDP at spending balance—the intersection of the aggregate expenditure line and the 45-degree line—depends negatively on the interest rate.

5. Central banks' actions to adjust the interest rate to maintain low inflation result in a relationship between interest rates and inflation. When inflation rises, the real interest rate rises. When inflation falls, the real interest rate falls.

6. The combined behavior of (1) the interest rate response to inflation and (2) the private sector adjusting spending in response to the interest rate generates an inverse relationship between real GDP and inflation—the aggregate demand/inflation curve.

7. Movements along the aggregate demand/inflation curve occur when inflation rises, causing the real interest rate to rise and real GDP to fall. Such movements along the curve also occur when inflation falls, the interest rate declines, and real GDP rises.

8. The aggregate demand/inflation curve shifts for many reasons, including a change in government purchases and a change in monetary policy to a different targe rate of inflation.

9. When adjusting prices, firms respond slowly to changes in demand and take account of expectations of inflation. So do workers when wages are being adjusted. As a result, inflation tends to increase when real GDP is above potential GDP and tends to decrease when GDP is below potential GDP.

10. The staggering of price and wage decisions tends to slow the adjustment of prices in the economy as a whole.

11. When combined with the aggregate demand/inflation curve, the price adjustment line provides us with a way to determine real GDP and inflation.

KEY TERMS

aggregate demand/inflation (*ADI*)
  curve

monetary policy rule
federal funds rate

target inflation rate
price adjustment (*PA*) line

QUESTIONS FOR REVIEW

1. How do we represent movements of inflation and real GDP in a single diagram?

2. Why are investment and net exports inversely related to the interest rate?

3. Why is real GDP inversely related to the interest rate in the short run?

4. Why does the interest rate rise when inflation begins to rise? Why may this rise be called a policy rule?

5. Why is real GDP inversely related to inflation in the short run? What is this relationship called?

6. What are examples of movements along the aggregate demand/inflation curve?

7. Why does a change in government purchases shift the aggregate demand/inflation curve to the right or left?

8. Why does a change in monetary policy shift the aggregate demand/inflation curve to the right or to the left?

9. Why does inflation increase when real GDP is above potential GDP?

10. What is the significance of expectations of inflation for price adjustment?

11. Why does staggered price setting slow down price adjustment in the economy?

PROBLEMS

1. Which of the following statements are true, and which are false? Explain your answers in one or two sentences.

  a) A decrease in the U.S. interest rate will cause the dollar exchange rate to decline.

  b) The central bank typically lowers the interest rate when inflation rises.

  c) A higher interest rate leads to greater net exports because the higher interest rate raises the value of the dollar.

  d) Investment is positively related to the interest rate.

2. Suppose that European interest rates are very high relative to those in the United States, and the Fed decides to lower the interest rate as inflation falls in the United States. What effect will this have on the value of the dollar relative to European currencies? Will the U.S. net exports be higher or lower? Why?

3. Suppose that the Fed makes a mistake in its implementation of policy: It increases the interest rate while the economy is already going into a recession. What effect will this increase in the interest rate have on real GDP and inflation in the short run?

4. Suppose the United States reaches an agreement with Japan that increases U.S. exports to Japan but has no effect on the U.S. imports of Japanese goods. Which way will the aggregate expenditure line shift? Will this cause a shift in the aggregate demand/inflation curve? Sketch the effect of this change in a diagram. What will happen to U.S. real GDP in the short run?

5. State which of the following changes causes a shift of the aggregate demand/inflation curve and which ones are a movement along it.

    a) A shift to a higher inflation target in the monetary policy rule

    b) An increase in government purchases

    c) An economic boom in Japan

    d) Being thrifty becomes fashionable

    e) An increase in the German interest rate

    f) A surprise inflationary shock hits the economy

6. Suppose you could use a change in either government purchases or monetary policy to increase real GDP in the short run. How would each policy affect consumption, investment, and net exports in the short run? Why?

7. Suppose the Fed is considering the two different policy rules, shown in the following table. Graph the policy rules. What economic factors will the Fed consider when deciding which policy rule to follow?

Inflation	Policy Rule 1 Interest Rate	Policy Rule 2 Interest Rate
0	1	3
2	3	5
4	4	7
6	7	9
8	9	11

If the Fed is currently following policy rule 1 and then shifts to policy rule 2, which way will the aggregate demand/inflation curve shift? What reasons might the Fed have for changing its policy? What effect will this change have on real GDP?

8. Suppose the government implements a policy that subsidizes business investment. How will this affect the relationship between investment and the interest rate? How will the aggregate demand/inflation curve shift? What will happen to real GDP in the short run?

9. Suppose you have the following information on the Fed's and the Bundesbank's policy rules:

Fed interest rate = 1.5 (inflation rate − 2) + 2

Bundesbank interest rate = 1.2 (inflation rate − 2) + 3

    a) Graph these policy rules. If the inflation rate is 2 percent in both countries, what will be the interest rate in each country?

    b) Some argue that Germany has a much lower tolerance for inflation than the United States. Can you tell—either from the diagram or from the equations—whether this is true?

10. The following table gives a numerical example of an aggregate demand/inflation curve.

Real GDP (percent deviation from potential GDP)	Inflation (percent per year)
3.0	2.0
2.0	2.5
1.0	3.0
0.0	4.0
−1.0	5.0
−2.0	7.0
−3.0	10.0

    a) Sketch the curve in a graph like Figure 27.3.

    b) What is the average rate of inflation in the long run?

    c) Suppose that the central bank increases the target inflation rate by 2 percent. What will happen to the average rate of inflation in the long run (assuming that potential GDP growth does not change)?

    d) Sketch a new aggregate demand/inflation curve corresponding to the new higher target inflation rate in part (c). How does the new curve compare to the old curve?

11. The following table gives a numerical example of a price adjustment line in the year 2000.

Real GDP (percent deviation from potential GDP)	Inflation (percent per year)
3.0	4.0
2.0	4.0
1.0	4.0
0.0	4.0
−1.0	4.0
−2.0	4.0
−3.0	4.0

    a) Sketch the line in a graph like Figure 27.10.

    b) If real GDP is above potential GDP in the year 2000, will the price adjustment line shift up or down in the year 2001? Explain.

    c) In the same graph as part (a), sketch in the aggregate demand/inflation curve given in Problem 10. Find the equilibrium level of real GDP and inflation in the year 2000.

    d) Show what happens to the price adjustment line if there is a sudden increase in inflation expectations.

12. Compare and contrast the microeconomic supply and demand model with the macroeconomic model with a price adjustment line and the aggregate demand/inflation curve.

28

Toward Recovery
and Expansion

The economic fluctuations model is one of the most powerful models in economics. Versions of this model are employed by business economists making forecasts for their clients, by regional economists in state capitals looking at the impact of changes in federal laws, by policy economists in Washington analyzing the effects of the president's economic policy proposals, and by international economists working at organizations like the International Monetary Fund trying to determine the effect of tax or spending changes in hundreds of countries around the world.

Now we are ready to use the economic fluctuations model as explained graphically in the previous chapter. We will focus on using the model to determine the path the economy takes toward recovery after a recession. We examine how that recovery brings real GDP back to potential GDP, where it then can expand along with potential GDP until the next boom or recession. Knowing

the likely speed of the economy toward recovery after a recession is important for choosing the correct economic policy. For example, both President Bush and President Clinton made proposals to speed up the recovery from the recession in the early 1990s. But in both cases the proposals were rejected by Congress. Were the presidents correct, or was Congress correct? On what economic basis are such proposals made or rejected?

In this chapter, we also look at how real GDP and inflation change over time after a shift in monetary policy, either to lower inflation or to higher inflation. We examine boom-bust theories of the business cycle, where monetary policy first errs in causing a boom with higher inflation and then overreacts to the error and causes a recession. We also study the effect of world oil price shocks like those experienced in the 1970s and again in the 1990s.

THE END OF RECESSIONS AND BOOMS

With the aggregate demand/inflation (*ADI*) curve and the price adjustment (*PA*) line as key elements of our model, we now examine the forces leading to a return of real GDP to potential GDP. To do so, we will focus on a particular example, a change in government purchases. In Chapter 25 we showed how a change in government purchases could push real GDP away from potential GDP in the short run. Now let us see the complete story.

Real GDP and Inflation over Time

Suppose the government cuts military purchases permanently. We want to examine the effects of this decrease in government purchases on the economy in the short run (about one year), the medium run (two to three years), and the long run (four to five years and beyond). These three lengths of time represent the average duration of recessions and recoveries, but remember that no two economic fluctuations are exactly alike. Some are longer and some are shorter than these time spans. We use the term *short run* to refer to the initial departure of real GDP from potential GDP, *medium run* to refer to the recovery period, and *long run* to refer to when real GDP is nearly back to potential GDP.

Figure 28.1 shows the aggregate demand/inflation curve and the price adjustment line on the same diagram. The intersection of the aggregate demand/inflation

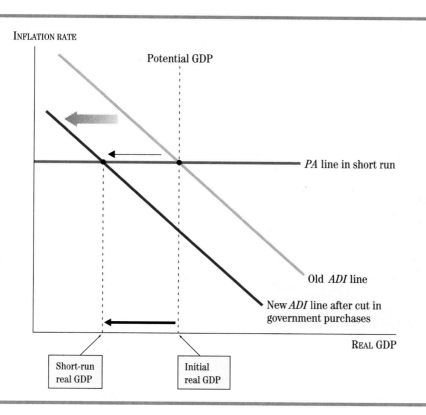

INFLATION RATE

Potential GDP

PA line in short run

Old *ADI* line

New *ADI* line after cut in government purchases

REAL GDP

Short-run real GDP

Initial real GDP

FIGURE 28.1
Short-Run Effects of a Reduction in Government Purchases
In the short run, the *PA* line does not move. Thus, in the short run, real GDP declines by the amount of the shift in the *ADI* curve, as noted on the horizontal axis.

curve and the price adjustment line determines a level of inflation and real GDP. Let us assume that we began with real GDP equal to potential GDP. Thus, the initial intersection of the aggregate demand/inflation curve and the price adjustment line occurs at a level of real GDP equal to potential GDP.

Now, recall from the previous chapter that a change in government purchases shifts the aggregate demand/inflation curve; in particular, a decline in government purchases shifts the aggregate demand/inflation curve to the left. Because the price adjustment line is flat, and because it does not move in the short run, a change in government purchases—shown by the shift in the aggregate demand/inflation curve from the "old" to the "new" in Figure 28.1—leads to a change in real GDP by the same amount as the shift in the aggregate demand/inflation curve. This is the short-run effect. The decrease in government purchases initially moves the aggregate demand/inflation curve to the left, and real GDP falls to the point indicated by the intersection of the price adjustment line and the new aggregate demand/inflation curve. At the new intersection real GDP is at a level below potential GDP.

Now consider what happens over time. The tendency for prices to adjust over time is represented by upward or downward shifts of the price adjustment line. Only in the short run does the price adjustment line stay put, reflecting the delay in the adjustment of price decisions. What is likely to happen over time when real GDP is below potential GDP? Inflation should begin to decline, because firms will increase their prices by smaller amounts. We represent a decline in inflation by shifting the price adjustment line down, as shown in Figure 28.2. The initial impact of the change in government spending took us to a point we label *SR,* for short run, in Figure 28.2. At that point, real GDP is lower than potential GDP. Hence, inflation will fall and the price adjustment line shifts down, as shown in the diagram. There is now a new point of intersection; we label that point *MR,* for medium run.

Note how real GDP has started to recover. At the point labeled *MR* in the diagram, real GDP is still below potential GDP but it is higher than the low (*SR*) point in the downturn. The reason real GDP starts to rise is that the lower inflation rate causes the central bank to lower the interest rate. The lower interest rate increases investment spending and causes net exports to rise. As a result, real GDP rises.

Because real GDP is still below potential GDP, there is still a tendency for inflation to fall. Thus, the price adjustment line continues to shift downward until real GDP returns to potential GDP. Figure 28.2 shows a third intersection at the point marked *LR* for the long run, where production has increased all the way back to potential GDP. At this point real GDP has reached long-run equilibrium in the sense that real GDP equals potential GDP. With real GDP equal to potential GDP, the price adjustment line stops shifting down. Inflation is at a new lower level than before the decline in government purchases, but at the final point of intersection in the diagram it is no longer falling. Thus, real GDP remains equal to potential GDP.

Note how successive downward shifts of the price adjustment line with intersections along the aggregate demand/inflation curve trace out values for real GDP and inflation as the economy first goes into recession and then recovers. In the short run, a decline in production comes about from the decrease in government spending; that

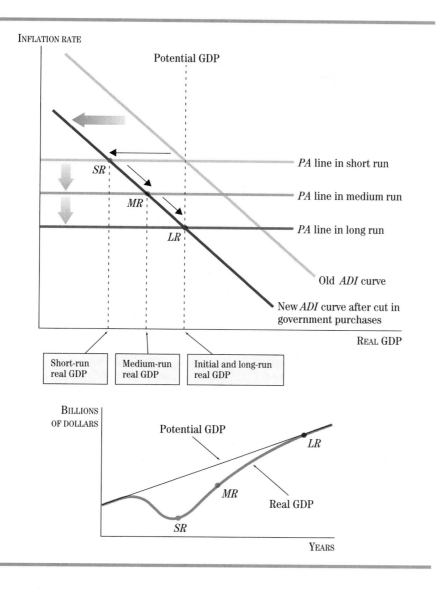

FIGURE 28.2
Dynamic Adjustment after a Reduction in Government Purchases
Initially, the reduction in government purchases shifts the *ADI* curve to the left. This reduces real GDP to the point labeled *SR,* or the short run. Then the *PA* line begins to shift down because real GDP is less than potential GDP. The *PA* line keeps shifting down until real GDP is back to potential GDP.

decline is followed by successive years of reversal as the economy recovers and real GDP returns to potential GDP. The behavior is shown in the sketch in the lower part of Figure 28.2. Thus, we have achieved one of the major goals of this chapter: showing how recessions end and recoveries take the economy back to normal.

A More Detailed Report: Economic Behavior Behind the Scenes

It is possible to give a more detailed report on what happens to consumption, net exports, and investment during this temporary departure from, and return to, potential GDP. To do so, we need to bring in some of our supporting diagrams to examine the source of the movements in real GDP and inflation that we have already summarized with the aggregate demand/inflation curve and the price adjustment line diagram in Figure 28.2.

Figure 28.3 includes these supporting diagrams. At first glance, it may look complicated, but it simply includes information we discussed in Chapter 27. The diagram in the lower right panel is identical to that in Figure 28.2. Thus, we are still examining the decline in government purchases. The monetary policy rule describing the response of interest rates to inflation in the upper-left panel is identical to that of Figure 27.5. The upper-right panel is the familiar aggregate expenditure line and 45-degree line diagram. The small table in the lower left summarizes how each component of real GDP changes in the short run and the long run. The arrows in the table indicate what happens compared with what would have happened in the absence of change in government purchases. The path of the economy in the absence of the hypothetical change is called the **baseline.** The term *baseline* is commonly used in public policy discussions to refer to what would have happened if a contemplated policy action were not taken; the arrows in the table tell whether a variable is up or down relative to the baseline. In this case, the baseline for real GDP is potential GDP. Thus, a downward-pointing arrow in the real GDP column means real GDP is below potential GDP; an upward-pointing arrow means real GDP is above potential GDP.

baseline: the path of an economic variable that would occur without the policy change under consideration.

Short Run

The decline in government spending gets things started. The aggregate expenditure (*AE*) line in the upper-right panel shifts down by the amount of the decrease in government spending. The new spending balance gives a lower level of real GDP. With lower income, people consume less. In the short run, investment does not change because interest rates have not yet changed, but net exports rise because the lower level of income in the United States means imports fall. That is, exports minus imports increase. This is all incorporated in the aggregate expenditure diagram.

The aggregate demand/inflation curve shifts to the left, and with no change in the price adjustment line, real GDP declines. This short-run effect is shown in the first row in the table. Real GDP and consumption are down *relative to the baseline.* Net exports are up *relative to the baseline.*

Medium Run

Price adjustment takes us to the medium run. We do not know exactly how long this takes, but we suppose as an approximation that two or three years is the medium run. We know the decline in real GDP below potential GDP causes inflation to fall; thus, we shift the price adjustment line down.

With the lower rate of inflation the central bank reduces the interest rate. This is shown in the upper left of Figure 28.3. The lower interest rate means that the aggregate expenditure line is moving back up again. The level of real GDP giving spending balance increases. The intersection of the aggregate demand/inflation curve and price adjustment line is at a higher level of real GDP. This medium-run level of real GDP is still below potential GDP, however.

Long Run

Now consider the long run, approximately four to five years. By this time real GDP has returned to potential GDP. Government spending is still lower than it was originally because we have assumed that this is a permanent decline in military

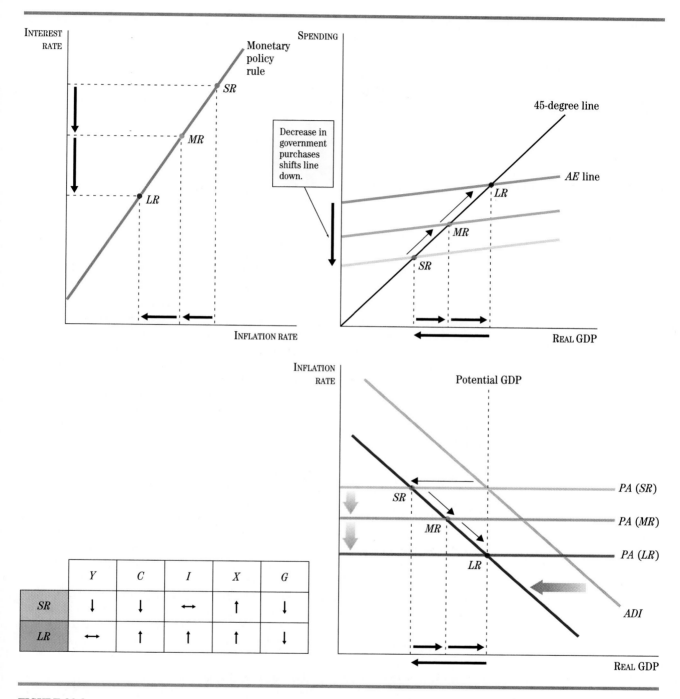

FIGURE 28.3

More Detailed Analysis of a Reduction in Government Purchases

The inflation–real GDP graph in the lower right diagram is the same as Figure 28.2. Also shown are the *AE* line, which shifts down by the amount government purchases are cut, and the monetary policy rule where interest rates fall as inflation falls. This decline in interest rates causes the *AE* line to move back up again. The arrows in the table keep track of the changes in the major variables relative to where they started.

FIGURE 28.4
Increase in Long-Term Growth after a Recession Caused by a Decrease in Government Purchases
A higher investment share of real GDP that results from the decline in government purchases leads to more capital and a higher growth of potential GDP. After the recession, real GDP will grow along, or fluctuate around, this higher growth path.

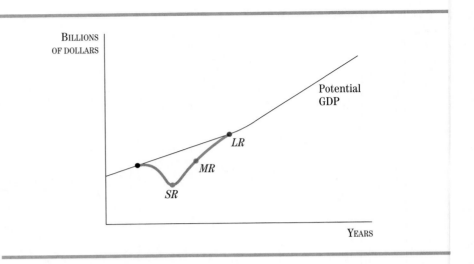

spending. Because real GDP is equal to potential GDP, aggregate income in the economy—which equals real GDP—is back to normal. Because income is back to normal, the effects of income on consumption and net exports are just what they would have been in the absence of the change in government purchases.

What about interest rates and their effect on consumption, investment, and net exports? We know that real GDP is back to potential GDP, so that the sum of consumption, investment, and net exports must be higher to make up for the decrease in government purchases. Interest rates must therefore remain lower. The summary table in Figure 28.3 shows consumption, investment, and net exports higher in the long run. We would expect that the consumption effects are small, however, because consumption is not very sensitive to interest rates. Most of the long-run impact of the decline in government purchases is to raise investment and net exports. The story is complete now. We have put all the pieces of the puzzle together.

To summarize, a decrease in government purchases has negative effects on the economy in the short run. Real GDP declines. Workers are laid off. Unemployment rises. In the long run, the economy is back to potential GDP, and consumption, investment, and net exports have gone up. In the long run, the decrease in government purchases permits greater private investment and more net exports. The increase in investment benefits long-run economic growth, as we know from Chapter 22; hence, the path of potential GDP over time has risen, and now real GDP is growing more quickly, as shown in Figure 28.4. In this sense, the decrease in government purchases is good for the long term despite its negative short-run effects.

The Return to Potential GDP after a Boom

Surprisingly, the adjustment of real GDP back to potential GDP after a boom can be explained using the same theory. For example, suppose an increase in real GDP above potential GDP is caused by an increase in government purchases for new highway construction. Starting from potential GDP, the aggregate demand/inflation curve would shift to the right. Real GDP would increase above potential GDP in the short run.

With real GDP above potential GDP, however, firms start to adjust their prices; inflation begins to rise. We would represent that as an upward shift in the price adjustment line. In the medium run real GDP would still be above potential GDP, and inflation would continue to rise. Eventually, real GDP would go back to potential GDP and the boom would be over. Thus, we predict that real GDP goes back to potential GDP. However, in this case, because government purchases have risen, the new long-run equilibrium will have a higher interest rate, and the sum of consumption, investment, and net exports will be lower.

Review

▶ With the price adjustment line and the aggregate demand/inflation curve, we can now explain both the initial steps of real GDP away from potential GDP and the return to potential GDP.

▶ In the short run a decline in government purchases, or any other change that shifts the aggregate demand/inflation curve to the left, will cause real GDP to fall below potential GDP.

▶ In the medium run, when the interest rate starts to fall, real GDP begins to increase again. Investment and net exports start to rise and partly offset the decline in government purchases.

▶ In the long run, real GDP returns to potential GDP. Interest rates are lower and consumption plus investment plus net exports have risen.

CHANGES IN MONETARY POLICY

A large change in government spending is, of course, not the only thing that can temporarily push real GDP away from potential GDP. Changes in taxes, consumer confidence, or foreign demand can also cause recessions or booms. But a particularly important factor is a change in monetary policy.

Consider, for example, a change in monetary policy that aims to lower the rate of inflation. Suppose that the inflation rate is about 10 percent and a new head of the central bank is appointed who has the objective of reducing inflation. Suppose the aim is to reduce the inflation rate to 4 percent. A reduction in the inflation rate is called **disinflation. Deflation** means declining prices, or a negative inflation rate, which is different from a declining inflation rate. To be sure, the aim of policy in this example is not deflation.

Figure 28.5 shows the short-run, medium-run, and long-run impact of such a change in the monetary policy. The focal point of the figure is the lower-right diagram. The other panels play supporting roles to help us keep track of the details. The upper-left panel shows the change in monetary policy. A shift to a lower target inflation rate means a leftward shift or, equivalently, an upward shift, in the monetary policy rule line, as we discussed in Chapter 27.

With inflation initially at 10 percent, the Fed's new policy indicates the need to increase the interest rate. Hence, the initial effect of the lower target inflation rate is an increase in the interest rate. This increase in the interest rate is shown in the upper-left panel of Figure 28.5.

One effect of the increase in the interest rate is to lower investment. In addition, the higher interest rate causes the dollar to appreciate, and this tends to reduce

disinflation: a reduction in the inflation rate.

deflation: a decrease in the overall price level, or a negative inflation rate.

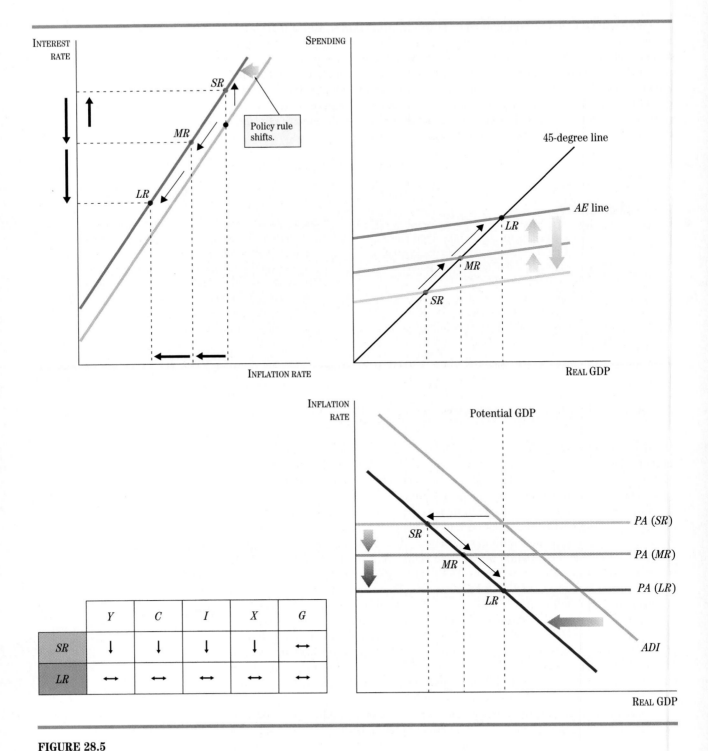

FIGURE 28.5
Disinflation: A Transition to Lower Inflation
The figure shows how a change in monetary policy to a lower target for inflation affects real GDP
over time. In the end, inflation is lower and real GDP is back to potential GDP.

net exports. The effect of the shift in investment and net exports is to shift the aggregate expenditure curve down and to reduce real GDP. The point labeled *SR* determines the new level of spending balance in the upper-right diagram and we therefore shift the aggregate demand/inflation curve, as shown in the lower-right diagram. Since prices are slow to adjust, we do not move the price adjustment line yet. Thus, inflation remains at 10 percent in the short run. The first row of the table summarizes the short-run effects. Note that consumption falls because real GDP is down and income is down. At this time things seem very grim. The short-run effect of the change to a new monetary policy is to cause real GDP to fall below potential GDP. If the disinflation is large enough, then this might mean a decline in real GDP, or a recession. If the disinflation is very small and gradual, then the decline in real GDP could result in a *temporary growth slowdown*. In a temporary growth slowdown, real GDP growth does not turn negative, as in a recession.

In any case, with real GDP below potential GDP, inflation will begin to decline. We show this in the lower-right diagram by moving the price adjustment line down. The lower price adjustment line, labeled *MR* for medium run, intersects the aggregate demand/inflation curve at a higher level of real GDP. Thus, the economy has begun to recover. The recovery starts because as inflation has come down, the Fed has begun to lower the interest rate. This is shown in the upper-left graph of Figure 28.5. As the interest rate declines, investment and net exports begin to rise again and the aggregate expenditure curve shifts up, as shown in the upper-right diagram.

However, at this medium-run situation, real GDP is still below potential GDP, so the inflation rate continues to decline. We show this in the diagram by shifting the price adjustment line down again. To make a long story short, we show the price adjustment line shifting all the way down to where it intersects the aggregate demand/inflation curve at potential GDP. Thus, in this long-run equilibrium, the economy has fully recovered, and the inflation rate is at its new lower target.

Note that the long-run equilibrium has consumption, investment, and net exports back to normal. However, inflation is changed, and it is lower. Moreover, with lower inflation the interest rate is also lower. It is interesting to note that to get this lower interest rate in the long run, the Fed first had to raise the interest rate, as shown in the upper-left graph in Figure 28.5.

The overall dynamic impacts of this change in monetary policy are very important. The initial impact of a monetary policy change is on real GDP. It is only later that the change shows up in inflation. Thus, there is a long lag in the effect of monetary policy on inflation.

Lower inflation would likely make potential GDP grow faster, perhaps because there is less uncertainty and productivity rises faster. If so, the return of real GDP to potential GDP will mean that real GDP is higher, and the long-run benefits of the disinflation to people in the economy may be great over the years. But such changes in the growth of real GDP will appear small in the span of years during which a disinflation takes place and will not change the basic story that a reduction in the rate of inflation, unless it is very gradual, usually results in a recession.

The Volcker Disinflation

The scenario we just described is very similar to the disinflation in the United States in the early 1980s under Paul Volcker, the head of the Fed from 1979 to 1987. First, interest rates skyrocketed as the disinflation began. The federal funds interest rate

Using Economics to Explain the Recovery from the Great Depression

The Great Depression was the biggest economic downturn in American history. There is simply no parallel either before or since. As shown in the figure, from 1929 to 1933, real GDP declined 35 percent. Between 1933 and 1937, real GDP rose 33 percent, then declined 5 percent in a recession in 1938. Real GDP increased by a spectacular 49 percent between 1938 and 1942. By 1942, real GDP had caught up with potential GDP, as estimated in the figure.

There is still much disagreement among economists about what caused the Great Depression, that is, the initial departure of real GDP from potential GDP. In their monetary history of the United States, Milton Friedman and Anna Schwartz argue that it was caused by an error in monetary policy, which implied a massive leftward shift in the aggregate demand/inflation curve. Unfortunately, it took several years of continually declining real GDP, declining inflation, and even deflation before the errors in monetary policy were corrected.

Another explanation is that there was a downward shift in consumption and investment spending that lowered the aggregate expenditures. Peter Temin of MIT has argued that such a spending shift was a cause of the Great Depression.

But whatever the initial cause, there seems to be more consensus that monetary policy was responsible for the belated recovery from the Great Depression. Interest rates (in real terms) fell precipitously in 1933 and remained low or negative throughout most of the second half of the 1930s. These low interest rates led to an increase in investment and net exports. Christina Romer of the University of California at Berkeley estimates that without the monetary response "the U.S. economy in 1942 would have been 50 percent below its pre-Depression trend path, rather than back to its normal level."*

Could the recovery from the Great Depression be associated with an increase in government purchases or a reduction in taxes? Evidently not. Romer shows that government purchases and tax policy were basically unchanged until 1941, when government spending increased sharply during World War II. By that time the economy had already made up most of the Depression decline in real GDP relative to potential GDP.

*Christina Romer, "What Ended the Great Depression?" *Journal of Economic History,* Vol. 52, December 1992, pp. 757–784.

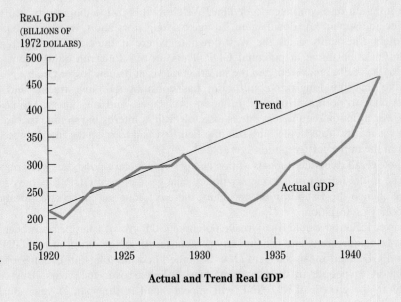

Actual and Trend Real GDP

went over 20 percent. By any measure, real GDP fell well below potential GDP in the early 1980s. Workers were laid off, the unemployment rate rose to 10.8 percent, investment declined, and net exports fell. Eventually, pricing decisions began to adjust and inflation began to come down. As inflation came down, the Fed began to lower the interest rate; the economy eventually recovered. In 1982, a recovery was under way and by 1985, the economy had returned to near its potential. The good news was that inflation was down from over 10 percent to about 4 percent, where it remained for several years before the economy entered a boom period in 1988. But that is another story.

Reinflation

The opposite of disinflation might be called **reinflation,** an increase in the inflation rate caused by a change in monetary policy. This could be analyzed with our theory simply by reversing the preceding process, starting with a change in monetary policy to a higher target inflation rate. This would cause the aggregate demand/inflation curve to shift right. There would be a temporary boom, but eventually inflation would rise and cut off the boom.

Although it would be unusual for central bankers to explicitly admit they were raising the target inflation rate, there could be political pressures that would lead to less concern about inflation. In this way there would be an implicit rise in the target for inflation.

Reinflation is one way to interpret the increase in inflation in the United States and other countries in the 1970s. But there were other things going on at that time, including a quadrupling of oil prices as petroleum-exporting countries, many of which are located in the Middle East, banded together and formed a cartel. We consider oil price shocks in the next section.

reinflation: an increase in the inflation rate caused by a change in monetary policy.

Review

▶ Disinflation is a reduction in inflation. It occurs when the central bank shifts monetary policy in the direction of a lower inflation target.

▶ According to the theory of economic fluctuations, disinflation has either a temporary slowing of real GDP growth or a recession as a by-product. A higher interest rate at the start of a disinflation

lowers investment spending and net exports. This causes real GDP to fall below potential GDP. Eventually the economy recovers. Inflation comes down and so does the interest rate.

▶ The large disinflation in the early 1980s in the United States was accompanied by a recession, as predicted by the theory.

THE CASE OF A PRICE SHOCK OR SUPPLY SHOCK

Shifts in the aggregate demand/inflation curve are called **demand shocks.** The change in government purchases and the change in monetary policy described in the previous two sections of this chapter are examples of demand shocks. However, shifts in the aggregate demand/inflation curve are not the only things that can push real GDP away from potential GDP. In particular, the price adjustment line can shift.

demand shock: a shift in one of the components of aggregate demand that leads to a shift in the aggregate demand/inflation curve.

What Is a Price Shock?

price shock: a change in the price of a key commodity such as oil, usually because of a shortage, that causes a shift in the price adjustment line; also sometimes called a supply shock.

Shifts in the price adjustment line are called **price shocks.** A price shock usually occurs when a temporary shortage of a key commodity, or group of commodities, drives up prices by such a large amount that it has a noticeable effect on the rate of inflation. Oil price shocks have been common in the last 25 years. For example, oil prices rose sharply in 1974, in 1979, and again in 1990. After such shocks there have been declines in real GDP and increases in unemployment. Hence, they appear to move real GDP significantly, though temporarily, away from potential GDP.

Price shocks are sometimes called *supply shocks* in an attempt to distinguish them from demand shocks due to changes in government spending or monetary policy. However, a shift in potential GDP—rather than a shift in the price adjustment line—is more appropriately called a supply shock. Shifts in potential GDP—such as a sudden spurt in productivity growth due to new inventions—can, of course, cause real GDP to fluctuate. Recall that *real business cycle theory* places great emphasis on shifts in potential GDP. Although a price shock might be accompanied by a shift in potential GDP, it need not be. Here we are looking at departures of real GDP from potential GDP and thus focusing on price shocks.

real business cycle theory: a theory of macroeconomics that stresses that shifts in potential GDP are a primary cause of fluctuations in real GDP; the shifts in potential GDP are usually caused by changes in technology. (Ch. 25)

The Effect of Price Shocks

How does our theory of economic fluctuations allow us to predict the effect of price shocks? The impact of a price shock can be illustrated graphically, as shown in Figure 28.6. In the case of a large increase in oil prices, for example, the price adjustment line will shift up to a higher level of inflation. Why? Because a large increase in oil prices will at first lead to an increase in the price of everything that

FIGURE 28.6
A Price Shock
Initially, inflation and the *PA* line rise because of a shock to oil or agricultural prices. This causes real GDP to fall. With real GDP below potential GDP, inflation begins to decline. As inflation declines, real GDP returns to potential GDP.

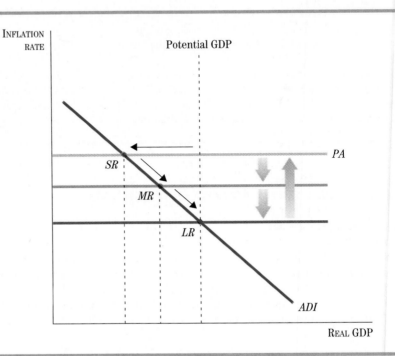

uses oil in production: home heating, gasoline, airplane fuel, airfares, plastic toys, and many other things. The overall price level is affected. As the price level rises, the price adjustment line, measuring inflation, must shift up.

The immediate impact of the shock is to lower real GDP as the intersection of the price adjustment line with the aggregate demand/inflation curve moves to the left. The reason this occurs is that interest rates rise, reducing investment spending and net exports.

With real GDP below potential GDP, however, the reduction in spending will put pressure on firms to adjust their prices. The lower prices bring about a lower rate of inflation. Thus, in the period following the rise of inflation, we begin to see a reversal. Inflation starts to decline. As inflation falls, interest rates begin to decline and the economy starts to recover again. If the central bank does not change its inflation target, the rate of inflation will return to where it was before the price shock started.

Temporary Shifts in the Price Adjustment Line

In this analysis of the price shock, the central bank raises interest rates, and the resulting decline in real GDP exerts countervailing forces to reduce inflation. It is possible for some price shocks to have only a temporary effect on inflation. Such a temporary effect can be shown graphically as a rise followed by a quick fall in the price adjustment line. In such a situation—where the price shock would be expected to automatically reverse itself—it would be wise for the central bank to delay raising the interest rate. Then if the price shock only has a temporary effect on inflation, the decline in real GDP can be avoided. In reality, whenever there is a price shock there is a great debate about whether it will have a temporary or permanent effect on inflation. The debate is rarely settled until after the fact.

Price shocks can also occur when commodity prices fall. For example, in 1986 there was a decline in oil prices. This resulted in a temporary decrease in inflation and a rise in real GDP, exactly what would be predicted by the theory of economic fluctuations.

Stagflation

An important difference between price shocks and demand shocks is that output declines while inflation rises in the case of a price shock. For demand shocks, inflation and output are positively related over the period of recession and recovery. The situation in which inflation is up and real GDP is down is called **stagflation.** As we have shown, price shocks can lead to stagflation.

stagflation: the situation in which high inflation and high unemployment occur simultaneously.

Review

▶ A price shock is a large change in the price of some key commodity like oil. Such shocks can push real GDP away from potential GDP and lead to a recession.

▶ In the aftermath of a price shock, the interest rate rises. Eventually, with real GDP below potential GDP, inflation begins to come down and the economy recovers.

COMBINING DIFFERENT SCENARIOS

The particular events or scenarios we have used thus far to illustrate the theory of economic fluctuations are isolated from each other. This has made it easier to explain what happens in the economy over time. However, in the real world, we rarely have one event occurring in isolation from others. Policymakers do not have the luxury of considering one event at a time. Fortunately, the economic fluctuations model is powerful enough to apply to such real-world situations. In this section, we show how.

A Monetary Policy Change with a Government Purchases Change

The case of a decrease in government purchases discussed earlier is an important example of where it is useful to combine different scenarios. In particular, it calls for combining such a change in government purchases with a change in monetary policy. This is shown in Figure 28.7. The leftward shift in the aggregate demand/inflation curve due to reduction in government purchases is counteracted by a rightward shift in the aggregate demand/inflation curve due to monetary policy. If the change in monetary policy is by just the right amount, there will be no short-run impact on real GDP.

This type of shift requires a complex coordination of the central bank policy with the change in government purchases. In practice, this is difficult because the timing of the changes is uncertain—Congress could delay cutting purchases, for example, or the president might have trouble getting enough votes to pass the legislation needed to reduce government purchases. Or, a new president with different ideas could come into office. It was just this type of coordination problem that arose several times in the United States during the efforts to reduce government spending in the 1990s. Proposals to reduce government spending were made in

FIGURE 28.7
Change in Monetary Policy to Accompany a Change in Government Purchases

If the central bank uses an interest rate rule for monetary policy, then a reduction in government purchases that lowers interest rates in the long run will end up reducing inflation. The central bank can avoid the reduction in inflation by shifting its policy rule, as shown in the figure.

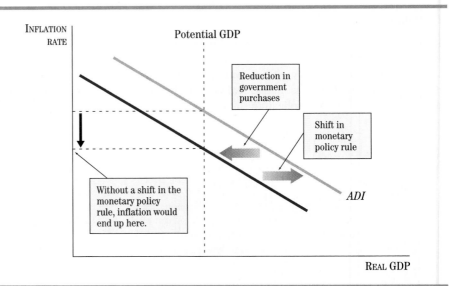

1990, 1993, and 1995. Each time the hope was that the Fed would adjust its monetary policy in a way consistent with a lower interest rate. This is an example of a combination of two scenarios: a reduction in government purchases and a change in monetary policy.

Monetary Errors and Reversals: A Boom-Bust Cycle

Another case where combining different scenarios leads to a more realistic description of reality is called a **boom-bust cycle,** which is illustrated in Figure 28.8. In this case, the central bank first makes a mistake and lowers the interest rate too much. Political pressure might be behind such a development. In any case we know

boom-bust cycle: a business cycle caused by a monetary policy in which interest rates are initially too low, causing a boom, and there is a subsequent increase in interest rates, which causes a recession.

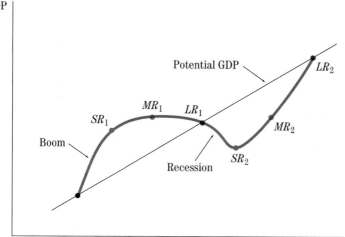

FIGURE 28.8
A Complete Boom-Bust Cycle
First, the central bank provides too much stimulus. The *ADI* curve shifts right, causing a boom. Inflation rises. Then the central bank notices the error and shifts the *ADI* curve back, causing a recession. Eventually, real GDP is brought to potential GDP. The short-run, medium-run, and long-run points for the boom and the recession are shown on both panels.

Brief History of Thought on Price Adjustment

Price adjustment has played a key role in theories of economic fluctuations since the beginning of economics. In the late 1700s, while Adam Smith was still working on the *Wealth of Nations,* David Hume, the Scottish economist and philosopher, wrote about slow price adjustment as a reason for economic fluctuations. Hume wrote, ". . . by degrees the price rises, first of one commodity, then of another."* More than 150 years later, John Maynard Keynes argued in the 1930s that unemployment occurs because prices or wages do not adjust enough, though he also worried that too rapid reductions in wages could reduce consumption demand and make a recession worse. Fifty years after Keynes wrote, Milton Friedman argued that "prices are sticky,"† and that slow price and wage adjustment is the reason why the economy returns gradually to potential GDP in the long run.

Today economists still focus on the slow adjustment of prices. However, views about price adjustment have not been stagnant for 200 years. Especially in the last 25 years, practical experience and improved methods to deal with expectations, limited information, and implicit contracts have led to an improved understanding of the role of price adjustment in fluctuations.

The price adjustment line reflects this experience and improved methods. It is a graphical representation of the effects of slow price adjustment on economic fluctuations. Due to slow price adjustment, the price adjustment line is flat and does not shift in the short run. After the short run, however, prices do start to adjust and the curve shifts either down, as in Figure 28.2, or up.

An alternative graph—shown in this box—has also been used by economists to represent the slow adjustment of prices. In this alternative graph the overall price level—rather than the inflation rate—is on the vertical axis and real GDP is on the horizontal axis. Potential GDP is shown by a vertical dashed line. The upward-sloping curve in the graph shows different combinations of the overall price level and real GDP. Along the flat region of the curve, the overall price level does not change as real GDP increases. This represents a range of sticky prices; some authors call this range the "Keynesian range" because real GDP was well below potential GDP during the Great Depression when Keynes argued that in such circumstances the price level would not change much when real GDP changed. The range where the curve becomes vertical is sometimes called the "classical range" because

Keynes argued that classical economists such as Hume and Smith implicitly assumed that the economy was near potential and that prices would be flexible, rising rapidly if real GDP increased further.

The upward-sloping curve in this diagram is sometimes called an "aggregate supply curve." It is possible to combine this aggregate supply curve with a downward-sloping "aggregate demand curve," much like the price adjustment line is combined with the aggregate demand/inflation curve.

Although such an aggregate supply curve highlights Keynes's distinction between his own theory and those of the classical economists, it does not reflect the experience and methods of the last several decades. For example, it predicts that the price level will fall when real GDP falls below potential GDP; but in reality the price level rarely falls in this situation. Instead, the inflation rate falls, as described by downward shifts in the price adjustment line in Figure 28.2. Moreover, the "Keynesian" and "classical" ranges are not accurate characterizations of the history of economic thought because many of the classical economists as well as many of today's non-Keynesian economists assume that prices are sticky.

If you continue your study of economics, you will find that there are still other graphical approaches used by authors of more advanced textbooks in macroeconomics. Some authors draw an aggregate supply curve that is flat through its whole range, others argue that an aggregate supply curve does not exist, and still others avoid the use of such graphs entirely, using only microeconomic supply curves.

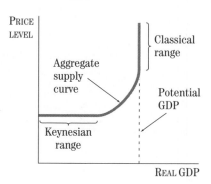

David Hume: Writings on Economics, ed. E. Rotwein (Madison, Wisc.: University of Wisconsin Press, 1955), p. 38.

†*Newsweek,* July 12, 1982, p. 64.

that such an error will cause a boom and a rise in inflation. The boom and the rise in inflation themselves might cause the central bank to see the error of its ways and to reverse its error. If so, the central bank will shift its policy again. This will then whipsaw the economy down, and a boom will quickly become a recession. Eventually the economy will recover from the recession, but the errors by the central bank—whether avoidable or unavoidable—have done damage. They have caused a complete economic fluctuation.

To illustrate a boom-bust cycle in Figure 28.8, we have patched two scenarios together. Scenario 1 is the mistaken shift in monetary policy that causes the aggregate demand/inflation curve to shift to the right with the reduction in interest rates causing the boom. Scenario 2 is the reversal, which causes the recession. Each scenario has a short run, a medium run, and a long run, as shown in the lower panel of Figure 28.8. Observe the path that real GDP would follow and how it corresponds to the points on the diagram.

Comparing the boom-bust cycle in Figure 28.8 with some actual economic fluctuations reveals a remarkable similarity. For example, compare the path of real GDP in Figure 28.8 with Figure 27.1 at the beginning of the previous chapter, which showed the economic fluctuations in real GDP and inflation in the United States economy from 1987 to 1994. This period fits into a boom-bust cycle very well.

Review

▶ The real world is characterized by combinations of scenarios rather than by isolated scenarios.

▶ One combination of scenarios is a coordinated change in monetary policy when government purchases change. This raises issues about the coordination of government spending and monetary policies.

▶ Typically, mistakes in monetary policy have been followed by reversals that have led to boom-bust cycles. A boom scenario is followed by a bust scenario.

CONCLUSION

Using the diagram with the aggregate demand/inflation curve and the price adjustment line, we can explain not only the first steps toward recessions and booms but also the recovery of the economy.

As we developed this model, we tested each piece of it. Each piece was shown to pass two tests: It fit the facts well, and it made economic sense. In conclusion, it is appropriate to ask how well the complete model fits the facts. How well does it explain actual behavior of real GDP and inflation in the economy? One basic test that the model passes is its consistency with the fact that inflation has remained greater than zero, year after year, without the price level declining even when real GDP returns to potential GDP after recessions. Any model that required the price level to fall in order for real GDP to return to potential GDP would be hopelessly wrong.

But the model also passes more stringent tests nearly as well. Figure 28.9 shows four actual patterns of fluctuations of real GDP and inflation. Each of the four episodes can be identified with a particular change in the economy that we

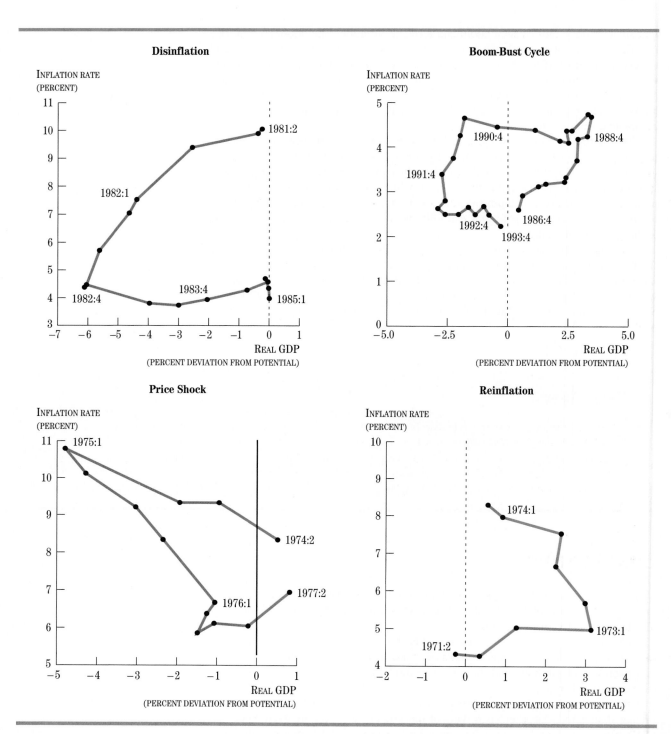

FIGURE 28.9
Four Different Types of Economic Fluctuations
Four different patterns of inflation and real GDP show the different types of economic fluctuations that can
be explained by the theory of economic fluctuations described in the text. (The number following the year
in the labeled points is the *quarter* of the year.)

have described in this chapter, either single scenarios or two spliced together. The episodes are labeled disinflation, boom-bust cycle, price shock, and reinflation. Although the pictures are not as smooth as in the theoretical diagrams, the theory works very well.

In the disinflation episode, real GDP falls below potential GDP and inflation declines, as would be predicted by a leftward shift of the aggregate demand/inflation curve followed by downward movement in inflation. The boom-bust cycle is easily explained by the combined monetary policy scenarios discussed in the previous section. In the price shock episode, inflation rises and real GDP declines, as would be predicted by an upward shift in the price adjustment line. In the reinflation episode, there is a boom and inflation rises, as would be predicted by the theory in the case of a demand shock.

The fact that real GDP returns toward potential GDP in the long run is also a test of the model because in reality all recessions and booms have ended. Real GDP appears to fluctuate around potential GDP rather than getting stuck forever in a boom or a recession. The tendency for real GDP to return toward potential GDP allows us to use the theory of long-run growth when discussing long-run trends in the economy. As the economy fluctuates, potential GDP gradually increases over time.

KEY POINTS

1. An increase in government purchases temporarily causes a boom, but as prices adjust, real GDP returns to potential GDP.

2. A decline in government purchases temporarily reduces real GDP, but over time the economy recovers as prices adjust.

3. Shifts in monetary policy, including explicit attempts to disinflate or reinflate, cause real GDP to depart from potential GDP temporarily. But eventually real GDP returns to potential GDP and only the inflation rate is changed.

4. Price shocks can also cause recessions. A price shock that raises the inflation rate will cause the interest rate to rise and real GDP to fall.

5. If the Fed follows its monetary policy rule, then it will raise interest rates following a price shock, and eventually inflation will come back down.

6. If a price shock is clearly temporary, then the Fed should not change the interest rate.

7. Boom-bust cycles that appear common in the history of economic fluctuations can be explained by monetary policy errors followed by attempts to reverse the errors.

8. Shifts of the price adjustment line and aggregate demand/inflation curve trace out actual observations fairly closely. Thus, the economic fluctuations model works well, but, like most models in economics and elsewhere, it is not perfect.

KEY TERMS

baseline	reinflation	stagflation
disinflation	demand shock	boom-bust cycle
deflation	price shock	

QUESTIONS FOR REVIEW

1. What causes the economy to recover after a recession? Does your answer depend on the cause of the recession?

2. What is the difference between the long-run and the short-run effects of a change in government spending?

3. What is disinflation, and how does the central bank bring it about?

4. What is reinflation, and what impact does it have on real GDP in the short run and long run?

5. What is a price shock, and why have price shocks frequently been followed by increases in unemployment?

6. What is the difference between a price shock and a supply shock?

7. Why do monetary policy errors seem to lead to boom-bust cycles?

8. When is it important to coordinate monetary policy with changes in plans for government spending?

PROBLEMS

1. Using the aggregate demand/inflation curve and the price adjustment line, describe what would happen to real GDP, consumption, investment, net exports, interest rates, and inflation in the short run, in the medium run, and in the long run if there were a permanent increase in government spending on highway construction. Be sure to provide an economic explanation for your results.

2. Suppose the central bank wants to revert to the original inflation rate before the increase in government spending in problem 1. How can it achieve its objective? Describe the proposed change in policy and its short-run, medium-run, and long-run effects on real GDP and inflation.

3. Using the aggregate demand/inflation curve and the price adjustment line, show what happens if the central bank reinflates the economy. Suppose the target inflation rate is changed from 2 percent to 5 percent. Consider the impact on the major components of spending in the short run, the medium run, and the long run.

4. The economy begins at potential GDP with an inflation rate of 4 percent. Draw this situation with an aggregate demand/inflation curve and a price adjustment line. Suppose there is a price shock that pushes inflation up to 6 percent in the short run, but the effect on inflation is viewed as temporary by the Fed. It expects the price adjustment line to shift back down by 2 percent next year, and in fact the price adjustment line does shift back down.

   a) If the Fed follows its usual policy rule, where will real GDP be in the short run? How does the economy adjust back to potential?

   b) Now suppose that since the Fed is sure that this inflationary shock is only temporary, it decides not to follow its typical policy rule but instead maintains the interest rate at its previous level. What happens to real GDP? Why? What will the long-run adjustment be in this case? Do you agree with the Fed's handling of the situation?

5. Use the following data to graph the aggregate demand/inflation curve:

Inflation (percent)	Real GDP (billions of dollars)
10	4,800
8	4,900
6	5,000
4	5,100
2	5,200

9. In what ways is the economic fluctuations model discussed in this chapter consistent with real-world observations?

   a) Suppose the current inflation rate is 4 percent, and potential GDP is $5,000 billion. Draw in the price adjustment line. What is the current deviation of real GDP from potential?

   b) In the long run, what will the inflation rate be if there is no change in economic policy? Explain how this adjustment takes place.

6. Continuing from problem 5, suppose that after the long-run adjustment back to potential, the Fed changes its policy rule so that the inflation target is 4 percent but potential GDP remains at $5,000 billion. What type of monetary policy is the Fed undertaking? Use the following data to show the shift in the aggregate demand/inflation curve.

Inflation (percent)	Real GDP (billions of dollars)
10	4,700
8	4,800
6	4,900
4	5,000
2	5,100

   a) How does the Fed accomplish this goal? What is the response of investment and net exports?

   b) In the short run, what is the deviation from potential GDP?

   c) How will the price adjustment line adjust in the medium and long run? Explain how this adjustment takes place.

7. Suppose that the GDP deflator in 2001 is 100, and in 2002 it is 105.

   a) Suppose the economy is at potential GDP in 2001 and 2002. What is the rate of inflation in 2002?

   b) Suppose instead that real GDP is below potential GDP in 2002. How is the adjustment back to potential made in this situation?

8. Suppose there are two countries that are very similar except that one has a much higher rate of money growth. They have identical potential GDP and are both at their long-run equilibrium. Draw this situation with an aggregate demand/inflation curve and a price adjustment line. Explain how these different equilibrium levels of inflation are possible. How do workers' and firms' expectations differ between the two countries?

9. Show in the shares of spending diagrams from Chapter 22 the effect of a decrease in government spending's share of GDP. Compare this case with the same situation using aggregate demand/inflation curves and price adjustment lines. Is the long-run effect the same in both models?

10. Recall from Chapter 27 that the Fed's policy rule shows different real interest rates for different levels of inflation.

    a) Graph the Fed's policy rule (as a solid line) along with that of a constant real interest rate (as a dashed line). What is the slope of the dashed line?

    b) Show the Fed's target rate of inflation on the graph.

    c) Recall from Chapter 22 that a permanent increase in government spending as a share of GDP will cause

the real interest rate to rise. If the government permanently increases its spending share in GDP, what will happen in the policy rule diagram? How does the dashed line shift? Show the new long-run inflation and interest rate at the intersection of the monetary policy rule and the dashed line.

    d) Now suppose that the Fed insists on maintaining the level of inflation that existed prior to the increase in government purchases. What does the Fed have to do to force this disinflation? Which way will the policy rule shift? Show in your diagram that the real interest rate is still permanently higher after the long-run adjustment to this new monetary policy.

7 part

Macroeconomic Policy

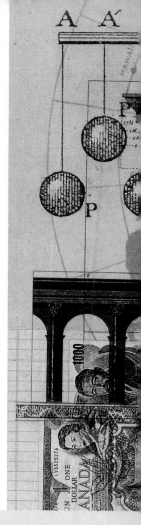

Using the macroeconomic theory developed in the previous two parts of the book, we now explore the fascinating world of macroeconomic policy in this last part. Macroeconomic policy, which includes both fiscal policy and monetary policy, has powerful effects on the economy.

Different countries have approached fiscal and monetary policy issues in various ways, and their approaches have changed over time. Some have successfully kept strict control over the government budget deficit. Others seem to have let the budget deficit grow out of control. As to monetary policy, some countries have given their central banks much independence; others require strict accountability. Some central banks are more concerned with the exchange rate than with the money supply; others focus on the money supply. As to policies that affect long-term

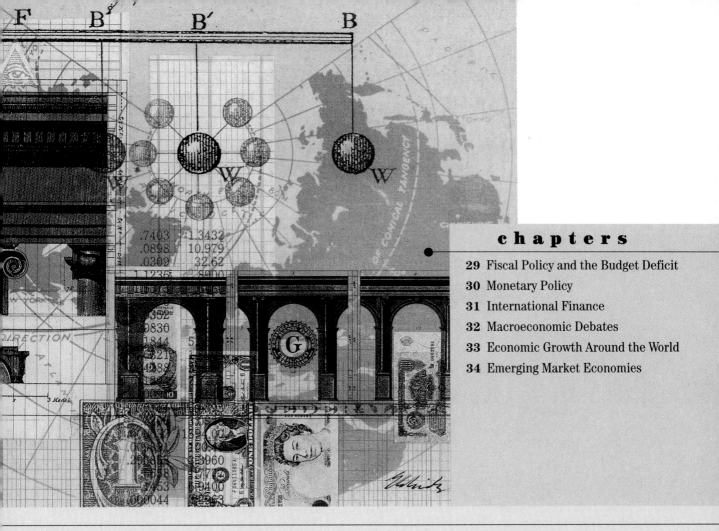

chapters

29 Fiscal Policy and the Budget Deficit

30 Monetary Policy

31 International Finance

32 Macroeconomic Debates

33 Economic Growth Around the World

34 Emerging Market Economies

growth, some countries have tax systems that encourage saving, whereas others seem to tax saving at a higher rate than consumption. These six chapters examine the pros and cons of the different approaches to monetary and fiscal policy. There are great differences of opinion on these issues but there are also important areas of agreement.

In Chapter 29 we look at how fiscal policy decisions are made and examine alternative methods for assessing the effects of the budget deficit on the economy. In Chapter 30 we explore the reasons for central bank independence and study alternative proposals for the conduct of monetary policy. In Chapter 31 we extend the analysis of monetary and fiscal policy to global issues. In Chapter 32 we discuss macroeconomic debates. In Chapter 33 we focus on economic growth around the world. In Chapter 34 we apply the tools of

economics to one of the most difficult policy problems in this age of emerging market economies: the transition from central planning to a market system.

From the disagreements between Malthus and Ricardo in the 1830s to the debates between Keynesians and monetarists in the 1960s to the disputes of the real business cycle school in the 1990s, macroeconomic policy issues have always been controversial. But macroeconomic models have had a great impact on economic policy outcomes. Exploring the policy issues in these chapters will prepare you for likely future debates over economic policy whether you are active in them or simply want to understand them as a citizen interested in the economic future of the world.

Fiscal Policy and the Budget Deficit

29

Fiscal policy is much easier to define than to carry out. Two of the fiscal activities of government are *spending*—on national defense, road building, schools, or transfer payments—and collecting *taxes* to pay for this spending. When spending is greater than taxes, there is a budget deficit, which must be financed by government *borrowing,* a third fiscal activity. *Policy* refers to a plan of action by the government. Hence, **fiscal policy** is defined as the government's plans for spending, for taxes, and for borrowing to finance the budget deficit, if one exists.

In previous chapters, we showed that changes in government spending and taxes affect the economy. An increase in government purchases or a cut in taxes will increase real GDP in the short run. In this chapter, we examine whether fiscal policy can make use of these short-run effects to reduce the size of economic fluctuations. For example, a policy of cutting taxes in a recession might reduce unemployment by ending the recession early or quickening the pace of recovery from recession. We also examine problems that arise in formulating and carrying out fiscal policy and discuss why economists frequently disagree about fiscal policy.

We also showed in previous chapters that changes in government spending and taxes affect the economy in the long run. For example, a decrease in government purchases as a share of GDP will lower interest rates and thereby increase incentives to invest and perhaps raise economic growth. Can a fiscal policy for spending and taxes be designed to improve long-term economic growth? If so, what problems exist in carrying out such a policy?

In the past two decades government spending increased more than taxes in the United States and many other countries. As a result, budget deficits and government borrowing rose sharply. But what exactly is the effect of the debt? Is the deficit harmful? These questions are also addressed in this chapter.

There have been attempts in recent years to make fiscal policy work better—legally limiting the size of the deficit, capping spending, changing the balance of power between the legislative and the executive branches. Have these measures improved the situation? Other ideas have also been proposed—limiting the terms of elected officials, amending the Constitution to require a balanced budget, and restricting campaign contributions. Would these improve the situation?

Essential to answering questions about fiscal policy is a careful assessment of the government budget, which contains the plans for spending, taxes, and the deficit each year, and that is where we begin.

fiscal policy: the government's plans for spending, for taxes, and for borrowing.

THE GOVERNMENT BUDGET: TAXES, SPENDING, THE DEFICIT, AND THE DEBT

The **federal budget** is the major summary document describing fiscal policy in the United States. The budget includes not only estimates of the deficit that get so much attention but also proposals for taxes and spending. Let's look at how the federal budget in the United States is put together.

federal budget: a summary of the federal government's proposals for spending, taxes, and the deficit.

Setting the Annual Budget

In the United States, the president submits a new budget to Congress each year for the following fiscal year. The fiscal year runs from October to October. For example, *The Budget of the United States: Fiscal Year 1998* applied to spending and taxes from October 1, 1997, through September 30, 1998. It was submitted by President Clinton to Congress in early 1997. The president typically devotes part of

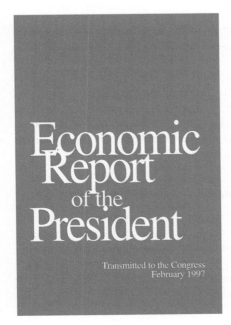

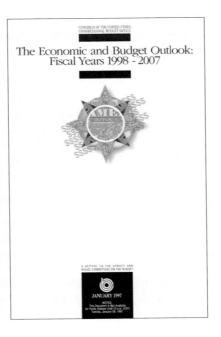

The CEA and CBO
The economic assumptions used for the federal budget are presented by the Council of Economic Advisers (CEA) in the *Economic Report of the President.* To assist the Senate and the House of Representatives in their deliberations on the president's fiscal policy proposals, the Congressional Budget Office (CBO) then does its own economic analysis, which is published each year in *The Economic and Budget Outlook.*

the State of the Union address to describing the budget and fiscal policy. Also at the start of each year, the *Economic Report of the President* is released, providing the economic assumptions underlying the budget prepared by the Council of Economic Advisers. The Congressional Budget Office makes its own economic assumptions. During the budget battles between President Clinton and the Congress in 1995, one of the main points of dispute was a discrepancy between the economic forecasts of the CEA and the CBO.

In putting together the federal budget, the president proposes many specific spending programs that fit into an overall philosophy of what government should be doing. President Bush proposed increased spending on scientific research and reduced spending on railroads, such as Amtrak. President Clinton proposed increased funding on training programs and reduced spending on defense. However, in any one year, most of the spending in the budget is determined by ongoing programs, which the president usually can do little to change. For example, payments of social security benefits to older people are a large item in the budget, but the amount of spending on social security depends on how many eligible people there are. If more people become eligible, then spending automatically goes up unless the social security law changes. Thus, in reality, the president can change only a small part of the budget each year.

A Balanced Budget versus a Deficit or Surplus

Recall the difference between **tax rate** and **tax revenues** discussed in Chapter 26. For the income tax, if the average tax rate is 20 percent and income is $3,000 billion, then tax revenues are $600 billion.

Taxes to pay for the spending programs are also included in the budget. As part of the budget, the president may propose an increase or a decrease in taxes. *Tax revenues* are the total dollar amount the government receives from taxpayers each year. When tax revenues are exactly equal to spending, there is a **balanced budget.** When tax revenues are greater than spending, there is a **budget surplus.** When spending is greater than tax revenues, there is a **budget deficit,** and the government must borrow to pay the difference.

balanced budget: a budget for which tax revenues equal spending.

budget surplus: the amount by which tax revenues exceed spending.

budget deficit: the amount by which government spending exceeds tax revenues.

Budget Deficit	Budget Balance	Budget Surplus
Tax revenues < spending	Tax revenues = spending	Tax revenues > spending

There is no requirement in the United States that the president submit a balanced budget. Presidents Reagan, Bush, and Clinton all submitted budgets to Congress that did not balance. Rather, they were in deficit. There are many reasons why proposed budgets do not balance. For example, as we will discuss later in this chapter, if the economy is in recession, increasing taxes or lowering spending to balance the budget could make the recession worse.

The Proposed Budget versus the Actual Budget

Keep in mind that the budget the president submits is only a *proposal.* The amount of tax revenues and spending, or expenditures, that actually occur during the fiscal year are much different from what is proposed. There are two main reasons for this difference.

First, the Congress usually modifies the president's budget, adding some programs and deleting others. Congress deliberates on the specific items in the president's budget proposal for months before the fiscal year actually starts. After the president's budget is debated and modified, it is passed by Congress. Only when the president signs the legislation is the budget enacted into law. Because of this congressional modification, the enacted budget is always different from the proposed budget.

Second, because of changes in the economy and other unanticipated events such as wars and natural disasters, the actual amount of spending and taxes will be different from what is enacted. After the fiscal year has begun and the budget has been enacted, various *supplementals* are proposed and passed. A supplemental is a change in a spending program or a change in the tax law that affects the budget in the current fiscal year. In addition, recessions or booms always affect tax revenue and spending to some degree.

Figure 29.1 shows the difference between proposed tax revenues, expenditures, and the deficit for the fiscal year 1991 budget (submitted in January 1990) and the actual tax revenues, expenditures, and deficit that occurred. The 1990–1991 recession was one reason why the difference was so large. In most years, the difference is smaller.

Figure 29.2 shows how the fiscal year 1997 budget moved from a proposal in early 1996 to enactment in late 1996 to completion in October 1997. The same **budget cycle** occurs every year. Because the whole cycle takes over two years, at any one time there are discussions about three budgets. For example, in September 1997, the budget for fiscal year 1997 was coming to a close, the budget for fiscal year 1998 was being considered by Congress, and the budget for fiscal year 1999 was being put together by the president's staff. The budget cycle does not always progress smoothly. In fiscal year 1996, President Clinton and the Congress did not settle on a budget until well into the fiscal year.

budget cycle: the more than two-year process in which the federal budget is proposed, modified, enacted, and implemented.

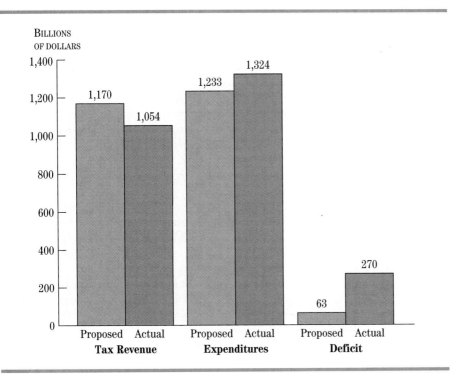

FIGURE 29.1
The Difference Between the Proposed and the Actual Budget in a Recession Year (billions of dollars)

When the fiscal year 1991 budget was submitted to Congress in early 1990, the 1991 deficit was forecast to be $63 billion. By the time the fiscal year was over—almost two years later—the deficit was $270 billion. Because of the 1990–1991 recession, tax revenues were smaller and spending was higher than in the proposed budget.

Source: Economic Report of the President, 1990, Table C-76; Economic Report of the President, 1994, Table B-77.

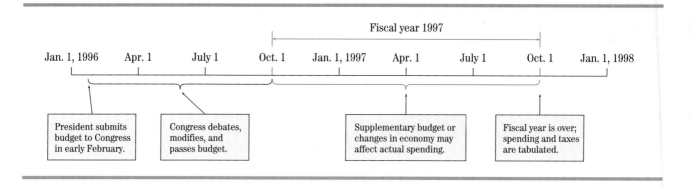

FIGURE 29.2
A Typical Budget Cycle: Fiscal Year 1997

The budget cycle begins about one year before the fiscal year begins. After considering various spending and tax options, the president submits a budget proposal to the Congress in February. The cycle is not complete until the end of the fiscal year. By then, a new budget is being enacted.

A Look at the Federal Budget

Table 29.1 contains summary totals from the federal budget for fiscal year 1995. The full budget, which is over 2,000 pages long, provides much more detail.

The Deficit

Table 29.1 shows tax revenues ($1,478 billion) were less than expenditures ($1,640 billion), so there was a deficit ($162 billion). Budget deficits are common in the United States. The last year without a deficit was 1969.

Taxes and Spending

The tax revenues of $1,478 billion include *personal income taxes* paid by individuals on their total income, *corporate income taxes* paid by businesses on their profits, *sales taxes* on items such as gasoline and beer, and *payroll taxes,* a percentage of wages paid by workers and their employers that supports government programs such as social security. Sales taxes are the smallest of the four components of total revenue, and corporate tax revenues are only slightly larger. Payroll taxes represent a large amount of revenues, nearly the same as personal income tax revenues. Payroll taxes have grown rapidly as a share of federal government revenues in recent years, while the other types of taxes have fallen in relative importance.

The expenditure side of the budget is divided into three basic classes of spending. One is called *purchases* of goods and services, the second is *transfer payments,* and the third is *interest payments.* Only purchases are included in the symbol *G* that we have been using in the text. Purchases represent *new* production, whether postal trucks, federal courthouses, or food for military troops. If you look at total expenditures by the federal government, which is $1,640 billion, a surprisingly small fraction—less than 40 percent—is for the purchase of goods and services. Excluding military, it is only about 10 percent of all spending.

The remaining share of government expenditures consists of transfer payments and interest. The major transfer programs are social security payments to retired people, welfare payments to the poor, unemployment compensation to the unemployed workers, Medicare to older people, and Medicaid to poor people. Transfer payments are a much larger portion of the budget than purchases of goods and services. In other words, the amount that government absorbs in new production is considerably smaller than the amount it transfers to individuals.

●────────────────────

TABLE 29.1
FY 1995 Federal Tax Revenues and Expenditures
(billions of dollars)

Tax Revenues	1,478	
Personal Income		615
Corporate Income		184
Sales Taxes		91
Payroll Taxes		588
Expenditures	1,640	
Purchases		453
Defense		302
Other		151
Transfers		958
Interest		229
Deficit	162	

Source: Economic Report of the President, 1997, Table B-80.

Interest payments are what the federal government pays every year on its borrowing from that year and from previous years. The government pays interest on its borrowings just like anyone else. In fiscal year 1995 interest payments amounted to $229 billion, which is much larger than all nondefense federal government purchases. Total interest payments equal the interest rate multiplied by the amount of government debt outstanding. For example, the interest rate on federal government debt averaged 6 percent in 1995, and total outstanding debt was about $3,783 billion ($229 billion in interest payments is approximately .060 times $3,783 billion). If interest rates come down, then interest payments on the debt go down. Because the United States has such a large amount of outstanding debt, interest payments remain high even when interest rates are low.

The U.S. Budget Deficit versus Other Countries

The United States is not the only country with a government deficit in recent years. Table 29.2 lists the deficits in many industrial countries in 1996, measured as a percentage of GDP. Greece had the largest deficit, and Japan had the smallest.

The Federal Debt

It is important to distinguish between the *federal deficit* and the *federal debt*. The two are frequently mixed up in popular discussions. **Federal debt** is the total amount of outstanding loans that the federal government owes. The deficit, you will recall, is the yearly amount by which spending exceeds taxes. Each year the deficit adds to the debt. If the government runs a surplus, the debt comes down by the amount of the surplus.

Consider an example with thousands of dollars rather than trillions of dollars. Think of it in terms of a student, Sam, who graduates from college with a $14,000 outstanding loan. In other words, he has a debt of $14,000. Suppose the first year that he works his income is $30,000 but he spends $35,000. Sam's deficit is $5,000 and his debt rises to $19,000. Assume that in the second year of work, he has income of $35,000 and spends $38,000; his deficit is $3,000 and his debt rises to $22,000. Each year debt rises by the amount of his deficit. If in the third year Sam earns $40,000 and spends $33,000, then he has a surplus of $7,000. This would reduce his debt to $15,000.

The laws of accounting we apply to Sam also apply to Uncle Sam. The federal government's deficit of $162 billion in 1995 required that the government borrow that amount from individuals, businesses, or foreigners. As a result, the outstanding government debt increased by $162 billion during fiscal year 1995. Figure 29.3 shows the difference between debt and deficit in the United States since 1950.

Long-Term and Short-Term Debt

The federal government borrows for both the short term and long term. With short-term borrowing, the government agrees to pay back the loan with interest in a short period of time, usually one year or less. Long-term government borrowing is for more than a year, up to 30 years. For example, in 1995 the federal government borrowed some funds long term and agreed to pay the loan back in the year 2025 at an interest rate of 7 percent.

The government borrows by selling government bonds. A **bond** is simply a contract (an IOU) that stipulates that the borrower will pay the person who owns

TABLE 29.2

Deficits in Developed Countries, 1996

(percentage of GDP)

Greece	10.0
Sweden	6.8
Italy	7.4
Finland	4.1
United Kingdom	2.4
Spain	3.9
Canada	3.5
France	3.7
Australia	3.9
United States	2.1
Germany	1.8
Austria	3.7
Netherlands	5.8
Norway	1.0
Ireland	2.5
New Zealand	1.6
Japan	0.9

Source: International Monetary Fund.

federal debt: the total amount of outstanding loans owed by the federal government.

bond: a financial contract that stipulates a specific repayment of principal plus interest on a loan at a given date in the future.

FIGURE 29.3
The Deficit and the Debt
When the deficit is zero, the debt does not change. When there is a deficit, the debt increases. When there is a surplus, the debt falls. Deficits and increasing debt have been the rule in recent years. The debt in 1950 was largely due to deficits during World War II.

Source: U.S. Department of Commerce; U.S. Department of the Treasury.

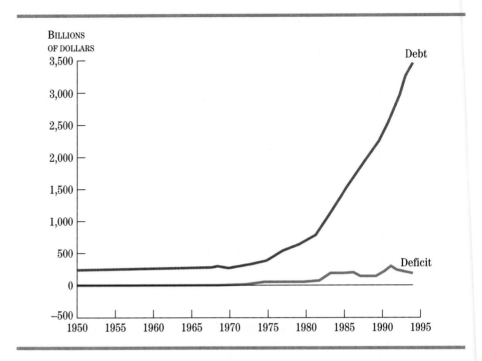

the bond a certain amount. The *maturity* of the bond is the number of years until the funds are paid back. For example, the government sells 30-year government bonds when it borrows funds for 30 years. It then uses the borrowed funds to pay for government spending in excess of tax revenues.

The average maturity on federal debt is about 6 years. Bonds that have a maturity of less than 1 year are called Treasury bills.

The Debt to GDP Ratio

When looking at the debt and the deficit over time, it is important to consider the size of the economy. For example, a $3 trillion debt may not be much of a problem for an economy with a GDP of $10 trillion but could be overwhelming for an economy with a GDP of $1 trillion. An easy way to compare the debt to the size of the economy is to measure the debt as a percentage of GDP—the **debt to GDP ratio.** It is appropriate to consider the debt as a ratio to nominal GDP rather than real GDP because the debt is stated in current dollars just as nominal GDP is.

debt to GDP ratio: the total amount of outstanding loans the federal government owes divided by nominal GDP.

Figure 29.4 shows the behavior of the debt as a percentage of GDP in the United States since 1950. Note that the debt was a high percentage of GDP at the end of World War II because the U.S. government borrowed large amounts to finance its military expenditures during the war. The debt to GDP ratio fell until the mid-1970s, when it began to increase again. The debt to GDP ratio is a good overall gauge of how a government is doing in managing its fiscal affairs.

Note that the ratio of debt to GDP can stay constant when the deficit is greater than zero. This occurs when GDP grows as fast as the debt grows. For example, if GDP grows by 5 percent per year in current dollars, then the debt to GDP ratio will stay constant if the debt grows by 5 percent per year. If the outstanding debt is $3,000 billion, then a deficit of $150 billion would increase the debt by 5 percent

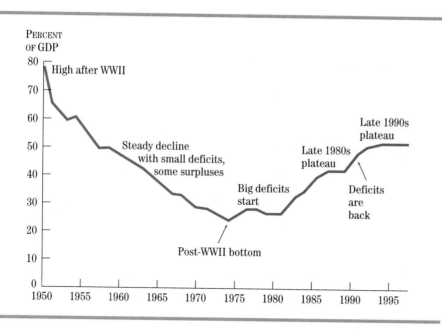

PERCENT OF GDP

High after WWII

Steady decline with small deficits, some surpluses

Post-WWII bottom

Big deficits start

Late 1980s plateau

Deficits are back

Late 1990s plateau

FIGURE 29.4
Debt As a Ratio to GDP
Relative to the size of GDP, the debt declined during the years after World War II. For the last 15 years, the debt has been rising as a ratio to GDP.

Source: U.S. Department of the Treasury.

(150/3000 = .05) and keep the debt to GDP ratio constant. If inflation rose by 5 percent per year so that GDP grew by 10 percent per year, then the deficit could be as large as $300 billion and the debt to GDP ratio would be constant. Robert Eisner, an economist at Northwestern University, emphasizes that the government's public infrastructure represents a public asset that can be viewed as a partial offset to the public debt.

State and Local Government Budgets

Much of government spending and taxation in the United States occurs outside of the federal government, in state and local governments. Although fiscal policy usually refers to the plans of the federal government, it is the combined action of federal, state, and local governments that has an impact on the overall economy. For example, in the 1990–1991 recession, many states cut back on spending and raised taxes; both actions would tend to reduce real GDP in the short run, just as reduced spending and higher taxes at the federal level would. Taken as a whole, state and local governments are a large force in the economy. Table 29.3 shows that in 1995 state and local government expenditures were about 55 percent as much as federal government expenditures.

Most of the expenditures are for public schools, local police, fire services, and roads. Observe that state and local government *purchases* of goods and services are larger than federal government purchases, especially when national defense is excluded.

The state and local governments as a whole ran a surplus in 1995. By running surpluses for many years, state and local governments have accumulated assets—mostly U.S. government bonds—on which they earn interest. Thus, interest payments are negative in Table 29.3, indicating that these governments received interest income. Note, however, that the surplus for state and local governments as a whole masks the deficits that loomed in some states and some cities.

TABLE 29.3
Combined Budgets of All State and Local Governments, 1995
(billions of dollars)

Tax Revenues	996	
Expenditures	901	
Purchases		683
Transfers		278
Interest		−60
Surplus	95	

Source: Economic Report of the President, 1997, Table B-83.

Review

▶ In the United States, the president submits a budget to Congress giving proposals for spending, for taxes, and for the deficit. The actual budget is different from the proposed budget because of congressional modifications and unforeseen events like wars and recessions.

▶ A budget deficit occurs when spending is greater than tax revenues. Virtually all major countries have had large deficits in recent years.

▶ The debt differs from the deficit. When a government or an individual runs a deficit, the debt increases. Surpluses reduce the debt.

▶ It is appropriate to consider the debt in relation to the size of the economy by measuring it as a percentage of GDP.

▶ Federal government expenditures are larger than state and local government expenditures, but state and local government purchases are larger than federal government purchases.

DISCRETIONARY AND AUTOMATIC COUNTERCYCLICAL FISCAL POLICY

Having seen how spending (purchases and transfers) and taxes fit together in the budget, let us now see whether plans for these—fiscal policy—can reduce the size of economic fluctuations.

Impacts of the Instruments of Fiscal Policy

We showed in Chapters 25 through 28 how changes in government spending and taxes affect real GDP. We now show how these changes might bring real GDP closer to potential GDP. Government purchases, transfers, and taxes are called the *instruments* of fiscal policy because they are the variables that directly affect the economy.

Changes in Government Purchases

We know that if there is a change in government purchases, real GDP will initially change by more than the change in government purchases. The exact amount depends on the size of the multiplier, which is uncertain, and depends on the marginal propensity to consume and the marginal propensity to import. If real GDP equaled potential GDP at the time of the change in government purchases, then real GDP will move away from potential GDP. Hence, a first lesson about fiscal policy is "do no harm." Erratic changes in government purchases can lead to fluctuations of real GDP away from potential GDP.

But suppose real GDP was already away from potential GDP. Then the change in government purchases could move real GDP closer to potential GDP. This is shown in Figure 29.5. In the top panel, real GDP starts out below potential GDP. An increase in government purchases shifts the aggregate demand/inflation curve to the right and moves real GDP back toward potential GDP. In the bottom panel, real GDP is above potential GDP, and a decrease in government purchases shifts the aggregate demand/inflation curve to the left, bringing real GDP back toward potential GDP. The important point is that a change in government purchases shifts the

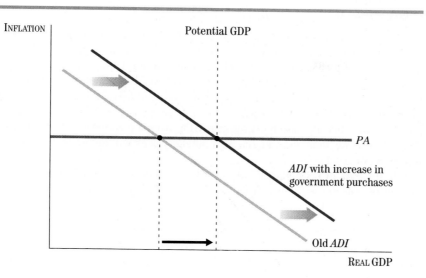

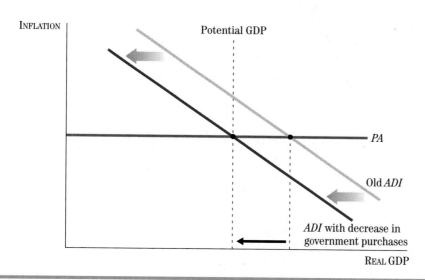

FIGURE 29.5
Effect of a Change in Government Purchases
If real GDP is below potential GDP, as in the top panel, an increase in government purchases, which shifts the *ADI* curve to the right, will move real GDP toward potential GDP. If real GDP is above potential GDP, as in the bottom panel, a decrease in government purchases will move real GDP toward potential. These are short-run effects.

aggregate demand/inflation curve from wherever it happens to be at the time of the change.

Now, these effects of government purchases are short term. Eventually, prices will adjust, and consumption, investment, and net exports will change and real GDP will return to potential GDP regardless of the change in government purchases. Nevertheless, as we will see, the short-run impacts of government purchases provide fiscal policy with the potential power to reduce the size of economic fluctuations.

A decrease in government purchases for defense is one example of a leftward shift in the aggregate demand/inflation curve. An increase in government purchases on roads and bridges works in the opposite direction. Because the changes in government spending affect investment, in the long run they may affect potential GDP. But for now, we focus on how they can move the economy closer to potential GDP.

Changes in Taxes

A change in taxes also affects real GDP in the short run. At any given level of real GDP, people will consume less if there is a tax increase because they have less income to spend after taxes. They will consume more if there is a tax cut. In either case, the aggregate demand/inflation curve will shift. The top panel of Figure 29.6 shows how a tax cut will shift the aggregate demand/inflation curve to the right and push real GDP closer to potential GDP if it is below potential GDP. The bottom panel shows a tax increase reducing real GDP from a position above potential GDP. Again, these are short-term effects. Eventually prices will adjust and real GDP will return to potential GDP.

In the case of tax changes, the size of the effect on real GDP is more uncertain than in the case of a change in government purchases. Recall that a temporary cut

FIGURE 29.6
Effects of a Change in Taxes
A decrease in taxes shifts the *ADI* curve to the right and can move real GDP toward potential GDP, as in the top panel. An increase in taxes moves real GDP toward potential in the lower panel.

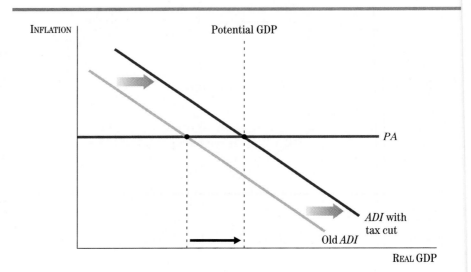

in taxes is unlikely to stimulate consumption by much, because the marginal propensity to consume is small. However, the marginal propensity to consume out of a permanent tax cut will be larger. In practice, people may be unsure how permanent a tax change will be.

Both increases and decreases in taxes can also affect potential GDP. For example, if an increase in tax rates causes some people to work less, then the labor supply will not be as large and potential GDP will be lower. But here our focus is on the departures of real GDP from potential GDP.

Countercyclical Fiscal Policy

Because government spending and taxes affect real GDP in the short run, fiscal policy can, in principle, offset the impact of shocks that push real GDP away from potential GDP. Such use of fiscal policy is called **countercyclical policy,** because the cyclical movements in the economy are being "countered," or offset, by changes in government spending or taxes. Both booms and recessions can be countered, in principle. Recessions require cuts in taxes or increases in spending; booms require increases in taxes or cuts in spending.

Figure 29.7 shows what such a policy would ideally do. A possible recession in the year 2001 is shown, perhaps caused by a drop in foreign demand for U.S. products. Without any change in government purchases or taxes, the economy would eventually recover, as shown in the figure. But suppose that the government quickly cuts taxes or starts a road-building program. The hope is that this will raise real GDP, as shown in the figure, and hasten the return to potential GDP.

How would this work when prices are adjusting and the inflation rate is changing as well? Figure 29.8 provides the analysis. The recession is seen to be caused by the leftward shift in the aggregate demand/inflation curve. But the cut in taxes or increase in spending shifts the aggregate demand/inflation curve in the opposite direction. The aggregate demand/inflation curve shifts back to the right. If these countercyclical measures are timely enough and neither too small nor too large—

countercyclical policy: a policy designed to offset the fluctuations in the business cycle.

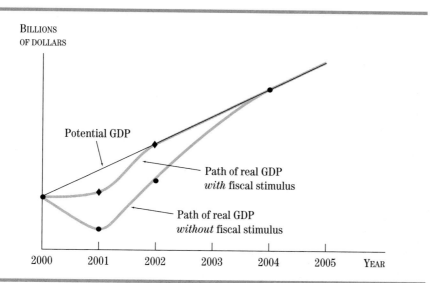

FIGURE 29.7
Effect of a Well-Timed Countercyclical Fiscal Policy
The figure shows a likely path of recovery from a recession caused by a decline in demand for U.S. products. A well-timed cut in taxes or increase in government purchases can reduce the size of the recession and bring real GDP back to potential GDP more quickly. The size of the economic fluctuation is smaller. The analysis is shown in Figure 29.8.

FIGURE 29.8
Analysis of a Well-Timed Countercyclical Fiscal Policy

A decline in demand—perhaps through a decrease in exports—shifts the *ADI* curve to the left. Without a countercyclical fiscal policy, real GDP recovers back to potential GDP, but a timely cut in taxes or increase in government purchases can offset the drop in demand and bring real GDP back to potential GDP more quickly.

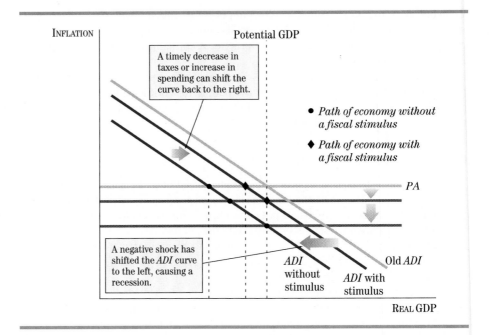

both big ifs—then the recession might be small and short lived. The example shows real GDP falling only slightly below potential GDP.

Figure 29.9 shows a less ideal case. Here government purchases are increased, but the response is too late. The increase occurs the year after the recession, during the recovery; it causes a boom.

Disagreements about the usefulness of fiscal policy boil down to an assessment of whether Figure 29.7 or Figure 29.9 is more likely. Let's first consider some examples.

FIGURE 29.9
Effect of a Poorly Timed Fiscal Policy

Here, in contrast to Figure 29.7, the fiscal stimulus comes too late, when the economy is already recovering. A boom is caused that could lead to inflation and perhaps another recession in later years.

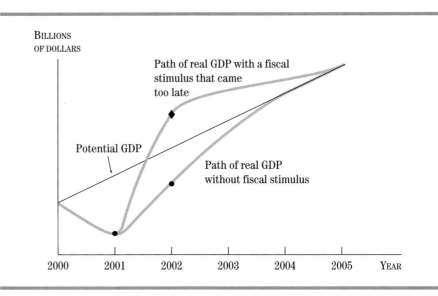

Discretionary Changes in the Instruments of Fiscal Policy

Discretionary fiscal policy refers to specific changes in laws or administrative procedures, such as a change in an existing program to speed up spending, the creation of a new program (such as a new welfare program), or a change in the tax system (such as higher tax rates). These changes in the law are discretionary changes because they require action on the part of the Congress or the president.

One of the most significant post–World War II discretionary fiscal policy actions was the 1964 tax cut, proposed by President John F. Kennedy and enacted after his death when Lyndon Johnson was president. The early 1960s were a period when real GDP was below potential GDP, and this large discretionary tax cut was a key factor in speeding the economic recovery. This cut in taxes also probably stimulated the growth of potential GDP and was therefore good for the long run.

Another example was the 1968 temporary income tax surcharge that raised tax rates. It was called a surcharge because 10 percent was added to any given tax rate. It was passed during the Vietnam War, when real GDP was above potential GDP. The aim was to bring real GDP back toward potential GDP. However, in this case, the boom continued. The tax increase came long after the boom had started. Perhaps because the surcharge was viewed as temporary, the marginal propensity to consume (MPC) was small and consumption did not change much.

Another large discretionary fiscal policy action was the Reagan tax cut of the early 1980s that lowered personal income tax rates by 25 percent. This tax cut helped the economy recover from the 1981–1982 recession. Like the Kennedy tax cut, this tax cut also probably raised the growth rate of potential GDP.

The impact of these examples of discretionary fiscal policy are neither as good as Figure 29.7 nor as bad as Figure 29.9. In none of these cases was the change in taxes speedy enough to offset a recession or a boom. The tax cuts came after the recessions and the tax increase came after the boom. At best, the tax cuts speeded up the recovery.

Automatic Changes in the Instruments of Fiscal Policy

Taxes and spending also change automatically as well as by discretionary actions of government. Income tax revenues expand when people are making more and fall when people are making less. Thus, tax revenues respond automatically to the economy. Tax payments rise when the economy is in a boom and more people are working. Tax revenues fall when the economy is in a slump and unemployment rises.

These changes in tax revenues are even larger with a progressive income tax. A **progressive tax** system means that individual tax payments *rise* as a proportion of income as income increases. With a progressive tax, a person earning $100,000 per year pays proportionately more in taxes than a person earning $20,000 per year. Because of this progressive tax system, as people earn more, they pay a higher tax rate, and when they earn less, they pay a lower tax rate.

Parts of government spending also change automatically. Unemployment compensation, through which the government makes payments to individuals who are unemployed, rises during a recession. When unemployment rises, so do payments to unemployed workers. Social security payments also increase in a recession because people may retire earlier if job prospects are bad. Welfare payments rise in a recession because people who are unemployed for a long period of time may qualify for welfare. As poverty rates rise in recessions, welfare payments increase.

These automatic tax and spending changes are called **automatic stabilizers** because they tend to stabilize the fluctuations of real GDP. How significant are

discretionary fiscal policy: changes in tax or spending policy requiring legislative or administrative action by the president or Congress.

progressive tax: a tax system in which an individual's tax payments rise as a proportion of income as the individual's income rises.

automatic stabilizers: automatic tax and spending changes that occur over the course of the business cycle that tend to stabilize the fluctuations in real GDP.

these automatic stabilizers? Consider the 1990–1991 recession. Real GDP in 1989 was above potential GDP. But by late 1990 and 1991, real GDP was dropping below potential GDP. As this happened, government spending went up and taxes went down.

The magnitude of these effects is quite large and can be seen by looking back at Figure 29.1. The difference between proposed and actual taxes and spending in the 1991 budget provides an estimate of the effect of the recession on taxes and spending. Tax revenue was $116 billion less than proposed before the recession. Thus, taxes were automatically reduced by this amount. However, spending was $91 billion more than proposed before the recession. Thus, spending rose by $91 billion in response to the recession. The combined effect of a $116 billion reduction in taxes and a $91 billion increase in spending is huge, and the timing was just about perfect. Since tax receipts went down in the recession and transfer payments went up, people's consumption was at a level higher than it would otherwise be. These automatic changes in tax revenues and government spending tended to stabilize the economy and probably made the recession less severe than it would have been. These changes did not completely offset other factors, however, because there still was a recession.

The Discretion versus Rules Debate for Fiscal Policy

For many years economists have debated the usefulness of discretionary and automatic fiscal policy. Automatic fiscal policy is an example of a fiscal policy rule. A **fiscal policy rule** describes how the instruments of fiscal policy respond to the state of the economy. Thus, the debate is sometimes called the "discretion versus rules" debate.

fiscal policy rule: a description of how the instruments of policy regularly respond to the state of the economy. Automatic stabilizers are an example of a fiscal policy rule.

The case for discretionary fiscal policy was made by President Kennedy's Council of Economic Advisers, which included Walter Heller and Nobel Prize–winning economist James Tobin. Proponents of discretionary fiscal policy argue that the automatic stabilizers would not be large or well-timed enough to bring the economy out of a recession quickly. Critics of discretionary policy, such as Milton Friedman, another Nobel Prize winner, emphasize that the effect of policy is uncertain and that there are long lags in the impact of policy. By the time spending increases and taxes are cut, a recession could be over; if so, the policy would only lead to an inflationary boom. Three types of lags are particularly problematic for discretionary fiscal policy: a *recognition lag,* the time between the need for the policy and the recognition of the need; an *implementation lag,* the time between the recognition of the need for the policy and its implementation; and an *impact lag,* the time between the implementation of the policy and its impact on real GDP.

Although lags and uncertainty continue to contribute to the discretion versus rules debate, other issues have also become central. Many economists feel policy rules are desirable because of their stability and reliability. A fiscal policy rule emphasizing the automatic stabilizers might make government plans to reduce the deficit more believable. Countercyclical fiscal policy raises the deficit during recessions. With discretionary policy, there is no guarantee that the deficit will decline after the recession. With an automatic policy rule, there is an expectation that the deficit will decline after the recession is over.

Since the end of the 1980s, there have been few discretionary fiscal policy actions to counter recessions or booms in the United States or Europe. For the most part, discretionary actions have not occurred because of high budget deficits and public concerns about the governments that caused these deficits in the first place.

ECONOMIC IMPACT OF THE BUDGET DEFICIT

What is the impact of the budget deficit on the economy? Because the budget deficit is equal to the difference between spending and taxes, the impact of the deficit is best understood by looking at the impact of spending and taxes, as we did in the previous section.

Short-Run and Long-Run Impact of the Deficit

Suppose the budget deficit increases because government purchases rise. Then the impact on the economy is precisely the same as our previous analysis of an increase in government purchases. The analysis of fiscal policy predicts that an increase in the budget deficit due to an increase in government purchases will cause real GDP to rise above potential GDP in the short run. Also, an increase in the budget deficit through a decrease in taxes will cause real GDP to rise temporarily above potential GDP.

In the long run, however, real GDP would return to potential GDP. If the increase in the deficit is caused by an increase in government purchases, investment and net exports would be lower as a share of GDP and interest rates would be higher. The higher interest rate and lower investment are the main harm of a long-lasting budget deficit. Moreover, the increase in government purchases would raise imports both because income rises and because the higher interest rate raises the exchange rate. The higher exchange rate would cause exports to fall. With imports rising and exports falling, net exports would decline, which means that the international trade deficit would be higher as a result of the increased budget deficit.

What if the budget deficit rises because of a cut in taxes? By raising disposable income, a cut in taxes will cause consumption to rise. Thus, in the long run the sum of investment and net exports will be lower as a share of GDP. Again, lower investment means lower long-term real GDP growth.

Ricardian Equivalence

Economists disagree on the long-run effects of a deficit due to a cut in taxes, however. Some economists argue that a decrease in taxes will not permanently increase consumption. According to this view, people realize that the lower taxes will mean a higher budget deficit and, therefore, higher debt and higher interest payments by the government in the future. With higher interest payments in the future, people will figure that their future taxes, or at least their children's taxes, will be higher than they otherwise would be. Forward-looking consumers, therefore, may not increase their consumption because they realize they will have to pay more in taxes in the future. If they are concerned about their children, they will figure that they need to pass more on to the next generation because the burden of the future deficit on their children has been increased.

Ricardian equivalence: the view that a change in taxes today will not affect consumption because people recognize that their, or their children's, future tax burden will change in an opposite direction.

The view that increases in the budget deficit through tax cuts will not affect consumption or the other components of GDP is called **Ricardian equivalence** after the nineteenth-century economist David Ricardo. Robert Barro, an economist at Harvard University, has done the most significant theoretical and empirical research in support of Ricardian equivalence. Many economists, however, including Martin Feldstein, also of Harvard University, do not find the evidence in support of Ricardian equivalence convincing. They think that an increase in the budget deficit through tax cuts will raise consumption and lower investment in the long run.

In any case, there is little disagreement among economists that an increase in the deficit as a share of GDP through higher government purchases will have a long-run impact of lower private investment.

The Burden of the Debt

Our discussion of Ricardian equivalence has focused on the higher debt that future generations incur as a result of the tax cut. The higher debt means that interest payments become an increased expenditure requirement of government. The federal budget, as shown in Table 29.1, already has a large portion of expenditures going to interest payments on the debt. Future interest payments represent a *burden of the debt* on future generations. If Ricardian equivalence holds, however, then an increase in the debt is not a burden on future generations because their parents or grandparents would have passed on additional inheritance to offset the burden.

Overall Assessment

If we sum up the economic arguments about the deficit, we see that the main long-run harmful effect is due to a reduction of private investment in the economy. This effect is likely to arise if the deficit persists for a long time and if it is due to an increase in government purchases; the harmful effect is also likely to arise if the deficit is due to a decline in tax revenues, though there is more disagreement about the effects of a change in tax revenue than a change in government purchases.

A reduction in investment is harmful to the economy because it lowers the growth of the capital stock and thereby lowers the growth of productivity. Lower productivity growth means a lower standard of living in the future.

Credible Deficit Reduction Plans

Because of the harmful long-term effects of the deficit, many economists feel that lowering the deficit is a good idea. But just as an increase in the deficit can raise real GDP in the short run, a decrease in the deficit can reduce real GDP below potential GDP in the short run. Thus, even though there is a long-term benefit from deficit reduction, there is possible short-term harm. Is there any way this harm can be reduced?

rational expectations assumption: the assumption that people forecast the future no better or no worse than economic forecasters. (Ch. 26)

In recent years economists have searched for ways to lessen the short-run impact of the budget deficit reductions on the economy. The idea of *rational expec-*

tations has helped in the search. The idea of rational expectations is that people, like economic forecasters, try to figure out what government actions will be. People also take these expectations of government actions into account in their personal decisions. Government policymakers have **credibility** if their announcements about future government actions are believable to people. If people's expectations are rational, then credibility can greatly influence how a change in the budget deficit affects the economy.

credibility: the believability of the government's intentions to carry out stated policies.

For example, if the government announces in advance its intention to reduce the deficit over a number of years in the future, and if the government's announcement is credible, then the negative short-run impact of the deficit reduction on the economy might be greatly reduced. Why?

We know that in the long run, the reduction in the budget deficit will lower interest rates. Thus, if the government announces plans to reduce the budget deficit in the future, people will expect that interest rates will decline in the future; this expectation of a future decline in interest rates may lower current interest rates.

Interest Rates and Expectations

Expectations of future declines in interest rates lower current interest rates because people have a choice between buying long-term bonds and short-term bonds. Consider the choice between a longer-term government bond with a maturity of 2 years and a shorter-term government bond that lasts 1 year. The choice is shown in Table 29.4. When you are deciding to buy the 2-year bond, your alternative is to buy the short-term bond. Rather than a 2-year bond, you could buy a 1-year bond and then buy another 1-year bond next year. The average interest rate over the two-year period should be about the same as the interest rate on the 2-year bond. Otherwise, no one would buy the bond with the lower average interest rate. If you expect interest rates to rise sharply next year, you will not buy the 2-year bond unless the current interest rate is higher. The interest rates on long-term bonds are thus affected by expectations of future interest rates. If people expect future interest rates to rise, then the interest rates on long-term bonds rise. If people expect future interest rates to fall, then interest rates on long-term bonds fall. The same analysis applies to 5-, 10-, or even 30-year bonds as well as to 2-year bonds.

The table shows the average interest rate for two alternatives:

▶A 2-year bond is held for 2 years and pays the current long-term interest rate of R percent each year.

▶A 1-year bond is held for 1 year and pays the current short-term interest rate of 5 percent; another 1-year bond is bought at the end of the first year with an *expected* interest rate of r percent.

TABLE 29.4
Effect of a Change in Expected Future Interest Rates

Type of Bond	Interest Rate in First Year	Interest Rate in Second Year	Average Interest Rate
Long term (2 years)	R	R	R
Short term (1 year)	5	r	$\dfrac{5 + r}{2}$

The average interest rate should be the same on the two so that

$$R = \frac{5 + r}{2}$$

Hence, if the expected future short-term interest rate (r) rises, so does the current long-term interest rate (R).

Using Economics to Explain a Rise in Long-Term Interest Rates

When faced with a large budget deficit, the government may hope that expectations of a credible multiyear plan of deficit reduction will lower interest rates. In Germany the reverse effect occurred in late 1989 and proved how powerful the expectations effect can be.

In 1989 it became more and more apparent that West Germany and East Germany would unite into one country. But as the inevitability of this event dawned on people, so did the likelihood that the German budget deficit would increase sharply. Unification would require large government expenditures, and it was unlikely that tax increases would be sufficient. Hence, by late 1989 people began to anticipate a large increase in the German budget deficit. The most credible thing anyone could say about German fiscal policy was that the budget deficit would increase.

This anticipation caused German long-term interest rates to jump sharply (see figure). People expected higher interest rates down

the road, and this caused interest rates to rise immediately in the bond market.

Because financial capital flows easily across the Atlantic, interest rates in the United States also rose in late

1989 and early 1990. In this case, the expectations proved remarkably accurate. The German budget shifted from a small surplus to a large deficit in one year.

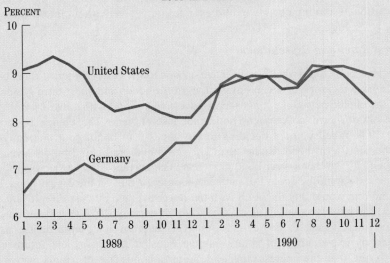

**Long-Term Interest Rates
in the United States and Germany;
1989 and 1990**

Source: Organization for Economic Cooperation and Development.

Now, suppose that the government announces a credible deficit reduction plan to take place over a 10-year period. People who buy and sell bonds will reason that future short-term interest rates will be lower as a result of the lower budget deficit. If they expect future interest rates to be lower, then the current long-term interest rate on bonds will decline. Now, long-term interest rates as well as short-term interest rates affect investment decisions. Hence, the lower long-term interest rates will reduce borrowing costs, and firms will begin to invest more. Note that the increase in investment is occurring in the short run, not only in the medium run and the long run, because interest rates have declined in the short run.

In the ideal case, the increased investment and net exports would just offset the decline in government purchases in the short run, and there would be no negative effect on real GDP. However, the ideal case is very hard to realize because it depends on the government announcements being very credible and on people adjusting their expectations to take account of the announcements. Moreover, the

Case of Little Credibility

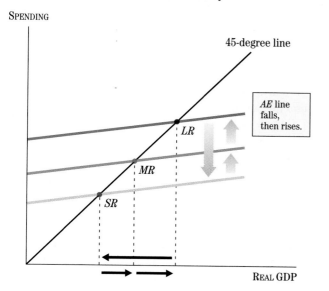

Ideal Case of Credible Deficit Reduction

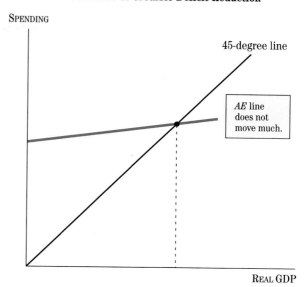

	Y	C	I	X	G	R
SR	↓	↓	↔	↑	↓	↔
LR	↔	↑	↑	↑	↓	↓

The interest rate (R) does not decline immediately.

	Y	C	I	X	G	R
SR	↔	↑	↑	↑	↓	↓
LR	↔	↑	↑	↑	↓	↓

Short-run output effects are mitigated by an immediate decline in the interest rate (R).

speed by which firms increase their investment must exactly match the speed of reduction in government purchases. Also, even if real GDP is unaffected, there may be different effects in different regions of the country because the lower government purchases and the increased investment would not necessarily occur in the same place.

Figure 29.10 illustrates the difference between such a credible deficit reduction plan and the more standard type of deficit reduction. The panel on the left is the standard case of deficit reduction through a cut in purchases that we have already analyzed. The panel on the right is the case of a credible deficit reduction. On the right, the aggregate expenditure (AE) line does not move much; the lower government purchases are offset by increased investment through the decline in interest rates. The tables illustrate the key interest rate difference in the two cases. On the left, the interest rate does not decline in the short run; hence, investment stays put. On the right, the interest rate falls in the short run because people foresee the interest rate declining in the long run and, immediately, current interest rates fall.

FIGURE 29.10
Benefits of Credible Budget Deficit Reduction
On the left, the budget deficit is reduced but the plan has no credibility. Interest rates do not change in the short run. On the right, a reduction in the interest rate in anticipation of budget deficit reduction stimulates investment and offsets the decline in government purchases.

The Structural versus the Cyclical Deficit

We noted earlier that taxes and spending change automatically in recessions and booms. These automatic changes affect the budget deficit, so in order to analyze the deficit it is important to try to separate out these automatic effects. The *structural,* or *full-employment, deficit* was designed for this purpose. The definition of **structural deficit** is the answer to the question, "What would the deficit be if real GDP equaled potential GDP?" Economists use the term *full-employment deficit* because full employment occurs when real GDP equals potential GDP; that is, the unemployment rate equals the natural rate, or the "full employment" unemployment rate.

structural deficit: the level of the government budget deficit under the scenario where real GDP is equal to potential GDP; also called the full-employment deficit.

Figure 29.11 introduces a graph to help explain the structural deficit. On the horizontal axis is real GDP. On the vertical axis is the budget deficit. The budget is balanced when the deficit is zero, which is marked by a horizontal line in the diagram. The region above zero represents a situation where taxes are less than spending and the government has a deficit. The region below zero is a situation where the government budget is in surplus. On the horizontal axis, letters *A, B,* and *C* represent three different levels of real GDP.

The downward-sloping line in Figure 29.11 says that as real GDP rises, the budget deficit gets smaller. More real GDP means a smaller deficit. Why? The automatic stabilizers are the reason. When real GDP rises, taxes rise, and spending on transfer programs falls. Because the deficit is the difference between spending and taxes, the deficit gets smaller. Conversely, when real GDP falls, tax receipts decline and spending on transfer programs increases, so the deficit rises. The downward-sloping line in Figure 29.11 pertains to a particular set of government programs and tax laws. A change in these programs or laws would *shift* the line. For example, an increase in tax rates would shift the line down.

Figure 29.12, a similar diagram, shows potential GDP and real GDP in 1991, a recession year when real GDP was below potential GDP. Imagine raising real GDP

FIGURE 29.11
The Effect of Real GDP on the Deficit

The deficit equals spending minus taxes. When real GDP falls, the deficit rises because spending rises and tax receipts fall. When real GDP rises, the deficit falls. When real GDP is at point *A,* there is a deficit; at point *B* the budget is balanced; and at point *C* there is a budget surplus (negative deficit).

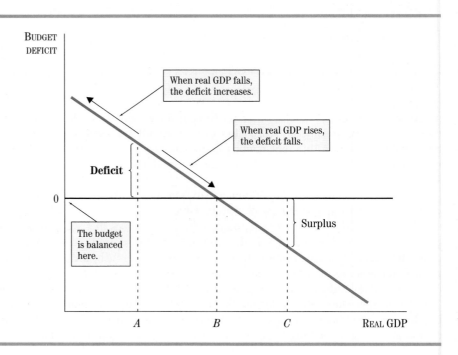

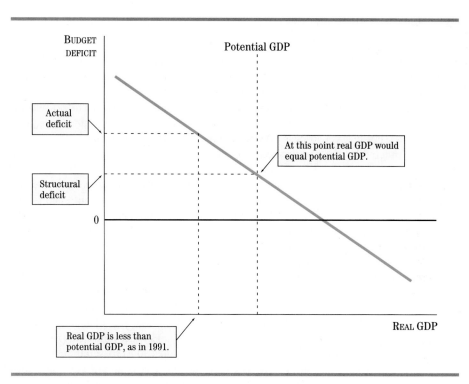

FIGURE 29.12

The Structural Deficit versus the Actual Deficit in a Recession Year

The deficit that would occur when real GDP is equal to potential GDP is called the structural deficit, as shown in the figure. The actual deficit rises above the structural deficit when real GDP falls below potential GDP, such as in 1991, a recession year.

up to potential GDP. We would predict that the deficit would go down, because tax receipts would rise as the economy grew and transfer payments would go down with fewer people unemployed, fewer people retiring, and fewer people on welfare. As we move to the right in the diagram, the deficit gets smaller. The structural deficit occurs when real GDP equals potential GDP.

The structural deficit provides a way to separate out cyclical changes in the budget caused by cyclical changes in the economy. The **cyclical deficit** is defined as the difference between the actual deficit and the structural deficit.

Figure 29.12 says that even if the U.S. economy were at full employment, there would still have been a deficit in 1991. Reducing the structural deficit would require changes in government programs to reduce spending or changes in the tax law to increase tax revenue. Such changes in government programs or the tax laws would shift the negatively sloped line down to give budget balance at full employment.

cyclical deficit: the difference between the actual deficit and the structural deficit.

Review

▶ The impact of a reduction in the deficit on the economy is best analyzed by looking at what happens to taxes and spending. A reduction in the deficit will temporarily reduce real GDP though, in the long run, real GDP returns to potential.

▶ A credible deficit reduction plan will result in smaller reductions in real GDP if interest rates fall in anticipation of the plan.

▶ The structural deficit adjusts the actual deficit for cyclical changes in the economy.

BUDGET REFORMS

Frustration with many failed attempts by the U.S. government to reduce the structural budget deficit to zero has led to proposals to reform the process under which the Congress and the president determine the budget.

The most widely discussed and popular proposal is the *balanced budget amendment to the U.S. Constitution.* Such an amendment has been voted on by Congress several times but has yet to pass. The amendment would require that the budget be balanced, much like the requirement for many state and local governments. The main advantage of the balanced budget amendment is that, if the law were adhered to, the budget deficit would be eliminated and the good long-term growth effects of a balanced budget would be reaped. However, there is some doubt that such a law could be enforced. What would the penalty be if the budget was not balanced? Another problem with a balanced budget amendment is that it would not permit the deficit to expand in a recession as part of the automatic stabilizers. Hence, recessions could be worse. Some versions of the balanced budget amendment focus only on keeping government spending within a percentage of GDP, allowing taxes to decline temporarily in a recession even if the deficit would rise. Others have escape clauses if there is a recession.

Another process reform gives the president more power to control spending. Starting in 1997, a new law authorized the president of the United States to veto separate items of legislation; this is called *line-item veto* authority. Under previous law the president could veto spending bills but not specific items in these bills. For the first time in U.S. history, President Clinton exercised the line-item veto in August 1997 by vetoing several spending and tax items in the 1997 budget agreement. The line-item veto is likely to be challenged in the courts, and it will take several years to assess the impact of this new law.

Other process reforms apply to the political system. Saying no to spending or yes to taxes is difficult for elected politicians who want to be reelected. *Term limits,* under which politicians could only serve for two or three terms, might make it easier for politicians to vote to cut spending on a program in their area. Alternatively, limiting political contributions from groups that have vested interests in government programs might make it easier for politicians to vote to limit the growth of such programs.

"In a compromise move to cut the budget, Congress and the president agreed to move the decimal one point to the left."

Review

▶ The balanced budget amendment to the U.S. Constitution, the line-item veto, and term limits are three reforms that could reduce the budget deficit.

▶ The line-item veto was given to the president in 1997, but the balanced budget amendment has failed in Congress several times.

CONCLUSION

Because the government is such a large player in the economy, its fiscal actions on spending, taxing, and borrowing exert a powerful influence on real GDP and employment. Such actions can cause real GDP to depart from potential GDP and can alter the long-term growth rate of potential GDP.

A first principle of fiscal policy, therefore, is that government not take actions that would harm the economy. Avoiding erratic changes in fiscal policy, making sure that taxes are not increased during recessions, and keeping budget deficits low when real GDP is equal to potential GDP are all part of this first principle. By running persistently large budget deficits in the 1980s and 1990s, fiscal policy in most countries has violated this first principle. Hence, budget reform aimed at reducing the budget deficit has been a high priority for fiscal policy. Changes in the way budget decisions are made—from balanced budget amendments to line-item vetoes—are possible reforms that have been suggested.

A second principle is that fiscal policy can be used to help smooth the economic fluctuations in the economy. Tax cuts and spending increases during recessions can help offset the declines in demand that cause recessions. Conversely, tax increases and spending cuts during booms can help offset forces leading to inflation in the economy.

There is debate among economists about whether the government is capable of taking discretionary actions with these effects. Policy lags and uncertainty make discretionary fiscal policy difficult. There is little disagreement, however, about the importance of automatic stabilizers under which tax and spending actions occur automatically without legislation. Automatic stabilizers cause the deficit to rise in recessions and fall during booms.

Another part of government policy that has powerful effects on the economy is monetary policy. We take up monetary policy in the next chapter.

KEY POINTS

1. Fiscal policy consists of the government's plans for spending, taxes, and borrowing to finance the deficit.

2. The government's budget is the primary document of fiscal policy. It gives the priorities for spending and taxes. In the United States, the president must submit a budget proposal to Congress.

3. Most industrial countries have had large deficits in the 1990s.

4. Because the Congress modifies the proposals and because of unanticipated events, the actual budget differs considerably from the proposed budget.

5. Changes in spending and taxes can move real GDP away from potential GDP in the short run. But in the long run, real GDP returns to potential GDP.

6. Discretionary changes in taxes and spending can be used to keep real GDP near potential GDP, but this requires excellent timing and flexibility. Lags and uncertainty make discretionary policy difficult.

7. The automatic stabilizers are an important part of fiscal policy. They are essentially a policy rule in which tax revenues automatically decline in recessions and rise in booms. Transfer payments move in the reverse direction.

8. A decrease in the budget deficit is likely to reduce real GDP in the short run. In the long run, real GDP returns to potential GDP, but investment and net exports are a larger share of GDP.

9. There is general agreement among economists about the effects of changes in the deficit due to changes in government purchases. In the case where the deficit is changed by changing taxes, economists who believe in Ricardian equivalence argue that the effects are small or zero in the long run.

10. A credible plan to reduce the budget deficit can reduce long-term interest rates and thereby counter the negative effects on real GDP even in the short run.

11. Budget reforms that aim to reduce the structural deficit should aim to preserve the automatic stabilizers. This will enable fiscal policy to play an important stabilization role as it moves to a zero structural budget deficit.

KEY TERMS

fiscal policy	federal debt	automatic stabilizer
federal budget	bond	fiscal policy rule
balanced budget	debt to GDP ratio	Ricardian equivalence
budget surplus	countercyclical policy	credibility
budget deficit	discretionary fiscal policy	structural deficit
budget cycle	progressive tax	cyclical deficit

QUESTIONS FOR REVIEW

1. Why is the actual budget deficit always different from the president's proposed deficit?

2. How does the government's debt differ from the government's budget deficit?

3. What are the differences between the short-run impact of a change in (a) purchases, (b) taxes, and (c) transfer payments?

4. Why is the long-run effect of a cut in government spending on investment less controversial than the effect of an increase in taxes?

5. What is Ricardian equivalence?

6. Why might interest rates fall when a credible program of budget deficit reduction is announced?

7. What is the difference between the structural deficit and the actual deficit?

8. What are the automatic stabilizers, and how do they help mitigate economic fluctuations?

9. What fiscal policy reform is needed in many countries?

10. Why has budget deficit reduction proved so difficult for so many countries?

PROBLEMS

1. Use a diagram with inflation on the vertical axis and real GDP on the horizontal axis to show the short-run, medium-run, and long-run effects of an increase in the budget deficit on the inflation rate and real GDP. Show how the aggregate demand/inflation curve and the price adjustment line shift over time.

2. Suppose you have the following data on projected and actual figures for the U.S. budget for 2001 (in billions of dollars):

	Projected Budget	Actual Budget
Taxes	2,150	2,100
Expenditures	2,250	2,400

a) What was the projected budget deficit? What was the actual budget deficit? Why did this happen?
b) If the government debt is $3,400 billion at the end of 2000, what is the debt at the end of 2001?

c) If GDP is $9,000 billion in 2001, what is the debt to GDP ratio? How does this compare to the debt to GDP ratio for 1992? (*Hint:* See Figures 29.3 and 29.4.)

3. Suppose the president of the United States promises to implement a program that reduces discretionary government spending in order to eliminate the budget deficit in five years. Progress is made for several years, but in the fourth year, there is a huge increase in oil prices. Output falls and the deficit rises. In the next election, the president's challenger campaigns on the apparent broken promise. Suppose you are advising the president during the reelection campaign. What should the president say? Write your advice in a half-page memo.

4. Suppose the economy is currently $100 billion below potential GDP, and the government wants to pursue discretionary fiscal policy to speed the recovery.
a) Show this situation using the aggregate demand/inflation curve. Indicate the effect of an increase in government purchases.

b) What are the long-run benefits to *not* increasing government purchases as a proportion of real GDP? (*Hint:* Think about the long-run growth model in Chapter 23.)

5. The federal budget deficit for the United States rose from about 3 percent of GDP in 1990 to about 5 percent of GDP in 1991.

a) Explain why at least part of this increase in the deficit occurred because of the recession in 1991.

b) Suppose real GDP was equal to potential GDP in 1990 and below potential GDP in 1991. Sketch a diagram that shows the responsiveness of the deficit to GDP and show the structural deficit. How large a share of GDP is the structural deficit?

c) Is it good or bad for the economy that the deficit increased as a result of the recession?

6. Examine the following hypothetical data (in billions of dollars):

Year	Budget Deficit	Government Debt as of Jan. 1	GDP
1996	100	1,000	4,000
1997	150	1,100	4,200
1998	—	—	4,800
1999	200	1,400	5,400

a) Fill in the missing values in the preceding table.

b) What is the percentage change in debt and GDP from 1997 to 1998?

c) What is the percentage change in the debt and GDP from 1998 to 1999?

d) Calculate the debt to GDP ratio for each year. How does this ratio change over time? Why?

7. Explain how a credible plan to decrease government expenditures ameliorates the downturn in the economy caused by the decrease in aggregate expenditures. Illustrate your answer with the aggregate expenditure curve.

8. Suppose that you are advising the prime minister of a country with budget deficit problems. You know that reducing the budget deficit will hurt production and employment in the short run but will be beneficial for the economy in the long run. The finance minister has a reputation of running large budget deficits and has little credibility. How would you recommend minimizing the negative short-run effects without compromising the budget deficit reduction? Explain.

9. State whether each of the following is true or false and explain your answer.

a) It is not possible to "grow out of" the government debt.

b) If the economy is already at potential GDP, then any increase in G will be inflationary.

c) It is possible to eliminate the deficit without eliminating the debt.

10. Suppose the government deficit is 3 percent of real GDP now, but economists say that the structural deficit is 2 percent.

a) Is real GDP currently above or below potential GDP? Why? Draw the diagram showing this situation.

b) In your diagram, show the situation where real GDP increases.

c) Draw the situation where there is a budgetary reform so that the structural deficit is zero. Does this mean that the current deficit goes to zero?

11. The Japanese government had a structural budget surplus in the late 1980s and real GDP was above potential GDP.

a) Draw this situation in a diagram like Figure 29.12.

b) Suppose Japanese citizens demand that their government get rid of the government surplus. Show what happens using the aggregate demand/inflation curve and the price adjustment line.

c) If the Japanese government has a credible, permanent increase in G, how does this affect the change in Japanese interest rates?

12. Suppose that real GDP is below potential GDP, and the Council of Economic Advisers is trying to evaluate various proposals for fiscal stimulus. They are uncertain about whether the multiplier is 1.7 or 2.5.

a) Draw the aggregate expenditure diagram for this situation. What is the slope of the aggregate expenditure line in each case?

b) Suppose the economic advisers decide the multiplier is 1.7, and they decide an increase in G of $50 billion would bring real GDP to potential GDP. Draw this in your diagram. If they are correct about the value of the multiplier, by how much does real GDP rise?

c) Suppose the Congress takes immediate action on the increase in G. If the multiplier is actually 2.5, by how much will they overshoot their target of potential GDP? Show this with the aggregate expenditure curve.

30

Monetary Policy

Monetary policy refers to the entirety of actions taken by the central bank that affect the money supply and thereby interest rates, exchange rates, inflation, unemployment, and real GDP. Monetary policy is a powerful force affecting our lives. Pivotal national events have been convincingly attributed to it, including the Great Depression of the 1930s, the Great Inflation of the 1970s, and the long back-to-back expansions of the 1980s and 1990s.

We showed in Chapters 27 and 28 why monetary policy affects real GDP. By taking actions that raise or lower interest rates, the central bank can affect investment, net exports, and consumption in the short run. It thus can cause the departure of real GDP from potential GDP during booms and recessions. Moreover, the way the central bank responds to developments in the econ-omy influences the speed at which real GDP returns to potential GDP during recoveries from recessions. Ultimately, monetary policy determines the rate of inflation; it thereby affects productivity and the growth of potential GDP in the long run.

In this chapter, we look at the independence of central banks and the rationale for this independence. We also show that people's demand for money depends on the interest rate, and we examine *how* central banks raise or lower interest rates in the short run by changing the money supply. Finally, we consider a number of alternative monetary policies, including simply keeping money growth constant. As with fiscal policy, there is disagreement among economists over monetary policy, and we will examine the reasons for this disagreement.

CENTRAL BANK INDEPENDENCE

The most important feature of a central bank, whether it is the Fed in the United States, the Bank of England in the United Kingdom, the Bundesbank in Germany, or the Bank of Japan in Japan, is the degree of independence the law gives it from the government.

The officials of the Fed are appointed by the president of the United States to long terms that may span several different governments; thus the term of the chair of the Fed does not coincide with the political terms of the president of the United States. For example, Paul Volcker served through most of the Reagan years, even though he was appointed by President Carter. Alan Greenspan served under Presidents Reagan, Bush, and Clinton. (The five Fed chairs who served during the past 40 years are shown below.) Therefore, like Supreme Court justices in the United States, Fed officials develop an independence.

Although it is difficult to measure independence objectively, the Fed seems to have more independence than the Bank of Japan and less independence than the Bundesbank. In 1997 the British Parliament gave the Bank of England greater independence; before 1997 the Bank of England had less independence than the Fed, but now it appears to have more. The advantage of **central bank independence** is that it prevents governments in power from using monetary policy in ways that appear beneficial in the short run but that harm the economy in the long run.

central bank independence: a description of the legal authority of central banks to make decisions on monetary policy with little interference by the government in power.

Short-Run Gain versus Long-Run Pain

We showed in Chapter 28 that a change in monetary policy can temporarily raise real GDP above potential GDP in the short run but that only inflation will be higher in the long run. Such a change in monetary policy toward higher inflation would first entail a reduction in interest rates and would shift the aggregate demand/inflation (*ADI*) curve to the right, as shown in Figure 30.1. Real GDP would rise along with investment, consumption, and net exports; unemployment would fall. In the short run, there would be no effect on inflation because of the slowness of firms to change their price decisions. The economic gain of such a temporary economic boom might help in a reelection, or it might raise the popularity needed to push legislation for new programs through the political system. However, the economic

William McChesney Martin
1951–1969

Arthur Burns
1969–1978

G. William Miller
1978–1979

Paul Volcker
1979–1987

Alan Greenspan
1987–

FIGURE 30.1
Short-Run Gain and Long-Run Pain from a Change in Monetary Policy

The Fed can temporarily stimulate the economy in the short run—real GDP rises above potential GDP. But in the long run the inflation rate is higher and this is harmful to the economy.

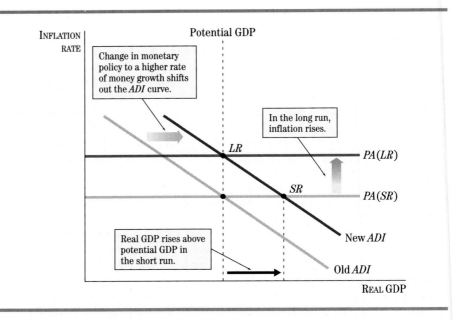

pain—higher inflation in the long run, also shown in Figure 30.1—would not be seen until after the election or after the legislation is passed.

Thus, there is a natural tendency toward higher inflation in the political system. If the government in power had complete control over the decisions of the central bank, it could take actions to make the economy look good in the short run for political purposes and not worry that it might look bad in the long run. Removing the central bank from the direct control of the government reduces this politically induced bias toward higher inflation because it is then more difficult for the government to get the central bank to take such actions. In fact, Figure 30.2 shows that central banks with more independence tend to have lower inflation performance.

FIGURE 30.2
Central Bank Independence and Inflation

The scatter plot shows that average inflation rates tend to be negatively related to the independence of central banks. The independence of the central bank is calculated by studying the laws of each country, including the length of the term of office of the head of the central bank (a longer term means more independence) and restrictions on the central bank lending to the government.

Source: Data from Alex Cukierman, *Central Bank Strategy, Credibility, and Independence* (Cambridge, Mass.: MIT Press, 1992).

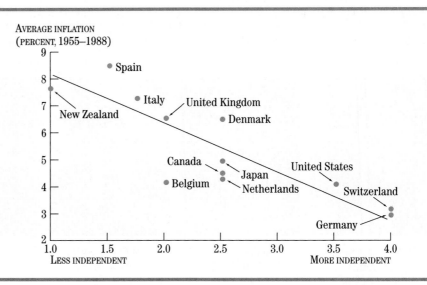

The Political Business Cycle

The **political business cycle** is the tendency of governments to use economic policy to cause an economic boom just before an election and then let the economy slow down right after the election. Because both fiscal and monetary policy raise real GDP above potential GDP in the short run, a political business cycle can be caused by either monetary or fiscal policy. Many economic and political studies have shown that the chances of an incumbent being reelected are increased greatly if the economy is doing well, as it always seems to in a boom. After the election, inflation could rise and cause a bust, but that would be long before the next election. By the time of the next election, policy could again be used to cause a boom, and the cycle is repeated.

Research in the 1970s by William Nordhaus of Yale University uncovered some evidence of a political business cycle in the United States. For example, some feel that the boom in the economy before the 1972 election may have been due to a monetary policy change pushing real GDP above potential GDP. On the other hand, the U.S. economy was near a recession in the 1980 and 1992 elections, the exact opposite of a political business cycle. Thus, the evidence of a political business cycle in the United States is no longer strong. In any case, political business cycles are harmful to the economy and especially to those who suffer from the higher inflation and unemployment at the end of the cycle. Preventing political business cycles is another reason for having a central bank that has some independence from the government in power.

political business cycle: a business cycle resulting from politicians' use of fiscal or monetary policy to affect the outcome of an election.

Time Inconsistency

The temptation of governments to use monetary policy for short-run gains despite the long-run costs is difficult to resist. Recent research has shown that even governments that aim solely to improve the well-being of the average citizen will say they want low inflation but then stimulate the economy to lower unemployment, fully aware of the inflationary consequences.

This temptation is known as **time inconsistency** because governments say they want low inflation but are later inconsistent by following policies that lead to higher inflation. They act like a teacher who tells the class there will be an exam to get the students to study, but then on the day of the exam, announces the exam is canceled. The students are happy to miss the exam and the teacher does not have to grade it. Everyone appears to be better off in the short run.

However, just as the teacher who cancels the exam will lose credibility with future classes, the central bank that tries the inconsistent policy will lose credibility. People will assume that the central bank will actually raise inflation even if it says it is aiming for low inflation. Credibility benefits monetary policy, as we show later in the chapter, and the costs of a loss of credibility are great.

time inconsistency: the situation in which policymakers have the incentive to announce one economic policy but then change that policy after citizens have acted on the initial, stated policy.

Government Borrowing from the Central Bank

There is yet another reason for the central bank to have a certain amount of independence from the government in power. If the government, rather than the central bank, had the ability to control the money supply, then the government might simply decide to print money to pay for its expenditures. The resulting increase in inflation could be large and harmful. For example, during the Revolutionary War, the American colonies printed paper money to pay for the war expenditures. The result was a huge inflation.

It is, of course, not unusual for governments to spend more than they receive in the form of tax revenue. We saw in the previous chapter that many industrialized countries have budget deficits and thus must borrow. But suppose the government could not borrow, perhaps because people were worried about political instability. During a war, for example, people might not want to lend to the government, worrying that the government would lose the war and would not pay back its borrowing. Similarly, political instability made it difficult for the newly elected government of Russia to borrow in the 1990s. In such a situation, if the government has control of the central bank it can simply instruct the central bank to print the money to pay for its deficit. If the deficit was large the inflation would be severe. Consider, for example, what would have happened if the U.S. central bank issued $236 billion in currency to make up for the difference between spending and taxes in the United States in 1993. This would have been a very large increase in the money supply in the United States and would have caused a horrible inflation. It would have increased the U.S. monetary base—currency plus bank reserves—from $386 billion to $622 billion, or about 61 percent in one year.

There are more subtle ways that a central bank with little independence can succumb to the needs of government finance. During World War II in the United States, the Fed agreed as part of the war effort to hold interest rates low in order to keep the interest rates on the government debt down. After World War II the Fed was able to remove itself from this agreement because of its independence; it recognized that holding interest rates too low would eventually lead to inflation.

The ramification of a central bank fully financing a huge government budget deficit is always inflation. That is why the inflation rate was so high in Russia and Brazil in the early 1990s. These cases illustrate another reason for central bank independence: to avoid the temptations to use the central bank to finance the government deficit and thereby cause inflation.

The importance of central bank independence has been stressed by many economists. Over 170 years ago, the great British economist David Ricardo described his idea of an ideal central bank:

> It is said that Government could not be safely entrusted with the power of issuing paper money; that it would most certainly abuse it. . . . There would, I confess, be great danger of this if the Government—that is to say the ministers—were themselves to be entrusted with the power of issuing paper money. But I propose to place this trust in the hands of Commissioners, not removable from their official situation but by a vote of one or both houses of Parliament. I propose also to prevent all intercourse between these Commissioners and the ministers, by forbidding every species of money transaction between them. The Commissioners should never, on any pretence, lend money to Government, nor be in the slightest degree under its control or influence.[1]

Possible Abuses of Independence

Central bank independence is no guarantee against monetary policy mistakes, however, and it could even lead to more mistakes. In principle, an independent central bank could cause more inflation than a central bank under control of the government. For example, those in charge of the central bank could—after they are appointed—succumb to arguments that high inflation is not so harmful after all. Or, at the other extreme, those in charge of the central bank could become so focused

---

Secrets of the Temple

This 1987 book raised questions about the independence of the Fed chair. By emphasizing the mystique of the Fed, the book attracted much popular attention. The picture on the cover is of the board table with several governors discussing monetary policy.

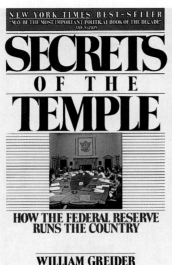

NEW YORK TIMES BEST-SELLER
"MAY BE THE MOST IMPORTANT POLITICAL BOOK OF THE DECADE"
THE NATION

SECRETS
OF THE
TEMPLE

HOW THE FEDERAL RESERVE RUNS THE COUNTRY

WILLIAM GREIDER

---

1. David Ricardo, *Plan for a National Bank,* 1824, pp. 10–11.

on inflation that they could be blinded to the effects of monetary policy on real GDP and employment and could either cause a recession or make an existing recession deeper or longer. Thus, a disadvantage of central bank independence is that it can be taken too far.

Whether independent or not, central banks need to be held *accountable* for their actions. If those in charge of the central bank do not perform their job well, it is appropriate that they not be reappointed. When the central bank of New Zealand was given greater independence in the late 1980s, its accountability was formalized very explicitly: If the head of the central bank does not fulfill low inflation goals agreed to in advance, the head is fired. But the central bank has independence in determining how to achieve these goals. This greater independence and accountability led to lower inflation in New Zealand. In fact, if you look back at Figure 30.2, you will see New Zealand *before* central bank independence; since independence, it has moved down and to the right toward lower inflation.

Review

▶ Central bank independence removes the central bank from short-run political pressures to lower interest rates, when doing so would ultimately raise inflation.

▶ Independent central banks need to be held accountable for their actions.

▶ Countries with more independent central banks have tended to have lower inflation than countries with less independent central banks.

MONEY DEMAND, MONEY SUPPLY, AND THE INTEREST RATE

Now that we have explored the rationale for the independence of Fed decisions, let's examine how the Fed carries out these decisions. If the Fed decides to raise interest rates, what action does it take to bring about this rise?

We will show how the interest rate is determined in a money market that consists of money demand and money supply. The Fed changes the interest rate by changing the money supply. To see how this works, we must first describe money demand and show that it depends on the interest rate.

Money Demand

Money demand is defined as a relationship between the interest rate and the quantity of money people are willing to hold at any given interest rate. As shown in Figure 30.3, the amount of money demanded is negatively related to the interest rate. One reason people hold money is to carry out transactions: buying and selling goods. Figure 30.3 shows that people will hold less money if the interest rate is high. That is, a higher interest rate reduces the amount of money people will want to carry around in their wallets or hold in their checking accounts. Conversely, a

money demand: a relationship between the interest rate and the quantity of money that people are willing to hold at any given interest rate.

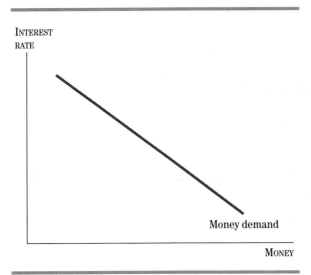

FIGURE 30.3
The Demand for Money

The interest rate is the opportunity cost of holding money. Higher interest rates on Treasury bills or other interest-bearing assets raise the opportunity cost of holding money and lower the quantity of money demanded.

lower interest rate will increase the amount of money people will want to hold. Why is money demand negatively related to the interest rate?

Remember that money (currency plus checking deposits) is only part of the wealth of most individuals. People usually hold some of their wealth in financial assets that pay interest. For example, some people hold securities, such as Treasury bills, as an alternative to money. If you bought Treasury bills in 1993, they would pay 3 percent interest; in 1996, they paid 5 percent interest. Holding money is different from holding Treasury bills because currency does not pay interest and checking deposits pay low, or no, interest. If you hold all your money in the form of cash in your wallet, clearly you do not gain any interest. Thus, an individual's decision to hold money is best viewed as an alternative to holding some other financial asset such as a Treasury bill. If you hold money, you get little or no interest; if you hold one of the alternatives, you earn interest.

The interest rate on the vertical axis in Figure 30.3 is the average interest rate on these other interest-bearing assets that people hold as alternatives to money. Now, if the interest rate on these alternatives rises, people will want to put more funds in those alternatives and hold less as money. If they hold the funds as currency, they get no interest on the funds. If they hold the funds in a checking account, they may get a small amount of interest but certainly less interest than would be gained on other securities. There is a lower quantity of money demanded at higher interest rates because putting the funds in interest-bearing securities becomes more attractive compared to keeping the funds in a wallet or purse.

In other words, the interest rate on the alternatives to holding money is the *opportunity cost* of holding money. When the opportunity cost increases, people hold less money. When the opportunity cost decreases, people hold more money.

Figure 30.3 represents money demand in the economy as a whole. The curve is obtained by adding up the money demanded by all the individuals in the economy at each interest rate. The money held by businesses—in cash registers or in checking accounts—should also be added in.

Money Supply

The Fed, of course, has no direct control over how much money as an individual you hold in your wallet or checking account, but it does control the supply of money in the whole economy. It does this by changing the monetary base—currency plus bank reserves, as we showed in Chapter 24. It changes the monetary base by either buying bonds or selling bonds.

On any given day the Fed buys and sells billions of dollars of government bonds. When the Fed buys government bonds, it has to pay for them with something. It pays for them with bank reserves—the deposits banks have with the Fed. For example, if the Fed wants to buy bonds held by Citibank, it says, "We want $1 billion worth of bonds, and we will pay for them by increasing Citibank's account with us by $1 billion." This is an electronic transaction. Citibank's deposits at the Fed (reserves) have increased by $1 billion and the Fed gets the bonds. They have exchanged bank reserves for the bonds. Now, the *monetary base* equals

monetary base: currency plus reserves. (Ch. 24)

currency plus reserves. By increasing reserves, the Fed increases the monetary base. Hence, *by buying bonds, the Fed increases the monetary base. By selling bonds, the Fed decreases the monetary base.* Buying and selling bonds is called an **open market operation.** The term *open market operation* is used because the market is open to anyone.

The *money multiplier,* as we studied in Chapter 24, provides a link between the money supply (M) and the monetary base (MB). The money multiplier is given by:

$$\frac{M}{MB} = \frac{1 + k}{r + k}$$

where r is the required reserve ratio and k is the currency to deposit ratio. Suppose r is .1 and the amount of currency people desire to hold as a fraction of deposits k is .2; then the money multiplier is $(1 + .2)/(.1 + .2) = 4$. Then an increase in the monetary base (MB) of $1 billion leads to increases in the money supply (M) of $4 billion.

Suppose the Fed buys bonds; this increases the monetary base, and according to the money multiplier the money supply in the economy increases. Similarly, if it sells bonds, it decreases the money supply.

Do not confuse the money multiplier with the government purchases multiplier described in Chapter 26. The government purchases multiplier tells us that an increase in government purchases of goods and services increases real GDP in the short run by a multiple of the increase in government purchases. The money multiplier has nothing to do with government purchases. The money multiplier tells us that an increase in the monetary base will increase the money supply by a multiple of the increase in the monetary base.

The Determination of the Interest Rate

We have now shown that money demand is determined by people in the economy deciding how much of their wealth to hold as money, and the money supply depends on the Fed. Now we put the two together to determine the interest rate, just as we combine the demand and supply for any good to determine the price. The quantity of money demanded must equal the quantity of money supplied. If the Fed supplies $300 billion in money, then people must hold that amount of money—no more and no less.

The interest rate brings the quantity of money demanded into equality with the quantity of money supplied. This is shown in Figure 30.4. The axes are the same as Figure 30.3, with the interest rate on the vertical axis and the quantity of money on the horizontal axis. We have added a vertical line to represent the money supply, as determined by the Fed. Observe how the interest rate plays the role of the price in this supply and demand diagram. There is only one place where this money supply line intersects the money demand curve. This intersection determines the interest rate in the money market, just as the intersection of the supply and demand curve for peanuts determines the price of peanuts in a peanut market. If the quantity of money supplied were above the quantity of money demanded, then people would put their excess money in interest-bearing accounts, driving down the interest rate on those accounts; the interest rate would fall. If the quantity of money supplied were below the quantity of money demanded, the interest rate would rise. There is only one value of the interest rate for which the money demand curve intersects the money supply line.

FIGURE 30.4
The Interest Rate and the Supply and Demand for Money
The interest rate in the money market is determined at the intersection of the money demand curve and the money supply line.

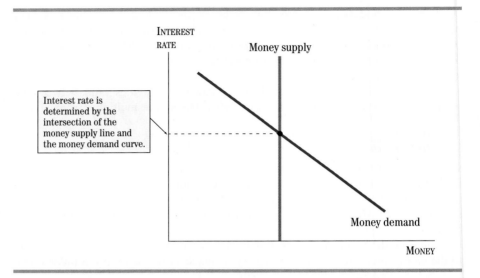

Review

▶ The demand for money depends inversely on the interest rate. A higher interest rate means a larger opportunity cost of holding money and therefore a lower amount of money demanded. Lower interest rates increase the amount of money demanded.

▶ The money supply is determined by the Fed. By buying bonds, the Fed increases the money supply.

By selling bonds, the Fed decreases the money supply.

▶ The interest rate is determined at the point where the money demand curve intersects the money supply line.

FED POLICY ACTIONS

We can now use the money demand and money supply diagram to show how the Fed affects the interest rate by changing the money supply.

Open Market Operations and Changes in the Federal Funds Rate

Let us describe what might happen on a typical day in the New York bond market to see how the Fed changes the interest rate. Suppose the Federal Open Market Committee (FOMC), the group at the Fed responsible for monetary policy, votes to lower the short-term interest rate by ¼ of a percentage point.

The situation facing the Fed is shown in the left panel of Figure 30.5, which shows money demand and money supply. To lower the interest rate the Fed must

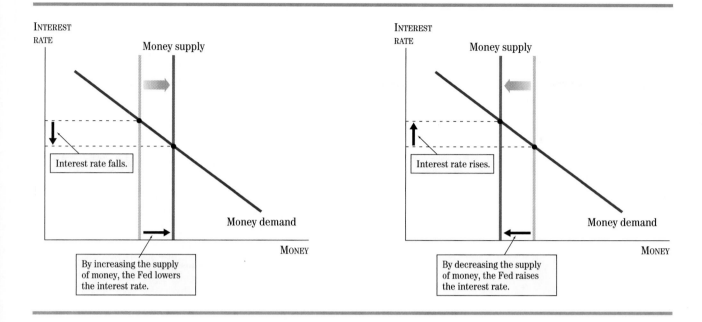

FIGURE 30.5
The Fed Can Change the Interest Rate by Changing the Money Supply

increase the money supply. This is shown in the diagram by shifting out the money supply line. At the higher money supply, there is a new intersection of the money supply and money demand curves. At this intersection, the interest rate is lower, which is exactly what the Fed wants.

In order to increase the money supply the Fed knows that, according to the money multiplier, it must increase the monetary base. In sum, if the Fed wants to lower the interest rate, it needs to increase the monetary base, and we know that this means it must buy bonds in the bond market.

Thus, the Fed buys the bonds from some bank, perhaps Citibank. The Fed pays for the bonds by increasing the amount of funds in Citibank's account so that bank reserves rise. With the rise in reserves we know that the monetary base rises, the money supply increases, and the interest rate falls; in our example the interest rate falls by ¼ percentage point.

The interest rate the Fed looks at in order to make sure that its actions are having the intended effect is called the *federal funds rate,* which is the short-term interest rate that banks charge each other on overnight loans. This interest rate is related to all other interest rates in the economy. (See Figure 30.6.) In particular, the federal funds rate is very closely related to interest rates on Treasury bills and other alternatives to holding money. The federal funds rate is also closely related to interest rates on bank loans, whether the loans are for construction, automobiles, or mortgages.

If the Fed wanted to raise the short-term interest rate, it would take action in precisely the opposite direction. It would sell bonds, which would lower bank reserves, lower the monetary base, lower the money supply, and raise interest rates. This case is illustrated in the panel on the right of Figure 30.5, which shows the money supply declining and the interest rate rising.

The Fed lowers the interest rate by increasing the supply of money, as in the graph on the left. The Fed can raise the interest rate by decreasing the supply of money, as in the graph on the right. The Fed changes the money supply by adjusting the monetary base through open market operations.

FIGURE 30.6
Short-Term Interest Rates
The federal funds rate is the interest rate the Fed focuses on when
deliberating about policy. Other
short-term interest rates move up
and down with the federal funds
rate. The rate on prime (low-risk)
bank loans is about 3 percentage
points above the federal funds rate.
Source: Federal Reserve Board.

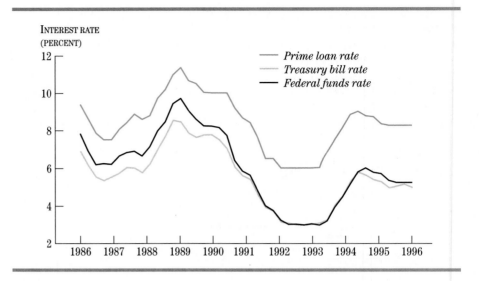

It is very important to remember that when the Fed changes the interest rate, it
also changes the money supply. When the Fed lowers the interest rate, for example,
it increases reserves, the monetary base, and thus the money supply. If the Fed
increases the money supply too much, then inflation will eventually rise. The Fed
must consider the impact of its actions on the money supply and on inflation each
time it considers raising or lowering interest rates.

The Monetary Transmission Channel

monetary transmission channel:
a description of how a change in
monetary policy eventually affects
real GDP.

The complete sequence of events through which a decision of the central bank to
buy bonds changes interest rates and shifts real GDP in the short run is called a
monetary transmission channel. The monetary transmission channel, from an
initial Fed bond purchase to a short-run rise in real GDP, can be summarized as
follows:

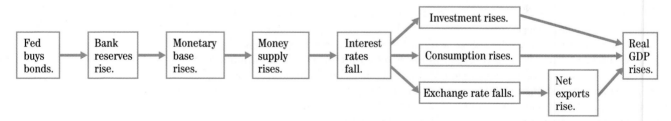

When the Fed buys bonds in the open market, the reserves at banks rise. Because
reserves are part of the monetary base, this causes the monetary base to rise. The
money multiplier tells us that the money supply is a multiple of the monetary base,
so this causes the money supply to rise. In order for people to hold the additional
money, the interest rate must fall; this stimulates investment and consumption.
Finally, the decline in the interest rate causes the exchange rate to fall, which raises
net exports. The increase in investment, consumption, and net exports raises real
GDP in the short run. (In the long run, however, as prices adjust, real GDP returns

to potential GDP, just as in Figure 30.1.) Remember that this all works in reverse: If the Fed sells bonds, real GDP will fall in the short run.

Economists have investigated the monetary transmission channel in great detail. For example, some economists like to focus on the role of *banks* in the monetary transmission channel. Recall that, as part of the multiplier process, banks expand their loans after an open market purchase. The loans are used to finance investment purchases, such as new equipment, and consumption purchases, such as new automobiles. The increase in loans provided by banks has a direct impact on aggregate spending and on real GDP.

Other Tools of Monetary Policy

Open market operations are a "tool" that the Fed uses to bring about changes in the money supply and interest rates. The Fed has two other tools it sometimes uses in conducting monetary policy.

The Discount Rate

The discount rate is one of these tools. The **discount rate** is the rate the Fed charges commercial banks when they borrow from the Fed. To understand why commercial banks borrow from the Fed, we must consider another role for central banks: the role of *lender of the last resort*. During recessions and depressions in the nineteenth and early twentieth centuries, there were frequently "runs" on banks in which people scrambled to withdraw their deposits for fear their bank was going under. Rumors caused runs even on sound banks. By agreeing to lend to banks if they experience a run, the Fed can bolster confidence in the bank. The mere existence of a central bank willing to lend reduces the chance of runs by raising confidence.

When commercial banks borrow from the Fed, economists say they "go to the discount window." Borrowings from the Fed are now very small. The Fed keeps the discount rate just a little below the federal funds rate. Because the discount rate is lower than the federal funds rate, the Fed then must discourage each bank from borrowing too much at the discount window.

Changes in Reserve Requirements

Another tool of monetary policy is the reserve requirement. Recall that the money multiplier depends on the required reserve ratio (r). If the Fed decreases the required reserve ratio—that is, decreases reserve requirements—then the money multiplier rises. For a given monetary base, therefore, a reduction in reserve requirements increases the money supply. Conversely, an increase in reserve requirements lowers the money supply.

In practice, however, the Fed very rarely changes reserve requirements; and when it does so its aim is not to change the money supply, because open market operations are sufficient to achieve any desired change in the money supply. Sometimes the Fed changes reserve requirements to affect the profits at banks. For example, in 1990, the Fed lowered reserve requirements in order to raise profits at banks and thereby reduce the chance that some banks would become insolvent during the 1990–1991 recession. Banks do not receive interest on reserves; thus, lower reserve requirements mean they can make more profits by making more interest-earning loans.

Keeping Track of the Monetary Transmission Channel

Here is a helpful memory device:

The Fed *Buys* bonds, and real GDP *Booms* in the short run.

The Fed *Sells* bonds, and real GDP *Slumps* in the short run.

discount rate: the interest rate that the Fed charges commercial banks when they borrow from the Fed.

In 1990, when the Fed lowered reserve requirements, it also lowered the monetary base so that the money supply was unaffected. In other words, the Fed used one of its other tools—open market operations—to exactly offset the effect of the reserve requirement tool on the money supply.

Review

▶ The Fed affects the short-term interest rate by changing the money supply. By buying bonds in the open market, the Fed increases the money supply and the interest rate falls. By selling bonds in the open market, the Fed decreases the money supply and the interest rate rises. These purchases and sales are called open market operations.

▶ In addition to open market operations, the Fed has two other tools: the discount rate and reserve requirements. By lowering reserve requirements, the Fed can increase bank profits, because banks do not receive interest on reserves.

ALTERNATIVE MONETARY POLICIES

We have now shown the actions the Fed must take when it decides to change the interest rate. Recall that the Fed usually decides to change the interest rate when inflation changes. For example, on March 25, 1997, the Fed announced that it was raising the interest rate from 5.25 percent to 5.50 percent because it was concerned that inflation was rising. We studied such a monetary policy response in Chapter 27. In this section we consider alternative ways the Fed might respond to changes in inflation as well as to changes in other variables.

In order to examine alternative Fed policy responses to inflation, look first at Figure 30.7, which shows an aggregate demand/inflation curve and a price adjustment line just as we derived them in Chapter 27. A rise in inflation is shown as an upward shift in the price adjustment line. Recall that the aggregate demand/inflation curve incorporates the Fed policy response to a rise in inflation. When inflation rises, the Fed raises the interest rate, and this tends to reduce real GDP relative to potential GDP in the short run, as shown in Figure 30.7. The decline in real GDP relative to potential GDP then puts downward pressure on inflation.

In Chapter 27 we described this Fed policy in terms of a monetary policy rule in which the Fed increases interest rates when inflation rises and decreases interest rates when inflation falls. That monetary policy rule is shown in Table 27.1 on page 732 and Figure 27.5 on page 733. In this section we show that many alternative monetary policy rules also imply a downward-sloping aggregate demand/inflation curve. However, alternative monetary policy rules imply different *slopes* of the aggregate demand/inflation curve. For example, a monetary policy rule that raises interest rates by more than shown in Table 27.1 will result in a flatter aggregate demand/inflation curve. Why? Because the larger change in the interest rate, for a given increase in inflation, will cause real GDP to decline by a larger amount, as shown for the flatter curve in Figure 30.7.

Now let's show why other monetary policy rules imply downward-sloping aggregate demand/inflation curves, though perhaps with different slopes.

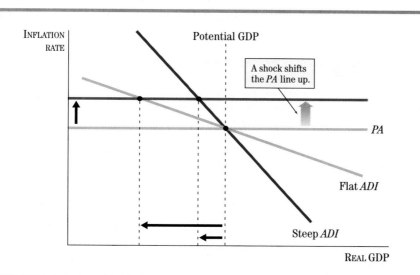

FIGURE 30.7
Alternative Monetary Policies
When a rise in inflation shifts the *PA* line up, the Fed's actions—incorporated into the *ADI* curve—affect the impact on real GDP. Many different monetary policy rules imply a downward-sloping *ADI* curve. They differ in how steep or flat the curve is.

The Constant Money Growth Rule

Historical studies by Milton Friedman and Anna Schwartz have led them to argue in favor of a monetary policy that simply holds the growth rate of the money supply constant from year to year. This is called a **constant money growth rule.**

A constant money growth rule would give good inflation performance in the long run. For example, from the quantity equation of money (Chapter 24), if the velocity growth rate is zero and the long-term real GDP growth rate is 3 percent, then setting money growth at 5 percent would keep inflation at 2 percent on average. If the Fed had a *target inflation rate* of 2 percent, then setting money growth at 5 percent would achieve this target over the long run.

constant money growth rule: a monetary policy in which the central bank keeps money growth constant.

Example. According to the quantity equation for money (see Chapter 24):

Inflation rate + real GDP growth = money growth + velocity growth

Thus,

> if money growth = 5 percent
> velocity growth = 0 percent
> real GDP growth = 3 percent

then the inflation rate = 2 percent.

Implications for the Aggregate Demand/Inflation Curve

Even with a constant money growth rule, inflation would not be perfectly stable from year to year. There would be shocks to the economy that would push the inflation rate around. However, with a constant money growth rule, if inflation picked up, whether because of an oil price shock or another shock, then interest rates would rise and real GDP would decline, just as described by the aggregate demand/inflation curve. Why would interest rates rise? With higher inflation, people would find they needed more money to carry out their transactions. For example, if inflation suddenly rose to 100 percent this year, the price level would double and people would need twice as much money. Money demand, as shown in Figure 30.4, would shift up. But with the constant money growth rule the Fed does not increase the money supply by enough to meet the increased demand. Hence, the amount of money demanded would be greater than the amount of money supplied; and, as Figure 30.4 suggests, the interest rate would rise. The higher interest rate would, in turn, reduce investment, consumption, and net exports. Hence, real GDP would fall. In sum, with higher inflation and lower real GDP, we trace out a downward-sloping aggregate demand/inflation curve.

The *slope* of the aggregate demand/inflation curve with a constant money growth rule would depend on how sensitive money demand is to the interest rate. This sensitivity to the interest rate determines how much the interest rate must change to bring the quantity of money demanded into equality with the quantity of money supplied by the Fed. If money demand were not very sensitive to the interest rate, then a big change in the interest rate would be required to bring the quantity of money demanded into equality with the fixed quantity of money supplied. This big change in the interest rate would have a large effect on real GDP and trace out a relatively flat aggregate demand/inflation curve.

Debates about Constant Money Growth Rules

Monetarists are economists who generally advocate a constant money growth rule. The monetarists argue that the main advantage of a constant money growth rule is that it prevents erratic shifts in monetary policy. We know that such shifts in monetary policy will cause real GDP to fluctuate and can cause boom-bust cycles. In other words, the constant money growth rule is attractive to monetarists because they feel it will do less harm to the economy. They worry about rules in which the Fed staff must decide each week or month how much to adjust the money supply in order to move interest rates around as determined by the FOMC. They agree with most other economists that the best policy is one that keeps the aggregate demand/inflation curve from shifting. They disagree about the best means of keeping it from shifting.

Those who object to the constant money growth rule do not differ with monetarists about the importance of keeping aggregate demand stable—that is, keeping the aggregate demand/inflation curve from shifting. They feel that uncertainty about measuring and defining the money supply will lead to poor performance with a constant money growth rule. In other words, they feel that a constant money growth rule will lead to more and larger shifts in the aggregate demand/inflation curve than would other rules. That is why they recommend the Fed focus more on interest rates, as in the policy rule discussed in Chapter 27.

Real GDP in the Monetary Policy Rule

Another monetary policy rule is a slight modification of the monetary policy rule described in Chapter 27. It formally adds in real GDP along with inflation as a variable influencing the Fed's interest rate decisions. For this rule, the central bank raises the interest rate when real GDP rises above potential GDP and lowers the interest rate when real GDP falls below potential GDP. Real GDP thus becomes another factor in the monetary policy rule along with the inflation rate.

If the central bank takes actions to raise the interest rate in this way when the economy goes into a boom, then the higher interest rate will slow the growth of real GDP and cut off the boom. Or, if the economy is in a recession, the central bank will reduce the interest rate. In this case, a lower interest rate could help bring about a more rapid recovery.

Table 30.1 shows a numerical example describing this type of policy rule. On the left is the inflation rate. On the top is the percent deviation of real GDP from potential GDP. The entries in the shaded part of the table show the interest rate. For example, the blue entry shows that when inflation is 2 percent and real GDP is equal to potential GDP (the percent deviation of real GDP from potential GDP is zero), the interest rate is 4 percent. When inflation rises to 4 percent, the interest

		Percent Deviation of Real GDP from Potential GDP		
		−2	0	2
Inflation Rate	0	.5	1	2
(percent)	2	3	4	5
	4	6	7	8
	6	9	10	11
	8	12	13	14

TABLE 30.1
A Numerical Example of Central Bank Interest Rate Policy Reacting to Both Real GDP and Inflation
(Compare with Table 27.1 on page 732.)

(The entries in the shaded area show the interest rate for each inflation rate and real GDP deviation.)

rate rises to 7 percent. Each column of Table 30.1 tells the same story: When inflation rises, the central bank raises the interest rate. Note that the interest rate rises more than inflation rises for every column in Table 30.1, just as in Table 27.1.

Now observe in Table 30.1 that the central bank's response to inflation also depends on what happens to real GDP. If real GDP is falling below potential GDP in a recession, the central bank reduces the interest rate. In other words, when real GDP falls below potential GDP, the central bank lowers the interest rate, and when GDP rises above potential the central bank raises the interest rate.

What are the reasons for the Fed to react to real GDP as well as to inflation in this way? First consider the case of a boom and then the case of a recession.

If the economy goes into a boom and real GDP rises above potential GDP, the Fed would raise the interest rate according to Table 30.1, even if the inflation rate had not started to increase. Such a policy response is sometimes called a **preemptive monetary strike** because the Fed increases the interest rate in anticipation of a rise in inflation, before the inflation rate actually rises. The interest rate response to higher real GDP may be based on an assessment by the Fed that the boom will soon bring higher inflation and, because monetary policy works with a lag, it is better to react sooner rather than later.

preemptive monetary strike: a Fed interest rate increase in anticipation of a rise in inflation.

If the economy goes into a recession, the rationale for reacting to real GDP is somewhat different. In the case of a recession, the decline of real GDP relative to potential GDP will call for a reduction of the interest rate, according to the policy rule in Table 30.1. The reduction in the interest rate will tend to stimulate real GDP and offset the recession, perhaps leading to a quicker recovery from the recession. Moreover, the decline in real GDP relative to potential GDP may be a signal of lower inflation in the future, another reason for the Fed to lower the interest rate.

In reality the Fed and other central banks appear to react to real GDP as well as to inflation in this way. In other words, Table 30.1 is a more accurate description of central bank behavior than Table 27.1, though Table 27.1 is a close approximation.

The monetary policy rule in Table 30.1 also leads to a downward-sloping aggregate demand/inflation curve, though the curve will be steeper than the simpler policy rule of Table 27.1, in which the Fed reacts only to inflation. Suppose that there is an increase in the inflation rate, as in Figure 30.7. Then the Fed will increase the interest rate and this will tend to reduce real GDP. However, as real GDP declines, the Fed keeps the interest rate below that level given by the policy rule without real GDP. Thus, for this policy rule, the Fed does not increase the interest rate as much for a given increase in inflation and, therefore, real GDP does not decline as much for any increase in inflation; in other words, the aggregate demand/inflation curve is steeper.

The Gold Standard

gold standard: a monetary standard in which the value of money is linked to gold.

For many years before the Fed was founded, much of the world operated under a monetary policy that was called the **gold standard.** When on a gold standard in the late nineteenth and early twentieth centuries, the U.S. Treasury had effective responsibility for monetary policy. Under the gold standard, the Treasury agreed to buy and sell gold at a fixed number of dollars per ounce. Also, the law tied the money supply in the economy to a multiple of the amount of gold at the Treasury. Such a policy would also tend to generate a downward-sloping aggregate demand/inflation curve. Why? If, for example, the price of gold began to rise above the fixed price, perhaps because of a general inflation that raised all prices, then the Treasury would start to lose gold. People would want to buy gold at the low fixed price, and the Treasury would have to sell it. But less gold at the Treasury would reduce the money supply. Thus, interest rates would rise and eventually would result in a decline in real GDP. Thus, the gold standard can be considered another example of a monetary policy rule.

The main advantage of a gold standard is that, as long as the relative price of gold does not change, there would be no inflation. The main disadvantage of a gold standard is that the relative price of gold could change. For example, when there were gold discoveries, the price of gold fell, and this led people to sell gold to the Treasury at the higher price. As the stock of gold at the Treasury rose, the money supply rose; this caused real GDP to rise in the short run, and eventually inflation rose. Thus, under the gold standard, changes in the price of gold added to fluctuations in real GDP.

Review

▶ Many alternative monetary policy rules imply a downward-sloping aggregate demand/inflation curve.

▶ The rules differ in how steep the aggregate demand/inflation curve is and how stable it is.

▶ Reacting to real GDP as well as to inflation allows the Fed to take preemptive strikes against inflation and better mitigate recessions.

▶ Monetarists prefer constant growth rate rules because such rules result in less erratic shifts in policy.

GAINS FROM CREDIBILITY

Central bank independence and clearly stated procedures for setting the interest rate, as described thus far in this chapter, are likely to bolster the credibility of monetary policy. What are the advantages of a credible monetary policy? There are two key advantages. One is a better understanding of Fed policy actions; the other is less costly disinflations. Let us consider each in turn.

Interpreting Policy Actions

An advantage of credibility for monetary policy is that the Fed can take actions that may appear contrary to its goals, but explain what it is doing and be believed. For

The Fed Chairman Speaks on Principles of Monetary Policy

Alan Greenspan was appointed to the chair of the Board of Governors of the Federal Reserve System by President Reagan, to a second term by President Bush, and to a third term by President Clinton. As part of the Senate confirmation process, Greenspan testified before the Senate Banking Committee. In doing so he gave a set of general principles of monetary policy that are excerpted here.

I see the fundamental task of monetary policy as fostering the financial conditions most conducive to the American economy performing at its fullest potential. As I have often noted before, there is every reason to believe that the main contribution the central bank can make to the achievement of this national economic objective over long periods is to promote reasonable price stability. Removing uncertainty about future price levels and eliminating the costs and distortions inevitably involved in coping with inflation will encourage productive investment and saving to raise living standards. Monetary policy is uniquely qualified to address this issue: Inflation is ultimately determined by the provision of liquidity to the economy by the central bank and, except through its effect on inflation, monetary policy has little long-term influence on the growth of capital and the labor force or the increase in productivity, which together determine long-run economic growth.

But a central bank must also recognize that the "long run" is made up of a series of "short runs." Our policies do affect output and employment in the short and intermediate terms, and we must be mindful of these effects. The monetary authority can, and should, lean against prevailing trends, not only when inflation threatens but also when the forces of disinflation seem to be gathering excessive momentum. That is, in fact, what has concerned us in recent months, and we have been taking actions designed to assist in returning the economy to a solid growth path.

However, the Federal Reserve, or any other central bank, must also be conscious of the limits of its capabilities. We can try to provide a backdrop for stable, sustainable growth, but we cannot iron out every fluctuation, and attempts to do so could be counterproductive. What we have learned about monetary policy since the beginnings of the Federal Reserve System is that the longer-term effect of a policy action may be quite different from its initial impact; what we do not know with precision is the size and timing of these effects, especially in the short run. Uncertainty about the near-term twists and turns of the economy, along with the awareness of the potential differences between long- and short-term effects, suggests both flexibility in the conduct of monetary policy and close attention to the longer-term context in conducting day-to-day operations.

Note how Greenspan touches on many of the issues discussed in this chapter: the difference between the long-run and short-run effects of monetary policy, the goal of price stability, inflation being ultimately determined by liquidity (another word for the money supply), and the uncertainty about the size and timing of the impacts of monetary policy.

Source: Federal Reserve Bulletin, 1991.

example, suppose the Fed sees that the relationship between money and the interest rate is currently going off track. Suppose that there is a shift in money demand, so that at every interest rate people demand more money. Such a shift is illustrated in Figure 30.8. To keep interest rates from changing in such a circumstance, the Fed would have to increase the money supply, as shown in the figure.

If the Fed had little credibility, then people might interpret such an increase in the money supply as an indication that the Fed was going to allow for more inflation. But with credibility the Fed could state its views—that it was increasing the money supply because of a shift in money demand—and people would not worry that the Fed was trying to raise the inflation rate.

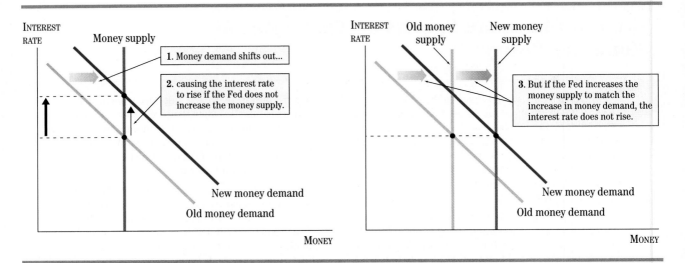

FIGURE 30.8
Shift in Money Demand and Fed Responses

The money demand curve shifts out. If the Fed does not increase the money supply, then the interest rate increases. If the Fed has credibility, it can increase the money supply without raising people's expectations of inflation.

FIGURE 30.9
Benefits of a Credible Disinflation

In the left graph, the *ADI* curve shifts to the new inflation target rapidly. The economy goes into a recession. In the right graph, the policy shift is announced, is credible, and occurs gradually. In the ideal case, there is little or no growth slowdown.

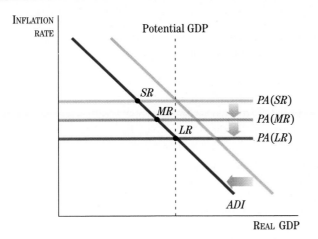

A sudden disinflation with no credibility: A recession occurs as interest rates jump and inflation does not change quickly.

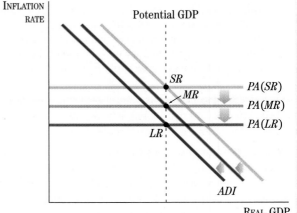

The ideal case of a more credible disinflation: Lower expectations of inflation and a more gradual shift in the *ADI* curve allow inflation to come down with little or no recession.

Expectations and Credible Disinflation

An important issue for monetary policy is how to reduce the inflation rate when it is too high. We considered this problem of disinflation in Chapter 28. We showed that a recession usually occurs when the Fed tries to reduce the rate of inflation. This is illustrated again in the left panel of Figure 30.9. However, if the Fed announces its disinflation path and is credible, then it is possible for disinflation to occur with a smaller decline in real GDP.

For example, in the right panel of Figure 30.9, the aggregate demand/inflation curve *and* the price adjustment line shift down together. With a credible policy of disinflation, the rate of inflation adjusts down because people expect lower inflation in the future. However, getting expectations of inflation down requires a great deal of credibility. If the Fed does not have much credibility, the disinflation will be as costly as shown in the left panel, regardless of what the Fed says.

Review

▶ If a central bank has credibility, it can take actions to offset shifts in money demand without adversely affecting inflation expectations.

▶ A credible disinflation has a smaller impact on output and employment than a disinflation that nobody believes will occur.

CONCLUSION

In this chapter we examined the reasons for central bank independence. We also showed how the Fed's actions to change the money supply affect the interest rate. Several different central bank policies—for example, keeping the growth rate of the money supply constant, or pegging the price of gold—effectively cause the interest rate to increase when inflation rises and to decrease when inflation falls. Thus, a policy rule can occur even without a central bank. Deciding which policy is a good one and how it can be implemented are the major questions about monetary policy.

In the next chapter we consider how monetary policy works in the global economy. We will see, for example, that different policies for exchange rates among countries involved in international trade affect the independence of monetary policy among those countries.

KEY POINTS

1. Monetary policy has a powerful effect on the economy. Large recessions and large inflations have been caused by monetary policy.

2. In most modern economies, monetary policy is the responsibility of the central bank.

3. Giving the central bank some independence is a way to avoid political business cycles and the temptation to change policy for short-term gain.

4. The Fed determines the money supply in the whole economy.

5. The demand for money is negatively related to the interest rate.

6. The Fed changes the interest rate by changing the supply of money.

7. The Fed can mitigate recessions by responding with lower interest rates.

8. Modern macroeconomic research suggests that the Fed should follow some kind of a policy rule in order to reduce uncertainty and gain credibility.

9. The Fed can reduce the costs of disinflation if it has such credibility.

10. The Fed's policy rule is responsive to real GDP as well as to inflation.

KEY TERMS

central bank independence
political business cycle
time inconsistency
money demand

open market operation
monetary transmission channel
discount rate
constant money growth rule

preemptive monetary strike
gold standard

QUESTIONS FOR REVIEW

1. What are some examples of the powerful effects of monetary policy?

2. What are the advantages and disadvantages of central bank independence?

3. What did monetary policy amount to before there were central banks?

4. Why is the demand for money inversely related to the interest rate?

5. What is the opportunity cost of holding money?

6. How does the Fed raise the interest rate?

7. How does a constant money growth rule determine the target inflation rate?

8. Why should real GDP be a variable in the monetary policy rule?

9. What are the advantages of a credible disinflation?

PROBLEMS

1. In recommending central banking reforms for Eastern European economies, the *Economic Report of the President, 1990,* p. 202, asserted, "It is widely agreed that the central bank should have a high degree of independence from the central government so that it can resist political pressures to finance government spending with money creation and can pursue the objective of price stability." Explain the reasoning behind this assertion. What are some counterarguments?

2. The original Federal Reserve Act of 1913 allowed the secretary of the Treasury to be a member of the Federal Reserve Board, but a later amendment prohibited this. How would such a change affect the conduct of monetary policy?

3. Suppose that the currency to deposit ratio (k) equals .2 and the monetary base is $300 billion. By how much does the money supply change when the reserve requirement ratio (r) is raised from .1 to .2?

4. Suppose the Fed wants to raise the federal funds rate. Describe in detail how it accomplishes this policy.

5. What is the discount rate? How does it differ from the federal funds rate? Describe how the Fed affects each of these interest rates.

6. Suppose there is an increase in money demand at every interest rate. Show this in a diagram. What effect will this have on the interest rate if the Fed does not increase the money supply?

7. Suppose there are two countries, identical except for the fact that the central bank of one country lets interest rates rise sharply when inflation rises and the other lets interest rates rise less when inflation rises. Draw the aggregate demand/inflation curve for each country. What are the benefits and the drawbacks of each country's policy?

8. During the early 1990s in Japan, there was deflation and real GDP was below potential GDP.
a) Draw a diagram showing the situation where there is deflation at potential GDP.
b) Suppose the Japanese central bank decides it must reinflate and sets a target inflation rate of 2 percent. How does it accomplish this? Show the short-, medium-, and long-run effects.
c) Is it possible that the central bank can have a fully credible reinflation? What are the benefits of immediate increases in the inflation rate?

9. Suppose that a government has a very bad credit rating (for example, there is serious default risk on the part of the government) and cannot sell bonds to finance its budget deficit. The only way it can finance the deficit is by issuing new money. As the deficit increases, what happens to inflation?

10. Suppose the velocity of money is constant, the growth rate of potential GDP is 2 percent per year, and the Fed's inflation target is initially 4 percent.

a) The Fed then increases its inflation target to 6 percent per year. Using the quantity equation of money in growth rates, calculate the growth rate of money both before the Fed changes its target and in the long run, after it changes its target.

b) Suppose, instead, that the Fed increases inflation to 10 percent, and the increase in uncertainty in the economy causes potential GDP to grow by 1 percent. What is the growth rate of money in the long run now?

11. Using the aggregate demand/inflation curve and the price adjustment line, show how real GDP would change over time if the Fed targeted a lower inflation rate and there was no change in fiscal policy. Suppose that real GDP was equal to potential GDP at the time of the change. Describe what happens to real GDP, investment, consumption, and net exports in the short run, medium run, and long run. Explain the role of interest rates and inflation in the adjustment of the economy.

12. Real GDP, consumption, and investment in the United States all declined from 1990 to 1991 and increased in 1992.

a) Using an aggregate demand/inflation curve and a price adjustment line, show how a change in monetary policy in 1991 could explain these developments.

b) Using a diagram with a monetary policy rule, describe what would happen to the interest rate and inflation in the short run (1991), the medium run (1992), and the long run according to the explanation in part (a) of this problem.

c) Net exports increased from 1990 to 1991. Is the explanation in part (a) consistent with this development? If not, what other factors may have explained the behavior of net exports?

International Finance

Countries are closely linked by trade. It is a rare day when we do not use or consume something made in another part of the world. In fact, advances in telecommunications and transportation and the removal of government restrictions on trade are transforming the world into one interconnected global market rather than separate national markets. Most commodity markets—including oil, copper, and wheat—are already world markets.

Trade between countries also requires another kind of market: the foreign exchange market, where one can obtain currency from another country in order to buy goods made in that country. The foreign currency market is itself a world market. Any time, day or night, the market in foreign currencies is open somewhere in the world. When the market closes for the day in Tokyo, it is just opening in London. When it closes in London, it is just opening in San Francisco. When the market closes in San Francisco, it is about to open in Tokyo again. The foreign currency market is huge. Foreign currency trading is more than forty times the amount of goods trading in the world.

In this chapter we show how trade imbalances, in which exports are not equal to imports, are a normal part of world trade, but that such trade imbalances require that the people in one country lend funds to people in other countries. We then examine how the exchange rate—the price of foreign currency—is determined in the global market in foreign currencies. Finally, we look at what happens when two or more countries decide to fix the exchange rate between their currencies.

The subject matter of this chapter is called *international finance* because it focuses on how trade deficits are financed and how international financial markets in foreign currencies function.

BALANCE OF TRADE AROUND THE WORLD

Net exports are defined as exports less imports. Another term for net exports is the trade balance. When net exports are negative, we say there is a trade deficit. If net exports are positive, there is a trade surplus. Some countries have trade surpluses, and some have trade deficits. However, the world as a whole has neither a trade deficit nor a trade surplus. Exports equal imports for the whole world.

The Trade Deficit

As shown in the top panel of Figure 31.1, the U.S. trade deficit grew rapidly in the 1980s. It then shrank rapidly in the late 1980s before starting to rise again. Because the world as a whole can have no deficit, countries outside the United States had a

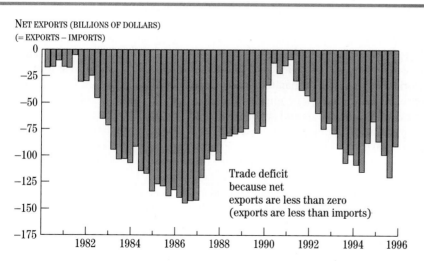

NET EXPORTS (BILLIONS OF DOLLARS)
(= EXPORTS – IMPORTS)

Trade deficit because net exports are less than zero (exports are less than imports)

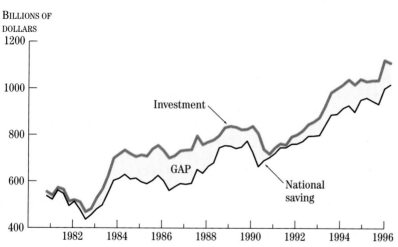

BILLIONS OF DOLLARS

Investment

GAP

National saving

FIGURE 31.1
The Trade Deficit and the Investment-Saving Gap
In the 1980s, the trade deficit in the United States rose. It narrowed in the late 1980s and then widened again. Observe that these swings in the trade deficit are closely associated with the gap between investment and saving.

Source: U.S. Department of Commerce.

821

reverse pattern: The rest of the world's trade surplus with the United States grew rapidly in the 1980s, declined rapidly in the late 1980s, and rose in the 1990s.

Why did these large swings occur? Sometimes trade barriers—*tariffs* and *quotas* in other countries—are offered as the reason for the United States trade deficit. But this clearly makes no sense as an explanation for the changes in the trade deficit in the 1980s and 1990s. For example, Europe, whose trade account with the United States moved from surplus to deficit and back to surplus again during this period, did not change its trade barriers.

The lower panel of Figure 31.1 provides a better explanation. It shows the pattern of (1) investment in new factories and equipment in the United States, and (2) saving by individuals, businesses, and governments in the United States. Although the levels of both investment and saving were increasing, the *gap* between them grew dramatically in the 1980s. The gap then diminished in the early 1990s before widening again. During the 1980s and again in the 1990s, investment rose very rapidly in the United States as investors took advantage of good profit opportunities to build new plants and invest in new machinery. But at the same time the amount of saving that Americans were doing did not increase as rapidly. Thus, a gap grew between the level of investment and the level of saving.

Observe the close relationship between the investment-saving gap and the trade deficit in Figure 31.1. When the investment-saving gap rose, the trade deficit got bigger. When the investment-saving gap fell, the trade deficit got smaller. This close connection is not a coincidence. When the people of a country invest more in new factories and equipment than they save, they have to import more from abroad than they export. The excess of imports over exports (the trade deficit) goes to fill the gap between investment and saving. Another way to state this association between the investment-saving gap and the trade deficit is through an equation: *Saving minus investment equals net exports.* For example, in 1996, saving was $1,017 billion and investment was $1,116 billion; the difference, −$99 billion, equaled net exports; in other words there was a trade deficit of $99 billion in 1996.

The gap between investment and saving is thus at the heart of the large trade deficits in the 1980s and again in the 1990s. As long as the United States is an attractive place to invest and U.S. saving is insufficient to provide for that investment, trade deficits are inevitable.

Example: Let
S = saving,
I = investment,
X = net exports,
then $S − I = X$.
If S = 1,017 and
I = 1,116, then
X = −99.

Both Merchandise Trade and Services Trade Are Important

merchandise trade: trade in goods that have physical form, such as oil, wheat, or computers.

services trade: trade in services, or things that do not have a physical form, such as consulting or telecommunications.

Both exports and imports can be divided into merchandise and services. **Merchandise trade** includes goods such as trucks, oil, televisions, wheat, textiles, and shoes. **Services trade** includes airplane passenger service, legal services, education, banking services, telephone services, business consulting services, and construction services. Although both merchandise and services are exported and imported, it is easier to imagine merchandise being shipped from one country to another. Examples of U.S. services exports would include an American telecommunications consultant going to Saudi Arabia to give assistance in using a new air traffic control system, or a Japanese graduate student in physics in the United States paying tuition and fees for room and board. Examples of U.S. services imports would include an American traveling on the French *Concorde,* or Apple Computer hiring a German lawyer for assistance in protecting its trademark.

Services trade is more difficult to measure than merchandise trade because the goods do not physically pass through customs booths at ports of entry. In recent years efforts to collect data on services have improved our understanding of the size and importance of services trade.

The **merchandise trade balance** is the difference between merchandise exports and merchandise imports. If merchandise exports are greater than merchandise imports, there is a merchandise trade surplus; if merchandise exports are less than merchandise imports, there is a merchandise trade deficit. Similarly, the **services trade balance** is the difference between services exports and services imports. Adding the services trade balance and merchandise trade balance together gives the total trade balance shown in the upper graph in Figure 31.1.

merchandise trade balance: the value of merchandise exports minus the value of merchandise imports.

Example: For 1996 in billions of dollars:

Merchandise exports	609
Merchandise imports	−795
Merchandise trade balance	−186

The U.S. Merchandise Trade Deficit

There has been a large U.S. merchandise trade deficit since the early 1980s. In 1996 the deficit was $186 billion. The merchandise trade balance is the most frequently reported trade statistic in the United States and in other countries. The merchandise data are easier to understand, and there is a tradition of looking at merchandise trade. Hence, many press reports still focus on the merchandise trade deficit. However, because of the growing importance of services, the merchandise trade deficit is too narrow a measure of a country's trade performance. Countries can gain as much in jobs and income from exporting services as they can gain from exporting merchandise.

services trade balance: the value of services exports minus the value of services imports.

Example: For 1996 in billions of dollars:

Services exports	238
Services imports	−151
Services trade balance	87

The U.S. Services Trade Surplus

The behavior of services trade is much different from merchandise trade in the United States. The United States has been running a surplus in services trade in recent years. As of 1996, the services trade surplus was $87 billion. The United States exported $238 billion of services in 1996 and imported $151 billion. Adding this services trade surplus to the merchandise trade deficit gives a radically different picture of the U.S. trade deficit. Without services, the trade deficit would have been $186 billion in 1996; with services, the trade deficit was about one-half as large— $99 billion.

Why is there a services trade surplus? A possible explanation is that the United States has a *comparative advantage* in the production of services. U.S. productivity in services is much higher than in other countries. Productivity in telecommunications services is greater in the United States than in Japan and Germany. Productivity in banking services is 50 percent greater in the United States than in the United Kingdom.

comparative advantage: a situation in which a person or country can produce one good more efficiently than another good in comparison with another person or country. (Ch. 2)

The Balance of Payments

Payments made from one country to another can take place for many reasons: Imports into the United States from Europe, for example, require payments to Europeans by Americans, and exports from the United States to Europe require payments by Europeans to Americans. But there are also transfer payments from foreign workers to family members at home, interest payments on loans, and payments of profits by foreign-owned firms. The **balance of payments** account keeps track of all these payments; it is a record of all the transactions between one country and the rest of the world. The balance of payments has two parts: the current account and the capital account.

balance of payments: the record of all the transactions between a country and the rest of the world; it includes information on the value of trade in goods and services as well as transfer payments.

The Current Account

The *current account* is a measure of all the payments made for currently produced goods and services plus *nontrade flows* of funds between a country and the rest of the world. All nontrade flows are lumped together in two categories: (1) interest, profits, and wages earned by the residents of another country, and (2) transfer payments received by the residents of another country.

In describing these two nontrade flows, we will look at Table 31.1, which shows the relationship between the *merchandise trade balance,* the *total (merchandise plus services) trade balance,* and the *current account balance* in the United States in 1996.

The first category of nontrade flows consists of interest payments, profits, and wages earned by businesses operating and people working in other countries. For example, if you live in Chicago and happen to have a deposit at a bank in London, your interest earnings on the bank deposit are a flow of funds from the United Kingdom to the United States. Another example is Blockbuster Video, headquartered in Ft. Lauderdale, Florida, which owns video rental stores in Australia (and many other countries); the profits earned in the Australian stores represent a flow of funds from Australia to the United States. This category of flows is called **factor income** because it represents earnings for a factor of production: for example, the store where Blockbuster videos are rented.

Factor income can either be paid or received by U.S. residents. If an American firm owns a business affiliate in Latin America or Europe, the interest payments and profits that the U.S. residents earn from the affiliate are called *receipt of factor income.* If a Japanese firm owns a business affiliate in the United States, the interest and profits that the affiliate pays to Japanese residents are *payment of factor income.* The difference between receipts of factor income and payments of factor income is called **net factor income from abroad.** Net factor income from abroad is one of the two items that must be added to the trade balance to get the current account balance.

As shown in Table 31.1, the United States received less factor income from abroad than it paid abroad in 1996; net factor income from abroad was −$9 billion. In other words, interest payments, profits, and wages of U.S. businesses and workers abroad were less than interest payments, profits, and wages of foreign affiliates and foreign workers in the United States. In 1996, receipts of factor income in the United States were $223 billion; payments of factor income were $232 billion.

The second category of nontrade flows consists of **international transfer payments,** which are humanitarian or military aid paid to other countries. International

---

factor income: earnings for a factor of production including wages and profits.

net factor income from abroad: the difference between receipts of factor income from foreign countries and payments of factor income to foreigners.

Example: For 1996, in billions of dollars:

Receipt of factor income	223
Payment of factor income	−232
Net factor income from abroad:	−9

international transfer payments: payments across international borders in the form of grants, remittances, and aid.

TABLE 31.1
Measures of the U.S. International Trade, 1996
(billions of dollars, surplus or deficit [−])

	1996
Merchandise trade balance	−186
Plus services trade balance	87
Equals total trade balance (net exports)	−99
Plus net factor income from abroad	−9
Plus net transfers from abroad	−39
Equals current account balance	−147

(Nontrade flows: *Plus* net factor income from abroad; *Plus* net transfers from abroad)

Source: U.S. Department of Commerce.

Desert Storm and the Current Account

Table 31.1 shows that net transfers to the United States were negative in 1996. That is the usual situation. Transfer payments made by foreigners to the United States have been much smaller than transfers made by the United States to foreigners for most of the last 70 years. The difference was largest as a share of GDP in the years immediately following World War II. Then, the Marshall Plan and other foreign assistance programs had the United States transferring abroad about 1.5 percent of GDP per year for several years as grants and technical assistance went to help rebuild Japan, Germany, and the rest of Europe. Since then the United States has continued to transfer more abroad in humanitarian and military aid than it has received from abroad. In a typical year the number is much smaller than during the Marshall Plan years—it was ½ percent of GDP in 1996.

However, 1991 was an exception. In 1991 the United States received more funds from foreign countries than it paid out to foreign countries. How did this happen? The U.S. military operation against Iraq—Desert Storm—was the reason. Other countries transferred funds to the United States as reimbursement for the U.S. military operation. Most of these funds came from Japan and Germany. The large receipt of payments was for expenses associated with conducting the air strikes, maintaining the civil defense systems, and sending the ground troops to drive the Iraqi forces from Kuwait.

The amount of funds transferred was large enough to have a very noticeable effect on the U.S. current account. As shown in Figure 31.2 (on page 826), the current account went into surplus in 1991. The year before, 1990, the current account was in deficit; the year after, 1992, it had returned to a deficit. The swing in the current account was largely due to these one-time transfers.

---

transfer payments can go both ways; **net transfers from abroad** are the difference between transfers received in the United States and transfer payments made by the United States. In 1996, net transfers from abroad in the United States were negative, as they are in most years because the United States gives more humanitarian and military aid than it receives. An important exception occurred during the 1991 military operation to drive Iraq from Kuwait. (See the box "Desert Storm and the Current Account.")

net transfers from abroad: the difference between transfer payments received and transfer payments made to other countries.

If we add net factor incomes from abroad and net transfers from abroad to the trade balance we get the **current account balance.** When the current account balance is negative, as in Table 31.1, we say there is a current account deficit. The behavior of the trade balance (net exports) and the current account balance has been fairly similar in recent years because the fluctuations in the trade deficit have been huge compared with fluctuations in net factor income or net transfers (see Figure 31.2).

current account balance: the value of exports minus the value of imports plus net factor income from abroad plus net transfers from abroad.

The Capital Account

A current account deficit in the United States means that Americans received fewer payments than they made to other countries. That is, payments to the United States for exports plus factor payments and transfer payments to the United States were less than payments by Americans for imports plus factor payments and transfer payments to other countries. If Americans receive less than they pay, then they must borrow from abroad, or equivalently, foreigners must increase their net assets in the

FIGURE 31.2
The Trade Deficit and the Current Account Deficit

The trade balance and the current account balance differ by two "nontrade" items: net factor payments from abroad and net transfers from abroad. In most recent years the United States has had both a trade deficit and a current account deficit; both deficits tend to move together because changes in net factor income and transfers are usually relatively small. (1991 was an exception.)

Source: U.S. Department of Commerce (quarterly data).

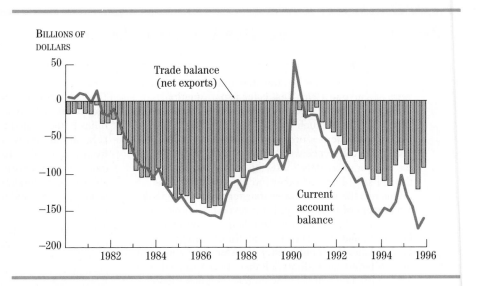

capital account: the part of the international accounts of a country that keeps track of the change in domestic assets owned by foreigners and foreign assets owned by citizens.

United States. In other words, if the current account deficit is $147 billion, foreigners must have made loans to Americans or bought assets in America for a net total of $147 billion.

The **capital account** measures these changes in loans and assets. For example, if the U.S. current account were in deficit by $100 billion, then the capital account would show an increase in foreign assets in the United States (net of an increase in U.S. assets in other countries) of $100 billion. If the United States were owed, say, $300 billion by foreigners, then the United States would now be owed $200 billion. If the United States already owed foreigners a net $500 billion, then it would now owe $600 billion. U.S. indebtedness to foreigners would go up by $100 billion because of the deficit. Thus, if the capital account is measured correctly, the net increase in foreign loans and foreign-owned assets in the capital account should equal the current account deficit.

Figure 31.3 shows what has happened to the capital account and net U.S. indebtedness in recent years. It shows that the value of assets held in the United States by foreigners is growing, as is the value of assets held in other countries by U.S. residents. But foreign assets in the United States have been growing faster than U.S. assets held abroad. The difference between U.S. assets held abroad and foreign assets held in the United States is **net foreign assets.** Net foreign assets have

net foreign assets: the difference between citizens' net assets held abroad and net assets in the domestic country held by foreigners.

declined from a positive value in the mid-1980s to a negative value in the mid-1990s. In other words, we might say that the United States shifted from a *net creditor* country to a *net debtor* country, as it borrowed from abroad year after year.

Although the change in net foreign assets each year should be exactly equal to the current account, there are errors and omissions in counting the assets. Generally, however, when the current account is in deficit, America's net foreign asset position declines. When the current account is in surplus, the net asset position increases.

Many people have expressed concern about the United States becoming a net debtor country, as shown in Figure 31.3. But the decline in the net foreign asset

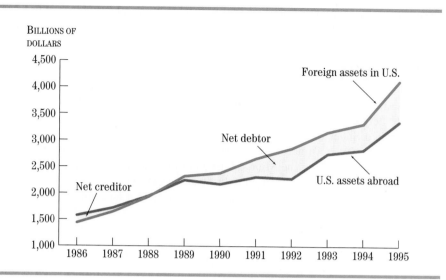

FIGURE 31.3
The Capital Account
Each year that the current account is in deficit, foreign assets in the United States grow by more than U.S. assets abroad. The capital account keeps track of these assets.

Source: U.S. Department of Commerce.

position may simply mean that the United States has more attractive investment opportunities than its citizens want to save up for and buy. In the late nineteenth century, the United States also had huge current account deficits. At that time, investing in U.S. railroads was viewed as an attractive opportunity for British investors. Thanks to that foreign investment, the railroads were built and many Americans prospered.

Bilateral Surpluses and Deficits

The **bilateral trade balance** is the trade surplus or deficit between *two* countries. That is, the bilateral trade balance of country A with country B equals the exports of country A to country B minus the imports of country A from country B. The U.S. bilateral trade balance with several countries is shown in Table 31.2. Note that the United States has a very large bilateral trade deficit with Japan.

Bilateral trade flow between countries depends on many factors. Consider, for example, the colonial period of American history. The trade across the Atlantic, sometimes called the "triangular trade flow" in the history books, represented the export of manufactured goods from England to America, the export of molasses

bilateral trade balance: the value of imports less the value of exports between two countries.

	Exports	Imports	Surplus or Deficit (−)
Australia	10	3	7
Canada	128	148	−20
Western Europe	132	147	−15
Japan	63	124	−61

TABLE 31.2
Bilateral Trade Between the United States and Several Other Countries in 1995
(billions of dollars)

Source: Economic Report of the President, 1997.

from America to the Caribbean, and the export of manufactured rum from the Caribbean to England. All these regions had huge bilateral trade deficits, but the deficits reflected the comparative advantage of England for manufacturing, America for agriculture, and the Caribbean for distilling.

More recently, many political figures in the United States pointed to the bilateral deficit between the United States and Japan as a sign of barriers to trade in Japan. Some people have even suggested taking actions to achieve balance of bilateral trade between the United States and Japan. Such actions would be a mistake for the United States or any other country. In the case of Japan, the large bilateral trade deficit with the United States occurs partly because Japan must import raw materials such as oil from the Middle East and other parts of the world. In order to obtain the funds to pay for the imported raw materials, Japan must export goods to other parts of the world. The United States, being such a large market, is an area ripe for importing goods from Japan. Thus, one reason the United States has a large bilateral trade deficit with Japan simply reflects Japan's need to import goods from other areas of the world.

Bilateral trade deficits are not indicators of how well a country is doing economically, or whether it is being affected by unfair trade practices in other countries. It is the nature of international trade that bilateral deficits and surpluses exist. Think of a personal example. Most people run a bilateral trade deficit with their grocery store. They buy goods from the store but do not sell goods to the store. This is perfectly natural and no one would even think to comment on it. Yet a bilateral trade deficit between countries is exactly the same. Americans buy more goods from Japan than the Japanese buy from Americans, just as you buy more from your grocer than you sell to your grocer.

Sectoral Deficits

sectoral trade balance: the value of exports less the value of imports in a particular sector or industry.

Also receiving political attention is the **sectoral trade balance,** the trade surplus or deficit in certain industries or sectors of the economy, such as automobiles, petroleum, and electronics. For example, one often hears that the United States not only has a bilateral deficit with Japan but also a deficit in the automobile sector.

The United States also has a deficit in the coffee industry, where it exports very little, clearly not having a comparative advantage. Making basketball and tennis shoes is labor intensive. Not surprisingly, therefore, the United States has a deficit in footwear, resulting from the import of shoes produced in countries with less expensive labor.

But other industries are in surplus, such as the pharmaceutical industry. The United States has a strong comparative advantage in pharmaceuticals because of high research and development expenditures, so it is not surprising that it has a large surplus in pharmaceuticals with other countries. The United States also has a large surplus in aircraft. The surplus in the services sector is also noteworthy. The U.S. surplus in business, professional, and technical consulting is about the same size as the U.S. deficit in footwear.

Sectoral deficits, like bilateral deficits, are influenced by comparative advantage. The United States currently has a comparative advantage in pharmaceuticals but not in shoes. Therefore, it has a sectoral trade deficit in footwear and a trade surplus in pharmaceuticals. Changes in the technology of shoe production and pharmaceuticals could change this comparative advantage in the future.

Review

▶ The gap between saving and investment determines whether there is a trade surplus or a trade deficit.

▶ The U.S. surplus in services reduced the trade deficit by about one-half in 1996.

▶ The current account includes two nontrade flows—net factor incomes and net transfers—as well as the trade account.

▶ The capital account measures purchases and sales of assets. In the 1980s the United States moved from a net creditor to a net debtor position.

▶ Bilateral deficits between countries and sectoral deficits for different types of goods are determined by comparative advantage.

EXCHANGE RATE DETERMINATION

When goods and services are traded across national boundaries, the buyer from one country must obtain the currency of the other country. For example, to buy a Braun coffeemaker manufactured in Germany, a U.S. retail store like Wal-Mart must pay in German marks. The German workers who produce the coffeemaker will want to be paid in marks because this is what they use to buy food and other goods in Germany. Thus, Wal-Mart must exchange its dollars for marks. The exchange rate, as we noted in Chapter 2, is the price of one currency in terms of another. On April 7, 1997, for example, the mark/dollar exchange rate was 1.71 marks per dollar. But it is not only trade in goods and services that results in the need for exchange of currencies. If you want to put some funds in a German bank account to use in a business you are opening in Germany, then you will also need to exchange your dollars for marks. What determines the exchange rate?

Like any price, the price between two currencies depends on demand and supply. If the demand for dollars goes up, then the price of dollars in terms of foreign currency will rise. For example, if the demand for dollars goes up, the dollar may rise from 1.71 marks per dollar to 2 marks per dollar, or from 100 yen per dollar to 130 yen per dollar. In practice, however, it is virtually impossible to determine the slopes and positions of supply and demand curves for foreign currency and to use them to predict exchange rates. Thousands of currency traders who are interested in obtaining foreign currency—not only to buy foreign goods but also to hold it to earn a higher interest rate, or to speculate—affect supply and demand. Hence, the supply and demand curves shift around by a large amount as expectations and interest rates change.

Nevertheless, the supply and demand model has implications that economists use to help analyze and predict the exchange rate. Two implications are that exchange rates reflect (1) purchasing power parity in the long run, and (2) interest rate differentials in the short run.

Purchasing Power Parity (PPP)

If transport costs are low and people are not prevented from buying whatever they want, the same commodity in two countries will sell for about the same amount; this is called the **law of one price.** The notion that exchange rates are determined so

law of one price: the notion that, with low transportation costs and no trade barriers, the same commodity is sold for the same price in two different countries when measured in the same currency.

purchasing power parity: the theory that exchange rates are determined in such a way that the prices of goods in different countries are the same when measured in the same currency.

tradable goods: goods for which transportation costs are not prohibitive.

that the price for the same commodity is the same around the world is sometimes called **purchasing power parity.** It provides us with a way to determine the exchange rate.

Tradable Goods

Consider first a situation where the cost of transporting a good is very low compared to the value of the good. Goods that can be traded without prohibitive transport costs are called **tradable goods.**

An example of a tradable good is a very expensive bottle of French wine—say, a 1978 Chateau Lafite-Rothschild, which costs about $825 for a 12-bottle case in San Francisco. That same type of wine costs 482 British pounds a case in London. Suppose the exchange rate between the British pound and the U.S. dollar is 1.7 dollars per pound. If you want to know how many dollars it would take to buy the case of wine in London, you simply multiply 482 pounds by 1.7 dollars per pound and get $819 for the dollar equivalent for the wine in London. That is about the same as the $825 a case in San Francisco. The difference is less than transport cost for a case of wine, which is probably about $20 dollars. In other words, the dollar price of the wine, whether it is purchased in San Francisco for $825 or in London for $819, is comparable.

In this example, purchasing power parity works quite well. If purchasing power parity did not hold closely for tradable goods, people would either buy or sell wine in London and ship the wine to San Francisco in order to make a nice profit. This would shift either supply or demand until purchasing power parity held. Hence, the exchange rate is such that the price of the wine in the two countries is almost the same.

Nontradable Goods

What about goods that are not tradable? Here purchasing power parity does not work well. Suppose, for example, you tried to ship a McDonalds' Big Mac purchased in the United States across the ocean. It would not be pleasant to eat. Even if you used an airplane, it would be stale and decayed by the time it arrived at its destination. The transport costs in this case are prohibitive, and purchasing power parity does not usually hold. For example, a Big Mac in Germany cost 4.90 marks in April 1997 and at the same time cost $2.42 in the United States. An exchange rate of 1.71 marks per dollar makes the Big Mac cost $2.86 in Germany. (Divide 4.90 marks by 1.71 marks per dollar and the answer is $2.86.) The $2.86 Big Mac in Germany is 20 percent more than the $2.42 Big Mac in the United States. Thus the exchange rate between the mark and the dollar is not given by purchasing power parity, according to the Big Mac. The purchasing power parity level works out to be 2.02 marks per dollar, because dividing 4.90 marks by 2.02 marks per dollar is about $2.42, the price in the United States.

Explaining Exchange Rates with PPP in Practice

How well does PPP work in explaining exchange rates if we use prices for both tradable goods and nontradable goods; that is, if we look at the price level for the whole economy? Not very well over short periods of time or for small changes in the price; but statistical studies of purchasing power parity show that it works very well in the long run or for large price changes.

The *Economist* magazine has popularized the idea of using the Big Mac to track purchasing power parity. Note the similarity between the PPP calculations in the text and this recent article on Big Mac PPP. Read the article and try to explain why the Big Mac is "not a perfect measure."

Source of article: Economist, April 12, 1997, p. 71. © 1997 The Economist Newspaper Group, Inc. Reprinted with permission. Further reproduction prohibited.

Big MacCurrencies

Can hamburgers provide hot tips about exchange rates?

. . . The Big Mac index is based upon the theory of purchasing-power parity (PPP)—the notion that a dollar should buy the same amount in all countries. In the long run, argue PPP fans, currencies should move towards the rate which equalises the prices of an identical basket of goods in each country. Our "basket" is a McDonald's Big Mac, which is now produced in over 100 countries. The Big Mac PPP is the exchange rate that would leave hamburgers costing the same in America as abroad. Comparing actual exchange rates with PPP provides one indication of whether a currency is under- or over-valued. . . .

The first column in the table shows local-currency prices of a Big Mac; the second converts them into dollars. The average American price (including tax) is $2.42. China is the place for bargain hunters: a Beijing Big Mac costs only $1.16. At the other extreme, Big Mac fans pay a beefy $4.02 in Switzerland. In other words, the yuan is the most undervalued currency (by 52%), the Swiss franc the most overvalued (by 66%).

The third column calculates big Mac PPPs. For example, dividing the German price by the American one gives a dollar PPP of DM2.02. The actual rate on April 7th was DM1.71, implying that the D-mark is 18% overvalued against the dollar. But over the past two years the dollar has risen nearer to its PPP against most currencies. The yen is now close to its PPP of ¥121. Two years ago the Big Mac index suggested that it was 100% overvalued against the dollar.

Some critics find these conclusions hard to swallow. Yes, we admit it, the Big Mac is not a perfect measure. Price differences may be distorted by trade barriers on beef, sales taxes, or large variations in the cost of non-traded inputs such as rents. All the same, the index tends to come up with PPP estimates that are similar to those based on more sophisticated methods.

Moreover, research by Robert Cumby, an economist at Georgetown University, suggests that a currency's deviation from Big Mac PPP can be a useful predictor of exchange rates. Over the past year, the Big Mac index has correctly predicted the direction of exchange-rate movements for eight of 12 currencies of large industrial economies. Of the seven currencies which changed by more than 10%, the Big Mac standard got the direction right in six cases. Better than some highly-paid currency forecasters. Investors who turned up their noses at the Big Mac index should now be feeling cheesed off.

The hamburger standard

	Big Mac prices		Implied PPP* of the dollar	Actual $ exchange rate 7/4/97	Local currency under(−)/over(+) valuation,† %
	In local currency	In dollars			
United States‡	**$2.42**	**2.42**	—	—	—
Argentina	Peso2.50	2.50	1.03	1.00	+3
Australia	A$2.50	1.94	1.03	1.29	−20
Austria	Sch34.00	2.82	14.0	12.0	+17
Belgium	BFr109	3.09	45.0	35.3	+28
Brazil	Real2.97	2.81	1.23	1.06	+16
Britain	‡1.81	2.95	1.34††	1.63††	+22
Canada	C$2.88	2.07	1.19	1.39	−14
Chile	Peso1,200	2.88	496	417	+19
China	Yuan9.70	1.16	4.01	8.33	−52
Czech Republic	CKr53.0	1.81	21.9	29.2	−25
Denmark	DKr25.75	3.95	10.6	6.52	+63
France	FFr17.5	3.04	7.23	5.76	+26
Germany	DM4.90	2.86	2.02	1.71	+18
Hong Kong	HK$9.90	1.28	4.09	7.75	−47
Hungary	Forint271	1.52	112	178	−37
Israel	Shekel11.5	3.40	4.75	3.38	+40
Italy	Lire4,600	2.73	1,901	1,683	+13
Japan	¥294	2.34	121	126	−3
Malaysia	M$3.87	1.55	1.60	2.50	−36
Mexico	Peso14.9	1.89	6.16	7.90	−22
Netherlands	Fl5.45	2.83	2.25	1.92	+17
New Zealand	NZ$3.25	2.24	1.34	1.45	−7
Poland	Zloty4.30	1.39	1.78	3.10	−43
Russia	Rouble11,000	1.92	4,545	5,739	−21
Singapore	S$3.00	2.08	1.24	1.44	−14
South Africa	Rand7.80	1.76	3.22	4.43	−27
South Korea	Won2,300	2.57	950	894	+6
Spain	Pta375	2.60	155	144	+7
Sweden	SKr26.0	3.37	10.7	7.72	+39
Switzerland	SFr5.90	4.02	2.44	1.47	+66
Taiwan	NT$68.0	2.47	28.1	27.6	+2
Thailand	Baht46.7	1.79	19.3	26.1	−26

*Purchasing-power parity; local price divided by price in the United States.   †Against dollar
‡Average of New York, Chicago, San Francisco and Atlanta   ††Dollars per pound
Source: McDonald's

FIGURE 31.4
Purchasing Power Parity,
1975–1995

As predicted by purchasing power parity, the U.S. dollar has appreciated against countries with high inflation (France, Italy, the U.K.) and depreciated against countries with low inflation (Japan, Germany).

Source: Economic Report of the President, 1997.

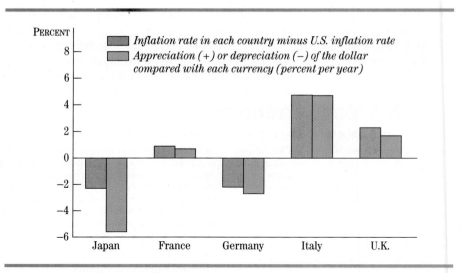

To see that *PPP* works well over long periods of time, it is helpful to introduce some notation. Let *P* be the price level in the United States and *P** the price level in Germany. Then the purchasing power exchange rate (*E*) would be given by $E \times P = P^*$. For example, if the price level in the United States is $10 and the price level in Germany is 30 marks, then the purchasing power exchange rate is 3 marks per dollar because $E \times P = (3 \times 10) = 30$ when $E = 3$. Now suppose that there is more inflation in the United States than in Germany so that *P* rises to $15 and *P** stays constant; then according to purchasing power parity, *E* must fall from 3 marks per dollar to 2 marks per dollar so that $E \times P = (2 \times 15)$ stays equal to *P**. Thus, the inflation in the United States will be matched by a depreciation of the dollar.

Such an association between inflation and the change in the exchange rate is exactly what happens over long periods, as shown in Figure 31.4. This figure shows (1) the inflation rate in several large countries compared to the United States, and (2) the change in the exchange rates of those different countries compared to the United States. For example, over this period from 1975 to 1995 the inflation rate in Italy was higher than in the United States. Over the same period of time the dollar appreciated relative to the lira, the Italian currency. The United Kingdom also had a higher inflation rate than the United States, and the dollar appreciated relative to the pound. Japan and Germany, on the other hand, had inflation rates that were on average lower than in the United States, and, as purchasing power parity would predict, the dollar depreciated relative to the yen and mark. Purchasing power parity works well in explaining exchange rates over this time span.

real exchange rate: a measure of the exchange rate between two currencies that adjusts for differences in inflation levels in the two countries.

One can adjust the exchange rate for inflation to get the **real exchange rate.** The change in the real exchange rate is given by the change in the actual exchange rate minus the difference in the inflation rates in the two countries. For example, over the 20-year period from 1975 to 1995, the dollar appreciated against the lira by about 4.7 percent per year. Over that same 20-year period, as shown in Figure 31.4, the inflation rate in Italy was 4.7 percent higher than in the United States (10.0 in Italy and 5.3 in the United States). Thus, the change in the real exchange rate is the change in the actual exchange rate (4.7 percent) minus the difference in the inflation rates (4.7 percent), which equals 0 percent. In other words, the real exchange rate between the dollar and the lira was unchanged. The entire 4.7 percent per year appreciation of the dollar was due to prices in Italy rising 4.7 percent per year faster than prices in the United States.

To summarize, if two countries have widely different inflation rates, the country with the lower inflation rate will have a currency that tends to appreciate over time relative to the country with the higher inflation rate. In this sense, the purchasing power parity theory works well. Over shorter periods of time, the purchasing power parity theory, however, does not work very well. For example, in the mid-1980s the U.S. dollar was much higher than could be explained by purchasing power parity. In the early 1990s, it was lower than purchasing power parity. What explains these deviations from PPP?

The Interest Rate: A Reason for Deviations from PPP

The most important reason for deviations of the exchange rate from purchasing power parity in the short run is the interest rate.

International investors operating in the global foreign exchange market decide where to place their funds to get the highest return. The capital they invest is highly mobile. The movement of funds around the world to receive the highest return creates a link between the interest rate and the exchange rate that can explain the departures from purchasing power parity.

For example, if the interest rate in the United States rises relative to interest rates abroad, then the U.S. dollar is more attractive to international investors. For an investor deciding whether to put funds in a bank in the United States or in Japan, a rise in the U.S. interest rate compared to Japan makes the United States more attractive, and this raises the price of the dollar. Similarly, if the U.S. interest rate falls relative to Japan's, the dollar will depreciate relative to the yen as international investors move their funds from the United States to Japan.

The chart in the margin shows how interest rates are correlated with the exchange rate. The rise of the dollar relative to other countries in the early 1980s and its subsequent decline in the late 1980s is highly correlated with the interest rate differential. In the early 1980s, interest rates in the United States rose relative to other countries, and then in the mid-1980s, interest rates in the United States declined relative to other countries.

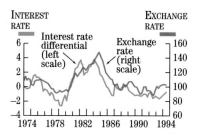

Review

▶ Purchasing power parity is a useful theory of exchange rates for tradable goods, for periods of high inflation, or for long periods of time.

▶ Short-run deviations from purchasing power parity are explained by interest rates. When the interest rate rises in the United States relative to another country, the exchange rate rises.

▶ The relationship between the interest rate and the exchange rate occurs because capital is very mobile around the world. Investors playing the global foreign exchange market shift their funds in response to interest rate differentials.

FIXED EXCHANGE RATE SYSTEMS

Throughout history, governments have chosen many times to use economic policy to influence the exchange rate. In the early nineteenth century, Britain adopted a gold standard under which the government pegged the price of gold at a fixed price of about 4 British pounds per ounce. The United States joined the gold standard in 1879, agreeing to buy and sell gold at about $20 an ounce. Because *both* currencies were tied to gold, the relative prices of the two currencies were tied together, at about $5 per pound at this time. If the exchange rate moved away from $5 per pound to, say, $4, gold traders could buy gold in London at $16 an ounce and sell gold in the United States at $20 an ounce. Such an easy profit could not last, and the exchange rate would quickly move back to $5 per British pound.

International Gold Standard

fixed exchange rate system: a system of international exchange rates in which the countries agree to maintain a predetermined value of their currencies in terms of other currencies.

When two or more countries are on a gold standard, the exchange rate between the countries is, therefore, fixed. A system like the international gold standard, where government actions prevent changes in the value of one currency compared to another, is called a **fixed exchange rate system.** In the case of the gold standard, the exchange rates were implicitly fixed because each country kept its exchange rate as close as possible to some particular price of gold. Note that when governments fix the price of gold, they do not set the price by decree, as with government price ceilings or floors discussed in Chapter 3. People are free to buy and sell gold and the price is determined in the gold market, but the government adjusts the supply of gold so that the government purchase price is the equilibrium price.

The gold standard keeps the price of currencies constant in terms of gold. One can also imagine a system without gold in which the countries agreed to peg their exchange rates to each other. For example, the French might agree to buy and sell French francs in exchange for German marks at a set exchange rate. That also is a fixed exchange rate system.

The Bretton Woods System

Bretton Woods system: the international monetary system put in place after World War II; it was based on fixed exchange rates. Infrequent adjustments of the exchange rates were permitted and did occur under the Bretton Woods System.

From the end of World War II through the early 1970s, the world's largest economies were linked in a fixed exchange system called the **Bretton Woods system.** As World War II was drawing to a close, a conference was held in Bretton Woods, New Hampshire, to decide on a good exchange rate system for the world economy. John Maynard Keynes was one of the theoreticians present at the conference. The key ingredient of the system was that exchange rates were to be fixed. In certain rare circumstances, provisions were made for decreases in the exchange rate (devaluations) or increases in the exchange rate (revaluations) of the currencies.

flexible exchange rate system: an international monetary system in which exchange rates are determined in foreign exchange markets and governments do not agree to fix them.

The Bretton Woods system lasted for about 25 years before it fell apart in the early 1970s. It was replaced by a **flexible exchange rate system,** whereby governments did not try to fix the value of their currencies in any particular way. Figure 31.5 shows the exchange rate between the German mark and the dollar and between the French franc and the dollar for the period that includes the Bretton Woods fixed exchange rate system and the subsequent flexible exchange rate system. The chart clearly shows that exchange rates were much more volatile in the flexible exchange rate period. Several changes in the exchange rates during the fixed exchange rate period are visible in Figure 31.5: two devaluations of the franc in the late 1950s, and one revaluation of the mark in the early 1960s.

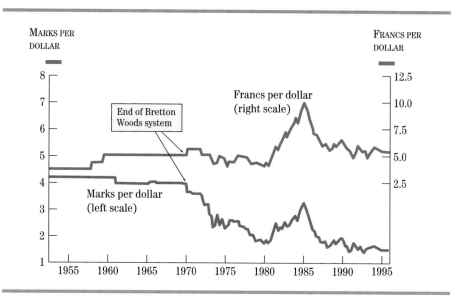

FIGURE 31.5
Francs and Marks per Dollar

These exchange rates and others have fluctuated since the end of the Bretton Woods fixed exchange rate system. From the mid-1980s through the 1990s, the fluctuations have been smaller.

Source: International Monetary Fund.

The European Monetary System

Within the overall flexible exchange rate system, the countries of Europe have attempted to fix their exchange rates among each other while jointly having flexible exchange rates with the rest of the world; this European system of fixed exchange rates is called the **European monetary system.** Through this exchange rate system, the value, for example, of the French franc in terms of the German mark could not change much. Figure 31.6 shows the behavior of the French franc relative to the mark. Notice that the franc and the mark did not have a significant change in relative value for most of the 1990s.

European monetary system:
a system of exchange rates in which European currencies are fixed relative to each other but are flexible against the dollar, the yen, and other currencies.

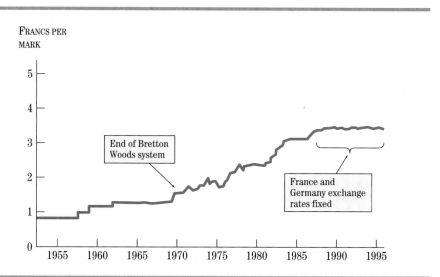

FIGURE 31.6
Exchange Rates in Europe

The French franc fluctuated little against the German mark until the 1970s, when the Bretton Woods system fell apart. In the 1970s and early 1980s, the franc depreciated against the mark, as Germany had relatively low inflation. In the late 1980s and 1990s, France and Germany fixed their exchange rates against each other.

Source: International Monetary Fund.

During the 1990s several European countries made plans to convert the European monetary system from a fixed exchange rate system with several currencies into a system where there is only a single currency. The single currency would be called the *euro,* which would eventually replace francs, marks, and the currencies of other countries that joined in. With a single currency, the exchange rate is effectively fixed for all time because there are no national currencies.

Review

▶ Governments have frequently fixed the exchange rate between currencies. In these fixed exchange rate systems, the government agrees to buy and sell gold or currencies in the market at a given price.

▶ Examples of fixed exchange rate systems are the international gold standard, the Bretton Woods system, and the European monetary system.

FIXED EXCHANGE RATES AND INTERNATIONAL INDEPENDENCE

A fixed exchange rate system has implications for economic policy. In this section we will first show that with a fixed exchange rate system, interest rates in different countries cannot be independent of each other. We will then look at some of the reasons why countries chose to fix exchange rates.

Loss of International Monetary Independence

Suppose the United States decides to set up or join a fixed exchange rate system with Japan and Europe. Suppose also that after the United States joins the system, a deep recession occurs in the United States, and policymakers look to a reduction in interest rates in the United States to help stimulate the economy. Such a reduction in interest rates, according to the exchange rate theory, will tend to lower the value of the dollar relative to other currencies. But if the dollar were fixed to the currencies of other countries, as it would be in a fixed exchange rate system, such a decline in the dollar would not be possible. Hence, if exchange rates were fixed, lower interest rates in the United States relative to interest rates in other countries would not be possible. There is a loss of **international monetary independence** because interest rates in the United States cannot change.

A real-life example of the conflict between fixed exchange rates and interest rate changes arose in Europe in the latter part of 1992. At that time, interest rates were rising in Germany because the German inflation rate was rising. But policy makers in Britain, which was facing hard economic times, did not want their interest rates to rise as German interest rates rose. The British faced a decision—either they could keep their interest rates near Germany's and, therefore, raise their interest rates, or they could let their interest rates fall. In the latter case, their exchange rate would depreciate. For much of 1991 and 1992, the British kept their exchange

international monetary independence: the idea that a flexible exchange rate system gives a country the ability to have much different interest rates than other countries.

rate stable and that required a rise in British interest rates. But by the end of 1992, increasingly poor conditions in Britain forced the British to devalue and to leave the European monetary system. Then interest rates in Britain could fall.

Interventions in the Exchange Market

Why wasn't it possible for the British government to go into the exchange market and buy and sell foreign exchange and thereby prevent these changes in the exchange rate? For example, if the British government purchased pounds it would increase the demand for pounds and thereby raise the pound exchange rate. Thus, if the high interest rates in Germany were reducing the value of the British pound, why couldn't the British government buy pounds to offset these pressures? Such buying and selling of foreign currency by governments is called **exchange market intervention.** Such intervention does occur, and it can affect the exchange rate for short periods of time. However, the world currency markets are so huge and fast moving that even governments do not have funds to affect the exchange rate for long by buying and selling foreign exchange.

    If there is a substantial interest rate advantage in favor of one currency, funds will flow into that currency, driving up the value; exchange market intervention by governments cannot do much about it. Empirical studies have shown that exchange market intervention—if it is not matched by a change in interest rates by the central bank—can have only small effects on the exchange rate.

exchange market intervention: purchases and sales of foreign currency by a government in exchange markets with the intention to affect the exchange rate.

Reducing Exchange Rate Risk

If fixed exchange rates lead to a loss of international monetary independence, then why do countries form fixed exchange rate systems? One reason to adopt a fixed exchange rate system is that exchange rate volatility can interfere with trade. This is certainly one of the reasons the European countries set up the European monetary system. Firms may not develop long-term relations and contacts in other countries if they are worried about big changes in the exchange rate.

    Innovations in financial markets in the 1970s and 1980s have made it easier for companies to **hedge,** or protect against, the risks associated with exchange rate volatility. The futures market in foreign currencies at the Chicago Mercantile Exchange is an example of one of these innovations. In a **futures market** one buys or sells a good for future delivery. There are futures markets for many items, including wheat, orange juice, and crude oil as well as French francs, German marks, and Japanese yen. Futures markets make it possible to ensure against changes in the exchange rate. The following example shows how.

    Consider the case of the mark/dollar exchange rate. One can buy a contract in the futures market through which one agrees to sell marks for dollars at some future date at a guaranteed price. It is thus possible for a company—like Mattel, the toy manufacturer—to hedge the revenue it might receive when it exports toys to Germany by taking out a futures contract in the Chicago Mercantile Exchange. Mattel can guarantee a price in dollars on those toys even if the mark/dollar exchange rate changes dramatically. By locking in a fixed dollar price in the futures market, firms can hedge the exchange rate risk.

    For example, Mattel's "price point" for one of its Masters of the Universe toys, Skeletor, is $3; this is the price it needs to make a profit selling this toy. Suppose that Mattel is currently manufacturing Skeletor toys and expects to sell these in

hedge: to reduce risk, usually by buying a futures contract to guarantee a price several months in the future.

futures market: a market that deals in commodities to be delivered in the future.

How the Masters of the Universe
overcame the attack of the Deutschemarks.

When a new toy sets out to conquer the world, its timing must be right. Its price-point must be perfect. There is no mercy from the marketplace.

So when the Masters of the Universe invaded Europe, Mattel Inc., like a lot of smart companies, locked in some key currency exchange rates in advance – at the Chicago Mercantile Exchange. And when the Deutschemarks rose up against them, Mattel was able to hold its ground.

The moral of the story is pretty clear. It pays to take control of as many sources of risk as possible. And the Chicago Mercantile Exchange has developed better ways for managers to control interest rate risk. Equities risk. And risks on some agricultural commodities. As well as international exchange-rate risk.

So look into the futures and options at The Merc. For over 100 years, we've helped smart businesses manage risk.

CHICAGO MERCANTILE EXCHANGE
International Monetary Market • Index and Option Market
The Exchange of Ideas.
1-800-331-3332
Chicago • New York • London • Tokyo

Foreign Currency Futures Advertisement

This is an advertisement for the futures market in exchange rates in Chicago. It mentions U.S. exporters of toys to Germany but also applies to U.S. exporters of other goods to other countries. The advertisement aims to entice exporters to use a market to hedge their risk.

Germany in about six months. It expects to sell each toy for 5 marks in Germany, and the exchange rate is currently $.62 per mark. Thus, the dollar price is $3.10; Mattel can make a profit because $3.10 is greater than $3.00. But suppose the mark falls to $.40. Then Mattel's dollar price falls to 5 marks times $.40, or $2.00, and Mattel has a losing operation on its hands. If Mattel hedges with a futures contract and locks in an exchange rate six months from now of $.61 per mark, then it ensures a profit because $5 \times (.61) = \$3.05$. Thus, futures markets in exchange rates can reduce the risk and uncertainty associated with exchange rate fluctuations.

Review

▷ A fixed exchange rate system means a loss of international monetary independence for countries in the system.

▷ Flexible exchange rates may cause uncertainty and reduce trade, but the development of futures markets in currencies can reduce the exchange rate risk and uncertainty.

CONCLUSION

This chapter focused on international trade flows and exchange rates. We have seen that the overall trade deficit, or trade surplus, can ultimately be traced to imbalances in national saving and investment. These imbalances and the resulting deficits and surpluses are not necessarily bad. If the investment opportunities in a country are greater than the saving of the people in the country—as in the railroad construction in America in the 1880s and 1890s—there will be a trade deficit, and foreigners provide the funds for investment by lending or buying real estate or shares in business enterprises. If the people of a country desire to save more than they invest in capital in the country—as in Japan in the 1980s and 1990s—they will lend or buy real estate or shares of businesses in other countries. None of this is bad. Indeed, the excess of saving over investment in relatively advanced countries can help spread the benefits of growth to developing countries.

However, if government policy acts to provide disincentives to save or invest, the resulting trade deficit can indeed be a serious concern. For example, a large and persistent government budget deficit that reduces a country's saving would lead to a trade deficit and be a cause for concern. A government policy that adds risk or creates disincentives to invest and thereby causes a trade surplus would also be a bad policy. But these policies are bad more because of the distortions to saving and investment they create than because of the trade deficit itself.

Bilateral deficits and sectoral deficits are also not necessarily a problem that needs to be addressed by policy. Such deficits are part of the normal operation of international trade between countries; they may be telling us that the international economy is working well, not poorly.

What about the exchange rate? What are the key ideas we have learned about the price of one currency in terms of another? First, a smoothly working foreign exchange market is essential for international trade. Because countries have different currencies, it is necessary to buy or sell foreign exchange when purchasing goods or services in other countries. Second, foreign exchange traders constantly move funds from one country to another electronically to get the highest rate of return. The amount of trading in the foreign exchange market is, therefore, huge; much more foreign exchange is traded each day than the value of the goods and services that are exported or imported. Third, exchange rates are determined by purchasing power parity and interest rates.

There are two basic approaches countries can take to the exchange rate, while not interfering with the freedom of buyers and sellers to obtain foreign exchange. They can agree to fix the exchange rate to another country's exchange rate, in which case the international currency market forces the country to lose its monetary independence—as was illustrated when British interest rates were held up by Germany in 1992. Or they can let their exchange rate be flexible, in which case interest rates can move independently. Both approaches have been tried many times throughout history. Currently the United States and Japan follow a flexible exchange rate system, while the countries within Europe have tried to use a fixed exchange rate system. Because of lack of agreement about what is the best approach, and because of changing circumstances, it is likely that we will continue to see flux in the choice of exchange rate systems.

KEY POINTS

1. Improvements in telecommunications and transportation and the removal of restrictions on trade are making the world economy more integrated.

2. The world as a whole cannot have a trade surplus or a trade deficit. As individual countries save more or less than they invest, overall trade deficits and surpluses are created.

3. Because of the importance of services, the merchandise trade deficit is much too narrow a measure of the deficit.

4. Bilateral deficits and sectoral deficits are influenced by comparative advantage.

5. The current account is the broadest measure of a country's balance with other countries.

6. The capital account measures changes in the net foreign asset position of a country.

7. Purchasing power parity explains exchange rates very well when goods are tradable, when inflation differences are high, or over a long period of time.

8. Interest rate differentials explain much of the short-term exchange rate movements.

9. Because capital flows freely around the world, interest rates are tied together for countries in a fixed exchange rate system.

10. However, fixed exchange rates can reduce uncertainty.

KEY TERMS

merchandise trade
services trade
merchandise trade balance
services trade balance
balance of payments
factor income
net factor income from abroad
international transfer payments
net transfers from abroad

current account balance
capital account
net foreign assets
bilateral trade balance
sectoral trade balance
law of one price
purchasing power parity
tradable goods
real exchange rate

fixed exchange rate system
Bretton Woods system
flexible exchange rate system
European monetary system
international monetary independence
exchange market intervention
hedge
futures market

QUESTIONS FOR REVIEW

1. Why can't the world have a trade surplus or deficit?

2. Why is the investment-saving gap so closely related to the trade deficit?

3. What is wrong with the merchandise trade deficit as a measure of trade imbalance?

4. What is the difference between net exports and the current account deficit?

5. Why has the net foreign asset position of the United States moved from positive to negative?

6. Of what use is purchasing power parity as a theory of the exchange rate?

7. Why is there a loss of international independence when countries join a fixed exchange rate system?

8. How can futures markets be used to hedge risk?

9. What is the difference between the Bretton Woods system and the European monetary system?

PROBLEMS

1. Calculate the trade deficit or surplus for the following data in billions of dollars:

Year	1998	2002
National saving	950	1,170
Investment	1,000	1,300

a) Has the deficit increased or decreased over this time period? Give some possible explanations.
b) Suppose net factor income and net transfers from abroad are zero. Is capital flowing into or out of the country in these years?

2. Transport costs relative to the value of most products have been falling throughout the history of world trade. How has this affected the validity of purchasing power parity? Suppose many countries impose trade taxes on goods going in or out of the country. How will this affect purchasing power parity?

3. The price of a fresh loaf of French bread in Paris is 5 francs, while the price of a fresh loaf of French bread (same quality) in San Francisco is $2. The price of gold is 2,000 francs per ounce in Paris, and the price of gold in San Fran-

cisco is $400 per ounce. What is your estimate of the exchange rate between dollars and francs? (State your answer in francs per dollar.) Explain your answer.

4. You are the chief financial officer of an American computer company. Your company wants to export computers to Great Britain, and market analysts predict that the systems could be sold at £2,000 each. At the current exchange rate of $1.50 for each pound, the company would make a 10 percent profit, which is considered normal for the industry. The marketing department plans to start selling the computers one year from now.

a) How can you, as chief financial officer, eliminate the exchange rate risk? Explain your answer.
b) Suppose you took the appropriate measures to eliminate the exchange rate risk, and at the moment of sale of the computers, the exchange rate is $2 per pound. Was your decision good or not? Why?

5. "It is possible to use purchasing power parity to explain appreciations or depreciations of the exchange rates because of inflation. Inflation in the home country minus inflation in the foreign country equals the decrease in the exchange rate when measured in terms of foreign currency per unit of home currency." Is this statement correct? Explain.

6. The consumer price index (CPI) in Italy was 60 in 1980 and 180 in 1992. The CPI in Japan was 80 in 1980 and 120 in 1992. The Italian-Japanese exchange rate was 4 lira per yen in 1980. If purchasing power parity held in 1980, what would purchasing power theory predict for the exchange rate in 1992?

7. Why would a European country want to drop out of the fixed exchange rate system? Why might the country want to join the fixed exchange rate system?

8. Compare and contrast the following:
a) merchandise trade balance and services trade balance
b) bilateral trade balance and sectoral trade balance
c) net factor income from abroad and net transfers from abroad
d) a fixed exchange rate system and a rent control system

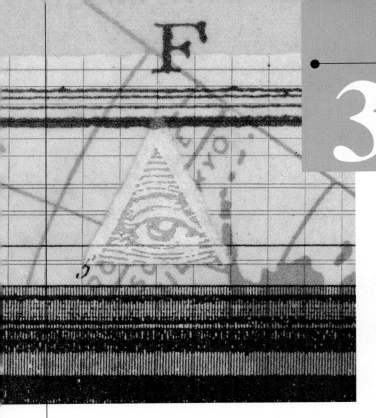

32

Macroeconomic Debates

Current theories of economic fluctuations and economic growth were developed from knowledge accumulated over many years. Practicing economists in business and government, including those who work at central banks like the Federal Reserve, draw on these theories when they analyze the economy and make policy decisions.

Macroeconomic theory, however, is by no means stagnant. Indeed, like many of our theories of the physical world—from explanations of how genes in our bodies work to theories of why black holes exist in outer space—macroeconomic theories change over time. Macroeconomic theories may change because a major economic event—such as the Great Depression of the 1930s or the Great Inflation of the 1970s—may reveal problems with a prevailing theory. Some economists may then propose new ideas challenging the prevailing theory. Defenders of the prevailing theory respond. Debate ensues. Eventually, the prevailing theory is usually modified.

There are also heated debates over the implementation of macroeconomic policy. Even economists who have the same basic view of how the macroeconomy works may disagree about the way the theories should be applied to solve current problems. A dispute about rules versus discretion, a difficulty in distinguishing short-term economic fluctuations from long-term economic growth, or an uncertainty about timing are examples of the many debates already mentioned in this book.

The purpose of this chapter is to review these debates and to place them in historical perspective. We look at the schools of thought that developed from the 1930s through the 1960s, including the work of John Maynard Keynes and the Keynesian school, the work of Milton Friedman and the monetarist school, and the work of Robert Solow and those in the neoclassical growth school. We also describe research from the 1970s through the present, including the new classical school, the new Keynesian school, the real business cycle school, and the supply side school. Figure 32.1 provides a visual summary of the schools. Although the theory of economic growth and fluctuations we have described in this book draws on all these schools, in this chapter we concentrate on which ideas come from which schools and on the key differences between the schools.

Much of the debate among macroeconomists has been about whether discretionary fiscal policy can be a useful way to reduce the harm from recessions. Discretionary fiscal policy was once the hallmark of Keynesian

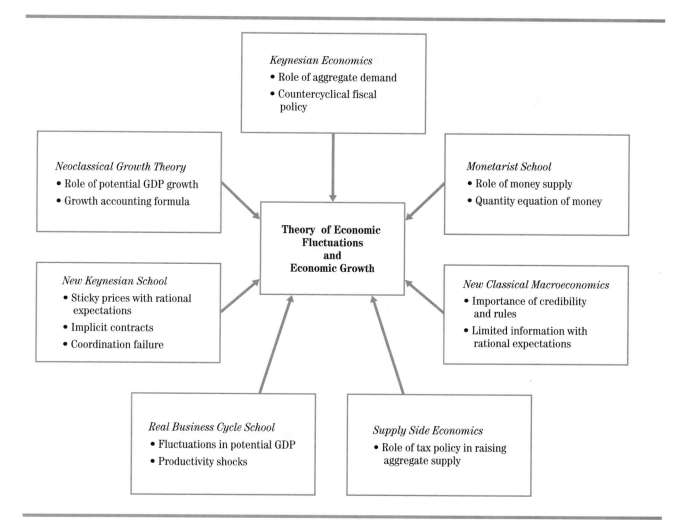

FIGURE 32.1

Spheres of Influence in Macroeconomic Thought

Different schools of thought have influenced the development of macroeconomics. Keynesian economics, the monetarist school, and neoclassical growth theory developed between the 1930s and the 1960s. New classical macroeconomics, the new Keynesian school, the real business cycle school, and supply side economics represent more recent developments. There has been—and still is—heated debate and controversy among the different groups.

economics. These policy debates have continued. In this chapter we therefore also look at the debates about the discretionary fiscal policy proposals made by Republican President Bush in 1992 and by Democratic President Clinton in 1993 to help speed the recovery from the 1990–1991 recession. Recessions have not disappeared from the economic landscape, and by looking at what was done in this recent recession, we can gain insight to alternative approaches to dealing with the effects of the next one.

SCHOOLS OF THOUGHT IN MACROECONOMICS

A large number of economic researchers have contributed to each school of thought summarized in Figure 32.1. For each school of thought, several key ideas or terms are also listed in the figure. Many of these key ideas are now incorporated into the theory of economic growth and fluctuations, and have been introduced in previous chapters of this book. Although learning about such a large number of schools of thought may seem like a daunting task, our goal here is to categorize and trace the history of these ideas rather than to explain them afresh.

Developments from the 1930s Through the 1960s

A good starting point for discussing the different schools of thought in macroeconomics is the economic research that emerged during and immediately after the Great Depression of the 1930s. This catastrophic world event helped cause a major shakeup in economic thinking—the **Keynesian revolution**—that eventually affected all economists, and thus their textbooks, their models, and their public policy advice. It was not until 40 years later, in the early 1970s, that a comparable change in the field of macroeconomics occurred.

Keynesian Economics

Keynesian revolution: a change in macroeconomic thinking, shaped by the Great Depression and the work of John Maynard Keynes, leading to a greater consideration of demand-side policies.

The publication in 1936 of John Maynard Keynes's book *The General Theory of Employment, Interest and Money* marks the beginning of the **Keynesian school** of macroeconomics. Current Keynesian economists include James Tobin of Yale University and Paul Samuelson of the Massachusetts Institute of Technology.

Keynesian school: a school of macroeconomic thought concerned with pursuing demand-side macro-economic policies—primarily fiscal policies working through the multi-plier—to reduce unemployment and encourage economic growth.

Keynes wrote the *General Theory* at a time when high unemployment and low production were causing severe distress in the world economy. Keynes's ideas had great appeal because they seemed to explain this catastrophe and to provide a way to end it. Keynes made a break with most previous economists by arguing that the level of total output or production in the economy was determined by aggregate demand: that is, by the total spending of consumers, businesses, government, and foreigners. Increases in government spending would raise aggregate demand and reduce unemployment, according to Keynes. Hence, the usefulness of countercyclical fiscal policy was explained by Keynes's theory.

The term *macroeconomics* as distinct from *microeconomics* arose during the early days of the Keynesian revolution, but it is incorrect to say that economists before Keynes had not worked on macroeconomic issues. The Scottish philosopher David Hume wrote a brilliant essay, "On Money," way back in 1752, which described the short-run impact of an increase in money, including a brief description of the slow adjustment of prices and the multiplier process. Adam Smith wrote about economic growth as well as the role of money in the economy. Many of the debates between Malthus and Ricardo were over macroeconomic issues: Using modern terminology, Malthus argued that deficient aggregate demand could bring real GDP below potential GDP, while Ricardo disagreed, arguing that supply will create its own demand—a principle called *Say's Law* after the French economist J. B. Say, who wrote about it—keeping real GDP equal to potential GDP.

However, these macroeconomic discussions had taken place more than 100 years before the Great Depression. Alfred Marshall, one of Keynes's teachers and author of the great microeconomic treatise *Principles of Economics,* wrote about macroeconomics, but it was clearly less of a priority for him. He chose to publish his macroeconomic book, *Money, Credit and Commerce,* very late in life (he was over 80 years old), and his macroeconomic theory was never as fully articulated as his microeconomic theory. Irving Fisher writing in the United States and Knut Wicksell writing in Sweden also worked on macroeconomic issues, focusing mainly on monetary policy issues.

Despite the work of Marshall, Fisher, and Wicksell, it is clear that macroeconomic issues had receded to the back burner for many economists and that the prevailing economic theories were inadequate to give a convincing or helpful explanation for the Great Depression. Keynes referred to this prevailing theory—"the atmosphere in which I was brought up"—as "the classical theory" and emphasized that he was making a transition away from that theory. Although historians of economic thought distinguish between the classical school of Smith and Ricardo and the neoclassical school of Marshall and his followers, Keynes used the term *classical* to mean "orthodox," referring to the prevailing theory at the time he wrote, including that of Marshall and Marshall's followers.

Keynes wrote little about inflation in the *General Theory,* though he did address inflation in his earlier writings in the 1920s. His analysis in the *General Theory* also deemphasized aggregate supply, or what we have called potential GDP in this book. Keynes also placed little emphasis on monetary policy, though in the *General Theory* he developed the idea that the demand for money depends on the interest rate. Many of Keynes's followers paid even less attention to inflation, aggregate supply, and monetary policy. Keynes's lack of attention to aggregate supply and inflation can almost certainly be explained by the conditions of his time: Real GDP was far below potential GDP, and inflation was a remote concern. Nevertheless, Keynes's inattention to aggregate supply, to inflation, and to monetary policy would be the cause of the most damaging attacks on Keynesian economics in later years.

Despite the criticism, Keynes's ideas have had a lasting effect on much of modern macroeconomics. By the late 1940s, Keynesian ideas were incorporated into introductory economics textbooks, such as the 1948 book by Paul Samuelson; by the 1950s, Keynesian economics had been incorporated into macroeconomic forecasting models. Finally, Keynesian economics was brought formally into national policymaking during the 1960s through the work of James Tobin and other members of President Kennedy's Council of Economic Advisers. In particular, the 1962 *Economic Report of the President* presented the arguments for the Keynesian view in a public policy context.

Key ideas traceable to Keynes's work include the theory that declines in real GDP during recessions are movements of real GDP below potential GDP due to *changes in aggregate demand.* Also attributable to Keynes is the use of the government spending multiplier to show the size of the impact on real GDP of a change in government purchases.

The Monetarist School

Milton Friedman mounted the earliest and most substantive attacks on Keynesian economics. In the 1950s, Friedman's work on the permanent income hypothesis of consumption was motivated by concerns that the Keynesian marginal propensity to consume and the multiplier were not stable. Friedman's permanent income hypothesis showed that the marginal propensity to consume was unlikely to be stable

HARRIS

Cartoonists & Writers Syndicate

monetarist school: a school of macroeconomic thought that holds that changes in the money supply are the primary cause of fluctuations in real GDP and the ultimate cause of inflation.

because people based their consumption more on their permanent income than on their actual income.

Friedman's criticism of the Keynesians' lack of attention to the effects of the money supply and to the power of monetary policy became the source of vociferous debates in macroeconomics in the 1960s. The **monetarist school,** for which Friedman's and Anna Schwartz's work on monetary history provided the foundation, argued that monetary policy was a powerful force—indeed, more powerful than fiscal policy. Friedman and Schwartz showed that declines in money growth were responsible for the prolonged duration of the Great Depression.

A long series of "radio," or "AM/FM," debates between the monetarists and the Keynesians ensued. (The debates were not broadcast over the radio; the term derives from the initials of the main protagonists in the debates, Albert Ando and Franco Modigliani [AM], versus Milton Friedman and David Meiselman [FM]). The main issue was whether changes in the money supply (the monetarist view) or changes in government spending (the Keynesian view) mattered more for changes in real GDP. The FM team argued the case for the money supply and offered proof in the form of empirical verification of the quantity equation of money. The AM team argued the case for government spending and offered proof in the form of empirical verification of the government spending multiplier. Today this debate seems rather pointless to many macroeconomists, because it is clear that aggregate demand can change because of both monetary policy *and* fiscal policy. Indeed, this is true of the theories of economic fluctuations presented in this book. However, before the debate monetary policy played only a small role in most Keynesian economic models; after the debate it played a much bigger role, so in this sense the monetarist criticism had a lasting influence on economic knowledge.

A second part of the monetarist attack on Keynesian economics was its criticism of the idea of a long-run tradeoff between inflation and unemployment that seemed to exist in most Keynesian models. Although Milton Friedman was one of the key figures in this debate, a nonmonetarist economist, Edmund Phelps of Columbia University, developed a similar criticism. In any case the idea that there is no long-run tradeoff between inflation and unemployment has now become part of the accepted assumption of most macroeconomists.

The Neoclassical Growth School

neoclassical growth school: an approach to macroeconomics that uses the aggregate production function and the growth accounting formula in describing long-term growth, emphasizing aggregate supply rather than aggregate demand.

While the battles between the monetarists and the Keynesians were heating up in the 1950s, another significant development in macroeconomics was beginning. This was the development of the **neoclassical growth school.** Robert Solow's 1956 paper entitled "A Model of Growth" was one of the first key works of the neoclassical growth school. At the time, this development received much less publicity than either Keynesian economics or monetarist economics, perhaps because it applied to the long run rather than to the short run, and long-run issues frequently get less public attention than short-run issues. The term *neoclassical* applies to this school because the framework for analysis is much like that used by neoclassical economists such as Alfred Marshall. Solow's *growth accounting formula* and the production function that underlies potential GDP are the heart of the neoclassical growth model. As stated by Solow, "The aggregate production function is only a little less legitimate a concept than, say, the aggregate consumption function, and for some kinds of long-run macro-models it is almost as indispensable as the latter is for the short-run."[1]

Despite its initial lack of attention, neoclassical growth theory has had a profound influence on modern macroeconomics. Most importantly it brought aggregate supply—that is, the production function and the growth of potential GDP—back into macroeconomics. Together, the monetarist school and the neoclassical growth school re-emphasized the three ingredients—inflation, money, and the growth of potential GDP—that were ignored by those Keynesians who had let aggregate demand and fiscal policy completely dominate macroeconomic theory and policy.

The neoclassical growth school also brought basic microeconomic principles, such as the notion of an equilibrium price and the importance of relative prices, into macroeconomics; these principles were frequently missing from the simple Keynesian theories. The emphasis of neoclassical growth theory on technology is more visible than ever in modern macroeconomics; growth economists such as Paul Romer of Stanford University have built new models of the technology process, examining what motivates the owners of "invention factories," as we discussed in the chapter "Technology and Economic Growth."

Developments from the 1970s Through the Present

By the mid-1970s—40 years after the start of the Keynesian revolution—signs of another dramatic change in macroeconomic thinking began to appear. These changes are referred to as the **rational expectations revolution,** and they may eventually turn out to be as dramatic in their impact as the Keynesian revolution. Rational expectations—the idea that people look ahead to the future using all available information—is central to this change in thinking in much the same way that the multiplier or the marginal propensity to consume (MPC) was central to the Keynesian revolution. However, just as the Keynesian revolution went well beyond the MPC and the multiplier, the rational expectations revolution went well beyond expectations.

There is no single treatise such as Keynes's *General Theory* that outlines the rational expectations approach. Much of the research on it is contained in articles published in economics journals by a number of economists. Most representative perhaps are the papers written by a number of researchers in the 1970s and collected in a 1981 book entitled *Rational Expectations and Econometric Practice,* edited by Robert Lucas and Thomas Sargent. Like Keynes's *General Theory,* the papers in this collection were addressed to other professional economists, not to the general public; they make for no easier reading than Keynes's classic.

The rational expectations revolution began as part of an effort to be more explicit about the ideas put forth by Edmund Phelps and Milton Friedman in their

rational expectations revolution: a change in macroeconomic thinking during the 1970s based on the assumption that people make rational, forward-looking decisions using all the information available to them.

---

1. R. M. Solow, "Technical Change and the Aggregate Production Function," *Review of Economics and Statistics,* Vol. 39, 1957, p. 312.

analysis of the tradeoff between inflation and unemployment (or the departures of real GDP from potential GDP). Expectations of inflation was the key mechanism that both Phelps and Friedman had used to show why there was no long-run tradeoff: Only the difference between inflation and expectations of inflation could affect the unemployment rate in the Phelps-Friedman theory. Hence, a permanent increase in inflation would raise people's expectations of inflation and thus leave unemployment unchanged in the long run.

But Phelps and Friedman were less specific about the short-run tradeoff. To be more explicit, economists needed to be more specific about what determined expectations. They used the rational expectations assumption to do so.

The rational expectations assumption itself has had a profound effect on macroeconomics. The important idea that budget deficit reduction might have only a small short-run negative impact was discovered as a result of using rational expectations in macroeconomics. For example, if people try to anticipate government actions (that is, if they have rational expectations), then when the government announces in advance a program to reduce the budget deficit, interest rates will fall and tend to offset the short-run negative impacts of budget deficit reduction.

New Classical Macroeconomics

policy ineffectiveness proposition: the proposition that anticipated monetary policy will have no effect on the economy.

new classical school: a school of macroeconomics that holds that prices are perfectly flexible, expectations are rational, and therefore anticipated monetary policy will have no effect on the economy.

One type of macroeconomic analysis with rational expectations assumes that prices are perfectly flexible. In the case where prices are perfectly flexible, the rational expectations assumption has another implication: Changes in monetary policy, if anticipated in advance, have no short-run effect on real GDP. This result is known as the **policy ineffectiveness proposition** and has been stressed by a school of economists called the **new classical school** (not to be confused with the similar-sounding neoclassical school!). Robert Barro of Harvard University, for example, has argued that only unanticipated changes in monetary policy cause changes in real GDP.

The policy ineffectiveness proposition can be illustrated with a supply curve for an individual firm, as shown in Figure 32.2. The price of the good that the firm sells is on the vertical axis, while the quantity supplied by the firm is on the horizontal axis. The relevant price for the firm's supply decision is the *relative price:* the price measured relative to all other goods and services in the economy. The firm will increase the quantity supplied if the price of the good rises relative to the price the firm perceives as prevailing in the economy. On the other hand, if the firm's price rises and the prices of all other goods also rise, then no relative price change will occur and the firms will not adjust the quantity supplied.

If prices are perfectly flexible, an increase in the money supply will immediately raise all prices in the economy. However, because of imperfect information the individual firm will not usually be aware that all other prices in the economy are changing. Thus, if the individual firm does not know that the money supply has increased (because the Fed did not announce the increase) then the firm will see only its own price rising. The firm guesses that the overall price does not rise, or at least does not rise as much as the individual firm's price rises. Thus, an unanticipated increase in the money supply will cause the firm to increase the quantity supplied. With other firms doing the same thing, real GDP will increase in the economy as a whole.

However, suppose that the central bank announces that it will increase the money supply. Then, when firms see their own prices rising, they will assume it is

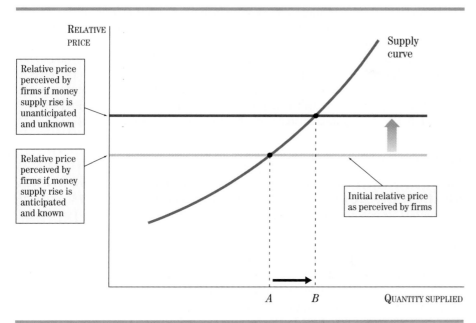

RELATIVE PRICE

Supply curve

Relative price perceived by firms if money supply rise is unanticipated and unknown

Relative price perceived by firms if money supply rise is anticipated and known

Initial relative price as perceived by firms

A   *B*   QUANTITY SUPPLIED

FIGURE 32.2
New Classical View of the Effects of Unanticipated versus Anticipated Increases in the Money Supply
If the central bank increases the money supply and all prices are flexible, then all prices will rise. However, if the increase in the money supply is unanticipated and unknown, then firms do not realize that all prices rise. Firms think that only their own prices rise; they are fooled into thinking that there is a relative price increase. Hence, they increase the quantity supplied from point *A* to point *B*. However, if the money supply increase is anticipated and known, then firms are not fooled into thinking there is a relative price increase; firms know all prices have risen and keep their quantity supplied at point *A*.

because all prices in the economy are rising. With no change in the relative price, they will, therefore, not change the quantity supplied. Hence, there will be no change in production. Thus, an anticipated change in the money supply has no effect on real GDP, which is the policy ineffectiveness proposition.

The New Keynesian School

The policy ineffectiveness proposition requires that prices be perfectly flexible. Another school of economics that grew out of the rational expectations revolution is called the **new Keynesian school.** A distinguishing feature of this school is that prices are assumed to be sticky, or slowly adjusting, rather than perfectly flexible. Stanley Fischer of MIT and Jo Anna Gray of the University of Oregon are two of the early contributors to this school, which, like the new classical school, began in the 1970s.

Thus, unlike the new classical models, anticipated monetary policy affects real GDP in the short run in the new Keynesian models. Much research of economists in the new Keynesian school has been devoted to explaining why prices are sticky.

One of the main contributions of the new Keynesian school has been to provide a way to combine the important aspects of the rational expectations revolution—including the important phenomena of credibility, time inconsistency, and policy rules—with a macroeconomic framework that includes the effects of aggregate demand, inflation, monetary policy, and potential GDP growth.

Another development sometimes associated with the new Keynesian school is the idea that the fluctuations in the economy are due to **coordination failure.** A coordination failure arises in circumstances where people's actions depend on what they expect other people will do. If you are running a firm and you expect business

new Keynesian school: a school of macroeconomics that holds that prices are sticky and expectations are rational to explain the effect of monetary and fiscal policy.

coordination failure: a situation where, because their actions are interdependent, people fail to act in a manner that is mutually beneficial.

to be good, then you will hire more workers and expand production. If you expect business to be bad, then you do not expand production. Thus, there are two possibilities: People expect bad times and, because of this expectation, times turn out to be bad—this is the case of coordination failure—or people expect good times and, because of this expectation, times turn out to be good. If people could agree to coordinate their production, then coordination failure, or bad times, might be eliminated. John Bryant of Rice University has been researching the possibility that periods of deficient aggregate demand might be due to coordination failures.

The Real Business Cycle School

real business cycle school: a group of economists who believe that shifts in potential GDP, largely due to changes in technology, are the primary cause of economic fluctuations.

Another outgrowth of the rational expectations revolution is the **real business cycle school.** The real business cycle school views the fluctuations in real GDP as due to fluctuations in potential GDP. Most typically it assumes the changes in potential GDP to be due to technological change in the production function. In terms of the growth accounting formula, therefore, the source of economic fluctuations is in the technological contribution to growth.

Finn Kydland of Carnegie Mellon University and Edward Prescott of the University of Minnesota are two of the originators of the real business cycle school, which has attracted many economists in recent years. An important contribution of the real business cycle school has been to focus the attention of macroeconomists more on the supply side of the economy. Clearly it is not correct to assume that all the fluctuations in real GDP are due to fluctuations of real GDP around potential GDP. The real business cycle school has provided a method for explaining the other sources of fluctuations in real GDP.

Supply Side Economics

supply side economics: the branch of economics that emphasizes that reducing marginal tax rates on investments and labor will increase aggregate supply, thereby stimulating the macroeconomy.

Like Keynesian economics and monetarist economics, supply side economics is almost a household term, widely discussed in recent years and appearing in many general-usage dictionaries. **Supply side economics** refers to the idea that by cutting taxes or reforming the tax system, the growth rate of aggregate supply, or potential GDP, can be increased.

Few economists would disagree that taxes affect incentives. But they disagree strongly over how large the effects are likely to be. In principle, there is an affinity between supply side economics and the real business cycle school because both emphasize the supply side of the economy, or potential GDP.

Macroeconomic Theory at the Turn of the Century

During the 1990s, economists came to use a catchy terminology when referring to the different schools of thought. They divided up economists into two broad camps: (1) the *freshwater* camp, including economists of the real business cycle school and the new classical school, many of whom happened to be located in the central regions of the United States (Great Lakes, Mississippi River), and (2) the *saltwater* camp, including economists of the new Keynesian school, many of whom happened to be located in either the eastern or western regions of the United States.

By the late 1990s a consensus of the two camps seemed to be developing. That consensus combined the sticky prices and implicit contracts of the saltwater camp with the careful treatment of information, policy rules, and equilibrium of the fresh-water camp. The consensus is represented by the papers collected in a book called the *Handbook of Macroeconomics*, a summary of modern macroeconomics written by many active researchers. The consensus is also evident in the rational expectations models with sticky prices used at the Federal Reserve Board, the International Monetary Fund, and other institutions with macroeconomic policy responsibility. But whether or not there is a consensus, if history is any guide to the future, macroeconomic debates will continue in the years ahead.

Review

▶ In examining developments in modern macroeconomics, it is helpful to focus on two periods: (1) the 1930s to the 1960s, which began with the Keynesian revolution and includes the work of the monetarist school and the neoclassical growth school; and (2) the 1970s to the 1990s, which began with the rational expectations revolution and includes

the work of the new classical school, the new Keynesian school, the real business cycle school, and the supply side school.

▶ The recent history of macroeconomic thought is one of heated debates in which the prevailing view gradually changes over time.

DEBATES ABOUT MACROECONOMIC POLICY

Having examined some of the debates about macroeconomic theory, let us look at the debates about policy. Consider the actions proposed by Presidents Bush and Clinton to help speed recovery from the 1990–1991 recession.

The Bush Fiscal Package

Table 32.1 summarizes President Bush's macroeconomic policy proposals, made in January 1992. The first proposal was to speed up government purchases. This meant that laws that had already been passed to build or improve roads or bridges would be implemented more quickly. As a result of this speedup, government purchases were to rise by $10 billion in the first six months of 1992.

Shift $10 billion in government purchases from the future into present.

Reduce the amount of tax withheld in the present.

Enact an investment tax credit (called an allowance) to encourage investment in 1992 and 1993 rather than in later years.

Reduce the capital gains tax.

TABLE 32.1
Key Parts of the Bush Stimulus Proposal

What would be the impact on the economy? The $10 billion increase in spending is only a small fraction of a percent of real GDP for one year. Hence, even with multiplier effects on consumption, this alone would not have had a big effect on the recovery, but it was some stimulus.

The second proposal was to decrease temporarily the amount of income taxes withheld by the government. Individuals who work must pay income taxes equal to a percentage of each paycheck to the government. This withholding of taxes is the way most income taxes are paid in the United States. On the average throughout the economy, taxes are overwithheld. For the year 1992, approximately $25 billion was to be refunded to taxpayers in April 1993. The Bush proposal was to reduce this withholding and help stimulate the economy in 1992. This meant that people would get more money during the year and less money in their refund the following year. Because this tax change was temporary, it was expected to have a fairly small effect on the economy. The effect would certainly be smaller than a permanent tax cut of this magnitude and probably even smaller than a temporary tax cut that was not completely offset by a higher tax the following year.

investment tax credit: a reduction in taxes for firms that buy new investment goods that is proportional to the expenditures on the good.

capital gains tax: a tax on the increase in the value of an asset.

How much additional consumption would there be if all of the $25 billion was received as income in 1992? Suppose that the marginal propensity to consume out of income is .6. The change in withholding would clearly have a smaller marginal propensity to consume (MPC), but how much smaller we do not know. Perhaps .3 would be a good guess. If you multiply .3 by $25 billion you get $7.5 billion. This is probably a reasonable guess of how much extra consumption would occur as a result of this kind of tax cut. People would have less withheld, their paychecks would be a little larger, and they could spend more. That would amount to less than a small fraction of a percent of real GDP. By adding both the speedup of construction spending and the delay in tax receipts, the effect is still less than ½ of a percent of real GDP.

"Do you blame the previous administration, the present administration or future administrations?"

The remaining parts of the Bush package required legislation that the Congress would have to pass. The **investment tax credit** meant that firms could reduce their taxes if they invested and purchased new investment goods in 1992. For example, a small business could get a tax break if it bought a delivery truck during 1992 rather than the following year. That would give firms an incentive to invest and stimulate demand in the economy.

Another part of the proposal requiring legislation was the capital gains tax reduction. The **capital gains tax** is a tax on the appreciation of assets. If you invest in a stock and its value increases, say by $100, you pay a tax on that capital gain. The Bush administration proposed that the tax be reduced. The aim was to stimulate investment and to help the economy by increasing aggregate demand in the short run and productive capacity in the long run.

The proposal to reduce the capital gains tax was controversial. Opponents of the reduction said that it was a giveaway to the rich. They argued that only 1 percent of the population gets two-thirds of the gains from the cut in capital gains tax. But proponents gave figures showing that 60 percent of the people who get the capital gains tax break earn less than $50,000 per year.

Debates about the Bush Proposals

As it turned out, none of the Bush stimulus proposals were enacted into law. Some lawmakers argued that the economy was already recovering. Others argued against the capital gains tax cut. The Congress voted positively on an alternative package with many of the president's proposals, but the package also included a tax increase, which President Bush said he would veto and did veto. His veto was sustained, so there was no stimulus package.

The only part of the stimulus proposals that actually took place were those that could be done without legislation—the adjustment of withholding and the speedup of purchases.

The Clinton Fiscal Package

After President Clinton was elected in November 1992, he also developed a stimulus program. His economic advisers recommended a large fiscal stimulus to help speed up the recovery from the 1991–1992 recession. The program is summarized in Table 32.2.

Note the similarities between the two proposals. The increase in government spending, the investment tax credit, and the reduction in the capital gains tax (though for a limited set of investments) were also on the Bush stimulus list. However, all the components of the Clinton proposal required congressional action.

Debate about the Clinton Proposals

Like the Bush proposals, the Clinton proposals received much criticism and were not enacted by Congress. The problem in this case was that the proposals would have increased the budget deficit. During this period, the concerns of many economists and the public had shifted to reducing the deficit rather than taking actions to stimulate the economy. Although the Democrats had a majority in both houses of Congress, some Democrats did not like the president's stimulus package because it would increase the deficit, so the plan failed. Because the package did not have an administrative component that could be put in place without legislation, there was no stimulus program at all.

Lessons

What can be learned from the failed Bush and Clinton discretionary stimulus proposals? Both cases illustrate some of the problems associated with implementing macroeconomic policy. First, there is a big difference between proposing a policy and enacting a policy, even when the president and both houses of Congress belong to the same party. Second, the examples illustrate that lags in getting discretionary

---

Increase government spending by $16 billion on items ranging from infrastructure to immunization programs.

Establish an incremental investment tax credit—to be temporary except for small firms.

Reduce the capital gains tax for investments in certain small companies held for five years or more.

TABLE 32.2
Key Parts of the Clinton Stimulus Proposal

policies enacted mean that they will most likely be too late to have the desired effect. In retrospect, even if the Clinton stimulus program had been enacted it would have been put in place in 1994. By 1996, data indicated that the economy was very close to full employment in 1994 and not in need of a fiscal stimulus.

Perhaps the most important lesson from this period is that both discretionary proposals were very small in comparison with the automatic stabilizer effects of fiscal policy. The budget deficit grew along with the unemployment rate in 1990 and 1991, just as it did in the 1981–1982 recession and all other recessions. The increase in the cyclical deficit was more than 2 percent of GDP, and it was well timed. The automatic stabilizers provided a substantial degree of fiscal stimulus to the economy, much larger than either of the discretionary action programs proposed.

Fortunately, the economy recovered from the 1990–1991 recession, and the expansion after this recession has been one of the longest in U.S. history. But when the next recession strikes there will undoubtedly be calls for the president to put forth another stimulus package. In doing so the delays in enactment and the power of the automatic stabilizers should be kept in mind.

Review

▶ Both President Bush and President Clinton proposed discretionary short-term stimulus packages to speed the recovery from the 1990–1991 recession. Both packages were vociferously debated.

▶ In the end, both proposals were defeated by Congress, though for much different

reasons. Both illustrate the great difficulties of using discretionary fiscal policy to reduce the fluctuations in the economy.

▶ In retrospect the automatic stabilizers had a much larger impact than either of the proposals would have had.

CONCLUSION

Newspaper articles and television programs frequently focus on current macroeconomic events—the threat of inflation, the reason for a recession, a president's budget plan, the Fed's interest rate strategy. As this chapter has shown, there are different schools of thought, and even those with the same views have debates about how to implement macroeconomic policy. It seems difficult to tell who is right in any particular instance. Hence, whether you are a casual observer, a concerned voter, or, like most of us, greatly affected by these events, you must make your own judgment.

This chapter has endeavored to provide you with some historical perspective on the different schools of thought so that you can form your own views about current policy problems. Recent case studies, such as the debates over macroeconomic policy discussed in this chapter, are useful for this purpose, but even now as you finish this chapter there are other interesting and important cases evolving. Try out your skills by reading and thinking about one of these—whether it is the next Fed interest rate decision, the next State of the Union address, a proposed reform of tax and budget policy, or simply the "informed opinion" about the macroeconomy from an economic expert.

KEY POINTS

1. Examining different schools of thought and case studies of macroeconomic policy decision-making provides a perspective on the relative importance of different debates and controversies.

2. The Keynesian revolution began in the 1930s. It emphasized the importance of aggregate demand and the role of fiscal policy in stabilizing aggregate demand.

3. The monetarist school criticized Keynesians for deemphasizing money and for the idea that there was a long-run tradeoff between inflation and unemployment.

4. Research on the neoclassical growth model focused attention on aggregate supply and the growth of potential GDP.

5. The rational expectations revolution started in the 1970s and brought increased attention to policy credibility,

time inconsistency, monetary independence, and policy rules.

6. The new classical school assumes that prices are perfectly flexible, leading to the policy ineffectiveness proposition.

7. The new Keynesian school incorporated sticky prices into models with rational expectations and explored the underlying reasons for sticky prices and wages.

8. The real business cycle school has shown that fluctuations in potential GDP may be a significant part of economic fluctuations.

9. Experience with discretionary policy in the 1990s was not favorable. Two fiscal packages proposed by two presidents were not enacted, leaving countercyclical policy to the automatic stabilizers.

KEY TERMS

Keynesian revolution
Keynesian school
monetarist school
neoclassical growth school
rational expectations revolution

policy ineffectiveness proposition
new classical school
new Keynesian school
coordination failure
real business cycle school

supply side economics
investment tax credit
capital gains tax

QUESTIONS FOR REVIEW

1. What economic event gave impetus to the Keynesian revolution?

2. What did Keynes mean by "the classical theory"?

3. What was the Keynesian-monetarist debate?

4. What was the impact of neoclassical growth theory on Keynesian economics?

5. What is the rational expectations revolution?

6. What is the policy ineffectiveness proposition?

7. What is the contribution of the real business cycle school to theories of economic fluctuations?

8. What was similar and different about the Bush and Clinton short-run stimulus plans? Why did both plans fail to pass Congress?

PROBLEMS

1. Contrast the Keynesian revolution of the 1930s with the rational expectations revolution of the 1970s, describing the contributions and schools of thought associated with each.

2. What was the impact of the AM/FM debates on the theory of economic fluctuations?

3. Explain why an anticipated *decrease* in the money supply would not affect real GDP if prices were perfectly flexible.

4. Compare and contrast new classical macroeconomics with the new Keynesian school.

5. Provide two explanations for the 1990–1991 recession, one based on real business cycles and the other based on

the assumption that real GDP departed from a steadily growing potential GDP.

6. What are some examples of fiscal policy actions that do not require legislation? Divide your answers into discretionary and automatic actions.

7. Suppose it is the year 2002, and the economy is just coming out of the 2001–2002 recession. There is pressure on the president to do something to help the recovery. Remember that there is a presidential election in the year 2004. Based on the experience of President Bush in 1992 and President Clinton in 1993, what would you recommend?

33

Economic Growth Around the World

Macroeconomics provides a pretty good framework for studying the steady upward climb of real GDP over time. In particular, the theory of economic growth tells us how technology and capital have provided workers with the means to raise their productivity and thereby achieve the modern miracle of economic growth.

Yet there is something disquieting about the theory when we look at all the facts. True, technological change can explain a good part of the economic growth miracle, but why exactly did improvements in technology suddenly start in the late 1700s in Europe? Moreover, as we compare living standards around the world, it is clear that people in some countries are much better off than people in other countries. Why has the theory applied so unevenly to different countries around the world, with some growing rapidly and some stuck in poverty, not growing at all? What will determine whether economic growth in the twenty-first century will be as great as the last two centuries or as terrible as the millennia before that?

In this chapter we look for answers to these crucial questions about the initial impetus to economic growth in the advanced countries, about the uneven patterns of economic growth in different countries, and about the prospects of future economic growth throughout the world. All the questions are interrelated and, surprisingly, they seem to have similar answers. We begin our quest for the answers by looking at patterns of growth in different parts of the world.

CATCHING UP OR NOT?

If technological advances can spread easily—as seems reasonable with modern communications—and if capital and labor have diminishing returns, then poorer regions with low productivity and, therefore, low income per capita will tend to catch up to richer regions by growing more rapidly. Why?

If the spread of new technology is not difficult, then we would expect regions with lower productivity to adopt the more advanced technology of other regions to raise their productivity. For example, the spread of technology appears to be easy in the states in the United States. Individual states have access to the same technology. People in all the states watch the same television networks, have access to the same national newspapers or wire services, and can read the same textbooks. Similar colleges and universities exist in all the states.

Diminishing returns would also tend to cause poor regions to catch up to the rich. Consider a relatively poor region where both capital per worker and output per worker are low. Imagine several hundred workers constructing a road with only rudimentary tools, such as picks, shovels, and perhaps jackhammers. With such low levels of capital, the returns to increasing the amount of capital would be very high. Diminishing returns to capital would not have set in. The addition of a few trucks and some earthmoving equipment to the construction project would bring huge returns in higher output. Regions with relatively low levels of capital per worker would, therefore, attract a great amount of investment; capital per worker would grow rapidly. The growth accounting formula tells us that output per worker grows rapidly when capital per worker grows rapidly. Thus, output per hour of work would grow rapidly in poorer regions where capital per worker is low.

A rich region where the capital per worker is high, however, would gain relatively little from additional capital per worker because diminishing returns have set in. Such a region would attract little investment and the growth rate of capital would be lower; the growth of output would also be lower.

Thus, economic growth theory predicts that regions with low productivity will grow relatively more rapidly than regions that are at the leading edge of technology and where the ratios of capital to labor are high. Regions with low productivity will tend to catch up to the more advanced regions by adopting existing technology and attracting capital.

Figure 33.1 illustrates this catch-up phenomenon. It shows the level of productivity on the horizontal axis and the growth rate of productivity on the vertical axis. The downward-sloping line is the **catch-up line.** A country or region on the upper left-hand part of the line is poor—with low productivity and, therefore, low income per capita—but growing rapidly. A country at the lower right-hand part of the line is rich—with high productivity and, therefore, high income per capita—but growth is relatively less rapid. That the catch-up line exists and is downward-sloping is a prediction of growth theory.

Catch-up Within the United States

Figure 33.2 examines how well the catch-up line works for the states within the United States. This picture presents the data on real income per capita and the growth rates of real income per capita for each of the states. Because productivity

Growth accounting formula:

$$\text{Growth rate of real} \atop \text{GDP per hour of work} =$$

$$\frac{1}{3}\left(\begin{array}{c}\text{growth rate of capital}\\ \text{per hour of work}\end{array}\right)$$

$$+\left(\begin{array}{c}\text{growth rate of}\\ \text{technology}\end{array}\right)$$

catch-up line: the downward-sloping relation between the level of productivity and growth of productivity predicted by growth theory.

FIGURE 33.1

The Catch-up Line

Growth theory with spreading technology and diminishing returns to capital and labor predicts that regions with lower productivity will have higher growth rates of productivity. The catch-up line illustrates this prediction. Because productivity is so closely related to income per capita, the catch-up line can also describe a relationship between income per capita and the growth rate of income per capita.

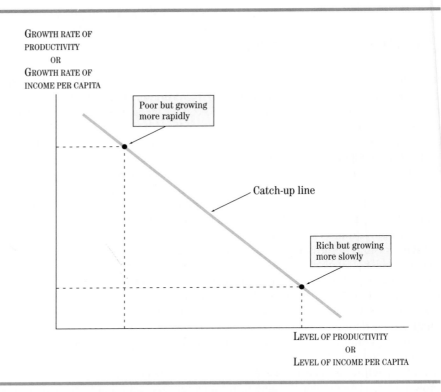

and real income per capita move closely together, we can examine the accuracy of the catch-up line with the real income per capita data. (Again, the adjective *real* means that the income data are adjusted for inflation.) Real income per capita in 1880 is on the horizontal axis, and the growth rate of real income per capita from 1880 to 1980 is on the vertical axis. Each point on the scatter diagram represents a state, and a few of the states are labeled. If you pick a state (observe Nevada, for example, down and to the right), you can read its growth rate by looking over to the left scale, and you can read its 1880 income per capita level by looking down to the horizontal scale.

The diagram clearly shows a tendency for states with low real income per capita in 1880 to have high growth rates. The state observations fall remarkably near a catch-up line. Southern states like Florida and Texas are in the high-growth group. On the other hand, in states that had a relatively high income per capita in 1880, income per capita grew relatively slowly. This group includes California and Nevada.

Thus, the theory of growth works quite well in explaining the relative differences in growth rates in the states of the United States. Where technological know-how is comparable, there is a tendency for relatively poor regions to grow more rapidly than relatively rich regions.

Catch-up in the Advanced Countries

What if we apply the same thinking to different countries? After all, communication is now global. Figure 33.3 is another scatter diagram with growth rate and income per capita combinations. It is like Figure 33.2 except that it plots real

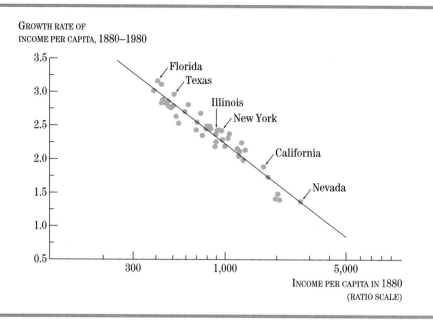

FIGURE 33.2
Evidence of Catch-up Within the United States

In the United States, those states that had low real income per capita 100 years ago grew relatively rapidly compared to states that had high income per capita. The poor states tended to catch up to the richer states. A catch-up line is drawn through the dots.

Source: Historical Statistics of the United States: Colonial Times to 1970, U.S. Department of Commerce, and *State Personal Income,* U.S. Department of Commerce, 1989.

income per capita in 1960 against growth in real income per capita from 1960 to 1990 for several advanced countries. These incomes are measured in U.S. dollars using the purchasing power parity method of comparing different countries discussed in Chapter 20.

Observe in Figure 33.3 that the richer countries, such as the United States, grew less rapidly. In contrast, relatively less rich countries, such as Greece, Portugal, Spain, and Italy, grew more rapidly. Canada and France are somewhere in

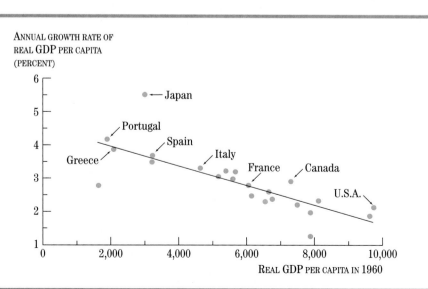

FIGURE 33.3
Evidence of Catch-up in More Advanced Countries, 1960–1990

For the advanced countries shown in the diagram, income per capita growth has been more rapid for those that started from a lower level of income per capita. Thus, there has been catching up, as shown by the catch-up line drawn through the points.

Source: International Comparison Project administered by the United Nations, World Bank, and International Monetary Fund. The data for 1960 are measured in 1985 dollars.

"According to figures released today, last month's gains in productivity were completely negated by this month's gains in counterproductivity."

between. These countries tend to display the catch-up behavior predicted by the growth theory. Apparently, technological advances are spreading and capital-labor ratios are rising more rapidly in countries where they are low and returns to capital are high. So far our look at the evidence confirms the predictions of growth theory.

Catch-up in the Whole World

However, so far we have not looked beyond the most advanced countries. Figure 33.4 shows a broader group of countries that includes not only the more advanced countries in Figure 33.3 but also countries that are still developing. It is apparent that there is little tendency for this larger group of countries to fall along a catch-up line. There may even be a decline in growth, with many poorer countries falling further behind over time.

The countries with very low growth rates, such as Bangladesh and Ethiopia, are also the countries with very low income per capita. On the other hand, many countries with higher growth rates had a much higher income per capita. Singapore and Hong Kong had higher growth rates even though their income per capita was above Sri Lanka and Ethiopia.

Comparing countries like Singapore and South Korea with countries like Bangladesh and Sri Lanka is striking. South Korea and Singapore had about the same real income per capita as Sri Lanka and Bangladesh in 1960, but South Korea and Singapore surged ahead with a more rapid growth rate over the last 30 years, leaving Bangladesh and Sri Lanka behind. But this is not the exception. Contrary to the predictions of the economic growth theory, which says that technological advances should spread and capital per hour of work should rise from low levels, Figure 33.4 shows little tendency for relatively poor countries to grow relatively rapidly. It appears that something has been preventing either the spread and the adoption of new technology or the increase in investment needed to raise capital-labor ratios. We examine possible explanations as this chapter proceeds.

FIGURE 33.4
Lack of Catch-up for Developing Countries, 1960–1990

Unlike the states in the United States or the advanced countries, there has been little tendency for poor countries to grow more rapidly than rich countries. The gap between rich and poor has not closed.

Source: International Comparison Project administered by the United Nations, World Bank, and International Monetary Fund. The data for 1960 are measured in 1985 dollars.

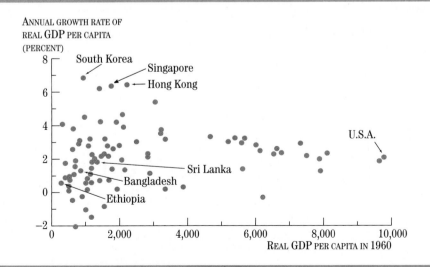

ECONOMIC DEVELOPMENT

Aside from raising questions about economic growth theory, the lack of catch-up evidenced in Figure 33.4 describes a disturbing situation. There are huge disparities in world income distribution, and billions of people in low-income countries lack the necessities those in high-income countries frequently take for granted.

Billions Still in Poverty

The richest countries in the world, with more than $10,000 income per capita, account for about 700 million people. The United States, with 250 million people, is among the richest, along with Japan and most of Western Europe. Another 600 million people live in countries that have an income per capita between $5,000 and $10,000. But the vast majority—about three-fourths of the world's people—live in countries with an income per capita of less than $5,000 per year. This is below the poverty level in advanced countries. Income per capita in South Korea, Venezuela, and Malaysia is only about one-third that of the United States. In China and Sri Lanka it is only one-eighth that of the United States. Income per capita for Ethiopia is a mere 2 percent of that in the United States.

Low income per capita is a serious economic problem, but the implications go well beyond economics. Large differences in income per capita and vast amounts of poverty can lead to war, revolution, or regional conflicts. Will these differences persist? Or is the lack of catch-up that has left so many behind a thing of the past?

Geographical Patterns

Figure 33.5 shows the location of the relatively rich and the relatively poor countries around the world. Notice that the higher-income countries tend to be in the northern part of the world. An exception to this rule is the relatively high income per capita in Australia and New Zealand. Aside from these exceptions, income disparity appears to have a geographical pattern—the North being relatively rich and the South relatively poor. Often people use the term **North-South problem** to describe world income disparities.

But whether it is North versus South or not, there do appear to be large contiguous regions where many rich or many poor countries are located together. The original increase in economic growth that occurred at the time of the Industrial

North-South problem: refers to the geographic dispersion of incomes: Northern countries tend to be relatively rich, and southern ones tend to be relatively poor.

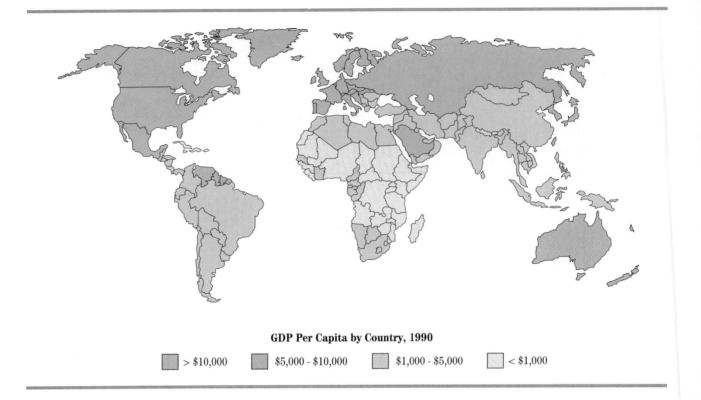

GDP Per Capita by Country, 1990

☐ > $10,000   ☐ $5,000 - $10,000   ☐ $1,000 - $5,000   ☐ < $1,000

FIGURE 33.5
Rich and Poor Countries Around the World
The highest-income regions tend to be located in North America, Europe, Japan, Australia, and the Middle East.

Source: International Comparison Project administered by the United Nations, World Bank, and International Monetary Fund.

economic development: the process of growth by which countries raise incomes per capita and become industrialized; also refers to the branch of economics that studies this process.

developing country: a country that is poor by world standards in terms of real GDP per capita.

industrialized country: a country with a large industrial base that is relatively well off by world standards in terms of real GDP per capita.

Revolution started in northwestern Europe—England, France, and Germany. It then spread to America, which industrialized rapidly in the nineteenth and twentieth centuries. It also spread to Japan during the late-nineteenth-century Meiji Restoration, one of the main purposes of which was to import Western technology into the Japanese economy.

Terminology of Economic Development

Economic development is the branch of economics that endeavors to explain why poor countries do not develop faster and to find policies to help them develop faster. Economists who specialize in economic development frequently are experts on the problems experienced by particular countries—such as a poor educational system, political repression, droughts, or poor distribution of food. The term **developing country** describes those countries that are relatively poor, and the term **industrialized country** describes the advanced or relatively well-off countries. Sometimes the term *less-developed country* (LDC) is used rather than *developing country*. There are also terms to distinguish between different developing countries. **Newly industrialized countries** such as Korea and Hong Kong are relatively poor countries that are growing rapidly. **Countries in transition** are relatively poor countries, such as Russia and Poland, that are moving from central planning to market economies.

Table 33.1 shows the shares of world GDP produced by the three classifications of countries: industrialized countries, developing countries, and countries in transition. Thus, this table looks at aggregate income (which equals GDP) rather than at income per capita. Over 50 percent of world GDP comes from the industrialized countries.

WORLD	100.00
Industrialized Countries	**54.6**
Major industrialized countries	46.8
United States	21.2
Japan	8.4
Germany	5.0
France	3.6
Italy	3.4
United Kingdom	3.3
Canada	1.9
Other industrialized countries	7.8
Developing Countries	**40.1**
By region	
Africa	3.3
Asia	23.1
Middle East and Europe	4.8
Western Hemisphere	8.9
Countries in Transition	**5.3**
Former Soviet Union	3.3
Central Europe	2.0

TABLE 33.1
Shares of World GDP

Source: World Economic Outlook, May 1995, p. 113. By permission of International Monetary Fund.

Most striking is the nearly 23 percent share of world GDP in Asia outside of Japan. This large share is due to the newly industrialized countries and to China. China's GDP is already larger than Japan's. Although income per capita is less, China is already a major force in the world economy.

Economic development economists working at universities, the World Bank, the International Monetary Fund, the United Nations, and of course in the developing countries themselves focus their research on reasons why poor countries have grown so slowly. We now proceed to examine these reasons and, in doing so, we will touch on some of the central issues of economic development. Our examination will consider the two key determinants of increasing productivity—improvements in technology and higher capital per worker. We consider technology in the next section and then go on to consider capital in the following sections.

newly industrialized country: a country that is growing rapidly and quickly developing its industrial base.

country in transition: a country that is transforming from a centrally planned economy to a market economy.

Review

▶ The slow productivity growth in poor countries has resulted in extreme income inequality around the world. The growth miracle has spread to parts of the world, but productivity in many developing countries of the world has remained low.

▶ With a few exceptions most of the rich countries are in the northern regions of the globe and most of the poor countries are in the southern regions, thus giving rise to the term *North-South problem.*

▶ About 75 percent of the world's population lives in countries with less than $5,000 income per capita.

OBSTACLES TO THE SPREAD OF TECHNOLOGY

We have now observed two essential facts about economic growth. First, a large and persistent growth wave began for the first time in human history about 200 years ago; this growth wave raised income per capita in some countries to many times that experienced throughout human history. Second, economic growth did not spread throughout much of the world, leaving people in many countries hardly better off than their ancestors. Could these two facts be linked? Could they have the same explanation? A number of ideas have been put forth to explain the increase in economic growth in the late 1700s, and some of these may help explain why growth has not accelerated in many developing countries.

Reduction in Restrictions in the Eighteenth and Nineteenth Centuries

Some economists and historians have pointed to developments in science as the explanation of the rapid increase in economic growth in Europe in the 1700s. But if that is the explanation, why did the Industrial Revolution not begin in China or in the Islamic nations, where scientific knowledge was far more advanced than in Europe? Others note the importance of natural resources, but these were available in many other countries where there was no Industrial Revolution and, since the mid-nineteenth century, growth in Japan has been high, yet Japan has almost no natural resources. Still others have focused on exploitation, slavery, colonialism, and imperialism, but these evils existed long before the Industrial Revolution.

What, then, is the reason for this increase in economic growth we associate with the Industrial Revolution? Historians of capitalist development from Karl Marx to Joseph Schumpeter have stressed that for the first time in human history, entrepreneurs in the 1700s were gaining the freedom to start business enterprises. Economic historian Angus Maddison shows in his book, *Phases of Capitalist Development,* that the Dutch were the first to lead in productivity, with the British and then the United States soon catching up. He also shows that in the 1700s many Dutch farmers owned their land, that there was a small, weak feudal nobility, and that potential power was in the hands of entrepreneurs. Hence there was greater freedom to produce and sell manufactured and agricultural products. By the late 1700s and early 1800s, similar conditions existed in the United Kingdom and the United States. Firms could ship their products to market and hire workers without political restrictions.

Moreover, these firms now were able to earn as much as they could by selling whatever they wanted at whatever price the market determined. They began to invent and develop new products that were most beneficial to individuals. The business enterprises could keep the profits. Profits were no longer confiscated by the nobles or kings. Individual property rights—including the right to earn and keep profits—were being established and recognized in the courts.

Karl Marx, one of the most knowledgeable historians of the Industrial Revolution, saw earlier than many others that the unleashing of business enterprises and entrepreneurs was the key to economic growth. He credited the business and entrepreneurial class—what he called the bourgeois class—with the creation of more wealth than was created in all of history.

In sum, the sudden increase in technology and productivity may have occurred when it did because of the increased freedom that entrepreneurs had to start businesses, to invent and apply new ideas, and to develop products for the mass of humanity where the large markets existed.

Remaining Restrictions in Developing Countries

If true, this explanation that the economic growth surge in the late 1700s and 1800s was caused by the removal of restrictions on business enterprises may have lessons for economic development. In many developing countries in this century, there have been heavy restrictions on businesses and a poor definition of individual property rights.

Good examples of these restrictions have been documented in the research of economist Hernando De Soto, who specializes in the economy of Peru. De Soto showed that there is a tremendous amount of regulation in the developing countries. This regulation is so costly that a huge informal economy has emerged. The **informal economy** consists of large numbers of illegal businesses that can avoid the regulations. Remarkably, 61 percent of employment in Peru is in the informal, unregulated, illegal sector of the economy. In the city of Lima, around 33 percent of the houses are built in this informal sector. About 71,000 illegal vendors dominate retail trade, and 93 percent of urban transportation is in the informal sector.

informal economy: the portion of an economy characterized by illegal, unregulated businesses.

This large informal sector exists because the costs of setting up a legal business are high. It takes 32 months—filling out forms, waiting for approval, getting permission from several agencies—for a person to start a retail business. It takes six years and 11 months to start a housing construction firm. Hence, it is essentially prohibitive for someone to try to start a small business in the legal sector. Therefore, the informal sector grows.

Why does it matter if the informal sector is large? How does this impede development? Precisely because the sector is informal. It lacks basic laws of property rights and contracts. These laws cannot be enforced in a sector that is outside the law. Bringing new inventions to market requires the security of private property so that one can capture the benefits from taking risks. Otherwise the earnings from the innovation might be taken away by the government or by firms that copy the idea illegally. For example, if a business in the informal sector finds that another firm reneges on a contract to deliver a product, then that firm has no right to use the courts to enforce the contract because the business itself is illegal.

Some economists feel that such restrictions are at the heart of poor economic development. The explanation given earlier for why the Industrial Revolution occurred in the Western countries seems to pinpoint a key reason why developing countries cannot achieve high growth rates. In Europe in the 1700s, a new freedom for businesses to operate in the emerging market economy led to new products and technology. These same types of freedoms and reliance on the market could raise the economic growth rate in the developing countries around the world today.

Perhaps the most pervasive form of restriction on entrepreneurs existed in the centrally planned economies of the former Soviet Union, central Europe, and China. The persistent differences in income per capita between the former East Germany and West Germany is evidence that such restrictions have been important in preventing low-income countries from catching up. As restrictions on the market have been removed, economic growth has increased rapidly in China and other countries of east Asia, such as Vietnam.

Many forecast continued rapid growth in China and the other emerging market economies well into the twenty-first century; if this occurs, a re-examination of the catch-up line 40 years from now for the whole world may show a much better fit for the countries of the world, perhaps as good as in Figures 33.2 and 33.3.

Human Capital

In order for existing technology to be adopted—whether in the form of innovative organizational structures of firms or as new products—it is necessary to have well-trained and highly skilled workers. For example, it is hard to make use of sophisticated computers to increase productivity when there are few skilled computer programmers.

Recall that human capital refers to the education and training of workers. Low investment in human capital is a serious obstacle to increasing productivity because it hampers the ability of countries that are behind to use new technology.

In fact, economists have found that differences in human capital in different countries can explain why some countries have been more successful at catching up than others. The developing countries that have been catching up most rapidly—in particular the newly industrialized countries like South Korea, Hong Kong, Taiwan, and Singapore—have strong educational systems in grade school and high school. This demonstrates the enormous importance of human capital for raising productivity.

Review

▶ The removal of restrictions on private enterprise may have been the key factor unleashing the growth of productivity at the time of the Industrial Revolution. Similar restrictions in developing countries may have tended to stifle development in recent years.

▶ An educated work force is also needed to adopt technology. Better-educated and more highly skilled workers—those with human capital—can also use available capital more efficiently.

OBSTACLES TO RAISING CAPITAL PER WORKER

In addition to obstacles to the spread and adoption of new technology, there are obstacles to the increase in capital per worker that can prevent poor countries from catching up.

High Population Growth

In order for the capital to labor ratio to increase, it is necessary to invest in new capital. However, the amount of investment in new capital must be larger than the increase in labor, otherwise capital would increase by less than labor and the ratio of capital to labor—the factor influencing productivity—would fall. Thus, high population growth raises the amount of investment needed to increase, or even maintain, a level of capital per worker. High population growth rates can, therefore, slow down the increase in capital per worker.

Population growth rates have declined substantially in countries where income per capita has risen to high levels, such as Europe, Japan, and the United States. Economic analysis of the determinants of population indicates that the high income per capita and resulting greater life expectancy may be the reason for the decline in population growth. When countries reach a level of income per capita where people can survive into their old age without the support of many children, or where there is a greater chance of children reaching working age, people choose to have fewer children. Hence, higher income per capita in developing countries would probably reduce population growth in these countries.

Insufficient National Saving

Capital accumulation requires investment, which requires saving. National saving equals investment plus net exports. National saving is the sum of *private saving* and *government saving.* In some developing countries where income per capita is barely above subsistence levels, the level of private saving—people's income less their consumption—is low. Government saving—tax receipts less expenditures—is also often low, perhaps because there is little income to tax and because governments have trouble controlling expenditures. Figure 33.6 shows the very low saving rates in the poorest countries of Africa and south Asia compared with the highest-saving countries.

For a poor country, it is natural for national saving to be less than investment and thus for imports to be greater than exports (net exports less than zero). In other words, a poor country naturally looks to net exports—that is, to foreign investment from abroad—as a source of capital formation for economic growth.

The Lack of Foreign Investment in Developing Countries

Investment from abroad can come in the form of **foreign direct investment,** such as when the U.S. firm Gap Inc. opens a store in Mexico. Technically, when a foreign firm invests in more than 10 percent of the ownership of a business in another country, that investment is defined as direct investment.

Foreign investment also occurs when foreigners buy smaller percentages (less than 10 percent) of firms in developing economies. For example, foreign investment in Mexico takes place when a German buys newly offered common stock in a Mexican firm. In that case, the foreign investment from abroad is defined as **portfolio investment,** that is, less than 10 percent of ownership in a company.

Another way investment can flow in from abroad is through borrowing. Firms in developing economies or their governments can borrow from commercial banks, such as the Bank of America, Dai-Ichi Kangyo, or Crédit Lyonnais. Sometimes the governments of developing economies obtain loans directly from the governments of industrialized economies. Borrowing can also occur from government-sponsored international financial institutions, such as the International Monetary Fund (IMF) and the World Bank.

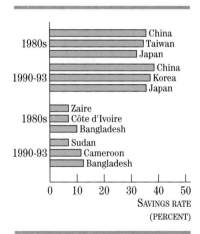

FIGURE 33.6
The Highest and Lowest Saving Countries
Very low national saving rates in poor countries impede capital accumulation and growth.

Source: World Economic Outlook, May 1995. By permission of International Monetary Fund.

National saving =
    investment + net exports
$$S = I + X$$

foreign direct investment: investment by a foreign entity of at least a 10 percent direct ownership share in a firm.

portfolio investment: investment by a foreign entity of less than a 10 percent ownership share in a firm.

Using Economics to Explain an Inadequacy of World Saving

Twice a year the International Monetary Fund (IMF) publishes a report—*World Economic Outlook*—on economic growth around the world. In the 1990s this report repeatedly expressed concern about the inadequacy of world saving, worrying that saving is insufficient for economic growth in the developing economies.

In particular, in May 1995 the IMF noted the following pertinent facts about saving rates and interest rates (because the IMF focuses on the whole world, it reports "world" saving rates and "world" interest rates, which are simply averages for all countries of the world):

	1973–1980	1981–1994
World real interest rate	1/2	5
World saving rate (percent)	25	23

The table shows that the interest rate is higher and the saving rate is lower in recent periods (the 1980s and 1990s) compared with earlier periods (the 1970s). Noting that "saving has to equal investment," the IMF concluded that "with current real interest rates high . . . there is at least prima facie evidence for a saving adequacy problem."

How did the IMF arrive at this conclusion? Is it warranted? How does the IMF know that the decline in saving is not due to a downward shift in investment demand in developing countries?

Let's examine the IMF's reasoning with the saving-investment diagram introduced in Chapter 22 and shown below. The world interest rate is measured on the vertical axis and world saving or investment as a share of world GDP is on the horizontal axis. Recall that, along the green saving curve, the saving rate rises as the interest rate rises because a higher interest rate gives people a greater incentive to save. Recall also that, along the purple investment curve, the investment rate declines as the interest rate rises because a higher interest rate discourages businesses from investing in plant and equipment. For the whole world, net exports must be zero, so that the world investment rate must equal the world saving rate; hence, the equilibrium interest rate is found at the intersection of the two curves. (Unlike Figure 22.12, we can conveniently ignore net exports in the analysis because $X = 0$.)

The interest rate/saving rate observations noted by the IMF are shown in the diagram. Observe that these observations can be explained by a leftward shift of the world saving rate in the direction of lower world saving. Such a shift *raises* the equilibrium interest rate and lowers the equilibrium amount of investment. In contrast, a shift in the world investment curve toward lower investment, perhaps because of a decline in investment demand in developing countries, *does not* raise the equilibrium interest rate. Hence, by using the interest rate/saving rate observations to identify a shift in the world saving curve, the IMF is correct to conclude that world saving is inadequate in the 1990s, at least compared with the 1970s.

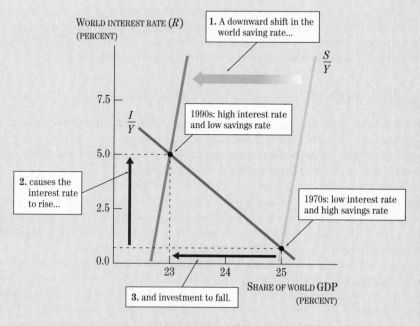

Source: *World Economic Outlook,* May 1995. By permission of International Monetary Fund.

Loans from International Financial Institutions

The **International Monetary Fund (IMF)** and the **World Bank** were established after World War II as part of a major reform of the international monetary system. Both institutions make loans to the developing economies. They serve as intermediaries, channeling funds from the industrialized countries to the developing countries. The IMF also makes loans to economies in transition, such as Poland and the former Soviet Union.

The IMF tries to help countries implement difficult economic reforms. Frequently it tries to induce the countries to make the reforms by making the loans conditional on the reforms; this is the idea of **conditionality.** Under conditionality, the IMF gives loans to countries only if the countries take on economic reform—such as eliminating price controls or privatizing firms. This conditionality is viewed as a way to encourage reforms that are difficult to undertake because of the various vested interests in each country.

The World Bank, which was originally set up to make loans to developing countries and thereby increase capital accumulation, actually consists of three different agencies. The first is the International Bank for Reconstruction and Development (IBRD). The second is the International Development Association (IDA), which specifically makes loans to the least well-off countries (the poorest of the poor, like Bangladesh), with the expectation that these loans have a lower probability of being repaid. Third is the International Finance Corporation (IFC), which makes loans to business firms.

Most of the loans of the IBRD and the IDA are for specific projects—such as the projects to build a $100 million dam for irrigation in Brazil and a $153 million highway in Poland. Some of the loans from the World Bank are for more general purposes, much as the IMF loans are, and these loans are conditional, as the IMF loans are, on good economic reform.

Where Is the Saving Coming From?

Despite the existence of these channels by which capital can flow to developing economies, there is a serious question whether the industrialized economies are saving enough to provide the increased capital. When an individual country saves more than it invests at home, it makes foreign investment abroad. A country can invest more than it saves by borrowing from abroad. In the whole world economy, saving must equal investment because (as of this writing) there seems to be no one in outer space to borrow from.

Figure 33.7 shows the percent of saving *supplied* to the world by countries with large trade surpluses and the percent of saving *used* by countries with large trade deficits during the early 1990s. The supply of Japanese saving to the rest of the world is very large; in fact, Japan is by far the largest supplier of capital to the world. In contrast, the United States and several other industrialized countries are users of capital.

International Monetary Fund (IMF): an international agency, established after World War II, designed to help countries with balance of payments problems and to ensure the smooth functioning of the international monetary system.

World Bank: an international agency, established after World War II, designed to promote the economic development of poorer countries through lending channeled from industrialized countries.

conditionality: stipulations on loans to countries from the International Monetary Fund that certain policy prescriptions, such as price reforms or reducing government budget deficits, must be met to receive funds.

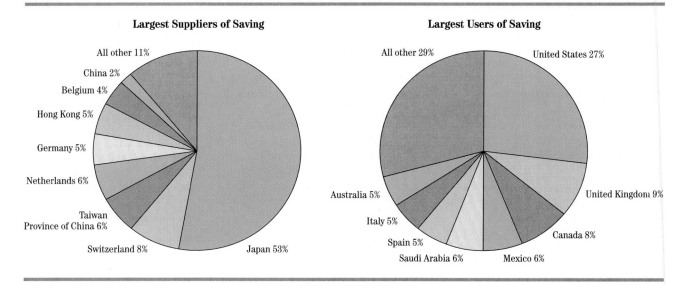

FIGURE 33.7
Suppliers and Users of Saving, 1989–1993
Japan is the largest supplier of saving, with its trade surplus, whereas the United States is the largest single user, with its trade deficit.

Source: World Economic Outlook, May 1995. By permission of International Monetary Fund.

Review

▶ High rates of population growth and low national saving are two of the obstacles to raising capital per worker in developing economies.

▶ The International Monetary Fund makes loans to developing countries. The loans are frequently conditional on an economic reform program.

▶ The World Bank makes loans mainly for specific projects. It consists of the International Bank for Reconstruction and Development, the International Development Association, and the International Finance Corporation.

INWARD-LOOKING VERSUS OUTWARD-LOOKING ECONOMIC POLICIES

One of the problems that developing countries face in trying to improve their growth rate is how to integrate their economies with the world economy. The basic question is whether they should encourage international trade with other countries or focus more on producing goods that substitute for international trade. There are two approaches.

In one approach, called the **import substitution strategy,** the developing country attempts to replace products that are imported from industrialized countries with products produced at home. This strategy tends to be inward-looking; laws

import substitution strategy: a trade policy designed to encourage local firms to produce goods that are normally imported into the country.

limiting imports coming from abroad are passed, and these are supplemented by subsidies to domestic industries. Taxes on imports—tariffs—are high. Firms may lobby their government to maintain or increase the subsidies or the tariffs which protect the firms from competition; such special interest lobbying is called *rent-seeking* by economists. An important example of this type of import substitution is the development of the steel industry in Brazil in the 1950s. The Brazilian government put tariffs on the import of foreign steel so that the Brazilian steel industry would have less competition.

An alternative way to increase growth is the **export-led strategy.** Under this strategy, the government of the developing country encourages international trade by expanding exports. Hence, the strategy tends to be outward-looking. Growth occurs through the manufacture and sale of products to other countries—shoes to America, black and white televisions to Europe, automobile tires to Japan. The aim of export-led growth is to increase trade rather than reduce trade. Although many countries that have followed export-led strategies have also had high tariffs on some commodities, such as agricultural goods, their strategies have been much more outward-looking than those of the import-substitution countries.

Table 33.2 shows the difference in economic growth in countries that have tried the import-substitution strategy compared to those that have tried the export-led growth strategy.

The table compares four countries: Brazil, Colombia, South Korea, and Tunisia (all developing countries) over a 23-year period. Brazil switched from an import-substitution strategy to an export-led growth strategy and saw increased economic growth. By the 1970s, economic growth in Brazil was in double digits, much higher than in the 1950s and early 1960s. The change was also dramatic in Colombia. The most dramatic is South Korea. The Korean success story, which began in the 1970s, seems related to the switch from an import-substitution strategy to one relying on trade and export growth. The same basic phenomenon is apparent in Tunisia as well as many other countries.

This experience indicates that a better strategy for increasing economic growth is to be outward-looking rather than inward-looking. A country's chance of catching up is greatly increased if it can adopt technology and use investment from abroad. By engaging in international trade, countries are able to learn more about technologies in other countries. For example, as South Korea's exports of electronic

export-led strategy: the government's encouragement of the economy's development by establishing an open trade policy and increasing exports.

Country	Period	Trade Strategy	Growth Rate
Brazil	1955–1960	Import substitution	6.9
Brazil	1960–1965	Import substitution	4.2
Brazil	1965–1970	Export-led	7.6
Brazil	1970–1976	Export-led	10.6
Colombia	1955–1960	Import substitution	4.6
Colombia	1960–1965	Import substitution	1.9
Colombia	1970–1976	Export-led	6.5
South Korea	1953–1960	Import substitution	5.2
South Korea	1960–1965	Export-led	6.5
South Korea	1970–1976	Export-led	10.3
Tunisia	1960–1970	Import substitution	4.6
Tunisia	1970–1976	Export-led	9.4

TABLE 33.2
Growth Rates for Different Trade Strategies in Four Countries, 1953–1976
(real GDP growth rate in percent per year)

equipment grew, the Koreans learned more about technology for producing electronic goods.

More countries appear to be changing their policies from inward-looking to outward-looking based on this experience. Mexico, for example, lowered its restrictions on imports in the mid-1980s and joined the United States and Canada in a free trade area in the 1990s. This approach to fewer restrictions on international markets parallels the developments that are removing restrictions on markets within the former centrally planned countries from Poland to China.

Review

▶ There are two alternative international strategies for developing economies: One is inward-looking, the other outward-looking.

▶ Import substitution replaces imports by domestic production: It limits imported goods and is inward-looking.

▶ Export-led growth tries to expand exports of manufactured products (textiles, shoes, clothing). It is outward-looking.

▶ The evidence shows that the export-led strategy works better; this is what would be predicted from economic growth theory.

CONCLUSION

In this chapter we have shown how productivity has increased in many countries because of higher capital per worker and technological change. In some countries there has been a convergence of productivity, with the poorer countries moving closer to the richer countries. However, for many developing countries, productivity has not been catching up and income per capita remains very low.

Among the possible explanations for the lack of catch-up are obstacles to the spread of technology, such as government restrictions on entrepreneurs and a shortage of human capital, and obstacles to higher capital per worker, such as low saving rates and low foreign investment. The removal of similar obstacles in Western Europe in the eighteenth century may have been the reason for the Industrial Revolution. Their removal today may result in another great growth wave in the developing economies.

In fact, there are already signs of the removal of such obstacles to economic growth. The movement from central planning to market systems in China, Vietnam, the countries of Eastern Europe and the former Soviet Union, and the greater reliance on markets in Latin America are examples. There are also signs of a resulting growth wave; growth in China and other countries of Asia has been particularly rapid as government restrictions on markets have been removed.

In the absence of retrenchments or setbacks from ethnic and military conflicts, we may see higher productivity growth in the poorer countries in the future than we have seen in the past. If so, the economic landscape of the world will be transformed.

Suppose, for example, that real GDP in the industrialized countries grows at a 2.5 percent pace for the next 50 years; this is higher than the 2 percent average rate of the 1990s. Suppose also that real GDP in all the other countries of the world grows at 5 percent per year; this is lower than the 6 percent pace of the developing Asian countries during the 1990s. With these growth rates, the countries we now classify as developing or in transition would produce 75 percent of world GDP in the year 2050; the countries we now classify as industrialized would produce 25 percent, a complete about-face from the current situation. This, of course, is an example, not a forecast, but it hints at some of the amazing possibilities for the future.

KEY POINTS

1. Economic growth theory pinpoints capital accumulation and technological change as the two key ingredients of productivity growth. In a world without obstacles to the spread of technology or to investment in new capital, growth theory predicts that poor regions will catch up to rich regions.

2. Catch-up has occurred in the states of the United States and among the industrialized countries but is distressingly absent from the developing countries.

3. Low incomes and poverty have persisted for the vast majority of the world's population while other countries get richer.

4. Insufficient capital accumulation in the poor countries, due to high population growth, low saving rates, or insufficient capital flows from the advanced countries, may have been part of the problem.

5. Higher population growth requires more investment in order to raise capital per worker.

6. Some countries may have poor growth performance because of restrictions on markets and the lack of property

rights. The lifting of those restrictions in Europe in the 1700s was a cause of the economic growth associated with the Industrial Revolution.

7. The removal of such restrictions may be a key to increased productivity and economic development.

8. Insufficient investment in human capital is another reason for low productivity growth in some countries.

9. Outward-looking economic policies that encourage the spread of technology and investment have worked better than inward-looking economic policies, as a comparison of different countries shows.

10. In many countries today, including Eastern Europe, Russia, Latin America, and China, there is great potential for higher economic growth as the market system is being encouraged and restrictions on entrepreneurs are being removed.

11. Another great growth wave would change the economic landscape of the whole world.

KEY TERMS

catch-up line
North-South problem
economic development
developing country
industrialized country

newly industrialized country
country in transition
informal economy
foreign direct investment
portfolio investment

International Monetary Fund (IMF)
World Bank
conditionality
import substitution strategy
export-led strategy

QUESTIONS FOR REVIEW

1. Why does economic growth theory predict that productivity and real income per capita will grow relatively more rapidly in poor countries?

2. Why is catch-up observed among the industrialized economies but not for the whole world?

3. Why is the identity that investment plus net exports equals saving important for understanding the flow of capital around the world?

4. What is the difference between foreign direct investment and portfolio investment?

5. Why is human capital important for the spread of technology?

6. What is the significance of conditionality for IMF loans?

7. What do government restrictions on entrepreneurs have to do with economic growth?

8. What harm does an informal economy cause?

9. Why does export-led growth appear to work better than import substitution?

PROBLEMS

1. Complete the following table assuming that the rate of growth of real GDP per capita stays constant. (*Hint:* see the appendix to Chapter 19.)

Country/ Region	Real GDP per Capita in 1999	Growth of Real GDP per Capita, 1999–2099 (annual percentage change)	Projected Real GDP per Capita in 2099
United States	$32,000	1.5	———
China	$ 3,400	7.5	———

2. What would be the effect of a decrease in the Japanese saving rate on the growth rate of developing countries? Why?

3. The rule of 72 gives the approximate doubling time of a variable if you know its rate of growth. For example, if the population of a country is 200 million and the rate of growth of the population is 2 percent per year, then it will take approximately 35 years for the country's population to reach 400 million. (See the appendix to Chapter 19 for a derivation.) Suppose real income per capita does not grow at all in the United States in the future. Suppose that the per capita growth rate is 4 percent per year in China. About how long will it take for China to catch up with the United States? What is likely to happen to the growth rates before this period of time passes? Use the per capita income data in problem 1.

4. Suppose a developing country does not allow foreign investment to flow into the country and, at the same time, it has a very low saving rate. Use the fact that saving equals investment and the growth accounting formula to explain why this country will have difficulty catching up with industrialized countries. What else can it do to improve its productivity if it does not allow capital in from outside the country?

5. Developed countries have shown that Malthus was wrong to ignore capital and technology, but he also ignored the possibility that people would have fewer children.

a) Examine the growth accounting formula to explain how a reduction in the growth rate of labor affects the growth rate of productivity. Assume that the proportion of the population that is in the labor force is constant.

b) In developing countries, people sometimes view children as a way to ensure that they have support in their old age. How will this attitude affect the growth rate of income per capita?

6. The states of the United States have moved toward each other in real income per capita over the past 100 years, but the countries of the world have not. What are the differences between state borders and country borders that might explain this problem?

7. Most developing countries have low saving rates and governments that run budget deficits. What will be required for such countries to have large increases in their capital stocks? What will happen if industrialized countries' saving rates decline as well? How does this affect the developing countries' prospects for catching up?

8. Which of the following will increase the likelihood of poor countries catching up to rich countries, and which will decrease the likelihood? Explain.

a) Industrialized countries do not allow their technology to be bought or leased by firms in developing countries.

b) Industrialized countries increase the conditional aid that is available for developing countries.

c) Worldwide saving rates fall.

d) Countries place high tariffs on importation of goods.

e) The legal system of developing countries is improved to protect the rights of entrepreneurs.

f) Governments in developing countries make use of their international aid to buy armaments from developed countries.

g) Investment in human capital increases in the developing countries.

9. Plot on a scatter diagram the data for the Asian countries that appears at the top of the next page. Does there appear to be a catch-up line in the scatter diagram?

Country	Per Capita Real GDP in 1965 (1984 U.S. dollars)	Average Annual Rate of Growth from 1965 to 1985 (%)
Thailand	360	4.0
Pakistan	210	2.4
Philippines	380	1.9
China	110	5.1
Malaysia	330	4.3
Indonesia	190	4.6

10. The International Monetary Fund (IMF) estimated that a decline in the world saving rate by 1 percentage point, due to a decline in Japanese saving, would increase the world interest rate by about 75 basis points.[1] Using a diagram like the one in the box on page 868, explain the reasoning behind the IMF's estimate. How large an interest rate rise would you predict from the diagram in the box?

1. *World Economic Outlook,* International Monetary Fund, May 1995, p. 88.

34

Emerging Market
Economies

There is perhaps no greater economic policy challenge and opportunity around the world today than the emergence of market economies. The tearing down of the Berlin Wall, the end of central planning in East Germany, and the unification of Germany are stirring symbols of this emergence. So is the end of central planning in Russia, the countries of central and Eastern Europe, and countries in the Transcaucasian and central Asian regions, such as Armenia, Georgia, and Mongolia. The emergence of market economies is also seen in China and Vietnam. A common feature of these countries is that a major transition is occurring—a transition from a *command economy,* or a centrally planned economy in which the government sets prices and decides *what, how,* and *for whom* goods should be produced, to a *market economy* that is based much more on markets and freely determined prices, in which most of these decisions are left to individuals.

Similar attempts to reduce government restrictions on markets are occurring in many other countries in Latin America and Asia. Although these economies were not formerly centrally planned, international and domestic trade was tightly restricted, and major parts of the economies were government owned. In recent years, Argentina, Chile, Mexico, and India have either reduced

government control of large segments of their economies or encouraged closer ties with market economies around the world, or both. Mexico recently joined a free trade agreement with the United States and Canada, while Chile and other countries of Latin America are anxious to join.

Table 34.1 provides a list of countries designated by *Economist* magazine as emerging market economies; clearly the list goes well beyond the former centrally planned economies. Even though the *Economist*'s list is not comprehensive (neither Mongolia, Ukraine, nor Vietnam are included), it demonstrates that the phenomenon of emerging markets is very widespread.

Although the long-run goals of the emerging market economies are to raise economic growth and improve living standards, the short-run problems of moving from a centrally planned economy to a market economy are particularly difficult. In fact, economic growth has faltered in some countries that are trying to make a transition from central planning to a market economy, especially in central and Eastern Europe and the former Soviet Union. People of these countries have shown signs of frustration and impatience with the transition.

In this chapter we take a special look at those emerging market economies that are making a transition from

TABLE 34.1

Emerging Market Economies as Defined by the *Economist*

	Population (millions)		Population (millions)		Population (millions)
China	1,260	Thailand	64	Portugal	11
Hong Kong	6	Argentina	36	South Africa	51
India	1,018	Brazil	170	Turkey	70
Indonesia	219	Chile	15	Czech Republic	11
Malaysia	22	Colombia	39	Hungary	10
Philippines	82	Mexico	103	Poland	40
Singapore	3	Venezuela	23	Russia	151
South Korea	48	Greece	11	**TOTAL**	**3,491**
Taiwan	22	Israel	6		

Source: Population figures are projections for the year 2000 from the *Statistical Abstract of the United States, 1995,* pp. 845–846.

central planning. To understand what is happening now, we need to look back at what economic life was like under central planning. We first show how central planning grew out of the communist revolutions that were induced by the Marxist criticism of market economies. We then examine the aim of market reforms, alternative approaches to reform, and the experience of several economies during the transition.

> **command economy:** an economy in which the government determines prices and production; also called a centrally planned economy. (Ch. 1)

> **market economy:** an economy characterized by freely determined prices and the free exchange of goods and services in markets. (Ch. 1)

CENTRALLY PLANNED ECONOMIES

With few exceptions, such as the North Korean economy, centrally planned economies no longer exist. But there are important economic lessons to be learned from the experience of the many countries that tried central planning during the twentieth century. A well-known expert on the ideas underlying communism, socialism, and the market economy, Robert Heilbroner, summarizes the lessons this way: "The Soviet Union, China and Eastern Europe have given us the clearest possible proof that capitalism organizes the material affairs of humankind more satisfactorily than socialism."[1]

A socialist economy, also called **socialism,** is an economic system in which the government owns the capital—factories, stores, farms, and equipment—and decisions about production and employment are made by those who run the government as part of a central plan for the economy. In contrast, in a market economy, also called **capitalism,** individuals own the capital, and decisions about production and

> **socialism:** an economic system in which the government owns and controls all the capital and makes decisions about prices and quantities as part of a central plan.

> **capitalism:** an economic system based on a market economy in which capital is individually owned, and production and employment decisions are decentralized.

1. See Robert Heilbroner, "The Triumph of Capitalism," *The New Yorker,* January 1993, pp. 98–109.

communism: an economic system in which all capital is collectively owned.

employment are decentralized and made by many individuals buying and selling goods in markets. The term **communism** refers to a theoretical situation where all the people of a country *collectively* own the capital and the land without direct government ownership. Those who advocated communism viewed collective ownership by the people as a long-term goal: A socialist economy would evolve into communism with the government gradually withering away. However, today most economists and historians use the word *communism,* to mean the same thing as *socialism,* as defined here.

Not all socialist economies are the same; there are different degrees of government ownership and centralization. For example, in some socialist economies, farmers could sell a portion of their agricultural output and use the proceeds to buy farm equipment or even consumer goods. Similarly, not all market economies are the same; in most market economies, the government owns the public infrastructure capital and is involved in the production of education, health services, and other goods. The degree of government involvement differs from market economy to market economy. For example, a much larger fraction of medical care is produced by the government in the United Kingdom than is produced by the government in the United States.

However, in reality the differences between socialist economies as a group and market economies as a group are much larger than the differences between the economies within each group. In other words, there is a "night-and-day" distinction between centrally planned economies with government ownership of firms that do not have to compete and market economies with private ownership of firms that do have to compete. To understand this distinction, we need to examine how centrally planned economies worked.

Central Planning in the Soviet Union

V. I. Lenin and the Bolshevik party (also known as the Communist party) gained control of the government of Russia in the October Revolution of 1917. At this time, the Russian economy was much less developed than most of Western Europe. GDP per capita in Russia was less than one-third that of the United Kingdom or the United States. The economy was mostly agricultural. Although large-scale manufacturing industries were growing, they were still much smaller than those in Germany, the United Kingdom, or the United States. For more than 1,000 years, before the communists gained control, Russia had been ruled by tsars, who held enormous power and resisted economic and political change.

For those reasons, the Russian people were dissatisfied with both their economy and their political system. Lenin and the Bolsheviks seized the opportunity, forcing through a completely new economic system. Most significantly, Lenin decreed that private firms would be taken over by the government, a process called **nationalization.** The Bolsheviks immediately nationalized the banking system, and by mid-1918, a massive nationalization of large- and small-scale industry was under way. Although the alleged reason for the Bolshevik takeover was to give workers control of the economy, Lenin soon rejected worker control. He argued that people like himself were needed to run the economy on behalf of the workers. He began controlling production from the center, appointing administrators to run each industry from offices in Moscow. In doing so he laid the foundation of a command economy—through which government *diktats,* or commands, rather than prices and decentralized markets, would determine what was produced. In 1921, **Gosplan,** the state planning commission, was established. In 1922 the Communist party

nationalization: the taking over of private firms by the government.

Gosplan: the planning agency of the former Soviet Union.

Karl Marx, 1818–1883

BORN:
Trier, Germany, 1818

EDUCATION:
University of Bonn, 1835
University of Berlin, 1836–1841
University of Jena, doctorate in philosophy, 1841

JOBS:
Editor, freelance journalist, Cologne, Paris, Brussels, 1842–1848
Independent study, freelance journalist, London 1849–1883

MAJOR PUBLICATIONS:
Communist Manifesto (with Friedrich Engels), 1848; *Das Kapital,* 1867
(Vol. I); Russian translation, 1868; English translation, 1886

What led to the rejection of markets and the acceptance of socialism in Russia, China, and Eastern Europe in the twentieth century? Although personal ambition, war, and political repression were factors, the economic writings of Karl Marx in the nineteenth century played a key role.

Karl Marx was an economist and social philosopher, but he was also an eloquent journalist and polemicist. Most of his work as an economist was spent analyzing capitalism. His most famous prediction was that capitalism would eventually die of its own internal contradictions.

Marx originally went to college to study law, but he soon was drawn to the writings of the philosopher Hegel, who characterized history as a struggle between conflicting forces; each idea (thesis) generated its opposite (antithesis), which it then had to contend with until a new thesis (synthesis) was created. This Hegelian view provided Marx with a framework to study the historical development of capitalism.

Marx soon became an outspoken critic of the existing economic and political system in Europe. He spent much of his adult life in London, studying and writing in the archives of the British Museum. Marx eked out a modest living—his wife and children struggling at the brink of poverty—through his journalistic writings and through financial assistance from his long-time friend and collaborator, Friedrich Engels.

Marx's polemical writings were influential. The widely read and often-quoted *Communist Manifesto* was a short pamphlet written in 1848 by Marx and Engels. It was nothing less than a stirring call for a revolution:

A specter is haunting Europe—the specter of communism. . . . Let the ruling classes tremble at a Communist revolution. The proletarians have nothing to lose but their chains. They have a world to win. Working men of all countries, unite!

Surprisingly, perhaps, Marx and Engels found much to admire in capitalism. They wrote that the *bourgeoisie*—the class that owned or ran the business firms

. . . has accomplished wonders far surpassing the Egyptian pyramids, Roman aqueducts, and Gothic cathedrals. . . . [D]uring its rule of scarcely one hundred years, [it] has created more massive and more colossal productive forces than have all preceding generations together.

It is in Marx's economic writings—longer and more ponderous—that his detailed criticism of capitalism is found. In particular, his treatise *Das Kapital* aimed to show why Adam Smith and David Ricardo were wrong in their praise of the market economy. For example, referring to Smith's idea that workers would benefit from increased labor productivity due to the division of labor or to more machinery, Marx wrote in *Das Kapital:*

Adam Smith, by a fundamentally perverted analysis, arrives at [this] absurd conclusion. . . . In truth, Adam Smith breaks his investigation off, just where its difficulties begin.

Marx argued instead that increases in labor productivity would not benefit workers; capitalists, trying to maintain their profits, would keep workers' wages from rising. But history shows that wages increased by huge amounts in the 150 years since Marx wrote.

Although socialism may have originally seemed like an attractive alternative to the market system, socialism's own severe problems eventually became obvious. Surprisingly, however, Marx wrote almost nothing about how a socialist economy would work. His writings focused entirely on capitalism.

Sources of quotes: Karl Marx and Friedrich Engels, *Communist Manifesto,* 1848, in *Essential Works of Marxism,* ed. A. P. Mendel (New York: Bantam Books, 1961), pp. 1, 44, and 16–17; Karl Marx, *Capital: A Critique of Political Economy* (New York: Modern Library, 1906), p. 647.

established the Soviet Union, incorporating Ukraine and other countries along with Russia into one large command economy.

At the very start, the experiment in central planning was unsuccessful. Production fell and inflation rose dramatically. Much of the blame for the early lack of success could be placed on the civil war between the communists (the Reds) and the anticommunists (the Whites). Moreover, Lenin had little guidance on how to set up a socialist economy. Karl Marx, whose analysis of capitalism provided the intellectual support for the communist revolution, wrote virtually nothing about how a socialist economy or central planning would work (see the box on Karl Marx). In any case, the early 1920s saw a retreat from central planning and a partial reinstatement of the market economy under Lenin's New Economic Policy. But with Lenin's death in 1924 and Joseph Stalin becoming leader of the Communist party's in 1928, central planning was reinstated with even more force than previously.

The Five-Year Plans

The goal of catching up with Western Europe and the United States came quickly to dominate Stalin's thinking about the economy. Catching up required raising the level of investment in factories and industrial equipment, increasing labor hours, and shifting workers out of agriculture into industry. Stalin wanted to do this rapidly and on a massive scale. To do so he needed to raise investment in heavy industry and reduce consumption. He saw a command economy as the only way to accomplish his goal.

five-year plan: a document that stated production goals for the entire Soviet economy for the succeeding five years.

Stalin, therefore, gave Gosplan much more authority to run the economy from the center. In 1928 Gosplan issued a **five-year plan** stipulating production goals for the entire economy. This five-year plan turned out to be the first of a succession of many more five-year plans, and the methods of central planning that would last for 60 years were put in place. Gosplan, under command of the Communist party leaders, controlled production not only for Russia but for the entire Soviet Union, which was spread over eleven time zones and covered one-sixth of the world's land area.

state enterprise: an organization, analogous to a firm in a market economy, that is owned and controlled by the government.

Production of most goods took place at **state enterprises**—organizations similar in function to business firms in market economies but owned and controlled by the government. Stalin also virtually abolished private property in agriculture in the Soviet Union. He created **collectivized farms,** through which the government took ownership of most farmland, farm equipment, and livestock.

collectivized farm: a farm in a planned economy that is in theory collectively owned by peasants, but controlled by the government.

By setting **production targets** for millions of products throughout the Soviet Union, Gosplan tried to control what and how much should be produced at each state enterprise and collectivized farm. Through this method Stalin was successful in raising the level of investment and reducing people's consumption and thereby rapidly expanding the number of machines and factories devoted to manufacturing. In order to make sure that the labor force was sufficient for this rapid industrialization, the communist government also placed restrictions on workers. For example, new graduates were assigned jobs in different parts of the country, and restrictions on moving to and living in certain areas made it difficult for workers to change jobs if they wanted to.

production target: a goal set for the production of goods and services in a planned economy.

Centrally Controlled Prices

Prices for individual goods were also set at the center, but Gosplan rarely set these prices at levels that would equate the quantity supplied with the quantity demanded. Shortages were typical. Food prices were set very low, resulting in food shortages.

The managers of state enterprises frequently found themselves having to wait for parts or inputs to production. At other times they produced an excess supply that no one could use. To be sure, when shortages got very severe, markets would develop: Enterprise managers in desperate need of materials would offer side payments, or bribes, to other managers or workers to get the materials. These markets operated outside of the normal central planning process and were called *gray* or *black markets*. Some economists feel that these markets enabled central planning to function by reducing crucial shortages.

Recall from Chapter 2 that prices have three roles: They transmit information, coordinate actions by providing incentives, and affect the distribution of income. In a market economy, a change in demand or supply causes a change in the price, which transmits information throughout the economy. Such changes in prices were thwarted by central planning. Central planners simply did not have enough information to know how to change the prices. Thus, the information transmission role of prices did not exist.

The coordination role of prices was deemphasized, although the central planners recognized that prices affected incentives. The managers of the state enterprises were given rewards for hitting production targets, but the rewards were not designed in a way that encouraged efficient management practices. To poke fun at Gosplan, a famous cartoon showed a picture of a nail factory producing *one* large but useless 500-ton nail in order to meet the factory's production target for 500 tons of nails. There were also few rewards for inventing new products or even for finding more efficient ways to produce the existing products. State enterprises thus became very inefficient. Competition between enterprises was discouraged, and production became highly concentrated in a few firms in each industry.

Gosplan did not ignore the role of prices in affecting the distribution of income. Prices were held low on most staple items and high on the few consumer durable items that were produced. By setting prices this way, Gosplan tried to make the distribution of goods and services more equal. But income distribution was by no means egalitarian under central planning. Communist party officials and enterprise managers were given extra payments in the form of better housing, transportation, and the opportunity to shop in stores that contained consumer goods unavailable to ordinary consumers. Because virtually all prices were set by the government, there was no measured inflation, although with prices set too low for many products the economy was frequently in a condition of shortage. The central bank (Gosbank) was the only bank in the country. It provided loans to state enterprises and collectivized farms in the amounts Gosplan instructed. Gosbank also issued currency (rubles) and accepted deposits from consumers.

Gosplan did not have to worry much about taxes because it could set the price of everything. For example, to finance the production of military goods, the central planners could set the price of inputs to defense production low and the price of defense goods high. They could also simply order increased production of military goods and reduced production of some other goods.

Trade Between the Soviet Union and Eastern Europe

After World War II when communist governments were installed in Poland, Hungary, Czechoslovakia, East Germany, Romania, and Bulgaria, Soviet-style central planning was extended to each of the countries of Eastern Europe. How did international trade take place between the Soviet Union and its close neighbors in the Soviet bloc?

Trade among these countries and the Soviet Union took place through a trading organization called the *Council for Mutual Economic Assistance.* The trade did not take place at world market prices. For example, the Soviet Union, rich in energy resources such as oil and natural gas, would supply energy to the Eastern European countries at prices well below the market prices prevailing throughout the world. The prices were established through political negotiations between the governments, which undoubtedly involved noneconomic considerations such as the placement of military troops and weapons. In exchange for the low-priced energy, the Eastern European countries would provide manufactured goods, though those were of a lesser quality than similar goods produced in the West. Prices for trade between the countries of Eastern Europe were similarly negotiated. Thus, neither domestic nor international trade between the centrally planned economies was market based.

Technological Change and the Quality of Goods

By most accounts Stalin's forced investment and forced labor strategy did increase economic growth in the 1930s in the Soviet Union. In the years after World War II both the Soviet Union and Eastern Europe grew rapidly. However, it eventually became apparent that great inefficiencies associated with central planning were starting to offset the high levels of investment and labor force participation. The growth of technology began to slow down. Investment rates and labor force participation rates had reached their limits, and technology growth was lagging seriously. Environmental pollution was severe in cities such as Warsaw and Bucharest.

State-owned retail shops had few consumer goods, and those they had were of very poor quality. Long lines were evident at stores, especially those selling anything special, such as candy bars or gasoline. The availability of goods was also poor.

One of the apparent puzzles about central planning was its success in certain areas. The space exploration achievements of the Soviet Union, for example, were outstanding enough for the United States to get involved in the space race. They were the source of President Kennedy's goal of a manned flight to the moon.

One explanation for this success was that an enormous amount of resources were put into defense production. Just as East German athletes dominated the Olympics because of all the resources that went into their training, a centrally planned economy could excel at certain things. Students with talents useful for defense production—mathematics, science, and engineering—were given excellent training in the Soviet Union. Even inefficiency can be offset by enough resources. Moreover, as mentioned previously, economists found that managers in defense production had ways to go outside the central planning system, essentially using gray markets to obtain parts or equipment in short supply. Such markets were tolerated more frequently in the defense industry than in consumer goods industries.

From Perestroika to the End of the Soviet Union

Pressures to reform the central planning system began in the 1960s and 1970s and gained momentum in the 1980s. In 1985, Mikhail Gorbachev became the leader of the Communist party. To deal with the problems of inefficiency, poor quality, and slow technology growth, he tried to change central planning in a process called **perestroika,** which translates as "restructuring." Perestroika changes were put into the twelfth five-year plan, formulated in 1985. For example, enterprise managers were to be made more accountable for their actions through worker and public criti-

perestroika: the restructuring of the Soviet economy by reforming the central planning process.

cism. By 1989, however, it was clear that perestroika was doing little to raise economic growth. Economists complained perestroika was piecemeal because it continued to rely on the central planning process to set prices. An alternative plan, called the Shatalin Plan, after one of Gorbachev's advisers, would have used the market much more. However, it was rejected by Gorbachev because it would have initiated a transition to a market economy and thereby done away with central planning.

But perestroika started a process that would not easily be stopped. The open criticism of the central planning process made it acceptable to criticize the political authorities. Soon people in Eastern Europe were criticizing their own governments and their close ties with the Soviet Union. Gorbachev decided to "let go" of the Eastern European countries in 1989, and by 1990 the republics of the Soviet Union also wanted their freedom. Gradually the Russian Republic began to take over the responsibility for the Soviet Union. After an aborted military coup in 1991, Gorbachev resigned and the Soviet Union ceased to exist. Boris Yeltsin, the president of Russia, disbanded central planning and began to follow a more comprehensive series of reforms aimed at creating a market economy. Yeltsin's own reforms have also been opposed, and a political struggle will determine how successful Russia is in implementing the reforms.

Soviet-Style Central Planning in China

The Chinese communists under Mao Zedong gained control of China in 1949. Mao's goals were similar to those of the Soviet Union—to rapidly industrialize. In fact, Mao originally viewed the Soviet Union as an economic model. He imported Soviet-style central planning to China. Under Mao and the Communist party, most economic production was controlled by the central government, just as in the Soviet Union. In the 1950s, growth was rapid due to heavy investment.

Starting in 1958, Mao began the "Great Leap Forward," which briefly raised economic growth by promoting a warlike work effort throughout the country calling for a massive expansion of production. But the Great Leap Forward could raise economic growth for only a short period. The communist spirit was not enough to make people work hard year after year. The Great Leap Forward ended in a huge decline in production.

A misguided attempt to revive the spirit of the communist revolution took place during the Cultural Revolution in the late 1960s. But the Cultural Revolution ended up severely hurting the Chinese economy. Productive managers and technicians were forced to leave their jobs and do manual labor. Universities were closed. By the late 1970s it was also clear that economic reform was necessary in China, a subject we will return to later in the chapter.

Review

▶ Central control of the economy began in Russia soon after the Bolsheviks rose to power. Central planning grew and dominated the Soviet economy under Stalin in the 1920s and 1930s and spread to Eastern Europe and China after World War II.

▶ Although the high investment and high labor force participation led to strong growth initially, central planning eventually broke down. Inefficiency, poor-quality goods, and slow growth of technology were the most obvious problems.

ALTERNATIVE PATHS TO A MARKET ECONOMY

How does a country change from central planning to a market economy? Recall that the first action of the Communists in Russia was to abolish private property rights and nationalize industry. One of the most difficult parts of reform has been to reverse this step, restoring private ownership and privatizing state enterprises.

The Goals of Reform

Defining the goals of reform is simple; getting there is what is difficult. The goals are simply the essential ingredients of a market economy, as defined in Chapter 2. To summarize, these are:

▶ *Freely determined prices* evolving out of decentralized markets rather than prices controlled by government.

▶ *Property rights and incentives,* which the Hungarian economist Janos Kornai argues in his book *The Road to a Free Economy* are the most important and frequently underemphasized part of a market economy: Decentralizing decisions without prices providing incentives through property rights will not create efficiency.

▶ *Competitive markets* so that the price system leads to an efficient allocation of goods, labor, and capital.

▶ *Freedom to trade at home and abroad,* which is needed in order to achieve the efficiencies associated with comparative advantage and economies of scale.

▶ *A role for government* in establishing a policy that keeps inflation in check and that efficiently collects taxes to pay for public goods and provides a social safety net.

▶ *A role for nongovernment organizations,* because in a market economy many transactions occur within organizations—as, for example, when an entrepreneur sets up a new firm to market a new product.

There is general agreement that any successful transition from central planning to a market economy must achieve these features of a market economy. A legal system specifying property rights and enforcing contracts must be set up. A banking and currency system must be established. A system of tax collection must be put in place. As is true of many areas of economics, however, there is disagreement about the speed of the transition.

Shock Therapy or Gradualism?

shock therapy: the abrupt introduction of free markets in a formerly centrally planned economy.

gradualism: the slow phasing-in of free market reforms.

A major question about the transition to a market economy is how fast it should be. The two basic alternatives are **shock therapy** and **gradualism.** Under shock therapy, or the *big bang* approach, all the elements of the market economy are put in place at once. Under gradualism, the reforms are phased in slowly.

One of the most remarkable aspects of the transition from central planning in the countries of Eastern Europe was the strong commitment to move to market economies on the part of government policymakers and the general public at the start of the reforms in 1989 and 1990. Most officials went out of their way to emphasize that they were not looking for a third way and to recognize the need to move to a Western-style market-based economic system in order to raise living standards.

Such positive attitudes about reform were part of the motivation behind shock therapy. Those in favor of a shock-therapy approach argue that such positive attitudes are probably temporary, creating a brief window of opportunity for reform. The enthusiasm for reform may diminish if, as is likely, the reforms do not bring noticeable improvements quickly. Thus, rather than see the reform movement aborted in midstream, it is better to sweep through the reforms quickly. This was one of the arguments for the shock-therapy approach that was used in Poland.

Another argument in favor of shock therapy is that all the elements of reform are interrelated. Making state enterprises private without competition, for example, could make things worse. And freeing up the price of energy products will reduce the government subsidy needed to finance the energy-producing enterprises. This will reduce the government budget deficit. Also, removing trade barriers and establishing a sound currency will be a guide to what the process should be as the free price system gropes for a new set of relative prices.

The arguments against shock therapy are that people require time to adjust to new circumstances. Enterprises producing medical supplies in Moscow might be used to getting cotton from central Asia, but if free trade makes it more attractive for central Asia to sell cotton in Japan, then production in Moscow will be disrupted.

Even though the production of low-quality black and white television sets in Warsaw is inefficient compared with imports from Malaysia, it might be better to move gradually to free trade. This would give the firms time to move into some other business and the workers time to find other jobs. The arguments against shock therapy are similar to the arguments against a fast disinflation strategy or against an immediate reduction in tariff barriers.

Review

▶ The goals of a transition to a market economy are much easier to state than to achieve; the goals can be defined in terms of the key ingredients of a market economy.

▶ Shock therapy and gradualism are two different paths to a market-based economy.

ECONOMIC REFORM IN PRACTICE

What has been the experience of those countries trying to make a transition from central planning to a market-based economy? Table 34.2 presents data on real GDP growth in the formerly centrally planned economies of central and Eastern Europe and the former Soviet Union. A quick glance at this table shows how difficult the transition has been. Although these countries had slow economic growth under communism, the period of transition has seen deep recession. In some countries the

●────────────────────

TABLE 34.2
Real GDP Growth for Some Economies in Transition

	Real GDP Growth (percent)	
	1992	1994
Central and Eastern Europe		
Albania	−9.7	7.4
Estonia	−21.6	6.0
Hungary	−4.3	2.6
Latvia	−35.2	2.0
Lithuania	−56.6	1.5
Poland	2.6	6.0
Romania	−10.1	3.4
Ukraine	−17.0	−23.0
Russia	−19.0	−15.0
Caucasus and Central Asia		
Azerbaijan	−22.1	−21.9
Georgia	−42.7	−10.0
Kazakhstan	−14.0	−25.0
Tajikistan	−30.0	−16.3
Uzbekistan	−11.1	−2.6

Source: World Economic Outlook, May 1995. By permission of International Monetary Fund.

decline in real GDP has been nearly as large as the decline in real GDP during the Great Depression in the United States. There are significant signs of improvement in the countries of central and Eastern Europe, except for Ukraine. But Russia and many of the central Asian countries continue to suffer transition problems.

To understand the problems of transition, we must look more carefully at the countries undertaking the transitions. Consider two countries—Poland and China—that have been undergoing a transition for several years and that have achieved positive economic growth.

Reforms in Poland

Poland was the first country in Eastern Europe to start a transition to a market economy. The Polish program has typified the shock-therapy approach.

Four months after the reform program was put in place in Poland, there were many visible signs of its effects, including a decline in inflation and a reduction of shortages. Inflation, which averaged 420 percent in 1989 and 1990, had fallen to 25 percent by 1992, but the adjustment costs, as evidenced by large declines in production and employment, were painful. Real GDP declined by 12 percent in 1990 and another 7 percent in 1991. However, by 1992 real GDP had stopped falling and showed a small increase. By 1994 economic growth was 6 percent, as shown in Table 34.2.

The Polish stabilization program made use of several policy initiatives. Government expenditures and the budget deficit were reduced sharply, largely through a reduction in government subsidies to state enterprises and a halting of public infrastructure investment. Most prices were deregulated at once and were left to be determined by state enterprises or private firms. Coal prices increased significantly, but internal transportation prices and rents remained low. Wage growth was controlled by government guidelines.

The result of these policies was a substantial decline in demand. There was also a reduction in shortages—the lines of people waiting to be served in butcher shops disappeared, for example. This reduction was brought on partly by the decline in demand, but also because free prices began to bring the quantity supplied into equality with the quantity demanded. Goods started appearing on the shelves, and firms could get intermediate inputs without long delays. Imported consumer goods, most noticeably fruit and vegetables, were more available. The trade account went into surplus in 1990 with exports increasing rapidly and imports declining rapidly.

At the start of the reform program, employment declined surprisingly little despite the large declines in production. The unemployment rate increased only to about 2 percent of the work force in the first few months of the program, but then unemployment increased sharply. Many workers were laid off because the state enterprises needed to reduce wage costs in order to avoid losses as the demand for their products dropped.

In order for a market economy to take root, it is necessary that existing state enterprises be privatized, a process called **privatization,** and that new private firms be able to start up. Moreover, private investment from abroad provides technological know-how. Privatization helps provide managers with the incentive to allocate resources efficiently and increase productivity.

privatization: the process of converting a government enterprise into a privately owned enterprise.

The Polish government submitted a privatization bill to the Parliament after the economic reforms began in 1990, but it moved slowly because of extensive debates. The main controversial issue was over who owned the state enterprises that were being sold. Hence, privatization was one part of the Polish reform program that was gradual.

A useful assessment of the Polish economic reforms comes from the person who implemented them firsthand on a day-to-day basis. Leszek Balcerowicz, who was the Polish finance minister in charge of the reforms, put it this way in 1993:

Even successful economic reforms generate some dissatisfaction. Such reforms transform hidden unemployment into open unemployment and produce shifts in the relative pay and prestige of many groups. New entrepreneurs, managers, lawyers, accountants, etc., are on the way up and—as a result—some powerful groups such as miners are on the way down. Not everybody can make a direct use of radically enlarged economic freedom, and those who can't often look with envy at the new ingroups.

But it is a mistake to reject the radical economic reforms simply because they produce these side effects. Postponing difficult steps is even more costly and risky socially, as a look at Ukraine or Russia shows. Radical reforms, as distinct from muddling through, also produce economic dynamism. Despite inherited hyperinflation and shortages, Poland has had a positive rate of growth since late 1991, and this year it is going to be the fastest growing country in Europe. Poland's decline in aggregate consumption in 1990–91 was by far the smallest among the Central and Eastern European countries.[2]

Reforms in China

Market-based reforms began in China earlier than in the former Soviet Union. The first reforms were in the agriculture sector. By the late 1970s, the Chinese government was leasing land back to individual farmers in order to give them more incentive to produce. The reform resulted in a huge increase in the growth rate of farm

2. From, "Why the Leftists Won the Polish Election, " from *The Wall Street Journal,* September 28, 1993, Section A, p. 10.

output. Agriculture production grew by 3 percent per year from 1952 to 1978; from 1978 (when the reforms began) to 1981, the growth rate was about 6 percent per year. Moreover, the increased efficiency in agriculture has increased the supply of labor in the industrial sector.

By the mid-1980s, about the same time as perestroika was starting in the Soviet Union, economic reforms were already spreading beyond the farm sector. Individual state enterprises were first given more discretion to experiment with new products and to use the profits generated from those products. As in the case of agriculture, industrial enterprises were leased to the managers, who could then keep part of the profits. As a result of these reforms, real GDP growth increased rapidly. Economic growth averaged a remarkably rapid 9.6 percent per year from 1987 to 1994. During the 1990s real GDP was falling in Russia.

China also reduced restrictions on foreign trade. In fact, much of China's growth has come from producing goods for foreign trade. Exports grew even more rapidly than real GDP. However, reform of exchange rates and monetary policy came much later in China. Free exchange of the local currency in terms of foreign currency was fully established only in 1993. And by the early 1990s, inflation was starting to become a problem in China. The inflation rate reached 22 percent in 1994.

To summarize, the overall reform in China has been much more gradual than in Poland. But economists continue to debate whether the gradual reform is better or worse than shock therapy.

Review

▶ Poland took the lead in major economic reform in Eastern Europe. Its reform program is the prototype of shock therapy.

▶ The transition has been hard on the Polish economy. However, real GDP growth started increasing in 1992 and reached 6 percent in 1994. Institutions have been put in place that will help foster the market economy in the future.

▶ China started its market-based reforms in the late 1970s by selling off a large amount of land to the farmers. Controls on state enterprises have been lifted more gradually.

ECONOMIC FREEDOM AND POLITICAL FREEDOM

Free markets and political freedom are not the same thing. Free markets, or economic freedom, allow people to engage freely in trade without restriction. Political freedom allows people to engage in free speech or to vote for their political representatives without restriction.

In principle a society can have political freedom without economic freedom—people could vote for central planning and price controls. Or a society could have economic freedom without political freedom: A dictator could allow people to trade without restrictions. Economists and political scientists have long debated whether there is a tendency for political freedom and economic freedom to exist together.

In abolishing private property and establishing central planning it is clear that Lenin and Stalin placed severe restrictions on people's political freedom. Indeed, millions who refused to go along with Stalin's program were imprisoned or executed. Thus, as practiced, socialism stifled both economic and political freedom. By abolishing private property it eliminated one of the key ingredients of a free market economy. But by abolishing democracy where it existed, or preventing its establishment through totalitarian dictatorship, it also restricted political freedom.

Central planning as practiced in the Soviet Union, China, and Eastern Europe resulted in a great loss of economic freedom along with a great loss of political freedom. Central planning was run by dictatorships. In order to carry out the collectivization of agriculture and forced investment and labor strategy of the 1930s the Soviet government had to imprison or execute many people. And the effort to restore a market economy and end central planning in Russia and Eastern Europe has been associated with an increase in democracy and political freedom.

However, the association of political and economic restrictions under communism does not prove that economic freedom and political freedom are necessarily connected. Throughout history there are examples where economic freedom has increased while political freedom has been repressed and vice versa. Many refer to China in the late 1980s as an example: A highly publicized and televised confrontation between dissident students and the government in Beijing indicated that the move toward free markets was not necessarily a move to political freedom.

Review

▶ The relationship between political freedom and economic freedom has long been of interest to economists and political scientists.

▶ History has shown that there is no causal relationship between democracy and free markets. There is, however, a close relationship between economic progress and political freedom. Most countries today with high real GDP per capita are also democracies with few restrictions on political freedom.

CONCLUSION

It was the economic failure of central planning and strict state control that led to socialism's demise. The failure of the centrally planned economy in East Germany in comparison with the success of the market economy in West Germany was as close as the real world ever gets to a controlled experiment. But if the emerging market economies do not deliver economic success for the people of these regions—a success that will be as obvious as was the failure of socialism—it is likely that there will be more changes, perhaps for the worse. And the success or failure of the market reforms in one country strongly influences what goes on elsewhere. Policymakers in Latin American countries say that the spirit of economic and political reform in those countries was stimulated by the "revolution of 1989" in Eastern Europe.

As we have seen in this chapter, the countries that are attempting a transition to a market economy have a difficult task before them. There have been setbacks, and there are likely to be more. The people of the United States, Japan, and Europe have a historic opportunity to participate and support the emerging market economies through developing links, investing, and providing technical cooperation, assistance, and advice. They have much to gain if the transition is successful.

KEY POINTS

1. The term *emerging market economies* usually refers to both former centrally planned economies making the transition to market economies and to developing economies that have recently increased privatization and reduced restrictions on trade.

2. Central planning and state control grew out of the communist revolutions under Lenin in Russia in 1917 and under Mao in China in 1949. Central planning was extended to central and Eastern Europe after World War II. At communism's height, over one-third of the world's population lived in centrally planned economies.

3. By mounting an intellectual criticism of the classical economists' model, Marx spearheaded the communist revolutions that eventually led to central planning.

4. Most centrally planned economies grew rapidly in their early stages due to heavy investment, but eventually productivity growth slowed down sharply and even declined.

5. The transition from central planning to a free market economy is much more difficult than the reverse transition. The road from socialism to free markets will be long, with the gains perhaps not noticeable for many years.

6. There are two different approaches to transition: shock therapy and gradualism.

KEY TERMS

socialism
capitalism
communism
nationalization
Gosplan

five-year plan
state enterprise
collectivized farms
production targets
perestroika

shock therapy
gradualism
privatization

QUESTIONS FOR REVIEW

1. When did central planning begin, and why?

2. What led to dissatisfaction with central planning and the end of socialism in Russia?

3. What comparison of countries is most useful for demonstrating the inefficiencies of central planning?

4. What are the six goals of an economic reform program?

5. What is the difference between shock therapy and

gradualism in the transition to a market economy?

6. What political argument favors shock therapy?

7. In what sense was the Polish reform program shock therapy, and in what sense was it more gradual?

8. Describe the difference between economic freedom and political freedom.

PROBLEMS

1. In 1960 Mao Zedong wrote, "The whole Socialist camp headed by the Soviet Union . . . now accounts for nearly 40 percent of the world's . . . gross industrial output . . . and it will not be long before it surpasses the gross industrial output of all the capitalist countries put together." Explain

why such a statement was believable at the time, and why the prediction turned out to be so inaccurate.

2. Why was central planning successful in increasing real GDP growth for a while? Why did real GDP growth eventually falter under central planning?

3. Design a gradual program for transition from central planning to a market-based economy. Explain how the basic features of a market economy will be achieved. Defend your plan against a proposal for a shock-therapy approach.

4. Explain why it may be easier to move from a market economy with private property to a command-and-control economy without private property than the other way around. Give a real-world example to prove your point.

5. Describe Gosplan's role during the period of central planning in the former Soviet Union.

6. Has Poland or China had an easier time with the transition from central planning? Why do you think this is the case?

7. "Economic freedom and political freedom necessarily go together." Is this statement valid? Explain.

8. Could state-owned firms be made to operate as if they were private firms? For example, suppose that the managers of the state enterprises were instructed to maximize profits with prices and wages set by the central planners. According to the Hungarian economist Janos Kornai, the answer to this question is no. In *The Road to a Free Economy,* he writes, "It is futile to expect a state-owned unit to behave as if it were privately owned." Provide an argument supporting Kornai's view. Be sure to mention the role of prices as well as the role of private property and incentives.

9. Compare and contrast how the three key questions— *how, what,* and *for whom* goods and services should be produced—are dealt with in a centrally planned economy versus in a market economy.

10. Comment on the validity of the following statement made by Fareed Zakaria in the *New York Times Book Review* on March 30, 1997. Support your answer with historical examples and economic reasoning: "Capitalism was and is a destructive and revolutionary phenomenon. It leveled European feudalism and aristocracy, then proceeded, in this century, to destroy statism, both fascist and communist. It has created a dynamic, materialistic, and dominating global culture with an aspiring middle class at its helm."

Glossary

ability-to-pay principle   the view that those with greater income should pay more in taxes than those with less income. (14)

absolute advantage   a situation in which a person or country is more efficient at producing a good in comparison with another person or country. (17)

accounting profits   total revenue minus total costs where total costs exclude the implicit opportunity costs; this is the definition of profits usually reported by firms. (9)

ad valorem tariff   a tax on imports evaluated as a percentage of the value of the import. (18)

ad valorem tax   a tax that is proportional to the value of expenditures. (7)

adverse selection   in insurance markets, a situation in which the people who choose to buy insurance will be the riskiest group in the population; analogous situations apply in other markets. (13)

aggregate demand   the total demand for goods and services by consumers, businesses, government, and foreigners. (19)

aggregate demand/inflation (*ADI*) curve   a line showing a negative relationship between inflation and the aggregate quantity of goods and services demanded at that inflation rate. (27)

aggregate expenditure line   the relation between the sum of the four components of spending ($C + I + G + X$) and aggregate income. (25)

aggregate hours   the total number of hours worked by all workers in the economy in a given period of time. (21)

aggregate income   the total income received by all factors of production in the economy; also simply called "income." (25)

aggregate supply   the total value of all goods and services produced in the economy by the available supply of capital, labor, and technology (also called potential GDP). (19)

antidumping duty   a tariff imposed on a country as a penalty for dumping goods. (18)

Antitrust Division of the Justice Department   the division of the Justice Department in the United States that enforces antitrust legislation, along with the Federal Trade Commission. (16)

antitrust policy   government actions designed to promote competition among firms in the economy; also called competition policy or antimonopoly policy. (16)

Arrow impossibility theorem   a theorem that says that no democratic voting scheme can avoid a voting paradox. (15)

ask   the price that sellers say they are willing to sell a good for in an auction market. (7)

asset   something of value owned by a person or a firm. (24)

asymmetric information   different levels of information available to different people in an economic interaction or exchange. (13)

automatic stabilizers   automatic tax and spending changes that occur over the course of the business cycle that tend to stabilize the fluctuations in real GDP. (29)

average fixed cost (*AFC*)   fixed cost divided by the quantity produced. (8)

average product of labor   the quantity produced divided by the amount of labor input. (8)

average revenue   total revenue divided by quantity. (10)

average tax rate   the total tax paid divided by the total taxable income. (14)

average total cost (*ATC*)   total costs of production divided by the quantity produced (also called cost per unit). (8)

average total cost pricing   a regulatory method that stipulates that the firm charge a price that equals average total cost. (16)

average variable cost (*AVC*)   variable costs divided by the quantity produced. (8)

backward-bending labor supply curve   the situation in which the income effect outweighs the substitution effect of an increase in the wage, causing the labor supply curve to bend back and take on a negative slope at higher levels of income. (12)

balance of payments   the record of all the transactions between a country and the rest of the world; it includes information on the value of trade in goods and services as well as transfer payments. (31)

balanced budget   a budget for which tax revenues equal spending. (29)

balanced budget multiplier   the ratio of the change in real GDP to a change in government purchases when the change in government purchases is matched by an equivalent change in taxes. (26)

bank   a firm that channels funds from savers to investors by accepting deposits and making loans. (24)

barriers to entry   anything that prevents firms from entering a market. (10)

barter   trade in goods or services without the use of money. (24)

baseline   the path of an economic variable that would occur without the policy change under consideration. (28)

bid   the price that buyers say they are willing to pay for a good in an auction market. (7)

bilateral monopoly   the situation in which there is one buyer and one seller in a market. (12)

bilateral trade balance   the value of imports less the value of exports between two countries. (31)

Board of Governors of the Federal Reserve System   the seven member governing board of the central bank of the United States. (32)

bond   a financial contract that stipulates a specific repayment of principal plus interest on a loan at a given date in the future. (29)

bond   a promise by a firm or government to pay a certain amount of money to the bondholder on a fixed date in the future. (24)

boom   unusually rapid increases in real GDP; frequently used to refer to the period when real GDP is greater than potential GDP. (28)

boom-bust cycle   a business cycle caused by a monetary policy in which interest rates are initially too low, causing a boom, and there is a subsequent increase in interest rates, which causes a recession. (28)

breakeven point   the point at which price equals the minimum of average total cost. (8)

Bretton Woods system   the international monetary system put in place after World War II; it was based on fixed exchange rates. Infrequent adjustments of the exchange rates were permitted and did occur under the Bretton Woods system. (31)

budget constraint   an income limitation on a person's expenditure on goods and services. (5)

budget cycle   the more than two-year process in which the federal budget is proposed, modified, enacted, and implemented. (29)

budget deficit   the amount by which government spending exceeds tax revenues. (29)

budget line   a line showing the maximum combinations of two goods that it is possible for a consumer to buy, given a budget constraint and the market prices of the two goods. (5ap)

budget surplus   the amount by which tax revenues exceed spending. (29)

business cycles   short-term fluctuations in real GDP and employment. (19)

business fixed investment   investment by firms in physical capital, such as factories and equipment. (20)

capital   the factories, improvements to cultivated land, machinery and other tools, equipment, and structures used to produce goods and services. (1, 19, 22)

capital abundant   a higher level of capital per worker in one country relative to another. (17)

capital account   the part of the international accounts of a country that keeps track of the change in domestic assets owned by foreigners and foreign assets owned by citizens. (31)

capital gain   the increase in the value of an asset through an increase in its price. (13)

capital gains tax   a tax on the increase in the value of an asset. (32)

capital income   the sum of profits, rental payments, and interest payments. (20)

capital intensive   production that uses a relatively high level of capital per worker. (17)

capital loss   the decrease in the value of an asset through a decrease in its price. (13)

capital-saving technological change   a technological innovation that reduces the amount of capital needed to produce a given amount of output with a given amount of labor. (23)

capitalism   an economic system based on a market economy in which capital is individually owned, and production and employment decisions are decentralized. (34)

cartel   a group of producers in the same industry who coordinate pricing and production decisions. (11)

Cartesian coordinate system   a graphing system in which ordered pairs of numbers are represented on a plane by the distances from a point to two perpendicular lines, called axes. (1ap)

catch-up line   the downward-sloping relation between the level of productivity and growth of productivity predicted by growth theory. (33)

causation   a relation of cause and effect between variables in which one variable is a determinant of another variable. (1)

central bank   the government institution that controls monetary policy in most countries. (24, 30)

central bank independence   a description of the legal authority of central banks to make decisions on monetary policy with little interference by the government in power. (30)

ceteris paribus   all other things being equal; refers to holding all other variables constant or keeping all other things the same when one variable is changed. (1)

chain weighted price index a price index using a changing basket of goods and services computed just as real GDP is computed, usually mentioned as a measure of inflation. (20)

checking deposit an account at a financial institution on which checks can be written; also called checkable deposit. (24)

choice a selection among alternative goods, services, or actions. (2)

Clayton Antitrust Act a law passed in 1914 in the United States aimed at preventing monopolies from forming through mergers. (16)

Coase theorem the idea that private negotiations between people will lead to an efficient resolution of externalities regardless of who has the property rights as long as the property rights are defined. (15)

coincidence of wants a condition required for exchange in a nonmonetary system; to accomplish a trade, it is necessary to find someone who has what you want and also wants what you have. (24)

collectivized farm a farm in a planned economy that is in theory collectively owned by peasants, but controlled by the government. (34)

command and control the regulations and restrictions that the government uses to correct market imperfections. (15)

command economy an economy in which the government determines prices and production; also called a centrally planned economy. (1, 34)

commerce clause the clause in the U.S. Constitution that prohibits restraint of trade between states. (17)

commodity money a good used as money that has some intrinsic value in a nonmonetary use. (24)

communism an economic system in which all capital is collectively owned. (34)

comparative advantage a situation in which a person or country can produce one good more efficiently than another good in comparison with another person or country. (2, 17, 31)

compensating wage differential a difference in wages for people with similar skills based on some characteristic of the job, such as riskiness, discomfort, or convenience of the time schedule. (12)

compensation all the pay a worker receives including fringe benefits. (12)

competitive equilibrium model a model that assumes utility maximization on the part of consumers and profit maximization on the part of firms, along with competitive markets and freely determined prices. (7)

competitive industry an industry characterized by many firms selling the same product and free entry and exit of firms. (10)

competitive market a market where no firm has the power to affect the market price of a good. (6)

complement a good that is usually consumed or used together with another good. (3)

conditional forecast a prediction that depends on assumed values for government purchases, taxes, or some other variable that affects the forecast. (25)

conditionality stipulations on loans to countries from the International Monetary Fund that certain policy prescriptions, such as price reforms or reducing government budget deficits, must be met to receive funds. (33)

conjectural variations approach a model that assumes that firms make decisions based on what they expect other firms to do in reaction to their decisions. (11)

constant money growth rule a monetary policy in which the central bank keeps money growth constant. (30)

constant returns to scale a situation in which long-run average total cost is constant as the output of a firm changes. (8)

consumer price index (CPI) a price index equal to the current price of a fixed market basket of consumer goods and services in a base year. (20)

consumer surplus the difference between what a person is willing to pay for an additional unit of a good—the marginal benefit—and the market price of the good; for the market as a whole, it is the sum of all the individual consumer surpluses or the area below the market demand curve and above the market price. (5, 7)

consumption purchases of final goods and services by individuals. (20)

consumption function the positive relationship between consumption and income. (25)

consumption share the proportion of GDP that is used for consumption; equals consumption divided by GDP, or C/Y. (22)

consumption smoothing the idea that, although their incomes fluctuate, people try to stabilize consumption spending from year to year. (26)

contestable market a market in which the threat of competition is enough to encourage firms to act like competitors. (10, 16)

contingent valuation an estimation of the willingness to pay for a project on the part of consumers who may benefit from the project. (15)

controlled experiments empirical tests of theories in a controlled setting in which particular effects can be isolated. (1)

convergence of positions the concentration of the stances of political parties around the center of citizens' opinions. (15)

cooperative outcome   an equilibrium in a game where the players agree to cooperate. (11)

coordination failure   a situation where, because their actions are interdependent, people fail to act in a manner that is mutually beneficial. (32)

corporate income tax   a tax on the accounting profits of corporations. (14)

corporation   a firm characterized by limited liability on the part of owners and the separation of ownership and management. (6)

correlation   the degree to which economic variables are observed to move together: If they move in the same direction, there is positive correlation; if they move in opposite directions, there is negative correlation. (1)

cost-benefit analysis   an appraisal of a project based on the costs and benefits derived from it. (15)

Council of Economic Advisers   a three-member group of economists appointed by the president of the United States to analyze the economy and make recommendations about economic policy. (1)

countercyclical policy   a policy designed to offset the fluctuations in the business cycle. (29)

country in transition   a country that is transforming from a centrally planned economy to a market economy. (33)

coupon   the fixed amount that a borrower agrees to pay to the bondholder each year. (13)

Cournot model   a model using the conjectural variations approach that assumes that each firm expects other firms to keep their production constant in response to actions the firm takes. (11)

craft union   a union organized to represent a single occupation, whose members come from a variety of industries. (12)

credibility   the believability of the government's intentions to carry out stated policies. (29)

cross-price elasticity of demand   the percentage change in the quantity demanded of one good divided by the percentage change in the price of another good. (4)

crowding out   the decline in private investment owing to an increase in government purchases. (22)

currency   money in its physical form: coin and paper money. (24)

currency to deposit ratio   the proportion of currency that people in the economy want to hold relative to their deposits; it equals currency divided by deposits. (24)

current account balance   the value of exports minus the value of imports plus net factor income from abroad plus net transfers from abroad. (31)

Current Population Survey   a monthly survey of a sample of U.S. households done by the U.S. Census Bureau; it measures employment, unemployment, the labor force, and other characteristics of the U.S. population. (14, 21)

customs union   a free trade area with a common external tariff. (18)

cyclical deficit   the difference between the actual deficit and the structural deficit. (29)

cyclical unemployment   unemployment due to a recession, when the rate of unemployment is above the natural rate of unemployment. (21)

deadweight loss   the loss in producer and consumer surplus due to an inefficient level of production. (7, 10)

debt contract   a contract in which a lender agrees to provide funds today in exchange for a promise from the borrower, who will repay that amount plus interest at some point in the future. (13)

debt to GDP ratio   the total amount of outstanding loans the federal government owes divided by nominal GDP. (29)

deferred payment contract   an agreement between a worker and an employer whereby the worker is paid less than the marginal revenue product when young, and subsequently paid more than the marginal revenue product when old. (12)

deflation   a decrease in the overall price level, or a negative inflation rate. (28)

demand   a relationship between price and quantity demanded. (3)

demand curve   a graph of demand showing the downward-sloping relationship between price and quantity demanded. (3)

demand schedule   a tabular presentation of demand showing the price and quantity demanded for a particular good, all else being equal. (3)

demand shock   a shift in one of the components of aggregate demand that leads to a shift in the aggregate demand/inflation curve. (28)

depreciation   the decrease in an asset's value over time; for capital, it is the amount by which physical capital wears out over a given period of time. (13, 20)

deregulation movement   begun in the late 1970s, the drive to reduce the government regulations controlling prices and entry in many industries. (16)

derived demand   demand for an input derived from the demand for the product produced with that input. (12)

developing country   a country that is poor by world standards in terms of real GDP per capita. (33)

diffusion   the spreading of an innovation throughout the economy. (23)

diminishing marginal utility the decline in additional utility from consumption of an additional unit of a good as more and more of the good is consumed. (5)

diminishing returns a situation in which successive increases in the use of an input, holding other inputs constant, will eventually cause a decline in the additional production derived from one more unit of that input. (23)

diminishing returns to labor a situation in which the incremental increase in output due to a unit increase in labor declines with increasing labor input; a decreasing marginal product of labor. (6)

discount rate an interest rate used to discount future payment when computing present discounted value. (13ap)

discount rate the interest rate that the Fed charges commercial banks when they borrow from the Fed. (30)

discounting the process of translating a future payment into a value in the present. (13ap)

discretionary fiscal policy changes in tax or spending policy requiring legislative or administrative action by the president or Congress. (29)

diseconomies of scale also called decreasing returns to scale; a situation where long-run average total cost increases as the output of a firm increases. (8)

disinflation a reduction in the inflation rate. (28)

disposable income income that households have to spend after taxes have been paid and transfers from the government have been received. (25)

dividend yield the dividend stated as a percentage of the price of the stock. (13)

division of labor dividing work into different tasks with groups of workers specializing in each task. (2, 23)

domestic content restriction a requirement that a fraction of the product must be produced within the area to qualify for zero tariffs between the countries in the free trade area. (18)

double-auction market a market in which several buyers and several sellers state prices at which they are willing to buy or sell a good. (7)

dual scale a graph that uses time on the horizontal axis and different scales on left and right vertical axes to compare the movements in two variables over time. (1ap)

dumping the selling of goods by foreign firms at a price below average cost or below the price in the domestic country. (18)

dynamic comparative advantage changes in comparative advantage over time from investment in physical and human capital and in technology. (17)

earned income tax credit (EITC) a part of the personal income tax through which people with low income who work receive a payment from the government or a rebate on their taxes. (14)

earnings accounting profits of a firm. (13)

economic development the process of growth by which countries raise incomes per capita and become industrialized; also refers to the branch of economics that studies this process. (33)

economic fluctuations swings in real GDP that lead to deviations of the economy from its long-term growth trend. (19)

economic growth an upward trend in real GDP, reflecting expansion in the economy over time; it can be represented as an outward shift in the production possibilities curve. (2, 19)

economic history the study of economic events and the collection of economic observations from the past. (1)

economic interaction exchanges of goods and services between people. (2)

economic model an explanation of how the economy or part of the economy works. (1)

economic profits total revenue minus total costs, where total costs include opportunity costs, whether implicit or explicit. (9)

economic regulation government regulation that sets prices or conditions on the entry of firms into an industry. (16)

economic rent the price of something that has a fixed supply. (13)

economic variable any economic measure that can vary over a range of values. (1)

economies of scale also called increasing returns to scale; a situation in which long-run average total cost declines as the output of a firm increases. (8, 16)

efficiency wage a wage higher than that which would equate quantity supplied and quantity demanded set by employers in order to increase worker efficiency, for example, by decreasing shirking by workers. (12, 21)

efficient market hypothesis the idea that markets adjust rapidly enough to eliminate profit opportunities immediately. (13)

elastic demand demand for which price elasticity is greater than 1. (4)

emission tax a charge made to firms that pollute the environment based on the quantity of pollution they emit. (15)

employment-to-population ratio the ratio (usually expressed as a percentage) of employed workers to the working-age population. (21)

equilibrium interest rate the interest rate that equates the sum of consumption, investment, and net export shares to the share of GDP available for nongovernment use. (22)

equilibrium price   the price at which quantity supplied equals quantity demanded. (3, 7)

equilibrium quantity   the quantity traded at the equilibrium price. (3)

equilibrium risk-return relationship   the positive relationship between the risk and the expected rate of return on an asset derived from the fact that, on average, risk-averse investors who take on more risk must be compensated with a higher return. (13)

equity contract   shares of ownership in a firm in which payments to the owners of the shares depend on the firm's profits. (13)

European monetary system   a system of exchange rates in which European currencies are fixed relative to each other but are flexible against the dollar, the yen, and other currencies. (31)

excess capacity   a situation in which a firm produces below the level that gives minimum average total cost. (11)

excess costs   costs of production that are higher than the minimum average total cost. (11)

exchange market intervention   purchases and sales of foreign currency by a government in exchange markets with the intention to affect the exchange rate. (31)

exchange rate   the price of one currency in terms of another. (2)

excise tax   a tax paid on the value of goods at the time of purchase. (14)

exclusive dealing   a condition of a contract by which a manufacturer does not allow a retailer to sell goods made by a competing manufacturer. (16)

exclusive territories   the region over which a manufacturer limits the distribution or selling of its products to one retailer or wholesaler. (16)

expansion   the period between the trough of a recession and the next peak, consisting of a general rise in output and employment. (19)

expected return   the return on an uncertain investment calculated by weighting the gains or losses by the probability that they will occur. (13)

experimental economics   a branch of economics that uses laboratory experiments to analyze economic behavior. (1)

explicit collusion   open cooperation of firms to make mutually beneficial pricing or production decisions. (11)

export supply curve   a curve showing the quantity of exports supplied at various prices. (18)

export-led strategy   the government's encouragement of the economy's development by establishing an open trade policy and increasing exports. (33)

export   the sale of goods and services abroad. (17)

exports   the total value of the goods and services that people in one country sell to people in other countries. (20)

external diseconomies of scale   a situation in which growth in an industry causes average total cost for the individual firm to rise because of some factor external to the firm; it corresponds to an upward-sloping long-run industry supply curve. (9)

external economies of scale   a situation in which growth in an industry causes average total cost for the individual firm to fall because of some factor external to the firm; it corresponds to a downward-sloping long-run industry supply curve. (9)

externality   the situation in which the costs of producing or the benefits of consuming a good spill over onto those who are neither producing nor consuming the good. (15)

face value   the principal that will be paid back when a bond matures. (13)

factor income   earnings for a factor of production including wages and profits. (31)

factor-price equalization   the equalization of the price of labor and the price of capital across countries when they are engaging in free trade. (17)

family support programs   transfer programs through which the federal government makes grants to states to give cash to certain low-income families. (14)

federal budget   a summary of the federal government's proposals for spending, taxes, and the deficit. (29)

federal debt   the total amount of outstanding loans owed by the federal government. (29)

federal funds rate   the interest rate on overnight loans between banks that the Federal Reserve influences by changing the supply of funds (bank reserves) in the market. (27)

Federal Open Market Committee (FOMC)   the committee, consisting of the seven members of the Board of Governors and the twelve presidents of the Fed district banks, that meets about eight times per year to decide monetary policy; only five of the presidents vote at any one time. (24)

Federal Reserve System (the Fed)   the central bank of the United States, which oversees the creation of money in the United States. (24)

Federal Trade Commission (FTC)   the government agency established to help enforce antitrust legislation in the United States; it shares this responsibility with the Antitrust Division of the Justice Department. (16)

final good   a new good that undergoes no further processing before it is sold to consumers. (20)

financial capital   funds used to purchase, rent, or build physical capital. (13)

financial intermediary   a firm that channels funds from savers to investors by accepting deposits and making loans. (24)

firm   an organization that produces goods or services. (6)

first theorem of welfare economics   the conclusion that a competitive market results in an efficient outcome; sometimes called the "invisible hand theorem"; the definition of efficiency used in the theorem is Pareto efficiency. (7)

fiscal policy   the government's plans for spending, for taxes, and for borrowing. (29)

fiscal policy rule   a description of how the instruments of policy regularly respond to the state of the economy. Automatic stabilizers are an example of a fiscal policy rule. (29)

five-year plan   a document that stated production goals for the entire Soviet economy for the succeeding five years. (34)

fixed costs   costs of production that do not depend on the quantity of production. (6, 8)

fixed exchange rate system   a system of international exchange rates in which the countries agree to maintain a predetermined value of their currencies in terms of other currencies. (31)

flat tax   a tax system for which there is a constant marginal tax rate for all levels of taxable income. (14)

flexible exchange rate system   an international monetary system in which exchange rates are determined in foreign exchange markets and governments do not agree to fix them. (31)

flexible price assumption   an assumption that prices adjust instantaneously in response to a change in supply or demand. (25)

food stamp program   a government program that pays coupons (food stamps) to people with low incomes in order to buy food. (14)

forecast   a prediction of an economic variable such as real GDP. (25)

foreign direct investment   investment by a foreign entity of at least a 10 percent direct ownership share in the firm. (33)

45-degree line   the line showing that aggregate expenditure equals aggregate income. (25)

forward-looking consumption model   a model that explains consumer behavior by assuming people anticipate future income when deciding on consumption spending today. (26)

free entry and exit   movement of firms in and out of an industry that is not blocked by regulation, other firms, or any other barriers. (9)

free trade   a complete lack of restrictions on international trade. (17)

free trade area (FTA)   an area that has no trade barriers between the countries in the area. (18)

freely determined price   a price that is determined by the individuals and firms interacting in markets. (2)

free-rider problem   a problem arising in the case of public goods because those who do not contribute to the costs of providing the public good cannot be excluded from the benefits of the good. (15)

frictional unemployment   short-term unemployment arising from normal turnover in the labor market, such as when people change occupations or locations, or are new entrants. (21)

fringe benefits   compensation that a worker receives excluding direct money payments for time worked: insurance, retirement benefits, vacation time, and maternity and sick leave. (12)

futures market   a market that deals in commodities to be delivered in the future. (31)

gains from trade   improvements in income, production, or satisfaction owing to the exchange of goods or services. (2, 17)

game theory   a branch of applied mathematics with many uses in economics including the analysis of the interaction of firms that take each other's actions into account. (11)

GDP deflator   nominal GDP divided by real GDP; it measures the level of prices of goods and services included in real GDP relative to a given base year. (20)

General Agreement on Tariffs and Trade (GATT)   an international treaty and organization designed to promote mutual reductions in tariffs and other trade barriers among countries. (18)

Gini coefficient   an index of income inequality ranging between 0 (for perfect equality) and 1 (for absolute inequality); it is defined as the ratio of the area between the Lorenz curve and the perfect equality line, divided by the area between the lines of perfect equality and perfect inequality. (14)

gold standard   a monetary standard in which the value of money is linked to gold. (24, 30)

Gosplan   the planning agency of the former Soviet Union. (34)

government failure   a situation in which the government makes things worse than the market, even though there may be market failure. (2)

government procurement   the process by which governments buy goods and services. (18)

government purchases   purchases by federal, state, and local governments of new goods and services. (20)

government purchases share   the proportion of GDP that is used for government purchases; equals government purchases divided by GDP, or *G/Y*. (22)

gradualism   the slow phasing-in of free market reforms. (34)

gross domestic product (GDP)   a measure of the value of all the goods and services newly produced in an economy during a specified period of time. (1)

gross investment   the total amount of investment, including that which goes to replacing worn out capital. (20)

growth accounting formula   an equation that states that the growth rate of real GDP per hour of work equals capital's share of income times the growth rate of capital per hour of work plus the growth rate of technology. (23)

Head Start   a government transfer program that provides day care and nursery school training for poor children. (14)

hedge   to reduce risk, usually by buying a futures contract to guarantee a price several months in the future. (31)

Herfindahl-Hirschman index (HHI)   an index ranging in value from 0 to 10,000 indicating the concentration in an industry; it is calculated by summing the squares of the market shares of each firm in the industry. (16)

horizontal merger   a combining of two firms that sell the same good or same type of good. (16)

hostile takeover   a situation in which investors buy a large share of a company and replace the management. (13)

housing assistance programs   government programs that provide subsidies either to low-income families to rent housing or to contractors to build low-income housing. (14)

human capital   a person's accumulated knowledge and skills. (12, 23)

implicit contract   an informal agreement between a firm and its customers or between a firm and its employees. (25)

implicit rental price   the interest payments on the funds borrowed to buy the capital plus the depreciation of the capital over a given period of time. (13)

import   the purchase of goods and services from abroad. (17)

import demand curve   a curve showing the quantity of imports demanded at various prices. (18)

import substitution strategy   a trade policy designed to encourage local firms to produce goods that are normally imported into the country. (33)

imports   the total value of the goods and services that people in one country buy from people in other countries. (20)

incentive   a device that motivates people to take action, usually so as to increase economic efficiency. (2)

incentive regulation   a regulatory method that sets prices for several years ahead and then allows the firm to keep any additional profits or suffer any losses over that period of time. (16)

income effect   the amount by which the quantity demanded falls because of the decline in real income from a price increase. (5)

income elasticity of demand   the percentage change in quantity demanded of one good divided by the percentage change in income. (4)

income inequality   disparity in levels of income among individuals in the economy. (7)

increasing opportunity cost   a situation in which producing more of one good requires giving up producing an increasing amount of another good. (2)

indifference curve   a curve showing the combinations of two goods that leave the consumer with the same level of utility. (5ap)

indirect business taxes   taxes, such as sales taxes, that are levied on products when they are sold. (20)

individual demand curve   a curve showing the relationship between quantity demanded of a good by an individual and the price of the good. (5)

industrial union   a union organized within a given industry, whose members come from a variety of occupations. (12)

industrialized country   a country with a large industrial base that is relatively well off by world standards in terms of real GDP per capita. (33)

industry   a group of firms producing a similar product. (9)

inelastic demand   demand for which the price elasticity is less than 1. (4)

infant industry argument   the view that a new industry may be encouraged by protectionist policies. (18)

inferior good   a good for which demand decreases when income rises and increases when income falls. (3)

inflation   an increase in the overall price level. (1)

inflation rate   the percentage increase in the overall price level over a given period of time, usually one year. (1, 19)

informal economy   the portion of an economy characterized by illegal, unregulated businesses. (33)

innovation   applications of new knowledge in a way that creates new products or significantly changes old ones. (23)

inputs or factors of production   labor, capital, and other resources used in the production of goods and services. (1)

insider   a person who already works for a firm and has some influence over wage and hiring policy. (21)

intellectual property laws laws that protect ownership rights over ideas and inventions; includes patent laws, copyright laws, and trademark laws. (23)

interest rate the amount received per dollar loaned per year, usually expressed as a percentage (e.g., 6 percent) of the loan. (19)

interindustry trade trade between countries in goods from different industries. (11, 18)

intermediate good a good that undergoes further processing before it is sold to consumers. (20)

internalize the process of providing incentives so that externalities are taken into account internally by firms or consumers. (15)

International Monetary Fund (IMF) an international agency, established after World War II, designed to help countries with balance of payments problems and to ensure the smooth functioning of the international monetary system. (33)

international monetary independence the idea that a flexible exchange rate system gives a country the ability to have much different interest rates than other countries. (31)

international trade exchange of goods and services between people or firms in different nations. (2, 17)

international transfer payments payments across international borders in the form of grants, remittances, and aid. (31)

intraindustry trade trade between countries in goods from the same or similar industries. (11, 17)

invention a discovery of new knowledge. (23)

inventory investment a change in the stock of inventories from one date to another. (20)

investment purchases of final goods by firms plus purchases of newly produced residences by households. (20, 22)

investment-saving gap the difference between the level of investment and the level of saving in the economy. (31)

investment share the proportion of GDP that is used for investment; equals investment divided by GDP or *I/Y*. (22)

investment tax credit a reduction in taxes for firms that buy new investment goods that is proportional to the expenditures on the good. (32)

invisible hand the idea that the free interaction of people in a market economy leads to a desirable social outcome; the term was coined by Adam Smith. (7)

iron law of wages the prediction that wages will always tend to equal the subsistence level. (23)

isocost line a line showing the combinations of two inputs that result in the same total costs. (8ap)

isoquant a curve showing the combinations of two inputs that yield the same quantity of output. (8ap)

job leavers people who are unemployed because they quit their previous job. (21)

job losers people who are unemployed because they lost their previous job. (21)

job rationing a reason for unemployment in which the quantity of labor supplied is greater than the quantity demanded because the real wage is too high. (21)

job search a reason for unemployment in which uncertainty in the labor market and workers' limited information requires people to spend time searching for a job. (21)

job vacancies positions that firms are trying to fill, but for which they have yet to find suitable workers. (21)

Keynesian revolution a change in macroeconomic thinking, shaped by the Great Depression and the work of John Maynard Keynes, leading to a greater consideration of demand-side policies. (32)

Keynesian school a school of macroeconomic thought concerned with pursuing demand-side macroeconomic policies—primarily fiscal policies working through the multiplier—to reduce unemployment and encourage economic growth. (32)

labor the number of hours people work in producing goods and services. (1, 19)

labor abundant a lower level of capital per worker in one country relative to another. (17)

labor demand the relationship between the quantity of labor demanded by firms and the wage. (12)

labor demand curve a downward-sloping relationship showing the quantity of labor firms are willing to hire at each wage. (21)

labor force all those who are either employed or unemployed. (21)

labor force participation rate the ratio (usually expressed as a percentage) of people in the labor force to the working-age population. (21)

labor income the sum of wages, salaries, and fringe benefits paid to workers. (20)

labor intensive production that uses a relatively low level of capital per worker. (17)

labor market the market in which individuals supply their labor time to firms in exchange for wages and salaries. (12)

labor market equilibrium the situation in which the quantity supplied of labor equals the quantity demanded of labor. (12)

labor productivity output per hour of work. (12, 19)

labor-saving technological change   a technological innovation that reduces the amount of labor needed to produce a given amount of output with a given amount of capital. (23)

labor supply   the relationship between the quantity of labor supplied by individuals and the wage. (12)

labor supply curve   the relationship showing the quantity of labor workers are willing to supply at each wage. (21)

labor union   a coalition of workers, organized to improve wages and working conditions of their members. (12)

law of demand   the tendency for the quantity demanded of a good in a market to decline as its price rises. (3)

law of one price   the notion that, with low transportation costs and no trade barriers, the same commodity is sold for the same price in two different countries when measured in the same currency. (31)

law of supply   the tendency for the quantity supplied of a good in a market to increase as its price rises. (3)

learning by doing   a situation in which workers become more proficient by doing a particular task many times. (23)

Leontief paradox   the inconsistency that Wassily Leontief found between the data on U.S. trade and the Heckscher-Ohlin model. (17)

liability   something of value a person or firm owes to someone else. (24)

life-cycle model   a type of forward-looking consumption model that assumes that people base their consumption decisions on their expected lifetime income rather than on their current income. (26)

limited information   a situation in which firms have incomplete knowledge about some market conditions, such as whether a change in demand for their product is temporary or permanent or whether the change is due to a recession or boom in the whole economy. (25)

linear   a situation in which a curve is straight, with a constant slope. (1ap)

liquidity constraint   the situation in which people cannot borrow to smooth their consumption spending when their income is low. (26)

loan   an interest-bearing asset to the bank that lends money to an individual or firm. (24)

long run   the minimum period of time during which all inputs to production can be changed. (8)

long-run average total cost curve   the curve that traces out the short-run average total cost curves, showing the lowest average total cost for each quantity produced as the firm expands in the long run. (8)

long-run competitive equilibrium model   a model of firms in an industry in which free entry and exit produce an equilibrium such that price equals the minimum of average total cost. (9)

long-run equilibrium   a situation in which entry and exit from an industry is complete and economic profits are zero with price (P) equal to average total cost (ATC). (9)

long-run industry supply curve   a curve traced out by the intersections of demand curves shifting to the right and the corresponding short-run supply curves. (9)

long-term employment contract   an agreement, either explicit or implicit, between employers and workers that sets conditions concerning the work relationship for a long period of time. (12)

Lorenz curve   a curve showing the relation between the cumulative percentage of the population and the proportion of total income earned by each cumulative percentage. It measures income inequality. (14)

M1   currency plus checking deposits plus travelers checks. (24)

M2   M1 plus savings, time, and limited checking deposits. (24)

macroeconomics   the branch of economics that examines the workings and problems of the economy as a whole—economic growth, inflation, unemployment, and economic fluctuations. (1)

Malthusian equilibrium   a situation in which production equals the subsistence level of output because population adjusts based on consumption of food. (23)

managed trade   a situation in which a government takes actions to promote or restrict trade in certain goods, usually by setting targets for exports or imports. (18)

mandated benefits   benefits that a firm is required by law to provide to its employees. (14)

marginal benefit   the increase in the willingness to pay to consume one more unit of a good. (5)

marginal cost   the change in total cost due to a one-unit change in quantity produced. (6, 8)

marginal cost pricing   a regulatory method that stipulates that the firm charge a price that equals marginal cost. (16)

marginal private benefit   the marginal benefit from consumption of a good as viewed by a private individual. (15)

marginal private cost   the marginal cost of production as viewed by the private firm or individual. (15)

marginal product of labor   the change in production due to a one-unit increase in labor input. (6, 12)

marginal propensity to consume (MPC)   the slope of the consumption function, showing the change in consumption that is due to a given change in income. (25)

marginal propensity to import (MPI)   the change in imports because of a given change in income. (26)

marginal propensity to save (MPS)   the change in saving due to a given change in income; MPS = 1 − marginal propensity to consume (MPC). (26)

marginal revenue   the change in total revenue due to a one-unit increase in quantity sold. (6)

marginal revenue product of capital   the change in total revenue due to a one-unit increase in capital. (13)

marginal revenue product of labor   the change in total revenue due to a one-unit increase in labor input. (12)

marginal social benefit   the marginal benefit from consumption of a good from the viewpoint of society as a whole. (15)

marginal social cost   the marginal cost of production as viewed by society as a whole. (15)

marginal tax rate   the change in total tax divided by the change in income. (14)

marginal utility   the additional utility from an additional unit of consumption of a good. (5)

market   an arrangement by which economic exchanges between people take place. (1, 2)

market definition   demarcation of a geographic region and a category of goods or services in which firms compete. (16)

market demand curve   the horizontal summation of all the individual demand curves for a good; also simply called the demand curve. (5)

market economy   an economy characterized by freely determined prices and the free exchange of goods and services in markets. (1, 34)

market equilibrium   the situation in which the price is equal to the equilibrium price and the quantity traded equals the equilibrium quantity. (3)

market failure   any situation in which the market does not lead to an efficient economic outcome and in which there is a potential role for government. (2, 15)

market power   a firm's power to set its price without losing its entire share of the market. (10)

maturity date   the date when the principal on a loan is paid back. (13)

means-tested transfer   a transfer payment that depends on the income of the recipient. (14)

median voter theorem   a theorem stating that the median or middle of political preferences will be reflected in the government decisions. (15)

Medicaid   a health insurance program designed primarily for families with low incomes. (14)

Medicare   a government health insurance program for the elderly. (14)

medium of exchange   an item that is generally accepted as a means of payment for goods and services. (2, 24)

mercantilism   the notion, popular in the 1700s, that the wealth of a nation was based on how much it could export in excess of its imports, and thereby accumulate precious metals. (17)

merchandise trade   trade in goods that have physical form, such as oil, wheat, or computers. (31)

merchandise trade balance   the value of merchandise exports minus the value of merchandise imports. (31)

microeconomics   the branch of economics that examines individual decision-making at firms and households and the way they interact in specific industries and markets. (1)

minimum efficient scale   the smallest scale of production for which long-run average total cost is at a minimum. (8)

minimum wage   a wage per hour below which it is illegal to pay workers. (3, 21)

minimum wage legislation   a law that sets a floor on the wage, or price of labor. (12)

mixed economy   a market economy in which the government plays a very large role. (1)

monetarist school   a school of macroeconomic thought that holds that changes in the money supply are the primary cause of fluctuations in real GDP and the ultimate cause of inflation. (32)

monetary base   currency plus reserves. (24, 30)

monetary policy rule   a description of how much the interest rate or other instruments of monetary policy respond to inflation or other measures of the state of the economy. (27)

monetary transmission channel   a description of how a change in monetary policy eventually affects real GDP. (30)

money   that part of a person's wealth that can be readily used for transactions; money also serves as a store of value and a unit of account. (24)

money demand   a relationship between the interest rate and the quantity of money that people are willing to hold at any given interest rate. (30)

money multiplier   the multiple by which the money supply changes due to a change in the monetary base. (24)

money supply   the sum of currency (coin and paper money) held by the public and deposits at banks. (24)

monopolistic competition   a market structure characterized by many firms selling differentiated products in an industry in which there is free entry and exit. (11)

monopoly   one firm in an industry selling a product for which there are no close substitutes. (10)

monopsony   a situation in which there is a single buyer of a particular good or service in a given market. (12)

moral hazard in insurance markets, a situation in which a person buys insurance against some risk and subsequently takes actions that increase the risks; analogous situations arise when there is asymmetric information in other markets. (13)

most-favored nation (MFN) the principle by which all countries involved in GATT negotiations receive the same tariff rates as the country with the lowest negotiated tariff rates. (18)

movement along the curve a situation in which a change in the variable on one axis causes a change in the variable on the other axis, but maintains the position of the curve. (1ap)

multilateral negotiation simultaneous tariff reductions on the part of many countries. (18)

multilateral trade trade among more than two persons or nations. (2)

multiplier the ratio of the change in real GDP to the shift in the aggregate expenditure line. (26)

national income the sum of labor income and capital income. (20)

national income and product accounts official government tabulation of the components of GDP and aggregate income. (20)

national saving aggregate income minus consumption minus government purchases. (20)

national saving rate the proportion of GDP that is saved, neither consumed nor spent on government purchases; equals national saving (S) divided by GDP, or S/Y. It also equals 1 minus the consumption share minus the government purchases share of GDP. (22)

nationalization the taking over of private firms by the government. (34)

natural monopoly a single firm in an industry in which average total cost is declining over the entire range of production and the minimum efficient scale is larger than the size of the market. (10, 16)

natural unemployment rate the unemployment rate that exists in normal times when there is neither a recession nor a boom and real GDP is equal to potential GDP. (21, 25)

negative externality the situation in which *costs* spill over onto someone not involved in producing or consuming the good. (15)

negative slope a slope of a curve that is less than zero, representing a negative or inverse relationship between two variables. (1ap)

negatively related a situation in which an increase in one variable is associated with a decrease in another variable; also called *inversely related*. (1)

neoclassical growth school an approach to macroeconomics that uses the aggregate production function and the growth accounting formula in describing long-term growth, emphasizing aggregate supply rather than aggregate demand. (32)

net exports the value of goods and services sold abroad minus the value of goods and services bought from the rest of the world; exports minus imports. (17, 20)

net exports share the proportion of GDP that is equal to net exports; equals net exports divided by GDP, or X/Y. (22)

net factor income from abroad the difference between receipts of factor income from foreign countries and payments of factor income to foreigners. (31)

net foreign assets the difference between citizens' net assets held abroad and net assets in the domestic country held by foreigners. (31)

net investment gross investment minus depreciation. (20)

net transfers from abroad the difference between transfer payments received and transfer payments made to other countries. (31)

new classical school a school of macroeconomics that holds that prices are perfectly flexible, expectations are rational, and therefore anticipated monetary policy will have no effect on the economy. (32)

new entrants people who are unemployed because they just entered the labor force and are still looking for work. (21)

new Keynesian school a school of macroeconomics that holds that prices are sticky and expectations are rational to explain the effect of monetary and fiscal policy. (32)

new trade theory models of international trade in which cost per unit declines as the international market grows. (17)

newly industrialized country a country that is growing rapidly and quickly developing its industrial base. (33)

nominal GDP gross domestic product without any correction for inflation; the same as GDP; the value of all goods and services newly produced in a country during some period of time, usually a year. (20)

nominal interest rate the interest rate uncorrected for inflation. (19)

nominal rigidities inflexibilities in wages and prices. (25)

noncooperative outcome an equilibrium in a game where the players cannot agree to cooperate and instead follow their individual incentives. (11)

nonexcludability the situation in which no one can be prevented from consuming a good. (15, 23)

nonrivalry the situation in which more people can consume a good without reducing the amount available for others to consume. (15, 23)

nontariff barrier any government action other than a tariff that reduces imports, such as a quota or a standard. (18)

normal good a good for which demand increases when income rises and decreases when income falls. (3)

normal profits the amount of accounting profits when economic profits are equal to zero. (9)

normative economics economic analysis that makes recommendations about economic policy. (1)

North-South problem refers to the geographic dispersion of incomes: Northern countries tend to be relatively rich, and southern ones tend to be relatively poor. (33)

oligopoly an industry characterized by few firms selling the same product with limited entry of other firms. (11)

on-the-job training the building of the skills of a firm's employees while they work for the firm. (12)

open-market operation the buying and selling of bonds by the central bank. (30)

opportunity cost the value of the next-best foregone alternative that was not chosen because something else was chosen. (2)

organization a human structure, such as a family, firm, government, or college, through which people may exchange goods and services. (2)

outsider someone who is not working for a particular firm, making it difficult for him or her to get a job with that firm although he or she is willing to work for a lower wage. (21)

overall price level an average of the prices of all goods and services with greater weight given to items on which more is spent. (1)

paper money currency made of paper that has no intrinsic value. (24)

Pareto efficiency a situation in which it is not possible to make someone better off without making someone else worse off. (7)

partnership a firm owned by more than one person in which the partners decide the division of the firm's income among them and are jointly liable for losses the firm incurs. (6)

part-time worker someone who works between 1 and 34 hours per week. (21)

patent a grant giving an inventor exclusive rights to use an invention for 17 years. (23)

payroll tax a tax on wages and salaries of individuals. (14)

peak the highest point in real GDP before a recession. (19)

per se rule a standard in antitrust cases in which it is only necessary to show that an action occurred, not also that there was intent or significant impact. (16)

perestroika the restructuring of the Soviet economy by reforming the central planning process. (34)

perfectly elastic demand demand for which the price elasticity is infinite, indicating an infinite response to a change in the price and therefore a horizontal demand curve. (4)

perfectly elastic supply supply for which the price elasticity is infinite, indicating an infinite response of quantity supplied to a change in price and thereby a horizontal supply curve. (4)

perfectly inelastic demand demand for which the price elasticity is zero, indicating no response to a change in price and therefore a vertical demand curve. (4)

perfectly inelastic supply supply for which the price elasticity is zero, indicating no response of quantity supplied to a change in price and thereby a vertical supply curve. (4)

permanent income model a type of forward-looking consumption model that assumes that people distinguish between temporary changes in their income and permanent changes in their income; the permanent changes have a larger effect on consumption. (26)

personal income income paid directly to individuals; includes labor income, transfer payments, and the part of capital income that is paid out to individuals. (20)

personal income tax a tax on all forms of income an individual or household receives. (14)

phaseout the gradual reduction of a government regulation or trade barrier. (17)

Phillips curve a downward-sloping relationship between inflation and unemployment; originally found by A. W. Phillips in data from the late 1800s and early 1900s. (24)

piece-rate system a system by which workers are paid a specific amount per unit they produce. (12)

policy ineffectiveness proposition the proposition that anticipated monetary policy will have no effect on the economy. (32)

political business cycle a business cycle resulting from politicians' use of fiscal or monetary policy to affect the outcome of an election. (32)

portfolio diversification spreading the collection of assets owned to limit exposure to risk. (13)

portfolio investment investment by a foreign entity of less than a 10 percent ownership share in the firm. (33)

positive economics economic analysis that explains what happens in the economy and why, without making recommendations about economic policy. (1)

positive externality the situation in which *benefits* spill over onto someone not involved in producing or consuming the good. (15)

positive slope a slope of a curve that is greater than zero, representing a positive or direct relationship between two variables. (1ap)

positively related a situation in which an increase in one variable is associated with an increase in another variable; also called *directly related*. (1)

potential GDP the economy's long-term growth trend for real GDP determined by the available supply of capital, labor, and technology. Real GDP fluctuates above and below potential GDP. (19, 25)

poverty line an estimate of the minimum amount of annual income required for a family to avoid severe economic hardship. (14)

poverty rate the percentage of people living below the poverty line. (14)

predatory pricing action on the part of one firm to set a price below its shutdown point to drive its competitors out of business. (16)

preemptive monetary strike a Fed interest rate increase in anticipation of a rise in inflation. (30)

present discounted value the value in the present of future payments. (13ap)

price refers to a particular good and is defined as the amount of money or other goods that one must pay to obtain the good. (3)

price adjustment (PA) line a flat line showing the level of inflation in the economy at a given point in time. It shifts up when real GDP is greater than potential GDP, and it shifts down when real GDP is less than potential GDP; it also shifts when expectations of inflation or raw materials prices change. (27)

price ceiling a government price control that sets the maximum allowable price for a good. (3)

price control a government law or regulation that sets or limits the price to be charged for a particular good. (3)

price discovery the process by which a market finds the equilibrium market price. (7)

price discrimination a situation in which different groups of consumers are charged different prices for the same good. (10)

price elasticity of demand the percentage change in the quantity demanded of a good divided by the percentage change in the price of that good. (4)

price elasticity of supply the percentage change in quantity supplied divided by the percentage change in price. (4)

price fixing the situation in which firms conspire to set prices for goods sold in the same market. (16)

price floor a government price control that sets the minimum allowable price for a good. (3)

price leader the price-setting firm in a collusive industry where other firms follow the leader. (11)

price level the average level of prices in the economy. (20)

price shock a change in the price of a key commodity such as oil, usually because of a shortage, that causes a shift in the price adjustment line; also sometimes called a supply shock. (28)

price-cost margin the difference between price and marginal cost divided by the price. This index is an indicator of market power, where an index of 0 indicates no market power and a higher price-cost margin indicates greater market power. (10, 11)

price-directed approach a management technique in which the instructions to a division of a firm are to maximize profits given transfer prices set by executives. (8)

price-earnings ratio the price of a stock divided by its annual earnings per share. (13)

price-maker a firm that has the power to set its price, rather than taking the price set by the market. (10)

price-taker any firm that takes the market price as given; this firm cannot affect the market price because the market is competitive. (6)

principal-agent relationship description of the relationship between the owners and managers of a firm in which the owners are viewed as the *principals* and the managers are viewed as *agents* for the owners. (6)

prisoner's dilemma a game in which individual incentives lead to a nonoptimal (noncooperative) outcome. If the players can credibly commit to cooperate, then they achieve the best (cooperative) outcome. (11)

private remedy a procedure that eliminates or internalizes externalities without government action other than defining property rights. (15)

privatization the process of converting a government enterprise into a privately owned enterprise. (15, 34)

producer surplus the difference between the price received by a firm for an additional item sold and the marginal cost of the item's production; for the market as a whole, it is the sum of all the individual firms' producer surpluses; or the area above the market supply curve and below the market price. (6, 7)

product differentiation the effort by firms to produce goods that are slightly different from other types of goods. (11)

production function a relationship that shows the quantity of output for any given amount of input. (6, 8)

production function the relationship that describes output as a function of labor, capital, and technology. (19)

production possibilities   alternative combinations of production of various goods that are possible, given the economy's resources. (2)

production possibilities curve   a curve showing the maximum combinations of production of two goods that are possible, given the economy's resources. (2)

production target   a goal set for the production of goods and services in a planned economy. (34)

productivity curve   a relationship stating the output per hour of work for each amount of capital per hour of work in the economy. (23ap)

profit maximization   an assumption that firms try to achieve the highest possible level of profits—total revenue minus total costs—given their production function. (6)

profit sharing   programs in which managers and employees receive a share of profits earned by the firm. (9, 13)

profits   total revenue received from selling the product minus the total costs of producing the product. (6)

progressive tax   a tax for which the amount of an individual's taxes rises as a proportion of income as the person's income increases. (14, 29)

property rights   rights over the use, sale, and proceeds from a good or resource. (2)

property tax   a tax on the value of property owned. (14)

proportional tax   a tax for which the amount of an individual's taxes as a percentage of income is constant as the person's income rises. (14)

protectionist policy   a policy that restricts trade to protect domestic producers. (18)

public choice models   models of government behavior that assume that those in government take actions to maximize their own well-being, such as getting reelected. (15)

public good   a good or service that has two characteristics: nonrivalry in consumption and nonexcludability. (15)

public infrastructure investment   purchases of capital by government for use as public goods, which add to the productive capacity of the economy. (22)

public infrastructure project   an investment project such as a bridge or jail funded by government designed to improve publicly provided services such as transportation or criminal justice. (15)

purchasing power parity   the theory that exchange rates are determined in such a way that the prices of goods in different countries are the same when measured in the same currency. (31)

purchasing power parity exchange rate   an exchange rate such that the prices of similar goods in different countries are the same when measured in the same currency. (20)

quantity demanded   the amount of a good that people want to buy at a given price. (3)

quantity equation of money   the equation relating the price level and real GDP to the quantity of money and the velocity of money: The quantity of money times its velocity equals the price level times real GDP; in terms of growth rates it states that money growth plus velocity growth equals inflation plus real GDP growth. (24)

quantity supplied   the amount of a good that firms are willing to sell at a given price. (3)

quantity-directed approach   a management technique in which decisions handed down by executives instruct a division to produce a given quantity. (8)

quintile   divisions or groupings of one-fifth of a population ordered by income, wealth, or some other statistic. (14)

quota   a governmental limit on the quantity of a particular good sold or imported. (3, 18)

rate of return   the return on an asset stated as a percentage of the price of the asset. (13)

rate of technical substitution   the rate at which one input must be substituted for another input to maintain the same production; it is the slope of the isoquant. (8ap)

rational expectations assumption   the assumption that people forecast the future no better or no worse than economic forecasters. (26, 29)

rational expectations revolution   a change in macroeconomic thinking during the 1970s based on the assumption that people make rational, forward-looking decisions using all the information available to them. (32)

real business cycle school   a group of economists who believe that shifts in potential GDP, largely due to changes in technology, are the primary cause of economic fluctuations. (32)

real business cycle theory   a theory of macroeconomics that stresses that shifts in potential GDP are a primary cause of fluctuations in real GDP; the shifts in potential GDP are usually caused by changes in technology. (25, 28)

real exchange rate   a measure of the exchange rate between two currencies that adjusts for differences in inflation levels in the two countries. (31)

real gross domestic product (real GDP)   a measure of the value of all the goods and services newly produced in a country during some period of time, adjusted for inflation. (1, 19, 20)

real interest rate   the interest rate minus the expected rate of inflation; it adjusts the nominal interest rate for inflation. (19)

real wage   the wage or price of labor adjusted for inflation; in contrast, the nominal wage has not been adjusted for inflation. (12, 21)

recession   a decline in real GDP that lasts for at least six months. (19)

Reciprocal Trade Agreement Act   passed in 1934 by the U.S. Congress, it allowed cuts in tariff rates based on similar cuts in tariff rates in European countries. (18)

recovery   the early part of an economic expansion, immediately after the trough of the recession. (19)

regressive tax   a tax for which the amount of an individual's taxes falls as a proportion of income as the person's income increases. (14)

reinflation   an increase in the inflation rate caused by a change in monetary policy. (28)

relative price   the price of a particular good compared to the price of other goods. (1)

relatively elastic   a situation in which the elasticity of one good is greater than the elasticity of another good. (4)

rent control   a government price control that sets the maximum allowable rent on a house or apartment. (3)

rent-seeking   behavior on the part of firms or individuals intended to preserve or obtain rights, privileges, or licenses through which above-normal profits (economic profits greater than zero) can be earned. (33)

rental price of capital   the amount that a rental company charges for the use of capital equipment for a specified period of time. (13)

required reserve ratio   the fraction of a bank's deposits that it is required to hold at the Fed. (24)

resale price maintenance   the situation in which a producer sets a list price and does not allow the retailer to offer a discount to consumers. (16)

research and development (R & D)   activities designed to further scientific knowledge and develop new products. (23)

reserves   deposits that commercial banks hold at the Fed. (24)

residential investment   purchases of new houses and apartment buildings. (20)

return   the income received from the ownership of an asset; for a stock, the return is the dividend plus the capital gain. (13)

revenue tariff   an import tax whose main purpose is to provide revenue to the government. (18)

Ricardian equivalence   the view that a change in taxes today will not affect consumption because people recognize that their, or their children's, future tax burden will change in an opposite direction. (29)

rule of reason   an evolving standard by which antitrust cases are decided, requiring not only the existence of monopoly power but also the intent to restrict trade and the existence of significant impact. (16)

sales tax   a type of excise tax that applies to total expenditures on a broad group of goods. (14)

savings deposit   an account at a financial institution that is very liquid but generally cannot be easily used for transactions. (24)

scarcity   the situation in which the quantity of resources is insufficient to meet all wants. (2)

scatter plot   a graph in which points in a Cartesian coordinate system represent the values of two variables. (1ap)

seasonal unemployment   unemployment that varies with the seasons of the year due to seasonal fluctuations in supply or demand for labor. (21)

sectoral trade balance   the value of exports less the value of imports in a particular sector or industry. (31)

services trade   trade in services, or things that do not have a physical form, such as consulting or telecommunications. (31)

services trade balance   the value of services exports minus the value of services imports. (31)

Sherman Antitrust Act   a law passed in 1890 in the United States to reduce anticompetitive behavior; Section 1 makes price fixing illegal, and Section 2 makes attempts to monopolize illegal. (16)

shift of the curve   a change in the position of a curve usually caused by a change in a variable not represented on either axis. (1ap)

shock therapy   the abrupt introduction of free markets in a formerly centrally planned economy. (34)

short run   the period of time during which it is not possible to change **all** inputs to production; only some inputs, such as labor, can be changed. (8)

shortage   the situation in which quantity demanded is greater than quantity supplied. (3)

shutdown point   the point at which price equals the minimum of average variable cost. (8)

slope   refers to a curve and is defined as the change in the variable on the vertical axis divided by the change in the variable on the horizontal axis. (1ap)

Smoot-Hawley tariff   a set of tariffs imposed in 1930 that raised the average tariff level to 59 percent by 1932. (18)

social insurance transfer   a transfer payment, such as social security, that does not depend on the income of the recipient. (14)

social regulation   government regulation, such as environmental, health, or safety regulation, that aims to overcome or correct externalities in which private costs differ from social costs. (16)

social security   the system through which individuals make payments to the government when they work and receive payments from the government when they retire or become disabled. (14)

socialism   an economic system in which the government owns and controls all the capital and makes decisions about prices and quantities as part of a central plan. (34)

sole proprietorship   a firm owned by a single person. (6)

specialization   the situation in which a resource, such as labor, concentrates and develops efficiency at a particular task. (2)

specific tariff   a tax on imports that is proportional to the number of units or items imported. (18)

specific tax   a tax that is proportional to the number of items sold. (7)

spending balance   the level of income or real GDP at which the 45-degree line and the aggregate expenditure line cross; also called equilibrium income. (25)

stagflation   the situation in which high inflation and high unemployment occur simultaneously. (28)

Standard Industrial Classification (SIC)   a taxonomy used to label and group industries for statistical purposes; each industry is given an SIC code. (9)

state enterprise   an organization, analogous to a firm in a market economy, that is owned and controlled by the government. (34)

statistical discrepancy   the discrepancy between calculations of GDP using the spending approach and the income approach due to unreported data or errors in data collection. (20)

sticky price assumption   an assumption that prices do not move quickly in response to a change in supply or demand; the assumption is used in the theory of economic fluctuations. (25)

store of value   something that will allow purchasing power to be carried from one period to the next. (24)

strategic behavior   firm behavior that takes into account the market power and reactions of other firms in the industry. (11)

strategic demand curve   a downward-sloping demand curve in which the firm incorporates its expectations of what other firms will do. (11)

strategic marginal revenue curve   the marginal revenue curve derived from a strategic demand curve. (11)

strategic trade policy   a set of government actions designed to encourage large firms to locate or start up in that country. (18)

structural deficit   the level of the government budget deficit under the scenario where real GDP is equal to potential GDP; also called the full-employment deficit. (29)

structural unemployment   long-term unemployment due to structural problems such as poor skills or longer term changes in demand or insufficient work incentives. (21)

structure-conduct-performance method   a method of analyzing the market power in an industry by looking at the structure of the industry. (11)

subsistence line   a line representing the minimum amount of production the population needs to survive or subsist. (23)

substitute   a good that has many of the same characteristics and can be used in place of another good. (3)

substitution effect   the amount by which quantity demanded falls when the price rises, exclusive of the income effect. (5)

supplemental security income (SSI)   a means-tested transfer program designed primarily to help the poor who are disabled or blind. (14)

supply   a relationship between price and quantity supplied. (3)

supply curve   a graph of supply showing the upward-sloping relationship between price and quantity supplied. (3)

supply schedule   a tabular presentation of supply showing the price and quantity supplied of a particular good, all else being equal. (3)

supply side economics   the branch of economics that emphasizes that reducing marginal tax rates on investments and labor will increase aggregate supply, thereby stimulating the macroeconomy. (32)

surplus   the situation in which quantity supplied is greater than quantity demanded. (3, 7)

systematic risk   the level of risk in asset markets that investors cannot reduce by diversification. (13)

tacit collusion   implicit or unstated cooperation of firms to make mutually beneficial pricing or production decisions. (11)

tangency point   the only point in common for two curves, showing the point where the two curves just touch. (5ap)

target inflation rate   the central bank's goal for the average rate of inflation over the long run. (27)

tariff   a tax on imports. (17)

tax bracket   a range of taxable income that is taxed at the same rate. (14)

tax incidence   the allocation of the burden of the tax between buyer and seller. (14)

tax rate   the percentage of income or the value of a good paid to the government in the form of taxes. (26)

tax revenue   the total amount the government receives in the form of taxes; equals the tax rate times income (also simply called taxes). (14, 26)

taxable income   a household's income minus exemptions and deductions. (14)

technological change   improvement in technology over time. (23)

technology   anything that raises the amount of output that can be produced with a given level of capital and labor. (19, 23)

terms of trade   quantity of imported goods a country can obtain in exchange for a unit of exported goods. (17)

time deposit   an account at a financial institution that requires that the money be left in the account for a specified period of time. (24)

time inconsistency   the situation in which policymakers have the incentive to announce one economic policy but then change that policy after citizens have acted on the initial, stated policy. (15, 30)

time-series graph   a graph that plots a variable over time, usually with time on the horizontal axis. (1ap)

total costs   the sum of variable costs and fixed costs. (6, 8)

total revenue   the price per unit times the quantity the firm sells. (6)

tradable goods   goods for which transportation costs are not prohibitive. (31)

tradable permit   a governmentally granted license to pollute that can be bought and sold. (15)

trade adjustment assistance   transfer payments made to workers who will be hurt by the move to free trade. (17)

trade balance   the value of exports minus the value of imports. (20)

trade creation   the increase in trade due to a decrease in trade barriers. (18)

trade diversion   the shifting of trade away from the low-cost producer toward a higher-cost producer because of a reduction in trade barriers with the country of the higher-cost producer. (18)

trade war   a conflict among nations over trade policies caused by imposition of protectionist policies on the part of one country and subsequent retaliatory actions by other countries. (18)

transaction cost   the cost of buying or selling in a market including search, bargaining, and writing contracts. (2, 15)

transfer payment   a grant of funds from the government to an individual. (14)

transfer price   a price that one department of an organization must pay to receive goods or services from another department in the same organization. (2)

treble damages   penalties awarded to the injured party equal to three times the value of the injury. (16)

trough   the lowest point of real GDP at the end of a recession. (19)

twin deficits   a term referring to a situation in which a government budget deficit and an international trade deficit occur simultaneously. (26)

unemployment insurance   a program which makes payments to people who lose their jobs. (14)

unemployment rate   the ratio (usually expressed as a percentage) of unemployed workers to the labor force. (19, 21)

unilateral disarmament   in trade policy, the removal of trade barriers by one country without reciprocal action on the part of other countries. (18)

unit elastic demand   demand for which price elasticity equals 1. (4)

unit of account   a standard unit in which prices can be quoted and values of goods can be compared. (24)

unit-free measure   a measure that does not depend on a unit of measurement. (4)

Uruguay Round   the most recent round of negotiations on the General Agreement on Tariffs and Trade, begun in 1986 in Uruguay. (18)

user fee   a fee charged for the use of a good normally provided by the government. (15)

utility   a numerical indicator of a person's preferences in which higher levels of utility indicate a greater preference. (5)

utility maximization   an assumption that people try to achieve the highest level of utility given their budget constraint. (5)

utility maximizing rule   a condition that a consumer maximizes utility by choosing to purchase a combination of two goods such that the ratio of marginal utilities for the two goods equals the ratio of the market prices or, alternatively, such that the ratio of the marginal utility to the price of each of the two goods is equal. (5)

value added   the value of the firm's production minus the value of the intermediate goods used in production. (20)

variable costs   costs of production that vary with the quantity of production. (6, 8)

velocity   a measure of how fast money is turned over in the economy: Velocity equals nominal GDP divided by the money supply. (24)

vertical merger   a combining of two firms in which one supplies goods to the other. (16)

voluntary import expansion (VIE)   a government agreement to expand imports from a particular country. (18)

voluntary restraint agreement (VRA)   a country's self-imposed government restriction on exports to a particular country. (18)

voting paradox   a decision-making dilemma caused by the fact that aggregate voting patterns will not consistently reflect citizens' preferences because of multiple issues on which people vote. (15)

wage   the price of labor defined over a period of time worked. (12)

welfare notch   a situation in which there is a decrease in total income for families on welfare when they increase the amount they work. (14)

working-age population   persons over 16 years of age who are not in an institution such as a jail or hospital. (21)

World Bank   an international agency, established after World War II, designed to promote the economic development of poorer countries through lending channeled from industrialized countries. (33)

World Trade Organization (WTO)   an international organization that can mediate trade disputes. (18)

yield   the annual rate of return on a bond if the bond were held to maturity. (13)

INDEX

Note: Page numbers followed by n indicate footnotes.

Ability-to-pay principle, 385–386
Absolute advantage, 463, 464
Academic wage gap, 332
Account, money as unit of, 646
Accounting profits, economic profits versus, 248–249
Acid rain, 416
Acquisitions, 224
    economies of scope and, 225–228, 226(table)
Acreage allotment programs, 189
ADI curve. *See* Aggregate demand/inflation (ADI) curve
ADM (Archer-Daniels Midland), 443
Ad valorem tariffs, 487
Ad valorem taxes, 188
Advanced countries, catch-up within, 858–860, 859(fig.)
Advanced Micro Devices, 262
Advantage
    absolute, 463, 464
    comparative. *See* Comparative advantage
Adverse selection, 363–364
    in insurance industry, 451
Advertising, product differentiation and, 295
AFDC (Aid to Families with Dependent Children), 386
AFL (American Federation of Labor), 338
Age, saving and, 545–546
Agents, principal-agent relationship and, 147
Aggregate demand, 525
    changes in, changes in output related to, 673–679, 674(fig.)
    economic fluctuations and, 525–526
Aggregate demand/inflation (ADI) curve, 728–739, 729(fig.)
    constant money growth rule's implications for, 811–812
    derivation of, 735–739, 736(fig.)
    interest rates and inflation and, 732–735
    interest rates and real GDP and, 728–731
    price adjustment line combined with, 744(fig.), 744–745
Aggregate expenditure line, 686–689, 687(fig.)
    multiplier and slope of, 707–708, 708(fig.)

multiplier for general shift in, 699–700
    shifts in, 688(fig.), 688–689
    slope of, 688
    when net exports depend on income, 712(table), 712–713, 713(fig.)
Aggregate hours of labor input, 570–572
    forecasts of, 571(table), 571–572
    unemployment and, 571
Aggregate income, 683
Aggregate supply, long-term economic growth and, 522–524
Aggregate supply curve, price adjustment and, 764
Agriculture, set-aside programs and, 189
Aid to Families with Dependent Children (AFDC), 386
Airbus, 497
Aircraft industry, 497
Airline industry
    deregulation of, 451, 452
    predatory pricing in, 439
    price discrimination in, 286
    product differentiation in, 297
Alcoa Aluminum, 438, 439
Allstate, 450
Altruism, 124
American Airlines, 286, 439
American Federation of Labor (AFL), 338
American Stock Exchange, 346
American Tobacco Company, 438, 439
"AM/FM" debates, 846
Amoco, 437
Ando, Albert, 846
Anheuser-Busch, 312
Anti-Corn League, 500
Antidumping duties, 494
Antitrust Division of the Justice Department, 439
Antitrust policy, 437–444
    existing monopolies and, 437–439
    mergers and, 439–443
    price fixing and, 443
    vertical restraints and, 443–444
Apple Computer, 438, 631, 822
Archer-Daniels Midland (ADM), 443
Arrow, 292, 293, 297
Arrow, Kenneth, 428–429
Arrow impossibility theorem, 429
Ask price, 176
Aspirin industry, 238, 239
    product differentiation in, 292–293

Assets, of commercial banks, 651, 652
Asymmetric information, 363–364
ATC. *See* Average total cost *(ATC) entries*
AT&T, 242(table), 280, 291, 438, 439
Automatic stabilizers, 785–786
Automobile industry
    globalization of, 242
    North American market and, 479–480
    trade restrictions and, 488, 490, 491
Average, geometric, 548n
Average costs, 204–205
    fixed *(AFC)*, 204, 205
    generic cost curves and, 209–211, 210(fig.)
    for individual firm, 208–211, 209(fig.)
    marginal versus average concepts and, 209
    total. *See* Average total cost *(ATC) entries*
    variable *(AVC)*, 204, 205
Average product of labor, 207
Average revenue, 269
Average tax rate, 376
Average total cost *(ATC)*, 204–205, 219(fig.), 219–221, 221(fig.)
    minimization of, 253–254
Average total cost pricing, 447

Backward-bending labor supply curve, 327, 329(fig.)
Balanced budget, 774
Balanced budget amendment to the U.S. Constitution, 794
Balanced budget multiplier, 718
Balance of payments, 823–827
    capital account and, 825–827, 827(fig.)
    current account and, 824(table), 824–825, 826(fig.)
Balance of trade, 821–829
    balance of payments and, 823–827
    bilateral surpluses and deficits and, 827(table), 827–828
    merchandise and services and, 822–823
    sectoral deficits and, 828
    trade deficit and, 821(fig.), 821–822
Balance sheet, of commercial banks, 651–652, 652(table)
Balcerowicz, Leszek, 887
Bangladesh, economic growth in, 860

Bank(s), 649, 694(fig.)
  central. *See* Central banks; Federal
    Reserve System (Fed)
  commercial. *See* Commercial banks
  money creation by, 652–655
  reserves and. *See* Reserves
BankBoston, 649
Bank of America, 450, 867
Bank of England, 799
Bank of Japan, 799
Bankruptcy, 200
Barriers, to trade. *See* Trade restrictions
Barriers to entry, 263, 283
Barro, Robert, 788, 848
Barter, 646
Baseball bat industry, 491
Baseline, 752
Base year, 549
Bastiat, Frédéric, 498
Bayer Company, 238
Becker, Gary S., 124
Benefit. *See* Cost-benefit analysis; Marginal benefit
Bertelsmann, 242(table)
Bid(s), bonds and, 353–354
Bid price, 176
Big bang approach, 884–885
Big Mac index, 831
Bilateral monopoly, labor unions and, 340
Bilateral trade balance, 827(table), 827–828
Biodiversity, externalities from, 420
Blau, Francine, 18
Blockbuster Video, 200, 296, 824
Blue Chip Economic Indicators, 680
Board(s) of directors, 147
Board of Governors, of Federal Reserve System, 649
Boeing, 458, 497
Bolshevik party, 878
Bonds, 652
  corporate, 345
  government, 346, 777–778
  prices and returns on, 353–355, 354(fig.)
Boom(s). *See also* Economic fluctuations
  end of, 749–755
  return to potential GDP after, 754–755
Boom-bust cycle, 763, 763(fig.), 765, 766(fig.)
Borrowing, by government, 801–802. *See also* Federal debt
Brazil, trade policy of, 871, 871(table)
Breakeven point, 214(fig.), 214–215
Bretton Woods system, 834, 835(fig.)

British Airways, 406
Budget constraint, 35–36, 117–123, 118(table)
  utility maximization subject to, 119(table), 119–123
Budget cycle, 775, 776(fig.)
Budget deficits, 716, 774, 776, 787–793
  credible plans for reducing, 788–791
  international comparisons of, 777, 777(table)
  short- and long-run impact of, 787–788
  structural versus cyclical, 792(fig.), 792–793, 793(fig.)
Budget line, 138(fig.), 138–139, 139(fig.)
  indifference curve and, 141, 141(fig.)
Budget surpluses, 774
Bundesbank, 799
Burger King, 345
Burns, Arthur, 799
Bush, George, 516, 649, 748, 774, 799, 815
  fiscal policy under, 851(table), 851–853, 853–854
Business cycles. *See* Economic fluctuations
Businesses. *See* Corporate *entries*; Firm(s)
Business fixed investment, 536
Business taxes, indirect, 540
Buyers, in double-auction markets, 177
B & W Riverview Estates, 262–263

Cadbury Schweppes, 312
CAFE (corporate average fleet efficiency), 419
California Public Utility Commission, 447
Canada, trade of, 491
Capacity
  excess, under monopolistic competition, 302
  normal utilization of, natural unemployment rate and, 675
Capital, 14, 523
  diminishing returns to, 625(fig.), 625–626, 626(fig.)
  efficient allocation among industries, 254
  financial. *See* Financial capital
  human. *See* Human capital
  investment in. *See* Investment
  labor and, economic growth and, 623, 624(fig.), 625–626
  marginal revenue product of, 347
  market demand for, 348, 349(fig.)

market supply of, 348, 349(fig.)
  mix with labor, 222, 232(table), 232–237, 233(fig.), 234(fig.)
  new, technology embodied in, 637
  physical. *See* Physical capital
  production function of firm and, 205–206
  rental price of, 346–347
  per worker, obstacles to raising, 866–870
Capital abundance, 472
Capital account, 825–827, 827(fig.)
Capital expansion
  average total costs and, 219(fig.), 219–220
  in long run, 221–222
  total costs and, 217–218, 218(fig.), 219(table)
Capital gains, 353, 374
Capital gains tax, 852
Capital goods, differentiation of, 293
Capital income, in GDP, 539–540
Capital intensiveness, 472
Capitalism, 877–878
Capital losses, 353
Capital markets, 344–365
  corporate governance and, 363–364
  for financial capital. *See* Financial capital
  for physical capital. *See* Physical capital
  risk in. *See* Risk
  terminology in, 345–346
Capital-saving technological change, 628
Card, David, 335
Carlyle, Thomas, 621
Cartels, 305
Carter, Jimmy, 649, 799
Cartesian coordinate system, 25
Casio, 458
Catch-up line, 857
Caterpillar, 293, 296, 302, 458
Causation, 12
CBO (Congressional Budget Office), 679, 773, 774
CBS Records, 225
CEA. *See* Council of Economic Advisers (CEA)
Ceccheti, Stephen, 676
Central banks, 649. *See also* Federal Reserve System (Fed); Monetary policy; Money supply
  government borrowing from, 801–802
  independence of, 799–803
  interest rates and inflation and, 732(table), 732–733

Centrally planned economies. *See* Command economies

CEOs (chief executive officers), 145–146

Ceteris paribus assumption, 17

Cetus, 630

Chain weighted price index, 552

Change in demand, 69, 70(fig.), 71
  changes in production and, 676–677

Charles Schwab, 450

Checking deposits, 647

Chevron, 437

Chicago Mercantile Exchange, 837

Chicago Police Department, 170

Chicken industry, 239

Chief executive officers (CEOs), 145–146

Children, poverty among, 399–400

China
  central planning in, 883
  economic reforms in, 887–888

Chips and Technologies, 262

Choice, 4, 34
  consumer decision and, 35–36
  for economy as a whole, 41–46
  producer decisions and, 37–38
  production possibilities curve and, 45–46, 46(fig.)

Chrysler, 242, 488

CIO (Congress of Industrial Organizations), 338

Circular flow diagram, 13–14, 14(fig.), 542(fig.)

Citibank, 450, 656, 804, 807

Claiborne, Liz, 290, 292

"Classical theory," 845

Clayton Antitrust Act (1914), 439

Clinton, Bill, 389, 515–516, 550, 649, 748, 773–774, 794, 799, 815
  fiscal policy under, 853(table), 853–854

Coase, Ronald, 50, 417, 418, 419

Coase theorem, 418

Cobden, Richard, 500

Coca-Cola, 36, 293, 302, 309–310, 312, 440

Coin(s), 647

Coincidence of wants, 646

Collectivized farms, 880

Collusion. *See also* Game theory; Oligopoly
  explicit, 305
  tacit, 305

Colombia, trade policy of, 871, 871(table)

Command and control remedies, 419–420, 423

Command economies, 20, 876, 877–883
  of China, 883
  economic questions in, 47–48
  of Soviet Union, 878, 880–883
  technological change and quality of goods and, 882
  transition to market economies. *See* Emerging market economies

Commerce clause, 459

Commerce Department, 407

Commercial banks, 649
  balance sheet of, 651–652, 652(table)

Commodity money, 645

Communism, 878

Communist Manifesto (Marx and Engels), 879

Communist party
  Chinese, 883
  Soviet, 878

Companies. *See* Corporate *entries;* Firm(s)

Comparable worth proposals, 334

Comparative advantage, 462–473, 467–471, 469(fig.)
  dynamic, 471–472
  factor abundance of countries and factor intensity of industries and, 472–473
  gains from trade and, 467–471, 469(fig.)
  opportunity cost and relative efficiency and, 463
  producer decisions and, 38
  relative prices and, 466–467, 467(table)

Compensating wage differentials, 331–332, 337

Compensation. *See* Wage *entries*

Competition
  as argument for trade restriction, 498
  increase by international trade, 461
  monopolistic. *See* Monopolistic competition
  monopolistic competition compared with, 302
  monopoly compared with, 275–276, 302

Competition policy. *See* Antitrust policy

Competitive Advantage (Porter), 296

Competitive equilibrium model, 170–195, 171(fig.)
  deadweight loss and. *See* Deadweight loss
  determining production, consumption, and price and, 172–176
  double-auction market and, 176–178
  efficiency and. *See* Efficiency; Inefficiency

long-run. *See* Long-run competitive equilibrium model
  predictions of, 178–180(fig.), 178–181

Competitive markets, 49, 148–149
  wage discrimination and, 333–334

Complements, 59

Compound growth, 531

Computer chip industry, 458

Computer industry, 239, 438, 631

Concentration ratios
  four-firm, 312, 312(table)
  as measures of market power, 312, 312(table)

Conditional forecasts, 681

Conditionality, 869

Congressional Budget Office (CBO), 679, 773, 774

Congress of Industrial Organizations (CIO), 338

Conjectural variations approach, 304, 308–311
  quantity and price determination and, 310
  strategic demand curves and, 309(fig.), 309–310, 310(fig.)

Constant money growth rule, 811–812
  debates about, 812
  implications for aggregate demand/inflation curve, 811–812

Constant returns to scale, 223, 223(fig.)

Consumer(s). *See also* Households
  expectations of, 58–59
  incomes of, 58
  information possessed by, 58
  number of, 58
  preferences of, 58

Consumer behavior, 110(fig.), 110–135
  consumer surplus and, 131(fig.), 131–133, 133(fig.)
  saving and, 133–135
  utility and. *See* Utility *entries*
  willingness to pay and. *See* Willingness to pay

Consumer decisions, 35–37
  gains from trade and, 36
  reallocation and, 36–37
  scarcity and choice and, 35–36

Consumer price index (CPI), 318, 552, 553(fig.)

Consumer products, differentiation of, 292–293

Consumer Product Safety Administration, 453

Consumer Reports magazine, 292, 293, 294, 295

Consumers Digest magazine, 292

Consumers Union, 454

Consumer surplus, 121–133, 131(fig.), 133(fig.), 175
maximizing sum of producer surplus plus, 186, 187(fig.)
monopoly and, 277–278
origin of, 132
Consumption. *See also* Marginal propensity to consume (MPC)
forward-looking model of. *See* Forward-looking consumption model
in GDP, 535, 535(fig.), 594, 595(fig.)
interest rates and, 596–598, 597(fig.), 684
interest rates and real GDP and, 730
marginal propensity to consume and, 683
shift in, investment and, 606–608, 607(fig.), 607(table)
two-way link between income and, 685–686
utility and, 111–112, 112(table), 113(table)
Consumption decisions, individual, 174–175
Consumption function, 682(table), 682–684
income measures and, 683–684, 684(fig.)
marginal propensity to consume and, 683, 683(fig.)
Consumption share line, movements along versus shifts in, 597–598
Consumption smoothing, 720
Contestable markets, 441
Contingent valuations, 411
Contracts
debt, 345
employment, long-term, 336–337
equity, 346
implicit, 677
Controlled experiments, 12–13
Convergence of positions, in two-party system, 427–428
Cooperative outcome, 305
Coordination failure, 849–850
Copyrights, 280, 282
Corn laws, 500
Corporate average fleet efficiency (CAFE), 419
Corporate bonds, 345
Corporate governance, 147, 363–364
asymmetric information and, 363–364
profit sharing and, 364
takeover threats and, 364
Corporate income taxes, 379
Corporations, 145–146
Correlation, 12

Cosmetics industry, 238–239
Cost(s)
average. *See* Average costs
changes in, industries and, 250, 252(fig.), 253
excess, under monopolistic competition, 301–302
fixed. *See* Fixed costs
in long run, 217–222
marginal. *See* Marginal cost
minimizing for given quantities, 235–236, 236(fig.)
opportunity. *See* Opportunity costs
private, marginal, 413–414, 414(fig.)
production decisions and, 152–154, 153(table)
production function of firm and, 205–207
in short run, 211–217, 212(fig.)
social, marginal, 413–414, 414(fig.)
total. *See* Total cost
transaction, 50, 418–419
per unit, number of firms related to, 476, 477(fig.), 478(fig.)
variable. *See* Variable costs
Cost-benefit analysis, 410–412
of economic versus social regulation, 453–455
marginal cost and marginal benefit and, 410–411
public infrastructure projects and, 411–412
of reducing externalities, 424
Council for Mutual Economic Assistance, 882
Council of Economic Advisers (CEA), 20, 25, 679, 773, 774, 786
aggregate hours of labor forecast by, 571(table), 571–572
Countercyclical policy, 783(fig.), 783–786, 784(fig.)
Countries in transition, 862
Coupons, of bonds, 353
Cournot, Augustin, 308
Cournot model, 308
CPI (consumer price index), 318, 552, 553(fig.)
Craft unions, 338
Creative destruction, 573
Credibility
of budget reduction plans, 789
of monetary policy, gains from, 814–817
Crédit Lyonnais, 867
Cross-price elasticity of demand, 101
Crowding out, 606
Currencies, 40. *See also* Money
definition of, 647

deposits versus, 656–657
exchange rates and. *See* Exchange rates
paper, 646–647
Currency to deposit ratio, 656–657
Current account, 824(table), 824–825, 826(fig.)
Desert Storm and, 825
Current account balance, 825
Current population survey, 394, 566
Curry Company, 282
Curves. *See also* Graphs; *specific curves*
movement along, 31–32
shift of, 32
slopes of, 30(fig.), 30–31, 31(fig.)
Customs unions, 502
Cyclical deficits, 793
Cyclical unemployment, 565

Dai-Ichi Kangyo, 867
Dairy industry, prices in, 83
Dango, 308
DARPA (Defense Advanced Research Projects Agency), 636
Darwin, Charles, 631
Days Inn, 239
Deadweight loss, 186, 188–192
managing divisions of large firms and, 227
from monopoly, 276–278
product variety versus, 302–303
set-aside programs and, 189
from taxation, 188–192
De Beers, 262, 263, 282–283
Debt. *See* Borrowing; Federal debt
Debt contracts, 345
Debt to GDP ratio, 778–779, 779(fig.)
Deductions, for income tax, 374
Defense Advanced Research Projects Agency (DARPA), 636
Deferred payment contracts, 337
Deficits
budget. *See* Budget deficits
trade. *See* Trade deficits
twin, 716
Deflation, 519, 666, 755
Demand, 55(table), 55–60. *See also* Supply and demand diagram
change in. *See* Change in demand
consumer behavior and. *See* Utility *entries;* Willingness to pay
cross-price elasticity of, 101
derived. *See* Derived demand
elastic, 93, 95(table)
for factors of production in general, 348
income elasticity of, 100(table), 100–101

increase in, effects on industry, 246–249, 247(fig.)
inelastic, 94, 95(table)
for labor. *See* labor demand
law of, 55
for money, 803–804, 804(fig.)
perfectly inelastic, 95, 95(fig.), 95(table)
price elasticity of. *See* Price elasticity of demand
relatively elastic, 94–95, 95(table)
shifts in. *See* Shifts in demand
unit elastic, 94, 95(table)
Demand curve, 55–56, 56(fig.)
for capital, 347–348, 348(fig.)
consumer behavior and. *See* Consumer behavior
elasticities and, 95
elasticity versus slope of, 93
graphical derivation of, 126–129, 127(fig.), 128(fig.)
import, 487
individual, 128
for labor, 578(fig.), 578–579
market. *See* Market demand curve
movements along versus shifts in, 59–60, 60(fig.), 120
strategic. *See* Strategic demand curves
Demand schedule, 55
Demand shocks, 759
Department of Commerce, 407
Department of Justice, Antitrust Division of, 439
Deposits
checking, 647
currency versus, 656–657
expansion of, 652–655
reserves linked to, 654–655
savings, 647–648
time, 648
Depreciation, 345, 592
in GDP, 540
Depressions. *See also* Economic fluctuations; Great Depression
recessions versus, 514(fig.), 514–515
Deregulation movement, 451–452, 452(table)
Derived demand, 320
fro labor, market demand and, 322–324, 323(fig.)
for physical capital, 346
De Soto, Hernando, 865
Developing countries, 862
human capital in, 866
lack of foreign investment in, 867, 869
obstacles to spread of technology in, 865–866
Diamond-water paradox, 123, 125

Diffusion, of innovation, 627
Digital Equipment, 438
Diktats, 878
Diminishing marginal benefit, 126
Diminishing marginal utility, 113–114
Diminishing returns to capital, 625(fig.), 625–626, 626(fig.)
Diminishing returns to labor, 152, 163, 618–619, 619(fig.)
Discount(s), quantity, 285, 286(fig.)
Discounting, 368
Discount rates, 368, 809
for public infrastructure projects, 411–412
Discouraged workers, 567
Discretionary fiscal policy, 785, 786
Discrimination, wage differentials and, 332–334
Diseconomies of scale, 223, 223(fig.)
external, 254–255, 255(fig.)
internal, 255
Disembodied technological change, 637
Disinflation, 519, 666, 755, 766(fig.)
credible, expectations and, 816(fig.), 817
Volcker, 757–759
Dismal science, economics as, 617, 621
Disposable income, 683–684
Disraeli, Benjamin, 500
Diversification, portfolio, to reduce risk, 360, 362(fig.)
Dividends, 146, 346
Dividend yield, 353
Division of labor, 628
international trade and, 461–462
producer decisions and, 38
Dole, Bob, 550
Domestic content restrictions, 502
Domestic policies, trade barriers related to, 491–492
Domestic trade, international trade versus, 38, 40
Double-auction markets, 176–178
Dow-Jones industrial average, 344, 360
Dr Pepper, 312, 440
Dumping, 494
Duopoly, 305–306, 306(fig.)
Dupuit, Jules, 132
Duties, antidumping, 494
Dynamic comparative advantage, 471–472

Earned income tax credit (EITC), 387–388
Earnings, 353. *See also* Income; Profit(s); Wage *entries*
Eastern Europe, trade between Soviet Union and, 881–882

Ebony magazine, 290
Econometric models, 692
Economic challenges, 4–5
The Economic Consequences of the Peace (Keynes), 709
Economic data, inaccurate, 13
Economic development, 861–863
geographical patterns of, 861–862, 862(fig.)
poverty and, 861
terminology of, 862–863, 863(table)
Economic fluctuations, 509, 511–515, 512(fig.), 513(table), 672–695, 673(fig.), 726–745, 727(fig.), 748–767
aggregate demand changes leading to output changes and, 673–679, 674(fig.)
aggregate demand/inflation curve and. *See* Aggregate demand/inflation (ADI) curve
consumption's response to income and, 682–684
end of recessions and booms and, 749–755
forecasting real GDP and, 679–681
government purchases changes and, 762(fig.), 762–763
monetary errors and reversals and, 763, 763(fig.), 765
monetary policy changes and, 755, 756(fig.), 757–759, 762(fig.), 762–763
policy and, 525–526
potential GDP changes and, 678
price adjustment and, 764
price adjustment line and. *See* Price adjustment *(PA)* line
price shocks and supply shocks and, 759–761
real GDP when consumption and income move together and, 685–691
spending balance and departures of real GDP from potential GDP and, 693–694
Economic fluctuations theory, 522
Economic growth, 509–511, 511(fig.), 616(table), 616–639
catch-up in whole world and, 860, 860(fig.)
catch-up within advanced countries and, 858–860, 859(fig.)
catch-up within United States and, 857–858, 859(fig.)
compound, 531
economic development and, 861–863
explanation of, 45

government size and, 612
growth accounting and, 632–635
inward-looking versus outward-look-
    ing economic policies and,
    870–872, 871(table)
with labor, capital, and technology,
    627–631. *See also* Technology
labor and capital only and, 623,
    624(fig.), 625–626
labor only and, 618–623
long-term. *See* Long-term economic
    growth
obstacles to raising capital per worker
    and, 866–870
obstacles to spread of technology and,
    864–866
potential GDP and, 638(fig.), 638–639
production possibilities curve and, 43,
    44(fig.), 45–46, 46(fig.)
slowdown in, 511
Economic growth theory, 522
Economic history, 6–7
Economic interaction, 34. *See also*
    Deadweight loss; Inefficiency;
    Pareto efficiency
Economic models, 15–19. *See also spe-
    cific models*
description of, 15(fig.), 15–17, 16(fig.)
development of, 19
graphs of. *See* Graphs
microeconomic versus macroeco-
    nomic, 17, 19
uses of, 19
Economic opportunities, 5
Economic policies. *See also* Antitrust
    policy; Fiscal policy; Monetary pol-
    icy; Technology policy
economics as science versus partisan
    policy tool and, 21
employment and unemployment and,
    582–585
industrial, 636
inward-looking versus outward-
    looking, 870–872, 871(table)
positive and normative economics
    and, 20–21
supply side, 524
tax, 385–386
Economic profits. *See also* Profit *entries*
accounting profits versus, 248–249
Economic questions, 2, 47–48
Economic reform. *See* Emerging market
    economies
Economic regulation, social regulation
    versus, 452–455, 453(table)
Economic rent, 348–350, 349(fig.)
Economic Report of the President, 773,
    774

of 1962, 845
Economics
as dismal science, 617, 621
positive and normative, 20–21
as science versus partisan policy tool,
    21
Economic variables, 11
Economies
command. *See* Command economies
informal, 865
market. *See* Market economies
mixed, 20
underground, omission from GDP,
    554–555
Economies of scale, 222–224, 223(fig.),
    224(fig.)
external, 255–258, 256(fig.)
natural monopolies and, 445, 445(fig.)
Economies of scope, 225–228,
    226(table)
Edison, Thomas, 629, 630, 631
Educational choice, explanation of, 45
Efficiency. *See also* Deadweight loss;
    Inefficiency; Market failures
of capital allocation among industries,
    254
comparative advantage and, 463
equality versus, taxes and, 385
informational, 192–194
minimum efficient scale and, 223,
    224(fig.)
Pareto, 182, 193
production possibilities curve and, 43
Efficiency wage, 337, 582
Efficient market(s), 182–186, 185(fig.)
conditions for, 183
definition of, 182
income inequality and, 185–186
Efficient market hypothesis, 362
E.I. Dupont de Nemours, 242(table)
EITC (earned income tax credit),
    387–388
Elastic demand, 93, 95(table)
Elasticity, 88–107. *See also* Price elastic-
    ity of demand; Price elasticity of
    supply
applications of, 105, 107
cross-price, of demand, 101
income, of demand, 100(table),
    100–101
Elderly people, poverty among, 399
Electronic scanners, 258
Electronics industry, comparative advan-
    tage and, 464(table), 464–467
Embodied technological change, 637
Emerging market economies, 884–889
in China, 887–888
goals of reform and, 884

in Poland, 886–887
political freedom and, 888–889
real GDP growth and, 885–886,
    886(table)
shock therapy versus gradualism in,
    884–885
Emission taxes, 423
Employment, 515–516. *See also* Labor
    entries; Unemployment *entries;*
    Wage *entries*
aggregate hours of labor input and,
    570–572
definition of, 567, 568(fig.)
long-term trends in, 579(fig.),
    579–580
in United States, 516(fig.), 516–517
Employment contracts, long-term,
    336–337
Employment-to-population ratio,
    568(fig.), 569, 569(table), 570,
    570(fig.)
Empowerment zones, 390, 392
Engels, Friedrich, 879
Enterprise zones, 390, 392
Entry. *See* Market entry
Environmental Protection Agency (EPA),
    420, 453, 454–455
Environmental quality, 556
Equality, efficiency and, taxes and, 385
Equilibrium
competitive. *See* Competitive equilib-
    rium model; Long-run competi-
    tive equilibrium model
in labor market, 330
long-run. *See* Long-run equilibrium
Malthusian, 621
market. *See* Market equilibrium
stochastic, in labor market, 582,
    583(fig.)
Equilibrium interest rate, saving invest-
    ment approach and, 609–610,
    610(fig.)
Equilibrium interest rates, 602–605
finding graphically, 603(fig.),
    603–604
graphing, 602, 602(fig.)
share of GDP available for nongovern-
    ment use and, 602–603
Equilibrium price, 68
number of firms related to, 478–479,
    479(fig.)
price adjustment to, 175–176
quantity produced and, 190–191
Equilibrium quantity, 68
Equilibrium risk-return relationship, 359
Equity contracts, 346
Essay on the Principle of Population
    (Malthus), 617, 622

Establishments, 145
Establishment survey, 576
Esteé Lauder, 238–239
Europe
 Eastern, trade between Soviet Union
  and, 881–882
 unemployment in, 584
European monetary system, 835(fig.),
 835–836
Excess capacity, under monopolistic
 competition, 302
Excess costs, under monopolistic compe-
 tition, 301–302
Exchange market interventions, 837
Exchange medium, 40
 money as, 646
Exchange rates, 40–41, 829–838
 fixed. *See* Fixed exchange rates
 interest rates and, 599–600, 833
 market, for GDP comparisons, 557
 net exports and, 600–601
 purchasing power parity, for GDP
  comparisons, 557–558
 purchasing power parity and, 829–833
 real, 832–833
Excise taxes, 378
Exclusive dealing, 444
Exclusive territories, 444
Exemptions, from income tax, 374
Exit. *See* market exit
Exit, Voice, and Loyalty (Hirschman),
 340
Expanded markets, gains from trade
 from, 474–480
Expansions, 512(fig.), 513
Expectations
 budget deficits and, 789(table),
  789–791, 791(fig.)
 changes in, price adjustment line and,
  742
 demand and, 58–59
 supply and, 64
Expected return, 357
Expected value, 357
Expedited package express industry, 238,
 239, 258
Expenditures. *See* Aggregate expenditure
 line; Federal budget; Fiscal policy;
 Government purchases
Experiment(s), controlled, 12–13
Experimental economics, 13
Explicit collusion, 305
Export(s), 460, 538, 711. *See also* Comparative advantage; International
 trade
 net. *See* Net exports
Export-led strategies, 871(table),
 871–872

Export supply curve, 487
External diseconomies of scale,
 254–255, 255(fig.)
External economies of scale, 255–258,
 256(fig.)
 internal economies of scale and, 258
Externalities, 412–425
 from biodiversity, 420
 command and control remedies for,
  419–420, 423
 costs versus benefits of reducing,
  424
 global, 416
 internalization of, 417
 negative, 413–414, 414(fig.)
 positive, 413, 414–416, 415(fig.)
 private remedies for, 417–419
 taxes and subsidies as remedy for,
  421(fig.), 421–423, 422(fig.)
 tradable permits as remedy for,
  423–424
Exxon, 437, 539

FAA (Federal Aviation Administration),
 453, 454
Face value, of bonds, 353
Factor income, 824
Factor-price equalization, 472–473
Factors of production, 148. *See also*
 Capital; Labor
 comparative advantage and, 472–473
 demand for, 348
 equality of prices in different coun-
  tries, 472–473
 prices of, 63
 short- and long-run costs of, 201–202
Families, definition of, 394
Family support programs, 386
Farm programs, 189
Faulty data, 13
FCC (Federal Communications Commission), 409, 436, 449–450
FDA (Food and Drug Administration),
 436, 453, 454, 492
FDIC (Federal Deposit Insurance
 Corporation), 450
Federal Aviation Administration (FAA),
 453, 454
Federal budget, 773–780
 balanced, versus deficits or surpluses,
  774
 deficits and, 776, 777, 777(table)
 federal debt and, 777–779, 778(fig.)
 proposed versus actual, 774–775,
  775(fig.), 776(fig.)
 reforms affecting, 794
 setting, 773–775
 taxes and spending and, 776–777

Federal Communications Commission
 (FCC), 409, 436, 449–450
Federal debt, 777–779, 778(fig.)
 burden of, 788
 debt to GDP ratio and, 778–779,
  779(fig.)
 long- and short-term, 777–778
 of United States, 25(table), 25–29,
  26–29(fig.), 27(table)
Federal Deposit Insurance Corporation
 (FDIC), 450
Federal Express, 238, 250, 253, 258,
 295, 344, 448
Federal funds rate, 520, 733, 807,
 808(fig.)
Federal Open Market Committee
 (FOMC), 650–651, 651(fig.),
 806
Federal Reserve System (Fed), 648–651,
 679, 799, 806–810. *See also*
 Monetary policy
 Board of Governors of, 450, 649
 discount rate and, 809
 district banks of, 650, 650(fig.)
 Federal Open Market Committee of,
  650–651, 651(fig.)
 interest rates and, 734
 monetary transmission channel and,
  808–809
 money supply control by, 655–658
 open market operations and changes
  in federal funds rate and,
  806–808, 807(fig.), 808(fig.)
 reserve requirement changes and,
  809–810
Federal Trade Commission (FTC), 436,
 439, 440, 442, 453
Federal Trade Commission Act (1914),
 439
Feldstein, Martin, 788
Fiat, 242
Final goods, 534
Financial capital, 345–346, 351–356
 bond prices and returns and, 353–355,
  354(fig.)
 stock prices and returns and, 351,
  352(fig.), 353
Financial intermediaries, 649. *See also*
 Bank(s)
Financial markets. *See also* Bonds;
 Financial capital; Stock
 regulation in, 450–451
Firm(s), 144(fig.), 144–168, 145(fig.),
 200–229. *See also* Competition;
 Corporations; Industries; Monopolistic competition; Monopoly; Oligopoly; *specific industries*
 acquisitions by, 224

capital, labor, and output decisions of, 351

costs of. *See* Cost(s); *specific costs*

derived demand for labor of, market demand and, 322–324, 323(fig.)

divisions of, managing, 227

economies of scale and, 222–224, 223(fig.), 224(fig.)

employment and production decisions of, labor demand and, 320–322

equilibrium number of, 249

legal forms of, 146–147

market prices and transfer prices and, 228

market supply curve and, 162–164, 164(fig.)

mergers of, 225–228, 226(table)

number of, 63, 147, 476, 477–479(fig.), 478–479

as price-taker, 148–149

producer surplus and, 165–167

product differentiation and, 296–297, 297(fig.)

production by. *See* Production

profits of. *See* Profit *entries*

shut downs of, 200

spin offs and, 224–225

tradable permits and, 423–424

translation of changes in demand to changes in quantity produced at, 677, 677(fig.)

First theorem of welfare economics, 185

Fiscal policy, 524, 772–787. *See also* Budget deficit; Federal budget

under Bush, 851(table), 851–853, 853–854

under Clinton, 853(table), 853–854

countercyclical, 783(fig.), 783–786, 784(fig.)

discretionary, 785, 786

discretion versus rules debate for, 786

federal budget and. *See* Federal budget

impact of instruments of, 780–783

instruments of. *See* Government purchases; Tax(es); Transfer payments

Fiscal policy rules, 786

Fischer, Stanley, 677, 849

Fisher, Irving, 647, 845

Five-year plans, 880

Fixed costs, 153, 201–203, 202(table), 203(fig.), 204(fig.)

in short and long runs, 201–202

Fixed exchange rates, 834–838

Bretton Woods system of, 834, 835(fig.)

European monetary system and, 835(fig.), 835–836

international gold standard and, 834

interventions in exchange market and, 837

loss of international monetary independence and, 836–837

reducing exchange rate risk and, 837–838

Fixed factors, 148

Fixed investment, business, 536

Fixed wage contracts, 336

Flat tax, 378

Flexible exchange rate system, 834, 835(fig.)

Flexible price assumption, 677

Flows, of inventories, 537

Fogel, Robert W., 7

FOMC (Federal Open Market Committee), 650–651, 651(fig.), 806

Food and Drug Administration (FDA), 436, 453, 454, 492

Food stamp program, 387

Ford, Henry, 628, 631

Ford Motor, 242, 488, 591

Forecasts, 679

conditional, 681

econometric models for, 692

forecasting industry and, 680

of real GDP, 679, 681

Foreign direct investment, lack of, in developing countries, 867, 869

ForEyes, 300, 301

Fort Ord, 685–686

Fortune 500 companies, 147

45-degree line, 686, 686(fig.)

Forward-looking consumption model, 719–722

consumption smoothing and, 720

permanent versus temporary changes in income and, 720, 721(fig.)

tests and applications of, 721–722

Four-firm concentration ratios, 312, 312(table)

Freedom, economic and political, 888–889

Free entry and exit, 245

Freely determined prices, 48

Freeman, Richard, 339

Free-rider problem, 407–408

avoiding, 408

property right assignment and, 419

Free trade, 461

transition to, 482

Free trade areas (FTAs), 502

Freshwater camp, 850–852

Frictional unemployment, 565

Friedman, Milton, 525, 611, 663–664, 720, 758, 764, 786, 845–846, 847–848

Fringe benefits, 317–318

in GDP, 539

FTAs (free trade areas), 502

FTC (Federal Trade Commission), 436, 439, 440, 442, 453

Full-employment deficits, 792(fig.), 792–793, 793(fig.)

Futures markets, 837

Gaebler, Ted, 431

Gains

capital, 353, 374

from reducing trade restrictions, 493–496

from voluntary exchange of existing goods, 461

Gains from trade, 36, 458–483

attack on mercantilism and, 460–462

comparative advantage and. *See* Comparative advantage

expanded markets and, 474–480

measuring in expanded markets, 475–481

producer decisions and, 38

sovereignty and, 459–460

talking points on, 476

transition to free trade and, 482

Galbraith, John Kenneth, 611

Games

positive-sum, 46

zero-sum, 46

Game theory, 303–308, 304(fig.)

duopoly game and, 305–306, 306(fig.)

incentives to cooperate and, 306

incentives to defect and, 306

secret defections and, 308

The Gap Inc., 444, 867

Gates, Bill, 436

GATT (General Agreement on Tariffs and Trade), 494, 500–501

GDP. *See* Gross domestic product (GDP); Potential GDP; Real GDP

GDP deflator, 549, 550–552, 553(fig.)

Gender, wage discrimination based on, 332–334

General Agreement on Tariffs and Trade (GATT), 494, 500–501

General Electric, 305, 443

General Motors, 147, 242, 242(table), 488, 539

The General Theory of Employment, Interest and Money (Keynes), 525, 709, 844, 845, 847

Geometric average, 548n

Germany, hyperinflation in, 661–662, 662(fig.)

Gini coefficient, 396–397, 397(fig.)

Global externalities, 416

Global industries, 242, 242(table)
Global warming, 416
Goldin, Claudia, 45
Gold standard, 647, 814
　international, 834
Goods. *See also* Product(s)
　capital, differentiation of, 293
　closely related, prices of, 59
　consumption of. *See* Consumption
　different prices for the same good and,
　　130
　final, 534
　importance in GDP, 533–534,
　　534(table)
　inferior, 58
　intermediate, 534
　multiple, utility from, 114–117,
　　116(table)
　normal, 58
　private, 407
　public. *See* Externalities; Public goods
　tax effects on, 379, 380(fig.), 381
　tradable, 830
Gorbachev, Mikhail, 882, 883
Gosplan, 878, 880, 881
Government. *See also* Regulation; Subsi-
　dies; Tax *entries*
　appropriateness of intervention by,
　　637
　borrowing by, 801–802
　federal. *See* Federal *entries*
　investment of, 593
　in market economies, 49
　monopolies and, 279–283
　monopolies run by, 448
　production by, 405(table), 405–406
Government bonds, 346, 777–778
Government budgets
　federal. *See* Federal budget
　state and local, 779, 779(table)
Government expenditures. *See* Federal
　budget; Fiscal policy; Government
　purchases
Government failure, 49, 425(fig.),
　425–431
　economic policy decisions through
　　voting and, 426–429
　incentives and, 430–431
　public choice models of, 426
　special interest groups and, 429
　time inconsistency and, 430
Government failures, 404–405
Government production, public goods
　and, 408, 410
Government purchases
　aggregate demand/inflation curve and,
　　737, 737(fig.)
　federal budget and, 776

in GDP, 537, 538(fig.), 595(fig.),
　595–596
　impact of changes in, 780–781,
　　781(fig.)
　investment and, 605–606, 606(fig.),
　　608
　monetary policy changes with changes
　　in, 762(fig.), 762–763
　printing money to finance, 665
Government saving, 546, 867
Government size, 611–612
　controversy over, 611
　economic growth and, 612
Gradualism, 884–885
Grape industry, change in, 242(fig.),
　242–243, 243(fig.)
Graphs, 25–32. *See also* Curves; *specific
　topics*
　of models with more than two vari-
　　ables, 31(fig.), 31–32
　pie charts, 29, 29(fig.)
　scatter plots, 29, 29(fig.)
　slopes of curves in, 30(fig.), 30–31,
　　31(fig.)
　time-series, 25(table), 25–29,
　　26–28(fig.), 27(table), 28(table)
Gray, Jo Anna, 849
Great Depression, 515
　recovery from, 758
　unemployment during, 517, 519(fig.)
Great Inflation, 519
Great Leap Forward, 883
Greenbacks, 647
Greenspan, Alan, 649, 799, 815
Gross domestic product (GDP), 6,
　533–543, 547–558
　definition of, 533–535
　income approach to, 539–541
　interest rate and debt as percentage of,
　　29, 29(fig.)
　international comparisons of, 556–558
　investment as share of, 594–596
　newspaper reporting of, 550–551
　nominal, 547, 549, 549(fig.)
　omissions from, 554–555
　potential. *See* Potential GDP
　production approach to, 541, 543,
　　543(fig.)
　ratio of federal debt to, 778–779,
　　779(fig.)
　real. *See* Real GDP
　revisions in, 554
　share available for nongovernment
　　use, 602–603
　spending approach to, 535(table),
　　535–538
　world, shares of, 29, 29(fig.)
Gross investment, 540, 591

Growth accounting, 632–635
　graphical illustration of, 633
Growth accounting formula, 632, 634,
　　641(fig.), 641–642, 642(fig.), 847
　case studies using, 634–635

Hamilton, Alexander, 426, 497
Handbook of Macroeconomics, 850–852
Haworth, Joan, 18
Hayek, Friedrich, 192
Head Start program, 387
Health-care industry
　prices in, 9, 10(fig.), 11, 11(table),
　　12(fig.)
　spending in, 7, 7(table), 8(fig.), 9
Heckscher, Eli, 472
Heckscher-Ohlin model, 472–473
Hedging, 837
Heilbronner, Robert, 877
Heller, Walter, 786
Herfindahl-Hirschman index (HHI),
　　439–441, 440(table), 441(table),
　　441–442
Hewlett, William, 591
Hewlett-Packard, 591, 592
HHI (Herfindahl-Hirschman index),
　　439–441, 440(table), 441(table),
　　441–442
Hirschman, Albert, 340
Hitachi, 242(table)
Hoffman, Felix, 238
Holiday Inn, 239
Home Depot, 200
Home work and production
　omission from GDP, 554
　work versus, 326–329
Homogeneous products, 292
Honda, 242
Hong Kong, economic growth in, 635
Horizontal mergers, 443
Hostile takeovers, 364
Households, 13. *See also* Consumer
　entries
　changing composition of, 397
　definition of, 394
　labor supply decisions of, 328
Housing assistance programs, 387
Howard Johnson Company, 282
Howe, Elias, 627–628
Human capital, 45, 629
　in developing countries, 866
　policy to encourage investment in,
　　636
　work versus obtaining, 329
Hume, David, 764, 844
Hyperinflation, 661–662, 662(fig.)
Hypotheses, 19
Hyundai, 242

IBM, 147, 170, 200, 225, 241, 242(table), 438
IBRD (International Bank for Reconstruction and Development), 869
IDA (International Development Association), 869
IMF (International Monetary Fund), 863, 867, 868, 869
Impact lag, 786
Imperfect information, 179, 227
Implementation lag, 786
Implicit contracts, 677
Implicit rental price, 350
Import(s), 460, 538, 711, 711(fig.). *See also* Comparative advantage; International trade; Marginal propensity to import (MPI); Net exports
    quotas on, 488–489, 489(fig.)
Import demand curve, 487
Import substitution strategy, 870–872, 871(table)
Inaccurate data, 13
Incentive(s)
    game theory and. *See* Game theory
    market-based, for better government, 430–431
    in market economies, 48
    problems with, in government, 430
    provided by prices, 51
    takeover threats as, 364
    through profit sharing, 364
Incentive regulation, 447, 448(fig.)
Income
    aggregate, 683, 683(fig.)
    capital, in GDP, 539–540
    demand and, 58
    dependence of, net exports on, 710–717
    disposable, 683–684
    factor, 824
    labor, in GDP, 539(table), 539–540
    low, zero tax on, 378
    mobility of, longer-term income inequality and, 397
    MPC for permanent versus temporary changes in, 720, 721(fig.)
    national, 541
    net, of foreigners, in GDP, 540–541
    personal, 541
    taxable, 374
    two-way link between consumption and, 685–686
Income approach to GDP, 539–541
Income changes
    budget constraint subject to utility maximization and, 120
    indifference curve and, 142, 142(fig.)

Income distribution, 394–400
    efficiency and, 185–186
    international, 398
    Lorenz curve and Gini coefficient and, 395–399, 396(fig.), 397(fig.)
    personal, 394(table), 394–395, 395(table)
    poverty and, 399(table), 399–400
    prices and, 51
    taxes and transfers and, 400
    wealth distribution versus, 397, 399
Income effect
    of price changes, 121
    work versus home work and leisure and, 327
Income elasticity of demand, 100(table), 100–101
Income inequality. *See also* Income distribution
    efficiency and, 185–186
Income taxes. *See also* Personal income taxes; Tax(es)
    corporate, 379
Incomplete specialization, 470–471
Increasing opportunity costs, 42
Index funds, 360
Indifference curve, 139–142, 140(fig.)
    budget line and, 141, 141(fig.)
    income changes and, 142, 142(fig.)
    price changes and, 141(fig.), 141–142
Indirect business taxes, 540
Individual demand curve, 128
Individual Retirement Accounts (IRAs), 606
Industrialized countries, 862
Industrial policy, 636
Industrial unions, 338
Industries, 238(fig.), 238–259, 239(fig.). *See also specific industries*
    broad groups of, 240, 240(table)
    change in, 239–243, 242(fig.), 243(fig.)
    in decline, 250, 251(fig.)
    efficient capital allocation and, 254
    external diseconomies of scale and, 254–255, 255(fig.)
    external economies of scale and, 255–258, 256(fig.)
    global, 242, 242(table)
    long-run competitive equilibrium model of. *See* Long-run competitive equilibrium model
    minimum costs per unit and, 253–254
    narrowly defined groups of, 240–241, 241(table)
    regulators as captives of industry and, 450

Industry supply curve, long-run, 255, 255(fig.), 257–258
Inefficiency, 186–188. *See also* Efficiency
    deadweight loss and, 186, 188
    maximizing sum of producer plus consumer surplus and, 186, 187(fig.)
    production possibilities curve and, 43
Inelastic demand, 94, 95(table)
Infant industry argument, for trade restriction, 497
Inferior goods, 58
Inflation, 9, 509, 519–520, 520(fig.), 659–666. *See also* Aggregate demand/inflation (ADI) curve
    disinflation and deflation and, 666
    expectations of, price adjustment line and, 740–741
    interest rates and, 732–735
    measurement of, 665–666
    money supply and, 659–662
    productivity growth and, 664–665
    real GDP and, over time, 749(fig.), 749–751, 751(fig.)
    reasons for, 665–666
    unemployment and, 663(fig.), 663–664, 664(fig.)
    wages and, 318
Inflation rate, 9, 519, 766(fig.). *See also* Deflation; Disinflation
    increase in, 759, 766(fig.)
    target. *See* Target inflation rate
Inflation tax, 665
Informal economy, 865
Information
    asymmetric, 363–364
    demand and, 58
    imperfect, 179, 227
    limited, implicit contracts and, 676–677
    product differentiation and, 295
    ways of processing, 172–173
Informational efficiency, 192–194
Infrastructure, investment in, 593
Innovation, 627
Inputs. *See* Capital; Factors of production; Labor
Insiders, employment and, 581–582
Insurance, social, 392
Insurance industry, regulation of, 451
Intel, 262, 458
Intellectual property laws, 631
Interest payments, in GDP, 539–540
Interest rates, 520–521, 596–605
    budget deficits and, 789(table), 789–791, 791(fig.)
    consumption and, 596–598, 597(fig.), 684

determination of, 805, 806(fig.)
discount rate, 809
equilibrium, 602–605
exchange rate deviations from pur-
    chasing power parity and, 833
exchange rates and, 599–600
federal funds, 733, 807, 808(fig.)
inflation and, 732–735
investment and, 598(fig.), 598–599
long-term rise in, 790
net exports and, 599(fig.), 599–600
nominal, 521
real. *See* Real interest rate
real GDP and, 728–731
types of, 520–521, 521(fig.)
Interindustry trade, 293, 295
    intraindustry trade versus, 474–475
Intermediate goods, 534
Internal diseconomies of scale, 255
Internal economies of scale, external
    economies of scale and, 258
Internalization, of externalities, 417
International Bank for Reconstruction
    and Development (IBRD), 869
International Development Association
    (IDA), 869
International gold standard, 834
International Monetary Fund (IMF), 863,
    867, 868, 869
International monetary independence,
    loss of, 836–837
International trade. *See also* Trade
    entries
    balance of. *See* Balance of trade
    definition of, 459
    domestic trade versus, 38, 40
    exchange rates and. *See* Exchange
        rates; Fixed exchange rates
    gains from. *See* Comparative advan-
        tage; Gains from trade
    by market economies, 49
    multilateral, 40–41
    quotas and, 75–77, 77(fig.)
    recent trends in, 459(fig.), 459–460
    restrictions on. *See* Trade restrictions
International Trade Commission (ITC),
    76
International transfer payments, 824–825
Intraindustry trade
    interindustry trade versus, 474–475
    product differentiation and, 293, 295
Intuit, 436
Invention, 627–628, 629–630
Inventories, stocks and flows and, 537
Inventory investment, 536
Investment, 590–613
    dependence on income, 717

fixed, business, 536
in GDP, 535–537, 536(fig.)
government, 593
government purchases and, 605–606,
    606(fig.)
government share of GDP and,
    611–612
gross, 540, 591
in human capital. *See* Human capital
interest rates and. *See* Interest rates
interest rates and real GDP and,
    729
inventory, 536
net, 540, 592
portfolio, 867
residential, 536
saving and, 608–611
saving related to, 544–546
shift in consumption and, 606–608,
    607(fig.), 607(table)
Investment share of GDP, 594–596
    changes in shares and, 595
    other shares versus, 594–595,
        595(fig.)
Investment tax credit, 852
Invisible hand, 170, 172
Iraq, Kuwaiti invasion by, 88, 105, 525
IRAs (Individual Retirement Accounts),
    606
Iron law of wages, 621
Isocost lines, 233, 234(fig.), 235,
    235(fig.)
Isoquants, 233
ITC (International Trade Commission),
    76

James, Frances M., 25
Japan
    GDP in, 557–558
    as supplier of saving, 869, 870(fig.)
    trade of, 490, 491, 492
Japan Travel Bureau, 242(table)
Jet magazine, 290
Job leavers, 572, 574–575
Job losers, 572–574, 574(fig.)
Job rationing, 580–582, 581(fig.)
Job search, 582, 583(fig.)
Job vacancies, 574
Johnson, John, 290, 292
Johnson, Lyndon B., 785
Justice Department, Antitrust Division
    of, 439

Kahn, R. F., 705
Das Kapital (Marx), 879
Kennedy, John F., 376, 385, 785, 786,
    882

Keynes, John Maynard, 106, 525, 682,
    705, 709, 764, 834, 844, 845, 847
Keynesian revolution, 844
Keynesian school, 844–845
KKR, 364
Klein, Lawrence, 692
Kmart, 200, 677
Kodak, 225
Komatsu, 293, 302
Kroger, 145
Krueger, Alan, 335
Kuwait, Iraqi invasion of, 88, 105, 525
Kuznets, Simon, 532
Kwik-Start, 145
Kydland, Finn, 850
Kyocera, 458

L.A. Gear, 298
Labor, 14, 523. *See also* Employment;
    Unemployment; Wage *entries*
    aggregate hours of labor input and,
        570–572
    average product of, 207
    capital and, economic growth and,
        623, 624(fig.), 625–626
    change in relative price of, 236(fig.),
        236–237
    diminishing returns to, 152, 163,
        618–619, 619(fig.)
    division of. *See* Division of labor
    economic growth and, 618–623
    firms' decisions about output and
        labor and, 351
    marginal product of, 151–152,
        320–321
    marginal revenue product of,
        321(table), 321–322
    mix with capital, 222, 232(table),
        232–237, 233(fig.), 234(fig.)
    production function of firm and,
        205–206
Labor abundance, 472
Labor demand, 316, 317(fig.), 319–326
    employment and production decisions
        of firm and, 320–322
    firm's derived demand and market
        demand and, 322–324, 323(fig.)
    MRP = W and marginal cost equals
        price rule compared and,
        324–325, 325(table)
Labor demand curve, 578(fig.), 578–579
Labor force, 566
    definition of, 567, 568(fig.)
    discouraged workers and, 567
Labor force participation rate, 568(fig.),
    569, 569(table), 570
Labor income, in GDP, 539, 539(table)

Labor intensiveness, 472
Labor market(s), 316–341, 317(fig.)
  categories of population in, 567,
    568(fig.)
  demand in. *See* Labor demand
  key indicators of conditions in,
    568(fig.), 569(table), 569–570,
    570(fig.)
  labor contracts in, 336–337
  supply in. *See* Labor supply
  unions and, 338–341
  wages and. *See* Wage(s)
Labor market equilibrium, 330
Labor productivity, 516
  increased, union/nonunion wage
    differential and, 339–340
  in United States, 516(fig.), 516–517
  wage differences and, 330–331
Labor-saving technological change, 628
Labor supply, 316, 317(fig.), 319–320,
    326–330
  of households, 328
  restricted, union/nonunion wage dif-
    ferential and, 339, 339(fig.)
  taxes and, 107
  work versus home work and leisure
    and, 326–329
  work versus human capital and, 329
Labor supply curve, 578(fig.), 578–579
Labor unions, 338–341
  monopsony and bilateral monopoly
    and, 340
  union/nonunion wage differentials
    and, 338–340
Lady Foot Locker, 225
Laissez faire system, 20
Lauder, Esteé, 238
Laws. *See also* Economic models; Legis-
    lation; *specific models*
  of demand, 55
  of one price, 829–830
  Say's, 844
  of supply, 61
LDCs (less-developed countries), 862
Learning by doing, 628–629
Legislation
  antitrust. *See* Antitrust policy
  labor, 338
  line-item veto and, 794
  minimum wage, 334–335, 335(fig.)
Leisure activity
  omission from GDP, 554
  work versus, 326–329
Lenin, V. I., 878
Lenscrafters, 292, 297, 300, 301
Leontief, Wassily, 472
Leontief paradox, 472
Less-developed countries (LDCs), 862

Levi Strauss, 444
Levitt, Arthur, 591
Lewis, John L., 338
Liabilities, of commercial banks,
    651–652
Liability, limited, of corporations, 146
Licenses, 282–283
Life-cycle model, 720
Limited information, implicit contracts
    and, 676–677
Limited liability, of corporations, 146
Limits to Growth (Meadows, et al.), 623
Lindbeck, Assar, 582
Linear curves, 31
Line-item veto, 794
Liquidity constraint, 720
Liz Claiborne, Inc., 290
Lloyd George, David, 709
Loans, 652. *See also* Borrowing; Federal
    debt
Lobbying, government failure and, 429
Local government budgets, 779,
    779(table)
Location, product differentiation and,
    296
Lockheed Martin, 242(table)
Long run
  capital and labor decisions in,
    232(table), 232–237, 233(fig.),
    234(fig.)
  capital expansion and production in,
    221–222
  costs in, 201–202, 217–222
  production in, 151, 217–222
  real interest rate in, 604
Long-run average total cost curve,
    220–221, 221(fig.)
Long-run competitive equilibrium
    model, 243–253
  entry and exit in, 245
  entry combined with individual firm
    expansion and, 250
  increase in demand and, 246–249,
    247(fig.)
  industries in decline and, 250, 251
  long-run equilibrium in, 245–246,
    254(fig.)
  new products and changes in costs
    and, 250, 252(fig.), 253
Long-run equilibrium, 245(fig.),
    245–246
  competitive. *See* Long-run competitive
    equilibrium model
  increase in demand and, 246, 428
  monopolistically competitive,
    301(fig.), 301–303
Long-run industry supply curve, 255,
    255(fig.), 257–258

Long-term economic growth
  aggregate supply and, 522–524
  government policy for, 524–525
Long-term employment contracts,
    336–337
Long-term unemployment, 575, 575(fig.)
Loral, 225
Lorenz curve, 395–399, 396(fig.),
    397(fig.)
Losses
  capital, 353
  deadweight. *See* Deadweight loss
Lucas, Robert, 525, 677, 847
Lumber industry, 491

McDonald's, 296, 345, 557, 830, 831
McDonnell Douglas, 573
Machine-tool industry, development of,
    257
Macroeconomic policy. *See also* Fiscal
    policy; Monetary policy
  debates about, 851–854
  for economic fluctuations, 526
Macroeconomics, 17, 19
  schools of thought in, 844–851
Macroeconomic theory, 522
Maddison, Angus, 864
Malthus, Thomas Robert, 481, 617,
    619–623, 622(fig.), 631, 844
Malthusian equilibrium, 621
Managed trade, 502
Managers, 145
Mandated benefits, 392–393, 393(fig.)
Mao Zedong, 883
Marginal benefit, 226
  cost-benefit analysis and, 410–411
  diminishing, 126
  greater than marginal cost, 278
  measuring, 125–126, 126(table)
  price equals marginal benefit rule and,
    129
  private, 415(fig.), 415–416
  social, 415(fig.), 415–416
Marginal cost, 153(fig.), 153–154,
    203–204
  cost-benefit analysis and, 410–411
  derivation of supply curve from,
    156–158
  graphical representation of, 155,
    155(fig.)
  marginal benefit greater than, 278
  marginal revenue and, 269–270,
    271(fig.)
  price equals marginal cost rule and,
    157–158
Marginal cost pricing, 446–447
Marginal private benefit, 415(fig.),
    415–416

Marginal private cost, 413–414, 414(fig.)
Marginal product (MP) of labor, 151–152, 320–321
wage discrimination and, 333, 333(fig.)
Marginal propensity to consume (MPC), 683, 683(fig.)
multiplier and, 701–703, 702(table), 703(table), 708, 710, 714, 714(table), 715(table)
for permanent versus temporary changes in income, 720, 721(fig.)
tax change and, 718, 719(fig.)
Marginal propensity to import (MPI), 711
multiplier and, 714, 714(table), 715(table)
tax change and, 718
Marginal propensity to save (MPS), multiplier and, 703–704
Marginal revenue, 156
declining, 266–267
less than price, 267–268
marginal cost and, 269–270, 271(fig.)
price elasticity of demand and, 268–269
price for price-takers and, 271
strategic, 310
Marginal revenue curves, strategic, 309
Marginal revenue product *(MRP)* of capital, 347
Marginal revenue product *(MRP)* of labor, 321(table), 321–322
marginal cost equals price rule and, 324–325, 325(table)
Marginal social benefit, 415(fig.), 415–416
Marginal social cost, 413–414, 414(fig.)
Marginal tax rate, 376–378, 377(fig.)
Marginal utility, 112–114, 114(fig.), 115(fig.)
diminishing, 113–114
Market(s), 14, 34–35. *See also specific markets*
competitive, 49, 148–149
contestable, 441
double-auction, 176–178
efficient. *See* Efficiency; Efficient market(s); Inefficiency
increasing size of, 479, 480(fig.)
number of firms in, 63
size of, gains from trade and, 474–480
Market definition, 441(table), 441–443
Market demand
for capital, 348, 349(fig.)
for labor, 324, 325(fig.)
Market demand curve, 129–130, 130(fig.)
preferences and, 129–130

Market economies, 20, 876
economic questions in, 47
emerging. *See* Emerging market economies
key elements of, 48–50
product differentiation in, 292–293
Market entry
barriers to, 263, 283
efficient market hypothesis and, 362
firm expansion and, 250
free, 245
under monopolistic competition, 300–301
Market equilibrium, 64–73
change in market and, 69–71
finding with supply and demand diagram, 68, 69(fig.)
market price determination and, 66–68, 67(table)
Market exit
efficient market hypothesis and, 362
free, 245
under monopolistic competition, 300–301
Market failures, 49, 404. *See also* Externalities
Market power, 263–265, 311–312
concentration ratios as measure of, 312, 312(table)
estimates of strategic demand curves as measure of, 311(table), 311–312
graph of, 265, 265(fig.)
price decisions and, 263–264
quantity and, 264
Market price, 79–84
determination of, 66–68, 67(table)
price ceilings and, 79, 80(fig.), 81
price floors and, 79, 81, 82(fig.), 83–84
as transfer prices, 228
Market supply, of capital, 348, 349(fig.)
Market supply curve, 144, 144(fig.), 162–164, 164(fig.)
shifts in, 164
slope of, 164
Marriage tax, 377
Marshall, Alfred, 64, 106, 132, 348, 709, 844–845, 847
Martin, William McChesney, 799
Marx, Karl, 20, 864, 879, 880
Matsushita, 438
Mattel, 145, 837–838
Maturity date, of bonds, 353
Mayflower, 676
MCI, 280, 291, 438
Meadows, D., 623
Means-tested transfers, 386–387, 387(table)

Measures, unit-free, 93
Median voter theorem, 427
Medicaid, 386, 776
Medicare, 392, 776
Medium of exchange, 40
money as, 646
Medoff, James, 339
Meiselman, David, 846
Mercantilism, attack on, 460–462
Merchandise trade, 822
Merchandise trade balance, 823
Merck & Co., 458, 629
Mergers, 439–443
economic analysis of, 439
economies of scope and, 225–228, 226(table)
government objections to, 442
Herfindahl-Hirschman index and, 439–441, 440(table), 441(table)
horizontal versus vertical, 443
legislation governing, 439
market definition and, 441(table), 441–443
Merrill Lynch, 450
MFA (Multifiber Agreement), 495
MFN (most-favored nation) policy, 501
Microeconomics, 17, 19
Microsoft, 436, 458, 631
Midpoint formulas, for calculating elasticity, 95–96
Milk industry, prices in, 83
Mill, John Stuart, 500
Miller, 312
Miller, G. William, 799
Mincer, Jacob, 335
Mini-Mart, 145
Minimum efficient scale, 223, 224(fig.)
Minimum wage, 79, 581
Minimum wage laws, 334–335, 335(fig.)
Mitsubishi, 242(table)
Mitsubishi Heavy Industries, 242(table)
Mixed economies, 20
M1 money supply measure, 647–648
M2 money supply measure, 648
Mobil, 437
Models. *See* Economic models; *specific models*
Modigliani, Franco, 720, 846
Monetarist school, 845–846
Monetary base, 657, 804–805
A Monetary History of the United States (Friedland and Schwartz), 525
Monetary policy, 524–525, 798–817. *See also* Central banks; Federal Reserve System (Fed)
changes in, 755, 756(fig.), 757–759, 762(fig.), 762–763

constant money growth rule and, 811–812
credible, gains from, 814–817
expectations and credible disinflation and, 816(fig.), 817
gold standard and, 814
interest rate determination and, 805, 806(fig.)
interpreting actions and, 814–815, 816(fig.)
money demand and, 803–804, 804(fig.)
money supply and. *See* Money supply
political business cycle and, 801
preemptive monetary strike and, 813
principles of, 815
real GDP in monetary policy rule and, 812–813, 813(table)
time inconsistency and, 801
Monetary policy rule, 732, 732(table)
Monetary transmission channel, 808–809
Money, 645–648
commodity, 645
creation of, 652–655
demand for, 803–804, 804(fig.)
form of, 646–647
functions of, 645–646
printing to finance government expenditures, 665
quantity equation of, 659–660, 660(fig.)
velocity of, 659–660
Money, Credit and Commerce (Marshall), 845
Money demand, 803–804, 804(fig.)
Money multiplier, 657(table), 657–658, 658(fig.)
Money supply, 804–805
definitions of, 647–648, 648(table)
Fed's control of, 655–658
inflation and, 659–662
Monopolistic competition, 290, 291, 298–303
entry and exit under, 300–301
long-run equilibrium under, 301(fig.), 301–303
monopoly and competition compared with, 302
in short run, 299–300
Monopoly, 149, 262–287. *See also* Antitrust policy
bilateral, labor unions and, 340
competition and monopolistic competition compared with, 302
competition compared with, 275–276
deadweight loss from, 276–278
experimental tests of model of, 277

generic diagram of, 273(fig.), 273–275
government-run, 448
licenses and, 282–283
marginal cost and price and, 278–279
market power of, 263–265
MC = MR rule and, 271–272
natural. *See* Natural monopolies
output and prices of, 274
patents and copyrights and, 280, 282
price discrimination and. *See* Price discrimination
profit-maximizing output and, 269–270
profits of, 274(fig.), 274–275
revenues and, 265–269, 266(table), 267(fig.)
Monopsony, labor unions and, 340
Moral hazard, 363
Mortgage(s), 345
Mortgage interest rate, 520
Most-favored nation (MFN) policy, 501
Motel franchising industry, 239
Motel 6, 239
Motley, Brian, 665
Motorola, 458
Movement along the curve, 31–32
MP. *See* Marginal product (MP) of labor
MPC. *See* Marginal propensity to consume (MPC)
MPI. *See* Marginal propensity to import (MPI)
MPS (marginal propensity to save), multiplier and, 703–704
MRP. See Marginal revenue product *(MRP)* of capital
MTV, 454
Multifiber Agreement (MFA), 495
Multilateral negotiations, for reducing trade barriers, 500–501
Multilateral trade, 40–41
Multiplier, 698–723
algebraic derivation of, 701–704, 702(table), 703(table)
balanced budget, 718
dependence of net exports on income and, 710–717
forward-looking consumption model and, 719–722
for general shift in aggregate expenditure line, 699–700
graphical derivation of, 699–701, 700(fig.)
marginal propensity to consume and, 708, 710
origins of, 705
slope of aggregate expenditure line and, 707–708, 708(fig.)

for tax change, 717–719, 719(fig.)
following through economy, 704–707, 705(table), 706(fig.), 714–716, 715(table)
uncertainty about size of, 710, 710(table)
Mutual funds, 360

NAFTA (North American Free Trade Agreement), 482, 501–502
National Highway and Traffic Safety Administration (NHTSA), 453
National income, 541
National income and product accounts, 534–535
Nationalization, 878
National Labor Relations Act, 338
National Labor Relations Board, 338
National park fees, 105
National saving, 544
insufficient, as obstacle to raising capital per worker, 867, 867(fig.)
National saving rate, 609, 609(fig.)
downward shift in, 610, 610(fig.)
National Science Foundation, 422
National security argument, for trade restriction, 497–498
Natural monopolies
economies of scale and, 445, 445(fig.)
regulation of, 279–280, 445–449
Natural unemployment rate, 565
normal capacity utilization and, 675
policies to reduce, 583, 585
NEC, 170
Negative correlation, 12
Negative externalities, 413–414, 414(fig.)
Negatively related variables, 16
Negative slope, 30, 30(fig.)
Neoclassical growth school, 846–847
Net exports, 460, 711–712, 712(table)
dependence on income, 710–717
exchange rates and, 600–601
in GDP, 538, 594, 595(fig.)
interest rates and, 599(fig.), 599–600
interest rates and real GDP and, 730
saving and, 544–546
Net factor income from abroad, 824
Net foreign assets, 826
Net income, of foreigners, in GDP, 540–541
Net investment, 540, 592
Net transfer from abroad, 825
New classical school, 848–849, 849(fig.)
New entrants, 572, 575
New Keynesian school, 849–850
Newly industrialized countries, 862

New products, industries and, 250, 252(fig.), 253
Newspapers
Federal Reserve System reporting in, 734
GDP reporting in, 550–551
unemployment information in, 576, 584
New trade theory, 480
New York City, 592
New York Stock Exchange, 346
New York Times Company, 170
NHTSA (National Highway and Traffic Safety Administration), 453
Nike, 298, 458
Nippon Steel, 242(table)
Nominal GDP, 547
real GDP versus, over time, 549, 549(fig.)
Nominal interest rate, 521
Nominal rigidities, 677
Nominal wage, 318
Noncooperative outcome, 305
Nonexcludability
public goods and, 407
in technology market, 631
Nongovernment organizations, in market economies, 49–50
Nonrivalry
public goods and, 407
in technology market, 630–631
Nontariff barriers, 495
Nordhaus, William, 801
Normal capacity utilization, natural unemployment rate and, 675
Normal goods, 58
Normal profits, 249
Normative economics, 20
North American Free Trade Agreement (NAFTA), 482, 501–502
North-South problem, 861
Northwest Airlines, 439

Observations, 5–15
documenting and quantifying, 6–11
graphing. *See* Graphs
interpreting, 11–14, 12(fig.)
OCC (Office of the Controller of the Currency), 450
Occupational Safety and Health Administration (OSHA), 453, 454, 455
Ocean Pacific, 458
Office Depot, 224, 442
Office of the Controller of the Currency (OCC), 450
Ohlin, Bertil, 472
Oil price(s)
deregulation of, 451
recessions due to, 513, 513(fig.)

Oil price changes
change in supply and, 90–92, 91(fig.)
elasticity and, 88, 105
OPEC and, 303
Oligopoly, 290–291
O'Neill, June, 18
"On Money" (Hume), 844
On-the-job training, 329, 629
On the Principles of Political Economy and Taxation (Ricardo), 481
OPEC. *See* Organization of Petroleum Exporting Countries (OPEC)
Open market operations, 805, 806–807, 807(fig.)
Opportunity costs, 36, 45
comparative advantage and, 463, 470–471
increasing, 42
Organization(s), 14, 34. *See also* Producer(s)
nongovernment, in market economies, 49–50
Organization of Petroleum Exporting Countries (OPEC), 303
defection from, 307
Osborne, David, 431
OSHA (Occupational Safety and Health Administration), 453, 454, 455
Output. *See also* Production; Real GDP
firms' decisions about capital and labor and, 351
monopoly, determining, 274
Outsiders, employment and, 581–582
Overall price level, 9, 10(fig.)
Owners, of firms, 145

Packard, David, 591
PA line. See Price adjustment *(PA)* line
Paper money, 646–647
Pareto, Vilfredo, 182
Pareto efficiency, 182, 193
Partnerships, 145
Part-time workers, 567
Patel, Marilyn Hall, 18
Patents, 280, 282, 630
Payroll subsidies, 392
Payroll survey, 576
Payroll taxes, 378
effect of, 382–384, 383(fig.)
Peaks, 512, 512(fig.)
Peanut market, prices in, 73–78, 74(fig.), 75(fig.)
Pearle Vision, 292, 300, 301
Peel, Robert, 500
Pencavel, John, 18
Pennsylvania Turnpike, 282
Pennzoil, 353, 356
Pepsi, 293, 302, 309–310, 441

PepsiCo, 312
Perestroika, 882–883
Perfectly elastic supply, 104, 104(fig.)
Perfectly inelastic demand, 95, 95(fig.), 95(table)
Permanent income model, 720
Permits, tradable, 423–424
Per se rule, 438
Personal income, 541
Personal income taxes, 374–378
computing, 374–376, 375(fig.)
effects of, 381–382, 382(fig.)
marginal tax rate and, 376–378, 377(fig.)
marriage tax and, 377
zero tax on low incomes and, 378
Petroleum industry. *See* Oil price changes; Oil price(s)
Pharmaceutical industry, comparative advantage and, 464(table), 464–467
Phaseout, of trade restrictions, 482
Phases of Capitalist Development (Maddison), 864
Phelps, Edmund, 663–664, 677, 846, 847–848
Philip Morris, 242(table)
Phillips, A. W., 663
Phillips curve, 663(fig.), 663–664, 664(fig.)
Physical capital, 345, 346–351
demand for, 346
firms' decisions about, 351
ownership of, 350
rental markets for, 346–350
Physical characteristics, product differentiation and, 296
Piece-rate system contracts, 336–337
Pie charts, 29, 29(fig.)
Pitt, William, 622
Pittsburgh Penguins, 540–541
Planck, Max, 15
Plott, Charles, 180
Poland, economic reforms in, 886–887
Policy effectiveness proposition, 848
Political business cycle, 801
Political economy, 20
Political freedom, economic freedom and, 888–889
Population growth, as obstacle to raising capital per worker, 866–867
Porter, Michael, 296
Portfolio diversification, to reduce risk, 360, 362(fig.)
Portfolio investment, 867
Positive correlation, 12
Positive economics, 20–21
Positive externalities, 413, 414–416, 415(fig.)

Positively related variables, 16
Positive slope, 30
Positive-sum games, 46
Potential GDP, 522–523
    changes in, economic fluctuations
        and, 678
    departure of real GDP from, price
        adjustment line and, 741–742
    economic growth and, 638(fig.),
        638–639
    movement away from, 693(fig.),
        693–694
    return to, after boom, 754–755
Poverty, 399(table), 399–400, 861
    taxes and transfers and, 400
Poverty line, 399, 399(table)
Poverty rate, 399, 400(fig.)
PPI (producer price index), 553
PPP. *See* Purchasing power parity (PPP)
Predatory pricing, 438–439
Prediction. *See also* Forecasts
    models for, 17
Preemptive monetary strike, 813
Preferences
    demand and, 58
    market demand curve and, 129–130
    utility and, 115–117
Prescott, Edward, 850
Present discounted value, 368–369
Price(s), 50–51. *See also* Inflation
    adjustment to equilibrium price,
        175–176
    ask, 176
    bid, 176
    of bonds, 354–355, 355(table)
    commodity, changes in, price adjust-
        ment line and, 742
    conjectural variations approach and,
        310
    demand and, 55, 59
    different, for same good, 130
    equality of marginal revenue with, 271
    equilibrium. *See* Equilibrium price
    expectations of, 64
    of factors, equality in different coun-
        tries, 472–473
    flexible, 677
    freely determined, 48
    importance of goods and services in
        GDP and, 533–534, 534(table)
    incentives provided by, 51
    income distribution and, 51
    law of one price and, 829–830
    market. *See* Market price
    market power and, 263–264
    monopoly, 274, 278–279
    number of firms related to, 478,
        478(fig.)

of oil. *See* Oil price(s); Oil price
        changes
    overall level of, 9, 10(fig.)
    price elasticity of demand and, 99
    quantity supplied at different prices
        and, 156(fig.), 156–157, 158(fig.)
    rationing function served by, 68
    relative. *See* Relative prices
    rental. *See* Rental price of capital
    shifts in supply and, 63
    as signals, 50–51
    Soviet, 880–881
    staggered setting of, price adjustment
        line and, 741
    sticky, 677, 764
    supply and, 61
    transfer, 50
Price adjustment *(PA)* line, 739–745
    aggregate demand/inflation curve com-
        bined with, 744(fig.), 744–745
    fit with facts, 742–743, 743(fig.)
    flatness of, 739–741
    shifts of, 741–742
    temporary shifts in, 761
Price ceilings, 79, 80(fig.), 81
    in insurance industry, 451
Price changes
    budget constraint subject to utility
        maximization and, 120
    income effect of, 121
    indifference curve and, 141(fig.),
        141–142
    oil prices and. *See* Oil price changes
    price elasticity of demand and,
        99–100
    in relative price of labor, 236(fig.),
        236–237
    stock and, 361
    substitution effect of, 121–122
Price controls, 79–84
    ceilings, 79, 80(fig.), 81, 451
    floors, 79, 81, 82(fig.), 83–84, 451
Price-cost margin, 278–279
    of oligopolistic firm, 310
Price-directed approach, for determining
        production level, 228
Price discovery, 181
Price discrimination
    different price elasticities of demand
        and, 284(fig.), 284–285
    in nonmonopolistic firms, 286
    quantity discounts as, 285, 286(fig.)
Price-earnings ratio, 353
Price elasticity of demand, 89–101
    change in supply and, 90–92, 91(fig.)
    definition of, 92–93
    demand curves and, 95
    differences in, 98–100, 99(table)

high versus low, 89–90
    importance of, 89–92, 90(fig.)
    long-run versus short-run, 100
    marginal revenue and, 268–269
    midpoint formulas for calculating,
        95–96
    price discrimination and, 284(fig.),
        284–285
    revenue and, 96–98, 97(fig.), 98(fig.),
        99(table)
    shifts in demand and, 100(table),
        100–101
    slope versus, 93, 94(fig.)
    terminology for, 93–95
Price elasticity of supply, 101–105
    definition of, 102–104, 104(fig.)
    importance of, 101–102, 102(fig.),
        103(fig.)
Price equals marginal benefit rule, 129
Price equals marginal cost rule, 157–158
Price fixing, 443
Price floors, 79, 81, 82(fig.), 83–84
    in insurance industry, 451
Price indexes, 552–553, 553(fig.)
Price leaders, 305
Price levels, 552
Price-makers, 149, 263
Price shocks, 760
Price-takers, 148, 181
    equality of marginal revenue with
        price and, 271
Pricing
    average total cost, 447
    marginal cost, 446–447
    predatory, 438–439
Principal-agent relationship, 147
Principles of Economics (Marshall), 106,
    709, 845
Principles of Political Economy (Mill),
    500
Prisoner's dilemma, 304(fig.), 304–305
Private benefit, marginal, 415(fig.),
    415–416
Private cost, marginal, 413–414,
    414(fig.)
Private goods, 407
Private remedies, for externalities,
    417–419
Privatization, 406, 887
Procter & Gamble, 242(table)
Producer(s). *See also* Organization(s)
    taxes paid by, shifts in supply curve
        and, 188, 190, 190(fig.)
Producer decisions, 37–38
    gains from trade and, 38
    scarcity and choice and, 37–38
    specialization, division of labor, and
        comparative advantage and, 38

Producer price index (PPI), 553
Producer surplus, 165–167, 175
  graphical representation of, 165, 165(fig.), 166(fig.)
  maximizing sum of consumer surplus plus, 186, 187(fig.)
  monopoly and, 277–278
  profits related to, 166–167, 167(table)
Product(s). *See also* Goods
  deadweight loss versus variety in, 302–303
  homogeneous, 292
  improvements in, omission from GDP, 555
  new, industries and, 250, 252(fig.), 253
Product differentiation, 292–297
  advertising and, 295
  amount of, 296–297, 297(fig.)
  consumer information services and, 295
  intraindustry trade and, 293, 295
  in market economy, 292–293
  methods of, 296
Production
  capital expansion in long run and, 221–222
  changes in, changes in demand and, 676–677
  factors of. *See* Factors of production
  in long run, 217–222
  in short run, 211–217, 212(fig.)
Production approach to GDP, 541, 543, 543(fig.)
Production decisions, individual, 174–175
Production function, 151(fig.), 151–152, 523–524
  of firm, costs and, 205–207
Production possibilities, 41–42, 42(table)
Production possibilities curve, 42–46, 43(fig.), 44(fig.)
  efficient, inefficient, and impossible points on, 43
  scarcity and choice and, 45–46, 46(fig.)
  shifts in, 43, 44(fig.), 45
  with trade, 469–470
  without trade, 468–469
Production targets, 880
Productivity. *See* Labor productivity
Productivity curve, 641, 641(fig.)
Productivity growth, inflation and, 664–665
Productivity slowdown, 634, 634(fig.), 634(table)
Profit(s), 149–155
  economic versus accounting, 248–249

monopoly, 273(fig.), 273–275, 274(fig.)
  normal, 249
  producer surplus related to, 166–167, 167(table)
  production and costs and, 150–155
  total revenue and, 150, 150(table)
Profit graphs, 160–161, 161(fig.)
Profit maximization, 149–150, 155–162
  output for, at monopoly, 269–270
  price equals marginal cost rule, 157–158
  profit graphs and, 160–161, 161(fig.)
  profit tables and, 159(table), 159–160
  quantity supplied at different prices and, 156(fig.), 156–157, 157(fig.)
Profit or loss rectangle, 211–214
  profits and losses and, 212, 213(fig.), 214
  total costs area of, 212
  total revenue area of, 211–212, 213(fig.)
Profit sharing, 147, 364
Profit tables, 159(fig.), 159–160
Progressive taxes, 378, 785
Property rights
  assigning, 417–419, 424
  in market economies, 48
Property taxes, 379
Proportional taxes, 378
Protectionist policies, 487. *See also* Trade restrictions
Public choice models, 426
Public goods, 406–410. *See also* Externalities
  actual government production and, 408, 410
  free riders and, 407–408
  new technology and, 408
Public infrastructure investment, 593
Public infrastructure projects, 411–412
  discount rates for, 411–412
Public policy, 20–21
  on taxes, 385–386
  voting and. *See* Voting
Purchases, government. *See* Government purchases
Purchasing power parity (PPP), 829–833
  Big Mac index and, 831
  exchange rates and, 830–833, 832(fig.)
  interest rates and, 833
  nontradable goods and, 830
  tradable goods and, 830
Purchasing power parity exchange rates, 557–558
Pure rent, 348–350, 349(fig.)

Quality of life, vital statistics on, 555–556
Quantity
  conjectural variations approach and, 310
  equilibrium, 68
Quantity demanded, 55
Quantity-directed approach, for determining production level, 228
Quantity discounts, 285, 286(fig.)
Quantity equation of money, 659–660, 660(fig.)
Quantity produced
  equilibrium price and, 190–191
  market power and, 264
Quantity supplied, 61
  at different prices, 156(fig.), 156–157, 158(fig.)
Quintiles, 394(table), 394–395
Quotas
  on imports, 488–489, 489(fig.)
  international trade and, 75–77, 77(fig.)

Race, wage discrimination based on, 332–334
Rain forests, of South America, 420
Rate of return, 353
  in reality, risk and, 359–360, 360(table)
  in theory, risk and, 358–359, 359(fig.)
Rate of technical substitution, 233
Rational expectations, budget reduction plans and, 789
Rational Expectations and Econometric Practice (Lucas and Sargent), 525, 847
Rational expectations assumption, 722
Rational expectations revolution, 847
Rationing, as function of price, 68
RCA, 629
R&D (research and development), policy to encourage, 636(fig.), 636–638
Reagan, Ronald, 385, 516, 649, 774, 785, 799, 815
Real business cycle school, 850
Real business cycle theories, 678
Real exchange rate, 832–833
Real GDP, 9, 509–515, 547–549
  aggregate demand changes leading to changes in, 673–679, 674(fig.)
  base year and, 549
  departure from potential GDP, price adjustment line and, 741–742
  determining through spending balance, 689(fig.), 689–690, 690(table)
  economic fluctuations and, 511–515, 512(fig.), 513(table)

economic growth and, 509–511, 511(fig.)
forecasting, 679, 681
growth between two years, 547–548
inflation and, over time, 749(fig.), 749–751, 751(fig.)
interest rates and, 728–731
nominal GDP versus, over time, 549, 549(fig.)
year-to-year chain of, 548
Real interest rate, 521
in long run, 604
Reallocation, consumer decisions and, 36–37
Real wage, 318, 578
Recessions, 512, 512(fig.). *See also* Economic fluctuations
aftermath of, 514
depressions versus, 514(fig.), 514–515
end of, 749–755
unemployment during, 517, 517(fig.), 519(fig.)
Reciprocal Trade Agreement Act (1934), 493–494
RECLAIM program, 424
Recognition lag, 786
Recoveries, 512(fig.), 513. *See also* Economic fluctuations
from Great Depression, 758
Reebok, 298
Re-entrants, 575
Regional trading areas, 501
Regressive taxes, 378
Regulation, 449–455
average total cost pricing for, 447
in borderline cases, 449–450
deregulation and, 451–452, 452(table)
economic versus social, 452–455, 453(table)
in financial markets, 450–451
incentive, 447, 448(fig.)
in insurance industry, 451
marginal cost pricing for, 446–447
of natural monopolies, 279–280, 445–449
regulators as captives of industry and, 450
supply and, 65
Reinflation, 759, 766(fig.)
Reinventing Government: How the Entrepreneurial Spirit Is Transforming the Public Sector (Osborne and Gaebler), 431
Relative efficiency, comparative advantage and, 463
Relatively elastic demand, 94–95, 95(table)
Relative prices, 9, 10(fig.), 11

comparative advantage and, 466–467, 467(table)
of labor, change in, 236(fig.), 236–237
Rent, economic (pure), 348–350, 349(fig.)
Rental markets, 346–350
demand curve for capital and, 347–348, 348(fig.)
fixed supply and, 348–350, 349(fig.)
market demand and supply and, 348, 349(fig.)
Rental payments, in GDP, 539
Rental price of capital, 346–347
implicit, 350
Rent control, 79
Report on manufactures (Hamilton), 497
Required reserve ratio, 652
Resale price maintenance, 444
Research and development (R&D), policy to encourage, 636(fig.), 636–638
Reserves, 652
changes in requirements for, 809–810
deposits linked to, 654–655
money supply and, 656
Residential investment, 536
Restructuring, 224–225
Retaliation, for trade restriction, 498
Retirement, 567
Returns
to capital, diminishing, 625(fig.), 625–626, 626(fig.)
expected, 357
to labor, diminishing, 618–619, 619(fig.)
rate of. *See* Rate of return
on stock, 351, 352(fig.), 353
Revenue(s)
average, 269
marginal. *See* Marginal revenue
monopoly and, 265–269, 266(table), 267(fig.)
price and, 96–98, 97(fig.), 98(fig.), 99(table)
tax. *See* Tax revenue
total. *See* Total revenue
Revenue tariffs, 493
Ricardian equivalence, 787–788
Ricardo, David, 462, 481, 499, 500, 622, 788, 802, 844
Risk, 356–362
aversion to, 356(table), 356–358, 357(table)
behavior under uncertainty and, 356(table), 356–358, 357(table)
diversification to reduce, 360, 362(fig.)
efficient market theory and, 362

exchange rate, reducing, 837–838
return in reality and, 359–360, 360(table)
return in theory and, 358–359, 359(fig.)
systematic, 360
Roadway Express, 220
Rockefeller, John D., 283, 436, 437
Romer, Christina, 758
Romer, Paul, 847
Roosevelt, Franklin D., 493
Roush, Carroll, 220
Roush, Galen, 220
Rule of reason, 438

Safeway, 364
Saint-Gobain, 242(table)
Salaries, in GDP, 539
Saltwater camp, 850–852
Samuelson, Paul, 844, 845
Sargent, Thomas, 525, 847
Sarnoff, David, 629
Saving, 133–135, 544–546. *See also* Marginal propensity to save (MPS)
age related to, 545–546
definition of, 544
equality with investment and net exports, 544–546
government, 546, 867
interest rate and, 134–135
investing related to, 546
investment and, 608–611
national. *See* National saving; National saving rate
price of future versus present consumption and, 134
Savings deposit(s), 647–648
Savings deposit interest rate, 520
Say, J. B., 844
Say's Law, 844
Scale
constant returns to, 223, 223(fig.)
diseconomies of. *See* Diseconomies of scale
economies of. *See* Economies of scale
minimum efficient, 223, 224(fig.)
Scarcity, 34
consumer decision and, 35–36
for economy as a whole, 41–46
producer decisions and, 37–38
production possibilities curve and, 45–46, 46(fig.)
Scatter plots, 29, 29(fig.)
Schumpeter, Joseph, 573, 864
Schwartz, Anna, 525, 758, 846
Scope, economies of, 225–228, 226(table)
Sears, 200

Seasonal unemployment, 575
Sectoral trade balance, 828
Securities and Exchange Commission (SEC), 450–451
Sellers, in double-auction markets, 177–178
Selway Bitterroot Wilderness, 126
Services, importance in GDP, 533–534, 534(table)
Services trade, 822–823
Services trade balance, 823
Set-aside programs, for farmers, 189
Seven-Up, 312, 441
Sherman Antitrust Act (1890), 437
Shift of the curve, 32
Shifts in demand, 56–59, 57(fig.)
    elasticities related to, 100(table), 100–101
Shifts in supply curve
    market, 164
    taxes paid by producers and, 188, 190, 190(fig.)
Shock therapy, 884–885
Shortages
    market price and, 67
    price ceilings and, 79, 80(fig.), 81
Short run
    costs and production in, 211–217, 212(fig.)
    costs in, 201–202
    labor input in, 205–206
    monopolistic competition in, 299–300
    production decisions in, 151
Short-term unemployment, 575, 575(fig.)
Shut down(s), 200
Shutdown point, 215(fig.), 215–217
SIC (Standard Industrial Classification), 241
Signals, prices ad, 50–51
Singapore, economic growth in, 635, 860
Singer Company, 628
Slopes, of curves, 30(fig.), 30–31, 31(fig.)
Smith, Adam, 20, 38, 39, 123, 170, 282, 460, 461–462, 481, 499, 500, 628, 844, 879
Smith, Fred, 238, 253
Smith, Vernon L., 180
Smoot-Hawley tariff, 493, 495(fig.)
Snower, Dennis, 582
Social benefit, marginal, 415(fig.), 415–416
Social cost, marginal, 413–414, 414(fig.)
Social insurance programs, 392
Socialism, 877, 878
Social regulation, economic regulation versus, 452–455, 453(table)

Social security, 392
Soft-drink industry, concentration ratio of, 312
Sole proprietorships, 145
Solow, Robert, 632, 641, 846
Sony Corporation, 225
South American rain forests, 420
South Korea
    economic growth in, 860
    trade policy of, 871(table), 871–872
Sovereignty, 459
Soviet Union, 878, 880–883
    central planning in, 878, 880–881
    decline in economic growth of, 634–635, 635(table)
    five-year plans in, 880
    after perestroika, 882–883
    prices in, 880–881
    technological change and quality of goods and, 882
    trade between Eastern Europe and, 881–882
Special interest groups, government failure and, 429
Specialization
    external economies of scale and, 256
    incomplete, 470–471
    producer decisions and, 38
Specific tariffs, 487
Specific taxes, 188
Spending approach to GDP, 535(table), 535–538
Spending balance
    determining real GDP through, 689(fig.), 689–690, 690(table)
    interest rates and real GDP and, 730–731, 731(fig.)
S&P (Standard & Poors) 500 Index, 360
Spin offs, 224–225
Sprint, 280, 291, 438
Sri Lanka, economic growth in, 860
SSI (supplemental security income), 386
Stagflation, 761
Stalin, Joseph, 880
Standard deduction, 374
Standard Industrial Classification (SIC), 241
Standard Oil Company, 283, 436, 437, 439
Standard & Poors (S&P) 500 Index, 360
Staples, 224, 442
State enterprises, 880
State government budgets, 779, 779(table)
Statistical discrepancy, 541
Stender v. Lucky Stores, 18
Sticky price(s), 764
Sticky price assumption, 677

Stigler, George, 450
Stochastic equilibrium, in labor market, 582, 583(fig.)
Stock, 146, 346
    portfolio diversification and, 360, 362(fig.)
    price changes and, 361
    prices and returns on, 351, 352(fig.), 353
Stock exchanges, 346
Stocks of inventories, 537
Store of value, money as, 646
Strategic behavior, 303–304
Strategic demand curves, 309(fig.), 309–310, 310(fig.)
    estimates of, as measures of market power, 311(table), 311–312
Strategic marginal revenue, 310
Strategic marginal revenue curves, 309
Strategic trade policy, 497
Structural deficits, 792(fig.), 792–793, 793(fig.)
Structural unemployment, 565
Structure-conduct-performance method, 312
Subsidies
    foreign, as argument for trade restriction, 498
    payroll, 392
    as remedy for externalities, 422(fig.), 422–423
    supply and, 64
Subsistence line, 619–623, 620(fig.), 621(fig.)
Substitutability, price elasticity of demand and, 99
Substitutes, 59
Substitution, technical, rate of, 233
Substitution effect
    of price changes, 121–122
    work versus home work and leisure and, 326
Sulfur dioxide emissions, 416
Sumitomo Chemical, 458
Sun Microsystems, 200
Supplemental security income (SSI), 386
Supply, 60–65, 61(table)
    aggregate. *See* Aggregate supply *entries*
    change in, 71, 71(table), 72(fig.), 90–92, 91(fig.)
    of labor. *See* Labor supply
    law of, 61
    perfectly inelastic, 104, 104(fig.)
    price elasticity of. *See* Price elasticity of supply
    shifts in, 62–65, 63(fig.)
    trade barriers to restrict, 496–497

Supply and demand diagram, finding
    equilibrium price with, 68, 69(fig.)
Supply and demand model, 54–84. *See
    also* Demand *entries;* Market equi-
    librium; Supply *entries*
    case study of, 73–78
Supply curve, 61(fig.), 61–62, 62
    derivation from firm's marginal cost,
        156–158
    export, 487
    industry, long-run, 255, 255(fig.),
        257–258
    for labor, 578(fig.), 578–579
    market. *See* Market supply curve
    movements along versus shifts in,
        64(fig.), 65
    shape of, work versus home work and
        leisure and, 327(fig.), 327–329,
        329(fig.)
    shifts in. *See* Shifts in supply curve
    shutdown curve and, 216
Supply schedule, 61
Supply shocks, 760(fig.), 760–761
Supply side economics, 850
Supply side policies, 524
Surpluses
    budget, 774
    consumer. *See* Consumer surplus
    market price and, 67
    producer. *See* Producer surplus
    trade. *See* Trade surpluses
Systematic risk, 360

Tacit collusion, 305
Takeovers, threats of, 364
Talking points, on gains from trade, 476
Tangency point, 141, 141(fig.)
Target inflation rate, 733, 733(fig.)
    changes in, 737, 738(fig.)
Tariffs, 461, 486, 487–488, 488(fig.)
    of abominations, 493
    ad valorem, 487
    revenue, 493
    Smoot-Hawley, 493, 495(fig.)
    specific, 487
    of United States, 493–495, 494(fig.)
Tax(es), 373(fig.), 373–386. *See also*
    Federal budget; Fiscal policy
    ad valorem, 188
    anticipating cuts or increases in,
        721–722
    business, indirect, 540
    capital gains, 852
    corporate, 146, 379
    deadweight loss from, 188–192
    economic theory of, 181
    effects of, 379–385
    emission, 423

employment and unemployment and,
    583, 585(fig.)
excise, 378, 379
federal budget and, 776
flat, 378
impact of changes in, 782(fig.),
    782–783
income distribution and poverty and,
    400
inflation, 665
labor supply and, 107
marriage, 377
multiplier for change in, 717–719,
    719(fig.)
payroll, 378
permanent versus temporary cuts in,
    721, 722(fig.)
personal. *See* Personal income taxes
progressive, 378, 785
property, 379
proportional, 378
regressive, 378
as remedy for externalities, 421(fig.),
    421–422, 423
sales, 379
shifts in supply curve due to, 188, 190,
    190(fig.)
specific, 188
supply and, 64
Taxable income, 374
Tax avoidance, 384
Tax brackets, 375
Tax credits, for research, 637
Tax evasion, 384–385
Taxi industry, licensing in, 282
Tax incidence, 380(fig.), 381
Tax policy, 385–386
Tax rates, 717–718
    average, 376
    marginal, 376–378, 377(fig.)
Tax revenue, 384(fig.), 384(table),
    384–385, 718
    perverse effects of taxes on, 384(fig.),
        384(table), 384–385
Teamsters Union, 450
"Technical Progress and the Aggregate
    Production Function" (Solow), 632
Technical substitution, rate of, 233
Technological change, 627
    capital-saving, 628
    embodied and disembodied, 637
    labor-saving, 628
    in Soviet Union, 882
Technology, 523, 627–631
    definition of, 627–629
    Industrial Revolution, 864–865
    new, public goods and, 408
    nonexcludability in market for, 631

nonrivalry in market for, 630–631
obstacles to spread of, 864–866
production of, 629–630
shifts in supply and, 62–63
Technology policy, 636–638
    to encourage investment in human
        capital, 636
    to encourage R&D, 636(fig.),
        636–637
    government intervention and, 637
    technology embodies in new capital
        and, 637
Telecommunications industry, 408, 409,
    438, 449–450, 451
Telemex, 406, 448
Teneo, 242(table)
Term limits, 794
Terms of trade, 467
Theories. *See* Economic models; *specific
    models*
The Theory of Moral Sentiments
    (Smith), 39
Thompson, Dan, 637
Thompson, Ross, 627–628
Thompson Bagel Machine Manufactur-
    ing Corporation, 637
3M, 147
Time
    discretion versus rules debate for
        fiscal policy and, 786
    product differentiation and, 296
Time deposits, 648
Time inconsistency, 801
    government failure and, 430
Time-series graphs, 25–29
    of one variable, 25(table), 25–28,
        26–28(fig.), 27(table)
    of two or more variables, 25(table),
        25–29, 26–29(fig.), 27(table)
Tit-for-tat strategy, 306
Tobin, James, 786, 845
Toronto Blue Jays, 541
Total cost, 153, 153(fig.), 201
    capital expansion and, 217–218,
        218(fig.), 219(table)
    graphical representation of, 154,
        154(fig.)
    profits and, 150–155
    total revenue and, under monopoly,
        269, 270(fig.)
Total revenue
    profits and, 150, 150(table)
    total costs and, under monopoly, 269,
        270(fig.)
Toyota, 242
Tradable goods, 830
Tradable permits, 423–424
Trade. *See also* International trade

domestic versus international, 38, 40
  gains from, 36
  interindustry. *See* Interindustry trade
  intraindustry. *See* Intraindustry trade
  by market economies, 49
  terms of, 467
Trade adjustment assistance, 482
Trade balance, 538
Trade creation, 502
Trade deficits, 716, 821(fig.), 821–822,
    823
  bilateral, 827(table), 827–828
  dependence of net exports on income
      and, 716
  sectoral, 828
Trade diversion, 501–502
Trade-Enhancement Initiative, 499
Trade policy, strategic, 497
Trade restrictions, 486–503
  arguments for, 496–499
  effects of, 487–492
  gains from reducing, 493–496
  history of, 493(fig.), 493–496
  phaseout of, 482
  political economy of protectionist
      pressures and, 496
  reduction of, 499–503
Trade surpluses, 823
  bilateral, 827(table), 827–828
Trade wars, 493, 495(fig.)
Trading periods, in double-auction mar-
    kets, 177, 177(table)
Trading rules, in double-auction markets,
    178
Tragedy of the commons, 418
Trammell Crow, 676
Transaction costs, 50
  for property right assignment,
      418–419
Transfer payments, 386–393
  earned income tax credit and,
      387–388
  exclusion from GDP, 537
  income distribution and poverty and,
      400
  international, 824–825
  mandated benefits and, 392–393,
      393(fig.)
  means-tested programs and, 386–387,
      387(table)
  social insurance programs and, 392
  welfare reform and, 388–392
Transfer prices, 50
  market prices as, 228
Treasury bill rate, 520
Treble damages, 443
Troughs, 512, 512(fig.)
Trucking industry, 449

Tunisia, trade policy of, 871, 871(table)
TWA, 286
Twin deficits, 716

Uchitelle, Louis, 515
Uncertainty, behavior under, 356(table),
    356–358, 357(table)
Underground economy, omission from
    GDP, 554–555
Unemployment, 564–585. *See also*
    Labor *entries*
  aggregate hours of labor input and,
      571
  cyclical, 565
  definition of, 567, 568(fig.)
  among different groups, 577,
      577(table)
  frictional, 565
  inflation and, 663(fig.), 663–664,
      664(fig.)
  long- versus short-term, 575, 575(fig.)
  measurement of, 566–567
  reasons for, 572–575
  during recessions, 517, 517(fig.),
      519(fig.)
  seasonal, 575
  structural, 565
Unemployment insurance, 392
Unemployment rate, 517, 565, 566(fig.),
    568(fig.), 569(table), 569–570,
    580–582
  job rationing and, 580–582, 581(fig.)
  job search and, 582, 583(fig.)
  natural. *See* Natural unemployment
      rate
Unilateral disarmament, for reducing
    trade barriers, 499
Unilever, 242(table)
Union(s). *See* Labor unions
Union Carbide, 200
United Airlines, 200, 286
United Nations, 863
United Parcel Service (UPS), 238, 250,
    253
United States
  budget deficits of, 777, 777(table)
  catch-up within, 857–858, 859(fig.)
  economic fluctuations in, 511–515,
      512(fig.), 513(table)
  economic growth in, 509–511,
      511(fig.)
  employment trends in, 579(fig.),
      579–580
  farm output of, 626, 626(fig.)
  GDP in, 557–558
  government debt in, 25(table), 25–29,
      26–29(fig.), 27(table)
  gross domestic product in, 6

income distribution in, 394–400
  inflation in, 519–520, 520(fig.)
  jobs and productivity in, 516(fig.),
      516–517
  monetary history of, 660–662,
      661(fig.), 662(fig.)
  as net debtor country, 826–827
  productivity slowdown in, 634,
      634(fig.), 634(table)
  tariffs of, 493–495, 494(fig.)
  taxes in. *See* Tax(es)
  trade deficits of, 821(fig.), 821–822
  trade of, 490, 491–492
  trade policy in, 486
  trade surpluses of, 823
  unemployment in, 517, 517(fig.),
      519(fig.), 564, 565–566, 566(fig.)
  as user of saving, 869, 870(fig.)
  wage trends in, 318–319, 319(fig.)
U.S. Constitution
  balanced budget amendment to, 794
  commerce clause of, 459
U.S. Department of Commerce, 407
U.S. Department of Justice, Antitrust
    Division of, 439
U.S. Postal Service, 238, 242(table),
    281, 282, 448
U.S. Weather Service, 407
United States Steel Company, 437
Unit elastic demand, 94, 95(table)
Unit-free measures, 93
Unit of account, money as, 646
University of California, 170
UPS (United Parcel Service), 238, 250,
    253
Uruguay Round, 501
User fees, 408
Utility, 111–117
  consumption and, 111–112,
      112(table), 113(table)
  marginal, 112–114, 114(fig.),
      115(fig.)
  from more than one good, 114–117,
      116(table)
  preferences and, 115–117
Utility maximization, 117–125
  diamond-water paradox and, 123, 125
  rules for, 122–123
  subject to budget constraint,
      119(table), 119–123
Utility maximizing rule, 122–123

Value
  of bonds, 353
  expected, 357
  money as store of, 646
Value added, 541, 543, 543(fig.)
Van Heusen, 292

Variable(s)
 economic, 11
 negatively related, 16
 positively related, 16
Variable costs, 153, 201–203, 202(table), 203(fig.), 204(fig.)
 in short and long runs, 201–202
Variable factors, 148
VCRs, 292
Velocity, of money, 659–660
Vencor, 147
Vernon, 347
Vertical mergers, 443
Vertical restraints, 443–444
VIE (voluntary import expansion), 491, 492(fig.)
Volcker, Paul, 649, 757–758, 799
Volcker disinflation, 757–759
Voluntary import expansion (VIE), 491, 492(fig.)
Voluntary restraint agreements (VRAs), 490(fig.), 490–491
Volvo, 242
Voting, 426–429
 convergence of positions in two-party system and, 427–428
 median voter theorem and, 427
 paradoxes and, 428(table), 428–429
 single issues with unanimity and, 427, 427(table)
Voting paradoxes, 428(table), 428–429
VRAs (voluntary restraint agreements), 490(fig.), 490–491

Wage(s), 317–319
 academic wage gap and, 332
 deferred, contracts with, 337
 efficiency, 337, 582

fixed, contracts with, 336
 fringe benefits and, 317–318
 in GDP, 539
 iron law of, 621
 minimum, 79, 581
 nominal, 318
 piece-rate, contracts with, 336–337
 real, 318, 578
 staggered setting of, price adjustment line and, 741
 time intervals and, 318
 trends in, 318–319, 319(fig.)
 work versus home work and leisure and, 326–327
Wage differentials, 330–335
 compensating, 331–332, 337
 discrimination and, 332–334
 labor productivity and, 330–331
 minimum wage laws and, 334–335, 335(fig.)
 union/nonunion, 338–340
Wal-Mart, 200, 253, 439, 677, 829
Walt Disney, 242(table)
Wants, coincidence of, 646
Waste, from inefficiency, measuring, 186–188
Wealth distribution, income distribution versus, 397, 399
Wealth of Nations (Smith), 20, 38, 39, 123, 460, 461–462, 481, 500, 628
Weather Service, 407
Welfare economics, first theorem of, 185
Welfare notches, 390, 390(fig.)
Welfare reform, 388–392
 payroll subsidies and empowerment zones and, 390, 392
 welfare notches and, 390, 390(fig.)

work disincentives and, 388–390, 389(fig.)
Wells Fargo Bank, 649
Westinghouse, 200, 305, 443
What Do Unions Do? (Freeman and Medoff), 339
Whitney, Eli, 257
Willingness to pay, 125–129
 graphical derivation of demand curve and, 126–129, 127(fig.), 128(fig.)
 measuring, 125–126, 126(table)
 price equals marginal benefit rule and, 129
Wilson, Kemmons, 239
Wilson, Woodrow, 709
Women, wage discrimination against, 332–334
Woods, Tiger, 4
Woolco, 225
Woolworth, 225
Working-age population, 567
World Bank, 863, 867, 869
World Economic Outlook, 868
World Trade Organization (WTO), 501
WTO (World Trade Organization), 501

Yellen, Janet, 20
Yellowstone National Park, 105
Yeltsin, Boris, 883
Yield
 on bonds, 354–355
 dividend, 353
Yosemite National Park, 105, 282
Young, Alwyn, 635

Zenith, 438
Zero-sum games, 46

PHOTO CREDITS *(continued from page iv)*

Chapter 4: p. 104, Raphael Caillarde/Gamma Liaison; p. 106, The Granger Collection. **Chapter 5:** p. 112, John Brooks/Gamma Liaison; p. 124, AP/Wide World Photos. **Chapter 6:** p. 152, De Richmond/The Image Works. **Chapter 7:** p. 193, Rande Delucal/Gamma Liaison. **Chapter 8:** p. 225 (top), Roger Kingston/ The Picture Cube; p. 225 (bottom), Andy Freeberg. **Chapter 9:** p. 258 (left), Paul Conklin/Photo Edit; p. 258 (right), Charles Gupton/Stock Boston. **Chapter 10:** p. 282, Courtesy of Mr. John Kramer. **Chapter 11:** p. 293 (left), John Coletti/The Picture Cube; p. 293 (right), Eric Carle/Stock Boston. **Chapter 12:** p. 337 (left), Courtesy of Henry Ford Museum; p. 337 (right), Dallas Morning News/Louis De Luca. **Chapter 13:** p. 347, Courtesy of Vernon Computer Rentals and Leasing; p. 363, Raymond Reuters/Sygma. **Chapter 14:** p. 374, Mark C. Burnett/ Stock Boston. **Chapter 15:** p. 409, Paul Conklin; p. 413, Jack Picone/Network Matrix. **Chapter 16:** p. 454 (left), Sara Krulivich/NYT Pictures; p. 454 (right), Jeff Greenberg/The Picture Cube. **Chapter 17:** p. 465 (left), Nathan Benn/Stock Boston; p. 465 (right), Bill Galley/Stock Boston; p. 481, The Bettmann Archive. **Chapter 19:** p. 523 (left), Andrew Sacks/Tony Stone Wide World; p. 523 (middle), Joe Caputo/Gamma Liaison; p. 523 (right), C. J. Pickerell/The Image Works. **Chapter 20:** p. 537, Sobel Klonsky/The Image Bank; p. 543, Mark Antman/ The Image Works. **Chapter 21:** p. 573 (left), Brent Jones/Stock Boston; p. 573 (middle), Mark Richards/Photo Edit; p. 573 (right), Anveal Vokra/The Picture Cube. **Chapter 22:** p. 592 (left), The Bettmann Archive; p. 592 (middle), The Bettmann Archive; p. 592 (right), Eric A. Weissmann/Stock Boston. **Chapter 23:** p. 618 (left), The Granger Collection; p. 618 (middle), The Granger Collection; p. 618 (right), Ed Lano/The Picture Cube; p. 622, The Bettmann Archive; p. 630 (left), The Bettmann Archive; p. 630 (right), Peter Menzel/Stock Boston. **Chapter 24:** p. 645 (top), The Granger Collection; p. 645 (bottom), The Bettmann Archive; p. 661, The Bettmann Archive; p. 662, The Bettmann Archive. **Chapter 25:** p. 676, Jack Spratt/The Image Works. **Chapter 26:** p. 709, The Bettmann Archive; p. 716 (top), Eric Sander/Gamma Liaison; p. 716 (bottom left), Bob Daemmrich/ The Image Works; p. 716 (bottom right), Bob Daemmrich/The Image Works. **Chapter 30:** p. 799 (left), The Bettmann Archive; p.799 (second from left), James Andanson/Sygma; p. 799 (center), John Coleman/Sygma; p. 799 (second from right), R. Maiman/Sygma; p. 799 (right), Jeffrey Markowitz/Sygma. **Chapter 31:** p. 838, Courtesy of Chicago Mercantile Exchange. **Chapter 34:** p. 879, The Bettmann Archive.

CARTOON CREDITS

Chapter 1: p. 21, P. Steiner. Cartoonists and Writers Syndicate. **Chapter 3:** p. 79, Toos. Cartoonists and Writers Syndicate. **Chapter 5:** p. 113, © 1994 Robert Mankoff from the Cartoon Bank, Inc. **Chapter 7:** p. 195, Drawing by Dana Fradon, © 1992 The New Yorker Magazine. **Chapter 8:** p. 226, Sidney Harris. Cartoonists and Writers Syndicate. **Chapter 9:** p. 241, Sidney Harris. Cartoonists and Writers Syndicate. **Chapter 10:** p. 285, The Keeping Up cartoon by William Hamilton is reprinted by permission of Chronicle Features, San Francisco, California. **Chapter 11:** p. 306, P. Steiner. Cartoonists and Writers Syndicate. **Chapter 12:** p. 329, The Far Side copyright 1990 Far Works, Inc./Dist. by Universal Press Syndicate. Reprinted with permission. All rights reserved. **Chapter 14:** p. 376,

World Trade with the United States

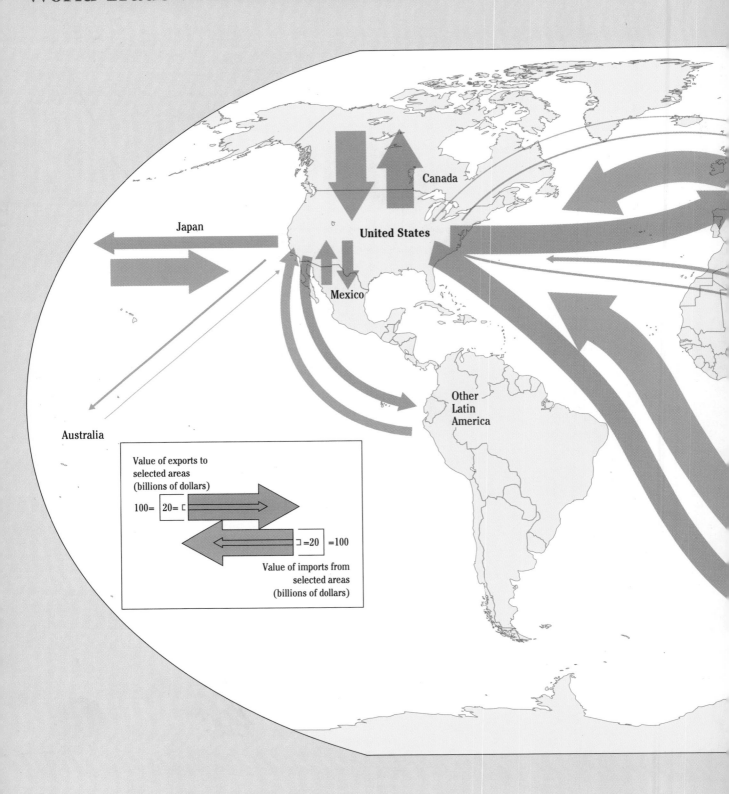

Japan

Canada

United States

Mexico

Australia

Other
Latin
America

Value of exports to
selected areas
(billions of dollars)

100 =   20 = ⊏

⊐ =20   =100

Value of imports from
selected areas
(billions of dollars)